Marketing Communications

Visit the *Marketing Communications, fifth edition* Companion Website at **www.pearsoned.co.uk/fill** to find valuable **student** learning material including:

- Regularly updated podcasts on the key concepts of marketing communications outline how the theory is related to contemporary practice
- Video case studies referred to at the start of each part contextualise your learning in the real world
- Links to key academic papers take your study further
- Practice multiple choice quizzes help assess your understanding

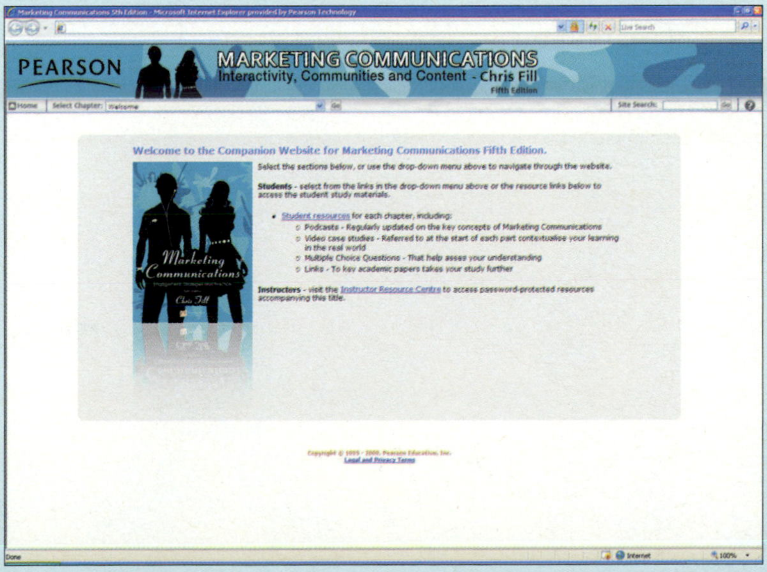

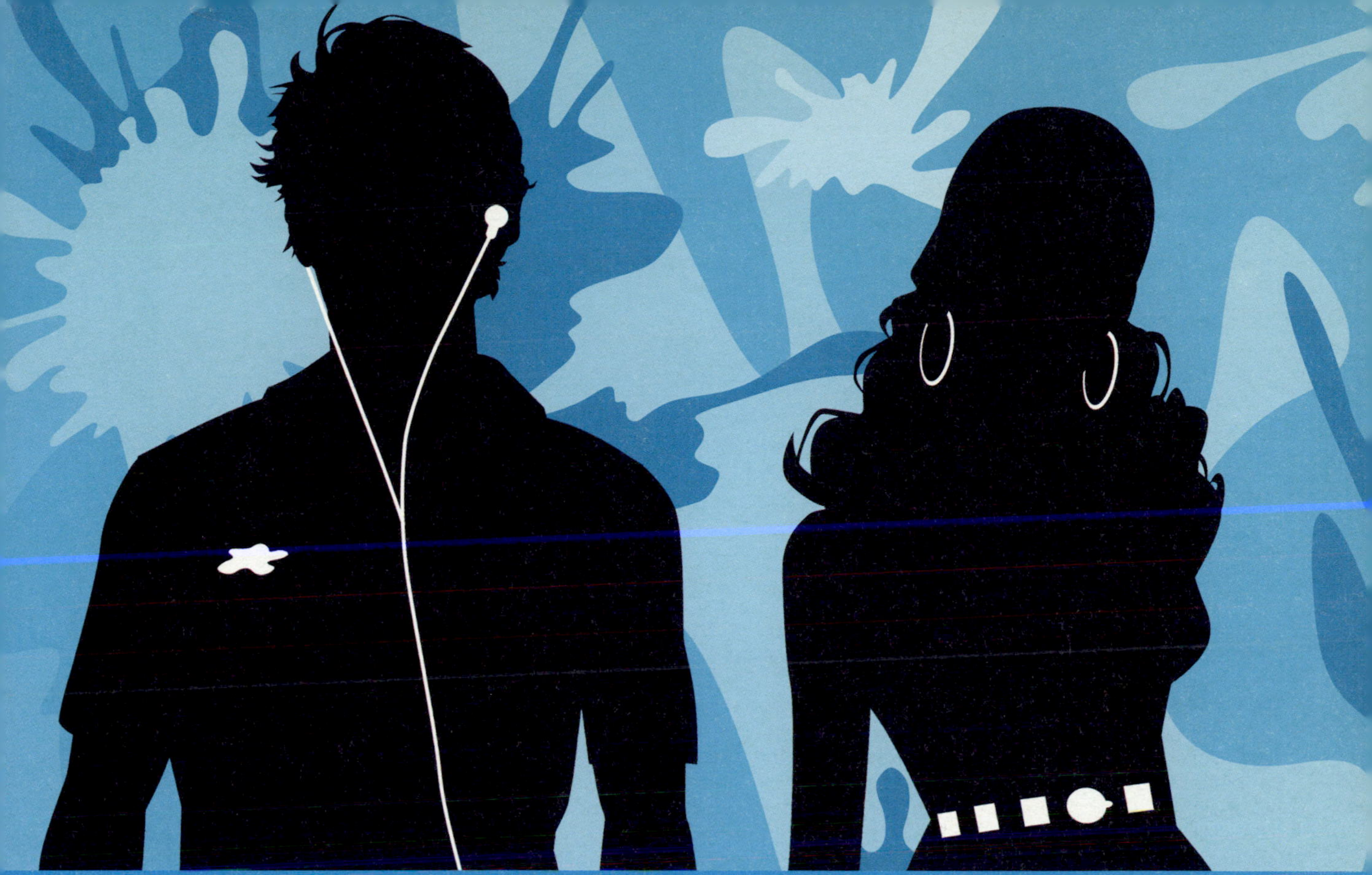

Marketing Communications

Interactivity, Communities and Content

Fifth Edition

Chris Fill

University of Portsmouth

FT Prentice Hall
FINANCIAL TIMES

An imprint of Pearson Education

Harlow, England • London • New York • Boston • San Francisco • Toronto • Sydney • Singapore • Hong Kong
Tokyo • Seoul • Taipei • New Delhi • Cape Town • Madrid • Mexico City • Amsterdam • Munich • Paris • Milan

Pearson Education Limited
Edinburgh Gate
Harlow
Essex CM20 2JE
England

and Associated Companies throughout the world

Visit us on the World Wide Web at:
www.pearsoned.co.uk

First published under the Prentice Hall Europe imprint 1995
Fourth Edition 2005
Fifth edition 2009

ISBN: 978-0-273-71722-5

British Library Cataloguing-in-Publication Data
A catalogue record for this book is available from the British Library

Library of Congress Cataloging-in-Publication Data
Fill, Chris.
Marketing communications : interactivity, communities, and content / Chris Fill. — 5th ed.
p. cm.
Includes bibliographical references and index.
ISBN 978-0-273-71722-5 (pbk. : alk. paper) 1. Communication in marketing. 2. Marketing channels. 3. Sales promotion. I. Title.
HF5415.123.F55 2009
658.8′02—dc22

2008046446

10 9 8 7 6 5 4 3 2 1
12 11 10 09 08

Typeset in 10/12pt Minion by 35
Printed and bound by Rotolito Lombarda, Italy

The publisher's policy is to use paper manufactured from sustainable forests.

For Karen, Johnny and Mike . . . our 'brilliant' family

Brief contents

Contents

Supporting resources

Visit **www.pearsoned.co.uk/fill** to find valuable online resources

Companion Website for students

- Regularly updated podcasts on the key concepts of marketing communications outline how the theory is related to contemporary practice
- Video case studies referred to at the start of each part contextualise your learning in the real world
- Links to key academic papers take your study further
- Practice multiple choice quizzes help asses your understanding

For instructors

- Complete, downloadable Instructor's Manual with sample answers to all the question material in the book
- PowerPoint slides that can be downloaded and used for presentations

Also: The **regularly maintained** Companion Website provides the following features:

- Search tool to help locate specific items of content
- E-mail results and profile tools to send results of quizzes to instructors
- Online help and support to assist with website usage and troubleshooting

For more information please contact your local Pearson Education sales representative or visit **www.pearsoned.co.uk/fill**

Guided tour

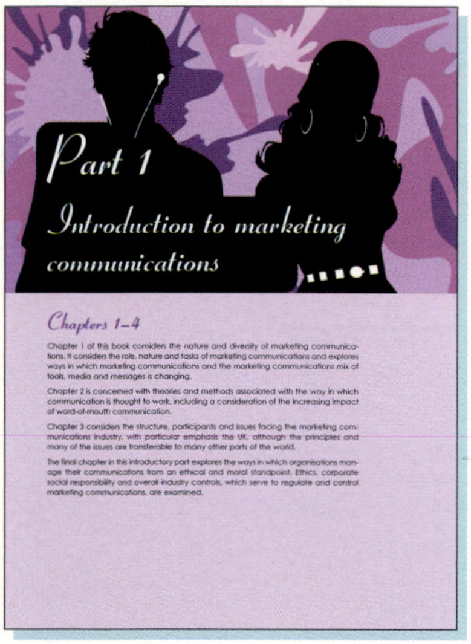

Part Openers summarise the key points in each chapter.

New to this edition!
A **Video Insight** opens each part of the book. These fascinating documentaries include interviews with top management teams from a variety of European companies who discuss a wide range of marketing communication decisions and their practical implications for business.

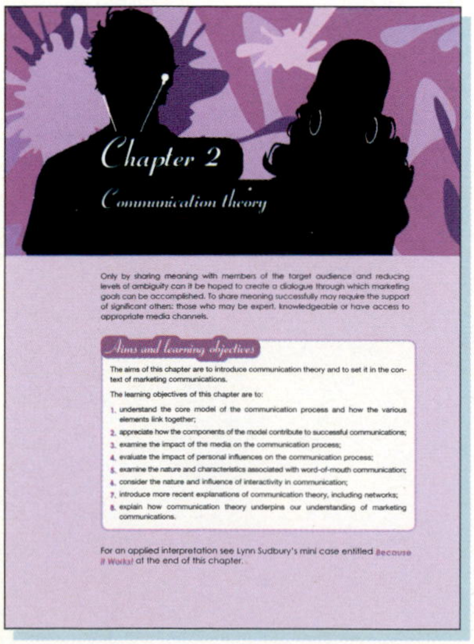

Aims and objectives enable you to focus on what you should have achieved by the end of the chapter.

Snappy **ViewPoints** boxes improve your understanding by providing different perspectives.

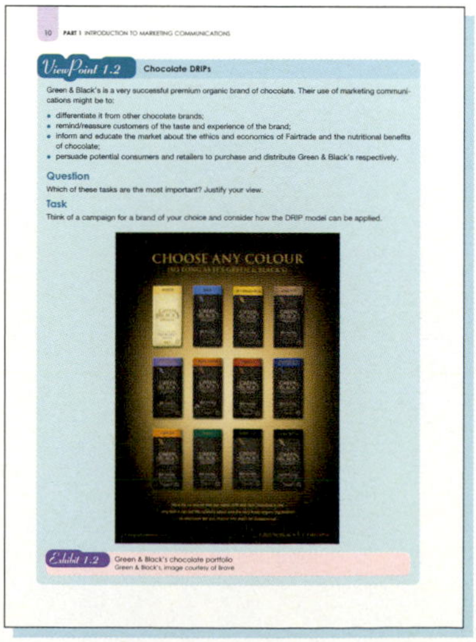

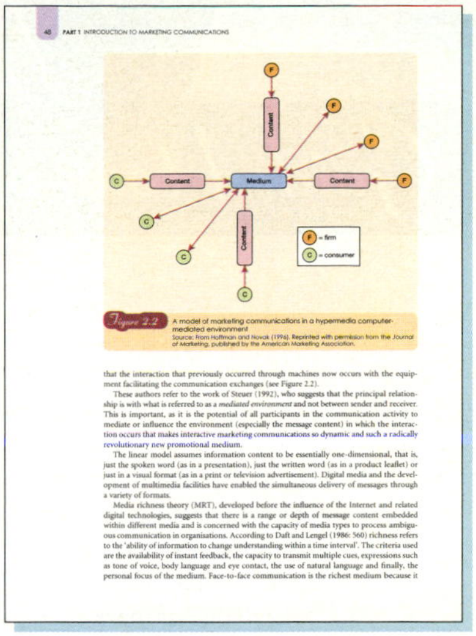

Figures and tables illustrate key points, concepts and processes visually to reinforce your learning.

Great **colour photography** from real, high-profile marketing campaigns is used throughout the book.

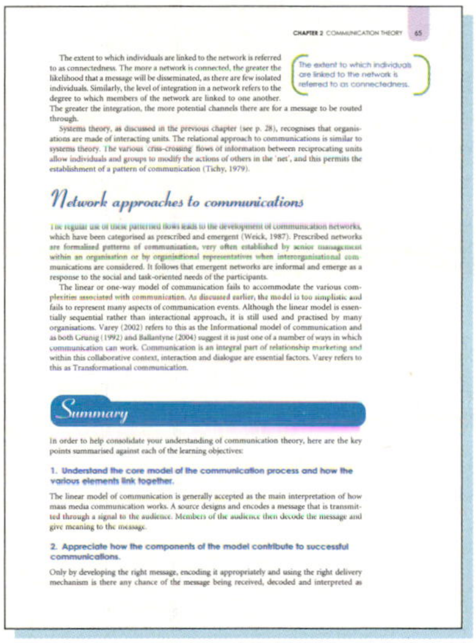

Margin notes help reinforce core concepts in the text body.

Summaries clinch the important concepts that have just been presented to reinforce the chapter.

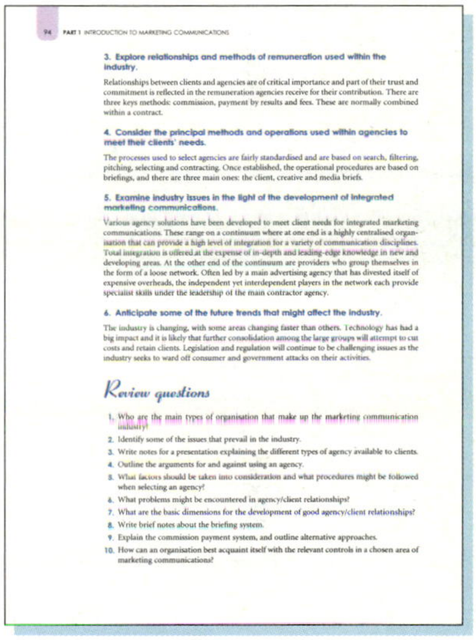

Every chapter ends with **Review questions** that test your understanding and help you to track your progress.

MiniCases encourage stimulating debates and class discussion.

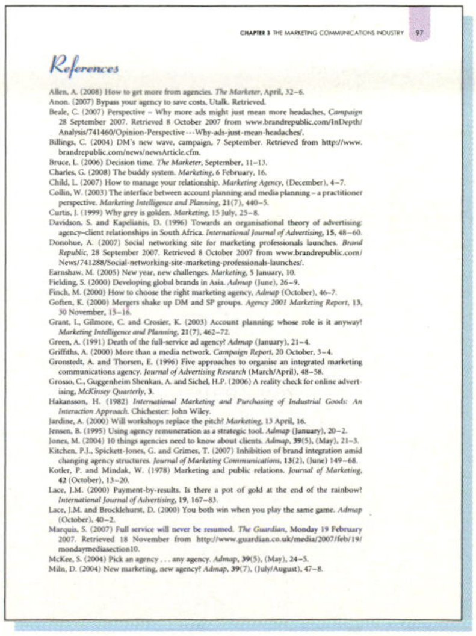

Each chapter is supported by a list of **References**, directing your independent study to both printed and electronic sources.

Guided tour of the web site

Visit the comprehensive web site **www.pearsoned.co.uk/fill** for a comprehensive collection of material to help you take your knowledge of marketing communications to a higher level. ▶

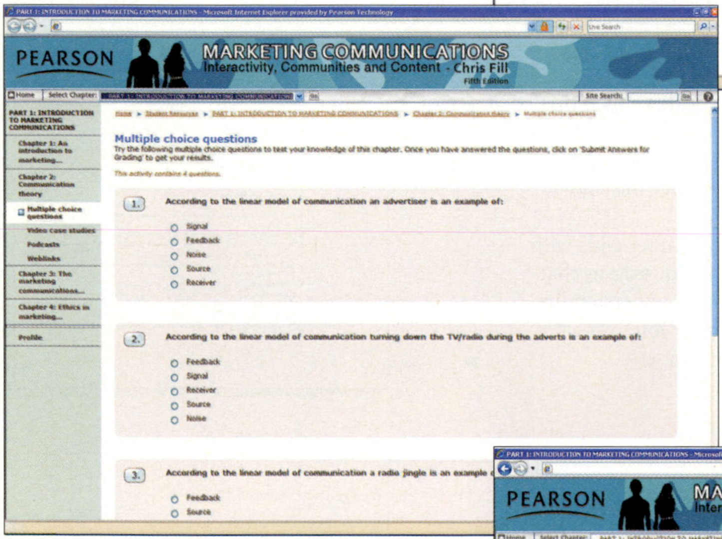

The **Multiple Choice Questions** will allow you to test your understanding. ◀

The **Video Case Studies** link in with the textbook and will provide provide visual examples of the marketing challenges that are constantly faced by businesses. ▶

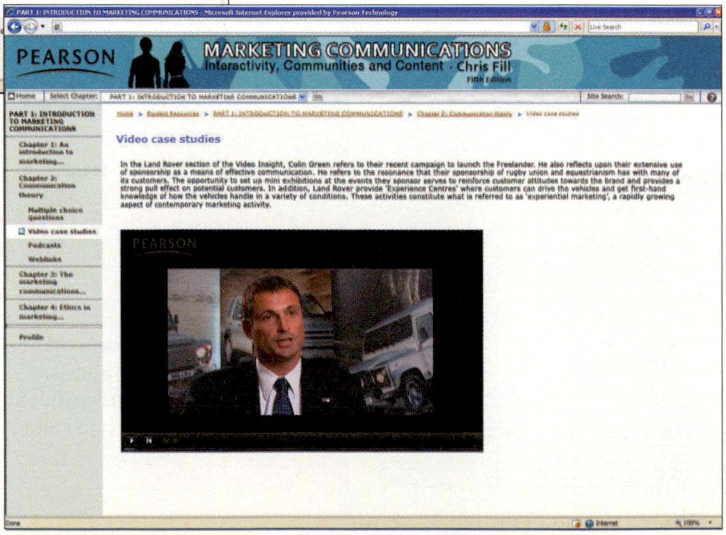

Preface

Thank you for reading the fifth edition of *Marketing Communications.* This book has been written to help you in three ways:

1. To understand and appreciate the variety of ways in which organisations use marketing communications
2. To identify and understand some of the key theories and concepts associated with marketing communications
3. To develop an insight into the reasoning behind the marketing communications activities used by organisations.

Marketing communications is a complex subject and draws on a variety of disciplines. This book has been written in the hope of disentangling some of the complexity so that you can enjoy the subject, be stimulated to want to know more and wish to engage further with the exciting and fast-changing world of marketing communications.

A world of marketing communications

All organisations, large and small, commercial, government, charities, educational and other not-for-profit organisations need to communicate with a range of stakeholders. This may be in order to get materials and services to undertake their business activities or to collaborate and coordinate with others to secure suitable distribution of their goods and services. In addition, there are consumers, you and me, people who are free to choose among the many hundreds and thousands of product offerings. Marketing communications provides a core activity so that all interested parties can understand the intentions of others and appreciate the value of the goods and services offered.

Traditionally, there are five main marketing communication tools: advertising, sales promotion, personal selling, public relations and direct marketing. In addition, there are media in which time and space can be bought or used to deliver messages to target audiences. For a long time the appropriate mix of these tools and the choice of media have been largely predictable. Distinct mixes could be identified for business-to-consumer (b2c) and business-to-business (b2b) audiences. There were variations reflecting particular brand circumstances, but essentially in the b2c market advertising was used to build brand values, sales promotions were used to encourage customer action and public relations sought to generate goodwill and interest in the company. Personal selling was regarded as the primary tool in b2b markets, but also had a role to play in retail environments, for example selling consumer durables. In the 1990s direct marketing became a more prominent tool in the mix because technology had enabled a form of communication by appealing personally and directly to the target customer. This change introduced new media formats and the subsequent development of the Internet and related digital technologies has accelerated change in the marketing communications industry. There are now a myriad of opportunities to reach audiences, with the Internet representing a new, yet challenging communication channel.

At the same time as the media world has splintered into many different parts so have the audiences with whom organisations need to communicate. Consumers now have a variety of different ways to spend their leisure time. Some of those who choose to incorporate the media as part of their relaxation now have not just three commercial television channels but nearly 200, all have access to an increasing number of general and specific interest magazines, a multitude of new cinema complexes and, of course, the Internet with an explosion of web sites offering a seemingly endless source of information, opportunities to buy online and a form of global entertainment and Web 2.0 offering an increasing range of social media opportunities. The world of marketing communications is bright, exciting, sometimes unpredictable, yet always challenging and evolving.

Managers are now not only required to find new ways to communicate, but are having to do so on reduced budgets and they must account for their communication spend. The development of long-term relationships with customers, whether in b2b or b2c markets, is now an essential aspect of marketing policy. Customer retention is crucial today and various devices, such as loyalty schemes, are used to shape long-term customer behaviour. Organisations now accept that the tools of the communication mix are not the only way brands communicate. All parts of the marketing mix communicate: the behaviour of employees and the performance of products, the actions of competitors all serve to influence the way in which each customer perceives a brand. Corporate branding is now recognised as an integral part of the overall communication effort. Corporate reputation and the actions undertaken by organisations are perceived not only in terms of brand values and profits but also in terms of their ethics and the impact organisations have on the environment.

Marketing communication agencies are trying to adjust the way they can best serve the interests of their clients. One of the results is structural realignment (mergers and takeovers) that can lead to consolidation. Clients themselves are fighting to generate superior value for their customers and to find new ways of establishing competitive advantage. Globalisation and the development of partnerships, alliances and networks all bear testimony to changing markets and expectations.

Where does this all lead? It leads to a new form and role for marketing communications and a vision that an organisation's entire marketing communications should be planned, coherent and consistent. This word consistency applies to internal policies and strategies, to messages to and from internal and external stakeholders, consistency with the values of their customers and with the relationships they forge with key suppliers and distributors.

This book introduces readers to this changing world of marketing communications and allows them to appreciate some of the conceptual underpinnings associated with marketing communications and associated aspects of integration. There are examples of the practical application of marketing communications and examples that demonstrate the application of theory in practice. This book does not just show how organisations use marketing communications, it also contains theoretical material to enable readers to understand why organisations use marketing communications in the ways they do.

Overview of the book

Despite the misuse and often laboured understanding of the terms, this book presents marketing communications from both a strategic and relational perspective. Marketing communications is a subject that can be presented in an overly simplistic and misleading way. This book recognises the complexity of the subject, considers the strategic, tactical and operational aspects and above all considers marketing communications from a contextual perspective, that is the way audiences frame and interpret marketing messages.

This book has been deliberately written from an academic perspective and seeks to provide a consistent appraisal of the ever-expanding world of marketing communications. The intention is to stimulate thought and consideration about a wide range of interrelated issues, and to help achieve this aim a number of theories and models are advanced. Some of these theories reflect marketing practice, while others are offered as suggestions for moving the subject forward. Many of the theories are abstractions of actual practice, some are based on empirical research and others are pure conceptualisation. All seek to enrich the subject, but not all need carry the same weight of contribution. Readers should form their own opinions based upon their reading, experience and judgement.

This book explores many topics and issues related to marketing communications. Of these, however, three stand out as representative of the whole text – engagement, interactivity and content. Effective marketing communications enables audiences to engage with products, services, brands and organisations. Relationships can develop through engagement and this enables customers, stakeholders and organisations to achieve their various goals. The degree to which engagement occurs can reflect audience perception, interpretation and the meaning of the messages delivered. Through engagement brand value and equity can be developed or reduced. Engagement, therefore, encompasses a range of marketing communication activities and is referred to throughout the text.

The second key issue concerns interactivity. Digital technology has enabled communication to advance substantially from being based primarily on the linear model, to embracing opportunities for all participants to respond and contribute to the communication process, often instantaneously. Interactivity is changing the way organisations choose to communicate with target audiences and is also changing the way audiences choose to interact with brands.

The third issue flows from the previous two. Consumers are now willing, motivated and able to contribute to marketing communications. Interactivity means that consumers are devising and delivering content through the messages they create. Referred to as user-generated-content, the increasing use of social networks and the volume of blogging, podcasting, viral and word-of-mouth communications for example, all bear witness to the changing importance of messages and communications content.

Marketing communications has traditionally been centred on the mix of tools. However, the expanding range of digital media, the development of interactivity, and the growing significance and changing source of messages and content have become an increasingly central aspect of marketing communications. The marketing communication mix has evolved to the point that it can be said to consist of three main elements: tools, media and messages. These issues are explored in the opening chapter.

In addition to these issues there are two overriding themes running through the text: relationship marketing and integrated communications. I am of the view that in the future organisations will perceive communications as a core strategic activity, central to strategic management and marketing thought. Corporate and marketing communications will inevitably merge and integrate, the need to build and sustain relationships with a variety of stakeholders both inside and outside the organisation will become paramount, and communications will be a vital source in making it all work. Witness the branding developments at the grocery giants Procter & Gamble and Unilever to understand this point. In this light, this text assumes relationship marketing to be essential and sees communication in the context of both transactional and relational exchanges.

The structure of the book has been revised from the previous edition. It is now in six parts with a new part devoted to the media. Here information about traditional and digital media is included plus a new chapter on interactive marketing communications. All chapters have been updated, new case studies included and the examples reflect contemporary practice.

For readers familiar with previous editions, the chapter concerning 'Stakeholders: supply chains and interorganisational relationships' has been removed from the text, in an attempt to create space for new material. I appreciate that some found this chapter particularly helpful and it was popular with several tutors. However, in an attempt to contain the size of the book this particular chapter has been removed from the physical hard copy, although it has been updated and made available on the web site that accompanies this book.

Structure of the text

There are six main parts to the book:

Part 1 introduces readers to the subject from a general perspective and then seeks to establish some of the key issues that are necessary in order to provide a foundation for the subject. These include communication theory, the structure and dynamics of the marketing communications industry and the means by which the industry serves its audiences. In addition, consideration is given to the way in which organisations behave and communicate their ethical, moral and environmental credentials. Legislation and voluntary controls provide the context within which organisations function with varying degrees of responsibility.

Part 2 considers the way in which marketing communications might work, commencing with two chapters on the important aspects of buyer behaviour and customer decision-making. These are followed by Chapter 7, which reviews relationship marketing concepts, and Chapter 8, which considers some of the ways in which marketing communications is thought to work.

Part 3 explores some of the managerial aspects associated with marketing communications. The core content concerns the various aspects of *strategy* and how organisations should develop their marketing communications in the light of their contextual positions. This part explores the concept of integrated marketing communications and moves on to examine strategy and planning concepts, objectives and positioning, product and corporate branding, financial and budgeting issues and the methods and issues associated with the evaluation and measurement of marketing communications.

Part 4 examines the individual disciplines or tools of marketing communications and the ways in which these can be applied in order to communicate and engage with target audiences. Attention is given to advertising, sales promotion, public relations, sponsorship, direct marketing and personal selling. The part concludes with an exploration of a range of other activities including exhibitions, product placement, packaging and field marketing.

Part 5 is new and has been written to help readers understand and focus on the variety and increasing importance of the media. There are four chapters that move through traditional and digital media, interactive marketing communications and media planning.

Part 6 examines marketing communications in the context of three specific audiences. In particular, consideration is given to international dimensions, business-to-business communications and the hugely important area of internal communications related to employee-based audiences.

Part 1: Introduction to marketing communications

This opening part serves to establish the scope of the book and provides a brief overview of the content and style adopted throughout the rest of the text. Chapter 1 provides an introductory perspective to marketing communications and sets out some important, key concepts. It provides an insight into how the configuration of the marketing communication mix has effectively changed over the last 10 years. Chapter 2 addresses issues concerning communication theory and in particular moves on from the simple linear interpretation of how communication works to one that recognises the influence of people, behaviour and interactional elements on the communication process. Chapter 3 is concerned with the nature and characteristics of the UK marketing communications industry and specifically examines the strategic and operational issues of advertising agencies and their interaction with client organisations. The content of Chapter 4 follows on directly from the previous chapter and examines some of the ethical and social issues for which organisations have responsibility in terms of what they say and how they say it.

Part 2: Understanding how marketing communications works

This part considers not only how marketing communications works but also explores some of the key contextual issues that influence the nature and form of marketing communications.

Chapters 5 and 6 consider the important aspects of buyer behaviour, upon which marketing communications should be developed. Only by understanding the market and the target audience can appropriate objectives, strategies, promotional methods, applications and resources be determined, allocated and implemented.

Chapter 7 considers ideas about relationship marketing and associated factors concerning the fundamental basis upon which marketing and marketing communications is now considered by many to work.

Chapter 8 discusses various approaches to understanding how marketing communications works. Although some of these ideas are borrowed from the world of advertising, the key notion is that effective marketing communications develops by establishing a level of engagement and delivering messages that provide significant value.

Part 3: Managing marketing communications

Part 3 of the book opens with Chapter 9. This chapter challenges ideas about the nature and validity of the 'integrated' view of marketing communications. This is a core chapter because it bridges the contextual elements and the application of the various disciplines. The notion that integrated marketing communications (IMC) is a valid and realistic concept is explored and readers are encouraged to consider the arguments for and against this approach.

Chapter 10 is concerned with the nature of communication strategy and considers the interrelationship between strategy and planning. The second section of the chapter introduces the marketing communications planning framework and works through the model highlighting issues and linkages and ends with an operational approach to devising, formulating and implementing a strategic marketing communications plan. The mini case at the end of this chapter is designed for readers to develop their planning skills.

Chapter 11 examines the nature of objectives and positioning in marketing communications and is followed by a chapter on branding. This chapter is significant in that it focuses on the role marketing communications can play in the development and maintenance of brands. The branding and positioning connection is significant, which is why these strategically significant elements are located next to each other.

Chapter 13 develops the branding theme and considers corporate identity, branding and reputational issues. The focus is again on the role of marketing, or rather corporate, communications in the identity and branding process rather than pure identity work alone. These elements are interrelated but it is intended to help readers recognise how communications can be a pivotal aspect of brand and corporate development.

Chapter 14 considers various budgeting approaches and issues concerning brand equity. Part 3 concludes with a chapter that examines the ways in which the performance of marketing communication activities can be evaluated. In effect these two chapters consider how much should be invested in the engagement process and how the engagement process should be measured.

Part 4: The tools of marketing communications

This part looks at the individual marketing communication disciplines that are available to organisations to communicate with their external and internal audiences.

There are eight chapters in this section with the first two considering advertising strategy and advertising messages. The first, Chapter 16, considers different advertising strategies and is developed out of Chapter 8, which considers how marketing communications might work. The chapter traces the development of advertising strategies and ends by considering some contemporary approaches. The following chapter builds on this base material and considers the importance of advertising messages and the different ways messages can be developed to achieve different goals. Chapter 18 considers the principles and techniques of sales promotion, and the subsequent chapters explore public relations, sponsorship, direct marketing and personal selling. Part 4 closes with a view of exhibitions, product placement, packaging and field marketing.

Part 5: The media

This new section brings together various chapters about the media and includes a new chapter on interactive marketing communications.

Chapter 24 considers traditional media, an important foundation upon which to consider the attributes of digital media, the subject of Chapter 25. This chapter commences with a consideration of the features of digitalisation and then explores the application and benefits that digital media offer marketing communications, including a section on web site design from a marketing perspective.

Chapter 26 examines interactive marketing communications. The first section considers interactivity in the context of each of the tools but then specifically examines search marketing and Web 2.0 applications.

Chapter 27 considers ideas and theories associated with media planning and the way in which people use media.

Part 6: Marketing communications for special audiences

This part of the book considers issues associated with marketing communications and special audiences. The audiences are themselves not so much special but display characteristics that deserve special attention. The first of these is the international audience and the issues arising when using marketing communications across two or more countries. The following chapter examines business-to-business marketing communications. Reference to both business-to-consumer (b2c) and business-to-business (b2b) are made throughout the book but here particular attention is paid to the special contextual conditions that arise through inter-organisational communications.

The final chapter considers the role of marketing communications within organisations where the employees are the target audience. Increasingly recognised as a key part of a brand, the importance of engaging with employees and using them as a means of engaging with external audiences is actively considered. This chapter should be read in conjunction with Chapter 13 that considers corporate branding and reputational issues.

Design features and presentation

In addition to the six-part structure of the book, there are a number of features that are intended to help readers navigate the material.

Chapter objectives

Each chapter opens with both the aims of what is to be covered and a list of learning objectives. This helps to signal the primary topics that are covered in the chapter and so guide the learning experience.

Navigation

Important key text is extracted and presented in the margin. This helps readers to locate relevant material quickly and highlight key issues. In addition, to assist readers through the various chapters, the left-hand page is used to identify the page number and in which part of the text it is located. To complement this, the right-hand page is used to flag the page number and the chapter title.

Visual supports

This book is produced in four colours and throughout the text there are numerous colour and black and white exhibits; figures (diagrams) and tables of information throughout the text serve to highlight, illustrate and bring life to the written word. The pictures used serve either to illustrate particular points by demonstrating theory in practice or they are used to complement individual examples. The examples are normally highlighted in the text as ViewPoints. These examples are easily distinguishable through the colour contrasts and serve to demonstrate how a particular aspect of marketing communications has been used by an organisation in a particular context. I hope you enjoy these ViewPoints of organisational practice.

Summaries and MiniCases

At the end of each chapter is a summary and a series of review and discussion questions. The chapter summaries are presented in the order of the learning objectives listed at the beginning of each chapter.

Readers are advised to test their own understanding of the content of each chapter by considering some or all of the discussion questions. In this sense the questions support self-study but tutors might wish to use some of these as part of a seminar or workshop programme. At the end of each chapter is a mini case study. Most of these have been written by marketing academics from a variety of universities and colleges and some have been written by leading marketing practitioners. These short cases can be used in class for discussion purposes and to explore some of the salient issues raised in the chapter. Students working alone can use the mini case to test their own understanding and they can use the questions that follow each mini case to consolidate their understanding.

Web support

Students and lecturers who adopt this text have a range of support materials and facilities to help them. Readers are invited to use the web site designed for *Marketing Communications*, not only as a source of additional material but also as an interactive forum to explore and discuss marketing communications issues, academic and practitioner developments and to improve learning. The site accommodates the needs of student readers and lecturers.

Student resources

- Additional learning materials including new chapters, adverts, podcasts
- Student forum for feedback, participation and networking
- Annotated weblinks
- Full online glossary
- Multiple choice questions
- Video cases from the start of each part
- Additional cases and examples
- Ask the author

Lecturer resources

- Instructor's guide
- PowerPoint slides for each chapter
- Additional case studies
- Full versions of video cases, on DVD.

There are various text files available for download, including answers to the case study in Chapter 10. A test bank of multiple-choice questions has also been developed for use by students and lecturers. In addition, there are hyperlinks to a range of related sites, an online glossary and chapters from previous editions that some readers have requested be made available.

This web site also enables readers to interact with their peers. This can be through discussion boards, posting articles and favourite ads, asking questions and making comments about academic and practical issues associated with marketing communications. The intention is that students make this their own marketing communications site. The site also includes a facility to 'ask the author' a question.

For lecturers and tutors not only is there an Instructor's Guide containing a range of teaching schemes, slides and exercises in downloadable format but there is also a password-protected section of the companion web site for their use. From this site a much larger range of PowerPoint slides, teaching schemes and case material can be downloaded.

Acknowledgements

This book could not have been written without the support of a wide range of brilliant people. Contributions range from those who provided information and permissions, those who wrote MiniCases, answered questions and those who tolerated my persistent nagging, sending through photographs, answering phone calls and emails and those who simply liaised with others. Finally, there are those who have read, reviewed drafts, made constructive comments and provided moral support and encouragement.

The list of individuals and organisations involved with this book is extensive. My thanks are offered to all of you. I have tried to list everyone but if anyone has been omitted then I offer my apologies.

MiniCase contributors

Many new contributors agreed to write a case study for this edition. To those established contributors and those new to this edition may I express my gratitude for the time and energy you gave to write your MiniCase.

David Bennison – Manchester Metropolitan University Business School
Peter Betts – University of Central Lancashire
Jim Blythe – Visiting Professor Plymouth University
Jill Brown – University of Portsmouth
Angela Carroll – Leeds University
Richard Christy – University of Portsmouth
Sofia Daskou – Hellenic American University
Janine Dermody – University of Gloucestershire
Tony Garry – DeMontfort University
Richard Godfrey – Aberystwyth University
Angela Hall – Manchester Metropolitan University
Simon Hardaker – Former Group Head of Internal Communication at Rolls-Royce
Mary Hedderman – University College Newport
Graham Hughes – Leeds Business School
Matt King – Media Safari
Poonam V. Kumar – TNS Asia Pacific & Middle East
Katy Lahiffe – DeMontfort University
Dominic Medway – Manchester Business School
Jeremy Miles – Silverdell
Mike Molesworth – Bournemouth University
Clive Nancarrow – Bristol Business School
Prasad Narasimhan – TVS Motor Company India
Nicola Robinsonova – Freelance Marketing Consultant
Yamin Sekhon – Bournemouth University
J. Graham Spickett-Jones – University of Hull
Stefan Schwarzkopf – Queen Mary College, University of London
Lorna Stevens – University of Ulster

David Stringer – Business Development Director
Lynn Sudbury – Liverpool John Moores University
Andrew Turnbull – Robert Gordon University
Gary Warnaby – University of Liverpool Management School
Peter Zissou – Marketing Manager Nestlé Hellas Ice cream SA

In addition I should like to acknowledge the contribution made by Kelly Page for writing the numerous online cases available at the book's website.

Other acknowledgements

Derek Adam-Smith – University of Portsmouth
Bruce Bowhill – University of Portsmouth
Richard Christy – University of Portsmouth
Nigel Markwick – Wolff Olins
Gordon Oliver – Horndean
Henry Lewis – Former postgraduate student of the University of Portsmouth
Debra Weatherley – FindPhoto

Above all perhaps are the various individuals at Pearson and their associates who have taken my manuscript, managed it and published it in this form. In particular I should like to thank David Cox for his enthusiasm, ideas, support and ability to get things done. In support has been Andrew Harrison and more recently Emma Violet who have both demonstrated a positive approach and have accommodated my predilection to circumnavigate procedures, or 'bend the rules'. In addition I should like to thank Mary Lince, Kelly Miller and Kay Holman for transforming the manuscript into the final product. Thank you all.

The biggest thank you is for my wife Karen. This book was not written overnight, yet Karen has supported me through the extended writing process. We have just celebrated our Pearl wedding anniversary and I should like to take this opportunity to express my love and thanks for the past 30 plus years that we have been together and she has put up with me.

Publisher's acknowledgements

We are grateful to the following for permission to reproduce copyright material:

Figures 1.1 and 1.5 from Redefining the nature and format of the marketing communications mix, *The Marketing Review*, 7, 1, reproduced by permission of Westburn Publishers Ltd. (Hughes, G. and Fill, C. 2007); Table 1.1 from *Marketing Communications, 3rd edn.*, Pearson Education Ltd. (Fill, C. 2002); Table 1.4 from *Marketing*, by permission of Oxford University Press (Baines, P. *et al.* 2008); Figure 2.2 from Marketing in hyper computer-mediated environments: conceptual foundations, *Journal of Marketing*, 60, July, American Marketing Association (Hoffman, D.L. and Novak, P.T. 1996); Table 2.2 reprinted from *Journal of Business Research*, Vol. 32, No. 3, March, P.F. Bone, Word-of-mouth effects on short-term and long-term product judgments, pp. 213–23, Copyright 1995, with permission from Elsevier (Bone, P.F. 1995); Table 2.3 derived from G.J. Johnson, C.G. Bruner II, and A. Kumar, Interactivity and its facets revisited, *Journal of Advertising* 35 (4) (Winter 2006): 35–52. Adapted with permission from M.E. Sharpe, Inc. (Johnson, G.J. *et al.* 2006); Table 2.4 reproduced with permission of Sage Publications, Inc. Books, from Communication in interpersonal relationships: social penetration theory by D. Taylor and I. Altman in *Interpersonal*

Processes: New Directions in Communication Research edited by M.E. Roloff and G.R. Miller, 1987; permission conveyed through Copyright Clearance Center, Inc. (Taylor, D. and Altman, I. 1987); Figure 2.6 from *Diffusion of Innovations, 3rd edn.*, reprinted with the permission of The Free Press, a Division of Simon & Schuster, Inc. (Rogers, E.M. 1983); Figure 2.7 from *Consumer Behaviour: Implications for Marketing Strategy, 4th edn.*, © 1989, pub. Richard D. Irwin, reproduced with permission of The McGraw-Hill Companies (Hawkins, D. *et al.* 1989); Table 3.1 from *Advertising Statistics Yearbook*, reproduced with permission from World Advertising Research Center, www.warc.com (Advertising Association 2007); Table 3.2 adapted from Marriage material, *The Marketer*, September, pp. 22–23, published by The Chartered Institute of Marketing (Sclater, I. 2006); Figure 3.3 from Marketing and public relations, *Journal of Marketing*, 42, October, American Marketing Association (Kotler, P. and Mindak, W. 1978); Figure 3.5 from Five approaches to organize an integrated marketing communications agency, *Journal of Advertising Research*, March/April, reproduced with permission from World Advertising Research Center, www.warc.com (Gronstedt, A. and Thorsen, E. 1996); Figure 5.7 adapted from *Understanding Attitudes and Predicting Social Behaviour, 1st*, © 1980. Electronically reproduced by permission of Pearson Education, Inc., Upper Saddle River, New Jersey (Ajzen, I. and Fishbein, M. 1980); Figure 6.2 adapted from A preliminary investigation into pre- and post-purchase risk perception and reduction, *European Journal of Marketing*, Vol. 28, Issue 1, pp. 56–71, © Emerald Group Publishing Limited, all rights reserved (Mitchell, V.-W. and Boustani, P. 1994); Figures 6.8 and 6.9 reproduced by permission of TNS; Figure 7.1 with kind permission from Springer Science+Business Media, *Journal of the Academy of Marketing Science*, Managing market relationships, Vol. 28, No. 1, 2000, pp. 24–30, G.S. Day, Copyright © 2000, Springer Netherlands (Day, G.S. 2000); Table 7.1 reprinted from *Business Horizons*, 45, 6, November-December, S.M. Wagner and R. Boutellier, Capabilities for managing a portfolio of supplier relationships, pp. 79–88, Copyright 2002, with permission from Elsevier (Wagner, S.M. and Boutellier, R. 2002); Figure 7.3 from *Perceived quality of business relationships*, Hanken – Swedish School of Economics and Business Administration (Holmlund, M. 1997); Figures 7.4 and 29.1 from The commitment-trust theory of relationship marketing, *Journal of Marketing*, 58, July, American Marketing Association (Morgan, M. and Hunt, S.D. 1994); Table 7.5 from The social function of trust and implications of e-commerce, *International Journal of Advertising*, 19, World Advertising Research Center (Morrison, D.E. and Firmstone, J. 2000); Figure 8.1 used with permission of Association for Consumer Research, from Attitude toward the ad as a mediator of advertising effectiveness: determinants and consequences, *Advances in Consumer Research* edited by R.P. Bagozzi and A.M. Tybout, 1983; permission conveyed through Copyright Clearance Center, Inc. (Lutz, R.J. *et al.* 1983); Table 8.3 from Dialogue and its role in the development of relationship specific knowledge, *Journal of Business and Industrial Marketing*, Vol. 19, No. 2, pp. 114–23, © Emerald Group Publishing Limited, all rights reserved (Ballantyne, D. 2004); Table 8.4 reprinted from *Public Relations Review*, 28 (1), February, M.L. Kent and M. Taylor, Toward a dialogic theory of public relations, pp. 21–37, Copyright 2002, with permission from Elsevier (Kent, M.L. and Taylor, M. 2002); Figure 9.2 from Revisiting the IMC Construct: a revised definition and four pillars, *International Journal of Advertising*, 27, 1, reproduced with permission from World Advertising Research Center, www.warc.com (Kliatchko, J. 2008); Table 9.3 adapted from *Open Planning: media neutral planning made simple* from www.openplanning.org/cases/openplanning/whitepaper.pdf, reprinted by permission of the authors (Jenkinson, A. and Sain, B. 2004); Table 9.4 derived from M. Reid. Performance auditing of integrated marketing communication (IMC) actions and outcomes, *Journal of Advertising* 34 (4) (Winter 2005): 41–54. Adapted with permission from M.E. Sharpe, Inc. (Reid, M. 2005); Table 10.3 from Benefit segmentation: A decision-oriented research tool, *Journal of Marketing*, 32, July, American Marketing Association (Haley, R.I. 1968); Table 10.6 reprinted from *Journal of Retailing and Consumer Services*, Vol. 15, No. 3, May, J.W.J. Weltevreden and R.A. Boschma, Internet strategies and performance of Dutch retailers, pp. 163–78, Copyright 2008, with permission from Elsevier (Weltevreden, J.W.J. and Boschma, R.A. 2008); Figure 12.1 from *The New Strategic*

Brand Management, Kogan Page Ltd. (Kapferer, J.-N. 2004); Table 12.1 adapted from *The New Strategic Brand Management*, Kogan Page Ltd. (Kapferer, J.-N. 2004); Figure 12.4 and Table 12.5 adapted from *Brand Management: A Theoretical and Practical Approach*, Pearson Education Ltd. (Riezebos, R. 2003); Table 12.4 from A practical framework for developing brand portfolios, *Admap*, July/August, reproduced with permission from World Advertising Research Center, www.warc.com (Walton, P. 2007); Figures 12.7 and 12.8 from Measurement and tracking of brand equity in the global marketplace – The PepsiCo experience, *International Marketing Review*, Vol. 18, No. 1, pp. 91–96, © Emerald Group Publishing Limited, all rights reserved (Kish, P. *et al.* 2001); Figure 12.9 from *ICAP Sector Study on Ice-Cream 2007*, Sector Study – ICAP Group S.A. (ICAP 2007); Figure 13.1 adapted from A new approach to the corporate image management process, *Journal of Marketing Management*, 5, 1, reproduced by permission of Westburn Publishers Ltd. (Shee, P.S.B. and Abratt, R. 1989); Table 13.3 adapted from The three virtues and seven deadly sins of corporate brand management, *Journal of General Management*, 27, 1, Braybrooke Press Ltd. (Balmer, J.M.T. 2001); Figure 13.6 from *Corporate image as an aid to strategic development*, unpublished MBA project, University of Portsmouth, reprinted by permission of the author (Markwick, N. 1993); Figures 14.2 and 14.3 from Ad spending: growing market share, *Harvard Business Review*, January/February, reprinted by permission of Harvard Business Review (Schroer, J. 1990); Table 14.3 from How to set digital media budgets, WARC Exclusive, retrieved 20 March 2008 from www.warc.com, reproduced with permission from World Advertising Research Center (Renshaw, M. 2008); Figure 14.4 from Ad spending: maintaining market share, *Harvard Business Review*, January/February, reprinted by permission of Harvard Business Review (Jones, J.P. 1990); Figures 14.5 and 14.6 from Managing advertising as an investment, *Admap*, 39, 7, July/August, reproduced with permission from World Advertising Research Center, www.warc.com (Farr, A. 2004); Figure 14.7 from www.PIMS-Europe.com, reprinted by permission of PIMS Associates (PIMS 2000); Figure 15.1 from Case Study: pre-testing mould-breaking ads, *Admap*, July/August, reproduced with permission from World Advertising Research Center, www.warc.com (Burden, S. 2007); Table 15.1 from Conceptualization and measurement of multidimensionality of integrated marketing communications, *Journal of Advertising Research*, September, reproduced with permission from World Advertising Research Center, www.warc.com (Lee, D.H. and Park, C.W. 2007); Table 15.7 adapted from The world wide web as an advertising medium: toward an understanding of conversion efficiency, *Journal of Advertising Research*, 6, 1, January/February, reproduced with permission from World Advertising Research Center, www.warc.com (Berthon, P. *et al.* 1996); Figure 16.1 from Does it pay to shock? Reactions to shocking and non-shocking advertising content among university students, *Journal of Advertising Research*, 43, 3, September, reproduced with permission from World Advertising Research Center, www.warc.com (Dahl, D.W. *et al.* 2003); Figure 16.3 adapted from An all-embracing theory of how advertising works?, *Admap*, February, reproduced with kind permission of Admap/WARC (Prue, T. 1998); Figure 16.4 from How advertising works: a planning model, *Journal of Advertising Research*, October, reproduced with permission from World Advertising Research Center, www.warc.com (Vaughn, R. 1980); Figures 16.5, 17.3, 17.4, 17.5 and 17.6 adapted from *Advertising Communications & Promotion Management, 2nd edn.*, pub. McGraw-Hill, reprinted by permission of John R. Rossiter (Rossiter, J.R. and Percy, L. 1997); Figure 17.1 from Message framing strategy for brand communication, *Journal of Advertising Research*, 47, 3, September, reproduced with permission from World Advertising Research Center, www.warc.com (Tsai, S.-P. 2007); Table 18.1 this article was published in *The Marketing Book, 3rd edn.* by M.J. Baker (ed.), S. Peattie and K.J. Peattie, Sales promotion, Copyright Elsevier 1994 (Peattie, S. and Peattie, K.J. 1994); Table 18.4 adapted from Loyalty trends for the 21st century, *Journal of Targeting Measurement and Analysis for Marketing*, Vol. 12, No. 3, Henry Stewart Publications (Capizzi, M. *et al.* 2004); Figure 18.5 from G. Hallberg, Is your loyalty programme really building loyalty? Why increasing emotional attachment, not just repeat buying, is key to maximizing programme success, *Journal of Targeting, Measurement and Analysis for Marketing*, 12 (3), Copyright © 2004,

Macmillan Publishers Ltd., reproduced with permission of Palgrave Macmillan (Hallberg, G. 2004); Figure 19.1 from *Managing Public Relations*, pub. Holt, Rinehart & Winston, reprinted by permission of James E. Grunig (Grunig, J. and Hunt, T. 1984); Table 19.1 from Toward public relations theory-based study of public diplomacy: Testing the applicability of the excellence study, *Journal of Public Relations Research*, Vol. 18, No. 4, reprinted by permission of Taylor & Francis Ltd., http://www.tandf.co.uk/journals (Yun, S.-H. 2006); Figure 19.5 reproduced with permission of Academy of Management (NY), from From crisis prone to crisis prepared: a framework for crisis management by C.M. Pearson and I. Mitroff, *Academy of Management Executive*, 7, 1, 1993; permission conveyed through Copyright Clearance Center, Inc. (Pearson, C.M. and Mitroff, I. 1993); Table 19.5 reprinted from *Public Relations Review*, 23, Summer, W.L. Benoit, Image repair discourse and crisis communication, pp. 177–86, Copyright 1997, with permission from Elsevier (Benoit, W.L. 1997); Figure 20.1 from A new framework for evaluating sponsorship opportunities, *International Journal of Advertising*, 25, 4, reproduced with permission from World Advertising Research Center, www.warc.com (Poon, D.T.Y. and Prendergast, G. 2006); Table 20.3 reprinted from *Industrial Marketing Management*, Vol. 35, No. 8, November, F. Farrelly, P. Quester and R. Burton, Changes in sponsorship value: Competencies and capabilities of successful sponsorship relationships, pp. 1016–26, Copyright 2006, with permission from Elsevier (Farrelly, F. *et al.* 2006); Table 21.4 adapted from *Permissions Marketing: Turning Strangers into Friends, and Friends into Customers*, reprinted with the permission of The Free Press, a Division of Simon & Schuster, Inc. (Godin, S. 2007); Figures 22.3 and 22.4 adapted from *Sales Management: Decisions, Strategies and Cases, 5th edn.*, Pearson Education, Inc. (Still, R. *et al.* 1988); Table 22.3 adapted from Marketing, business process and shareholder value: an organizationally embedded view of marketing activities and the discipline of marketing, *Journal of Marketing*, 63, American Marketing Association (Srivastava, R.K. *et al.* 1999); Figure 22.5 from Examining the antecedents of sales organization effectiveness: an Australian study, *European Journal of Marketing*, 33, 9/10, reprinted by permission of MCB University Press Ltd. (Grant, K. and Cravens, D.W. 1999); Table 22.5 adapted from Infusing technology into personal selling, *Journal of Personal Selling and Sales Management*, 22, 3, Summer, Copyright PSE National Educational Foundation, used by permission of M.E. Sharpe, Inc. (Widmier, S.M. *et al.* 2002); Figures 22.9 and 22.10 from *Sales Force Management, 3rd edn.*, © 1990, pub. Irwin, reproduced with permission of The McGraw-Hill Companies (Churchill, G.A. *et al.* 1990); Figure 23.1 from Branded entertainment: A new advertising technique or product placement in disguise?, *Journal of Marketing Management*, 22, 5–6, reproduced by permission of Westburn Publishers Ltd. (Hudson, S. and Hudson, D. 2006); Table 23.2 adapted from Fighting for a new view of field work, *Marketing*, 9 March, reproduced from *Marketing* magazine with the permission of the copyright owner, Haymarket Business Publications Limited (McLuhan, R. 2000); Table 23.3 from Which way forward?, *Marketing*, 13 December, reproduced from *Marketing* magazine with the permission of the copyright owner, Haymarket Business Publications Limited (Bashford, S. 2007); Table 24.2 from *Advertising Statistics Yearbook*, World Advertising Research Center (Advertising Association 2003); Figure 25.1 from The impact of information technology deployment on trust, commitment and value creation in business relationships, *Journal of Business and Industrial Marketing*, Vol. 19, No. 3, pp. 197–207, © Emerald Group Publishing Limited, all rights reserved (Ryssel, R. *et al.* 2004); Table 25.1 adapted from *The Experience Economy: Work is theatre and every business is a stage*, reprinted by permission of Harvard Business School Press (Pine, J. and Gilmore, J. 1999); Table 25.3 from Web site characteristics and business performance: some evidence from international business-to-business organizations, *Marketing Intelligence and Planning*, Vol. 21, No. 2, pp. 105–14, © Emerald Group Publishing Limited, all rights reserved (Karayanni, D.A. and Baltas, G.A. 2003); Figure 26.1 from Internet community bonding: the case of macnews.de, *European Journal of Marketing*, Vol. 38, 5/6, pp. 626–40, © Emerald Group Publishing Limited, all rights reserved (Szmigin, I. and Reppel, A.E. 2004); Table 26.1 from Advertising on the web: is there response before click-through?, *Journal of Advertising Research*, March/April, reproduced with permission from World Advertising Research Center, www.warc.com (Briggs, R. and Hollis, N. 1997); Figure 26.2 reprinted from *European Management Journal*, Vol. 17, No. 3, June, R.V. Kozinets, E-tribalized marketing?: the strategic implications of virtual communities of consumption, pp. 252–64, Copyright 1999, with permission from Elsevier (Kozinets, R.V. 1999); Table 27.2 adapted from Putting the 'Group' back into group support systems: some theoretical issues about dynamic processes in groups with technological enhancements, *Group Support Systems: New Perspectives* edited by L.M. Jessup and J.S. Valacich, reprinted by permission of W.H. Freeman and Company/Worth Publishers (McGrath, J.E. and Hollingshead, A.B. 1993); Table 27.5 from Regency planning, *Admap*, February, www.admapmagazine.com, World Advertising Research Center (Ephron, E. 1997); Table 27.6 reproduced from an article by C. Beale in the 28 November 1997 edition of *Campaign* magazine with the permission of the copyright owner, Haymarket Business Publications (Beale, C. 1997); Table 27.7 from Media consumption and consumer purchasing, © Copyright 2006 by ESOMAR® - The World Association of Research Professionals. This paper first appeared in *Worldwide Multi-Media Measurement (WM3)*, Shanghai, June 2006, published by ESOMAR (Shultz, D. E. *et al.* 2006); Table 29.2 and Figure 29.3 reprinted from *Industrial Marketing Management*, Vol. 26, No. 1, January, D.I. Gilliland and W.J. Johnston, Toward a model of business-to-business marketing communications effects, pp. 15–29, Copyright 1997, with permission from Elsevier (Gilliland, D.I. and Johnston, W.J. 1997); Table 29.3, Figures 29.4 and 29.5 from Communication strategies in marketing channels, *Journal of Marketing*, October, American Marketing Association (Mohr, J. and Nevin, J.R. 1990); Table 29.5 updated from From key account selling to key account management, *Journal of Marketing Practice: Applied Marketing Science*, 1 (1), reprinted by permission of Emerald Group Publishing Ltd. (Millman, T. and Wilson, K. 1995); Figure 30.1 and Table 30.2 from Rethinking internal communication: a stakeholder approach, *Corporate Communications: An International Journal*, Vol. 12, No. 2, pp. 177–98, © Emerald Group Publishing Limited, all rights reserved (Welch, M. and Jackson, P.R. 2007); Figure 30.3 reprinted with permission from Advertising's internal audience, *Journal of Marketing*, published by the American Marketing Association, M.C. Gilly and M. Wolfinbarger, Vol. 62, January 1998, pp. 69–88 (Gilly, M.C. and Wolfinbarger, M. 1998); Table 30.3, this article was published in *Research in Organizational Behavior*, Vol. 7, L.L. Cummings and B.M. Staw (eds), S. Albert and D.A. Whetten, Organisational identity, pp. 263–95, Copyright Elsevier 1985 (Albert, S. and Whetten, D.A. 1985); Figure 30.5 from *The Corporate Image: Strategies for Effective Identity Programme, rev. edn.*, pub Kogan Page Ltd., reprinted by permission of the author (Ind, N. 1992).

Viewpoint 4.2 reproduced by permission of Advertising Standards Authority, www.asa.org.uk; Viewpoint 12.3 reproduced by permission of Procter and Gamble UK.

Exhibits

(Key: b-bottom; c-centre; l-left; r-right; t-top)
Exhibit 1.1 The London Eye; Exhibit 1.2 Green & Black's, image courtesy of Brave; Exhibit 1.3 Tim Cuff/Alamy; Exhibit 1.4 Pepsi Co; Exhibits 2.1, 4.3, 5.1, 5.2, 5.3, 8.5, 8.6, 11.5, 12.5, 15.3, 17.1, 20.1, 28.1 and 28.2 courtesy of The Advertising Archives; Exhibit 2.2 Aga, www.aga-web.co.uk; Exhibits 2.3 and 8.3 reproduced with the kind permission of Ronseal Ltd.; Exhibit 2.4 StrawberryFrog and Onitsuka Tiger; Exhibit 4.1 Pictorial Press Ltd/Alamy; Exhibit 4.2 Brand X/Corbis; Exhibit 4.4 Guy Christian/Hemis/Corbis; Exhibit 5.4 Birds Eye Ltd; Exhibit 5.5 Department for Transport; Exhibit 6.1 Direct Wines Ltd; Exhibit 6.2 Ralph Lauren Fragrances; Exhibit 7.1 Paul Gapper/Alamy; Exhibit 7.2 used by permission of Unilever; Exhibit 8.1 reproduced by permission of AA driving school; Exhibit 8.2 National Motor Museum, Beaulieu and The AA; Exhibit 8.7 reproduced with the kind permission of Cadbury Trebor Bassett; Exhibit 9.2 courtesy of Boots; Exhibit 10.1 courtesy of B&Q; Exhibit 10.2 courtesy of Saatchi & Saatchi, London and Carlsberg UK; Exhibit 10.3 Ski Rossendale; Exhibit 11.1

Environment Agency copyright. All rights reserved; Exhibit 11.2 reproduced with the kind permission of No More Nails on behalf of Henkel Consumer Adhesives and BDHTBWA; Exhibit 11.3 Lowe Worldwide/InBev; Exhibit 11.4 National Westminster Bank Plc © 2006; Exhibit 12.1 SCPhotos/Alamy; Exhibit 12.2 Gianni Muratore/Alamy; Exhibits 12.3 and 12.4 David Cox; Exhibit 12.6 reproduced with the kind permission of JCB; Exhibit 13.1 Shell Brands International AG; Exhibit 13.2 Accenture/ Young and Rubicam New York; Exhibit 13.3 Shell Brands International AG; Exhibit 14.1 Cruciform (Standard) © and Trade Marks of Royal Mail Group Ltd. Reproduced by kind permission of Royal Mail Group Ltd. All rights reserved; Exhibit 15.1 Newspaper Marketing Agency/ VCCP Ltd; Exhibit 15.2 Helen King/Corbis; Exhibit 16.1 AFP/Getty Images; Exhibit 16.2 reproduced by permission of Amnesty International; Exhibit 16.3 Reckitt Benckiser/Cillit Bang; Exhibit 17.2(l) Jim Smeal/WireImage/ Getty Images; 17.2(r) Leon Neal/AFP/Getty Images; Exhibit 17.3 © Duracell 2006, reproduced by permission of Duracell; Exhibit 17.4(b) Paul Mogford/Alamy; Exhibit 17.4(t) Danone; Exhibits 17.5, 17.6 and 17.7 TVS Motor Company Ltd; Exhibit 18.1Fujifilm UK; Exhibit 18.2 Premier Foods; Exhibit 18.3 AMVBBDO/Walkers; Exhibit 18.4 Virgin Atlantic; Exhibit 18.5 Tesco Stores Ltd; Exhibit 19.1 Brent Stirton/Getty Images; Exhibit 19.2 reproduced with the kind permission of Dyson; Exhibit 19.3 PA Photos/PA Wire; Exhibit 19.4 courtesy of Cisco Systems, Inc. Unauthorised use not permitted; Exhibit 20.2 courtesy of B&Q and Benoit Stichelbaut/DPPI/Offshore Challenges; Exhibit 20.3 courtesy of Toyota (GB) Ltd/CHI and Partners; Exhibit 20.4 Tim Mosenfelder/Corbis; Exhibit 21.1 Brilliant Media/ Thomas Sanderson; Exhibit 21.2 reproduced by permission of Direct Line; Exhibit 21.3 ING Direct; Exhibit 21.4 Stan Gamester/Photofusion; Exhibit 23.1 ING MEDIA; Exhibit 23.2 Kraft Foods; Exhibit 24.1 courtesy of Land Rover; Exhibit 24.2 Pretty Polly; Exhibit 24.3 Thornton's; Exhibit 24.4 Freud Communications/Vue Cinemas; Exhibit 25.1 from Crack the Code, *Marketing*, 6 February, reproduced from *Marketing* magazine with the permission of the copyright owner, Haymarket Business Publications Limited (Murphy, D. 2008); Exhibit 26.1 Manchester Utd Ltd; Exhibit 26.3 Sherbet; Exhibit 26.4 reproduced by permission of Tourism Ireland; Exhibit 27.1 Michael Prince/Corbis; Exhibit 27.2 JCDecaux Airport; Exhibit 27.3 GSK Nutritional Healthcare U.K.; Exhibit 29.1 reproduced by permission of Barclaycard; Exhibit 29.2 Redactive Media Group; Exhibit 30.1 reproduced by permission of B&Q; Exhibit 30.2 Marks & Spencer; Exhibits 30.3 and 30.4 © Rolls-Royce plc.

In some instances we have been unable to trace the owners of copyright material, and we would appreciate any information that would enable us to do so.

Part 1

Introduction to marketing communications

Chapters 1–4

Chapter 1 of this book considers the nature and diversity of marketing communications. It considers the role, nature and tasks of marketing communications and explores ways in which marketing communications and the marketing communications mix of tools, media and messages is changing.

Chapter 2 is concerned with theories and methods associated with the way in which communication is thought to work, including a consideration of the increasing impact of word-of-mouth communication.

Chapter 3 considers the structure, participants and issues facing the marketing communications industry, with particular emphasis the UK, although the principles and many of the issues are transferable to many other parts of the world.

The final chapter in this introductory part explores the ways in which organisations manage their communications from an ethical and moral standpoint. Ethics, corporate social responsibility and overall industry controls, which serve to regulate and control marketing communications, are examined.

Video Insight Part 1

The video Insight accompanying Part 1 features two very different, yet well known brands. The first is about the Swedish brand Ikea, who as we know market household furniture, or to put it bluntly, products. The other video features the City of Birmingham, whose marketers are trying to market a city, or a service. Both products and services require the use of marketing communications but they are not always used in the same way, nor do they use the same tools, media and messages, the marketing communications mix.

The Ikea case provides some interesting material because it serves to complement some important points made in the opening chapter. Marketing communications should be an audience centred activity designed to engage customers. Here we hear about Ikea developing their marketing around their customers and always using their campaigns to engage their customers, whether they are online browsing the catalogue on instore touching, feeling and experiencing the brand.

The material featuring the City of Birmingham provides a helpful introduction to some of the general issues and techniques associated with marketing communications, a theme that runs through the opening part of the book. In this video reference is made to the campaigns and the use of tools and media designed to help change the way people perceive Birmingham. Their campaigns are not just about how wonderful Birmingham may be but they also include a call to action, often through the web site, to encourage people to change not only the way their perceive Birmingham, but to also change their behaviour towards the city.

Go to **www.pearsoned.co.uk/fill** to watch the Video Insight, and then answer the following questions:

1. Having read the chapter, view the video and write brief notes about Birmingham's use of the marketing communication mix.
2. What are the tasks that marketing communications are used for by the City of Birmingham?
3. How do Ikea use marketing communications to engage their audiences?

Chapter 1

Introduction to marketing communications

Marketing communications is concerned with the methods, processes, meanings, perceptions and actions associated with the ways in which organisations (and their brands) engage with their target audiences.

Aims and learning objectives

The aims of this introductory chapter are to explore some of the concepts associated with marketing communications and to develop an appreciation of the key characteristics of the main tools of the communications mix and the way in which the mix is changing.

The learning objectives of this chapter are to:

1. examine the concept of exchange in the marketing context;
2. assess the role of communication in the context of the marketing mix;
3. consider the nature of the marketing communications mix;
4. identify the key characteristics of each major tool in the communications mix;
5. examine the effectiveness of each communication tool;
6. appreciate the importance of understanding the significance of context in marketing communications;
7. compare the use of marketing communications in consumer and business markets.

For an applied interpretation see Gary Warnaby, David Bennison and Dominic Medway's MiniCase entitled ***Hadrian's Wall – marketing the Roman frontier*** at the end of this chapter.

Introduction

Organisations engage with a variety of audiences in order to pursue their marketing and business objectives. Engagement refers to the nature of the communication that can occur between people and between people and machines. It refers to the use of communication tools, media and messages in order to captivate an audience, often achieved through a blend of intellectual and emotional engagement or stimulation. Engagement may last seconds, such as the impact of a stunning ad, the sight of a beautiful person or the emotion a piece of music might bring to an individual. Alternatively, engagement may be protracted and last hours, days, weeks, months or years, depending on the context and the level of enjoyment or loyalty felt towards the event, object or person.

> Engagement refers to the use of communication tools, media and messages in order to captivate an audience, often achieved through a blend of intellectual and emotional engagement or stimulation.

There is no universally agreed definition of the term engagement, but there can be no doubt that organisations seek to engage their audiences to help achieve their marketing and communication objectives.

Organisations such as Apple, Tesco, Santander, Haier, Nokia, Ryanair, BBC, Gillette, Microsoft, Chanel, Boeing, Shelter and Disney all operate across a number of sectors, markets and countries and use a variety of marketing communications tools to engage with their various audiences. These audiences consist not only of people who buy their products and services but also of people and organisations who might be able to influence them, who might help and support them by providing for example, labour, finance, manufacturing facilities, distribution outlets and legal advice or who are interested because of their impact on parts of society or the business sector in particular.

The organisations mentioned earlier are all well-known brand names, but there are hundreds of thousands of smaller organisations that also need and use marketing communications to convey the essence of their products and services and to engage their audiences. Each of these organisations, large and small, is part of a network of companies, suppliers, retailers, wholesalers, value-added resellers, distributors and other retailers, which join together, often freely, so that each can achieve its own goals.

At a basic level marketing communications, or promotion as it was originally known, is used to communicate elements of an organisation's offering to a target audience. This offer might refer to a product, a service or the organisation itself as it tries to build its reputation. However, this represents a broad view of marketing communication and fails to incorporate the various issues, dimensions and elements that make up this important communication activity. A leading Scandinavian marketing academic, Gronroos (2004) provides a useful insight into this when he suggests that in addition to these 'planned' events there are marketing communications experienced by audiences relating to both their experience from using products (how tasty is this smoothie?) or the consumption of services (just how good was the service in that hotel, restaurant or at the airport?). In addition to these there are communications arising from unplanned or unintended experiences (empty stock shelves or accidents). These dimensions of marketing communications are all represented at Figure 1.1 (Hughes and Fill, 2007).

> In addition to these 'planned' events there are marketing communications experienced by audiences relating to their experience from using products.

Figure 1.1 helps demonstrate the breadth of the subject and the inherent complexity associated with managing communication with audiences and the way they engage with a brand. Although useful in terms of providing an overview, this framework requires elaboration in order to appreciate the detail associated with each of the elements, especially planned marketing communications. This book builds on this framework and in particular considers issues associated with both planned and unplanned aspects of marketing communications.

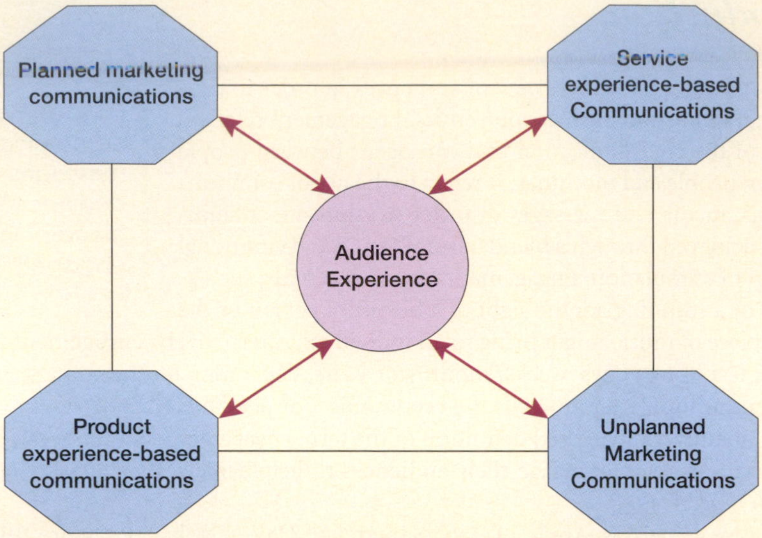

Figure 1.1 A macro-framework of marketing communications
Source: Hughes and Fill (2007). Used with permission.

Planned marketing communications incorporates three key elements: tools, media and messages. The main communication tools are advertising, sales promotion, public relations, direct marketing, personal selling and added-value approaches such as sponsorship. Messages can be primarily informative or emotional but are usually a subtle blend of both dimensions reflecting the preferences and needs of the target audience. To help get these messages through to their audiences, organisations use two main types of media. One refers to traditional media such as print and broadcast, cinema and outdoor. The other refers to the increasing use of digital media, and the Internet in particular, in order to listen to and converse with their audiences.

ViewPoint 1.1 The London Eye's Easter communications

> The London Eye is the world's tallest cantilevered observation wheel.

The London Eye is the world's tallest cantilevered observation wheel at 135m high. Located on the banks of the River Thames it offers unrivalled views over London. Since opening at the turn of the century, the London Eye has become an iconic landmark, with a status that can be compared to Tower Bridge, Big Ben, Eros and the Tower of London. It has been used as a backdrop in countless films and for innumerable television programmes. A source of pride for the whole country as well as the capital, the London Eye is the most distinctive addition this century to the world's greatest city, loved by Britons and tourists alike.

In fact, in its short life, it has become the most popular paid for UK visitor attraction, visited by over 3.5 million people a year (an average of 10,000 a day). A breathtaking feat of design and engineering, passengers in the London Eye's capsules can see up to 40 kilometres in all directions, in complete comfort and safety.

The London Eye needs to communicate with a range of audiences, not just visitors. It also needs to communicate different messages to achieve different goals. To achieve all of these goals it uses various campaigns at different times of the year. For example, the Easter campaign in 2007 was used to drive visitor numbers and enhance the customer experience. This involved the use of sales promotion in the form of a 'Spring'-oriented competition to win an electric car. Advertising through newspapers, magazines and posters to inform people of the competition, leaflets and the London Eye web site were all used to communicate the event. The site itself was decorated to reflect the Spring theme and the gift shop was used to provide related souvenirs. Press releases were also used to create publicity about the London Eye competition.

Question

To what extent should the London Eye work with other London attractions to encourage visitors to the capital city?

Task

Make a list of other ways in which the London Eye might have used marketing communications to promote this and other campaigns. Is this a planned or unplanned marketing communication activity?

Exhibit 1.1 Press ad used to publicise the London Eye Easter promotion
Courtesy of The London Eye.

Unplanned marketing communications involve communications that have not been anticipated.

Many leading organisations recognise the influence of word-of-mouth communication and are actively seeking to shape the nature, timing and speed with which it occurs.

Unplanned marketing communications involve communications that have not been anticipated. These may be both positive and negative but here the emphasis is more on how the organisation reacts to and manages the meaning attributed by audiences. So, comments by third-party experts, changes in legislation or regulations by government, the actions of competitors, failures in the production or distribution processes or perhaps the most potent of all communications, word-of-mouth comments between customers, all impact on the way in which organisations and brands are perceived and the images and reputations that are developed. Many leading organisations recognise the influence of word-of-mouth communication and are actively seeking to shape the nature, timing and speed with which it occurs. This topic is discussed in more detail in Chapter 2 and again in Chapter 26.

Increasingly digital media, the Internet in particular, are used to 'talk' with customers, potential customers, suppliers, financiers, distributors, communities and employees, among others.

The concept of marketing as an exchange

It is generally accepted that there are two main forms of exchange: transactional and relational (or collaborative) exchanges.

The concept of exchange, according to most marketing academics and practitioners, is central to our understanding of marketing. For an exchange to take place there must be two or more parties, each of whom can offer something of value to the other and who are prepared to enter freely into the exchange process, a transaction. It is generally accepted that there are two main forms of exchange: transactional and relational (or collaborative) exchanges.

Transactional (or market) exchanges (Bagozzi, 1978; Houston and Gassenheimer, 1987) occur independently of any previous or subsequent exchanges. They have a short-term orientation and are primarily motivated by self-interest. When a consumer buys a 'meal' from a burger van they have not used before, then a market exchange can be identified. Burger and chips in exchange for money. In contrast to this, *collaborative* exchanges have a longer-term orientation and develop between parties who wish to build and maintain long-term supportive relationships (Dwyer *et al.*, 1987). So, when someone frequents the same burger van on a regular basis, perhaps on their way home after lectures, or an evening's entertainment, relational or collaborative exchanges are considered to be taking place.

These two types of exchange represent the extremes in a spectrum of exchange transactions. This spectrum of exchanges, as depicted at Figure 1.2, is underpinned by relational theory. This

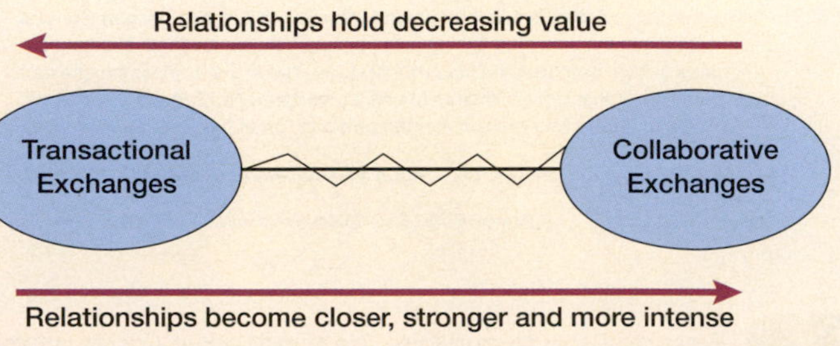

Figure 1.2 A spectrum of marketing exchanges

means that elements of a relationship can be observed in all exchanges (Macneil, 1983). Relationships become stronger as the frequency of exchanges increases. As exchanges become more frequent so the intensity of the relationship increases so that the focus is no longer on the product or price within the exchange but on the relationship itself.

In industrial societies transactional exchanges have tended to dominate commercial transactions, although recently there has been a substantial movement towards establishing collaborative exchanges. In other words, a mixture of exchanges occur and each organisation has a portfolio of differing types of exchange that it maintains with different customers, suppliers and other stakeholders. Communication is similar to oil in that it lubricates these exchanges and enables them to function. However, just as different types of oil are necessary to lubricate different types of equipment, so different types of communication are necessary to engage with different audiences.

Collaborative exchanges form the basis of the ideas represented in relationship marketing. Many organisations use the principles of relationship marketing manifest in the form of customer relationship marketing or loyalty marketing programmes. However, it is important to note that short-term relationships are also quite common and a necessary dimension of organisational exchange. This book is developed on the broad spectrum of relationships that organisations develop directly with other organisations and consumers and indirectly on a consumer-to-consumer and interorganisational basis.

Collaborative exchanges form the basis of the ideas represented in relationship marketing.

The tasks of communication in exchange transactions

Bowersox and Morash made a significant contribution in their 1989 paper when they demonstrated how marketing flows, including the information flow, can be represented as a network that has the sole purpose of satisfying customer needs and wants. Communication is important in these exchange networks as it can help achieve one of four key tasks:

- It can *inform* and make potential customers aware of an organisation's offering.
- Communication may attempt to *persuade* current and potential customers of the desirability of entering into an exchange relationship.
- Communications can also be used to *reinforce* experiences. This may take the form of *reminding* people of a need they might have or reminding them of the benefits of past transactions with a view to convincing them that they should enter into a similar exchange. In addition, it is possible to provide *reassurance* or comfort either immediately prior to an exchange or, more commonly, post-purchase. This is important as it helps to retain current customers and improve profitability, an approach to business that is much more cost-effective than constantly striving to lure new customers.
- Finally, marketing communications can act as a *differentiator*, particularly in markets where there is little to separate competing products and brands. Mineral water products, such as Perrier and Highland Spring, are largely similar: it is the communications surrounding the products that have created various brand images, enabling consumers to make purchasing decisions. In these cases it is the images created by marketing communications that enable people to differentiate one brand from another and position them so that consumers' purchasing confidence and positive attitudes are developed. Therefore, communication can inform, persuade, reinforce and build images to differentiate a product or service, or to put it another way, DRIP (Fill, 2002) (see Table 1.1).

Communication can inform, persuade, reinforce and build images to differentiate a product or service.

ViewPoint 1.2 Chocolate DRIPs

Green & Black's is a very successful premium organic brand of chocolate. Their use of marketing communications might be to:

- differentiate it from other chocolate brands;
- remind/reassure customers of the taste and experience of the brand;
- inform and educate the market about the ethics and economics of Fairtrade and the nutritional benefits of chocolate;
- persuade potential consumers and retailers to purchase and distribute Green & Black's respectively.

Question

Which of these tasks are the most important? Justify your view.

Task

Think of a campaign for a brand of your choice and consider how the DRIP model can be applied.

Exhibit 1.2 Green & Black's chocolate portfolio
Image courtesy of Brave.

Table 1.1 DRIP elements of marketing communications

DRIP element	Examples
Differentiate	Cravendale milk is better for us than ordinary milk because it is finely filtered, making it purer for a fresher taste.
Reinforce	McCain used communications to reassure consumers about the nutritional content of its products.
Inform/make aware	The Environment Agency and Flood Action Week inform various organisations, such as the Met Office, local media and the general public of the new flood warning codes.
Persuade	This isn't just food, this is M&S food.

Source: Fill (2002).

At a higher level, the communication process not only supports the transaction, by informing, persuading, reinforcing or differentiating, but also offers a means of exchange itself, for example communication for entertainment, for potential solutions and concepts for education and self-esteem. Communications involve intangible benefits, such as the psychological satisfactions associated with, for example, the entertainment value of television advertisements or the experiences within a sponsored part of a social network. Communications can also be seen as a means of perpetuating and transferring values and culture to different parts of society or networks. For example, it is argued that the way women are portrayed in the media and stereotypical images of very thin or 'size zero' women are dysfunctional in that they set up inappropriate role models. The form and characteristics of the communication process adopted by some organisations (both the deliberate and the unintentional use of signs and symbols used to convey meaning) help to provide stability and continuity.

> Communications involve intangible benefits, such as the psychological satisfactions associated with, for example, the entertainment value of television advertisements.

Other examples of intangible satisfactions can be seen in the social and psychological transactions involved increasingly with the work of the National Health Service (NHS), charities, educational institutions and other not-for-profit organisations, such as housing associations. Not only do these organisations recognise the need to communicate with various audiences, but also they perceive value in being seen to be 'of value' to their customers. There is also evidence that some brands are trying to meet the emerging needs of some consumers who want to know the track record of manufacturers with respect to their environmental policies and actions. For example, the growth in 'Fairtrade' products, designed to provide fairer and more balanced trading arrangements with producers and growers in emerging parts of the world, has influenced Kraft that they should engage with this form of commercial activity. Typhoo claims on its packaging, 'care for tea and our tea pickers'.

The notion of value can be addressed in a different way. All organisations have the opportunity to develop their communications to a point where the value of their messages represents a competitive advantage. This value can be seen in the consistency, timing, volume or expression of the message. Heinonen and Strandvik (2005) argue that there are four elements that constitute communication value. These are the message content, how the information is presented, where the communication occurs and its timing, in other words, the all-important context within which a communication event occurs. These elements are embedded within marketing communications and are referred to throughout this book.

> Organisations have the opportunity to develop their communications to a point where the value of their messages represents a competitive advantage.

Communication can be used for additional reasons. The tasks of informing, persuading and reinforcing and differentiating are primarily activities targeted at consumers or end-users. Organisations do not exist in isolation from each other, as each one is a part of a wider system of corporate entities, where each enters into a series of exchanges to secure raw material inputs or resources and to discharge them as value-added outputs to other organisations in the network.

The exchanges that organisations enter into require the formation of relationships, however tenuous or strong. Andersson (1992) looks at the strength of the relationship between organisations in a network and refers to them as 'loose or tight couplings'. These couplings, or partnerships, are influenced by the communications that are transmitted and received. The role that organisations assume in a network and the manner in which they undertake and complete their tasks are, in part, shaped by the variety and complexity of the communications in transmission throughout the network. Issues of channel or even network control, leadership, subservience and conflict are implanted in the form and nature of the communications exchanged in any network.

Collaborative exchanges are supported by more frequent communication activity.

Within market exchanges, communications are characterised by formality and planning. Collaborative exchanges are supported by more frequent communication activity. As Mohr and Nevin (1990) state, there is a bi-directional flow to communications and an informality to the nature and timing of the information flows.

Marketing communications and the process of exchange

The exchange process is developed and managed by:

- researching customer/stakeholder needs;
- identifying, selecting and targeting particular groups of customers/stakeholders who share similar discriminatory characteristics, including needs and wants;
- developing an offering that satisfies the identified needs at an acceptable price, which is available through particular sets of distribution channels;
- making the target audience aware of the existence of the offering. Where competition or other impediments to positive consumer action exist, such as lack of motivation or conviction, a promotional programme is developed and used to communicate with the targeted group.

Where competition or other impediments to positive consumer action exist, such as lack of motivation or conviction, a promotional programme is developed and used to communicate with the targeted group.

Collectively, these activities constitute the marketing mix (the 4Ps as the originator of the term McCarthy (1960) referred to them), and the basic task of marketing is to combine these 4Ps into a marketing programme to facilitate the exchange process. The use of the 4Ps approach has been criticised as limiting the scope of the marketing manager. The assumption by McCarthy was that the tools of the marketing mix allow adaptation to the uncontrollable external environment. It is now seen that the external environment can be influenced and managed strategically, and the rise and influence of the service sector is not easily accommodated within the original 4Ps. To do this, additional Ps such as Processes, Political Power and People have been suggested. A marketing mix of 20Ps has even been proposed but the essence of the mix remains the same, namely that it is product-focused and reflects an inside/out mentality. That is, inside the organisation looking out on the world (or customer). This deterministic approach has raised concerns about its usefulness in a marketing environment that is so different from that which existed when the 4Ps concept was conceived.

Promotion therefore, is one of the elements of the marketing mix and is responsible for the communication of the marketing offer to the target market. While recognising that there is implicit and important communication through the other elements of the marketing mix (through a high price, for example, symbolic of high quality), it is the task of a planned and integrated set of communication activities to communicate effectively with each of an organisation's stakeholder groups.

At a fundamental level it is possible to interpret the use of marketing communications in two different ways. One of these ways concerns the attempt to develop brand values. Historically, advertising has been used to focus on establishing a set of feelings, emotions and beliefs about a brand or organisation. In this way brand communication is used to help consumers think positively about a brand, helping them to remember and develop positive brand attitudes in the hope that when they are ready to buy that type of product again, Brand *x* will be chosen because of the positive feelings.

The other, and perhaps more contemporary use of marketing communications is to help shape behaviour, rather than feelings. In an age where short-term results and managerial accountability are increasingly critical, investment in brands is geared to achieve a fast return on investment (ROI). This does not allow space and money to build positive attitudes towards brands. Now the urgency is to encourage people to behave differently. This might be by driving them to a web site, buying the product or making a telephone call. This behaviour change can be driven by using messages that provide audiences with a reason to act or what is referred to as a 'call-to-action'.

So, on the one hand communications can be used to develop brand feelings and on the other to change or manage the behaviour of the target audience. These are not mutually exclusive, for example, many television advertisements are referred to as direct-response ads because not only do they attempt to create brand values but they also carry a web site address, telephone number or details of a special offer (sales promotion). In other words, the two goals can be mixed into one – a hybrid approach.

On the one hand communications can be used to develop brand feelings and on the other to change or manage the behaviour of the target audience.

At this point it is worth pointing out that marketing communications should not be used just to reach audiences external to the organisation. Good communications with internal stakeholders, such as employees, are also vital if, in the long term, successful favourable images, perceptions and attitudes are to be established. This book considers the increasing importance of suitable internal communications (Chapter 30) and their vital role in helping to form a strong and consistent corporate identity (Chapter 13).

ViewPoint 1.3 Tony the Tiger bows to social forces

It is commonly assumed that the use of digital media enhances communications for the benefit of all concerned. This is not necessarily true in all cases, as Kellogg's and other food manufacturers have experienced.

Kellogg's has used online chat, web ads, mobile-based competitions and desktop characters but none of these approaches has proved entirely satisfactory.

In fact, Kellogg's spend very little online with a budget of just 1 per cent of the company's £60 million marketing budget. By far the majority of the budget is channelled through television, press and radio as these provide the level of returns that Kellogg's expect, a level that so far is not realisable online.

One of the ironies facing breakfast cereal manufacturers is that not so long ago these products were perceived as a health food. Now public concern is directed at what exactly is in these products, namely the sugar, preservatives and flavourings. In addition, there has been growing social concern about advertising to children, and in particular the role of food manufacturers in this process. These changes impact on Kellogg's as much as any other manufacturer in this sector.

Kellogg's response was that it was better to take charge of the situation and be in control rather than be instructed by a third party to work in a different way. So, in 2007 they took down all of their brand specific web sites, many of which contained games for kids. Rather than attempt to reach children much of Kellogg's advertising and communications are now targeted at adults, or the 16–24-year-old group to whom most of Frosties are sold. The animated character used to promote Frosties, Tony the Tiger, has become an adult tiger.

Source: Dorrell (2007).

Question

Would it be better for companies such as Kellogg's if they were not allowed to advertise these types of food products before 2100 hrs each day?

Task

Visit the Kellogg's web site and determine the degree to which Tony the Tiger is targeted at adults.

New forms of communication have been developed in response to changing market and environmental conditions. For example, public relations is now seen by some to have a marketing and a corporate dimension (Chapters 13 and 19). Direct marketing is now recognised as an important way of developing closer relationships with buyers, both consumer and organisational (Chapters 10, 12, 13, 21 and 27), while new and innovative forms of communication through sponsorship (Chapter 20), floor advertising, video screens on supermarket trolleys and check-out coupon dispensers (Chapters 24 and 25) and the Internet and associated technologies (Chapters 25 and 26) mean that effective communication requires the selection and integration of an increasing variety of communication tools, media and messages. Figure 1.3 attempts to reflect the interrelationships between the tools, media and audiences.

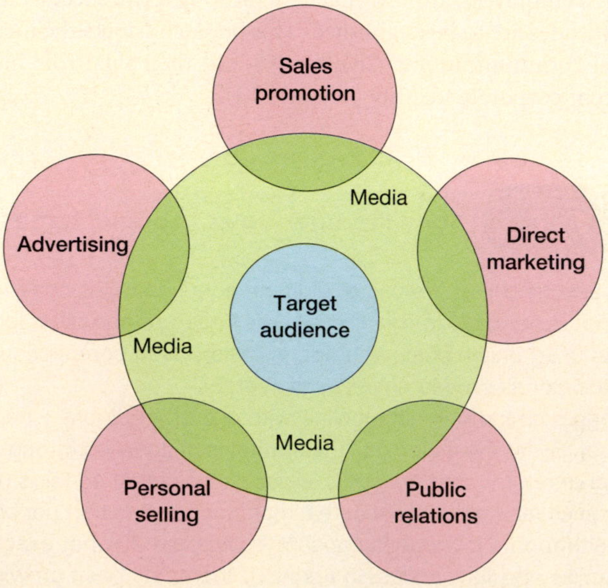

Figure 1.3 The interrelationships between tools, media and audiences

Defining marketing communications

There is no universal definition of marketing communications and there are many interpretations of the subject. Table 1.2 depicts some of the main orientations through which marketing communications has evolved. The origin of many definitions rests with a promotional outlook where the purpose was to use communications to persuade people to buy products and services. The focus was on products, one-way communications, and the perspective was short term. The expression marketing communications emerged as a wider range of tools and media evolved and as the scope of the tasks these communications activities were expected to accomplish expanded.

In addition to awareness and persuasion, new goals such as developing understanding and preference, reminding and reassuring customers became accepted as important aspects of the communications effort. Direct marketing activities heralded a new approach as one-to-one, two-way communications began to shift the focus from mass to personal communications efforts. Now a number of definitions refer to an integrated perspective. This view has gathered momentum since the mid 1990s and is even an integral part of the marketing communications vocabulary. This topic is discussed in greater depth in Chapter 9. However, this transition to an integrated perspective raises questions about the purpose of marketing communications. For example, should the focus extend beyond products and services, should corporate communications be integrated into the organisation's marketing communications, should the range of stakeholders move beyond customers, what does integration mean and is it achievable? With the integrative perspective a stronger strategic and long-term orientation has developed, although the basis for many marketing communication strategies appears still to rest with a promotional mix orientation.

Some of these interpretations fail to draw out the key issue that marketing communications provides added value, through enhanced product and organisational symbolism. They also fail to recognise that it is the context within which marketing communications flows that impacts upon the meaning and interpretation given to such messages. Its ability to frame and associate offerings with different environments is

The word 'integration' is used to express a variety of marketing and communication-related activities.

Table 1.2 The developing orientation of marketing communications

Orientation	Explanation
Information and promotion	Communications are used to persuade people into product purchase using mass media communications. Emphasis on rational, product-based information.
Process and imagery	Communications are used to influence the different stages of the purchase process that customers experience. A range of tools is used. Emphasis on product imagery and emotional messages.
Integration	Communication resources are used in an efficient and effective way to enable customers to have a clear view of the brand proposition. Emphasis on strategy, media neutrality and a balance between rational and emotional communication.
Relational	Communication is used as an integral part of the different relationships that organisations share with customers. Emphasis on mutual value and meaning plus recognition of the different communication needs and processing styles of different stakeholder groups.

powerful. Today, in an age where the word 'integration' is used to express a variety of marketing and communication-related activities, where corporate marketing is emerging as the next important development within the subject (Balmer and Gray, 2003) and where interaction is the preferred mode of communication and relationship marketing is the preferred paradigm (Gronroos, 2004) marketing communications now embraces a wider remit, one that has moved beyond the product information model and now forms an integral part of an organisation's overall communications and relationship management strategy. This perspective embraces communications as a one-way, two-way, interactive and dialogic approach necessary to meet the varying needs of different audiences. The integration stage focuses on the organisation, whereas the next development may have its focus on the relationships that an organisation has with its various audiences. Above all else, marketing communications should be an audience-centred activity.

Marketing communications is a management process through which an organisation engages with its various audiences.

Marketing communications is a management process through which an organisation engages with its various audiences. Through an understanding of an audience's preferred communication environments, organisations seek to develop and present messages for its identified stakeholder groups, before evaluating and acting upon any responses. By conveying messages that are of significant value, audiences are encouraged to offer attitudinal, emotional and behavioural responses.

This definition has three main themes. The first concerns the word *engages*. By recognising the different transactional and collaborative needs of the target audience, marketing communications can be used to engage with a variety of audiences in such a way that one-way, two-way, interactive and dialogic communications are used (Chapters 2 and 9) that meet the needs of the audience. It is unrealistic to believe that all audiences always want a relationship with your organisation/brand, and for some, one-way communication is fine. However, messages should encourage individual members of target audiences to respond to the focus organisation (or product/brand). This response can be immediate through, for example, purchase behaviour or use of customer care lines, or it can be deferred as information is assimilated and considered for future use. Even if the information is discarded at a later date, the communication will have attracted attention and consideration of the message.

ViewPoint 1.4 Chivas engagement . . . thisisthelife

Over the past 50 years Chivas Regal Whisky has developed a reputation and set of values associated with quality, sociability and special shared experiences when drinking Chivas. However, their goal was to reach a global audience and to do so in such a way that they could engage and offer audiences something of value that would enhance their lives.

To help achieve this an independent web site was created. This was called thisisthelife.com and was sponsored by Chivas. The site is a social network and it invites people to share travel experiences, whether they be about mountains, beaches, cities, islands or journeys. The site is about user content, designed to help people map the experiences they have and those they want to enjoy. The site has a single banner saying it is sponsored by Chivas but otherwise it is devoid of commercial messaging. Without having to message consumers directly with brand information, this approach adds value and serves to engage audiences and enable them to share experiences.

Source: Beeching and Wood (2007).

Question

How does this site demonstrate engagement?

Task

What would you post on the thisisthelife.com site if this had been you on the mountain?

Exhibit 1.3 Some travel experiences just have to be shared
Tim Cuff/Alamy.

The second theme concerns the *audiences* for marketing communications. Traditionally marketing communications has been used to convey product-related information to customer-based audiences. Today, a range of stakeholders have connections and relationships of varying dimensions, and marketing communications needs to incorporate this breadth and variety. Stakeholder audiences, including customers, are all interested in a range of corporate issues, sometimes product-related and sometimes related to the policies, procedures and values of the organisation itself. Marketing communications should be an audience-centred activity and in that sense it is important that messages be based on a firm understanding of both the needs and environment of the audience. To be successful, marketing communications should be grounded in the behaviour and information-processing needs and style of the target audience. This is referred to as understanding the context in which the communications event is to occur (Chapters 5, 6 and 12). From this base it is easier to present and position brands in order that they are perceived to be different and of value to the target audience.

The third theme from the definition concerns the *response*. This refers to the outcomes of the communication process, and can be used as a measure of whether a communication event has been successful. There are essentially two key responses, cognitive and emotional. Cognitive responses assume an audience to be active problem-solvers and that they use marketing

Cognitive responses assume an audience to be active problem-solvers.

communications to help them in their lives, in purchasing products and services and in managing organisation-related activities. For example, brands are developed partly to help consumers and partly to assist the marketing effort of the host organisation. A brand can inform consumers quickly that, among other things, 'this brand means *x* quality', and through experience of similar brand purchases consumers are assured that their risk is minimised. If the problem facing a consumer is 'which new soup to select for lunch', by choosing one from a familiar family brand the consumer is able to solve it with minimal risk and great speed. Cognitive responses assume audiences undertake rational information processing.

Emotional responses assume decision-making is a result of emotional reaction to a communication stimulus.

Emotional responses on the other hand, assume decision-making is not made through active thought processing but as a result of emotional reaction to a communication stimulus. Hedonic consumption concerns the purchase and use of products and services to fulfil fantasies and to satisfy emotional needs. Satisfaction is based on the overall experience consuming a product. For example, sports cars and motorbikes are not always bought because of the functionality and performance of the vehicle, more due to the thrill of independence, power and a feeling of being both carefree and in danger. Marketing communications, and content in particular, should be developed in anticipation of an audience's cognitive or emotional response.

Marketing communications therefore, can be considered from a number of perspectives. It is a complex activity and is used by organisations with varying degrees of sophistication and success. However, it is now possible to clarify both the roles and the tasks of marketing communications. The role of marketing communications is to engage audiences and the tasks are to differentiate, reinforce, inform or persuade audiences to think, feel or behave in particular ways.

ViewPoint 1.5 O_2 Audience orientation

As if to emphasise the need to be audience-oriented, O_2 developed a campaign called 'A world that revolves around you'. The campaign was based on the insight that pre-pay customers felt neglected. This helped establish the campaign objectives, namely to improve retention and loyalty, and in doing so demonstrate that O_2 regarded pre-pay customers as important. Customers were offered the opportunity of a 10 per cent refund of their top-ups every three months.

By understanding the media used by this customer segment it became possible to develop a media mix that was oriented around the target audience. The first phase of the campaign was based around creating awareness and for this traditional media, such as broadcast, outdoor and print media were sufficient. However, this alone would not encourage retention, interaction with the audience was necessary and this required an understanding of which media they use and when they use it. This was achieved by first plotting the path a typical customer took each day and then second, selecting media that fitted with this pattern. Information was gathered by talking to customers online, when on their mobiles, during top-ups, or in O_2 stores. The result of this was a media plan that involved email, postcards, SMS, MMS, a WAP site, a seeded message in online chatrooms and brand street events. Approximately 50 per cent of O_2's customers took part in the campaign.

Source: Bashford (2007).

Question

How does this O_2 example demonstrate an audience orientation?

Task

Track the route you follow each day (to work, college, university), work out your media behaviour at home and then work out the media opportunities that a brand of your choice, has to reach you.

The marketing communications mix

Marketing communications involves a mix of three elements: tools, media and messages. See Figure 1.4 for a depiction of the traditional configuration of the mix. The primary element of the mix has customarily been the mix of tools (or disciplines) that can be used in various combinations and different degrees of intensity in order to communicate with a target audience. There are five principal marketing communications tools: advertising, sales promotion, public relations, direct marketing and personal selling.

Marketing communications involves a mix of three elements: tools, media and messages.

In addition to these tools or methods of communication, there are the media, or the means by which advertising and other marketing communications messages are conveyed. Tools and media should not be confused as they have different characteristics and seek to achieve different goals. Also, just in case you were thinking something is missing, the Internet is a medium not a tool.

To complete the trilogy, messages need to be conveyed to the target audience. The marketing communications mix therefore consists of tools, media and messages.

Since the mid 1990s, however, there have been some major changes in the environment and in the way organisations communicate with their target audiences. New technology has given rise to a raft of different media while people have developed a variety of ways to spend their leisure time. This is referred to as media and audience fragmentation and organisations have developed fresh combinations of the communication mix in order to reach their audiences effectively. For example, there has been a dramatic rise in the use of direct-response media as direct marketing has become a key part of the marketing plan for many products. The Internet and digital technologies have enabled new interactive forms of communication, where the receiver has greater responsibility for their part in the communication process. An increasing number of organisations are using public relations to communicate messages about the organisation (corporate public relations) and also messages about their brands (marketing public relations).

The Internet and digital technologies have enabled new interactive forms of communication, where the receiver has greater responsibility for their part in the communication process.

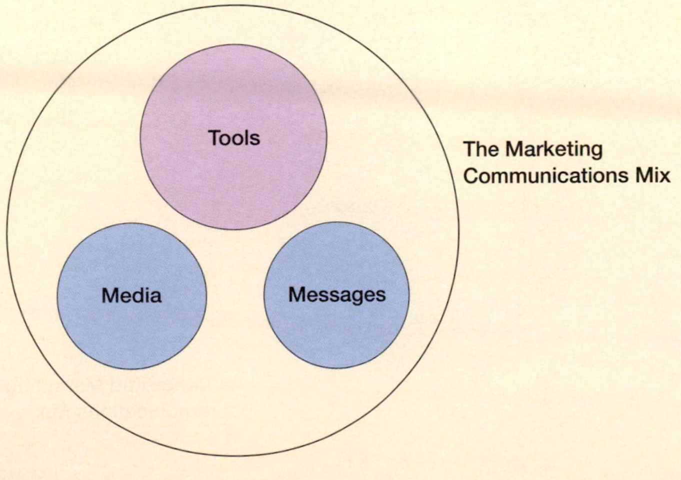

Figure 1.4 A traditional model of the marketing communications mix

The traditional mix has evolved dramatically. Originally brands were developed through the use of advertising to generate 'above-the-line' mass communication campaigns. The strategy was based around buying advertising time (called spots) in major television programmes that were watched by huge audiences (20 million plus people). The alternative approach was to buy space in newspapers and magazines. This strategy required media owners to create programmes (content) that would attract brand owners because of the huge, relatively passive audiences. By interrupting the audience's entertainment brand owners could talk to their markets in order to sell their brands.

However, since the days of just two commercial television programmes there has been a proliferation of media. Audiences no longer use the television as their main form of information or entertainment and newspaper readership has fallen steadily over the past decade. Moore (2007) suggests that consumers now use media to satisfy four additional needs:

- to discover;
- to participate;
- to share;
- to express themselves.

Rather than passive media involvement, these motivations, as he refers to it, require active engagement with media. Consumers now have a choice of media and leisure activities, they decide how and when to consume information and entertainment. Consumers are now motivated and able to develop their own content, be it through text, music or video and consider topics that they can share with friends on virtual networks. Thus, media and messages are the key to reaching consumers today, not the tools. More direct and highly targeted, personalised communication activities using direct marketing and the other tools of the mix predominate, and to use the jargon, through-the-line and below-the-line communications tools are much more prevalent today. Figure 1.5 brings these elements together and shows that no longer are the tools the primary focus of the communications, that media and content are now a major concern and that the three elements are mixed in an integrated manner. This serves to reinforce the effect of the mix as a whole.

The shift is towards *permission*-based communications.

The new mix represents a shift in approach. The traditional format represents an *intervention*-based approach to marketing communications, one based on seeking the attention of a customer who might not necessarily be interested. The shift is towards *permission*-based communications,

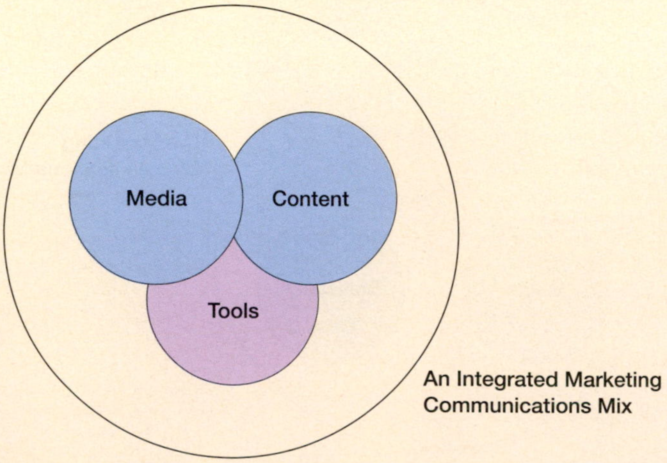

Figure 1.5 A contemporary model of the marketing communications mix
Source: Hughes and Fill (2007).

where the focus is on communications with members of an audience who have already expressed an interest in a particular offering. In other words with permission-based communications the seedlings for a closer relationship are signalled by the audience, not the brand owner. This has a particular impact on direct marketing, interactive communications and, to some extent, personal selling. Ideas concerning different levels of permission marketing are explored in this book, particularly in Chapter 21.

Advertising

Advertising is a non-personal form of mass communication that offers a high degree of control for those responsible for the design and delivery of advertising messages. However, the ability of advertising to persuade the target audience to think or behave in a particular way is suspect. Furthermore, the effect on sales is extremely hard to measure. Advertising also suffers from low credibility in that audiences are less likely to believe messages delivered through advertising than they are messages received through some other tools and word-of-mouth communication.

Advertising is a non-personal form of mass communication.

The flexibility of this tool is good because it can be used to communicate with a national audience or a particular specialised segment. Although the costs can be extremely high, a vast number of people can be reached with a message, so the cost per contact can be the lowest of all the tools in the mix. Advertising and related media are considered in some depth in Chapters 16, 17 and 24 to 27.

Sales promotion

Sales promotion comprises various marketing techniques, which are often used tactically to provide added value to an offering. The aim is to accelerate sales and gather marketing information. Like advertising, sales promotion is a non-personal form of communication but has a greater capacity to target smaller audiences. It is controllable and, although it has to be paid for, the associated costs can be much lower than those of advertising. As a generalisation, credibility is not very high, as the sponsor's goals are easily identifiable. However, the ability to add value and to bring forward future sales is strong and complements a macroeconomic need, which focuses on short-term financial performance. Sales promotion techniques and approaches are the subject of Chapter 18.

The aim is to accelerate sales and gather marketing information.

Personal selling

Personal selling is traditionally perceived as an interpersonal communication tool that involves face-to-face activities undertaken by individuals, often representing an organisation, in order to inform, persuade or remind an individual or group to take appropriate action, as required by the sponsor's representative. A salesperson engages in communication on a one-to-one basis where instantaneous feedback is possible. The costs associated with interpersonal communication are normally very high.

This tool, the focus of Chapter 22, differs from the previous two in that, while still lacking in relative credibility and control, the degree of control is potentially lower, because the salesperson is free at the point of contact to deliver a message other than that intended (Lloyd, 1997). Indeed, many different messages can be delivered by a single salesperson. Some of these messages may enhance the prospect of the salesperson's objectives being reached (making the sale), or they may retard the process and so incur more time and hence costs. Whichever way it is viewed, control is lower than with advertising.

Many different messages can be delivered by a single salesperson.

Public relations

Public relations is concerned with establishing and maintaining relationships with various stakeholders and with enhancing the reputation of the organisation. This indicates that public relations should be a part of the wider perspective of corporate strategy, something that is discussed at length in Chapter 19. The increasing use of public relations, and in particular publicity, is a reflection of the high credibility attached to this form of communication. Publicity involves the dissemination of messages through third-party media, such as magazines, newspapers or news programmes. There is no charge for the media space or time but there are costs incurred in the production of the material. (There is no such thing as a free lunch or free promotion.) There is a wide range of other tools used by public relations, such as event management, public affairs, sponsorship and lobbying. It is difficult to control a message once it is placed in the media channels, but the endorsement offered by a third party can be very influential and have a far greater impact on the target audience than any of the other tools in the promotional mix.

ViewPoint 1.6 Associating with extreme Red Bulls

The energy drink Red Bull was first launched in the mid 1980s but its development in Britain continues to be strong, with sales increasing 14 per cent in 2007 on the previous year and a 27 per cent market share. There are several factors contributing to this performance, not least of them being the quality of the product and the perceived value consumers derive from drinking the brand.

The brand makes use of a wide range of marketing communications tools and media, with a message that is based around the distinctive, slim silver can, that it is cool to drink Red Bull. The brand uses television, print and cinema as key media channels to reach their 14–19-year-old target audience and build brand awareness. However, this is not enough to sustain contemporary brands and so they use other activities to build a brand experience for users, based around excitement, adrenalin, danger and youth culture. To achieve this Red Bull associate themselves with extreme sports (e.g. Formula 1, the Red Bull Air Race World Series, street culture and music events). This builds credibility that in turn fosters word-of-mouth communication.

Source: Turner (2008) www.redbull.com.

Question

To what extent is the brand experience a more important driver of sales than the quality of the product and its various attributes?

Task

Make a list of five events with which Red Bull might associate themselves.

This non-personal form of communication offers organisations a different way to communicate, not only with consumers but also with many other stakeholders.

The four elements of the communications mix discussed so far have a number of strengths and weaknesses. As a response to some of the weaknesses that revolve around costs and effectiveness, direct marketing emerged in the 1990s as a new and effective way of building relationships with customers over the long term.

Direct marketing

Direct marketing is now a standard form of marketing communication used by organisations in a variety of ways. It represents a shift in focus from mass to personalised communications. In particular, the use of direct mail, telemarketing and the fast-developing area of interactive marketing communications represents through-the-line communications. By removing the face-to-face aspect of personal selling and replacing it with an email communication, a telephone conversation or a direct mail letter, many facets of the traditional salespersons' tasks can be removed, freeing them to concentrate on their key skill areas.

Direct marketing seeks to target individual customers with the intention of delivering personalised messages and building a relationship with them based on their responses to the direct communications. In contrast to conventional approaches, direct marketing attempts to build a one-to-one relationship, a partnership with each customer, by communicating with the customers on a direct and personal basis. If an organisation chooses to use direct marketing then it has to incorporate the approach within a marketing plan. This is because distribution is different and changes in the competitive environment may mean that prices need to change. For example, charges for packing and delivery need to be incorporated. The product may also need to be altered or adapted to the market. For example, some electrical products are marketed through different countries on home shopping channels and web sites. The electrical requirements of each country or region need to be incorporated within the product specification of each country's offering. In addition to these changes, the promotion component is also different, simply because communication is required directly with each targeted individual. To do this, direct-response media must be used.

Direct marketing seeks to target individual customers.

In many cases, direct-response media are a derivative of advertising, such as direct mail, magazine inserts and television and print advertisements that use telephone numbers and web addresses to encourage a direct response. However, direct response can also be incorporated within personal selling through telemarketing and sales promotions with competitions to build market knowledge and develop the database, which is the key to the direct marketing approach.

Direct response can also be incorporated within personal selling through telemarketing and sales promotions.

This text regards direct marketing as a management process associated with building mutually satisfying customer relationships through a personal and intermediary-free interaction and dialogue. Direct-response media are the primary communication tools when direct marketing is an integral part of the marketing plan. Further discussion of direct marketing and direct-response communications can be found in Chapters 21 and 26.

The Internet is both a distribution channel and communication medium, one that enables consumers and organisations to communicate in radically different ways. It allows for interactivity and is possibly the best medium to enable dialogue. Communication is two-way, often interactive, and very fast, allowing businesses and individuals to find information and enter exchange transactions in such a way that some traditional communication practices and shopping patterns are being reconfigured.

Finally, reference has been made to above- and below-the-line communications. Above-the-line refers to advertising. Where advertising is bought agencies are remunerated (paid) partly by a commission charged as a percentage of the value of media bought by the client. All the other tools do not involve media purchases and so there is no commission to be paid and are referred to as below-the-line. See Chapter 14 for more detail.

The key characteristics of the communication tools

Each of the tools of the communication mix performs a different role and can accomplish different tasks. This reflects their different capabilities, their various attributes and key characteristics. These are the extent to which each of the tools is controllable, whether it is paid for by the sponsor and whether communication is through mass media or undertaken personally. One additional characteristic concerns the receiver's perception of the credibility of the source of the message. If the credibility factor is high then there is a greater likelihood that a message from that source will be accepted by receivers.

Each of the tools of the communication mix performs a different role and can accomplish different tasks.

The 4Cs framework set out at Table 1.3, depicts the key characteristics and shows the relative effectiveness of the communication tools across a number of different characteristics. These are the ability of each to communicate, the credibility they bestow on messages, the costs involved and the control that each tool can maintain.

Table 1.3 The 4Cs framework – a summary of the key characteristics of the tools of marketing communications

	Advertising	Sales promotion	Public relations	Personal selling	Direct marketing
Communications					
Ability to deliver a personal message	Low	Low	Low	High	High
Ability to reach a large audience	High	Medium	Medium	Low	Medium
Level of interaction	Low	Low	Low	High	High
Credibility					
Given by the target audience	Low	Medium	High	Medium	Medium
Costs					
Absolute costs	High	Medium	Low	High	Medium
Cost per contact	Low	Medium	Low	High	High
Wastage	High	Medium	High	Low	Low
Size of investment	High	Medium	Low	High	Medium
Control					
Ability to target particular audiences	Medium	High	Low	Medium	High
Management's ability to adjust the deployment of the tool as circumstances change	Medium	High	Low	Medium	High

Effectiveness of the communication tools

Each element of the marketing communications mix has different capacities to communicate and to achieve different objectives. The effectiveness of each tool can be tracked against the purchase decision process. Here consumers can be assumed to move from a state of unawareness through product comprehension to purchase. Advertising is better for creating awareness, and personal selling is more effective at promoting action and purchase behaviour.

Readers are encouraged to see the elements of the mix as a set of complementary ingredients, each drawing on the potential of the others. The tools are, to a limited extent, partially interchangeable and in different circumstances different tools are used to meet different objectives. For example, network marketing organisations, such as Avon Cosmetics, use personal selling to complete the majority of activities in the purchase decision sequence. The high cost of this approach is counterbalanced by the effectiveness of the communications. However, this aspect of interchangeability only serves to complicate matters. If management's task was simply to identify problems and then select the correct precision tool to solve the problem, the issue of the selection of the 'best' communications mix would evaporate (Figure 1.6).

The five tools of the communication mix are supplemented by one of the most effective forms of marketing communication, *word-of-mouth* recommendation. As developed, word-of-mouth recommendation is one of the most powerful marketing communication tools and, if an organisation can develop a programme to harness and accelerate the use of personal recommendation (advocacy) effectively, there is a far greater likelihood that the marketing programme will be successful.

The five elements of the communication mix are supplemented by one of the most effective forms of marketing communication, *word-of-mouth* recommendation.

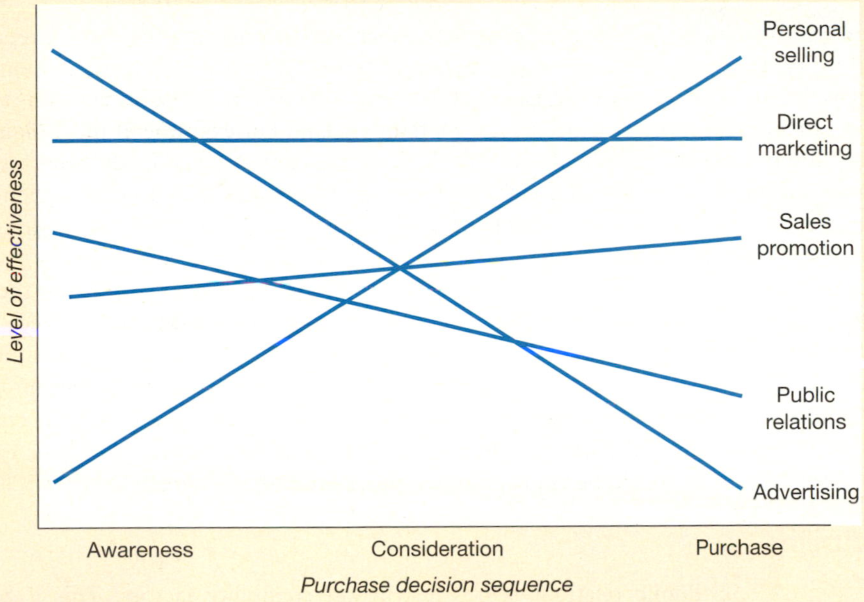

Figure 1.6 The relative effectiveness of the tools of the marketing communications mix

Criteria when selecting the mix

Using the key characteristics it is possible to determine the key criteria organisations should consider when selecting communication tools. These are as follows:

- the degree of control required over the delivery of the message;
- the financial resources available to pay a third party to transmit messages;
- the level of credibility that each tool bestows on the organisation;
- the size and geographic dispersion of the target audiences;
- the communication tasks each tool is best at satisfying.

Control

Control over the message, particularly in traditional mass media communication, is necessary to ensure that the intended message is transmitted to and received by the target audience. Furthermore, this message must be capable of being understood in order that the receiver can act appropriately. Message control is complicated by interference or negative 'noise' that can corrupt and distort messages. For example, an airline's advertising may be discredited by a major news story about safety checks or even an accident.

> Control over the message is necessary to ensure that the intended message is transmitted to and received by the target audience.

Advertising and sales promotion allow for a high level of control over the message, from design to transmission. Interestingly, they afford only partial control or influence over the feedback associated with the original message.

Control can also be an important factor when considering online and digital-based communications. For example, the ability to place banner ads, to bid for sponsored links and determine keyword rankings in search engines requires control and deliberation.

Financial resources

Control is also a function of financial power. In other words, if an organisation is prepared to pay a third party to transmit the message, then long-term control will rest with the sponsor for as long as the financial leverage continues. However, short-term message corruption can exist if management control over the process is less than vigilant. For example, if the design of the message differs from that originally agreed, then partial control has already been lost. This can happen when the working relationship between an advertising agency and the client is less than efficient and the process for signing off work in progress fails to prevent the design and release of inappropriate creative work.

Advertising and sales promotion are tools that allow for a high level of control by the sponsor, whereas public relations, and publicity in particular, is weak in this aspect because the voluntary services of a third party are normally required for the message to be transmitted.

There is a great variety of media available to advertisers. Each media type (for example television, radio, newspapers, magazines, posters and the Internet) carries a particular cost, and the financial resources of the organisation may not be available to use particular types of media, even if such use would be appropriate on other grounds.

Credibility

Public relations scores heavily on credibility factors.

Public relations scores heavily on credibility factors. This is because receivers perceive the third party as unbiased and to be endorsing the offering. They view the third party's comments as objective and trustworthy in the context of the media in which the comments appear.

At a broad level, advertising, sales promotion and, to a slightly lesser extent, personal selling are tools that can lack credibility, as perceived by the target audience. Because of this, organisations often use celebrities and 'experts' to endorse their offerings. The credibility of the spokesperson is intended to distract the receiver from the sponsor's prime objective, which is to sell the offering. Credibility, as we see shall later, is an important aspect of the communication process and of marketing communications.

Dispersion – size and geography

The size and geographic dispersion of the target audience can be a significant influence on the choice of tools.

The size and geographic dispersion of the target audience can be a significant influence on the choice of tools. A national consumer audience can only be reached effectively if tools of mass communication are used, such as advertising and sales promotion. Similarly, various specialist businesses require personal attention to explain, design, demonstrate, install and service complex equipment. In these circumstances personal selling – one-to-one contact – is of greater significance. The tools of marketing communications can enable an organisation to speak to vast national and international audiences through advertising and satellite technology, or to single persons or small groups through personal selling and the assistance of word-of-mouth recommendation.

Communication tasks

One of the reasons direct marketing has become so successful is that it delivers a call-to-action.

Figure 1.6 provides a visual demonstration of the effectiveness of the tools across the purchase decision process. This is important because each of the tools excels at particular DRIP tasks. One of the reasons direct marketing has become so successful is that it delivers a call-to-action and is therefore a very good persuasive tool as well as being good at reinforcing messages. Advertising on the other hand is much better at differentiating offerings and informing audiences about key features and benefits.

Table 1.4 Key selection criteria for the tools of the marketing communication mix

		Advertising	Sales promotion	Public relations	Direct marketing	Personal selling
Level of control		Medium	High	Low	High	Medium
Level of cost		High	Medium	Low	Medium	High
Level of credibility		Low	Medium	High	Medium	Medium
Level of dispersion	*High*	Low	Medium	High	High	Medium
	Low	Medium	High	High	Medium	High
Primary tasks		Differentiating Informing	Persuading	Differentiating Informing	Persuading Reinforcing	Persuading

Source: Baines *et al.* (2008) *Marketing*. By permission of Oxford University Press.

Context and marketing communications

Traditionally, each of the communication tools has been regarded as the domain of particular groups within organisations. For example:

- Personal selling is the domain of the sales director, and traditionally uses an internally based and managed sales force.
- Public relations is often the domain of the chairperson and is frequently administered by a specialist PR agency.
- Advertising and sales promotion are the domain of the marketing director or brand manager. Responsibility for the design and transmission of messages for mass communications is often devolved to an external advertising agency.

For a number of reasons, many organisations have evolved without marketing being recognised as a key function, let alone as a core philosophy. First, the organisation may have developed with a public relations orientation in an environment without competition, where the main purpose of the organisation was to disperse resources according to the needs of their clients. The most obvious examples are to be drawn from the public sector, local authorities and the NHS in particular. A second reason would be because a selling perspective ('our job is to sell it') dominated. There would invariably be no marketing director on the board, just a sales director representing the needs of the market.

It is not surprising that these various organisational approaches have led to the transmission of a large number of different messages. Each function operating with good intent, but stakeholders receiving a range of diverse and often conflicting messages.

Organisations can be seen as open social systems (Katz and Kahn, 1978) in which all of the components of the unit or system are interactive and interdependent (Goldhaber, 1986). Modify one part of a system and adjustments are made by all the other components to accommodate the change. This effect can be seen at the micro and macro levels. At the macro level the interdependence of organisations has been noted by a number of researchers. Stern and El-Ansary (1995) depict distribution channels as 'a network of systems', thereby recognising organisations as interdependent units. At the micro level, the individual parts of an organisation accommodate each other as the organisation adjusts to its changing environment. By assembling the decisions associated with the development and delivery of a marketing communications strategy (Figure 1.7), it becomes possible to see the complexity and sensitivity of each of the decision components.

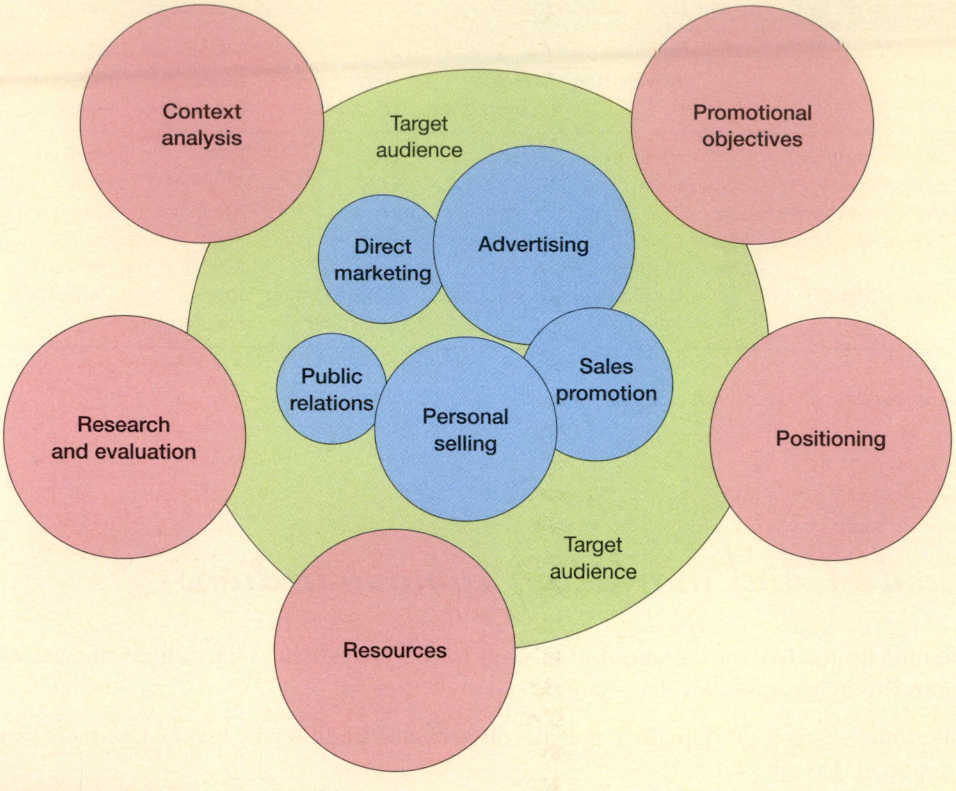

Figure 1.7 The system of marketing communications

> marketing communications undertaken by organisations within these systems can be regarded as a series of communication episodes.

The marketing communications undertaken by organisations within these systems can be regarded as a series of communication episodes. These episodes can often be construed as a form of interaction, some of which can become a dialogue. The amount of time between episodes may vary from the very small, such as those associated with many major FMCG (fast-moving consumer goods) brand campaigns, which run and run, to the very large, such as those associated with some business-to-business campaigns or one-off events associated with a single task, for instance the UK government's drink-driving campaigns held annually during each Christmas period.

These episodes occur within situations where specific factors can be identified and where the circumstances are characteristically individual. Indeed, it is unlikely that any two episodes will occur within the exact same circumstances. The use of marketing communications as a means of influencing others is therefore determined by the specific circumstances or the context in which the episode is to occur. Marketing communications thus become part of the context, both influencing and being influenced by the particular circumstances.

> It is important when considering the elements and factors that contribute to marketing communications, to account for the context in which the communications will contribute.

It is important therefore, when considering the elements and factors that contribute to marketing communications, to account for the context in which the communications will contribute. For example, falling sales often provoke a response by management to increase or change the advertising. The perception of the brand by the target audience might be inaccurate or not what was intended, or a new product might be launched into a competitive market, where the positions adopted by competitors are well established. These contexts contain a set of specific circumstances in which a marketing communication episode might (will) occur. It should be borne in mind that the list of possible contexts is endless and that the task facing marketing communications managers is to identify the key aspects of any situation and deliver promotional messages that complement the context. This enables audiences to interpret messages correctly and maintain a dialogue.

The main tasks facing the management team responsible for marketing communications are to decide the following:

- who should receive the messages;
- what the messages should say;
- what image of the organisation/brand receivers are to form and retain;
- how much is to be spent establishing this new image;
- how the messages are to be delivered;
- what actions the receivers should take;
- how to control the whole process once implemented;
- determining what was achieved.

These tasks are undertaken within a context within which there may be many episodes or only a few. Note that more than one message is often transmitted and that there is more than one target audience. This is important, as recognition of the need to communicate with multiple audiences and their different information requirements, often simultaneously, lies at the heart of marketing communications. The aim is to generate and transmit messages that present the organisation and its offerings to their various target audiences, encouraging them to enter into a dialogue and relationship. These messages must be presented consistently and they must address the points stated above. It is the skill and responsibility of the marketing communications manager to blend the communication tools and create a mix that satisfies these elements.

It should also be borne in mind that the list of possible contexts is endless and that the task facing marketing communications managers is to identify the key aspects of any situation and deliver promotional messages that complement the prevailing context. This enables audiences to interpret messages correctly and to provide them with opportunities for interactivity and assist them to enter into dialogue.

ViewPoint 1.7 Cola contexts

Cola sales in North America declined in 2000 and 2001 as some cola consumers switched to variety flavoured carbonated soft drinks. Coca-Cola capitalised on this market development by introducing Vanilla Coke. This new product was launched into the market with a great deal of marketing communications activity, including a $12m TV advertising campaign. Market share grew quickly and soon Vanilla Coke dominated the new category.

Pepsico needed to respond but their task was made harder by the fact that Vanilla Coke had established the market's taste and flavour for vanilla cola drinkers. To be successful Pepsico needed a point of differentiation and they had no research data or quantifiable taste claim that they could use legitimately. Anecdotal evidence suggested that Vanilla Coke was perceived as particularly sweet. Using the Pepsi brand imagery as a younger and cooler brand, Pepsi Vanilla was launched as 'the not-so-vanilla vanilla', implying that it had a superior taste and repositioning Vanilla Coke as a has-been brand.

The launch of Pepsi Vanilla, a product not available outside North America, was partly a competitive reaction to the launch of Vanilla Coke. The 'not-so-vanilla vanilla' launch was led by a $25m media advertising programme with the goal of achieving substantial reach in a short period of time. The launch was timed to burst on a public holiday, Labor Day, and was then scheduled to appear during the season's television premieres of programmes such as *ER*, *Scrubs* and *Las Vegas*, all of which attract large audiences.

Other media included the use of outdoor in high population and key influencer locations such as Times Square, print in terms of a 4-week placement in *USA Today*, plus appearances in *Rolling Stone* and *Sports Illustrated*. Online pop-ups and banners were used to drive traffic to a new dedicated Pepsi Vanilla web site together with email to loyal Pepsi drinkers, making them aware and encouraging trial of the new drink.

Product placement was used in the popular programme *The Batchelor*, while merchandising and sampling activity were featured in-store and at the 2003 NFL football festival. Finally, public relations were used around one of the television ads that compared the two competing brands. Comment and opinion appeared in a range of media including the *Wall Street Journal*.

In just four weeks from launch Pepsi Vanilla reached 96 per cent distribution, achieved 65 per cent consumer awareness in five weeks (the goal was 50 per cent) and exceeded all its volume share targets, outpacing Vanilla Coke that at the time, lost 1 per cent market share (*Beverage Post*).

Sources: Bhatnager (2003); Effie Awards; www.nyama.org.

Question

If you were the marketing manager for Vanilla Coke, how might you respond to Pepsi's new product launch?

Task

Which communication tools and how many types of media can you identify in the Pepsi Vanilla launch campaign?

Exhibit 1.4 Vanilla Pepsi
Courtesy of Pepsi Co.

Communication differences

Having identified the need to communicate with a number of different audiences, it seems appropriate to conclude this opening chapter by examining the differences between communications used by and targeted at two very different and specific audiences. These are organisations (commonly referred to as business-to-business) and those aimed at consumer markets. Some writers (Brougaletta, 1985; Gilliland and Johnston, 1997) have documented a variety of differences between consumer and business-to-business markets. The following is intended to set out some of the more salient differences (see also Table 1.5):

Message reception

The contextual conditions in which messages are received and ascribed meanings are very different. In the organisational setting the context is much more formal, and as the funding for the purchase is to be derived from company sources (as opposed to personal sources for consumer market purchases) there may be a lower orientation to the price as a significant variable in the purchase decision. The item is intended for company usage, whereas products bought in a consumer context are normally intended for personal consumption.

Number of decision-makers

In consumer markets a single person very often makes the decision. In organisational markets decisions are made by many people within the buying centre. This means that the interactions

Table 1.5 Differences between consumer and business-to-business marketing communications

	Consumer-oriented markets	Business-to-business markets
Message reception	Informal	Formal
Number of decision-makers	Single or few	Many
Balance of the promotional mix	Advertising and sales promotions dominate	Personal selling dominates
Specificity and integration	Broad use of communications mix with a move towards integrated mixes	Specific use of below-the-line tools but with a high level of integration
Message content	Greater use of emotions and imagery	Greater use of rational, logic and information-based messages although there is evidence of a move towards the use of imagery
Message origin	Increasing use of user-generated-content	Limited use of user-generated materials
Length of decision time	Normally short	Longer and more involved
Negative communications	Limited to people close to the purchaser/user	Potentially an array of people in the organisation and beyond
Target marketing and research	Great use of sophisticated targeting and communication approaches	Limited but increasing use of targeting and segmentation approaches
Budget allocation	Majority of budget allocated to brand management	Majority of budget allocated to sales management
Evaluation and measurement	Great variety of techniques and approaches used	Limited number of techniques and approaches used

of the participants should be considered. In addition, a variety of different individuals need to be reached and influenced and this may involve the use of different media and message strategies.

The balance of the communications mix

The role of advertising and sales promotions in business-to-business communications is primarily to support the personal selling effort.

The role of advertising and sales promotions in business-to-business communications is primarily to support the personal selling effort. This contrasts with the mix that predominates in consumer markets. Personal selling plays a relatively minor role and is only significant at the point of purchase in some product categories where involvement is high (cars, white goods and financial services), reflecting high levels of perceived risk. However, the increasing use of direct marketing in consumer markets suggests that personal communications are becoming more prevalent and in some ways increasingly similar to the overall direction of business-to-business communications.

The constituents of the marketing communications mix

Business-to-business markets have traditionally been quite specific in terms of the promotional tools and media used to target audiences. While the use of advertising literature is very important, there has been a tendency to use a greater proportion of below-the-line activities. This compares with consumer markets, where a greater proportion of funds have been allocated to above-the-line activities. It is interesting that the communications in the consumer market are moving towards a more integrated format, more similar in form to the business-to-business model than was previously considered appropriate.

Message content

Generally, there is high involvement in many business-to-business purchase decisions, so communications tend to be much more rational and information-based than in consumer markets. However, there are signs that businesses are making increased use of imagery and emotions in the messages (see Chapters 17 and 29).

Message Origin

Increasingly, consumers are taking a more active role in the creation of content.

Increasingly, consumers are taking a more active role in the creation of content. Blogging for example, is important in both consumer and business markets, but the development of user-generated-content and word-of-mouth communication is becoming a significant part of consumer-based marketing communications activities.

Length of purchase decision time

The length of time taken to reach a decision is much greater in the organisation market. This means that the intensity of any media plan can be dissipated more easily in the organisational market.

Negative communications

The number of people affected by a dissatisfied consumer, and hence negative marketing communication messages, is limited. The implications of a poor purchase decision in an organisational environment may be far-reaching, including those associated with the use of the product, the career of participants close to the locus of the decision and, depending on the size and spread, perhaps the whole organisation.

Target marketing and research

The use of target marketing processes in the consumer market is more advanced and sophisticated than in the organisational market. This impacts on the quality of the marketing communications used to reach the target audience. However, there is much evidence that the business-to-business markets organisations are becoming increasingly aware and sophisticated in their approach to segmentation techniques and processes.

The use of target marketing processes in the consumer market is more advanced and sophisticated than in the organisational market.

Budget allocation

The sales department receives the bulk of the marketing budget in the organisation market and little is spent on research in comparison with the consumer market.

Measurement and evaluation

The consumer market employs a variety of techniques to evaluate the effectiveness of communications. In the organisation market, sales volume, value, number of enquiries and market share are the predominant measures of effectiveness.

There can be no doubt that there are a number of major differences between consumer and organisational communications. These reflect the nature of the environments, the tasks involved and the overall need of the recipients for particular types of information. Information need, therefore, can be seen as a primary reason for the differences in the way communication mixes are configured. Advertising in organisational markets has to provide a greater level of information and is geared to generating leads that can be followed up with personal selling, which is traditionally the primary tool in the promotional mix. In consumer markets, advertising used to play the primary role with support from the other tools of the promotional mix. This is not always true today as organisations use other tools such as public relations, combined with digital media, to reach particular audiences. Interestingly, digital media appear to be helping to reconfigure the marketing communications mix and perhaps reducing the gulf and distinction between the mix used in business-to-business and consumer markets. Throughout this book, reference will be made to the characteristics, concepts and processes associated with marketing communications in each of these two main sectors.

There are a number of major differences between consumer and organisational communications.

Summary

In order to help consolidate your understanding about this introduction to marketing communications, here are the key points summarised against each of the learning objectives:

1. Examine the concept of exchange in the marketing context.

The concept of exchange transactions underpins the marketing concept. Of the different types of exchange, market and collaborative exchanges are the two that can be observed most often in industrial societies. Relationships become stronger as exchanges move from market towards a collaborative status. This is regarded as a relational approach.

2. Assess the role of communication in the context of the marketing mix.

Marketing communications has an important role to play in communicating and positioning products and services, not only for consumers but also with regard to the business-to-business sector and other organisations that represent other stakeholders. The role of communications is to engage audiences with a view to differentiate products and services, reinforce beliefs and experiences, inform on availability and finally, persuade audiences to behave in particular ways.

3. Consider the nature of the marketing communications mix.

The configuration of the marketing communications mix is changing. For a long time the mix was assumed to be just about the tools, with the media playing a secondary role. Now, with a proliferation of media and content being created by consumers, the tools no longer dominate mix decisions and all three elements play important roles.

4. Identify the key characteristics of each major tool in the communications mix.

The key tools consist of advertising, public relations, sales promotion, direct marketing and personal selling. Each has particular characteristics but they can all be considered in terms of four key parameters: their ability to communicate; the level of control that management may use; the costs involved in their use; and the credibility each is perceived to have. These are brought together within the 4Cs framework.

5. Examine the effectiveness of each communication tool.

All of the tools are effective means of delivering communication. However, their effectiveness varies at different points, best observed through the purchase decision sequence. For example, advertising is good at raising awareness and personal selling is best at closing orders. Neither excels at the other's strengths.

6. Appreciate the importance of understanding the significance of context in marketing communications.

Marketing communication activities occur within a specific set of circumstances, referred to as a context. Managers need to identify the key aspects of any context and deliver messages that complement the prevailing conditions. This enables audiences to interpret messages correctly and assists them in developing interaction and dialogue.

7. Compare the use of marketing communications in the consumer and business markets.

The way in which the marketing communication mix is configured for consumer markets is very different from the mix used for business markets. The tools, media and messages used are all different as the general contexts in which they operate require different approaches.

Review questions

1. Briefly compare and contrast the two main types of exchange transaction.
2. How does communication assist the exchange process?
3. What is the role of marketing communications and identify the key tasks that it is required to undertake?
4. Name the three main elements that make up the marketing communications mix.
5. How do each of the tools compare across the following criteria: control, communication effectiveness and cost?
6. How does direct marketing differ from the other tools of the mix?

7. Identify five different advertisements that you think use direct-response media. How effective do you think they might be?
8. Explain contexts and episodes. Describe the main tasks facing the management team responsible for marketing communications.
9. What is systems theory and how might it apply to marketing communications?
10. Explain how marketing communications supports the marketing and business strategies of the organisation.

MiniCase Hadrian's Wall – marketing the Roman frontier

Gary Warnaby: University of Liverpool Management School
David Bennison: Manchester Metropolitan University Business School
Dominic Medway: Manchester Business School

Introduction

Hadrian's Wall dates from AD 122 and is the most spectacular and best known Roman *limes* or frontier system (Dudley, 1970), stretching across the narrowest part of England, from the River Tyne in the east to the Solway Firth in the west – a distance of 80 Roman miles (122km or 76 modern miles) (Crow, 1989). It 'stood as a dramatic gesture of Roman power and superior technology over the barbarian peoples to the north and south of the frontier' (Crow, 1989: 39). It has been described as 'the greatest monument to Roman achievement in Britain' (Hunter Blair, 1963: 74).

Although much of the original Wall has since disappeared, in 1987 Hadrian's Wall was designated as a World Heritage Site by UNESCO,[1] in recognition of its attributes. The Wall, and the larger forts in its vicinity (the best known of which are Housesteads and Vindolanda), are recognised as '*magnet attractions*' in the North East England Tourism Strategy for 2005–10 developed by One NorthEast,[2] the regional development agency. '*Magnet attractions*' are those that '*generate the highest visitor numbers and expenditure in the North East*' and '*play a vital role as catalysts in themed campaigns and in drawing visitors to our more dispersed attractions*' (One NorthEast, 2005: 16). Indeed, walking the length of Hadrian's Wall has long been popular, and a cross-country footpath from Wallsend in Newcastle to Bowness-on-Solway was designated an official National Trail in May 2003 with many new sections of path following the wall itself.[3] However, this has raised concerns about the destruction of valuable archaeology as a consequence of increased erosion caused by walkers (British Archaeology, 2005).

Research commissioned by the two regional development agencies One NorthEast and NorthWest RDA (ONE/NWDA, 2004) indicated that in 2003, the estimated number of visitors to 'Hadrian's Wall Country' (HWC) stood at 776,000. Of this total 458,000 were visiting the museums and historic sites along the Wall, on average visiting 1.3 sites. Thirty-one thousand visitors were estimated to be serious walkers but not visiting any of the sites, and the remainder (287,000) were estimated to be general sightseers (i.e. not visiting any particular Roman site or walking). However, visitor numbers are on a long-term downward trend and there is a perception that more could be made of this unique asset. Consequently, in 2003, a major study was commissioned, the aim of which was to assess the potential of Hadrian's Wall, and according to the chief executive of One NorthEast, '*take an independent view on how best this status can be developed through a Vision that all partners can be part of and one that will maximise the economic potential of the Wall in terms of visitor spending and job creation*' (NorthWest RDA/One North East, Press Release, 6 September 2004).

Perceptions of Hadrian's Wall[4]

The first stage of the major study process was to implement research into the perceptions of the Wall among consumers and key stakeholder organisations.

Consumer research reported in the major study report indicated that expectations of the Hadrian's Wall 'experience' were modest. Non-visitors felt that there was not enough there to warrant a visit. Previous visitors remembered the Wall in terms of the individual sites visited, not as a holistic entity. Research indicated that visitors had low expectations in advance of their visit, although the actual experience was perceived fairly positively, despite '*requiring a high level of effort from the visitor*', and not having '*the sort of "wow" factor that leads to recommendations to friends and family to visit*' (ONE/NWDA, 2004: 1). Visitors perceived that there was little effort made to link individual sites together in the context of the bigger Hadrian's Wall 'story'.

Stakeholders in the development of the Wall recognised that significant improvements were required – not only to the Wall itself, but also to the supporting infrastructure. Convincing local businesses and communities of the benefits that could accrue from increased tourism levels (particularly after the outbreak of foot and mouth disease in 2001, which had a severe impact on the rural economy of many areas of Britain), was regarded as key to achieving this. However, existing unwieldy organisational arrangements were seen as a potential obstacle as there was a requirement to represent *all* the interests involved. Consequently, no single organisation had clear authority and it was felt that the overall management of the Wall suffered as a result.

Vision and objectives

The second stage of the major study was the development of a vision for the Wall in order to guide the partners in their actions in delivering a world-class visitor experience. Branding consultants were hired to develop and test a draft vision. The 'audacious' goal was:

> To move Hadrian's Wall from a Northern 'ought to see' to a Global 'must see, stay and return for more'.

This was to be achieved by positioning the Wall as the 'Greatest Roman Frontier' (ONE/NWDA, 2004, p. 4).

It was recognised that the ambitious nature of the goal had significant implications – organisational structures that were capable of directing substantial capital investment budgets and managing the future direction of the Wall needed to be in place. The creation of a visitor experience that could deliver the 'Greatest Roman Frontier' positioning was complicated by the geography of the Wall and the existing management structure. The main visitor sites are geographically disconnected because of the physical length of the Wall, limiting the potential for visiting more than one site in a single trip. Weak linkages between the individual sites mean that it is difficult consistently to communicate what the Wall has to offer. Moreover, the individual sites are owned and operated by different organisations, each with its own style of presentation and quality of interpretation. Inevitably there is a degree of competition between the individual sites. In addition, the development of a suitable supporting visitor infrastructure is a crucial dimension. While this was outside the remit of the major study, it is recognised that it is a crucial part of the visitor experience that will need to be addressed if the vision is to be achieved.

The next stage was the development of a strategy for delivering the vision of the 'Greatest Roman Frontier' in such a way as to support economic regeneration in the region. Here, the specific requirements of the different sections of the Wall need to be recognised:

- Central section
  This is the most developed and best-recognised section of the Wall, which passes through environmentally sensitive landscapes. The articulated strategic objective is to grow visitor revenues in ways that recognise and address existing, as well as potential future visitor management issues.
- Cumbria section
  This section of the Wall is less developed, with little customer awareness. Knowledge of the links between Roman sites on the Cumbrian coast and Hadrian's Wall is largely limited to those with a particular interest in Roman archaeology.
- Tyne and Wear section
  This urban section of the Wall in Newcastle-upon-Tyne includes two popular visitor sites, Segedunum and Arbeia, along with the less well-known Museum of Antiquities which is located on the university campus. There are existing plans to relocate the Museum of Antiquities to incorporate it into a proposed larger museum in Newcastle. The objective for this section is to establish the existing and planned sites as part of the 'Greatest Roman Frontier' with the aim of broadening their visitor market.

These three sections of the wall have been explicitly highlighted in the Hadrian's Wall Country logo, which is featured in subsequent marketing communications. The logo incorporates a cartographic representation of the wall, with the three squares relating to the sections of the Wall outlined above. A recent modification of the logo has extended the line of the Wall in the Cumbria section (i.e. the left-hand square) to incorporate the Cumbrian coastline in its entirety.

The aim of the strategy is to increase the number of visitors to Hadrian's Wall Country to 1,038,000 by 2011, with visitors to sites growing from the current level of 665,000 and the number of sites visited increasing to just over 1.8. This inevitably has implications for marketing communications activities, and the following communications tasks were articulated in the major study document:

1. Raise public awareness of the new interpretation and experiences along the Wall, including its little-known existence along the West Cumbria coast.

2. Convert the awareness into visits to the Wall for whatever type of experience particular tourists enjoy, whether it be an intensive single visit to one particular site, a day visiting several sites, a walk on part of the Trail, or a staying visit that can involve an extended version of any of the above.

Developing management structures

Another conclusion of the major study report was the need to develop successful partnership working, given the multitude of stakeholders involved – for example the production of the Hadrian's Wall Management Plan (which is a condition of achieving World Heritage Site status), has its own committee of 52 stakeholders. Drawing on the experience of similar contexts, it was ascertained that the management structure of the most successful locations appeared to be a formal central organisational structure with devolved powers in order to facilitate coordinated development activities. A further report on how this might be achieved was produced in April 2005, and subsequently Hadrian's Wall Heritage Limited (HWHL) was created in May 2006, the aim of which is:

> To realise the economic, social and cultural regeneration potential of the Hadrian's Wall World Heritage Site and the communities and environment through which it passes by sustainable tourism development, management and conservation activities, which benefit local communities and the wider region. And all that done in a way that reflects the values embodied in the World Heritage Site Management Plan.
> (HWHL, n/d)

It is envisaged that HWHL will be a catalyst for the economic and cultural regeneration of the Hadrian's Wall corridor and will facilitate a ten-year programme of capital and revenue projects that will deliver economic and conservation benefits to communities from West Cumbria to Tyneside. It will act as the lead agency for the delivery of investment and conservation projects associated with the Wall and its surrounding communities – in other words it '*will be a Hadrian's Wall one-stop shop*'. As part of this function, it will be the main point of contact for people wanting information about the Wall (HWHL, n/d).

Marketing communications activities

Marketing – and particularly marketing communications – activity will be a crucial element of achieving the above objectives, and in its first 18 months of operation HWHL has undertaken numerous initiatives in order, '*to build brand awareness, encourage more and prolonged visits, and grow the longer term visitor economy*' (HWHL, 2007b: 24).

Crucial in this has been the development of a web site – www.hadrians-wall.org. According to HWHL's marketing strategy, the web site represents

> a multi-dimensional way of presenting the offer: [it] can present content in a more inspirational way, across different formats so that the HWC offer can be brought to life [and it] will be a main tool in repositioning the HWC offer, diversifying from the main theme of the wall as part of the Roman frontier, as well as providing deeper, richer and more interactive content on that part of the area's history.
> (HWHL, 2007a: 6)

Linked to this, in 2007, the summer marketing campaign was built around the theme 'Plan your invasion'. The main focus of this was a stand-alone web-based journey planner, with an interface that actively promoted the various destinations, facilities and attractions of 'Hadrian's Wall Country'. In addition, there were full colour press adverts which ran in July and August. These adverts emphasised the range of activities, facilities and attractions that were located in the area – not only those explicitly linked to the Roman heritage, but also those with a more tangential relationship (e.g. art galleries, cafes, restaurants, etc.), which nevertheless contribute to the overall visitor experience.

In addition, this activity was supported by promotional literature designed to be used by visitors before and during their visit. The existing Hadrian's Wall World Heritage Site newsletter has been relaunched as *Frontier*, with features and stories aimed at those with an interest in the Wall and Roman heritage, which is available both as a printed version and as an e-zine with added online content. Other important publications include a *Roman Attractions* leaflet and accommodation mini guide, an updated *Essential Guide to Hadrian's Wall Path National Trail* and a booklet entitled *Walking in Hadrians' Wall Country* (incorporating 15 circular walks). Thirty-five thousand copies of this last publication were tactically distributed throughout the corridor and its access points, and copies sent to numerous travel and walking journalists, with several walking press trips set up for Spring 2008.

Indeed, HWHL has been actively engaged in public relations activities designed to stimulate and maintain media interest in the area at local, regional and national level through national and local print and broadcast media as well as relevant web sites, with a view to aligning coverage to marketing campaigns and key messages. The web site has an image library that best represents Hadrian's Wall Country.

Initial evaluation of these activities has been positive. Approximately 2.1 million people saw the press advertising, and the online journey planner has received over 1 million hits to date (and was named 'Website of the Week' by *New Media Age* magazine). Media relations activity has been successful, with coverage in various print media vehicles and also in national broadcast media including television programmes such as *Timewatch*, *Britain's Best* (Hadrian's Wall was shortlisted in this programme, showcasing some of Britain's finest heritage sites and encouraging viewers to vote for their choice), *Britain's Favourite View*, *Written Britain*, and a six-part series entitled *The Wall*, scheduled for Spring 2008. This covered the story of the Wall and the communities living in and around it, 'then and now' (HWHL, 2007b).

These activities seem set to ensure that the profile of Hadrian's Wall will be raised both regionally and nationally into the future, and a positive start has been made in achieving the articulated vision for the locale.

MiniCase references

British Archaeology (2005) New body to promote endangered Roman wall, *British Archaeology*, 82, May/June. Available at http://www/britarch.ac.uk/ba/ba82/news.shtml. Retrieved 1 August 2005.

Carman, J. (2002) *Archaeology & Heritage: An Introduction*. London & New York: Continuum.

Crow, J.G. (1989) *Housesteads Roman Fort*. London: English Heritage.

Dudley, D. (1970) *Roman Society*. Harmondsworth: Penguin Books.

Hadrian's Wall Heritage Ltd (2007a) *Hadrian's Wall Heritage marketing Strategy 2007–2010*. Hexham: HWHL.

Hadrian's Wall Heritage Ltd (2007b) *Annual Review 2006–07: Bringing History and Landscape to Life*. Hexham: HWHL.

Hadrian's Wall Heritage Ltd (n/d) *New Opportunities, A New Company, 2000 Years of History*. Hexham: HWHL.

Hunter Blair, P. (1963) *Roman Britain and Early England 55B.C. – A.D.871* New York & London: W.W. Norton & Company.

One NorthEast (2005) *North East England Tourism Strategy Final Report*.

One NorthEast/North West Development Agency (2004) *Hadrian's Wall Major Study Report Summary September 2004*.

MiniCase notes

1. UNESCO is the United Nations Educational, Scientific and Cultural Organisation. Its remit is to contribute to peace and security in the world by promoting collaboration among nations through education, science, culture and communication. More detail of the remit of UNESCO with particular reference to heritage is given by Carman (2002). It operates the World Heritage list of monuments, groups of buildings or sites considered to be 'of outstanding universal value' as defined by various criteria, which are provided at http://whc.unesco.org/criteria/htm.
2. One NorthEast is the Regional Development Agency for the north east of England. It was established in April 1999 and is responsible for setting and implementing the agenda for economic and business development, regeneration and improvement in that area. More detail about the organisation can be found at http://www.onenortheast.co.uk/page/aboutone/index.cfm.
3. More details can be found at http://www.ramblers.org.uk/info/paths/hadrianswall.html.
4. The primary source is the *Hadrian's Wall Major Study Report Summary September 2004* (ONE/NWDA, 2004) produced by One NorthEast and its counterpart in the north west of England, the NorthWest Regional Development Agency.

MiniCase questions

1. What issues may potentially impact on the achievement of the vision for Hadrian's Wall and its positioning as the 'Greatest Roman Frontier', and consequently would need to be taken into account in the planning process?
2. What are the implications of the 'Greatest Roman Frontier' positioning for the 'product' being marketed, initially by the two regional development agencies, and now by Hadrian's Wall Heritage Limited?
3. How might the chosen positioning be communicated to relevant target audiences into the future?

References

Andersson, P. (1992) Analysing distribution channel dynamics. *European Journal of Marketing*, **26**(2), 47–68.

Bagozzi, R. (1978) Marketing as exchange: a theory of transactions in the market place. *American Behavioral Science*, **21**(4), 257–61.

Baines, P., Fill, C. and Page, K. (2008) *Marketing*, Oxford: Oxford University Press.

Balmer, J.M.T. and Gray, E.R. (2003) Corporate brands: what are they? What of them? *European Journal of Marketing*, **37**(7/8), 972–97.

Bashford, S. (2007) Collaboration is imperative. *Marketing*, 13 December, 4–5.

Beeching, P. and Wood, J. (2007) The rise and fall of the advertising agency. *Admap*, (January), Issue 479, 48–9.

Bhatnagar, P. (2003) Joy of (Vanilla) Pepsi? *CNN Money*, 8 September Retrieved 27 September, 2007 from www/money.cnn.com/2003/08/07/news/companies/pepsi_vanilla/.

Bowersox, D. and Morash, E. (1989) The integration of marketing flows in channels of distribution. *European Journal of Marketing*, **23**, 2.

Brougaletta, Y. (1985) What business-to-business advertisers can learn from consumer advertisers. *Journal of Advertising Research*, **25**(3), 8–9.

Dorrell, E. (2007) Changing tack. *NMA*, 5 July, 21.

Dwyer, R., Schurr, P. and Oh, S. (1987) Developing buyer–seller relationships. *Journal of Marketing*, **51** (April), 11–27.

Effie Awards (2003) Pepsi Vanilla: 'the not-so-vanilla vanilla' Retrieved 27 September 2007 from http://effie.org.ua/files/Pepsi_Vanilla._the_notsovanilla_vanilla.pdf.

Fill, C. (2002) *Marketing Communications*, 3rd edn. Harrow: Financial Times Prentice-Hall.

Gilliland, D.I. and Johnston, W.J. (1997) Toward a model of business-to-business marketing communications effects. *Industrial Marketing Management*, **26**, 15–29.

Goldhaber, G.M. (1986) *Organisational Communication*. Dubuque, IA: W.C. Brown.

Gronroos, C. (2004) The relationship marketing process: communication, interaction, dialogue, value. *Journal of Business and Industrial Marketing*, **19**(2), 99–113.

Heinonen, K. and Strandvik, T. (2005) Communication as a element of service value. *International Journal of Service Industry Management*, **16**(2), 186–98.

Houston, F. and Gassenheimer, J. (1987) Marketing and exchange. *Journal of Marketing*, **51** (October), 13–18.

Hughes, G. and Fill, C. (2007), Redefining the nature and format of the marketing communications mix. *The Marketing Review*, 7(1), 45–57.

Katz, D. and Kahn, R.L. (1978) *The Social Psychology of Organisations*, 2nd edn. New York: Wiley.

Lloyd, J. (1997) Cut your rep free. *Pharmaceutical Marketing* (September), 30–2.

McCarthy, E.J. (1960) *Basic Marketing: A Managerial Approach*. Homewood, IL: Irwin.

Macneil, I.R. (1983) Values in Contract: internal and external. *Northwestern Law Review*, **78**(2), 340–418.

Mohr, J. and Nevin, J. (1990) Communication strategies in marketing channels. *Journal of Marketing*, **54** (October), 36–51.

Stern, L. and El-Ansary, A. (1995) *Marketing Channels*, 5th edn. Englewood Cliffs, NJ: Prentice-Hall.

Turner, C. (2008) How Red Bull invented the 'cool' factor, *UTALK Marketing*. Retrieved 12 February 2008 from www.utalkmarketing.com/pages/article.

Chapter 2

Communication theory

Only by sharing meaning with members of the target audience and reducing levels of ambiguity can it be hoped to create a dialogue through which marketing goals can be accomplished. To share meaning successfully may require the support of significant others: those who may be expert, knowledgeable or have access to appropriate media channels.

Aims and learning objectives

The aims of this chapter are to introduce communication theory and to set it in the context of marketing communications.

The learning objectives of this chapter are to:

1. understand the core model of the communication process and how the various elements link together;
2. appreciate how the components of the model contribute to successful communications;
3. examine the impact of the media on the communication process;
4. evaluate the impact of personal influences on the communication process;
5. examine the nature and characteristics associated with word-of-mouth communication;
6. consider the nature and influence of interactivity in communication;
7. introduce more recent explanations of communication theory, including networks;
8. explain how communication theory underpins our understanding of marketing communications.

For an applied interpretation see Lynn Sudbury's MiniCase entitled ***Because it Works!*** at the end of this chapter.

An introduction to the process of communication

It was established in the previous chapter that marketing communications is partly an attempt by an organisation/brand to create and sustain a dialogue with its various constituencies. Communication itself is the process by which individuals share meaning. Therefore, for interaction and even dialogue to occur, each participant in the communication process needs to be able to interpret the meaning embedded in the others messages, and be able to respond. For this overall process to work, information needs to be transmitted to and from all participants. It is important, therefore, that those involved with marketing communications understand the complexity of the transmission process. Through knowledge and understanding of the communications process, participants are more likely to achieve their objective of sharing meaning with each member of their target audiences and so have an opportunity to enter into a dialogue.

Communication itself is the process by which individuals share meaning.

In the previous chapter the point was established that there are a variety of reasons why organisations need to communicate with various groups. Of these, one of the more prominent is the need to influence or persuade. As an initial observation, persuasive communications can be seen in three different contexts. These are set out in Table 2.1.

These three perspectives focus upon the use of persuasion, but there is a strong need for organisations also to inform and remind. Furthermore, these approaches are too specific for general marketing purposes and fail to provide assistance to those who wish to plan and manage particular communication activities.

Table 2.1 Forms of persuasion

Form of persuasion	Explanation
Negotiation	Individuals use a variety of overt and subtle rewards and punishments to persuade the other of the superiority of their point of view.
Propaganda	Organisations seek to influence their target audiences through the use of symbols, training and cultural indoctrination.
Use of speakers	When a speaker addresses a large group influence is achieved through the structure of the material presented, the manner in which the presentation is delivered and the form of evidence used to influence the group.

A linear model of communication

Wilbur Schramm (1955) developed what is now accepted as the basic model of mass communications (Figure 2.1). The components of the linear model of communication are:

1. Source: the individual or organisation sending the message.
2. Encoding: transferring the intended message into a symbolic style that can be transmitted.
3. Signal: the transmission of the message using particular media.
4. Decoding: understanding the symbolic style of the message in order to understand the message.
5. Receiver: the individual or organisation receiving the message.

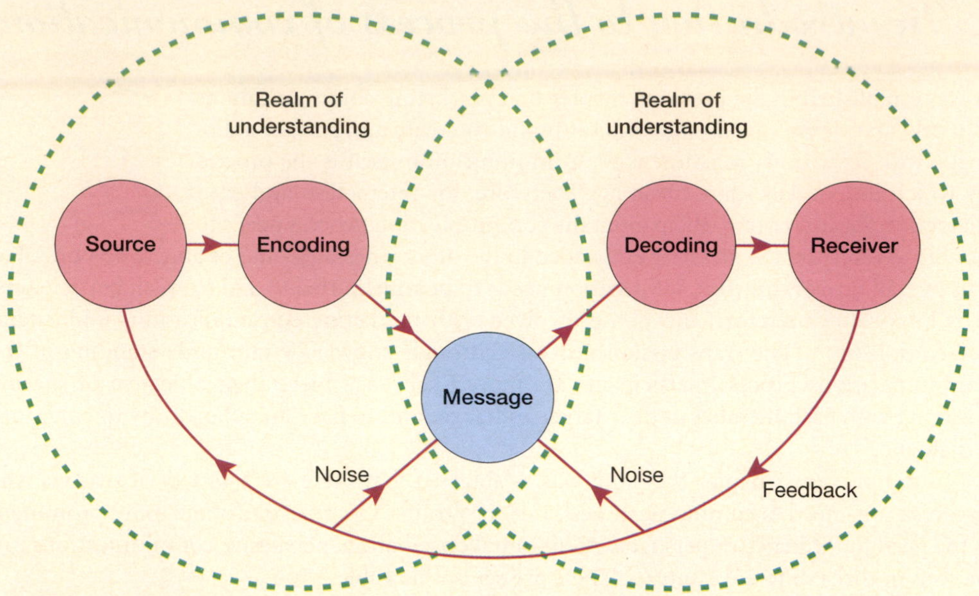

Figure 2.1 A linear model of communication
Source: Based on Schramm (1955) and Shannon and Weaver (1962).

6. Feedback: the receiver's communication back to the source on receipt of the message.
7. Noise: distortion of the communication process, making it difficult for the receiver to interpret the message as intended by the source.

It is the quality of the linkages between the various elements in the process that determine whether a communication event will be successful.

This is a linear model that emphasises the 'transmission of information, ideas, attitudes, or emotion from one person or group to another (or others), primarily through symbols' (Theodorson and Theodorson, 1969). The model and its components are straightforward, but it is the quality of the linkages between the various elements in the process that determine whether a communication event will be successful.

Source/encoding

The source, an individual or organisation, identifies a need to transmit a message and then selects a combination of appropriate words, pictures, symbols and music to represent the message to be transmitted. This is called encoding. The purpose is to create a message that is capable of being understood by the receiver.

There are a number of reasons why the source/encoding link might break down. For example, the source may fail to diagnose a particular situation accurately. By not fully understanding a stakeholder's problem or level of knowledge, inappropriate information may be included in the message, which, when transmitted, may lead to misunderstanding and misinterpretation by the receiver. By failing to appreciate the level of education of the target receiver, a message might be encoded in words and symbols that are beyond the comprehension of the receiver.

The source of a message is an important factor in the communication process.

Some organisations spend a great deal of time and expense on marketing research, trying to develop their understanding of their target audience. The source of a message is an important factor in the communication process.

Delightful honey and acacia blossom.
Finished with a hint of freshly toasted brioche.
A simply superb Champagne.
And at BUY 2 GET 3RD FREE.
It's a £%@#ing Christmas cracker!
Wines you can swear by
threshers

Exhibit 2.1 A magazine ad for Threshers demonstrating linear communication
Image courtesy of The Advertising Archives.

A receiver who perceives a source lacking conviction, authority, trust or expertise is likely to discount any message received from that source, until such time as credibility is established.

Most organisations spend a great deal of time and expense recruiting sales representatives. The risk involved in selecting the wrong people can be extremely large. Many high-tech organisations require their new sales staff to spend over a year receiving both product and sales training before allowing them to meet customers. From a customer's perspective, salespersons who display strong product knowledge skills and who are also able to empathise with the individual members of the decision-making unit are more likely to be perceived as credible. Therefore, an organisation that prepares its sales staff and presents them as knowledgeable and trustworthy is more likely to be successful in the communication process than one that does not take the same level of care.

The source is a part of the communication process, not just the generator of detached messages. Patzer (1983) determined that the physical attractiveness of the communicator, particularly if it is the source, contributes significantly to the effectiveness of persuasive communications.

This observation can be related to the use, by organisations, of spokespersons and celebrities to endorse products. Spokespersons can be better facilitators of the communication process if they are able to convey conviction, if they are easily associated with the object of the message, if they have credible expertise and if they are attractive to the receiver, in the wider sense of the word.

This legitimate authority is developed in many television advertisements by the use of the 'white coat', or product-specific clothing, as a symbol of expertise. By dressing the spokesperson in a white coat, they are immediately perceived as a credible source of information ('they know what they are talking about'), and so are much more likely to be believed.

Signal

Once encoded, the message must be put into a form that is capable of transmission. It may be oral or written, verbal or non-verbal, in a symbolic form or in a sign. Whatever the format chosen, the source must be sure that what is being put into the message is what is required to be decoded by the receiver. The importance of this aspect of the communication process will be developed later when different message strategies are examined in Chapter 17.

The channel is the means by which the message is transmitted from the source to the receiver.

The channel is the means by which the message is transmitted from the source to the receiver. These channels may be personal or non-personal. The former involves face-to-face contact and word-of-mouth communications, which can be extremely influential. Non-personal channels are characterised by mass media advertising, which can reach large audiences.

Information received directly from personal influence channels is generally more persuasive than information received through mass media. This may be a statement of the obvious, but the reasons for this need to be understood. First, the individual approach permits greater flexibility in the delivery of the message. The timing and power with which a message is delivered can be adjusted to suit the immediate 'selling' environment. Second, a message can be adapted to meet the needs of the customer as the sales call progresses. This flexibility is not possible with mass media messages, as these have to be designed and produced well in advance of transmission and often without direct customer input.

ViewPoint 2.1 Is this what you really meant?

When developing names or taglines for global brands it is important to choose a name that translates appropriately into all the languages. The encoding process, the name of the car, cleaner, biscuit or fashion accessory should be well researched and capable of being decoded by the target audience in such a way that there is meaning, sense and value. The following are examples where the encoding process had not been properly considered:

- When the European hardware store chain 'Götzen' opened in Istanbul they had to change the name as 'Göt' means 'ass' in Turkish.
- 'Traficante' is an Italian brand of mineral water. In Spanish, it means drug dealer.
- Clairol's 'Mist Stick', curling iron had problems when launched in Germany because 'Mist' is slang for manure.
- A main-stream UK bank informed audiences in a recent advertising campaign that to show the soles of your feet in Thailand is a very rude gesture and, to give the thumbs up sign in Turkey, has quite the opposite meaning to its symbolism of cool acceptance here in Britain.
- Finally, workers in an African port saw a consignment with the international symbol for 'fragile' (a wine glass with snapped stem) on the side. They assumed it meant that they had been sent a cargo of broken glass and immediately pitched all the cases overboard into the harbour.

Sources: Adapted from: www.i18nguy.com/translations and http://www.sourceuk.net/indexf.html?03590.

Question

To what extent should the encoding process be researched?

Task

Search the web and find your own examples of communications where different meanings have emerged.

Decoding/receiver

Decoding is the process of transforming and interpreting a message into thought. This process is influenced by the receiver's realm of understanding, which encompasses the experiences, perceptions, attitudes and values of both the source and the receiver. The more the receiver understands about the source and the greater their experience in decoding the source's messages, the more able the receiver will be to decode the message successfully.

Exhibit 2.2 Decoding a print ad

Shows a lady relaxing in the foreground and something resembling a cooker (the AGA), in the background. How are these two focal parts of the image related? The copy helps the reader decipher the code.

Aga, taken from their Love Aga Compaign, www.aga-web.co.uk.

Feedback/response

Feedback is that part of the response that is sent back to the sender, and it is essential for successful communication.

The set of reactions a receiver has after seeing, hearing or reading the message is known as the response. These reactions may vary from the extreme of dialing an enquiry telephone number, returning a coupon or even buying the product, to storing information in long-term memory for future use. Feedback is that part of the response that is sent back to the sender, and it is essential for successful communication. The need to understand not just whether the message has been received but also which message has been received is vital. For example, the receiver may have decoded the message incorrectly and a completely different set of responses may have been elicited. If a suitable feedback system is not in place then the source will be unaware that the communication has been unsuccessful and is liable to continue wasting resources. This represents inefficient and ineffective marketing communications.

The evaluation of feedback is vital if sound communications are to be developed. Only through evaluation can the success of any communication be judged. Feedback through personal selling can be instantaneous, through overt means such as questioning, raising objections or signing an order form. Other means, such as the use of gestures and body language, are less overt, and the decoding of the feedback needs to be accurate if an appropriate response is to be given. For the advertiser, the process is much more vague and prone to misinterpretation and error.

Feedback through mass media channels is generally much more difficult to obtain, mainly because of the inherent time delay involved in the feedback process. There are some exceptions, namely the overnight ratings provided by the Broadcasters' Audience Research Board to the television contractors, but as a rule feedback is normally delayed and not as fast. Some commentators argue that the only meaningful indicator of communication success is sales. However, there are many other influences that affect the level of sales, such as price, the effect of previous communications, the recommendations of opinion leaders or friends, poor competitor actions or any number of government or regulatory developments. Except in circumstances such as direct marketing, where immediate and direct feedback can be determined, organisations should use other methods to gauge the success of their communications activities, for example, the level and quality of customer inquiries, the number and frequency of store visits, the degree of attitude change and the ability to recognise or recall an advertisement. All of these represent feedback, but, as a rough distinction, the evaluation of feedback for mass communications is much more difficult to judge than the evaluation of interpersonal communications.

Noise

A complicating factor, which may influence the quality of the reception and the feedback, is noise. Noise, according to Mallen (1977), is 'the omission and distortion of information', and there will always be some noise present in all communications. Management's role is to ensure that levels of noise are kept to a minimum, wherever it is able to exert influence.

Noise occurs when a receiver is prevented from receiving all or part of a message in full.

Noise occurs when a receiver is prevented from receiving all or part of a message in full. This may be because of either cognitive or physical factors. For example, a cognitive factor may be that the encoding of the message was inappropriate, thereby making it difficult for the receiver to decode the message. In this circumstance it is said that the realms of understanding of the source and the receiver were not matched. Another reason noise may enter the system is that the receiver may have been physically prevented from decoding the message accurately because the receiver was distracted. Examples of distraction are that the telephone rang, or someone in the room asked a question or coughed. A further reason could be that competing messages screened out the targeted message.

Some sales promotion practitioners are using the word 'noise' to refer to the ambience and publicity surrounding a particular sales promotion event. In other words, the word is being used as a positive, advantageous element in the communication process. This approach is not adopted in this text.

Realms of understanding

Successful communications are more likely to be achieved if the source and the receiver understand each other.

The concept of the 'realm of understanding' was introduced earlier (see p. 42). It is an important element in the communication process because it recognises that successful communications are more likely to be achieved if the source and the receiver understand each other. This understanding concerns attitudes, perceptions, behaviour and experience: the values of both parties to the communication process. Therefore, effective communication is more likely when there is some common ground – a realm of understanding between the source and receiver.

Some organisations, especially those in the private sector, spend a huge amount of money researching their target markets and testing their advertisements to ensure that their messages can be decoded and understood by the target audience. The more organisations understand their receivers, the more confident they become in constructing and transmitting messages to them. Repetition and learning, as we shall see later, are important elements in marketing communications. Learning is a function of knowledge and the more we know, the more likely we are to understand.

Influences of the communication process

The linear, sequential interpretation of the communication process fails to accurately represent all forms of communication. Indeed, it is probable that there is no single model or framework that is entirely satisfactory and capable of covering all forms of communication. However, there are two particular influences on the communication process that need to be considered. First, the media used to convey information and second, the influence of people on the communication process. These are considered in turn.

The influence of the media

The dialogue that marketing communications seeks to generate with audiences is partially constrained by an inherent time delay based on the speed at which responses are generated by the participants in the communication process. Technological advances now allow participants to conduct marketing communication-based 'conversations' at electronic speeds. The essence of this speed attribute is that it allows for interactively based communications, where enquiries are responded to more or less instantly (see Chapters 25 and 26).

New, digital-based technologies, and the Internet in particular, provide an opportunity for interaction and dialogue with customers. With traditional media the tendency is for monologue or at best delayed and inferred dialogue. One of the first points to be made about these new, media-based communications is that the context within which marketing communications occurs is redefined. Traditionally, dialogue occurs in a (relatively) familiar context, which is driven by providers who deliberately present their messages through a variety of communication devices into the environments that they expect their audiences may well pass or recognise. Providers implant their messages into the various environments of their targets. Yuan *et al.* (1998) refer to advertising messages being 'unbundled', such as direct marketing, which has no other content, or 'bundled' and embedded with other news content such as television, radio and web pages with banner ads. Perhaps more pertinently, they refer to direct and indirect online advertising. Direct advertising is concerned with advertising messages delivered to the customers (email) while indirect advertising is concerned with messages that are made available for customers to access at their leisure (web sites).

> New, digital-based technologies, and the Internet in particular, provide an opportunity for interaction and dialogue with customers.

Digital media-based communications tend to make providers relatively passive. Their messages are presented in an environment that requires targets to use specific equipment to actively search them out. The roles are reversed, so that the drivers in the new context are active information seekers, represented by the target audience (members of the public and other information providers such as organisations), not just the information providing organisations.

A further development resulting from the use of digital media in marketing communications is the target of the communication activity. Interactivity, as stated above, has increased in speed, but interactivity can occur not only between people as a result of a message conveyed through a particular medium but also with machines or cyberspace. As Hoffman and Novak (1996) state, people interactivity is now supplemented by machine interactivity. This means

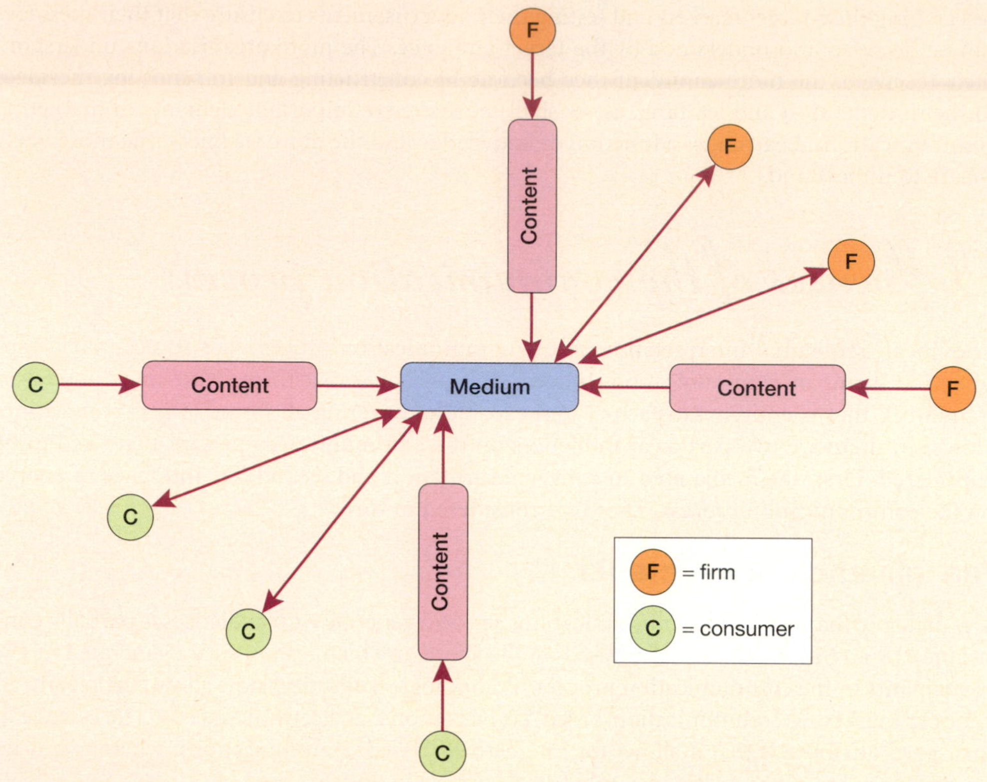

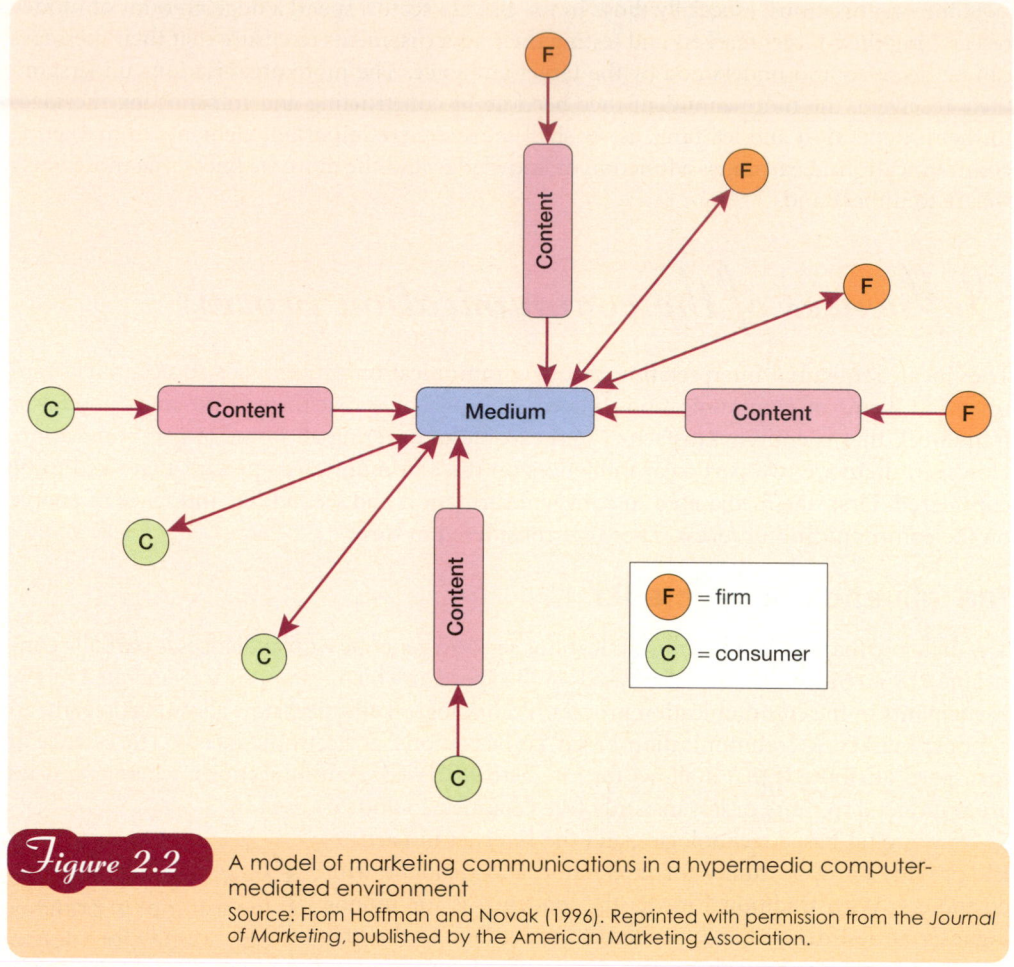

Figure 2.2 A model of marketing communications in a hypermedia computer-mediated environment

Source: From Hoffman and Novak (1996). Reprinted with permission from the *Journal of Marketing*, published by the American Marketing Association.

that the interaction that previously occurred through machines now occurs with the equipment facilitating the communication exchanges (see Figure 2.2).

These authors refer to the work of Steuer (1992), who suggests that the principal relationship is with what is referred to as a *mediated environment* and not between sender and receiver. This is important, as it is the potential of all participants in the communication activity to mediate or influence the environment (especially the message content) in which the interaction occurs that makes interactive marketing communications so dynamic and such a radically revolutionary new promotional medium.

The linear model assumes information content to be essentially one-dimensional, that is, just the spoken word (as in a presentation), just the written word (as in a product leaflet) or just in a visual format (as in a print or television advertisement). Digital media and the development of multimedia facilities have enabled the simultaneous delivery of messages through a variety of formats.

Media richness theory (MRT), developed before the influence of the Internet and related digital technologies, suggests that there is a range or depth of message content embedded within different media and is concerned with the capacity of media types to process ambiguous communication in organisations. According to Daft and Lengel (1986: 560) richness refers to the 'ability of information to change understanding within a time interval'. The criteria used are the availability of instant feedback, the capacity to transmit multiple cues, expressions such as tone of voice, body language and eye contact, the use of natural language and finally, the personal focus of the medium. Face-to-face communication is the richest medium because it helps establish a personal connection. At the other end of the scale, numeric and formal written communication is slow, often visually limited and impersonal. Such media is said to be leaner. The scale starts with face-to-face and is followed by the telephone, email, letter, note, memo, special report, fliers and bulletins. It is argued that rich media have a greater capacity to reduce ambiguity and allow for more complex and difficult communications. Lean media are more cost-effective for simple or routine communications. By fitting the right media to the right type of task, it is argued that managerial performance can be improved or optimised. Media richness theory provides a scale or ranking of different media concerning the richness of information each medium is capable of communicating. With the advent of digital technologies it might be expected that new media would be relatively rich and hence impact positively on task performance.

The scale starts with face-to-face and is followed by the telephone, email, letter, note, memo, special report, fliers and bulletins.

However, although intuitively appealing, there is little empirical evidence to support MRT. Dennis and Kinney (1998) found that new media did allow for quicker decision-making but they argue that MRT is an old theory and not necessarily relevant in the digital age. Other, subsequent theories have evolved and these will be considered in greater depth in Chapter 24.

The influence of people

The traditional view of communication holds that the process consists essentially of one step. Information is directed and shot at prospective audiences, rather like a bullet is propelled from a gun. The decision of each member of the audience to act on the message or not is the result of a passive role or participation in the process (Figure 2.3). Organisations can communicate with different target audiences simply by varying the message and the type and frequency of channels used. The one-step model has been criticised for its oversimplification, and it certainly ignores the effect of personal influences on the communication process and potential for information deviance.

Two-step flow of communication

This model depicts information flowing via media channels to particular types of people (opinion leaders and opinion formers; see p. xx) to whom other members of the audience refer for information and guidance. Through interpersonal networks, opinion leaders not only reach

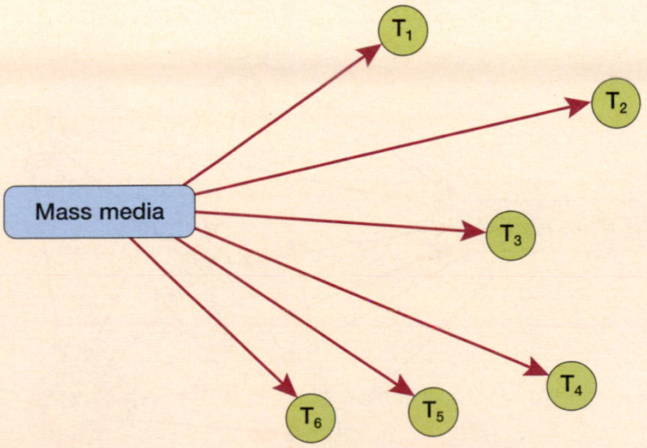

Figure 2.3 One-step model of communication. T = member of the target audience

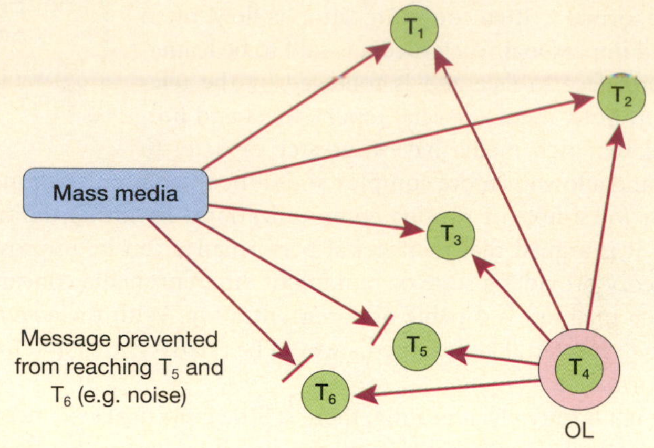

Figure 2.4 Two-step model of communication. OL = opinion leader

members of the target audience who may not have been exposed to the message, but may reinforce the impact of the message for those members who did receive the message (Figure 2.4). For example, editors of travel sections in the Sunday press and television presenters of travel programmes fulfil the role of opinion former and can influence the decision of prospective travellers. It can be seen that targets 5 and 6 were not exposed to the original message, so the opinion leader (OL; T_4) acts as an original information source for them and as a reinforcer for targets 1, 2 and 3.

> The implication of the two-step model is that the mass media do not have a direct and all-powerful effect over their audiences.

The implication of the two-step model is that the mass media do not have a direct and all-powerful effect over their audiences. If the primary function of the mass media is to provide information, then personal influences are necessary to be persuasive and to exert direct influence on members of the target audience.

Multi-step flow of communications

This model proposes that the process involves interaction among all parties to the communication process (see Figure 2.5). This interpretation closely resembles the network of participants who are often involved in the communication process.

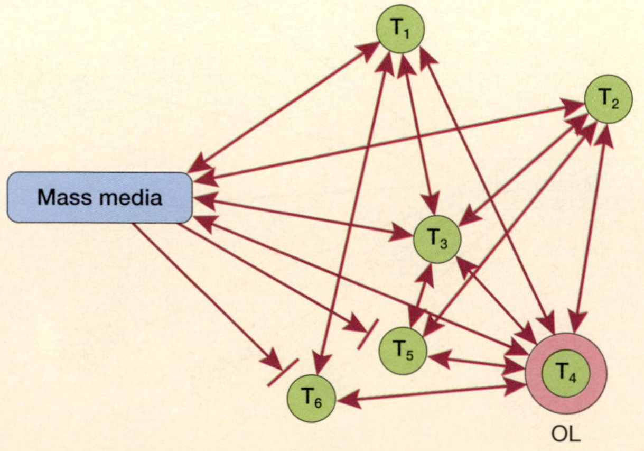

Figure 2.5 Multi-step model of communication

"I wanted a beautiful natural wax finish, so naturally I used Ronseal Quick & Easy Brushing Wax."
After
Before
Ronseal Quick & Easy Brushing Wax is the quick and easy way to create a beautiful natural wax finish.
It's so simple, just brush it on, leave to dry for 10 -20 minutes, then buff off to provide natural colour and protection for interior wood.
Find out more online with colours and step-by-step guides at www.brushingwax.co.uk
RONSEAL
Brushing wax
RONSEAL® DOES EXACTLY WHAT IT SAYS ON THE TIN®

Exhibit 2.3 Brushing Wax print ad. This uses the principles of opinion leadership (a representative of the target audience) to convey product benefits

Word-of-mouth communications

The multi-step model suggests that opinion leaders/formers and members of the target audience all influence each other. Indeed, successful communication is characterised by interaction and word-of-mouth (WoM) communications can assist and enrich this communication process. It might be assumed therefore, that personal influence is important and can enrich the communication process.

Customers use word-of-mouth recommendations to provide information and to support and reinforce their purchasing decisions.

Customers use word-of-mouth recommendations to provide information and to support and reinforce their purchasing decisions. At the heart of this approach is the source credibility that is assigned to people whose opinions are sought after and used in the purchase decision process. In comparison to advertising messages, word-of-mouth communications are considerably more robust (Berkman and Gilson, 1986).

WoM has been related to many aspects of marketing. For example, Woodside and Delozier (1976: 12) link WoM with consumer risk, while others establish links with complaining behaviour (Blodgett *et al.*, 1995: 32), product judgements (Bone, 1995: 214), consumer attitudes (Bickart and Schindler, 2001: 31) and as an integral aspect of the customer relationship (Wangenheim, 2005: 154) to name but a few.

Stokes and Lomax (2002) define word-of-mouth communication as 'interpersonal communication regarding products or services where the receiver regards the communicator as impartial'. This simple definition was developed from some of the more established interpretations that failed to accommodate contemporary media and the restrictions concerning the perceived independence of the communicator. For example, Helm and Schlei (1998: 42) refer to WoM as 'verbal communications (either positive or negative) between groups such as the product provider, independent experts, family, friends and the actual or personal consumer'. Organisations now use WoM techniques commercially in order to generate a point of differentiation.

People like to talk about their product (service) experiences, for a variety of reasons that are explored in the next section. However, by talking with a neighbour or colleague about the good experiences associated with a new car, for example, the first-hand 'this has actually happened to someone I know' effect will be instrumental in the same views being passed on to other colleagues, irrespective of their validity or overall representation of similar cars. Mazzarol *et al.* (2007) identify the 'richness of the message' and the 'strength of the implied or explicit advocacy' as important triggers for WoM.

Viral marketing (see Chapter 26) is an electronic version of the spoken endorsement of a product or service where messages, screen savers and other information are targeted at key individuals who then voluntarily pass the message to friends and colleagues and in doing so bestow, endorse and provide the message with much valued credibility.

But why do people want to discuss products or advertising messages? Bone (1995) cited by Stokes and Lomax (2002) refers to three elements of WoM (see Table 2.2).

Dichter (1966) determined that there were four main categories of output WoM.

1. *Product involvement*

   People, he found, have a high propensity to discuss matters that are either distinctly pleasurable or unpleasurable. Such discussion serves to provide an opportunity for the experience to be relived, whether it be the 'looking for' or the 'use' experience, or both.

Table 2.2 Elements of word-of-mouth communication

Element of WoM		Explanation
Direction	Input WoM	Customers seeking recommendation prior to purchase
	Output WoM	Expression of feelings as a result of the purchase experience
Valence		The positive or negative feelings resulting from the experience
Volume		The number of people to which the message is conveyed

Source: After Bone (1995).

2. *Self-involvement*
   Discussion offers a means for ownership to be established and signals aspects of prestige and levels of status to the receiver. More importantly, perhaps, dissonance can be reduced as the purchaser seeks reassurance about the decision.
3. *Other involvement*
   Products can assist motivations to help others and to express feelings of love, friendship and caring. These feelings can be released through a sense of sharing the variety of benefits that products can bestow.
4. *Message involvement*
   The final motivation to discuss products is derived, according to Dichter, from the messages that surround the product itself, in particular the advertising messages and, in the business-to-business market, seminars, exhibitions and the trade press, which provide the means to provoke conversation and so stimulate word-of-mouth recommendation.

It is interesting to note that Dichter's various forms of involvement, in particular the 'self' and 'other' categories, bare a strong similarity to the market exchanges and collaborative exchanges explored in Chapter 1. However, people who identify very closely with a brand and who might be termed brand advocates often engage in word-of-mouth communications. Advocacy can be demonstrated not only through word-of-mouth communications but also through behaviour, for example, by wearing branded clothing or using tools and equipment. The issue of advocacy is explored further in Chapter 7 in the section on loyalty and retention schemes.

People who identify very closely with a brand and who might be termed brand advocates often engage in word-of-mouth communications.

ViewPoint 2.2 Hotel speak

A hotel manager noticed that input WoM for his hotel given by travel agents was much stronger than the output WoM, even though the overseas guests reported very favourable satisfaction levels. In order 'to align the input WoM needs of potential customers with activities designed to encourage appropriate output WoM', a range of activities were introduced to prompt WoM opportunities.

One of these strategies required guests to tell the agents of their experience and he also communicated with the agents by sending them copies of the guest comment cards. He also provided complimentary rooms for the agents so that they could experience the hotel first-hand and then sent them teddy bears (a reminder of England) when they made a certain number of bookings. Later he sent them jars of honey. Guests were also given teddy bears on departure.

One other notable activity included restoring one of the hotel rooms to how it would have been when the hotel opened in 1860. People perceived this as novel, interesting and it gave rise to extensive positive output WoM. This activity also gave rise to a number of public relations activities.

Source: Stokes and Lomax (2002).

Question

If WoM communication is so important why is it not a core activity within marketing communications for all brands?

Task

When you next visit a leisure or entertainment complex make a mental note of the ways in which the brand owner encourages visitors to talk about the brand.

These motivations to discuss products and their associative experiences vary between individuals and with the intensity of the motivation at any one particular moment. There are two main persons involved in this process of word-of-mouth communications: a sender and receiver. Research indicates that the receiver's evaluation of a message is far from stable over time and accuracy of recall decays (expectedly) through time. What this means for marketing communications is that those people who have a positive product experience, especially in the service sector, should be encouraged to talk as soon as possible after the event (Christiansen and Tax, 2000). For example, Pepsi Raw was launched in pubs and bars in order to reach young affluent consumers. The goal was to encourage this target audience to talk about the brand and in doing so imbue the brand with social group associations and then roll the brand out across supermarkets (Simms, 2007).

There are three particular groups based on their type of word-of-mouth endorsement: promoters, passively satisfied and detractors.

According to Reichheld (2003) cited by Mazur (2004) organisations should measure word-of-mouth communication because those who speak up about a brand are risking their own reputation when they recommend a brand. Looking at the financial services sector, Reichheld argues that measures based on customer satisfaction or retention rates can mask real growth potential because they are measures of defection, and switching barriers may induce inertia. He found three particular groups based on their type of word-of-mouth endorsement: promoters, passively satisfied and detractors. In particular he identified a strong correlation between an organisation's growth rate and the percentage of customers who are active promoters.

For organisations it is important to target messages at those individuals who are predisposed to such discussion, as this may well propel word-of-mouth recommendations and the success of the communications campaign. The target, therefore, is not necessarily the target market, but those in the target market who are most likely to volunteer their positive opinions about the offering or those who, potentially, have some influence over members. There are three types of such volunteers: opinion leaders, formers and followers.

Opinion leaders

Katz and Lazerfeld (1955) first identified individuals who were predisposed to receiving information and then reprocessing it to influence others. Their studies of American voting and purchase behaviour led to their conclusion that those individuals who could exert such influence were more persuasive than information received directly from the mass media. These opinion leaders, according to Rogers (1962), tend 'to be of the same social class as non-leaders, but may enjoy a higher social status within the group'. Williams (1990) uses the work of Reynolds and Darden (1971) to suggest that they are more gregarious and more self-confident than non-leaders. In addition, they have a greater exposure to relevant mass media (print) and as a result have more knowledge/familiarity and involvement with the product class, are more innovative and more confident of their role as influencer (leader) and appear to be less dogmatic than non-leaders (Chan and Misra, 1990).

Opinion leaders, according to Rogers (1962), tend 'to be of the same social class as non-leaders, but may enjoy a higher social status within the group'.

Opinion leadership can be simulated in advertising by the use of product testimonials. Using ordinary people to express positive comments about a product to each other is a very well-used advertising technique.

The importance of opinion leaders in the design and implementation of communication plans should not be underestimated. Midgley and Dowling (1993) refer to *innovator communicators*: those who are receptive to new ideas and who make innovation-based purchase decisions without reference to or from other people. However, while the importance of these individuals is not doubted, a major difficulty exists in trying to identify just who these opinion leaders and innovator communicators are. While they sometimes display some distinctive characteristics, such as reading specialist media vehicles, often being first to return coupons, enjoying attending exhibitions or just involving themselves with new, innovative techniques or products, they are by their very nature invisible outside their work, family and social groups.

ViewPoint 2.3 Singalong a blogger

In today's digital environment opinion leaders are often revealed due to their propensity to blog. Bloggers may have strong opinions but they are able to lead and shape the opinion of mainstream audiences. For example, the agency 'Strawberry Frog' developed a campaign for the very cool sports shoe brand Onitsuka Tiger.

A new shoe was launched in World Cup year 2006, and featured video clips on the web site of staff in Japan singing a 'Lovely Football' song. The site also featured the world's first online Karaoke machine that empowered people at home to sing along and record themselves. The site received millions of hits and the shoe sold out in weeks. The total cost of the campaign . . . just $300k.

The reason for the success of the campaign was that Strawberry Frog had identified just 20 superstar bloggers who, it is alleged, have a strong influence over the European sports shoe market. By offering these 20 individuals exclusive access and content, these bloggers relayed positive messages to their 100K followers. These in turn introduced the brand to the mainstream and so the new shoe was a success.

Source: Adapted from Grant (2006).

Question

Should opinion leaders be rewarded for their contribution to a brand's marketing communications?

Task

Find a blogger and ask them why they blog.

Exhibit 2.4 Onitsuka Tiger

Electric Light Shoe is the dramatic centerpiece for Onitsuka Tiger's integrated global brand campaign for 2008. It is a one-metre long sculpture based on an Onitsuka Tiger sneaker shape. The sculpture is a tribute to Tokyo's vibrant city lights, and takes much of its inspiration from the underground cult of *Dekotora* (decorated trucks). For more information go to the companion web site for this book.

Image title: Electric Light shoe; Agency: Amsterdam Worldwide; Creative Director: Andrew Watson; Account Director: Nicolette Lazarus.

Opinion formers

Opinion formers are individuals who are able to exert personal influence because of their authority, education or status associated with the object of the communication process.

Opinion formers are individuals who are able to exert personal influence because of their authority, education or status associated with the object of the communication process. Like opinion leaders, they are acknowledged and sought out by others to provide information and advice, but this is because of the formal expertise that opinion formers are adjudged to have. For example, community pharmacists are often consulted about symptoms and medicines, and film critics carry such conviction in their reviews that they can make or break a new production.

ViewPoint 2.4 Skin tight

When BBC2 broadcast the *Horizon* programme on 27 March 2007, Boots were not to realise the storm that was to be created. The programme was about the accentuated claims made by cosmetic houses and the benefits their products offered. However, of all the products tested, one product was found to meet the claims made for it. This was an across-the-counter anti-ageing cream called No7 Protect & Perfect serum. The report found that the serum did improve skin appearance and that it did reduce fine wrinkles, just as the promotional messages claimed.

Within 24 hours sales had increased by 2,000 per cent and not a single, 30ml jar of Boots No7 Protect & Perfect serum could be found in the country. Boots had shipped in 21 weeks' supplies into the stores the night before but these were sold the day following the programme at a rate of one jar every 10 seconds. Stores developed four-figure waiting lists, online the company's web site had 4,000 requests in an evening while a single jars of the £16.75 serum were being bought and sold for £100 on eBay (Craig, 2007).

The trust afforded to the BBC and the authority of the programme *Horizon* provided such strong levels of source credibility that people regard the programme and its presenters as opinion formers. Boots did not have to resort to any further marketing communications other than to inform customers that stocks had been replenished.

Sources: Bainbridge (2007); Craig (2007).

Question

Is it right that an independent organisation such as the BBC should be allowed to act as a covert marketing organisation for a third-party brand?

Task

For a more detailed insight to this event see the mini case at the end of this chapter.

The BBC radio programme *The Archers*, an everyday story of country folk, has been used to deliver messages about farming issues. The actors in the programme are opinion formers and they direct messages to farmers about farming techniques and methods. The educational use was very important after the Second World War.

Popular television programmes, such as *Eastenders*, *Brookside* and *Coronation Street*, all of which attract huge audiences, have been used as vehicles to draw attention to and open up debates about many controversial social issues, such as contraception, abortion, drug use and abuse, and serious illness and mental health concerns.

The influence of opinion formers can be great. For example, the editor of a journal or newspaper may be a recognised source of expertise, and any offering referred to by the editor in the media vehicle is endowed with great credibility. In this sense the editor acts as a gatekeeper, and it is the task of the marketing communicator to ensure that all relevant opinion formers are identified and sent appropriate messages.

However, the credibility of opinion formers is vital for communication effectiveness. If there is a suspicion or doubt about the impartiality of the opinion former, then the objectivity of their views and comments are likely to be perceived as tainted and not believed so that damage may be caused to the reputation of the brand and those involved.

Many organisations constantly lobby key members of parliament in an effort to persuade them to pursue 'favourable' policies. Opinion formers are relatively easy to identify, as they need to be seen shaping the opinion of others, usually opinion followers.

Opinion followers

The vast majority of consumers can be said to be opinion followers. The messages they receive via the mass media are tempered by the opinions of the two groups of personal influencers just discussed. Some people actively seek information from those they believe are well informed, while others prefer to use the mass media for information and guidance (Robinson, 1976). However, this should not detract from the point that, although followers, they still process information independently and use a variety of inputs when sifting information and responding to marketing stimuli.

Ethical drug manufacturers normally launch new drugs by enlisting the support of particular doctors who have specialised in the therapy area and who are recognised by other doctors as experts. These opinion formers are invited to lead symposia and associated events to build credibility and activity around the new product. At the same time, public relations agencies prepare press releases with the aim that the information will be used by the mass media (opinion formers) for editorial purposes and create exposure for the product across the target audience, which, depending upon the product and/or the media vehicle, may be GPs, hospital doctors, patients or the general public. All these people, whether they be opinion leaders or formers, are active influencers or talkers (Kingdom, 1970).

Types of word-of-mouth communication

Organisations use WoM communication because it is an effective way of delivering messages. It provides a way to cut through the clutter of advertising and media-based messages. However, current and recent practice suggests that two forms of WoM communications are emerging. The original concept is based on the idea that people talk voluntarily and in doing so convey messages about their product, service and associated experiences. Often organisations will target known opinion leaders and provide them with information and materials in the hope they will talk about them to their friends. These conversations can be positive or negative and the control organisations have on these messages is virtually nil.

In recent years some organisations have started to use the principles of WoM to stimulate their marketing communications, but without the voluntary element. In other words, certain opinion leaders and formers are being coerced into a simulated WoM communication process. This is achieved by deliberately paying or rewarding 'talkers' in advance, in the expectation that they will talk about their positive experience. Here the voluntary element is lost and organisational control re-established, simply through the provision of rewards and payments. Referred to as word-of-mouth advertising, this approach distorts the original meaning of word-of-mouth communication.

Some organisations have started to use the principles of WoM to stimulate their marketing communications, but without the voluntary element.

ViewPoint 2.5 Mouthy taxi drivers? Never

Taxi drivers have a reputation for having opinions on a wide range of matters and issues. They are also prepared to talk about various topics, even if the customer is not that interested. This propensity to talk has not been lost to the Tourism Authority of Thailand who have targeted some cab drivers as part of a new campaign to boost tourism.

The Tourism Authority of Thailand has paid for several cab drivers to experience an all expenses five day visit to Bangkok. The cab drivers claim that no one has asked them to talk about their holiday experience but it is fairly certain that they will talk about their experience and in doing so persuade some people to visit. Especially when their taxis are repainted to represent images of Thailand. One driver reported by Pavia (2008) had also enjoyed ten days in Melbourne, courtesy of the city's tourist board.

Taxi Promotions UK are one of the first agencies to actively promote this new form of communication. They refer to their cabbies as 'ambassador drivers' and perhaps they will be endorsing events, exhibitions, airlines, theatres and may be even shops in the future.

Source: Pavia (2008).

Question

To what extent are 'paid' opinion leaders such as these taxi drivers, viable forms of marketing communication?

Task

When you are next in a taxi make a note of any brands the taxi driver refers to.

Process of adoption

An interesting extension to the concept of opinion followers and the discussion on word-of-mouth communications is the process by which individuals become committed to the use of a new product. Rogers (1983) has identified this as the process of adoption and the stages of his innovation decision process are represented in Figure 2.6. These stages in the adoption process are sequential and are characterised by the different factors that are involved at each stage (e.g. the media used by each individual).

1. *Knowledge*
   The innovation becomes known to consumers, but they have little information and no well-founded attitudes. Information must be provided through mass media to institutions and people whom active seekers of information are likely to contact. Information for passive seekers should be supplied through the media and channels that this group habitually uses to look for other kinds of information (Windahl *et al.*, 1992).
   Jack cleans his teeth regularly, but he is beginning to notice a sensitivity to both hot and cold drinks. He becomes aware of an advertisement for Special Paste on television.
2. *Persuasion*
   The consumer becomes aware that the innovation may be of use in solving known and potential problems. Information from those who have experience of the product becomes very important.
   Jack notices that the makers of Special Paste claim that their brand reduces the amount of sensitive reaction to hot and cold drinks. Special Paste has also been recommended to him by someone he met in the pub last week. Modelling behaviour predominates.
3. *Decision*
   An attitude may develop and may be either favourable or unfavourable, but as a result a decision is reached whether to trial the offering or not. Communications need to assist this part of the process by continual prompting.

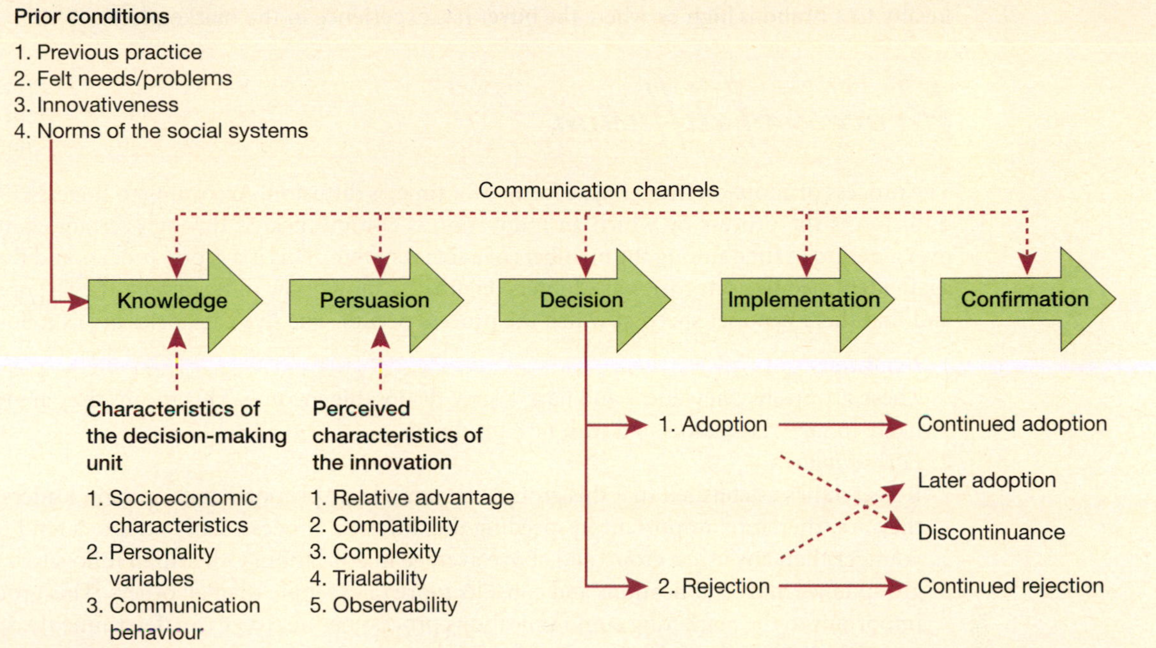

Figure 2.6 Stages in the innovation decision process of adoption
Source: Reprinted with the permission of The Free Press, a division of Simon & Schuster, Inc., from *Diffusion of Innovations*, Third Edition by Everett M. Rogers. Copyright © 1962, 1971, 1983 by The Free Press. All rights reserved.

Jack is prepared to believe (or not to believe) the messages and the claims made on behalf of Special Paste. He thinks that Special Paste is potentially a very good brand (or not). He intends trying Special Paste because he was given a free sample (or because it was on a special price deal).

4. *Implementation*
For the adoption to proceed in the absence of a sales promotion, buyers must know where to get it and how to use it. The product is then tested in a limited way. Communications must provide this information in order that the trial experience be developed.
Jack buys 'Special Paste' and tests it.
5. *Confirmation*
The innovation is accepted or rejected on the basis of the experience during trial. Planned communications play an important role in maintaining the new behaviour by dispelling negative thoughts and positively reaffirming the original 'correct' decision. McGuire, as reported in Windahl *et al.* (1992), refers to this as post-behavioural consolidation.
It works, Jack's teeth are not as sensitive to hot and cold drinks as they were before he started using 'Special Paste'. He reads an article that reports that large numbers of people are using these types of products satisfactorily. Jack resolves to buy 'Special Paste' next time.

This process can be terminated at any stage and, of course, a number of competing brands may vie for consumers' attention simultaneously, so adding to the complexity and levels of noise in the process. Generally, mass communications are seen to be more effective in the earlier phases of the adoption process for products that buyers are actively interested in, and more interpersonal forms are more appropriate at the later stages, especially trial and adoption. This model assumes that the stages occur in a predictable sequence, but this clearly does not happen in all purchase activity, as some

Mass communications are seen to be more effective in the earlier phases of the adoption process.

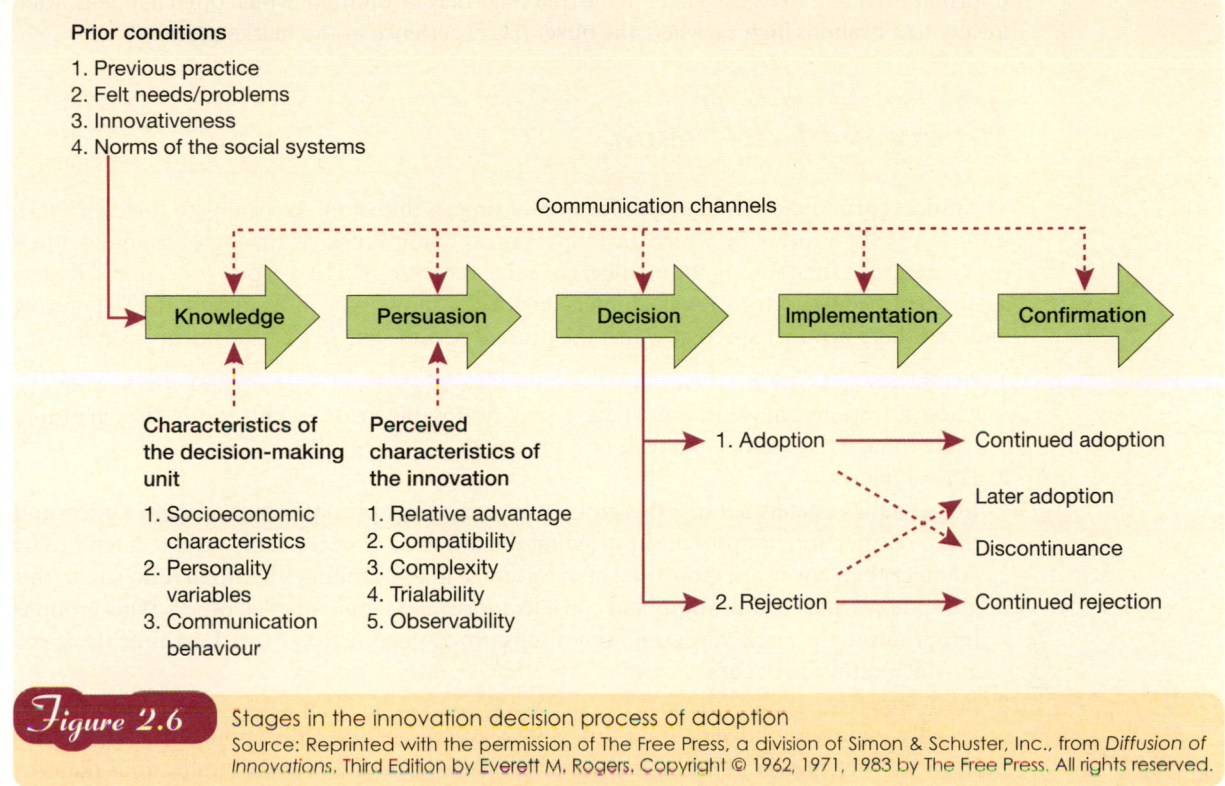

information that is to be used later in the trial stage may be omitted, which often happens when loyalty to a brand is high or where the buyer has experience in the marketplace.

Process of diffusion

The process of adoption in aggregate form, over time, is diffusion. According to Rogers (1983), diffusion is the process by which an innovation is communicated through certain channels over a period of time among the members of a social system. This is a group process and Rogers again identified five categories of adopters. Figure 2.7 shows how diffusion may be fast or slow and that there is no set speed at which the process occurs. The five categories are as follows:

1. *Innovators*
   These groups like new ideas and have a large disposable income. This means they are more likely to take risks associated with new products.
2. *Early adopters*
   Research has established that this group contains a large proportion of opinion leaders and they are, therefore, important in speeding the diffusion process. Early adopters tend to be younger than any other group and above average in education. Other than innovators, this group takes more publications and consults more salespeople than all others. This group is important to the marketing communications process because they can determine the speed at which diffusion occurs.
3. *Early majority*
   Usually, opinion followers are a little above average in age, education, social status and income. They rely on informal sources of information and take fewer publications than the previous two groups.
4. *Late majority*
   This group of people is skeptical of new ideas and only adopts new products because of social or economic factors. They take few publications and are below average in education, social status and income.

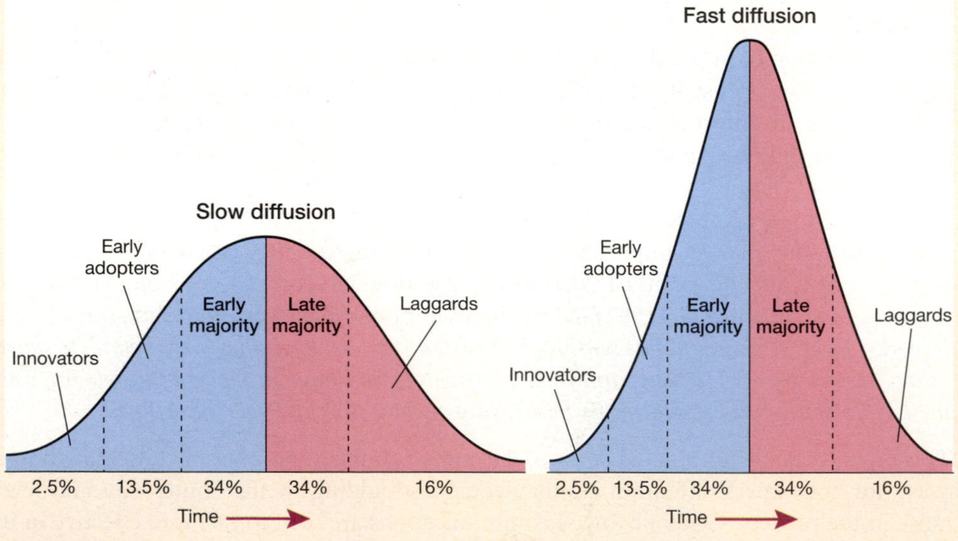

Figure 2.7 Fast and slow diffusion of an innovation
Source: From Hawkins *et al.* (1989) *Consumer Behaviour*, 4th Edition. Used with permission of the McGraw-Hill Companies.

5. *Laggards*
   A group of people who are suspicious of all new ideas and set in their opinions. Lowest of all the groups in terms of income, social status and education, this group takes a long time to adopt an innovation.

This framework suggests that, at the innovation stage, messages should be targeted at relatively young people in the target group, with a high level of income, education and social status. This will speed word-of-mouth recommendation and the diffusion process. Mahajan *et al.* (1990) observe that the personal influence of word-of-mouth communications does not work in isolation from the other communication tools. Early adopters are more likely to adopt an innovation in response to 'external influences' and only through time will the effect of 'internal influences' become significant. In other words, mass media communications need time to work before word-of-mouth communications can begin to build effectiveness.

A major difficulty associated with the use of this framework, however, is the inability to define which stage of the diffusion process is operating at any time. Furthermore, Gatignon and Robertson (1985) suggest that there are three elements to the diffusion process, which need to be taken into account, particularly for the fast-moving consumer goods sector:

1. The rate of diffusion or speed at which sales occur.
2. The pattern of diffusion or shape of the curve.
3. The potential penetration level or size of the market.

Care should be taken to ensure that all three of these elements are considered when attempting to understand the diffusion process. It can be concluded that if a promotional campaign is targeted at innovators and the early majority, and is geared to stimulating word-of-mouth communications, then the diffusion process is more likely to be successful than if these elements are ignored.

ViewPoint 2.6 Digital influencers

When Sony wanted to launch its BRAVIA LCD television it was a faced with an audience that was essentially cynical towards advertising and promotional messages and hard to reach with telling branded messages. The success of the launch was partly due to its use of a key part of the audience, Digital Influencers.

Digital Influencers are people who understand, appreciate and enjoy technology. They are effectively digital opinion leaders and they represent an important target audience. The key for Sony was to encourage these influencers to spread the word about BRAVIA to the early majority and reach the mass market.

The original BRAVIA television ad was based round 250,000 coloured balls fired out of a cannon in San Francisco. During filming, local residents shot their own video footage. This found its way onto the Internet, which in turn provoked significant comment and interest. Quite transparently, Sony started to feed the digital influencers with blogging 'blog fodder', and they in turn used the material to develop conversations with other much broader audiences. Sony also slowly released official film that helped to create links from the Sony site to the original amateur images posted on Flickr. As the mainstream audiences, who are less technologically able than influencers, tuned into the BRAVIA interest so simpler content was made available, for example, screen savers and mobile phone wallpapers.

Source: Whitton and Ryan (2006).

Question

Do you believe the increasing use of opinion leaders is due to cost cutting or because it is superior form of communication?

Task

Think about buying a new laptop, make a note of who or what you would consult prior to purchase.

Interaction and interactivity in communications

The models and frameworks of the communication process discussed to date can be interpreted as an abstraction. The one-step model is linear and unidirectional, and it suggests that the receiver plays a passive role in the process. The two-step and multi-step models attempt to account for the interactive nature of communication and they proffer a mutually participative role for all parties to the communication process. These models emphasise individual behaviour and exclude the social behaviour implicit in the process. Goffman (1969) advocates an 'interactional' approach which focuses on the roles adopted by the players in the communication process. Through mutual understanding of each other's behaviour, the rules of the communication process are established. McEwan (1992) suggests that this permits formal and informal communication procedures to be established, and that mutual understanding (Rogers and Kincaid, 1981) and increased levels of trust can be developed by the participants.

This is an interesting perspective, as strands of the importance of source credibility can be identified in this approach. Evidence of Goffman's approach can be seen in personal selling. Sellers and buyers, meeting for the first time, often enter negotiations at a formal level, each adopting a justifiable, self-protective position. As negotiations proceed, so the two parties adjust their roles, and, as the likelihood of a mutual exchange increases, so the formal roles give way to more informal ones.

Interactivity

The interactional approach has increased currency as the influence and use of interactivity within commercially oriented communications develops. The emergence of digital media has helped change the primary mode of communication from one based on mass one-way communication, to one that is essentially individual, transformational and one that enables interaction.

A key question emerges, what is interaction and what are its key characteristics? If we can understand the dynamics and dimensions of interactivity then it should be possible to develop more effective marketing communications. In the context of marketing communications, interactivity can be considered from one of two perspectives. One is the technology, tools and features (e.g. multimedia, www, online gaming) that provide for interaction. The second, according to Johnson *et al.* (2006) is the added value that interactivity is perceived to bring to the communication process. These researchers point out that interaction should not be seen as technology specific, simply because face-to-face interaction has a considerably longer history. These two forms of interaction are referred to in the literature as mediated (technology) and non-mediated (human) interaction.

> In the context of marketing communications, interactivity can be considered from one of two perspectives.

Johnson *et al.* (2006) identify four dimensions, or facets as they refer to them, of interactivity. These are set out in Table 2.3.

The dimensions are considered to apply to both mediated and non-mediated interactive situations. Of these dimensions, three have the largest impact on an individual's perception of interactivity in a communication episode. In decreasing order of importance these are, non-verbal, level of responsiveness, speed of response and reciprocity.

The implications for marketing communications can be far-reaching. For example, the researchers suggest that the perception that non-verbal information is more influential than speed of response might mean that decisions about whether to increase a site's graphics (non-verbal) or its speed (of response) need to consider that the former might well reduce the latter in areas where there are bandwidth restrictions.

> Three dimensions have the largest impact on an individual's perception of interactivity in a communication episode: non-verbal, level of responsiveness, speed of response and reciprocity.

Table 2.3 The facets of interactivity

Dimensions of interactivity	Explanation
Reciprocity	The extent to which communication allows mutual action
Responsiveness	The extent to which responses are perceived to be appropriate, relevant and resolve the information requirements of the episode
Speed of response	The extent to which a response is immediate or without delay
Nonverbal information	The extent to which there is nonverbal information in the communication episode

Source: Derived from Johnson *et al.* (2006).

ViewPoint 2.7 Tetra Pak: expert interaction

Tetra Pak have been developing their position with regard to recycling issues for many years. Their web site acts as a fulcrum for Tetra Pak's efforts to encourage recycling and environmental awareness.

Working with their agency they actively engage with bloggers who either misunderstand or lack clarity in their messaging about recycling issues. Links are provided into www.tetrapakrecycling.co.uk to provide clarity about how and where its products can be recycled.

One novelty about the site is that Tetra Pak openly encourages visitors to tell others about the site and recycling issues. This it achieves by using a video featuring a woman with a loud-hailer informing the world that 'cartons are recyclable'.

Source: Gray (2007).

Question

Why do Tetra Pak focus on bloggers? How do they identify them in the first place?

Task

Visit the **www.tetrapakrecycling.co.uk** and consider the extent to which the company extols recycling.

Relational approaches to communications

The previous model accounts for social behaviour but does not account for the context within which the behaviour occurs. Communication events always occur within a context (Littlejohn, 1992) or particular set of circumstances, which not only influence the form of the communication but also the nature and the way the communication is received, interpreted and acted upon. There are a huge number of variables that can influence the context, including the disposition of the people involved, the physical environment, the nature of the issue, the history and associated culture, the goals of the participants and the expected repercussions of the dialogue itself.

Communication events always occur within a context.

Littlejohn identifies four main contextual levels: interpersonal, group, organisational and mass communication. These levels form part of a hierarchy whereby higher levels incorporate the lower levels but 'add something new of their own'.

The relational approach means that communication events are linked together in an organised manner, one where the events are 'punctuated' by interventions from one or more of the participants. These interventions occur whenever the participants attempt cooperation or if conflict arises.

Soldow and Thomas (1984), referring to a sales negotiation, state that a relationship develops through the form of negotiations rather than the content. An agreement is necessary about who is to control the relationship or whether there will be equality. Rothschild (1987) reports that 'sparring will continue' until agreement is reached or the negotiations are terminated. In other words, without mutual agreement over the roles of the participants, the true purpose of the interaction, to achieve an exchange, cannot be resolved.

An interesting aspect of relational communication theory is social penetration (Taylor and Altman, 1987). Through the disclosure of increasing amounts of information about themselves, partners in a relationship (personal or organisational) develop levels of intimacy, which serve to build interpersonal (interorganisational?) relationships. The relationship moves forward as partners reveal successive layers of information about each other and, as a greater amount or breadth of information is shared, confidence grows. These levels can be seen to consist of orientation, exploratory affective exchange, affective exchange and stable exchange; see Table 2.4. These layers are not uncovered in a logical, orderly sequence. It is likely that partners will return to previous levels, test the outcomes and rewards and reconsider their positions as the relationships unfolds through time. This suggests that social penetration theory may lie at the foundation of the development of trust, commitment and relational exchanges between organisations.

Table 2.4 Layers of social penetration

Orientation	The disclosure of public information only.
Exploratory affective exchange	Expansion and development of public information.
Affective exchange	Disclosure, based upon anticipated relationship rewards, of deeper feelings, values and beliefs.
Stable exchange	High level of intimacy where partners are able to predict each other's reactions with a good level of accuracy.

Source: *Interpersonal Processes: New Directions in Communication Research* by Taylor, D. and Altman, I. Coyright 1987 by Sage Publications Inc. Books. Reproduced with the permission of Sage Publications Inc. Books in the format Textbook via copyright Clearance Centre.

Relationships need not be just dyadic, as the interactional approach suggests, but could be triadic or even encompass a much wider network or array of participants. Through this perspective a 'communication network' can be observed, through which information can flow. Participants engage in communication based upon their perception of the environment in which the communication occurs and the way in which each participant relates to each other.

Rogers (1986) identifies a communication network as 'consisting of interconnected individuals who are linked by patterned communication flows'. This is important, as it views communication as transcending organisational boundaries. In other words, it is not only individuals within an organisation that develop patterned communication flows but also individuals across different organisations. These individuals participate with one another (possibly through exchanges) and use communication networks to achieve their agenda items.

The extent to which individuals are linked to the network is referred to as connectedness. The more a network is connected, the greater the likelihood that a message will be disseminated, as there are few isolated individuals. Similarly, the level of integration in a network refers to the degree to which members of the network are linked to one another. The greater the integration, the more potential channels there are for a message to be routed through.

The extent to which individuals are linked to the network is referred to as connectedness.

Systems theory, as discussed in the previous chapter (see p. 28), recognises that organisations are made of interacting units. The relational approach to communications is similar to systems theory. The various 'criss-crossing' flows of information between reciprocating units allow individuals and groups to modify the actions of others in the 'net', and this permits the establishment of a pattern of communication (Tichy, 1979).

Network approaches to communications

The regular use of these patterned flows leads to the development of communication networks, which have been categorised as prescribed and emergent (Weick, 1987). Prescribed networks are formalised patterns of communication, very often established by senior management within an organisation or by organisational representatives when interorganisational communications are considered. It follows that emergent networks are informal and emerge as a response to the social and task-oriented needs of the participants.

The linear or one-way model of communication fails to accommodate the various complexities associated with communication. As discussed earlier, the model is too simplistic and fails to represent many aspects of communication events. Although the linear model is essentially sequential rather than interactional approach, it is still used and practised by many organisations. Varey (2002) refers to this as the Informational model of communication and as both Grunig (1992) and Ballantyne (2004) suggest it is just one of a number of ways in which communication can work. Communication is an integral part of relationship marketing and within this collaborative context, interaction and dialogue are essential factors. Varey refers to this as Transformational communication.

Summary

In order to help consolidate your understanding of communication theory, here are the key points summarised against each of the learning objectives:

1. Understand the core model of the communication process and how the various elements link together.

The linear model of communication is generally accepted as the main interpretation of how mass media communication works. A source designs and encodes a message that is transmitted through a signal to the audience. Members of the audience then decode the message and give meaning to the message.

2. Appreciate how the components of the model contribute to successful communications.

Only by developing the right message, encoding it appropriately and using the right delivery mechanism is there any chance of the message being received, decoded and interpreted as intended. The strength of the linkages are important for successful communication. The realm of understanding or the context for the communication needs to be understood and accommodated by all parties to the communication process.

3. Examine the impact of the media on the communication process.

Each type of media provides varying levels of information richness. However, digital media now enable interactivity and have transformed the nature and form of communications. Mass communications, although important has given way to increasing levels of interactive and personal communications.

4. Evaluate the impact of personal influences on the communication process.

Communications do not work in isolation from people. Indeed people, in the form of opinion leaders and formers can be an integral part of much of the communications in which we are all involved, either offline or online.

5. Examine the nature and characteristics associated with word-of-mouth communication.

Word-of-mouth communication, whether offline or online, represents a highly credible form of communication and one which an increasing number of organisations are seeking to use as part of their marketing communications.

6. Consider the nature and influence of interactivity in communication.

The use of interactivity in mediated environments has grown, as has the understanding of how the use of the dimensions of interactivity, namely, nonverbal, responsiveness, speed of response and reciprocity can improve perceptions of interaction and quality of communication.

7. Introduce more recent explanations of communication theory, including interactional networks.

The linear model has had to be adapted in order to accommodate the influence of people on communications. The two-step and multi-step models help to explain this dimension but these are all essentially individual interpretations. However, the interactional approach considers the roles people adopt within communications; the relational perspective examines the social context; and network theories consider the different patterns of communications that can occur within groups of participants.

8. Explain how communication theory underpins our understanding of marketing communications.

Communication is about shared meaning. It is critically important, therefore, that those responsible for their organisation's marketing communications, whether that be for a grocery product, building materials or a charity, attempt to communicate messages so that the intended meaning is actually understood by all recipients.

Review questions

1. Name the elements of the linear model of communication and briefly describe the role of each element.
2. Make brief notes explaining why the linear interpretation of the communication process is not entirely valid.

3. Discuss the nature and characteristics of media richness theory.
4. Discuss the differences between one-step, two-step and multi-step communications.
5. How do opinion leaders differ from opinion formers and opinion followers?
6. Why is word-of-mouth communication so important to marketing communications?
7. What are the three elements of word-of-mouth communication identified by Bone?
8. Draw a graph to show the difference between fast and slow diffusion.
9. What is the relational approach to communications? How might social penetration theory assist our understanding of this interpretation of how communication works?
10. Identify two forms of communication networks.

MiniCase **Because it works!**

Lynn Sudbury: Liverpool John Moores University

The array of beauty lotions and potions that claim to ward off wrinkles and other signs of ageing that women – and increasingly men – can choose from, is extensive. Indeed, in an overall industry reputed to be worth £25 billion world-wide and £6.2bn in Britain, Boots N°7 'Protect & Perfect' serum, retailing at £16.75 for 30ml and being on the shelves for three years already, was an unlikely contender for the title 'Magic Cream' that was to spark a wave of near hysteria that reached as far as the USA and Australia. Yet, that's exactly what happened after the product was featured on BBC's science programme *Horizon*.

The *Horizon* programme featured Lesley Regan, a 50-year-old professor of obstetrics and gynaecology at St Mary's Hospital in London, who went in search of 'The Holy Grail' – otherwise known as an anti-ageing product that scientifically worked. Her search led her to the cream perfected by scientist Steve Barton and his team in Nottingham. Mr Barton has been using the serum for several years, and had conducted his own trials with what he described as 'fantastic' results. However, it was only when the product was examined by a team of expert dermatologists at Manchester University that the claims became more believable. Professor Chris Griffiths, who heads the team at Manchester, explained that although they were initially sceptical, their independent research spanning 10 months and investigating a range of anti-ageing creams – many of which retail for far more than £17 – scientifically proved that N°7's Protect & Perfect actually worked. The cream was found to contain protecting and renewing agents associated with the production of collagen and elastin, as well as silicone and antioxidants, and was compared to prescription drugs used to treat severe acne and sun damage to skin. Professor Griffiths was reported to say 'At both basic science and clinical levels Boots N°7 Protect & Perfect has been shown scientifically to repair photo-aged skin and improve the fine wrinkles associated with photo-ageing.'

Boots had expected demand to rise once the programme had aired, and had prepared by shipping in 21 weeks supply of the product prior to the *Horizon* programme. Yet, despite the fact that the serum was only shown on camera for a few seconds, within 24 hours of the programme being aired, sales rose by 2,000 per cent, the shelves in Boots up and down the country were empty, waiting lists reportedly comprising four figures were opened, Boots' web store received 4,000 requests in one evening, and within days the product was being traded on ebay for up to £100. Some stores reported women charging behind counters, convinced that there would be hidden supplies there, others raced each other down aisles to get to the 'Magic Cream', and one store reported a near-riot when a single customer bought up their entire stock.

These events were only the beginning of the frenzy, however. While Boots switched most of their production to the Protect & Perfect line in an effort to cope with demand, the shortage fuelled further demand, as the news of the cream spread and more and more people wanted to buy it. The serum was a major conversation topic among mums outside schools and between friends. When stores received stock, they would telephone customers on the waiting lists telling them to be quick, and these customers would tell their friends, so stocks continued to disappear from shelves almost as fast as they could be filled, despite the product then being limited to one purchase per customer. Media reports of queues developing in the early hours outside Boots stores when stocks were expected fuelled even more demand. Many men also waited outside stores from 5a.m., some of them claiming to be under strict instructions from females to get their hand on the cream. Others, however, admitted to wanting to try the cream for themselves. Young girls queued up, some of them to buy for their mothers who had been trying to get hold of the cream for some time; others because they had heard from older friends that it actually worked.

Protect & Perfect was also big news on the web. Blogging gave individuals an outlet to share their thoughts, while an extraordinary number of on-line beauty forums such as 'Hey, Dollface!' focused on the serum. The 'Beauty Community Forum' of the magazine *Good Housekeeping*, for example, which has almost 44,000 members and can have many non-member guests on line at any one time as well, contained entries from scores of women sharing their experiences, beliefs and knowledge about the product. Many asked for advice on how to get hold of the cream, and the magazine's Beauty Director was asking women to share their results with the forum after using the product for at least 8 weeks – the time she believed it took to see results. The product even featured on plastic surgery blogs, and on-line discussions about the brand could be found from doctors in Australia to beauty editors in America.

Not all communication about the brand was positive. Both *The Guardian* and The *Independent on sunday* contained pieces from journalists pouring scorn on the women who queued half the night for the product, labelling their reaction as 'madness' and 'a case study of human perversity . . . another instance of the growing phenomenon we might call hysteria marketing'. Others, of course, might just call it word-of-mouth.

MiniCase questions

1. Discuss the reasons why in the first instance the *Horizon* programme caused such a reaction among consumers.
2. Identify the opinion formers and opinion leaders in the case.
3. Discuss the variables that influenced the word-of-mouth communications around *Protect & Perfect*.

References

Bainbridge, J. (2007) To embellish or conceal, *Marketing*, 8 August, 15.

Ballantyne, D. (2004) Dialogue and its role in the development of relationship specific knowledge, *Journal of Business and Industrial Marketing*, **19**(2), 114–23.

Berkman, H. and Gilson, C. (1986) *Consumer Behaviour: Concepts and Strategies*. Boston, MA: Vent.

Bickart, B. and Schindler, R.M. (2001) Internet forums as influential sources of consumer information, *Journal of Interactive Marketing*, **15**(3), 31–40.

Blodgett, J.G., Wakefield, K.L. and Barnes, J.H. (1995) The effects of customer service on complaining behaviour. *Journal of Services Marketing*, **9**(4), 31–42.

Bone, P.F. (1995) Word of mouth effects on short-term and long term product judgments. *Journal of Business Research*, **21**(3), 213–23.

Chan, K.K. and Misra, S. (1990) Characteristics of the opinion leader: a new dimension. *Journal of Advertising*, **19**(3), 53–60.

Christiansen, T. and Tax, S.S. (2000) Measuring word of mouth: the questions of who and when, *Journal of Marketing Communications*, **6**, 185–99.

Craig, O. (2007) Why girls love Steve, *Sunday Telegraph*, 7 June 2007. Retrieved 11 October 2007 from www.telegraph.co.uk/news/main.jhtml?xml=/news/2007/04/08/nrsteve08.xml&page=3.

Daft, R.L. and Lengel, R.H. (1986) Organizational information requirements, media richness and structural design. *Managerial Science*, **32**, 554–71.

Dennis, A.R. and Kinney, S.T. (1998) Testing media richness theory in the new media, *Information Systems Research*, **9**(3), 256–74.

Dichter, E. (1966) How word-of-mouth advertising works. *Harvard Business Review*, **44** (November/December), 147–66.

Gatignon, H. and Robertson, T. (1985) A propositional inventory for new diffusion research. *Journal of Consumer Research*, **11**, 849–67.

Goffman, E. (1969) *Strategic Interaction*. New York: Doubleday.

Grant, J. (2006) The future is small, *The Marketer*, (September), 27–9.

Gray, R. (2007) Rapid response, *Marketing*, (November), 48–9.

Grunig, J. (1992) Models of public relations and communication. In *Excellence in Public Relations and Communications Management* (eds J.E. Grunig, D.M. Dozier, P. Ehling, L.A. Grunig, F.C. Repper and J. Whits), 285–325. Hillsdale, NJ: Lawrence Erlbaum.

Hawkins, D.I., Best, R.J. and Coney, K.A. (1989) *Consumer Behaviour: Implications for Marketing Strategy*. Homewood, IL: Richard D. Irwin.

Helm, S. and Schlei, J. (1998) Referral potential – potential referrals: An investigation into customers' communication in service markets. Proceedings from 27th EMAC Conference, *Marketing Research and Practice*, 41–56.

Hoffman, D.L. and Novak, P.T. (1996) Marketing in hyper computer-mediated environments: conceptual foundations, *Journal of Marketing*, **60** (July), 50–68.

Johnson, G.J., Bruner II, G.C. and Kumar, A. (2006) Interactivity and its facets revisited, *Journal of Advertising*, **35**(4) (Winter), 35–52.

Katz, E. and Lazarfeld, P.F. (1955) *Personal Influence*. Glencoe, IL: Free Press.

Kingdom, J.W. (1970) Opinion leaders in the electorate. *Public Opinion Quarterly*, **34**, 256–61.

Littlejohn, S.W. (1992) *Theories of Human Communication*, 4th edn. Belmont, CA: Wadsworth.

Mahajan, V., Muller, E. and Bass, F.M. (1990) New product diffusion models in marketing. *Journal of Marketing*, **54** (January), 1–26.

Mallen, B. (1977) *Principles of Marketing Channel Management*. Lexington, MA: Lexington Books.

Mazur, L. (2004) Keep it simple, *Marketing Business*, (March), 17.

Mazzarol, T., Sweeney, J.C. and Soutar, G.N. (2007) Conceptualising word-of-mouth activity, triggers and conditions: an exploratory study. *European Journal of Marketing*, **41**(11/12), 1475–94.

McEwan, T. (1992) Communication in organisations. In *Hospitality Management* (ed. L. Mullins). London: Pitman.

McGuire, W.J. (1989) 'Theoretical foundations of campaigns'. In *Public communication campaigns*, (eds R.E. Rice and C.K. Atkin), 2nd edn, 43–65. Newbury Park, CA: Sage Publications.

Midgley, D. and Dowling, G. (1993) Longitudinal study of product form innovation: the interaction between predispositions and social messages. *Journal of Consumer Research*, **19** (March), 611–25.

Patzer, G.L. (1983) Source credibility as a function of communicator physical attractiveness. *Journal of Business Research*, **11**, 229–41.

Pavia, W. (2008) Spiel at the wheel?, *The Times*, 14 January. Retrieved 20 January from www.taxipromotions.com/news,-events-and-pr/spiel-at-the-wheel_.php.

Reichheld, F.F. (2003) The one number you need to grow. *Harvard Business Review*, (December), 47–54.

Reynolds, F.D. and Darden, W.R. (1971) Mutually adaptive effects of interpersonal communication. *Journal of Marketing Research*, **8** (November), 449–54.

Robinson, J.P. (1976) Interpersonal influence in election campaigns: two step flow hypothesis. *Public Opinion Quarterly*, **40**, 304–19.

Rogers, E.M. (1962) *Diffusion of Innovations*, 1st edn. New York: Free Press.

Rogers, E.M. (1983) *Diffusion of Innovations*, 3rd edn. New York: Free Press.

Rogers, E.M. (1986) *Communication Technology: The New Media in Society*. New York: Free Press.

Rogers, E.M. and Kincaid, D.L. (1981) *Communication Networks: Toward a Paradigm for Research*. New York: Free Press.

Rothschild, M. (1987) *Marketing Communications*, Lexington, MA: D.C. Heath.

Schramm, W. (1955) How communication works. In *The Process and Effects of Mass Communications* (ed. W. Schramm), 3–26. Urbana, IL: University of Illinois Press.

Shannon, C. and Weaver, W. (1962) *The Mathematical Theory of Communication*. Urbana, IL: University of Illinois Press.

Simms, J. (2007) Bridging the gap, *Marketing*, 12 December 2007, 26–8.

Soldow, G. and Thomas, G. (1984) Relational communication: form versus content in the sale interaction. *Journal of Marketing*, **48** (Winter), 84–93.

Steuer, J. (1992) Defining virtual reality: dimensions determining telepresence. *Journal of Communication*, **42**(4), 73–93.

Stokes, D. and Lomax, W. (2002) Taking control of word of mouth marketing: the case of an entrepreneurial hotelier. *Journal of Small Business and Enterprise Development*, **9**(4), 349–57.

Taylor, D. and Altman, I. (1987) Communication in interpersonal relationships: social penetration theory. In *Interpersonal Processes: New Directions in Communication Research* (eds M.E. Roloff and G.R. Miller), 257–77. Newbury Park, CA: Sage.

Theodorson, S.A. and Theodorson, G.R. (1969) *A Modern Dictionary of Sociology*. New York: Cromwell.

Tichy, N. (1979) Social network analysis for organisations, *Academy of Management Review*, **4**, 507–19.

Varey, R. (2002), Requisite communication for positive involvement and participation: A critical communication theory perspective, *International Journal of Applied Human Resource Management*, **3**(2), 20–35.

Wangenheim, F.V. (2005) Post switching negative word of mouth, *Journal of Service Research*, **8**, 67–78.

Weick, K. (1987) Prescribed and emergent networks. In *Handbook of Organisational Communication* (ed. F. Jablin). London: Sage.

Williams, K. (1990) *Behavioural Aspects of Marketing*. Oxford: Heinemann.

Windahl, S., Signitzer, B. and Olson, J.T. (1992) *Using Communication Theory*. London: Sage.

Whitton, F. and Ryan, L. (2006) Sony BRAVIA LCD TV-Balls, *IPA Effectiveness Awards*, Institute of Practitioners in Advertising. Retrieved 18 January 2008 from http://www.warc.com/ArticleCenter/Default.asp?CType=A&AID=WORDSEARCH82662&Tab=A.

Woodside, A.G. and Delozier, M.W. (1976) Effects of word of mouth advertising on consumer risk taking, *Journal of Advertising*, **5**(4), 12–19.

Yuan, Y., Caulkins, J.P. and Roehrig, S. (1998) The relationship between advertising and content provision on the Internet, *European Journal of Marketing*, **32**(7/8), 667–87.

Chapter 3

The marketing communications industry

New technology and increasing competition have been the main drivers of change within the marketing communications industry. Client needs have evolved particularly as they search for lower costs and facilities to support integrated marketing communications. The media and communication agencies have been adapting to the changing environment, albeit very slowly at times.

Aims and learning objectives

The aim of this chapter is to introduce the communications industry, the various organisations involved and some of the issues affecting the operation of the industry.

The learning objectives of this chapter are to:

1. provide an introductory understanding of the nature of the communications industry;
2. consider the nature and role of the main types of organisations involved in the industry;
3. explore relationships and methods of remuneration used within the industry;
4. consider the principal methods and operations used within agencies to meet their clients' needs;
5. examine industry issues in the light of the development of integrated marketing communications;
6. anticipate some of the future trends that might affect the industry.

For an applied interpretation see Mike Molesworth's MiniCase on ***Branding the Tasu 24/2 subnotebook*** at the end of this chapter.

Introduction

The marketing communications industry consists of four principal actors.

The marketing communications industry consists of four principal actors. These are the media, the clients, the agencies (historically, the most notable of which are advertising agencies) and finally the thousands of support organisations, such as production companies and fulfilment houses, who enable the whole process to function. It is the operations and relationships between these organisations that not only drive the industry but also form an important context within which marketing communications can be understood. Figure 3.1 sets out the main actor organisations in the industry.

Only through outsourcing can organisations experience increased levels of flexibility and gain access to the special skills and expertise necessary to engage audiences in competitive environments.

There is an argument that organisations should manage and develop their marketing communications 'in-house', that is, do it themselves. This could enable better control and lower costs. However, this argument is now very weak due to the increasing complexity and diversity of communication activities and the restructuring of organisations aimed at de-layering and hollowing out their organisations. It can only be through outsourcing that organisations experience increased levels of flexibility and gain access to the special skills and expertise necessary to engage audiences in competitive environments.

There is little or no room to maintain people with skills and expertise that are only drawn upon infrequently and where the notion of critical mass is important for media buying. Most observers argue that it could only be accomplished by agencies and others who are dealing with a large number of clients and who are, by definition, in constant touch with developments in the industry. In the field of media buying, for example, many would argue that it is unlikely that the necessary expertise could be developed in-house. The increased emphasis on accountability and efficiency means that it is necessary to outsource such activities in order to use expertise, specialised resources and take advantage of collective discounts from media houses. Marketing practitioners, therefore, need to use some of the other organisations in the communications industry. A level of interdependence exists which requires cooperative and collaborative behaviour if the system is to function efficiently.

The number of relationships that can be developed in this industry, as with others, is enormous. To further complicate matters, the slow yet enduring move towards integrated marketing communications (Chapter 9) requires participants to form new relationships and acquire new skills.

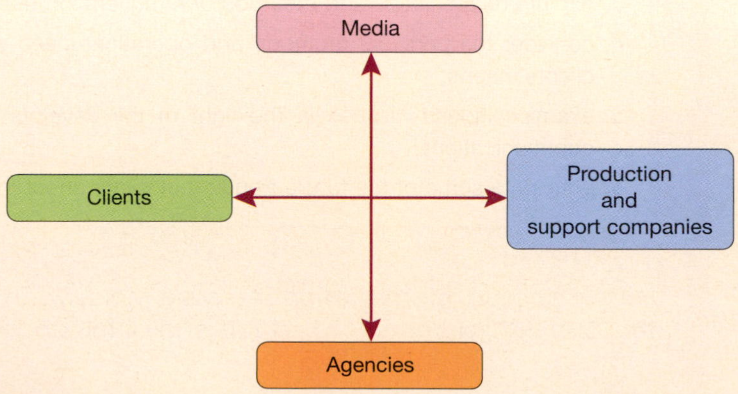

Figure 3.1 The principal organisations in the marketing communications industry

Dimensions of the UK marketing communications industry

It is useful to consider the size and value of the industry by considering the sums of money spent by clients on marketing communications. Some of these figures are acknowledged to be estimates, and there is some evidence of 'double counting' (one or more sectors claiming part of the overall spend for itself), so any figures produced cannot be seen as being totally accurate. That said, however, the total spend for advertising, as can be seen from Table 3.1, was £19 billion in 2006.

ViewPoint 3.1 Industry issues

In an article in 2005 the Director-General of the Incorporated Society of British Advertisers, Malcolm Earnshaw, referred to three main issues facing the marketing industry.

The first of these was the need for advertisers to defend their rights to advertise responsibly and not to be constrained by increasing legislation and government regulations. In particular, he referred to a then recent Government White Paper regarding food advertising and public health (obesity).

The second issue concerned the continuing consolidation in the media and the possible negative impact on clients in the advertising market.

The third issue referred to clients using the services of procurement specialists in order to drive down advertising costs with the consequent impact on agency margins and overall profitability. His argument is based on the need for agencies to offer better value to clients rather than to win pitches based on price alone.

At a more fundamental level consideration has been given to changing the number of minutes in each hour that ads can be screened on TV. The current average is seven minutes but Ofcom, the industry tzar, is thinking about raising this to nine minutes on the main commercial channels, ITV1, Channel 4 and Channel 5. Those in the industry are generally in favour as this will lower prices and attract a new raft of organisations who are able to advertise on television. Beale, (2007) reports that those outside the industry are not so keen, typified by headlines such as 'ad nauseam' (*The Sun*), and 'It's time to put the kettle on – again' (*The Times*).

Sources: Earnshaw (2005); Beale (2007).

Question

If you had to write a fourth issue for Earnshaw to refer to, what would it be?

Task

Make a list of three reasons to support the extension to 9 minutes' advertising in every hour and three against such a move.

The Institute of Sales Promotion claims that the growth of sales promotion has been 'explosive', but measuring the growth is difficult because there are no rate cards (price lists) and the breadth of activities that are attributable to sales promotion are many and varied. However, the Institute estimates that expenditure on sales promotion has grown from £9 billion in 1996, perhaps to £15 billion in 2003 and to £20 billion in 2006. Although not yet formally exceeding the spend on advertising, this area of activity is fast catching up and, despite published figures, it is widely believed inside the industry that sales promotion has already overtaken advertising in terms of the proportion of client spend, in particular sectors.

It is widely believed inside the industry that sales promotion has already overtaken advertising.

Table 3.1 Total UK advertising expenditure (including direct mail) £m

	2006 (£m)	2003 (£m)	2000 (£m)
Press	8,346	8,382	8,604
Television	4,594	4,374	4,646
Direct mail	2,322	2,431	2,049
Outdoor and transit	1,084	901	810
Radio	534	582	595
Cinema	188	180	128
Internet	2,016	376	155
Total	**19,084**	**17,227**	**16,988**

Source: Advertising Association (2007) *Advertising Statistics Yearbook*. Used with kind permission from WARC.

Growth in direct marketing has continued, with expenditure on direct mail, the dominant aspect of the industry.

Estimates vary, mainly because of problems of definition, but of the other areas in the industry sponsorship has grown significantly. Estimates suggest that sponsorship was worth around £1 billion in 2007. Direct marketing spend had increased steadily as confidence has grown in the industry, although a downturn in the economy brought this increase to an abrupt halt with two years of little or no growth. However, Goften (2000) predicted a recovery and since 2005 investment and growth in direct marketing has continued, with expenditure on direct mail, the dominant aspect of the industry, rising to £2,322 billion (Direct Mail Information Service (DMIS)).

Other areas of the industry include public relations, which has experienced steady development and was worth approximately £4.0 billion in 2007 and exhibitions of which there were 944 in 2005, each over 2,000 sq ft and in total worth approximately £2.0 billion.

Expenditure patterns do change, albeit at different rates, and, given the domination of advertising and sales promotion, the overall balance is unlikely to change dramatically in the short term. However, it is clearly important for those responsible for the future and current planning of marketing communications activities to monitor trends, particularly those in the fastest growing sectors of the industry, in order to identify and target creative opportunities.

Structure and development of the UK marketing communications industry

Adaptation to the environment is important for survival.

As with any industry, growth and development spawn new types and structures. Adaptation to the environment is important for survival. The same applies to the marketing communications industry, where, to take the advertising industry as an example, many different organisational configurations have evolved. Before considering some of the structural issues it is useful to understand the main types of organisation that populate the industry. These are set out at Figure 3.1. As with any industry, growth and development spawn new types and structures.

Clients can decide to undertake the communications functions in-house. However, this is both costly and inefficient, and most outsource their requirements. Of the four main groups the production and media houses require that the clients and agencies agree and specify campaigns in order that they are able to contribute. So, to some extent therefore, agencies and clients are the lead players in this industry.

Agency types and structures

The marketing communications industry consists of a number of different types of organisations whose purpose is to enable clients to communicate effectively and efficiently with their target audiences. Originally these organisations acted as agents on behalf of media owners who wanted to sell media time and space. The agents bought large chunks of media space at a discounted price and then resold it, in separate smaller parts, at much higher prices. This was basically a production and selling role but one that has changed drastically. These agents learned to work more closely with their clients and in doing so became more customer-oriented. As will be seen later, agents undertook two main roles, creative message design and media planning and buying. The media component has subsequently been spun off to specialist agencies and might be regarded as direct function of the media owners yet again. However, the interest and drive towards integrated communications, including media neutrality, means that agents will probably assume new, more independent roles in the shape of the communications industry in the future. In addition to this White (2007) identifies several pressures working on agencies. These are the growth in importance of direct marketing, the increasing range of media and the need among large organisations for quasi-global ad networks. The result of this development is that a number of different types of agencies have emerged, all of which fulfil particular roles.

Agents bought large chunks of media space at a discounted price and then resold it, in separate smaller parts, at much higher prices.

Full-service agencies

The first and most common type of agency (advertising) is the full-service agency. This type of organisation offers the full range of services that a client requires in order to advertise its products and services. Agencies such as J. Walter Thompson and Leo Burnett offer a full service consisting of strategic planning, research, creative development, production, interactive and media planning and buying. Very often these services are offered on a global basis but this does not mean a full service agency needs to be large, employing thousands of people. Some mid size agencies employing a couple of dozen people can offer a full service. Whatever the size, some of these activities may be subcontracted, but overall responsibility rests with the full-service agency. Further discussion of some of the issues concerning full-service agencies follows later.

Boutiques

A derivative of this type of agency is the boutique or creative shop, which often forms when creative personnel (teams) leave full service agencies to set up their own business. Boutiques provide specialist or niche services for clients such as copyrighting, developing creative content and other artistic services. These agencies provide clients with an alternative source of ideas, new ways of thinking about a problem, issue or product. Clients choose to use them because they either wish to use particular styles and approaches for their creative work or they want to generate a raft of creative ideas.

Boutiques provide specialist or niche services for clients.

ViewPoint 3.2 **It's not advertising, it's communication**

Many aspects of the marketing communications industry have changed and are continuing to change. Some of these concern the nature and size of agencies. Many large dominant groups are emerging such as the four major organisations who recently pitched for Samsung's worldwide branding account. These four – Interpublic's using its FCB operation), Omnicom (using BBDO agency), WPP (using J. Walter Thompson and Red Cell) and Publicis Groupe (using Leo Burnett and Saatchi & Saatchi).

The fact that WPP won the account is not the point. These organisations evolved as advertising agencies but now they have transformed themselves into 'communication partners'. This reflects the increasing attention given to relationship marketing, the development of integrated marketing communications and the relative decline in the dominance of advertising within the communications mix. Organisations now seek to communicate different messages and this involves using a variety of (neutral) media. The term 'communication agencies' or partners, suggests variety and flexibility and reflects a change in core business.

Apart from structural and name change the industry launched Social Professional in September 2007. This is a social network site designed specifically for all people working in the marketing communications industry. The free-to-use site was developed so that the industry had a facility in which to collaborate, network and communicate in a secure, moderated environment.

Among the main features are forums on a wide range of topics, including advertising, direct marketing, branding, sponsorship, reverse chronological ordering of blogs, an option to create an alter ego to encourage more honest debate and an RSS feed service to help users keep up-to-date with market developments.

Sources: Donohue (2007) plus various.

Question

Is use of the term 'communication partners' disingenuous when advertising continues to be core business?

Task

Visit the web site of one of the big four and determine the spread of their business activities.

Media specialists

Similarly, media specialists provide clients with media services expertise. These organisations deliver media strategy and consulting services for both client advertisers as well as agencies. Their core business however, is focused on the planning, scheduling buying and monitoring of a client's media schedule. Child (2007) reports that advertisers believe the role of strategic media planning is 50 per cent more important today than it was seven years ago. The key advantage of using a media specialist is that they have the capacity to buy media time and space at rates far lower than a client or advertising agency can procure them. This is because of the sheer volume of business that media specialists buy. Child also believes that there are some indications that clients believe it is more important to have a global media network rather than a global advertising agency.

Two main forms of media specialist have emerged: media independents and media dependents.

Two main forms of media specialist have emerged: media independents, where the organisation is owned and run free of the direction and policy requirements of a full service agency, and media dependents, where the organisation is a subsidiary of a creative or full service organisation. The largest dependent in Britain is ZenithOptimedia, owned originally by Saatchi & Saatchi, and the largest independent is Carat.

Digital media

Digital media agencies have developed as a result of the huge and rapid growth of the digital media industry. The growth has come from two main areas. The first concerns the surge of online brands that hit the market full of expectation of transforming the way business is conducted. The second concerns established offline brands seeking to reach customers by adding interactive capabilities to their marketing channels.

The provision of Internet facilities has been the main area of work, mainly communication and business operations activities. This has been followed by WAP technology activity,

Web 2.0 and interactive television (see Chapters 25 and 26). The market appears to have formed into three main parts of a spectrum of activities. At one end are those agencies that are marketing-oriented and at the other are technology-based organisations. Real growth is likely to develop in the middle with organisations referred to as 'interactive architects' who can offer a blend of skills and consultancy services. Merger and acquisition activity has been intense, mainly a reaction to rapid industry growth, which was not capable of being sustained. The move towards what is referred to as 'integrated marketing communications' (see Chapter 9) has been accelerated by the greater efficiency and harmonisation that digital technology brings. However, one trend emerging from this changing environment is a polarisation on either traditional or digital work. There is a general absence of agencies that can work in both arenas (Grosso *et al.*, 2006) and one of the outcomes of this skill shortage is that spending on online ads might slow.

A la carte

Partly in response to the changing needs of clients and consumers, many organisations require greater flexibility in the way their advertising is managed. Consequently these clients prefer to use the services of a range of organisations. So, the planning skills of a full service agency, the creative talent of a particular boutique and the critical mass of a media-buying independent provide an *à la carte* approach. This approach requires the client advertiser to manage the entire marketing communication process, an 'in-house' arrangement. This process enables improved flexibility yet demands strong management coordination and control as the process is more complex and problematic.

Many organisations require greater flexibility in the way their advertising is managed.

Other communication agencies

The agencies and organisations set out so far in this chapter have their roots and core business firmly set within the advertising part of the communications industry. In addition to these there are a swathe of other agencies each specialising in a particular aspect of the marketing communications industry. So, there are agencies that provide sales promotion, public relations, sponsorship, field marketing and direct marketing. Their structure and operations reflect the needs of their market specialism but they are based on the principles through which the advertising agencies operate.

Direct marketing agencies

Direct marketing has become a significant and influential part of the marketing communications industry. Direct marketing and direct response agencies create and deliver campaigns through direct mail, telemarketing or through a variety of offline and online media, which is referred to as direct response media.

One of the distinguishing elements of a direct marketing agency is the database. These agencies maintain large databases that contain mailing lists. This data can be merged and reconstructed to reflect a client's target market. The agency helps to develop promotional materials and then implements the campaign through the data list. Direct agencies will either own or have access to a fulfilment house. These organisations fulfil customer orders, that is, process the order and take payment resulting from the direct marketing campaign, send out the ordered products and deal with after sales services as necessary.

Industry structure

The structure of the industry has inevitably changed through time. Some may argue that it has not changed enough, but the shape and size of the industry has developed. Over the last 20 years the size of the industry has increased in response to changes in technology, the

The structure of the industry has inevitably changed through time.

growth in the number of marketing communications activities and with it the real value of advertising, sales promotion, public relations and direct marketing. The rate of growth among these tools has been variable with only direct marketing showing consistent levels of real growth.

The configuration of the agency services industry partly reflects the moves made by the larger agencies to consolidate their positions. They have attempted to buy either smaller, often medium-sized competitors, in an attempt to protect their market shares or provide an improved range of services for their clients. See the section below on one-stop shopping. This has led to an industry characterised by a large number of very large agencies and an even larger number of very small agencies. These smaller agencies have formed as the result of people formerly employed in large agencies becoming frustrated with having to work within tight margins and increased administration leaving and setting up their own fledgling businesses. This is currently evident in the direct marketing part of the industry, according to Billings (2004). She argues that there are now two distinct structural models emerging: those DM agencies who are attached to advertising agencies (for example Elvis and Hall Moore CHI) and those which are entirely independent (for example, Barraclough Edwards Chamberlain and Nitro). This pattern was observed previously when media planning houses developed. Some were entirely independent and others, such as Zenith, were dependent upon a parent organisation.

As a broad interpretation the industry consists of some large agencies, a large number of very small agencies and relatively few medium-sized agencies. Although ownership has been an important factor driving industry development, the current preference for loose, independent networks has enabled some large organisations to offer clients an improved range of services (IMC) and the small agencies a chance to work with some of the bigger accounts. Miln (2004) speculated that structural changes to the way in which clients and agencies work together would give rise to what he referred to as 'new agencies' who would provide a limited range of specific communication services, most commonly involved with the thinking around the creative or media elements, but would outsource or delegate the implementation to a third-party organisation. These organisations possess the core skills associated with project management and are better placed to fulfil this specialist role. The agency will remain responsible to the client for the implementation, but would be in a better position to continue advising about the overall communication strategy and media imperatives. The extent to which this has happened is questionable but the principles behind this thinking remain interesting, even if they require a change of cultural awareness and strategic reorientation.

One-stop shopping

As with most industries, the structure of the communications industry has evolved in response to changes in the environment. However, if there is a holy grail of communications it is an agency's ability to offer clients a single point from which all of their integrated communication needs can be met. In search of this goal, WPP and Saatchi & Saatchi set about building the largest marketing communications empires in the world. According to Green (1991), Saatchi & Saatchi attempted to become the largest marketing services company in the world. The strategy adopted in the early 1980s was to acquire companies outside its current area of core competence, media advertising. Organisations in direct marketing, market research, sales promotion and public relations were brought under the Saatchi banner.

By offering a range of services under a single roof, rather like a 'supermarket', the one-stop shopping approach made intrinsic sense. Clients could put a package together, rather like eating from a buffet table, and solve a number of their marketing requirements – without the expense and effort of searching through each sector to find a company with which to work.

Green also refers to the WPP experience in the late 1980s. J. Walter Thompson and Ogilvy and Mather were grouped together under the umbrella of WPP and it was felt that synergies were to be achieved by bringing together their various services. Six areas were identified: strategic marketing services, media advertising, public relations, market research, non-media advertising and specialist communications. A one-stop shopping approach was advocated once again.

The recession of the early 1990s brought problems to both of these organisations, as well as others. The growth had been built on acquisition, which was partly funded from debt. This required considerable interest payments, but the recession brought a sharp decline in the revenues of the operating companies, and cash flow problems forced WPP and Saatchi & Saatchi to restructure their debt and their respective organisations. As Phillips (1991) points out, the financial strain and the complex task of managing operations on such a scale began to tell.

However, underpinning the strategy was the mistaken idea that clients actually wanted a one-stop shopping facility. It was unlikely that the best value for money was going to be achieved through this, so it came as no surprise when clients began to question the quality of the services for which they were paying. There was no guarantee that they could obtain from one large organisation the best creative, production, media and marketing solutions to their problems. Many began to shop around and engage specialists in different organisations (*à la carte*) in an attempt to receive not only the best quality of service but also the best value for money. Evidence for this might be seen in the resurgence of the media specialists whose very existence depends on their success in media planning and buying. By 1990 it was estimated that in Britain 30 per cent of market share in media buying was handled by media specialist companies.

It is no wonder then that clients, and indeed many media people working in agencies who felt constrained, decided to leave and set up on their own account, feeling that full-service agencies were asking too much of their staff, not only in terms of providing a wide range of integrated marketing services generally, but also in giving full attention and bringing sufficient expertise to bear in each of the specific services they had to offer (account management, creative, production, media research, etc.).

The debate about whether or not to use a full-service agency becomes even more crucial, perhaps, for those in specialist areas.

The debate about whether or not to use a full-service agency becomes even more crucial, perhaps, for those in specialist areas.

The debate about whether or not to use a full-service agency becomes even more crucial, perhaps, for those in specialist areas. For example, a large number of business-to-business communication agencies have been set up by people leaving full-service agencies. They spotted opportunities to provide specialist services in a market area that at the time was under resourced, often marginalised or even ignored. In many ways it comes back to the quality of relationships. Arguments for the specialist agency were based on the point that, while there may be some convergence of approaches between consumer goods marketing and business-to-business advertising, it can be easier for a business-to-business advertising agency to do consumer advertising than it is to do the reverse.

As a general view, business-to-business shops survive on their ability to execute some very fundamental techniques for clients, such as direct mail or sales promotion. In contrast, the large, consumer goods-oriented shops, whose traditional skills are market research, planning and media advertising, often lack the core skills, initiative or expertise to deliver business-to-business marketing services.

The same has been said of direct marketing where there appears to be the same sort of disenchantment with the full-service agency. Criticisms include the exclusion of direct marketing experts from presentations to clients, a lack of education among mainstream agency types as to what direct marketing actually does or the complaint that clients do not want to be force fed a direct marketing subsidiary that may be incompetent or inappropriate. The experience of those involved in direct marketing has been further destabilised by the growth in the Internet. Direct mail has gained rather than lost because many online brands have used direct mail as off-line promotion to drive web site traffic. Telemarketing has flourished because call centres have repositioned themselves as multimedia contact centres and have extended their range of services.

There is a spectrum of approaches for clients. They can find an agency that can provide all of the required marketing communication services under one roof, or find a different agency for each of the services, or mix and match. Clearly the first solution can only be used if the budget holder is convinced that the best level of service is being provided in *all* areas, and the second only if there are sufficient gains in efficiency (and savings in expenditure) to warrant the amount of additional time they would need to devote to the task of managing marketing communications.

One area that has experienced significant change has been in media.

One area that has experienced significant change has been in media. Industry concentration and the development of global networks has shifted the structure and composition of the industry. Clients have responded by centralising their business into a single media network agency in search of higher discounts and improved efficiency. As a general rule, the stronger the competitive forces, the lower the profitability in the market. An organisation needs to determine a competitive approach that will allow it to influence the industry's competitive rules, protect it from competitive forces as much as possible and give it a strong position from which to compete. At the turn of the century media networks had yet to find a competitive form of differentiation although some were beginning to offer additional services as a way of trying to enhance brand identities (Griffiths, 2000). At the time the power of the media agencies, the low switching costs of buyers and the large threat of substitute products made this a relatively unattractive industry in its current form. This has changed. Media are now perceived to be much more important, much more significant than they used to be and as a result have developed increased market value.

ViewPoint 3.3 Growth engine

In the 1980s full-service agencies employed creatives and media specialists. They rarely got on, with the media specialists eventually leaving to develop their own companies. The major agencies soon realised that this disintegration was not in their best interests and so promptly set about creating (buying) their own 'dependent' media companies. These were still kept separate from the creative agencies but remained wholly-owned, technically a full-service operation (once again) but never referred to as such.

Marquis (2007) observes the irony of Engine, an agency group who are looking to acquire a media planning and buying business. Engine consists of a collection of specialist businesses dealing in a range of communication activities. It might be argued that the core business is the advertising agency WRCS but the range of associated companies encompass a spectrum of marketing communication activities. These range from consumer PR, public affairs and digital to sales promotion, direct marketing, experiential marketing and sponsorship (www.theenginegroup.com/). The two key elements not in the portfolio are media planning and buying and this, Marquis argues, is critical if Engine is to have any credibility as a marketing communications 'supermarket'.

Whether the full-service agency model of the 1980s is a suitable structure through which to deliver integrated marketing communications in the twenty-first century, is a separate debate. However, it is probable that the commercial sophistication of media agencies today precludes the reinstatement of a truly full-service operation. Engine is thriving as a group and demonstrates not only the need for new models of operation but also reflects the redundancy of the full-service approach.

Source: Adapted from Marquis (2007).

Question

How do you think the acquisition of a media planning agency would add value to Engine's operations?

Task

Search and list the top three media houses in your country or region.

Finer segmentation to determine markets that permit higher margins and a move to provide greater differentiation among agencies, together with a policy to reduce the threats from substitute products, perhaps through more visible alliances and partnerships, has helped to enable the industry to recover its position and provide greater stability. It is interesting to note that many leading agencies have moved into strategic consultancy, away from the reliance on mass media, where a substantially higher margin can be generated. Many direct marketing companies have evolved out of sales promotion agencies. According to Goften (2000), both have tried to reposition themselves with the sales promotion houses adopting a wide variety of promotional activities and direct marketing agencies moving their focus of business activity to one that is either oriented towards ecommerce or customer relationship management. The signs are in 2008 that these two disciplines are moving towards each other again, many undertaking tasks in each other's traditional domain.

Selecting an agency

In the areas that have traditionally dominated marketing communications, advertising and sales promotion, there has never been a shortage of advice on how to select an agency. Articles informing readers how to select an agency (Young and Steilen, 1996; Woolgar, 1998; Finch, 2000; McKee, 2004; Bruce, 2006) appear regularly, and there are a large number of publications and organisations to assist in the process.

The process of selecting an agency that is set out below appears to be rational and relatively straightforward. Readers should be aware that the reality is that the process is infused with political and personal issues, some of which can be contradictory. Logically the process commences with a *search*, undertaken to develop a list of potential candidates. This is accomplished by referring to publications such as *Campaign Portfolio* and the *Advertising Agency Roster*, together with personal recommendations. The latter is perhaps the most potent and influential of these sources. As many as 10 agencies could be included at this stage although six or seven are to be expected.

> The reality is that the process is infused with political and personal issues, some of which can be contradictory.

ViewPoint 3.4 Relationships matter more than pitches

When Rob Murray was appointed as Marketing Director for Wickes, the building and DIY supplies store, he had to appoint an advertising agency to help bring about the changes he had determined needed to happen. In his previous position at Ryvita he had used the agency MWO who had proved successful for all parties.

Murray appointed MWO to the Wickes account, worth £10m a year, without a pitch, and just a little bit of support from procurement consultants. Based on the successful relationship and the known operations and processes, Murray felt the strength of the relationship was important and was not something that could be replicated by the many other agencies, all of whom could also produce good ads.

Martin Glenn at Birds Eye Iglo is reported to have appointed Abbot Mead Vickers BBDO with whom he worked when at PepsiCo, while Jim Hytner appointed Walker Media when at Channel 5 and Barclays. Agency/client relationships do matter.

Source: Charles (2008).

Question

Should it be mandatory that all agency appointments be made as a result of a fair and equal pitching process?

Task

Pick two brands of your choice, go to their web sites and find out how long their current agency has been with the brand.

Next, the client will visit each of the short-listed candidates in what is referred to as a *credentials presentation*. This is a crucial stage in the process, as it is now that the agency is evaluated for its degree of fit with the client's expectations and requirements. Agencies could develop their web sites to fulfil this role, which would save time and costs. The agency's track record, resources, areas of expertise and experience can all be made available on the Internet from which it should be possible to short-list three or possibly four agencies for the next stage in the process: the pitch.

In the PR industry agencies are selected to pitch on the basis of the quality and experience of the agency people, its image and reputation and relationships with existing clients. In addition, Pawinska (2000) reports that the track record of the agency and the extent of its geographical coverage are also regarded as important.

To be able to make a suitable bid the agencies are given a brief and then required to make a formal presentation (the *pitch*) to the client some 6–8 weeks later. This presentation is about how the agency would approach the strategic and creative issues and the account is awarded to whichever produces the most suitable proposal. Suitability is a relative term, and a range of factors need to be considered when selecting an organisation to be responsible for a large part of a brand's visibility. A strategic alliance is being formed and therefore a strong understanding of the strategic objectives of both parties is necessary, as is an appreciation of the structure and culture of the two organisations. The selection process is a bringing together of two organisations whose expectations may be different but whose cooperative behaviour is essential for these expectations to have any chance of materialising. For example, agencies must have access to comprehensive and often commercially confidential data about products and markets if they are to operate efficiently. Otherwise, they cannot provide the service that is expected. However, it should be noted that pitches are not mandatory, and as Jones (2004) reports, nearly one-third of clients move their accounts without involving pitches. One of the reasons for this is the increasing cost involved in running the whole process, as much as £50,000 according to Jones. Indeed Wethey (2006) questions the whole validity and efficacy of the pitching process. He argues that many pitches are a waste of resources (time and money), that too many agencies devote too much of their resources chasing new business, that pitches do not solve client problems and that the whole process is often unrealistic.

It should be noted that pitches are not mandatory.

The immediate selection process is finalised when terms and conditions are agreed and the winner is announced to the contestants and made public, often through press releases and the use of trade journals such as *Campaign*, *Marketing* and *Marketing Week*.

The immediate selection process is finalised when terms and conditions are agreed.

This formalised process is now being questioned as to its suitability. The arrival of new media firms and their need to find communication solutions in one rather than eight weeks has meant that new methods have had to be found. In addition, agencies felt that they were having to invest a great deal in a pitch with little or no reward if the pitch failed. Their response has been to ask for payment to pitch which has not been received well by many clients. The tension that arises is that each agency is required to generate creative ideas over which they have little control once a pitch has been lost. The pitching process also fails to give much insight into the probable working relationships and is very often led by senior managers who will not be involved in the day-to-day operations. One solution adopted by Iceland and Dyson (Jardine, 2000) has been to invite agencies to discuss mini-briefs. These are essentially discussion topics about related issues rather than the traditional challenge about how to improve a brand's performance. Issuing the mini-brief on the day eliminates weeks of preparation and associated staff costs, and enables the client to see agency teams working together.

Agency operations

Most communications agencies are generally organised on a functional basis. There have been moves to develop matrix structures utilising a customer orientation, but this is very inefficient and the low margins prohibit such luxuries. There are departments for planning, creative and media functions coordinated on behalf of the client by an account handler or executive.

The account executive fulfils a very important role in that these people are responsible for the flow of communications between the client and the agency. The quality of the communications between the two main parties can be critical to the success of the overall campaign and to the length of the relationship between the two organisations. Acting at the boundary of the agency's operations, the account executive needs to perform several roles, from internal coordinator and negotiator to presenter (of the agency's work), conflict manager and information gatherer. Very often account executives will experience tension as they seek to achieve their clients' needs while trying to balance the needs of their employer and colleagues. These tensions are similar to those experienced by salespersons and need to be managed in a sensitive manner by management.

Account executives are responsible for the flow of communications between the client and the agency.

ViewPoint 3.5 Online creative marketplaces

New technology has been used to assist different aspects of campaign management. A large majority has been supplier-driven but more recent contributions have attempted to enable both clients and agencies to participate more equally in the campaign development process. For example, an online marketplace called BootB has been developed with the express intention of enabling clients to reach a whole range of creative talent around the world. The site enables clients to bypass agencies and to make direct contact with a whole range of creative talent, not accessible through a single or roster agency.

Clients post their briefs on the site, in 12 languages, for a range of marketing communications activities, including viral, PR, advertising and direct mail campaigns. Anyone in the world, individuals, groups and even agencies, are then free to submit their creative designs to the site and if chosen, are paid professional fees from an account holding the budget.

This site signals a change in the way creative work is developed and has ramifications for agency structures and operations.

Kickfire developed one of the first marketing resource management (MRM) systems, designed specifically to enable organisations to manage the development processes associated with campaigns.

The software application provides for a large degree of ubiquity and freedom as suppliers and clients can work on marketing projects regardless of location. Using a specific password-protected web site, parties can share data and documents, develop schedules, allocate individuals to particular tasks, check project progress and produce relevant and timely reports.

The system uses digital asset management functionality to store logos, images and copy that can be utilised by all participants. Public relations activities are also assisted as there are templates for writing press releases. This helps develop coordinated marketing communications through the promotion of image consistency and usage.

Sources: Adapted from Anon. (2007); Murphy (2002).

Question

To what extent should agencies use amateur advertising content?

Task

Visit BootB. Can you make a contribution?

Project management – Provide basic project details, e.g. timescales, contacts and people, project numbers

Where are we now? – Describe current brand details, e.g. background, position, competitors, key issues

Where do we want to be? – What needs to be achieved in terms of goals, e.g. sales, market share, ROI, shareholder value, awareness, perception, etc.

What are we doing to get there? – What is the context in terms of the marketing strategy, overall communication strategy and campaign strategy?

Who do we need to talk to? – What is understood about the audiences the communications are intended to influence?

How will we know if we have arrived? – What will be measured, by whom, how and when to determine whether the activity has been successful?

Practicalities – Budgets, timings and schedules, creative and media imperatives

Approvals – Who has the authority to sign off the brief and the agency work?

Figure 3.2 A new briefing structure

Once an account has been signed, a client brief is prepared that provides information about the client organisation (Figure 3.2). It sets out the nature of the industry it operates in together with data about trends, market shares, customers, competitors and the problem that the agency is required to address. This is used to inform agency personnel. In particular, the account planner will undertake research to determine market, media and audience characteristics and make proposals to the rest of the account team concerning how the client problem is to be resolved.

Briefing is a process that is common across all client–agency relationships in the communication industry.

Briefing is a process that is common across all client–agency relationships in the communication industry. Regardless of whether working in direct marketing, sales promotion, advertising, public relations, media planning and buying or other specialist area, the brief has a special importance in making the process work and the outcomes significant. However, the importance of preparing a brief of suitable quality has for some been underestimated. With agencies having to brief themselves and some briefs insufficiently detailed, a recent joint industry initiative sought to establish common working practices. The outcome of the process was a briefing template intended to be used by all across the communications agencies in the industry. Eight key headings emerged from the report and these can be seen at Figure 3.2.

In addition to the role of account handler, which might be regarded as one of traffic management, is the role undertaken by account planners (or creative planners). The role of the account planner has been the subject of a recent flurry of debate (Collin, 2003; Grant *et al.*, 2003; Zambarino and Goodfellow, 2003). The general conclusion of these papers is that the role account planner, which has been evolving since the beginning of the 1960s, has changed as the communications industry has fragmented and that a new role is emerging in response to integrated marketing communication and media neutral planning initiatives (see Chapter 9 for details about these concepts).

The traditional role of the account planner, which began in full-service agencies, was to understand the client's target consumers and develop strategies for the creative and media departments. As media broke away from full-service agencies so the role of the account planner shifted to the creative aspect of the agency work. Media planners assumed the same type of work in media companies although their work focused on planning the right media mix to reach the target audience. With the development of integrated perspectives and the move towards a broader view of a client's communication needs so there is an expectation that the planning role will evolve into a strategic role. The role will be to work with a broad range of marketing disciplines (tools) and media but not to brief creatives or media planners directly (Collin, 2003). As media broke away from full-service agencies so the role of the account planner shifted to the creative aspect of the agency work.

As media broke away from full-service agencies so the role of the account planner shifted to the creative aspect of the agency work.

Creative teams comprise a copywriter and an art director, supported by a service team. This team is responsible for translating the proposal into an advertisement. In a full-service agency, a media brief will also be generated, informing the media planning and buying department of the media and the type of media vehicles required. However, the vast majority of media planning work is now undertaken by specialist media agencies, media independents, and these will be briefed by the client, with some support from those responsible for the creatives.

In recent years, partly as a response to the growth of new media, a raft of small entrepreneurial agencies has emerged, to exploit the new opportunities arising from the digital revolution. Many of these are run without the control and structures evident in large, centralised agencies. While dedicated teams might theoretically be the best way to manage a client's project, the reality in many cases is the use of project teams comprising expert individuals working on a number of projects simultaneously. This is not a new phenomenon, but as a result many people are multi-tasking and they assume many roles with new titles. For example, the title head of content has arisen to reflect the significance of content issues in the new media market. Project managers assume responsibility for the implementation phase and the coordination of all aspects of a client's technological facilities. In addition, there are positions such as head of marketing, mobile (increasing focus on WAP technology), production and technology. The result is no hierarchies, flat structures and flexible working practices and similar expectations.

Relationships

The nature of the relationships that exist in the industry shapes and influences the strategies and operations. There are a vast number of relationships that form between various clients and agencies, disciplines and within individual organisations.

Client/agency relationships

If the briefing process provides the mechanism for the agency operations, it is the relationship between the agency and the client that very often determines the length of the contract and the strength of the solutions advanced for the client.

The relationship between the agency and the client very often determines the length of the contract and the strength of the solutions advanced for the client.

There are a number of agency/client relationships that have flourished over a very long period of time, and some for several decades. Sclater (2006) refers to the agency BBH, which was established in 1982. The agency started with three key clients, Audi, Levi's and Whitbread (now InBev UK) and all three are still working together over two decades later. Similarly WCRS has had a long-term relationship with BMW, since 1979. There are a huge number of other

Table 3.2 Longer-lasting agency/client relationships

Agency	Clients since
Abbott Mead Vickers BBDO	Volvo (1985), Sainsbury's (1981), *The Economist* (1986), Homebase (1991) BT (1994)
Grey Advertising	GlaxoSmithKline (1955, 21 brands), Procter & Gamble (1956, 31 brands)
Lowe Worldwide	Unilever/Lever Faberge (1963) Unilever/Best Foods (1964) Stella Artois (1981), Vauxhall (1983), Johnson & Johnson (1986)
Ogilvy & Mather	Unilever (1952), Mattel (1954) Kraft Foods (1954), Nestlé (1959) American Express (1963), Ford (1975)
Saatchi & Saatchi	Carlsberg (1973), Pepsi, (1981), Procter & Gamble (1983), NSPCC (1984) Toyota (1992)

Source: Adapted from Sclater (2006).

accounts who have excellent relationships that have lasted a long time, see Table 3.2 for a snapshot of some of the more longer public agency/client relationships.

However, these appear to be in the minority, as many relationships appear to founder as clients abandon agencies and search for better, fresher solutions, because a contract expires, the client needs change or owing to takeovers and mergers between agencies, which require that they forfeit accounts that cause a conflict of interest.

Clients and agencies enter into a series of interactions or exchanges through which levels of trust and commitment develop.

From a contextual perspective these buyer/seller relationships can be seen to follow a pattern of formation, maintenance and severance, or pre-contract, contracting process and post-contract stages (Davidson and Kapelianis, 1996). Clients and agencies enter into a series of interactions (West and Paliwoda, 1996) or exchanges through which levels of trust and commitment develop. Hakansson (1982) identified different contexts or atmospheres within which a relationship develops. These contexts had several dimensions: closeness/distance, cooperation/conflict, power/dependence, trustworthiness and expectations. Therefore, the client/agency relationship should be seen in the context of the network of organisations and the exchanges or interactions that occur in that network. It is through these interactions that the tasks that need to be accomplished are agreed, resources made available, strategies determined and goals achieved. The quality of the agency/client relationship is a function of trust, which is developed through the exchanges and which fosters confidence. Commitment is derived from a belief that the relationship is worth continuing and that maximum effort is warranted to maintain the relationship (Morgan and Hunt, 1994). The development of new forms of remuneration (see p. 89) based around payment by results, also signifies a new client focus and a willingness to engage with clients and to be paid according to the success and contribution the agency can provide (Lace and Brocklehurst, 2000).

The way in which clients use multiple agencies to fulfil the whole range of communication tasks does not encourage the establishment of strong relationships nor does it help the cause of integrated marketing communications. The use of roster agencies means that marketing teams have to manage more agencies, often with reduced resources. This means that agencies get a smaller share of the available budget, which in turn does not help agencies feel comfortable (Child, 2007).

Poor relationships between agencies and clients are likely to result from a lack of trust and falling commitment.

Poor relationships between agencies and clients are likely to result from a lack of trust and falling commitment. As it appears that communication is a primary element in the formation and substance of relational exchanges, clients might be advised to consider the agencies in their roster as an extended department of the core organisation and use internal marketing communication procedures to assist the development of identity and belonging.

One last point to be made is the increasing age gap between those in the industry, both agency and client, and their audiences. Those people that produce marketing communications tend to be under 35 and the average age of those targeted to receive the communications is rising. Curtis (1999) reports that Reg Starkey, a creative partner of Prime Advertising, Marketing and Research, claims that this may increase the chance of misunderstanding older consumers and that this error of interpretation can become a self-fulfilling prophecy.

ViewPoint 3.6 Some come and some go

When Maleon, a building services company searched for agencies to help them with their various marketing tasks, it was word-of-mouth that led them to one agency to fulfil one role and the credentials/pitching selection route that found another. Part of the process involved asking the agencies whether they understood the brief and the client proposition. In many cases the larger agencies had not taken the proposition on board correctly, a sign perhaps, that they were not fully engaged with their prospective client and not a good sign for future relationships. Maleon found greater success with mid-sized agencies who empathised with Maleon's needs.

At the other end of the spectrum Timex, the well-known watch brand, held a 30 per cent market share in the United States, where it sells more watches than the next 18 best-selling brands combined. In 2002, Timex USA decided to end its 16-year relationship with its lead agency Fallon Worldwide. According to Timex spokesman Jim Katz: 'After 16 years, we feel we wanted to see what else is out there.' The account was thought to be worth around £6m at the time of the dissolution.

Sources: Various, including Allen (2008).

Question

Should clients be advised to only seek agencies of a similar size and market standing?

Task

Make a list of the characteristics you feel make for a longer-lasting client/agency relationship.

Marketing and public relations

A further example of the potential problems that can arise in the industry concerns the role and structural position within organisations of public relations, relative to the marketing function. The issue concerns where in an organisation public relations should be located and more importantly, to whom they should report.

The role that public relations should assume and its structural position within an organisation have become increasingly complex and a source of much debate. Traditionally, public relations has been regarded as a function of public affairs or corporate communication, which reports directly to the CEO. Control over the activities of public relations is direct and the purpose is to convey appropriate information about the corporate entity and to create goodwill and understanding with other stakeholders. To that end, public relations was seen as separate to and distinct from marketing. A publication by the Public Relations Educational Trust (1991) declared that 'PR is NOT Marketing'. The substantiation for this is based on an interpretation of marketing, one that is strictly profit-oriented. This does not reflect reality, as self-help groups and organisations such as the NHS and charities would not be able to practise marketing if such a narrow perspective were supported.

The role that public relations should assume and its structural position within an organisation have become increasingly complex.

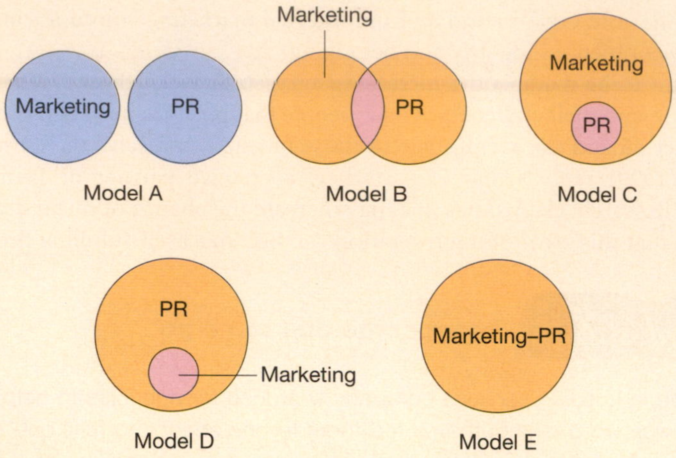

Figure 3.3 Relationships between marketing and public relations
Source: Kotler and Mindak (1978). Used with kind permission of the American Marketing Association.

Kotler and Mindak (1978) set out five ways in which organisations can manage the marketing and public relations functions. These are depicted in Figure 3.3. It can be seen that the structural relationship of marketing and public relations can range from the traditional view, where they are separate and totally unconnected, fulfilling different roles, through various other forms where one subsumes the other, to model E. Here, both share an equal and mutually supportive relationship. In this form, both recognise the need to segment markets and to provide different satisfactions. Each function needs the support of the other and both have similar needs in terms of understanding the attitudes, perceptions and awareness held by each market or stakeholder. Internal conflict is effectively reduced, and this in turn facilitates the transmission of consistent, positive and coordinated messages to all stakeholders.

Kotler and Mindak highlight these key relationships well, but the models can also be used to depict the development of public relations and marketing in organisations. For example, local authorities have for a long time had a public relations department, but only recently have they begun to appoint marketing managers in response to their changing responsibilities, environments and new competitive orientation. Hospitals are having to focus on market needs rather than the needs of internal experts. Many are increasing the level of public relations activities and are also introducing marketing as a distinct function, partly to assist the necessary change in culture.

Many private sector organisations are making a transition from model C to model D or E, depending upon their experiences and organisational culture, market environments and the perspective of the CEO and senior management team towards the roles of public relations and marketing.

The level of interest and strength of voice given to integrated marketing communications has been a force for bringing these two disciplines together. Increasingly campaigns are being used in a coordinated way and public relations is used in conjunction with the other marketing communication instruments. Clients are not normally structured internally so that they have an integrated communications department, and until the benefits of this type of approach are recognised, it is likely that the gulf between these two functions will continue.

The level of interest and strength of voice given to integrated marketing communications has been a force for bringing these two disciplines together.

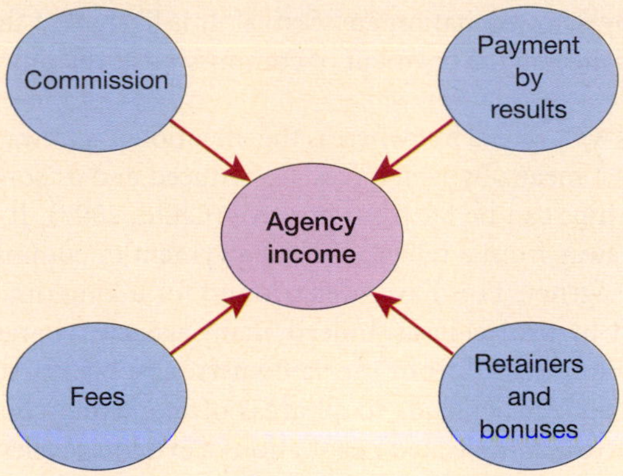

Figure 3.4 Remuneration methods in the marketing communications industry

Agency remuneration

One factor that has a significant impact on the quality of the relationship between the parties is the remuneration or reward for the effort (added value) the agency makes in attempting to meet and satisfy the needs of its client. One major cause for concern and complaint among marketing managers is the uncertainty over how much their marketing communications programmes will finally cost and the complexity surrounding the remuneration system itself.

There are three main ways in which agencies are paid. These are *commission*, *fees* and *payment by results* (PBR). These are often supplemented by bonuses (see Figure 3.4). Very rarely is a single method used within a contract.

Traditionally, advertising agencies were paid a commission by media owners for selling space in their publications. A figure of 15 per cent emerged as the norm and seemed a fair reward for the efforts of the agency. However, as relationships between agencies and clients strengthened, it seemed only reasonable that the clients should feel that agencies should act for them (and in their best interests), and not for the media owners. A number of questions were raised about whether the agency was actually being rewarded for the work it did and whether it was being objective when recommending media expenditure. As media independents emerged, questions started to be asked about why media agencies received 3 per cent and the creative agency received 12 per cent.

Traditionally, advertising agencies were paid a commission by media owners for selling space in their publications.

Client discontent is not the only reason why agency remuneration by commission has been called into question, and alternatives are being considered. In times of recession marketing budgets are inevitably cut, which means less revenue for agencies. Increasing competition means lower profit margins if an agency is to retain the business, and if costs are increasing at the same time, the very survival of the agency is in question. As Snowden stated as long ago as 1993, 'Clients are demanding more for less.' She went on to say, 'It is clear to me that the agency business needs to address a number of issues; most important amongst them, how agencies get paid. It is the key to the industry's survival.'

During the early 1990s there was a great deal of discussion and energy directed towards non-commission payment systems. This was a direct result of the recession, in which clients cut budgets and there was a consequent reduction in the quantity of media purchased and hence less revenue for the agencies. Fees became more popular, and some experimented with payment by results. Interestingly, as the recession died and the economy lifted, more revenue resulted in larger commission possibilities, and the death throes of the commission system were quickly replaced by its resuscitation and revival. It is likely that there will continue to be a move away from a reliance on the payment of commission as the only form of remuneration to the agency.

The use of bonuses is widespread but whereas the intention is to reward excellent work, some agencies see bonuses as a means by which fees are reduced and as some clients refuse to pay the impact on relationships can be far from positive (Child, 2007). It is likely that there will continue to be a move away from a reliance on the payment of commission as the only form of remuneration to the agency. Fees have been around for a long time, either in the form of retainers or on a project-by-project basis. Indeed, many agencies charge a fee for services over and above any commission earned from media owners. The big question concerns the basis for calculation of fees (and this extends to all areas of marketing communications, not just advertising), and protracted, complicated negotiations can damage client/agency relationships.

Payment by results seems a good solution.

For many, payment by results seems a good solution. There are some problems, however, in that the agency does not have total control over its performance and the final decisions about how much is spent and which creative ideas should be used are the client's. The agency has no control over the other marketing activities of the client, which might determine the degree of success of the campaign. Indeed, this raises the very thorny question of what 'success' is and how it might be measured. Despite these considerations, it appears that PBR is starting to become an established form of remuneration with over 30 per cent of agency–client contracts containing an element of PBR. Lace (2000) explains that this is due to the inadequacies of both commission- and fee-based systems in the 'new age of cost cutting and accountability'.

A different way of looking at this is to consider what the client thinks the agency does, and from this evaluate the outcomes from the relationship. Jensen (1995) proposed that advertising agencies should be regarded as an *ideas business* that seeks to build brands for clients. An alternative view is that agencies are *advertising factories*, where the majority of the work is associated with administration, communication, coordination and general running around to ensure that the advertisement appears on the page or screen as desired.

Advertising agencies should be regarded as an *ideas business* that seeks to build brands.

If the 'ideas business' view is accepted then the ideas generated add value for the client, so the use the client makes of the idea should be rewarded by way of a royalty-type payment. If the 'factory concept' is adopted, then it is the resources involved in the process that need to be considered and a fee-based system is more appropriate. Both parties will actively seek to reduce costs that do not contribute to the desired outcomes. These are different approaches to remuneration and avoid the volume of media purchased as a critical and controversial area.

Agency structures and IMC

The development of integrated marketing communications has been mentioned earlier and although the concept is subject to considerable debate and uncertainty the underlying good sense inherent in the concept resonates with clients and agencies. As a result the influence of IMC on agencies and clients should not be underestimated.

In order for messages to be developed and conveyed through an integrated approach, the underlying structure supporting this strategy needs to be reconsidered. Just as the structure of the industry had a major impact on the way in which messages were developed and communicated as the industry developed, so the structural underpinning needs to adapt to the new and preferred approaches of clients. Kitchen *et al.* (2007) report that a survey incorporating well-established PR and advertising agencies, found resistance towards the integration of certain working practices. These, the authors conclude, need to be refashioned in order that

Table 3.3 Integrated agency options

Type of agency	Explanation
Integrated agency	A single agency that provides the full range of communication disciplines.
Complementary agencies	The client selects a range of different agencies, each from a different discipline and self manages or appoints a lead agency.
Networked agencies	A single group agency is appointed (e.g. WPP or Interpublic) who then appoints agencies within their own profit-oriented network.
Mini-group agencies	Clusters of small independent specialist agencies who work on a non-competitive basis for a client.

the agencies working practices enable all the promotional disciplines to be incorporated in an integrated manner.

The use of outside agencies that possess skills, expertise and purchasing advantages that are valued by clients is not new and is unlikely to change. However, the way in which these outsourced skills are used and how they are structured has been changing. Aspects of client–agency relationships are important and are considered in Chapter 7. What is important at this stage is a consideration of the way in which those organisations who provide outsourcing facilities and contribute to a client's IMC can be configured to provide optimal servicing and support.

Clients who seek a marketing communications campaign which draws on more than one marketing communications discipline, have a basic choice of four main options. These are set out in Table 3.3.

None of these four approaches can provide a perfect solution and the variety of integrated possibilities reflects the different client structures and cultures and consequently the different needs and relationships that need to be satisfied (Murphy, 2004). The mini-group option is a relatively recent development and can include the use of product development, research, design and interactive services. This means that this approach serves a broad range of needs, typical of smaller client organisations whose budgets do not match those of mainstream firms.

Gronstedt and Thorsen (1996) suggest five ways in which agencies could be configured to provide integrated marketing communications. The research is centred upon US-based advertising agencies, so, while not immediately transferable to the European, Asian or other regional markets, their proposals provide a base from which other agencies might evolve in other geographic markets.

The models are presented in Figure 3.5, and although the authors acknowledge that a mix of forms could be identified, one particular form tended to dominate each agency. The forms denote a continuum, at one end of which is a highly centralised organisation that can provide a high level of integration for a variety of communication disciplines. Staffed by generalists with no particular media bias, these organisations are structured according to client needs, not functional specialisms. Total integration is offered at the expense of in-depth and leading-edge knowledge in new and developing areas.

> The forms denote a continuum, at one end of which is a highly centralised organisation that can provide a high level of integration.

At the other end of the continuum are those providers who group themselves in the form of a network. Often led by a main advertising agency that has divested itself of expensive overheads, the independent yet interdependent network players each provide specialist skills under the leadership of the main contractor agency. One of the two main weaknesses associated with this model concerns the deficiency associated with communications across the players in the

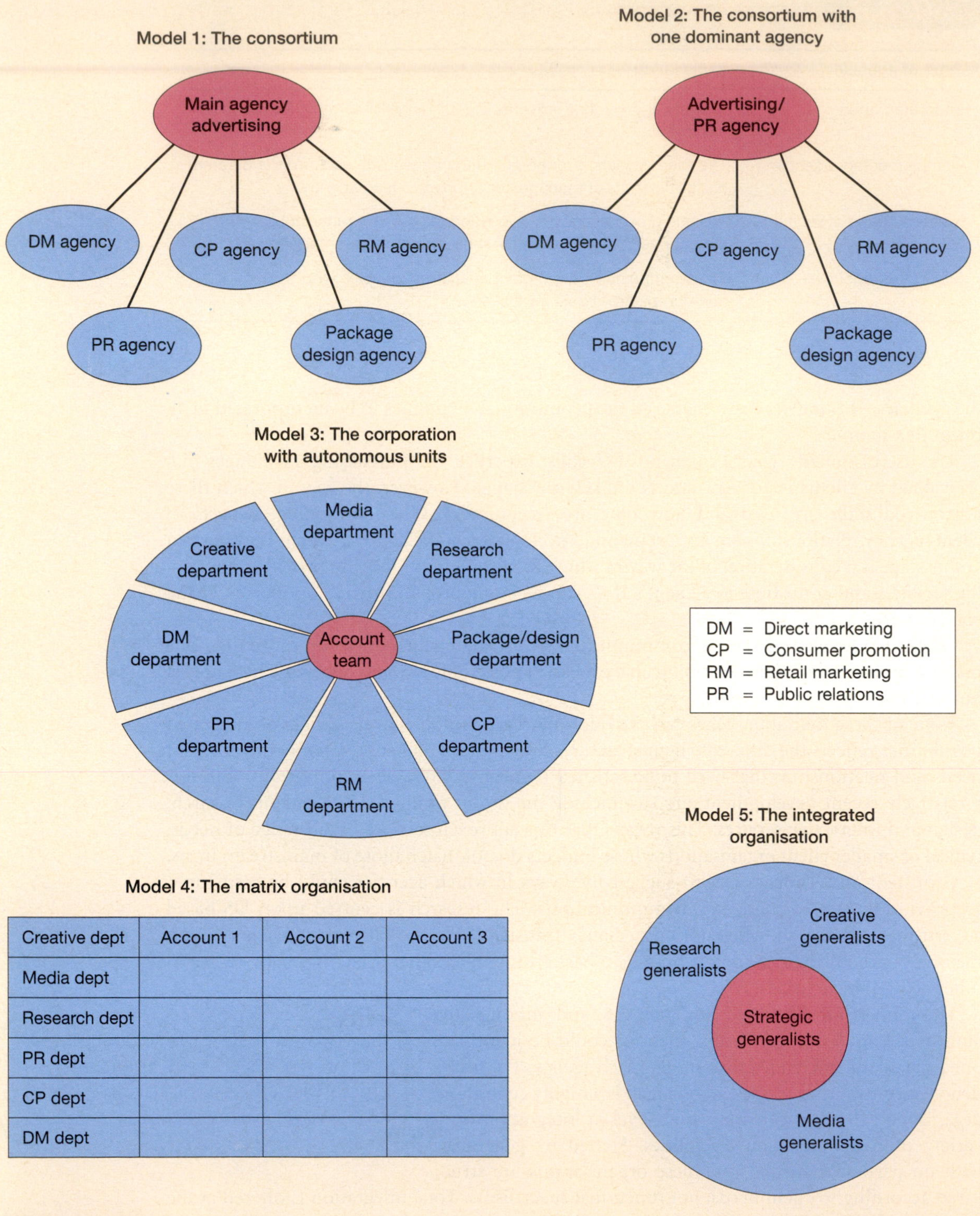

Figure 3.5 An overview of the five agency structures
Source: Gronstedt and Thorson (1996). Used with kind permission from WARC.

network. This horizontal aspect means that individual members of the network tend to identify with their own area of expertise and advance their specialism, possibly at the expense of the client's overriding requirements. The other main weakness concerns the transitory or temporary nature of a member organisation's involvement within such networks. Therefore, the level of potential integration is possibly weakest in this model, although the level of expertise available to clients is highest at this end of the continuum.

One of the essential points emerging from this research is that there seems to be a trade-off between levels of integration and the expertise provided by different agencies. Clients who want to retain control over their brands and to find an integrated agency where all the required services are of the exact level and quality demanded may be expecting too much. The inevitability of this position is that clients may choose to select marketing communication expertise from a variety of sources, and the integrated agency may well lose out.

Furthermore, environmental factors should not be ignored, and it may be that clients in the future will state their preferred structural requirements at the pitching or client briefing stage of the agency–client relationship. Increasingly, agencies may well be required to mix and match their structures and provide structural flexibility to meet the varying needs of their clients.

A further point concerns global branding and the standardisation/adaptation debate when considered in the light of IMC. One argument is that standardisation is the only way in which IMC can be achieved. However, as it is generally accepted that there are few examples of truly standardised global brands, does that suggest that IMC is not possible for global brands? A strong counter-view is that globalisation encourages integration where it matters, at the point of implementation. Furthermore, to have adaptation, there must be strong internal integration between head office (and business/marketing strategies) and those responsible for local adaptation and implementation. For example, Fielding (2000) shows that many Japanese and Korean advertising messages emphasise product-related information, whereas many Western brands require an emphasis on the development of brand personality and character. If such a difference is to be overcome and IMC is to succeed, a consistent core message and local or regional flavour need to be delivered.

Summary

In order to help consolidate your understanding of the marketing communication industry, here are the key points summarised against each of the learning objectives:

1. Provide an introductory understanding of the nature of the communications industry.

The structure of the industry is similar in most countries but the relationships and operations will inevitably vary. However, the marketing communication industry in Britain has evolved slowly, with the large agencies seeking to bring a range of communication skills and facilities together within a single group. Mid size and small agencies still maintain a functional orientation (e.g. advertising, promotion or public relations).

2. Consider the nature and role of the main types of organisations involved in the industry.

The agencies broker or facilitate the communication needs of clients, while media houses plan, buy and monitor media purchases for their clients. Production facilitators ensure the processes work by making videos, providing fulfilment or staging events. All deliver specific value to the industry and have different roles to play.

3. Explore relationships and methods of remuneration used within the industry.

Relationships between clients and agencies are of critical importance and part of their trust and commitment is reflected in the remuneration agencies receive for their contribution. There are three keys methods: commission, payment by results and fees. These are normally combined within a contract.

4. Consider the principal methods and operations used within agencies to meet their clients' needs.

The processes used to select agencies are fairly standardised and are based on search, filtering, pitching, selecting and contracting. Once established, the operational procedures are based on briefings, and there are three main ones: the client, creative and media briefs.

5. Examine industry issues in the light of the development of integrated marketing communications.

Various agency solutions have been developed to meet client needs for integrated marketing communications. These range on a continuum where at one end is a highly centralised organisation that can provide a high level of integration for a variety of communication disciplines. Total integration is offered at the expense of in-depth and leading-edge knowledge in new and developing areas. At the other end of the continuum are providers who group themselves in the form of a loose network. Often led by a main advertising agency that has divested itself of expensive overheads, the independent yet interdependent players in the network each provide specialist skills under the leadership of the main contractor agency.

6. Anticipate some of the future trends that might affect the industry.

The industry is changing, with some areas changing faster than others. Technology has had a big impact and it is likely that further consolidation among the large groups will attempt to cut costs and retain clients. Legislation and regulation will continue to be challenging issues as the industry seeks to ward off consumer and government attacks on their activities.

Review questions

1. Who are the main types of organisation that make up the marketing communication industry?
2. Identify some of the issues that prevail in the industry.
3. Write notes for a presentation explaining the different types of agency available to clients.
4. Outline the arguments for and against using an agency.
5. What factors should be taken into consideration and what procedures might be followed when selecting an agency?
6. What problems might be encountered in agency/client relationships?
7. What are the basic dimensions for the development of good agency/client relationships?
8. Write brief notes about the briefing system.
9. Explain the commission payment system, and outline alternative approaches.
10. How can an organisation best acquaint itself with the relevant controls in a chosen area of marketing communications?

MiniCase Branding the Tasu 24/2 subnotebook

Mike Molesworth: Bournemouth University

Four months ago Tasu's first laptop computer, the 24/2 – initially developed as a cheap computer for schools, but never sold as such – was successfully launched as a consumer product in Europe. This was just three months after going on sale in Taiwan where it is manufactured and where Tasu are based. The laptop's name comes from its tiny dimensions (just 24cm wide and 2cm high) and despite having all the functions of a 'full-size' laptop, it costs just under £200 (€250). Prior to this product Tasu were manufacturers of PC components, often sold under different brand names, and so outside Taiwan the Tasu brand was almost unheard off prior to the 24/2's launch.

The international rollout was rapid and focused on distribution, mainly through specialist online retailers (Tasu have no retail distribution systems of their own). However, supply of the computer to Europe was extremely limited. Marketing activities for the European launch were also limited with no real launch budget and little time to prepare. In fact the whole European 24/2 team, who are based in a small office in the United Kingdom, had been set up in a rush. The launch focused on the development of the dedicated multi-language European web site that shows specifications, price and retailers, and allows warranty registration (with the offer of email product updates). The web site also contains a series of press releases – about one every two weeks – mainly relating to stock levels and units sold. A press launch was also organised, with 100 review machines being sent to major newspapers, technology magazines and high-profile technology websites. Most of these resulted in favourable reviews (even *The Register*, a site that is renowned for its cynicism, has been largely positive about the 24/2).

However, even before the European launch online buzz generated huge anticipation among technology enthusiasts. Actually, the online hype was so great that many Taiwanese versions of the 24/2 found their way to Europe via eBay prior to the European launch, so there was an established and growing number of blog posts from owners before the official launch date. At launch there was even a dedicated and independent UK-based '24/2user forum' (set up by an entrepreneurial IT specialist) with over 2,000 registered members and content in four European languages (although English dominates). This grew to nearly 20,000 members and nearly 200,000 posts at the end of the first European quarter. At the same time *Youtube* had over 700 videos of the 24/2 including reviews 'unboxings' and 'how to' guides. And there was also an established 24/2 'fan group' set up on *Facebook* by a user. Most computing and technology forums had an established thread discussing the 24/2 well before the machines were available to order in Europe.

After the first quarter European sales approached 500,000 units and everyone in the European office thought that the launch had been a tremendous success. Although stock was arriving weekly, supply was still short and most retailers still had a waiting list of eager customers. Blog activity continued and was generally positive and the independent 24/2 user forum was growing daily, providing amazing product support and valuable feedback to the Tasu marketing team.

Following the euphoria of the launch success the European team started discussions about future marketing communication strategy. Sam Brandt, the European sales manager made it clear that he saw no reason to spend money on advertising given the low stock and continued demand. However Elsbeth Quest, the marketing director was less convinced that sales would remain buoyant and pushed for a larger marketing budget and a large online campaign. Things came to a head at a heated strategy meeting. Elsbeth highlighted the imminent arrival of competition in the form of other cheap, small subnotebooks as a key reason to spend money, positioning Tasu as a market leader and innovator. She also presented evidence from online research that she had commissioned that showed that although awareness and reputation was high among innovators, most European computer users had still not heard of Tasu and the 24/2. She noted that an analysis of the log files for Tasu's web site seemed to confirm that most traffic came from specialist technology sites that 'ordinary' users are unlikely to visit. She pointed out that there are future product launches planned for the year and beyond, and that Tasu therefore needed to focus on building the brand in Europe. She stated that she wanted an online awareness campaign based on banners on key sites, and more complex sponsorship arrangements to aid branding. In particular she suggested sponsoring the independently run user forum, after all the money is there and profits are good.

Elsbeth claimed that a budget of £500,000 (€700,000) for the rest of the year would be a reasonable amount based on margins and sales.

Sam remained unconvinced. His technical background and regular use of the sites that discuss the 24/2 suggested to him that sponsorship was likely to undermine the reputation that had been gained among the tech-savvy users. His belief was that it was the customers that had built this brand and that it was best left that way. He argued that if anything, marketing effort should go into supporting retailers to ensure that they continue to stock and promote the 24/2. He noted that some were concerned by the lack of supply and outstanding customer orders that might potentially damage their reputation with their customers, and he pointed out that increasing demand at this stage would only compound such problems. He dismissed the need for marketing, highlighting that on several occasions he had been approached while using his 24/2 in cafes and on the train. He felt that because it was used in public and was highly visible the machine 'sold itself'. He pointed to forum discussion and even a *Youtube* video ('how my 24/2 got me a date') to show that word-of-mouth and word of 'mouse' are all that are needed. He was therefore convinced that sales would continue to grow without intervention. He again stated his belief that money should go into increasing the sales force, into improving distribution, and into new product development for the local market.

After an hour of increasingly heated argument Sam and Elsbeth became openly hostile. Sam suggested that the marketing role was pointless and that Elsbeth did not understand the product, the market or its users. Elsbeth replied by suggesting that 24/2s only 'sold themselves' because of the PR launch and web site, and that Sam clearly had no idea how to build a brand – like all salespeople he was only interested in short-term gain. Eventually the director of European operations intervened. Winston Chen suggested that a specialist consultant should be employed to review the situation and then to prepare a strategy document. Elsbeth and Sam were both convinced that such a report would support their view, so the two managers agreed.

However Winston thought that both managers had done a good job and was worried about the potential consequences of the consultant's report. He did not want to lose either manager over this. So fearing the damage to relationships that the results of the consultancy might cause he secretly briefed the consultant not to 'humiliate' either manager.

Today, two weeks later, the consultant, Janice Merrit presents her initial analysis. Sam and Elsbeth are both pleased, but slightly disappointed at the same time. Janice suggests that they are both right! She suggests that Sam's sensitivity to blogs, to trade reviewers, to the retailers, and especially to online communities, is very important. But she also agrees with Elsbeth that Tasu should not leave branding and awareness entirely to the user and that it would be useful to take a longer-term view of Tasu's online strategy including long-term relationships with customers and brand building activities, in particular among potential customers who do not necessarily get involved with technology blogs and forums. Winston is delighted, the heat taken out of the discussion, the team can now prepare a strategy together.

MiniCase questions

1. Following the consultant's conclusion, what type of agency might be best suited to meet Tasu's needs?
2. How should Tasu select an agency and what are the key issues that the newly appointed agency should address?
3. How might Tasu reward the agency for their hard work?

References

Allen, A. (2008) How to get more from agencies. *The Marketer*, April, 32–6.

Anon. (2007) Bypass your agency to save costs, Utalk. Retrieved.

Beale, C. (2007) Perspective – Why more ads might just mean more headaches, *Campaign* 28 September 2007. Retrieved 8 October 2007 from www.brandrepublic.com/InDepth/Analysis/741460/Opinion-Perspective---Why-ads-just-mean-headaches/.

Billings, C. (2004) DM's new wave, campaign, 7 September. Retrieved from http://www.brandrepublic.com/news/newsArticle.cfm.

Bruce, L. (2006) Decision time. *The Marketer*, September, 11–13.

Charles, G. (2008) The buddy system. *Marketing*, 6 February, 16.

Child, L. (2007) How to manage your relationship. *Marketing Agency*, (December), 4–7.

Collin, W. (2003) The interface between account planning and media planning – a practitioner perspective. *Marketing Intelligence and Planning*, **21**(7), 440–5.

Curtis, J. (1999) Why grey is golden. *Marketing*, 15 July, 25–8.

Davidson, S. and Kapelianis, D. (1996) Towards an organisational theory of advertising: agency–client relationships in South Africa. *International Journal of Advertising*, **15**, 48–60.

Donohue, A. (2007) Social networking site for marketing professionals launches. *Brand Republic*, 28 September 2007. Retrieved 8 October 2007 from www.brandrepublic.com/News/741288/Social-networking-site-marketing-professionals-launches/.

Earnshaw, M. (2005) New year, new challenges. *Marketing*, 5 January, 10.

Fielding, S. (2000) Developing global brands in Asia. *Admap* (June), 26–9.

Finch, M. (2000) How to choose the right marketing agency, *Admap* (October), 46–7.

Goften, K. (2000) Mergers shake up DM and SP groups. *Agency 2001 Marketing Report*, **13**, 30 November, 15–16.

Grant, I., Gilmore, C. and Crosier, K. (2003) Account planning: whose role is it anyway? *Marketing Intelligence and Planning*, **21**(7), 462–72.

Green, A. (1991) Death of the full-service ad agency? *Admap* (January), 21–4.

Griffiths, A. (2000) More than a media network. *Campaign Report*, 20 October, 3–4.

Gronstedt, A. and Thorsen, E. (1996) Five approaches to organise an integrated marketing communications agency. *Journal of Advertising Research* (March/April), 48–58.

Grosso, C., Guggenheim Shenkan, A. and Sichel, H.P. (2006) A reality check for online advertising, *McKinsey Quarterly*, **3**.

Hakansson, H. (1982) *International Marketing and Purchasing of Industrial Goods: An Interaction Approach*. Chichester: John Wiley.

Jardine, A. (2000) Will workshops replace the pitch? *Marketing*, 13 April, 16.

Jensen, B. (1995) Using agency remuneration as a strategic tool. *Admap* (January), 20–2.

Jones, M. (2004) 10 things agencies need to know about clients. *Admap*, **39**(5), (May), 21–3.

Kitchen, P.J., Spickett-Jones, G. and Grimes, T. (2007) Inhibition of brand integration amid changing agency structures. *Journal of Marketing Communications*, **13**(2), (June) 149–68.

Kotler, P. and Mindak, W. (1978) Marketing and public relations. *Journal of Marketing*, **42** (October), 13–20.

Lace, J.M. (2000) Payment-by-results. Is there a pot of gold at the end of the rainbow? *International Journal of Advertising*, **19**, 167–83.

Lace, J.M. and Brocklehurst, D. (2000) You both win when you play the same game. *Admap* (October), 40–2.

Marquis, S. (2007) Full service will never be resumed. *The Guardian*, Monday 19 February 2007. Retrieved 18 November from http://www.guardian.co.uk/media/2007/feb/19/mondaymediasection10.

McKee, S. (2004) Pick an agency . . . any agency. *Admap*, **39**(5), (May), 24–5.

Miln, D. (2004) New marketing, new agency? *Admap*, **39**(7), (July/August), 47–8.

Morgan, R.M. and Hunt, S.D. (1994) The commitment–trust theory of relationship marketing. *Journal of Marketing*, **58** (July), 20–38.
Murphy, C. (2004) Small but perfectly formed? *Marketing*, 15 December, 12.
Murphy, D. (2002) Automation assists business efficiency. *Marketing*, 30 May, 23.
Pawinska, M. (2000) The passive pitch. *PR Week*, 12 May, 14–15.
Phillips, W. (1991) From bubble to rubble. *Admap* (April), 14–19.
Public Relations Educational Trust (1991) *The Place of Public Relations in Management Education*. London: Institute of Public Relations.
Sclater, I. (2006) Marriage material, *The Marketer*, September, 22–3.
Snowden, S. (1993) The remuneration squeeze, *Admap* (January), 26–8.
Starkey, R. (1999) cited in Curtis (1999).
West, D.C. and Paliwoda, S.J. (1996) Advertising client–agency relationships. *European Journal of Marketing*, **30**(8), 22–39.
Wethey, D. (2006) The shocking truth about the pitch. *The Marketer*, September, 7–8.
White, R. (2007) Structuring the (ad) agency. *Admap*, March, 14–15.
Woolgar, T. (1998) Choosing an agency. *Campaign Report*, 9 October, 6–7.
Young, M. and Steilen, C. (1996) Strategy-based advertising agency selection: an alternative to 'spec' presentation. *Business Horizons*, **39** (November/December), 77–80.
Zambarino, A. and Goodfellow, J. (2003) Account planning in the new marketing and communications environment (has the Stephen King challenge been met?). *Marketing Intelligence and Planning*, **21**(7), 424–34.

Chapter 4

Ethics in marketing communications

Richard Christy

Ethical considerations – questions of right and wrong – are an inseparable part of real-life marketing communications. Any part of an organisation's marketing communications can send messages about its ethical stance, either intentionally or otherwise. Organisations need to cultivate an active awareness of the ethical consequences of their marketing communications.

Aims and learning objectives

The aims of this chapter are to introduce ideas of business ethics and to review how they are relevant to marketing communications.

The objectives of this chapter are to:

1. review briefly the main ideas in ethics and the way they are applied to business in general;
2. discuss the differing viewpoints of the ethics of marketing communications as a whole;
3. understand how ethical considerations, such as truth-telling, respect for personal privacy, the treatment of vulnerable groups and questions of taste and decency, affect specific issues in marketing communications;
4. introduce frameworks and models that can help managers to think through these issues in planning their marketing communications.

For an applied interpretation see Richard Christy's MiniCase entitled ***Pure and simple fashions*** at the end of this chapter.

Introduction

Something that is functionally effective may or may not be ethically acceptable.

In this book, the word 'good' is probably used dozens of times, often in the sense of 'likely to contribute to effective marketing communications', or something similar. 'Good', however, can also have a moral, or ethical (the two words are used interchangeably here), connotation, which may be quite distinct: something that is functionally effective may or may not be ethically acceptable. This chapter looks at how ethical questions of good and bad or right and wrong might be applied to marketing communications.

Familiar concerns

How do these questions make themselves felt in real life? Everyone will have their own list, but common concerns include:

- misleading or false advertising;
- shocking, tasteless or indecent material in marketing communications;
- high-pressure sales techniques, particularly when applied to vulnerable groups;
- telesales calls, or 'spam' emails that seem to intrude on personal privacy;
- PR communications that seem to distract and obfuscate, rather than inform;
- the payment of bribes to win business.

Why is it worth paying attention to these matters? For many, the main reason for wanting to understand how ethics may bear upon marketing communications will be a natural desire to know how good things can be promoted and bad things avoided. For others, interest in these questions will result from a realisation that if a company conducts its marketing communications (or any other aspect of its business) in a way that others find unethical, then it may have negative consequences which can outweigh any functional benefits. Finally, many may believe that there is no necessary contradiction between being effective in business and behaving ethically, and perhaps even that true, long-term effectiveness in business is more likely to be achieved by companies that set and stick to high ethical standards.

Importance of judgement and experience

There has been a growing emphasis on business ethics in recent years, partly as a consequence of an increased public interest in how businesses behave (i.e. not just in the products and services they produce) and a more skeptical and less respectful attitude to the place of business and business people in society. This growing awareness has also been fuelled by a far wider availability of information about corporate actions: it is much more difficult to keep things permanently secret in the Internet age. As a subject, business ethics addresses itself to the complete range of activities of an organisation, part of which concerns the ethical implications of the way an organisation approaches its marketing communications. As we shall see, many of the issues that arise are not simple 'black-and-white' questions, but more complex situations in which judgement and experience have to be applied to arrive at an ethically acceptable solution.

Many of the issues that arise are complex situations in which judgement and experience have to be applied to arrive at an ethically acceptable solution.

For example, most people would presumably object to a sales presentation, the content of which was designed to mislead consumers about a product or deliberately make false claims about its benefits, but few would go as far as to require every marketing communication to provide full 'warts and all' detail about the advantages and possible disadvantages of buying and using the product. Finding the balance between these two extremes is not wholly an ethical question – practical and legal issues, for example, are also likely to intrude – but one in which an understanding of ethics as applied to the conduct of business can be very valuable.

This chapter provides a brief introduction to some of the main ideas in ethics and to the way in which ethical thinking can be applied to business. For all that common sense plays a major role in the resolution of many real-life ethical questions, these issues can be highly complex, with solutions sometimes depending strongly on the approach adopted to analysis. Understanding moral concepts may help a decision-maker to analyse the ethical ramifications of a situation in order to make a better ethical choice. Sometimes, in real-life business situations, resolving to do the right thing can be easier than determining what the right thing actually *is*.

Resolving to do the right thing can be easier than determining what the right thing actually *is*.

Ideas in business ethics

Ethics is the study of morality: those practices and activities that are importantly right and wrong (De George, 1999); business ethics considers the application of ethical principles to the conduct of business. This distinction may seem obvious, but it makes an important point: just as medical ethics considers the application of ethics to medicine, business ethics is about the way general ethical principles should be applied to business. In particular, business is not 'exempt' from the moral considerations that apply to human affairs in general, nor should a separate set of moral standards be developed for the set of human activities that fall under the heading of business (or marketing communications in particular).

Ethics is the study of morality: those practices and activities that are importantly right and wrong.

Questions of right and wrong have occupied thinkers and writers over many millennia, and it is impossible to provide anything but a superficial overview in the space available here. Those who wish to follow up in more detail some of the theoretical ideas mentioned here should consult a specialist business ethics text: Crane and Matten's (2007) book, for example, is one of many in the field that provide a clear and accessible account of the application of ethical principles to business.

Duties and consequences

Two major schools of thought can be distinguished in ethical thinking in Western philosophy, which broadly lie on either side of the means/ends debate:

- The first is concerned with *duties, rights and principles*, and argues that some actions are always bad and others always good.
- The second approach focuses on *consequences*, holding that whether an act is good or bad depends on what happens as a result of taking that action, no matter what the action is. Utilitarianism is a well-known form of this approach, seeking to identify actions that (very broadly) can be expected to result in the greatest good of the greatest number.

Problems of the main approaches

To make this distinction is to oversimplify a very complex and long-running debate and also to overlook the many sophisticated variants and hybrid theories that have been developed. In the course of this debate, the problems inherent in either approach have been well rehearsed – an approach to ethics based on duty alone is likely to be inflexible and difficult to put into practice in a complex real world. By contrast, the alternative approach of considering only outcomes seems unsatisfactory to many. Crude utilitarianism, for example, is (by definition) 'unprincipled' and insufficiently concerned with the idea of justice. Also, in practical terms, it can also be very difficult to arrive at a satisfactory assessment of 'the greatest good', however that is defined.

Neither approach on its own seems to offer a practical and foolproof guide to ethical business decision-making. As has been suggested above, a simple and apparently unarguable duty-based rule such as 'Always tell the truth in marketing communications', may cause problems as soon as we start to plan an advertising campaign. Is it our duty to provide a detailed and reasoned discussion of all of the reasons for and against buying the product, whatever the medium we are using? Must we refrain from using ironic statements that are plainly designed to entertain, rather than inform?

Basing the ethical evaluation of our actions only on the expected consequences brings a separate set of problems. If, for example, a company designs an advertising campaign that most people will find mildly amusing but which a small religious minority will find highly offensive, then the publication of research data showing a weighted average calculation of approval for the adverts will be unlikely to reassure most people's intuitive concerns about the campaign. In practical terms, it can also be extraordinarily difficult to forecast all of the consequences of a proposed action, however concerned one may be to achieve a balanced assessment.

Table 4.1 Ethical theories – a summary

Ethical theory	Distinctive characteristic	Example
Duties or principles	Good or bad is evident in the act itself, irrespective of the consequences	'Never tell lies'
Consequences	Whether an act is good or bad depends on what happens as a result of the act	Utilitarianism: 'take the action that results in the greatest good for the greatest number'
Virtues	Virtues are good qualities in a person's character that lie between undesirable extremes	'Study and imitate the behaviours of those who are judged to be good'
Teleological	Goodness or badness judged against the purpose of the organisation	'A business should not do things that are not consistent with the business purpose'

Other approaches to business ethics

These practical difficulties in applying simple rules or methods to complex, real-life situations have caused many writers in business ethics to leave the theoretical ends/means argument to one side and to propose alternative bases for judging the ethical implications of proposed business actions. Jackson (1996), for example, explains how a focus on moral virtues in business life can provide a much more practical basis for assessing good conduct in business. The concept of virtues seeks to express those qualities and dispositions in a person that will help to ensure a good life, often seeking a 'mean' between two undesirable poles. Finding the 'mean', however, is far from straightforward. Murphy (1999) argues that a virtues approach is appropriate and useful in analysing the ethics of organisations as well as individuals, and discusses five virtues that are particularly relevant to the ethical conduct of international marketing: integrity, fairness, trust, respect and empathy.

A different alternative is proposed by Sternberg (2000), in which the assessment of business ethics is based upon a definition of the *purpose* of the company (for this reason, her approach to business ethics is described as teleological):

> *To be an ethical business, an organisation must be a business and must conduct its activities ethically. An organisation is a business if its objective is maximising long-term owner value; a business acts ethically, if its actions are compatible with that aim and with distributive justice and ordinary decency.*
> *(p. 93)*

In this definition, 'distributive justice' refers to the principle by which rewards are allocated in proportion to the contribution made to organisational ends, while the constraint of 'ordinary decency' obliges a firm to refrain from coercion, lying, cheating and so on, whether or not they appear at the time to further the business purpose. These two restrictions acknowledge the vital importance of confidence and trust in the business world.

'Distributive justice' refers to the principle by which rewards are allocated in proportion to the contribution made to organisational ends.

In adopting this approach, a manager would be mainly concerned with the consequences of a proposed action, but would concentrate on those consequences that are directly or indirectly relevant to the firm's long-term interests, rather than seeking to judge what is in the general interest. On first reading, this may seem to some to be nothing more than a formal statement of the 'Greed is good' values that are sometimes associated with the aggressive 'Anglo-Saxon' model of capitalism of the 1980s. The teleological approach, however, is importantly different from the excesses of that era:

- The concept of 'long-term owner value' is not the same thing as that of short-term rewards: the pursuit of long-term value may require very different actions from a policy designed to maximise, say, the next dividend payment.
- The requirement to behave with 'common decency' firmly excludes actions on the part of the firm such as lying, cheating, stealing and coercion, no matter how expedient or financially attractive they may seem in the short term: these things are always unethical.
- An intelligently self-interested firm will generally not wish to pursue activities that give it a bad reputation among customers, suppliers, potential recruits and so on, because to do so would be to fail to maximise long-term owner value. As real-life corporate behaviour suggests, a concern for company reputation is sometimes not a guarantee of ethical behaviour, but the teleological principle provides a powerful reason to behave ethically in business.

An intelligently self-interested firm will generally not wish to pursue activities that give it a bad reputation.

This teleological principle, and the primacy it accords to the interests of the shareholders, has been criticised as incomplete by some (see, for example, Crane and Matten, 2007) and many argue for a much more extensive view of corporate social responsibility. However, thinking broadly and clearly about the long-term interests of a business can in many cases help to identify the ethical way forward, as will be argued in this chapter.

Stakeholder theories

Although it is framed in terms that may seem to be disconcertingly stark – even provocative – this teleological principle may help to illuminate the difference between the ideas of 'stakeholder' theory and the seemingly narrower concerns of what De George (1999) refers to as the organisational view of business. One example of this view is provided by Milton Friedman's (1970) suggestion that the social responsibility of business is to use its resources to engage in activities designed to increase its profits, within the 'rules' of free competition and without deception or fraud. This type of approach views directors and managers as agents of the owners, with a prime duty to maximise their wealth. By contrast, some forms of stakeholder theory define a far wider set of external interests, to which the firm is in some way 'accountable' (see Chapter 8 for a fuller discussion of the implications of stakeholder theory).

Whatever view is taken of a firm's relationship with, and duties towards, its various stakeholders, the mere acknowledgement of complexity and plurality does not of itself help managers to know what to *do* about this plurality in practice. Managers seeking to 'balance' stakeholder interests will quickly encounter the very practical problem of *how* that balance should be defined. Consider, for example, opportunities for a firm to contribute to, or become involved with, charitable causes. The available range of local, national and global causes will in total outweigh any conceivable budget. What is needed is an ethical basis for deciding whether to lend support at all and, if so, which causes to support. Asking the question 'Which actions best support the long-term goals of this firm?' in an intelligent and enlightened way may well help to illuminate the complex ethical issues facing firms today. The word 'enlightened' is used here to describe an outlook that deliberately considers the long term as well as the short term, which thinks more broadly than the immediate transactions carried out by the firm and is active and searching, rather than passive.

The teleological principle requires that stakeholder interests be acknowledged and taken into account.

The teleological principle requires that stakeholder interests be acknowledged and taken into account, because not to do so would be a violation of the principle. Importantly, it also provides guidance on *how* those interests are to be taken into account (i.e. by assessing their impact on the long-term interests of the owners of the firm).

The scope of ethical issues in marketing communications

Before looking at the application of these ideas to marketing communications, one or two things need to be clarified. The first of these is the importance of distinguishing between:

- those critiques of marketing communications that are based upon a belief that the activity as a whole is undesirable;
- criticisms of some aspects of marketing communications in practice that are based on an acceptance that the activity is in principle justifiable.

The next section provides a brief review of some of the first type of critique, not least because these arguments are frequently encountered in public debate; in effect, they are part of the world in which marketing takes place. The rest of the chapter, however, concerns itself with the second category of criticisms – ethical issues that are raised by the practice of marketing communications, with a clear implication that advertising, selling, PR and so on are things that can be done ethically or unethically, depending upon the choices that are made.

It is also important to clarify that the discussion here concentrates on marketing communications in particular, rather than marketing in general, meaning that many issues relating to marketing as a whole have been excluded. It is certainly unethical to advertise a product that is known to be so badly designed or manufactured as to be dangerous, for example, but the ethical issue in this case has more to do with the practice of product management than advertising. Those interested in ethical issues affecting marketing in general should consult a specialised text such as Schlegelmilch (1998), or the reviews of the literature presented in Nill and Schibrowsky (2007) or Tsalikis and Fritzsche (1989).

The final clarification is to point out that the main ethical questions in marketing communications are considered one by one in this chapter, rather than looking at the individual elements of the promotional mix in turn. Questions of truth-telling, decency, privacy and so on have some bearing on every part of the promotional mix, although the context of each medium may affect the way in which ethical considerations have to be applied.

Marketing communications: a diabolical liberty?

In Stanley Donen's 1967 comedy film *Bedazzled* Peter Cook plays a jaded, weary devil, who complains that since introducing the seven deadly sins he has done very little except invent advertising. The line is just a joke, of course, but does rely on one familiar view of advertising:

Exhibit 4.1 Peter Cook: joke based on a popular view of advertising as manipulative and bad
Pictorial Press Ltd/Alamy.

that it is inherently bad, manipulative or corrupting. Nor is this disapproval confined to advertising: the image of the smooth, fast-talking 'snake oil' salesman is an enduring one, with many modern counterparts. Similarly, the public relations industry has suffered from some extremely *poor* PR in recent years: the term 'PR' sometimes seems to be used in a way that is almost synonymous with half-truths, insincerity and manipulation. In contemporary politics, the term 'spin' is generally pejorative, suggesting a growing impatience with slick presentation at the expense of candour and truth.

If these views – in effect, that marketing communications is inherently undesirable and unworthy – are taken seriously, then the ethical response must presumably be to indulge in these activities as little as possible, if at all. Happily, however, this is not the only view that can be taken: an alternative view regards marketing communications as playing a key role in the market economy, assisting the process through which consumer needs are identified and satisfied. From this perspective, the ethics of advertising, PR and so on, depend upon how they are carried out: in themselves, these activities are ethically neutral. Most of this chapter takes the latter perspective, but it is certainly worth briefly highlighting the more fundamental critiques of advertising.

Advertising as mass manipulation?

Vance Packard's famous book on mass communications, *The Hidden Persuaders* (1960), had a major impact. His concern was what he saw as the manipulative, widespread use of psychological techniques in advertising, PR, politics and so on:

> *[M]any of us are being influenced and manipulated – far more than we realise – in the patterns of our everyday lives. Large-scale efforts are being made, often with impressive success, to channel our unthinking habits, our purchasing decisions, and our thought processes by the use of insights gained from psychiatry and the social sciences. Typically these efforts take place beneath our level of awareness, so that the appeals which move us are often, in a sense, 'hidden'.*
> *(p. 11)*

Today's hard-pressed advertisers, trying to engage the attention of a sophisticated, knowing and demanding public, might be forgiven for wryly wishing that anything like that level of influence could be achieved. However, Packard's book provided a powerful expression of a point of view that is often found in press and academic commentaries on advertising, sometimes linked to more fundamental political critiques of the capitalistic society in which advertising takes place. Forty years later, a similar concern was evident in Klein's (2000) account of the anti-capitalist protests that took place in several cities internationally. One of the strands of this diverse movement has been concern about the dominance of global brands in everyday life.

Pollay's (1986) review of social science commentaries on advertising drew together a wide range of material into a general framework. This synthesis suggested that advertising was seen – by social scientists – as a powerful and intrusive means of communication and persuasion, whose (unintended) effects could be to reinforce materialism, cynicism, irrationality, selfishness and a number of other undesirable outcomes. Holbrook's (1987) reply to this paper challenged some of its implicit assumptions (e.g. that advertising is monolithic, somehow acting in concert; that it appeals to a mass audience; that it manipulates social values; that it relies mainly upon emotional impact) and suggested that the 'conventional wisdom or prevailing opinion' represented in the Pollay model was unfairly destructive of a much more diverse reality.

Space does not permit anything like an adequate discussion of these serious and important arguments. The important point to be taken forward is that this discussion of ethics in marketing communications takes for granted a number of much broader issues to do with the ethical acceptability of marketing as an activity and of the capitalist system which engendered it. As Robin and Reidenbach (1993) point out:

> *The degree to which the basic marketing functions are seen to be ethical or unethical must . . . be measured within our understanding of their history, the times in which they are applied, the context in which they are applied, the expectations of society, the requirements of capitalism and our best understanding of human behaviour.*
> *(p. 104)*

Truth-telling

> The general ethical requirement to tell the truth is one that bears upon every type of marketing communication.

The general ethical requirement to tell the truth is one that bears upon every type of marketing communication. Reflecting the widespread public distaste for lying and deceit, there are plenty of legal and other regulatory deterrents to this type of unethical conduct in advertising, selling, public relations and so on. Clearly, no responsible business will wish to be found on the wrong side of these requirements, but there remains plenty of scope for judgement in respect of which aspects of the truth are to be presented in marketing communications and how they are to be put across.

As discussed at the beginning of this chapter, we expect a salesperson not to lie to us, but few would require from a salesperson a full and balanced account of the advantages and disadvantages of our entering into the proposed transaction. There are perhaps two reasons. Mainly, it is unreasonable to expect the salesperson or advertiser to have enough information about us to be able to carry this out; also, however, there is a general acceptance that the principle of *caveat emptor* (let the buyer beware) should play some sort of moderating role.

As Sternberg (2000) observes, the aim of a salesperson is to sell the company's products, not to provide consumer guidance. Both buyer and seller have their own interests and it is normally up to either party to look after these interests during the purchase process. Thus, there is no ethical requirement that customers should ensure that the transaction is profitable for the seller, nor – in every case – that the seller must go to great lengths to ensure that the buyer is making a wise and prudent purchase (although many sellers will choose to provide some advice of this nature, in order to appeal more effectively to customers). Much depends on the context of the sales dialogue: the nature of the product or service, the awareness and expectations of the customer and so on (see also Smith's (1995) 'consumer sovereignty' test discussed below). It is also usually important for the seller to make it plain in some way that selling is actually taking place: the Market Research Society, for example, defines the unacceptable practice of 'sugging' – selling under guise (of conducting research). The distinction between selling and giving independent advice is also embodied in the regulations relating to the marketing of financial services in Britain.

Misrepresentation and 'puffery'

Some way short of the extreme of deceit or lying, but nonetheless the wrong side (for most people) of the ethical divide, is the problem of deliberate or reckless misrepresentation in selling. Chonko (1995) defines misrepresentation as occurring when salespeople make incorrect statements or false promises about a product or service. The dividing line is not always absolutely clear: a salesperson can be generally expected to show enthusiasm for the product, which may result in some degree of exaggeration. Up to a point, of course, a sales negotiation can be seen as a performance in which both buyer and seller may make some claims that do not represent their actual or final position. Most, however, would accept this as perfectly normal, perhaps even seeing it as an effective way of identifying and delineating the area within which both buyer and seller are prepared to participate.

> Misrepresentation in advertising is likely to be condemned by codes of practice, if not by actual statute.

Misrepresentation in advertising is likely to be condemned by codes of practice, if not by actual statute. The American Marketing Association's code of ethics, for example, is clear that it is the responsibility of members to avoid false and misleading advertising and sales promotions that use deception or manipulation (American Marketing Association, n.d.). Much advertising, however, contains some degree of what might be called 'embellishment' or 'puffery' – the enthusiastic use of language and images to convey the most optimistic view of the product or service being portrayed. Those who find embellishment to be a natural, obvious and harmless aspect of advertising language will have some difficulty in providing a firm dividing line between harmless embellishment and deception. Chonko (1995) points out that the American Federal Trade Commission regards puffery as acceptable because such statements are not likely to be relied upon by consumers in making their choice. However, this approach seems itself to place great reliance on being able to identify those parts of a marketing communication that *are* likely to be relied upon. Similar issues are raised by the visual images created for advertising, which naturally seek to show the product as appealingly as possible – there will be little serious concern about using mashed potato to represent easily melted ice-cream in an advertising photo session. However, for some products aimed at some audiences – and children's toys are often mentioned in this context – exaggerated images may have a greater potential to delude. These questions are complex in detail: the extent to which consumers should be held responsible for critically evaluating the commercial messages is not a simple issue, since so much depends on the circumstances of an individual case. For Attas (1999), for example, it is preferable to think about the effects of deceptive advertising in terms of the effect on society as a

> It is preferable to think about the effects of deceptive advertising in terms of the effect on society as a whole.

Exhibit 4.2 If this advertising image of ice cream is actually mashed potato, does it matter?
© Brand X/Corbis.

whole (i.e. as if deception at a particular level were commonplace), rather than seeking to make firm statements about the possible effects on an individual.

The importance of context: selling complex products

The importance of context in judging ethical behaviour can be seen in the debate in Britain over the problems arising from the selling of private pensions during the 1980s. In many cases customers were persuaded by salespeople to switch out of existing pension schemes into new schemes whose subsequent performance left them worse off. In these cases the complex nature of the services, together with the unfamiliarity of many of the customers with the various types of product and how to choose between them, led them to place an unusually great reliance on the advice provided by the salesperson. Put another way, the extent to which the buyer was foreseeably *able* to 'beware' in these cases was very limited, which in turn should have placed a greater than normal ethical duty on the salesperson to ensure that the customers were properly informed of the consequences and implications of the switch. The fact that these ethical standards were clearly not met in a large number of cases has caused a great deal of loss, anxiety and inconvenience for the customers who lost out, but also a great deal of difficulty, expense and embarrassment for the pensions industry as a whole. By contrast, while we may view with considerable unease the unfolding consequences of the 2007 'credit crunch' in world markets, we are much less likely to view with sympathy the financial services organisations who bought into the financial derivative products that fell so alarmingly in value.

Writing about ethical issues in insurance selling in general, Diacon and Ennew (1996) point out that marketing transactions in retail financial services have greater than normal potential for ethical complications. The unavoidable complexity of many financial services products is heightened by the fact that the evaluation may depend upon individual calculations carried out for the customer by the salesperson; also, risk for the customer may be significant, in that the actual benefits received will often depend upon the performance of the economy over a long period. The authors highlight a number of other ethical issues relevant to insurance selling, including:

- the issue of 'fitness for purpose' in both the design of the products and the way in which they are matched to customer needs;
- the transparency of the price for these products, such that any commissions payable to the intermediary organisation or individual salesperson are clearly visible;
- the need for truth in promotion, not only in terms of strict factual correctness, but also in terms of what the consumer might be expected to understand from a phrase;
- the effect of the sales targeting and reward systems of the selling organisation on the behaviour of salespeople, particularly in view of the important advisory component of this type of selling.

In their survey of the industry, the authors found some awareness of these ethical issues and also evidence of initial moves to address the main cause of problems: the potentially dangerous combination of commission-based selling and imperfect information on the part of customers.

The serious problems arising from personal pension selling during the 1980s provide an example of how important it is for businesses to maintain an active awareness of the likely effects of their actions. It is difficult to escape the conclusion that a more enlightened assessment of the long-term interests of the business on the part of financial service providers would have helped to avert many of the problems, to the great benefit of all involved. This is easy to conclude with hindsight: the effective ethical businesses are those that manage to cultivate this type of *foresight*.

The relational context and expectations

The importance of the buyer/seller context in which the statement is made is also reflected in Gundlach and Murphy's (1993) paper on the ethics of relational marketing exchanges. In these exchanges the value of the arrangement for both sides depends critically upon the mutual maintenance of trust, equity, responsibility and commitment (as opposed to the more contractual regulation of shorter-term transactional relationships). Clearly, the expectations as regards the content and openness of marketing communications in the former would be different from the latter. A customer might, for example, feel upset if a car salesperson with whom he had dealt for many years failed to tell him that the model he was buying was about to be superseded, because that would seem to be inconsistent with the trust built up over the years. The same customer might not be at all upset to find the same thing happen with a personal computer bought from a discount store in London, not only because computers are known to date more quickly than models of cars, but also because there was no long-term relationship to be brought into question.

In relational marketing exchanges the value of the arrangement for both sides depends critically upon the mutual maintenance of trust, equity, responsibility and commitment.

Truth-telling and PR

The practice of public relations (PR) is also likely to raise many truth-telling issues. The purpose of PR is to create and manage relationships between the firm and its various publics and there must always be a temptation in so doing to place undue emphasis on the positive aspects of the firm's actions. The question of what is 'due' emphasis is no easier in this area of marketing communications than in selling or advertising: a firm must strike an ethical balance, based on its understanding of its impact on others and its own long-term interests and reputation. Firms that make a habit of using PR techniques to mislead stakeholder groups are in effect consuming in the short term the trust upon which their long-term profitable existence may depend.

Botan (1997) distinguishes between the 'monologic' and 'dialogic' approaches to PR, suggesting that dialogue is a more ethical basis for planning PR campaigns, particularly in an information society. More pragmatically, Barton (1994) warns that, following the major business scandals of the 1980s, courts may increasingly hold PR firms liable for making false or misleading statements on behalf of their clients, placing a prudential burden of proof and research on the PR firms themselves. Onerous though such burdens may turn out to be, they appear to be little different from that which an enlightened view of long-term self-interest on the part of PR firms might indicate – PR firms above all must rely upon a basic level of public trust in their activities if they are to do any good for their clients at all.

ViewPoint 4.1 Business and sustainability: extending the dialogue

One clear trend over the last few years has been the broadening of the range of topics handled in the dialogue between companies and their various publics (or stakeholder groups). Many prominent companies were used to publishing accounts of their activities under the heading of corporate social responsibility: involvement in social projects, charitable donations and so on. With the emerging public concern about the truly global issue of climate change, however, businesses are starting to communicate the actions they are taking to respond to these challenges. In 2007, leading UK retailer Marks & Spencer published its 'Plan A (because there is no Plan B)', which detailed a major programme of investments over the next five years that are designed to reduce the impact of the M&S business on the natural environment. As the company's web site[1] puts it:

> Plan A is our five-year, 100-point 'eco' plan to tackle some of the biggest challenges facing our business and our world. It will see us working with our customers and our suppliers to combat climate change, reduce waste, safeguard natural resources, trade ethically and build a healthier nation.
>
> We're doing this because it's what you want us to do. It's also the right thing to do. We're calling it Plan A because we believe it's now the only way to do business.
>
> There is no Plan B.

The second sentence of this quote suggests that both consequentialist and duty-based motivations are at play here: the company expects to win greater respect and affection from its customers by making these investments (which may have competitive significance, of course), but also believes that it should behave in this way anyway. It may also be prudently preparing for more demanding general regulatory requirements in the medium term: by choosing to make these investments early, it will be better placed than companies that wait until they are obliged by governments. In terms of the dialogue between the company and its public, M&S is going to some lengths to raise expectations and to provide regular progress reports against its 'Plan A' targets. As the world continues to wake up to the all-pervasive effects of climate change, we can expect this type of dialogue to become increasingly common.

Question

Review the M&S 'Plan A' web pages. Why, in your view, has M&S embarked upon this programme and what is the evidence for this conclusion?

Task

On the basis of web site evidence, find out what similar initiatives by UK High Street multiple retailers can be observed?

Vulnerable groups

The question of truth-telling leads directly to the special requirements for the treatment of vulnerable groups in marketing communications campaigns. Many countries, for example, have much stricter controls on the content and timing of advertising to children than on advertising in general, based upon an enhanced concern for the potential of advertisements and other promotional material to delude and disturb this audience. From 2008, the UK communications regulator Ofcom banned adverts for junk food from TV programmes aimed at children under the age of 16, reflecting growing concern about the effects on health and the growing levels of obesity in children.[2] It is perhaps a wholly natural impulse to wish to protect the vulnerable from being led astray, but it would be wrong to see commercial advertising for food products as necessarily dangerous. As Strachan and Pavie-Latour (2008) suggest, those concerned for the well-being of children should take care not to over-insulate children from marketing messages: as adults, they will need to be able to deal with this information in making their own choices about important subjects such as food and nutrition. Responsible advertisers from the food industry could play an important part in that educational process.

These special regulatory actions, however, should not distract attention from the general ethical requirement to design marketing communications that show an enlightened understanding of, and concern for, the needs of the recipient of the communication. The often-discussed tragic problems resulting from the sale of baby milk products in some developing countries had much to do with marketing and other communications from the seller that simply did not take adequate account of the reality of life in developing countries. As De George (1999) observes:

> *In an attempt to increase sales, Nestlé, as well as other producers of infant formula [milk], extended the sale of their product to many countries in Africa. They followed some of the same marketing techniques that they had followed with success and without customer complaint elsewhere.*
>
> *One standard technique was advertising on billboards and magazines. A second was the distribution of free samples in hospitals to new mothers as well as to doctors. In themselves, these practices were neither illegal nor unethical. Yet their use led to charges of following unethical practices and to a seven-year worldwide boycott of all Nestlé products.*
>
> *(p. 264)*

In retrospect, it is easy to point out that the company should have paid greater attention to the likelihood in this environment of the product being made up with water from a contaminated source or of the product being over-diluted by users who were unfamiliar with it. Again, firms that cultivate an enlightened awareness of their impact on their surroundings will have a greater chance of perceiving and anticipating these issues before they become problems.

Firms that cultivate an enlightened awareness of their impact on their surroundings will have a greater chance of perceiving and anticipating these issues before they become problems.

Privacy and respect for persons

One aspect of the duty-based view of ethics referred to at the beginning of this chapter is the importance of treating others as ends in themselves, rather than merely as means: in other words, not merely using others, but treating them with the respect they deserve as fellow human beings. This ethical requirement finds a number of potential applications in the world of marketing communications, for example:

- avoiding the annoyance and harassment that can result from the inappropriate application of high-pressure sales techniques;

- respecting the wish that some may have at some times to be private, not to be approached with sales calls and – for some – not to be sent unsolicited direct mail or email communications;
- refraining from causing unwarranted distress or shock by ensuring that the content of any marketing communication remains within generally accepted boundaries of taste and decency.

The first of these issues is perhaps easiest to deal with here: harassment is something that can be subjectively defined (i.e. by the recipient of the unwelcome attention) and no ethical business will wish to cross that line. The fact that sales harassment does take place does not undermine the principle, but rather suggests that some businesses have a flawed view of their long-term interest, or, in the most opportunistic cases, that they are making no plans to have a long-term future. As in some of the other cases discussed above, the need for regulation is primarily to support and reinforce the action that an ethical company would be likely to choose anyway.

Responding to individual preferences for privacy

The issue of privacy is a little more complex, especially if it is treated as a question of 'rights'. It is not very easy to define a separate and defensible right to privacy in respect of direct marketing approaches. Privacy is essentially a subjective concept, to do with not being perceived or disturbed at a particular time or while engaged in a particular activity. To express this as a right seems to involve a corresponding obligation on the part of others to sense in some way that a person is in a private state and then not to disturb that person, which sounds impractical in many circumstances. In the context of a capitalist society, it is also difficult to think about general prohibitions on the making of commercial approaches.

This is not at all to argue that concerns about privacy in respect of direct marketing have no basis, but rather to suggest that they can be more productively addressed by regarding them as a reasonable request (rather than the assertion of a right) and then considering how an ethical firm ought to respond (Christy and Mitchell, 1999). Privacy-related concerns in this area seem to fall into two main categories: unwelcome sales approaches (e.g. teleselling calls in the evening) and a more general concern about the implications of large amounts of personal data being collected, stored and processed for sale to those involved in direct and database marketing. The latter concern is one that is becoming more prominent in the mass Internet age: the great convenience and value-for-money available from on-line shopping is increasingly tempered by fears of fraud and the new worry about identity theft.

> Ethical firms will refrain as far as possible from making unwelcome approaches, for reasons of enlightened self-interest.

In the first case, the ethical response is the same as for sales harassment: ethical firms will refrain as far as possible from making unwelcome approaches, for reasons of enlightened self-interest. They will, for example, support and encourage the development of general schemes through which individuals can signify their general wish not to be contacted. They will also seek out and use mailing lists that are a very close match with their target segments, which will both make the mailing more effective and also reduce the chance of the mailing piece being seen as 'junk'. They will also provide a clear means for those who do not wish to be contacted to indicate their wish.

An ethical company can also respond to the second and more general concern about privacy, both by offering clear opportunities to individuals to have their details excluded from files and also by ensuring as far as possible that information about individuals used in direct marketing has been ethically collected, processed and stored (e.g. such that it is still up-to-date, thus minimising the risk of, say, causing distress by inadvertently mailing to deceased people). Sometimes, even these efforts may not be enough to avoid causing offence inadvertently, and an ethical firm will ensure that it has in place clear and effective systems to receive and respond to the complaint.

Taste and decency

The question of taste and decency in the content of marketing communications is also one that may have an ethical aspect. This is not only to do with the use of 'pin-up' images in corporate calendars and trade advertising; separate, but related concerns may apply to the use by a charity of particularly distressing images in order to raise funds or even the apparently innocent use of stereotypical images in advertising.

Images of women and men in advertising

The first point to be made is that public standards of what is acceptable in this area clearly change over time. The portrayal of women in early television advertisements, for example, now often seems so obviously inappropriate as to be hilarious: no advertiser adopting a similar tone today could expect to communicate effectively (except perhaps as a spoof). The extent to which contemporary images of women and men in advertising may also be creating stereotypes is beyond the scope of this chapter, but it should be clear that an advertisement that annoys or alienates its target audience is unlikely to be effective. Effective (and ethical) advertisers will wish to treat their prospective audiences with respect, if only because in a competitive market they cannot afford to behave otherwise. David Ogilvy's (1963: 96) often-quoted remark that: 'the consumer isn't a moron; she is your wife', provided a much-needed reminder to fellow advertisers of the need to avoid insulting the intelligence of their audiences. The fact that this (no doubt entirely well-intentioned) advice would probably be expressed differently today also underlines the point that standards and expectations do change over time. Concerns are

Exhibit 4.3 Domestic bliss or cynical stereotyping?
Image courtesy of The Advertising Archives.

expressed not only about the portrayal of women in advertising, but also about the relative exclusion of other groups. In Britain, concern is sometimes expressed in the press about the relative exclusion of ethnic minorities from advertising images in general and from specialised sectors such as the fashion industry.[3] Carrigan and Szmigin (2003) comment on the under-representation of older consumers in marketing images, and call on advertisers to avoid giving offence through negative stereotyping and to seek to promote age diversity in their work. More broadly, Borgerson and Schroeder (2002) discuss the way in which advertising images may carelessly stereotype people, groups, cultures and regions for narrow commercial purposes. Ethical advertisers will seek to understand their target audiences well enough to be able to communicate effectively, without giving inadvertent offence.[4] Building up this level of understanding is also very important in a cross-cultural context, where the risk of giving offence inadvertently is much higher. The point is obviously true for international or global marketing, but many domestic markets are also increasingly multicultural in nature.

Advertising images may carelessly stereotype people, groups, cultures and regions for narrow commercial purposes.

ViewPoint 4.2 Types of public complaint

The annual report of the Advertising Standards Authority (ASA) provides a crude barometer of public attitudes towards advertising images. For example, its annual report for 2007 states:

> In 2007, the ASA received 24,192 complaints about a record 14,080 advertisements. The total number of complaints received increased by 7.9 per cent in comparison with 2006. Although this figure is lower than the all-time high of 2005 when 26,236 complaints were received, the number of ads complained about continued to rise: 2007's total represented an increase of 9.6 per cent on the year before.

Over the years, the most significant cause of complaint about ads has been to do with untruthfulness or dishonesty. There were 12,083 complaints about misleading ads in 2007, 8,946 about offensiveness and 2,452 related to harm. The great majority of complaints came from the public, rather than from industry.

The ten most complained-about campaigns included a diverse mixture of types of advertising: there were complaints about provocative newspaper images, misleading statements about products and services on offer and offensive stereotyping.

On the other hand, the report gives details of a number of cases in which the ASA had decided that the complaint was 'not justified' – six of the ten most complained-about campaigns had received this verdict. Although the general reasons for complaint may not change much from year to year, the adjudication reports on the ASA website do provide an interesting barometer of public concerns.

Source: ASA web site (www.asa.org.uk); accessed 17 November 2008.

Question

Consider the statements made by the ASA on its web site about its approach to dealing with complaints about advertising. Discuss the interplay of ethics based on duties/principles and ethics based on consequences in this approach.

Task

Standards and expectations about things such as taste and decency do change over time. Make notes about the sort of things an organisation like the ASA would need to do to in order to remain sensitive to those changes.

Images designed to shock

The question of the use of shocking images in marketing communications is one in which an organisation would do well to consider its own long-term interest as broadly as possible. In the short term, a shocking image may be effective, but used to excess the tactic will be counter-productive for a growing number of recipients of the message. The controversy resulting from Benetton's famous poster campaigns in the 1990s certainly succeeded in gaining publicity for the knitwear company. As the images used in successive waves of the campaign became increasingly uncomfortable, however, mounting criticism from both the public and from business partners led to the abandonment of the campaign by the company.

ViewPoint 4.3 Finding the balance – good causes

Recent examples of shocking images illustrate the tension between the desire to make a point powerfully and the need to avoid undue offence. In April 2000 Barnardo's, the children's charity, ran a press advertisement featuring a baby sitting alone in a filthy flat and holding a syringe. The advert was headed 'John Donaldson, age 23' and the copy explained how the work of the charity sought to prevent child abuse victims from the bleak future that could await them. Protestors objected that the advertisement was shocking and offensive, but the Advertising Standards Authority did not uphold the complaints, noting that the advertiser had behaved responsibly in researching the advert among its target audience in order to ensure that the message was understood and was unlikely to cause offence.

Three years later, the ASA reported that a subsequent Barnardo's advert – showing a baby with a cockroach (rather than a silver spoon) in its mouth – had generated 475 complaints, which was more than any other national press campaign in the ASA's history. The ASA upheld these complaints, finding that the charity 'had used unduly shocking images and that the photographs used were likely to cause serious or widespread offence'. Barnardo's were saddened by this finding and commented:

> While the adverts may have shocked some sensibilities, they succeeded in highlighting the very serious issue of child poverty in the UK and challenging the blinkered views of those who claim that it does not exist. Barnardo's has always fought for the nation's most disadvantaged children and its commitment to do so will continue undaunted.

The purpose of these examples is not to comment on the decisions made, but rather to illustrate the complex issues that have to be weighed in these situations in marketing communications. Barnardo's and other cause-promoting organisations are not businesses in the normal sense, but they do need to make similarly broad and balanced judgements in deciding how to communicate their ideas. The issue remains a live one for advertisers and advertising regulators: in 2007, the Committee of Advertising Practice (CAP) published a special report entitled 'Social good ads can't always rely on shock tactics' (CAP, 15 May 2007). This report reviewed some recent campaigns, including the 'get unhooked' series of ads issued by the Department of Health in the run-up to the ban on smoking in public places, as well as campaigns by the British Heart Foundation, Save the Children Fund and Barnardo's. Some of the complaints had been upheld by the ASA and others not: the report gives some valuable insights into how judgements are made in what will no doubt continue to be a challenging area.

Sources: ASA web site (http://www.asa.org.uk), accessed 16 February 2008; Barnardo's web site (http://www.barnardos.org.uk), accessed 16 February 2008; CAP web site (http://www.cap.org.uk) accessed 16 February 2008.

Question

Summarise the factors that charities and public service advertisers need to consider in order to ensure that their marketing communications are properly effective, without causing unjustifiable offence.

Task

Review the CAP report 'Social good ads can't always rely on shock tactics' (CAP, 15 May 2007) and discuss the findings of this report.

The same concerns may apply to a charity: those appealing for funds to help alleviate distressing problems around the world may be tempted to make use of shocking, real-life images of the situations that they encounter. Being aware of the ever-present risk of 'compassion fatigue' on the part of donors, as well as the possibility of causing unwarranted distress to some recipients of the message, most charity fund-raising communications remain within limits of taste and decency for what are likely to be purely prudential reasons.

Public service organisations can also consider the use of shocking imagery to communicate important messages.

Public service organisations can also consider the use of shocking imagery to communicate important messages: adverts against drinking and driving have for many years been deliberately hard-hitting, for reasons that most would accept as justifiable. In 2004, London's Metropolitan Police published a series of very shocking photographs on posters, beer mats and nightclub flyers.[5] The images showed the physical decline over several years of real-life drug addicts, in the hope of deterring young people from choosing to go down the same road.

Hospitality, incentives, inducements, and bribery and extortion

The ethical questions surrounding the payment of bribes in business feature prominently in most textbooks on business ethics. These difficult issues need to be mentioned here both because they are important and because they may well involve sales staff. Bribes are unofficial – and usually illegal – payments to individuals 'to procure services or gain influence' (*Collins Concise English Dictionary*). These payments may be to secure orders, for example, or to expedite deliveries.

Distinguishing between bribery and extortion

It is useful to draw a distinction between extortion and bribery: the former is demanded by the would-be receiver, while the latter is offered by the individual or organisation wishing to buy the influence. In a situation in which informal payments of this nature are thought to be commonplace, a company's decision to go along with extortion is ethically different from a decision to offer a bribe. But in either case, the familiar distinction between short-term and long-term benefits is important.

Difficult choices

The ethical company will need to take account of the effects on its image and wider relationships of taking part in bribery or extortion: these illegal practices have harmful effects on local economies and are likely to be regarded negatively by most stakeholders. The normal conduct of business relies heavily upon trust and the rule of law, both of which are undeniably jeopardised by corruption.

For Sternberg (2000), offering a bribe is an attempt to cheat and a violation of ordinary decency, while taking a bribe is a violation of distributive justice: decisions are made because of the bribe, rather than the relevant merits of the business offering. These are difficult questions in practice, which may involve hard choices, including the choice of whether to take part in markets in which corruption is endemic. Dunfee *et al.* (1999) examine the question of bribery in some detail from a social contract theory point of view (based upon a multilayered analysis of what affected parties and society might agree to), arguing that acceptability can only be judged by such a broad analysis. The campaigning organisation Transparency International provides a range of resources on its web site[6] that help to illustrate the scale and extent of the problems caused by corruption, including the corrosive effects on economic development.

Corporate hospitality: what are the limits?

Far less serious than actual bribery, but arguably on the same continuum, is the question of the scale of entertainment and hospitality that should be provided by the selling organisation to the buying organisation. It is entirely natural for a company to seek to build up closer relationships with its major customers, and corporate hospitality would normally be seen as an entirely legitimate part of this process. Even here, however, sales staff may be conscious of 'grey areas', in which the lavishness of the hospitality or gift-giving may seem to be out of proportion to the purpose of building a business relationship. Many companies recognise this potential hazard by providing guidelines to staff on what is to be regarded as acceptable in taking and offering corporate hospitality. Those guidelines will naturally take account of normal practice within the industry and may well differ from one industry to another and – within any given industry – from one period to another.

Again, however, the appropriate judgement about corporate entertainment is likely to be the one that maximises the company's long-term interests, within the limits of common decency and distributive justice. Hospitality expenditure, like any other business expense, needs to be assessed in terms of its intended purpose and in the context of the long-term aims of the business. At one extreme, to ban all corporate entertainment would damage a firm's commercial relationships and hence its interests in most situations; at the other end of the scale, however, a different type of damage to the firm's long-term interests would be caused by practising over-lavish hospitality.

Exhibit 4.4 Decisions regarding the level of hospitality afforded to customers can be problematic if not clearly defined by the organisation
© Guy Christian/Hermis/Corbis

Ethical influence of supervisory and reward systems in sales management

The previous section mentioned the beneficial role that company codes can play in promoting and facilitating ethical decision-making on the part of sales and other staff. It is also worth highlighting that the management framework itself can also exert a powerful positive or negative influence on the ethical decision-making environment. Sales recruitment, training and briefing systems, for example, can be designed to encourage ethical behaviours on the part of sales staff, but equally may (e.g. through neglect) provide an uncertain context for individual employees, in which inexperienced or opportunistic staff may start to take decisions that are against the long-term interest of the company.

Fostering ethical behaviour by the sales force

Ethical companies design sales motivation and reward systems that encourage sales behaviour that maximises the long-term company interest.

The same is true of the approach taken to sales motivation and reward: a sales targeting and reward system that has been designed without due consideration of the long-term reputation of the company may have the effect of encouraging and rewarding some highly damaging behaviours on the part of staff, especially in the run-up to year-end with everyone under pressure to meet targets. Ethical companies design sales motivation and reward systems that encourage sales behaviour that maximises the long-term company interest. In an empirical study in this area, Hunt and Vasquez-Parraga (1993) found that sales managers did consider both the behaviours of sales staff and the consequences of those behaviours: unethical behaviour was likely to be more severely disciplined, for example, if the consequences were negative for the organisation. The authors suggest that:

> *A culture emphasising ethical values may be best developed and maintained by having sales people and their supervisors internalising a set of [duty-based] norms proscribing a set of behaviours that are inappropriate, 'just not done', and prescribing a set of behaviours that are appropriate, 'this is the way we do things'. In both cases, sales people and their supervisors should know that when ethical issues are involved, rewards (or punishments) flow from following (or violating) the [duty-based] norms, not from organisationally desirable or undesirable outcomes.*
> *(Hunt and Vasquez-Parraga, 1993: 87)*

This suggestion, with its emphasis on duties for salespeople, rather than consequences, may at first sight seem to be at odds with Sternberg's (2000) general recommendation that a business should take that course of action which is consistent with maximising long-term owner value within the constraints of common decency and distributive justice. There is, however, no necessary contradiction: the recommended sales management framework may well be the best way for the firm to maximise long-term owner value, reflecting, for example, the difficulty that individual salespeople may have in reliably judging the long-term interests of the firm. It will also be very helpful to create a culture in which individual salespeople feel able to report unexpected difficulties that they encounter in applying the ethical code of practice as they understand it, either because the code seems inappropriate or because a new type of problem has arisen. In this way, a company can help to ensure that its good intentions concerning ethical behaviour are realised in practice. A recent review of the literature on sales ethics by Ferrell *et al.* (2007) discusses the interplay of factors such as organisational culture, the sales 'ethical climate' and individual factors (for example, age, gender, education) in identifying and dealing with ethical issues.

Ethical decision-making models in marketing

A number of contributions to the literature have proposed models to facilitate ethical decision-making in business in general and in marketing in particular. In looking at these models, we necessarily stray beyond the specific topic of this chapter: the models offer approaches to decision-making that are certainly applicable to marketing communications, but can also be applied more widely in business affairs.

Chonko (1995) characterises the ethical decision-making process in marketing as comprising:

- the ethical situation itself (e.g. the opportunity, or scope for action, the ethical decision history and the moral intensity of the situation);
- characteristics of the decision-maker (for example, knowledge, experience, achievement, motivation, need for affiliation);
- significant influences (e.g. the organisation, the law, economics, technology);
- the decision itself;
- the outcomes of the decision (e.g. in terms of performance, rewards, satisfaction, feedback).

From a different point of view, Smith (1995) suggests that marketing ethics can be seen as depending upon the prevailing outlook, ranging along a continuum from *caveat emptor* (let the buyer beware) at one end, moving through intermediate points of industry standards, ethics codes and consumer sovereignty to the position of *caveat venditor* (let the seller beware). In his view, ethics in marketing has for some time been moving away from the simple *caveat emptor* position towards the position of consumer sovereignty. He proposes a consumer sovereignty test for companies to apply:

- *Consumer capability:* is the target market vulnerable in ways that limit consumer decision-making?
- *Information:* are consumer expectations at purchase likely to be realised? Do consumers have sufficient information to judge?
- *Choice:* can consumers go elsewhere? Would they incur substantial costs or inconvenience in transferring their loyalty?

The answers to these test questions in any situation will help the firm to realise what actions it needs to take in order to behave ethically.

Laczniak and Murphy (2006) propose a set of seven 'basic propositions' that should govern ethical decision-making in marketing, as follows:

1. Ethical marketing puts people first.
2. Ethical marketers must achieve a behavioural standard in excess of the law.
3. Marketers are responsible for whatever they intend as a means or ends with a marketing action.
4. Marketing organisations should cultivate better (i.e. higher) moral imagination in their managers and employees.
5. Marketers should articulate and embrace a core set of ethical principles.
6. Adoption of a stakeholder principle is essential to ethical marketing decisions.
7. Marketing organisations ought to delineate an ethical decision-making protocol.

As discussed above, the 'stakeholder principle' in the sixth proposition is not one that is shared by all commentators in the field and the article provides an interesting discussion of these views.

In these decision models, the literature provides a checklist of questions or characteristics that aim to help a firm think its way through ethical issues. As should be clear, the answers to the questions are very much up to the judgement made by the managers involved in the process.

Regulating marketing communications

As discussed above, advertising and other forms of marketing communications have the potential to offend, mislead or cause distress. An important question in this area is what – if anything – should be done to lessen this potential harm. This question has a range of possible answers, ranging from minimal or non-existent controls to extensive and detailed statutory regulation. At one end of this scale, the libertarian view of the world places ethical priority on the freedom of individuals to choose how to behave (provided that they do not unacceptably compromise the liberty of others). A libertarian argument might assert that the 'off' switch provides all of the control of television advertising content that is needed. Individuals and groups with different views of what is acceptable or desirable must learn to tolerate each other. A libertarian would also view with caution any proposal to allow governmental control of advertising content. As has already been suggested, companies that create and publish offensive advertising are running some risk of material loss, since those who are offended may choose to buy from a less offensive competitor instead. However, a completely libertarian stance would be unsatisfactory for many: rightly or wrongly, governments are generally expected to have some sort of involvement in a wide range of choices in everyday life – what we eat and drink, what we view and so on. In the case of marketing communications, there are a number of reasons why the self-interest of advertisers and of consumers may not be a completely reliable guarantor of harm-free content:

- Not all advertisers have competitors.
- Marketing communications may offend or harm those who are not customers of the advertiser and who therefore cannot respond by buying elsewhere.
- Whether the effect is experienced by customers or third parties, the offence caused in a particular case may be so profound and lasting as to outweigh any conceivable benefit.
- Some businesses may have little interest in the longer-term effects of their marketing communications messages, if – for example – they only plan to take part in a market for a short time and then withdraw.
- Advertisers may fail to forecast the effects of their choices properly and so cause inadvertent harm or offence.

Concerns such as these underlie the case for some form of regulation – the idea that society will be better served by regulating marketing communications than by a free-for-all. This is essentially a utilitarian ethical perspective, arguing that the greatest good of the greatest number is achieved by a system of regulation, despite the cost to some forms of individual liberty. Regulation could be statutory (based upon laws) or voluntary, based upon codes and processes run by the marketing industry. Usually, a country's regulation of marketing communications will involve elements of both types, with an emphasis on self-regulation for most day-to-day questions. As Harker (1998) suggests, following a review of approaches to regulation in five countries, the legal and voluntary approaches can complement each other very well: an effective combined approach seems more likely to result in acceptable advertising for the society concerned.

The legal and voluntary approaches can complement each other very well: an effective combined approach seems more likely to result in acceptable advertising for the society concerned.

In the United Kingdom, a major change to the regulation of marketing communications was introduced from November 2004. The main thrust of the reform was to introduce a 'one-stop shop' for consumer complaints, with the Advertising Standards Authority taking responsibility for advertising content regulation in both broadcast and non-broadcast advertising (the former by delegation from Ofcom, the general regulator for the communications industry, and the latter by continuance of the ASA's former role). For this purpose the ASA, which continues to be funded by levies from advertising, administers a set of codes of advertising practice

Self-regulation in practice

In the UK, a range of specialised codes have been developed to provide guidance on the production of acceptable marketing communications in particular circumstances. The web site of the Advertising Standards Authority (ASA) (http://www.asa.org.uk) provides access to full-text versions of these codes. The ASA's main code for non-broadcast advertising (the Code of Advertising, Sales Promotion and Direct Marketing, published by the Committee of Advertising Practice) begins with a set of general principles. The first two in particular set the tone for the whole code:

- All marketing communications should be legal, decent, honest and truthful.
- All marketing communications should be prepared with a sense of responsibility to consumers and to society.

(ASA Code of Advertising, Sales Promotion and Direct Marketing (2003: 6.)

Notably, political advertising is exempt from this Code (section 12.1), although government communications are bound by it. The general rules of the Code discuss the requirements of legality, decency, honesty and truthfulness in more detail and also provide guidance on, for example, the protection of privacy, the use of testimonials and endorsements, on competitor comparisons and product availability.

Later sections of the main Code focus on sales promotion (sections 27 to 40) and direct marketing (sections 41 to 45), with guidance on specific issues such as free offers and free trials (section 32) and the increasingly important area of database practice (section 43). The Code also offers detailed guidance on specific marketing communications contexts, such as:

- alcoholic drinks;
- children;
- motoring;
- health and beauty products and therapies;
- weight control;
- financial products;
- tobacco.

This 37-page document has been developed by representatives of the advertising world over many years. Besides the advice and guidance, it defines the processes through which advertisers should comply with the Code and the sanctions that can be applied. Although very detailed, its text is characterised by clarity and a strong practical emphasis: after all, a key aim of the Code is to help those in the industry to produce 'marketing communications that are welcomed and trusted' (p. 3).

Since the broadening of its responsibilities in 2004 (see below), the ASA also now maintains a range of Codes on broadcast advertising:

- The Radio Advertising Standards Code;
- The TV Advertising Standards Code;
- Advertising Guidance Notes (concerning, for example, the identification of programmes likely to appeal to children and young people);
- Rules on the Scheduling of television advertisements;
- Code for Text Services;
- Guidance on Interactive TV.

As can be seen from this list, the self-regulatory regime is having to encompass the technology-fuelled proliferation of broadcast entertainment and information services. Keeping up to date with this rapid development, as well as remaining sensitive to changes in public sensitivity or taste is a major challenge for any organisation and the ASA's library of advertising codes can be expected to continue to evolve in future.

for the various types of advertising (see www.asa.org.uk for further details). The system is aimed at providing clearer arrangements for consumers, as well as a better and more consistent structure for dealing with the much more diverse range of communications media that has developed in recent years. Although Ofcom retains backstop powers over the new arrangements for broadcast advertising, the system remains effectively self-regulatory[7] in approach, building on the ASA's more than four decades of experience as the regulator of non-broadcast advertising content.

Ethics and marketers

In closing this chapter, it is perhaps worth highlighting some of the research that has been conducted into the ethical behaviour of real-life marketing people. As Goolsby and Hunt (1992) point out, marketing as a function is often linked in the public mind with ethical abuse, mainly because of the way marketing operates at the boundary between the firm and its customers. In their study, however, the authors found that marketing people (and especially marketing women) compared favourably with those from other functions in terms of cognitive moral development (broadly, an individual's capacity for independent moral reasoning).

Singhapakdi *et al.* (1995) concluded from a survey of US marketing professionals that marketers seem to believe that ethics and social responsibility are important components of organisational effectiveness. The survey also partly indicated that ethical corporate values seem to sensitise marketers to the need to include ethics and social responsibility in marketing decisions. This view is supported by Creyer and Ross (1997), who found that many consumers do take a company's ethics into account in making purchase decisions and that they may pay a higher price to a firm whose behaviour they approve of. Clear, readily accessible and credible information about corporate behaviour is an essential element in this relationship.

These findings would seem to indicate that there may be a positive reception within the marketing profession for Thompson's (1995) suggestion:

> *For marketers, adopting a more caring orientation offers an opportunity to become ethical innovators within their organisation. In most firms, those in marketing positions are closest to consumers, in terms of direct interaction and knowledge of their lifestyles. One role for marketers would be to regard themselves as more explicit advocates of consumer interests – both immediate and long-term.*
> *(p. 188)*

This general proposal about the role of marketing in general has special relevance for the activities of marketing communications.

Summary

In order to help consolidate your understanding of ethics in marketing communciations, here are the key points summarised against each of the learning objectives:

1. Review briefly the main ideas in ethics and the way they are applied to business in general.

This chapter has provided a brief introduction to the main ideas in business ethics and looked at some of the implications of these ideas for the practice of marketing communications. Just as there are no special ethical rules for business in general, ethics in marketing communications is a matter of applying normal ethical principles to the practice of marketing communications. Some of the difficulties in business of deciding between general ethical systems based upon duties and those based upon consequences may be avoided by taking a teleological or purpose-based approach, seeking to identify actions that will have the effect of maximising the long-term interest of the firm and its owners, remaining always within the important constraints of common decency and distributive justice. Done properly, this approach obliges managers to take an intelligent and enlightened view of the likely consequences of their actions on others.

2. Discuss the differing viewpoints of the ethics of marketing communications as a whole.

It is sometimes argued that practices such as advertising are inherently undesirable: powerful means of manipulation with destructive consequences. This chapter, however, has taken the view that ethics in marketing communications need to be considered in the context of a market economy, meaning that advertising, selling and so on are activities which are in themselves ethically neutral, but can be carried out in ethical or unethical ways.

3. Understand how ethical considerations, such as truth-telling, respect for personal privacy, the treatment of vulnerable groups and questions of taste and decency affect specific issues in marketing communications.

The chapter has has looked at the way ethical anaysis can help to understand and resolve many problems in marketing communications, including those to do with truth-telling, behaviour towards vulnerable groups, privacy and respect for persons, taste and decency, inducements and approaches to sales supervision and reward. Regulation of marketing communications content is also an important aspect of ethical decision-making: regulation may be statutory, imposed by a government, or voluntary, coordinated by the industry. Advertising regulation in most countries contains elements of both.

4. Introduce frameworks and models that can help managers to think through these issues in planning their marketing communications.

The chapter has reviewed a range of practical frameworks from the literature that can assist in ethical decision-making. Marketing communications managers, with their special responsibility for the dialogue between the firm and the outside world, have every reason to take business ethics seriously (and generally, in fact, seem to do so) and may well have the opportunity to play an influential role in this respect within the firm as a whole.

Review questions

1. What are the practical problems of adopting a simple duties-based or consequences-based approach to ethics in marketing communications?
2. Explain why a practical approach to ethical business has to be based upon a clear idea of the purpose of a business.
3. What are the limitations, if any, of the principle *caveat emptor* (let the buyer beware) as a guide to ethics in personal selling?
4. What guiding principles can help a company to decide about the proposed use of a shocking image in its advertising?
5. Why is it both difficult and important for a company to take account of individual privacy in designing and implementing its marketing communications?
6. What ethical lessons for marketing communications managers in financial services companies should be learned from the private pensions scandal in Britain in the 1980s?

7. What is the difference between lying, misrepresentation and puffery in advertising? What tests should an advertiser apply to avoid misrepresentation?
8. What evidence would help to differentiate between legitimate corporate hospitality and unethical inducements, such as bribery?
9. Describe, with examples, the way in which Smith's consumer sovereignty test can help a company to design ethical marketing communications.
10. Explain the benefits of the one-stop shop arrangements for advertising complaints handling in the United Kingdom.

Notes

1. http://plana.marksandspencer.com/?action=PublicAboutDisplay.
2. http://news.bbc.co.uk/1/hi/health/7166510.stm
3. See, for example, http://www.independent.co.uk/news/uk/home-news/fashion-is-racist-insider-lifts-lid-on-ethnic-exclusion-782974.html.
4. For example, the author of this chapter is not dismayed to see images of younger people in the advertising of the products and services he buys. Like most baby boomers, he currently prefers the mild, but harmless delusion that he still looks like someone in his thirties.
5. Source: BBC News web site (http://news.bbc.co.uk). Accessed 12 November 2004.
6. http://www.transparency.org/.
7. Strictly speaking, the new system is co-, rather than self-regulatory, in that Ofcom, with its statutory powers, has delegated the responsibility for maintaining and applying codes of practice approved by the regulator (see www.ofcom.org.uk).

MiniCase Pure and Simple Fashions

Richard Christy

It was late in the evening and marketing director Jane Carson was reflecting on how quickly difficult situations seemed to develop in the business environment of the twenty-first century. It was only last month that she had organised a very successful launch of the new season's designs, coupled with the relaunch of her company's redesigned and upgraded web site, which would provide much greater ease of use. Recent events, however, had demonstrated that modern communications media could just as effectively carry bad news.

Pure and Simple Fashions (PSF) was a familiar retail brand on the high street, providing mid-priced fashions aimed at younger women. From its launch 10 years earlier, its competitive positioning had also been pure and simple, as reflected in its advertising line: 'Fashion that doesn't cost the earth'. Pure and Simple clothes were made from natural fibres, grown organically and processed in ways that supported the environmental notion of 'sustainability': working with natural resources without reducing the future availability of those resources. This idea – coupled with some inspired and widely praised innovative designs – had connected very effectively with PSF's target segment and the organisation had built up a loyal following over the years. Indeed PSF's positioning seemed to appeal just as strongly to the new generation of young women customers as to the organisation's original clients, many of whom had stayed with PSF. The company had grown steadily, with retail outlets in most UK cities and large towns, and an enviable profit growth record, based upon its well-established positioning. This business development had been supported by extensive and very popular press and poster advertising, based upon appealing natural images from ecosystems around the world. Two years ago, PSF had initiated an expansion into continental Europe, based upon franchised outlets in a growing number of major cities. This had now been complemented by the introduction of an upgraded web site, whose design had been nominated for a national award for ease of access and use.

Customers could view the ranges in three dimensions, match colours and order clothes manufactured to exactly their own sizes. The new distribution channel was underpinned by extensive customer relationship management software, which PSF hoped would enable it to build a closer relationship with its individual customers, as well as providing the basis for increasing growth into international markets.

The current crisis for PSF had its roots in a television documentary programme broadcast two weeks earlier. The documentary had set out to investigate what some saw as the negative effects of increasing globalisation. The agenda was a familiar one, focusing on the enormous economic power wielded by very large multinational corporations in smaller developing countries. Part of the programme had focused on working conditions in factories in developing countries, showing the manufacture of branded clothing and other products for world markets. Pure and Simple was one of many well-known brands mentioned in this part of the programme, in a sequence that also contrasted bright and appealing advertising images from Europe with distressing views of unpleasant and oppressive working environments and interviews with employees about their experiences. No specific allegations about PSF or any other brand were made in the programme, although allusions were made to earlier, well-documented allegations about the use of child labour by some manufacturers. Street interviews with shoppers in London were used to suggest a disparity between the promoted image of branded goods and the reality of life for those who made them.

In the days following the broadcast of the programme, newspapers and magazines took up the themes of the programme, resulting in a flood of emails and letters from readers and heated discussions on the various news web sites and blogs. It was clear that the programme had – at least on an emotional level – been very effective. Soon, PSF branch managers began to report increasing numbers of hostile questions from customers about the company's sourcing policy; the levels of telephone and email enquiries into PSF's headquarters confirmed this development. The problem had escalated to a new level with the threat from a previously little-known anti-capitalist lobbying group to 'jam' the communications of a number of brand-owning organisations, including PSF, by flooding their web sites with vast amounts of communications traffic. The experiences of other organisations in the recent past had shown that threats of this nature needed to be taken seriously: the effect for PSF at the beginning of the present season could be disastrous, particularly given the strength and clear focus of its present environmentalist positioning.

Although Pure and Simple had never made any public statement about its policy concerning the manufacture of its products, Jane Carson knew that PSF had always insisted that working conditions in its suppliers were in line with – and in many cases significantly better than – local 'best practice', although of course actual wage rates were low by European standards. Objectively, PSF could argue strongly that its suppliers maintained high standards and that its participation in developing countries was of clear benefit to those economies. However, the present public debate was not being conducted objectively and Jane wondered how to regain the initiative. What seemed to be happening was that those customers who had been attracted to Pure and Simple because of its environmental commitment were those who were now expressing the greatest concern about the issues raised by the televison programme. For some time it had been possible to see the growing links between previously disparate specialist lobbying organisations, together with the increasing interest on the part of affluent and well-educated customers in the values embodied in the brands they chose. Had Pure and Simple sat on its environmental laurels in recent years and been caught napping by these new developments? Or was it PSF's very strong public image and accessibility that rendered it vulnerable to these protests, whatever the reality of its case? The textbook injunction to 'balance stakeholder interests' seemed to be particularly problematic this evening, as Jane worked on her company's response.

Note: this case is wholly imaginary; no reference is intended to actual organisations or people.

MiniCase questions

1. What ethical issues for Pure and Simple Fashions arise in this case?
2. How would an evaluation of these ethical issues based on broad stakeholder theory differ from one based on Sternberg's teleological perspective?
3. Outline a possible marketing communications strategy for PSF that will allow it to respond to its current difficulties and continue its successful and profitable growth as a fashion retailer.
4. What lessons might PSF learn concerning the management of its relationship with its various stakeholders?

References

American Marketing Association (n.d.) Code of ethics. http://www.ama.org/. Accessed 1 March 2001.

ASA (2008) ASA Code of Advertising, Sales Promotion and Direct Marketing 2003. Retrieved 24 August 2008 from www.asa.org.uk/cap/codes/cap_code/.

Attas, D. (1999) What's wrong with deceptive advertising? *Journal of Business Ethics*, **21**, 49–59.

Barton, L. (1994) A quagmire of ethics, profit and the public trust: the crisis in public relations services. *Journal of Professional Services Marketing*, **11**(1), 87–99.

Borgerson, J.L. and Schroeder, J. (2002) Ethical issues of global marketing: avoiding bad faith in visual representation. *European Journal of Marketing*, **36**(5–6), 570–94.

Botan, C. (1997) Ethics in strategic communication campaigns: the case for a new approach to public relations. *Journal of Business Communication*, **34**(2), 188–202.

Carrigan, M. and Szmigin, I. (2003) Regulating ageism in UK advertising: an industry perspective. *Marketing Intelligence and Planning*, **21**(4), 198–204.

Chonko, L.B. (1995) *Ethical Decisions in Marketing*. Thousand Oaks, CA: Sage.

Christy, R. and Mitchell, S.M. (1999) Direct marketing and privacy. *Journal of Targeting, Measurement and Analysis for Marketing*, **8**(1), 8–20.

Crane, A. and Matten, D. (2007) *Business Ethics*, 2nd edn. Oxford University Press.

Creyer, E.H. and Ross, W.T. (1997) The influence of firm behaviour on purchase intention: do consumers really care about business ethics? *Journal of Consumer Marketing*, **14**(6), 421–33.

De George, R.T. (1999) *Business Ethics*, 5th edn. Englewood Cliffs, NJ: Prentice-Hall.

Diacon, S.R. and Ennew, C.T. (1996) Ethical issues in insurance marketing in the UK. *European Journal of Marketing*, **30**(5), 67–80.

Dunfee, T.W., Smith, N.C. and Ross, W.T. (1999) Social contracts and marketing ethics. *Journal of Marketing*, **63**(3), 14–32.

Ferrell, O.C., Johnston, M.W. and Ferrell, L. (2007) A framework for personal selling and sales management ethical decision making, *Journal of Personal Selling and Sales Management*, **27**(4), 291–99.

Friedman, M. (1970) The social responsibility of business is to increase its profits. *New York Times Magazine*, 13 September, 32 ff.

Goolsby, J.R. and Hunt, S.D. (1992) Cognitive moral development and marketing. *Journal of Marketing*, **56** (January), 55–68.

Gundlach, G.T. and Murphy, P.E. (1993) Ethical and legal foundations of relational marketing exchanges. *Journal of Marketing*, **57** (October), 35–46.

Harker, D. (1998) Achieving acceptable advertising. An analysis of advertising regulation in five countries. *International Marketing Review*, **15**(2), 101–18.

Holbrook, M.B. (1987) Mirror, mirror, on the wall, what's unfair in the reflections on advertising? *Journal of Marketing*, **51** (July), 95–103.

Hunt, S.D. and Vasquez-Parraga, A.Z. (1993) Organisational consequences, marketing ethics and salesforce supervision. *Journal of Marketing Research* (February), 78–90.

Jackson, J.C. (1996) *An Introduction to Business Ethics*. Oxford: Blackwell.

Klein, N. (2000) *No Logo*. London: Flamingo.

Laczniak, G.R. and Murphy, P.E. (2006) Normative perspectives for ethical and socially responsible marketing, *Journal of Macromarketing*, **26**(2), 154–77.

Murphy, P.E. (1999) Character and virtue ethics in international marketing: an agenda for managers, researchers and educators. *Journal of Business Ethics*, **18**, 107–24.

Nill, A. and Schibrowsky, J. A. (2007) Research on marketing ethics: a systematic review of the literature. *Journal of Macromarketing*, **27**, 256–73.

Ogilvy, D. (1963) *Confessions of an Advertising Man*. London: Longman.

Packard, V. (1960) *The Hidden Persuaders*. Harmondsworth: Penguin.

Pollay, R.W. (1986) The distorted mirror: reflections on the unintended consequences of advertising. *Journal of Marketing*, **50** (April), 18–36.

Robin, D.P. and Reidenbach, R.E. (1993) Searching for a place to stand: toward a workable ethical philosophy for marketing. *Journal of Public Policy and Marketing*, **12**(1), 97–105.

Schlegelmilch, B. (1998) *Marketing Ethics: An International Perspective*. London: International Thomson Business Press.

Singhapakdi, A., Kraff, K.L., Vitell, S.J. and Rallapalli, K.C. (1995) The perceived marketing. *Journal of the Academy of Marketing Science*, **23**(1), 49–56.

Smith, N.C. (1995) Marketing strategies for the ethics era. *Sloan Management Review* (Summer), 85–97.

Sternberg, E. (2000) *Just Business*, 2nd edn. Oxford: Oxford University Press.

Strachan, J. and Pavie-Latour, V. (2008) Food for thought. *International Journal of Market Research* **50**(1), 13–27.

Thompson, C.J. (1995) A contextualist proposal for the conceptualization and study of marketing ethics. *Journal of Public Policy and Marketing*, **14**(2), 177–91.

Tsalikis, J. and Fritzsche, D.J. (1989) Business ethics: a literature review with a focus on marketing ethics. *Journal of Business Ethics*, **8**, 695–743.

Part 2

Understanding how marketing communications works

Chapters 5–8

This part of the book is concerned with the contextual aspects of marketing communications.

Chapters 5 and 6 explore fundamental issues concerning information processing and buyer behaviour, important elements if marketing communication messages are to be effective.

Chapter 7 explores the nature and characteristics of relationships and then reviews the impact marketing communications can have on relationship marketing and its development. This provides a platform for the way in which the rest of the book is developed.

The final chapter in Part 2 develops ideas about how marketing communications might work and traces some important models and concepts that again are reflected in later parts of this text.

For readers with access to the companion web site that accompanies this book, there is a supplementary chapter available in PDF format. This examines the influence and potential impact on marketing communications, of an organisation's different stakeholders and the interrelationships that organisations form with them.

Video Insight Part 2

Part 2 of the book is concerned with issues relating to how marketing communications might work. Broadly, marketing communications work partly by understanding audiences, their perceptions and attitudes and then using marketing communications to change, develop or build on these elements.

The video material of the City of Birmingham focuses on how the marketing team measure people's perceptions of the city and how they have tried to make their communications interactive, encouraging people to share their feelings about the city, with the city. This involves extensive use of their web site.

HSBC provide an insight into another important dynamic of marketing communications, the development of customer and supplier relationships. This part of the Video Insight allows you to hear about the way in which this bank considers the importance of customer relationships and how they use marketing communications to develop them.

Part 2 of the book also addresses issues concerning the way customers buy products and services and how marketing communications needs to be used in a complementary way, if it is to function effectively. In the video we see how Land Rover has changed their products as a result of changes in the marketplace. We then hear about how they account for the way their customers make buying decisions and how they use marketing communications in the knowledge of how their customers use their brand.

Go to **www.pearsoned.co.uk/fill** to watch the Video Insight, and then answer the following questions:

1. How have the City of Birmingham used marketing communications to change peoples' perceptions of the city? Why do you think they have had to do this?
2. If you were responsible for HSBC's marketing how would you use marketing communications to build customer trust?
3. How might advertising be used to influence a potential customer's decision making process?

Chapter 5

Understanding how customers process information

Understanding the way in which customers perceive their world, the way they learn, develop attitudes and respond to marketing communication stimuli is fundamental if effective communications are to be developed.

Aims and learning objectives

The aim of this chapter is to provide an introduction to the main elements of buyer information processing, in order that readers develop an appreciation of the way marketing communications can be built on an understanding of buyer behaviour.

The learning objectives of this chapter are to:

1. introduce cognitive theory as an important element in the development of planned communications;
2. examine personality as a main factor in the determination of successful communications;
3. explore perception in the context of marketing communications;
4. understand the main differences between conditioning and cognitive learning processes;
5. appraise the role of attitudes and the different ways in which attitudes are thought to be developed;
6. appreciate the importance of understanding an individual's intention to act in a particular way and its part in the decision process;
7. understand how marketing communications can be used to influence these elements of buyer behaviour and in particular change attitudes;
8. provide a brief overview of the other environmental influences that affect the manner in which individuals process information.

For an applied interpretation see Janine Dermody's MiniCase entitled ***The lost generation? The challenge of communicating with politically cynical British youth*** at the end of this chapter.

Introduction

This chapter explores the elements that influence the information processing behaviour of two different types of buyer: consumers and organisational buyers. It will then establish how the identification of different behaviour patterns can influence marketing communications.

Marketing is about many things, but one of its central themes is the management of behaviour. This behaviour may be seen in the context of an exchange, in which case actions prior to, during and after a purchase will be important. In a relationship context, it is the series of behaviours manifest at the beginning, in the middle and during the decline and termination of a relationship that will be pertinent. Whichever perspective is adopted, it makes sense to underpin marketing activities with an understanding of buyer behaviour, in order that marketing strategies and communication plans in particular be more effective. It is not the intention to provide a deep or comprehensive analysis of buyer behaviour, since there are many specialist texts that readers can refer to (for example, Solomon *et al.*, 2007 or Evans *et al.*, 2006). However, this book considers the context in which buyers process information, the way they behave, their decision-making processes and the ways in which such knowledge can be utilised for effective marketing communications.

> It makes sense to underpin marketing activities with an understanding of buyer behaviour.

There are a number of theoretical approaches that have been developed to assist our understanding of human behaviour, but the majority have their roots in one of three psychological orientations. These three (Freud's psychoanalytical theory, reinforcement theory and cognitive theory) can be seen to have influenced thinking about buyer behaviour over the last 50 years (see Table 5.1). This book explores cognitive theory in the context of marketing communications and also acknowledges the influence of emotional and hedonic consumption perspectives.

Table 5.1 Summary of three main psychological orientations

Theoretical approach	Explanation
Psychoanalytical theory	First developed by Freud, this approach is based on the way an individual develops over time within the context of a family and their interactions with mother and father and later with their siblings. Freud was the first to think in this way and to consider the unconscious as an important influence on behaviour. These are now referred to as psychodynamic theories and they hold that human behaviour is primarily the function of reactions to internal (thus mostly unconscious) stimuli: instincts, urges, thoughts.
Reinforcement theory	People behave in the knowledge of what will happen as a result of their behaviour. Therefore, behaviour is dependent upon the expected outcomes or consequences: Rules of Consequences. The three Rules describe the logical outcomes that typically occur after consequences: 1. Consequences that lead to Rewards increase a behaviour. 2. Consequences that lead to Punishments decrease a behaviour. 3. Consequences that lead to neither Rewards nor Punishments extinguish a behaviour.
Cognitive theory	Assumes individuals use and process information derived from external and internal sources, to solve problems and make considered decisions. See text below. Social cognitive theory considers the interaction of an individual's environment, behaviour and various personal factors such as cognitive, affective and biological events.

Cognitive theory

Mainstream psychology has moved from a behavourist to a cognitive orientation. Similarly, the emphasis in understanding and interpreting consumer behaviour has progressed from a reinforcement to a cognitive approach.

Cognitive theory is based on an information-processing, problem-solving and reasoning approach to human behaviour.

Cognitive theory is based on an information-processing, problem-solving and reasoning approach to human behaviour. Individuals use information that has been generated by external sources (e.g. advertisements) and internal sources (e.g. memory). This information is given thought, processed, transferred into meanings or patterns and then combined to form judgements about behaviour (based on Rumelhart in Belk, 1975).

The cognitive orientation considers consumers to be adaptive problem solvers, people who use various processes to reason, form concepts and acquire knowledge. There are several determinants that are important to the understanding of the cognitive orientation because they contribute to the way in which individuals process information. These are personality, perception, learning, attitudes, certain environmental influences and issues pertinent to an individual's purchase situation (Figure 5.1). Each of these will now be considered.

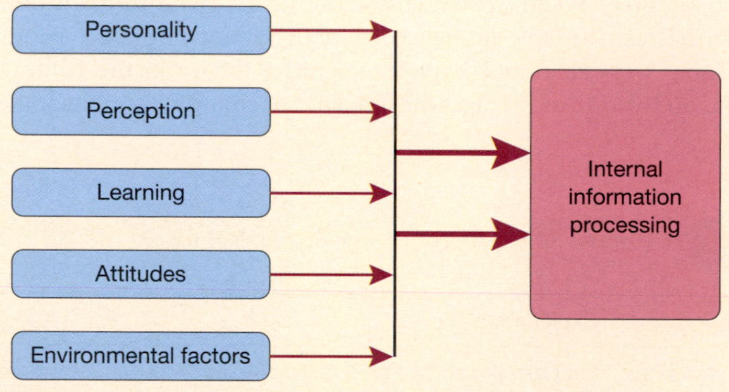

Figure 5.1 Elements of information processing

ViewPoint 5.1 Thinking adrenaline with Red Bull

As consumers become more aware and interested in healthy eating and drinking so food and drink manufacturers have tried to adapt their products and communications to meet the needs of this new market.

The world of sports and energy drinks is relatively complex as there are clear yet different attributes associated with brands in these two markets. Energy drinks are designed to provide a boost to a person's system and they contain caffeine and sugar to provide the stimulation. Red Bull and Lucozade Energy are the two market leaders.

Sports drinks on the other hand are designed to replenish nutrients, water and sugar lost through exercise. In this market Lucozade and Powerade lead the market and it is this part of the market that has benefited most from the interest in healthier lifestyles.

Marketing communications in this market need to communicate the benefits of use and this requires some cognitive thought on behalf of consumers. Bainbridge (2007) reports that Red Bull spends 30 per cent of its turnover on promotional activity. Much of this is spent associating the brand with sports activities and the accompanying adrenaline rush. This is supported by using testimonials from key sports personalities across a range of activities from football and cricket through to golf, water and snow sports.

Source: Bainbridge (2007) www.redbull.co.uk.

Question

How might a competitor to Red Bull in the energy drinks market communicate their brand's attributes if not allowed to use sports activities?

Task

Visit www.redbull.co.uk and make a list of the range of sports that they associate themselves with.

Personality

Personality is, essentially, concerned with the inner properties of each individual, those characteristics that differentiate each of us. Consideration is given to two main approaches: the Freudian and Trait theories of personality.

Personality is, essentially, concerned with the inner properties of each individual, those characteristics that differentiate each of us.

Psychoanalytic theory

Freud believed that the needs that motivate human behaviour, are driven by two primary instincts: life and death. The life instincts are considered to be predominantly sexual in nature, whereas the death instincts are believed to be manifested through self-destructive and/or aggressive behaviour.

The personality of the individual is assumed to have developed in an attempt to gratify these needs, and consists of the id, superego and ego; this approach is termed psychoanalytic theory. The id is the repository for all basic drives and motivations. Its function is to seek pleasure through the discharge of tension. The superego acts to restrain the id, to inhibit the impulses of the pleasure-seeking component, partly by acting within the rules of society. These two are obviously in conflict, which the ego attempts to mediate by channelling the drives of the id into behaviour acceptable to the superego.

The application of psychoanalytic theory to buyer behaviour suggests that many of the motives for purchase are driven by deeply rooted sexual drives and/or death instincts. These can only be determined by probing the subconscious, as demonstrated by the work undertaken by motivation researchers, the first of whom were Dichter and Vicary. Motivation research attempts to discover the underlying motivations for consumer behaviour. A variety of techniques have been developed, including in-depth interviews, projective techniques, association tests and focus groups.

Psychoanalytic theory has been criticised as too vague, unresponsive to the environment and too reliant on the early development of the individual. Furthermore, because the samples used are very often small and because of the emphasis on the unconscious, verification and substantiation of the results of experiments are often difficult – some say impossible.

Psychoanalytic theory has been criticised as too vague, unresponsive to the environment and too reliant on the early development of the individual.

However, the psychoanalytic approach has been used as the basis for many advertising messages, aimed at deeply rooted feelings, hopes, aspirations and fears. For example, many life assurance companies use fear in their advertising messages to motivate people to invest in life and pension policies. Advertisements for cars often depict symbols: those of life and death (e.g. Audi), safety (e.g. Volvo) and virility (e.g. Ferrari or Porsche).

We also know that buyers can be motivated by symbolic as well as functional motives in their purchases. Thus the use of sexual appeals and symbols in advertisements is often undertaken with this information in mind. In addition, many commentators agree that motivation research is the forerunner of the psychographics research often used for market segmentation.

Trait theory

In contrast with the largely qualitative approach of the Freudian school is the empirical perspective. Under this approach, personality is measured and quantified. What is being measured are the traits or 'distinguishing, relatively enduring ways in which one individual differs from another' (Guildford, 1959). Personality tests invariably seek to measure individual differences in respect of specific traits. The end result is a label that is applied to the particular traits observed in the individuals being tested. These labels, for example, consider aspects such as the degree of assertiveness, responsiveness to change or the level of sociability an individual might exhibit.

Of specific interest to marketing communicators is the relationship between broad personality traits and general styles of behaviour.

Of specific interest to marketing communicators is the relationship between broad personality traits and general styles of behaviour. Consumer psychologists, working on behalf of advertising agencies in particular, have spent a great deal of time trying to identify specific traits and then develop consumer profiles, which enable a distinct market segment to be determined. One of the early attempts was the 4Cs programme, developed by Young and Rubicam in the late 1980s. Four distinct types of consumer were identified: aspirers, succeeders, mainstreamers and reformers, each of whom have particular psychographic characteristics.

Mainstreamers are motivated by a basic need for security and belonging. To satisfy that drive, they tend to buy established products and manufacturers' brands, as they perceive purchase risk to be lower. Aspirers seek status and self-esteem and this is directed through identification with materialism. Aspirers are able to express themselves through the possession of goods, which act as symbols of achievement, such as the latest hi-fi or designer clothes. Succeeders are people who are successful but who need to control the events in their lives. Typically they read the *Financial Times* or the *Daily Telegraph* and consume products that have proven quality. Reformers are the antithesis of the aspirers, in that they seek self-fulfilment rather than status. Own brands and natural products are sought by them, as it is the quality of life that is their underlying motivation (*QED*, 1989).

The use of personality within marketing communications is both well established and important, as demonstrated through the use of celebrities for the purposes of brand endorsement.

ViewPoint 5.2 Disguising personality with silhouettes

Some brands are deliberately stripped of personality as this enables them to appeal to a wider audience and avoid being labelled or stereotyped. For example, BMW's long running advertising campaign is based on the functional excellence of their cars. BMW's advertising is characterised by the lack of people in their advertising. For many years the driver was never seen and there are no passengers or children, so viewers cannot categorise certain types of drivers as typically BMW.

DeBeers have used the strapline, 'a diamond is forever' because they feel it has universal appeal. One of their more successful campaigns, 'Shadows' presented couples in silhouette form progressing through various stages in their lives. The ad was designed to reach and appeal to a wide range of people, signifying that a diamond was for everyone.

In much the same way Apple used a silhouette of a person wearing/using an iPod. Although the visual suggested male, female and age-group characteristics, the silhouette focused attention on the product, not the type of person who should use it.

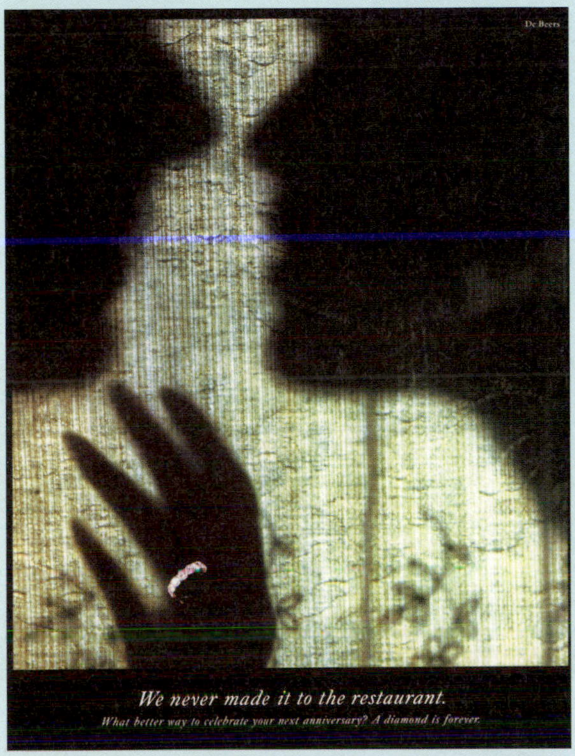

Exhibit 5.1 DeBeers – Shadows
Image courtesy of The Advertising Archives.

Exhibit 5.2 iPod Silhouette
Image courtesy of The Advertising Archives.

In all of these cases the absence of clearly defined users or the use of a silhouette devoid of personality, invited viewers to superimpose themselves and their own personalities into the car, relationship and music environment respectively. By not presenting a particular type of person and their distinguishing personality traits, these brands have been able to reach and appeal to diverse audiences.

Sources: Adapted from Cobau (2000); Anon. (2004).

Question

To what extent do you think potential purchasers might find it difficult to associate with these brands, when there is nobody to identify with?

Task

Get copies of these three ads. Apart from the silhouette, is there anything else that they have in common?

By combining the qualitative approach of the motivational researchers with the quantitative approach of the trait theorists, psychographic variables can be determined. Over the last 20 years this has developed into a popular segmentation technique, called psychographics.

Perception

Perception is concerned with how individuals see and make sense of their environment.

Perception is concerned with how individuals see and make sense of their environment. It is about the selection, organisation and interpretation of stimuli by individuals so that they can understand the world.

Each day, individuals are exposed, to a tremendous number of stimuli. De Chernatony (1993) suggests that each consumer is exposed to over 550 advertisements per day while Lasn (1999) estimated that this should be 3,000 advertisements per day (cited by Dahl *et al.*, 2003). In addition, there are thousands of other non-commercial stimuli that each individual encounters. To cope with this bombardment, our sensory organs select those stimuli to which attention is given. These selected stimuli are organised in order to make them comprehensible and are then given meaning. In other words, there is an interpretation of the stimuli that is influenced by attitudes, values, motives and past experiences as well as the character of the stimuli themselves. Stimuli, therefore, are selected, organised and interpreted.

Perceptual selection

The vast number of messages mentioned earlier need to be filtered, as individuals cannot process them all. The stimuli that are selected result from the interaction of the nature of the stimulus with the expectations and the motives of the individual. Attention is an important factor in determining the outcome of this interaction: 'Attention occurs when the stimulus activates one or more sensory receptor nerves and the resulting sensations go to the brain for processing' (Hawkins *et al.*, 1989).

The nature of the stimuli, or external factors such as the intensity and size, position, contrast, novelty, repetition and movement, are factors that have been developed and refined by marketing communicators to attract attention. Animation is used to attract attention when the product class is perceived as bland and uninteresting, such as margarine or teabags. Unexpected camera angles and the use of music can be strong methods of gaining the attention of the target audience, as used successfully in the Bacardi Breezer and Renault commercials. Sexual attraction can be a powerful means of capturing the attention of audiences and

Sexual attraction can be a powerful means of capturing the attention of audiences.

Exhibit 5.3 Diet Coke

The hugely successful Diet Coke television ads depict office workers timing their work break to coincide with the presence of certain attractive males.

Images courtesy of The Advertising Archives.

when associated with a brand's values can be a very effective method of getting attention (for example, the Diet Coke advertisement, Exhibit 5.3).

The expectations, needs and motives of an individual, or internal factors, are equally important. Individuals see what they expect to see, and their expectations are normally based on past experience and preconditioning. From a communications perspective the presentation of stimuli that conflict with an individual's expectations will invariably receive more attention. The attention-getting power of erotic and sexually driven advertising messages, is understood and exploited. For example, jeans manufacturers such as Levi 501s, Wranglers and Diesel, often use this type of stimulus to promote their brands. However, advertising research based on recall testing often reveals that the attention-getting stimulus (e.g. the male or female) generates high recall scores, but the product or brand is very often forgotten. Looked at in terms of Schramm's model of communication (Chapter 2), the process of encoding was inaccurate, hence the inappropriate decoding.

Of particular interest is the tendency of individuals to select certain information from the environment. This process is referred to as selective attention. Through attention, individuals avoid contact with information that is felt to be disagreeable in that it opposes strongly held beliefs and attitudes.

Through attention, individuals avoid contact with information that is felt to be disagreeable.

Individuals see what they want or need to see. If they are considering the purchase of a new car, there will be heightened awareness of car advertisements and a correspondingly lower level of awareness of unrelated stimuli. Selective attention allows individuals to expose themselves to messages that are comforting and rewarding. For example, reassurance is often required for people who have bought new cars or expensive technical equipment and who have spent a great deal of time debating and considering the purchase and its associated risk. Communications congratulating the new owner on their wise decision often accompany post-purchase literature such as warranties and service contracts. If potentially harmful messages do get through this filter system, perceptual defence mechanisms help to screen them out after exposure.

Perceptual organisation

For perception to be effective and meaningful, the vast array of selected stimuli needs to be organised. The four main ways in which sensory stimuli can be organised are figure–ground, grouping, closure and contour.

Figure–ground

Each individual's perception of an environment tends to consist of articles on a general background, against which certain objects are illuminated and stand proud. Williams (1981) gives the examples of trees standing out against the sky and words on a page. This has obvious implications for advertisers and the design and form of communications, especially advertisements, to draw attention to important parts of the message, most noticeably the price, logo or company/brand name.

Grouping

Grouping can be used to encourage associations between a product and specific attributes.

Objects that are close to one another tend to be grouped together and a pattern develops. Grouping can be used to encourage associations between a product and specific attributes. For example, food products that are positioned for a health market are often displayed with pictures that represent fitness and exercise, the association being that consumption of the food will lead to a lifestyle that incorporates fitness and exercise, as these are important to the target market.

Closure

When information is incomplete individuals make sense of the data by filling in the gaps. This is often used to involve consumers in the message and so enhance selective attention. Advertisements for American Express charge cards or GM credit cards ('if invited to apply'), for example, suggest that ownership denotes membership, which represents exclusiveness and privilege.

Television advertisements that are run for 60 seconds when first launched are often cut to 30 or even 15 seconds later in the burst. The purpose is two-fold: to cut costs and to remind the target audience. This process of reminding is undertaken with the assistance of the audience, who recognise the commercial and mentally close the message even though the advertiser only presents the first part.

Contour

Contours give objects shape and are normally formed when there is a marked change in colour or brightness. This is an important element in package design and, as the battle for shelf space in retail outlets becomes more intense, so package design has become an increasingly important aspect of attracting attention. The Coca-Cola bottle and the packaging of the Toblerone bar are two classic examples of packaging that convey the brand.

These methods are used by individuals in an attempt to organise stimuli and simplify their meanings. They combine in an attempt to determine a pattern to the stimuli, so that they are perceived as part of a whole or larger unit. This is referred to as gestalt psychology.

Perceptual interpretation

Interpretation is the process by which individuals give meaning to the stimuli.

Interpretation is the process by which individuals give meaning to the stimuli once they have been organised. As Cohen and Basu (1987) state, by using existing categories, meanings can be given to stimuli. These categories are determined from the individual's past experiences and they shape what the individual expects to see. These expectations, when combined with the strength and clarity of the stimulus and the motives at the time perception occurs, mould the pattern of the perceived stimuli.

The degree to which each individual's ascribed meaning, resulting from the interpretation process, is realistic, is dependent upon the levels of distortion that may be present. Distortion may occur because of stereotyping: the predetermined set of images which we use to guide our expectations of events, people and situations. Another distortion factor is the halo effect that occurs when a stimulus with many attributes or dimensions is evaluated on just a single attribute or dimension. Brand extensions and family branding strategies are based on the understanding that if previous experiences with a different offering are satisfactory, then risk is reduced and an individual is more likely to buy a new offering from the same 'family'.

Marketing and perception

Individuals, therefore, select and interpret particular stimuli in the context of the expectations arising from the way they classify the overall situation. The way in which individuals perceive, organise and interpret stimuli is a reflection of their past experiences and the classifications used to understand the different situations each individual frames every day. Individuals seek to frame or provide a context within which their role becomes clearer. Shoppers expect to find products in particular situations, such as rows, shelves or display bins of similar goods. They also develop meanings and associations with some grocery products because of the utility and trust/emotional satisfaction certain pack types evoke. The likelihood that a sale will be made is improved, if the context in which a purchase transaction is undertaken does not contradict a shopper's expectations.

> Individuals select and interpret particular stimuli in the context of the expectations arising from the way they classify the overall situation.

Marketing communications should attempt to present products (objects) in a frame or 'mental presence' (Moran, 1990) that is recognised by a buyer, such as a consumption or purchase situation. A product has a much greater chance of entering an evoked set if the situation in which it is presented is one that is expected and relevant. However, a new pack design can provide differentiation and provoke people into reassessing their expectations of what constitutes appropriate packaging in a product category.

Javalgi *et al.* (1992) point out that perception is important to product evaluation and product selection. Consumers try to evaluate a product's attributes using the physical cues of taste, smell, size and shape. Sometimes no difference can be distinguished, so the consumer has to make a judgement on factors other than the physical characteristics of the product. This is the basis of branding activity, where a personality is developed for the product which enables it to be perceived differently from its competitors. The individual may also set up a separate category or evoked set in order to make sense of new stimuli or satisfactory experiences. Consumer perception of salon- and shop-based haircare products shows important differences and indicates the different roles that marketing communication needs to play (see Figure 5.2). Within each of these sectors many brands are developed that are targeted at different segments based upon demographic, benefit and psychographic factors.

Goodrich (1978) discusses the importance of perception, which can be seen in terms of the choices tourists make when deciding which destination to visit. The decision is influenced by levels of general familiarity, levels of specific knowledge and perception. It follows that the more favourable the perception of a particular destination, the more likely it is to be selected from its competitors.

Finally, individuals carry a set of enduring perceptions or images. These relate to themselves, to products and to organisations. For example, many consumers perceive the financial services industry negatively. This is simply because of the inherent complexity associated with the product offerings and the rumble of negative publicity caused by the debate over account-charges and the Northern Rock issue (Nottage, 2007). The concept of positioning the product in the mind of the consumer is fundamental to marketing strategy and is a topic that will be examined in greater depth in Chapter 11. The image an individual has of an organisation is becoming

> Individuals carry a set of enduring perceptions or images. These relate to themselves, to products and to organisations.

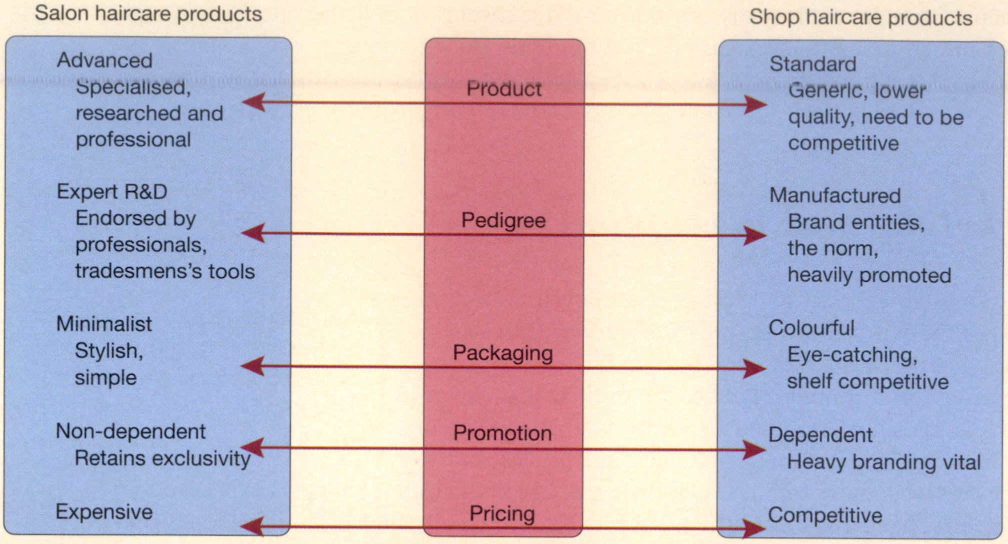

Figure 5.2 Comparison of salon and shop haircare products

recognised as increasingly important, judging by the proportion of communication budgets being given over to public relations activities and corporate advertising in particular.

Organisations develop multiple images to meet the positioning requirements of their end-user markets and stakeholders. They need to monitor and adjust their identities constantly in respect of the perceptions and expectations held by the other organisations in their various networks. For example, the level of channel coordination and control can be a function of the different perceptions of channel members. These concern the perception of the channel depth, processes of control and the roles each member is expected to fulfil. Furthermore, the perception of an organisation's product quality and its associated image (reputation) is becoming increasingly important. Both end-user buyers and channel members are attempting to ensure that the intrinsic and extrinsic cues associated with their products are appropriate signals of product quality (Moran, 1990).

ViewPoint 5.3 Frozen images

Sales of frozen food had been falling, by as much as 12 per cent in 2005, as consumers' preference moved to the chiller cabinet. Research by Mintel in 2004, cited by Jones (2007), found that people perceived dog food as a more desirable product than a frozen ready meal. Consumers perceived frozen food to be of poor quality, that there was little variety, it scored low on taste, it was seen to be not as good for you as fresh food and that frozen ready meals and both fruit and vegetables are a compromise purchase. Overall this was a challenging situation for frozen food manufacturers including the market leader Bird's Eye.

Bird's Eye's approach was to first introduce the 'Store Cupboard'. This represented a place for food that is free of preservatives, artificial flavours, colours and other additives. Their second was to launch an advertising campaign where the goal was to convey the truth about various aspects of chilled and frozen food. One truth was to convey the message that Bird's Eye fish was frozen as soon as it was caught, unlike some wet fish sales where the fish can be up to 10 days old. Another truth is that Bird's Eye only use wild Alaskan salmon unlike competitors who use farmed salmon, which is fed synthetically-produced astaxanthin in order to ensure the preferred pink colour.

The campaign helped to arrest and reverse the fall in sales while the growth for products featured in the advertising was exceptional. Bird's Eye had changed the way frozen food was perceived, they had provided consumers with facts and relevant information, an opportunity to see a different point of view and in doing so presented the brand as truthful and trustworthy.

Source: Jones (2007).

Question

If you were a competitor of Bird's Eye what would be your reaction to this campaign?

Task

Visit the Bird's Eye site and determine how important freshness appears to be in their frozen foods pages.

Exhibit 5.4 This ad by Birds Eye was part of a campaign to change the way frozen food was perceived by consumers
Courtesy of Birds Eye Ltd.

Learning

There are two mainstream approaches to learning: behavioural and cognitive.

Table 5.2 Types of learning

Type of learning		Explanation
Behavioural	Classical	Individuals learn to make associations or connections between a stimulus and their responses. Through repetition of the response (the behaviour) to the stimulus, learning occurs.
	Operant	Learning occurs as a result of an individual operating or interacting with the environment. The response of the individual is instrumental in getting a positive reinforcement (reward) or negative reinforcement (punishment). Behaviour that is rewarded or reinforced will be continued, whereas behaviour that is not rewarded will cease.
Cognitive		Assumes that individuals attempt to actively influence their immediate environments rather than be subject to it. They try to resolve problems by processing information from past experiences (memory) in order to make reasoned decisions based on judgements.

Behavioural learning

There are three factors important to behavioural learning: association, reinforcement and motivation.

The behavourist approach to learning views the process as a function of an individual's acquisition of responses. There are three factors important to behavioural learning: association, reinforcement and motivation. However, it is the basic concept of the stimulus–response orientation that will be looked at in more detail.

It is accepted that for learning to occur all that is needed is a 'time–space proximity' between a stimulus and a response. Learning takes place through the establishment of a connection between a stimulus and a response. Marketing communications are thought to work by the simple process of people observing messages and being stimulated/motivated to respond by requesting more information or purchasing the advertised product in search of a reward. Behaviour is learned through the conditioning experience of a stimulus and response. There are two forms of conditioning: classical and operant.

Classical conditioning

Classical conditioning assumes that learning is an associative process that occurs with an existing relationship between a stimulus and a response. By far the best-known example of this type of learning are the experiments undertaken by the Russian psychologist Pavlov. He noticed that dogs began to salivate at the sight of food. He stated that this was not taught, but was a reflex reaction. This relationship exists prior to any experimentation or learning. The food represents an unconditioned stimulus and the response (salivation) from the dogs is an unconditioned response.

Pavlov then paired the ringing of a bell with the presentation of food. Shortly the dogs began to salivate at the ringing of the bell. The bell became the conditioned stimulus and the salivation became the conditioned response (which was the same as the unconditioned response).

From an understanding of this work it can be determined that two factors are important for learning to occur:

- To build the association between the unconditioned and conditioned stimulus, there must be a relatively short period of time.
- The conditioning process requires that there be a relatively high frequency/repetition of the association. The more often the unconditioned and conditioned stimuli occur together, the stronger will be the association.

Classical conditioning can be observed operating in each individual's everyday life. An individual who purchases a new product because of a sales promotion may continue to buy the product even when the promotion has terminated. An association has been established between the sales promotion activity (unconditioned stimulus) and the product (conditioned stimulus). If product quality and satisfaction levels allow, long-run behaviour may develop despite the absence of the promotion. In other words, promotion need not act as a key purchase factor in the long run.

Advertisers attempt to associate their products/services with certain perceptions, images and emotions that are known to evoke positive reactions from consumers. Image advertising seeks to develop the associations that individuals have when they think of a brand or an organisation, and hence its reputation. Messages of this type show the object with an unconditioned stimulus that is known to evoke pleasant and favourable feelings. The product becomes a conditioned stimulus eliciting the same favourable response. The advertisements for Bounty Bars use images of desert islands to evoke feelings of enjoyment and pleasure and associations with coconuts.

Advertisers attempt to associate their products/services with certain perceptions, images and emotions that are known to evoke positive reactions.

ViewPoint 5.4 Conditioned stimuli

Gary Lineker became closely associated as the face of Walker's crisps. Alan Hansen is developing the role of spokesperson for Morrisons, and Jamie Oliver and Penelope Cruz are becoming brand ambassadors for Sainsbury's and L'Oréal Paris respectively.

For several years Citroën UK and Citroën France both used Claudia Schiffer in their car advertising. In Britain the international model is only associated with a single product, the Xara in two separate executions. However, research indicates that across all segments she became the face of Citroën and an association has developed between the two.

The car becomes the conditioned stimulus and the celebrity model acts as an unconditioned stimulus. See the model, think of the Xara or perhaps think of Citroën.

Question

If frequency of pairing between the conditioned and the unconditioned stimulus is necessary for learning to occur, why do many brands keep changing their ambassadors?

Task

Find another brand where this type of relationship has developed.

Operant conditioning

In this form of conditioning, sometimes known as instrumental conditioning, learning occurs as a result of an individual operating or acting on some part of the environment. The response of the individual is instrumental in getting a positive reinforcement (reward) or negative reinforcement (punishment). Behaviour that is rewarded or reinforced will be continued, whereas behaviour that is not rewarded will cease.

B. F. Skinner was a pioneer researcher in the field of operant conditioning. His work, with rats who learned to press levers in order to receive food and who later only pressed the lever when a light was on (discriminative stimulus), highlights the essential feature of this form of conditioning: that reinforcement follows a specific response.

Many organisations use reinforcement in their communications by stressing the benefits or rewards that a consumer can anticipate receiving as a result of using a product or brand. For example, Tesco offer 'Reward Points' and Nectar offer a reward of money savings which 'makes the difference'. Reinforcement theories emphasise the role of external factors and exclude the individual's ability to process information internally. Learning takes place either through direct reinforcement of a particular response or through an associative conditioning process.

Operant conditioning is a mechanistic process that is not realistic, as it serves only to simplify an extremely complex process.

However, operant conditioning is a mechanistic process that is not realistic, as it serves only to simplify an extremely complex process.

Cognitive learning

This approach to our understanding of learning assumes that individuals attempt to control their immediate environments. They are seen as active participants in that they try to resolve problems by processing information that is pertinent to each situation. Central to this process is memory. Just as money can be invested in short-, medium- and long-term investment accounts, so information is memorised for different periods of time. These memories are sensory, short-term and long-term (see Figure 5.3).

Sensory storage refers to the period in which information is sensed for a split second, and if an impression has been made the information will be transferred to short-term memory where it is rehearsed before transfer to long-term memory. *Short-term* memory lasts no longer than approximately eight seconds and a maximum of four or five items can be stored in short-term memory at any one time. Readers will probably have experienced being introduced to someone at a social event only to forget the name of the guest when they next meet them at the same event. This occurs because the name was not entered into *long-term* memory. Information can be stored for extended periods in long-term memory. This information is not lying dormant, however, it is constantly being reorganised and recategorised as new information is received.

There are four basic functions by which memory operates.

There are four basic functions by which memory operates. These are, first, *rehearsal*, where information is repeated or related to an established category. This is necessary so that the second function, *encoding*, can take place. This involves the selection of an image to represent the perceived object. Once in long-term memory it is *categorised and stored*, the third function. *Retrieval* is the final function, a process by which information is recovered from storage.

Cognitive learning is about processing information in order that problems can be resolved. These information-handling processes can range from the simple to the complex. There are three main processes: iconic, modelling and reasoning.

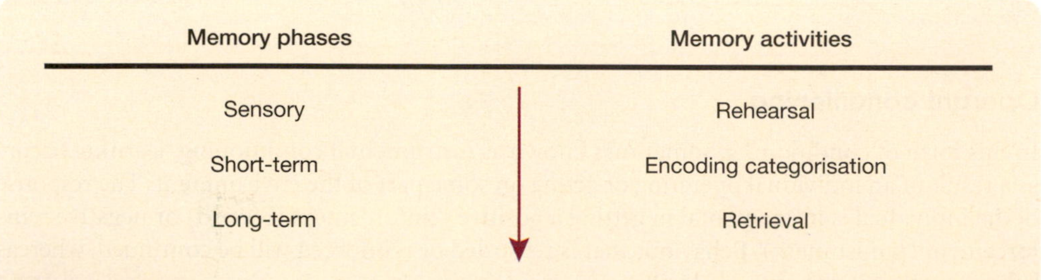

Figure 5.3 Aspects of internal information processing

Iconic rote learning involves understanding the association between two or more concepts when there is an absence of a stimulus. Learning occurs at a weak level through repetition of simple messages. Beliefs are formed about the attributes of an offering without any real understanding of the source of the information. Advertisers of certain products (low value, frequently purchased) will try to remind their target audiences repeatedly of the brand name in an attempt to help consumers learn. Through such repetition, an association with the main benefits of the product may be built, if only via the constant reminders by the spokesperson.

Learning through the *modelling* approach involves the observation and imitation of others and the associated outcomes of their behaviour. In essence, a great deal of children's early learning is developed in this way. Likewise, marketing communicators use the promise of rewards to persuade audiences to act in a particular way. By using positive images of probable rewards, buyers are encouraged to believe that they can receive the same outcome if they use the particular product. For example, clothing advertisements often depict the model receiving admiring glances from passers-by. The same admiration is the reward 'promised' to those who wear the same clothing. A similar approach was used by Kellogg's to promote their Special K breakfast cereal. The commercial depicted a (slim) mother and child playing on a beach. The message was that it is important to look after yourself and to raise your family through healthy eating, an outdoor life and exercise.

Reasoning is perhaps the most complex form of cognitive learning. Through this process, individuals need to restructure and reorganise information held in long-term memory and combine it with fresh inputs in order to generate new outputs. Financial services providers have to convey complex information, strictly bounded by the Financial Services legislation and the Financial Services Authority. So, brands such as Nationwide and Hiscox convey key points about simplicity and specialist services respectively, to differentiate their brands. This enables current and potential customers to process detailed information about these brands and to make judgements or reason that these brands reach acceptable (threshold) standards.

Reasoning is perhaps the most complex form of cognitive learning.

Of all the approaches to understanding how we learn, cognitive learning is the most flexible interpretation. The rational, more restricted approach of behavioural learning, where the focus is external to the individual, is without doubt a major contribution to knowledge. However, it fails to accommodate the complex internal thought processes that individuals utilise when presented with various stimuli.

It is useful to appreciate the way in which people are believed to learn and forget as there are several issues which are useful to media planners in particular.

Interference theory

Burke and Srull (1988) suggest that learning and brand recall can be interfered with. This may be caused either by new material affecting previously stored information or by old information being retrieved and interfered with by incoming messages. The first case, where the last message has the strongest recall, is similar to the recency effect discussed in the context of message design (Chapter 17).

In a competitive environment, where there are many messages being transmitted, each one negating previous messages, the most appropriate strategy for an advertiser would be to separate the advertisements from those of its competitors. This reasoning supports much of the positioning work undertaken by brand managers.

Decay

The rate at which individuals forget material assumes a pattern, as shown in Figure 5.4. Many researchers have found that information decays at a negatively decelerating rate. As much as 60 per cent of the initial yield of information from an advertisement has normally decayed within six

Information decays at a negatively decelerating rate.

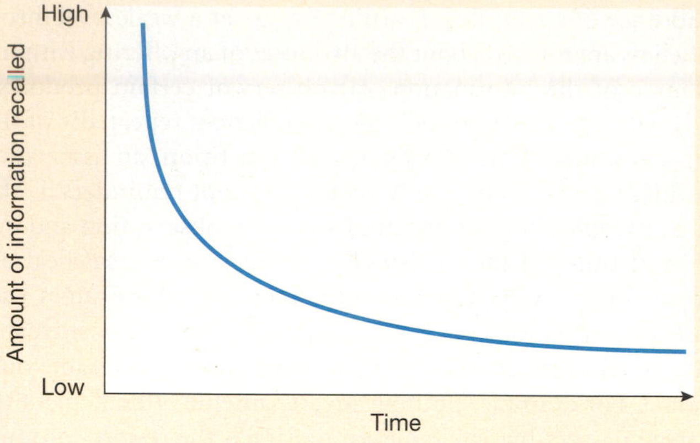

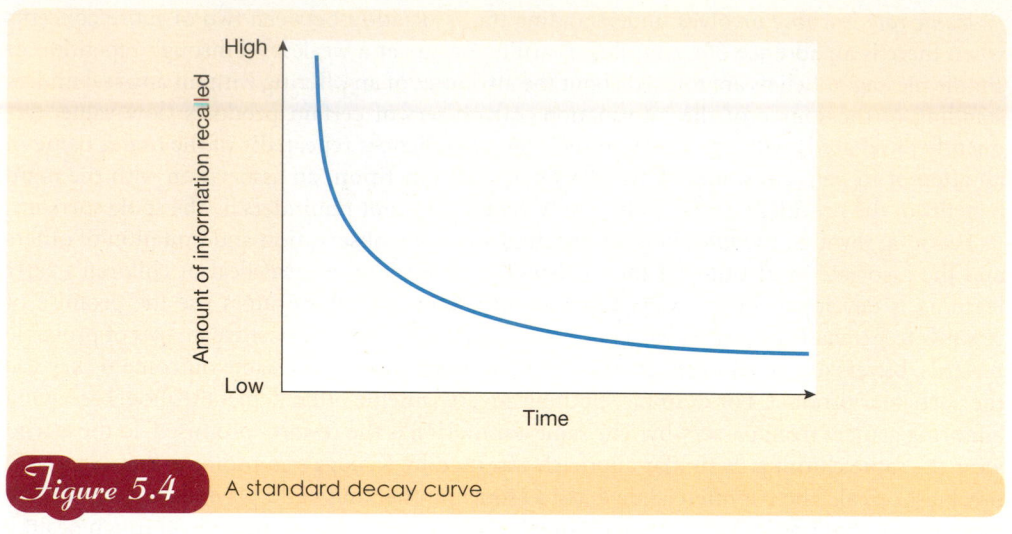

Figure 5.4 A standard decay curve

weeks. This decay, or wear-out, can be likened to the half-life of radioactive material. It is always working, although it cannot be seen, and the impact of the advertising reduces through time. Like McGuire's (1978) retention stage in his hierarchy of effects model (see Chapter 16), the storage of information for future use is important, but with time, how powerful will the information be and what triggers are required to promote recall?

Advertising wear-out is thought to occur because of two factors.

Advertising wear-out is thought to occur because of two factors. First, individuals use selective perception and mentally switch off after a critical number of exposures. Second, the monotony and irritation caused by continued exposure lead to counter-argument to both the message and the advertisement (Petty and Cacioppo, 1979). Advertisements for alcoholic drinks such as Carlsberg and Artois attempt to prevent wear-out by using variations on a central theme to provide consistency yet engage audiences through interest and entertainment.

Cognitive response

Learning can be visualised as following either of the curves set out in Figure 5.5. The amount learnt 'wears out' after a certain repetition level has been reached. Grass and Wallace (1969) suggest that this process of wear-out commences once a satiation point has been reached. A number of researchers (Zielske, 1959; Strong, 1977) have found that recall is improved when messages are transmitted on a regular weekly basis, rather than daily, monthly or in a concentrated or dispersed format.

An individual's ability to develop and retain awareness or knowledge of a product will, therefore, be partly dependent not only on the quality of the message but also on the number and quality of exposures to a planned message. To assist the media planner there are a number of concepts that need to be appreciated and used within the decisions about what, where and when a message should be transmitted. There are a number of other concepts that are of use to media planners: these are reach and coverage, frequency, gross rating points, effective frequency, efficiency and media source effects.

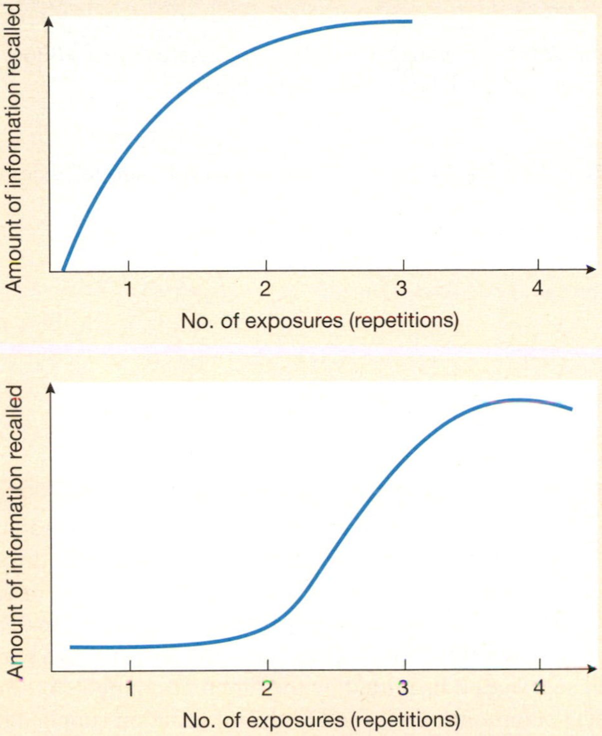

Figure 5.5 Learning curves

ViewPoint 5.5 Cognitive or emotional cats?

The differences between the cognitive and emotional approaches can be clearly seen in the battle to feed British cats. The two main competitors, Whiskas (owned by Mars) and Felix (owned by Purina) have used communications which appeal directly to the cognitive and emotional needs of cat owners.

For a long time in the 1980s Whiskas was market leader with a 53 per cent market share. To help establish this position the brand used a well-tried advertising formula. This consisted of a middle-class housewife who was shown with a perfect cat. This scene was followed by one in which a scientist, in a white coat, explained the nutritional ingredients and value of feeding the 'animal' Whiskas. The rationality of this approach could not be challenged.

At this time Felix, with just 5 per cent market share, was a struggling brand. However, research commissioned to accompany a relaunch found that cat owners could not recognise the perfect cat proclaimed by Whiskas. Their cats were scruffy, naughty, cheeky and very demanding and they were loved because of their fun loving spirit and mischievous personalities.

Felix was developed to reflect this perception, to remind owners of their cats and the ads made no reference at all to meat, nutrition or well-being. Communications were designed to engage audiences (cat owners) on an emotional level and appeal to the relationship they have with their pets (not animals). Felix's market share rose sharply and the brand became the second largest brand in the category and forced Whiskas to drop their rational approach and use more emotional communications.

Source: Challis *et al.* (2006).

Question

Do you believe the use of a emotional approach would have been successful in the 1980s. In other words, is the use (and success) of these of these approaches culturally determined?

Task

Choose two dog food brands and determine the level of emotion and rationality in their respective communications.

Attitudes

Attitudes are learned through past experiences and serve as a link between thoughts and behaviour.

The perceptual and learning processes may lead to the formation of attitudes. These are predispositions, shaped through experience, to respond in an anticipated way to an object or situation. Attitudes are learned through past experiences and serve as a link between thoughts and behaviour. These experiences may relate to the product itself, to the messages transmitted by the different members of the channel network (normally mass media communications) and to the information supplied by opinion leaders, formers and followers.

Attitudes tend to be consistent within each individual: they are clustered and very often interrelated. This categorisation leads to the formation of stereotypes, which is extremely useful for the design of messages as stereotyping allows for the transmission of a lot of information in a short time period (30 seconds) without impeding learning or the focal part of the message.

Attitude components

Attitudes are hypothetical constructs, and classical psychological theory considers attitudes to consist of three components:

1. *Cognitive component (learn)*
   This component refers to the level of knowledge and beliefs held by individuals about a product and/or the beliefs about specific attributes of the offering. This represents the learning aspect of attitude formation.
2. *Affective component (feel)*
   By referring to the feelings held about a product – good, bad, pleasant or unpleasant – an evaluation is made of the object. This is the component that is concerned with feelings, sentiments, moods and emotions about an object.
3. *Conative component (do)*
   This is the action component of the attitude construct and refers to the individual's disposition or intention to behave in a certain way. Some researchers go so far as to suggest that this component refers to observable behaviour.

   This three-component approach (Figure 5.6) to attitudes is based upon attitudes towards an object, person or organisation. The sequence of attitude formation is generally considered to be learn, feel and do. However, this approach to attitude formation is limited in that the components are seen to be of equal strength. A single-component model has been developed where the attitude only consists of the individual's overall feeling towards an object. In other words, the affective component is the only significant component.

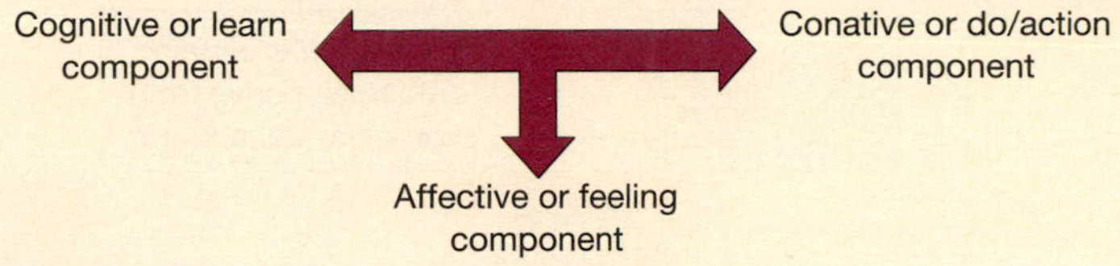

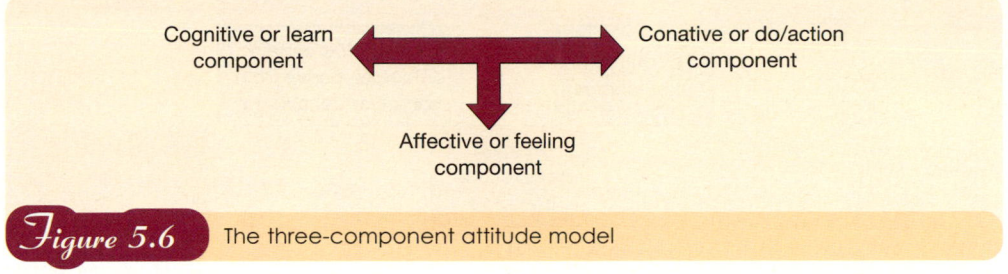

Figure 5.6 The three-component attitude model

Intentions

Of the many advances in this area, those made by Ajzen and Fishbein (1980) have made a significant contribution. They reasoned that the best way of predicting behaviour was to measure an individual's intention to purchase (the conative component). Underlying intentions are the individual's attitude towards the act of behaviour and the subjective norm. In other words, the context within which a proposed purchase is to occur is seen as important to the attitude that is developed towards the object.

The subjective norm is the relevant feelings others are believed to hold about the proposed purchase, or intention to purchase. Underpinning the subjective norm are the beliefs held about the people who are perceived to 'judge' the actions an individual might take. Would they approve or disapprove, or look favourably or unfavourably upon the intended action?

Underpinning the attitude towards the intention to act in a particular way are the strengths of the beliefs that a particular action will lead to an outcome. Ajzen and Fishbein argue that it is the individual's attitude to the act of purchasing, not the object of the purchase, that is important. For example, a manager may have a positive attitude towards a particular type of expensive office furniture, but a negative attitude towards the act of securing agreement for him to purchase it.

Underpinning the attitude towards the intention to act in a particular way are the strengths of the beliefs that a particular action will lead to an outcome.

The theory of reasoned action (Ajzen and Fishbein, 1980; Figure 5.7) shows that intentions are composed of interrelated components: subjective norms, which in turn are composed of beliefs and motivations about relevant others, towards a particular intention, and attitudes, which in turn are made up of beliefs about the probable outcomes that a behaviour will lead to.

This approach recognises the interrelationship of the three components of attitudes and that it is not attitude but the intention to act or behave that precedes observable behaviour that should be the focus of attention. It should be understood that attitudes do not precede behaviour and cannot be used to predict behaviour, despite the attempts of a number of researchers. Attitudes are important, but they are not the sole determinant of behaviour, and intentions may be a better indicator of behaviour.

Attitudes impact on consumer decision-making, and the objective of marketing communications is often to create a positive attitude towards a product and/or to reinforce or change existing attitudes. An individual may perceive and develop a belief that British Airways has a friendly and informal in-flight service and that the service provided by Lufthansa is cold and formal. However, both airlines are perceived to hold a number of different attributes, and each individual needs to evaluate these attributes in order that an attitude can be developed. It is necessary, therefore, to measure the strength of the beliefs held about the key attributes of different products. There are two main processes whereby beliefs can be processed and measured: compensatory and non-compensatory models.

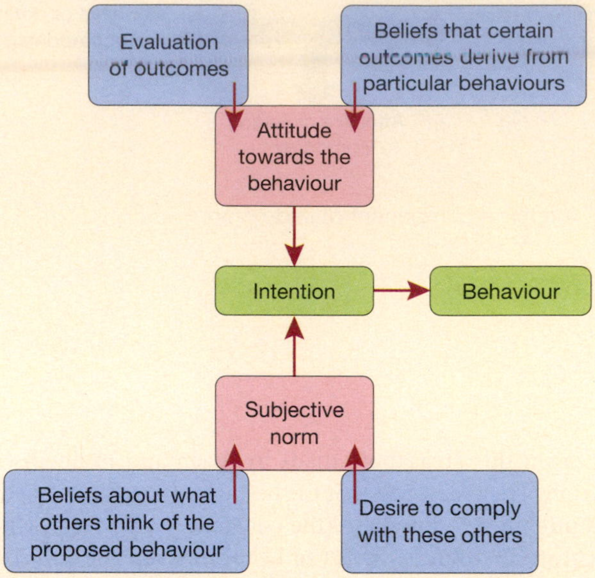

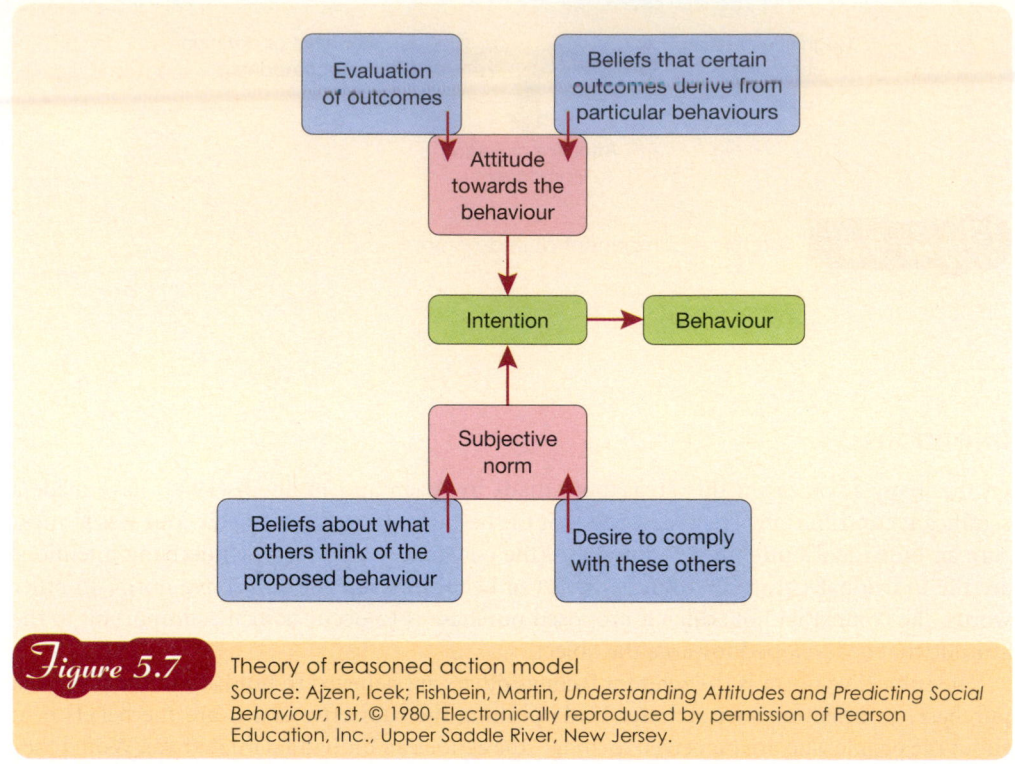

Figure 5.7 Theory of reasoned action model
Source: Ajzen, Icek; Fishbein, Martin, *Understanding Attitudes and Predicting Social Behaviour*, 1st, © 1980. Electronically reproduced by permission of Pearson Education, Inc., Upper Saddle River, New Jersey.

Compensatory models

Through this approach, attributes that are perceived to be weak can be offset by attributes that are perceived to be strong. As a result, positive attitudes are determined in the sense that the evaluation of all the attributes is satisfactory. For example, Table 5.3 sets out a possible evaluation of three package holidays. Despite the weakness on hotel cleanliness, the strength of the other attributes in package 2 scores this one the highest, so the strongest attitude is formed towards this product. Some individuals make decisions about products on the basis that their attributes must not contain any weaknesses. Therefore package 2 would not be considered, as it fails to reach a minimum level of expected satisfaction on cleanliness, thus, despite its strengths, it is relegated from the decision alternatives.

Table 5.3 Compensatory and non-compensatory models

	Weighting	Package 1		Package 2		Package 3	
Attribute		Rating	Score	Rating	Score	Rating	Score
Price	5	5	25	6	30	5	25
Hotel cleanliness	3	3	9	2	6	4	12
Travel times	2	7	14	9	18	4	8
Attitude rating			48		54		45
Possible decisions							
Compensatory model		Not considered		*Winner*		Not considered	
Non-compensatory model		*Winner*		Not considered		Considered	

An understanding of attitude components and the way in which particular attributes can be measured not only enables organisations to determine the attitudes held towards them and their competitors but also empowers them to change the attitudes held by different stakeholders, if it is thought necessary.

Using marketing communications to influence attitudes

Marketing communications can be used to influence the attitudes held by a target audience. When developing campaigns, consideration needs to be given to the current and desired attitudes of the target audience. The focus of a campaign can be on whether the audience requires information (learning), an emotional disposition (feeling) or whether the audience need to be encouraged to behave in a particular way (doing).

> Marketing communications can be used to influence the attitudes held by a target audience.

In today's competitive environment in which product lifecycles are shortening, innovation is increasingly critical and organisations require marketing staff to be accountable for their investments, there is greater urgency to encourage potential customers to test, use or behave towards a product in particular ways. Marketing communications can induce behavioural change by getting people to buy a brand and this might require the use of direct marketing, sales promotions and personal selling. When the emphasis of a campaign is on driving behaviour and action, direct-response advertising can be effective. It is said that 40 per cent of television ads have a telephone number or web site address.

In some circumstances change might be in the form of motivating customers to visit a web site, to fill in an application form, call for a brochure, download a document or just encourage them to visit a shop and sample the brand free of money and any other risks. This 'doing' component of the attitude construct is commonly referred to as a 'call-to-action'.

Changing attitudes

Marketing communications is important to either maintain or change attitudes held by stakeholders. Attitudes can be changed in other ways, for example through changes to product and service elements, pricing and channel decisions. However, marketing communications have a pivotal role in conveying each of these aspects to the target audience. Branding (Chapter 11) is a means by which attitudes can be established and maintained in a consistent way and it is through the use of the tools of the communications mix that brand equity can be sustained. The final point that needs to be made is that there is a common thread between attributes, attitudes and positioning (Chapters 10 and 11). Attributes provide a means through which brands can be differentiated from competitors' products (DRIP Chapter 1). Marketing communications are used to convey information about these attributes. People form attitudes as a result of their interpretation of the associated marketing communications, and from that they position brands in their minds.

> Attributes provide a means through which brands can be differentiated from competitors' products.

Environmental influences on the attitudes people hold towards particular products and services are partly a reflection of the way they interpret the marketing communications surrounding them, partly as a result of their direct experience of using them and partly as a result of the informal messages received from family, friends and other highly credible sources of information. These all contribute to the way people position products and services and the way they understand them relative to competing products.

Managing attitudes (towards an offering) is therefore very important but before marketing communications can be used it may be necessary to change the product offering (its attributes) to ensure credibility and to enable promises to be delivered.

1. *Change the physical product or service element*
   At a fundamental level, attitudes might be so ingrained that it is necessary to change the product or service. This may involve a radical redesign or the introduction of a significant new attribute. Only once these changes have been made should marketing communications be used to communicate the new or revised object. When the fruit juice drink 'Sunny Delight' was sold by Procter & Gamble the first thing the new owners did was to change the drink itself. It raised the level of fruit juice and added vitamins and reduced the number of colourants, additives and preservatives. Only then was the drink relaunched, proclaiming the nature of the reconstituted drink.

Attitudes might be so ingrained that it is necessary to change the product or service.

2. *Change misunderstanding*
   In some circumstances people might misunderstand the benefits of a particularly important attribute and marketing communications are required to correct the beliefs held. This can be achieved through product demonstration of functionally based communications. Packaging and even the name of the product may need to be revised.
3. *Build credibility*
   Attitudes towards a brand might be superficial and lack sufficient conviction to prompt conative behaviour. This can be corrected through the use of an informative strategy, designed to build credibility. Product demonstration and hands-on experience (e.g. through sampling) are effective strategies. Skoda support a rally team to convey durability, speed and performance.
4. *Change performance beliefs*
   Beliefs held about the object and the performance qualities of the object can be adjusted through appropriate marketing communications. For example, by providing accurate information it is possible to change the perceptions held about the attributes, and so it is possible to change the attitudes about the object. See ViewPoint 5.3 about how Bird's Eye changed the way people perceived frozen food.
5. *Change attribute priorities*
   By changing the relative importance of the different attributes and ratings it is possible to change attitudes. Therefore, a strategy to emphasise a different attribute can change the attitude not only to a brand but to a product category. By stressing the importance of travel times, it might raise the importance of this attribute in the minds of potential holiday-makers and so give package 2 an advantage over its rivals, using the non-compensatory decision rule. Dyson changed attitudes to carpet cleaning equipment by stressing the efficiency of their new cyclone technology rather than the ease of use, aesthetic design or generic name (Hoover) associations used previously.

A strategy to emphasise a different attribute can change the attitude not only to a brand but to a product category.

6. *Introduce a new attribute*
   Opportunities might exist to introduce a radically different and new (or previously unused) attribute. This provides a means for clear differentiation until competitors imitate and catch up. The solution for package 3 may be to introduce a fourth attribute, one in which the suppliers of package 3 know they have an advantage over the competition. This may be that they have a no-surcharge guarantee and packages 1 and 2 do not. By making prominent the new no-surcharge guarantee in the promotional messages transmitted by package 3, the introduction of a new significant attribute may lead to greater success.
7. *Change perception of competitor products*
   By changing the way competitor products are perceived it is possible to differentiate your own brand. For example, by changing the perception of packages 1 and 2 or changing the association of their packages with the others, package 3 might gain an advantage. This

could be achieved by using messages that set the package apart from its rivals, suggesting, for example, that not all package holidays are the same. This is a theme that was used by Thomson Holidays, when their copy read, 'We go there, we don't stay there'.

8. *Change or introduce new brand associations*
   By using celebrities or spokespersons with whom the target audience can identify, it might be possible for package 3 to change the way the product is perceived on an emotional basis rather than relying on attributes and a more rational argument.
9. *Use corporate branding*
   By altering the significance of the parent brand relative to the product brand, it is possible to alter beliefs about brands and their overall value. In some situations there is little to differentiate competitive brands and little credible scope to develop attribute-based attitudes. By using the stature of the parent company it is possible to develop a level of credibility and brand values that other brands cannot copy, although they can imitate by using their parent brand. Procter & Gamble have introduced their name to the packs of many of their brands.
10. *Change the number of attributes used*
   Many brands still rely on a single attribute as a means of providing a point of differentiation. This was popularly referred to as a unique selling proposition (USP) at a time when attribute- and information-based communications reflected a *feature*-dominated understanding of branding. Today, two or even three attributes are often combined with strong emotional associations in order to provide a point of differentiation and a set of *benefit*-oriented brand values.

> Many brands still rely on a single attribute as a means of providing a point of differentiation.

In order to make sense of these different approaches, and to understand how marketing communications can be used to bring about attitudinal change, it is helpful to consider the three attitude components considered earlier in this chapter; the cognitive, affective and conative components.

Cognitive component

When an audience lacks information, misunderstands a brand's attributes or whose perception of a brand is inappropriate, the essential task of marketing communications is to give the audience the right, or up-to-date, information. This enables perception, learning and attitude development based on clear truths. This is a rational, informational approach, one that appeals to a person's ability to rationalise and process information in a logical manner. It is therefore important that the level and quality of the information provided is appropriate to the intellectual capabilities of the target audience. Other tasks include showing the target audience how a brand differs from those of competitors, establishing what the added value is and suggesting who the target audience is by depicting them in the message.

Both advertising and public relations are key tools and television, print and the Internet are key media used to deliver information and influence the way people perceive a brand. Rather than provide information about a central or popular attribute or aspect of an offering, it is possible to direct the attention of an audience to different aspects of the object and so shape their beliefs about the brand in different ways to competitors. So, some crisp and snack food manufacturers used to communicate the importance of taste. Now in an age of chronic social obesity, many of these manufacturers have changed the salt and fat content and now appeal to audiences on the basis of nutrition and health. They have changed the focus of attention from one attribute to another.

Although emotion can be used to provide information, the overriding approach is informational.

Affective component

Having established that a product might be useful it is important that the audience develop positive attitudes towards a brand based on an emotional attachment or set of values.

Marketing communications is used to convey a set of emotional values.

Marketing communications is used to convey a set of emotional values that will appeal to and hopefully engage the target audience.

When attitudes to a brand or product category are discovered to be either neutral or negative it is common for brands to use an emotional rather than rational or information-based approach. This can be achieved by using messages that are unusual in style, colour and tone and because they stand out and get noticed they can change the way people feel and their desire to be associated with that object, brand or product category. There is great use of visual images and the appeal is often to an individual's senses, feelings and emotional disposition. The goal is help people feel, 'I (we) like, I (we) desire (aspire to), I (we) want or I (we) belong to' whatever is being communicated. Establishing and maintaining positive feelings towards a brand can be achieved through reinforcement and to do this it is necessary to repeat the message.

Creating positive attitudes used to be the sole preserve of advertising but today a range of tools and media can be used. For example, product placement within films and music videos, helps to show how a brand fits in with a desirable set of values and lifestyles. The use of suitable music, characters that reflect the values of either the current target audience or an aspirational group, a tone of voice, colours and images all help to create a particular emotional disposition and understanding about what the brand represents or stands for.

Perhaps above all else the use of celebrity endorsers to create desire through association is one of the main ways attitudes are developed, based on an emotional disposition. This approach focuses on changing attitudes to the communication (attitudes to the ad) rather than the offering. Fashion brands are often presented using a celebrity model and little or no text. The impact is visual, inviting the reader to make positive attitudes and associations with the brand and the endorser. See the successful ads for Marks & Spencer and TopShop.

Marmite use an emotional approach based on challenging audiences to decide whether they love or hate the unique taste. The government have used a variety of approaches to change people's attitude to drink/driving, smoking, vaccinations, tax, pensions and the use of rear seat belts to name but a few of their activities. They will often use an information approach, but in some cases use an affective approach based on dramatising the consequences of a particular behaviour to encourage the audience to change their attitudes and behaviour. The overriding strategy is therefore emotional.

Exhibit 5.5 The Government's *THINK!* Seat belts campaign used to change behaviour towards using belts in the rear seats of cars
Department for Transport/Abbott Mead Vickers BBDO.

Conative component

In some product categories people are said to be inert because they are comfortable with a current brand, have little reason to buy into a category, do not buy any brand or are just reluctant to change their brand. In this situation attitude change should be based on provoking behaviour. As explained later in this book, the growth and development of direct marketing and web-based communications is based on the desire to encourage people to do something rather than undertake passive attitude change that does not necessarily result in a sale. So, a conative approach stimulates people to try, test, trial, visit (a showroom or web site) a brand, usually free and often without overt commitment.

> A conative approach stimulates people to try, test, trial, visit.

Sales promotion, personal selling and direct marketing are the key tools used to drive behavioural change. For example, sales promotions are geared to driving behaviour by getting people to try a brand, direct marketing seeks to encourage a response and hence engage in interaction and salespeople will try to close a customer to get a sale. Advertising can be used to raise awareness and direct people to a store or web site.

In addition to these approaches, experiential marketing has become very popular as it is believed that direct experience of touching, feeling or using a product helps establish positive values and develop commitment. So, many car manufacturers offer opportunities to test drive a car not only for a few hours but several days. They have test circuits where drivers can spend time driving several different cars in the range across different terrain.

The overriding strategy in this context is to provoke customers into action.

ViewPoint 5.6 branching out as NatWest change attitudes

The banking system is a classic example of market inertia. Customers see little reason to move or change their banks unless provoked by gross inefficiency or their accounts are mishandled. At the same time many banks have closed a large proportion of their UK branch network and moved their call centres off shore to reduce costs, they have moved away from a human approach to customer service to one based on mechanics. There has since been a 'consumer backlash against foreign call centres [that] has led some companies to return operations to the UK' (Winterman, 2007).

When the Royal Bank of Scotland bought NatWest in 2000 it reversed the strategy of closing branches and using overseas call centres. A policy of refurbishing all the branches has since been implemented, new branches opened and all call centre operations are now UK-based.

As a result, NatWest have used this initiative as the backbone of their communication strategy. By positioning themselves against an attribute that had been discarded by competitors, NatWest have been able to establish a clear point of differentiation. By focusing their marketing and communications on their branch network in order to provide customers the opportunity for personal contact by just walking into a local branch, they have been able to add considerable value to the brand and given inert customers a reason to change to NatWest.

Sources: Winterman (2007); www.natwest.com/.

Question

As all banks provide a service, how feasible is it for them to use service as a basis for differentiation?

Task

Find two other banks and determine the attributes they use for differentiation.

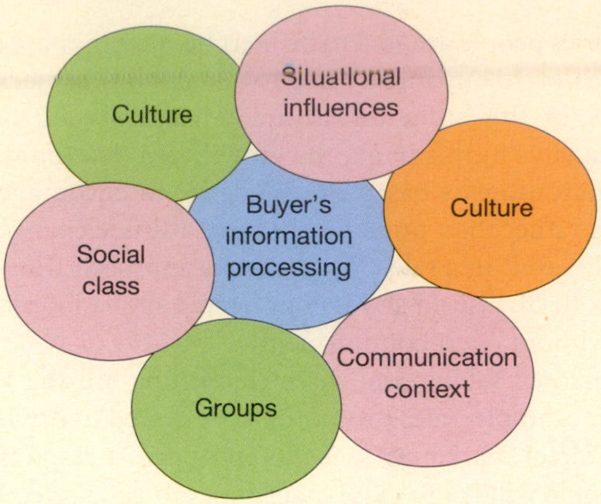

Figure 5.8 Environmental influences on buyer information processing

Environmental influences on buyer information processing

Neither organisations nor consumers exist in a vacuum. They exist in an 'open' system and therefore act upon and are affected by various environmental factors (Figure 5.8). There are a number of externally generated influences that impact upon buyer information processing and decision-making. The main factors are considered in the final section of this chapter.

Culture

Culture encompasses the norms, beliefs, artefacts and customs that are learned from society and that constitute its values.

Culture has been referred to as the unique characteristics that identify the acceptable patterns of behaviour and social relations within a particular society. Culture encompasses the norms, beliefs, artefacts and customs that are learned from society and that constitute its values. It is these values that influence consumer behaviour and are of increasing importance to the international advertiser. Indeed, a more detailed consideration of the role of culture on marketing communications can be found in Chapter 28.

Culture is learned and acquired, it is not instinctive. Culture defines acceptable behaviour within a society and so sets the rules for all members who belong to the culture. For marketing communications, culture should be seen as a communication system in its own right. Through verbal and non-verbal actions a society is able to maintain stability, to bind all members with a sense of identity and to provide them with a means of continuity.

Sub-cultures

There are a number of sub-cultures within any given culture. These include age, geography, race, religion and ethnic groupings and they can all influence the way marketing communications are perceived, interpreted and understood.

Social class

Virtually all societies are stratified by class, based upon power, wealth and prestige. Society values individuals and groups on criteria such as education, occupation and level of income. This information is distilled into a social class system, such as upper, middle and lower class, which for a long time has been a main characteristic of UK society.

Marketers have developed a socioeconomic categorisation that is used as a primary means of segmenting markets. Creative designers have always used symbols to reflect the values, lifestyles, norms and family roles associated with each perceived stratum. Among the many benefits this brings is the ability to transfer a lot of information relatively quickly and so communicate effectively. The process also allows for the continuity of the core values of society.

However, this traditional approach to segmentation is becoming increasingly difficult to utilise as consumers' purchasing habits become more complex and their lifestyles become less rigid and more open. Advertisers recognise the speed at which consumers can move between purchasing styles, even in the space of a single shopping trip. This is because the requirements of each purchase can be so different that tailor-made segmentation by product is necessary. For example, Dulux recognises that its market for paints consists of 'sloshers' and 'craftsmen'. Paint can be bought for the attic, where it will be 'sloshed', or for the lounge, where it will be applied by the same person like a 'craftsman'.

Groups

Groups are one of the primary factors influencing learning and socialisation. An individual may simultaneously be a member of several groups, each having a different degree of effect. These groups can be categorised as follows:

Groups are one of the primary factors influencing learning and socialisation.

1. Ascribed groups: one automatically belongs, e.g. family.
2. Primary/secondary groups: where interaction is on a one-to-one basis, e.g. family and friends.
3. Formal/informal groups: where the presence or absence of structure and hierarchy defines the group activity.
4. Aspirational/membership groups: groups to which the individual wishes to belong or does belong.

All these act as reference groups for the individual and influence the individual's behaviour.

Situational influences

The design, encoding and media channels used to transmit communication messages must take into account that buyers are influenced by factors that are unique to each buying situation and are not related specifically to the product or the individual. The situational context impacts on the information-processing capabilities of the buyer. For example, the amount of light in the store or the level of store traffic can influence the amount of time given to decision-making. While this factor will normally have been accounted for in the formulation of the marketing strategy, it must be revisited if the communications are to be effective.

When considering the impact that situational influences might have on information processing, the type of situation needs to be considered. A situational determinant is a factor that is unique to each buying act. These situational influences are connected neither to the purchase object nor to the buyer, and are independent of them. Hansen (1972) identified three types of situation: usage, purchase and communications.

Usage situation

It is important to understand when and where an offering is to be consumed, whether its consumption is a largely a private act, oriented to the individual (such as chocolate bars) or part

Communications need to encapsulate the situation in which consumption occurs.

of a social activity (such as beer). For example, some manufacturers of breakfast cereals have been repositioning (Chapter 11) their brands in an attempt to encourage use at other times of the day. Communications need to reflect this strategy and encapsulate the situation in which consumption occurs.

ViewPoint 5.7 Breakfast culture in New York

As food and drink manufacturers have had to adapt their product offerings and change key attributes, in the light of growing concerns about obesity, so the juice market has benefitted and grown. However, most brands need to fight hard to provide a point of differentiation, as juice is natural and the category is perceived more as a commodity.

For many years Tropicana performed well but with the arrival of own label brands that copied Tropicana's gable top carton and undercut its premium price so market share fell in a rising market.

Research identified three key interrelated points. One was an upmarket audience who preferred fresh, premium quality foods. The second was that Tropicana was the number one grocery brand in New York, bigger than Coca-Cola. The third point was that this audience perceived New York as strongly aspirational.

As New York has a strong breakfast culture incorporating waffles, muffins, pancakes, eggs and coffees, all available from restaurants, hotels and diners, a campaign was devised to incorporate Tropicana as a key ingredient in a typical New York breakfast. The television ad used Dean Martin's 'How do you like your eggs in the morning'.

Sales rose immediately the ads were aired and volume grew by 25 per cent in 2005 and sales value grew three times the rate of the previous year. By cross-referencing an audience to a known and desired cultural set Tropicana arrested a decline in sales and reinvigorated the brand.

Sources: Hui (2005); Huzzey *et al.* (2006).

Question

Associating a food/drink with an occasion (in this case breakfast) is not new. To what extent might such an association restrict the development of a brand?

Task

Identify two other brands that are strongly associated with a major city.

Purchase situation

The act of purchase and the associated environment can influence the behaviour of the target individual. Is shopping a monthly, biannual, weekly or last-minute activity? Mothers shopping with children are more likely to be influenced by product preferences of their children than when shopping without them. This may be due not only to the amount of time available to complete the physical act of shopping but also to the time to process the information. Engel *et al.* (1990) cite information load, format and form as important criteria. Too much information (information overload) can reduce the accuracy of an individual's decision-making, whereas the order in which information is presented both on packages and in terms of store layout can seriously retard the amount of time taken to process information, and this can also influence the motivation of the shopper.

The way in which information is presented will affect the decision style.

The way in which information is presented will affect the decision style. For example, the ease of comparing brands, perhaps on an individual attribute basis (e.g. diabetics determining the amount of sugar or carbohydrate in competing brands), will influence both perception and purchase behaviour. The development of online buyer comparison sites means that a number of attributes can be compared at the same time.

What is the environment of the shop like? Are there opportunities to influence the target with in-store promotions and advertising messages? Different individuals prefer different supermarkets and price is not the sole criterion. Store loyalty is a function of a number of issues, among them convenience, layout, product range, car-parking facilities and whether packers are available. Associated with this is the concept of corporate image. Each of the supermarket chains has a particular range of images held by its consumers. Consumer perception of store efficiency and value for money and the totality of corporate communications need to reflect, deflect or reinforce particular images. This element is pursued in greater depth in Chapter 15.

Communications situation

The settings in which marketing communications are received will affect the degree to which the message is understood and acted upon. For example, salespersons cold-calling on organisations (arriving at an organisation and requesting a sales interview without a prior appointment) are not usually received in a positive way. Furthermore, having gained an appointment through a prior arrangement does not mean that the information provided during the visit will be received as intended. The buyer may have been advised of some bad news prior to the meeting and their thoughts are not focused on the object of the sales meeting or presentation. Television commercials may be zipped or zapped, clutter may prevent key points of the message getting home or general noise in the form of conversation may also affect the effectiveness of the message. One of the central issues concerning the situation in which communications are received is the need to gain the attention of the receiver.

The settings in which marketing communications are received will affect the degree to which the message is understood and acted upon.

Having determined that there are particular types of situations where the consumption process occurs, Belk (1975) proposes that there are five main situation variables that should be considered. These are the physical aspects, the social surroundings, the time, the task and the antecedent states.

Physical aspects refer to the store design and layout, the location, the lighting, music, smells and sounds associated with the situation. The *social surroundings* refer to all those involved in the purchase, usage or communications. For example, a child was described in one type of situation as accompanying a mother on the shopping activity, and children have a degree of influence on such an event.

Time was considered in the context of the time available to complete the activity, but it could also be considered in the context of time of day, year or season, or time elapsed since the last purchase. The *task* itself is pertinent. Is the purchase for a third party as a present, or is it for personal consumption? Finally, *antecedent states* are the influences each individual experiences, but state is transitional. For example, states of high elation, despondency, bitterness or pleasure are experienced by all individuals, but they are not enduring characteristics.

The particular impact of various environmental influences can affect the behaviour of buyers during purchase activity, during usage and when information is being processed. Understanding the impact of the physical, time and social influences, together with the nature of the task and antecedent states, provides the marketing communications planner with fresh inputs to the exercise of positioning the product appropriately.

Summary

1. Introduce cognitive theory as an important element in the development of planned communications.

Cognitive theory is based upon an information-processing, problem-solving and reasoning approach to human behaviour. Individuals use information that has been generated by external sources (e.g. advertisements) and internal sources (e.g. memory). This information is given thought, processed, transferred into meanings or patterns and then combined to form judgements about behaviour.

The cognitive orientation considers consumers to be adaptive problem solvers, people who use various processes to reason, form concepts and acquire knowledge.

2. Examine personality as a main factor in the determination of successful communications.

Personality is, essentially, concerned with the inner properties of each individual, those characteristics that differentiate each of us. There are two main approaches: the Freudian and Trait theories of personality.

Freudian theory is based on the beliefs that human behaviour is driven by two primary instincts: life and death. The personality of the individual is assumed to have developed in an attempt to gratify these needs, and consists of the id, superego and ego; this approach is termed psychoanalytic theory.

Trait theory is a quantitative approach where the distinguishing and relatively enduring ways in which one individual differs from another is measured and quantified. Personality tests invariably seek to measure individual differences in respect of specific traits such as the degree of assertiveness, responsiveness to change or the level of sociability an individual might exhibit.

3. Explore perception in the context of marketing communications.

Perception is concerned with how individuals see and make sense of their environment. The way in which individuals perceive, organise and interpret stimuli is a reflection of their past experiences and the classifications used to understand the different situations each individual frames every day.

Marketing communications are used to position brands using a variety of stimuli so that consumers understand and recognise them.

4. Understand the main differences between conditioning and cognitive learning processes.

The Behavourist approach to learning considers the process to be a function of an individual's acquisition of responses. There are three factors important to learning: association, reinforcement and motivation. Behaviour is learned through the conditioning experience of a stimulus and response.

Cognitive learning considers learning to be a function of an individual's attempt to control their immediate environment. They are seen as active participants in that they try to resolve problems by processing information that is pertinent to each situation. Central to this process is memory. Cognitive learning is about processing information in order that problems can be resolved. These information-handling processes can range from the simple to the complex. There are three main processes: iconic, modelling and reasoning.

5. Appraise the role of attitudes and the different ways in which attitudes are thought to be developed.

Attitudes are predispositions, shaped through experience, to respond in an anticipated way to an object or situation. Attitudes are learned through past experiences and serve as a link between thoughts and behaviour. Attitudes tend to be consistent within each individual: they are clustered and very often interrelated. Attitudes consist of three interrelated elements; the cognitive, affective and conative, otherwise referred to as learn, feel, do.

6. Appreciate the importance of understanding an individual's intention to act in a particular way and its part in the decision process.

Underlying intentions are the individual's attitude towards the act of behaviour and the subjective norm. In other words, the context within which a proposed purchase is to occur is seen as important to the attitude that is developed towards the object.

The theory of reasoned action shows that intentions are composed of interrelated components: subjective norms, which in turn are composed of beliefs and motivations about relevant others, towards a particular intention, and attitudes, which in turn are made up of beliefs about the probable outcomes that a behaviour will lead to.

7. Understand how marketing communications can be used to influence these elements of buyer behaviour and in particular change attitudes.

Marketing communications can be used to influence the attitudes held by a target market. When developing campaigns consideration needs to be given to the current and desired attitudes to be held by the target audience. The focus of a campaign can be on whether the audience requires information (learning), an emotional disposition (feeling) or whether the audience needs to be encouraged to behave in a particular way (doing).

8. Provide a brief overview of the other environmental influences that affect the manner in which individuals process information.

There are a number of externally generated influences that impact upon buyer information processing and decision-making. These concern culture and sub-cultures, groups, situational influences, the usage situation and the purchase and communications situations.

The particular impact of these environmental influences can affect the behaviour of buyers during purchase activity, during usage and when information is being processed. Understanding the impact of the physical, time and social influences, together with the nature of the task and antecedent states, provides marketing communications opportunities to position products and services appropriately.

Review questions

1. Write a short description of cognitive theory. How does it differ from behaviourism?
2. What are the main elements of information processing?
3. How does Trait theory differ from Freudian theories of personality?
4. Describe a purchase repertoire (or evoked set) and suggest how marketing communications might assist perceptual selection.
5. To what extent are perception and positioning interlinked?
6. Choose three print advertisements where the user is promised a reward.
7. Attitudes are believed to comprise three elements. Name them.
8. Write a brief explanation of the theory of reasoned action.
9. How might the environment influence marketing communications?
10. Identify the different types of situational influences on the purchase process.

MiniCase The lost generation? The challenge of communicating with politically cynical British youth

Dr Janine Dermody, University of Gloucestershire

In this case study you are invited to explore what may be described as part of a global paradox, which illustrates the complexities involved in understanding an audience's attitudes and behaviour and the challenges of trying to communicate with them.

The political landscape in Britain

Within this paradox democracy is triumphant throughout the world with new waves of democracy occurring in Eastern Europe, Latin America and Asia; but in contrast fewer people are willing to turn out and vote in many Western democracies, most notably in Britain and the United States. Consequently there are increasing concerns about changes in society that are undermining the effectiveness of democratic institutions such as government and causing the public to turn away from them. These changes include a growing public cynicism about politics and a widespread disaffection with political institutions, a decline in the institutions that underpin civic society and democracy such as political parties, and the long-term decline in electoral turnout in the majority of democratic countries.

This political disengagement is highly evident within British society, where public attitudes in the first decade of the twenty-first century appear to revolve around fear and distrust, with cynicism and suspicion abounding on the integrity of politicians and their styles of governance. As a nation, Britain is becoming more distrustful of its politicians and government and electoral participation appears to be in 'meltdown'. In the 2001 British election turnout reached an all-time low, with 59.4 per cent of the British public voting (Mori figures). In the 2005 election, when turnout might have been expected to be higher because of public anger over the Iraq war, turnout only increased to 61 per cent. Of particular concern though are the attitudes of young people towards electoral politics – most visible through the high proportion of them failing to vote in elections.

Young people in Britain have been lambasted by journalists for their continuing failure to vote, for example Polly Toynbee has described them as 'airheads' and 'know-nothings' and Nigella Lawson has argued they 'should be treated with contempt'. Politicians, keen to catch their votes have tried a number of initiatives including *'Rock the Vote'* (1997) – a cross-party alliance that aimed to encourage young people to register to vote, and more recently Labour's personal text messages to the mobile phones of young people to remind them to vote. The filmic qualities of Labour's 2001 advertising campaign were also perceived by young people as specifically designed for them (even though they were not).

So what are young peoples' attitudes and behaviour towards electoral politics?

Youth electoral attitudes and behaviour

We will start by examining their electoral behaviour. In the 1997 British general election, 43 per cent of 18–24 year olds did not vote, in 2001 this increased to 61 per cent abstention, and in 2005 63 per cent abstained (Mori figures). Research indicates this abstention is not confined to national elections; it also includes local and European elections where youth turnout at each election point is progressively deteriorating. An evaluation of the evidence on youth electoral attitudes and behaviour signifies some alarming trends, and signals very strongly that young people are very isolated compared with other electoral segments in Britain:

- Turnout at elections is lower for 18–24 year olds than older voters, and the drop in turnout indicates an increasing predisposition among this younger age group not to vote in elections.
- Young people are less interested in national political issues than older adults; and they know less about the election process.
- Young people perceive politicians and governments as dishonest and inefficacious – contributing to their belief that voting is a 'worthless' act or creating anger resulting in the withholding of their vote.
- Young people feel alienated from British society, and are therefore not voting.
- Globalisation is undermining the credibility and authority of national governments – destabilising faith in a nation's elected officials and reinforcing youth electoral apathy.
- Electoral civic-mindedness is less strong in young people than it is in older adults, contributing to non-voting behaviour, or more self-centred voting behaviour.

These trends reflect negative attitudinal positions – revolving around trust, cynicism and personal political efficacy.

Trust involves a positive evaluation of the performance of governments, parties and leaders, combined with optimism and confidence in their intentions to do 'good'. Cynicism involves a negative evaluation – the expectation that these bodies will not act in the public's best interests, and may intentionally harm them. The negative evaluations of young people signals that their appraisals are not positive, and that they are not hopeful or certain of the 'good' intentions of these bodies. Indeed, recent research confirms that young people are highly cynical of politicians and leaders; with significant proportions of them agreeing that 'politicians lie to the media and the public', 'candidates for office are only interested in people's votes not their opinions' and 'politicians lose touch with the people once elected'. These negative evaluations, can, however, be counterbalanced by a strong sense of personal political efficacy. Personal political efficacy is the feeling that the political action of individuals can influence the behaviour and policies of government, parties and politicians – it is a feeling of empowerment. The strength of personal political efficacy is derived from individuals' political competence, essentially their level of political interest and knowledge, executed through their political experiences. Thus, a strong sense of personal political efficacy evolves from successful experiences that cultivate confidence and expertise, for example successfully petitioning for a Marine Conservation Bill, while unsuccessful experiences, for example the failure of the anti-war and anti-tuition fees protests, can reduce individuals strength of political efficacy, increase their cynicism and decrease their trust. In order to help you understand the consequences of these attitudes, you need to be aware of the nature of our consumer culture, which has generated individuals who believe they are empowered, self-knowingly unique and enterprising. As a result increasing numbers of young people who choose to vote will act as consumers who seek choices that offer high personal efficacy for them. This means they will vote *if* they think that their vote will make a positive difference to their lives and those of their friends and family, and possibly, more widely to elements of British and global society that they care about – and as 'empowered voter-consumers', they will vote even if they are highly cynical.

Figure 5.9 portrays *some* of the relationships between trust, cynicism and personal efficacy and electoral engagement and political alienation. For example, low trust, high distrust, high cynicism and low personal efficacy feed young peoples' feelings of alienation from electoral politics, thereby contributing to non-voting behaviour. Essentially such politically alienated individuals have no political hope, faith or confidence; they are politically sceptical, highly cynical and ever wary and watchful of government, politicians and parties. It is therefore not surprising that so many young people feel very politically estranged and are therefore not voting. Yet as you can see from this model, high personal efficacy is important because it can overcome highly cynical attitudes to facilitate voting behaviour.

So should politicians just give up on this generation and focus their attention on active voters? Are they completely lost? While there is some merit in this suggestion, from a marketing perspective that focuses on gaining 'winnable' customers, this is not an option for regenerating civic society. While marketers would not normally advocate trying to win 'angry customers', this is exactly what politicians need to do if they are to restore young peoples' confidence in them.

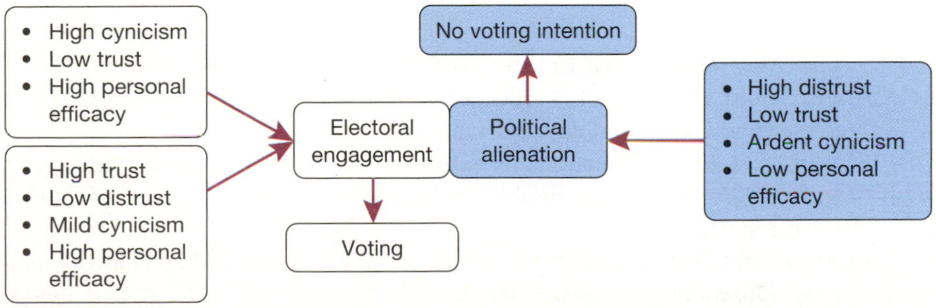

Figure 5.9 Dimensions of electoral engagement and alienation

Yet how can this be achieved?

Well, while this generation are angry, their cynicism will not always prevent them from voting if their personal political efficacy is high. Personal political efficacy is therefore very important in any efforts to reconnect with this disengaged age group. The marketing communications challenge therefore becomes one of designing campaigns to build the personal political efficacy of young people in order to increase their trust in parties and leaders and consequently reduce their feelings of political alienation. The difficulty of this task, however, should not be underestimated!

MiniCase questions:

1. For the majority of you, you will just have read an account of people in the same age group as yourself (18–24 year olds).
   a) How closely does the account above reflect yourself and your attitudes towards politicians and voting? If you are different, why are you different? Could it be your personality? The way you perceive the world? The way you learn?
   b) In order to represent this group more fully, create a pictorial representation of them – using visuals and text from magazines, newspapers, web sites, photographs, print ads, etc. You may create a multiple image that includes both genders, ethnicity, etc., or individual pictures of different segments. Support your pictures with accompanying explanations.
2. What forms of personal political efficacy do you think should be encouraged? How would your suggestions increase young peoples' trust in government, the prime minister, parties and politicians? How could the building of personal political efficacy influence cynicism? Can you envisage any problems if personal political efficacy is increased among this age group (18–24)? Are there examples where the personal efficacy of this age group has been developed in other contexts and/or countries? Elaborate on your findings in drawing your conclusions.
3. Role play: You work within a premiere marcoms agency and have just won the account for (please choose one):
   a) The Labour Party
   b) The Conservative Party
   c) The Electoral Commission.

   In teams, develop a marcoms campaign for 18–21-year-olds eligible to vote for the first time that you believe will increase their personal political efficacy and, in so doing, overcome the obstacles created by their cynicism and low trust, resulting in a very positive disposition towards voting in a forthcoming British general election. Your campaign should include objectives, segmentation, positioning and communications and media strategies as well as creative work. Your ideas must be realistic and you must work to the budget given to you by your tutor. It is critical that you justify your campaign.

   You may include your pictorial representations from question (1b) and the conclusions you have drawn from question (2).

References

Anon. (2004) Apple Computer: iPod Silhouettes. *New York American Marketing Association*, Effie Awards, Retrieved 12 February 2006 from www.nyama.org.

Ajzen, I. and Fishbein, M. (1980) *Understanding Attitudes and Predicting Social Behavior*. Englewood Cliffs, NJ: Prentice-Hall.

Bainbridge, J. (2007) Functionality extends reach. *Marketing*, 19 September, 34–5.

Belk, R. (1975) Situational variables in consumer behaviour. *Journal of Consumer Research*, **2** (December), 57–64.

Burke, R. and Srull, T.K. (1988) Competitive interference and consumer memory for advertising. *Journal of Consumer Research*, **15** (June), 55–68.

Challis, G., Lustig, B., Wood, J., Bisnet, L. and Carter, S. (2006) Felix – continuity saved the cat. *Institute of Practitioners in Advertising*, IPA Effectiveness Awards.

Cobau, S. (2000) DeBeers Consolidated Mines Ltd: a diamond is forever campaign. *Encyclopedia of Major Marketing Campaigns*, **1**. Retrieved 10 August 2007 from: http://www.warc.com/ArticleCenter/Default.asp?CType=A&AID=WORDSEARCH84137&Tab=A.

Cohen, J. and Basu, K. (1987) Alternative models of categorisation. *Journal of Consumer Research* (March), 455–72.

Dahl, D.W., Frankenberger, D. and Manchanda, R.V. (2003) Does it pay to shock? *Journal of Advertising Research*, **43**(3), September, 268–80.

de Chernatony L. (1993) The seven building blocks of brands. *Management Today* (March), 66–7.

Engel, F., Blackwell, R. and Minniard, P. (1990) *Consumer Behaviour*, 6th edn. New York: Dryden Press.

Evans, M., Jamal, A. and Foxall, G. (2006) *Consumer Behavior*, Chichester: Wiley.

Goodrich, J.N. (1978) The relationship between preferences for and perceptions of vacation destinations: application of a choice model. *Journal of Travel Research*, **17**(2), 8–13.

Grass, R.C. and Wallace, H.W. (1969) Satiation effects of TV commercials. *Journal of Advertising Research*, **9**(3), 3–9.

Guildford, J. (1959) *Personality*. New York: McGraw-Hill.

Hansen, F. (1972) *Consumer Choice Behaviour: A Cognitive Theory*. New York: Free Press.

Hawkins, D., Best, R. and Coney, K. (1989) *Consumer Behavior*. Homewood, IL: Richard D. Irwin.

Hui, B. (2005) Tropicana – 'Breakfast in New York', *Marketing*, 11 May 2005. Retrieved 17 October 2007 from www.brandrepublic.com/News/474954/.

Huzzey, A., Wood, J., Leaver, R., Garcia, M. and Binet, L. (2006) Tropicana – how Big Apple helped sell orange juice, *IPA Effectiveness Awards*, Institute of Practitioners in Advertising. Retrieved 10 August 2007 from http://www.warc.com/ArticleCenter/Default.asp?CType=A&AID=WORDSEARCH82627&Tab=A.

Javalgi, R., Thomas, E. and Rao, S. (1992) US travellers' perception of selected European destinations. *European Journal of Marketing*, **26**(7), 45–64.

Jones, H. (2007) Cool operator. *The Marketer*, September, 25–9.

Lasn, K. (1999) *Culture Jam: The Uncooling of America*, New York: Eagle Brook.

McGuire, W. (1978) An information processing model of advertising effectiveness. In *Behavioral and Management Science in Marketing* (eds H.J. Davis and A.J. Silk), 156–80. New York: Ronald Press.

Moran, W. (1990) Brand preference and the perceptual frame, *Journal of Advertising Research* (October/November), 9–16.

Nottage, A. (2007) Clarity will boost consumer trust. *Marketing*, 10 October, 21.

Petty, R.E. and Cacioppo, J.T. (1979) Effects of message repetition and position on cognitive responses, recall and persuasion. *Journal of Personality and Social Psychology*, **37** (January), 97–109.

QED (1989) It's not easy being a dolphin. BBCTV.

Schiffman, L. and Kanuk, L. (1991) *Consumer Behavior*. Englewood Cliffs, NJ: Prentice-Hall.

Skinner, B.F. (1953) *Science and Human Behavior*. New York: Macmillan.

Solomon, M., Bamossy, G., Askegaard, S. and Hogg, M.K. (2007) *Consumer Behaviour: A European Perspective*, 2nd edn, Harlow: Prentice-Hall.

Strong, E.C. (1977) The spacing and timing of advertising. *Journal of Advertising Research*, **17** (December), 25–31.

Williams, K.C. (1981) *Behavioural Aspects of Marketing*. London: Heinemann.

Winterman, D. (2007) Just returning your call . . . to the UK, *BBC News Magazine* Wednesday, 14 February 2007. Retrieved 15 January 2008 from http://news.bbc.co.uk/1/hi/magazine/6353491.stm

Zielske, H.A. (1959) The remembering and forgetting of advertising. *Journal of Marketing*, **23** (January), 239–43.

Chapter 6

Customer decision-making

Customers make product purchase-related decisions in different ways. Understanding the ways in which buyers make decisions and the factors that impact upon the decision process can affect the effectiveness of marketing communications. In particular, it can influence message structure, content and scheduling.

Aims and learning objectives

The aim of this chapter is to consider some of the different processes consumers and organisational buyers use to make purchase decisions and relate these to marketing communications.

The learning objectives of this chapter are to:

1. explain the general process through which purchase decisions are made;
2. examine the sequence and methods used by consumers to make decisions;
3. explore the components of perceived risk;
4. introduce and explain involvement theory and relate it to planned communication activities;
5. consider the different types of individual who contribute to purchase decisions made by organisations;
6. understand the stages that organisations use to make purchase decisions;
7. appreciate the differences in the approaches and content of marketing communications between consumer and organisational buying.

For an applied interpretation see Poonam V. Kumar and Prasad Narasimhan's MiniCase entitled ***Understanding consumers' needs: the success of the Apache motorcycle in India*** at the end of this chapter.

Introduction

An understanding of the contextual elements that impact upon individual purchase decision-making and the overall process through which individuals behave and ultimately make decisions is an important first stage in the development of any marketing communications plan. Knowledge of a buyer's decision-making processes is vital if the correct type of information is to be communicated at the right time and in the right or appropriate manner. There are two broad types of buyer: consumers and organisational buyers. First, consideration will be given to a general decision-making process and then an insight into the characteristics of the decision-making processes for consumers and organisational buyers will be presented. The chapter concludes with a consideration of the differences between the two main approaches.

Knowledge of a buyer's decision-making processes is vital if the correct type of information is to be communicated at the right time.

A general buying decision-making process

Figure 6.1 shows that there are five stages to the general process whereby buyers make purchase decisions and implement them. Marketing communications can impact upon any or all of these stages with varying levels of potential effectiveness.

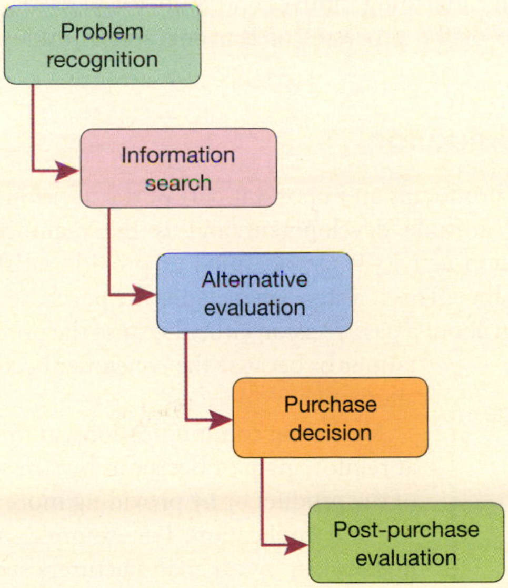

Figure 6.1 Five general stages of a buyer's purchase decision process

Problem recognition

Problem recognition occurs when there is a perceived difference between an individual's ideal state and reality. Advertisers often induce 'problem recognition' by suggesting that the current state is not desirable or by demonstrating how consumers can tell whether they have a similar problem (e.g. 'Is your hair dull and lifeless?'). The

Problem recognition occurs when there is a perceived difference between an individual's ideal state and reality.

difficulty in getting buyers to recognise that they have a problem invites the question, do they actually have a problem? If there is no identified need, then it is not marketing but selling that is being practised.

Information search

Having identified a problem a prospective buyer will search for information in an attempt to resolve it. There are two main areas of search activity: the internal search involves a memory scan to recall experiences and knowledge, utilising the perceptual processes to see whether there is an 'off-the-shelf' solution. If there is no 'off-the-shelf' solution, the prospective buyer will resort to an external search. This will involve family and friends, the web, reference sources and commercial guides and advertising.

Alternative evaluation

Potential solutions need to be evaluated in order that the optimum choice be made. Products considered feasible constitute the *preference set*, and it is from these seven or eight products that a smaller group of products is normally assembled. This is referred to as the *evoked set* (or repertoire) and it is from this that consumers make a choice. Attributes used to determine the sets are referred to as evaluative criteria. Very often these attributes are both objective and subjective in nature.

Purchase decision

Having evaluated various solutions, the buyer may develop a predisposition to make a purchase. This will involve matching motives and evaluative criteria with product attributes. This necessitates the use of the processes of learning and attitude formation, discussed in Chapter 5.

Post-purchase evaluation

Direct experience of the product is an important part of the decision process. Feedback from use helps learning and attitude development and is the main contributor to long-run behaviour. Communication activity must continue to provide satisfaction and prevent the onset of cognitive dissonance. This is a state where, after the purchase decision has been made, a buyer might feel tension about a past decision either because the product fails to reach expectations or because the consumer becomes aware of a superior alternative.

Marketing communications, at this stage, should be aimed at reinforcing past decisions by stressing the positive features of the product or by providing more information to assist its use and application.

Marketing communications, at this stage, should be aimed at reinforcing past decisions by stressing the positive features of the product or by providing more information to assist its use and application. For example, much of the advertising undertaken by car manufacturers seeks to prevent the onset of tension and purchase dissatisfaction.

Types of consumer decision-making

Buyers do not follow the general decision sequence at all times. The procedure may vary depending upon the time available, levels of perceived risk and the degree of involvement a buyer has with the type of product. Perceived risk and involvement are issues that will be covered later. At this point three types of problem solving behaviour (extended problem solving, limited problem solving and routinised response) will be considered.

Extended problem solving (EPS)

Consumers considering the purchase of a car or house undertake a great deal of external search activity and spend a lot of time reaching a solution that satisfies, as closely as possible, the evaluative criteria previously set. This activity is usually associated with products that are unfamiliar, where direct experience and hence knowledge are weak, and where there is considerable financial risk.

Marketing communications should aim to provide a lot of information to assist the decision process. The provision of information through sales literature, such as brochures and leaflets, web sites for determining product and purchase criteria in product categories where there is little experience, access to salespersons and demonstrations and advertisements are just some of the ways in which information can be provided.

Marketing communications should aim to provide a lot of information to assist the decision process.

Limited problem solving (LPS)

Having experience of a product means that greater use can be made of internal memory-based search routines, and the external search can be limited to obtaining up-to-date information or ensuring that the finer points of the decision have been investigated.

Marketing communications should attempt to provide information about any product modification or new attributes and convey messages which highlight those key attributes known to be important to buyers. By differentiating the product, marketing communications provide the buyer with a reason to select that particular product.

ViewPoint 6.1 Boots deep into magazines

One of the advantages of publishing an own brand magazine, as proclaimed by the customer publishing industry, is that customers spend on average 25 minutes (not seconds) reading a magazine. They are often used to prevent brand switching and as part of a coordinated marketing communications strategy, they serve to engage readers and keep them interested in the brand. They provide opportunities to present new products, a reason to visit the web site or store and can be perceived as a thank you for previous custom.

Boots publish Health & Beauty, six times a year, targeted at women 25–55 who hold the brand's Advantage Card. They claim that the magazine is used to meet three key objectives. These are to communicate brand values, reward its most valuable customers and drive sales, not necessarily in that order.

The magazine has produced some remarkable results. Over £10 million in incremental sales, 65 per cent of readers say it makes them more interested in visiting the store while products featured in the magazine experience an average sales increase of 35 per cent.

Source: Fry (2006).

Question

To what extent do you think customer magazines help extended or limited decision making?

Task

Get a copy of two customer magazines for brands competing in the same market. How do they compare and which do you prefer?

Routinised response behaviour (RRB)

For a great number of products the decision process will consist only of an internal search. This is primarily because the buyer has made a number of purchases and has accumulated a great deal of experience. Therefore, only an internal search is necessary, so little time or effort will be spent on external search activities. Low-value items which are frequently purchased fall into this category, for example toothpaste, soap, tinned foods and confectionery.

Some outlets are perceived as suitable for what are regarded as distress purchases. Tesco Express and many petrol stations position themselves as convenience stores for distress purchases (for example, a pint of milk at 10 p.m.). Many garages have positioned themselves as convenience stores suitable for meeting the needs of RRB purchases. In doing so they are moving themselves away from the perception of being only a distress purchase outlet.

Communicators should focus on keeping the product within the evoked set.

Communicators should focus on keeping the product within the evoked set or getting it into the set. Learning can be enhanced through repetition of messages, but repetition can also be used to maintain attention and awareness.

Perceived risk

Risk concerns the uncertainty of a proposed purchase and the outcomes that will result from a decision to purchase a product.

An important factor associated with the purchase decision process is the level of risk perceived by the buyer. This risk concerns the uncertainty of a proposed purchase and the outcomes that will result from a decision to purchase a product.

Risk is perceived because the buyer has little or no experience of the performance of the product or the decision process associated with the purchase. Buyers may lack the ability to make what they see as the right decision and they may be forced to trade the decision to purchase one product in lieu of another because resources, such as time and money, are restricted. Risk is related to not only brand-based decisions but also to product categories, an especially important aspect when launching new technology products, for example. The level of risk an individual experiences varies through time and across products, and is often a reflection of an individual's propensity to manage risk. Risk is related to involvement, trust and other buyer behaviour concepts.

There are five main forms of risk.

Settle and Alreck (1989) suggest that there are five main forms of risk that can be identified; the purchase of a hi-fi unit demonstrates each element. These are set out in Table 6.1 with respect to the purchase of a hi-fi system.

A sixth element, time, is also considered to be a risk factor (Stone and Gronhaug, 1993). Using the hi-fi example, will purchase of the unit lead to an inefficient use of my time? Or can I afford the time to search for a good hi-fi so that I will not waste my money?

Table 6.1 Types of perceived risk

Type of perceived risk	Explanation
Performance	Will the unit reproduce my music clearly?
Financial	Can I afford that much or should I buy a less expensive version?
Physical	Will the unit damage my other systems or endanger me in any way?
Social	Will my friends and colleagues be impressed?
Ego	Will I feel as good as I want to feel when listening to or talking about my unit?

What constitutes risk is a function of the contextual characteristics of each situation, the individuals involved and the product under consideration:

What constitutes risk is a function of the contextual characteristics of each situation, the individuals involved and the product under consideration.

1. Each situation varies according to perceptions of the shopping experience, the time the purchase is to be made in the context of the other activities that need to be completed (last chance to buy a birthday present, only 15 minutes left before meeting my partner), and the image different stores have and the risk that is associated with the products offered by the store.
2. Each individual has a propensity to higher or lower levels of risk. These levels may vary according to their experience of purchasing particular products, demographic factors such as age, level of education and religion, and various personality factors.
3. The product may, if only for price, convey a level of risk to the purchaser. For example, the purchase of a car is not only a large financial commitment for most people, but is also a highly emotive decision that has significant ego and social risks attached to it.

Perceived risk need not be constant throughout the decision process. Mitchell and Boustani (1994) suggest that the level of perceived risk may vary as depicted in Figure 6.2, although more work is required to determine the validity of their initial findings.

The main question is, how can buyers be helped to alleviate high levels of risk during the pre- and post-purchase stages in the decision process? The main method used by buyers is the acquisition of information. Information through the mass media, through word-of-mouth communications and through personal selling (usually sales representatives) is used to set out the likely outcomes and so reduce the levels of risk. Brand loyalty can also be instrumental in reducing risk when launching new products. The use of guarantees, third-party endorsements, money-back offers (some car manufacturers offer the opportunity to return a car within 30 days or exchange it for a different model) and trial samples (as used by many hair care products) are well-used devices to reduce risk.

ViewPoint 6.2 Back page risk reducers

Many print-based direct response advertisements use a variety of ways to reduce the risk inherent in buying 'off the back page'. Holiday companies, direct wine and book clubs use a variety of sales channels but web-based companies and direct response magazine advertisements provide a rich source of business.

Magazine advertisements, often to be found on or near the back of magazines and Sunday newspaper supplements, allow for a large amount of text as well as the eye-catching visual work. The text is often used to reduce functional risk by explaining the features and extolling the benefits of the product or service. Social and ego risks are reduced by setting the right visual scene and depicting people using the product who may be seen as either aspirational or represent the target market.

Financial risk is reduced through opportunities to buy now at a reduced or discounted price (credit card) and promises of warrantees and money back guarantees further reduce the uncertainty of this form of exchange. Finally, time risk is reduced through buy now opportunities and delivery to the door, negating the need to travel, park, browse, compare, decide and carry home the purchase.

Question

With so many different forms of risk, can advertising be used to eliminate them all?

Task

Get a copy of a magazine that accompanies many weekend newspapers, look at the direct response ads and identify the ways in which perceived risk is reduced.

THE SUNDAY TIMES WINE Club
The Perfect Festive Dozen – plus 3 Rioja FREE!
SAVE £21
100% Money Back GUARANTEE
The Club's guarantee is total. If you don't like any wine, for any reason, we'll refund you. No problem.
The Perfect Festive Dozen
£71.88 £49.99 (+ £5.99 delivery) SAVE £21.89
call 0870 444 7200
www.sundaytimeswineclub.co.uk/ZK31
Quote: ZK31 Weekdays 8am–11pm Weekends 8am–9pm
As the festive season approaches, we've picked 12 stunning wines (with a £21.89 saving!) for you to savour with friends and family over the indulgent dinners ahead ...
The Club's Perfect Festive Dozen is yours for JUST £49.99 and comes with three magnicent Rioja FREE. What's more, in-depth tasting notes are also included to help you savour each wine to the full – and impress your dinner party guests!
The case opens with tongue-tingling Sauvignon Blanc from Chile that makes a mouthwatering apéritif. Crisp Italian Pinot Grigio is simply superb with smoked salmon and your lively Chardonnay, made by a master of French winemaking, is a worthy accompaniment to your Christmas turkey.
For a rich main course you have luxurious claret from the extraordinary 2005 vintage. Then there's powerful, spicy Shiraz from a hotshot Aussie winemaker for sipping by the reside, plus plummy Chilean Merlot that was recommended by Decanter magazine and goes surprisingly well with dark chocolate!
Don't forget your three bottles of Rioja (worth £19.95). They come from a respected family-run winery and are free with your Perfect Festive Dozen.
Hurry! You must order by December 17th for guaranteed Christmas delivery – Don't delay!
LIMITED STOCKS – ORDER TODAY
YES, please send me the Perfect Festive Dozen for JUST £49.99 (+ £5.99 delivery)
Title Initials Surname
Address
Postcode
Kindly indicate a safe place to leave if out
Daytime Telephone Evening Telephone
e-mail address
Ref: ZK31
Valid from date: Expiry date: Maestro issue number:
Signature Date

Exhibit 6.1

Sunday Times Direct Wine

This offer went out on 8 December 2007 in the *Saturday Times Magazine*. The circulation was approximately 750k and the ad generated a response that was 60 per cent ahead of forecast with a total of 216 new customers applying for the offer.

Direct Wines Ltd.

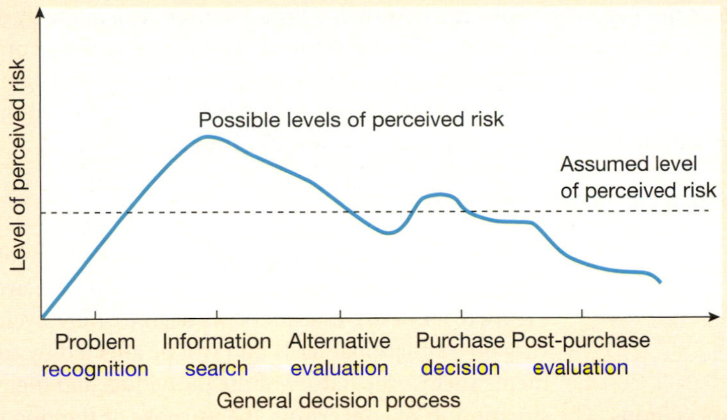

Figure 6.2 Varying levels of perceived risk through the purchase decision process
Source: Adapted from Mitchell and Boustani (1994). © Emerald Group Publishing Limited. All rights reserved.

Appreciating the level and types of risk buyers perceive is important for many marketing activities. As Mitchell (1999) points out, new product development, segmentation, targeting, positioning and marketing communications can all be influenced by understanding perceived risk. Services, he points out, have been shown to carry higher levels of risk, mainly because of their characteristics of heterogeneity, perishability, inseparability and intangibility which serve to undermine buyer confidence. For example, Ashford *et al.* (2000) refer to the perceived risk associated with dental care and mention fear and anxiety, the internal environment of the practice, dentists' social and communication skills and patient satisfaction as important elements that may interrelate and influence attitudes and behavioural intentions.

Many direct marketing advertisements in magazines seek to reduce a number of different types of risk (see Exhibit 6.1). Companies offering wine for direct home delivery, for example, try to reduce performance risk by providing information about each wine being offered. Financial risk is reduced by comparing their 'special' prices with those in the High Street, social risk is approached by developing the brand name associations trying to improve credibility, and time risk is reduced through the convenience of home delivery.

Many direct marketing advertisements in magazines seek to reduce a number of different types of risk.

Involvement theory

A central framework, critical to understanding consumer decision-making behaviour and associated communications, is involvement theory. Purchase decisions made by consumers vary considerably, and one of the factors thought to be key to brand choice decisions is the level of involvement (in terms of importance and relevance) a consumer has with either the product or the purchase process.

A central framework, critical to understanding consumer decision-making behaviour and associated communications, is involvement theory.

The term 'involvement' has become an important concept in the consumer behaviour literature. The concept has its roots in social psychology, but its current form and interpretation by researchers is both interesting and revealing. There is no consensus on a definition of involvement. Kapferer and Laurent (1985) argue that involvement has five different facets. These are interest, risk importance, risk probability, sign value and hedonic value. Their approach tends to be all-consuming, whereas Ratchford (1987), quoting Zaichkowsky (1985) and others, does not perceive involvement as such a broad matter. The majority of researchers do not recognise the importance of hedonic and sign value elements in this context. To some, involvement is about the ego, perceived risk and purchase importance – a cognitive perspective. To those who favour a behavioural perspective, the search for and evaluation of product-oriented information is pertinent (Schiffman and Kanuk, 1991).

Involvement: characteristics

> The various characteristics associated with the involvement concept can be considered in three phases.

The various characteristics associated with the involvement concept can be considered in three phases. These are depicted at Figure 6.3. Phase 1 considers the degree of involvement that will vary on a situational basis and will be affected by contextual elements such as the nature of the individual and their experiences, values and expectations. The situation itself concerning the purpose of the purchase (e.g. gift or own consumption) will also affect the level of involvement. The product or service will also be a factor taking account of whether the individual has direct or indirect experience of the object. In addition, the nature of the stimulus to purchase will also be an important factor, whether this be an advertisement, friend or general need.

Phase 2 is characterised by three main factors. The intensity of involvement reflects the level or degree of personal relevance and is normally seen as either high or low involvement. The focus of the involvement refers to whether the object or the communications surrounding the product are of primary importance. The third factor concerns the duration of the involvement. Essentially this may be temporary (e.g. if motivated by an advertisement seen for the first time, or buying a gift) or it may be longer lasting or enduring, reflecting some form of loyalty, commitment or interest in the object or product category.

Phase 3 concerns the outcomes or responses individuals give as a consequence of the involvement they experience. The manner and speed at which information is processed (as a result of the level of involvement) leads primarily to either attitudes being formed prior to behaviour (high involvement) or attitudes being formed after product experience or behaviour (low involvement).

The implications for those responsible for marketing communications are many and varied. However, where high involvement is present messages should stress attributes and

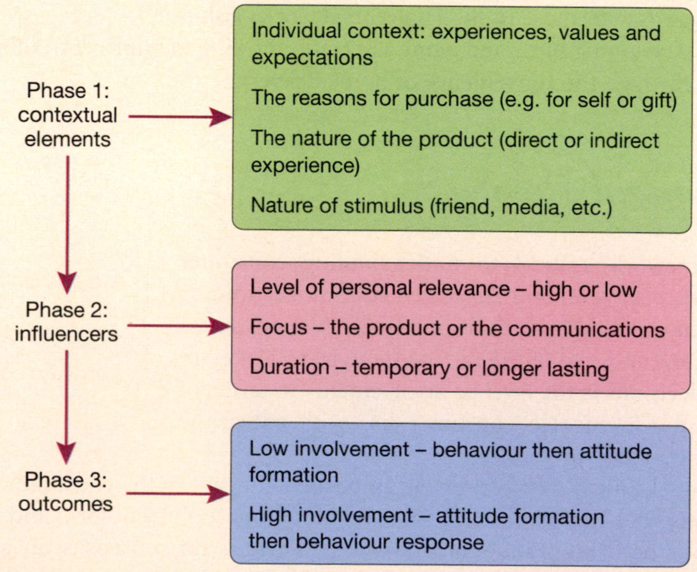

Figure 6.3 Three phases of individual involvement and attitude development

benefits (functional) so that they feed the more rational, considered information processing style that accompanies this position. Where there is low involvement it is better to use more emotional (expressive) messages simply because individuals do not expend any considered or conscious effort in processing the information.

Following this analysis of the involvement process, it is interesting to consider Laaksonen's (1994) interpretation where he draws upon three perspectives of involvement from the literature. These are the cognitive, predisposition to act and response-based interpretations.

He proposes that the *cognitive view* of involvement regards the perceived personal relevance of an object to an individual as of paramount importance. This approach refers to the strength or extent of the cognitive/attitude structure towards an object. The strength of the psychological linkage between an individual and a stimulus object determines the intensity of involvement. How important is it to purchase a Wii? This intensity of attitude is seen to have originated from social judgement theory, where involvement is seen as a variable affected by how others might interpret a purchase; that is, their predisposition to respond to a Wii.

The second perspective regards involvement as an individual state or *predisposition to act*. Here, involvement focuses on the mental state of an individual, evoked by a stimulus. It is the degree of perceived importance, the interest or level of emotional attachment, arousal, drive or motivation that defines the intensity of involvement, either present in an individual or present in any given situation. Using the previous analogy, how motivated is the individual to purchase a Wii? Therefore, involvement refers to the motivational state of an individual in a specific situation. The goals and their importance (hierarchy) defined by individuals determine the direction (towards an object/advertisement or perhaps the act of purchasing) and the level (high, medium, low) of involvement. Again, involvement is regarded as a mediating variable in information processing and a predisposition to act.

Involvement is regarded as a mediating variable in information processing and a predisposition to act.

The third perspective is the *response view*. Here involvement is regarded as a reaction to an external stimulus or stimuli such as marketing communications. These responses are typically characterised by the form of cognitive and behavioural processing (learn–feel–do) directed to accomplishing a task. So the response view of involvement is based on the reaction of an individual to a stimulus, which will affect the learn–feel–do sequence and the depth to which processing occurs. Therefore, the impact of promotional messages for the Wii is likely to be most important in determining the direction and purchase intentions of potential game station purchasers. Here, involvement is considered as a cognitive response to the marketing communication messages (Batra and Ray, 1983). These views do not see involvement as a mediating variable, simply because involvement is regarded as 'an actualised response in itself' (Laaksonen, 1994).

Of these three, no one view can be determined as a correct interpretation. In a way all are wrong and all are right simultaneously. There is agreement among many researchers that involvement should be seen in the context of three main states. These are high, low and zero involvement. The last of these is self-explanatory and requires no additional comment. The other two states are portrayed as two discrete ends of a continuum. Consumers are thought to move along this continuum, from high to low, as purchase experience increases, perceived risk is reduced and levels of overall knowledge improve.

The approach taken here is that involvement is about the degree of personal relevance and risk perceived by members of the target market in a particular purchase situation (Rossiter *et al.*, 1991). This implies that the level of involvement may vary through time as each member of the target market becomes more (or less) familiar with the purchase and associated communications. At the point of decision-making, involvement is either high or low, not some point on a sliding scale or a point on a continuum between two extremes. Involvement is a cognitively bound concept, the strength and depth of which varies among and between individuals.

Involvement is about the degree of personal relevance and risk perceived by members of the target market in a particular purchase situation.

High involvement

High involvement occurs when a consumer perceives an expected purchase that is not only of high personal relevance but also represents a high level of perceived risk. Cars, washing machines, houses and insurance policies are seen as 'big ticket' items, infrequent purchases that promote a great deal of involvement. The risk described is financial, but, as noted earlier, risk can take other forms. Therefore, the choice of perfume, suit, dress or jewellery may also represent high involvement, with social risk dominating the purchase decision. Consumers therefore, devote a great deal of time to researching the intended purchase and collecting as much information as possible in order to reduce, as far as possible, levels of perceived risk.

Low involvement

A *low-involvement* state of mind regarding a purchase suggests little threat or risk to the consumer. Low-priced items such as washing powder, baked beans and breakfast cereals are bought frequently, and past experience of the product class and the brand cues the consumer into a purchase that requires little information or support. Items such as alcoholic and soft drinks, cigarettes and chocolate are also normally seen as low involvement, but they induce a strong sense of ego risk associated with the self-gratification that is attached to the consumption of these products.

ViewPoint 6.3 Using sporting heroes to groom men

Men's grooming products have traditionally been regarded as evoking low involvement but the sector has started to change in recent years, especially within the younger male age groups.

Early in 2007 Gillette announced that Tiger Woods, Thierry Henry and Roger Federer had been appointed as their new brand ambassadors. All three have been used across global print and broadcast advertising, consumer promotions, point-of-sale materials, online and public relations in support of Gillette premium shaving products. The choice of these particular ambassadors is said to complement the brand values, as they were selected not only for their outstanding sporting accomplishments, but also for their behaviour away from sport in terms of their charitable actions, support of social causes and for their reputations upholding sporting values. In January 2008 Gillette launched their first TV campaign featuring the three champions supported by a web site, magazine and outdoor work.

Encouraged by these types of key sporting and celebrity endorsers men are becoming more overtly involved with their appearance, health and fitness. As a result some parts of the sector are now becoming more involved with the products and the category.

In a sector where brands such as Nivea, King of Shaves, Easy4men and the recently launched Gillette Fusion have grown to satisfy this new market opportunity, care over the presentation of these products is important. Care over the packaging, naming and merchandising of these products is necessary in order to communicate effectively with those men who prefer to be 'involved' with grooming products. It is necessary to use male vocabulary and to avoid effeminate or softer suggestive words. The focus should be on the functionality and performance of the product and to convey masculinity through acronyms such as DDS (for Dual Delivery Systems) rather than phrases such as natural herbs, essence or plant extracts. Brand names such as Perfector, Enhancer, Defender and Improver are more likely to resonate well with modern man. LabSeries Skincare for Men for example, uses the line 'High-tec, high performance, high results' on its web site.

Sources: Gray (2004); Davidson (2008); Tungate (2008). www.pg.com/news/gillette_champions.jhtml.

Question

Why do many men appear reluctant to involve themselves in grooming products?

Task

David Beckham used to endorse Gillette. Which brands does he support now?

Hedonic consumption

There is a range of products and services that can evoke high levels of involvement based on the emotional impact that consumption provides the buyer. This is referred to as hedonic consumption, and Hirschmann and Holbrook (1982) describe this approach as 'those facets of consumer behaviour that relate to the multi sensory, fantasy and emotive aspects of one's experience with products'. With its roots partly in the motivation research and partly in the cognitive processing schools, this interpretation of consumer behaviour seeks to explain how and why buyers experience emotional responses to the act of purchase and consumption of particular products. *Historical imagery* occurs when, for example, the colour of a dress, the scent of a perfume or cologne, or the aroma of a restaurant or food

There is a range of products and services that can evoke high levels of involvement based on the emotional impact that consumption provides the buyer.

Exhibit 6.2 Romance by Ralph Lauren
An example of romantic fantasy used for fragrance advertising.
Courtesy of Ralph Lauren Fragrances.

can trigger an individual's memory to replay an event. In contrast, *fantasy imagery* occurs when a buyer constructs an event, drawing together various colours, sounds and shapes to compose a mental experience of an event that has not occurred previously. Consumers imagine a reality in which they derive sensory pleasure. Some smokers were encouraged to imagine themselves as 'Marlboro Men': not just masculine, but as idealised cowboys (Hirschmann and Holbrook, 1982).

The advertising of fragrances and luxury brands is often based on images that encourage individuals to project themselves into a desirable or pleasurable environment or situation.

The advertising of fragrances and luxury brands is often based on images that encourage individuals to project themselves into a desirable or pleasurable environment or situation, for example, those which foster romantic associations. Some people form strong associations with particular fragrances and use this to develop and maintain specific images. Advertising is used to create and support these images and in doing so enhance the emotional benefits derived from fragrance brand associations. As Retiveau (2007) indicates, hedonics are closely related and influence the simultaneous perception of fragrances. The Ralph Lauren *Romance* ad (Exhibit 6.2) is an excellent example of a romantic/fantasy message. The visual depicts strong sensory and masculinity properties designed to appeal to a particular female target market. The ad evokes a sense of nostalgia contemporised by the choice of rugged footwear.

There are a number of challenges with this approach, namely measurement factors of reliability and validity, but, nevertheless, appreciating the dreams, ideals and desires of the target audience can be an important contribution to the creation of promotional messages.

Consumer decision-making processes

From this understanding of general decision-making processes, perceived risk and involvement theory, it is possible to identify two main approaches to consumer decision-making.

High-involvement decision-making

If an individual is highly involved with the initial purchase of a product, EPS is the appropriate decision sequence, as information is processed in a rational, logical order. Individuals who are highly involved in a purchase are thought to move through the process shown in Figure 6.4. When high-involvement decision-making is present, individuals perceive a high level of risk and are concerned about the intended purchase. The essential element in this sequence is that a great deal of information is sought initially and an attitude is developed before a commitment or intention to trial is determined.

Information search is an important part of the high-involvement decision-making process.

Information search is an important part of the high-involvement decision-making process. Because individuals are highly motivated, information is actively sought, processed and evaluated. Many media sources are explored, including the mass media, word-of-mouth communications and point-of-sale communications. As individuals require a lot of information, print media are more appropriate as a large volume of detailed information can be transmitted and this allows the receiver to digest the information at a speed which they can control.

Evaluation of the information and of the alternatives that have been derived from the information search needs to be undertaken. By comparing and implicitly scoring the different attributes of each alternative, a belief about the overall competitiveness of each alternative can be established. In Chapter 5 a compensatory model was examined. In this approach, individuals do not reject products because an attribute scores low; rather, a weakness is offset or compensated for by the strength and high scores accredited to other attributes. An individual's

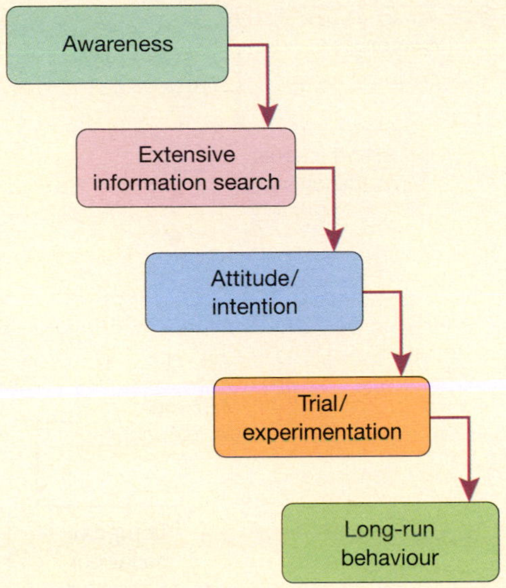

Figure 6.4 High-involvement decision-making process

attitude to a purchase is the sum of the scores given to the range of evaluative criteria used in the decision-making process. As observed in Chapter 5, Fishbein states that an attitude towards the act of purchasing and the subjective norm (the perceived attitude of others to the act being considered) combine to form an *intention* to act in a particular way. This part of the process is facilitated by the use of credible sources of information. Therefore, personal selling is important to bring individuals closer to the product, in order that it may be demonstrated and allow intense learning to occur.

Trial behaviour will follow if the perceived quality of the product is satisfactory and sufficient triggers, from internal searches, stimulate experimentation. Likewise, long-run behaviour, the goal of all marketing activities, will be determined if the guarantees and product quality combine to meet the expectations of the individual, generated by the information search.

Low-involvement decision-making

If an individual has little involvement with an initial purchase of a product, LPS is the appropriate decision process. Information is processed cognitively but in a passive, involuntary way. Information is processed using right-brain thinking so information is stored as it is received, in sections, and this means that information is stored as a brand association (Heath, 2000). An advertisement for Andrex toilet tissue featuring the puppy is stored as the 'Andrex Puppy' without any overt thinking or reasoning. Because of the low personal relevance and perceived risk associated with this type of processing, message repetition is necessary to define brands and create meaningful brand associations. Individuals who have a low involvement with a purchase decision choose not to search for information and are thought to move through the process shown in Figure 6.5.

Message repetition is necessary to define brands and create meaningful brand associations.

Communications can assist the development of awareness in the low-involvement decision-making process. However, as individuals assume a passive problem-solving role, messages need to be shorter than in the high-involvement process and should contain less information. Broadcast media are preferred as they complement the passive learning posture adopted by the

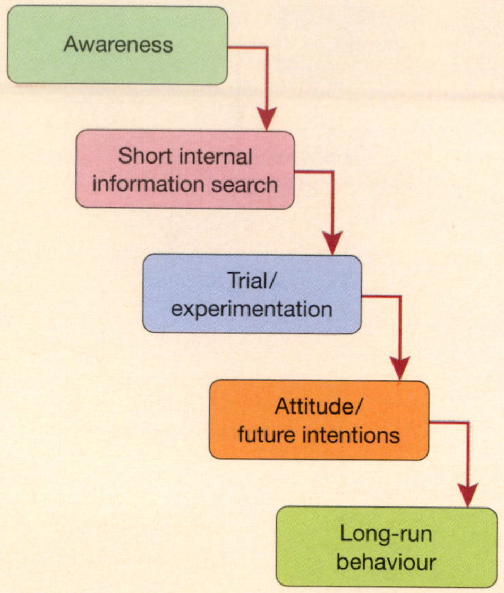

Figure 6.5 Low-involvement decision-making process

individual. Repetition is important because the receiver has little or no motivation to retain information, and their perceptual selection processes filter out unimportant information. Learning develops through exposure to repeated messages, but attitudes do not develop at this part of the process (Harris, 1987).

Where low involvement is present, each individual relies upon internal, rather than external, search mechanisms, often prompted by point-of-purchase displays. Using non-compensatory decision rules (Chapter 5), where product weaknesses are not offset by strengths, individuals make decisions, often at the point of purchase, to try established or new brands.

Price can be a very important factor by which individuals can discriminate between low-involvement purchase decisions. In high-involvement decisions there is a wide variety of attributes that individuals can use to discriminate between purchase decisions. In low-involvement purchases, price, packaging, point-of-purchase displays and promotions work together to cue and stimulate an individual into trying a product.

As a direct result of trying a product (or experimenting) and hence product experience, an attitude develops. By judging the quality of the experience, an attitude is formed which acts as the basis for future decisions. Long-run behaviour is a function of promotional messages, product quality and the degree of loyalty that can be sustained towards the brand.

Subsequent purchase activity

The initial purchase decision process frames all subsequent decisions in the product category. If a high-involvement decision process ends satisfactorily, then levels of brand loyalty are normally high, which means that subsequent decisions can be processed much more quickly. Routinised response behaviour occurs safely, as any risk associated with a purchase can be dispelled through the security associated with a brand. Brand loyalty is the normal outcome of a successful high-involvement decision-making process.

Brand loyalty is the normal outcome of a successful high-involvement decision-making process.

If the high-involvement process ends in partial satisfaction, then, depending upon the nature and extent of the outstanding risk, the next decision may also be EPS. For example, if the purchase of a first savings or investment product results in total dissatisfaction, any second purchase of a similar or financially related product will require a review of the critical attributes to provide up-to-date product and provider information, but not necessarily to inform about what a savings/investment policy is.

If the initial decision was motivated by a low level of involvement and the outcome was satisfactory, then subsequent decisions will be based upon a state of brand ambivalence. This means that individuals relegate these decisions to a habitual process but will consider a number of different brands, and will switch to one of them if they perceive that the circumstances in which the decision is being made are changing. For example, a typical habitual decision concerns the purchase of tinned tomatoes. Most consumers will decide upon their usual brand until they notice a price promotion, special offer or incentive to purchase a different brand. A switch may also be actuated by different merchandising and positioning within the store, different personal requirements (e.g. dietary changes) and levels of brand awareness.

Repeat purchase decisions are often unstable on the grounds that buyers are content to switch between products in their evoked set unless there is a high level of brand loyalty. Manufacturers of products that are associated with low-involvement decision-making are required to engage in promotional activities that keep the awareness of the brand at the top of each individual's mind-set. Otherwise there is a danger that a competitor may change the circumstances in which an individual makes a decision and trigger a motivation to try its offering.

Impact on marketing communications

Involvement is a theory central to our understanding of the way in which information is processed and the way in which consumers make decisions about product purchases. It was established that there are two main types of involvement: high and low. This concept of involvement leads to two orderings of the hierarchy of effects. In decisions where there is high involvement, attitude precedes trial behaviour. In low-involvement cases this position is reversed. In the former a positive and specific position is assumed by the consumer, whereas in the latter attitudes to the product (not the product class) develop after product use.

> In decisions where there is high involvement, attitude precedes trial behaviour.

As discussed earlier, where there is high involvement, consumers seek out information because they are concerned about the decision processes and outcomes. Because they have these concerns, consumers develop an attitude prior to behaviour. Products that evoke high-involvement decision processes tend to be high cost, to be bought relatively infrequently, to be complex, to elicit feelings of risk and to be visible to others.

Where there is low involvement, consumers are content to select any one of a number of acceptable products and often rely on those that are in the individual's evoked set. Low involvement is thought to be a comfortable state, because there are too many other decisions in life to have to make decisions about each one of them, so an opportunity not to have to seek information and make other decisions is welcome.

This suggests that high and low positions are neither static nor permanent. Involvement is said by some (Vaughn, 1980; Ratchford, 1987) to be a continuum where consumers can move from a high- to a low-involvement position, as their experience of a product increases and their perceived risk is reduced. Figure 6.6 indicates the advertising and promotion strategies best suited for each level within both involvement spectra.

> High and low positions are neither static nor permanent.

Involvement impacts therefore on what is said, how it is said and when it is said. Readers are advised that other material relating to involvement and the strategic implications for marketing communications can be found in Chapters 11 and 16.

> Involvement impacts on what is said, how it is said and when it is said.

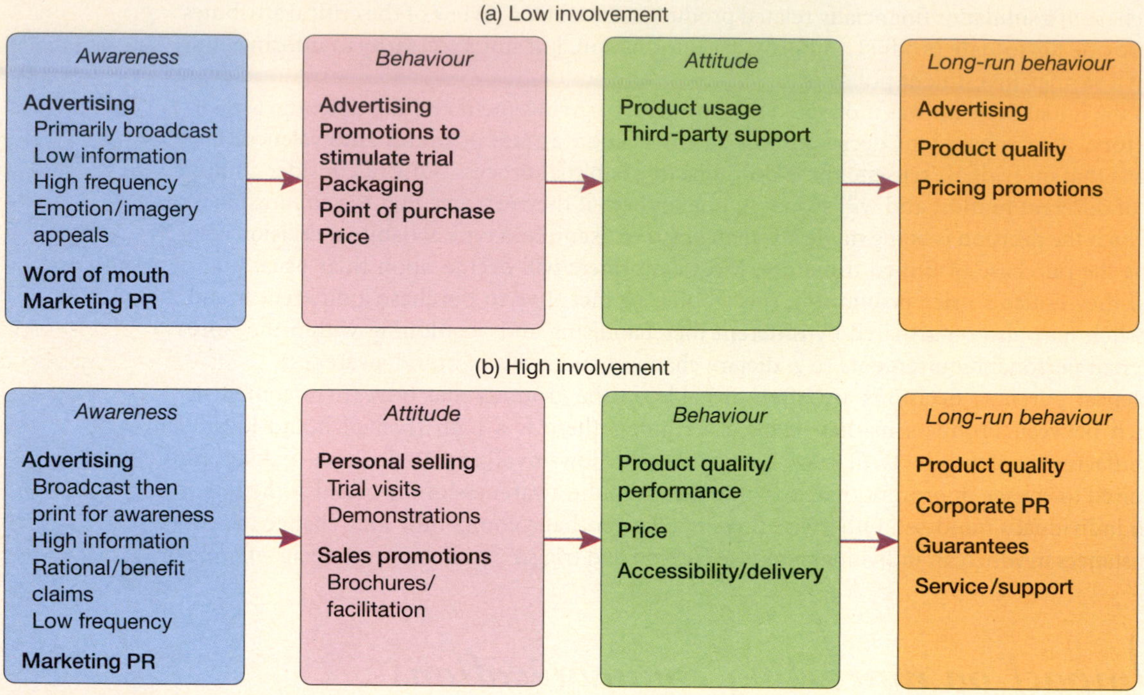

Figure 6.6 Promotional strategies for different levels of involvement

Organisational buying decision processes

Organisations have so far been viewed in the context of sellers, but in order to function they need to buy materials, parts, general supplies and services from a range of other organisations. Some texts refer to this as industrial marketing or, in the more current terminology, business-to-business marketing, reflecting the growth and importance of the public sector and the increasing use of the services sector within mature economies. However, the term 'organisational marketing' is used here to reflect the wide range of organisations involved with such activities.

Organisational buying processes need to be understood, just as consumer buying processes do, in order that appropriate and effective communication plans can be developed to complement and support the marketing mix.

Organisational buying, according to Webster and Wind (1972), is 'the decision making process by which formal organisations establish the need for purchased products and services and identify, evaluate and choose among alternative brands and suppliers'. Of particular significance is the relationship that develops between organisations that enter market exchange transactions. As mentioned previously, the various networks that organisations belong to will influence the purchase decisions that other organisations in the network make. However, before exploring these issues, it is necessary to review the context in which organisational decisions are made.

> There are far fewer buyers in the organisational context than in the consumer market.

One way of examining the context is to compare organisational decisions with those made in consumer markets. There are far fewer buyers in the organisational context than in the consumer market, although there can be a number of people associated with a buying decision in an organisation. Orders are invariably larger and the frequency with which they are placed is much lower. It is quite common for agreements to be made between organisations for the supply of materials over a number of years. Similarly, depending upon the complexity of the product (photocopying paper or a one-off satellite), the negotiation process may also take a long time.

ViewPoint 6.4 Hospital buying decisions

The purchase of medical supplies and equipment by hospitals is an important decision, if only because of the implications of the decisions made with regard to patient welfare. However, the wide variety of people involved in the process can lead to buying decisions becoming overly complex, sometimes over budget and delayed. For example, purchasing decisions regarding infusion pumps are influenced by various stakeholder groups: medical experts (such as doctors and consultants), administrators (such as general managers and purchasing administrators), those with financial responsibilities, purchasing agents and of course certain direct government representatives, Primary Care Trusts and other influential stakeholders.

Question

What are the implications for manufacturers and suppliers in order that they communicate effectively with this range of influencers?

Task

Draw up a list of communication tools and media that you might use to communicate your infusion pumps. Prioritise them and justify your decisions.

Many of the characteristics associated with consumer decision-making processes can be observed in the organisational context. However, organisational buyers make decisions which ultimately contribute to the achievement of corporate objectives. To make the necessary decisions, a high volume of pertinent information is often required. This information needs to be relatively detailed and is normally presented in a rational and logical style. The needs of the buyers are many and complex, and some may be personal. Goals, such as promotion and career advancement within the organisation, coupled with ego and employee satisfaction combine to make organisational buying an important task, one that requires professional training and the development of expertise if the role is to be performed optimally.

Organisational buyers make decisions that vary with each buying situation and buyclass. Buyclasses, according to Robinson *et al.* (1967), comprise three types: new task, modified rebuy and straight rebuy (Table 6.2):

Table 6.2 Main characteristics of the buyclasses

Buyclass	Degree of familiarity with the problem	Information requirements	Alternative solutions
New buy	The problem is fresh to the decision-makers	A great deal of information is required	Alternative solutions are unknown, all are considered new
Modified rebuy	The requirement is not new but is different from previous situations	More information is required but past experience is of use	Buying decision needs new solutions
Rebuy	The problem is identical to previous experiences	Little or no information is required	Alternative solutions not sought or required

1. *New buy*
   As the name implies, the organisation is faced with a first-time buying situation. Risk is inevitably large at this point, and partly as a consequence there are a large number of decision participants. Each participant requires a lot of information and a relatively long period of time is required for the information to be assimilated and a decision to be made.
2. *Modified rebuy*
   Having purchased a product, the organisation may request through its buyer that certain modifications be made to future purchases, for example, adjustments to the specification of the product, further negotiation on price levels or perhaps the arrangement for alternative delivery patterns. Fewer people are involved in the decision process than in the new task situation.
3. *Straight rebuy*
   In this situation, the purchasing department reorders on a routine basis, very often working from an approved list of suppliers. No other people are involved with the exercise until different suppliers attempt to change the environment in which the decision is made. For example, they may interrupt the procedure with a potentially better offer.

These phases bear a strong resemblance to the extended, limited and routinised response identified earlier with respect to the consumer market.

Reference has been made on a number of occasions to organisational buyers, as if these people are the only representatives of an organisation to be involved with the purchase decision process. This is not the case, as very often a large number of people are involved in the purchase decision. This group is referred to as either the decision-making unit (DMU) or the buying centre.

Buying centres vary in size and composition in accordance with the nature of each individual task.

Buying centres vary in size and composition in accordance with the nature of each individual task. Webster and Wind (1972) identified a number of people who make up the buying centre.

Users are people who not only initiate the purchase process but also use the product, once it has been acquired, and evaluate its performance. *Influencers* very often help set the technical specifications for the proposed purchase and assist the evaluation of alternative offerings by potential suppliers. *Deciders* are those who make purchasing decisions. In repeat buying activities the buyer may well also be the decider. However, it is normal practice to require that expenditure decisions involving sums over a certain financial limit be authorised by other, often senior, managers. *Buyers* (purchasing managers) select suppliers and manage the process whereby the required products are procured. As identified previously, buyers may not decide which product is to be purchased but they influence the framework within which the decision is made.

Gatekeepers have the potential to control the type and flow of information to the organisation and the members of the buying centre. These gatekeepers may be technical personnel, secretaries or telephone switchboard operators.

The size and form of the buying centre is not static. It can vary according to the complexity of the product being considered and the degree of risk each decision is perceived to carry for the organisation. Different roles are required and adopted as the nature of the buying task changes with each new purchase situation (Bonoma, 1982). It is vital for seller organisations to identify members of the buying centre and to target and refine their messages to meet the needs of each member of the centre.

Each member of the buying centre is an active problem solver and processes information so that personal and organisational goals are achieved.

The task of the marketing communications manager and the corresponding sales team is to decide which key participants have to be reached, with which type of message, with what frequency, and to what depth should contact be made. Just like individual consumers, each member of the buying centre is an active problem solver and processes information so that personal and organisational goals are achieved.

Table 6.3 Major influences on organisational buying behaviour

Stakeholder influences	Organisational influences	Individual influences
Economic conditions	Corporate strategy	Personality
Legislation	Organisational culture and values	Age
Competitor strategies	Resources and costs	Status
Industry regulations	Purchasing policies and procedures	Reward structure and systems
Technological developments	Interpersonal relationships	
Social and cultural values		
Interorganisation relationships		

Source: Based on Webster and Wind (1972).

Influences on the buying centre

Three major influences on organisational buyer behaviour can be identified as stakeholders, the organisational environment and those aspects which the individual brings to the situation. (see Table 6.3).

Stakeholders develop relationships between the focus organisation and other stakeholders in the network. The nature of the exchange relationship and the style of communications will influence buying decisions. If the relationship between organisations is trusting, mutually supportive and based on a longer-term perspective (a relational structure) then the behaviour of the buying centre may be seen to be cooperative and constructive. If the relationship is formal, regular, unsupportive and based on short-term convenience (a market, structure-based relationship) then the purchase behaviour may be observed as courteous yet distant.

Without doubt the major determinant of the organisational environment is the cost associated with switching from one supplier to another (Bowersox and Cooper, 1992). When an organisation chooses to enter into a buying relationship with another organisation, an investment is made in time, people, assets and systems. Should the relationship with the new supplier fail to work satisfactorily, then a cost is incurred in switching to another supplier. It is these switching costs that heavily influence buying decisions. The higher the potential switching costs, the greater the loss in flexibility and the greater the need to make the relationship appropriate at the outset.

Behaviour within the buying centre is also largely determined by the interpersonal relationships of the members of the centre. Participation in the buying centre has been shown to be highly influenced by individuals' perceptions of the personal consequences of their contribution to each stage in the process. The more that individuals think they will be blamed for a bad decision or praised for a good decision, the greater their participation, influence and visible DMU-related activity (McQuiston and Dickson, 1991). The nature and dispersal of power within the unit can influence the decisions that are made. Power is increasingly viewed from the perspective of an individual's ability to control the flow of information and the deployment of resources (Spekman and Gronhaug, 1986). This approach reflects a network approach to, in this case, intraorganisational communications.

Behaviour within the buying centre is largely determined by the interpersonal relationships of the members of the centre.

From a communications perspective there is strong evidence that the provision/collection of information is a major contributor to risk reduction (Mitchell, 1995). Figure 6.7 sets out some of the more common approaches used by organisations to reduce risk.

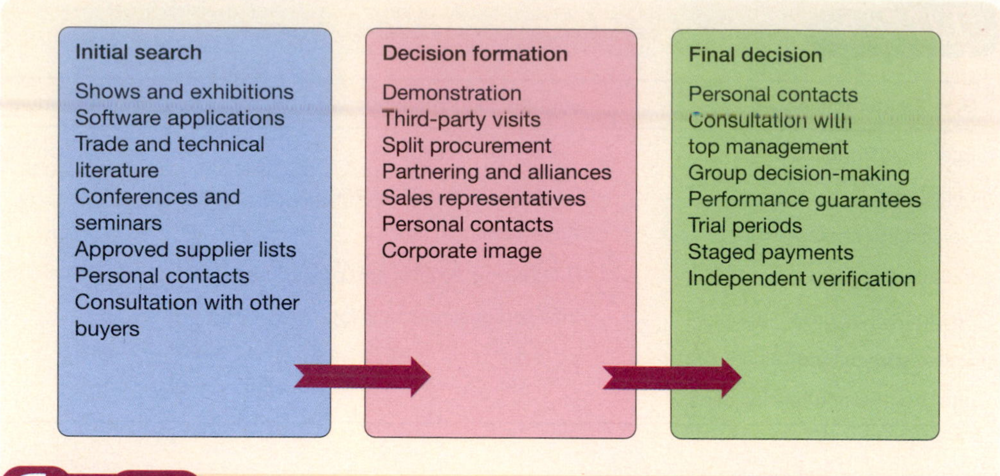

Figure 6.7 Risk reduction approaches for organisational purchase decisions

Buyphases

The organisational buying decision process consists of several stages or buyphases (Robinson *et al.*, 1967). The following sequence of six phases or events is particular to the new task buyclass. Many of these buyphases are ignored or compressed when either of the other two buyclasses is encountered.

Need/problem recognition

Products or services are purchased because of two main events (Cravens and Woodruff, 1986). Difficulties may be encountered first as a result of a need to solve problems, such as a stock-out or new government regulations, and, second, as a response to opportunities to improve performance or enter new markets. Essentially, the need/recognition phase is the identification of a gap. This is the gap between the benefits an organisation has now and the benefits it would like to have. For example, when a photocopier breaks down or fails to meet the needs of the organisation, the communication benefits it offers are missed by the users. This gap can be bridged by using a different machine on a temporary basis or by buying a new machine that provides the range of benefits required.

Product specification

As a result of identifying a problem and the size of the gap, influencers and users can determine the desired characteristics of the product needed to resolve the problem. This may take the form of a general description or may require a much more detailed analysis and the creation of a specification for a particular product. What sort of photocopier is required? What is it expected to achieve? How many documents should it copy per minute? Is a collator or tray required? This is an important part of the process, because if it is executed properly it will narrow the supplier search and save on the costs associated with evaluation prior to a final decision.

As a result of identifying a problem and the size of the gap, influencers and users can determine the desired characteristics of the product needed to resolve the problem.

Supplier and product search

At this stage the buyer actively seeks organisations that can supply the necessary product. There are two main issues at this point. Will the product reach the required performance standards and will it match the specification? Second, will the potential supplier meet the other organisational requirements? In most circumstances organisations review the market and their internal sources of information and arrive at a decision that is based on rational criteria.

Organisations, as we have seen before, work wherever possible to reduce uncertainty and risk. By working with others who are known, of whom the organisation has direct experience and who can be trusted, risk and uncertainty can be reduced substantially. This highlights another reason why many organisations seek relational exchanges and operate within established networks and seek to support each other.

The quest for suppliers and products may be a short task for the buyer; however, if the established network cannot provide a solution, the buying organisation has to seek new suppliers, and hence new networks, to be able to identify and short-list appropriate supplier organisations.

Evaluation of proposals

Depending upon the complexity and value of the potential order(s), the proposal is a vital part of the communication plan and should be prepared professionally. The proposals of the short-listed organisations are reviewed in the context of two main criteria: the product specification and the evaluation of the supplying organisation. If the organisation is already a part of the network, little search and review time need be allocated. If the proposed supplier is new to the organisation, a review may be necessary to establish whether it will be appropriate (in terms of price, delivery and service) and whether there is the potential for a long-term relationship or whether this is a single purchase that is unlikely to be repeated.

Once again, therefore, is the relationship going to be a market exchange or a relational exchange? The actions of both organisations, and of some of the other organisations in the network to the new entrant, are going to be critical in determining the form and nature of future relationships.

Supplier selection

The buying centre will undertake a supplier analysis and use a variety of criteria depending upon the particular type of item sought. This selection process takes place in the light of the comments made in the previous section. A further useful perspective is to view supplier organisations as a continuum, from reliance on a single source to the use of a wide variety of suppliers of the same product.

The buying centre will undertake a supplier analysis.

Jackson (1985) proposed that organisations might buy a product from a range of different suppliers, in other words a range of multiple sources are maintained (a practice of many government departments). She labelled this approach 'always a share', as several suppliers are given the opportunity to share the business available to the buying centre. The major disadvantage is that this approach fails to drive cost as low as possible, as the discounts derived from volume sales are not achieved. The advantage to the buying centre is that only a relatively small investment is required and little risk is entailed in following such a strategy.

At the other end of the continuum are organisations that only use a single-source supplier. All purchases are made from the single source until circumstances change to such a degree that the buyer's needs are no longer being satisfied. Jackson referred to these organisations as 'lost for good', because once a relationship with a new organisation has been developed, they are lost for good to the original supplier. An increasing number of organisations are choosing to enter alliances with a limited number of, or even single-source, suppliers. The objective is to build a long-term relationship, work together to build quality and help each other achieve their goals.

Outsourcing manufacturing activities for non-core activities has increased, and this has moved the focus of communications from an internal to an external perspective.

Evaluation

The order is written against the selected supplier and immediately the supplier is monitored and performance is evaluated against such diverse criteria as responsiveness to enquiries and modifications to the specification and timing of delivery. When the product is delivered it may reach the stated specification but fail to satisfy the original need. This is a case where the specification needs to be rewritten before any future orders are placed.

Organisational buying has shifted from a one-to-one dyadic encounter, salesperson to buyer, to a position where a buying team meets a selling team. The skills associated with this process are different and are becoming much more sophisticated, and the demands on both buyers and sellers are more pronounced. The processes of buying and selling are complex and interactive.

Developments in the environment can impact on a consumer or organisation buyer and change both the way decisions are made and their nature. For example, the decision to purchase new plant and machinery requires consideration of the future cash flows generated by the capital item. Many people will be involved in the decision, and the time necessary for consultation may mean that other parts of the decision-making process are completed simultaneously.

ViewPoint 6.5 Influences on pump buying

There are a large number of influences that impact on purchasing decisions. These can be classified as macro and micro, or external and internal. However, in certain purchasing situations, and in certain sectors, there are a variety of ongoing costs that also need to be considered.

In Viewpoint 6.4, infusion pumps were considered as a focus for hospital buying. In addition to the various political, social and technological influences that affect the various decision-makers and members of the DMU, there are economic factors associated with running these pumps. For example, the Royal United Hospital Bath NHS Trust disclosed that they saved £35,000 on consumables by adopting a lifecycle costing approach when deciding on the supplier of their next pump order. In a sense this saving represents added value, especially in a purchasing environment that is increasingly subject to tighter controls, stricter procedures and a culture that stresses value for money. The pump supplier who lost the hospital's business would do well to consider the influences, benefits and value that they need to offer in future.

Question

In this situation, do you believe that marketing communications should be strictly about the functionality and performance of infusion pumps or is there scope to incorporate more emotional messages?

Task

List the different influences that might affect the decision to buy medical equipment.

There are a number of other issues concerned with the manner in which the members of a buying centre interact and make choices. An interesting new approach to strategic management considers the subjective, cognitive thoughts of the strategist to be more important than has been considered previously. Porter (1980), Ansoff and McDonnell (1990) and others in what is referred to as the design school of thought, assume that strategic decisions result from rational, logical analysis and interpretation of the environment.

An alternative view is that as environments are too complex and dynamic for objective analysis to be any practical use (Simon, 1976), then strategy or choices are fashioned from individuals' interpretations of their environment. Projections of historical data in uncertain, highly unpredictable environments mean that strategists, or members of the buying centre in this case, will rely more on knowledge and experience as the main platform for decision-making.

Unifying models of buyer decision-making

The models of decision-making presented here and in the literature are important because they focus attention on key issues and bring out the priorities. They help the development of marketing communications by segregating audiences according to their situational needs. However, two points of contention concern the implied rationality of decision-making, particularly in organisational contexts and the assumption that consumer decision-making is different from organisational decision-making.

For example, there is immediate similarity between the EPS, LPS and RRB consumer-related purchase states and the new task, modified rebuy and rebuy states associated with organisational buying. Risk and involvement are relevant to both categories and, although the antecedents may vary, the marketing communications used to alleviate or reduce these conditions are essentially the same, just deployed in different ways. Wilson (2000) explores the issues related to rationality and implied differences. For example, consumers make product-related purchase decisions based on a wide array of inputs from other people and not just those in the immediate family environment. This is akin to group buying dynamics associated with the DMU. He argues that the rationality normally associated with organisational decision-making is misplaced, suggesting that in some circumstances the protracted nature of decision-making is more a reflection of organisational culture and the need to follow bureaucratic procedures and to show due diligence. In addition, issues concerning established behaviour patterns, difficulties and reluctance to break with established (purchasing) practices, intra- and interorganisational politics and relationships, and the costs associated with supplier switching all contribute to a more interpretive understanding of organisational decision-making. Further support for this view is given by Mason and Gray (1999), who refer to the characteristics of decision-making in the air business passenger travel market and note some strong similarities between the two main groups.

> The protracted nature of decision-making is more a reflection of organisational culture and the need to follow bureaucratic procedures and to show due diligence.

What needs to be considered is that many of the characteristics of both consumer and organisational decision-making show greater similarities than normally assumed (or taught). The implication for marketing communications is that a richer deeper understanding of these processes and characteristics may encourage the development of more effective communications.

Summary

In order to help consolidate your understanding of customer decision-making, here are the key points summarised against each of the learning objectives:

1. Explain the general process through which purchase decisions are made.

There are five stages to the general process whereby buyers make purchase decisions and implement them. These are problem recognition, information search, alternative evaluation, purchase decision and post-purchase evaluation. Organisations use marketing communications in different ways in order to influence these different stages.

2. Examine the sequence and methods used by consumers to make decisions.

Buyers do not follow the general purchase decision sequence at all times and three types of problem solving behaviour are experienced by consumers. These are extended problem solving, limited problem solving and routinised response. The procedure may vary depending upon the time available, levels of perceived risk and the degree of involvement a buyer has with the type of product.

3. Explore the components of perceived risk.

Consumers experience risk when making purchasing decisions. This risk is perceived and concerns the uncertainty of the proposed purchase and the outcomes that will result from a decision to purchase a product. The level of risk an individual experiences varies through time, across products and is often a reflection of an individual's propensity to manage risk. Risk is related to involvement, trust and other buyer behaviour concepts. Five types of perceived risk can be identified. These are ego, social, physical, financial and performance risks.

4. Introduce and explain involvement theory and relate it to planned communication activities.

Involvement is about the degree of personal relevance and risk perceived by individuals in a particular purchase situation. Individuals experience involvement with products or services to be purchased. The products and services themselves should not be classified as high or low involvement. The level of involvement may vary through time as each member of the target market becomes more (or less) familiar with the purchase and associated communications. At the point of decision-making, involvement is either high or low.

5. Consider the different types of individual who contribute to purchase decisions made by organisations.

There are a wide variety of individuals involved in organisational purchase decisions. There are *Users*, *Influencers*, *Deciders*, *Buyers* and *Gatekeepers*. All fulfil different functions, all have varying degrees of impact on purchase decisions and all require different marketing communications in order to influence their decision-making.

6. Understand the stages that organisations use to make purchase decisions.

The organisational buying decision process consists of six main stages or buyphases. These are need/problem recognition, product specification, supplier and product search, the evaluation of proposals, supplier selection and evaluation.

7. Appreciate the differences in approaches and content of marketing communications between consumer and organisational buying.

There are several points of similarity and differentiation between the way consumers and organisations make purchasing decisions. All affect the way marketing communications should be used. However, two points of contention concern the implied rationality of decision-making, particularly in organisational contexts and the assumption that consumer decision-making is different from organisational decision-making.

Review questions

1. Describe the general decision-making process.
2. What are EPS, LPS and RRB?
3. Select a product and a service which you have used recently and relate the six elements of perceived risk to both of them. How do the elements of risk differ?

4. Explain the three broad interpretations of involvement. How does involvement differ from perceived risk?
5. Describe the high- and low-involvement decision-making processes.
6. Highlight the differences between consumer and organisational buying.
7. What are buyclasses and buying centres?
8. How might a salesperson successfully utilise knowledge about the buying centre?
9. Explain the components of the various buyphases.
10. What are the main communication differences between consumer-oriented and business-to-business-oriented marketing communications?

MiniCase Understanding consumers' needs: the success of the Apache motorcycle in India

Poonam V. Kumar: TNS – Asia Pacific & Middle East
Prasad Narasimhan: TVS Motor Company India
Adapted by
Clive Nancarrow: University of the West of England

Introduction

The motorcycle market in India was originally a sellers' market with enormous waiting lists of buyers, but it has now become much more competitive. The focus had been on producing technically better machines – better fuel efficiency being the key differentiation. Segmentation was based on price and branding limited to reassurances about quality and after sales service – all of this based on the assumption that consumer motives were largely rational.

Changing lanes

The TVS motor company took the decision to look beyond improving functional performance for a solution. TVS decided to attempt a better understanding of what the market needed through consumer research. With the best technical and design consultants in the world, they were confident that once market gaps were identified and understood, creating a suitable product would not be difficult.

The research tool box

The research consisted of several stages. The first was a qualitative exploratory phase to uncover the need structure of the market. This was followed by quantitative need-based segmentation to validate the need structure and measure the sizes of the need segments. Mapping and measuring of existing brands on the needs landscape helped to identify where the opportunity lay. Concepts were developed and tested and then finally the technical design team given the direction to develop/identify a suitable product that expressed the desired brand positioning. This represented a complete paradigm shift in the method of client working and thinking, where most of the earlier launches (the successful ones as well as not so successful) had emerged from the engineering and draftsman drawing boards.

NeedScope®, TNS' proprietary system, was identified as the most suitable solution.

The TNS NeedScope® system

Two concepts form the theoretical basis of NeedScope – a marketing model and an archetypal framework. The marketing model describes how brands and needs are two sides of an equation and should fit together. The outer, most easily accessible, layer of consumer needs is the rational layer and is satisfied by the functional benefits the product delivers. The only route to competitive advantage seemed to be engineering innovation, leading to long new product development cycles, high risk launches without any means to secure long-term advantage as all the big three had equal access to international state-of-the-art technology.

The second layer has to do with social psychology – the need to identify with particular groups in society. These needs are met by the social values or character of the brand – a brand for young people, for women, upscale, etc.

And finally, at the heart of the model are the emotive needs. These are the core drivers of brand choice, the engine that powers the consumer's relationship with the brand.

The marketing model is therefore not just an emotive model. It recognises that consumers have needs at all levels, and that the rational or functional level serves as a screener, the first stop, which if not satisfied, will keep the brand out of the consumer's consideration set. However, this is not the layer at which loyalty can be built and it is necessary to go below the surface. Starting with the rational, the model systematically uncovers the inner need layers. There is also no hierarchy – no layer is considered more important than the other. The needs are interlinked and only when cohesively met across all three layers, will a powerful connection be struck with the consumer.

The second concept is the NeedScope archetypal framework (see Figure 6.8). Two axes are the fundamental anchors of the framework. The horizontal is the 'I' versus 'We' axis. The right side represents the drive for individualism and self-assertion. The left side is about the fundamental sense of belonging – the need for acceptance, togetherness, friendship and warmth. The vertical dimension divides the model into the extroverted and introverted poles. The top is about energy directed outwards – release, stimulation, freedom. The bottom is about energy that is inwards – more contained and controlled and therefore less visible. While these are opposites, there are no hierarchies or negatives. Consumers are multi-faceted and have multiple needs, depending on the context of the category and occasion.

We can identify six basic archetypes. Archetypes are the unchanging constant in human beings that hold over time, across different geographies and cultures. For example, everyone recognises and connects with the nurturing care of the Mother, the appealing purity of the Innocent or the determined courage of the Winning Hero beating odds and with the irresistible sensuality of the Seductress. Over millennia, powerful stories have been told and written about them. They take different faces and names, but they still strike the same deep chord within all human beings. They are reflected in our gods and goddesses, in our mythologies and it does not matter if one is one is Greek or Indian, Chinese or Nordic. Uncannily, cultures that have evolved thousands of miles from each other and with no real contact, developed the same stories. These archetypes are found in culture after culture, they anchor our worlds and our belief systems. Carl Jung calls this the collective unconscious.

The quantitative stage of research involved segmentation based on needs. There were six need states identified and each need state was detailed on all layers of needs as well as other demographic and behavioural parameters to enable targeting (see Figure 6.9).

The size of the need states indicates the dynamic shift of the market towards more modernity and individualism.

Brands were then mapped on the needs landscape based on how consumers perceived them. Pulsar, the big success in the market, was in Potency. The TVS brands were *all* clustered in the lower part of the affiliative section of the map. Clearly, all of them

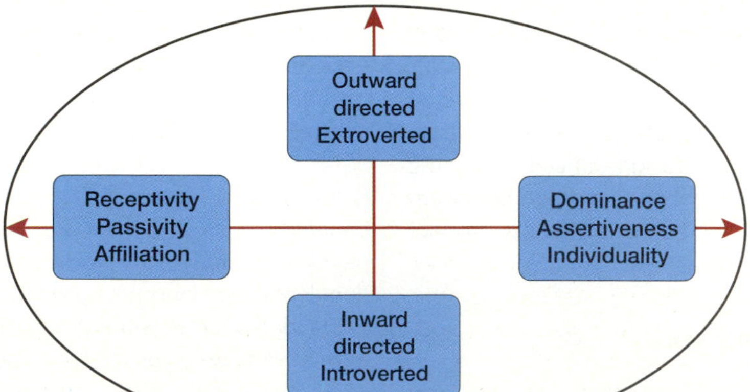

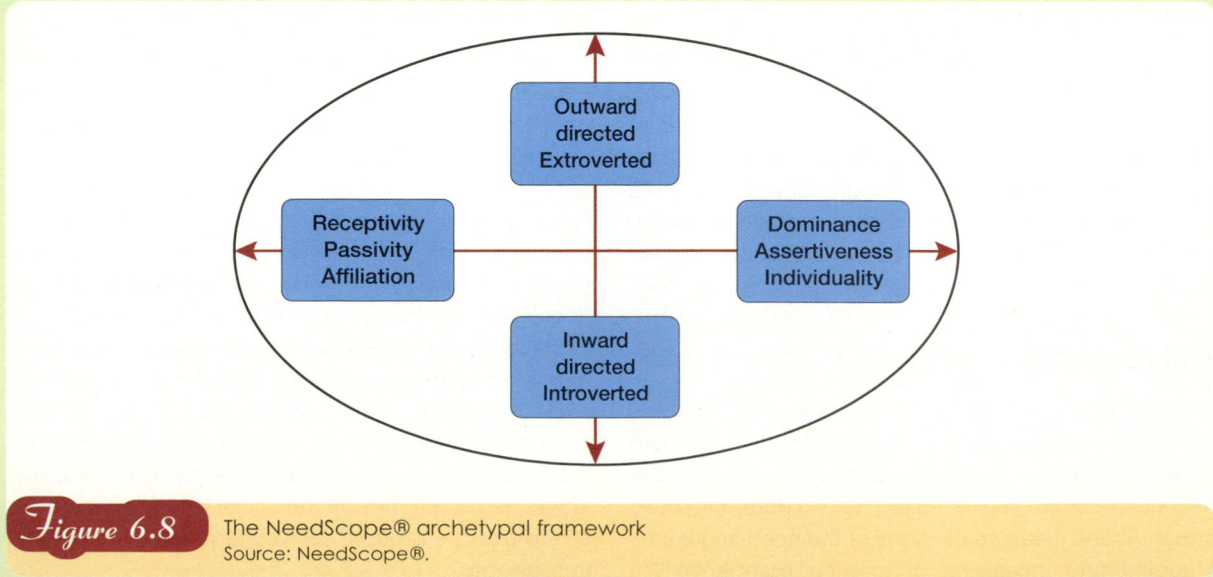

Figure 6.8 The NeedScope® archetypal framework
Source: NeedScope®.

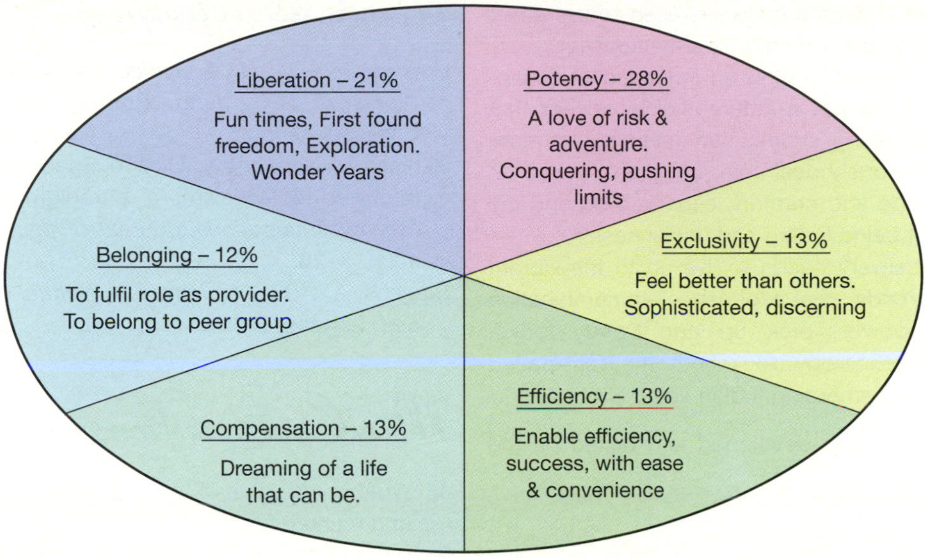

Figure 6.9 Six need segments
Source: NeedScope®.

were drawing imagery and symbology from the affiliative, reliable image of the corporate brand. The position of the TVS brands indicated sub-optimal utilisation of the portfolio and the absence from the more dynamic and growing part of the market was a cause for concern. TVS clearly had to get back into the action.

From the analysis Potency and Liberation were identified as the opportunity. An in-depth need state–brand fit analysis showed that Liberation, rather than Potency was a more optimal target for several reasons:

- Potency, while larger and exciting, already had a formidable competitor in Pulsar. There was a high risk of becoming a me-too launch unless something dramatically different was created.
- While the need to create a new brand rather than a new TVS model was recognised, it was also clear that the auto being a high-ticket buy, the signature of an established company would be needed for market acceptance and consequently there would be some company brand influence. The Potency need state with its macho, rugged individualism was just too distant to be targeted credibly with TVS's affiliative imagery.
- Liberation had a younger skew, which opened up the opportunity to target a new social group – the first-time bike buyer. With the market size growing, the profile of the buyer was getting younger and this segment was expected to grow even further as the older, middle-class consumers had begun to shift towards four-wheelers.

Liberation – Life, Here I come!!!

The first step was to understand Liberation on all levels of need.

- Emotively, Liberation represents the wonder years in a man's life. The first taste of freedom, the first venture into adulthood. A time of freedom, fun, exploration of the world and experiences before responsibility and the realities of life take over. The bike in this need state symbolises a rite of passage – the boy becomes a man – and is the ideal partner to explore spaces, both physically and emotively. In the physical sense it is about mobility. Emotionally it is about reaching places you have never been.
- Liberation evokes the heady kick and excitement of youth, the exciting discovery of adulthood and the bike is integral as a source of pleasure.
- There was a definite younger demographic skew, but the need also extended to the 'young at heart'. For the young man, the motorbike is a symbol to flaunt his adult status. With older men it is about recapturing moments gone by, the longing for eternal youth.
- The social values of the need state are reflected in younger men in the golden period between boys and

adult men. The need for affiliation is typically strong at this stage and so the bike is used to represent togetherness – a buddy to share the fun with.

- With every brand boasting an international collab oration, this was not a differentiating, nor for that matter a motivating, proposition. International technology is obviously desirable, but there is also an emerging pride and comfort, especially among the youth, about being Indian and 'Indianness'.
- Functional delivery needs to live up to the vibrant need for a trendy, cool experience – a combination of speed, power, pick up and trendy looks. Advanced technology to reflect the fast-paced lifestyles of the emerging Indian youth.

Two concepts were developed and tested on the same frame of reference.

Source: Based on a paper given at ESOMAR Annual Congress, Berlin, September 2007 by Poonam Kumar, Motivational Research, APAC Region, TNS Asia, India; Prasad Narsimhan TVS Motor Company, India (ESOMAR Copyright)

Note: The full paper is available on www.pearsoned.co.uk/fill.

MiniCase references

Hopcke, R.H. (1992) *A Guided Tour of The Complete Works of C.G. Jung*, Boston, MA: Shambhala Publications Inc.

Barker, A., Nancarrow, C. and Spackman, N. (2001) Informed eclecticism: a paradigm for the 21st century. *International Journal of Market Research*, **43**(1), 3–28.

Stevens, A. (1994) *Archetype: A Natural History of the Self*. London: Biddles Ltd.

MiniCase questions

1. What is the value of the TNS NeedScope® system to a marketer?
2. What is the value of NeedScope to the creative department of an advertising agency.
3. Why is research, and this type of research in particular, so important?

References

Ansoff, H.I. and McDonnell, E.J. (1990) *Implanting Strategic Management*, 2nd edn. Hemel Hempstead: Prentice-Hall.

Ashford, R., Cuthbert, P. and Shani, N. (2000) Perceived risk and consumer decision making related to health services: a comparative study. *International Journal of Nonprofit and Voluntary Sector Marketing*, **5**(1), 58–72.

Batra, R. and Ray, M.L. (1983) Operationalizing involvement as depth and quality of response. In *Advances in Consumer Research* (eds R.P. Bagozzi and A.M. Tybout), **10**, 309–13 Ann Arbor, MI: Association for Consumer Research.

Bonoma, T.V. (1982) Major sales: who really does the buying? *Harvard Business Review* (May/June), 113.

Bowersox, D. and Cooper, M. (1992) *Strategic Marketing Channel Management*, New York: McGraw-Hill.

Cravens, D. and Woodruff, R. (1986) *Marketing*, Reading, MA: Addison-Wesley.

Davidson, D. (2008) Gillette unveils TV ad with Woods, Henry and Federer. *Brandrepublic*, 18 January, Retrieved 20 March 2008 from www.brandrepublic.com/News/MostRead/777804/Gillette-unveils-TV-ad-Woods-Henry-Federer/.

Fry, A. (2006) Customer publishing: worth the reading, *Marketing*, 19 April, http://www.brandrepublic.com/News/554712/Customer-publishing-Worth-reading/.

Gray, R. (2004) The changing faces of man, *Marketing*, 27 October, 28–30.

Harris, G. (1987) The implications of low involvement theory for advertising effectiveness, *International Journal of Advertising*, **6**, 207–21.

Heath, R. (2000) Low-involvement processing, *Admap* (March), 14–16.

Hirschmann, E.C. and Holbrook, M.B. (1982) Hedonic consumption: emerging concepts, methods and propositions. *Journal of Marketing*, **46** (Summer), 92–101.

Jackson, B. (1985) Build customer relationships that last, *Harvard Business Review*, **63**(6), 120–8.

Kapferer, J.N. and Laurent, G. (1985) Consumer involvement profiles: a new practical approach to consumer involvement. *Journal of Advertising Research*, **25**(6), 48–56.

Laaksonen, P. (1994) *Consumer Involvement: Concepts and Research*. London: Routledge.

Mason, K.J. and Gray, R. (1999) Stakeholders in a hybrid market: the example of air business passenger travel. *European Journal of Marketing*, **33**(9/10), 844–58.

McQuiston, D.H. and Dickson, P.R. (1991) The effect of perceived personal consequences on participation and influence in organisational buying. *Journal of Business*, **23**, 159–77.

Mitchell, V.-M. (1995) Organisational risk perception and reduction: a literature review. *British Journal of Management*, **6**, 115–33.

Mitchell, V.-M. (1999) Consumer perceived risk: conceptualisations and models. *European Journal of Marketing*, **33**(1/2), 163–95.

Mitchell, V.-M. and Boustani, P. (1994) A preliminary investigation into pre and post-purchase risk perception and reduction. *European Journal of Marketing*, **28**(1), 56–71.

Porter, M.E. (1980) *Competitive Strategy: Techniques for Analysing Industries and Competitors*. New York: Free Press.

Ratchford, B.T. (1987) New insights about the FCB grid. *Journal of Advertising Research* (August/September), 24–38.

Retiveau, A. (2007) The Role of Fragrance in Personal Care Products, retrieved 26 October 2008 from www.sensoryspectrum.com/presentations/Fragrances.

Robinson, P.J., Faris, C.W. and Wind, Y. (1967) *Industrial Buying and Creative Marketing*. Boston, MA: Allyn & Bacon.

Rossiter, J.R., Percy, L. and Donovan, R.J. (1991) A better advertising planning grid. *Journal of Advertising Research* (October/November), 11–21.

Schiffman, L. and Kanuk, L. (1991) *Consumer Behavior*. Englewood Cliffs, NJ: Prentice Hall.

Settle, R.B. and Alreck, P. (1989) Reducing buyers' sense of risk. *Marketing Communications* (January), 34–40.

Simon, H.A. (1976) *Administrative Behavior: A Study of Decision Making Processes in Administrative Organizations*. New York: Free Press.

Spekman, R.E. and Gronhaug, K. (1986) Conceptual and methodological issues in buying centre research. *European Journal of Marketing*, **20**(7), 50–63.

Stone, R.N. and Gronhaug, K. (1993) Perceived risk: further considerations for the marketing discipline. *European Journal of Marketing*, **27**(3), 39–50.

Tungate, M. (2008) Because he's worth it too, *Marketing*, 13 February, 24–7.

Vaughn, R. (1980) How advertising works: a planning model. *Journal of Advertising Research* (October), 27–33.

Webster, F.E. and Wind, Y. (1972) *Organizational Buying Behavior*. Englewood Cliffs, NJ: Prentice-Hall.

Wilson, D.F. (2000) Why divide consumer and organisational buyer behaviour? *European Journal of Marketing*, **34**(7), 780–96.

Zaichkowsky, J. (1985) Measuring the involvement constraint. *Journal of Consumer Research*, **12**, 341–52.

Chapter 7

Marketing: relationships and communications

The importance of relationship marketing is now recognised as a central aspect of both consumer and business marketing. There are a number of dimensions associated with organisational and consumer relationships, many of which encompass established concepts such as trust, commitment and loyalty. The role that marketing communications can play in establishing and nurturing key relationships is pivotal, yet the ways in which marketing communications might best be deployed depend to a large extent on the context in which both the relationship and the communications are configured.

Aims and learning objectives

The aim of this chapter is to explore concepts and ideas concerning marketing relationships and the role marketing communications can play in developing and sustaining such relationships.

The learning objectives of this chapter are to:

1. explore the concept of value and its role in developing marketing relationships;
2. consider the characteristics of relationship marketing;
3. appraise the theoretical concepts underpinning relationship marketing;
4. consider the importance of customer retention and the use of loyalty programmes to reduce customer defection;
5. examine ways in which marketing relationships can be developed;
6. explore issues concerning the development of trust in online environments;
7. explore ways in which marketing communications can help organisations develop relationships.

For an applied interpretation see Angela Carroll's MiniCase entitled ***Reggae Reggae Sauce*** at the end of this chapter.

Introduction

Value has become an increasingly significant concept to marketing practitioners as well as academics. Indeed, many believe that the only viable marketing strategy should be to deliver improved shareholder value (Doyle, 2000). However, the importance of providing value for customers is not a new idea. Concepts of differentiation, unique and emotional selling propositions (USPs and ESPs) and positioning are founded on the idea that superior perceived value is of primary significance to customers.

It has been long understood that customers buy benefits not features, that they buy products and services as solutions that enable them to achieve their goals. The majority of women buy lipstick because of a mixture of both tangible and intangible attributes or even features and benefits. They buy particular brands because they feel different as a result of using them. What they do buy will vary from person to person, but in terms of tangible attributes they prefer to buy colour and smudge-free lips (no bleed), that they stay on lips, prevent dryness, are long-lasting and smooth (Puth *et al.*, 1999). However, among the intangible attributes are self-confidence, a coordinated fashion accessory, trust, perhaps an alter-ego or, as Revlon once claimed, hope.

The same principle applies to organisational marketing. Business customers buy solutions to business problems, not just stand-alone products. These benefits and solutions constitute added value for the customer, and represent the reason for one offering being selected in preference to another. For both consumers and business customers, value is determined by the net satisfaction derived from a transaction, not the costs incurred to obtain it.

So, if customers seek to satisfy their needs through their purchase of specific products and services then it can be said that the satisfaction of needs is a way of delivering value. Kothandaraman and Wilson (2001) argue that the creation of value is dependent upon an organisation's ability to deliver high performance on the benefits that are important to the customer and this in turn is rooted in their competency in technology and business processes, or core competences. Doyle (2000) regards the creation of customer value as being based on three principles:

It can be said that the satisfaction of needs is a way of delivering value.

- Customers will choose between alternative offerings and select the one that (they perceive) will offer them the best value.
- Customers do not want product or service features, they want their needs met.
- It is more profitable to have a long-term relationship between a customer and a company than a one-off transaction.

Value is the customer's estimate of the extent to which a product or service can satisfy their needs. However, there are normally costs associated with the derivation of benefits such that a general model of value would identify the worth of the benefits received for the price paid (Anderson and Narus, 1998). Therefore, value is relative to customer expectations and experience of competitive offerings within a category and can be derived from sources other than products, such as the relationships between buyers and sellers (Simpson *et al.*, 2001).

Value is the customer's estimate of the extent to which a product or service can satisfy their needs.

The value concept

The value chain concept developed by Porter (1985), is based on the premise that organisations compete for business by trying to offer enhanced value, which is developed, internally, through a coordinated chain of activities. The value chain was devised as a tool to appraise an organisation's ability to create what Porter terms differential advantage. It consists of nine activities, five primary and four support, all of which incur costs but together can (and should) lead to the creation of value. The primary activities are those direct actions necessary to bring materials into an organisation, to convert them into final products or services, to ship them out to customers and to provide marketing and servicing facilities. Support activities facilitate the primary activities. Customers perceive they are getting superior value when these activities are linked together. These linkages can be achieved through systems and processes such as those offered by new technology. Doyle refers to three processes:

- Innovation processes to generate a constant stream of new products and hence ability to maintain margins.
- Operations processes to deliver first-class performance and costs.
- Customer creation and support processes to provide a consistent and positive cash flow.

ViewPoint 9.1 Added value OnAir

As part of its customer development Airbus has developed facilities for airlines to offer a range of consumer communications while in flight. The system enables passengers to use email and text messages, send and receive voice messages and browse the web all through the use of their own phones, laptops and PDAs.

Airbus has identified a major opportunity in the market and believes the system, branded as OnAir, represents significant added value for major premium travel airlines to offer their passengers. It is expected that Boeing will offer a similar system with both manufacturers recognising the need for their customers to offer passengers additional value in what is a highly competitive market.

Question

Consider the view that the speed at which Boeing nullified Airbus' OnAir system suggests that added value has to be protected and long term to be of significance.

Task

Make a note of two ways in which a rail operator might provide added value to attract and retain travellers?

The processes used by an organisation become a critical part of the way in which they can add value. Customers, however, lie at the heart of the value chain. Only by understanding particular customer needs and by focusing value chain activities on satisfying them, can superior value be generated. Value might be perceived in terms of price, low cost and accessibility. For others, price may be relatively inconsequential and the other benefits associated with a brand or organisation such as continuity of supply, innovation and prestige are signals that a longer-term association is of greater value to them. However, according to Ryssel *et al.* (2004) there is an increasing amount of evidence that the relationships organisations form are themselves a generator of value and hence an important aspect of contemporary marketing.

The relationships organisations form are themselves a generator of value and hence an important aspect of contemporary marketing.

Development of relationship marketing

Interaction between customers and sellers is based around the provision and consumption of perceived value. However, the quality, duration and level of interdependence between customers and sellers can vary considerably. The reasons for this variance are many and

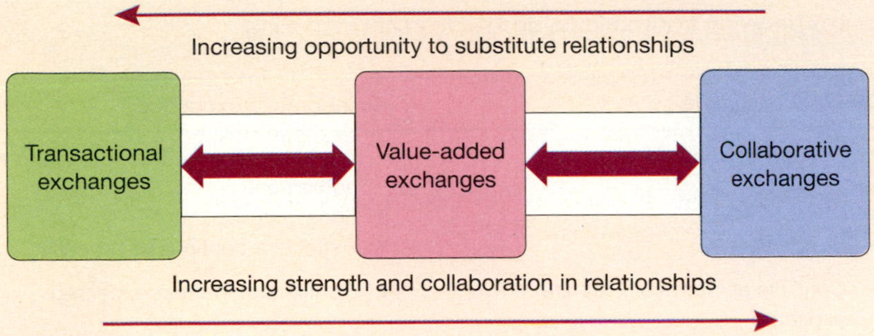

Figure 7.1 A continuum of value-oriented exchanges
Source: Adapted from Day (2000).

wide-ranging but at the core are perceptions of shared values and the strength and permanence of any relationship that might exist. Relationship value can be visualised as a continuum (see Figure 7.1).

Relationship value can be visualised as a continuum.

At one end of the continuum are transactional exchanges, characterised by short-term, commodity or price-oriented exchanges, between buyers and sellers coming together for one-off exchanges independent of any other or subsequent exchanges. Both parties are motivated mainly by self-interest. Movement along the continuum represents increasingly valued relationships. Interactions between parties are closer and stronger. The focus moves from initial attraction to retention and mutual understanding of each other's needs.

The focus moves from initial attraction to retention and mutual understanding.

At the other end of the continuum are relational exchanges, or what Day (2000) refers to as collaborative exchanges. These are characterised by a long-term orientation, where there is complete integration of systems and processes and the relationship is motivated by partnership and mutual support. Trust and commitment underpin these relationships and these variables become increasingly important as relational exchanges become established.

Perceived value may take many forms and be rooted in a variety of attributes, combined in different ways to meet segment needs. However, the context in which an exchange occurs between a buyer and a seller provides a strong reflection of the nature of their relationship. If the exchange is focused on the product (and the price) then the exchange is considered to be essentially transactional. If the exchange is focused around the needs of both the customer and the seller then the exchange is considered to be relational. The differences between transactional and collaborative exchanges are set out in Table 7.1 and provide an important starting point in understanding the nature of relationship marketing.

The product marketing approach is rooted in the traditional 4Ps model of marketing and to a large extent reflects the transactional approach. For a long time consumer marketing has been regarded as something that generally takes place between anonymous individuals. Relationship marketing considers the value inherent in a longer-term series of exchanges that occur between individuals who are, in general, known to each other. Relationship marketing acknowledges the changing lifetime needs of customers and emphasises the importance of both the product and customer lifecycles. This in turn leads to a focus on customer retention.

Relationship marketing is also characterised by the frequency and intensity of the exchanges between customers and sellers. As these exchanges become more frequent and more intense so the strength of the relationships between buyers and sellers improves. It is this that provided the infrastructure for a new perspective of marketing, one based on relationships (Spekman, 1988; Rowe and Barnes, 1998), rather than the objects of a transaction, namely products and services.

Relationship marketing is characterised by the frequency and intensity of the exchanges between customers and sellers.

Table 7.1 Key differences between transactional and relationship marketing

Attribute	Discrete exchange	Collaborative exchange
Chronological aspects of exchange	• Defined beginning • Short-term • Sudden end	• Beginning can be traced back to earlier agreements • Long-term • Reflects a continuous process
Expectations of the relationship	• Conflicts of interest/goals are expected • Immediate settlement ('cash payment') • No problems expected in future	• Conflicts of interest expected • Future problems are overcome by trust and joint commitment
Communication	• Minimal personal relations • Ritual-like communication predominates	• Both formal and informal communication used
Transferability	• Totally transferable • It makes no difference who performs contractual obligations	• Limited transferability • Exchanges are highly dependent on the identity of the parties
Cooperation	• No joint efforts	• Joint efforts at both planning and implementation stages • Modifications endemic over time
Division of burden and benefit	• Sharp distinction between parties • Each party has its own, strictly defined obligations	• Burden and benefits likely to be shared • Division of benefits and burdens likely to vary over time

Source: Wagner and Boutellier (2002).

However, a word of caution is necessary as not everyone believes relationship marketing is an outright success. For example, Rapacz and Reilly (2008: 22) suggest that the current view of relationship marketing has become 'stuck in a rut'. They argue that audits of the relationship marketing practices used to support many leading brands indicate that relationship marketing is not working. The goal, Rapacz and Reilly suggest, should be commitment to the brand rather than the relationship itself. They refer to the over promise of one-to-one marketing, the difficulties and inefficiencies associated with databases and CRM technology and issues concerning loyalty programmes. The result of their critique is that they advocate the greater use of a variety of marketing communications techniques to generate increased brand commitment. They use the Jack Daniels brand to make their point about good practice, highlighting communications that, if disciplined, entertaining, benefit-oriented and multifaceted, serve to bring greater commitment to a brand.

It is better to consider the prevailing contextual conditions as the key dynamics that shape relationships.

The notion that relationships will improve as they evolve across a continuum is not accepted by all. The expectation that relationships can be enhanced through the application of marketing programmes is not one that is always experienced in practice. For example, Palmer (2007) believes that the continuum perspective is too simplistic and unrealistic. Better to consider the prevailing contextual conditions as the key dynamics that shape relationships, which inevitably wax and wane over time.

Rao and Perry (2002) cited by Palmer, suggest that relationship development can be considered in terms of stages theory or states theory. Stages theory reflects the notion of incremental development (along the continuum) while stages theory suggests that relationship development does not conform to the processional interpretation because of the complexity and sheer unpredictability of relationship dynamics.

Palmer offers a compromise, namely a 'stages-within-a-state' interpretation. He draws on the work of Anderson and Narus (1999) and Canning and Hammer-Lloyd (2002) to make his point. There may be some validity in this view but the notion that all exchanges reflect a degree of relational commitment (Macneil, 1983) should not be ignored.

ViewPoint 7.2 Collaborative sausages

The small market town of Ludlow in Shropshire has five independent butchers, and when Tesco were granted permission to build a supermarket in the town, these butchers and other retailers felt their businesses to be under threat. As part of a method to protect these established businesses, the mayor encouraged them to collaborate, and in doing so expand their businesses.

The first step was to create the Ludlow Marches Food and Drink Festival. Of the many events the pub and sausage trails proved to be popular with customers. It is quite usual for customers to shop at a single butchers, so the trail aimed to stimulate local customers to frequent all the butchers. The trick of the trail was that different butchers had different products and this was a way for customers to sample the range of products on offer. Although initially reluctant, the butchers became allies and they now produce and cook over 3,000 sausages just for the festival.

The festival is a now a well-established gastronomic event and the collaborative venture has been taken a step further. By creating a trading identity for them, the Ludlow Sausage Company, the butchers now serve customers through Internet trading. At first the products offered were small hampers of sausages but now the range has become more extensive and there is further collaboration with the local brewery, Hobson's. This enhanced the product range with a Hobson's sausage (beer-flavoured), but the reach and distribution for both parties was important.

Source: Cox (2004); www.theludlowsausage.co.uk/.

Question

How did the independent butchers of Ludlow add value?

Task

How do you judge the value offered by one of your local retailers?

Exhibit 7.1 Sausages at an exhibition
Paul Gapper/Alamy.

Principles of retention

Marketing has been characterised by its potential to influence and attract customers. Indeed, early ideas considered marketing to be a social anathema due to the perception that it persuaded and manipulated people into purchasing goods and services they did not want. While these fears and misgivings have generally been overcome, a further fallacy concerned the notion that all customers are good customers. As most commercial organisations will now agree, some customers are far more attractive than other customers on the grounds that some are very profitable, others are marginally profitable but offer great potential while others offer little and/or incur losses.

Some customers avoid costly switching costs that are associated with finding new suppliers.

Through the use of relationship cost theory it was possible to identify the benefits associated with stable and mutually rewarding relationships. Some customers avoid costly switching costs that are associated with finding new suppliers, while suppliers experience reduced quality costs incurred when adapting to the needs of new customers. Reichheld and Sasser (1990) identified an important association between a small (e.g. 5 per cent) increase in customer retention and a large (e.g. 60 per cent) improvement in profitability. Therefore, a long-term relationship leads to lower relationship costs and higher profits. Since this early work there has been general acceptance that customers who are loyal not only improve an organisation's profits but also strengthen its competitive position (Day, 2000) because competitors have to work harder to dislodge or destabilise their loyalty. It should be noted that some authors suggest the link between loyalty and profitability is not that simple (Dowling and Uncles, 1997), while others argue that much more information and understanding is required about the association between profitability and loyalty, especially when there may be high costs associated with customer acquisition (Reinartz and Kumar, 2002).

By undertaking a customer profitability analysis it is possible to identify those segments that are worth developing, and hence build a portfolio of relationships, each of varying dimensions and potential. These relationships provide mutually rewarding benefits and provide a third dimension in the customer dynamic, namely customer development.

The duration and intensity of each relationship phase will inevitably vary.

Customer relationships can be considered in terms of a series of relationship development phases: customer acquisition, development, retention and decline. The duration and intensity of each relationship phase will inevitably vary and it should be remembered that this representation is idealistic. A customer relationship cycle is represented at Figure 7.2.

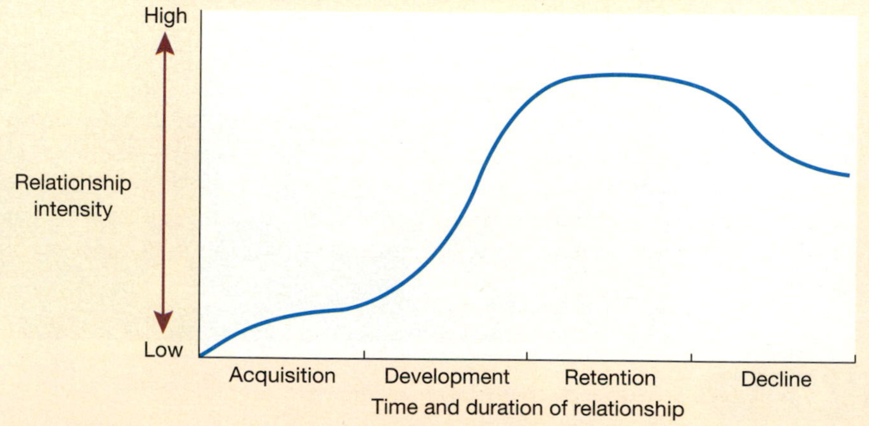

Figure 7.2 Customer relationship life cycle

Table 7.2 Customer acquisition events

Acquisition event	Explanation
Search	Buyers and sellers search for a suitable pairing
Initiation	Both parties seek out information about the other before any transaction occurs
Familiarisation	The successful completion of the first transaction enables both parties to start revealing more information about themselves

Customer acquisition

The acquisition phase is characterised by three main events: search, initiation and familiarisation (see Table 7.2).

The logical sequence of acquisition activities moves from search and verification through the establishment of credentials. The length of this period of initiation will depend partly on the importance of the buying decision, the complexity of the products and partly upon the nature of the introduction. If the parties are introduced by an established and trusted source then certain initiation rights can be shortened. Once a transaction occurs the buyer and sellers start to become more familiar with each other and gradually begin to reveal more information about themselves. The seller receives payment, delivery and handling information about the buyer and as a result is able to prepare customised outputs. The buyer is able to review the seller's products and experience their service quality.

Customer development

The development phase is characterised by the seller attempting to reduce buyer risk and enhance credibility. This is achieved by encouraging cross-selling whereby the buyer consumes other products, by improving the volume of purchases, by engaging the buyer with other added-value services and by varying delivery times and quantities. The buyer's acquiescence is dependent upon their specific needs and the degree to which the buyer wishes to become more involved with the supplier. Indeed, it is during this phase that the buyer is able to determine whether or not it is worth developing deeper relationships with the seller.

Customer retention

The retention phase is the most profitable one where the greatest level of relationship value is experienced. The retention phase will generally last as long as both the buyer and seller are able to meet their individual and joint goals. If the relationship has become more involved greater levels of trust and commitment between the partners will permit increased cross-buying and product experimentation, and b2b relationships, joint projects and product development. However, the very essence of relationship marketing is for organisations to identify a portfolio of customers with whom they wish to develop a range of relationships. This requires the ability to measure levels of retention and also to determine when resources are to be moved from acquisition to retention and back to acquisition.

> The retention phase is the most profitable.

Customer decline

Customer decline is concerned with the closure of a relationship. Termination may occur suddenly as a result of a serious problem or episode between the parties. The more likely process is that the buying organisation decides to reduce their reliance on the seller because their needs have changed or an alternative supplier, who offers superior added value, has been found. The

ViewPoint 7.3 Retaining office accounts

The office products division of the Cantrell Corporation had been an important part of the company's overall performance with 40 per cent of its revenue derived online. However, office products customers rely on flawless e-commerce performance from their suppliers to help reduce their administrative overheads, and as a result competition within this sector is strong.

One of the challenges facing Cantrell was that their web site was not integrated with customer account information, so customers with questions about order status or account balances flooded the call centres. Costs were rising, customers were leaving and performance targets were being missed with increased regularity. Cantrell resolved to reassert their prominence in the market by creating a world-class shopping experience, with CRM capabilities, automatic fulfilment and integration with their largest customers. The company developed a new web site and as a result customers are now able to research their questions online, and the company no longer needs to fund an additional call centre.

Customers can now shop online for office supplies, order online training courses and read online newsletters that are customised for them. They can quickly and efficiently find the items they need in the online catalogue, order them and check stock. Cantrell's order fulfilment system now reads web orders just as if they had been generated from the call centre, and fulfils them automatically. As a result, instead of customers leaving, new accounts are being registered at record levels, order fulfilment cycles have been reduced and costs lowered, all in the name of using technology to improve customer management and retention.

Question

To what extent do you believe customer retention is function of the trade-off between trust and the switching costs associated with finding and establishing a relationship with a different supplier?

Task

List and prioritise the top four attributes you believe the supplier of office equipment must possess.

buyer either formally notifies the established supplier or begins to reduce the frequency and duration of contact and moves business to other, competitive organisations.

Theoretical concepts of relationship marketing

There have been numerous theoretical attempts to explain relationship marketing. Three are presented here: social exchange, social penetration and interaction theories.

Social exchange theory

The central premise associated with social exchange theory (Blau, 1964) is that relationships are based upon the exchange of values between two or more parties. Whatever constitutes the nature of an exchange between the participants, equality or satisfaction must be felt as a result. An absence of equality means that an advantage might have been gained by one party and this will automatically result in negative consequences for another. Therefore, in a b2b context, organisations seeking to maintain marketing channel relationships should not raise prices past threshold levels or allow levels of service output to fall below those of competitors. If channel partners perceive a lack of added value from these exchanges they are more likely to compare performance with other potential suppliers, and even withdraw from the relationship by establishing alternative sources of supply.

> The central premise associated with social exchange theory is that relationships are based upon the exchange of values between two or more parties.

Exchanges can occur between two parties, three parties in sequence, or between at least three parties within a wider network and not necessarily sequentially. Relationships evolve from exchange behaviour that serves to provide the rules of engagement. They are socially constructed and have been interpreted in terms of marriage and social relationships (Tynan, 1997). Social norms drive exchange reciprocity within relationships, and serve to guide behaviour expectations.

Whether in personal or interorganisational relationships, exchanges are considered to consist of two main elements. First, there are value exchanges, which are based on the exchange of resources (goods for money) and second, there are symbolic exchanges where, in an interorganisational context, goods are purchased for their utility plus the feelings and associations that are bestowed on the user.

Social exchange theory serves to explain customer retention on the basis that the rewards derived through exchanges exceed the associated costs. Should expectations about future satisfaction fall short of the levels established through past exchanges, or alternative possibilities with other organisations suggest potentially improved levels of satisfaction, then the current partner may be discarded and a new relationship encouraged.

Social exchange theory serves to explain customer retention on the basis that the rewards derived through exchanges exceed the associated costs.

Social penetration theory

This theory is based on the premise that as relationships develop individuals begin to reveal more about themselves. Every encounter between a buyer and seller will allow each party to discover more about the other and make judgements about assigning suitable levels of relationship confidence. Consequently, the behaviour and communications exhibited between parties may well change from a very formal and awkward introduction to something more knowledgeable, relaxed and self-assured.

As relationships develop individuals begin to reveal more about themselves.

Altman and Taylor (1973) refer to personality depth and personality breadth as two key aspects of the social penetration approach. Personality breadth is concerned with the range of topics (or categories) discussed by the parties and the frequency with which organisations discuss each topic. Unsurprisingly, products and customer needs are two main categories that are discussed by organisations. The analogy of an onion is often used to describe the various layers that make up the depth of a personality. The outer layers are generally superficial, contain a number of elements (of personality) and are relatively easy to determine. However, the key personality characteristics, those that influence the structure of the outer levels, are embedded within the inner core. The term personality depth refers to the difficulties associated with penetrating these inner layers, often because of the risks associated with such revelations.

Personality depth can be interpreted in terms of the degree to which a seller understands each of its customers. This client knowledge will vary but may include the way they use the products, their strategies, resources, culture and ethos, difficulties, challenges, successes and other elements that characterise buying organisations. Through successive interactions each organisation develops more knowledge of the other, as more information is gradually exposed, revealed or made known. At the outset of relationships, buyers tend to restrict the amount of information they reveal about themselves, but as confidence and trust in the other party develops so the level of openness increases. Likewise, as relationships develop so the degree of formality between the parties decreases, becoming more informal. This relationship intensity impacts on the quality of the relationship between two or more organisations.

As relationships develop so the degree of formality between the parties decreases, becoming more informal.

Deconstructing a relationship reveals that it is composed of a series, or layers, of interactions. Each interaction results in judgements about whether to terminate or proceed with the

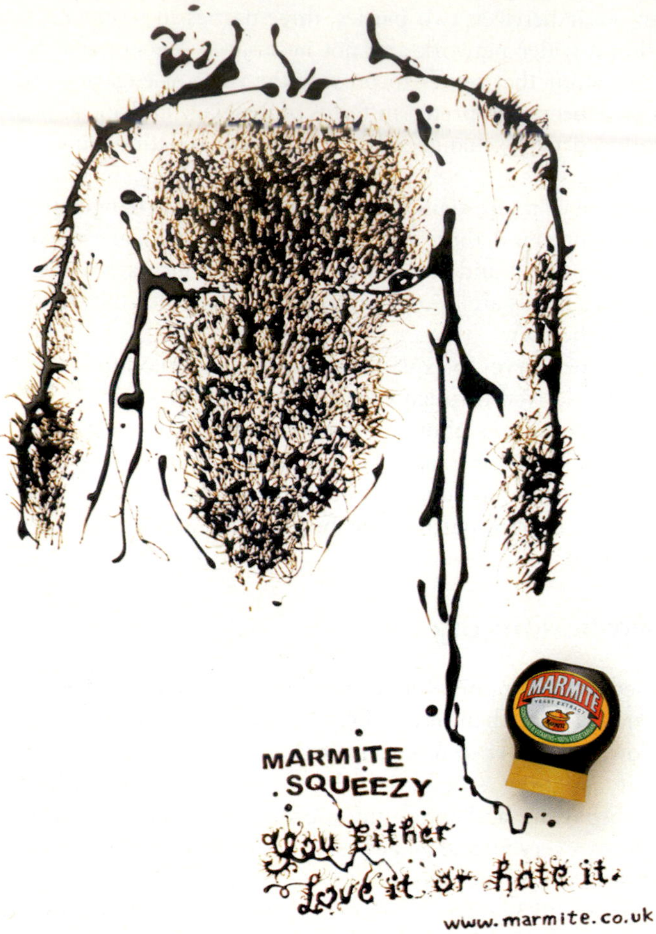

Exhibit 7.2 Marmite – love it or hate it. Brand personality that openly proclaims contrasting consumer preferences and brand relationships
Courtesy of Unilever and Marmite.

relationship. The judgement is based on the accumulation of interactions, the history of the relationship and the level of customer knowledge that has been revealed.

Interactional theory

The development of relationship marketing appears to coincide with the emergence of network approaches to interorganisational analysis. This is referred to as industrial network analysis, and has evolved from the original focus on dyadic relationships (Araujo and Easton, 1996). The International Marketing and Purchasing Group (IMP), a significantly strong and influential research group, focuses on the interaction between members of a network. The IMP Group analyses relationships, rather than transactions between buyers and sellers but, unlike relationship marketing theorists, they believe that both parties are active participants. Relationships between buyers and sellers are regarded as long-term, close and complex, and through episodes of exchange the links between organisations become institutionalised. Processes and roles become established, ingrained and expected of one another. It is particularly significant in this interactional approach that other organisations are considered to influence the relationship between a buyer and a seller. This incorporates ideas concerning network interpretations of business-to-business and channel configuration, considered in Chapter 8.

The Interactional approach is based on relational exchanges with a variety of organisations within interlocking networks. An important aspect of network operation is the high degree of cooperation and reciprocity necessary between participants. This cooperation is manifest through the various exchanges that organisations undertake. McLoughlin and Horan (2000) identify five main exchange elements, while the IMP Group determine four. These are set out in Table 7.3:

The Interactional approach is based on relational exchanges with a variety of organisations within interlocking networks.

Table 7.3 Elements of exchange episodes

McLoughlin and Horan (2000)	IMP Group
Financial and economic exchange	Product/service exchange
Technological exchange	Information exchange
Information exchange	Financial exchange
Knowledge exchange	Social exchange
Legal exchange	

These two lists are largely similar and both encompass formal and informal exchanges. These occur over time, with varying levels of intensity between two or more organisations.

Building marketing relationships

As discussed earlier, relationships are developed through interaction and dialogue. Exchanges that occur as a result of interaction are influenced by four main factors: technology; organisational determinants (size, structure and strategy); organisational experience; and individuals. The result of this is an atmosphere in which a relationship exists and which reflects issues of power-dependence, the degree of conflict or cooperation and the overall closeness or distance of the relationship.

Relationships consist of much more than just interaction or a series of exchanges so deconstruction of a relationship can provide a deeper understanding of the nature of relationships and, in doing so, indicate how marketing communications might best be used. Holmlund (1997), cited by Gronroos (2004) suggests that an on-going relationship can be considered to consist of four components. These are set out in Figure 7.3.

Holmlund states that an on-going relationship consists of various sequences, which in turn consist of episodes constructed from a series of acts. Phone calls and email, factory and site visits, service calls and the provision of information are examples of *acts*, which represent interaction. An *episode* is developed from a series of interrelated acts. The delivery of an order consists of a number of actions such as the placement of the order, the credit checking, fulfilment, delivery and unloading and each of these are *acts*. Interrelated episodes are referred to as *sequences*, which are time-specific. For example, an advertising or sales promotion campaign, a construction project, a training programme or all activities experienced during a holiday or visit to a hotel. Relationships, therefore, are composed of sequences, many of which might overlap. Marketing activities, including communications, can therefore be better understood and deployed within this structured approach to understanding relationship development.

An *episode* is developed from a series of interrelated acts.

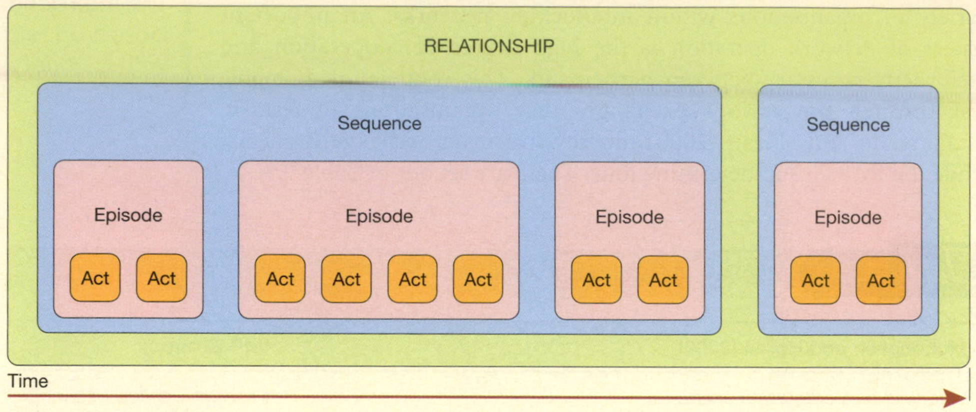

Figure 7.3 Interaction levels in a relationship
Source: Holmlund (1997): 96.

ViewPoint 7.4 Building relationships for 'You & Us'

UBS is one of the world's leading financial firms and claim to operate in two locations: 'Everywhere, and right next to you'.

A few years ago they launched a major corporate advertising campaign under a single brand. It represented a clear change of direction from their traditional advertising strategy based around the promotion of the various merits of UBS' products and services. The theme of their new campaign 'You & Us' highlights the importance of UBS' client relationships.

The campaign used global television and print advertising to focus on the importance and strength of UBS' client relationships that are backed by the powerful resources of the firm. The campaign's strapline, 'You & Us' is used to represent the intimacy of the relationship between individual clients and their advisors. It is used on all communication materials, including their home page. All of the advertisements feature just two people, a client and advisor, meeting in familiar situations. For example, sitting at a restaurant table, meeting in a conference room or an aerial shot of them crossing a road. The messages are reinforced by the voiceover that tries to be reassuring and natural, similar to the voice of a trusted friend, and definitely not corporate. The background to the ads carry images of skyscrapers, offices and mountains. These were used to reinforce the message that each UBS advisor has the support of a large, powerful organisation with all the resources necessary to meet a client's needs.

UBS provide a sophisticated business-to-business service so the advisors (actors) in the ads play a crucial role as they effectively become the face of UBS. Through their advisors, clients can access the 'UBS universe' of products, services, tools and resources. The 'You & Us' line is a promise that only the firm's employees keep through their day-to-day contact with clients.

Source: www.ubs.com/1/e/media_overview/media_americas/virtualpresskits/.

Question

Apart from the impact on customers, who else might be affected by this new positioning?

Task

Find two other global finance corporations and note how they position themselves.

Related relationship concepts

Among the many concepts associated with relationship marketing, three stand out. *Trust* and *commitment* and *loyalty* are considered in turn.

Trust

Many writers contend that one of the crucial factors associated with the development and maintenance of interorganisational relationships is trust (Morgan and Hunt, 1994; Doney and Cannon, 1997). However, Cousins and Stanwix (2001) believe that the concepts, although important, are difficult to define, and suggest that many authors fail to specify clearly what they mean when using them. A review of the literature indicates that trust is an element of personal, intraorganisational and interorganisational relationships, and is both necessary for and results from their perpetuation. As Gambetta (1988) argues, trust is a means of reducing uncertainty in order that effective relationships can develop.

Cousins and Stanwix (2001) also suggest that, although trust is a term used to explain how b2b relationships work, often it actually refers to ideas concerning risk, power and dependency and these propositions are used interchangeably. From their research of vehicle manufacturers, it emerges that b2b relationships are about the creation of mutual business advantage and the degree of confidence that one organisation has in another.

Interorganisational trust is based on two main dimensions: credibility and benevolence. Credibility concerns the extent to which one organisation believes (is confident) that another organisation will undertake and complete its agreed roles and tasks. Benevolence is concerned with goodwill, that the other organisation will not act opportunistically, even were the conditions for exploitation to arise (Pavlou, 2002). In other words, interorganisational trust involves judgements about another organisation's reliability and integrity.

Interorganisational trust is based on two main dimensions: credibility and benevolence.

ViewPoint 7.5 Losing trust in television?

Both the BBC and ITV faced criticisms in 2007 concerning the way they ran some phone-in programmes. The first scandal to break concerned the previously crystal-clean children's show *Blue Peter*. It was revealed that following a technical fault with the phone lines, they used a studio guest to phone-in to claim a prize. The 40,000 viewers who had called the premium-rate line were disbarred from the competition as they had no chance of winning. Unfortunately, the joy associated with the researcher whose 'quick thinking' enabled the programme to proceed, turned sour when the producers and the programme's editor failed to report the incident (deception) to BBC management.

Both GMTV and Channel 4 (*Richard and Judy*) were found by Ofcom to have rigged phone-in competitions by picking winners before the phones lines were switched off. Later it was found that programmes such as *Ant and Dec's Saturday Night Takeaway*, *Gameshow Marathon* and *Soapstar Superstar*, all on ITV, were also rigged and effectively defrauded customers.

These scams resulted in large fines and many people having to resign their positions. Perhaps the more significant outcome was the public's loss of trust and faith in television programmes, the competitions they offer and the messages they deliver.

Sources: Byrne (2007); Robinson (2007); Sherwin (2007).

Question

To what extent should the control of all competitions be regulated by legislation?

Task

Find another phone-in scandal. How did the promoter respond when first approached about the issue?

Table 7.4 Elements of institutional trust

Element of institutional trust	Key aspect
Perceived monitoring	Refers to the supervision of transactions by, for example, regulatory authorities or owners of b2b market exchanges. This can mitigate uncertainty through a perception that sellers or buyers who fail to conform with established rules and regulations will be penalised.
Perceived accreditation	Refers to badges or symbols that denote membership of externally recognised bodies that bestow credibility, authority, security and privacy on a selling organisation.
Perceived legal bonds	Refers to contracts between buyers, sellers and independent third parties, so that the costs of breaking a contract are perceived to be greater than the benefits of such an action. Trust in the selling organisation is therefore enhanced when bonds are present.
Perceived feedback	Refers to signals about the quality of an organisation's reputation and such feedback from other buyers about sellers, perhaps through word-of-mouth communication, can deter sellers from undertaking opportunistic behaviour.
Perceived cooperative norms	Refers to the values, standards and principles adopted by those party to a series of exchanges. Cooperative norms and values signal good faith and behavioural intent, through which trust is developed.

Source: Based on Pavlou (2002).

It has been suggested that interorganisational trust consists of three main elements (Zucker (1986); Luo (2002)). *Characteristic* trust, based on the similarities between parties, *process* trust, developed through familiarity and typically fostered by successive exchange transactions, and *institutional* trust, see below. This third category might be considered to be the most important, especially at the outset of a relationship when familiarity and similarity factors are non-existent or hard to discern respectively.

Pavlou (2002) argues that there are six means by which institutional trust can be encouraged (see Table 7.4).

Institutional trust is clearly vital in B2C markets where online perceived risk is present and known to prevent many people from purchasing online. In the B2B market, institutional trust is also important but more in terms of the overall reputation of the organisation. The development and establishment of trust is valuable because of the outcomes that can be anticipated. Three major outcomes from the development of trust have been identified by Pavlou, namely satisfaction, perceived risk and continuity. Trust can reduce conflict and the threat of opportunism, which in turn enhances the probability of buyer satisfaction, an important positive outcome of institutional trust.

Perceived risk is concerned with the expectation of loss and is therefore tied closely with organisational performance. Trust that a seller will not take advantage of the imbalance of information between buyer and seller effectively reduces risk. Continuity is related to business volumes, necessary in online B2B marketplaces, and the development of both on- and offline enduring relationships. Trust is associated with continuity and, when present, is therefore indicative of long-term relationships. Ryssel *et al.* (2004: 203) recognise that trust (and commitment) have a 'significant impact on the creation of value and conclude that value creation is a function of the atmosphere of a relationship rather than the technology employed'.

Table 7.5 Components of trust

Trust component	Explanation
Reputation	Provides a summary statement of the likelihood that purchase and experience expectations will not disappoint.
Familiarity/closeness	Personal or human trust is a significant component witnessed by organisations recruiting people with skills and experience that potential buyers can identify with. Sales force representatives and slice of life advertising typify ways in which organisations seek to establish familiarity.
Performance	The performance of the product or service becomes regularised and habitual.
Accountability	The use of trade associations, credit agencies and professional organisations to underwrite and enforce performance standards give consumers the necessary confidence to trust and can be important in areas where consumers have limited specialised knowledge.

Source: Morrison and Firmstone (2000). Used by permission of WARC.

Trust within a consumer context is equally important as a means of reducing uncertainty. In particular, brands are an important means of instilling trust, mainly because they are a means of condensing and conveying information so that they provide sufficient information for consumers to make calculated purchase decisions in the absence of full knowledge. In a sense, consumers transfer their responsibility for brand decision-making, and hence brand performance, to the brand itself. Through extended use of a brand, purchasing habits develop, or what is termed routinised response behaviour. This is important not just because complex decision-making is simplified, but because the amount of communication necessary to assist and provoke purchase is considerably reduced.

The establishment of trust can be based around the existence of various components (Morrison and Firmstone, 2000). These are set out in Table 7.5.

According to Young and Wilkinson (1989) the presence of trust within a relationship is influenced by four main factors: the duration of the relationship; the relative power of the participants; the presence of cooperation; and various environmental factors that may be present at any one moment. Extending these ideas into what is now regarded by many as a seminal paper in the relationship marketing literature, Morgan and Hunt (1994) argue, and support with empirical evidence, that the presence of both commitment and trust leads to cooperative behaviour and this in turn is conducive to successful relationship marketing.

The presence of both commitment and trust leads to cooperative behaviour.

Online trust and security

These components can be substantiated through experience but in terms of information systems technology (IST) and the Internet in particular, problems arise when attempting to apply these criteria. There is a total lack of accountability on the Internet that may explain why a certain proportion of the population are reluctant to engage in online transactions. Many consumers do not understand the performance characteristics of the Internet and of various aspects of the digital world, which suggests to Morrison and Firmstone that there is too much missing knowledge for a sufficient level of trust to be present.

This factor may dissipate as successive generations become more conversant and confident in technology and its performance characteristics, as the proportion of digital natives outweighs the number of digital immigrants. However, at the moment a lack of familiarity might partly explain why sufficient numbers of consumers do not place their trust when there is so much that is unknown. In addition, the cues by which trust is established offline have yet to become established in the online world. Symbols, trade marks and third-party endorsements need to be available so that the trust-inducing cues can be interpreted and relied on. Finally, brand reputation is a summary statement of performance and reputation conveys signals that others do, and for long-established brands, have in the past trusted the brand. Morrison and Firmstone (2000: 621) argue that 'existence confers an invitation to trust and a long existence gives strength to the presumption that one should trust'. This means that pure play operations will have a more challenging task to establish reputation than bricks and clicks operations that are able to transfer part of their offline reputation into their online world.

Technology is available to provide virtually secure online transactions and, despite the relatively small amount of online crime, there is a strong consumer perception that online transactions are not safe, even though many of these same people willingly give their credit card details over the telephone to complete strangers. eRetailers should use marketing communications to reduce levels of perceived risk associated with online shopping and to provide a strong level of consumer reassurance. Thomas (2000) suggests that there are a number of things that can be done to provide such reassurance:

1. Strong offline brands immediately provide recognition and an improved level of security, although care needs to be taken to convince audiences that the operator's online work is as effective as that of the offline brand.
2. Ensure that the web pages where sensitive data are stored are hosted on a secure server. Use the most up-to-date security facilities and then tell consumers the actions you have taken to create a feel-good association and trust with the online brand. It is also worthwhile listing any physical, tangible addresses the company might have in order that consumers feel they are dealing with a modern yet conventional business.
3. Provide full contact details, fax, telephone, postal addresses and the names of people they can refer to. Again, this enables a level of personalisation and may soften the virtual atmosphere for those hesitant to immerse themselves in online transactions.
4. Provide an opportunity for the consumer to lock into the online brand by registering and subscribing to the site. Many organisations offer an incentive such as a free email newsletter or introductory offer.
5. By satisfying criteria associated with transparency, security and customer service it is possible to earn accreditation or cues that signal compatibility and compliance. The Academy of Internet Commerce operates a best practice called the Academy Seal of Approval. The logo appears on the site and when clicked provides a full text of the charter itself, a powerful form of reducing functional and financial risk.

Post-purchase communications are just as important in the online as well as the offline environment.

Post-purchase communications are just as important in the online as well as the offline environment. Email acknowledgement of an order provides reassurance that the company actually exists and prompt (immediate next day) delivery or, if on extended delivery, an interim progress report (email) will provide confidence. Online order tracking is now quite common, making it possible to see the exact location of an order.

ViewPoint 7.6 Making an omelette out of credit

The world of personal finance has become increasingly complex. Part of this complexity is due to increased consumer wealth but it also because much of the business has moved online. The digital era has changed the relationship between banks and their customers. Consumers no longer rely on newspapers and expert comment. They now go online and search for information to either substantiate or develop views about products and services. Consumers now expect 24/7 access, and social networking sites enable people to share brand experiences, good and bad, more quickly and away from the influence of the expert and the bank.

Trust can be easily eroded in the digital environment even by events offline. The collapse of Northern Rock in late 2007 hit the industry hard as people queued to withdraw their savings while the Northern Rock web site ground to a halt.

In February 2008 the Citigroup bank announced that it was withdrawing the credit cards from 161,000 of their 'Egg' customers. This action was taken in attempt to offload customers who were reported by the bank to have a 'higher than acceptable risk profile'. Many customers complained, claiming they paid off their credit balances each month and could not be deemed to be credit risk customers. However, it might be seen that they were relatively unprofitable customers and the bank would rather work with customers who ran balances up to their credit levels and only paid the minimum amount each month.

The bank has now cancelled an agreement entered into with their customers, some of whom may not have transgressed the terms and conditions. The issue concerns whether this action is in the best interests of the bank's long-term relationships with its stakeholders and whether it will impact on its reputation. This realignment by the bank may send signals to prospective customers that this organisation is not to be trusted.

Sources: Nottage (2007); Ashton and Watts (2008).

Question

Does the *Egg* case suggest that bad publicity is so short-lived that it is deemed acceptable to work in this way?

Task

What sort of relationship do you have with your bank and how does this differ from the relationship you have with other financial providers . . . why?

Commitment

Morgan and Hunt regard commitment as the desire that a relationship continue (endure) in order that a valued relationship be maintained or strengthened. They postulated that commitment and trust are key mediating variables between five antecedents and five outcomes (see Figure 7.4).

Commitment and trust are key mediating variables.

According to the KMV model the greater the losses anticipated through the termination of a relationship the greater the commitment will be expressed by the exchange partners. Likewise, when these partners share the same values commitment increases. Trust is enhanced when communication is perceived to be of high quality but decreases when one organisation knowingly takes action to seek to benefit from the relationship, which will be to the detriment of the other.

Kumar *et al.* (1994) distinguish between *affective* and *calculative* commitment. The former is rooted in positive feelings towards the other party and a desire to maintain the relationship. The latter is negatively oriented and is determined by the extent to which one party perceives it is (not) possible advantageously to replace the other party.

The centrality of the trust and commitment concepts to relationship marketing has thus been established and they are as central to marketing channel relationships as to other b2b relationships (Achrol, 1991; Goodman and Dion, 2001).

Customer loyalty and retention

Implicit within this customer relationship cycle is the notion that retained customers are loyal. However, this may be misleading as 'loyalty' may actually be a term used to convey

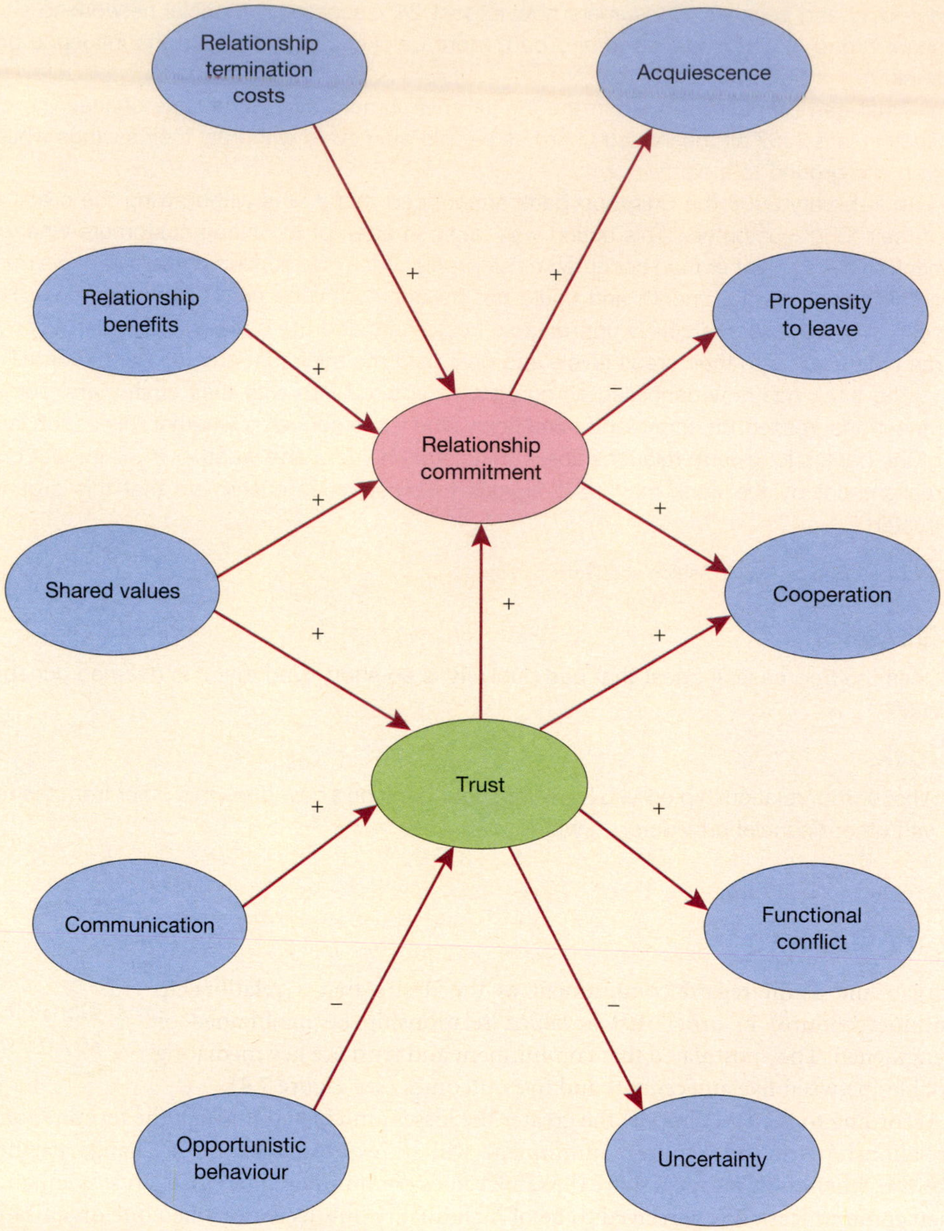

Figure 7.4 The KMV model of commitment and trust
Source: Morgan and Hunt (1994). Used with kind permission of the American Marketing Association.

convenience or extended utility. Loyalty, however presented, takes different forms, just as there are customers who are more valued than others. Christopher *et al.* (2002) depict the various types of relationships as stages or steps on a ladder, the 'Relationship marketing ladder of loyalty' (Figure 7.5).

A prospect becomes a purchaser, completed through a market or discrete exchange. Clients emerge from several completed transactions but remain ambivalent towards the seller organisation. Supporters, despite being passive about an organisation, are willing and able to

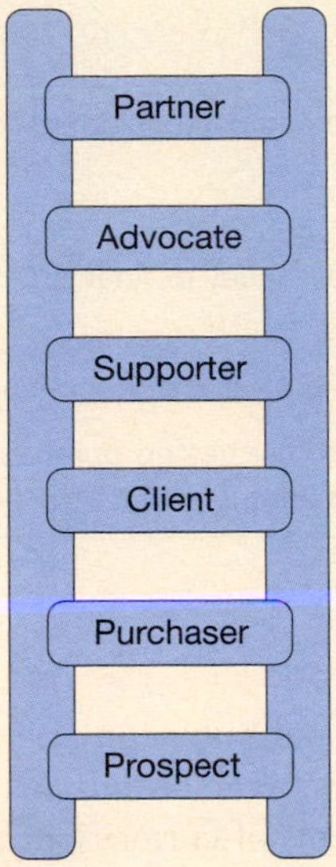

Partner: someone who has the relationship of a partner with you

Advocate: someone who actively recommends you to others, who does your marketing for you

Supporter: someone who likes your organisation, but only supports you passively

Client: someone who has done business with you on a repeat basis but may be negative, or at best neutral, towards your organisation

Purchaser: someone who has done business just once with your organisation

Prospect: someone whom you believe may be persuaded to do business with you

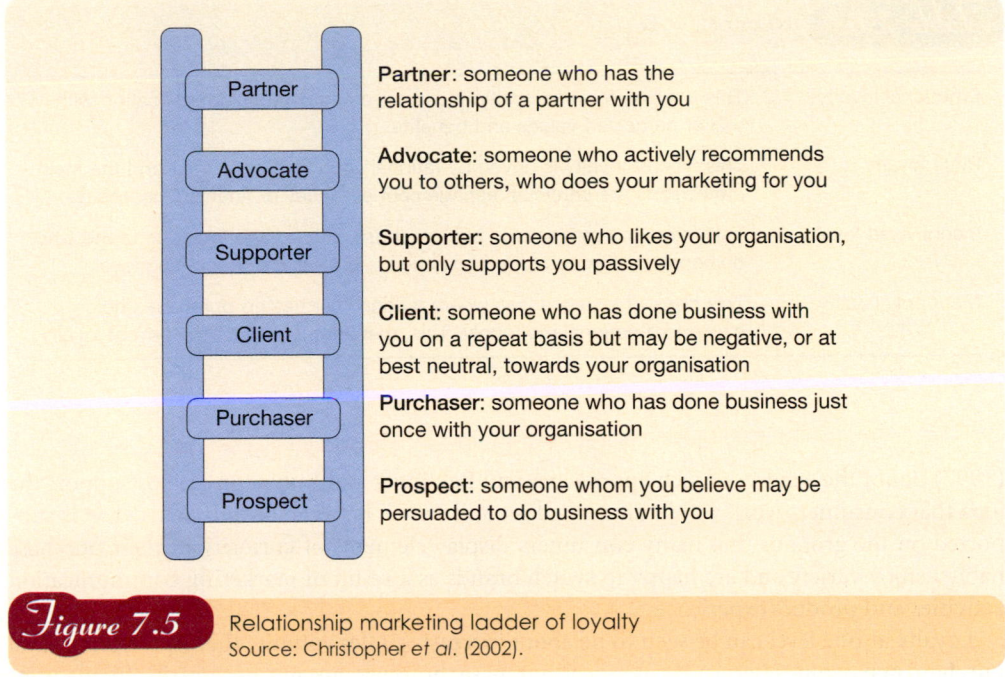

Figure 7.5 Relationship marketing ladder of loyalty
Source: Christopher *et al.* (2002).

enter into regular transactions. Advocates represent the next and penultimate step. They not only support an organisation and its products but actively recommend it to others by positive, word-of-mouth communications. Partners, who represent the top rung of the ladder, trust and support an organisation just as it trusts and supports them. Partnership status, discussed in greater detail later in this chapter, is the embodiment of relational exchanges and interorganisational collaboration.

Partnership status is the embodiment of relational exchanges and interorganisational collaboration.

This cycle of customer attraction (acquisition), development, retention and decline represents a major difference to the 4Ps approach. It is, above all else, customer-focused and more appropriate to marketing values. However, even this approach is questionable as, although the focus of analysis is no longer the product but the relationship, the focus tends to be oriented towards the 'customer relationship' rather than the relationship per se. In other words there is a degree of asymmetry inherent in the relationship marketing concept.

The simplicity of the loyalty ladder concept illustrates the important point that customers represent different values to other organisations, and that perceived value (or worth) may or may not be reciprocated, thus establishing the basis for a variety and complexity of different relationships. The theoretical development of relationship marketing encompasses a number of different concepts. These involve a greater emphasis on cooperation rather than competition and the identification of different development phases within customer relationships, namely customer acquisition, development and retention.

Types and levels of loyalty

The concept of loyalty has attracted much research attention if only because of the recent and current popularity of this approach. Table 7.6 represents some of the more general types of loyalty that can be observed.

These hierarchical schemes suggest that consumers are capable of varying degrees of loyalty. This type of categorisation has been questioned by a number of researchers. Fournier and Yao

Table 7.6 Types of loyalty

Emotional loyalty	This is a true form of loyalty and is driven by personal identification with real or perceived values and benefits.
Price loyalty	This type of loyalty is driven by rational economic behaviour and the main motivations are cautious management of money or financial necessity.
Incentivised loyalty	This refers to promiscuous buyers: those with no one favourite brand who demonstrate through repeat experience the value of becoming loyal.
Monopoly loyalty	This class of loyalty arises where a consumer has no purchase choice owing to a national monopoly. This, therefore, is not a true form of loyalty.

(1997) doubt the validity of such approaches and Baldinger and Rubinson (1996) support the idea that consumers work within an evoked set and switch between brands. This view is supported on the grounds that many consumers display elements of curiosity in their purchase habits, enjoy variety and are happy to switch brands as a result of marketing communication activities and product experience.

Loyalty at one level can be seen to be about increasing sales volume, that is, fostering loyal purchase behaviour. High levels of repeat purchase, however, are not necessarily an adequate measure of loyalty, as there may be a number of situational factors determining purchase behaviour, such as brand availability (Dick and Basu, 1994).

> There is plenty of evidence to show that many satisfied customers buy a variety of brands.

At another level, loyalty can be regarded as an attitudinal disposition. O'Malley (1998) suggests that customer satisfaction has become a surrogate measure of loyalty. However, she points out that there is plenty of evidence to show that many satisfied customers buy a variety of brands and that polygamous loyalty, as suggested by Dowling and Uncles (1997), may be a better reflection of reality.

Another interesting perspective on relationship marketing concerns the role of consumer satisfaction. Garbarino and Johnson (1999) researched the attitudes and motivations of people who held long-term subscriptions to a theatre. While this group might be said to hold a strong relationship with the theatre, it was possible to determine two sub-groups of customers. Some had a functional orientation towards the service provider and others were determined as holding partnership characteristics. These they termed low and high relational customers respectively. Their research found that the long-term intentions of the low relational customers are driven by overall satisfaction measures. In contrast, high relational customers are driven by trust and commitment which means that satisfaction is an irrelevance for this customer group. They will continue subscribing regardless of whether the plays and performances are entertaining and enjoyable. The implication for the design of marketing communication programmes is that transactional-based communications that focus on developing measures of satisfaction will be suitable for customers who have a functional yet long-term relationship with a brand. For those more passionately involved, communications should focus on building trust and commitment.

The Institute of Practitioners in Advertising (IPA) published a report that indicated that as little as 9 per cent of loyalty schemes were significantly profitable. When schemes are successful, this is not achieved by retaining customers but through the attraction of new ones (McLuhan, 2007). In other words the whole notion that loyalty schemes serve to retain customers is possibly flawed.

At whichever level of loyalty, customer retention is paramount and neither behavioural nor attitudinal measures alone are adequate indicators of true loyalty. O'Malley suggests that a combination of the two is of greater use and that, when used together, the twin parameters relative attitudes (to alternatives) and patronage behaviour (the recency, frequency and monetary model), as suggested by Dick and Basu (1994), offer more accurate indicators of loyalty (see Chapter 21 for a consideration of loyalty programmes).

The role of marketing communications in relationships

Having considered ideas about relationship marketing and established its centrality within contemporary marketing thought, it now remains to explore ways in which marketing communications can contribute to relationship marketing. Transaction marketing, where the focus is product and price, uses mass communications with persuasion as a central element. Relationship marketing, with its focus on the relationship between the participants, encourages interaction and dialogue. This is compatible with the concepts of integrated marketing communications (IMC). Gronroos (2004) suggests that although IMC cannot be synonymous with relationship marketing, it is an important aspect of relationship marketing. He argues that within an interaction and planned communication context customer messages can be divided into five groups. These are set out in Table 7.7.

Gronroos develops the view that there are two main types of message that customers receive, process and use to determine the extent to which a relationship delivers value. The first of these types is the planned marketing communication message, which is predetermined and delivered through various media and tools of the communication mix. Planned messages set out an organisation's promises. In addition, there are messages generated through the product and service aspects of the interaction that occurs between organisations and their customers. The degree to which these two streams of messages support or counter each other will influence the type of unplanned communications that ensue. See Figure 1.1 in Chapter 1 for a graphical representation of these types of marketing communication message.

The greater the degree that the two sets of messages support or reinforce one another, the more favourable the unplanned communication that should result in positive word-of-mouth communication (Gronroos and Lindberg-Repo, 1998). This can lead to the establishment of two-way communication, an increasing propensity to share information, a process of

Table 7.7 Source of messages about an organisation.

Message Source	Explanation
Planned marketing communications	Make promises about how solutions to customer problems should occur – for example, mass communications, brochures, sales, direct response, WWW pages
Product messages	For example: the design, technical features, utility, appearance, production process, durability and distribution
Service messages	Derived from interactions with an organisation's customer service – deliveries, invoicing, claims handling, product documentation
Unplanned messages	News stories, references, gossip, Internet chat groups, word-of-mouth communications
Absence	A lack of communication or silence following service breakdown

Source: Derived from Gronroos (2000) who acknowledges the work of Calonius (1989) and Duncan and Moriarty (1997).

Through shared meaning trust increases.

reasoning and ultimately dialogue. Reasoning is important because it enables a sharing of values and a deeper understanding of the other party's needs and position. Through shared meaning trust increases. Gronroos (2004) argues that relationship marketing develops not from planned marketing communications, but through the interaction and personal experience of products and services and the degree to which these two sets of messages and meanings complement the promises and messages transmitted previously. He suggests that when these two processes come together a single, two-way communication process emerges. Put precisely he says, (p. 107) 'the two processes merge into a relationship dialogue'.

Communication during the customer lifecycle

Marketing communications can play an important role throughout all relationship phases and at all stages of the customer lifecycle. Indeed, marketing communications should be used to engage with audiences according to the audiences' needs, whether transactional and remote, or relational and close. According to Ryssel *et al.* (2004) the use of IST, which enables communication to be timely, accurate and direct, has a positive impact on trust. During the acquisition phase, marketing communications needs to be geared towards creating awareness and access to the brand. Included within this period will be the need to help potential customers become familiar with the brand and to help them increase their understanding of the key attributes, possible benefits from use and to know how the brand is different and represents value that is superior to the competition. Indeed, marketing communications has to work during this phase because it needs to fulfil a number of different roles and it needs to be targeted at precise audiences. Perhaps the main overriding task is to create a set of relevant brand values, which represent significant value for the target audience. In DRIP terms differentiation and information will be important and in terms of the promotional mix, advertising and direct marking in the b2c market and personal selling and direct marketing in the b2b market.

The main goals during the development phase are for the selling organisation to reduce buyer perceived risk and to simultaneously enhance their own credibility.

The main goals during the development phase are for the selling organisation to reduce buyer perceived risk and to simultaneously enhance their own credibility. In order to reduce risk a number of messages will need to be presented though marketing communications. The selection of these elements will depend upon the forms of risk that are present either in the market sector or within individual customers. Marketing communications needs to engage by communicating messages concerning warranties and guarantees, finance schemes, third-party endorsements and satisfied customers, independent testing and favourable product performance reports, awards and the attainment of quality standards, membership of trade associations, delighted customers, growth and market share, new products and alliances and partnerships, all of which seek to reduce risk and improve credibility. In DRIP terms information and persuasion will be important and in terms of the promotional mix, public relations, sales promotion and direct marketing in the b2c market, and personal selling, public relations and direct marketing in the b2b market will be significant.

The length of the retention phase will reflect the degree to which the marketing communications is truly interactional and based on dialogue. Messages need to be relational and reinforcing. Incentive schemes are used extensively in consumer markets as a way of retaining customers and minimising customer loss or churn. They are also used to cross-sell products and services and increase a customer's commitment and involvement with the brand. Through the use of an integrated programme of communications value can be enhanced for both parties and relational exchanges are more likely to be maintained. In business markets personal contact and key account management are crucial to maintaining interaction, understanding and mutual support.

Through the use of an integrated programme of communications value can be enhanced for both parties and relational exchanges are more likely to be maintained.

Electronic communications have the potential to automate many routine transactions and allow for increased focus on one-to-one communications. In DRIP terms reinforcement and information will be important and in terms of the promotional mix, sales promotion and direct marking in the b2c market, and personal selling (and key accounts), public relations and direct marketing in the b2b market will be significant.

The final phase of decline concerns the process by which a relationship is eventually terminated. This process may be sharp and sudden or slow and protracted. Marketing communications plays a minor role in the former but is more significant in the latter. During an extended termination, marketing communications, especially direct marketing in the form of telemarketing and email, can be used to deliver orders and profits. These forms of communication are beneficial because they allow for continued personal messages but do incur the heavy costs associated with field selling (b2b) or advertising (b2c). In DRIP terms reinforcement and persuasion will be important and in terms of the promotional mix, direct marketing in both markets and sales promotion in the b2c market will be significant.

Customer relationship management

One technological approach, designed specifically to enable better customer service and retention, is customer relationship management, more commonly referred to as CRM systems. Establishing what constitutes CRM is far from easy based on the various interpretations that have been placed on the term. Ang and Buttle (2003) suggest that there are three main approaches: *strategic*, where CRM is seen as a core business strategy; *operational*, where CRM is about automating different aspects of an organisation's selling, marketing and service functions; and, finally, *analytical*, where CRM is about manipulating data to improve the efficiency and effectiveness of each phase of the customer relationship lifecycle. From this it is possible to consider CRM as the delivery of customer value through the strategic integration of business functions and processes, using customer data and information systems and technology.

Early CRM applications were designed for supplier organisations to enable them to manage their end-user customers and consequently they became regarded as a front-end application. Originally developed as sales force support systems (mainly sales force automation – see Chapter 22) they have subsequently evolved as a more sophisticated means of managing customers, using real-time customer information.

CRM applications typically consist of call management, lead management, customer record, sales support and payment systems. These are necessary in order to respond to questions from customers (e.g. about products, deliveries, prices and order status) and questions from internal stakeholders about issues such as strategy, processes, operations and sales forecasts.

CRM applications typically consist of call management, lead management, customer record, sales support and payment systems.

These systems should be used at each stage of the customer lifecycle, in order to develop an understanding about customer attitudes and behaviour that the organisation desires. Theoretically, CRM should be used to assist in making decisions about whom to target, which customer differences should be taken into account and what impact this will have on profitability. It is this aspect of profitability, or relative profitability of individual customers, that is important and which is a core aspect of relationship marketing. As Nancarrow and Rees (2003) suggest, only by understanding the actual, potential, current and lifetime forms of individual customer profitability can different strategies be developed for different profit segments. Low-profit-generating customers may need to be treated differently from those customers that are highly profitable, and those customers who incur losses for the organisation may need to be dropped.

The conceptual idea of using customer and transactional data in order to proactively shape customer relationships is appealing. IST now enables much of this to happen. However, many client organisations have voiced disappointment and even criticism when such systems fail to meet their expectations, while Rigby *et al.* (2002) report that very few CRM investments have proved to be successful. Table 7.8 lists some of the more prominent reasons.

Table 7.8 Reasons for CRM disappointment

Author	Reasons for CRM underachievement
Wightman, 2000	Failure to adopt CRM within a strategic orientation
Stone, 2002	CRM is regarded as a mere add-on application that is expected to resolve all customer interface difficulties
Sood, 2002	Failure of systems to accommodate the wide array of relationships that organisations seek to manage
O'Malley and Mitussis, 2002	Internal political issues concerning ownership of systems

Most of the reasons cited in Table 7.8 are based on the failure of a large number of organisations, both clients and vendors, to understand the central tenets of a customer-focused business philosophy. If CRM systems are to work then a central business strategy, one based on the importance of trust, commitment and customer satisfaction, has to be agreed and led by the senior managers. Only within this context can it be expected that the installation of databases, data warehouses and associated software will help influence the quality of an organisation's relationships with its customers and stakeholders. Good customer management requires attention to an organisation's culture, training, strategy, propositions and processes. Regretfully, too many organisations focus on the interface or fail to understand the broader picture.

Summary

In order to help consolidate your understanding of the role of marketing communications within relationship marketing, here are the key points summarised against each of the learning objectives:

1. Explore the concept of value and its role in developing marketing relationships.

Value is the customer's estimate of the extent to which a product or service can satisfy their individual needs. Value is relative to customer expectations and experience of competitive offerings within a category, and can be derived from sources other than products, such as the relationships between buyers and sellers.

The development of customer perceived value is now regarded not only as crucial for commercial success but there is an increasing amount of evidence that indicates that the relationships organisations form, with a range of stakeholders, not just customers, are themselves a generator of value and hence an important aspect of contemporary marketing.

2. Consider the characteristics of relationship marketing.

Interaction between customers and sellers is based around the provision and consumption of perceived value. Relationship value can be visualised as a continuum.

At one end of the continuum are transactional exchanges, characterised by short-term, commodity or price-oriented exchanges, between buyers and sellers coming together for one-off exchanges independent of any other or subsequent exchanges. Both parties are motivated mainly by self-interest.

At the other end of the continuum are relational or collaborative exchanges. These are characterised by a long-term orientation, where there is complete integration of systems and processes and the relationship is motivated by partnership and mutual support. Trust and commitment underpin these relationships and these variables become increasingly important as collaborative exchanges become established.

3. Appraise the theoretical concepts underpinning relationship marketing.

There have been numerous theoretical attempts to explaining relationship marketing. Three are presented here: social exchange, social penetration and interaction theories.

4. Consider the importance of customer retention and the use of loyalty programmes to reduce customer defection.

By undertaking a customer profitability analysis it is possible to identify those segments that are worth developing, and hence build a portfolio of relationships, each of varying dimensions and potential. These relationships provide mutually rewarding benefits and provide a third dimension in the customer dynamic, namely customer development.

At the heart of many relationship marketing strategies are loyalty or customer retention programmes. Whether these are loyalty or perhaps convenience programmes may be debatable but organisations in the b2c market should always question whether consumers really desire a relationship with a brand and whether their actions are bred of loyalty or inertia. Questions concerning trust and commitment have far-ranging implications for marketing communications whether these are delivered offline or in an online context.

5. Examine ways in which marketing relationships can be developed.

Exchanges that occur as a result of interaction are influenced by four main factors: technology; organisational determinants (size, structure and strategy); organisational experience; and individuals. The result of this is an atmosphere in which a relationship exists and which reflects issues of power-dependence, the degree of conflict or cooperation and the overall closeness or distance of the relationship.

Relationships consist of much more than just interaction or a series of exchanges so deconstruction of the relationship construct can provide a deeper understanding of the nature of relationships and in doing so indicate how marketing communications might best be used. Customer relationships can be considered in terms of a series of relationship development phases: customer acquisition; development; retention; and decline.

6. Explore issues concerning the development of trust in online environments.

The cues by which trust is established offline have yet to become fully established in the online world. Symbols, trade marks and third-party endorsements need to be available so that the trust-inducing cues can be interpreted and relied on.

Strong offline brands provide immediate recognition and an improved level of security, although care needs to be taken to convince audiences that the operator's online work is as effective as that of the offline brand. By satisfying criteria associated with transparency, security and customer service it is possible to earn accreditation or cues that signal compatibility and compliance.

7. Explore ways in which marketing communications can help organisations develop relationships.

Where transaction marketing is predominant, one where the focus is product and price, the use of mass communications with persuasion as a central element is recommended. Where collaborative exchanges prevail, personal communications that emphasise the relationship with its focus on interaction and dialogue is important.

Marketing communications can play an important role throughout all relationship phases and at all stages of the customer lifecycle. Indeed, marketing communications should be used to engage with audiences according to the audiences' needs, whether transactional and remote, or collaborative and close.

Review questions

1. Discuss the view that the notion of customer value is too abstract to be of worth to organisations when loyalty is so hard to establish.
2. Identify the three principles Doyle established for the development of customer value.
3. Without looking back, draw the figure depicting the range of value-oriented exchanges.
4. Make a list of the main differences between transactional and relationship marketing.
5. Write brief notes explaining relationship marketing in terms of social exchange, penetration and interaction theories.
6. Explain the concepts trust and commitment and outline the linkages between them.
7. Evaluate reasons why it has been difficult for organisations to establish online customer trust.
8. Identify two different commercial loyalty programmes and consider the marketing communications used to support them.
9. Prepare brief notes explaining different types of loyalty.
10. Discuss ways in which marketing communications can be used to develop relationships with customers.

MiniCase Reggae Reggae Sauce

Angela Carroll: University of Leeds

Background

The Reggae Reggae Sauce brand was invented by entrepreneur, chef and singer Levi Roots. Born in Clarendon, Jamaica, Levi learnt to cook from his grandmother who taught him how to mix Caribbean flavours and the importance of natural ingredients in her kitchen. She passed onto him an old family recipe which had been handed down from generation to generation. When he came to England to join the rest of his family, Levi used cooking to combat homesickness, spending hours in the kitchen preparing his grandmother's recipes including jerk sauce. He perfected and refined the secret recipe to create Reggae Reggae Sauce, a marinade which is popular for barbequed food and which can also be used on its own as a dip or condiment.

Jerk is a Jamaican style of cooking which traditionally used a mixture of dry-rubbed spices called Jamaican Jerk. Jerk spice must contain two essential ingredients to get the right level of flavours: Jamaican pimento (otherwise known as allspice) and scotch bonnet peppers, which give it a kick. In addition, a range of other ingredients such as cinnamon, garlic, cloves, tomatoes and nutmeg may be included. Jerked meat dates back centuries to the end of the 15th century when Columbus visited Jamaica but Jerk-stands are a very popular feature of modern-day Jamaica. Traditionally, jerk spice was always used with pork but today chicken, fish and tofu are also used.

For a number of years Levi made batches of the sauce in his kitchen in Brixton and sold it at Brixton market out of a bag on his back. The popularity of the sauce among Brixton's community persuaded Levi to set up a web site to promote and sell it. In addition, he regularly had a stall at the annual Notting Hill carnival which was called the Rasta'raunt because it was much more than a food experience. Levi's other passion in life is music and as a reggae musician he was nominated for best reggae singer at the 1998 MOBO awards. Through Reggae Reggae Sauce Levi felt that he could combine his two great passions and create a fusion between the food he was cooking and the music he was singing.

In 2006 Levi was spotted at the World Food Market by a BBC researcher who invited him to appear on the BBC2 programme *Dragon's Den*. In the programme aimed at aspiring entrepreneurs, individuals compete for investment from the panel of successful business figures in exchange for a share in the business. Two of the panel, Peter Jones and Richard Farleigh, were won over by his presentation during which he sang a reggae tune 'Proper Tings' and claimed that the sauce 'puts music in your food'. They agreed to invest £25,000 each in the business for a 20 per cent return share.

Following the programme's airing in February 2007, an excusive deal was secured with Sainsbury's who agreed to stock the product in 607 stores at a retail price of £1.49. The weeks that followed *Dragon's Den* were a testing time for Levi: he had to distribute a product that had previously been made in his own kitchen to a national market in a very short space of time. A licence was granted to a company in South Wales to manufacture the product to Levi's secret recipe and to meet the demand from Sainsbury's. In addition packaging decisions had to be taken including shape of the bottle and label design. Media interest in Levi escalated with requests for interviews, television appearances and music performances. His web site was flooded with orders and the brand became Sainsbury's fastest selling product in the category. He has subsequently developed a loyal customer base who are fond of both the product and the man behind it.

Despite the pressures created by the brand launch, Levi continued with his music career. He launched 'Proper Tings' as a single under the title 'The Reggae Reggae Sauce Song', with proceeds donated to Comic Relief. He is currently working on a new album with legendary producer Mad Professor while also compiling an album entitled 'The Best of Levi Roots'.

Determined to combine his love of food and music Levi said, 'I'm not in this to be the next Heinz Ketchup. I just want to bring the sweet, sweet flavour of reggae music to the world.'

In June 2007, Levi also opened a take away outlet in London, Papine Jerk Centre, serving traditional West Indian food. The ethos is to prepare fresh, healthy food in front of customers in a fun, vibrant atmosphere.

In terms of market, Reggae Reggae Sauce competes most directly in the bottled sauce sector rather than the cooking sauce sector due to its versatility and the fact that it does not have to be heated. The bottled category was worth £362m in 2006 with the manufacturer brands of table sauce such as tomato ketchup accounting for 65 per cent of the market. Dish-specific sauces such as Reggae Reggae Sauce account for 16 per cent of the market. Growth has been moderate in this category with a 5.3 per cent increase between 2003 and 2006. However, the development of the barbeque market, fuelled by higher temperatures in the United Kingdom, is forecast to create a strong year-round presence for such sauces. In addition, there is evidence that some consumers are seeing established sauce products as boring and seeking more adventurous flavours, adopting a more experimental approach. Advertising expenditure in the sector has fluctuated over the past five years but is currently around £8m per annum. Traditional table sauce brands such as Heinz account for a significant level of expenditure. Competitors to Reggae Reggae Sauce include Nandos who have a range of spicy sauces including a sweet and sticky marinade and Encona, an Afro-Caribbean range produced by WT Foods, which was relaunched in 2006 with the aim of emphasising the Caribbean heritage.

MiniCase references

Bottled sauces, UK, Mintel, November 2006
www.itzcaribbean.com.
www.reggae-reggae.co.uk.

MiniCase questions

1. Discuss what factors Levi might consider when developing relationships with retailers such as Sainsbury's and independent food retailers.
2. Outline how the brand might use marketing communications to develop relationships with both retailers and consumers.
3. Consider how consumers could be encouraged to buy Reggae Reggae Sauce for the first time and then repeatedly in the future.

References

Achrol, R.S. (1991) Evolution of the marketing organisation: new forms for turbulent environments. *Journal of Marketing*, **55**(4), 77–93.

Altman, I. and Taylor, D.A. (1973) *Social Penetration: The Development of Interpersonal Relationships*. New York: Holt, Rinehart & Winston.

Anderson, J.C. and Narus, J.A. (1998) Business Marketing: understand what customers value. *Harvard Business Review*, **76** (June), 53–65.

Anderson, J.C. and Narus, J.A. (1999) *Business Market Management*. Upper Saddle River, NJ: Prentice-Hall.

Ang, L. and Buttle, F.A. (2003) ROI on CRM: a customer journey approach. *CRM Today*. Retrieved 16 August 2004 from www.crm2day.com/library/EpFlupuEZVRmkpZCHM.php.

Araujo, L. and Easton, G. (1996) Networks in socioeconomic systems: a critical review. In *Networks in Marketing* (ed. D. Iacobucci). Thousand Oaks, CA: Sage.

Ashton, J. and Watts, R. (2008) Good payers face being axed by credit card firms. *Sunday Times*, 3 February 2008. Available online at http://www.timesonline.co.uk/tol/money/borrowing/article3295315.ece.

Baldinger, A. and Rubinson, J. (1996) Brand loyalty: the link between attitude and behaviour. *Journal of Advertising Research*, **36**(6) (November–December), 22–34.

Blau, P. (1964) *Exchange and Power In Social Life*. New York: John Wiley & Sons.

Byrne, C. (2007) Serious Fraud Office reviews evidence in ITV phone-in scandal. *The Independent*, 20 October 2007. Retrieved 20 October from www.news.independent.co.uk/media/article3078884.ece.

Calonius, H., Aviontis, G.L., Papavasiliou, N.K. and Kouremeos, A.G. (eds) (1989) *Market communication in service marketing, Marketing Thought and Practice in the 1990s, Proceedings from the XVIIIth Annual Conference of the European Marketing Academy, Athens*.

Canning, L. and Hammer-Lloyd, S. (2002) Modelling the adaptation process in interactive business relationships. *Journal Business and Industrial Marketing*, **17**(7), 615–36.

Christopher, M., Payne, A. and Ballantyne, D. (2002) *Relationship Marketing: Creating Stakeholder Value*. Oxford: Butterworth Heinemann.

Cousins, P. and Stanwix, E. (2001) Its only a matter of confidence! A comparison of relationship management between Japanese and UK non-owned vehicle manufacturers. *International Journal of Operations and Production Management*, **21**(9) (October), 1160–80.

Cox, J. (2004) The Ludlow Sausage Company – winning the 'coopetition' game. Retrieved 19 October 2004 from wisdomnetwork.com.

Day, G. (2000) Managing market relationships. *Journal of the Academy of Marketing Science*, **28**(1) (Winter), 24–30.

Dick, A.S. and Basu, K. (1994) Customer loyalty: toward an integrated framework. *Journal of the Academy of Marketing Science*, **22**(2), 99–113.

Doney, P.M. and Cannon, J.P. (1997) An examination of the nature of trust in buyer–seller relationships. *Journal of Marketing*, **62**(2), 1–13.

Dowling, G.R. and Uncles, M. (1997) Do customer loyalty programmes really work? *Sloan Management Review* (Summer), 71–82.

Doyle, P. (2000) *Value Based Marketing*. Chichester: Wiley.

Duncan, T. and Moriarty, S. (1997) *Driving Brand Value*. New York: McGraw-Hill.

Fournier, S. and Yao, J.L. (1997) Reviving brand loyalty: a reconceputalisation within the framework of consumer–brand relationships. *International Journal of Research in Marketing*, **14**(5), 451–72.

Gambetta, D. (1988) *Trust: Making and Breaking Co-operative Relations*. New York: Blackwell.

Garbarino, E. and Johnson, M.S. (1999) The different roles of satisfaction, trust and commitment in customer relationships. *Journal of Marketing*, **63** (April), 70–87.

Goodman, L.E. and Dion, P.A. (2001) The determinants of commitment in the distributor–manufacturer relationship. *Industrial Marketing Management*, **30**(3) (April), 287–300.

Gronroos, C. (2000) Creating a relationship dialogue: communication, interaction, value. *Marketing Review*, **1**(1), 5–14.

Gronroos, C. (2004) The relationship marketing process: communication, interaction, dialogue, value. *Journal of Business and Industrial Marketing*, **19**(2), 99–113.

Gronroos, C. and Lindberg-Repo, K. (1998) Integrated marketing communications: the communications aspect of relationship marketing. *IMC Research Journal*, **4**(1), 3–11.

Holmlund, M. (1997) *Perceived quality of business relationships*. Helsingfors: Hanken Swedish School of Economics, Finland/CERS.

Kothandaraman, P. and Wilson, D. (2001) The future of competition: value creating networks. *Industrial Marketing Management*, **30**(4) (May), 379–89.

Kumar, N., Hibbard, J.D. and Stern, L.W. (1994) *The Nature and Consequences of Marketing Channel Intermediary Commitment*. Working paper. Cambridge, MA: Marketing Science Institute, 94–115.

Luo., X. (2002) A framework based on relationship marketing and social exchange theory. *Industrial Marketing Management*, **31**(2) (February), 111–18.

Macneil, I.R. (1980) *The New Social Contract*. New Haven, CT: Yale University Press.

Macneil, I.R. (1983) Values in contract: internal and external. *Northwestern Law Review*, **78**(2), 340–418.

McLoughlin, D. and Horan, C. (2000) Perspectives from the markets-as-networks approach. *Industrial Marketing Management*, **29**(4), 285–92.

McLuhan, R. (2007) Is loyalty a myth? *Marketing*, 15 August, 29–30.

Morgan, R.M. and Hunt, S.D. (1994) The commitment-trust theory of relationship marketing. *Journal of Marketing*, **58** (July), 20–38.

Morrison, D.E. and Firmstone, J. (2000) The social function of trust and implications of e-commerce. *International Journal of Advertising*, **19**, 599–623.

Nancarrow, C. and Rees, S. (2003) Market research and CRM. Retrieved 21 August 2004 from http://www.wnim.com/issue21/pages/crm.htm.

Nottage, A. (2007) Clarity will boost consumer trust. *Marketing*, 10 October, 21.

O'Malley, L. (1998) Can loyalty schemes really build loyalty? *Marketing Intelligence and Planning*, **16**(1), 47–55.

O'Malley, L. and Mitussis, D. (2002) Relationships and technology: strategic implications. *Journal of Strategic Marketing*, **10**(3) (September), 225–38.

Palmer, R. (2007) The transaction–relational continuum: conceptually elegant but empirically denied. *Journal of Business and Industrial Marketing*, **22**(7), 439–51.

Pavlou, P.A. (2002) Institution-based trust in interorganisational exchange relationships: the role of online B2B marketplaces on trust formation. *Journal of Strategic Information Systems*, **11**(3–4) (December), 215–43.

Porter, M.E. (1985) *Competitive Advantage: Creating and Sustaining Superior Performance*, New York: Free Press

Puth, G., Mostert, P. and Ewing, M. (1999) Consumer perceptions of mentioned product and brand attributes in magazine advertising. *Journal of Product Brand Management*, **8**(1), 38–50.

Rao, S. and Perry, C. (2002) Thinking about relationship marketing: where are we now? *Journal of Business and Industrial Marketing*, **17**(7), 598–614.

Rapacz, D. and Reilly, M. (2008) The new view of relationship marketing. *Journal of Integrated Marketing Communications*, 19–25. http://jimc.medill.northwestern.edu/JIMCWebsite/2008/RelationshipMarketing.pdf.

Reichheld, F.F. and Sasser, E.W. (1990) Zero defections: quality comes to services, *Harvard Business Review*, (September), 105–11.

Reinartz, W.J. and Kumar, V. (2002) The mismanagement of customer loyalty. *Harvard Business Review*, (July), 86–94.

Rigby, D.K., Reichheld, F.F. and Schefter, P. (2002) Avoid the four perils of CRM. *Harvard Business Review*, February, 101–9.

Robinson, J. (2007) Phone fiasco gives BBC a wake-up call. *The Observer*, 18 March 2007, 12.

Rowe, W.G. and Barnes, J.G. (1998) Relationship marketing and sustained competitive advantage. *Journal of Market-Focused Management*, **2**(3), 281–97.

Ryssel, R., Ritter, T. and Gemunden H.G. (2004) The impact of information technology deployment on trust, commitment and value creation in business relationships. *Journal of Business and Industrial Marketing*, **19**(3), 197–207.

Sherwin, A. (2007) BBC fined £50,000 for Blue Peter scandal. *The Times*, 10 July 2007. Retrieved 18 October from www.timesonline.co.uk/tol/news/uk/article2051044.ece.

Simpson, P.M., Sigauw, J.A. and Baker, T.L. (2001) A model of value creation: supplier behaviors and their impact on reseller-perceived value. *Industrial Marketing Management*, **30**(2) (February), 119–34.

Sood, B. (2002) CRM in B2B: developing customer-centric practices for partner and supplier relationships. Retrieved 28 April 2003 from http://www.intelligentcrm.com/020509/508feat2r2.shtml.

Spekman, R. (1988) Perceptions of strategic vulnerability among industrial buyers and its effect on information search and supplier evaluation. *Journal of Business Research*, **17**, 313–26.

Stone, M. (2002) Managing public sector customers. *What's New in Marketing*, (October). Retrieved October 2002 from www.wnim.com/.

Thomas, R. (2000) How to create trust in the net. *Marketing*, 2 March, 35.

Tynan, C. (1997), A review of the marriage analogy in relationship marketing. *Journal of Marketing Management*, **13**, 695–703.

Wagner, S. and Boutellier, R. (2002) Capabilities for managing a portfolio of supplier relationships. *Business Horizons*, **45**(6), 79–88.

Wightman, T. (2000) E-CRM: the critical dot-com discipline. *Admap*, April, 46–8.

Young, L.C. and Wilkinson, I.F. (1989) The role of trust and co-operation in marketing channels: a preliminary study. *European Journal of Marketing*, **23**(2), 109–22.

Zucker, L. (1986) Production of trust: institutional sources of economic structure 1840–1920. *Research in Organisation Behaviour*, **8**(1), 53–111.

Chapter 8

How marketing communications might work

Understanding how marketing communications might work with its rich mosaic of perceptions, emotions, attitudes, information and patterns of behaviour is challenging in itself. Any attempt to understand how marketing communications might work must be cautioned by an appreciation of the complexity and contradictions inherent in this complicated commercial activity.

Aims and learning objectives

The aims of this chapter are to explore some of the theoretical concepts associated with ideas about how marketing communications might work and to consider the complexities associated with understanding how clients can best use marketing communications.

The learning objectives of this chapter are to:

1. explore ideas concerning the strategic context of marketing communications;
2. explain how marketing communications has emerged;
3. discuss the role and tasks of marketing communications;
4. suggest ways in which marketing communications might work;
5. examine the concept of significant value;
6. consider the strengths and weaknesses of a model explaining of how marketing communications might work.

For an applied interpretation see Andrew Turnbull's MiniCase entitled ***'Get on your bike!' Mountain biking tourism in the Cairngorms National Park (CNP)*** at the end of this chapter.

Introduction

This chapter considers ways in which marketing communications might work and introduces a number of concepts and frameworks that have contributed to our understanding. This chapter should be read prior to Chapters 9 and 16 which explore ideas about integrated marketing communications and ways in which advertising are considered to work. In addition, Chapter 17 complements this chapter as it considers the content of advertising messages, or what is to be conveyed.

Ideas about how advertising works dominate the literature whereas ideas about how marketing communications are thought to work are often regarded as of secondary consideration. Although it is recognised that both these approaches are important it is necessary to change this priority, if only in recognition of the principles of integrated marketing communications. This chapter therefore, deals with ideas concerning ways to explain and interpret how marketing communications might work.

The strategic context

For a long time many considered marketing communications to be a purely operational issue, one which worked by delivering messages about products, to audiences who then, if the communication was effective, purchased the product. No real consideration was given to combining and synchronising the tools, reinforcing messages, understanding the target audience or keying the communications into an overall organisational strategy.

This silo approach has changed. Propelled by the emerging focus on a wider range of stakeholders, the excitement about relationship marketing (Chapter 7), surging developments in digital technology and media applications (Chapter 25) and the emerging controversy over integrated marketing communications (Chapter 9), have raised the profile and importance of a strategic orientation for marketing communications.

The corporate strategy that organisations pursue should be supported by business, operational and functional level strategies. Therefore, to be effective marketing communications should be used to complement the marketing, business and corporate strategies. Such complementarity serves to reinforce core messages, reflect the mission and provide a means of using resources efficiently yet at the same time provide reinforcement for the whole business strategy.

> To be effective marketing communications should be used to complement the marketing, business and corporate strategies.

ViewPoint 8.1 AA's friendly strategy

The relationship between corporate strategy and marketing communications can be observed quite clearly at the UK market leader for roadside assistance, the AA.

The AA used to position itself as the 'fourth emergency service' and in doing so conveyed very clearly its main business activity and key values for audiences. Centrica, whose core business rests with providing a range of household services, bought the organisation partly because it saw value in the 14.8 million members and the opportunities to cross-sell their products. This strategy was reflected in the new strapline 'Just AAsk', introduced in 2002 (see Exhibit 8.1). This drew attention not just to the breakdown facilities, but to insurance, publishing, driving lessons, retailing and other travel-related services.

However, CVC Capital Partners, in partnership with Permira, bought the AA out of Centrica, partly because they could see opportunities to exploit unrealised value. Their business strategy was about splitting the company into independent businesses, and selling off parts because they are not core to roadside assistance. As a result the 'Just AAsk' strategy was abandoned and the centralised marketing department collapsed.

Following research that identified that it was the perception of the quality of the patrols that acted as a key decision criterion for customers, the AA decided to refocus its communications on its core breakdown business. By putting the AA patrol at the very heart of the brand and its communication strategy, the AA repositioned itself as the customers' 'friend', that is someone who can be relied on to help whenever and wherever they are called upon. Carole King's classic song' 'You've Got A Friend', was used to reinforce the emotionally laden message. Here it is possible to interpret a relationship marketing orientation in the shift of

Exhibit 8.1 AA Poster 'Learn to Drive' demonstrates the Just AAsk Strapline and its invitation to solve the problems of a particular target audience

Exhibit 8.2 'Fourth emergency service'
National Motor Museum, Beaulieu and The AA.

emphasis in the AA's communications, and a move away from pure attribute performance. This new campaign is in use at the time of writing and incorporates a wide range of media including television, press, cinema, radio and online for brand-building and a complete range of direct media channels on- and offline for acquisition.

Sources: Bold (2004); Anon. (2008); www.theAA.com.

Question

What might be the consequence for the AA's marketing communications if its business strategy changed to a value-for-money orientation?

Task

Identify another road-side breakdown organisation and determine its business strategy and marketing communications. Are they compatible?

Marketing communications works when it effectively reflects the corporate level strategy and supports the marketing plan.

It could be argued that marketing communications works when it effectively reflects the corporate level strategy and supports the marketing plan and other related activities. It does not work simply because it complements strategy but it certainly will not work unless it does reflect the marketing and business imperatives.

The emergence of marketing communications

It is important to appreciate how marketing communications has developed in order to understand how it might work. Before marketing communications there was promotion and before that separate individual promotional tools, and one overriding tool, advertising. The broad task of advertising was to deliver the unique selling proposition (USPs) that all products were considered to have. These USPs were based on product features and related to particular attributes that differentiated one product from another. If this uniqueness was of value to a consumer then the USP alone was thought sufficient to persuade consumers to purchase.

However, the reign of the USP was short lived when technology enabled me-too and own label brands to be brought to market very quickly and product lifecycles became increasingly shorter. The power of the USP was eroded and with it the basis of product differentiation as it was known then. In addition, the power and purpose of advertising's role to differentiate was challenged.

ViewPoint 8.2 USP with Ronseal

Ronseal have a range of products in the specialist paint sector. One of their major products is called No Rust, which, unlike other paints, can be applied directly to rust and its 3 in 1 formulation means – no primer, no undercoat, no fuss.

They claim that the unique formulation contains 'anti-rust agents, anti-sag agents and advanced silicone technology to create a paint that locks out moisture to give superior, long lasting protection'.

This USP is reflected in their hard-hitting advertising and universally applied message: RONSEAL – Does exactly what it says on the tin® (see Exhibit 8.3).

Question

Is the role of the USP strong in all markets?

Task

Find another brand, in any category, and determine whether it uses USPs.

Exhibit 8.3 Ronseal USP

What emerged were emotional selling propositions or ESPs. Advertising's role became more focused on developing brand values, ones that were based on emotion and imagery. This approach to communication builds brand awareness, desire and aspirational involvement.

However, it often fails to provide customers with a rationale or explicit reason to purchase, what is often referred to as a 'call to action'.

Other tools were required to provide customers with an impetus to act and sales promotions, event marketing, roadshows and, later, direct marketing evolved to fulfil this need. These tools are known collectively as below-the-line communication tools and their common characteristic is that they are all capable of driving action or creating behavioural change. For example, sales promotions can be used to accelerate customer behaviour by bringing forward sales that might otherwise have been made at some point in the future. Methods such as price deals, premiums and bonus packs are all designed to change behaviour by calling customers into action. This may be in the form of converting or switching users of competitive products, creating trial use of newly introduced products or encouraging existing customers to increase their usage of the product.

ViewPoint 8.3 Dental ESPs

Toothpaste, the biggest part of the oral hygiene market (including dental floss, mouthwashes, dental gum and dental cleaners and fixatives) has experienced declining sales. This is due in part to competitive price deals, bonus packs and the increasing use of electronic toothbrushes that require less toothpaste.

Toothpaste has traditionally been presented on an attribute basis with each brand focusing on a particular USP. For example, Sensodyne for sensitive teeth and gums and Colgate for decay prevention and tartar control.

In the 1990s manufacturers started to move towards using ESPs, principally whitening agents with cosmetic benefits. The use of ESPs in this market is becoming increasingly common as products are launched for smokers, children and, for example, Crest's 'Revitalise' that is targeted at women and used celebrities such as Ulrika Jonsson in their advertising. The focus is now about lifestyle and how teeth contribute to an individual's overall beauty, appearance and feelings about oneself. Growing interest in the cosmetic benefits of toothpaste has led Crest's owners, Procter & Gamble, to move the brand from the oral care to the beauty division.

Source: Bainbridge (2004).

Question

Discuss the notion that to be really effective messages should include both USPs and ESPs.

Task

Find out the USPs or ESPs used in the cosmetics, fruit juice, digital cameras and PDA categories

The shift in focus away from mass communications towards more personalised messages delivered though different media has been demonstrated by the increased use of direct marketing by organisations over the past ten years. It can also be argued that the development of direct marketing is a response to some of the weaknesses, to do with cost and effectiveness of the other tools, most notably advertising.

> The communication mix has expanded and become a more complex managerial instrument.

The communication mix has expanded and become a more complex managerial instrument, but essentially it is now capable of delivering two main solutions. On the one hand it can be used to develop and maintain brand values, and on the other it could be used to change behaviour through the delivery of calls to action. From a strategic perspective, the former is oriented to the long term and the latter to the short term. It is also apparent that the significant rise of the below-the-line tools within the mix is partly a reflection of the demise of the USP, but it is also a reflection of the increasing financial pressures experienced by organisations to improve performance and improve returns on investment.

Organisations, therefore, are faced with a dilemma. On the one hand they need to create brands that are perceived to be of value, but on the other they need to prompt or encourage customers into purchase behaviour. To put it another way, marketing communications should be used to encourage buyers along the purchase decision path but how many resources should be used to create brand values and how many should be used to prompt behaviour?

Role of marketing communications

Extending these ideas about values and action leads to a consideration of the role of marketing communications. In Chapter 1 the notion of engagement was introduced to explain the different forms of marketing communication. Engagement, or buy-in as referred to by Thomson and Hecker (2000), when considering employee-oriented communications, consists of two main components, an intellectual and an emotional element. The intellectual element is concerned with audiences engaging with a brand on the basis of processing rational, functional information. The emotional element is concerned with audiences engaging and aligning themselves with a brand's values on the basis of emotional and expressive information. It follows that communication strategies should be based on the information processing styles of audiences and their access to preferred media. Communications should reflect a suitable balance between the need for rational information to meet intellectual needs and expressive types of communication to meet emotional needs in an organisation's different audiences. The better the quality of communication, the higher the level of engagement.

Communications should reflect a suitable balance between the need for rational information to meet intellectual needs and expressive types of communication to meet emotional needs.

The DRIP tasks of marketing communications were also introduced in Chapter 1. The idea that marketing communications can be used to differentiate, reinforce, inform or persuade audiences to think or behave in a particular way reveals not only the inherent complexity in this subject but also the wide expectation associated with the use of this aspect of marketing.

Table 8.1 Aspects of DRIP

Role	Tasks	Explanation
Differentiate	Attribute Whole product	To make a product or service stand out in the category
Reinforce	Remind Reassure	To consolidate and strengthen previous messages and experiences
Inform	Make aware Educate	To make known and advise of availability and features
Persuade	Purchase Further enquiry	To encourage further positive purchase-related behaviour

Marketing communications are used extensively to enable individuals to progress through the decision-making process. The first task is to *inform* or make potential customers aware of a product's availability, of its new attributes or its revised facilities. However, this element has other tasks that may need implementing. Indeed, information may be necessary to instruct audiences about *how* to use products, or to advise *when* a product should be used or to suggest *who* might be the optimal users. In other words, marketing communications is used to engage audiences intellectually.

In addition to informing, customers need to know how a product differs from other competitor brands. This differentiation task of marketing communications has two sub-tasks attached to it. The first task is to clarify for audiences, either directly or indirectly, the degree to which certain attributes are unique or superior to other competing brands. The second task is to convey how the product (service) as a whole is superior to other brands in the category. When customers perceive and believe in the strength of both of these claims, a sense of conviction and preference can develop.

One of the more popular perceptions of marketing communications is that it can be used to *persuade* customers to purchase products or to behave in new ways. Packard (1958) wrote about the 'Hidden Persuaders' and regarded advertising as an undesirable force that relentlessly drove customers to buy products they did not want or need. Echos of this are to be found in a more recent book by Klein (2005). However, although this is no longer a widespread or popular view, there can be no doubt that marketing communications has a task to *persuade* current and potential customers to act in particular, desirable ways. Readers should remember that product purchase is just one of several tasks that marketing communications might persuade individuals to undertake. For example, new behaviour might be to visit a web site, engage in word-of-mouth (or mouse) communications, send for a brochure, phone a number or download wallpaper or ringtones. Persuasion might be achieved intellectually or emotionally depending on the product offering and the degree of uncertainty felt by the audience towards the purchase.

Persuasion might be achieved intellectually or emotionally.

ViewPoint 8.4 Changing the times for consumption

Many seasonal products try to deseasonalise their sales by reminding markets of their products and demonstrating new ways or fresh occasions when their customers can buy and consume their brands. For a long time ice-cream was a summer food but Walls and then the super premium brands such as Haagen Dazs and Ben and Jerry's used communications to extend consumption across the year.

Liqueur brands are heavily oriented to the Christmas market but summer barbecues, parties and Father's Day have been used by liqueur brands to stimulate new reasons to buy (Solley, 2004). Baileys have made extensive use of television to show younger age groups enjoying the brand and have also sponsored the Channel 4 series *Sex in the City*, in order to reinforce the repositioning and develop new brand associations.

Camelot seek to remind players of the benefits of playing the National Lottery, both personal and social. As if to demonstrate this neatly, one recent campaign was based on the good causes that lottery money has been used to fund and this was replaced at the end of 2004 with an umbrella theme called 'Be lucky': from the social to the individual.

Question

Discuss the idea that by changing the time for consumption, competitor brands are given a cost-free chance to expand to their market.

Task

Find one other category in which a brand has attempted to deseasonalise consumption.

A further task is to reassure audiences.

In an era when customer retention and loyalty are dominant marketing goals, the use of planned and coordinated communications to reinforce previous messages and product experiences is of vital importance. The two main sub-tasks are to remind people of a need they might have or to remind them of the benefits of past transactions and so convince them that they should enter into a similar exchange. A further task is to reassure audiences, to comfort them by reaffirming the correctness of their original thoughts or purchase decisions. Through reassurance in particular, marketing communications can be used to retain current customers. This approach to business is much more cost-effective than constantly striving to lure new customers.

How does marketing communications work?

For a message to be communicated successfully, it should be meaningful to the recipient. Messages need to be targeted at the right audience, be capable of gaining attention, be understandable, relevant and acceptable. For effective communication to occur, messages should be designed that fit the cognitive capability of the target audience and follow the 'model' of how marketing communications works.

Unfortunately, there is no such single model, despite years of research and speculation by a great many people. However, from all the work undertaken in this area, mainly with regard to advertising, a number of views have been expressed, and the following sections attempt to present some of the more influential perspectives. For an interpretation of how advertising might work, this chapter should be read in conjunction with Chapter 16.

Sequential models

Various models have been developed to assist our understanding of how these promotional tasks are segregated and organised effectively. Table 8.2 shows some of the better-known models. These models were developed primarily to explain how advertising worked. However, the principle of these hierarchical models also applies to marketing communications.

AIDA

Developed by Strong (1925), the AIDA model was designed to represent the stages that a salesperson must take a prospect through in the personal selling process. This model shows the prospect passing through successive stages of attention, interest, desire and action. This expression of the process was later adopted, very loosely, as the basic framework to explain how persuasive communication, and advertising in particular, was thought to work.

Table 8.2 Sequential models of advertising

Processing	AIDA sequence[a]	Hierarchy of effects sequence[b]	Information sequence[c]
		Awareness	Presentation
			↓
Cognitive			Attention
		↓	↓
	Attention	Knowledge	Comprehension
	↓	↓	↓
	Interest	Liking	Yielding
		↓	
Affective		Preference	
	↓	↓	↓
	Desire	Conviction	Retention
Conative	↓	↓	↓
	Action	Purchase	Behaviour

Sources: [a] Strong (1925); [b] Lavidge and Steiner (1961); [c] McGuire (1978).

Hierarchy of effects models

An extension of the progressive, staged approach advocated by Strong emerged in the early 1960s. Developed most notably by Lavidge and Steiner (1961), the hierarchy of effects models represent the process by which advertising was thought to work and assume that there is a series of steps a prospect must pass through, in succession, from unawareness to actual purchase. Advertising, it is assumed, cannot induce immediate behavioural responses; rather, a series of mental effects must occur with fulfilment at each stage necessary before progress to the next stage is possible.

The information processing model

McGuire (1978) contends that the appropriate view of the receiver of persuasive advertising is as an information processor or cognitive problem solver. This cognitive perspective becomes subsumed as the stages presented reflect similarities with the other hierarchical models, except that McGuire includes a retention stage. This refers to the ability of the receiver to retain and understand information that is valid and relevant. This is important, because it recognises that marketing communication messages are designed to provide information for use by a prospective buyer when a purchase decision is to be made at some time in the future.

Difficulties with the sequential approach

For a long time the sequential approach was accepted as the model upon which advertising was to be developed. However, questions arose about what actually constitute adequate levels of awareness, comprehension and conviction and how it can be determined which stage the majority of the target audience has reached at any one point in time.

The model is based on the logical sequential movement of consumers towards a purchase via specified stages. The major criticism is that it assumes that the consumer moves through the stages in a logical, rational manner: learn, then feel and then do. This is obviously not the case, as anyone who has taken a child into a sweet shop can confirm. There has been a lot of research that attempts to offer an empirical validation for some of the hierarchy propositions, the results of which are inconclusive and at times ambiguous (Barry and Howard, 1990). Among these researchers is Palda (1966), who found that the learn–feel–do sequence cannot be upheld as a reflection of general buying behaviour and provided empirical data to reject the notion of sequential models as an interpretation of the way advertising works.

> There is evidence that a positive attitude is not necessarily a good predictor of purchase behaviour.

The sequential approach sees attitude towards the product as a prerequisite to purchase, but, as discussed earlier (Chapter 5), there is evidence that a positive attitude is not necessarily a good predictor of purchase behaviour. What is important, or more relevant, is the relationship between attitude change and an individual's intention to act in a particular way (Ajzen and Fishbein, 1980). Therefore, it seems reasonable to suggest that what is of potentially greater benefit is a specific measure of attitude *towards* purchasing or *intentions* to buy a specific product. Despite measurement difficulties, attitude change is considered a valid objective, particularly in high-involvement situations.

A great deal of time and money must be spent on research, determining what needs to be measured. As a result, only large organisations can utilise the model properly: those with the resources and the expertise to generate the data necessary to exploit this approach fully.

All of these models share the similar view that the purchase decision process is one in which individuals move through a series of sequential stages. Each of the stages from the different models can be grouped in such a way that they are a representation of the three attitude components, these being cognitive (learn), affective (feel) and conative (do) orientations. This could be seen to reflect the various stages in the buying process, especially those that induce high involvement in the decision process but do not reflect the reality of low-involvement decisions.

Cognitive processing

Reference has already been made to whether buyers actively or passively process information. In an attempt to understand how information is used, cognitive processing tries to determine 'how external information is transformed into meanings or patterns of thought and how these meanings are combined to form judgements' (Olsen and Peter, 1987).

Cognitive processing tries to determine 'how external information is transformed into meanings or patterns of thought'.

By assessing the thoughts (cognitive processes) that occur to people as they read, view or hear a message, an understanding of their interpretation of a message can be useful in campaign development and evaluation (Greenwald, 1968; Wright, 1973). These thoughts are usually measured by asking consumers to write down or verbally report the thoughts they have in response to such a message. Thoughts are believed to be a reflection of the cognitive processes or responses that receivers experience and they help shape or reject a communication.

Researchers have identified three types of cognitive response and have determined how these relate to attitudes and intentions. Figure 8.1 shows these three types of response, but readers should appreciate that these types are not discrete; they overlap each other and blend together, often invisibly.

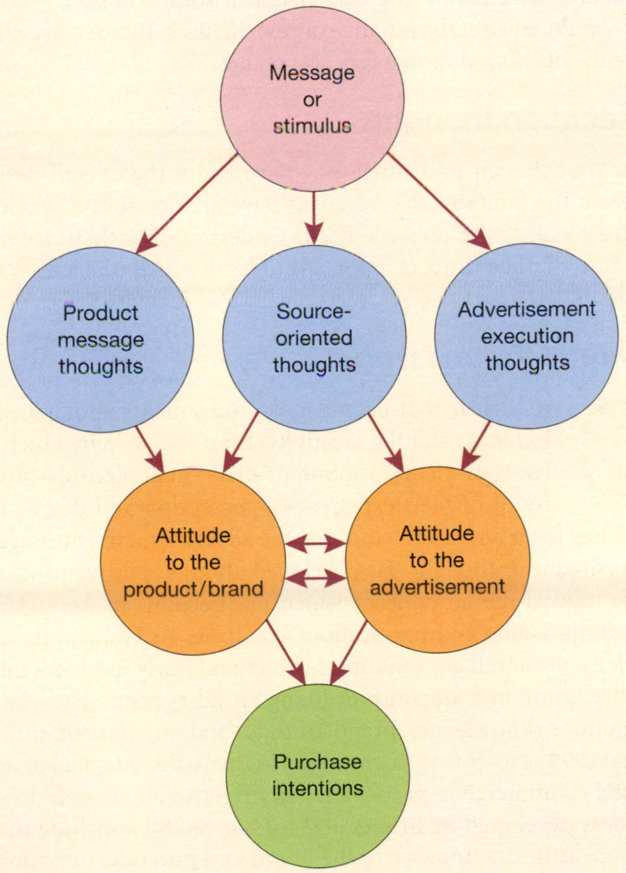

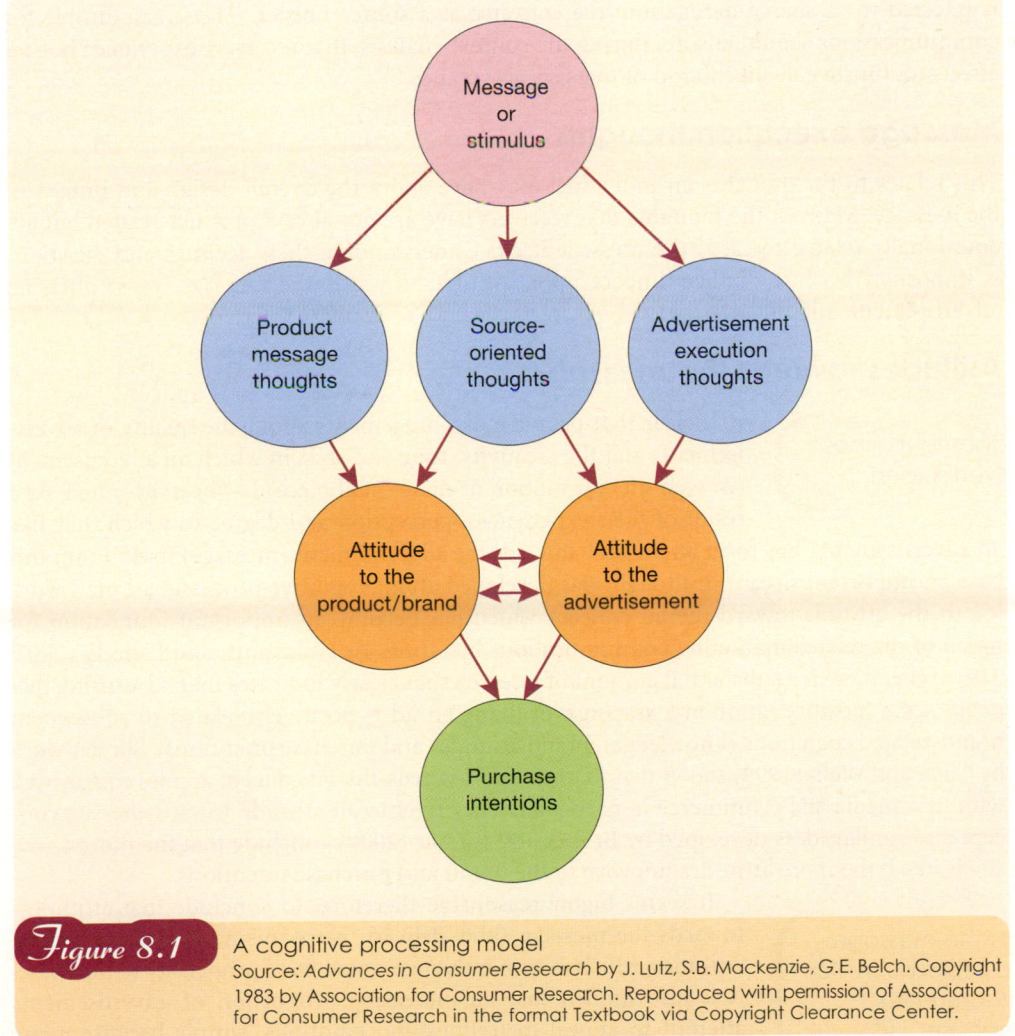

Figure 8.1 A cognitive processing model

Source: *Advances in Consumer Research* by J. Lutz, S.B. Mackenzie, G.E. Belch. Copyright 1983 by Association for Consumer Research. Reproduced with permission of Association for Consumer Research in the format Textbook via Copyright Clearance Center.

Product/message thoughts

These are thoughts that are directed to the product or communication itself. Much attention has been focused on the thoughts that are related to the message content. Two particular types of response have been considered: counter-arguments and support arguments.

A counter-argument occurs when the receiver disagrees with the content of a message. According to Belch and Belch (2004),

> *The likelihood of counter-argument is greater when the message makes claims that oppose the beliefs or perceptions held by the receiver. Not surprisingly, the greater the degree of counter-argument, the less likely the message will be accepted. Conversely, support-arguments reflect acceptance and concurrence with a message. Support-arguments, therefore, are positively related to message acceptance.*

Advertisements and general communications should encourage the generation of support arguments.

Source-oriented thoughts

A further set of cognitive responses is aimed at the source of the communication. This concept is closely allied to that of source credibility, where, if the source of the message is seen as annoying or distrustful, there is a lower probability of message acceptance. Such a situation is referred to as source derogation; the converse as a source bolster. Those responsible for communications should ensure, during the context analysis, that receivers experience bolster effects to improve the likelihood of message acceptance.

Message execution thoughts

This relates to the thoughts an individual may have about the overall design and impact of the message. Many of the thoughts that receivers have are not always product-related but are emotionally related towards the message itself. Understanding these feelings and emotions is important because of their impact upon attitudes towards the message, most often an advertisement, and the offering.

Attitudes towards the message

People make judgements about the quality of advertisement.

It is clear that people make judgements about the quality of advertisements and the creativity, tone and style in which an advertisement (or web site, promotion or direct mail piece) has been executed. As a result of their experiences, perception and degree to which they like an advertisement, they form an attitude towards the advertisement (message) itself. From this base an important stream of thought has developed about cognitive processing. Lutz's work led to the attitude-toward-the-ad concept which has become an important foundation for much of the related marketing communications literature. As Goldsmith and Lafferty (2002: 319) argue, there is a substantial amount of research that clearly indicates that advertising that promotes a 'positive emotional response of liking an ad is positively related to subsequent brand-related cognitions (knowledge), brand attitudes and purchase intentions'. Similar work by Chen and Wells (1999) shows that this attitude-towards-the-ad concept applies equally well with new media and ecommerce in particular. They refer to an attitude-toward-the-site concept and similar ideas developed by Bruner and Kumar (2000) conclude that the more a web site is liked, the more attitudes improve to the brand and purchase intentions.

Attitudes-towards-the-message impact on brand attitudes, which in turn influence consumers' propensity to purchase.

It seems highly reasonable therefore, to conclude that attitudes-towards-the-message (and delivery mechanism) impact on brand attitudes, which in turn influence consumers' propensity to purchase. It is also known that an increasing proportion of advertisements attempt to appeal to feelings and emotions, simply because many researchers believe that attitudes towards both the advertisement and the product should be encouraged and are positively correlated with purchase intention. Similarly, time and effort is placed with the design of sales promotion instruments, increasing attention is given to the design of packaging in terms of a pack's communication effectiveness and care is taken about the wording in advatorials and press releases. Perhaps above all else, more and more effort is being made to research and develop web sites with the goal of designing them so that they are strategically compatible, user-friendly and functional, or to put it another way – liked. Any model developed to explain how marketing communications works should therefore be based around the important concept, attitude-towards-the-message.

Elaboration likelihood model

What should be clear from the preceding sections is that neither the purely cognitive nor the purely emotional interpretation of how marketing communication works is realistic. In effect, it is probable that both have an important part to play in the way the various tools, and advertising in particular, works. However, the degree of emphasis should swing according to the context within which the marketing communication message is expected to work.

One approach to utilise both these elements has been developed by Petty and Cacioppo (1983). The Elaboration Likelihood Model (ELM) has helped to explain how cognitive processing, persuasion and attitude change occur when different levels of involvement are present. Elaboration refers to the extent to which an individual needs to develop and refine information necessary for decision-making to occur. If an individual has a high level of motivation or ability to process information, elaboration is said to be high. If an individual's motivation or ability to process information is poor, then their level of elaboration is said to be low. The ELM distinguishes two main cognitive processes, as depicted in Figure 8.2

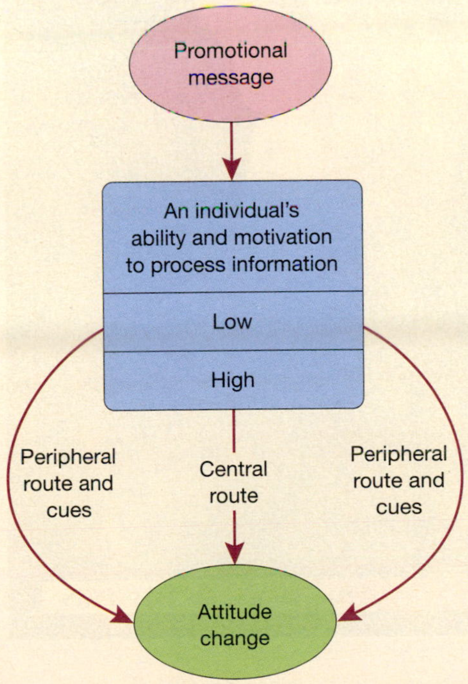

Figure 8.2 The elaboration likelihood model
Source: Based on Aaker *et al.* (1992).

Under the central route the receiver is viewed as very active and involved.

Under the central route the receiver is viewed as very active and involved. As the level of cognitive response is high, the ability of the message (advertisement) to persuade will depend on the quality of the argument rather than executional factors. For example, the purchase of a consumer durable such as a car or washing machine normally requires a high level of involvement. Consequently, potential customers would be expected to be highly involved and willing to read brochures and information about the proposed car or washing machine prior to demonstration or purchase. Their decision to act would depend on the arguments used to justify the model as suitable for the individual. For the car purchase these might include the quiet and environmentally friendly engine, the relatively excellent fuel consumption and other safety and performance indicators, together with the comfort of the interior and the effortless driving experience. Whether the car is shown as part of a business executive's essential 'kit' or the commercial is flamboyant and rich will be immaterial for those in the central route.

ViewPoint 8.5 Peripheral tea

Consumers tend to stay with their preferred brands of food and drink and will only switch if their preferred brand fails to reach threshold levels of satisfaction or a new brand offers sufficient curiosity and engagement that trial is induced. Many brands in the tea market for example, use peripheral cues in order to get the brand noticed, remembered and enjoyed. Twinings used a Jack-in-the Box to symbolise the stimulating effects of their breakfast tea and as an easy means for customers to make associations with the Twinings brand.

Spring into
life
with a brisk,
full-bodied tea
ENGLISH
BREAKFAST
www.twinings.com
There's more to tea with TWININGS

Exhibit 8.4 Through the use of peripheral cues, Twinings have been able to enrich the way their brand is perceived while at the same time improve the level of awareness

The Brooke Bond tea brand, PG Tips, used chimpanzees in what was one of the longest running ad campaigns, 45 years. The chimpanzees were used to bring humour to a brand of tea and in doing so helped consumers associate the brand with fun. The chimps were used to parody James Bond, removal men trying to get a piano downstairs, Tour de France cyclists and even housewives doing the ironing and they all (pretended) to drink their favourite cup of tea. After their introduction PG became the number one brand and sales fluctuated according to whether the ads featuring the chimps were on air.

However, complaints by animal welfare groups eventually saw the demise of the Chimps. They have been replaced with Monkey, a knitted version, who appears with Al (Johnny Vegas). The subsequent success of this pairing continues to emphasise the importance of peripheral cues in particular product categories.

Sources: Blackstock (2002); Carter (2008).

Question

To what extent is the use of peripheral cues a positive or negative comment on the intellectual capacity of the target audience?

Task

Find a brand that you like that uses peripheral cues.

Exhibit 8.5 PG Tips – chimpanzees perform as peripheral cues
Image courtesy of The Advertising Archives.

Exhibit 8.6 PG Tips now with Monkey as a peripheral cue
Image courtesy of The Advertising Archives.

Under the peripheral route, the receiver is seen to lack the ability to process information and is not likely to engage cognitive processing.

Under the peripheral route, the receiver is seen to lack the ability to process information and is not likely to engage cognitive processing. Rather than thinking about and evaluating the message content, the receiver tends to rely on what have been referred to as 'peripheral cues', which may be incidental to the message content. Twinings use peripheral cues to attract attention to their brand (see Exhibit 8.5).

In low-involvement situations, a celebrity may serve to influence attitudes positively. This is based upon the creation of favourable attitudes towards the source rather than engaging the viewer in the processing of the message content. For example, Gary Lineker was the celebrity spokesperson used to endorse Walkers crisps for many years. Gary Lineker, former Tottenham and England football hero and now BBC sports presenter, was an important peripheral cue for Walkers crisps (more so than the nature of the product), in eventually persuading a consumer to try the brand or retaining current users. Think crisps, think Gary Lineker, think Walkers. Where high involvement is present, any celebrity endorsement is of minor significance to the quality of the message claims.

Communication strategy should be based upon the level of cognitive processing that the target audience is expected to engage in and the route taken to affect attitudinal change.

Communication strategy should be based upon the level of cognitive processing that the target audience is expected to engage in and the route taken to affect attitudinal change. If the processing level is low (low motivation and involvement), the peripheral route should dominate and emphasis needs to be placed on the way the messages are executed and on the emotions of the target audience (Heath, 2000). If the central route is expected, the content of the messages should be dominant and the executional aspects need only be adequate.

Interaction, dialogue and relationships

Marketing communications is traditionally perceived and developed as a planned managerial activity. This in itself is perfectly fine, to be encouraged and is a central platform for the development of integrated marketing communications (see Chapter 9). However, much of marketing practice and theory has moved towards a more relational rather than transactional perspective (see Chapter 7). Marketing communications is in transition as it adapts in order to complement this new approach. Therefore, any explanation about how it works should be articulated in the light of relationship marketing principles.

Digital media offer opportunities for audiences to respond to the messages they receive.

As a generalisation, mass media-based communications generate one-way communication and is based on informing, telling and educating audiences with a view to persuading them to act in a particular way, ultimately to purchase a product (Ballantyne, 2004). Digital media and digital technologies have given organisations radically different methods to communicate with audiences. Digital media offer opportunities for audiences to respond to the messages they receive and give rise to opportunities for people to interact with those organisations with whom they wish to be involved and to whom they grant permission to continue sending messages. One-way communication begins to look like two-way communication.

Digital technology has further enabled the interaction process.

Interaction is about actions that lead to a response, and in the 1990s direct marketing helped make significant inroads in the transition from one-way to two-way and then interactive-based communication. Digital technology has further enabled this interaction process. However, interaction alone is not a sufficient goal simply because the content of the interaction could be about a radical disagreement of views, an exchange of opinion or a social encounter.

Table 8.3 Communication matrix

Direction	Mass markets	Portfolio/mass-customised	Networks
One-way Planned communications designed to inform and persuade Medium to high wastage	*Communication 'to'* Planned persuasive messages aimed at securing brand awareness and loyalty; e.g. *communication of USPs and ESPs*	*Communication 'for'* Planned persuasive messages with augmented offerings for target markets; e.g. *communicating targeted lifecycle products, guarantees, loyalty programmes*	
Two-way Formal and informal with a view to listening and learning Minimal wastage		*Communication 'with'* Integrated mix of planned and interactively shared knowledge; e.g. *face to face, direct (database), contact centres, interactive b2b Internet portals*	*Communication 'between'* Dialogue between participants based on trust, learning and adaptation with co-created outcomes; e.g. *key account liaison, expansion of communities, staff teamwork*

Source: Ballantyne (2004).

Dialogue occurs through mutual understanding and a reasoning approach to interactions, one based on listening and adaptive behaviour. Dialogue is concerned with the development of knowledge that is specific to the relationship of the parties involved. Ballantyne refers to this as 'learning together' (Ballantyne, 2004: 119) and it is referred to by Gronroos (2004) as a critical aspect of marketing communication's role within relationship marketing (see Chapter 7).

Ballantyne refers to two-way communication with audiences in two ways. First, as a '*with*' experience, as manifest in face-to-face encounters and contact centres. He also distinguishes a higher order of two-way communication based on communication '*between*' parties. It is this latter stage that embodies true dialogue where trust, listening and adaptive behaviour are typical. These are represented diagrammatically in Table 8.3.

The adoption of dialogue as the basis for communication changes an organisation's perspective of its audiences. Being willing and able to enter into a dialogue indicates that there is a new emphasis on the relationships organisations hold with their stakeholders. Kent and Taylor (2002) argue that there are five main features of a dialogical orientation. These are presented in Table 8.4.

Table 8.4 The five features of a dialogical orientation

Role	Explanation
Mutuality	The recognition of the presence of organisational stakeholder relationships
Propinquity	The temporality and spontaneity of organisation–stakeholder interactions
Empathy	Support for stakeholder interests and their goals
Risk	Willingness to interact with others on their terms
Commitment	The extent to which an organisation actually interprets, listens to and practises dialogical communications

Source: Kent and Taylor (2002). Used with permission.

It can be seen in Table 8.4 that many aspects of dialogue require interaction as a precursor. In other words, for dialogue to occur there must first be interaction and it is the development and depth of the interaction that leads to meaningful dialogue.

Ideas about how marketing communication works must be founded, in part, on the notion and significance of the level of interaction and dialogue that the organisation and their stakeholders desire. One-way communication, as reflected in traditional, planned, mass media-based communication still plays a significant role, especially for audiences who prefer transactional exchanges. Two-way communication based on interaction with audiences who desire continuing contact, or dialogue for those who desire a deeper more meaningful relationship, will form an increasingly important aspect of marketing communications strategy in the future.

Developing significant value

The message proclaims something that is personally significant to the individual in their current context.

Marketing communications consists of a set of tools and media that are used in varying ways to convey messages to audiences. Depending upon the context in which the message is created, delivered and interpreted, the brand and the individual have an opportunity to interact. Marketing communication messages normally pass individuals unobserved. Those that are remembered contain particular characteristics (Brown, 1991; Fletcher, 1994). These would appear to be that the product must be different or new, that the way the message is executed is different or interesting and that the message proclaims something that is personally significant to the individual in their current context. The term 'significance' means that the message is meaningful, relevant (e.g. the individual is actually looking to buy a new car or breakfast cereals tomorrow or is planning to gather information on a new project) and is perceived to be suitably credible. These three characteristics can be tracked from the concept of ad likeability (Chapter 16), which many researchers believe is the only meaningful indicator of the effectiveness of an advertisement.

To be successful therefore, it is necessary for marketing communication messages to:

- present an object that is new to the receiver;
- be interesting and stimulating;
- be personally significant.

The object referred to in the first element refers to both products and services (or an offering that is substantially different from others in the category) and to organisations as brands. The net effect of all these characteristics might be that any one message may be *significantly valuable* to an individual.

Messages announcing new brands or new attributes may convey information that is perceived to be significantly different. As a result, individuals may be intrigued and interested enough to want to try the brand at the next purchase opportunity. For these people there is a high level of personal relevance derived from the message, and attitude change can be induced to convince them that it is right to make a purchase. For them the message is significantly valuable and as a result may well generate a purchase decision, which will, from a market perspective, drive a discernible sales increase.

The vast majority of marketing communications are about products that are not new.

However, the vast majority of marketing communications are about products that are not new or that are unable to proclaim or offer anything substantially different. These messages are either ignored or, if interest is aroused, certain parts of the message are filed away in memory for use at a later date. The question is, if parts are filed away, which parts are filed and why and how are they retrieved?

Marketing communications can provide a rationale or explanation for why individuals (cognitive processors) have bought a brand and why they should continue buying it. Normally, advertising alone does not persuade – it simply reminds and reassures individuals. Or, to put it another way, individuals use advertising and public relations to remind themselves of preferred brands or to reassure themselves of their previous (and hence correct) purchase behaviour. Sales promotions, personal selling and direct marketing are then used by organisations to help consumers behave in particular ways.

Consumers, particularly in fast-moving consumer goods (FMCG) markets, practise repertoire buying based on habit, security, speed of decision-making and to some extent self-expression. The brands present in any single individual repertoire normally provide interest and satisfaction. Indeed, advertising needs to ensure that the brand remains in the repertoire or is sufficiently interesting to the individual that it is included in a future repertoire. Just consider the variety of messages used by mobile phone operators, such as O_2, T-Mobile, Vodafone, 3 and Orange. These are continually updated and refreshed using particular themes all of which are intended to be visually and cognitively engaging.

ViewPoint 8.6 Remembering Flaky ads

Work undertaken through the research agency Millward Brown attempted to understand how much and which parts of an ad individuals perceive and remember. Part of their work concerned ads for Cadbury's Flake. This chocolate bar crumbles easily when bitten and this feature has been developed as a point of differentiation for the brand.

An advertisement was devised that depicted the bar being eaten by three different people in three different contexts. The first was a secretary, who collected the crumbs in the wrapping paper. The second was a man on a train, who collected the crumbs on a plate, and the third was a small boy, who used a straw to suck up the crumbs. Each character was shown for 10 seconds, but in the tracking studies that followed it was the small boy who was recalled most, in disproportion to the time of the message exposure (see Figure 8.3 and Exhibit 8.7).

Source: Brown (1991).

Question

The message is clear, successful ads are interesting ads . . . true?

Task

Ask a group of friends which ad they remember and then ask them why they think they remember that particular one.

Exhibit 8.7 Cadbury's Flake bar

Messages, in particular advertising messages, that are interesting, immediately relevant or interpreted as possessing a deep set of personal meanings (all subsequently referred to as 'likeable' (see Chapter 16) will be stored in long-term memory (Chapter 5).

Research shows repeatedly that only parts of an advertisement are ever remembered – those parts that are of intrinsic value to the recipient and are sometimes referred to as 'the take-out'. The Brown (1991) example provided at Viewpoint 8.5 provides suitable evidence of this phenomenon. This selectivity, or message take-out, is referred to as the *creative magnifier* effect. Figure 8.3 illustrates the effect that parts of a message might have on the way a message is remembered.

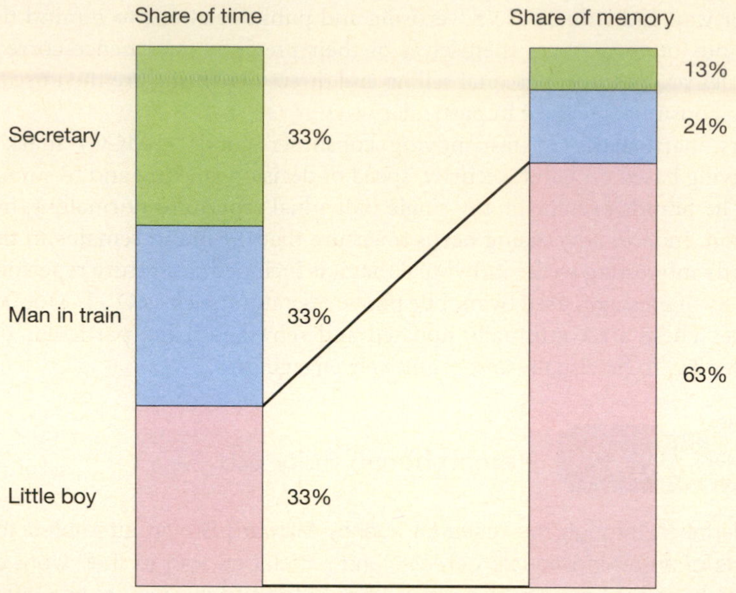

Figure 8.3 The creative magnifier
Source: Brown (1991).

The implication of this is that messages work best through the creation of interest and likeable moments, from which extracts are taken by individuals and stored away in memory. However, it might also be reasonable to suggest that the other tools of the mix are also capable of enabling individuals to take extracts. For example, the size of a sales promotion offer, or the tone of a sales presentation, the professionalism of a direct mail piece or the immediacy of an online promotion might all give due reason for an individual to generate a take-out. Interest is generated through fresh relevant ideas where the brand and the messages are linked together in a meaningful and relevant way. This in turn allows for future associations to be made, linking brands and marketing communication messages in a positive and experiential way.

Advertising is used to trigger brand associations and experiences.

Advertising is used to trigger brand associations and experiences for people, not only when seated in front of a television, or PC, when reading a magazine or reading text messages but also when faced with product purchase decisions. Seventy per cent of low-value FMCG purchase decisions are said to be made at the point of purchase. All forms of marketing communication, but principally advertising, can be used to generate brand associations, which in turn are used to trigger advertising messages or, rather, 'likeable' extracts. The other tools of the mix can benefit from the prior use of advertising to create awareness so that the call-to-action brought about through below-the-line communications can occur naturally, unhindered by brand confusion or uncertainty.

This last point is of particular importance because advertising alone may not be sufficient to trigger complete recall of brand and communication experiences. The brand, its packaging, sales promotion, digital media, POP and outdoor media all have an important role to play in providing consistency and interest and prompting recall and recognition. Integrated marketing communications is important, not just for message take-out or likeable extracts, but also for triggering recall and recognition and stimulating relevant brand associations.

Messages that customers perceive as being of significant value to them as individuals, are key to developing effective marketing communications. In order to create such messages, a complex array of disciplines, media, people, technology and intuition need to be coordinated and deployed. These principles apply equally to consumer and business markets, it is just that the mix of marketing communication elements changes with each context.

Towards a model of marketing communications

Marketing communications is a complex subject, if only because of the large number of variables, the nature of customer and stakeholder behaviour and the dynamic nature of markets, organisations and information processing. So far in this chapter, a number of issues have been presented which, taken independently, are interesting but lack overall coherence and direction and do not necessarily deal with the complexity or advance our understanding about how marketing communications works. The following represents an attempt to bring these different elements together and to offer a general framework to depict how marketing communications might work.

Any descriptive model of a process should be considered as a generalisation and intended only to represent the key elements, the flow between them and the outcomes and possible consequences. The model that follows is intended to bring together the key elements associated with the way in which the marketing communications process works.

The starting point for any model or framework depicting how marketing communications may work, should be the audience or individual person receiving messages. The context therefore, is an important aspect of marketing communications not the message itself, the media or the tools used.

The context is an important aspect of marketing communications, not the message itself, the media or the tools used.

This model seeks to accommodate marketing communications in both consumer and b2b markets. It attempts to reflect the different marketing communications needs of those individuals who are engaged in both transactional and relationship exchanges, although it does not indicate how marketing communications might assist transition from the former to the latter.

The task of marketing communications is to present key messages in such a way that the meanings that people (the target audience) ascribe to them are relevant and capable of being memorised, acted upon and recalled at some point in the future. Advertising can be regarded as a potentially powerful means of enabling buyers to attribute meanings to messages they receive about brands. Messages conveyed through the below-the-line communications enable people to decide if and *how* they should respond to the message. Lannon (1992) argues that we should be concerned with what people do *with* advertising, how they assign meaning and Gronstedt (1997) echoes this thought with respect to public relations. He suggests that the focus should be on what stakeholders do with messages as opposed to what the message does to the stakeholder.

Customers are problem solvers and their capability is partly determined by their level of elaboration. They can be regarded as active information processors (to varying degrees) in all product categories. Advertising is a convenient and often cost-effective way of conveying information about brands to people, who then have an opportunity to reappraise their understanding of the brand and its related elements. Advertising can either make people aware or promote interest in a new brand or remind buyers of the values and experiences of previous usage. More direct forms of communication may enable people to make brand associations but are more likely to pose challenges with regard to persuasion and how they should act in response to a message. These marketing communication messages are processed internally and are used to achieve two main outcomes: one is to update an individual's knowledge about a brand and/or the generic category of products as they see it ('Oh, that is a different type of ice cream'). The second is to prompt individuals into further action, either to seek more information or to purchase.

One of the main outcomes is to prompt individuals into further action, either to seek more information or to purchase.

Our understanding of perception suggests that people organise filtered and selected stimuli according to the context of their current situation and past experiences. Therefore, marketing communication messages need to be consistent in order that people can organise information about a brand in the same way as they processed the information the last time they perceived the stimuli. As suggested above, the stimulus need not be just an advertisement – it could be any element of the promotional or marketing mix, or indeed the brand itself. Therefore, the presence of either the product or the communication event may act as a stimulus. It is not surprising that integrated marketing communications require that, whatever the contact with a brand, the message should be the same and be expected in the context with which information was processed previously.

The model presented in Figure 8.4 attempts to bring together those elements that influence the way in which marketing communications might be considered to work. Stimuli are considered in the context of the probable exchange environment that will reflect a transactional or relational emphasis. These stimuli will act upon levels of elaboration, which in turn determine levels of cognitive processing. Likeable extracts are taken out of the messages and stored for future use. Marketing communication messages and/or brand experiences then allow for these extracts to be recalled. This impacts on the attitude to the brand and towards the message, which affects purchase intentions. Therefore, brands and all the tools of the marketing communication mix work together – each is capable of reinforcing the other and triggers are required to establish or recall brand values and then prompt the action processes and reinforce previous behaviour.

For marketing communications to work and for messages to be effective, they must be likeable and must be contextually compatible.

For marketing communications to work and for messages to be effective, they must be likeable (interesting, meaningful and relevant to the brand and the target audience) and must therefore be contextually compatible with the target audience and the

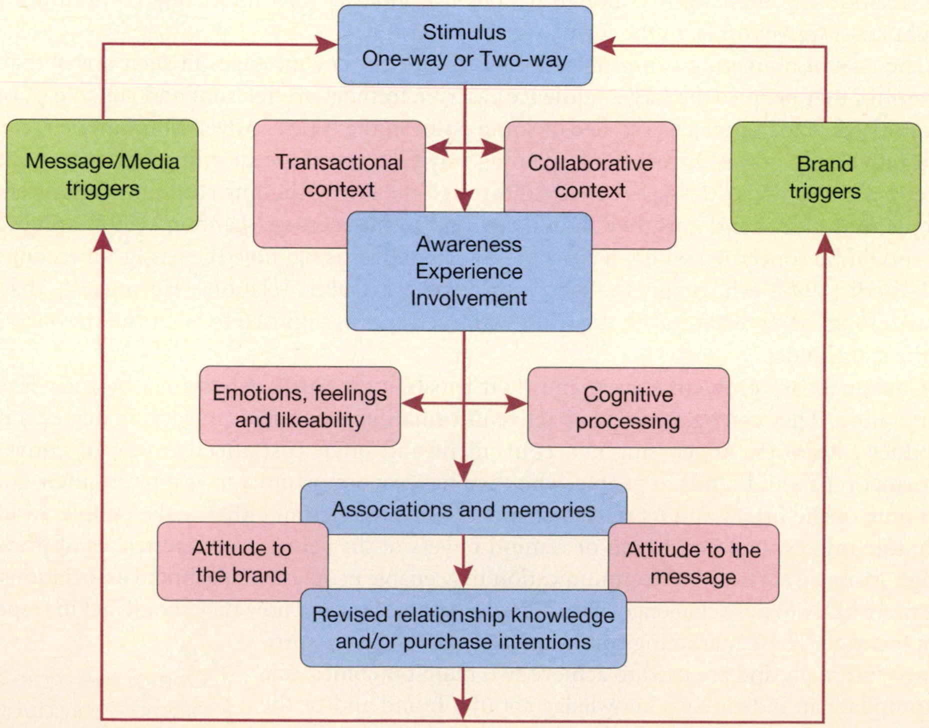

Figure 8.4 A model of how marketing communications might work

brand. If these twin factors (likeability and contextual compatibility) are established then positive emotional attitudes towards the message may form, which in turn lead to positive influences on purchase intentions.

Summary

In order to help consolidate your understanding of the ideas concerning how marketing communications might work, here are the key points summarised against each of the learning objectives:

1. Explore ideas concerning the strategic context of marketing communications.

The corporate strategy that organisations pursue should be supported by business-, operational- and functional-level strategies. To be effective, marketing communications should be used to complement the marketing, business and corporate strategies. Such complementarity serves to reinforce core messages, reflect the mission and provide a means of using resources efficiently, while at the same time providing reinforcement for the whole business strategy.

2. Explain how marketing communications has emerged.

The communication mix has expanded and become a more complex managerial instrument, but essentially it is now capable of delivering two main solutions. On the one hand, it can be used to develop and maintain brand values and on the other, it can be used to change behaviour through the delivery of calls-to-action. From a strategic perspective, the former is oriented to the long term and the latter to the short term. It is also apparent that the significant rise of the below-the-line tools within the mix is partly a reflection of the demise of the USP but it is also a reflection of the increasing financial pressures experienced by organisations to improve performance and improve returns on investment.

USPs have given way to ESPs and industry and commerce have shifted the focus of marketing spend away from above- to below-the-line activities, as if to emphasise the need to affect behavioural change. Therefore, it is now more important to understand the way marketing communications works rather than just the way advertising works.

3. Discuss the role and tasks of marketing communications.

The role of marketing communications is to engage audiences, and this can be achieved principally through the use of intellectual and/or emotional messages. Marketing communications can achieve particular tasks. These are to differentiate, reinforce, inform and persuade audiences to think or behave in particular ways.

4. Suggest ways in which marketing communications might work.

For a message to be communicated successfully, it should be meaningful to the recipient. Messages need to be targeted at the right audience, be capable of gaining attention, be understandable, relevant and acceptable. For effective communication to occur, messages should be designed that fit the cognitive capability and relationship orientation of the target audience.

There is no single model that explains how marketing communications might work, despite years of research and speculation by a great many people. Several sequential models have been proposed but these are no longer deemed applicable. Ideas involving cognitive processing, the elaboration likelihood model and interactive and dialogic forms of communication provide a basis for considering ways in which marketing communication works.

5. Examine the concept of significant value.

Marketing communication messages normally pass individuals unobserved. Those that are remembered contain particular characteristics. These would appear to be that the product must be different or new, that the way the message is executed is different or interesting and that the message proclaims something that is personally significant to the individual in their current context. The term 'significance' means that the message is meaningful, relevant and is perceived to be suitably credible. These three characteristics can be tracked from the concept of ad likeability (Chapter 16), which many researchers believe is the only meaningful indicator of the effectiveness of an advertisement.

6. Consider the strengths and weaknesses of a model explaining how marketing communications might work.

The starting point for any model or framework depicting how marketing communications may work, should be the audience or individual person receiving messages. The context therefore, is an important aspect of marketing communications, rather than the message itself, the media or the tools used.

For marketing communications to work and for messages to be effective, they must be likeable (interesting, meaningful and relevant to the brand and the target audience) and must therefore be contextually compatible with the target audience and the brand. If these twin factors (likeability and contextual compatibility) are established, then positive emotional attitudes towards the message may form which in turn lead to positive influences on purchase intentions.

Review questions

1. Explain the role that marketing communications plays within relationship marketing.
2. Write brief notes outlining the difference between three sequential models and evaluate the ways in which they are considered to work.
3. Which element in McGuire's model separates it from other similar models?
4. Explain the concepts of USPs and ESPs.
5. Discuss the primary roles of marketing communications.
6. Cognitive processing consists of three main elements. Name them.
7. Give examples of peripheral and central route cues to attitude change using the elaboration likelihood model.
8. Describe the creative magnifier effect. Why is it important?
9. What is the likely impact of triggers and brand associations in determining how advertising works?
10. Evaluate the concept of significant value.

MiniCase 'Get on your bike!' Mountain biking tourism in the Cairngorms National Park (CNP)

Andrew Turnbull: Aberdeen Business School, Robert Gordon University

Interest in mountain biking is currently undergoing rapid growth in Scotland and mountain biking tourism offers a means to use the Scottish landscape to attract several, largely untapped, target audiences, including thrill seekers, mountaineers, mountain bike owners, holidaymakers and families. These groups represent a small but growing proportion of the nearly 20 million visitors each year to Scotland from the UK, as well as those from abroad. The question is, however, how can these audiences, with their differing requirements, be engaged and what communications strategies might be employed to reach them most cost effectively?

Areas in Scotland such as the CNP can potentially benefit significantly from successful diversification and provision of facilities for the sport, but a number of stakeholders will need to be satisfied in the process, not least those concerned about the effects on the environment. Certainly mountain biking fits in well with some of the principal aims of the park, for example to promote understanding and enjoyment of the special qualities of the area and to contribute to the social development of the area's communities. The issue is whether this can be successfully linked to the promotion of sustainable use of the park's natural resources. For the long term, it is critical that any new mountain biking facilities do not have a detrimental impact upon fragile landscapes or rare wildlife.

Before considering how to communicate, profiles of the receivers must be drawn up. The interest groups here can be summarised as users, divided into the sub-segments above, environmentalists, the media and both local authorities and the Scottish Executive. It is not enough simply to communicate with actual and potential customers when considering such a high profile and environmentally sensitive location. A clear conflict in each group's desires and objectives represents a major obstacle to a successful communications plan.

So the strategy put forward, which stems from primary research activity, included a mix of communications tools taking into account potential resources, the complexity of the messages to be conveyed and the diversity of the audiences, as well as the nature, size and location of the market. Above all, it should be realised that mountain biking trails in the Cairngorms are in their infancy, so awareness creation is the key.

To start with however, advertising will be limited, in part because the audiences are geographically spread and in part because of the expense. Specialist publications such as *Cycling World* and *Men's Health* can be used, however, and other titles will be considered in or immediately pre-season, including local press in the CNP area. Inserts, as a form of direct marketing, also represent an option and information leaflets, including sales promotional offers, will be distributed to all visitor centres, attractions and accommodation outlets, including Guest Houses, B&Bs, hostels and hotels. These can be targeted not just within the CNP area, but in any location within a two-hour drive time.

Cinema, in all the major cities in Scotland, is a medium that has potential when the right films are on screen, as the cost is significantly lower than broadcast media, the impact is high and audiences can be easily matched to the mountain biker user profiles identified above. The disadvantage, of course, is that unlike press ads and leaflets, no direct response is possible, only the inclusion of a web address.

The importance of new media, in particular the Internet, cannot be underestimated given the young, educated and well-off customer profile. Dialogue allows interactivity and feedback can give competitive advantage! Web sites (such as http://cycling.visitscotland.com/mountain_biking/mb_centre/mountain_biking_cairngorms) providing maps and giving information regarding the newest facilities, the latest trails and access routes will be vital too, in encouraging word-of-mouth among a close-knit group who will frequently communicate between themselves. Receivers in such a market will be easily influenced by opinion and style leaders.

Inevitably, in a campaign with limited finances, publicity gained through public relations activities are expected to form the central part of the communications strategy involving traditional media. Apart from the use of press releases concerning events such as mountain biking championships, advertorials and competitions will be placed in relevant press titles and stands reserved at selected UK exhibitions. Costs can be shared by entering alliances with bike manufacturers and other joint promotional activities are potentially available with equipment and clothing providers, retail outlets and even the ordnance survey map producers.

All these organisations are in a position to help each other and combined activity through the pooling of resources will prove mutually beneficial.

Joining forces with other businesses looking to serve the mountain bike community will also assist with presenting a united front to the environmental lobby and the authorities. A socially responsible, environmentally aware message that nevertheless emphasises the financial benefits to the area, allows the media too to support mountain biking initiatives, rather than seek to find fault and take issue with the influx of new people and new activities that potentially conflict with more traditional pursuits such as hill walking and climbing.

An evaluation focus is always critical when measuring the reaction to initiatives targeted so precisely at niche audiences. As with all communications activities, measurement involves both 'hard' factors, which can be precisely quantified, and 'soft' factors, that must then be interpreted to assess their value.

So, for example, the number of new mountain bike trails is known exactly, the number of visitors using them can be estimated and expenditure associated with each visitor group can also be calculated from market research. The share of visits that mountain bikers represent to the area can also be determined as can uplift of, and response to, leaflets left in accommodation establishments and 'hits' on web sites, together with pages viewed and time spent browsing. Visitors to exhibition stands, as well as numbers leaving contact details, are further measures of success. Where media are utilised, then cover, reach and frequency, as well as a profile of the media user, give a good indication of who has been reached and how often.

Nevertheless, it is not just quantifiable measures that demonstrate effectiveness of a campaign. Qualitative measures, including attitudes towards the messages conveyed, the imagery associated with the creative execution, and values expressed, will all contribute to the overall impact.

The way is clear to allow CNP to diversify into mountain biking tourism. Given a good product, with the establishment of trails and facilities, then a focused communications campaign should overcome conservative values and capitalise on the opportunities this relatively new sport provides. The region's economy will benefit, Scotland's reputation will grow and a country that breathes history will further embrace the modern tourist market place.

MiniCase questions

1. For any marketing communications programme to work, it is essential that the messages sent reach the target audience(s). Summarise all the audiences identified in the case and consider the segmentation criteria that have been applied.
2. Critically analyse the communications process in the case, in the context of at least two models identified earlier in the text book. For example, the process of adoption model and the original Schramm *et al.* linear model.
3. Identify and critically examine the choice and balance of communications activities and media planned and determine first, the reasons for their selection and second, how well you believe they will work together.

References

Aaker, D.A., Batra, R. and Myers, J.G. (1992) *Advertising Management*. 4th edn. Englewood Cliffs, NJ: Prentice-Hall.

Ajzen, I. and Fishbein, M. (1980) *Understanding Attitudes and Predicting Social Behavior*. Englewood Cliffs, NJ: Prentice-Hall.

Anon. (2008) Superbrands case studies: the AA. *Brand Republic* 3 January. Retrieved 14 January 2008 from www.brandrepublic.com/InDepth/Analysis/774861/Superbrands-case-studies-AA/.

Bainbridge, J. (2004) Dental diversification. *Marketing*, 12 September, 36–7.

Ballantyne, D. (2004) Dialogue and its role in the development of relationship specific knowledge. *Journal of Business and Industrial Marketing*, **19**(2), 114–23.

Barry, T. and Howard, D.J. (1990) A review and critique of the hierarchy of effects in advertising. *International Journal of Advertising*, **9**, 121–35.

Belch, G.E. and Belch, M.A. (2004) *Advertising and Promotion: An Integrated Marketing Communications Perspective*, 6th edn. Homewood, IL: Richard D. Irwin.

Blackstock, C. (2002) Tea party over as PG Tips chimps are given the bird. *The Guardian*, 12 January. Retrieved 12 February 2008 from www.monkeyworld.co.uk/press.php?ArticleID=59

Bold, B. (2004) AA turns its back on £22m 'JustAAsk' campaign. *Marketing*, 13 October 2004. Retrieved 4 February 2005 from http://www.brandrepublic.com/News/224662/.

Brown, G. (1991) *How Advertising Affects the Sales of Packaged Goods Brands*. Warwick: Millward Brown.

Bruner, G.C. and Kumar, A. (2000) Web commercials and advertising hierarchy of effects. *Journal of Advertising Research*, January/April, 35–42.

Carter, M. (2008) Monkey Business, *The Independent*, 17 March, 8–9

Chen, Q. and Wells, W.D. (1999) Attitude toward the site. *Journal of Advertising Research*, September/October, 27–37.

Fletcher, W. (1994) The advertising high ground. *Admap* (November), 31–4.

Goldsmith, R.E. and Lafferty, B.A. (2002) Consumer response to web sites and their influence on advertising effectiveness. *Internet Research: Electronic Networking Applications and Policy*, **12**(4), 318–28.

Greenwald, A. (1968) Cognitive learning, cognitive response to persuasion and attitude change. In *Psychological Foundations of Attitudes* (eds A. Greenwald, T.C. Brook and T.W. Ostrom), 197–215. New York: Academic Press.

Gronroos, C. (2004) The relationship marketing process: communication, interaction, dialogue, value. *Journal of Business and Industrial Marketing*, **19**(2), 99–113.

Gronstedt, A. (1997) The role of research in public relations strategy and planning. In *The Handbook of Strategic Public Relations and Integrated Communications* (ed. C.L. Caywood), 34–59. Boston, MA: McGraw-Hill.

Heath, R. (2000) Low involvement processing, *Admap* (April), 34–6.

Kent, M.L. and Taylor, M. (2002) Toward a dialogic theory of public relations. *Public Relations Review*, **28**(1) (February), 21–37.

Klein, N. (2005) *No Logo*, London: Flamingo.

Lannon, J. (1992) Asking the right questions: what do people do with advertising? *Admap* (March), 11–16.

Lavidge, R.J. and Steiner, G.A. (1961) A model for predictive measurements of advertising effectiveness. *Journal of Marketing* (October), 61.

Lutz, J., Mackensie, S.B. and Belch, G.E. (1983) Attitude toward the ad as a mediator of advertising effectiveness. *Advances in Consumer Research*, **X**. Ann Arbor, MI: Association for Consumer Research.

McGuire, W.J. (1978) An information processing model of advertising effectiveness. In *Behavioral and Management Science in Marketing* (eds H.L. Davis and A.J. Silk), 156–80. New York: Ronald/Wiley.

Olsen, J.C. and Peter, J.P. (1987) *Consumer Behavior*. Homewood, IL: Irwin.

Packard, V. (1958) *The Hidden Persuaders*, Harmondsworth: Penguin.

Palda, K.S. (1966) The hypothesis of a hierarchy of effects: a partial evaluation. *Journal of Marketing Research*, **3**, 13–24.

Petty, R.E. and Cacioppo, J.T. (1983) Central and peripheral routes to persuasion: application to advertising. In *Advertising and Consumer Psychology* (eds L. Percy and A. Woodside), 3–23. Lexington, MA: Lexington Books.

Solley, S. (2004) Not just for Christmas. *Marketing*, 4 August, 34–5.

Strong, E.K. (1925) *The Psychology of Selling*. New York: McGraw-Hill.

Thomson, K. and Hecker, L.A. (2000) The business value of buy-in. In *Internal Marketing: Directions for Management* (eds R.J. Varey and B.R. Lewis), 160–72. London: Routledge.

Wright, P.L. (1973) The cognitive processes mediating the acceptance of advertising. *Journal of Marketing Research*, **10** (February), 53–62.

Part 3 Managing marketing communications

Chapters 9–15

The main theme of this part of the book concerns the management of marketing communications.

This part opens with a consideration of a core concept, integrated marketing communications (IMC). It explores ideas concerning the nature and validity of this concept and suggests that the concept is used in a number of ways by both academics and practitioners. This chapter adopts a strategic perspective, one that is extended into the following chapter. Here, in Chapter 10, issues about strategy and planning are discussed and readers are encouraged to consider the interaction between the two elements. The marketing communications planning framework is introduced at this point.

Chapter 11 examines the nature and role of objectives in marketing communications and then considers the importance of positioning activities. This is an important strategic aspect of this subject and one that is supported by product and corporate branding issues that are the focus of the following two chapters. The main point within these chapters is not branding itself but the role marketing communications plays in the branding process.

The final two chapters in this part review matters concerning the allocation of financial resources and how communications and campaigns should be evaluated. Chapter 14 looks at the various techniques used by organisations to develop suitable budgets for marketing communications and debates the efficiency and effectiveness of these approaches. Chapter 15 is important because it looks at the evaluation of marketing communications activities from both a campaign and promotional tool perspective. It is important because evaluation is often overlooked in terms of its impact and contribution to the overall process.

Video Insight Part 3

Part 3 of the book is concerned with the issues associated with managing marketing communications. This includes developing marketing communications strategy, planning and integrating campaigns, devising and managing budgets and evaluating the effectiveness of marketing communications activities. In addition to these aspects, marketing communications plays an important role in developing and maintaining brands.

Marketing India is a demanding task considering the diversity of potential tourist experiences. The Video Insight shows how understanding target markets and adopting a planned approach can lead to effective communications. It refers to India as a brand and brands need to be managed if they are to be developed successfully. In a similar way the interview with Canon Precentor, Lucy Winkett provides an interesting perspective on the way St. Paul's Cathedral can be considered a brand.

The Land Rover contribution considers some of the strategic issues and responds to criticisms that this brand is essentially an environmental hazard. Issues concerning CSR are critical aspects of an organisation's communications and these are demonstrated well in this Video Insight.

Marketing communications can be used to reflect the prevailing or dominant corporate or country/region culture, especially if it can be used to provide an emotional selling point or a means of sustainable differentiation. The strength of the Swedish culture and its influence on purchasing and customer experiences is examined by the interview with Ikea.

Most marketing professionals will recognise the importance of measuring marketing activities. Research shows that some organisations are reluctant to invest in this activity, at least to the extent they should. Here, Dave Hodgson, Marketing Manager for Marketing Birmingham advocates the need to evaluate marketing communications activities on the basis that if it is not measurable (an activity) then it is not worth doing in the first place.

Go to **www.pearsoned.co.uk/fill** to watch the Video Insight, and then answer the following questions:

1. What are the difficulties associated with branding India?
2. How do Ikea segment their markets and how do the use push, pull and profile strategies?
3. How do Birmingham measure their marketing communications?

Chapter 9

Integrated marketing communications

Integrated marketing communications are more likely to occur when organisations attempt to interact with their various internal and external audiences. The communication mix used in any interaction should be audience-centred and internally consistent with the organisation's objectives and strategies. Target audiences should perceive these communications and associated cues as relevant, likeable, timely and of value.

Aims and learning objectives

The aims of this chapter are to explore the nature and characteristics of integrated marketing communications and to understand the complexities associated with developing and implementing this form of marketing communications.

The learning objectives of this chapter are to:

1. introduce the concept of integrated marketing communications (IMC) and explore what it is that is integrated;
2. understand the different perspectives of IMC;
3. consider the background and reasons for the development and interest in IMC;
4. explore some of the issues associated with managing and implementing IMC;
5. explain variants of the IMC concept: media-neutral planning and open planning approaches;
6. consider how the structures and frameworks of advertising and communication agencies might need to change so that they are better able to work with IMC;
7. examine ideas concerning an incremental approach to IMC.

For an applied interpretation see J. Graham Spickett-Jones' MiniCase entitled ***IMC – richer consumer engagement*** at the end of this chapter.

Introduction

To appreciate the essence of integrated marketing communications (IMC) it is helpful to understand its origins and the key factors that have helped shape its development. For many years agencies and clients believed that to deliver messages to particular audiences it was necessary to use specific tools of the communications mix. At the time it was a common belief that to achieve specific communication effects *on* buyers it was necessary to use particular tools. So for example, clients were recommended to use advertising to create awareness, sales promotions to generate immediate sales uplifts and public relations to create interest and goodwill towards a brand. This view held that each tool has specific characteristics and particular communication abilities. As a result clients were required to deal with a variety of functionally different and independent agencies in order to complete their communication requirements with their various audiences.

It was a common belief that to achieve specific communication effects *on* buyers it was necessary to use particular tools.

This 'specialisation' resulted in a proliferation of advertising agencies and the development of sales promotion houses. Public relations specialists stood off from any direct association with marketing. Personal selling had already evolved as a discrete function within organisations. This approach was also legitimised by the development of trade associations and professional management groups (for example, the Institute of Practitioners in Advertising (UK) and the Institute of Sales Promotion (UK)) that seek to endorse, advance, protect and legitimise the actions of their professions and members. One of the outcomes of this silo perspective and functional development of the marketing communications industry has been entrenchment and the inevitable opposition to change.

Now that clients have begun to re-orient their communications away from mass media approaches to increased levels of interaction with customers, the structural inadequacies of the marketing communication industry have served to constrain them. IMC has emerged partially as a reaction to this structural inadequacy and the realisation by clients that their communication needs can (and should) be achieved more efficiently and effectively than previously. In other words, just as power has moved from brand manufacturers to multiple retailers and now to consumers, so power is moving from agencies to clients.

This trend away from traditional communication strategies based on mass communications, directing generalised messages to huge segmented audiences has played a part in the development of IMC. Contemporary strategies are based more on personalised, customer-oriented and technology-driven approaches, and are often referred to as integrated marketing communications (IMC). Duncan and Everett (1993) recall that this new, largely media-oriented approach, has been referred to variously as *orchestration, whole egg* and *seamless communication*. More recent notions involve the explicit incorporation of corporate communications, reflected in titles such as integrated marketing and integrated communications (see Cornelissen (2000)).

More recent notions involve the explicit incorporation of corporate communications.

It is interesting that the rapid development of direct marketing initiatives since the second half of the 1980s and the impact the Internet has made have coincided with a move towards what has become regarded as integrated marketing communications. A further significant development has been the shift in marketing philosophies, from transaction to relationship marketing, as introduced in Chapter 1 and considered in more detail in Chapter 7.

What is to be integrated?

The notion that some aspects of marketing communications should be integrated begs the question, what is it that needs to be integrated? While the origins of IMC might be found in

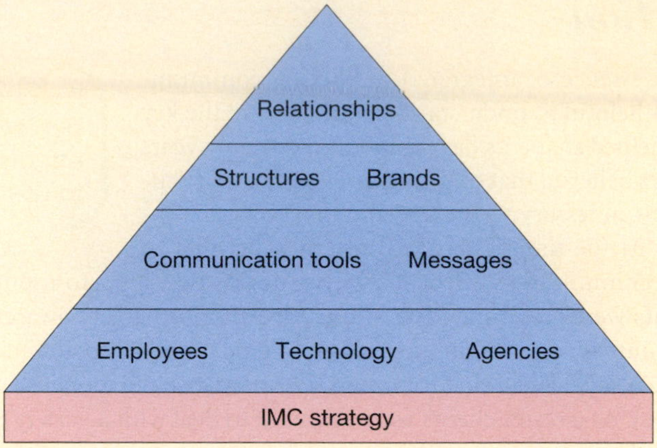

Figure 9.1 Elements for integration

the prevailing structural conditions and the needs of particular industry participants, an understanding of what elements should be integrated in order to achieve IMC needs to be established.

The problem with answering this question is that unless there is an agreement about what IMC is then identifying appropriate elements is far from easy, practical or in any one's best interests. Figure 9.1 shows some of the elements that need integrating.

The following represents some of the fundamental elements, but readers are advised to consider some of the other issues that have been raised in this chapter before confirming their views about this stimulating yet relatively young concept.

Communication tools

The key visual triggers used in advertising should be replicated across the range of promotional tools used.

One of the early and more popular views of IMC was that the messages conveyed by each of the 'promotional' tools should be harmonised in order that audiences perceive a consistent set of meanings within the messages they receive. One interpretation of this perspective, is that the key visual triggers (design, colours, form and tag line) used in advertising should be replicated across the range of promotional tools used, including POP and the sales force. At another level, integration is about bringing together the communication tools (Pitta *et al.* 2006). One such combination is the closer alliance of advertising with public relations. Increasing audience fragmentation means that it is more difficult to locate target audiences and communicate with them in a meaningful way. By utilising the power of public relations to get advertisements talked about, what the trade refer to as media equivalents, so a form of communications consistency, or integration to some, becomes possible.

The rapid development of direct marketing approaches has helped some organisations bring together the different tools such that they undertake more precise roles and reinforce each other. For example, the use of direct mail and telemarketing to follow through on an ad campaign is common place, but now web-enabled communications, customer care centres and sales promotions can be linked together through database applications, and all are designed to communicate the same core message.

ViewPoint 9.1 Integrated crumbs

Two of McVitie's core brands are Hobnobs and Milk Chocolate Digestives and a campaign was required to reinforce the credentials of the McVitie's umbrella brand with consumers and to convey the message that their biscuits are made 100 per cent from UK wheat and oats.

To deliver this message they developed an integrated campaign based around the core message 'share the goodness'.

The campaign, which was advertising-led, consisted primarily of a £2m poster. In addition they used direct marketing to reinforce brand values. Public relations were used to support the campaign. Here the goal was to create media interest and comment about the brand. This was achieved through an art exhibition held at Leeds, Bristol and Birmingham city centres. The exhibition featured two 5ft bales of wheat covered with Milk Chocolate Digestives wrappers.

The events drew extensive broadcast and print media interest and the whole campaign saw sales rise a massive 9 per cent compared to the same period in the previous year.

Source: Cowlett (2007).

Question

Is this an example of integrated marketing communications or just good practice?

Task

Which other tools and media could have been used in the McVitie's campaign?

Messages

A further interpretation, at a deeper level, is that the theme and set of core messages used in any campaign should first be determined and then deployed as an integrated whole across the communication mix (sometimes referred to as synergy). One of the differences is the recognition that mass media advertising is not always the only way to launch consumer or business-to-business promotional activities, and that a consideration of the most appropriate mix of communication tools and media might be a better starting point when formulating campaigns.

> The theme and set of core messages used in any campaign should first be determined and then deployed as an integrated whole across the communication mix.

Another perspective of IMC, provided by Duncan and Moriarty (1998), is that stakeholders (including customers) automatically integrate brand messages. This suggests that as long as the gap between the different messages (in content and meaning) are acceptable, then management's task is to manage the process and seek to narrow these gaps that may be perceived.

What runs through both these approaches is the belief that above-the-line and below-the-line communications need to be moulded into one cohesive bundle, from which tools can be selected and deployed as conditions require.

Marketing mix

The elements of the marketing mix, however configured, also need to be integrated because they also communicate (Smith, 1996). The price and associated values, the product, in terms of the quality, design and tangible attributes, the manner and efficiency of the service delivery people and where and how it is made available, for example the location, web site, customer contact centres, retailer/dealer reputation and overall service quality need to be perceived by customers as a coordinated and consistent whole. These touch points with brands are aspects of a consumer's brand experience and are used to develop images that through

> The elements of the marketing mix, however configured, need to be integrated.

time may shape brand reputations. Traditionally the marketing mix was expected to deliver the brand proposition. Now it is expected that all these elements will be coordinated to maximise impact and enable customers to experience the brand through pre-, actual and post-product use.

Branding

Brands are themselves a form of integration.

Brands are themselves a form of integration. This means that internally organisations need to be sufficiently coordinated so that the brand is perceived externally as consistent and uniform. However, this proposition is based on the view that a brand is prepared and delivered for a single target audience but audience and media fragmentation make this task more challenging. Audience sizes are shrinking, which means that in many situations a single audience is no longer economically viable. Brands therefore, need to appeal to a number of different audiences (White, 2000) and to do this it is necessary to develop brands that appeal to diverse consumer groups. White refers to these new brands as 'chameleon' brands. They are characterised by their ability to adapt to different situations (audiences and media) yet retain a core proposition that provides a form of continuity and recognition. For example, a top of the range music system may be seen by the owner as prestigious and technically superb, by a guest at a party as ostentatiously outrageous and overpriced and by a friend as a product of clever design and marketing. All three might have developed their attitudes through different sources (e.g. different print media, exhibitions, the Internet, retail stores, word-of-mouth) but all agree that the brand has a common set of values and associations that are important to each of them.

ViewPoint 9.2 Integration to promote conservation

When ZSL London Zoo launched Gorilla Kingdom in 2007 it used a wide range of communication tools and media and had to integrate their use if their sales and communication objectives were to be achieved.

Advertising, for example, outdoor such as billboards and London Underground poster sites.
Sales promotion, for example, included train promotion offers to encourage visitors from outside London.
Direct marketing, for example, direct mail to groups within the travel trade industry.
Public relations, for example, press releases, events, receptions for journalists and sponsorship of radio programme Magic FM.
Personal selling, for example, to people in the travel trade.

By integrating them within the new ZSL London Zoo brand and by timing and coordinating with each other, this marketing communications achieved significant impact and achieved its goals.

Question

How do we know a campaign is integrated?

Task

ZSL London Zoo subsequently launched the new Blackburn Aviary. Make brief notes about how would you use marketing communications to assist the launch?

The presentation of chameleon brands requires high levels of integration, a need to develop a series of innovative messages based around a core proposition. The use of a single ad execution needs to be replaced by multiple executions delivered through a variety of media, each complementing and reinforcing the core brand proposition. This means that the audience is more likely to be surprised or reminded of the brand (and its essence) through a series of refreshingly interesting messages, thereby raising the probability that the likeability factor (see Chapter 17) will be strengthened, along with the brand and all relevant associations.

A further dimension of the branding factor concerns the role of corporate brands and issues of corporate communications. Should these be integrated with product brand communications, and if so what are the branding strategies that should be followed?

Strategy

IMC is regarded by some as a means of using the tools of the communication mix in a more efficient and synergistic manner. At some level this can be true but IMC requires a deeper understanding of how and where messages are created. At a strategic level, IMC has its roots in the overall business strategy of an organisation. Using Porter's (1980) generic strategies, if a low-cost strategy (e.g. Asda) is being pursued, it makes sense to complement the strategy by using messages that either stress any price advantage that customers might benefit from or at least do not suggest extravagance or luxury. If using a differentiation focus strategy (e.g. Waitrose), price should not figure in any of the messages and greater emphasis should be placed on particular attributes that convey the added value and enable clear positioning. There is no right way (or formula) to establish IMC but there is a need to recognise that it is a developmental exercise and that it should have a strategic orientation as well as strategic outputs.

There is no right way (or formula) to establish IMC.

Employees

The next element that should be integrated concerns the recognition that IMC cannot be sustained unless it is supported by all customer-facing employees. It is generally agreed that all employees should adopt a customer focus and 'live' the brand. While this can be achieved partially through the use of training courses and in-house documentation (including electronic forms), this usually requires a change of culture and that means a longer-term period of readjustment and the adoption of new techniques, procedures and ways of thinking and behaving.

Once the internal reorientation has begun (not completed), it is possible to take the message to external audiences. As long as they can see that employees are starting to act in different ways and do care about them as customers and do know what they are talking about in support of the products and services offered, then it is likely that customers (and other stakeholders) will be supportive. IMC should be concerned with blending internal and external messages so that there is clarity, consistency and reinforcement of the organisation's (or brand's) core proposition.

ViewPoint 9.3 'Try something integrated today'

The development and launch of Sainsbury's highly successful 'Try something new today' campaign, is regarded by many as a good example of a form of integrated marketing communications. The root of the campaign was in the business strategy, one which aimed to boost sales by £2.5bn by March 2008. At a store level this was translated into getting shoppers to put an extra £1.40 into their shopping baskets on each visit to a Sainsbury's store.

From this strategic goal the communications strategy took shape. From a positioning based on 'Making life taste better' to one which read, 'Try something new today', the £10m campaign, led by Jamie Oliver, sought to awake shoppers from what Sainsbury's referred to as 'Sleep Shopping', where people tend to buy the same products on a routine basis, to one where they are prepared to experiment a little.

The strength of the basic idea enabled the message to be used in various media, across channels and adapted for different target segments. Not only was the campaign rooted in business strategy but it also encouraged staff participation.

Staff were given two days' training and then provided with various ingredients and recipes so that they could try them out at home. The thinking was that they could pass ideas onto customers and in doing so provide credibility and enhance the in store experience for shoppers.

Sources: Adapted from Anon. (2005); Brook (2005); Reed (2006); www.sainsburys.co.uk.

Question

Can IMC be achieved without having to incorporate a strategic orientation?

Task

Find out what each of the other main supermarkets regard as IMC.

Exhibit 9.1 Celebrity chef Jamie Oliver working with Sainsbury's to help us all 'try something new today'
Image courtesy of The Advertising Archives.

Technology

The interest and debate about IMC has been accelerated by developments in technology. The use of technology, and in particular database technologies, has enabled marketing managers a vastly improved view of customer behaviour, attitudes and feelings towards brands. This has allowed more precise and insightful communications to be generated and the subsequent feedback and measurement facilities have further developed the overall quality of customer communications. However, the mere presence of technology does not result in effective marketing communications. Technology needs to be integrated into not just the overall information systems strategy but also the marketing strategies of organisations. Technology is an enabler and to use it effectively requires integration. The effective use of technology can touch a number of areas within the IMC orbit. For example, technology can be used to develop effective web sites, extranets and intranets, customer contact centres, databases, advertising campaigns, fulfilment processes, CRM and sales force automation. If each of these applications is deployed independently of the others their impact will be limited. Developed within an integrated framework the potential for marketing and customer service can be tremendous.

Technology needs to be integrated into not just the overall information systems strategy but also the marketing strategies of organisations.

Associated with the use of technology are issues concerning the measurement and evaluation of IMC activities. One of the criticisms of IMC is that no evaluation system has yet been proposed or implemented so that the claims made about IMC delivering superior returns can be validated (Swain, 2004). This is part of the planning process and so integration of all aspects of the campaign planning process is necessary.

Agencies

Reference has been made earlier and in Chapter 3 to some of the structural issues involving agencies in the marketing communications industry and with the development of IMC. Agencies play a critical role in marketing communications and if IMC is to be established it cannot be accomplished without the explicit involvement of all those working on the supply side.

Apart from questions concerning the range of promotional services offered by individual agencies and whether these are all delivered by a single agency or through a network of interacting agencies, two particular issues arise. The first concerns leadership and the other remuneration.

With regard to leadership should the agency or the client lead the process of developing IMC? The consensus appears to be that this is the client's role (Swain, 2004), mainly because clients are better positioned to make integration happen across their own organisation. However, Swain then points out that there is no agreement about who in the client organisation should be responsible for implementing IMC. Indeed, Kitchen *et al.* (2007) confirm the reluctance of both advertising and public relations agencies to provide for integrative working practices.

A similar question concerns the implementation of integrated campaigns. Most major brands operate with several agencies, each providing different skills. These are known as roster agencies simply because different agencies can be brought into different campaigns to provide support when necessary. Herein lies the problem for clients implementing an integrative programme: how best to manage an integrative approach? One way is to appoint a lead agency that assumes responsibility for integration. Another way, used by AOL, who work with 12 agencies, is for the client to drive the programme forward and to involve the roster agencies (Gray, 2007). However, many client organisations, such as Shell, prefer to appoint a lead agency and very often it is the generalist ad agency that is appointed.

> A move to IMC requires a change in agency performance measures.

The second issue, remuneration, should be regarded as interrelated to the measurement factor (Swain, 2004). This is because clients see reward as a derivative of performance. The traditional remuneration system is based on activities (Spake *et al.* (1999) cited by Swain). Commission earned from the use of media to gain awareness or change attitudes is not measured against revenue or profit performance, and is referred to as 'an activity'. Results- or 'outcome'-based systems are considered a performance measure. A move to IMC requires a change in agency performance measures and consequently, a change in their method of remuneration. Closer integration of agencies within the IMC process will, among other things, bring changes in structure, operations, performance measures, remuneration and new responsibilities within the client relationship.

This list of elements that need to be integrated is not exclusive. There are other influences that are particular to individual organisations that could have been included. However, consideration of these various elements suggests strongly that what is being integrated is far more than just the communication tools. Indeed, viewed holistically integration is a strategic concept that strikes at the heart of an organisation's marketing and business orientation.

The development of IMC

The word integration has been used in various ways and it is the interpretation of the word integration that determines whether integrated marketing communications is real, achievable or even practised. In many ways, reality suggests that the claims many organisations and the communications industry make in the name of IMC are simply a reflection of improved management and coordination of the communication tools. The recent interest in media-neutral planning (MNP) may be a good thing for the cause of improved communications and relationship development but MNP does not address the wider strategic issues, the importance of internal communications or the structural issues of IMC on both the client and agency sides.

As established above, early interpretations of IMC were constructed around the idea that what was to be integrated were the promotional tools and media. Scholars such as Shultz (1993) and Duncan and Everett (1993) led much of the IMC activity and many organisations were enthusiastic about the new ideas, driven by the desire to restructure internally, reduce costs and deliver consistent messages. Kitchen *et al.* (2004) refer to this as the inside-out IMC approach.

The next phase was characterised by an exploration of the nature, direction and content typified by definitions that introduced management, strategy and brand development into the IMC process. Shimp (2000) among others, supported the explicit introduction of these aspects to IMC.

The current interpretation has moved the IMC concept forward, this time as an audience- or customer-driven process, one that incorporates ideas concerning relationship marketing. Duncan and Mulhern (2004) cited by Reid (2005), Gronroos (2004) and Duncan (2002) have provided valuable insights into this dimension of IMC, one which Kitchen *et al.* (2004) refer to as the outside-in IMC approach.

It should be noted that while many writers, such as Kitchen and Shultz (1997 and 1998) and Duncan (2002), have written positively and consistently promoting ideas about IMC, other authors such as Cornelissen and Lock (2000), Percy *et al.* (2001) and Spotts *et al.* (1998), to name but a few, have been critical of the concept and have doubted the merits inherent in the concept. This dichotomy of views reveals the inherent instability of the IMC concept. Readers interested in a fuller appraisal of IMC are referred to Kitchen *et al.* (2004) and Cornelissen (2003).

As part of his critique Cornelissen (2003) distinguishes two different themes running through the IMC literature. The first is that IMC is regarded as a predominantly *process*-oriented concept and the second is that it is a *content*-oriented concept. These are examined in the following section.

> Unsurprisingly, there is no agreement about what IMC is, what it encompasses or how it should be measured.

> IMC is a not a proven marketing theory – there is no empirical evidence to support the concept.

Unsurprisingly therefore, there is no agreement about what IMC is, what it encompasses or how it should be measured. Indeed, there is no universally agreed definition and, apart from some anecdotal comment, there is little practical evidence of the application of a strategic, customer-oriented IMC programme. There are numerous claims of IMC practice but these are little more than coordinated promotional mix activities using themed messages (inside-out).

IMC is a not a proven marketing theory (Cornelissen, 2003). There is no empirical evidence to support the concept, yet the ideas inherent in the overall approach appear to hold value. Although Cornelissen refers to the IMC concept as only worthy of symbolic value, a view later refuted by Kitchen, it does appear that what is integration to one person (or agency) may be coordination or simply good professional practice to another.

Perspectives on IMC

Cornelissen argues that the literature indicates that there are two main interpretations of IMC: a content and a process perspective respectively.

The *content* perspective assumes that message consistency is the major goal in order to achieve the 'one voice, one look' position. IMC works when there is consistency throughout the various materials and messages. However, this is not a new practice as Cornelissen points out that practitioners having been doing this long before the term IMC surfaced. This view is also associated with the zero-based planning approach that holds that the choice of tools and media should be based on effectiveness criteria rather than the specialist functions for which the planners and managers are responsible. This means that the various agencies and personnel responsible for campaign design and deployment do so without prejudice or bias towards a preferred tool or media. This approach is discussed later in this chapter.

The *content* perspective assumes that message consistency is the major goal in order to achieve the 'one voice, one look' position.

ViewPoint 9.4 Integrated toilet tissue

Velvet is a major toilet tissue brand bought by SCA Hygiene from Procter & Gamble. When SCA launched their Triple Velvet brand they referred to their integrated campaign. The £15m television campaign was supported with direct mail, sampling and touch-test panels in shopping centres, designed to help customers feel the softness of the brand.

Later that year SCA launched an interactive web site accompanied by an online campaign. This campaign extended the theme of the television ad as it features a virtual Velvet factory in which 'Baby MD' advises consumers about various product developments and promotions, while encouraging visitors to download various branded games. Aimed at mothers and children, the site is reported to replicate social networking experiences whose goal is to encourage return visits.

Source: Jones (2007).

Question

Are these primarily a process or content perspective of IMC?

Task

Visit the Velvet web site and comment on whether you believe the site appears to be part of an integrated approach. www.velvet-tissues.co.uk/.

The second interpretation offered by Cornelissen is referred to as a *process* perspective. Here the emphasis is on a structural realignment of the communication disciplines within organisations, even to the point of collapsing all communications into a single department. Even if this extreme interpretation is not a valid goal for an organisation, cross-functional systems and processes are regarded as necessary to enable integrated marketing communications.

The process perspective of IMC is rooted in the belief that real IMC can only be generated through an organisational structure that brings the various communication disciplines together in a single body or unit. By creating a single department out of which advertising, public relations and the other disciplines operate, so cross-functional coordination between the disciplines is enabled. Some argue that the process view needs to incorporate a series of intervening stages as systems, processes and procedures are brought together incrementally to enable the cross-functionality to work.

The process perspective of IMC is rooted in the belief that real IMC can only be generated through an organisational structure that brings the various communication disciplines together.

Research suggests that organisations have made little attempt to restructure their marketing communications disciplines and that public relations and marketing remain as a clear divide. What has happened, however, is that there are much closer cross-functional relationships and systems and processes to support them. Some organisations are moving incrementally towards a process perspective of IMC.

ViewPoint 9.5 Integrated cigarettes

Imperial Tobacco Ltd (ITL) is Canada's largest tobacco manufacturer and its leading brand, Player's has experienced a growth in market share from 37 per cent in 1973 to over 68 per cent in 1998. The brand was targeted at males under 25 years old and used messages set in mountainous or aquatic settings using sports themes.

What is interesting about ITL is that they abandoned the brand management structure and adopted a brand planning process structure. This involves a cross-functional approach that is regarded as a more strategic approach to brand development and brand defence. The company also developed a detailed insight into product and image positioning.

The brand strategy was clearly articulated internally and it was used to provide a platform for a consistent approach to messages and media selection. Consistency across their marketing communications and brand imagery was also achieved through the division head of brand marketing who considered activities across all brands and functional areas.

Source: Dewhirst and Davis (2005).

Question

Is this primarily a process or content perspective of IMC?

Task

Read the paper by Dewhirst and Davis (2005) and learn more about ITL's approach to IMC.

In an attempt to develop our understanding of IMC, Lee and Park (2007) proposed a multidimensional model of IMC based on four key dimensions. These have been drawn from the literature and, unlike Cornelissen's work, represent an attempt to measure IMC. Their four dimensions are concerned with a single message, multiple customer groups, database marketing and the need to use IMC to build customer relationships. A fuller account of these dimensions can be seen in Chapter 15.

Kliatchko (2008) suggests that IMC has several distinctive attributes and he refers to them as the 'four pillars of IMC'. These are stakeholders, content, channels and results. Figure 9.2 sets out the constituent elements within each of the pillars.

His argument is that these four elements can be observed at different levels of IMC and that at each level one of the elements tends to dominate.

It may be that a suitable theoretical basis upon which to develop IMC is emerging through the relationship marketing literature. We know that a relationship orientation requires a multidisciplinary approach to trigger interaction and dialogue (Gronroos, 2004). So, it may be

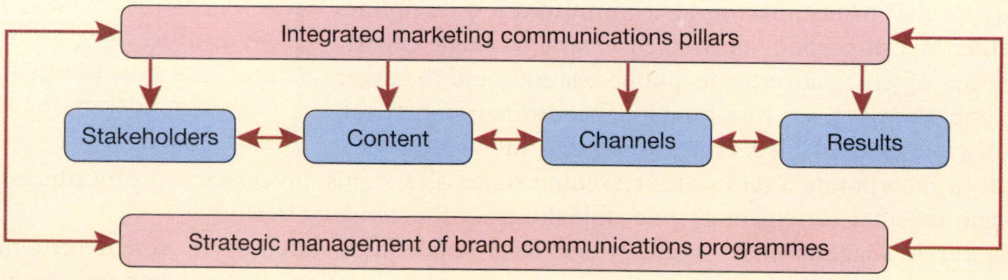

Figure 9.2 The Elements of the four pillars of IMC
Source: Kliatchko (2008). Used with permission from WARC.

that a deeper understanding of relational theory will help to advance the IMC concept and provide researchers with a surer footing upon which to explore the topic.

However, whether a content or process perspective is adopted, the position remains that until there is empirical evidence to support a theoretical base upon which to build IMC strategy and operations, the phrase will probably continue to be misused, misunderstood and used in a haphazard and inconsistent way.

From this review and bearing in mind that no single form of IMC can be identified, the following general definition of IMC is offered:

> *IMC can represent both a strategic and tactic approach to the planned management of an organisation's communications. IMC requires that organisations coordinate their various strategies, resources and messages in order that they enable meaningful engagement with target audiences. The main purposes are to develop a clear positioning and encourage stakeholder relationships that are of mutual value.*

This definition serves to link IMC with business-level strategies and relationships. The importance of coherence within the organisation is made, whether this be through systems or structural change. Implicit is the underpinning notion that IMC is necessary for the development of effective relationships and that not all relationships need be collaborative and fully relational, as so often assumed to be the case in many contemporary interpretations.

Implicit is the underpinning notion that IMC is necessary for the development of effective relationships.

Reasons for the developing interest in IMC

The explosion of interest in IMC has resulted from a variety of drivers. Generally they can be grouped into three main categories: those drivers (or opportunities) that are market-based, those that arise from changing communications, and those that are driven from opportunities arising from within the organisation itself. These are set out in Table 9.1.

The opportunities offered to organisations that contemplate moving to IMC are considerable and it is somewhat surprising that so few organisations have been either willing or able to embrace the approach. One of the main organisational drivers for IMC is the need to become increasingly efficient. Driving down the cost base enables managers to improve profits and levels of productivity. By seeking synergistic advantages through its communications and associated activities and by expecting managers to be able to account for the way in which they consume marketing communication resources, so integrated marketing communications becomes increasingly attractive. At the same time, organisation structures are changing more frequently and the need to integrate across functional areas reflects the efficiency drive.

From a market perspective, the predominant driver is the reorientation from transaction-based marketing to relationship marketing. The extension of the brand personality concept into brand relationships (Hutton, 1996) requires a customer consideration in terms of asking not only 'What do our customers want?', but also 'What are their values, do they trust us and are we loyal to them?' By adopting a position designed to enhance trust and commitment, an organisation's external communications need to be consistent and coordinated, if only to avoid information overload and misunderstanding.

From a market perspective, the predominant driver is the reorientation from transaction-based marketing to relationship marketing.

From a communication perspective, the key driver is to provide a series of triggers by which buyers can understand the values a brand stands for and a means by which they can use certain messages to influence their activities within the relationships they wish to develop. By differentiating the marketing communications, often by providing clarity and simplicity, advantages can be attained.

Table 9.1 Drivers for IMC

Organisational drivers for IMC
- Increasing profits through improved efficiency
- Increasing need for greater levels of accountability
- Rapid move towards cross-border marketing and the need for changing structures and communications
- Coordinated brand development and competitive advantage
- Opportunities to utilise management time more productively
- Provide direction and purpose for employees

Market-based drivers for IMC
- Greater levels of audience communications literacy
- Media cost inflation
- Media and audience fragmentation
- Stakeholders' need for increasing amounts and diversity of information
- Greater amounts of message clutter
- Competitor activity and low levels of brand differentiation
- Move towards relationship marketing from transaction-based marketing
- Development of networks, collaboration and alliances

Communication-based drivers for IMC
- Technological advances (Internet, databases, segmentation techniques)
- Increased message effectiveness through consistency and reinforcement of core messages
- More effective triggers for brand and message recall
- More consistent and less confusing brand images
- Need to build brand reputations and to provide clear identity cues

An integrated approach should attempt to provide a uniform or consistent set of messages. These should be relatively easy to interpret and to assign meaning. This enables target audiences to think about and perceive brands within a relational context and so encourages behaviour as expected by the source. Those organisations that try to practise IMC understand that buyers refer to and receive messages about brands and companies from a wide range of information sources. Harnessing this knowledge is a fundamental step towards enhancing marketing communications.

It seems useful to itemise the advantages and disadvantages associated with IMC. These are set out in Table 9.2. General opinion suggests that the advantages far outweigh the disadvantages and that increasing numbers of organisations are seeking to improve their IMC resource. As stated earlier, database technology and the Internet have provided great impetus for organisations to review their communications and to implement moves to install a more integrated communication strategy.

Managing IMC

The development and establishment of IMC by organisations has not been as widespread as the amount of discussion around the subject has suggested. Recent technological advances and the benefits of the Internet and related technologies have meant that organisations have had a reason to reconsider their marketing communications and have re-evaluated their approach. Whatever route taken, the development of IMC requires change, a change in thinking, a change in actions and a change in expectations. The changes required to achieve IMC are large and the barriers are strong. What can be

The development of IMC requires change, a change in thinking, a change in actions and a change in expectations.

Table 9.2 Advantages and disadvantages of IMC

Advantages of IMC
Provides opportunities to cut communication costs and/or reassign budgets
Has the potential to produce synergistic and more effective communications
Can deliver competitive advantage through clearer positioning
Encourages coordinated brand development with internal and external participants
Provides for increased employee participation and motivation
Has the potential to cause management to review its communication strategy
Requires a change in culture and fosters a customer focus
Provides a benchmark for the development of communication activities
Can lead to a cut in the number of agencies supporting a brand
Disadvantages of IMC
Encourages centralisation and formal/bureaucratic procedures
Can require increased management time seeking agreement from all involved parties
Suggests uniformity and single message
Tendency to standardisation might negate or dilute creative opportunities
Global brands restricted in terms of local adaptation
Normally requires cultural change from employees and encourages resistance
Has the potential to severely damage a brand's reputation if incorrectly managed
Can lead to mediocrity as no single agency network has access to all sources of communications

observed are formative approaches to IMC and that organisations have experimented and tried out various ideas within their resource and cultural contexts.

As with many aspects of change, there is nearly always resistance to the incorporation of IMC, and, if sanctioned, only partial integration has been achieved. This is not to say that integration is not possible or has not been achieved, but the path to IMC is far from easy and the outcomes are difficult to gauge with great confidence. However, it is the expectation (what level of IMC) that really matters, as it signals the degree of change that is required.

Resistance to integration

Resistance to change is partly a reflection of the experiences and needs of individuals for stability and the understanding of their environments. However, it is also a reflection, again, of the structural conditions in organisations and industry, which have helped determine the expectations of managers and employees.

Eagle and Kitchen (2000) set out four principal areas or themes concerned with barriers to IMC programmes:

- power, coordination and control issues;
- client skills, centralisation/organisation and cultural issues;
- agency skills/talent and overall time/resource issues;
- flexibility/modification issues.

While these provide a useful general overview, the following represent some of the more common, more focused reasons for the resistance to the incorporation of IMC.

Financial structures and frameworks

Resistance through finance-led corporate goals, which have dominated industry performance and expectations, has been particularly significant. The parameters set around it and the extent to which marketing communications is often perceived as a cost rather than an investment, have provided a corporate environment where the act of preparing for and establishing integrative activities is perceived negatively. Furthermore, the period in which communication activities are expected to generate returns is often too short and works against the principles of IMC and the time needed for the effects to take place.

Opposition/reluctance to change

The attitudes and opinions of staff are often predictable in the sense that any move away from tried and proven methods to areas that are unknown and potentially threatening is usually rejected. Change has long been regarded with hostility and fear, and as such is normally resisted. Our apparent need for stability and general security has been a potent form of resistance to the introduction of IMC. This is changing as change itself becomes a familiar aspect of working life. Any move towards IMC therefore, represents a significantly different approach to work, as not only are the expectations of employees changed but so also are the working practices and the associated roles with internal customers and, more importantly, those providing outsourcing facilities.

Traditional hierarchical and brand management structures

Part of the reluctance to change is linked with the structure and systems inherent in many organisations. Traditional hierarchical structures and systems are inflexible and slow to cope with developments in their fast-adapting environments. These structures can stifle the use of individual initiative, can slow the decision-making process and encourage inertia. The brand management system, so popular and appropriate in the 1970s and early 1980s, focuses upon functional specialisms, which is reflected in the horizontally and vertically specialised areas of responsibility. Brands now need to be managed by flexible teams of specialists, who are charged with responsibilities and the resources necessary to coordinate activities across organisations in the name of integration.

Attitudes and structure of suppliers and agencies

> Advertising agencies have maintained their traditional structures and methods of operating, while their clients have begun to adapt and reform themselves.

One of the principal reasons often cited as a barrier to integration is the relationship that clients have with their agencies, and in particular their advertising agencies. Generally, advertising agencies have maintained their traditional structures and methods of operating, while their clients have begun to adapt and reform themselves. The thinking behind this is that for a long time advertising agencies have tried to maintain their dominance of mass advertising as the principal means of brand development. In doing so they seek to retain the largest proportion of agency fee income, rather than having these fees diluted as work is allocated below the line (to other organisations).

The establishment of IMC threatens the current role of the main advertising agencies. This is not to say that all agencies think and act in this way. They do not, as witnessed by the innovative approaches to restructuring and the provision of integrated resources for their clients by agencies such as St Lukes. So, while clients have seen the benefits of integrated marketing communications, their attempts to achieve them have often been thwarted by the structures of the agencies they need to work with and by the attitudes of their main agencies.

Perceived complexity of planning and coordination

The complexity associated with integrating any combination of activities is often cited as a means for delaying or postponing action. Of greater significance are the difficulties associated with coordinating actions across departments and geographic boundaries. IMC requires the cooperation and coordination of internal and external stakeholder groups. Each group has an agenda that contains goals that may well differ from or conflict with those of other participants.

For example, an advertising agency might propose the use of mass media to address a client's needs, if only because that is where its specialist skills lie. However, direct marketing might be a more appropriate approach to solving the client's problem, but because there is no established mechanism to coordinate and discuss openly the problem/solution, the lead agency is likely to have its approach adopted in preference to others.

Implementing IMC

The restraints that prevent the development of IMC need to be overcome. Indeed, many organisations that have made significant progress in developing IMC have done so by instigating approaches and measures that aim to reduce or negate the impact of the barriers that people put up to prevent change. The main approaches to overcoming the barriers are as follows.

Adopting a customer-focused philosophy

The adoption of a customer-focused approach is quite well established within marketing departments. However, this approach needs to be adopted as an organisation-wide approach, a philosophy that spans all departments and results in unified cues to all stakeholders. In many cases, agencies need to adopt a more customer-oriented approach and be able and willing to work with other agencies, including those below the line.

Training and staff development programmes

A move towards IMC cannot be made without changes in the expectations held by employees within the client and agency sectors. Some of the key processes necessary for change need to be used. For example, the involvement and participation of all staff in the process is in itself a step towards providing motivation and acceptance of change when it is agreed and delivered.

> A move towards IMC cannot be made without changes in the expectations held by employees.

Appointing change agents

The use of change agents, people who can positively affect the reception and implementation of change programmes, is important. As IMC should span an entire organisation, the change agent should be a senior manager, or preferably director, in order to signal the importance and speed at which the new perspective is to be adopted.

Some organisations have experimented with the appointment of a single senior manager who is responsible for all internal and external communications.

Planning to achieve sustainable competitive advantage

In order to develop competitive advantages, some organisations have restructured by removing levels of management, introduced business reprocessing procedures and even set up outsourcing in order that they achieve cost efficiencies and effectiveness targets. Prior to the implementation of these delayering processes, many organisations were (and many still are) organised hierarchically.

Back in 1997 Brown foresaw that the emergence and establishment of IMC would only be successful once the industry matures, becomes market-oriented and leaves behind issues concerning client–agency complications. In addition, traditional brand management systems, most of which were designed to prevent the development of synergies or shared knowledge, need to be overhauled. These issues have not yet been fully resolved and IMC in practice remains ill-defined, and superficial. What is required therefore, is a restructuring and redesignation of who manages communications and this requires a planned approach. It is evident that current systems, processes, procedures and structures are not suitable to support and sustain a planned approach to enable the full development and delivery of IMC.

> IMC in practice remains ill-defined, and superficial.

Media-neutral planning

The media-neutral planning (MNP) approach emerged partly as a response to criticism of IMC and partly as an attempt to articulate the potential practice of IMC. For many MNP is integration under a different guise but one of the strengths of the concept is that it openly focuses on the needs of clients and agencies. It attempts to stimulate the use of a communication mix that is driven by the needs of a target audience and not those of the communication industry. This means that rather than keep recommending that clients use mass media communications, which have traditionally rewarded agencies through a more than generous commission system, a more balanced mix of tools and media should be adopted in order to be more effective and efficient.

One of the main reasons for the interest in IMC is the potential to reduce costs. The rise in some media costs, most notably television through the 1990s, the specialised and independent nature of the agency side of the industry, the proliferation of media opportunities and the splintering of audiences, the increasing clamour for measures of return on investment in communications have led to a reappraisal of the role and nature of marketing communications and the emergence of MNP ideas. As clients have tried to reduce costs they have made greater use of both through and below-the-line tools.

Agencies interested in preserving margins have attempted to maintain the prominence of advertising in their media plans but have reduced the emphasis on television advertising or have sought better deals through use of multiple television channel mixes, improved negotiation and more alliances. Some client organisations (e.g. Kraft, Kellogg's, Unilever and Procter & Gamble) have moved, if unintentionally, towards a form of coordinated marketing communication activity. These organisations have reduced their reliance on above-the-line media and have attempted to move towards the use of below-the-line tools in order to reduce costs and deliver consistent messages in an attempt to cut through the increasing clutter. Ray (2002) refers to organisations such as Nike, Reebok and Alliance & Leicester who have practiced MNP, however, he also refers to some of the problems, such as structures, areas of expertise and attitudes, faced by agencies attempting to offer a more neutral media approach for their clients.

ViewPoint 9.6 Boots use MNP

The launch by Boots of their Intelligent Colour Foundation was an important opportunity to support the contemporary, fashionable image of the No. 7 brand. The revolutionary product blends to the colour of an individual's skin and only requires the user to decide between three shades of light, medium and dark.

As part of the planning process, Boots decided to explore the use of MNP and formed a cross-disciplinary team to improve the level of interaction between departments and to optimise planning. The MNP team consisted of representatives of the brand, consumer insight, direct and relationship marketing (through the Advantage Card), PR and communication channel planning.

It was generally accepted that PR would play a critical role but rather than rely on television and magazine advertising, it was decided to augment the plan with direct mail using the Boots Advantage Card database. It was thought this would be more cost-effective than to invest further in other media, particularly television.

In order to measure the impact of this neutral approach, the planning team used two key measurement tools to avoid the misleading sales and awareness measures.

The first of these was a store-based model that could identify sales effect on a store-by-store basis thereby enabling the identification of stores by campaign area, e.g. with/without television, with/without mail, with/without in-store promotions etc. The second was a tracking study that would identify actual exposure to different media by means of a combination of viewing/reading questions together with the establishment of two matched samples to enable real comparisons of mailed versus non-mailed respondents. The tracking study measured awareness, product understanding, interest and image.

The detailed results are confidential but showed clearly that by including mail in the mix it also added value and Boots became more supportive of integrated communications and a media neutral approach.

For more information about this case readers should visit www.brandrepublic.com/think/.

Question

Is MNP just IMC under another name?

Task

Visit the www.brandrepublic.com/think/ and make a note of the key issues and MNP.

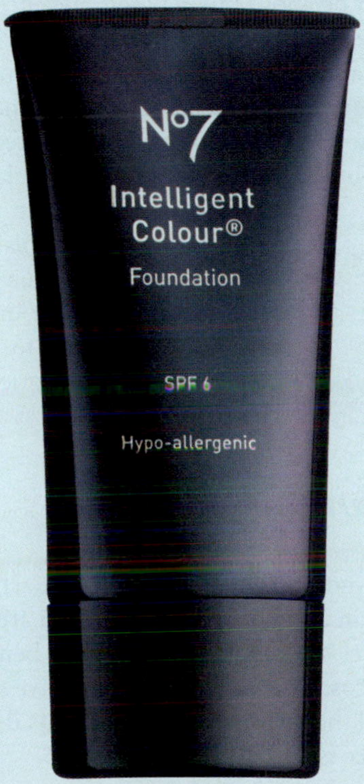

Exhibit 9.2 Boots Intelligent Colour foundation
Courtesy of Boots.

The drive behind the development of MNP appears to be concerned more with reducing the emphasis that television advertising plays in media plans, rather than the formulation of distinct media plans that deliver advertising messages in the most effective way, regardless of media selection. Many of those that support media-neutral approaches are often quoted using examples that involve a mix of tools and media.

The drive behind the development of MNP appears to be concerned more with reducing the emphasis that television advertising plays in media plans.

MNP recognises that mass media advertising is not always the most appropriate way to launch or develop consumer or business-to-business promotional activities, and that a consideration of the most suitable mix of communication tools might be a better starting point when formulating campaigns. Advertising alone cannot carry the weight of a brand necessary to build and sustain the desired associations. Public relations, sales promotions and field marketing (merchandising) for example, have increasingly important roles to play in establishing and sustaining a brand. However, where advertising is used, the changing media landscape and the increasing penetration of new technology means that a greater use of cross-media planning approaches is likely to enhance the effectiveness of a campaign and reduce costs, especially if previous campaigns used television as the primary medium. The traditional model of media planning, whereby a primary medium and perhaps two or three secondary media are scheduled over a five-week campaign has now to be surpassed by a more contemporary mix that uses a cross-media plan combining new and old media and that is appropriate to target audience preferences and the context of the marketing communications activities.

Therefore, it might be interpreted that media-neutral mixes represent the response of the agency side of the marketing communications industry while IMC represents the client side approach to managing their marketing communications in a more effective and strategic manner. MNP should not be about mixing tools and media but should be regarded as an integral part of IMC. However, IMC is not the same as MNP.

The development and delivery of a marketing communications programme that repeatedly delivers significant value cannot be based solely on media-neutral planning or loose notions of IMC. What is necessary is the development of a strategic marketing communications approach that delivers a total brand experience (Tobaccowala and Kugel, 2001). This requires a coordinated approach to the selection and implementation of the right promotional tools and media that will deliver messages that are of significant value to the target audience. However, it also requires the integration of a cross-functional, multi-audience strategic approach to marketing communications, one that delivers a brand experience for the target audience.

What is necessary is the development of a strategic marketing communications approach that delivers a total brand experience.

Open planning

In many ways media-neutral planning is an approach to planning where all media have equal probability of selection and those that are chosen are deemed the best vehicles to achieve the media plan's objectives. Although there are many benefits, such as changing attitudes and perhaps reducing some costs, the neutrality perspective seeks to address industry issues about the planning process and the thinking the incumbents undertake, rather than demonstrate direct concern with audience issues.

In an attempt to move thinking a step forward the open planning concept was developed by Jenkinson, who in 2002/03 coordinated a panel of leading marketers who shared a goal to simplify the media-neutral planning concept. The main goal was to reappraise the way organisations consider their processes and thinking about marketing communication activities with a view to optimising their communication potential. The MNP group argue that this requires rethinking the way communication disciplines (tools) and media are used, to develop new methods of evaluating communication activity and to accelerate the speed at which organisations are able to integrate their communications with their business and marketing strategies.

The main goal was to reappraise the way organisations consider their processes and thinking about marketing communication activities with a view to optimising their communication potential.

The MNP group have proposed a series of new approaches based mainly on ideas concerning open planning. Open planning is concerned with eight action areas, each of which contributes to the process of MNP. These action areas are set out in Table 9.3. Readers wishing to know more should visit www.openplanning.org.uk.

Thinking in terms of these action areas should promote marketing communications that are audience-centred rather than promulgate the previous model that focused on the needs of the communication industry (see Figure 9.3).

Table 9.3 Action areas within the Open Planning approach

Action area	Explanation
Disciplines	Any promotional tool (i.e. discipline) can be used with any medium to achieve stated business and marketing objectives.
Media	Any medium can be used, by any tool (i.e. discipline), in almost all mixes. This means redefining media to mean anything that conveys a message to an audience. A salesperson becomes a medium.
Channels	Any mix of disciplines within a single medium becomes an open channel.
Process	All agencies (and others) should be involved with the thinking and planning process at the outset, to determine the message and goals before any resources are allocated (i.e. budgets).
Structure	The communication process should be driven by the communication preferences of a target audience (or community) rather than the silo structure-based functional specialisation present in much of the industry today.
Relationships	The relationship between client and agency should be open and functional. Agency remuneration should be based on the achievement of brand goals and not commission based on media choice.
Results	Defining more precise communication goals that enable a level playing field for all disciplines, media and agencies to maximise their contribution.
Tools	Use of media planning tools that embrace all touch points with customers.

Source: Adapted from Jenkinson and Sain (2004).

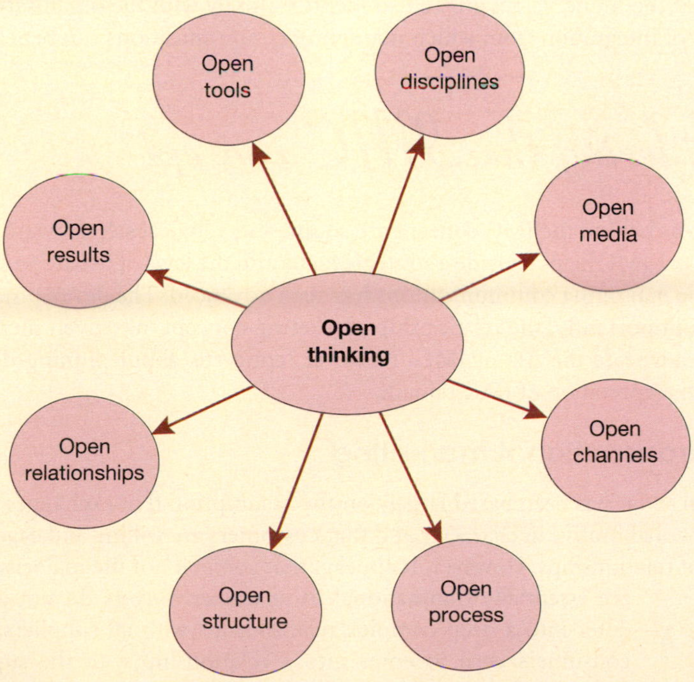

Figure 9.3 The eight action areas of open planning

Client structures and IMC

Clients have also embraced IMC and its influence on their structures. The hierarchical structures common in many organisations in the period up to the 1970s have been subject to attack. In search of survival in recession and increasing profits and dividends in times of plenty, organisations have sought to restructure and realign themselves with their environment. Hierarchies delivered a management structure that delegated authority in compartmentalised units. The brand management system that accompanied this structural approach provided a straitjacket and gave only partial authority to incumbents. At the same time, responsibility for pricing, channel management, personal selling and public relations activities was split off and allocated to a number of others. It follows from this that the likelihood of internal integration has been hampered by the structure of the organisation and the way in which structural units were assembled.

The restructuring process has resulted in organisations that are delayered and leaner.

The restructuring process has resulted in organisations that are delayered and leaner. This means that the gap between senior management and those within the operating core (Mintzberg *et al.*, 2003) is both smaller and now capable of sustaining viable internal communications that are truly two-way and supportive.

Increasingly, organisations are operating in overseas or cross-border markets. For a deeper account of the issues concerning international marketing communications, readers are referred to Chapter 28. However, as organisations develop structurally, from international to multinational to global and transnational status, so the need to coordinate internally and to integrate internal communications becomes ever more vital to sustain integrated marketing communications (Grein and Gould, 1996). Internal marketing (Chapter 30) is becoming more popular with clients (and agencies) as it is realised that employees are important contributors to corporate identity programmes and invaluable spokespersons for the products they market. Internal communications can help not only to inform and remind/reassure but also to differentiate employees in the sense that they understand the organisation's direction and purpose, appreciate what the brand values are and so identify closely with the organisation as a whole. This is a form of integration from which marketing communications can benefit.

Reconsidering the IMC concept

The central ideas behind the IMC concept are sound and a logical step forward for marketing communications. IMC helps provide a strategic focus and the level of debate and interest about how best to use marketing communications has been advanced. The development of technology and more importantly, the relationship marketing concept, has given increased impetus to those who advocate the use of IMC. However, concerns about pinning down the exact meaning and interpretation of IMC remain.

IMC and transactional marketing

The discussion so far has been based largely on the assumption that exchanges are (or should be) essentially collaborative in character and that customers are willing and eager to enter into a wide range of relationships. However, it appears that some, if not the majority of exchanges, are essentially transactional in character. Buyers do not always wish to enter into a deep complex relationships with all suppliers, nor do some consumers wish to enter into a relationship with the supplier of their favourite chocolate bar, dishwasher tablets or frozen peas. As a result these convenience-based exchanges are oriented towards a value based on the

Buyers do not always wish to enter into a deep complex relationships with all suppliers.

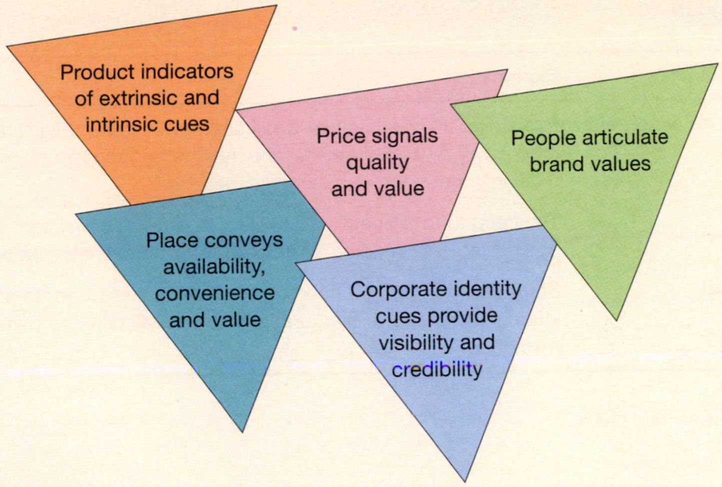

Figure 9.4 The marketing mix communicates

product, its price and overall availability and convenience. Depending upon the product category, after-sales and service support will be important but, by definition, customers in transactional mode do not wish to enter into any serious interaction, let alone dialogue.

The target marketing process requires the development and implementation of a distinct marketing mix to meet the requirements of selected target markets. The elements are mixed together in such a way that they should meet the needs of the target segment. Each element of the marketing mix has a variable capacity to communicate (see Figure 9.4).

Therefore, it may be that traditional forms of marketing communications are sufficient to reach transactional customers. Messages that focus mainly on attributes, features and benefits, emotional values, price and availability will continue to be valid and improved if delivered though a coordinated mix of tools and media that are customer-oriented. By using communications that use a coordinated communications mix, which makes greater use of a range of tools and media that are neutral and seek to cut waste and improve efficiency, will be advantageous.

IMC and relationship marketing

> The relationship marketing paradigm has developed at the same time as IMC.

As stated already, there is no universally agreed definition of IMC and the development of this relatively new, embryonic concept is strewn with attempts to pin it down and label it. What can be observed however is that the relationship marketing paradigm has developed at the same time as IMC and that there are areas where the two concepts intertwine and reinforce each other. One of the difficulties associated with the IMC view, and with its half-sister, media-neutral planning, is that successful marketing communications results from an entirely planned approach. Planning is an essential aspect of managing marketing communications but customers interact with products and services in different ways. They experience brands through their observation of others consuming them, through their own use, as well as through planned, unplanned and word-of-mouth communications. It is the totality of this communication experience that impacts on relationship development. IMC therefore has a critical role in the development of relationship marketing. This is because it is an important process, one that seeks to generate a response from customers, provoke interaction and then dialogue, which is a key characteristic of relationship marketing (Gronroos, 2004). These ideas are explored in greater depth in Chapter 7.

Table 9.4 Duncan-Moriarty categories of relationship drivers

Relationship drivers	Explanation
Relationship development	Everything an organisation does and says is seen, heard and interpreted by stakeholders. The need is to provide a consistent relational focus through all messages
Processes	The need for a process and system to provide consistent strategic positioning and in doing so help support the identity and reputation
Organisational	Structural and cross-functional cohesion is necessary to support internal marketing and an unbiased use of all communication resources

Source: Derived from Reid (2005).

The Duncan and Moriarty IMC miniaudit has been designed to help assess an organisation's IMC relationship-building practices. It recognises the influence of organisational structure and marketing communication strategies and objectives and attempts to measure the strategic consistency of the brand messages. Many of the elements considered earlier in the section 'what is to be integrated' can be identified in the nine drivers identified by Duncan and Moriarty. These can be grouped into three categories, as presented in Table 9.4.

IMC therefore has a potentially greater role to play within collaborative transactions and with customers who wish to become involved within mutually rewarding relationships. To date IMC has been regarded as a concept that needs to be applied across an organisation's entire marketing communications and customer base. The suggestion is that aspects of IMC should be applied to both transactional and collaborative customers but greater emphasis on interaction and dialogue should be given to communication with current and potential relationship-driven customers and other stakeholders.

Aspects of IMC should be applied to both transactional and collaborative customers.

An incremental approach to IMC

Integrated marketing communications means different things to different people. Opportunities to develop IMC appear to vary according to a variety of factors, including organisation size and development. Low (2000) suggests that IMC is more likely to be successful in smaller rather than large organisations. This is because they have fewer brands to be integrated, lower levels of hierarchical complexity and departmental formalisation and are inherently more adaptive. However, Reid (2005) found that large organisations were more likely to adopt IMC principles, suggesting this was due to their more sophisticated planning systems, greater number of formal mechanisms for managing customer data, and the fact that they are already experienced at managing internal functional groups and external agencies. He also found that the greater the level of market orientation within an organisation the more likely IMC practices would be successful. Both Low and Reid appear to agree that IMC is positively related to the intensity of competitive activity experienced by an organisation.

It is clear therefore, that the successful implementation of IMC needs to be founded on an audience-centred (outside-in) orientation. However, IMC also means different things to different organisations and the level of IMC implemented and experienced by organisations is bounded by their context. There

The successful implementation of IMC needs to be founded on an audience-centred (outside-in) orientation.

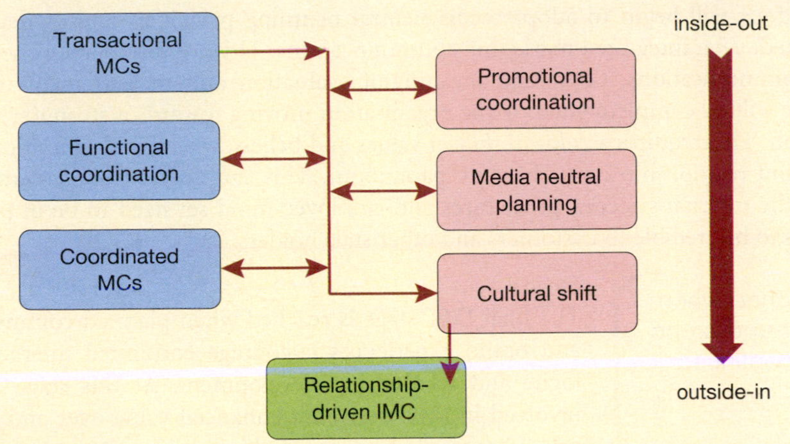

Figure 9.5 An incremental approach to the establishment of IMC

is an emerging belief that although organisations should embrace the marketing mix and the communications mix in the name of IMC they should use cross-functional systems and processes to incorporate internal communications and all those outsourced providers who contribute to the overall marketing communication process. As Figure 9.5 demonstrates, all of these elements should be linked to the overall purpose of the organisation, normally encapsulated and framed in the strategy, philosophy and mission of the organisation.

It seems logical that moves towards the establishment of IMC must be undertaken in steps as it cannot be accomplished overnight, an incremental approach is required (Fill, 2001). Organisations experience an incremental approach to the implementation and establishment of IMC. What they achieve at any one moment is a function of their context, and may be recognised as forms of coordination. Different organisations have coordinated various aspects of their communications activities. Many organisations have focused upon their promotional activities and have tried to bring together their communications to provide consistency and thematic harmonisation. Others have developed more sophisticated systems and procedures to interlink their activities internally.

Organisations experience an incremental approach to the implementation and establishment of IMC.

Stage 1

Therefore, it seems that the starting point in the move towards IMC needs to reflect the context within which exchanges occur. In the majority of cases these will be transactional, where the focus is on product and price. The move from this point will be towards coordinating the tools, media and messages of the mix and this will gradually take place both internally and externally with the organisation's various agencies.

Stage 2

In order to make this work and to move forward, organisations need to create a technology platform necessary to provide a stream of information upon which it is possible to interact coherently with customers. The technology will be used internally to provide an operational tie between the different departments and functional areas. This is an important part of the process as different sections of the organisation are introduced to the ideas of being market-oriented. To support this, the notion that internal marketing relationships and internal marketing communications play an important role in the overall orientation process is also introduced.

Stage 3

Organisations will begin to adopt media-neutral planning principles and/or develop fully coordinated, even integrated marketing communications. This will be characterised by data-driven communications, CRM and meaningful evaluation and measurement techniques. This stage will be complemented by the organisation moving towards a strong(er) customer orientation. This requires a *cultural shift* of values and beliefs, whereby organisational, brand identity and relationship issues become paramount. This can only be implemented at this stage, as the internal systems, procedures and employee mind set need to be in place if the strategy is to be credible to customers and other stakeholders.

The final IMC stage is reached when planned communications and brand experiences encourage continued interaction, dialogue and relationship development.

Stage 4

The final IMC stage is reached when planned communications and brand experiences encourage continued interaction, dialogue and relationship development. At this stage all parties involved in IMC derive an enhanced value over and above the value that would have been achieved without the integration.

In order for these incremental stages to be undertaken and completed satisfactorily, managers must be clear and agreed about what it is they wish to achieve and communicate their intent to all those it involves, both inside and outside the organisation.

This sequential depiction sets out various incremental stages and does not require that they all be followed in strict order, and nor is it intended that all organisations should or do progress to the end. For many, perhaps small and medium-sized organisations, especially those with many transactional customers, promotional coordination or coordinated marketing communications stages may suffice.

One of the key issues encouraging the establishment of IMC has been the willingness of some public relations practitioners to move closer to the marketing department. When IMC began to emerge, Miller and Rose (1994) commentated that the previously held opposition to integration by public relations practitioners had begun to dissolve as the more enlightened agencies see it as 'a reality and a necessity'. Although this movement has not surged forward, many public relations agencies now proclaim that they provide IMC, particularly web and direct and database marketing services. Apart from this, the marketing communications industry has yet to come together and provide clients with the fully integrated services they desire.

Summary

In order to help consolidate your understanding of integrated marketing communications, here are the key points summarised against each of the learning objectives:

1. Introduce the concept of integrated marketing communications (IMC) and explore what it is that is integrated.

Integrated marketing communications (IMC) is concerned with the development, coordination and implementation of an organisation's various strategies, resources and messages. The role is to enable coherent and meaningful engagement with target audiences. In an age when consumers can touch brands across a range of channels it is important that each contact reinforces previous messages and facilitates the development of valued relationships. While the concept of IMC is attractive, to date the development of the approach in practical terms has not been very encouraging. There has been a great deal of debate about the meaning and value of an integrated approach and some attempt to coordinate the content and delivery of marketing communication messages. Most organisations have yet to achieve totally integrated marketing communications; only partial or coordinated levels of activity have so far been achieved.

A wide range of elements needs to be integrated. These include the communication tools, media and messages, plus the elements of the marketing mix, brands, strategy, employees, agencies and technology.

2. Understand the different perspectives of IMC.

Cornelissen identified two main perspectives of IMC running through the literature. He refers to one of these as a predominantly *process*-oriented concept and the second is that IMC is a *content*-oriented concept.

The *content* perspective holds that IMC works when there is a consistency throughout the various materials and messages. The *process* perspective of IMC is rooted in the belief that real IMC can only be generated through an organisational structure that brings the various communication disciplines together in a single body or unit.

3. Consider the background and reasons for the development and interest in IMC.

The interest in IMC has resulted from three main drivers. These include market-based drivers, those that arise from changing communications, and those that are driven from opportunities arising from within the organisation itself.

4. Explore some of the issues associated with managing and implementing IMC.

The management of IMC has been shown to be a challenging task and one that does not always result in a successful outcome. There is much resistance to the development of IMC, again based on a range of factors, some of them found in many situations regardless of what it is that is to be changed. There are several ideas concerning the best way to implement IMC but perhaps the most important point is that IMC can only be achieved by incremental change, not a one-off wholesale change.

5. Explain variants of the IMC concept: media-neutral planning and open planning approaches.

Media-neutral planning is an element of IMC but IMC is not the same as MNP. With increasing levels of fragmentation and rising media (television) costs the need for media-neutrality has increased. The main thrust of MNP is to reduce the emphasis on television and make increased use of other tools and media that are more audience-focused than traditional marketing communications practice has been to date.

Open planning is concerned with eight action areas, each of which contribute to the process of MNP. Working with action areas is designed to promote marketing communications that are audience-centred rather than perpetuate a focus on the communication industry.

6. Consider how the structures and frameworks of advertising and communication agencies might need to change so that they are better able to work with IMC.

Many organisations that have sought to develop IMC have had to restructure their organisations and provide new systems and processes to enable integration at a process level to develop. In much the same way, agencies have been faced with structural change in order to remain competitive to meet the needs of their clients. Their difficulty is that there is not an optimal structure. Agencies need to trade off between the need to provide expertise and the need to control and provide a central source of IMC.

7. Examine ideas concerning an incremental approach to IMC.

Integrated marketing communications means different things to different people. Opportunities to develop IMC appear to vary according to a variety of factors, including organisation size and development.

The development of IMC appears to best achieved when an incremental approach is adopted. *Stage 1* considers the transactional elements and any move forward should be based on coordinating the tools, media and messages of the mix. This will gradually take place both internally and externally with the organisation's various agencies. *Stage 2* requires a technology platform necessary to provide a stream of information upon which it is possible to interact coherently with customers. *Stage 3* is characterised by data-driven communications, CRM and meaningful evaluation and measurement techniques. This stage is often complemented by a strong(er) customer orientation. This requires a *cultural shift* of values and beliefs, whereby organisational, brand identity and relationship issues become paramount. Finally, *Stage 4* is reached when planned communications and brand experiences encourage continued interaction, dialogue and relationship development.

Review questions

1. Discuss the main reasons for the development of IMC.
2. Prepare brief notes explaining four different elements that should be part of the integration process.
3. Explain how various definitions of IMC have evolved.
4. What are the reasons for interest in IMC and is it a valid concept?
5. Appraise the main reasons offered for the failure of organisations to develop IMC.
6. What is the incremental approach to establishing IMC?
7. Explain the ideas concerning media-neutral planning and what is open planning?
8. Explain the meaning of process and content perspectives of IMC.
9. Discuss the view that IMC is essentially the same as relationship marketing.
10. Prepare the outline for an essay arguing whether IMC is a strategic approach or just a means to correct internal operational difficulties and reduce media costs.

MiniCase IMC – richer consumer engagement

J. Graham Spickett-Jones, University of Hull

IMC seeks to optimise the use of resources in the way campaign elements are combined, but it is not new or easy to describe. As communication technologies and agency skills advance, optimum campaign solutions may be both context specific and evolving. As early as the 1970s Stephen King (2007) recognised the power of a *coherent totality* in marketing propositions. He suggested this totality should be traced through the advertising, the pack and even the physical elements of a product to express an *integrated* brand personality. Back then, adverting was often a primary means of encapsulating this brand personality. So advertising agencies liked to think of themselves as brand guardians, and they used processes that integrated advertising messages across different media platforms. Cost-effective advertising combinations, drawing on the relative strengths of outdoor, print and radio media, were often used to amplify television campaigns. However, as marketing communication disciplines have expanded and embraced new technology, the challenge of how to manage integration across the communication landscape has grown.

Debate remains over what IMC involves in practise, perhaps because IMC is a moving target. As the range of potential campaign resources expands and the media habits of consumers shift, the judgements about which campaign elements to integrate for optimal effectiveness may also change. One of the challenges of managing IMC remains the measurement of isolated elements within an integrated campaign framework. IMC requires ways to measure campaigns that can combine above-the-line and below-the-line activity and off-line and on-line channels. This is an area Google are keen to develop but their UK Managing Director, Mark Howe, regards this as a distant goal, 'It won't happen this year, but that is the Holy Grail' (McCormick, 2008).

An expanding range of potential campaign elements available to communication planners provides a creative palette for combining a range of contact points with different markets. This offers new and traditional 'touch points' as ways to reach people in different ways and with specific messages that suit each touch point. Intercepting people in ways that understand their responsiveness in different environments and particular media contexts can help to integrate campaign activity. It can help map an optimum *media journey* for different types of target groups so that a combination of touch points can be used to orchestrate the *brand journey* sought by a campaign. The tools may change but the task remains similar to one Stephen King would have recognised 30 years ago, the development of a *coherent totality* in the marketing proposition, and the coordinated effort to make cost-effective and optimal use of promotional resources.

What is different, however, is the growing complexity of the communication landscape, the ever more competitive pressure on organisations and the growing media literacy of the public. This means large IMC programmes may need to employ *communication planning* at an early stage of a campaign cycle to interpret the best type of campaign solution and the sort of communication agencies that might be needed to help. Often this communication planning service has been provided by one of the specialist media agencies but other large communication agencies have started to offer this service too, to try to retain a strong strategic campaign role. Communication planning can help develop a campaign brief, which may prepare to involve an integrated cocktail of professional communication services well before approaching these other agencies.

An example where communication planning was used early on to help coordinate a major integrated campaign can be seen in the work of the communication planning agency, Naked, for the directory enquiry service, 118 118. The service was launched in Britain in 2003 for the US directory enquiries provider, InfoNXX. The launch campaign involved a wide range of integrated communication activities and Naked worked on the campaign plan from an early stage, well ahead of the launch date, with the advertising agency WCRS, who developed the creative proposition used across the campaign.

The IMC campaign aimed to take people on a brand journey so that 118 118 would become the natural inheritor of the previous number associated with the directory enquiry service in the UK, 192. This was a time of forced market disruption because the telecommunications regulator at the time was keen to weaken the near monopoly on this lucrative service by the previously state-owned company, British Telecom (BT). To do this the established directory enquiry number was to be scrapped and replaced, and a number of companies had decided to enter the market. The challenge for all competitors would be similar, to become a *top of mind* number in a low involvement but potentially large and therefore lucrative market. Naked planned to take the market on a brand journey in stages. *Stage 1, Advertising*, starting to develop recognition of the brand. *Stage 2, Conversations*, planned to develop buzz so people would share information about the brand to give it legitimacy. *Stage 3, Experiential*, was designed to encourage participation and involvement with the brand. While *Stage 4, Personal*, was designed to create a sense of ownership, where the brand became a consumer's own service.

The media journey closely mapped these stages using carefully selected symbols to give continuity, a pair of men as spoof athletes decked out in running vests with the same 'competitor number' repeated on each vest: '118' and '118'. A zany personality for the two athletes was portrayed at Stage 1, using advertising across a wide range of platforms. This was anticipated to resonate with the UK public because of a love of nostalgia, humour and irreverence. The adverting helped established the symbol (two wacky runners, each with a 118 vest) as a potential public icon. With the catch phrase, '*got your number*', this iconography was used as a vehicle to manage the rest of the brand journey. The media landscape employed both

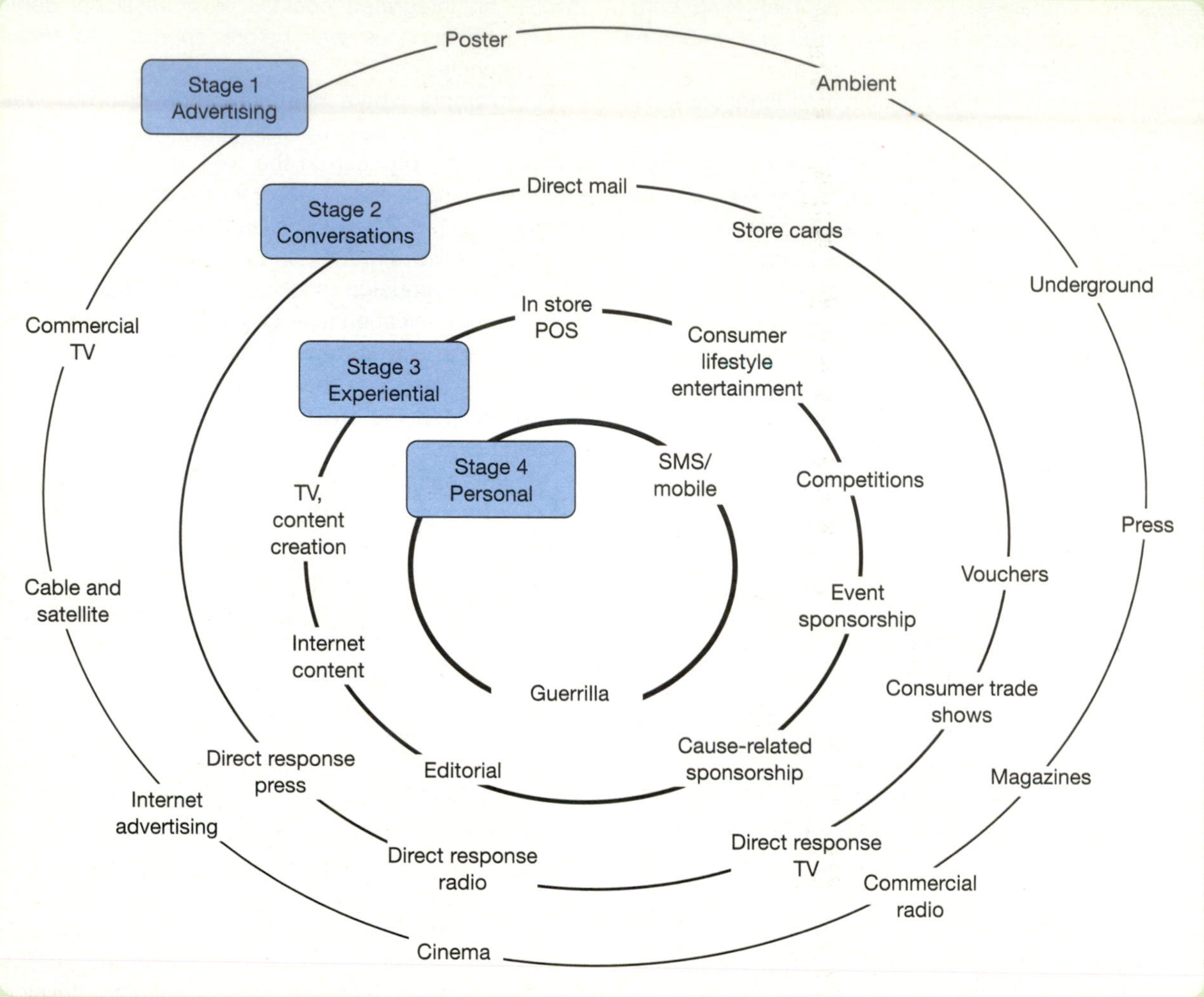

Figure 9.6 A media map of the launch campaign for '118 118'
Source: Adapted from presentation by agencies Naked, WCRS and Huge to D&AD's Xchange (2004) (London School of Fashion, 1 September 2004).

traditional channels and novel media spaces (e.g. fly-posting, street-hawkers [selling 118 shirts in the centre of major UK cities], washing-line stunts using 118 shirts and barber shop window promotions – seeming to advertise hair cuts like the spoof athletes used as brand symbols).

The campaign involved novel experiential elements, especially at Stage 3 of the programme. This made some of the tracking and measurement a particular challenge. However, the nature of the product behind the brand meant that the service requests could be tracked. Therefore the agencies involved agreed to work partly on a performance-based remuneration system, where they were rewarded for the success of the campaign measured by the volumes of traffic driven to use the directory enquiry service.

Within less than a year of the service going live 118 118 had a close to 50 per cent market share. This was achieved in an otherwise cluttered and competitive market that had been previously dominated by a near monopoly provider.

MiniCase references

King, S. (2007) What is a brand?. In *A Master Class in Brand Planning: The Timeless Works of Stephen King* (eds J. Lannon and M. Baskin), 27–40. London: John Wiley & Sons.

McCormick, A. (2008) Google looks for media's Holy Grail. *Media Week*, 12–19 February, 18.

MiniCase questions

1. In the campaign above, what might have been the role for consumer-driven content and social networks web sites?
2. In terms of the use of large-scale IMC, how might a launch campaign differ from the ongoing campaign activity needed to support a brand after launch?
3. Which participants involved in a campaign plan are best placed to coordinate IMC activity and why?
4. In what ways might IMC benefit from a network of service providers found in industry clusters, such as that found in Central London?

References

Anon. (2005) Sainsbury's polishes up its image, 19 September, retrieved 5 November 2007 from www.news.bbc.co.uk/1/hi/business/4259224.stm

Brook, S. (2005) Sainsbury's unveils new slogan, *MediaGuardian*, 19 September 2005. Retrieved 5 November 2007 from http://www.guardian.co.uk/media/2005/sep/19/business.advertising.

Brown, J. (1997) Impossible dream or inevitable revolution: an exploration of integrated marketing communications. *Journal of Communication Management*, **12**(1), 70–81.

Cornelissen, J. (2000) Integration in communication management: conceptual and methodological considerations. *Journal of Marketing Management*, **16**, 597–606.

Cornelissen, J.P. and Lock, A.R. (2000) Theoretical concept or management fashion? Examining the significance of IMC. *Journal of Advertising Research*, **50**(5), 7–15.

Cornelissen, J.P. (2003) Change, continuity and progress: the concept of integrated marketing communications and marketing communications practice. *Journal of Strategic Marketing*, **11** (December), 217–34.

Cowlett, M. (2007) Nexus gives biscuits a classic crunchy edge, *PR Week*, 16 May. Retrieved 19 February 2008 from http://www.prweek.com/uk/.

Dewhirst, T. and Davis, B. (2005) Brand strategy and integrated marketing communications (IMC): A case study of Player's cigarette brand marketing. *Journal of Advertising*, **34**(4), (Winter), 81–92.

Duncan (2002) *IMC: using advertising and promotion to build brand* (International edition). New York: McGraw-Hill.

Duncan, T. and Everett, S. (1993) Client perceptions of integrated marketing communications. *Journal of Advertising Research*, **3**(3), 30–9.

Duncan, T. and Moriarty, S. (1998) A communication-based marketing model for managing relationships. *Journal of Marketing*, **62** (April), 1–13.

Duncan, T. and Mulhern, F. (2004) *A white paper on the status, scope and future of IMC programs.* (From the IMC symposium by the IMC programs at Northwestern University and University of Denver.) New York: McGraw-Hill.

Eagle, L. and Kitchen, P. (2000) IMC, brand communications, and corporate cultures. *European Journal of Marketing*, **34**(5/6), 667–86.

Fill, C. (2001) Essentially a matter of consistency. *Marketing Review*, **1**(4), (Summer), 409–25.

Gray, R. (2007) Unity of purpose, *Marketing*, 13 December, 6.

Grein, A.F. and Gould, S.J. (1996) Globally integrated communications. *Journal of Marketing Communications*, **2**, 141–58.

Gronroos, C. (2004) The relationship marketing process: communication, interaction, dialogue, value. *Journal of Business and Industrial Marketing*, **19**(2), 99–113.

Hutton, J.G. (1996) Integrated relationship-marketing communications: a key opportunity for IMC. *Journal of Marketing Communications*, **2**, 191–9.

Jenkinson, A. and Sain, B. (2004) Open planning: media neutral planning made simple. Retrieved 14 November 2004 from www.openplanning.org/cases/openplanning/whitepaper.pdf.

Jones, G. (2007) Velvet makes digital debut, *Marketing*, 21 March, 14.

Kitchen, P.J. and Shultz, D.E. (1997) Integrated marketing communications in US advertising agencies: an exploratory study. *Journal of Advertising Research*, **37**(5), 7–18.

Kitchen, P.J. and Shultz, D.E. (1998) IMC – a UK ads agency perspective. *Journal of Marketing Management*, **14**(2), 465–85.

Kitchen, P., Brignell, J., Li, T. and Spickett-Jones, G. (2004) The emergence of IMC: a theoretical perspective. *Journal of Advertising Research*, **44** (March), 19–30.

Kitchen, P.J., Spickett-Jones, G. and Grimes, T. (2007) Inhibition of brand integration amid changing agency structures. *Journal of Marketing Communications*, **13**(2), 149–68.

Kliatchko, J. (2008) Revisiting the IMC construct: a revised definition and four pillars. *International Journal of Advertising*, **27**(1), 133–60.

Lee, D.H. and Park, C.W. (2007) Conceptualization and measurement of multidimensionality of integrated marketing communications. *Journal of Advertising Research*, (September), 222–36.

Low, G.S. (2000) Correlates of integrated marketing communications. *Journal of Advertising Research*, **40**(3), 27–39.

Miller, D.A. and Rose, P.B. (1994) Integrated communications: a look at reality instead of theory. *Public Relations Quarterly* (Spring), 13–16.

Mintzberg, H., Lampel, J.B., Quinn, J.B. and Ghoshal, S. (2003) *The Strategy Process*, 4th edn. Englewood Cliffs, NJ: Pearson Education.

Percy, L., Rossiter, J.R. and Elliot, R. (2001) *Strategic Advertising Management*, New York: Oxford University Press.

Pitta, D.A., Weisgal, M. and Lynagh, P. (2006) Integrating exhibit marketing into integrated marketing communications. *Journal of Consumer Marketing*, **23**(3), 156–66.

Porter, M.E. (1980) *Competitive Strategy: Techniques for Analyzing Industries and Competitors*. New York: Free Press.

Ray, A. (2002) How to adopt a neutral stance. *Marketing*, 27 June, 27.

Reed, D. (2006) Media rivalry barring integrated path. *Precision Marketing*, 25 August, 6.

Reid, M. (2005) Performance auditing of integrated marketing communication (IMC) actions and outcomes. *Journal of Advertising*, **34**(4) (Winter), 41–54.

Schultz, D. (1993) *Integrated Marketing Communications: Putting It Together and Making It Work*. Lincolnwood, IL: NTC Business Books.

Shimp, T.A. (2000) *Advertising Promotion: Supplemental Aspects of Integrated Marketing Communications*, 5th edn. Fort Worth, TX: Dryden Press, Harcourt College Publishers.

Smith, P. (1996) Benefits and barriers to integrated communications. *Admap* (February), 19–22.

Spake, D.F., D'Souza, G., Crutchfield, T.N. and Morgan, R.M. (1999) Advertising agency compensation: an agency theory explanation. *Journal of Advertising*, **28**(3), 53–72.

Spotts, H.E., Lambert, D.R. and Joyce, M.L. (1998) Marketing déjà vu: the discovery of integrated marketing communications. *Journal of Marketing Education*, **20**(3), 210–18.

Swain, W.N. (2004) Perceptions of IMC after a decade of development: who's at the wheel, and how can we measure success? *Journal of Advertising Research*, **44**(1) (March), 46–65.

Tobaccowala, R. and Kugel, C. (2001) Planning and evaluating cross-media programs. *Admap*, February, 33–6.

White, R. (2000) Chameleon brands: tailoring brand messages to consumers. *Admap*, (July/August), 8–40.

Chapter 10

Marketing communications: strategies, tactics and planning

A marketing communications strategy refers to an organisation's overall positioning orientation and their preferred approach to communicating with customers and stakeholders. Marketing communications strategies are contingent on the business and marketing strategies the organisation is pursuing. Tactics are concerned with the communication mix developed to deliver the positioning strategy.

Marketing communication plans are concerned with programmes and campaigns designed to articulate an organisation's marketing communication tactics and strategy.

Aims and learning objectives

The aims of this chapter are to explore the nature of strategy and marketing communications strategies in particular. The goal is to enable readers to appreciate the elements and concepts associated with marketing communication strategy, tactics and planning, and to introduce the marketing communications planning framework.

The learning objectives of this chapter are to:

1. establish the differences between strategy, tactics and planning;
2. appreciate the essence of marketing communications strategy;
3. consider three main marketing communication strategies: pull, push and profile;
4. explain the notion of strategic balance;
5. explore different approaches to Internet-based communication strategies;
6. present a planning framework and consider the different elements involved in the development of marketing communication plans;
7. highlight the importance of the linkages and interaction between the different elements of the plan.

For an applied interpretation see Angela Hall's MiniCase entitled ***Ski Rossendale*** at the end of this chapter.

Introduction

In essence IMC represents a strategic approach to marketing communications.

This chapter follows on from the previous chapter that explored integrated marketing communications. In essence IMC represents a strategic approach to marketing communications, yet its application by many organisations is invariably more consistent with a tactical rather than strategic perspective. Various issues implicit in the previous discussion are relevant in this chapter and, although not developed further, should be considered by readers.

It is assumed by many that marketing communication strategy is simply the combination of tools of the communications mix. In other words, strategy is about the degree of direct marketing, personal selling, advertising, sales promotion and public relations that is incorporated within a planned sequence of communication activities.

This is important but this is tactical, and is not the essence of marketing communications strategy. From a strategic perspective, key decisions concern the overall direction of the programme and target audiences, the fit with marketing and corporate strategy, the key message and desired positioning the brand is to occupy in the market, the resources necessary to deliver the position and overall goals.

The chapter begins with a consideration of some fundamental ideas concerning the nature of strategy. From this a contextual and customer perspective is developed on which to build marketing communications strategy. This is used in preference to a production orientation, which is founded on the resource base. This customer orientation requires revisiting ideas concerning market segmentation and the characteristics and buying behaviour of the different target audiences. From here various dimensions of communications strategy are developed.

Understanding strategy

In order to appreciate the role and nature of communication strategy it is useful to appreciate the dimensions of the strategy concept. The management literature on strategy is extensive yet there seems to be little agreement or consensus about what it is, what it means or how it should be developed. A full discussion of this topic is beyond the scope of this book but what follows is a brief overview of some of the more general views about management strategy.

The disparity of views about strategy is due to the multidimensional nature of the strategy concept.

Hambrick (1983) suggested that the disparity of views about strategy is due to the multidimensional nature of the strategy concept, that strategy is situational and that it varies according to industry and the environment in which it operates. In other words contextual issues determine the nature of strategy. This may be true but it does not help us understand what strategy is.

The one main area wherein most authors find agreement concerns the hierarchical nature of strategy within organisations (Kay, 1993; Johnson *et al.*, 2008; Mintzberg and Ghoshal, 2003). This refers to the notion that there are three main levels of organisational strategy; corporate, competitive and functional. Corporate strategy is considered to be directional and sets out the broad, overarching parameters and means through which the organisation operates in order to realise its objectives. Strategies at the functional level, for example, marketing, finance and production, should be integrated in such a way that they contribute to the satisfaction of the higher-level competitive strategies, which in turn should satisfy the overall corporate goals. Competitive-level strategies are important because not only do they set out the way in which the organisation will compete and use resources, but they should also provide clear messages about the way in which the organisation seeks to manage its environment.

Chaffee (1985) identifies several themes associated with the various strategic interpretations. The first is that strategy is used by organisations as a means of adjusting to changing environmental conditions and the second is that strategy is often referred to in terms of decision making, actions and implementation. Apart from the hierarchical element mentioned previously, one of her other significant observations concerned the point that strategy could take various forms, most notably, deliberate, emergent and realised formats.

Two main strategy schools of thought can be identified, namely the planning and the emergent approaches. The planning school is the pre-eminent paradigm and is based on strategy development and implementation, which is explicit, rational and planned as a sequence of logical steps. Andrews (1987) comments that strategy is concerned with a company's objectives, purpose and policies and its plans to satisfy the goals using particular resources with respect to a range of internal and external stakeholders. The organisation interacts with and attempts to shape its environment in pursuit of its goals. This perspective of strategy was first formulated in the 1950s and 1960s when the operating environments of most organisations were simple, stable and thus predictable. However, these conditions rarely exist in the twenty-first century and the validity of the rational model of strategy has been questioned.

Two main strategy schools of thought can be identified, namely the planning and the emergent approaches.

The emergent school of thought considers strategy to develop incrementally, step-by-step, as organisations learn, sometimes through simple actions of trial and error. The core belief is that strategy is comprised of a stream of organisational activities that are continuously being formulated, implemented, tested, evaluated and updated. Chaffee suggests that strategy should be considered in terms of a linear, adaptive or interpretive approach, each one reflecting a progressively sophisticated perspective. While the linear approach reflects the more traditional and deliberate approach to strategy (Ansoff, 1965; Andrews, 1987), the adaptive strategy is important because it reflects the view that organisations flex and adjust to changing environments while the interpretive or higher-order point of view considers strategy to be a reflection of the influence of social order on strategic decision making.

The emergent school of thought considers strategy to develop incrementally, step-by-step, as organisations learn, sometimes through simple actions of trial and error.

Two other strategic authors to be mentioned are Mintzberg (1994) and Whittington (1993). Mintzberg argues that strategy can be regarded as one or more of 5Ps of strategy. These are strategy as a Plan, Position, Perspective, Ploy and Pattern. Whittington (1993) offers four generic strategies: Classical, Evolutionary, Processual and Systemic (see Table 10.1).

Table 10.1 Views of strategy

Author	Type of Strategy	Explanation
Mintzberg	Plan	A predetermined, deliberate course of action, implementation and evaluation.
	Position	An attempt to locate an organisation within a market.
	Perspective	A collective view of the world, one that is ingrained within the organisation and its position within it.
	Ploy	A scheme or manoeuvre to sidestep or outwit competitors.
	Pattern	A stream of actions in which there are consistent patterns of behaviour.
Whittington	Classical	Planned, rational and deliberate.
	Evolutionary	Darwinian in outlook, this strategy perceives a manager's task as trying to survive by fitting as closely as possible to the prevailing environmental conditions.
	Processual	An essentially incremental perspective whereby strategy is concerned with learning from past actions and experience. Little emphasis is given to long-term planning and horizons.
	Systemic	Strategy is a reflection of the social systems in which strategists participate.

Sources: Whittington (1993); Mintzberg (1994).

There are a number of common points shared within these various views and perspectives of strategy. Chaffee, Mintzberg and Whittington all agree that strategy can be considered to be deliberate in nature as reflected in their respective linear, planned and classical approaches. They also agree that strategy can be emergent and can evolve from the actions of the organisation. This can be seen in their adaptive, pattern and processual approaches. They also develop views on the extent to which an organisation interacts with its environment or seeks to directly influence it. Chaffee refers to interpretive strategies, Mintzberg to strategy as a perspective and Whittington to systemic interpretations.

ViewPoint 10.1 Strategic Apples

According to Rumelt, an eminent US academic and strategy consultant, most corporate strategic plans are concerned with maintaining market share and rolling forward three- or five-year resource budgets. There is little strategy in the corporate strategies he sees.

For him, strategy is about exploiting change in the environment, change in terms of technological advances, resource prices, consumer tastes or competitive behaviour. Strategy is about how these changes are developed and the positions that firms adopt with regard to these changes. Rumelt refers to a discussion with Steve Jobs at Apple following his successful return to the company in 1998. Rumelt observed at the time that Apple, no matter how well they performed, were still operating in a small niche within the personal computer business. So, the question he posed was what was Jobs trying to achieve, what was the longer-term strategy? The unexpected answer was . . . 'I am going to wait for the next big thing'.

For Jobs, strategy is not about 'cutting costs and forming alliances', a disparaging phrase used by Rumelt when referring to common interpretations of corporate strategy. His role was to seize opportunities presented by the environment, evidenced through the subsequent success of Pixar, iPod and probably iPhone.

Source: Adapted from Lovallo and Mendonca (2007).

Question

How would you interpret Apple's approach to strategy – is it planning or emergent?

Task

Go to the web sites for Boeing and Airbus. What are their strategies?

Strategy is about the means, speed and methods by which organisations adapt to and influence their environments.

Views on strategy have evolved as our understanding has developed. Strategy is not just about a deliberate, planned approach to business development, although it can be at the functional and competitive levels. Strategy is about the means, speed and methods by which organisations adapt to and influence their environments in order that they achieve their goals. What is also clear is that the demarcation between an organisation and its environment is less clear than it used to be. An imaginary line was once used to refer to a border between an organisation and its environment. This line is no longer deemed valid as organisations are now viewed as boundary-free. The implications of this borderless concept for marketing communications are potentially enormous. Not only do contemporary views of strategy amplify the significance of the interaction between strategy and an organisation's environment but they also stress the importance for strategy, at whatever level, to be contextually oriented and determined.

Market segmentation

The planned and deliberate perspective of strategy has had a long-term impact on marketing management. The process of market analysis and evaluation leading to planned strategies designed to meet prescribed and measurable goals is well established. It is argued that this approach enables finite resources to be used more efficiently as they can be directed towards markets that hold, potentially, greater value than other markets. Market segmentation is a part of this approach and is both a functional and competitive-level strategy. More importantly, the process of market segmentation is the means by which organisations define the broad context within which their strategic business units (SBUs) and products are offered.

Market segmentation is the division of a mass market into identifiable and distinct groups or segments, each of which has common characteristics, needs and display similar responses to marketing actions. Through this process specific target segments can be selected and marketing plans developed to satisfy the individual needs of the potential buyers in these chosen segments. The development, or rather identification, of segments can be perceived as opportunities, and, as Beane and Ennis (1987) suggest, 'a company with limited resources needs to pick only the best opportunities to pursue'. The most common bases upon which markets can be segmented are set out in Table 10.2.

> Segmentation is necessary because a single product is unlikely to meet the needs of all customers in a mass market.

This process of segmentation is necessary because a single product is unlikely to meet the needs of all customers in a mass market. If it were, then a single type of toothpaste, chocolate bar or car would meet all of our needs. This is not so, and there are a host of products and brands seeking to satisfy particular buyer needs. For example, ask yourself the question, 'Why do I use toothpaste?' The answer, most probably, is one of the following:

- You want dental hygiene.
- You like fresh breath and you do not want to offend others.

Table 10.2 Bases for segmenting markets

Segmentation base	Explanation
Demographic	Key variables concern age, sex, occupation, level of education, religion, social class and income characteristics, many of which determine, to a large extent, a potential buyer's ability to enter into an exchange relationship or transaction.
Geographic	In many situations the needs of potential customers in one geographic area are different from those in another area. For example, it is often said that Scottish beer drinkers prefer heavy bitters, Northerners in England prefer mild, drinkers in the West prefer cider, and in the South lager is the preferred drink.
Geodemographic	This type of segmentation is based on the assumption that there is a relationship between the type of housing people live in and their purchasing behaviours. At the root of this approach is the ability to use postcodes to send similar messages to similar groups of households, on the basis that where we live determines how we live. The most well-known commercial applications are Acorn (a classification of residential neighbourhoods), Mosaic and Pinpoint.
Psychographic	Through an analysis of consumers' activities, interests and opinions (AIO) it is possible to determine lifestyles or patterns of behaviour. These are a synthesis of the motivations, personality and core values held by individuals. These AIO patterns are reflected in the buying behaviour and decision-making processes of individuals. By identifying and clustering common lifestyles, a correlation with a consumer's product and/or media usage patterns becomes possible.
Behaviouristic	Usage and lifestage segments are derived from analysing markets on the basis of customer behaviour. Usage of soft drinks can be considered in terms of purchase patterns (two bottles per week), usage situations (parties, picnics or as an alcohol substitute) or purchase location (supermarket, convenience store or wine merchant). Lifestage analysis is based on the principle that people have varying amounts of disposable income and different needs at different stages in their lives. Their priorities for spending change at different trigger points and these points or lifestages do not occur at the same time.

Table 10.3 Benefit segments for the toothpaste market

Segment name	The sensory segment	The sociables	The worriers	The independents
Principal benefit sought	Flavour, product appearance	Brightness of teeth	Decay prevention	Price
Demographic strengths	Children	Teens, young people	Large families	Men
Special behavioural characteristics	Users of spearmint-flavoured toothpaste	Smokers	Heavy users	Heavy users
Brands disproportionately favoured	Colgate, Stripe	Macleans, Plus White, Ultra Brite	Crest, Sensodyne	Brands on sale
Personality characteristics	High self-involvement	High sociability	High hypochondriasis	High autonomy
Lifestyle characteristics	Hedonistic	Active	Conservative	Value oriented

Source: Haley (1968). Used with kind permission of the American Marketing Association.

- You want white, shining teeth to appear attractive and approachable.
- You like the fresh oral sensation.
- Other products (e.g. water, soap) are not so effective and do not taste very nice.

Whatever the reason, it is unlikely that given a choice everyone would all choose the same product. In what is now regarded as a classic study, Russell Haley (1968) undertook some pioneering research in this field and from it established four distinct types of customer. Even after over 35 years have elapsed this typology remains a potent practical example of market segmentation: those who bought toothpaste for white teeth (sociables); those who wished to prevent decay (worriers); those who liked the taste and refreshment properties (sensors); and finally those who bought on a price basis (independents). Each of these groups has particular demographic, behaviouristic and psychographic characteristics that can be seen in Table 10.3.

It is not surprising that a range of toothpaste products has been developed that attempts to satisfy the needs of different buyers, for example, Macleans for fresh breath, Crest for dental hygiene, Sensodyne for those sensitive to hot and cold drinks and numerous others promoted on special offers for those independent buyers looking for a low price. There are others who are not very interested in the product and have continued using a brand that others in their current or past households are comfortable with.

ViewPoint 10.2 Ethically Segmented

As the move towards ethical and environmental awareness grows, a study by Henley Centre reveals the extent to which the United Kingdom is becoming green. The report identifies five segments:

- **Onlookers** Moderately concerned but have no intention of making small changes or living ethically, 26 per cent of the population.
- **Conveniently conscious** Fairly concerned about the environment, think brands should act responsibly and they make easy lifestyle changes, 35 per cent of the population.
- **Positive choosers** Highly aware, very concerned and try hard to live ethically, 31 per cent of the population.

- Principled pioneers — The most committed group, happy to install alternative energy sources and calculate their carbon footprint, just 4 per cent of the population.
- Vocal activists — Very similar to the positive choosers but they vocalise their concerns about unethical brands, 4 per cent of the population.

This suggests there are opportunities for brands to develop strategies to appeal to these segments. In doing so, such ethical positioning appears to lead consumers to perceive brands to be of higher quality.

Source: Tiltman (2007).

Question

How might this information affect an electronics manufacturer and a management consultancy?

Task

Using a search engine, locate a solar energy equipment supplier and see how they might segment their markets.

Therefore, target segments constitute the environment and the context for the marketing communications strategy and activities. It is the characteristics of the target segment and their perception that should shape an audience-centred marketing communication strategy.

Marketing communications strategy

Many organisations do not develop and implement a communication strategy. They may develop brand strategies, advertising strategies and indeed some form of integrated marketing communication strategies but there is little evidence of organisations developing corporate-led communication strategies. Steyn (2003) believes that this might be because practitioners do not fully understand the word *strategy*, while Moss and Warnaby (1998) suggest that academics have neglected the role of corporate communication in the strategy process. Holm (2006) reported that the programmes at two leading Swedish communication schools contained 90 per cent communication-related material and just 10 per cent on leadership matters. In contrast, the programme at Sweden's leading management school designed to deliver strategic education, devotes just 3 per cent of the time to communication issues. The general conclusion Holm draws is that those responsible for organisation, strategic leadership and decision making appear to lack insight, awareness and the skills regarding communication. Undoubtedly ideas concerning communication and strategy have not always been well articulated or taught together, are often tactical and there is certainly little agreement on what constitutes corporate communication and marketing communication strategies.

Marketing communications strategy is concerned with two key dynamics. The first dynamic is concerned with who, in broad terms, is the target audience? End-user customers need to derive particular benefits based on perceived value, from the exchange process. These benefits are very different from those that intermediaries expect to derive, or indeed any other stakeholder who does not consume the product or service. The second dynamic concerns the way in which an audience understands the offering they are experiencing either through use or through communications. The way in which people interpret messages and frame objects in their mind is concerned with positioning.

> The way in which people interpret messages and frame objects in their mind is concerned with positioning.

Marketing communications strategy therefore, is concerned with audiences and positioning.

Audiences

The prevailing approach to marketing communications (advertising) strategy has traditionally been founded upon the configuration of the 'promotional' mix. Strategy was an interpretation of the mix and hence the resources an organisation deployed. This represents a production rather than market orientation to marketing communications and is intrinsically misplaced. This inside-out form of strategy is essentially resource-driven. However, a market orientation to strategy requires a consideration of the needs of the audience first and then a determination of the various messages, media and disciplines to accomplish the strategy, an outside-in approach.

Consumer purchase decisions are characterised (very generally and see Chapter 6) by a single-person buying centre whereas organisational buying decisions can involve a large number of different people, fulfilling different roles and all requiring different marketing communication messages. It follows from this that the approach to communicating with these two very different target sectors should be radically different, especially in terms of what, where, when and how a message is communicated. Once communication objectives have been established, it is necessary to formulate appropriate strategies.

Communication objectives that are focused on consumer markets require a different strategy from those formulated to satisfy the objectives that are focused on organisational customers. In addition, there are circumstances and reasons to focus communications on the development of the organisation with a corporate brand and range of other stakeholders. Often, these corporate brands need to work closely with the development of product brands.

Positioning

Positioning is the key strategic framework for an organisation's brand-based communications.

As noted in the earlier discussion about strategy, positioning is an integral concept, and for some the essence of strategy. Wind (1990) stated quite clearly that positioning is the key strategic framework for an organisation's brand-based communications, as cited by Jewell (2007). All products and all organisations have a position in the minds of audiences. The task, therefore, is to actively manage the way in which audiences perceive brands. This means that marketing communications strategy should be concerned with achieving effective and viable positions so that the target audience understands what the brand does, what it means (to them) and can ascribe value to it. This is particularly important in markets that are very competitive and where mobility barriers (ease of entry into and exit from a market, e.g. plant and production costs) are relatively low.

Positioning is about visibility and recognition of what a product/service/organisation represents to a buyer. In markets where the intensity of rivalry and competition are increasing and buyers have greater choice, identification and understanding of a product's intrinsic values become critical. Channel members have limited capacities, whether this is the level or range of stock they can carry or for retailers, the amount of available shelf space that can be allocated. An offering with a clear identity and orientation to a particular target segment's needs will not only be stocked and purchased, but can warrant a larger margin through increased added value.

Marketing communications strategy is essentially about positioning.

It is generally accepted that positioning is the natural conclusion to the sequence of activities that constitute a core part of the marketing strategy. Market segmentation and target marketing are prerequisites to successful positioning. It has also been established that marketing communications should be an audience-centred rather than product-centred activity. From this it can be concluded that marketing communications strategy is essentially about positioning. For new products and services, marketing communications needs to engage target audiences so that they can understand what the brand means, how it differs from similar offerings and as a result position it in their minds. For the vast majority of products and services that are already established, marketing communications strategy should be concerned with either maintaining a strong position or repositioning it in the minds of the target audiences. Chapter 11 provides more information about the positioning concept and the different strategies used by organisations to position their brands.

The 3Ps of marketing communications strategy

As a result of understanding the broad nature of the target audience and the way we want them to position the offering in their minds, it is possible to identify three main marketing communication strategies:

- Pull-positioning strategies – these are intended to influence end-user customers (consumers and b2b);
- Push-positioning strategies – these are intended to influence marketing (trade) channel buyers;
- Profile-positioning strategies – these are intended to influence a wide range of stakeholders, not just customers and intermediaries.

These are referred to as the 3Ps of marketing communications strategy. Push and pull relate to the direction of the communication to the marketing channel: pushing communications down through the marketing channel or pulling consumers/buyers into the channel via retailers, as a result of receiving the communications. They do not relate to the intensity of communication and only refer to the overall approach. Profile refers to the presentation of the organisation as a whole and therefore the identity is said to be 'profiled' to various other target stakeholder audiences, which may well include consumers, trade buyers business-to-business customers and a range of other influential stakeholders. Normally, profile strategies do not contain or make reference to specific products or services that the organisation offers (see Table 10.4).

This may be blurred where the name of a company is the name of its primary (only) product, as is often the case with many retail brands. For example, messages about B&Q are very often designed to convey meaning about the quality and prices of its consumer products and services, however, they often reflect on the organisation itself, especially when its advertising shows members of staff in workwear, doing their work (see Exhibit 10.1).

All three of these strategies are intended to position the offering, in particular ways, in the minds of the target audience. Within each of these overall strategies, individual approaches should be formulated to reflect the needs of each particular case. So, for example, the launch of a new shampoo product will involve a push-positioning strategy to get the product on the shelves of the appropriate retailers. The strategy would be to gain retailer acceptance of the new brand and to position

All three strategies are intended to position the offering, in particular ways, in the minds of the target audience.

Table 10.4 Marketing communications strategy options

Strategy	Target audience	Message focus	Communication goal
Pull	Consumers	Product/service	Purchase
	End-user b2b customers	Product/service	Purchase
Push	Channel intermediaries	Product/service	Developing relationships and distribution network
Profile	All relevant stakeholders	The organisation	Building reputation

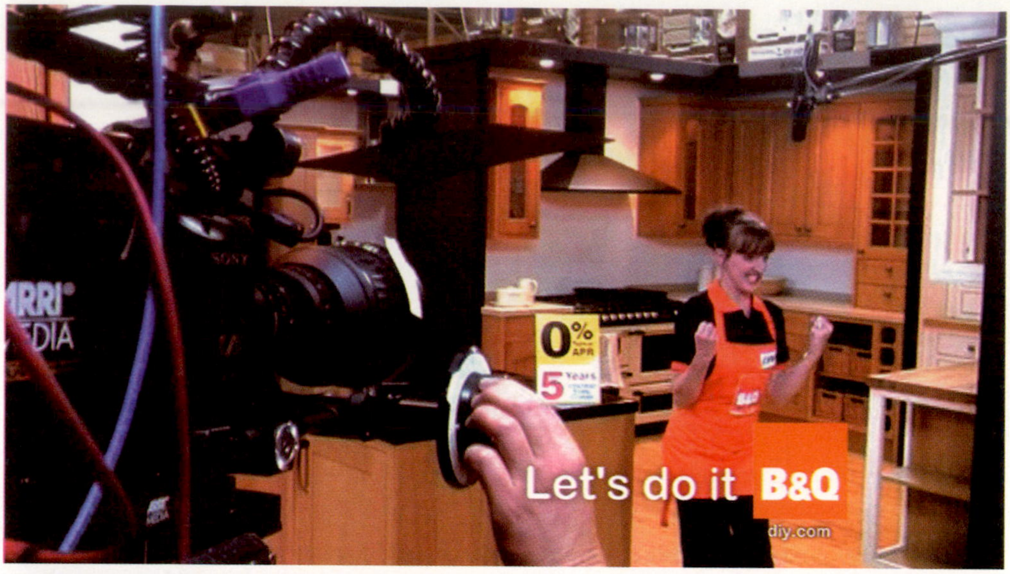

Exhibit 10.1 B&Q use their staff in advertising campaigns as brand ambassadors. This serves to communicate brand values and to recognise the value of staff to the marketing programme
Courtesy of B&Q.

it as a profitable new brand to gain consumer interest. Personal selling supported by trade sales promotions will be the main marketing communications tools. A pull-positioning strategy to develop awareness about the brand will need to be created, accompanied by appropriate public relations work. The next step will be to create particular brand associations and thereby position the brand in the minds of the target audience. Messages may be primarily functional or expressive but they will endeavour to convey a brand promise. This may be accompanied or followed by the use of incentives to encourage consumers to trial the product. To support the brand, care lines and a web site will need to be put in place to provide credibility as well as a buyer reference point and an opportunity to interact with the brand.

The degree to which these plans are developed varies.

In order that these strategies are implemented, it is normal procedure to develop a marketing communications plan. The degree to which these plans are developed varies across organisations and some rely on their agencies to undertake this work for them. However, there can be major benefits as a result of developing these plans in-house, for example, by involving and discussing issues internally and developing a sense of ownership.

As noted earlier, planning is not necessarily the same as strategy, although the two are often used interchangeably. Strategy is about the direction, positioning and implementation of an organisation's desired marketing communications (in this case) in order that it positions the brand in the minds of particular target audiences. Tactics are concerned with detail associated with campaigns to deliver the position. Planning, on the other hand, is usually about the formalisation of the strategy, tactics and ideas into a manageable sequence of activities that are linked, coherent and capable of being implemented in the light of the available resources. Marketing communications strategy is about the way an organisation positions its products and services in the minds of its customers and stakeholders. It must do this in the light of its business and marketing strategies and the prevailing contextual conditions, in order to encourage a degree of interaction and dialogue with selected stakeholders.

A marketing communications plan is concerned with the development and managerial processes involved in the articulation of an organisation's marketing communication strategy. This will be considered later in this chapter.

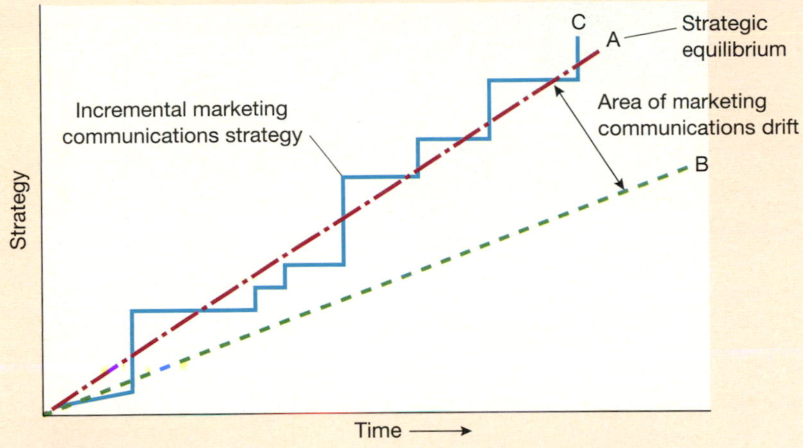

Figure 10.1 Drift in marketing communications strategy

There is little doubt that planning, tactics and strategy are interlinked but it is useful to consider strategy as something that needs to be attended to on a regular basis. With so many variables and an external environment that is subject to tremendous change, marketing communications strategy can be seen to drift, to move away from the original promises that framed its central message and lose the strength of the position gained. The only way to correct drift is to change the marketing communications strategy by at least an amount according to the degree to which messages have drifted. This might be best observed in Figure 10.1.

Planning, tactics and strategy are interlinked.

Line B suggests that if current marketing communications remain as they are, then the size of the gap with the central theme of marketing communications will widen and any attempt to get back will be large and expensive. Line C depicts a brand that has adapted its marketing communications and positioning on a more frequent basis (than B) and as a result follows an emergent strategy, one that results in a more consistent message. This concept might be interpreted in terms of positioning and repositioning brands and the changing of agencies in order to revitalise and change the direction of the communications strategy currently being pursued.

A pull-positioning strategy

If messages designed to position a brand are to be directed at targeted, end-user customers, then the intention is invariably to generate increased levels of awareness, change and/or reinforce attitudes, reduce risk, encourage involvement and ultimately provoke a motivation within the target group. This motivation is to stimulate action so that the target audience expects the offering to be available to them when they decide to enquire, experiment or make a repeat purchase. This approach is a *pull-(positioning)* strategy and is aimed at encouraging customers to 'pull' products through the channel network (see Figure 10.2). This usually means that consumers go into retail outlets (shops) to enquire about a particular product and/or buy it, or to enter a similar transaction direct with the manufacturer or intermediary through direct mail or the Internet. B2b customers are encouraged to buy from dealers and distributors while both groups of consumers and b2b customers have opportunities to buy through direct marketing channels where there is no intermediary.

A *pull-(positioning)* strategy is aimed at encouraging customers to 'pull' products through the channel network.

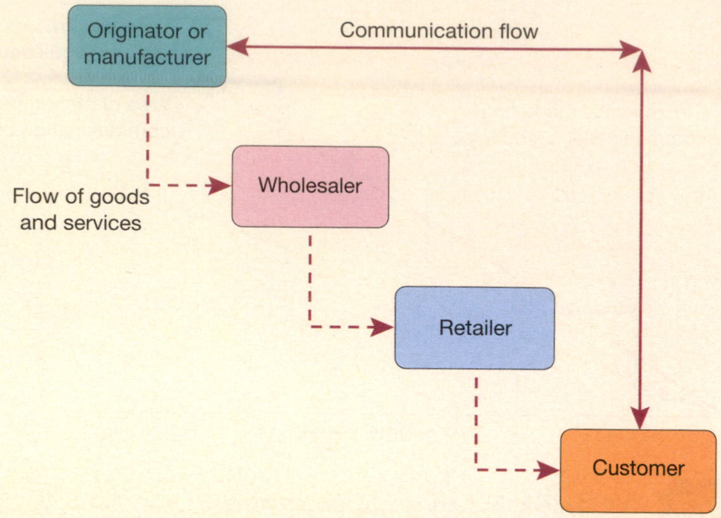

Figure 10.2 The direction of communication in a pull strategy

To accomplish and deliver a pull-positioning strategy, the traditional approach has been to deliver mass media advertising supported by below-the-line communications, most notably sales promotions. There has been greater use of direct marketing in non-fast-moving consumer goods sectors and use of the Internet presents opportunities to reach audiences in new ways, thereby reducing any reliance on the old formulaic approach to pull-based strategies. The decision to use a pull strategy has to be supported by a core message proposition. This will vary according to the outcomes of the context analysis and the needs of the target audience. However, it is probable that the core message will seek to differentiate (position), remind or reassure, inform or persuade the audience to think, feel or behave in a particular way. Agencies and clients have their own approach to this labelling activity.

ViewPoint 10.3 Probably the best pull strategy in the world

Carlsberg, just like many other consumer brands, are competing in a Western European market that is characterised by a proliferation of channels, media and customer segments. They use a wide communication mix, incorporating a full range of tools and media. For example, their consumer advertising uses television, outdoor, in-store, digital and print media. In addition, they use public relations, sponsorship and product placement, and they support local events and festivals to gain visibility.

As 10 per cent of their brands drive 80 per cent of their profits (that is one power brand in each of the ten European markets), so they have started to focus more of their resources on a reduced number of brands.

Pull strategies are configured around developing relationships with customers and Carlsberg refer to this development process as a 'funnel'. When building awareness they use sponsorship, festivals and events. When building on the awareness to generate increased loyalty they use media such as television as they believe they can communicate their messages more effectively this way. The final stage in the funnel process is to provide visibility in pubs and restaurants, and to activate brands in-store. This seemingly simple process can be complex because of the timing, costs and effectiveness associated with the move from one stage to another.

Source: Adapted from Riiber Knudsen (2007).

Question

How do Carlsberg position their brand?

Task

Find three drinks brands in the same category (e.g. alcohol, juice, water or carbonated) and determine how they want to be perceived.

Exhibit 10.2 This still from a Carlsberg ad uses humour to convey the message that if Carlsberg ran a football team it would probably provide the best goal celebration in the world.
Courtesy of Saatchi & Saatchi, London and Carlsberg UK. Director: Daniel Kleinman.

ASDA has developed a strong market share in the United Kingdom based mainly on price competition or on what is referred to as everyday low pricing (pull/price). Tesco runs everyday low pricing but uses sales promotions as a form of complementary positioning (pull/price/promotions). In their wake, Sainsbury's and Morrisons have used differing pull strategies to try and regain share, increase profitability and stave off takeover threats.

Although Sainsbury's uses EDLP (everyday low pricing) on 1,000 selected lines, it has adopted a classic branding campaign, based around the celebrity chef Jamie Oliver. Making heavy use of television, the brand is positioned around a quality proposition emphasised by the personality and the associated redesign of major stores.

The level and degree of involvement, explored at some depth in Chapter 5, has some implications for pull strategies. Marketing communication messages can be considered to be a stimulus that in some situations will have a strong impact on the level of involvement enjoyed by the target audience. A strategic response to this would be to adapt marketing communication messages so that they are effective at different levels of involvement, a form of differentiation.

Another approach would be to turn low-involvement decisions into high-involvement ones that, through communications, encourage members of the target audience to reconsider their perception of a brand or of the competition. Again, this represents a form of differentiation. A third approach is to segment the market in terms of the level of involvement experienced by each group and according to situational or personality factors, and then shape the marketing communication messages to suit each group.

A pull strategy therefore, refers to marketing communications (the use of tools, media and messages) designed to position an offering in the minds of particular end-user customer audience(s). This positioning can be achieved in many ways, and Chapter 11 considers a range of positioning techniques and opportunities.

A push-positioning strategy

A second group or type of target audience can be identified, based first on their contribution to the marketing channel, and second because these organisations do not consume the products and services they buy, but add value before selling the product on to others in the demand chain. The previous strategy was targeted at customers who make purchase decisions related largely to their personal (or organisational) consumption of products and services. This second group buys products and services, performs some added-value activity and moves the product through the marketing channel network. This group is a part of the b2b sector, and the characteristics and issues associated with trade channel marketing communications are explored in greater detail in Chapter 29.

The role of marketing communications is to develop and support the relationships that exist.

Trade channel organisations, and indeed all b2b organisations, are actively involved in the development and maintenance of interorganisational relationships. The degree of cooperation between organisations will vary and part of the role of marketing communications is to develop and support the relationships that exist.

The 'trade' channel has received increased attention in recent years as the strategic value of intermediaries has become both more visible and questioned in the light of the Internet. As the channel networks have developed, so has their complexity, which impacts upon the marketing

ViewPoint 10.4 Makita use below-the-line branding

Black & Decker discovered that they were losing sales in the trade sector because their products were perceived to be more suitable for consumers and the do-it-yourself market. Their response was to develop a separate brand for this particular trade sector. They used a new name 'Makita', identified the product range through the colour, marine blue and made it available through different trade channels. The promotional materials and support documentation needed a different 'tone of voice' to reflect a more rugged and stronger position. The messages were integrated in order to reinforce the desired positioning and targeted at trade customers through intermediaries, such as ScrewFix and Toolsdirect that served to reinforce the new positioning.

Question

To what extent does this type of repositioning require the use of advertising?

Task

Find a competitor to Makita. How do they use marketing communications?

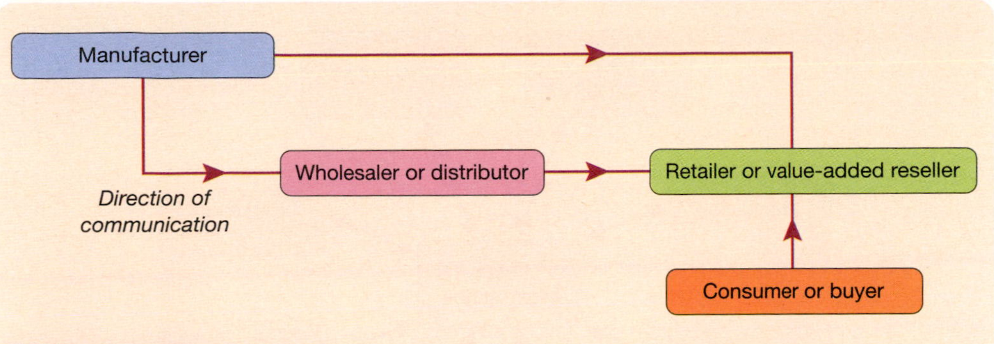

Figure **10.3** The direction of communication in a push strategy

communications strategies and tools used to help reach marketing goals. The expectations of buyers in these networks have risen in parallel with the significance attached to them by manufacturers. The power of multiple retailers, such as Tesco, Sainsbury's, Morrisons, Waitrose and Asda, is such that they are able to dictate terms (including the marketing communications) to many manufacturers of branded goods.

A *push-positioning* communication strategy involves the presentation of information in order to influence other trade channel organisations and, as a result, encourage them to take stock, to allocate resources (e.g. shelf space) and to help them to become fully aware of the key attributes and benefits associated with each product with a view to adding value prior to further channel transactions. This strategy is designed to encourage resale to other members of the network and contribute to the achievement of their own objectives. This approach is known as a *push* strategy, as it is aimed at pushing the product down through the channel towards the end-users for consumption (see Figure 10.3).

Push-positioning communication strategy involves the presentation of information in order to influence other trade channel organisations.

The channel network consists of those organisations with whom others must cooperate directly to achieve their own objectives. By accepting that there is interdependence, usually dispersed unequally throughout the network, it is possible to identify organisations that have a stronger/weaker position within a network. Communication must travel not only between the different levels of dependence and role ('up and down' in a channel context) and so represent bidirectional flows, but also across similar levels of dependence and role, that is horizontal flows. For example, these may be from retailer to retailer or wholesaler to wholesaler.

Marketing communications targeted at people involved in organisational buying decisions are characterised by an emphasis on personal selling. Trade advertising, trade sales promotions and public relations all have an important yet secondary role to play. Direct marketing has become increasingly important and the development of the Internet has had a profound impact on b2b communications and interorganisational relationships. However, personal selling has traditionally been the most significant part of the communication mix where a push strategy has been instigated.

Finally, just as it was suggested that the essence of a pull strategy could be articulated in brief format, a push strategy could be treated in a similar way. The need to consider the core message is paramount, as it conveys information about the essence of the strategy. Push/inform, push/position or push/key accounts/discount might be examples of possible terminology. Whether or not this form of expression is used, it is important that marketing communication strategy be referred to more than just push; what is to be achieved also needs to be understood.

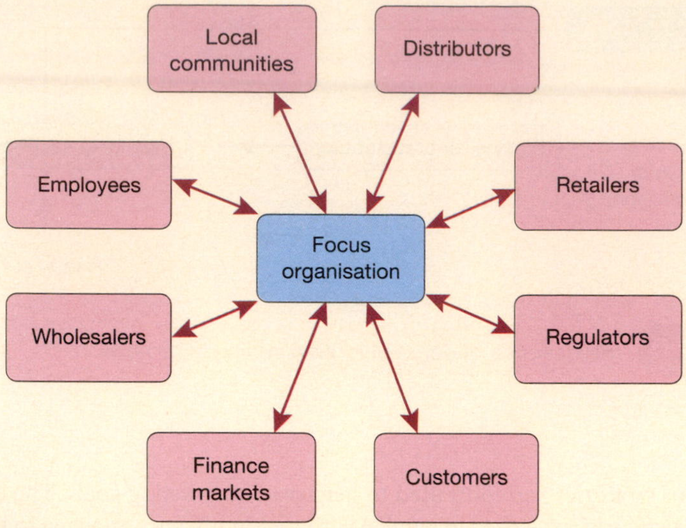

Figure 10.4 The direction of communication in a profile strategy

A profile-positioning strategy

The strategies considered so far concern the need for dialogue with customers (pull) and trade channel intermediaries (push). However, there is a whole range of other stakeholders, many of whom need to know about and understand the organisation rather than actually purchase its products and services (see Figure 10.4). This group of stakeholders may include financial analysts, trade unions, government bodies, employees or the local community. It should be easy to understand that these different stakeholder groups can influence the organisation in different ways and, in doing so, need to receive (and respond to) different types of messages. Thus, the financial analysts need to know about financial and trading performance and expectations, and the local community may be interested in employment and the impact of the organisation on the local environment, whereas the government may be interested in the way the organisation applies health and safety regulations and pays corporation, VAT and other taxes. It should also be remembered that consumers and business-to-business customers may also be more interested in the organisation itself and so help initiate an umbrella branding strategy, which is considered in Chapters 13 and 16.

Traditionally these organisational-oriented activities have been referred to as corporate communications, as they deal more or less exclusively with the corporate entity or organisation. Products, services and other offerings are not normally the focus of these communications. It is the organisation and its role in the context of the particular stakeholders' activities that is important. However, it should be noted that as more corporate brands appear, the distinction between corporate and marketing communications begins to become much less clear. Indeed, when considered in the light of the development and interest in internal marketing (and communications), it may be of greater advantage to consider corporate communications as an organisation's umbrella communications approach, with marketing communications activities a subpart of corporate communications (see Chapter 13 and van Riel, 1995).

> As more corporate brands appear, the distinction between corporate and marketing communications begins to become much less clear.

Communications used to satisfy this array of stakeholder needs and the organisation's corporate promotional goals are developed through what is referred to as a profile strategy, a major element of which is corporate branding, the subject of Chapter 13.

The awareness, perception and attitudes held by stakeholders towards an organisation need to be understood, shaped and acted upon. This can be accomplished though continual dialogue, which will normally lead to the development of trust and commitment and enable relationships to grow. This is necessary in order that stakeholders act favourably towards an organisation and enable strategies to flourish and objectives be achieved.

ViewPoint 10.5 So, who are we?

Organisations need to raise their profile for different reasons and at different times. These might reflect changing market conditions, trading circumstances, poor trading results, threat of takeover or a general repositioning.

G4S had to raise its profile because of a series of takeovers and mergers, which required the company to restructure, rebrand and reposition itself. Group 4 merged with Danish Falck in 2000, merged with Securicor in 2004, and then rebranded as G4S in 2006.

The first part of the rebranding incorporated staff. Through the use of a relaunch event day, 15,000 contracted staff were given information about the new company name, structure, board composition, new uniforms and livery. In addition, internal staff received information through desk drops, magazines, new letters and question–answer sessions.

Externally oriented communications revolved around the new logo. Fresh, clean and a break from the previous visual identity.

Source: Anon. (2008).

Question

What do you believe are the main differences between rebranding and raising profile?

Task

Make a list of all the reasons an organisation might choose to deliberately raise its profile.

To build corporate brands, organisations must develop modern integrated communication programmes with all of their key stakeholder groups. Audiences demand transparency and accountability and instant on-line access to news, developments, research and networks means that inconsistent or misleading information must be avoided. As if to reinforce this, a survey reported by Gray (2000) found that CEOs rated the reputation of their organisations as more important than that of their products. However, the leading contributor to the strength of the corporate brand is seen to be their products and services, followed by a strong management team, internal communications, PR, social accountability, change management and the personal reputation of the CEO.

Stakeholder analysis is used in the development of strategic plans, so if an organisation wants its communications to support the overall plan, it makes sense to communicate effectively with the appropriate stakeholders. Rowe *et al.* (1994) point out that, because of the mutual interdependence of stakeholders and the focus organisation, 'each stakeholder is in effect an advocate of any strategy that furthers its goals'. It follows, therefore, that it is important to provide all stakeholders with information that enables them to perceive and position the organisation, so as to generate the desired corporate image. This requires a communication strategy that addresses these particular requirements, even though there may not be any immediately recognisable shift in performance.

It is important to provide all stakeholders with information that enables them to perceive and position the organisation.

However, it would be incorrect to perceive corporate communications as just a means of shaping or influencing the attitudes and behaviour of other stakeholders. Organisations exist within a variety of networks, which provide a context for the roles and actions of member organisations (Chapter 7). Bidirectional communication flows exist and organisations adapt themselves to the actions and behaviour of others in the network. Therefore, corporate communications provides a mechanism by which it can learn about the context(s) in which it exists and is itself shaped and influenced by the other stakeholders with whom it shares communications. Reference is made to the work of Grunig and Hunt (1984), considered in Chapter 19.

A *profile-positioning* strategy focuses an organisation's communications upon the development of stakeholder relationships, corporate image and reputation, whether that be just internally, just externally or both. To accomplish and deliver a profile strategy, public relations, including sponsorship and corporate advertising, become the pivotal tools of the marketing communications mix. Personal selling may remain a vital element delivering both product/service and corporate messages.

A *profile-positioning* strategy focuses an organisation's communications upon the development of stakeholder relationships, corporate image and reputation.

Strategic balance

While the pull, push and profile strategies are important, it should be remembered that they are not mutually exclusive. Indeed, in most organisations it is possible to identify an element of each strategy at any one time. In reality, most organisations are structured in such a way that those responsible for communications with each of these three main audiences do so without reference to, or coordination with, each other. This is an example of how integrated marketing communications, which is examined in Chapter 9, needs to have one senior person responsible for all the organisational communications. Only through a single point of reference is it realistically possible to develop and communicate a set of brand values that are consistent and credible.

Recognising these limitations that organisations often place on themselves, the 3Ps should be considered as part of a total communication approach. Figure 10.5 depicts how the emphasis of a total communication strategy can shift according to changing contextual elements, for example, the needs of the various target audiences, resources and wider elements such as the environment and the competition. The marketing communications eclipse provides a visual interpretation of the balance between the three strategic dimensions. The more that is revealed

The marketing communications eclipse provides a visual interpretation of the balance between the three strategic dimensions.

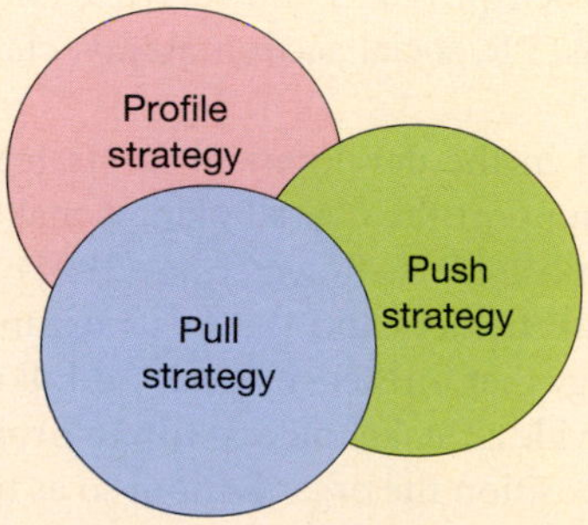

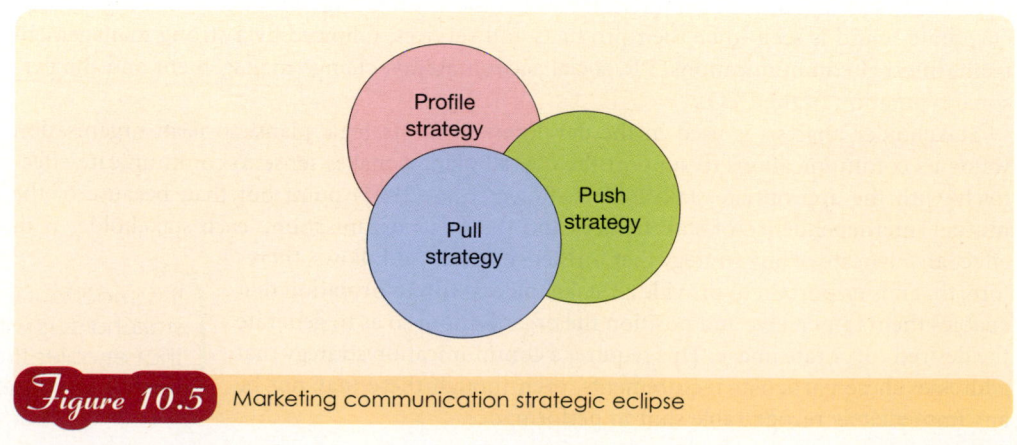

Figure 10.5 Marketing communication strategic eclipse

Table 10.5 Issues to be considered when developing marketing communications

Element	Issue
Target audiences	Which type of audience do we need to reach and why?
Channel strategies	How do we make our products/services available – direct or indirect?
Objectives	What do we need to achieve – what are our goals?
Positioning	How do we want to be perceived and understood?
Branding	How strong is our brand and what values and associations do stakeholders make with it?
Integration	How consistent are our communications, internally and externally?
Competitors	How do our communications compare with those of our key competitors?
Resources	What resources do we have and which do we need to secure?

of any one single strategy, the greater its role in any single campaign. Conversely, the less that is revealed, the smaller the contribution. In any one campaign, one or two of the three strategies might be used in preference to another and will often reflect branding approaches. For example, a brand manager's use of a profile strategy at Procter & Gamble or Mars will be virtually zero and will almost certainly be entirely pull in order to support the marketing channel or trade customers.

The role of each element of the marketing communications mix is important in communication strategy. Each tool has different strengths and should be used accordingly. For example, direct marketing and sales promotion are more likely to be effective in persuading consumer audiences, while personal selling is likely to be more effective in b2b situations. A profile strategy designed to change perception and understanding of the organisation is more likely to utilise public relations and corporate advertising.

Marketing communication strategy, regardless of the overall focus, is normally composed of a number of different elements. When considering strategy there are a number of key issues that need to be considered. These are shown in Table 10.5.

Strategy needs to be understood in terms of the answers given in response to several critical questions. First, how are the communication goals that have been set going to be achieved? Second, how they are going to be accomplished in terms of complementing the business and marketing strategies? Third, can current resources and opportunities support the strategy and do they encourage target audiences to respond to the communications?

Answers to these questions are not always easy to find and very often there will be conflicting proposals from different coalitions of internal stakeholders. In other words, there is a political element that needs to be considered and there may also be a strong overriding culture that directs the communication strategy and that may hinder innovation or the development of alternative methods of communication. Everyone who is involved with the development of marketing communications campaigns (internally and externally) should agree and prioritise necessary activities. The development of a marketing communications plan facilitates this process and enables the strategy to be articulated in such a way that the goals are achieved in a timely, efficient and effective manner.

Internet strategies

The development of Internet-based facilities is now quite commonplace for organisations and consumers. The function and speed of development of Internet facilities within organisations is a function of many factors, such as the size and core skills of the organisation. For example, it is normally easier for an IST organisation than a transport organisation to develop ecommerce facilities. Other factors include the nature of the product offering and the market and competitor conditions. It cannot, therefore, be concluded that there is a fixed pathway for the development and incorporation of the Internet within an organisation, nor should there be one, as the flexibility and adaptability to meet individual organisational requirements needs to be retained.

However, it is useful to understand the basic types of online facilities in order to appreciate the strategic thinking that needs to be undertaken. The Internet can become an integral part of the way an organisation operates, the way it sees its future and the way others see it, and not just be used to supplement the organisation's promotional programme. Having said that, it is this technology factor, more than any other, that has done so much to accelerate moves towards integrated marketing communications and to encourage managers to consider the totality of their activities rather than focus on an individual aspect.

The Internet can become an integral part of the way an organisation operates, the way it sees its future and the way others see it.

The different Internet-related phases through which an organisation usually passes needs to be considered alongside the technological platform that the organisation wishes to operate. Essentially the Internet provides web site access for everyone. An extranet platform enables an organisation to restrict access to a number of selected organisations/people. For example, end-user customers, intermediaries and suppliers all might use an extranet to provide benefits that all can share and through which the host might develop competitive advantage. An intranet platform enables the use of the same browser-based technology but access is restricted to the employees of an organisation.

The strategic choice of platform requires consideration of the different stakeholders and communities with which the organisation wishes to interact. The management of these groups is then necessary in order to ensure optimum usage and the development of suitable relationships. Management need to encourage stakeholder communities to grow and to interact with one another and this requires that users be empowered, encouraged to innovate and be reviewed on a regular basis.

While the ability to reach customers directly, avoiding channel intermediaries and reducing transaction costs is attractive, strategies must be decided upon for attracting customers to a web site (or TV-based 'shop'). Reliance on online communications alone is too limiting and unlikely to be successful, so a combination of off-line and on-line communications is necessary to attract sufficient traffic.

The variety of offline communications used by organisations varies according to their budgets and their overall strategy. Many online brands use television and outdoor advertising to promote not only the web site but, more importantly for them, the brand name to drive shareholder interest as these new entities seek stock market listings. As a result of this activity, outdoor advertising spend has grown substantially. Sponsorship is also used to promote web site addresses as well as a host of corporate literature such as company reports, brochures, calling cards and letterheads. Online communications vary from banner ads and pop-ups to viral marketing and public relations. However, research indicates that the most important factor driving first-time visits is word-of-mouth and recommendations by significant others. In other words, people are more disposed to having their web site behaviour directed by those they trust rather than risk time and effort seeking information based on communications that lack inherent credibility.

Many online brands use television and outdoor advertising to promote not only the web site but, more importantly for them, the brand name to drive shareholder interest.

The balance between offline and online generated traffic will also vary depending upon the nature of the brand itself. If a brand is being developed by a bricks-and-mortar company as an additional distribution and communications channel, but there is to be no visible tie to the parent company (e.g. Egg and Citibank), then the offline branding development will need to be considerable. However, if the brand is to be tied in closely to the current channels (e.g. Argos), the initial branding can be constrained to converting current customers to the new product and to stimulating word-of-mouth recommendations, a much lower communications investment.

However, whatever the reason or branding strategy used to generate traffic, thought should be given to capitalising on the facilities to personalise the experience through the use of underlying data capture, storage, retrieval and processing abilities of integrated technologies. The ability to start with some knowledge of a customer's preferences, previous purchases, their already secure financial details and delivery address, for example, should be a major source of advantage. In addition, the interactive communications strategy needs to be thought through all points of customer interaction. Many companies have addressed the need to capture customers and even extract critical personal information but have failed to think through the total process and consider how the behaviour of the company communicates attitudes and degree of care. The use of email to confirm receipt and despatch details of a customer's order goes a long way to developing trust and positive customer attitudes, but unless the whole fulfilment exercise is compatible (and fulfilling), the whole of the investment in the front end of the exercise will be wasted.

Weltevreden *et al.* (2005) have determined a typology of Internet strategies used by retailers. In particular, they identify nine strategies employed by retailers with active web sites. These are shown at Table 10.6.

Four of these are 'information-only-strategies' where there are varying levels of product information available or services designed to assist customer relationships. The remaining five are referred to as 'online-sales-strategies' each tied in various ways to the organisation's physical outlets, or in one case not at all.

Weltevreden and Boschma (2008) conclude from a study of Danish retailers that adopting an Internet strategy invariably has positive effects on performance in terms of more customers, improved customer relationships, increased competitiveness and overall sales growth. They also found that adopting an Internet sales strategy was more beneficial for

Adopting an Internet strategy invariably has positive effects on performance.

Table 10.6 Internet strategies used by retailers

Strategy	Explanation	Product information	Online sales
Billboard	Web site used to make customers aware of their existence	None	No
Brochure	Limited product information and services	Limited	No
Catalogue	Web site provides detailed product information but limited services	Extensive	No
Service	Web site used to provide additional services to improve relationships (e.g. help desks)	Limited/extensive	No
Export	Web site used to expand into new areas without affecting their physical outlets	Extensive	Yes
Mirror	Web site used as an additional virtual outlet but few linkages with physical outlets and no additional services	Extensive	Yes
Synergy	Customer interaction between web site physical outlets encouraged through cross-promotions, ordering/pickup, full availability	Extensive	Yes
Anti-mirror	Web site the dominant channel and the role of the physical outlets is to support the web site	Extensive	Yes
Virtual	Web site is the only organisational presence	Extensive	Yes

Source: Adapted from Weltevreden and Boschma (2008).

independent retailers than it was for multiple retailers. The researchers speculate that this may be due to the independents being able to reach a wider market than previously, whereas multiples already serve a wide market.

Developing a marketing communications plan

> The intended positioning can be missed if the marketing communication is not entirely effective.

The context in which a communication event is to occur shapes not only what and how messages are developed and conveyed, but also influences the interpretation and meaning ascribed to the communication. In other words the intended positioning can be missed if the marketing communication is not entirely effective. The development of marketing communication plans helps to minimise errors and provide for efficiency and effectiveness.

There are a number of contexts that influence or shape marketing communications. All marketing managers (and others) need to understand these contextual elements and appreciate how they contribute and influence the development of marketing communication programmes. In addition, there are a number of other elements and activities that need to be built into a programme in order that it can be implemented. These elements concern the goals, the resources, the communication tools to be used and measures of control and evaluation. Just like the cogs in a clock, these elements need to be linked together if the plan is to work. The marketing communications planning framework (MCPF) aims to bring together the various elements that constitute marketing communications into a logical sequence of activities. The rationale for promotional decisions is built on information generated at previous levels in the framework. It also provides a checklist of activities that need to be considered.

To help students and managers comprehend the linkages between the elements and to understand how these different components complement each other, the rest of this chapter deals with the development of marketing communication plans. To that extent it will be of direct benefit to managers seeking to build plans for the first time or for those familiar with the activity to reconsider current practices. Second, the material should also be of direct benefit to students who are required to understand and perhaps prepare such plans as part fulfilment of an assessment or examination in this subject area.

> The MCPF represents a way of bringing together the different components in the communication process.

The MCPF represents a way of bringing together the different components in the communication process, of appreciating the way in which they relate to one another and is a means of writing coherent marketing communications plans for work or for examinations, such as those offered by the Chartered Institute of Marketing.

The marketing communications planning framework

It has been established (Chapter 1) that the principal tasks facing marketing communications managers are to decide:

1. Who should receive the messages.
2. What the messages should say.
3. What image of the organisation/brand receivers are expected to retain.
4. How much is to be spent establishing this new image.

5. How the messages are to be delivered.
6. What actions the receivers should take.
7. How to control the whole process once implemented.
8. What was achieved.

Note that more than one message is transmitted and that there is more than one target audience. This is important, as recognition of the need to communicate with multiple audiences and their different information requirements, often simultaneously, lies at the heart of marketing communications. The aim is to generate and transmit messages which present the organisation and their offerings to their various target audiences, encouraging them to enter into a dialogue. These messages must be presented consistently and they must address the points stated above. It is the skill and responsibility of the marketing communications planner to blend the communication tools and to create a mix that satisfies these elements.

A framework for integrated marketing communications plans

To enable managers and students to bring together the various promotional elements into a cohesive plan, which can be communicated to others, an overall framework is required.

The MCPF (Figure 10.6) seeks to achieve this by bringing together the various elements into a logical sequence of activities where the rationale for marketing communications decisions is built upon information generated at a previous level in the framework. Another advantage of using the MCPF is that it provides a suitable checklist of activities that need to be considered.

The MCPF represents a sequence of decisions that marketing managers undertake when preparing, implementing and evaluating communication strategies and plans. It does not mean that this sequence reflects reality; indeed, many marketing decisions are made outside any recognisable framework. However, as a means of understanding the different components, appreciating the way in which they relate to one another and bringing together various aspects for work or for answering examination questions such as those offered by the Chartered Institute of Marketing, this approach has many advantages and has been used by a number of local, national and international organisations.

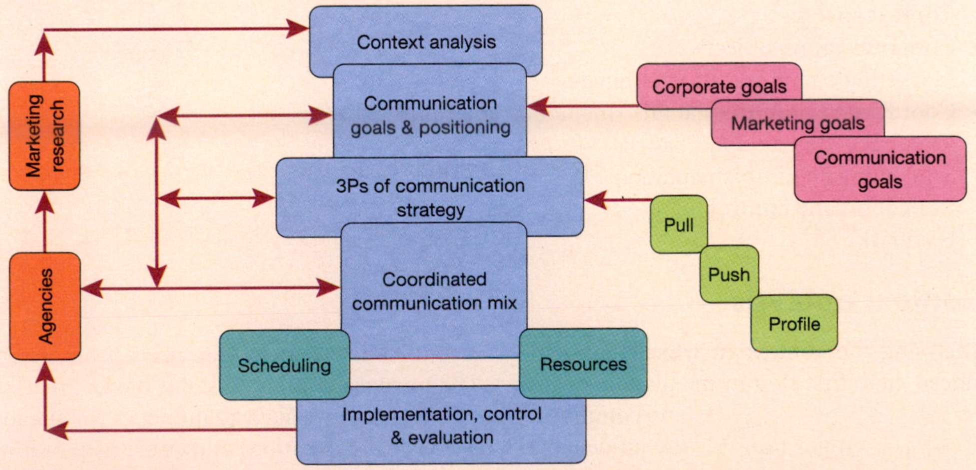

Figure 10.6 The marketing communications planning framework

Marketing communications requires the satisfaction of communication objectives.

Marketing communications requires the satisfaction of communication objectives through the explicit and deliberate development of communication strategy. The MCPF will be used to show first, the key elements, second, some of the linkages and third, the integrated approach that is required.

This framework reflects the deliberate or planned approach to strategy marketing communications. The process of marketing communications, however, is not linear, as depicted in this framework, but integrative and interdependent. To that extent, this approach is a recognition of the value of stakeholder theory and of the requirement to build partnerships with buyers and other organisations networked with the organisation.

Other 'decision sequences' have been advanced, in particular one by Rothschild (1987) and another by Engel *et al.* (1994). One of the difficulties associated with their frameworks is that they fail to bring strategy into the development of the promotional mix. Their frameworks rely on the objective and task approach, whereby plans are developed for each of the individual promotional tools, and then aggregated to form strategy.

Another more recent framework is the SOSTAC (situation, objectives, strategy, tactics, action, control) approach. This is essentially a sound system and moves closer than most of the others to achieving suitable marketing communication plans. However, as the framework is multipurpose and is intended for application to a variety of planning situations, there is a strong danger that the communication focus is lost at the situation analysis phase. This can lead to a reiteration of a SWOT (strengths, weaknesses, opportunities, threats) and/or a general marketing plan, with subsequent problems further down the line in terms of the justification and understanding of the communications strategy and promotional mixes that need to be deployed. In addition, the SOSTAC model does not give sufficient emphasis to the need to identify and understand the characteristics of the target audience, which is so important for the development of a coherent marketing communications plan.

The MCPF approach presented here is not intended to solve all the problems associated with the formulation of such plans, but it is robust enough to meet the needs of employers and examiners, and is recommended.

Elements of the plan

Marketing communications plans consist of the following elements. These elements will now be considered in turn.

- Context analysis
- Communication objectives
- Marketing communications strategy
- Coordinated promotional mix (methods, tools and media)
- Resources (human and financial)
- Scheduling and implementation
- Evaluation and control
- Feedback

Context analysis

The purpose is to understand the key market and communication drivers that are likely to influence a brand.

Analysing the context in which marketing communication episodes occur is a necessary, indeed vital, first step in the planning process. The purpose is to understand the key market and communication drivers that are likely to influence (or already are influencing) a brand (or organisation) and either help or hinder its progress towards meeting its long-term objectives. This is different from a situation analysis, because the situation analysis considers a range of wider organisational factors, most of which

Table 10.7 The main elements of the context analysis

Context element	Dimensions
The customer context	Segment characteristics Levels of awareness, perception and attitudes towards the brand/organisation Level of involvement Types of perceived risk DMU characteristics and issues
The business context	Corporate and marketing strategy and plans Brand/organisation analysis Competitor analysis
The internal context	Financial constraints Organisation identity Culture, values and beliefs Marketing expertise Agency availability and suitability
The external context	Who are the key stakeholders and why are they important? What are their communication needs? Social, political, economic and technological restraints and opportunities.

are normally considered in the development of marketing plans (while the communication focus is lost). Duplication is to be avoided, as it is both inefficient and confusing.

The compilation of a context analysis (CA) is very important, as it presents information and clues about what the promotional plan needs to achieve. Information and market research data about target audiences (their needs, perception, motivation, attitudes and decision-making characteristics), the media and the people they use for information about offerings, the marketing objectives and time-scales, the overall level of financial and other resources that are available, the quality and suitability of agency and other outsourced activities, and the environment in terms of societal, technological, political and economic conditions, both now and at some point in the future, all need to be considered.

At the root of the CA is the marketing plan. This will already have been prepared and contains important information about the target segment, the business and marketing goals, competitors and the time-scales in which the goals are to be achieved. The rest of the CA seeks to elaborate and build upon this information so as to provide the detail in order that the plan can be developed and justified.

The CA provides the rationale for the plan. It is from the CA that the marketing objectives (from the marketing plan) and the marketing communications objectives are derived. The type, form and style of the message are rooted in the characteristics of the target audience, and the media selected to convey messages will be based on the nature of the tasks, the media habits of the audience and the resources available. The main components of the context analysis are set out in Table 10.7.

Communication objectives

The role of promotional objectives in the planning process is important for a number of reasons. First, they provide a balance to the plan and take away the sole emphasis on sales that inevitably arises. Second, they indicate positioning issues, third, they highlight the required balance of the promotional mix, fourth, they

Promotional objectives provide a balance to the plan and take away the sole emphasis on sales that inevitably arises.

provide time parameters for campaigns, and finally, they provide a crucial means by which particular marketing communication activities are evaluated.

Ideally, communication objectives should consist of three main elements:

Corporate objectives

These are derived from the business or marketing plan. They refer to the mission and the business area that the organisation believes it should be in.

Marketing objectives

These are derived from the marketing plan and are output-oriented. Normally these can be considered as sales-related objectives, such as market share, sales revenues, volumes, ROI and profitability indicators.

Marketing communication objectives

These are derived from an understanding of the current context in which a brand exists and the future context in the form of where the brand is expected to be at some point in the future. These will be presented as awareness levels, perception, comprehension/knowledge, attitudes towards and overall degree of preference for the brand. The choice of communication goal depends on the tasks that need to be accomplished. In addition, most brands need either to maintain their current brand position or reposition themselves in the light of changing contextual conditions.

These three elements constitute the promotional objectives and they all need to be set out in SMART terminology (see Chapter 11). What also emerges is a refinement to the positioning that managers see as important for success. Obviously, not all plans require express attention to positioning (e.g. government information campaigns) but most commercial and brand-oriented communication programmes need to communicate a clear position in their market. Thus, at this point the positioning intentions are developed and these will be related to the market, the customers or some other dimension. The justification for this will arise from the CA.

Marketing communications strategy

It is imperative that the strategy be geared to the communication needs of the target audience.

The communication strategy should be customer- not method/media-oriented. Therefore, the strategy depends on whether the target audience is a consumer segment, a distributor or dealer network or whether other stakeholders need to be reached. In addition, it is imperative that the strategy be geared to the communication needs of the target audience that is revealed during the customer and business context analyses. This will show what the task is that marketing communications needs to fulfil. Having established who the audience is, push-, pull- or profile-dominated strategies can be identified. The next step is to determine the task that needs to be accomplished. This will have been articulated previously in the marketing communications objectives, but the approach at this stage is less quantitative and softer.

The DRIP tasks of marketing communications can be used to suggest the strategy being pursued. For example, if a new brand is being launched, the first task will be to inform and differentiate the brand for members of the trade before using a pull strategy to inform and differentiate the brand for the target, end-user customers. An organisation wishing to signal a change of strategy and/or a change of name following a merger or acquisition may choose to use a profile strategy and the primary task will be to inform of the name change. An organisation experiencing declining sales may choose to remind customers of a need or it may choose to improve sales through persuasion.

Coordinated communication mix

Having formulated, stated and justified the required position, the next step is to present the basic form and style of the key message that is to be conveyed. Is there to be a lot of copy or just a little? Is there to be a rational or emotional approach or some weighting between the two? What should be the tone of the visual messages? Is there to be a media blitz (e.g. a Microsoft-type day, as used for the launch of Windows 95, or Cable & Wireless yellow saturation)? It is at this point that those responsible for the development of these plans can be imaginative and try some new ideas. Trying to tie in the message to the strategic orientation is the important part, as the advertising agency will refine and redefine the message and the positioning.

From this the promotional mixes need to be considered *for each* of the strategies proposed, that is, a mix for the consumer strategy, a mix for the trade strategy and a distinct mix for the communications to reach the wider array of stakeholders.

The choice of promotional methods should clearly state the methods and the media to be used. A short paragraph justifying the selection is very important, as the use of media in particular is to a large extent dependent upon the nature of the goals, the target audience and the resources. The key is to provide message consistency and a measure of integration.

Resources

This is a vitally important part of the plan, one that is often avoided or forgotten about. The resources necessary to support the plan need to be determined and these refer not only to the financial issues but to the quality of available marketing expertise and the time that is available to achieve the required outcomes.

Gantt charts and other project planning aids are best used to support this part of the plan. The cost of the media and methods can either be allocated in a right-hand column of the chart, or a new chart can be prepared. Preferably, actual costs should be assigned, although percentages can be allocated if examination time is at a premium. What is important is the relative weighting of the costs and a recognition and understanding of the general costs associated with the proposed individual activities.

It must be understood that a television campaign cannot be run for less than £1.5 million and that the overall cost of the strategy should be in proportion to the size of the client organisation, its (probable) level of profitability and the size and dynamics of the market in which it operates.

Scheduling and implementation

The next step is to schedule the deployment of the methods and the media. This is best achieved by the production of a Gantt chart.

Events should be scheduled according to the goals and the strategic thrust. So, if it is necessary to communicate with the trade prior to a public launch, those activities tied into the push strategy should be scheduled prior to those calculated to support the pull strategy.

Similarly, if awareness is a goal then, if funds permit, it may be best to use television and posters first before sales promotions (unless sampling is used), direct marketing, point of purchase and personal selling.

Evaluation and control

Unless there is some form of evaluation, there will be no dialogue and no true marketing communications. There are numerous methods to evaluate the individual performance of the tools and the media used, and for examination purposes these should be stated. In addition, and perhaps more meaningfully, the most important measures are the communication objectives set in the first place. The success of a promotional strategy and the associated plan is the degree to which the objectives set are achieved.

Feedback

The planning process is completed when feedback is provided. Not only should information regarding the overall outcome of a campaign be considered but so should individual aspects of the activity. For example, the performance of the individual tools used within the campaign, whether sufficient resources were invested, the appropriateness of the strategy in the first place, any problems encountered during implementation and the relative ease with which the objectives were accomplished are all aspects that need to be fed back to all internal and external parties associated with the planning process.

Feedback is vitally important because it provides information for the context analysis that anchors the next campaign.

This feedback is vitally important because it provides information for the context analysis that anchors the next campaign. Information fed back in a formal and systematic manner constitutes an opportunity for organisations to learn from their previous campaign activities, a point often overlooked and neglected.

Links and essential points

It was mentioned earlier that there are a number of linkages associated with different parts of the marketing communications plan. It is important to understand the nature of these links as they represent the interconnections between different parts of the plan and the rationale for undertaking the contextual analysis in particular. The contextual analysis (CA) feeds the items shown in Table 10.8. For example, research undertaken by Interbrand for Intercontinental Hotels to find out what influenced the brand experience of hotel guests, discovered that one of the key factors was the hotel concierge. As a result the role of the concierge became a central character in the communication strategy, influencing the campaign goals, positioning and message strategy (Gustafson, 2007). The promotional objectives derived from the CA feed decisions concerning strategy, tools and media, scheduling and evaluation.

The marketing communications strategy is derived from an overall appreciation of the needs of the target audience (and stakeholders) regarding the brand and its competitive position in the market. The communication mix is influenced by the previous elements and the budget that follows. However, the nature of the tools and the capacity and characteristics of the media influence scheduling, implementation and evaluation activities.

To help explain the MCPF and the linkage, a mini case study follows the chapter summary and review questions. You are required to prepare a marketing communications plan. It is

Table 10.8 Linkages within the MCPF

Objectives	From the marketing plan, from the customer, stakeholder network and competitor analysis and from an internal marketing review
Strategic balance between push, pull and profile	From an understanding of the brand, the needs of the target audiences, including employees and all other stakeholders, and the marketing goals
Brand positioning	From users' and non-users' perceptions, motivations, attitudes and understanding about the brand and its direct and indirect competitors
Message content and style	From an understanding about the level of involvement, perceived risk, DMU analysis, information-processing styles and the positioning intentions
Promotional tools and media	From the target audience analysis of media habits, involvement and preferences, from knowledge about product suitability and media compatibility, from a competitor analysis and from the resource analysis

suggested that you prepare one using the material in this chapter as a guide. An answer is available at the web site www.booknets/fillc that you can use to compare with your own response. The prepared answer is not the only possible answer – there are other plans that could be of equal significance and use.

Summary

In order to help consolidate your understanding of marketing communications strategy, here are the key points summarised against each of the learning objectives:

1. Establish the differences between strategy, tactics and planning.

Two main strategy schools of thought can be identified, namely the planning and the emergent approaches. The planning school is the pre-eminent paradigm and is based on strategy development and implementation, which is explicit, rational and planned as a sequence of logical steps.

The emergent school of thought considers strategy to develop incrementally, step-by-step, as organisations learn, sometimes through simple actions of trial and error. The core belief is that strategy is comprised of a stream of organisational activities that are continuously being formulated, implemented, tested, evaluated and updated.

Strategy should be considered to be about the means, speed and methods by which organisations adapt to and influence their environments in order to achieve their goals.

2. Appreciate the essence of marketing communications strategy.

Marketing communications strategy is concerned with two key dynamics. The first dynamic is concerns who, in broad terms, is the target audience? End-user customers need to derive particular benefits based on perceived value from the exchange process. These benefits are very different from those that intermediaries expect to derive, or indeed any other stakeholder who does not consume the product or service. The second dynamic concerns the way in which an audience understands the offering they are experiencing either through use or through communications. The way in which people interpret messages and frame objects in their mind is concerned with positioning.

Marketing communications strategy is concerned with audiences and positioning.

3. Consider three main marketing communication strategies: pull, push and profile.

The 3Ps of marketing communications strategy are:

- Pull-positioning strategies – these are intended to influence end-user customers (consumers and b2b);
- Push-positioning strategies – these are intended to influence marketing (trade) channel buyers;
- Profile-positioning strategies – these are intended to influence a wide range of stakeholders, not just customers and intermediaries.

Push, pull and profile strategies can be combined in different ways to meet the needs of different communication tasks. In addition to the broad target, it is important to express strategy in terms of the differentiation (positioning), reminding/reassuring, informing and persuading of audiences.

4. Explain the notion of strategic balance.

The 3Ps are a part of a total communication approach. The pull, push and profile strategies are not mutually exclusive and it is possible to identify an element of each strategy operating at any one time.

The marketing communications eclipse provides a visual interpretation of the balance between the three strategic dimensions. The more that is revealed of any single strategy, the greater its role in any single campaign. Conversely, the less that is revealed, the smaller the contribution.

5. Explore different approaches to Internet-based communication strategies.

Internet communication strategies need to be developed on a variety of factors. These include the marketing strategy; whether the operation is a bricks extension or a pure play operation; the relationship to be held with any parent brand; the relationships with intermediaries; the methods to be used to drive site traffic; and perhaps the most important of these is probably the need to consider all points where customers interact with the brand.

6. Present a planning framework and consider the different elements involved in the development of marketing communication plans.

A marketing communications planning framework (MCPF) consists of the following elements.

- Context analysis
- Communication objectives
- Marketing communications strategy
- Coordinated communication mix (methods, tools and media)
- Resources (human and financial)
- Scheduling and implementation
- Evaluation and control
- Feedback.

The MCPF aims to bring together the various elements that constitute marketing communications into a logical sequence of activities. The rationale for promotional decisions is built on information generated at previous levels in the framework. It also provides a checklist of activities that need to be considered.

This framework reflects the deliberate or planned approach to strategy marketing communications. The MCPF represents a way of understanding the different promotional components, of appreciating the way in which they relate to one another and is a means of writing coherent marketing communications plans for work or for examinations.

7. Highlight the importance of the linkages and interaction between the different elements of the plan.

Just as the strength of the value chain lies in the internal linkages so the strength of a marketing communication plan is to be found within the various linkages that bind the components together. It is important to understand the nature of these links as they represent the interconnections between different parts of the plan and the rationale for undertaking the contextual analysis in particular.

Review questions

1. Write brief notes explaining some of the key approaches to understanding strategy.
2. Explain the role strategy plays in marketing communications.
3. Compare strategy with planning. In what ways might planning be the same as strategy?
4. What are the 3Ps of marketing communications strategy? Explain the differences between each of them and use the marketing communications eclipse to support your answer.
5. Explain the key characteristics associated with a pull strategy.
6. Draw two diagrams depicting the direction of communications in both the push and the pull strategies.
7. Describe what the 'core message' is and provide four examples.
8. Sketch the marketing communications planning framework – from memory.
9. Following on from the previous question, check your version of the MCPF with the original and then prepare some bullet-point notes, highlighting the critical linkages between the main parts of the framework.
10. Discuss the extent to which Internet strategies should be considered a part of marketing communication strategies as a whole.

MiniCase 'Ski Rossendale'

Angela Hall: Manchester Metropolitan University Business School

Introduction

Ski Rossendale is located on a hillside in the Rossendale Valley, Lancashire, 20 miles north of Manchester. It has excellent travel links, just off the end of the M66 motorway, and with buses from Manchester every 15 minutes stopping within 1 mile.

Ski Rossendale's slopes are divided into three main areas. The main slope is 200m × 25m (with 2 button tows), the fun slope is 70m × 15m (with 1 button tow and big air and railslide feature), and the nursery slope is 35m × 40m (with 2 rope tows and a travelator lift). Currently the fun slope and nursery slope are made from SNOWFLEX virtual snow, the main slope was upgraded during the last year to incorporate part SNOWFLEX and also a half-pipe was added to the bottom of the main slope.

There is also an on-site cafe that is owned and run by Ski Rossendale, and this is open while the slope is open. The cafe offers drinks, breakfast, lunch and dinner. While no formal research has taken place on usage and views of the cafe, it is generally considered to be under-utilised by the users of the slope. Currently the cafe has a general seating area, the back section of which can be used as a separate small function area for children's parties, and an outside area where patrons can view the main slope while enjoying their refreshments.

Rossendale Leisure Trust (RLT) is a charitable trust and includes a number of business units within it. These take the form of five facilities: Haslingden Sports Centre, Haslingden Swimming Pool, Marl Pits Swimming Pool, Bacup Leisure Hall and Ski Rossendale. A sixth business unit operates under the title 'Lifestyles Team' and encompasses Sports Development, Arts Development and Healthy Communities.

Aims/objectives

Their vision is 'to establish Rossendale Leisure Trust as a benchmark organisation of its type in the UK' (www.rltrust.co.uk), with a mission of 'getting Rossendale on the move'. Seven trust values are presented:

- ensure every resident can access our services;
- help to bring our community together;

Exhibit 10.3 Ski Rossendale
Ski Rossendale.

- deliver better opportunities through partnership working;
- use resources effectively at all times;
- build on our achievements and learn from our mistakes;
- develop knowledge and understanding in sport and arts;
- provide a long-term legacy for the community of Rossendale.

No marketing objectives, or marketing communications objectives have been formalised by Ski Rossendale, and there are no formal marketing or marketing communications plans in place currently.

There is a business development manager at Ski Rossendale who took up position in July 2007. This person will develop business and focus on marketing activities, although they are from a sports science background, and currently has little marketing expertise.

Target audience

No detailed analysis of those using the slope has taken place. However, all those attending the slope are asked to give their postcode, this is recorded in paper form when hiring the equipment. Currently some very basic analysis of this is undertaken. The main geographical areas customers are from are Greater Manchester and Lancashire, with smaller numbers from Cumbria down to North Wales and into Yorkshire. Ski Rossendale would like to look at how to capture data on current users and build relationships with these people. Data on usage figures are available, but it is recognised that this information needs to be improved. Retaining existing customers and getting them to use the slope more is seen as a key objective in the immediate future. This is especially important bearing in mind competition from the Chill Factor e (a new indoor real snow development near the Trafford Centre, Manchester), which may well try to take customers away.

Potentially, anyone interested in keeping fit and interested in outdoor activities could be targeted. Research indicates that outdoor activity participants are sporting all-rounders, with many taking part in three or more sports overall (Mintel, 2004). There is a much higher interest in extreme sports (such as snowboarding and extreme skiing) among the 15–24 year olds (Mintel, 2003). Although 1.2 per cent of UK adults go on snowsports holidays (2003), some 3.7 per cent consider themselves leisure snowsports participants (Mintel, 2003). It is estimated that there will be a 7 per cent projected growth of 18–30 year olds between 2005 and 2010 who are seen as a key target audience (Mintel, 2005). While skiing and snowboarding are seen as minority sports, there are currently 1.6 million skiers and 0.5 million snowboarders aged 15+ within the United Kingdom (Mintel, 2006).

Ski Rossendale see one of their key target markets as being those people who are going on winter ski/snowboard holidays. The ski slope is at its busiest during the December to March period, as many people prepare themselves for their winter holiday, and lessons tend to be at full capacity during this peak period.

Currently Ski Rossendale acknowledges that they have poor links with local schools and consider this as an area for growth. However, one of the issues here is the cost of transporting children to the slope. The government has been encouraging further participation in sport with a number of plans (e.g. Plan for Sport March 2001, Game Place strategic view). Long term, the government see the promotion of sport in schools as especially important. The strengthening of links between schools and community sports clubs and the re-establishment of sport as an extra-curricular activity could be crucial in motivating schoolchildren to maintain their participation after they leave education, by introducing them to methods and venues for playing outside school. Also, increased sports participation in general is likely to encourage greater participation in extreme sports (Mintel, 2003). During the school summer holidays Ski Rossendale offered a number of holiday courses for children and this also allowed free use of the ski slope for the remainder of the school holidays.

Good links have been established with disabled groups, and the Uphill Ski Club is based at Ski Rossendale. Disabled groups are catered for much better than competitors, with disabled adaptive instruction, groups allowed to store specialist equipment there, and concessionary rates provided.

Saturday morning Kids' Club is popular, especially during the peak season. They cater for children from the age of 3 (Kindergarten classes run for 3–5 year olds). Two sessions 9.30 to 11a.m. and 11.30 to 1p.m. run every Saturday, but tend to be quieter and not running to full capacity outside the peak season. The summer Sunday race league is also aimed at children and getting them to engage with the ski slope on a more regular basis.

A key objective is to increase the level of usage of the slope at times outside peak season, especially with regard to lessons with instructors. The aim would be to offer incentives for individuals, families and other groups (e.g. schools) to increase their usage of the slope and lessons outside peak season. As the months of January and February are especially busy, they would also like to encourage people to start preparing for their holiday earlier.

Furthermore, the opening of the Chill Factor e at Trafford Park in Manchester is likely to take away some of Ski Rossendale's existing customers. Therefore, an increase in marketing communications in order to retain existing customers is also essential.

Children's parties have become increasingly popular for Ski Rossendale. This involves the use of large tubes that are sat on to come down the nursery slope, followed by a meal in the cafe. It is felt that there is potential for this to be developed further, especially during the summer months when the weather is better, and the slope quieter.

Adult parties are also starting to become popular. The use of the tubes is not restricted to the nursery slope, and therefore allows adults to go at a much faster speed. Party bookings allow for customers to bring their own alcohol and food. This allows the slope to be used outside normal opening times, and there appears to be potential to bring in increased revenue.

Prices 2008

Use of slope and hire of equipment only

Adult:	Standard Ticket (up to 2 hours)	£17
	Super Ticket (over 2 hours)	£19
Child:	Standard Ticket (up to 2 hours)	£10
	Super Ticket (over 2 hours)	£12
Adult Concession (students and over 60s)		
	Standard Ticket (up to 2 hours)	£10
	Super Ticket (over 2 hours)	£12

Special passes

Child:	Full year pass	£140
	Full year pass, direct debit	£13 per month
Adult:	Full year pass	£280
	Full year pass, direct debit	£25 per month

Ski lessons (including equipment hire)

Ski/board taster session (50 minutes)	
Adult:	£14
Child:	£8
Ski/board lessons (1 hour 45 minutes, range of levels offered)	
Adult:	£25.00
Child:	£17.50

A variety of full-day courses, ½ day courses, holiday courses etc. are offered in addition to the above. Instructors can also be hired for exclusive use by an individual or group. See www.ski-rossendale.co.uk for further information.

Ski/snowboard party (includes equipment hire and use of slope) 50 minute lesson with an Instructor, followed by a party meal in restaurant (minimum 6 in group)	£15.00 per person
Snow Tube party, with party meal	£10.00 per person

Competitors

At the moment, the main competitors are seen as Castleford, Sheffield and Halifax and the new facility next to the Trafford Centre in Manchester from November 2007.

Xscape Castleford (www.xscape.co.uk): This is the only real snow slope competitor currently, and therefore prices are much more expensive (e.g. 1 hour £21, 2 hours £31, lessons from £27 for 1 hour adult, and £23 per child). A wide range of facilities are available at the slope.

Sheffield Ski Village (www.sheffieldskivillage.co.uk): This is not seen as a main competitor, due to its distance, although facilities there are excellent, especially for skiing. A more complicated pricing structure exists here, although they offer a number of children's activities and 'piste & feast' events also.

Halifax (www.ridehalifax.co.uk): Closer than Sheffield, although the slope is smaller. It is more attractive to snowboarders, with a wide range of jumps (e.g. main 20ft kicker, side kicker, small learner jump, 10ft quarter pipe).

Manchester The Chill Factor e (www.chilfactore.com) opened in November 2007. It is next to the Trafford Centre, Manchester, and is a ski complex offering snowboarding, skiing, ice wall for climbers, tobogganing facilities, along with a rock-climbing wall and a children's play area. There are three ski slopes, the longest being 180 metres long. There is also an après-ski area with alpine-themed bars and restaurants. This is Britain's biggest indoor ski slope. Prices are £22 per adult and £18 for children at peak times for 1½ hours, and £17 adult/£14 children at off-peak times (although these prices do not cover hire of equipment, unlike Ski Rossendale).

Marketing communications

Ski Rossendale has recently out-sourced the production of a web site, which contains basic information concerning opening times, courses and costs, and allows for electronic queries to be raised.

Generally, little marketing communications is undertaken. A variety of leaflets is produced and these are available at the ski slope or at the other organisations within the trust. Some leaflets have been inserted into local newspapers, and some leaflet drops have been undertaken in some of the local areas, but this only happens very occasionally. Some local newspaper advertising has been undertaken, as well as limited PR through a small number of press releases. Representatives from Ski Rossendale also attend the annual Ski Show in Manchester, which takes place in October, and run ski lessons on the ski slope at the event. Some mutually beneficial marketing communications has been undertaken with Jaguar at Bolton and Blackburn, which involved Ski Rossendale banners and information being put up in its showrooms, while Jaguar brought demonstration cars to Ski Rossendale for a weekend. The first annual open day is being held this October where use of the facilities will be free for the day. The Marketing Manager feels that far more marketing communications could be undertaken. Innovative ideas are sought that will help to stretch the budget of £40,000 per annum. Although small, this is a substantial increase in the £10,000 available two years ago.

There is an opportunity to build relationships with existing customers, although at the moment, they do not have a full, useable database of these existing customers. Very few PR activities have been undertaken, and with such a small budget there is potential here to stretch this. Over the next year the key groups to target are: existing customers (retain them and increase their usage); better links and usage by schools; increase in use as a party destination (children and adults). In the longer term more users need to be attracted and usage for corporate events increased (although at the moment, they do not have the facilities to cater for this market).

MiniCase references

Mintel (2003) *Extreme Sports – UK* – November.
Mintel (2004) *Snow Sports – UK* – September.
Mintel (2005) *Extreme Sports – UK* – October.
Mintel (2006) *Snow Sports – UK* – September.

MiniCase questions

Your brief

The assignment is based on the Ski Rossendale case study. You are to take on the role of a marketing communications consultant to the Trust. Your task is to provide an analysis of the marketing communications problems and issues, set objectives and develop a new communications strategy for the club. This is to be implemented over the next 12 months.

Tasks

1. Analysis

You should provide a thorough, logically structured analysis of the facts as reported in the case, using other information to support your analysis. You will need to consider internal and external influences and use the figures, where appropriate, to provide evidence to support your analysis. This should include a summary of what you believe the key issues are that the Trust faces. These should be focused on areas that come under your remit as a consultant in marketing communications.

2. Objectives

These should be specific; they should relate to the 12-month period; you may include longer-term objectives. You should include some numerate objectives.

3. Marketing communications strategy

The final part of your report will provide strategic direction for the organisation. Define target segments. How should the organisation position itself? Which elements of the communications mix should be utilised and to what purpose? You should include a schedule of the methods and media to be used. You should also present an outline budget indicating the cost and allocation of budget to your communications proposals. Sources should be clearly quoted for all costs.

4. Evaluation of the marketing communications plan

Discuss how you would measure the effectiveness of the plan, and how this would be monitored and evaluated. Ensure you refer to appropriate theory in this area.

References

Andrews, K. (1987) *The Concept of Corporate Strategy*. Homewood, IL: Richard D. Irwin.

Anon. (2008) Guarding her patch. *The Marketer*, February, 27–9.

Ansoff, H.I. (1965) *Corporate Strategy*. New York: McGraw-Hill.

Beane, T.P. and D.M. Ennis (1987) Market segmentation: a review. *European Journal of Marketing*, **21**(5), 20–42.

Chaffee, E. (1985) 'Three models of strategy'. *Academy of Management Review*, **10**(1), 89–98.

Engel, J.F., Warshaw, M.R. and Kinnear, T.C. (1994) *Promotional Strategy*, 8th edn. Homewood, IL: Richard D. Irwin.

Gray, R. (2000) The chief encounter. *PR Week*, 8 September, 13–16.

Grunig, J. and Hunt, T. (1984) *Managing Public Relations*. New York: Holt, Rineholt & Winston.

Gustafson, R. (2007) Best of all worlds. *Marketing: Brands by Design*, 14 November, 11.

Haley, Russell I. (1968) Benefit segmentation: a decision-oriented research tool. *Journal of Marketing*, **32** (July), 30–5.

Hambrick, D.C. (1983) High profit strategies in mature capital goods industries: a contingency approach. *Academy of Management Journal*, **26**, 687–707.

Holm, O. (2006) Integrated marketing communication: from tactics to strategy, *Corporate Communications: An International Journal*, **11**(1), 23–33.

Jewell, R.D. (2007) Establishing effective repositioning communications in a competitive marketplace. *Journal of Marketing Communications*, **13**(4), 231–41.

Johnson, G., Scholes, K. and Whittingham, R. (2008) *Exploring Corporate Strategy*, 8th edn. Harlow: Pearson Education.

Kay, J. (1993) The structure of strategy. *Business Strategy Review*, **4**(2) (Summer), 17–37.

Lovallo, D.P. and Mendonca, L.T. (2007) Strategy's strategist: an interview with Richard Rumelt, *McKinsey Quarterly*, **4**. Retrieved 30 September 2007 from www.mckinseyquarterly.com/strategy/strategic-thinking/Strategys

Mintzberg, H. (1994) *The Rise and Fall of Strategic Planning*. Englewood Cliffs, NJ: Prentice-Hall.

Mintzberg, H. and Ghoshal, S. (2003) *Strategy Process: Concepts, Context and Cases*. Global edn. Englewood Cliffs, NJ: Financial Times/Prentice-Hall.

Moss, D. and Warnaby, G. (1998) Communications strategy? Strategy communication? Integrating different perspectives. *Journal of Marketing Communications*, **4**(3), 131–40.

van Riel, (1995) *Principles of Corporate Communication*, Harlow: Financial Times/Prentice-Hall.

Riiber Knudsen, T. (2007) Confronting proliferation . . . in beer: an interview with Carlsberg's Alex Myers, *McKinsey Quarterly*. Retrieved 28 July 2007 from www.mckinseyquarterly.com/marketing/confronting-proliferation

Rothschild, M. (1987) *Marketing Communications*. Lexington, MA: DC Heath.

Rowe, A.J., Mason, R.O., Dickel, K.E., Mann, R.B. and Mockler, R.J. (1994) *Strategic Management: A Methodological Approach*, 4th edn. Reading, MA: Addision-Wesley.

Steyn, B. (2003) From strategy to corporate communication strategy; a conceptualisation, *Journal of Communication Management*, **8**(2), 168–83.

Tiltman, D. (2007) Who is the ethical consumer? *Marketing*, 11 July, 28–30.

Weltevreden, J.W.J., Atzema, O.A.L.C. and Boschma R.A. (2005) The adoption of the Internet by retailers: a new typology of strategies. *Journal of Urban Technology* **12**(3), 59–87.

Weltevreden, J.W.J. and Boschma, R.A. (2008) Internet strategies and performance of Dutch retailers. *Journal of Retailing and Consumer Services*, **15**(3) (May), 163–78.

Whittington, R. (1993) *What is Strategy and Does it Matter?* London: Routledge.

Wind, Y.J. (1990) Positioning analysis and strategy. In *The Interface of Marketing and Strategy* (eds G. Day, B. Weitz and R. Wensley), 387–412 (Greenwich, CT: JAI Press).

Chapter 11

Marketing communications: objectives and positioning

The formal setting of marketing communication objectives is important because they provide guidance concerning what is to be achieved and when. These objectives form a pivotal role between the business/marketing plans and the marketing communications strategy. The way in which a product or service is perceived by buyers is the only positioning that really matters.

Aims and learning objectives

The aims of this chapter are to establish the nature and importance of the role that objectives play in the formulation of marketing communication strategies and to explore the concept of positioning.

The learning objectives of this chapter are to:

1. examine the need for organisational objectives;
2. specify the different types of organisational goals;
3. examine the relationship between corporate strategy and promotional objectives;
4. determine the components of SMART-determined promotional objectives;
5. examine the differences between sales- and communication-based objectives;
6. evaluate the concept of positioning;
7. understand the importance of perceptual mapping;
8. explain the main types of positioning strategies.

For an applied interpretation see Richard Godfrey's MiniCase entitled ***Unlocking the secrets of the male shopper*** at the end of this chapter.

Introduction

There are many different opinions about what it is that marketing communications seeks to achieve. The conflicting views have led some practitioners and academics to polarise their thoughts about what constitutes an appropriate set of objectives. First, much effort has been spent trying to determine what promotion and marketing communication activities are supposed to achieve; second, how should the success of a campaign be evaluated?; and finally, how is it best to determine the degree of investment that should be made in each of the areas of the promotional mix?

The most common marketing communications objectives set by managers are sales-related.

The process of resolving these different demands that are placed on organisations has made the setting of promotional objectives very complex and difficult. It has been termed 'a job of creating order out of chaos' (Kriegel, 1986). This perceived complexity has led a large number of managers to fail to set promotional objectives or to set the wrong ones. Many of those who do set them, do so in such a way that they are inappropriate, inadequate or merely restate the marketing objectives. The most common marketing communications objectives set by managers are sales-related. These include increases in market share, return on investment, sales volume increases and improvements in the value of sales made after accounting for the rate of inflation.

Such a general perspective ignores the influence of the other elements of the marketing mix and implicitly places the entire responsibility for sales performance with the promotional mix. This is not an accurate reflection of the way in which businesses and organisations work. In addition, because sales tests are too general, they would be an insufficiently rigorous test of promotional activity and there would be no real evaluation of promotional activities. Sales volumes vary for a wide variety of reasons:

1. competitors change their prices;
2. buyers' needs change;
3. changes in legislation may favour the strategies of particular organisations;
4. favourable third-party communications become known to significant buyers;
5. general economic conditions change;
6. technological advances facilitate improved production processes;
7. economies of scale, experience effects and, for some organisations, the opportunity to reduce costs;
8. the entry and exit of different competitors.

These are a few of the many reasons why sales might increase and conversely why sales might decrease. Therefore, the notion that marketing communications is entirely responsible for the sales of an offering is clearly unacceptable, unrealistic and incorrect.

The role of objectives in corporate strategy

Objectives play an important role in the activities of individuals, social groups and organisations because:

1. They provide direction and an action focus for all those participating in the activity.
2. They provide a means by which the variety of decisions relating to an activity can be made in a consistent way.
3. They set out the time period in which the activity is to be completed.
4. They communicate the values and scope of the activity to all participants.
5. They provide a means by which the success of the activity can be evaluated.

It is generally accepted that the process of developing corporate strategy demands that a series of objectives be set at different levels within an organisation (Johnson and Scholes (2006), and Quinn *et al.* 2003). This hierarchy of objectives consists of mission, strategic business unit (SBU) or business objectives and functional objectives, such as production, finance or marketing goals.

> The process of developing corporate strategy demands that a series of objectives be set at different levels within an organisation.

The first level in the hierarchy (mission) requires that an overall direction be set for the organisation. If strategic decisions are made to achieve corporate objectives, both objectives and strategy are themselves constrained by an organisation's mission. Thompson and Strickland (1990) claim that mission statements are a vision that management have of what the organisation is trying to achieve in the long term. A mission statement outlines who the organisation is, what it does and where it is headed. A clearly developed, articulated and communicated mission statement enables an organisation to define whose needs are to be satisfied, what needs require satisfying and which products and technologies will be used to provide the desired levels of satisfaction.

Conventionally, setting the mission answers the question 'What business are we in?' (Levitt, 1960). Obvious answers such as 'engineering', 'food processing', 'import and export' or 'retailing' miss the point. These are merely activities. Missions must be linked, explicitly, first and foremost to the needs met, rather than to markets or industries (Rosen, 1995). According to IBM, its original success was tied to its founder's principle of 'offering the best customer service in the world', not to technological innovation. The mission then, should clearly identify the following:

- the customers'/buyers' to be served;
- the needs to be satisfied;
- the products and/or technologies by which these will be achieved.

In some organisations these points are explicitly documented in a mission statement. These statements often include references to the organisation's philosophy, culture, commitment to the community and employees, growth, profitability and so on, but these should not blur or distract attention from the organisation's basic mission. The words mission and vision are often used interchangeably, but they have separate meanings. Vision refers to the expected or desired outcome of carrying out the mission over the agreed period of time.

The mission provides a framework for the organisation's objectives, and the objectives that follow should promote and be consistent with the mission. While the word 'mission' implies a singularity of purpose, organisations have multiple objectives because of the many aspects of the organisation's performance and behaviour that contribute to the mission, and should, therefore, be explicitly identified. However, as Rosen points out, many of these objectives will conflict with each other. In retailing, for example, if an organisation chooses to open larger stores, then total annual profit should rise, but average profit per square metre will probably fall. Short-term profitability can be improved by reducing investment, but this could adversely affect long-term profitability. Organisations therefore have long-term and short-term objectives.

> The mission provides a framework for the organisation's objectives.

At the SBU level, objectives represent the translation of the mission into a form that can be understood by relevant stakeholders. These objectives are the performance requirements for the organisation or unit, which in turn are broken down into objectives or targets that each functional area must achieve, as their contribution to the unit objectives. Marketing strategies are functional strategies, as are the strategies for the finance, human resource management and production departments. Combine or aggregate them and the SBUs overall target will, in reductionist theory, be achieved.

The various organisational objectives are of little use if they are not communicated to those who need to know what they are. Traditionally, such communication has focused on employees, but there is increasing recognition that the other members of the stakeholder network need to understand an organisation's purpose and objectives. The marketing objectives developed for the marketing strategy provide important information for the communications strategy. Is the objective to increase market share or to defend or maintain the current situation? Is the product new or established? Is it being modified or slowly withdrawn? The corporate image is shaped partly by the organisation's objectives and the manner in which they are communicated. All these impact on the objectives of the communications plan.

Promotional objectives consist of three main components. The first component concerns issues relating to the buyers of the product or service offered by the organisation. The second concerns issues relating to sales volume, market share, profitability and revenue. The third relates to the image, reputation and preferences that other stakeholders have towards the organisation. Each of these three streams is developed later in this chapter.

Promotional objectives consist of three main components.

The role of promotional objectives and plans

Many organisations, including some advertising agencies, fail to set realistic (if any) promotional objectives. There are several explanations for this behaviour, but one of the common factors is that managers are unable to differentiate between the value of promotion as an expenditure and as an investment. This issue is addressed later (Chapter 16), but for now the value of promotional objectives can be seen in terms of the role they play in communications planning, evaluation and brand development.

The setting of promotional objectives is important for three main reasons. The first is that they provide *a means of communication and coordination* between groups (e.g. client and agency) working on different parts of a campaign. Performance is improved if there is common understanding about the tasks the promotional tools have to accomplish. Second, objectives constrain the number of options available to an organisation. Promotional objectives act as *a guide for decision-making* and provide a focus for decisions that follow in the process of developing promotional plans. The third reason is that objectives provide *a benchmark* so that the relative success or failure of a programme can be evaluated.

Performance is improved if there is common understanding about the tasks the promotional tools have to accomplish.

There is no doubt that organisations need to be flexible to be able to anticipate and adjust to changes in their environments. This principle applies to the setting of promotional objectives. To set one all-encompassing objective and expect it to last the year (or whatever period is allocated) is both hopeful and naive; multiple objectives are necessary.

The content of promotional objectives has also been the subject of considerable debate. Two distinct schools of thought emerge: those that advocate sales-related measures as the main factors and those that advocate communication-related measures as the main orientation.

The sales school

As stated earlier, many managers see sales as the only meaningful objective for promotional plans. Their view is that the only reason an organisation spends money on promotion is to sell its product or service. Therefore, the only meaningful measure of the effectiveness of the promotional spend is in the sales results.

These results can be measured in a number of different ways. Sales turnover is the first and most obvious factor, particularly in business-to-business markets. In consumer markets and the fast-moving consumer goods sector, market share movement is measured regularly and is used as a more sensitive barometer of performance. Over the longer term, return on investment measures are used to calculate success and failure. In some sectors the number of products sold, or volume of product shifted, relative to other periods of activity, is a common measure. There are a number of difficulties with this view. One of these has been considered earlier, that *sales result from a variety of influences*, such as the other marketing mix elements, competitor actions and wider environmental effects, such as the strength of the currency, changing social preferences or the level of interest rates.

A second difficulty rests with the concept of *adstock or carryover*. The impact of promotional expenditure may not be immediately apparent, as the receiver may not enter the market until some later date, but the effects of the promotional programme may influence the eventual purchase decision. This means that, when measuring the effectiveness of a campaign, sales results will not always reflect its full impact.

When measuring the effectiveness of a campaign, sales results will not always reflect its full impact.

Sales objectives *do little to assist the media planner, copywriters and creative team* associated with the development of the communications programme, despite their inclusion in campaign documents such as media briefs.

Sales-oriented objectives are, however, applicable in particular situations. For example, where direct action is required by the receiver in response to exposure to a message, measurement of sales is justifiable. Such an action, a behavioural response, can be solicited in direct-response advertising. This occurs where the sole communication is through a particular medium, such as television or print.

The retail sector can also use sales measures, and it has been suggested that packaged goods organisations, operating in mature markets with established pricing and distribution structures, can build a databank from which it is possible to isolate the advertising effect through sales. For example, Sainsbury's was able to monitor the stock movements of particular ingredients used in its 'celebrity recipe' commercials. This enables it to evaluate the success of particular campaigns and particular celebrities. Its use of celebrity chef Jamie Oliver is so successful that it can stock ingredients in anticipation of particular advertisements being screened. However, despite this cause-and-effect relationship, it can be argued that this may ignore the impact of changes in competitor actions and changes in the overall environment. Furthermore, the effects of the organisation's own corporate advertising, adstock effects and other family brand promotions need to be accounted for if a meaningful sales effect is to be generated.

ViewPoint 11.1 Privileged sales objectives

RBS, previously the Royal Bank of Scotland, has three main brands in the car insurance market, Direct Line, Churchill and Privilege. The first two have been enormously successful while Privilege has had varying levels of success being targeted at, Londoners, the over 50s and performance car drivers. However, the market was relatively static in terms of the number of people taking out new car policies. New entrants are able to use the Internet at low cost and people are able to switch providers at little cost. Indeed, the car insurance market was becoming characterised by a salience factor (the one that stands out wins). RBS' business strategy was to create a portfolio of brands so when people were thinking about car insurance they had a better chance of picking up the business.

Two business/sales objectives were set:

- Grow sales of the Privilege brand by 100 per cent in two years.
- *Invest heavily in advertising to build the brand and sacrifice short-term profits to hit five-year income and profitability targets.*

(See Viewpoint 11.2.)

Source: Adapted from IPA, Anon. (2006).

Question

What other objectives could have been set?

Task

Make a short list of the key activities necessary to achieve these goals.

The sales school advocates the measure on the grounds of simplicity. Any manager can utilise the tool, and senior management does not wish to be concerned with information which is complex or unfamiliar, especially when working to short lead times and accounting periods. It is a self-consistent theory, but one that may misrepresent consumer behaviour and the purchase process (perhaps unintentionally), and to that extent may result in less than optimal expenditure on marketing communications.

The communications school

Promotional efforts are seen as communication tasks, such as the creation of awareness or positive attitudes towards the organisation or product.

There are many situations, however, where the aim of a communications campaign is to enhance the image or reputation of an organisation or product. Sales are not regarded as the only goal. Consequently, promotional efforts are seen as communication tasks, such as the creation of awareness or positive attitudes towards the organisation or product. To facilitate this process, receivers have to be given relevant information before the appropriate decision processes can develop and purchase activities established as a long-run behaviour.

Various models have been developed to assist our understanding about how these promotional tasks are segregated and organised effectively. AIDA and other hierarchy of effects models are considered in Chapter 8 at some length and need not be repeated here. However, one particular model was developed deliberately to introduce clear objectives into the advertising development process: Dagmar.

Dagmar

Russell Colley (1961) developed a model for setting advertising objectives and measuring the results. This model was entitled 'Defining Advertising Goals for Measured Advertising Results – Dagmar'. Colley's rationale for what is effectively a means of setting communications-oriented objectives was that advertising's job, purely and simply, is to communicate to a defined audience information and a frame of mind that stimulates action. Advertising succeeds or fails depending on how well it communicates the desired information and attitudes to the right people at the right time and at the right cost.

Colley proposed that the communications task be based on a hierarchical model of the communications process: awareness – comprehension – conviction – action.

Table 11.1 Hierarchy of communications

Stage	Explanation
Awareness	Awareness of the existence of a product or brand is necessary before any purchase will be made.
Comprehension	Audiences need information and knowledge about the product and its specific attributes. Often the audience needs to be educated and shown either how to use the product or how changes (in attributes) might affect their use of the product.
Conviction	By developing beliefs that a product is superior to others in a category or can confer particular rewards through use, audiences can be convinced to trial the product at the next purchase opportunity.
Action	Potential buyers need help and encouragement to transfer thoughts into behaviour. Providing call-free numbers, Web site addresses, reply cards, coupons and sales people helps people act upon their convictions.

Source: Based on Colley (1961).

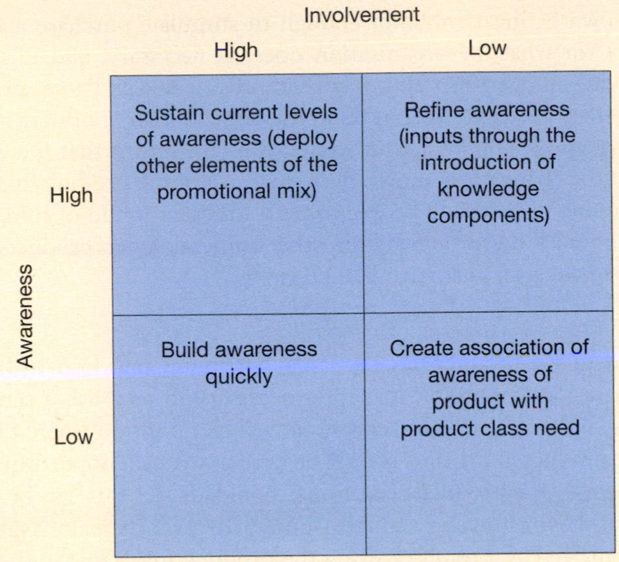

Figure 11.1 An awareness grid

Awareness

Awareness of the existence of a product or an organisation is necessary before purchase behaviour can be expected. Once awareness has been created in the target audience, it should not be neglected. If there is neglect, an audience may become distracted by competing messages and the level of awareness of the focus product or organisation may decline. Awareness, therefore, needs to be created, developed, refined or sustained, according to the characteristics of the market and the particular situation facing an organisation at any one point in time (see Figure 11.1).

Awareness of the existence of a product or an organisation is necessary before purchase behaviour can be expected.

In situations where the buyer experiences high involvement and is fully aware of a product's existence, attention and awareness levels need only be sustained, and efforts need to be applied to other communication tasks, which may be best left to the other elements of the communications mix. For example, sales promotion and personal selling are more effective at informing, persuading and provoking purchase of a new car once advertising has created the necessary levels of awareness.

Where low levels of awareness are found, getting attention needs to be a prime objective so that awareness can be developed in the target audience. Where low involvement exists, the decision-making process is relatively straightforward. With levels of risk minimised, buyers with sufficient levels of awareness may be prompted into purchase with little assistance of the other elements of the mix. Recognition and recall of brand names and corporate images are felt by some (Rossiter and Percy, 1987) to be sufficient triggers to stimulate a behavioural response. The requirement in this situation would be to refine and strengthen the level of awareness in order that it provokes interest and stimulates a higher level of involvement during recall or recognition.

Where low levels of awareness are matched by low involvement, the prime objective has to be to create awareness of the focus product in association with the product class. It is not surprising that organisations use awareness campaigns and invest a large amount of their resources in establishing their brand or corporate name. Many brands seek to establish 'top of mind awareness' as one of their primary objectives for their advertising spend.

Many brands seek to establish 'top of mind awareness' as one of their primary objectives.

Comprehension

Awareness on its own is, invariably, not enough to stimulate purchase activity. Knowledge about the product (or what the organisation does) is necessary, and this can be achieved by providing specific information about key brand attributes. These attributes and their associated benefits may be key to the buyers in the target audience or may be key because the product has been adapted or modified in some way. This means that the audience needs to be educated about the change and shown how their use of the product may be affected. For example, in attempting to persuade people to try a different brand of mineral water, it may be necessary to compare the product with other mineral water products and provide an additional usage benefit, such as environmental claims.

Conviction

Having established that a product has particular attributes that lead to benefits perceived by the target audience as important, it is then necessary to establish a sense of conviction. By creating interest and preference, buyers are moved to a position where they are convinced that one particular product in the class should be tried at the next opportunity. To do this, the audience's beliefs about the product need to be moulded, and this can be accomplished by using messages that demonstrate a product's superiority over its main rival or by emphasising the rewards conferred as a result of using the product, for example, the reward of social acceptance associated with many fragrance, fashion clothing and accessory advertisements, and the reward of self-gratification associated with many confectionery messages (Cadbury's Flake).

Low-involvement decisions rely on the strength of advertising messages, packaging and sales promotion to secure conviction.

High-involvement decisions are best supported with personal selling and sales promotion activities, in an attempt to gain conviction. Low-involvement decisions rely on the strength of advertising messages, packaging and sales promotion to secure conviction.

Action

A communications programme is used to encourage buyers to engage in purchase activity. Advertising can be directive and guide buyers into certain behavioural outcomes, for example, to the use of free phone numbers (0800 in the United Kingdom), direct mail activities and reply cards and coupons. However, for high-involvement decisions the most effective tool in the communications mix at this stage in the hierarchy is personal selling. Through the use of interpersonal skills, buyers are more likely to want to buy a product than if the personal prompting is absent. The use of direct marketing activities by Avon Cosmetics, Tupperware, Betterware and suppliers of life assurance and double-glazing services has been instrumental in the sales growth experienced by organisations in these markets.

Colley's dissatisfaction with the way in which advertising agencies operated led him to specify the components of a good advertising objective: 'A specific communications task to be accomplished among a defined audience to a given degree in a given period of time' (Dutka, 1995). An analysis of this statement shows that it is made up of four distinct elements:

- a need to specify the communications task;
- a need to define the audience;
- a need to state the required degree of change;
- a need to establish the time period in which the activity is to occur.

Colley's statement is very clear – it is measurable and of assistance to copywriters. Indeed, Dagmar revolutionised the approach taken by advertisers to the setting of objectives. It helped to move attention from the sales effect to the communication effect school and has led to improved planning processes, as a result partly of a better understanding of advertising and promotional goals.

Many of the difficulties associated with sequential models, as presented in Chapter 8, are also applicable to Dagmar. In addition to problems of hierarchical progression, measurement

ViewPoint 11.2 Privileged communication objectives

The ambitious sales objectives set out previously in Viewpoint 11.1 for the relaunch of Privilege, could only be achieved through effective communications. The product itself was not subject to any radical change although the web site and the sales team were retrained. The success of the relaunch depended on communications and this required setting appropriate communication objectives and achieving a strong positioning in the market (the strategic element).

The first main goal was to make people aware of the brand and the second was to invoke a behavioural response and drive people to the web site to be converted into a sale. The awareness goal would not be cheap as at least nine brands in the market had already invested in excess of £10m per annum. RBS invested £22m over 18 months and although they were not the biggest investors, their sales increased 226 per cent and they doubled their market share inside two years.

(See Viewpoint 11.1.)

Source: Anon. (2006).

Question

To what extent do you think the awareness goal was more important than the behavioural goal?

Task

Find out the messages used by Privilege to achieve this result.

and costs are issues concerning the sales orientation, restrictions upon creativity and short-term accountability.

Sales orientation

This criticism is levelled by those who see sales as the only valid measure of effectiveness. The sole purpose of communication activities, and advertising in particular, is to generate sales. So, as the completion of communications tasks may not result in purchases, the only measure that need be undertaken is that of sales. This point has been discussed earlier and need not be reproduced here.

Restrictions upon creativity

Dagmar is criticised on the grounds that creative flair can be lost as attention passes from looking for the big idea to concentration on the numbers game, of focusing on measures of recall, attitude change and awareness. It is agreed that the creative personnel are held to be more accountable under Dagmar and this may well inhibit some of their work. Perhaps the benefits of providing direction and purpose offset the negative aspects of a slight loss in creativity.

Short-term accountability

To the above should be added the time period during which management and associated agencies are required to account for their performance. With accounting periods being reduced to as little as 12 weeks, the communications approach is impractical for two reasons. The first is that the period is not long enough for all of the communication tasks to be progressed or completed. Sales measures present a much more readily digestible benchmark of performance.

The second concerns the unit of performance itself. With the drive to be efficient and to be able to account for every communication pound spent, managers themselves need to use measures that they can understand and that they can interpret from published data. Sales data and communications spend data are consistent measures and make no further demands on managers. Managers do not have enough time to spend analysing levels of comprehension or preference and to convert them into formats that are going to be of direct benefit to them and their organisations. Having said that, those organisations that are prepared to invest in a more advanced management information system will enable a more sophisticated view to be taken.

The approach adopted by the communication school is not universally accepted. Those who disagree, argue that it is too difficult and impractical to translate a sales objective into a series of specific communications objectives. Furthermore, what actually constitutes adequate levels of awareness and comprehension and how can it be determined which stage the majority of the target audience has reached at any one point in time? Details of measurement, therefore, throw a veil over the simplicity and precision of the approach taken by the communication orientation school.

The approach adopted by the communication school is not universally accepted.

From a practical perspective, it should be appreciated that most successful marketing organisations do not see the sales and communications schools as mutually exclusive. They incorporate both views and weight them according to the needs of the current task, their overall experience, the culture and style of the organisation and the agencies with whom they operate.

Derivation of promotional objectives

It has been established that specific promotional objectives need to be set up if a suitable foundation is to be laid for the many communication decisions that follow. Promotional objectives are derived from understanding the overall context in which the communications will operate. Comprehending the contexts of the buyer and the organisation allows the objectives of the planned communications to be identified: the *what* that is to be achieved. For example, objectives concerning the perception that different target customers have of a brand, the perception that members of a performance network have of the organisation's offerings, the reactions of key stakeholders to previous communications and the requirements of the current marketing plan all impact upon the objectives of the communication plan. Therefore, promotional objectives evolve principally from a systematic audit and analysis of the key communication contexts, and specifically from the marketing plan and stakeholder analysis.

Promotional objectives evolve principally from a systematic audit and analysis of the key communication contexts.

It was established earlier that there are three main streams of objectives. These are set out in Figure 11.2. The first concerns issues relating to the buyers of the product or service offered by the organisation. The second concerns issues relating to market share/sales volume,

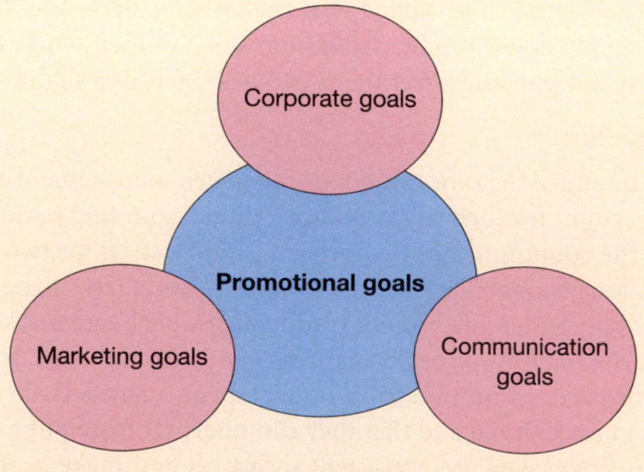

Figure 11.2 The three elements of promotional goal setting

profitability and revenue. The third stream relates to the image, reputation and preferences that other stakeholders have towards the organisation.

All these objectives are derived from an analysis of the current situation. The marketing communication brief that flows from this analysis should specify the sales-related objectives to be achieved, as these can be determined from the marketing plan. Sales-related objectives might concern issues such as market share and sales volume.

Customer-related objectives concern issues such as awareness, perception, attitude, feelings and intentions towards a brand or product. The exact issue to be addressed in the plan is calculated by analysing the contextual information driven by the audit.

Issues related to the perception of the organisation are often left unattended or, worse, ignored. Research may indicate that the perception of particular stakeholders, in either the performance or the support network, does not complement the current level of corporate performance or may be misplaced or confused. Objectives will need to be established to correct or reinforce the perception held of the organisation. The degree of urgency may be directly related to the level of confusion or misunderstanding or be related to competitive or strategic actions initiated by competitors and other members of the network. Corporate strategy may have changed and, as identified earlier, any new strategy will need to be communicated to all stakeholders.

Objectives will need to be established to correct or reinforce the perception held of the organisation.

The need for realism when setting promotional objectives

Hierarchy of effects models which specify stages of development were first proposed as far back as 1898 by E. St Elmo Lewis (Barry and Howard, 1990) and similar views were expressed by Colley (Dagmar) in 1961. Yet despite the passage of time since their publication, a large number of organisations still either fail to set any promotional objectives or confuse objectives with strategy. Organisations seeking to coordinate their communications need to recognise the necessity of setting multiple objectives at different times in the campaign period and of being prepared to adjust them in the light of environmental changes. These changes may be due to ever-decreasing product lifecycles or technological developments that may give a competitor comparative advantage, and perhaps legislative developments (or the timing of management's interpretation and implementation of certain legislation) may bring about a need to reconfigure the promotional mix.

Management's failure to set objectives is often the result of a lack of awareness of the current position, or a lack of understanding of how and why appropriate objectives need to be established. With increasingly competitive and turbulent environments, a greater number of organisations are turning their attention to ways in which they can communicate more effectively with their stakeholders. Furthermore, as more executives undertake management education programmes, so a higher level of skill is being transferred to organisations, and this in turn will bring a higher incidence of better practice.

The overall objective of any promotional programme is to increase the level of sales. While it seems unreasonable to expect the communication mix to bear total responsibility for this, it is also unreasonable and impractical to expect the communications approach to bear total responsibility. It is imperative that organisations are willing and prepared to set promotional objectives that utilise basic communications tasks, such as awareness and intentions, and that they utilise sales benchmarks as means of determining what has been achieved and how. Promotional objectives are a derivative of both marketing and corporate strategies. Just as revenue and income targets are part of marketing strategy, so they should form part of the

Promotional objectives are a derivative of both marketing and corporate strategies.

promotional objectives. They cannot be separated and they cannot be neglected. Figure 11.2 shows the different types of objectives that can be set for a promotional strategy.

The choice depends on the situation facing each manager and, in particular, whether the product or organisation is new. Establishing and maintaining levels of awareness is, however, paramount to any communications programme, and must be considered one of the primary communication objectives.

ViewPoint 11.3 Norwich Union flood maps

Early in 2004, Norwich Union launched its flood maps, a digital method of gauging the flood danger to individual properties. This new system sought to replace the previous postcode approach to risk evaluation that failed to discriminate potential flood risk properties from high rise flats.

The launch of the new product aimed to achieve two different objectives. The first was communication-related and geared to raising awareness of the maps to property owners, especially in high-risk parts of the country. The second was sales-related as Norwich Union wanted to sell more property insurance policies.

Source: Various, including **www.environment.agency.gov.uk.**

Question

Was awareness raising alone a sufficient goal?

Task

Find a flood map for area. If your home is in a flood risk area, what other information would you like to know?

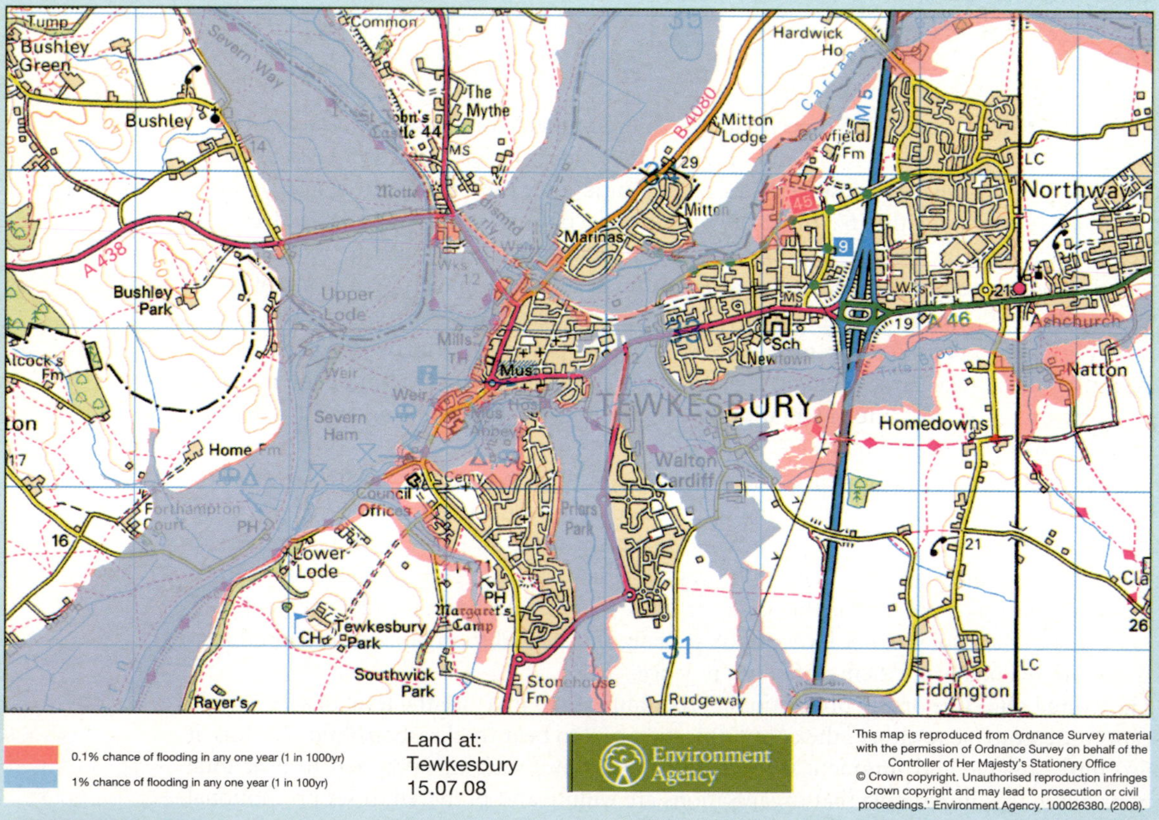

Exhibit 11.1 Flood map for the Tewkesbury area. Used functionally to inform people about potential flooding problems and to assist the selling of property insurance.

Promotional objectives need to be set that reflect the communication and sales tasks that the product or organisation needs to accomplish. It should be appreciated that promotional objectives are vitally important, as they provide the basis for a string of decisions that are to be taken at subsequent stages in the development of the communication plan.

Management's next task is to make decisions regarding which of these different promotional objectives will receive attention first. In order that decisions can be made regarding promotional strategy, the communications mix and the level of resources allocated to each promotional tool, it is necessary to rank and weight the objectives at this stage in the management process. The criteria used to weight the different objectives will inevitably be subjective, because they reflect each manager's perception, experience and interpretation of their environment. However, it is also their skill and judgement that are the important elements, and as long as the criteria are used and applied in a consistent manner the outcome of the communication plan is more likely to be successful.

SMART objectives

To assist managers in their need to develop suitable objectives, a set of guidelines has been developed, commonly referred to as SMART objectives. This acronym stands for specific, measurable, achievable, relevant, targeted and timed.

The process of making objectives SMART requires management to consider exactly what is to be achieved, when, where and with which audience. This clarifies thinking, sorts out the logic of the proposed activities and provides a clear measure for evaluation at the end of the campaign:

> The process of making objectives SMART requires management to consider exactly what is to be achieved, when, where and with which audience.

- *Specific*
  What is the actual variable that is to be influenced in the campaign? Is it awareness, perception, attitudes or some other element that is to be influenced? Whatever the variable, it must be clearly defined and must enable precise outcomes to be determined.
- *Measurable*
  Set a measure of activity against which performance can be assessed. For example, this may be a percentage level of desired prompted awareness in the target audience.
- *Achievable*
  Objectives need to be attainable, otherwise those responsible for their achievement will lack motivation and a desire to succeed.
- *Realistic*
  The actions must be founded in reality and be relevant to the brand and the context in which they are set.
- *Targeted and timed*
  Which target audience is the campaign targeted at, how precisely is the audience defined and over what period are the results to be generated?

Having determined what levels of awareness, comprehension or preference are necessary or how attitudes need to be developed, the establishment or positioning of these objectives as a task for the organisation to accomplish should be seen as a primary communication objective. The attitude held or what individuals in the target market perceive, comprehend or prefer is a focus for campaign activity and subsequent evaluation.

An introduction to positioning

The final act in the target marketing process of segmentation and targeting is positioning. Following on from the identification of potential markets, determining the size and potential of market segments and selecting specific target markets, positioning is the process whereby information about the organisation or product is communicated in such a way that the object is perceived by the consumer/stakeholder to be differentiated from the competition, to occupy a particular space in the market. According to Kotler (2003), 'Positioning is the act of designing the company's offering and image so that they occupy a meaningful and distinct competitive position in the target customers' minds.'

Positioning is not about the product but what the buyer thinks about the product or organisation.

This is an important aspect of the positioning concept. Positioning is not about the product but what the buyer thinks about the product or organisation. It is not the physical nature of the product that is important for positioning, but how the product is perceived that matters. This is why part of the context analysis (Chapter 10), requires a consideration of perception and attitudes and the way stakeholders see and regard brands and organisations. Of course, this may not be the same as the way brand managers intend their brands to be seen or how they believe the brand is perceived.

ViewPoint 11.4 Now, please adjust your clothing

Asda has used the George brand of clothing for several years but after a period of relatively slow growth decided that the market it was currently serving did not offer the long-term growth it was seeking. At the time it competed against Primark and TK Maxx in what is referred to as the discount market. A new strategy was developed to enable it to compete against M&S and Next among others in the mid market sector. This required that the George brand be repositioned. This was necessary in order that the target market perceived and understood what the George brand presents and what the brand promise is.

In order to reposition the brand successfully, changes are necessary in order that the range of clothes offered match the needs of the target market, in terms of style, quality and price. So, as a first step Asda had to adjust the brand architecture (see Chapter 12). The George brand itself, positioned for the 25- to 45-year-old market, and G21, positioned for consumers aged 25 and under, remained. However, Asda replaced the Collections, Fast Fashion and the Must Haves sub-brands, aimed at fashion-conscious young shoppers. In their place they introduced two new sub-brands: Boston Crew for men, which was already in the Asda portfolio, and Moda aimed at women. Both of these labels are positioned to attract the over-45s.

Thus, once the right brand structure is in place the brands can be communicated. At the time of writing Asda used Coleen McLoughlin as the face of the brand but this celebrity may not fit the mid-market position Asda are aiming for, and to compete with Twiggy, who fronts the M&S brand, someone who appeals to the new segment may be required. In order to compete against its new competitors Asda will need (with their agencies) to detemine a message strategy that will add value to the George brand and thereby motivate shoppers to try the brand because they percieve that it offers them something better than its immediate competitors.

Source: Bokaie (2008).

Question

Why is it necessary to organise the brand architecture when positioning a brand?

Task

Who would you chose to front the new Asda brand and help its repositioning?

This audience orientation is emphasised by Blankstson and Kalafatis (2007). They considered the positioning strategies of several leading credit card providers from three perspectives. These were the banks' executives, the positioning strategies that were implemented, and finally but most importantly, the perception of the target audiences of the positioning strategies. In the words of the researchers; presumed practice, actual practice and perceived practice. One of the outcomes of their work was the need to manage the potential gulf that may occur when the presumed and actual positioning strategies drift away from the way audiences actually perceive the brand.

In the consumer market, established brands from washing powders (Ariel, Daz, Persil) and hair shampoos (such as Wash & Go, Timotei), to cars (for example, Peugeot, Saab, Nissan) and grocery multiples (Sainsbury's, Tesco) each carrys communications that enable receivers to position them in their respective markets.

The positioning concept is not the sole preserve of branded or consumer-oriented offerings or indeed those of the business-to-business market. Organisations are also positioned relative to one another, mainly as a consequence of their corporate identities, whether they are deliberately managed or not. The position an organisation takes in the mind of consumers may be the only means of differentiating one product from another. King (1991) argues that, given the advancement in technology and the high level of physical and functional similarity of products in the same class, consumers' choices will be more focused on their assessment of the company they are dealing with. Therefore, it is important to position organisations as brands in the minds of actual and potential customers.

The position an organisation takes in the mind of consumers may be the only means of differentiating one product from another.

One of the crucial differences between the product and the corporate brand is that the corporate brand needs to be communicated to a large array of stakeholders, whereas the product-based brand requires a focus on a smaller range of stakeholders, in particular, the consumers and buyers in the performance network.

Whatever the position chosen, either deliberately or accidentally, it is the means by which customers understand the brand's market position, and it often provides signals to determine a brand's main competitors, or (as is often the case) customers fail to understand the brand or are confused about what the brand stands for.

The development of the positioning concept

This perspective was originally proposed by Ries and Trout (1972). They claimed that it is not what you do to a product that matters; it is what you do to the mind of the prospect that is important. They set out three stages of development: the product era, the image era and the positioning era.

The product era occurred in the late 1950s and early 1960s and existed when each product was promoted in an environment where there was little competition. Each product was accepted as an innovation and was readily accepted and adopted as a natural development. In the pharmaceutical market, drugs such as Navidex, Valium and Lasix became established partly because of the lack of competition and partly because of the ability of the product to fulfil its claims. This was a period when the features and benefits of products were used in communications – the unique selling proposition was of paramount importance.

The image era that followed was spawned by companies with established images, which introduced new me-too products against the original brands. It was the strength of the perceived company image that underpinned the communications surrounding these new brands that was so important to their success. Products such as Amoxil, Tagamet and Tenormin were launched on an image platform.

The positioning era has developed mainly because of the increasingly competitive market conditions, where there is now little compositional, material or even structural difference between products within each class. Consequently, most products are now perceived relative to each other. In most markets the level and intensity of 'noise' drives organisations to establish themselves and their offerings in particular parts of the overall market. It is now the ability of an offering to command the attention of buyers and to communicate information about how an offering is differentiated from the other competitive offerings that helps to signal the relative position the offering occupies in the market.

The positioning concept

From the research data and the marketing strategy, it is necessary to formulate a positioning statement that is in tune with the promotional objectives.

Clear, consistent positioning is an important aspect of integrated marketing communication.

One of the roles of marketing communications is to convey information so that the target audience can understand what a brand stands for and differentiate it from other competing brands. Clear, consistent positioning is an important aspect of integrated marketing communication. So the way in which a brand is presented to its audience influences the way it is going to be perceived. Therefore, accepting that there are extraneous reasons why the perception of a brand might not be the same as that intended, it seems important that managers approach the positioning task in an attentive and considered manner. Coke Zero was originally positioned as a male-oriented brand, whereas Diet Coke targeted women. 'Girls Aloud' singer Cheryl Tweedy was used to front the launch of Coke Zero while footballer Wayne Rooney acted as brand ambassador. Unsurprisingly Coke Zero quickly became dubbed Bloke Coke. However, this was changed in 2008 and the brand was repositioned on its benefits (Bokaie, 2007).

Generally there are two main ways in which a brand can be positioned, these are functional and expressive (or symbolic) positioning. Functionally positioned brands stress the features and benefits, and expressive brands emphasise the ego, social and hedonic satisfactions that a brand can bring. Both approaches make a promise, a promise to deliver a whiter, cleaner and brighter soap powder (functional) or clothes that we are confident to hang on the washing line (for all to see), dress our children in and send to school and not feel guilty, or dress ourselves in and complete a major business deal (symbolic).

Functionally positioned brands stress the features and benefits, expressive brands emphasise the ego, social and hedonic satisfactions.

ViewPoint 11.5 Functional positioning: stuck, not nailed

Marketing communications in the consumer and trade adhesives market places heavy reliance on demonstrating the performance of the individual brands. Solvite, for example, presents a man glued to a board and suspended in dangerous situations (above sharks, towed into the sky and at a theme park on a 'vertical drop ride'). Another brand, 'No More Nails', uses a similar functional approach. One execution shows a man sitting on a chair that has been glued half-way up a wall inside a house (see Exhibit 11.2).

Adhesives provoke low-involvement decision-making and there is generally little consumer interest in the properties of each brand. The essential information that consumers require is that the brand has strong performance characteristics. This sets up umbrella brand credibility so that sub-brands for different types of glue are perceived to have the same properties as the umbrella brand and that will do the 'job'.

Advertising should use drama in order to attract attention and to build up a store of images that enable people to recall a brand of adhesives that actually do stick.

Exhibit 11.2 A still from a TV ad promoting the strength of the adhesive 'No More Nails'

Question

Is it important to stress one key attribute or should several be presented in a brand's communications?

Task

Find a competitor brand to 'Solvite' and 'No More Nails'. How do they position themselves?

ViewPoint 11.6 Expressive positioning: croaked

Anheuser-Busch is one of the three top brewers in the United States and all of them were experiencing declining sales. One of the reasons for this decline was that consumers in the 21–27-year age rage preferred more specialist beers produced by smaller breweries.

Anheuser-Busch was a traditional brewer and sought to reverse the decline using its flagship brand, Budweiser. Its agency, with whom it had worked for 79 years, D'Arcy, Masius, Benton, & Bowles, had used campaigns featuring scantily dressed women and blue-collar workers. While the formula had limited success and was used by all three competitors, the approach had drawn complaints from different stakeholders. Anheuser-Busch wanted a big change and started by firing the agency.

In order to re-establish itself with core consumers the new agency, DDB Needham develop an idea based on hawking frogs. The Budweiser 'Frogs' campaign was introduced at the 1995 Super Bowl with the amphibians on lily pads. They croaked to each other, at first it was indistinguishable but then three words emerged . . . Bud . . . Weis . . . Er. A neon Budweiser sign reinforced the brand name but this constituted the entire message. Subsequent campaigns based on the amphibian theme were introduced including a lady frog and eventually lizards.

The campaign was an instant success as the ads provided entertainment especially as they were laced with irony. The sexist labels attached to its previous campaigns stopped and the buzz and publicity surrounding the Frogs was enormous. Far from functional this campaign demonstrated how beer could be communicated expressively, and in doing so reverse the sales decline. The Frogs campaign was eventually withdrawn. Some believe this was partly because school children began to believe there was an association between frogs and beer.

Sources: Lane (2007), www.galegroup.com.

Question

Is expressive positioning always going to offend or threaten a group?

Task

Find an expressive positioning campaign of your choice. What do you like about it and does it work?

Managing positions

The development and establishment of a position is a core strategic marketing communications activity. Positioning is one of two dynamics considered within communications strategy, considered previously in Chapter 10. The first dynamic is concerned with who, in broad terms, is the target audience? End-user customers need to derive particular benefits based on perceived value, from the exchange process. These benefits are very different from those that intermediaries expect to derive, or indeed any other stakeholder who does not consume the product or service. The second dynamic concerns the way in which an audience understands the offering they are experiencing either through use or through communications. The way in which people interpret messages and frame objects in their mind is concerned with positioning. Therefore, positioning is an integral part of marketing communications strategy.

In order that suitable positions be set, managers wishing to develop a position can be guided by the following process:

1. Determine the positions held by competitors? This will almost certainly require research to determine attitudes and perceptions and possibly the key attributes that consumers perceive as important. Use perceptual mapping.
2. From the above, will it be possible to determine which position, if any, is already held by the focus brand.
3. From the information gathered so far, will it be possible to determine a positioning strategy, that is, what is the desired position for the brand?
4. Is the strategy feasible in view of the competitors and any budgetary constraints? A long-term perspective is required, as the selected position has to be sustained.
5. Implement a programme to establish the desired position.
6. Monitor the perception held by consumers of the brand, and of their changing tastes and requirements, on a regular basis.

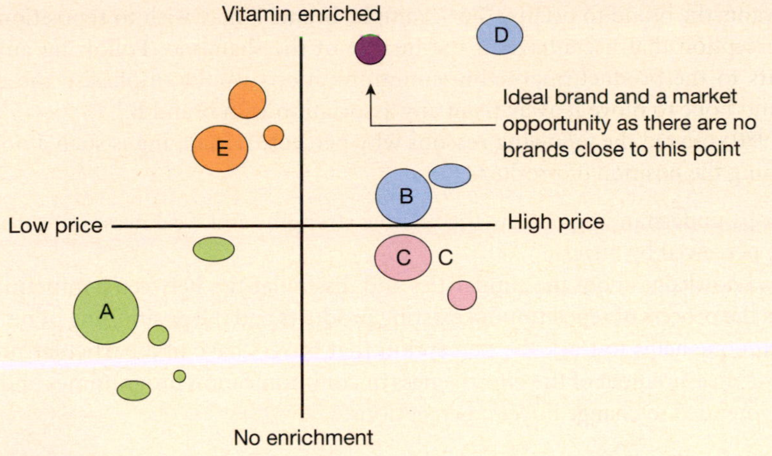

Figure 11.3 A perceptual map for a shampoo market

Perceptual mapping

In order to determine how the various offerings are perceived in a market, the key attributes that stakeholders use to perceive products in the market need to be established. A great deal of this work will have been completed as part of the research and review process prior to developing a communications plan. The next task is to determine perceptions and preferences in respect of the key attributes as perceived by buyers.

The objective of the exercise is to produce a perceptual map (brand and multidimensional maps) where the dimensions used on the two axes are the key attributes, as seen by buyers. This map represents a geometric comparison of how competing products are perceived (Sinclair and Stalling, 1990). Figure 11.3 shows that the key dimensions for consumers in the shampoo market could be price and enrichment. Each product is positioned on the map according to the perception that buyers have of the strength of each attribute of each product. By plotting the perceived positions of each brand on the map, an overall perspective of the market can be developed.

Each product is positioned on the map according to the perception that buyers have of the strength of each attribute.

The closer products are clustered together, the greater the competition. The further apart the positions, the greater the opportunity to enter the market, as competition is less intense. From the map, it can be seen that brand A dominates the bottom left-hand sector where a low price and little enrichment have attracted a number of buyers and competitive brands. Brands B and C are in direct competition, positioned closely together on a fairly high price yet medium level of enrichment. Brand D is isolated and may need to be repositioned as it may start losing share to a competitor, especially if the ideal position is occupied by B or any of the brands clustered around brand E.

Substitute products are often uncovered by their closeness to each other (Day *et al.*, 1979). It is also possible to ask buyers and other stakeholders what an ideal brand would consist of. This perfect brand can then be positioned on the map, and the closer an offering is to the ideal point, the greater its market share should be, as it is preferred over its rivals. These maps are known as preference maps.

By superimposing the position of an ideal brand on the map, it is possible to extend the usefulness of the tool. Perceptions of what constitutes the right amount of each key attribute can assist management in the positioning exercise. Marketing communications can, therefore, be designed to convey the required information about each attribute and so adjust buyers' perceptions so that they are closer to the ideal position, or to the position on the map that management wants the brand to occupy. For example, brand C may wish to reposition by changing the perception that users have of the quality of the shampoo. Following any necessary adjustments to the product, marketing communications would emphasise the enrichment attribute and hope to move it away from any association with brand B.

Neal (1980) offered the following reasons why perceptual mapping is such a powerful tool for examining the position of products:

1. It develops understanding of how the relative strengths and weaknesses of different products are perceived by buyers.
2. It builds knowledge about the similarities and dissimilarities between competing products.
3. It assists the process of repositioning existing products and the positioning of new products.
4. The technique helps to track the perception that buyers have of a particular product, and assists the measurement of the effectiveness of communication programmes and marketing actions intended to change buyers' perceptions.

Promotional strategy enables brand managers to identify gaps and opportunities in the market and allows organisations to monitor the effects of past marketing communications.

Perceptual mapping is an important tool in the development and tracking of promotional strategy. It enables brand managers to identify gaps and opportunities in the market and allows organisations to monitor the effects of past marketing communications. For example, in the early 1980s, none of the available brands in the newly emerging lager market was seen as refreshing. All brands were perceived as virtually the same. Heineken saw the opportunity and seized the position for refreshment, and has been able to occupy and sustain the position ever since.

Positioning strategies

The development of positions that buyers can relate to and understand is an important and vital part of the marketing communications plan. In essence, the position adopted is a statement about what the brand is, what it stands for and the values and beliefs that customers (hopefully) will come to associate with the particular brand. The visual images or the position statement represented in the strapline may be a significant trigger that buyers use to recall images and associations of the brand.

There are a number of overall approaches to developing a position. These can be based on factors such as the market, the customer or redefining the appeal of the brand itself (see Table 11.2).

To implement these three broad approaches, various strategies have been developed. The list that follows is not intended to be comprehensive or to convey the opinion that these strategies are discrete. They are presented here as means of conveying the strategic style, but in reality a number of hybrid strategies are often used.

Product features

This is one of the easier concepts and one that is more commonly adopted. The brand is set apart from the competition on the basis of the attributes, features or benefits that the brand has relative to the competition. For example, Volvos are safe; Weetabix contains all the vitamins needed each day; and the Royal Bank of Scotland promotes its credit card by extolling the benefits of its interest rate compared with those of its competitors.

Price/quality

This strategy is more effectively managed than others because price itself can be a strong communicator of quality. A high price denotes high quality, just as a low price can deceive buyers

Table 11.2 Positioning approaches

Approach	Type of application
Market-related	*First into a market* Heineken was first to take the refreshment position *Redefine the market* Carlsberg claims to be 'Probably the best beer in the world' British Airways as 'The way to fly' Miller Lite said the *lite* meant not heavy; not low alcohol *Importance/leadership claim* H. Samuel claims to be 'The nation's favourite jeweller'
Customer-related	*A unique buying reason* Ronseal, because 'It does exactly what it says on the tin' *Particular type of buyer* Glenfiddich: 'Independently minded. Independently made'
Appeal-related	*Distinct personality* Pepperami became a crazy/mad 'bit of an animal' *Decision criteria* Virgin Upper Class was presented as a sensible, rational business decision, not a whim or a risk *Imaginative or interesting* Castrol made oil into liquid engineering Dyson, because it uses cyclone technology

into thinking a product to be of low quality and poor value. Retail outlets such as Harrods and Aspreys use high prices to signal high quality and exclusivity. At the other end of the retail spectrum, Matalan, BHS and Woolworth's position themselves to attract those with less disposable income and to whom convenience is of greater importance. The price/quality appeal used to be best observed in Sainsbury's, 'where good food costs less' before it was changed and with the alcoholic lager Stella Artois, which was positioned as 'refreshingly expensive'.

Exhibit 11.3 shows a series of print ads which depict the various stages involved in pouring the perfect glass of Stella Artois. The art of pouring, presenting and serving Stella Artois in the right way, enables the colour, aroma and flavour of each beer to be fully appreciated, in much the same way as the French appreciate their wine. These ads are intended to enhance the perception of the overall drinking experience and to help position the brand as a premium quality beer. One of the outcomes of this positioning has been the development of various 'pouring competitions', not only in Belgium where the brand is brewed, but also as far away as New Zealand.

Use

By informing markets of when or how a product can be used, a position can be created in the minds of the buyers. For example, Kellogg's, the breakfast cereal manufacturer, has repositioned itself as a snack food provider. Its marketing strategy of moving into new markets was founded on its over dependence on breakfast consumption. By becoming associated with snacks, not only is usage increased, but the opportunity to develop new products becomes feasible. The launch of Pop Tarts is a testimony to this strategy. Milky Way, 'the sweet you can eat between meals', informs just when it is permissible to eat chocolate and After Eight chocolate mints clearly indicate when they should be eaten. The hair shampoo Wash & Go positions the brand as a quick and easy to use (convenience) product, for those whose lifestyles are full and demanding.

I
The Purification
The perfect beer deserves a spotless glass. Which is precisely why we like barmen to thoroughly rinse and clean your Stella Artois chalice prior to serving. Doing so prevents the head of foam from disappearing too quickly, leaving the beer unprotected. It's also just one of nine meticulous steps involved in a ritual we like barmen to follow when pouring our beer. Regrettably, you won't find this attention to detail everywhere. But you'll always find it at our Stella Artois Gold Standard Establishments. Handpicked from a selection of thousands of bars and restaurants, each of these venues serves Stella Artois exactly as it's meant to be: perfectly. Learn more at StellaArtois.com.
II
The Sacrifice
III
The Liquid Alchemy Begins
The chalice glass is held at a 45 degree angle. When the beer hits the chalice and begins to circulate, it creates the ideal proportion of foam relative to liquid.
IV
The Head
ALTHOUGH "CROWN" WOULD BE MORE APPROPRIATE.
The natural creation of the foam head occurs by straightening and lowering the glass. This initial foam is important as it prevents the beer from coming into contact with the air and losing any flavour.
V
The Removal
Your bartender then closes the tap in one quick action and moves the glass away from the font to prevent any drops from falling into the glass. These drops come into contact with the air, and oxidise, making them unworthy of your glass of Stella Artois.
VI
The Beheading
Pouring a Stella Artois takes patience and a little skill with a knife. In other words, as the frothy head foams over the edge of the chalice, your barman should gently cut it off. Doing so prevents the beer from going flat too quickly. It's also just one of nine steps involved in an age-old ritual we like barmen to observe when pouring it. Regrettably, you won't find this attention to detail everywhere. But you'll always find it at our Stella Artois Gold Standard Establishments. Handpicked from a selection of thousands of bars and restaurants, each of these venues ensures that your Stella Artois tastes exactly as it should: perfect. Learn more at StellaArtois.com.
VII
The Judgment
Perfection is in the details. Specifically, it's in just the right amount of foam. Three centimeters. No more. No less. This head creates a protective "cap" that keeps your Stella Artois from going stale. It's also just one of nine steps involved in a meticulous ritual we like barmen to follow when pouring our beer. Regrettably, you won't find this attention to detail everywhere. But you'll always find it at our Stella Artois Gold Standard Establishments. Handpicked from a selection of thousands of bars and restaurants, each of these venues serves Stella Artois exactly as it's meant to be: perfectly. Learn more at StellaArtois.com.
VIII
The Cleansing
Your bartender then rinses the bottom and sides of the glass.
This step keeps the outside of the chalice clean and comfortable to hold.
IX
The Bestowal
Finally, your Stella Artois is served to you on a coaster, accompanied by the drip catcher at the base.
Behold the perfect glass of Stella Artois. Cheers to you, and for your patience, a refreshing reward.

Exhibit 11.3 Stella Artois – Pouring rituals
With kind permission of InBev and Lowe Worldwide.

Product class dissociation

Some markets are essentially uninteresting, and most other positions have been adopted by competitors. A strategy used by margarine manufacturers is to disassociate themselves from other margarines and associate themselves with what was commonly regarded as a superior product, butter. The moisturising bar Dove is positioned as 'not a soap'. The UK-based bank, NatWest, position themselves with the strapline, 'Another way', which suggests that their

Promotional offer for 5-Year Young Persons Railcard runs from 12 June until 31 October 2006 and is available to first year students entering higher education for the first time who will be aged 16 or over at the time of issue and 26 or under at the expiry of the Railcard. £100 is the value based on purchasing the Railcard from a train company each year for 5 years at a cost of £20 per year. Your Railcard will be re-issued each year provided your account has been used during the previous 3 month period. Railcard is only available when a Student account is opened. See In-branch leaflet for full details. Textphone users call 0800 917 0789.
Student banking
another way
FREE
5-Year Young Persons Railcard
worth £100
At last, freebies worth having
NatWest
Young Persons Railcard
VALID UNTIL
25 SEP 2011
NAME
MR A. MAWSON
NWB 000001
TO BE CARRIED ON ALL RAIL JOURNEYS
Apply online and get a FREE MSN Webcam
Windows Live Messenger
NatWest
Apply online at natwest.com/students
or visit your local branch today

Exhibit 11.4 Nat West – Another Way
Reproduced with permission of National Westminster Bank Plc © 2006.

The position sets out to promise customers that they are different from other banks.

approach is different from their competitors. The foundation for their claim is based on their prominent use of local branches and use of UK-based call centres. This is to counteract the threat of Internet banking and the perception of poor quality that many international call-centres receive. The position therefore sets out to promise customers that they are different from other banks and offer better services and customer care.

User

A sensible extension of the target marketing process is to position openly so that target users can be clearly identified. Flora margarine was for men, and then it became 'for all the family'. American Express uses several leading celebrities, including Sir Terence Conran, Beyonce, and Jose Mouriniho, to suggest that users can have a lifestyle profile that complements those who use and endorse the Amex card. Some hotels position themselves as places for weekend breaks, as leisure centres or as conference centres. The cookware brand Le Creuset repositioned itself to appeal to a younger customer segment.

Exhibit 11.5 Jose Mourinho endorsing American Express
Image courtesy of The Advertising Archives.

Competitor

For a long time, positioning oneself against a main competitor was regarded as dangerous and was avoided. Avis, however, performed very successfully 'trying even harder' against Hertz, the industry number one. Saab contested the 'safest car' position with Volvo and Qualcast took on its new rival, the hover mower, by informing everyone that 'it is a lot less bovver than a hover', because its product collected the grass cuttings and produced the manicured lawn finish that roller-less mowers cannot reproduce.

Benefit

Positions can also be established by proclaiming the benefits that usage confers on those who consume. Sensodyne toothpaste appeals to all those who suffer from sensitive teeth, and a vast number of pain relief formulations claim to smooth away headaches or relieve aching limbs, sore throats or some offending part of the anatomy. Daewoo entered the UK market offering car buyers convenience by removing dealerships and the inherent difficulties associated with buying and maintaining cars.

Heritage or cultural symbol

An appeal to cultural heritage and tradition, symbolised by age, particular heraldic devices or visual cues, has been used by many organisations to convey quality, experience and knowledge. Kronenbourg 1664, 'Established since 1803', and the use of coats of arms by many universities to represent depth of experience and a sense of permanence are just some of the historical themes used to position organisations.

Whatever the position adopted by a brand or organisation, both the marketing and communication mixes must endorse and support the position so that there is consistency throughout all communications. For example, if a high-quality position is taken, such as that of the Ritz Carlton Hotel Group, then the product quality must be relatively high compared with competitors, the price must be correspondingly excessive and distribution synonymous with quality and exclusivity. Sales promotion activity will be minimal in order not to convey a touch of inexpensiveness, and advertising messages should be visually affluent and rich in tone and copy, with public relations and personal selling approaches transmitting high-quality, complementary cues.

> Both the marketing and communication mixes must endorse and support the position.

The dimensions used to position brands must be relevant and important to the target audience and in the image cues used must be believable and consistently credible. Positioning strategies should be developed over the long term if they are to prove effective, although minor adaptions to the position can be carried out in order to reflect changing environmental conditions.

> The dimensions used to position brands must be relevant and important to the target audience.

Repositioning

Technology is developing quickly, consumer tastes evolve and new offerings and substitute products enter the market. This dynamic perspective of markets means that the relative positions occupied by offerings in the minds of consumers will be challenged and shifted on a frequent basis. If the position adopted by an offering is strong, if it was the first to claim the position and the position is being continually reinforced with clear simple messages, then there may be little need to alter the position originally adopted.

However, there are occasions when offerings need to be repositioned in the minds of consumers/stakeholders. This may be due to market opportunities and development, mergers and acquisitions or changing buyer preferences, which may be manifested in declining sales. Research may reveal that the current position is either inappropriate or superseded by a competitor, or that attitudes have changed or preferences surpassed; whatever the reason, repositioning is required if past success is to be maintained. However, repositioning is difficult to accomplish, often because of the entrenched perceptions and attitudes held by buyers towards brands and the vast (media) resources required to make the changes.

ViewPoint 11.7 It's not golf, it's a community

The World Golf Village is a residential and retail resort development in Florida. As the name suggests it is built on and around a golf course complex. Indeed, it was created by the 'PGA Tour' to be a base for the World Golf Hall of Fame.

Unfortunately, the project failed to get going and soon investors and prospects began to reduce their commitment, negative comments emerged in the press and soon a perception of the village as a ghost town were heard among stakeholders.

The real problem was that the original scheme had been overly ambitious with regard to purchase rates and village attendance. The complex was positioned as a golf only male-oriented domain. The quality of the homes themselves were not in doubt but negative perceptions and images of the community did not entice people to want to buy into the village ambiance. Even the brokers and press perpetuatod this negative perception.

To rescue the project a repositioning strategy for the village was developed. However, instead of targeting male golfers the campaign was targeted at women, known to be the decision-makers when selecting communities. The focus was on promoting a premium, yet well-rounded community of people of all ages, including families, not just empty nesters. The village was presented as fashionable, stylish and aspirational. Rather than push the functionality of golf, an emotional personality position was adopted.

Since the repositioning strategy was implemented sales grew for the next two years. The number of people enquiring (traffic) about the community grew by 11 per cent, while all other indices became positive and attitudes to the community and its facilities improved enormously.

Source: New York American Marketing Association Effie Awards 2005. www.nyama.org.

Question

Should repositioning only be undertaken when things go wrong?

Task

Find an example of another brand that has been successfully repositioned.

Jewell (2007) draws attention to the need to consider repositioning from a customer's perspective, something neglected in the literature. He also shows that two key tasks need to be accomplished during a repositioning exercise. First, the old positioning needs to be suppressed so that customers no longer relate to it and second, consumers need to learn the new position. These twin tasks are complementary, as interference or rather the deliberate weakening of the old position will help strengthen acceptance of the new position.

Green & Black's, the UK's fastest-growing confectionery brand, launched a £1.2m national advertising campaign – 'Green & Black's . . . it deserves a little respect' as part of its programme to consolidate its repositioning from an organic to luxury chocolate brand and as a result almost trebled its value in two years.

The Defence Establishment and Research Agency (DERA) was required to change its name when it ceased being a government-owned organisation and was privatised. The name QinetiQ represented a radical change of name but it needed to reflect its new position in a new commercial market.

Summary

In order to help consolidate your understanding about the role of objectives and positioning within marketing communications, here are the key points summarised against each of the learning objectives:

1. Examine the need for organisational objectives.

Objectives play an important role in the activities of individuals, social groups and organisations for a variety of reasons. These include providing direction and an action focus for all those participating in the activity, a means by which the variety of decisions relating to an activity can be made in a consistent way, and they set out the time period in which the activity is to be completed. In addition, they communicate the values and scope of the activity to all participants and finally, they provide a means by which the success of the activity can be evaluated.

2. Specify the different types of organisational goals.

The use of objectives in the management process is clearly vital if the organisation's desired outcomes are to be achieved. Each of the objectives, at corporate, unit and functional levels, contributes to the formulation of the promotional objectives. They are all interlinked, interdependent, multiple and often conflicting.

3. Examine the relationship between corporate strategy and promotional objectives.

The various organisational objectives are of little use if they are not communicated to those who need to know what they are. Traditionally, such communication has focused on employees, but there is increasing recognition that the other members of the stakeholder network need to understand an organisation's purpose and objectives.

The major task for communication objectives is twofold: first, to contribute to the overall direction of the organisation by fulfilling the communication requirements of the marketing mix; second, to communicate the corporate thrust and values to various stakeholders so that they understand the organisation, can respond to its intentions and help develop appropriate relationships.

4. Determine the components of SMART-determined promotional objectives.

Promotional objectives are derived from an initial review of the current situation and the marketing plan requirements. They are not a replication of the marketing objectives but a distillation of the research activities that have been undertaken subsequently.

There are three main streams of objectives. The first concerns issues relating to the buyers of the product or service offered by the organisation. The second concerns issues relating to market share/sales volume, profitability and revenue. The third stream relates to the image, reputation and preferences that other stakeholders have towards the organisation.

To assist managers in their need to develop suitable objectives, a set of guidelines has been developed, commonly referred to as SMART objectives. This acronym stands for specific, measurable, achievable, relevant, targeted and timed.

5. Examine the differences between sales- and communication-based objectives.

Promotional objectives consist of two main elements: sales-oriented and communication-oriented. A balance between the two will be determined by the situation facing the organisation, but can be a mixture of both product and corporate tasks. These objectives, once quantified, need to be ranked and weighted in order that other components of the plan can be developed.

6. Evaluate the concept of positioning.

The position adopted is a statement about what the brand is, what it stands for and the values and beliefs that customers (hopefully) will come to associate with the particular brand. Visual and text/copy images or the position statement represented in a strapline may be a significant trigger that buyers use to recall images and associations of the brand.

There are two main ways in which a brand can be positioned, these are functional and expressive (or symbolic) positioning. Functionally positioned brands stress the features and benefits, and expressive brands emphasise the ego, social and hedonic satisfactions that a brand can bring.

7. Understand the importance of perceptual mapping.

A perceptual map represents a geometric comparison of how competing products are perceived by customers, based on important attributes. Each product is positioned on the map according to the perception that buyers have of the strength of each attribute of each product. By plotting the perceived positions of each brand on the map, an overall perspective of the market can be developed and strategies formed to develop clearer, more rewarding positions.

8. Explain the main types of positioning strategies.

There are a number of overall approaches that can be used to develop a position. These can be based on factors such as the market, the customer or redefining the appeal of the brand itself. To implement these three broad approaches, various strategies have been developed. These include product features, price/quality, use, product class dissociation, user, competitor, benefit and heritage or use of cultural symbols.

Review questions

1. Why do organisations use objectives as part of their planning processes?
2. What should a mission statement clearly identify?
3. Suggest three reasons why the setting of promotional objectives is important.
4. Write a brief report arguing the case both for and against the use of an increase in sales as the major objective of all promotional activities.
5. Repeat the exercise as for the previous question but this time focus on communication-based objectives.
6. How and from where are promotional objectives derived?
7. Why is positioning an important part of marketing communications?
8. What is perceptual mapping?
9. Select four print advertisements for the same product category and comment on the positions they have adopted.
10. What are the main positioning strategies?

MiniCase Unlocking the secrets of the male shopper

Richard Godfrey: School of Management and Business, Aberystwyth University

Men have been a marketing afterthought for more than a century. Starting in the late 1800s, when *Good Housekeeping* and *Cosmopolitan* began teaching generations of women how to be Type A wives and mothers, brand managers painted a giant bull's-eye on the female consumer. They have taken relentless aim ever since. 'He makes. She buys.' That's the calculation that turned women into shoppers and men into providers.
(Byrne, 2006).

All this began to change following the Second World War, and has quickened apace in the last 30 years. Men are now actively forced/encouraged into a way of being in which they too have become increasingly objectified, measured through their own practices of consumption: by what they wear; their body image; their material possessions etc. This can be seen through the emergence and spread of men's magazines, High Street stores and forms of popular entertainment that encourage men to take greater interest in their appearance, to adopt consumption-led lifestyles.

The importance of men as (a market of) consumers has been marked by numerous attempts at classification and careful targeting by marketers. A recent issue of *Business Week* (4 September 2006) ran with the cover story 'Secrets of the Male Shopper' in which Nanette Byrne attempted to categorise male shopping habits into five distinct groups, based on a range of shared traits, attitudes and consuming behaviours. The first, the 'Metrosexual', who might be conceived of as the successor to the 1980s yuppie, is the quintessential 'feminised' male consumer. For him, consumption is all about style and the completion of self through designer brands and services. Against this she situates the 'Retrosexual', rejecting all things feminine, and reasserting a notion of masculinity through consumption of alcohol, sports (viewing) and junk food. There is also 'Modern Man', called by others 'New Man', who sits at something of a halfway point between the metro- and retrosexual. He has a vested interest in his appearance but does not subscribe to some of the vanity practices of the metrosexual: 'Moisturizer and hair gel are perfectly ordinary to him; a manicure is a tougher call' (Byrne, 2006). Then there is the 'Maturiteen' – the current cohort of teenagers – far more sophisticated in their consumption habits than previous teen generations and, thanks to their literacy with the Internet and other forms of telecommunications, far more influential over family decision-making than their predecessors. Finally, there is the 'Dad', for the most part something of a marketing undesirable but with new-found interest in fatherhood, increasingly the target of marketing communications. Byrne cites the example of the Bugaboo baby stroller, with its black and chrome frame, front and rear suspension and off-road wheels, as indicative of the targeted offerings now made towards such men.

Despite differences among these trait-based typologies, these men share a number of consuming habits. Perhaps one of the most significant of these is the increased attention paid to physical appearance. Most notably this occurs in relation to increased care and attention paid to one's body in terms of grooming, body modification and in the selection of clothing and accessories (of course, through these processes and practices, such body routines become 'masculinised'; that is to say, they become legitimate forms of masculine behaviour).

This changing attitude towards and among men has resulted in the rapid growth of a range of 'self-presentation' industries including fashion, cosmetic surgery and, markedly, in the market for men's grooming products, which was estimated to be worth more than £780 million in 2006. This market is now saturated with offerings all vying for a slice of this lucrative pie. Reflecting prevailing trends in the female grooming markets, many of the competitors in this industry position and communicate their brands using common (masculine) themes, such as use of sex appeal (especially at the higher end of the market), aspirational celebratory endorsers (such as Gillette's use, since 2004, of David Beckham), and, in the packaging of their goods, through the use of masculine colours and materials such as strong blues, black, red and brushed steel or silver. This makes for a cramped and, at times, undifferentiated drugstore shelf.

However, against this trend a number of competitors, recognising that not all men are alike, have started to move away from such standardised positioning in order to reflect the increasingly fragmented male audience. Lynx, for example, has focused on the social benefits of its brand. By combining sex with humour, campaigns over the last few years, such as the highly successful 'Pulse' campaign have sought to almost parody the communications activities of more exclusive brands. The Pulse ad demonstrated that even a 'nerdy' guy, with little going for him, can ooze sex appeal and get the girls, thanks to the 'Lynx effect'! The tongue-in-cheek ad, which sought to break down some of the established norms of communicating in this industry, not only proved a commercial success but also spawned a new dance craze and saw the track 'Make Luv', which was used in the ad, re-enter the singles chart at number one. The spread of the ad into popular culture was invaluable in helping to reposition a brand that had come to be associated, primarily, with the declining 'lad' culture of the 1990s.

Elsewhere, 'King of Shaves' has attempted to sidestep many of the brands that adopt a more aspirational appeal by focusing on the functional (or technical) value of the brand. Playing on male traits that turn around the control and mastery of technology it deploys overt masculine language in its branding such as in the use of the slogan: 'The World's Best shaving and skincare "software"'. It offers brands such as the XCD Defender, where XCD stands for 'Enhance', 'Camouflage', 'Defend' and also offers a web site offering 'expert' shaving tips and techniques.

A new entrant, Bulldog, launched in 2007, perhaps going after the 'Modern Man' or 'Dad's offers a range of grooming products using all natural ingredients but at supermarket prices. As noted in a recent edition of *Marketing Week*:

> They decided that they would not pitch their brand at an exclusive, niche market but instead aim Bulldog at mainstream consumers, giving them, they claim, a natural choice at a reasonable price for the first time. They gave the brand a strong masculine identity, taking a risk with the potentially polarising name Bulldog. Clean, white packaging with a bold typeface was chosen to make the range look markedly different from the market leaders such as Lynx, Nivea, Gillette and L'Oréal.
> (Jack, 2008)

With the spread of the tweenager phenomenon and boys as young as 10 or 12 now using grooming products, these consuming behaviours look set to continue well into the future.

MiniCase references

Byrne, N. (2006) 'Secrets of the Male Shopper', *Business Week*, 4 September 2006. Last accessed on 14 March 2008.

Jack, L. (2008) 'Analysis: Bulldog aims to see off men's skincare competition', *Marketing Week*, 13 March 2008. Last accessed on 14 March 2008.

MiniCase questions

1. Identify the social and cultural changes that have led to the rise of the male shopper.
2. How might an understanding of 'perception theory' be used in the targeting of male consumers?
3. Identify the different male consumer typologies outlined in the case. What are their key personality traits? How could a marketing communicator use this information in order to position a brand?

References

Anon. (2006) Privilege – Making dosh by being posh: how selling car insurance different made a positive difference to profitability, IPA Effectiveness Awards 2006. Retrieved 17 November 2007 from http://www.warc.com/ArticleCenter/Default.asp?CType=A&AID=WORDSEARCH82653&Tab=A.

Barry, T. and Howard, D.J. (1990) A review and critique of the hierarchy of effects in advertising. *International Journal of Advertising*, **9**, 121–35.

Blankstson, C. and Kalafatis, S.P. (2007) Positioning strategies of international and multicultural-orientated service brands. *Journal of Services Marketing*, **21**(6), 435–450.

Bokaie, J. (2007) Coke Zero to drop 'bloke coke' advertising theme. *Marketing*, 7 November, 1.

Bokaie, J. (2008) George eyes mid-market domain. *Marketing*, 26 March 2008, 4.

Colley, R. (1961) *Defining Advertising Goals for Measured Advertising Results*. New York: Association of National Advertisers.

Day, G., Shocker, A.D. and Srivastava, R.K. (1979) Customer orientated approaches to identifying product markets. *Journal of Marketing*, **43**(4), 8–19.

Dutka, S. (1995) *Defining Advertising Goals for Measured Advertising Results*, 2nd edn. New York: Association of National Advertisers.

Jewell, R.D. (2007) Establishing effective repositioning communications in a competitive marketplace. *Journal of Marketing Communications*, **13**(4), 231–41.

Johnson, G. and Scholes, K. (2006) *Exploring Corporate Strategy: Text and Cases*, 7th edn. Harlow: Prentice-Hall.

King, S. (1991) Brand building in the 1990s. *Journal of Marketing Management*, **7**, 3–13.

Kotler, P. (2003) *Marketing Management – Analysis, Planning, Implementation and Control*, 11th edn. Englewood Cliffs, NJ: Prentice-Hall.

Kriegel, R.A. (1986) How to choose the right communications objectives. *Business Marketing* (April), 94–106.

Lane, M. (2007) Anheuser-Busch Comaines, Inc.: Frogs Campaign. *Encyclopedia of Major Marketing Campaigns*, 2, www.gale.group.com.

Levitt, T. (1960) Marketing myopia. *Harvard Business Review* (July/August), 45–56.

Neal, W.D. (1980) Strategic product positioning: a step by step guide. *Business (USA)* (May/June), 34–40.

Quinn, J.B., Mintzberg, H., James, R.M., Lampel, J.B and Ghosal, S. (2003) *The Strategy Process*, 4th edn. New York: Prentice-Hall.

Ries, A. and Trout, J. (1972) The positioning era cometh. *Advertising Age*, 24 April, 35–8.

Rosen, R. (1995) *Strategic Management: An Introduction*. London: Pitman.

Rossiter, J.R. and Percy, L. (1987) *Advertising and Promotion Management*. Lexington, MA: McGraw-Hill.

Sinclair, S.A. and Stalling, E.C. (1990) Perceptual mapping: a tool for industrial marketing: a case study. *Journal of Business and Industrial Marketing*, **5**(1), 55–65.

Thompson, A. and Strickland, A.J. III (1990) *Strategic Management*. Homewood, IL: BPI Irwin.

Chapter 12

Branding and the role of marketing communications

The images, associations and experiences that customers make with brands, and the brand identities that managers seek to create, need to be closely related if long-run brand purchasing behaviour is to be achieved. Marketing communications can play an important and integral part in the development of positive brand associations that have meaning and purpose for customers.

Aims and learning objectives

The aims of this chapter are to explore the nature and characteristics of branding and to identify the way in which marketing communications can be used to develop and maintain brands that engage their respective target audiences.

The learning objectives of this chapter are to:

1. introduce and explore the nature of branding;
2. examine the common characteristics of brands;
3. determine the benefits to both buyers and owners of brands;
4. identify the different types of brands and the relationships they can have with the parent organisation;
5. appreciate the strategic importance of brands;
6. understand the way in which marketing communications can be used to build and support brands;
7. explain the role of branding in business-to-business markets;
8. explore some of the issues associated with branding online and in virtual brand communities;
9. appraise the nature and characteristics of brand equity.

For an applied interpretation see Sofia Daskou and Peter Zissou's MiniCase entitled ***Rebranding Greek ice-cream: the case of Nestlé ice-cream*** at the end of this chapter.

Introduction

Successful brands create strong, positive and lasting impressions, all of which are perceived by audiences to be of value to them personally. Individuals perceive brands without having to purchase or have direct experience of them. The elements that make up this impression are numerous, and research by Chernatony and Dall'Omo Riley (1998a) suggests that there is little close agreement on the definition of a brand. They identified 12 types of definition; among them is the visual approach adopted by Assael (1990), that a brand is the name, symbol, packaging and service reputation. The differentiation approach is typified by Kotler (2000), who argues that a brand is a name, term, sign, symbol or design or a combination of these intended to identify the goods or services of one seller or group of sellers, and to differentiate them from those of competitors.

Successful brands create strong, positive and lasting impressions.

What these researchers have identified is that brands are a product of the work of managers who attempt to augment their products with values and associations that are recognised by, and are meaningful to, their customers. In other words, brands are a composite of two main constructs, the first being an identity that managers wish to portray and the second being images, construed by audiences, of the identities they perceive. The development of Web 2.0 and user-generated-content in the form of blogs, wikis and social networks have added a new dimension to the managerial-driven perspective of brands. Consumers are assuming a greater role in defining what a brand means to them and now they are prone to sharing this with their friends, family and contacts rather than with the organisation itself. As Gray (2006) points out, this means that brand managers have reduced levels of influence over the way their brands are perceived and this in turn impacts on the influence they have managing corporate reputation.

It is important, therefore, to recognise that both managers and customers are involved in the branding process. In the past the emphasis and control of brands rested squarely with brand owners. Today, this influence has shifted to consumers as they redefine what brands mean to them and how they differentiate among similar offerings and associate certain attributes or feelings and emotions with particular brands.

The influence has shifted to consumers as they redefine what brands mean to them.

Consistent quality, fulfilled brand promises and customer satisfaction through time can help buyers to learn to trust a brand. This may lead customers to prioritise a brand within their evoked set for that product category. The acceptance of buyers as active problem-solvers means that branding can be seen as a way in which buyers can reduce the amount of decision-making time and associated perceived risk. This is because brand names provide information about content, taste, durability, quality, price and performance, without requiring the buyer to undertake time-consuming comparison tests with similar offerings or other risk-reduction approaches to purchase decisions. In some categories, brands can be developed through the use of messages that are entirely emotional or image-based. Many of the 'products' in FMCG categories base their communications on imagery, assuming low involvement and the use of peripheral cues. Other sectors, such as cars or pharmaceuticals, require rational, information-based messages supported by image-based messages (Boehringer, 1996). In other words, a blend of messages may well be required to achieve the objectives and goals of the campaign.

Branding is a task that requires a significant contribution from marketing communications and is a long-term exercise. Organisations that cut their brand advertising in times of recession reduce the significance and power of their brands. The Association of Media Independents claims, not surprisingly, that the weaker brands are those that reduce or cut their advertising when trading conditions deteriorate.

In line with moves towards integrated marketing communications and media-neutral planning (see Chapter 9), many organisations are moving the balance of their communication mix away from an emphasis on advertising (especially offline)

Many organisations are moving the balance of their communication mix away from an emphasis on advertising.

towards the other tools and media. For example, mobile phone companies have used advertising to develop brand awareness and positioning and have then used sales promotion and direct marketing activities to provide a greater focus on loyalty and reward programmes. These companies operate in a market where customer retention is a problem. Customer loss (or churn rate) used to exceed 30 per cent and there was a strong need to develop marketing and communications strategies to reduce this figure and provide for higher customer satisfaction levels and, from that, improved profitability.

Brand characteristics

The essence of a strong brand is that it is sufficiently differentiated to the extent that it cannot be easily replicated by its competitors. This level of differentiation requires that a brand possess many distinctive characteristics and to achieve this it is important to understand how brands are constructed.

> Brands consist of two main types of attributes: intrinsic and extrinsic.

Brands consist of two main types of attributes: intrinsic and extrinsic. Intrinsic attributes refer to the functional characteristics of the product such as its shape, performance and physical capacity. If any of these intrinsic attributes were changed, it would directly alter the product. Extrinsic attributes refer to those elements that are not intrinsic and if changed do not alter the material functioning and performance of the product itself: devices such as the brand name, marketing communications, packaging, price and mechanisms that enable consumers to form associations that give meaning to the brand. Buyers often use the extrinsic attributes to help them distinguish one brand from another because in certain categories it is virtually impossible for them to make decisions based on the intrinsic attributes alone.

Biel (1997) refers to brands being composed of a number of elements. The first refers to the functional abilities a brand claims and can deliver. The particular attributes that distinguish a brand are referred to as brand skills. He refers to cold remedies and their skill to relieve cold symptoms, for 6 hours, 12 hours or all day.

The second element is the personality of a brand and its fundamental traits concerning lifestyle and perceived values, such as being bland, adventurous, exciting, boring or caring. The idea of brand personification is not new, but it is an important part of understanding how a brand might be imagined as a person and how the brand is different from other brands (people). Linda Barker endorses the DFS brand and, in doing so, makes a strong measure of association between the DFS brand (and its values) and the effervescent personality of the designer and TV presenter.

ViewPoint 12.1 Luxury brands

The focus of luxury brand communications is not on the intrinsic but on the extrinsic attributes. Strategies are often based on developing brand-name associations that appeal to the aspirational needs and social and psychological motivations of the target audiences.

Luxury brands such as Dior, Rolex, Gucci, Cartier and Donna Karan have been developed mainly through a combination of advertising, public relations, craftsmanship, word-of-mouth and a touch of mythology. For example, 'I found this material in a Scandinavian shop in Bath', claimed shoe designer Manolo Blahnik.

In order to grow and to reach new target markets, luxury brands are faced with a dilemma. They can lower their prices to attract new customers, but this threatens to impact the perception of the main brand by undermining its values and reputation, the one important point of differentiation that has made the brand successful.

Exhibit 12.1 Luxury brand – Gucci
SCPhotos/Alamy.

Exhibit 12.2 Luxury brand – Dior
Gianni Muratore/Alamy.

The route forward is to introduce sub-brands that cannot be seen to be part of the main brand. Thus, Klein Cosmetics splits its business into two, classic brands and the CK franchise line that includes CkOne and CkB fragrances. Tudor is a sub-brand of Rolex and Donna Karan uses Signature and DKNY as associate labels (see Exhibit 12.1).

Sources: Various including Brooke and Nottage (2008); Lovett (2008).

Question

To what extent can luxury brands be personified?

Task

Choose a luxury brand and try to collect as many communication artefacts relating to that brand as you can. Now, perform a mini content analysis to isolate core approaches and branding approaches.

The third branding element is about building a relationship with individual buyers. People are said to interact with brands. A two-way relationship can be realistically developed when it is recognised that the brand must interact with the consumer just as much as the consumer must interact with the brand. Blackston (1993) argues that successful branding depends on consumers' perceptions of the attitudes held by the brand towards them as individuals. He illustrates the point with research into the credit card market, where different cards share the same demographic profile of users and the same conventional brand images. Some cards provide recognition or visibility of status, which by association are bestowed upon the owner in the form of power and authority. In this sense the card enhances the user. This contrasts with other cards, where the user may feel intimidated and excluded from the card because as a person the attitudes of the card are perceived to be remote, aloof, condescending and hard to approach. For example, respondents felt the cards were saying, 'If you don't like the conditions, go and get a different card', and 'I'm so well known and established that I can do as I want.'

The implications for brand development and associated message strategies become clearer. In line with this thinking, Biel cites Fournier (1995), who considers brand/consumer relationships in terms of levels of intimacy, partner quality, attachment, interdependence, commitment and love.

Biel sees brands as being made up of three elements: brand personality, brand skills and brand relationships.

Therefore, Biel sees brands as being made up of three elements: brand personality, brand skills and brand relationships. These combine to form what he regards as 'brand magic', which underpins added value.

A more recent approach to brand development work involves creating a brand experience. Tango was an early pioneer of this approach. They used roadshows to create indirect brand-related experiences, such as bungee jumping, trampolining and other out-of-the-norm activities. FujiFilm underpin a great deal of their UK marketing communications on events, if only because they provide opportunities to provide direct experiences, in this case of the features and benefits of Fujifilm's brand values. Their events are grouped under three main headings exhibitions, product launches and sponsorship. The first two of these enable contact with trade customers and consumers, who can handle the products and become immersed in the brand. They can also provide direct feedback.

Kapferer (2004) refers to a brand identity prism and its six facets (see Figure 12.1). The facets to the left represent a brands-outward expression, while Kapferer argues that those to

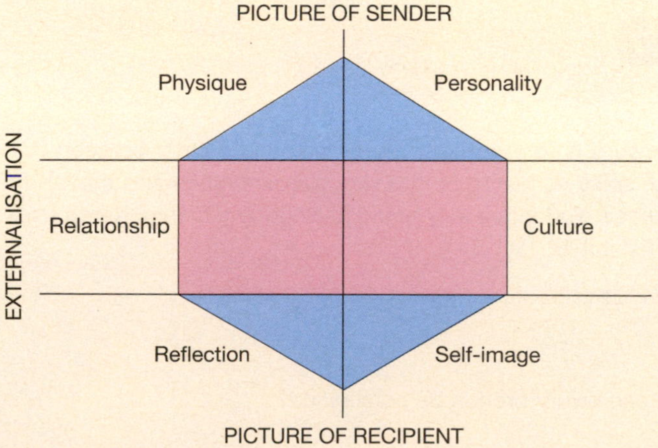

Figure 12.1 Brand identity prism
Source: Kapferer (2004). Used with permission.

Table 12.1 Brand facets

Brand facet	Explanation
Physique	Refers to the main physical strength of the brand and its core added value. What does the brand do and what does it look like? E.g. the Coca-Cola bottle.
Personality	Those human characteristics that best represent the identity, best understood by the use of celebrity spokespersons who provide an instant personality.
Culture	A set of values that are central to a brand's aspirational power and essential for communication and differentiation.
Relationship	A brand's relationship defines the way it behaves and acts towards others. Apple exudes friendliness, IBM orderliness and Nike provocation. Important in the service sector.
Customer reflection	Refers to the way customers see the brand . . . for old people, for sporty people, clever people, people who want to look younger. This is an outward reflection.
Self-image	Refers to how an individual feels about themselves, relative to the brand. This is an inner reflection.

Source: Adapted from Kapferer (2004). Used with permission.

the right are incorporated within the brand, an inner expression or spirit as he refers to it. These facets represent the key dimensions associated with building and maintaining brand identities and are set out in Table 12.1; they are interrelated and define a brand's identity, while also representing the means by which brands can be managed, developed and even extended.

All brands consist of a mixture of intrinsic and extrinsic attributes and management's task is to decide on the balance between them. Indeed, this decision lies at the heart of branding in the sense that it is the strategy and positioning that lead to strong brands.

Benefits of branding

As a brand becomes established with a buyer, so the psychological benefits of ownership are preferred to competing offerings, and a form of relationship emerges. Brands are said to develop personalities and encapsulate the core values of a product. They are a strong means by which a product can be identified, understood and appreciated. Marketing communications plays an important role in communicating the essence of the personality of the brand and in providing the continuity for any relationship, a necessity for a brand to be built through time. This can be achieved through the development of emotional links and through support for any product symbolism that might be present.

Just as brands can provide benefits for buyers, so important direct benefits for manufacturers or resellers also exist. Brands provide a means by which a manufacturer can augment its product in such a way that buyers can differentiate the product, recognise it quickly and make purchase decisions that exclude competitive products in the consideration set. Premium pricing is permissible, as perceived risk is reduced and high quality is conveyed through trust and experience formed through an association with the brand. This in turn allows for loyalty to be developed, which in turn allows for cross-product promotions and brand extensions. Integrated marketing communications becomes more feasible as buyers perceive thematic ideas and messages, which in turn can reinforce positioning and values associated with the brand. For a summary of the benefits of branding, see Table 12.2.

Integrated marketing communications becomes more feasible as buyers perceive thematic ideas and messages, which in turn can reinforce positioning and values associated with the brand.

Table 12.2 Benefits of branding

Customer benefits	Supplier benefits
Assists the identification of preferred products	Permits premium pricing
Can reduce levels of perceived risk and so improve the quality of the shopping experience	Helps differentiate the product from competitors
Easier to gauge the level of product quality	Enhances cross-product promotion and brand
Can reduce the time spent making product-based decisions and in turn reduce the time spent shopping	Encourages customer loyalty/retention and repeat-purchase buyer behaviour
Can provide psychological reassurance or reward	Assists the development and use of integrated marketing communications
Provides cues about the nature of the source of the product and any associated values	Contributes to corporate identity programmes
	Provides for some legal protection
	Provides for greater thematic consistency and uniform messages and communications

Brand portfolios: architecture and forms

The way in which an organisation structures and manages its brands not only affects its overall success but also influences the marketing communications used to support them. The development of brand portfolios is a means of gaining and protecting brand advantage. The fundamental structure of a brand portfolio consists of three main levels: the architecture, the form and the individual brand (see Figure 12.2).

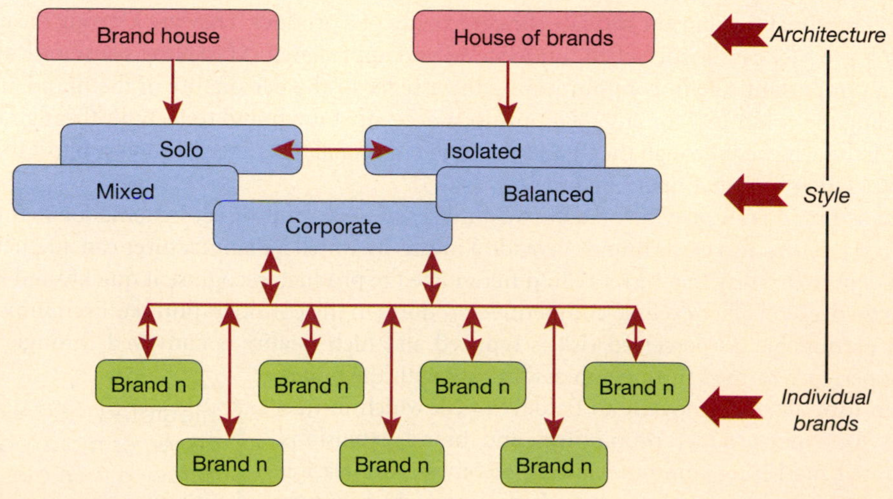

Figure 12.2 Basic structure of brand portfolio

Brand architecture

An organisation's brand architecture represents the overall marketing interface with the community of stakeholders. Petromilli *et al.* (2002) identify the two most common types of brand architecture as branded house and the house of brands. These were formerly known as family brands and multi-brand structures.

Branded house architecture uses a single (master) brand to cover a series of offerings that may operate within descriptive sub-brand names. This approach is used by companies such as Boeing, IBM, Virgin and Disney. Each seeks to dominate entire markets and categories through their single, highly relevant and highly leveraged master corporate brand, typical of the branded house structure. Tesco use the classic branded house architecture. All of its brands are tied into the Tesco name. However, when it entered the US market it broke away from this strategy and used the name 'Fresh and Easy'. US consumers have a different set of needs compared with the UK market and what Ritson (2007) refers to as their parochial nature led Tesco to break away from their established brand approach.

The *house of brands* architecture is characterised by a group or collection of brands that have no outward connections and operate independently of each other. These are brands that stand alone. General Motors and Procter & Gamble use this brand architecture. These two approaches represent the two extremes of a spectrum. Many organisations operate a mix of these two architectures, and their brand architecture lies somewhere between the two, indicating that neither strategy is inherently superior.

Many organisations operate a mix of these two architectures.

ViewPoint 12.2 The House of Dove and Lynx

For a long time Unilever supported their fmcg brands through a branded house strategy. This enabled them to protect the individual identity of brands within the portfolio, which in turn meant that the actions or circumstances affecting any one brand could not hurt others.

This strategy was fine at a time when the number of available media was relatively limited. Today there are a growing number of media channels and so it is important that brands are presented consistently across all consumer touchpoints. In addition to this Unilever decided to move away from a house of brands architecture to one that was based on endorsement. Through the use of a corporate logo on all of their products Unilever effectively linked all of the brands.

Unilever own Dove and Lynx. Dove's communication platform is based on natural beauty and uses a range of 'normal' women to promote the brand. This is in stark contrast to the celebrities and beautiful people used in most cosmetic and fragrance advertising. Dove also claim to protect girls from the messages many beauty ads promote.

As if in complete contradiction, Lynx uses a flagrant sexist platform to reach their teenage market. Had the endorsed brand architecture not been implemented Ritson (2007) suggests this hypocritical positioning would not have been exposed.

Source: Ritson (2007).

Question

Are Unilever guilty of hypocrisy, ignorance or is their commercial right to position brands in contradictory ways?

Task

Visit the two sites for Dove and Lynx. Which of these is the more effective and why?

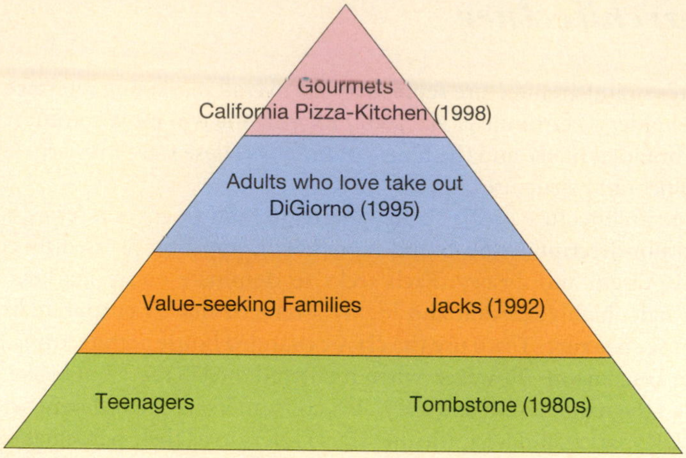

Figure 12.3 Kraft's integrated pizzas brand structure

Pierce and Moukanas (2002) claim that most large companies organise their portfolio of brands as a disparate collection of individual brands. This strategy becomes more effective when these brands are integrated.

This spectrum of brand architectures is a reflection of an organisation's corporate strategy, culture and inter-product, or brand relationships. The approach each organisation adopts not only influences the deployment of resources to support the brands but also shapes the messages and media used within the marketing communications. Five main relationships can be identified: solo, isolated, mixed, balanced and corporate styles (See Table 12.3).

Table 12.3 Organisation/product brand relationships

Relationship	Explanation
Solo style	Organisations whose brand offer is a single product type. Images of the organisation and the product tend to be the same; for example: Kwik-Fit, Pirelli, Coca-Cola.
Isolated style	Essentially a multi-product branding approach that requires promotional expenditure to support each individual brand. Should a particular brand be damaged, the other brands in the portfolio and the corporate name are protected.
Balanced style	The identity of each individual product is related to the parent organisation; for example Ford UK, where each car brand is prefixed by Ford. The Ford Fiesta 1.3L, Ford Focus and Ford Transit all convey the balance between the corporate name and the individual brands.
Mixed style	There is no pattern of relationship between the products and the parent organisation. For example, the German organisation Bosch GmbH identifies its spark plugs and power tools range under the Bosch name, but uses the name Blaupunkt for its radios.
Corporate style	Although an organisation may operate in a number of different strategic business areas, this approach requires all communications to be targeted at reinforcing the corporate image. IBM, Mars, Hewlett-Packard and Black & Decker are examples of this form.

Source: Based on Gray and Smeltzer (1985).

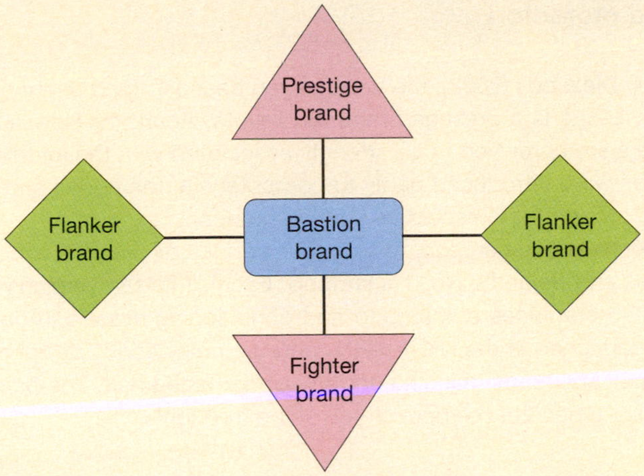

Figure 12.4 Portfolio of brands
Source: After Riezebos (2003).

The way in which an organisation structures its portfolio of brands influences the strategic development and leverage of the assets it owns. One primary source of motivation to manage the portfolio is the desire to protect the most profitable brands from competitive attack. Riezebos (2003) identifies a range of different types of brand based on the role they each play within an overall portfolio. Bastion brands are of major importance to an organisation, usually because they are the most valuable in terms of profit, revenue and market share, consequently they are prone to attack. One major form of strategic response is to develop other brands in order to protect the premier brand (see Figure 12.4).

The role of flanker brands is to protect the bastion brand by warding off competitors. By charging a slightly lower price and by offering a different set of attributes these brands make it more difficult for competitor brands to enter the market. Rather than lose sales to competitors, it is better to lose sales to an internal brand, even if the retained profits are not as high as those generated by the bastion brand.

Fighter brands are used to fend off competitors who compete on discounted prices. Prices of fighter brands are set between the bastion brand and the competitor's low-cost offering, while the quality is adjusted to be perceived as lower than that of the bastion brand. Marketing communications should focus on name awareness, not price.

Fighter brands are used to fend off competitors who compete on discounted prices.

Prestige brands can also be aimed at niche markets but this time the focus is on high quality and luxury. Prices are set high but marketing communications needs to focus on the high quality and status associated with ownership (see Viewpoint 12.3).

Brand forms

There are many forms of branding but primarily there are four key types: manufacturer, distributor, price and generic brands.

Manufacturers' brands help to identify the producer of a brand at the point of purchase. For example, Cadbury's chocolate, Ford cars and Coca-Cola are all strong manufacturers' brands. This type of brand usually requires the assistance of channel intermediaries for wide distribution. Marketing communications are driven by the manufacturer in an attempt to

ViewPoint 12.3 Brand protectors

According to the ideas proposed by Riezebos (2003), the Volkswagen bastion brand might be protected by Seat and Skoda as fighter brands. Lexus is a prestige brand for Toyota, Acura for Honda and Infinity for Nissan. These vehicle manufacturers are perceived to be strongly associated with the middle-range vehicle market. Each of these luxury brands were introduced partly to compete with Mercedes and BMW but also to provide a prestige brand and so protect their respective bastion brands.

Procter & Gamble market a portfolio of shampoo brands. These include head & shoulders, an anti dandruff shampoo, which is the UK and Ireland's No. 1 shampoo. Each of its ten versions is designed to give dandruff protection. Wash & Go combines a shampoo and conditioning system in one product, the first 2 in 1 shampoo. Pantene was launched in the UK in 1991, and the collection is designed to combat a range of common hair issues such as split ends, thinning and dry or damaged hair. The brand offers shiny healthy looking hair whatever the hair type: 'Let the best of you shine through'.

Source: Riezebos (2003: 198–200).

Question

If brand protectors were not used to influence and deliberately shape the market, what would happen to the market and its associated dynamics?

Task

Using the material provided in this ViewPoint, which of the hair care brands might be designated the bastion and flanker brands? What do you think their structural roles might be?

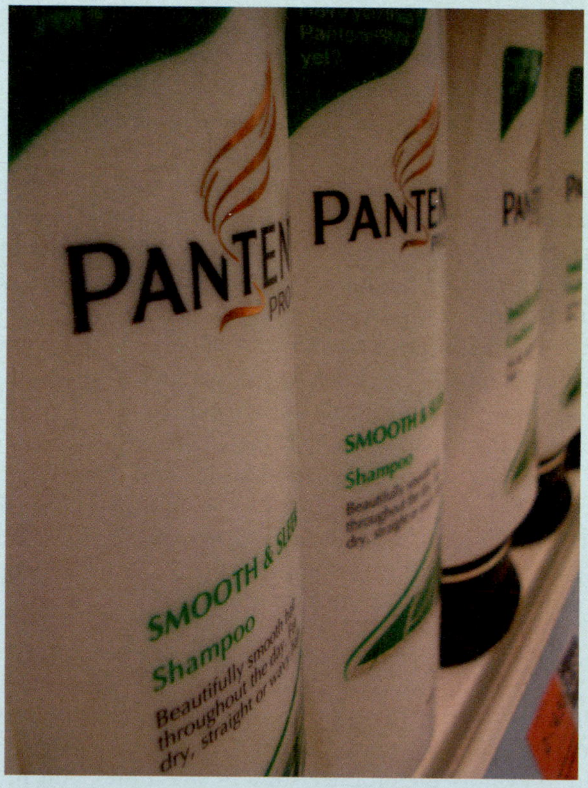

Exhibit 12.3 Pantene offers shiny healthy looking hair whatever the hair type

Exhibit 12.4 Wash & Go and Head & Shoulders, P&G's Number 1 shampoo brand in the UK and Ireland

persuade end-users to adopt the brand, which in turn stimulates channel members to stock and distribute the brand.

Distributor (or own-label) brands do not associate the manufacturer with the offering in any way. Distributor brands are owned by channel members, typically a wholesaler, such as Nurdin & Peacock, or a retailer, such as Tesco, Boots and Woolworths. This brand form offers many advantages to both the manufacturer, who can use excess capacity, and retailers, who can earn a higher margin than they can with manufacturers' branded goods and at the same time develop organisational (e.g. store) images. Channel members have the additional cost of promotional initiatives, necessary in the absence of a manufacturer's support. Some manufacturers refuse to make distributor products in an attempt to restrict availability and number of brands from which consumers can choose. There have been occasions where multiple grocers have launched products that are alleged to be too similar to key manufacturer brands. Often this leads to channel conflict as the name and/or packaging of the distributor brand is alleged to resemble too closely that of the brand leader.

The growth of distributor brands at the expense of manufacturer brands need not be expected to continue unchecked. Consumers value or expect a certain level of brand choice in stores, and as some store traffic and spend per visit rates have declined, some grocery multiples have taken steps to stem the volume of their distributor brand provision and increased the volume of manufacturer brands on their shelves.

Some grocery multiples have taken steps to stem the volume of their distributor brand provision.

Price brands are produced by manufacturers in an attempt to compete with private brands. Tesco has used this approach to respond to the arrival of a number of low-cost retailers such as Kwik Save and Aldi. The product is low-priced and is further characterised by an absence of any promotional support. The effect on the other brands in the manufacturer's portfolio may be to stimulate promotional support to prevent the less loyal buyers from trading over to the low-priced offering.

The fourth and final form is the *generic brand*. This is sold without any promotional materials and the packaging displays only information required by law. Manufacturers are even less inclined to produce these 'white carton' products than price brands. They are often sold at prices 40 per cent below the price of normal brands. They consume very few promotional resources, for obvious reasons, but their popularity, after a burst in the 1970s, has waned considerably, particularly in the supermarket sector where they gained their greatest success. However, generics are significant in some markets. In the early 1990s the pharmaceuticals industry experienced growth in the use of generic products, spurred by the government's NHS reforms (Blackett, 1992) but outside the pharmaceuticals industry generic brands have had minimal influence.

The strategic role of branding

Walton (2007) suggests that there three dimensions to brand strategy: meaning, space and expression (see Table 12.4).

From a strategic perspective, brands play one of three significant roles. In broad terms, they can be used to defend market share or a group of brands by protecting established positions. They can be used to attack competitor brands and win market share or they can provide a way of deterring potential competitors from entering the market. In other words, they act either as a market entry barrier or as an aid to customer retention. To enable these strategic roles to be accomplished there are three elements that need to be attended to. These are integration, which in turn can lead to differentiation and deliver added value (see Figure 12.5 and the following discussion).

Integration

For a brand to be maintained and to work, it is important that the communications used to develop and maintain the brand are consistent and meaningful. Part of the essence of integrated marketing communications is that the mix used to support a brand, including the messages that are used to convey brand values, must be consistent, uniform and reinforcing. Therefore, successful branding is partly the result of effective integrated marketing communications.

When Levi Strauss attempted to prevent Asda from selling its clothing it was attempting to protect the way it wanted to be perceived, that is, its positioning. If Asda had continued to sell

Table 12.4 Brand dimensions

Brand dimension	Explanation
Meaning	Refers to how consumers perceive a brand. This may be functional, emotional or symbolic.
Space	This concerns the actual product and the category in which it operates.
Expression	How the brand projects its identity through marketing communications in order that it relates to the target market in terms of its 'look and feel'.

Source: Walton (2007). Used with kind permission from WARC.

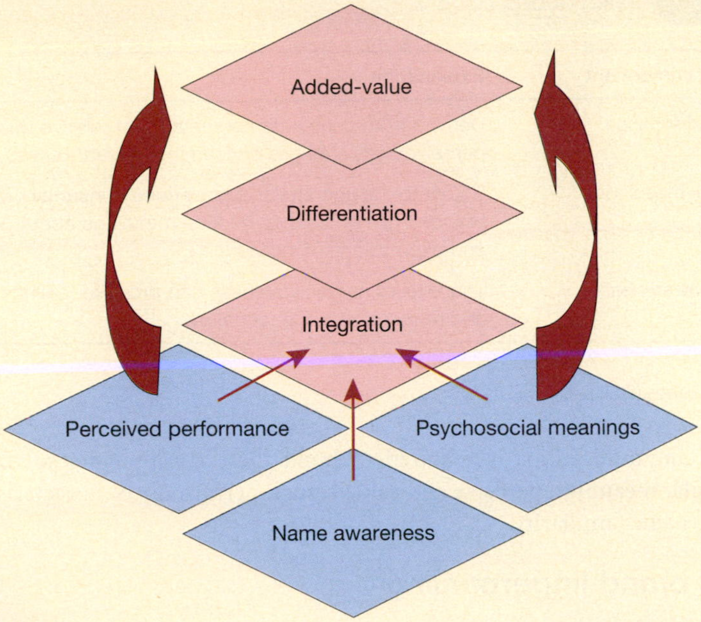

Figure 12.5 The strategic dimensions of branding

Levi Strauss products, market forces would ultimately have determined whether the positioning determined by Levi Strauss was of value to customers.

Differentiation

Brands that are integrated provide opportunities to be perceived as different, relative to a competitor's product. Branding is a method of separation and positioning so that customers can recognise and understand what a brand stands for, relative to other brands. However, not all brands choose to be different as there is some strategic advantage for smaller, new-entry brands to associate themselves closely with the market leader. This is witnessed by the disagreements between distributors and manufacturers over the packaging, names and type faces used for some products (e.g. Coca-Cola and Sainsbury's Cola, Penguin and Asda's Puffin bars).

Added value

The final key element is added value. Brands enable customers to derive extra benefits as one brand can provide different advantages to another. These advantages might be in the form of rational attribute-based advantages (e.g. whiter, stronger or longer) or they may be more emotionally based advantages derived through the augmented aspects of the products (e.g. the way you feel about a brand). This issue is evidenced by the vigour with which Levi Strauss resisted the distribution of its jeans through price-oriented distributors such as Asda. One of the arguments proposed by the company was that the inherent brand value was effectively removed through this form of distribution.

Value is added to brands through three main components: perceived performance, psycho-social meaning and the extent of brand-name awareness (Riezebos, 2003) (see Table 12.5). Added value is developed using different combinations of these three components.

Value is added to brands through three main components: perceived performance, psycho-social meaning and the extent of brand-name awareness.

Table 12.5 Brand added value

Added value component	Explanation
Perceived performance	Derived from consumer perceptions of relative quality and perceived associations concerning key attributes.
Psycho-social meanings	Refers to the immaterial associations consumers make about brands from which they deduce meanings about personality and expressions of individuality.
Brand-name awareness	The level of name awareness can provoke feelings of familiarity and reduced risk or uncertainty.

Source: After Riezebos (2003).

Marketing communications is required to build these components so that consumers deduce particular meanings, perceive and value certain performance characteristics and build awareness and name familiarity.

Individual brand fingerprinting

One of the main branding tasks is to reinforce the brand's presence, position and quality in the market. However, it is important that all branding activities extend across all key consumer contact points, a policy that needs to be pursued when developing integrated marketing communications (Chapter 9).

When developing a marketing communications plan it is vitally important to consider the information arising from a brand audit and then develop a brand fingerprint, as Vyse (1999) refers to it. The management and development of a brand require resources and processes to ensure that the brand associations that customers make are as intended and that the gap between managers' and buyers' expectations is acceptable. The completion of a brand audit should result in an improved consumer insight, but understanding consumers is worthless unless the information is in a form that can be read and understood by everyone involved in the brand development process.

Brands suffer mid-life crises, they lose friends and need to be vigorously rejuvenated, often through exceptional creativity (Tango, Sainsbury's, British Airways). Vyse comments that brands need to be up to date and speak the current language. Gap has a look and feel that travels across its store design, its through-the-line communications, and on packaging which expresses the visual, tactile, emotional and functional values of the clothes. Brand fingerprinting is about developing a single document that can be used by everyone involved with the brand development process. The benefits are as follows:

- It allows for continuity when brand managers move on in their careers.
- When the retail environment changes in a radical manner (e.g. ecommerce).
- It focuses on the consumer and so helps maintain the relationship.
- It fosters good team practice.

A brand fingerprint consists primarily of a document that summarises the essential character of the brand. According to Vyse, this comprises the following elements:

- *Target*: a description of the person for whom the brand is always the first choice by defining their attitudes and values.
- *Insight*: a description defining the elements about the consumer and their needs upon which the brand is founded.
- *Competition*: a picture of the market and alternative choices as seen by the consumer and the relative values the brand offers in the market.

- *Benefits*: the various functional and emotive benefits that motivate purchase.
- *Proposition*: the single most compelling and competitive statement the target consumer would make for buying the brand.
- *Values*: what the brand stands for and believes in.
- *Reasons to believe*: the proof we offer to substantiate positioning.
- *Essence*: the distillation of the brand's generic code into one clear thought.
- *Properties*: the tangible things of which the merest glimpse, sound, taste, smell or touch would evoke the brand.

For a brand to grow and be sustained, the functional aspects of the product must be capable of meeting buyer expectations. If the quality of the physical and functional aspects of the product is below acceptable standards, marketing communications activities alone cannot create and sustain a brand. Jaguar cars were rejected when first exported to the United States, because the first buyers of Jaguars (innovators in the process of adoption) experienced a variety of problems. These included overheating, because thermostats failed to work, and gearboxes and clutches, that needed replacing too quickly. This led to a poor perception and hence image of Jaguar, which meant that market penetration was slow, at least until the product defects were corrected. A quality initiative at the production plant resulted in a car that performed at exceptionally high levels on all functions. Marketing communications then built upon the new credibility, so that Jaguar became one of the most sought-after prestige cars in the United States.

The role of marketing communications in branding

Marketing communications plays a vital role in the development of brands and is the means by which products become brands. The way in which marketing communications is used to build brands is determined strategically by the role that the brand is expected to play in achieving an organisation's goals. Chernatony and Dall'Olmo Riley (1998b) argue that there are several roles that marketing communications can play in relation to brand development. For example, they suggest the role during brand extensions is to show buyers how the benefits from the established brand have been transferred or extended to the new brand. It may be that some of the problems experienced by Lego in 2003/04 were due to a brand extension strategy that has not been suitably supported by marketing communications. Alternatively, the poor financial situation may have been be due to a move away from core brand values (Lee, 2004).

> The way in which marketing communications is used to build brands is determined strategically.

Another role, based on the work of Ehrenberg (1974), is to remind buyers and reinforce their perceptions and in doing so defend the market. Whatever the role, one major determinant that applies to all organisations is the size of the financial resources that are made available. Should the budget be high, advertising will often be the main way through which brand name associations are shaped. The brand name itself will not need to be related to the function or use experience of the brand as the advertising will be used to create and maintain brand associations.

However, when financial resources are restricted, a below-the-line approach is necessary. In particular, the brand name will need to be closely related to the function and use experience of the product, while packaging will also play a significant role in building brand associations.

Brand building through advertising

When advertising is used to help consumers to make brand associations, two main approaches can be used: a rational or an emotional approach. When a rational approach is used

When a rational approach is used the functional aspects of a brand are emphasised.

the functional aspects of a brand are emphasised and the benefit to the consumer is stressed. Very often product performance is the focus of the message and a key attribute is identified and used to position the brand. Typically, unique selling propositions were often used to draw attention to a single superior functional advantage that consumers found attractive. For example, a washing powder that washes clothes whiter, drinks that have the highest percentage of fruit juice content and paint that covers more square metres than any other paint.

Many brands now try to present two or even three brand features as the USP has lost ground. For example, when Britvic launched *Juice Up* into the chilled fruit juice sector to compete with *Sunny Delight*, it used the higher fruit juice and lower sugar attributes as the main focus of the communication strategy. The rational approach is sometimes referred to as an informative approach (and complements functional positioning, see Chapter 11). In terms of added value (see above) this approach complements the perceived performance criteria identified by Riezebos (2003).

ESPs can enable consumers to make positive brand associations based on both psychological and socially acceptable meanings, a psychosocial interpretation.

When an emotional approach is used, advertising should provide emotional selling points (ESPs). These can enable consumers to make positive brand associations based on both psychological and socially acceptable meanings, a psychosocial interpretation. Product performance characteristics are dormant while consumers are encouraged to develop positive feelings and associations with the brand. A further goal can be to create positive attitudes towards the advertising itself, which in turn can be used to make associations with the brand. In other words, the role of likeability, discussed later in Chapter 15, becomes paramount when using an emotional advertising approach. Therefore, these types of advertisements should be relevant and meaningful, credible, and be of significant value to the consumer. In essence, therefore, emotional (or transformational) advertising is about people enjoying the advertisement (and complements expressive positioning, see Chapter 11).

ViewPoint 12.4 The Famous Grouse does it above the line

The UK whisky market experienced major changes during the 1990s. At one time the blended sector was dominant but the market had been eroded through the growth of own label brands, Irish and American spirits and single malts. These pressures combined to create difficult trading conditions for blended whisky brands. Not only was the market in decline but also many brands such as Famous Grouse, were suffering long-term declining sales, in this case 36 per cent in 16 years. Even Bells, the market leader, had suffered declining volume sales. The question was how could advertising revive a brand in this context?

Some brands for example, Teachers and Grants, withdrew all advertising support and effectively treated their brands as cash cows, draining their residual profits. This was not seen as a strategy that could deliver long-term value so it was decided to invest and build the Famous Grouse brand through advertising. The key was to build a brand that not only consumers could become engaged with, but also one that would enable the brand to stand out and retain on trade distribution. This was achieved through a creative that used the iconic bird depicted on the label. In real life the grouse is a shy and retiring bird. Not so with The Famous Grouse who was used to demonstrate cheekiness, fun and even a slight irreverence.

Over the decade since the advertising campaign began, the strength of the brand has increased considerably. The above-the-line campaign cost £15.4 million between 1996 and 2006 and it is claimed that it has generated an additional £513 million of value. Of the brands in the blended sector, only Bells and Famous Grouse have increased the strength of their brands. It is interesting to note that they were the only two to invest in advertising.

Source: Barnett *et al.* (2006).

Question

Is it too late for Teachers and Grants to develop their brands and add value?

Task

Try to collect five different ads of the Famous Grouse and identify three strengths and three weaknesses associated with the brand's advertising.

Exhibit 12.5 The Famous Grouse
Image courtesy of The Advertising Archives.

Brand building through below-the-line techniques

When the marketing communications budget is limited or where the target audience cannot be reached reasonably or effectively through advertising, then it is necessary to use various other communication tools to develop brands. Although sales promotion is traditionally perceived as a tool that erodes rather than helps build a brand, as it has a price rather than a value orientation, it can be used strategically. In recent years, new technology has enabled innovative sales promotion techniques to be used as a competitive weapon and to help build brand presence.

Direct marketing and public relations are important methods used to build brand values, especially when consumers experience high involvement. However, experience suggests that the sole use of direct marketing in FMCG markets has been less than satisfactory from those that have experimented (e.g. Heinz in the mid 1990s). The Internet offers opportunities to build new dot-com brands and the financial services sector has tried to harness this method as part of a multichannel distribution policy. What appears to be overridingly important for the development of brands operating with limited resources are the brand name and the merchandising activities, of which packaging, labelling and POP are crucial. In addition, as differentiation between brands becomes more difficult in terms of content and distinct symbolism, the nature of the service encounter is now recognised to have considerable impact on brand association. The development of loyalty schemes and carelines for FMCG, durable and service-based brands is a testimony to the importance of developing and maintaining positive brand associations.

When advertising is the main source of brand development consumers develop associations about the content and positioning of the brand through advertising messages.

When advertising is the main source of brand development consumers develop associations about the content and positioning of the brand through advertising messages. As a substitute for advertising, it is the merchandising, packaging and the brand name itself that need to convey the required symbolism in such a way that the content and positioning are understood by the target audience. Indeed, the brand name needs to be closely aligned with the brand's primary function, more so than when advertising is able to convey the product's purpose and role. So, the name O_2 *Arena* rebrands, identifies and repositions the controversial structure, the name *Sensodyne* says something about the functionality of the toothpaste and *Netrank* conveys ideas that this might be (and is) a search engine optimisation agency.

ViewPoint 12.5 Sula Vineyards do it below-the-line

Beer is currently India's preferred alcoholic drink but the rapid growth of the wine industry is threatening to challenge beer's overall supremacy.

Sula Vineyards are a typical new winery seeking to establish their brand in the emerging market. Faced with a market where taxes are extremely heavy (except on beer), new entrants need to find a strong point of differentiation.

However, there is one big problem that faces all producers of alcohol, namely that advertising of alcohol is not allowed. Some major global brands are able to create brand awareness using television and outdoor media to promote their names using their other brands such Kingfisher mineral water and Smirnoff CDs.

The marketing communications used to support brands such as Sula Vineyards therefore need to be below-the-line and closely oriented to help consumers learn and experience their brands. Sula Vineyards use sales promotion (sampling and tastings), experiential marketing (winery tours), public relations (media relations and lobbying) and word-of-mouth recommendation. Sampling is important, especially within the trade. Once restaurant, hotel and bar staff and distributors appreciate the quality of their brand they are in a better position to recommend the brand. Lobbying helps raise the profile of the brand but is also undertaken to get the rules relating to alcohol relaxed and available through supermarkets and accessible to more women, who currently prefer not to frequent traditional liquor shops.

Source: Durston (2008).

Question

Does the ban on advertising alcohol prevent consumers from having full knowledge of brand availability?

Task

How might Sula name their brands to assist brand identification?

The below-the-line route needs to achieve a transfer of image. Apart from the clarity of the brand name (which needs to describe the product functions) and the shape, nature and information provided through the packaging and associated labelling, there are additional mechanisms through which brand associations can be developed. There are five such devices: co-branding, geographical identifiers, the use of ingredient brands, support services and award symbols.

There are many occasions where advertising funds are not available to develop brand associations and where the brand name and merchandising needs to be the predominant force in enabling buyers to develop managed and positive brand associations. An increasing number of organisations in the b2b sector are using branding approaches and recognise the benefits of co-branding in particular. Charities and organisations in the not-for-profit sector are increasingly using commercial organisations to co-brand. The former receive commercial expertise and funding while the latter gain in terms of association with good deeds, giving (rather than taking) and being seen to care.

Marketing communications is the means by which products become brands. Buyers make associations immediately they become aware of a brand name. It is the brand manager's task to ensure that the associations made are appropriate and provide a means of differentiation. By communicating the key strengths and differences of a brand, by explaining how a brand brings value to a customer and by reinforcing and providing consistency in the messages transmitted, a level of integration can be brought to the way a brand is perceived by the target market.

Finally in this section, the importance of branding as a part of integrated marketing communications should not be forgotten, and to do this internal brand education is crucial. The way a brand relates internally to departments and individuals and the way the brand is articulated by senior management are important parts of brand education. Brands are not just external elements – they should form part of the way in which an organisation operates, part of its cultural configuration.

Business-to-business branding

Branding has been used by a number of manufacturers (e.g. Intel, Teflon, Nutrasweet) to achieve two particular goals. Rich (1996) reports that the first goal is to develop an identity which final end-users perceive as valuable. For example, Intel has developed its microprocessors such that PCs with the Intel brand are seen to be of high quality and credibility. This provides the PC manufacturer with an added competitive advantage. The second goal is to establish a stronger relationship with the manufacturer. Nutrasweet works with food manufacturers advising on recipes simply because the final product is the context within which Nutrasweet will be evaluated by end-users.

A b2b brand is often tied closely to the company itself, as opposed to b2c brands, which often distance themselves from the manufacturer or company name. For example, a Rolls-Royce power turbine is branded Rolls-Royce because of the perception of tradition, high quality, performance and global reach that are associated with the Rolls-Royce name. Marketing communications should be developed so that they incorporate and perpetuate the personality of the brand. Thus, all the Rolls-Royce advertising materials should be in corporate colours and contain the logo. All copy should be in the house style and reinforce brand perceptions.

A b2b brand is often tied closely to the company itself.

Beverland *et al.* (2007) offer an alternative model to Kapferer's (2004) prism (above) in order to address the needs of the business market. Their approach, depicted at Figure 12.6 uses five main dimensions upon which business brands are built: product, service, adaptation, logistics and advice.

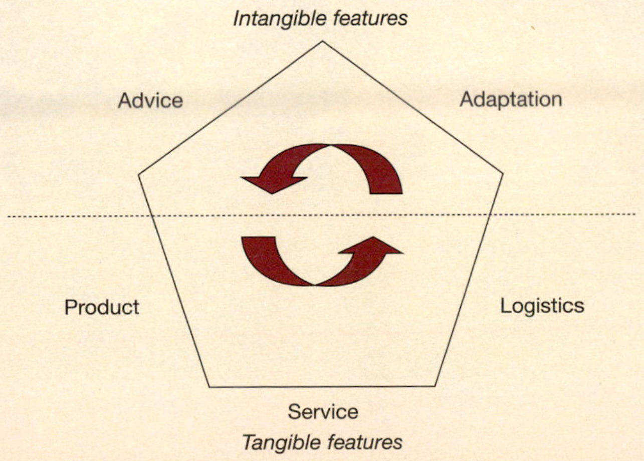

Figure 12.6 Five pillars of business branding
Sources: Beverland *et al.* (2007). Adapted from Ford *et al.* (2002): 122.

ViewPoint 12.6 Dancing Diggers with JCB

JCB is Europe's leading manufacturer of construction equipment and has developed a unique promotional style based on demonstrating the features and versatility of its products in an entertaining way. The JCB Dancing Diggers consists of a series of trick routines that the company's demonstration team performs. The Dancing Diggers perform at exhibitions and draw huge crowds as the capabilities of the giant earth-moving equipment are shown off. This activity feeds advertising, sales literature and, of course, public relations work, providing a strong means of arresting attention and building tremendous levels of credibility.

One little touch of personal selling and publicity skill can be observed in the development and launch of a machine called the 3D. The owner, Joe Bamford, designed the cab so that the operator could make a cup of tea. He promised to personally deliver the first 100 orders with a free kettle, which he did for each purchaser.

Source: www.jcb.co.uk. Used with permission.

Question

To what extent do the use of exhibitions, events and storytelling really build business brands?

Task

Go to www.caterpillar.com/ and find signs of the way they brand themselves?

Exhibit 12.6 JCB
The Dancing Diggers are an important part of the company's publicity strategy.
Picture reproduced with the kind permission of JCB.

The researchers argue that the tangible elements (product benefits) are normally more prominent at the beginning of a business relationship. However, as the relationship develops and as the decision-making becomes increasingly complex so there is a shift away from the tangible to the intangible aspects and abstract associations.

The use of event sponsorship, whereby an organisation provides financial support for a conference or exhibition, has become increasingly popular (Miller, 1997). Mainly because of the costs involved, event organisers have sought sponsorship aid. For sponsors, events provide a means of promoting visibility within a narrowly focused target market. In addition, they provide a means of highlighting their own particular contribution within the conference or their exhibition stand.

The use of joint promotional activities between manufacturers and resellers will continue to be an important form of communication behaviour. The desire to build networks that provide cooperative strength and protection for participants is likely to continue. Manufacturers will use joint promotional activities as a means of forging close relationships with retailers and as a means of strengthening exit barriers (routes away from relationships).

The desire to build networks that provide cooperative strength and protection for participants is likely to continue.

Online branding

The major difference between online and offline branding is the context in which the brand associations are developed and sustained. Both forms of branding are about developing and sustaining valuable relationships with consumers, but online branding occurs in a virtual context. This context deprives consumers of many of the normal cues used to sense and interpret brands. Opportunities to touch and feel, to try on and physically feel and compare products are largely removed and a new set of criteria has to be used to convey and interpret brand associations.

One of the strengths of the Internet is its ability to provide copious amounts of regularly updated information, available '24/7'. As a result online brands tend towards the use of rational messages, using product attributes, quality and performance measures, third-party endorsements, comparisons and price as a means of brand differentiation and advantage. However, it should be remembered that online branding strategies are influenced by the nature of the brand itself. If the brand has a strong offline presence then the amount of online branding work will be smaller than if it is a pure-play brand. Branding should be a part of an overall communications strategy, where online and offline work are coordinated. Breen (1999) argues that online brands are stronger if the following hold true:

- There is an overall communications strategy.
- It is not expected to establish consumer relationships through a single web site visit. The development of a personalised pathway for continued dialogue, such as that used by Amazon.com (which sends regular emails to customers about the status of their purchases and details of potentially interesting offers), is important.
- A record is kept of the changing needs and interests of their consumers.
- They attempt to be seen as a trustmark, not a trademark.
- They try to integrate relationship-building activities with the real world. For example, financial services broker Charles Schwab opens 70 per cent of its accounts in branches where there is a face-to-face-based relationship from which account details are put online. The feeling that there is a personal element to the online relationship appears to add comfort and security.

In 2007/08 the online reliance on rational, informational approaches started to give way as brands became more interactive and capable of emotional engagement. Brand building, once the preserve of offline communications is now an online expectation.

Each web site provides a focus for the brand identity and it is the experience consumers have with a site that determines whether a site will be revisited. The web site acts as a prime means of differentiating online brands and those that fail to develop differential advantage will probably learn that visitors are only one click away from leaving a site (Oxley and Miller, 2000). These commentators refer to a site's 'stickiness' and ability to retain visitors, which in turn can increase advertising rate card costs. However, as they point out, a long visit does not necessarily mean that the experience was beneficial as the site may try to facilitate customer transactions quickly, or enable them to find the information they need without difficulty; in other words, reduced levels of stickiness may be appropriate in some circumstances.

All online branding activities need to extend across all key consumer contact points, in both offline and online environments.

All online branding activities need to extend across all key consumer contact points, in both offline and online environments. Internet users generally exhibit goal-directed behaviour and experiential motivations. Goal-directed behaviour that is satisfied is more likely to make people want to return to a site. Therefore, it can be concluded (broadly) that satisfying experiential motivations makes people stay, and in doing so boosts the potency of an online brand.

Virtual brand communities

Virtual brand communities (VBC) have emerged in recent years as a result of the positive interaction generated through the use of several online tools, most notably chat rooms, forums and discussion areas. Firms such as Procter & Gamble have developed VBCs not only to engage with target audiences but to also enable interaction among their audiences. The two main benefits are that VBCs enable increased brand exposure in a semi-clean environment and also provide rich opportunities to learn about the motivations, feelings and issues related to buyer behaviour and market trends (Pitta and Fowler, 2005).

A VBC is a group of individuals who interact online in order to share their interest in a brand or product.

A VBC is a group of individuals who interact online in order to share their interest in a brand or product. Muniz and O'Guinn (2001) suggest that there are three core components within a community:

- a consciousness of kind (a feeling or passion that binds participants);
- rituals and traditions (shared codes of behaviour and values plus memories of significant events);
- a sense of moral responsibility (moral commitment among members to enable survival of the community).

Casaló *et al.* (2008) undertook one of the first empirical research exercises to determine the effectiveness of community participation. They found that trust in the community itself may increase participation levels, with satisfaction with previous interactions and perceived levels of communication as key factors driving trust. They also discovered that involvement in these communities also had a positive effect on the participants' commitment to the brand. In other words, VBCs can increase the strength of the ties felt towards the brand, which in turn can improve loyalty and drive higher levels of retention.

Brand equity

Brands represent a value to both organisations and shareholders.

The concept of brand equity has arisen from the increasing recognition that brands represent a value to both organisations and shareholders. Brands as assets can impact heavily on the financial well-being of a company. Indeed, Pirrie (2006: 40) refers to the evidence that organisations with strong brands 'consistently outperform their markets'.

According to Ehrenberg (1993), market share is the only appropriate measure of a brand's equity or value and, as a result, all other measures taken individually are of less significance, and collectively they come together as market share. However, this view excludes the composition of brands, the values that consumers place in them and the financial opportunities that arise with brand development and strength.

Lasser *et al.* (1995) identify two main perspectives of brand equity, namely a financial and a marketing perspective. The financial view is based on a consideration of a brand's value as a definable asset, based on the net present values of discounted future cash flows (Farquahar, 1989). The marketing perspective is grounded in the beliefs, images and core associations consumers have about particular brands. Richards (1997) argues that there are both behavioural and attitudinal elements associated with brands and recognises that these vary between groups and represent fresh segmentation and targeting opportunities. A further component of the marketing view is the degree of loyalty or retention a brand is able to sustain. Measures of market penetration, involvement, attitudes and purchase intervals (frequency) are typical. Feldwick (1996) used a three-part definition to bring these two approaches together. He suggests brand equity is a composite of:

- *brand value*, based on a financial and accounting base;
- *brand strength*, measuring the strength of a consumer's attachment to a brand;
- *brand description*, represented by the specific attitudes customers have towards a brand.

In addition to these, Cooper and Simmons (1997) offer *brand future* as a further dimension. This is a reflection of a brand's ability to grow and remain unhindered by environmental challenges such as changing retail patterns, alterations in consumer buying methods and developments in technological and regulative fields. As if to reduce the increasing complexity of these measures Pirrie (2006) argues that brand value needs to be based on the relationship between customer and brand owner and this has to be grounded in the value experienced by the customer, which is subsequently reflected on the company. For consumers the brand value is about 'reduction'; reducing search time and costs, reducing perceived quality assurance risks, and making brand associations by reducing social and ego risks (see Chapter 6 for more information about perceived risks). For brand owners, the benefits are concerned with 'enablement'. She refers to enabling brand extensions, premium pricing and loyalty.

Brand value needs to be based on the relationship between customer and brand owner and this has to be grounded in the value experienced by the customer.

Attempts to measure brand equity have to date been varied and have lacked a high level of consensus, although the spirit and ideals behind the concept are virtually the same. Table 12.6 sets out some of the approaches adopted. As a means of synthesising these approaches the following are considered the principal dimensions through which brand equity should be measured:

- *brand dominance*: a measure of its market strength and financial performance;
- *brand associations*: a measure of the beliefs held by buyers about what the brand represents;
- *brand prospects*: a measure of its capacity to grow and extend into new areas.

Brand equity is considered important because of the increasing interest in trying to measure the return on promotional investments. This in turn aids the valuation of brands for balance sheet purposes. A brand with a strong equity is more likely to be able to preserve its customer franchise and so fend off competitor attacks. From the BrandZ Top 100 model Farr (2006) determined that the top brands are characterised by four factors. They are all strong in terms of innovation, great customer experience, clear values and strong sector leadership. Kish *et al.* (2001) refer to PepsiCo's attempt to build its model of brand equity, called Equitrak (see Viewpoint 12.7).

Table 12.6 Five approaches to measuring brand equity

Source	Factors measured
David Aaker	Awareness, brand associations, perceived quality and market leadership, loyalty, market performance measures.
BrandDynamics, BrandZ (Millward Brown)	Presence, relevance to consumer needs, product performance, competitive advantage, bonding.
Brand asset valuator (Young and Rubicam)	Strength (differentiation and relevance), stature (esteem and knowledge).
Interbrand Global Top 100 (Omnicom)	Intangible future earnings, the role of the brand, brand strength.

Sources: Adapted from Cooper and Simmons (1997); Haigh (1997); Pirrie (2006). http://www.brandassetvaluator.com.au/, www.millwardbrown.com/Sites/, http://www.interbrand.com/best_brands_2006_FAQ.asp

ViewPoint 12.7 Determining value at PepsiCo

PepsiCo determined that it needed to define brand equity so that it could track the development of its various brands, benchmark them against 'icon stature' brands and enable comparisons to be made within the PepsiCo portfolio (Kish *et al.*, 2001).

The Equitrak model developed by PepsiCo. consists of two main elements: brand recognition and brand regard (see Figure 12.7). Brand recognition refers to the depth and breadth of awareness levels. Brand

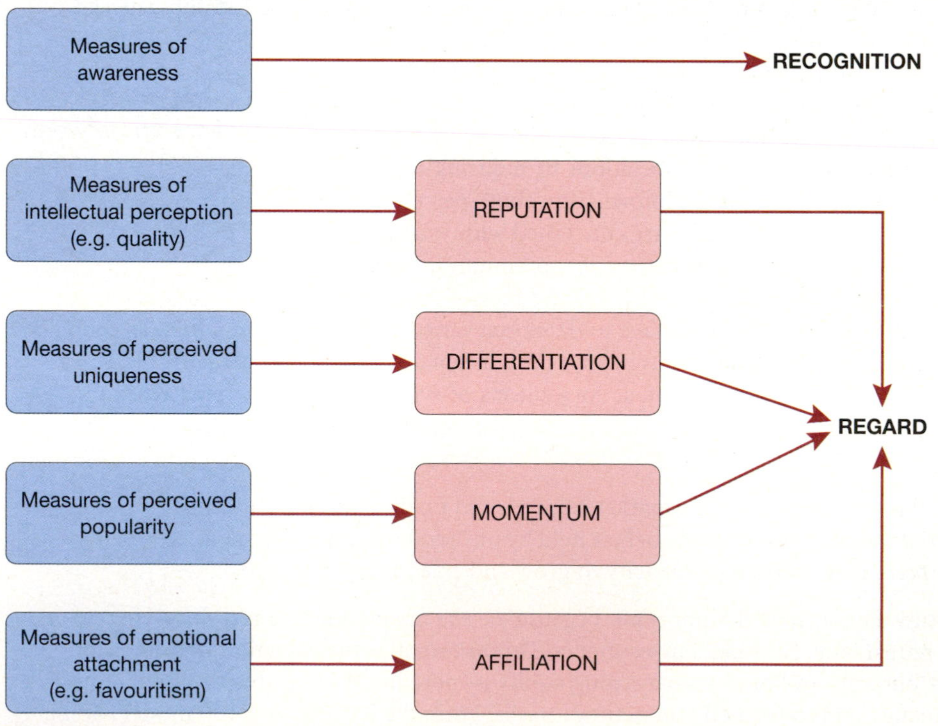

Figure 12.7 The structure of PepsiCo's brand equity model Equitrak
Source: Kish *et al.* (2001).

regard is about how people feel about a brand and measures a number of dimensions. The dimensions are weighted and then multiplied by the recognition score to provide an overall brand equity score.

By plotting the scores on a map it is possible to see how a brand is performing in particular regions, competitive analysis can be undertaken and strategic brand decisions made (see Figure 12.8).

Source: Kish *et al.* (2001).

Question

To what extent should brand valuation incorporate measures of both financial- and market-related factors. What might be the right balance between these two factors?

Task

Go to **www.interbrand.com/portfolio_service.asp?services=1002** and read the short case studies about brand equity and associated valuation.

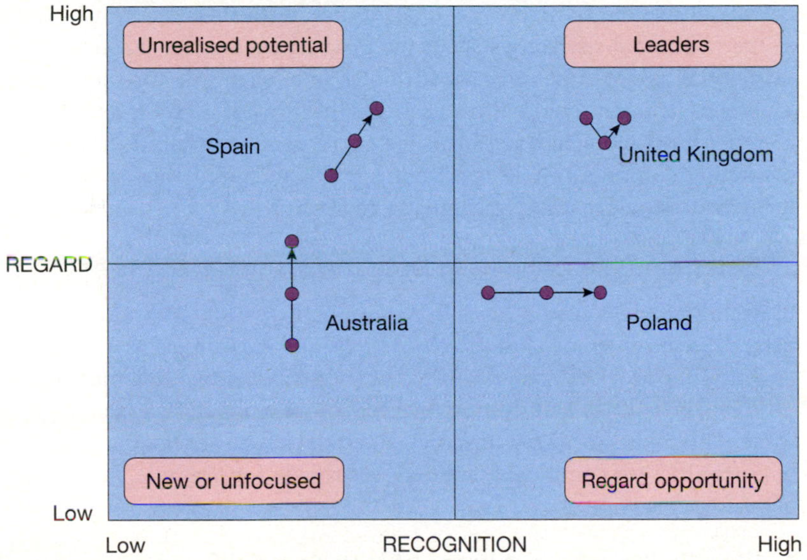

Figure 12.8 Brand equity development trend for a snack brand over time by country
Source: Kish *et al.* (2001). © Emerald Group Publishing Limited. All rights reserved.

Developing brand equity is a strategy-related issue and whether a financial, marketing or twin approach is adopted, the measurement activity can help focus management activity on brand development. However, there is little agreement about what is measured and how and when it is measured. Ambler and Vakratsas (1998) argue that organisations should not seek a single set of measures simply because of the varying circumstances and contextual factors that impinge on brand performance. In reality, the measures used by most firms share many common elements.

Summary

In order to help consolidate your understanding of branding and the role of marketing communications, here are the key points summarised against each of the learning objectives:

1. Introduce and explore the nature of branding.

Branding is a strong means by which a product can be identified, understood and appreciated. Brands are a composite of two main constructs: **1**) an identity that managers wish to portray, and **2**) images, construed by audiences, of the identities they perceive. The development of Web 2.0 and user-generated-content in the form of blogs, wikis and social networks have added a new dimension to the managerial-driven perspective of brands. It is important therefore to recognise that both managers and customers are involved in the branding process.

2. Examine the common characteristics of brands.

Brands consist of two main types of attributes: intrinsic and extrinsic. Intrinsic attributes refer to the functional characteristics of the product such as its shape, performance and physical capacity. If any of these intrinsic attributes were changed, it would directly alter the product. Extrinsic attributes refer to those elements that are not intrinsic and if changed do not alter the material functioning and performance of the product itself: devices such as the brand name, marketing communications, packaging, price and mechanisms which enable consumers to form associations that give meaning to the brand.

3. Determine the benefits to both buyers and owners of brands.

Branding provides customers with a quick and easy way of understanding what a product is, what value it represents and can also represent a measure of psycho-social reassurance.

Branding provides manufacturers and distributors with a means of differentiating their products in order to gain competitive advantage in such a way that customers perceive added value. This allows for premium pricing and the improved margin can be used to invest in new opportunities for commercial initiatives through, for example, innovation or improved levels of customer service.

4. Identify the different types of brands and the relationships they can have with the parent organisation.

An organisation's brand architecture represents the overall marketing interface with the community of stakeholders. The way in which an organisation structures and manages its brands not only affects its overall success but also influences the marketing communications used to support them. The two most common types of brand architecture as branded house and the house of brands.

The development of brand portfolios is a means of gaining and protecting brand advantage. The fundamental structure of a brand portfolio consists of three main levels: the architecture, the form and the individual brand.

5. Appreciate the strategic importance of brands.

Branding is a key strategic communication issue and not only affects FMCG products but is increasingly used by b2b organisations as a means of differentiation and added value.

6. Understand the way in which marketing communications can be used to build and support brands.

Marketing communications has an important role to play in brand development and maintenance. In many circumstances advertising is used to develop strong brands. To help customers make associations with brands either a rational, information-based approach might be adopted or alternatively a more emotional relationship might be forged, one based more on imagery and feelings.

Brands can be developed through the use of above-the-line techniques, namely advertising, or through below-the-line approaches.

7. Explain the role of branding in business-to-business markets.

In a large number of cases the opportunity to use advertising is restricted and many smaller and b2b organisations need to rely on a below-the-line approach. In these circumstances, the brand name is important as it needs to symbolise or convey meaning about the functionality of the brand. In addition, merchandising, packaging and other POP elements will be prominent in brand development.

Branding has been used by a number of manufacturers (e.g. Intel, Teflon, Nutrasweet) to achieve two particular goals. The first goal is to develop an identity that final end-users perceive as valuable. The second goal is to establish a stronger relationship with the manufacturer.

8. Explore some of the issues associated with branding online and in virtual brand communities.

The major difference between online and offline branding is the context in which the brand associations are developed and sustained. Both forms of branding are about developing and sustaining valuable relationships with consumers, but online branding occurs in a virtual context. This context deprives consumers of many of the normal cues used to sense and interpret brands. Opportunities to touch and feel, to try on and physically feel and compare products are largely removed and a new set of criteria has to be used to convey and interpret brand associations.

All online branding activities need to extend across all key consumer contact points, in both offline and online environments. A VBC is a group of individuals who interact online in order to share their interest in a brand or product. VBCs can increase the strength of the ties felt towards the brand, which in turn can improve loyalty and drive higher levels of retention.

9. Appraise the nature and characteristics of brand equity.

Brands as assets can impact heavily on the financial well being of a company. Indeed, Pirrie (2006: 40) refers to the evidence that organisations with strong brands 'consistently outperform their markets'. There are two main ways of considering brand equity, namely a financial and a marketing perspective.

Review questions

1. Write brief notes explaining what branding is.
2. How do brands assist customers and brand owners?
3. Summarise Biel's concept of 'brand magic'.
4. Select five consumer brands and evaluate their characteristics.
5. Explain the concept of a brand portfolio and set out what you understand by the terms architecture, bastion and fighter brands.
6. Discuss the relative importance of the three elements that determine the strategic aspect of branding.
7. Explain advertising's role in the development of brands.

8. Find three non-FMCG brands and evaluate how their brand strength has been developed without the aid of advertising. How might you improve the strength of these brands?
9. Explain how business-to-business markets might benefit from adopting a branding approach.
10. Discuss two approaches to brand equity.

MiniCase Rebranding Greek ice-cream: the case of Nestlé ice-cream

Sofia Daskou: Hellenic American University
and
Peter Zissou: Marketing Manager, Nestlé Hellas Ice cream S.A.

Introduction

In 2008, Nestlé Hellas Ice Cream SA was the biggest ice-cream firm in Greece. It was created in 2006 with the acquisition of Delta Ice-Cream, by Nestlé Hellas. The firm links its available technology and international-level know-how with the reliability, the quality and the knowledge of the Hellenic taste palette to offer high-quality ice-creams to Greek consumers.[1] In 2003, Nestlé US merged with Dreyer's ice-cream business, which resulted in Nestlé owning 67 per cent of the combined company. Taking into account the acquisition of Delta Ice-Cream, Nestlé strengthened its position as one of the largest ice-cream producers in the world.[2]

The international ice-cream industry

In 2007, the ice-cream market globally accounted for $50 billion. Examples of the annual per capita consumption of ice-cream was 18.7 litres in the United States, 13.3 litres in Finland, 11.81 in Sweden, 8.91 in Denmark, 8.51 in Germany and 4.3 in Greece in 2006.[3] Globally the largest ice-cream competitors were Nestlé, Unilever (Algida/Walls), Haagen Dazs, Dreyers, Lotte and McDonald's. In Greece, Nestlé Hellas Ice-Cream SA, EVGA, Unilever (Algida) and Kri Kri shared almost 80 per cent of the market in terms of volume and 92 per cent in terms of value. In 2007, Nestlé Hellas Ice-cream SA held the leading position in the market.

The story of Delta Ice-Cream

Delta ice-cream brands have traditionally been favoured by Greek consumers. Greeks preferred Delta brands because of the firm's Greek identity, taste, innovation and quality. These ice-cream brands had also become popular outside Greece. In the year 2000, Delta Ice-Cream SA, was selling through subsidiaries in Serbia, Romania, and Bulgaria. By 2001, a gross €70 million was invested by Delta Holdings in the Balkans, which allowed the firm to reach a market share of almost 50 per cent across these countries. However, even at that time, the firm was interested in collaborating with a strategic partner in the ice-cream market in the wider Balkan region.[4]

By 2004, Delta Ice-Cream held a leading market position in Greece, Romania, FYROM, Montenegro, Serbia, Hungary and Bulgaria. Balkan ice-cream markets tend to grow faster than western European markets.[5] This growth was good news for Delta Holdings whose market share in the region continued to grow in the period 2001–05.

The Greek ice-cream market

Unlike other Europeans, Greeks associate ice-cream consumption exclusively with summer months, so the seasonal consumption of ice-cream in Greece begins in March, peaks in the summer months[6] and drops in October. During the period 1994–2002 Greek domestic consumption of ice-cream showed fluctuations with most consumers interested in individual and family packs of ice-cream (see Figure 12.9).[7] In 2007, impulse- and family-size packs of ice-cream accounted for 76 per cent of the market. The majority of consumers tended to prefer impulse-size ice-creams and mainly ice-cream sticks, to consume preferably at home,[8] yet most Greeks purchased ice-creams from street kiosks rather than supermarkets.

The Greek ice-cream market had a turnover of €250 million in 2007, and a growth rate of anything between 1–3 per cent was forecast for 2008.[9] In 2007, ICAP[10] forecast a rising trend in the sales of own-label

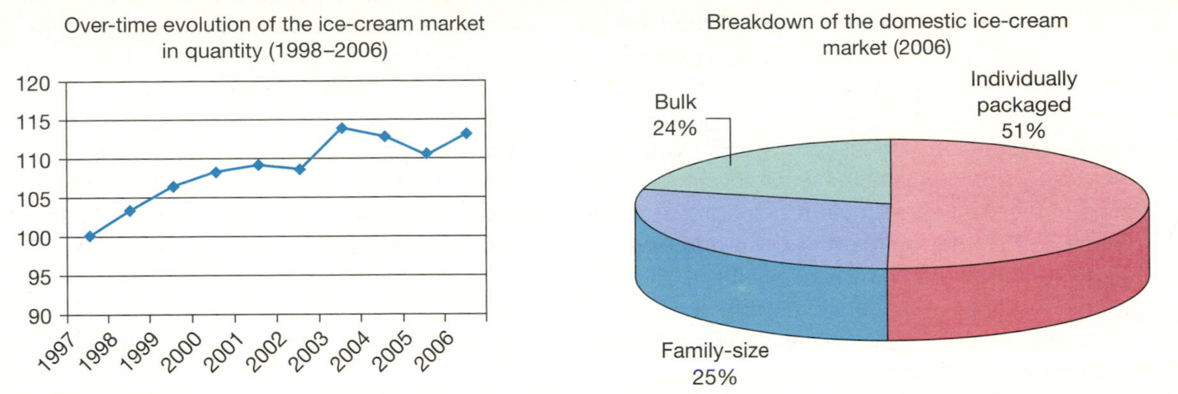

Figure 12.9 Ice-cream consumption in Greece
Source: ICAP Sector Study on Ice-Cream (2007).

ice-creams, as well as an increase in the at-home consumption, irrespective of the point of purchase selected by consumers. ICAP justified this trend by explaining that children and young people (who comprise an important segment of the ice-cream market) spend an increasing amount of their free time at home, while the average person's free time is constantly shrinking.[11] Greeks obtain 'impulse' ice-creams principally from kiosks, but also from supermarkets, corner stores, restaurants and cafes. All these points of sale display ice-creams in branded firm refrigerators.

Branding the product mix

In 2007, the product mix of Nestlé Hellas Ice Cream SA comprised ice-cream on sticks, ice lollies, ice-cream cups, ice-cream cones, ice-cream bars, multipacks and ice-cream sandwiches.

The Greeks favourite ice-cream cup is the firm's Nirvana brand, which comes in various flavours such as strawberry cheesecake, chocolate chip, coffee liqueur, cookies and cream, pralines and cream. The positioning of Nirvana presented in TV advertisements signalled the association of the brand with indulgence and a premium quality product. In 2006, the campaign for Nirvana included product tastings, outdoor and TV adverts, PR events and a contest. Artists were invited to produce artwork inspired by the mood that Nirvana generated in consumers. The best piece of work was offered the Nirvana award.

The Boss brand is the leading premium stick ice-cream product of the firm. Over the years the real-chocolate-coated Boss stick exuded indulgence and sensuality in its TV adverts. That image had always been projected via above- and below-the-line marketing communications of the brand. In 2007, the brand was extended with the additional flavours Boss Brownies and Boss Almond Vanilla. Multi-packs represent an ice-cream category with a high growth rate that attracts consumers who are interested in smaller portions without sacrificing their enjoyment. This type of product also interests consumers who prefer consumption of individual ice-cream units at home. In 2007, the firm created three new flavours for this line.

By 2008, Nestlé Hellas Ice Cream SA was identifiable by a renewed corporate image, that in 2007 had already appeared at the points of sale. The basic characteristics of the renewed image were the maintenance of the green colour of the refrigerators that hosted the product, but also augmented with a tone of renewal and freshness.[12] As the Greek ice-cream market is a mature market (characterised by intense seasonality and fluctuating demand), the firm paid attention to the improvement of the presentation of the product at the point of sale. In 2006, Nestlé aimed to develop the image of its ice-cream brands to be as attractive as possible, by allocating updated and well-presented refrigerators, with new and original promotional material attached to them at the points of sale. The branding strategy for 2007 was two-fold:

1. to combine the Delta ice-cream product mix with the international Nestlé ice-cream product mix.
2. to display the Nestlé logo alongside the Delta lego on the refrigerators, signalling the identification of the corporate Nestlé brand with the popular Delta brands.

In 2007, Nestlé renewed the representation of its identity by providing its distributors with new refrigerators illustrating combined brand imagery from both

Delta and Nestlé. The objective was to secure the taste that Greek ice-cream consumers demand from their ice-cream suppliers, by signalling the 'new identity' of the ice-creams. The visual representation of the 2007 refrigerators retained the green base colour that Greek consumers were familiar with at the points of sale, however, the refrigerators were revamped. In marketing terms the firm adopted a brand integration multi-stage process to 'merge' the Delta and Nestlé ice-cream brand personalities. Subsequently, all the TV adverts for Nestlé ice-cream brands stressed the fact that the brands were available from the *green* refrigerators (of Nestlé and Delta).

The marketing challenge

Nestlé aimed to retain its leading position in the Greek ice-cream market without losing the customers who had been fans of the old Delta brands. The firm attempted to phase the rebranding over a period of several years. In 2007, the firm decided to retain the familiar green refrigerators, but include the Nestlé logo on them. In 2008, the firm stopped using the Delta logo in one area of its communications, but retained Delta's successful brands in its contemporary product mix. In addition, in 2008 the firm removed the Delta logo from the packaging of the products. In the future the firm will need to find ways to complete the rebranding of the old Delta ice-creams by assigning them a Nestlé identity. The challenge is to effect this rebranding without offending Greek consumers by transforming a Greek brand into an international one. How should Nestlé proceed to fulfil the rebranding of its ice-creams?

MiniCase endnotes/references

1. Nestlé and Delta Green refrigerators press release, published in the newspaper *Eleftheros Typos*.
2. http://www.nestle.com/MediaCenter/PressReleases/AllPressReleases/. 'Nestlé achieves full ownership of Dreyer's and becomes world leader in ice cream', Vevey, 19 January 2006.
3. http://grhomeboy.wordpress.com/2007/07/14/greek-ice-cream-market-to-extend/. 'Greek ice cream market to extend', 14 July 2007.
4. Korfiatis, C. (2001) 'Proposal of entry in the subsidiary company of Greek group Delta that dominates the Balkans', Newspaper *To Vima*, 8 July 2007, 14. Article code: B13307D141.
5. www.food-business-review.com, 19 December 2005. 'Nestlé/Delta: Freezing out European Rivals'.
6. http://grhomeboy.wordpress.com/2007/07/14/greek-ice-cream-market-to-extend/. 'Greek ice cream market to extend', 14 July 2007.
7. http://www.icap.gr/news/index_uk_2355.asp. ICAP Sector Study on Ice Cream, 26 June 2003.
8. http://grhomeboy.wordpress.com/2007/07/14/greek-ice-cream-market-to-extend/. 'Greek ice cream market to extend', 14 July 2007.
9. http://grhomeboy.wordpress.com/2007/07/14/greek-ice-cream-market-to-extend/. 'Greek ice cream market to extend', 14 July 2007.
10. ICAP is the largest Hellenic Organization of Economic Information, Publications. The firm also offers Advising & Consulting Services to Enterprises in Greece.
11. http://www.icap.gr/news/index_uk_8040.asp. 'Limited growth margins in the domestic market of ice cream', 11 July 2007.
12. Nestlé and Delta Green refrigerators press release, published in the newspaper *Eleftheros Typos*.

MiniCase questions

1. Discuss the branding issues of Nestlé Hellas Ice-Cream SA.
2. What are the advantages and disadvantages of the rebranding strategy adopted by Nestlé?
3. Design an integrated communications campaign to rebrand and reposition the Nestlé ice-cream product mix in Greece and in the wider Balkans region.

References

Ambler, T. and Vakratsas, D. (1998) Why not let the agency decide the advertising. *Market Leader*, **1** (Spring), 32–7.

Assael, H. (1990) *Marketing: Principles and Strategy*. Orlando, FL: Dryden Press.

Barnett, A., Davidson, M. and Dias, S. (2006) The Famous Grouse. *IPA Advertising Effectiveness Paper*. Institute of Practitioners in Advertising. Retrieved 10 December 2007 from http://www.warc.com/ArticleCenter/Default.asp?CType=A&AID=WORDSEARCH82620&Tab=A.

Beverland, M., Napoli, J. and Yakimova, R. (2007) Branding the business marketing offer: exploring brand attributes in business markets. *Journal of Business and Industrial Marketing*, **22**(6), 394–9.

Biel, A. (1997) Discovering brand magic: the hardness of the softer side of branding. *International Journal of Advertising*, **16**, 199–210.

Blackett, T. (1992) Branding and the rise of the generic drug. *Marketing Intelligence and Planning*, **10**(9), 21–4.

Blackston, M. (1993) A brand with an attitude: a suitable case for treatment. *Journal of Market Research Society*, **34**(3), 231–41.

Boehringer, C. (1996) How can you build a better brand? *Pharmaceutical Marketing* (July), 35–6.

Breen, B. (1999) Building stronger internet identities. *Marketing*, 16 September, 25–6.

Brooke, S. and Nottage, A. (2008) Luxe in flux, *Marketing*, 13 February, 30–1.

Casaló, V., Flavián, C. and Guinalíu, M. (2008) Promoting consumers' participation in virtual brand communities: a new paradigm in branding strategy. *Journal of Marketing Communications*, **14**(1) (February), 19–36.

Chernatony de, L. and Dall'omo Riley, F. (1998a) Defining a brand: beyond the literature with experts' interpretations. *Journal of Marketing Management*, **14**, 417–43.

Chernatony de, L. and Dall'omo Riley, F. (1998b) Expert practitioners' views on roles of brands: implications for marketing communications. *Journal of Marketing Communications*, **4**, 87–100.

Cooper, A. and Simmons, P. (1997) Brand equity lifestage: an entrepreneurial revolution. TBWA Simmons Palmer. Unpublished working paper.

Durston, J. (2008) How to turn Indians into wine drinkers: the case of Sula Vineyards, *WARC.com*, February. Retrieved 16 March 2008 from www.warc.com.

Ehrenberg, A.S.C. (1974) Repetitive advertising and the consumer. *Journal of Advertising Research*, **14** (April), 25–34.

Ehrenberg, A.S.C. (1993) If you are so strong why aren't you bigger? *Admap* (October), 13–14.

Farquahar, P. (1989) Managing brand equity. *Marketing Research*, **1**(9) (September), 24–33.

Farr, A. (2006) Soft measure, hard cash, *Admap*, November, 39–42.

Feldwick, P. (1996) What is brand equity anyway, and how do you measure it? *Journal of Market Research*, **38**(2), 85–104.

Fournier, S. (1995) A consumer–brand relationship perspective on brand equity. Presentation to Marketing Science Conference on Brand Equity and the Marketing Mix, Tucson, Arizona, 2–3 March. Working paper 111, 13–16.

Gray, R. (2006) Wake up to digital danger, *Marketing*, 13 December, 52.

Gray, E.R. and Smeltzer, L.R. (1985) SMR Forum: corporate image – an integral part of strategy. *Sloan Management Review* (Summer), 73–8.

Haigh, D. (1997) Brand valuation: the best thing to ever happen to market research. *Admap* (June), 32–5.

Kapferer, J.-N. (2004) *The New Strategic Brand Management*. London: Kogan Page.

Kish, P., Riskey, D.R. and Kerin, R. (2001) Measurement and tracking of brand equity in the global marketplace: the PepsiCo experience. *International Marketing Review*, **18**(1), 91–6.

Kotler, P. (2000) *Marketing Management: The Millennium Edition.* Upper Saddle River, NJ: Prentice-Hall.

Lasser, W., Mittal, B. and Sharma, A. (1995) Measuring customer based brand equity. *Journal of Consumer Marketing*, **12**(4), 11–19.

Lee, J. (2004) Lego calls review of £35m European media. *Campaign*, Retrieved 23 December 2004 from www.brandrepublic.com/news/.

Lovett, L. (2008) Why the shoe fits. *The Times Luxx Magazine*, 22.

Miller, R. (1997) Make an event of it. *Marketing*, 5 June, 28.

Muniz, A. and O'Guinn, T.C. (2001) Brand communities. *Journal of Consumer Research*, 27, (March), 412–32.

Oxley, M. and Miller, J. (2000) Capturing the consumer: ensuring website stickiness. *Admap* (July/August), 21–4.

Petromilli, M., Morrison, D. and Million, M. (2002) Brand architecture: building brand portfolio value. *Strategy and Leadership*, **30**(5), 22–8.

Pierce, A. and Moukanas, H. (2002) Portfolio power: harnessing a group of brands to drive profitable growth. *Strategy and Leadership*, **30**(5), 15–21.

Pirrie, A. (2006) What value brands? *Admap*, (October) 40–2.

Pitta, D.A. and Fowler, D. (2005) Online communities and their value to new product developers. *Journal of Product and Brand Management*, **14**(5), 283–91.

Rich, M. (1996) Stamp of approval. *Financial Times*, 29 February, 9.

Richards, T. (1997) Measuring the true value of brands. *Admap* (March), 32–6.

Riezebos, R. (2003) *Brand Management: A Theoretical and Practical Approach.* Harlow: Pearson.

Ritson, M. (2007) Welcome to the house of brands. *Marketing*, 12 December 2007, 21.

Vyse, K. (1999) Fingerprint clues identify the brand. *Marketing*, 30 September, 38.

Walton, P. (2007) A practical framework for developing brand portfolios. *Admap*, (July/August), 33–5.

Chapter 13

Managing corporate reputation: identity and branding

The awareness, perception and attitudes held by an organisation's various stakeholders will vary in intensity and need to be understood and acted upon. This can be accomplished through a strategy that develops the profile of an organisation, one that seeks continual dialogue and leads to the development of trust-based relationships. This is necessary in order that stakeholders think and act favourably towards an organisation and enable the organisation to develop strategies that are compatible with the environment and its own objectives.

Aims and learning objectives

The aim of this chapter is to consider those communications that are designed to encourage a dialogue with stakeholders, with a view to influencing the image and reputation of the organisation.

The learning objectives of this chapter are to:

1. examine the key concepts associated with corporate identity;
2. understand the difference between corporate branding and corporate identity;
3. consider some of the ideas and issues associated with corporate communications;
4. understand the core elements associated with corporate identity;
5. explain the meaning and importance of corporate reputation;
6. introduce a framework incorporating corporate identity into the process of strategic management.

For an applied interpretation see Karl Milner and Graham Hughes' MiniCase entitled ***Just how branded is the NHS?*** at the end of this chapter.

Introduction

This chapter is concerned with the way in which organisations are presented and perceived, and how they interact with their various stakeholder audiences. It is also concerned with the images that people form as a result of interpreting the various identity signals that organisations transmit and any interaction that may ensue. Melewar (2003) derived the following definition from a consideration of the literature. For him, corporate identity is concerned with 'the set of meanings by which an organisation allows itself to be known and through which it enables people to describe, remember and relate to it'.

People form images of an organisation based on the cues or signals that organisations transmit.

All organisations use corporate communications to deliver their corporate identity. It is through the identity that stakeholders form images of the organisation and, through time, corporate reputations are built. People form images of an organisation based on the cues or signals that organisations transmit. These cues may be sent deliberately or they may be accidental or unintended. Whatever the source, these cues can be critical because the way they are interpreted shapes the way organisations are regarded and even whether transactions occur.

Hatch and Schultz (2000) refer to two schools of thought about strategic identity management. The 'visual' school, which is concerned with operational aspects, and a 'strategic' school, which is concerned with an organisation's aims and how it positions and distinguishes itself. This demarcation is useful because not only does it help identify the scope of the topic but it also shows how identity management, indeed reputation management, has evolved. These two aspects of identity management are referred to later in this chapter.

Organisations are said to have a personality, a persona that reflects the inner spirit and heart of the organisation. From this cultural core identities are developed and presented to the outside world. The management of the corporate identity is vital if the image held of the organisation, by all stakeholders, is to be consistent and accurately represent the personality of the organisation (Dowling, 1993).

Gorb (1992) refers to a continuum of differentiation where at one end there is a total loss of personality and at the other end a schizoid position is achieved. The trick is to change with the environment and maintain a differentiated position by providing continuity in the way the identity is represented and perceived. He quotes Shell, whose logo, established over a century ago, appears to have been preserved unchanged. Exhibit 13.1 shows that in reality it has undergone many changes and what we see today is nothing like the original. This has occurred through careful continuity of the idea of the seashell and adaptation of it to the various contexts through time.

There are a number of identity-related topics, including visual identity, strategic corporate identity, social identity and organisational identity (He and Balmer, 2007). These are set out at Table 13.1.

Table 13.1 Perspectives on identity schools of thought

Form of identity		Explanation
Corporate identity	Visual	Using visual expression for organisational self-presentation.
	Strategic	Using an organisation's characteristics, traits and attributes as cues to express how an organisation wants to be seen.
Social identity		How members see themselves as a social part of the organisation.
Organisational identity		The identity of an organisation as perceived by the members.

Exhibit 13.1 Shell have evolved their logo over a long time to the point that the current logo shows little similarity to the original
Shell Brands International AG.

Although He and Balmer separate the visual and strategic forms of corporate identity they are often considered to be part of the same area of study. The social and organisational forms of identity are part of the organisational behaviour school of thought. However, there is evidence to suggest that the organisational and corporate identity schools are showing signs of overlap, a view shared by Cornelissen *et al.* (2007) and Anisimova (2007). Although reference is made to organisational identity, this chapter concentrates on corporate identity that encapsulates both the visual and strategic perspectives.

Corporate identity or corporate branding?

Some researchers, authors and marketing practitioners prefer the term 'corporate branding' and are using it to replace the expression 'corporate identity'. Balmer (1998) suggested that corporate identity was the accepted terminology in the 1980s and early 1990s, and that this gave way to corporate branding at the turn of the century. However, it can be argued that there are some intrinsic differences in this terminology. Balmer and Gray (2003) claim that there are strong and fundamental differences between these two concepts. All organisations have a need to address identity-related issues, such as those posed by Albert and Whetten (1985) who said the three key questions that organisations need to find answers to are, 'Who are we?', 'What business are we in?', and 'What do we want to be?' However, if corporate identity is a necessity for all organisations, corporate branding is not. Corporate brands are developed from their identity and, unlike traditional

Corporate brands are developed from their identity and primarily concerned with the delivery of specific corporate promises.

approaches to corporate messages, are primarily concerned with the delivery of specific corporate promises. These promises are often conveyed through a short strapline or 'mantra' (Keller, 1999). Balmer and Gray (2003) use Disney and Nike as examples: 'fun, family entertainment' and 'authentic athletic performance' respectively. These brands are seen to consist of certain criteria, which are set out in Table 13.2.

Table 13.2 Corporate brand criteria

Corporate brand criteria	Explanation
Rarity	Corporate brand values (functional and emotional) developed over time that cannot be easily imitated.
Durability	The value of the brand depreciates slowly, relative to product brands.
Inappropriability	Only the owning organisation can derive performance-related outcomes.
Imperfect imitability	It is very difficult for a competitor to copy or replicate the brand.
Imperfect substitutability	Strong corporate brands maintain their position through continuous improvement and protect themselves from competitors and from being overtaken.

Source: Based on Balmer and Gray (2003).

ViewPoint 13.1 ITN Source of rebranding

ITN Source offers moving-image content for its customers in a wide range of television, film, advertising, education online and many other creative media sectors. The company claims to provide access to the largest collection of moving-image libraries in the world, housing over 800,000 hours of footage captured over three centuries. It adds 15 hours of content each day and is growing its revenue at 35 per cent per annum.

To signify its position as a major global multimedia-content business it changed its name from ITN Archive to ITN Source and rebranded each of its six divisions with individual identities while unifying them under a fresh, new global identity.

A bulk email was personalised and sent to 14,000 customers. It included a call-to-action encouraging respondents to click through to a microsite. The launch was preceded with a major technical update to the web site. This allows for enhanced interactive capabilities and the ability to demonstrate footage work. It is claimed that the system enhanced the communication of the rebranding exercise and drove higher than expected traffic levels back to the site. The campaign emails alone achieved a click through rate of 7 per cent.

Sources: Williams, (2006); www.itnsource.com/en/About_Us/PressOffice/.

Question

To what extent is this rebranding exercise a visual or strategic task and what business is ITN Source in?

Task

Visit www.itnsource.com and find out what the company's strapline is.

Table 13.3 Differences between product and corporate brands

	Product brand	Organisation brand
Focus of attention on . . .	The product	The organisation
Managed by . . .	Middle management	CEO/top management
Attract attention and gain support of . . .	Customers	Multiple stakeholders
Delivered by . . .	Marketing	Whole organisation
Communicated by . . .	Marketing communications	Multiple communications, activities, and contacts
Time horizon . . .	Short (product life)	Long (organisation life)
Importance to organisation . . .	Tactical for function	Strategic for organisation

Source: Adapted from Balmer (2001). Used with permission.

Balmer and Gray developed these criteria based on the 'resource-based view of the firm', which is grounded in the brand, having considerable resources and capabilities that can be used as a major source of sustainable value. The basis therefore, of a strong corporate brand and its ability to deliver its promise is the organisation's ability to continually leverage its resources to deliver superior value.

> A strong corporate brand and its ability to deliver its promise is the organisation's ability to continually leverage its resources to deliver superior value.

Corporate brands are a complex form of identity, but not all organisations need a corporate brand, if, for example, they are a public utility, monopoly or work in commodities. Even though this area is of increasing interest to academics and organisations, issues concerning the development and criticality of corporate reputation appear to be of greater importance to organisations.

Before proceeding it is worth establishing the differences between product and corporate branding. Although some argue that the two are intrinsically the same and it is only the implementation and context that differs, there is a generally held view that corporate and product brands are different. Anisimova (2007) suggests that corporate branding represents a blend of the perspectives held by those corporate identity and the organisational theorists. Dunnion and Knox (2005) offer the following table (Table 13.3) that sets out clearly the key points of difference.

The corporate identity process

Shee and Abratt (1989) are acknowledged to be the first to attempt to disentangle the confusion surrounding identity and image. They identify three main elements that are central to the development of corporate image (see Figure 13.1). These are corporate personality, identity and image. Individuals and organisations project their

> Three main elements are central to the development of corporate image: corporate personality, identity and image.

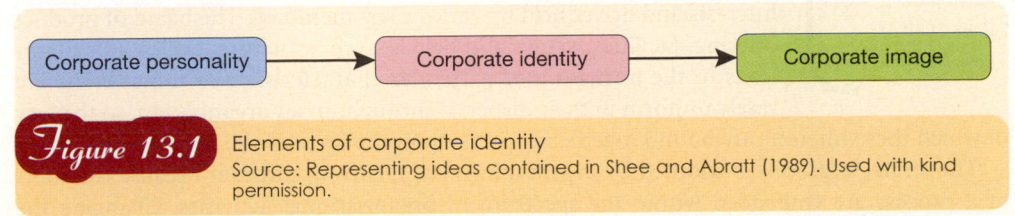

Figure 13.1 Elements of corporate identity
Source: Representing ideas contained in Shee and Abratt (1989). Used with kind permission.

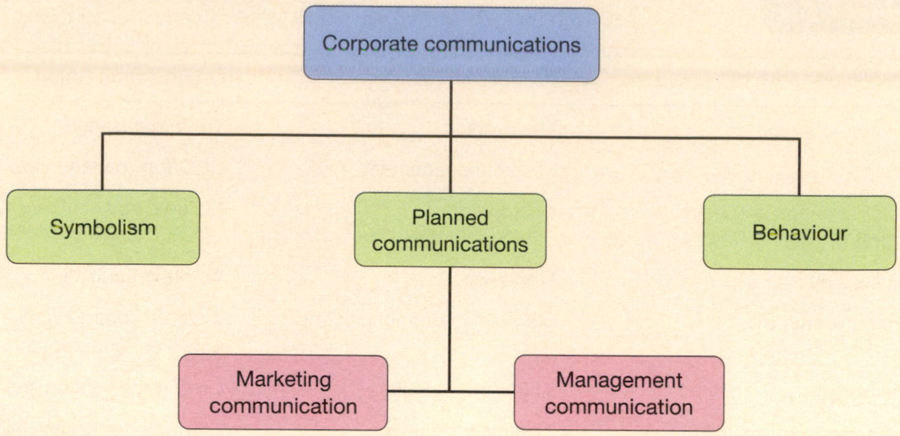

Figure 13.2 Dimensions of corporate communications

personalities through their identity. The identity is communicated through corporate communications that include symbolism, behaviour and marketing communications. The audience's perception of the identity is the image they have of the object, in this case, the corporate body. This process is discussed in the next sections and is represented in Figure 13.2.

Corporate personality

The first of these elements requires the recognition and acceptance that organisations have personalities, or at least significant characteristics. As Bernstein (1984) states, just as individuals have personalities, so do organisations. Corporate personalities are derived partly from the cultural characteristics of the organisation: the core values and beliefs that in turn are part of a corporate philosophy. Essential to corporate personality is the strategy process adopted by the organisation. The degree to which the strategic process is either formalised and planned or informal and emergent, and whether strategy is well communicated, play major roles in shaping the personality of the organisation.

For example, management now recognises the powerful influence that an organisation's corporate objectives have in informing and guiding the operations of each of the functional departments. The formulation of the mission statement requires management and employees to understand what the organisation seeks to achieve. To understand what the organisation wants to achieve requires understanding what the organisation values and believes in, which in turn involves and reflects the involvement of all members of the organisation, either deliberately or involuntarily. Indeed, the stated philosophy and values that are articulated through the mission statement (and other devices) are important in establishing the preferred relationship it has with its various constituencies (Leuthesser and Kohli, 1997).

Corporate personality can be considered to be composed of two main facets: the culture and overall strategic purpose.

The corporate personality can be considered to be composed of two main facets: the culture and overall strategic purpose (Markwick and Fill, 1997). Organisational culture is a composite of the various sectional interests and drives held by various key members. The blend of product offering, facilities, values and beliefs, staff, structure, skills and systems leads to the formation of particular characteristics or traits. Traits are rarely uniform in their dispersal throughout an organisation, so the way in which these interests are bound together impacts upon the form of the primary culture.

The strategic processes adopted by organisations are relatively constant because the roots of a process are embedded within the spectrum of organisational activities. Changing the strategic process is very different from changing the content of a strategy. Stuart (1999a) refers specifically to the contribution the organisational structure can make to an organisation's corporate identity. Interestingly she considers Mintzberg's typology of organisational structures Mintzberg and Quinn, (1988), but what can be gathered is that structure impacts on strategy, which informs the identity process.

There was a great deal of merger activity in the late 1990s but management appears to be guilty of not paying enough attention to a vision of what the new culture will be like and how it will be expressed through the identity. The merger between Mannesmann, which was over 100 years old, and Vodafone, a mere 18 years old, was made on the basis of share value and global expansion, not cultural fit. The evidence suggests that it is the financial business model that dominates and not the brand model. Mergers do not result in amalgamated cultures, as experience shows that one will be pre-eminent, usually as a result of one or two key individuals reaching top positions. People also leave because they do not like the new way of doing things.

Corporate personality is the totality of the characteristics that identify an organisation. Consider the values held by organisations such as easyJet, HSBC, the NHS, Tesco and Oxfam. Not only are the images different but so are the values and the personalities.

The BBC and Channel 5 are interesting organisations to consider from a personality perspective. The BBC is a mature organisation where stability, security and reliability have long been regarded as important characteristics. However, these are now regarded by some as impediments to progress and innovation, not helped by the events surrounding the Hutton inquiry. Channel 5 is young and vibrant, where programme quality is measured differently from the BBC and where innovation is seen as an important part of challenging the rules of standard broadcasting.

Corporate personality is what an organisation actually is.

Corporate identity

The second element in the image process is corporate identity. This is the formation of the cues by which stakeholders can recognise and identify the organisation. In recent years, many organisations have chosen to pay more attention to their identity and have tried to manage these cues more deliberately.

ViewPoint 13.2 Rocky identities

Many financial services organisations offer online banking. The chance to reduce costs and reach new customer groups has been a major force behind this development. What is interesting, however, is that many have chosen to rebrand their online offering and create a separate identity.

The Halifax uses 'If', the Cooperative Bank 'Smile' and Citi 'Egg'. Abbey National chose to use the name 'Cahoot' in order to reach a more affluent customer, one which research shows would not normally bank with Abbey National.

The disguise of the online brand identity therefore enables organisations to use communications to be directed to particular customer segments without having to overcome the negative values associated with the parent brand.

The chaos that surrounded the wrecked Northern Rock bank resulted in a change of strategy. This involved downsizing the operation and converting from a lender (of mortgages) to become, principally, a savings bank (Odoi, 2008). One of the key questions, therefore, is should the name of the bank be changed?

Question

Would you change the name of the Northern Rock bank?

Task

Make a list of the possible names you would consider using if a new name had been required. Would the new name contain the words Northern and Rock in it?

Identity is a means by which an organisation differentiates itself from other organisations.

Identity is a means by which an organisation differentiates itself from other organisations. Bernstein (1984) makes an important point when he observes that all organisations have an identity, whether they like it or not. Some organisations choose deliberately to manage their identities, just as individuals choose not to frequent particular shops or restaurants, drive certain cars or wear specific fabrics or colours. Other organisations take less care over their identities and the way in which they transmit their identity cues, and as a result confuse and mislead members of their networks and underperform in the markets in which they operate.

According to Olins (1989), management of the identity process can communicate three key ideas to its audiences. These are what the organisation is, what it does and how it does it. Corporate identity is manifested in four ways. These, he says, can be interpreted as the products and services that the organisation offers, where the offering is made or distributed, how the organisation communicates with stakeholders and, finally, how the organisation behaves.

The marked development of the corporate brand has been noticeable in recent years. Organisations have used it as a means of differentiating their products from competitors' products and have recognised the power of the characteristics that delineate one organisation from another. These characteristics are embodied by the organisation's personality, values and culture. The corporate brand is a means of presenting these characteristics to various audiences, such as financial markets, suppliers, employees, channel network partners, trade unions, competitors and customers.

Corporate communications

Corporate communication refers to the process that translates corporate identity into corporate image.

According to Ind (1992) corporate communication refers to the process that translates corporate identity into corporate image. As mentioned above, increasingly organisations are taking an active interest in corporate identity and branding (Cowlett, 2000) mainly because of the benefits that can be achieved across the organisation. By attempting to control the messages that it transmits, an organisation can inform and motivate stakeholders concerning what it is, what it does and how it does it in a credible and consistent way. Traditionally, the bulk of this communication work has been the responsibility of public relations.

Corporate communications consists of three main elements: symbolism, behaviour and different forms of planned communication. These planned communications consist of management communication and marketing communication. The former is concerned with line and functional communications necessary to ensure functional activities are completed appropriately. This also includes management communications undertaken with external stakeholders. Marketing communications involve product- and service-oriented communications and organisational communication, normally undertaken through a range of public relations activities and corporate advertising, plus internal communications aimed at building commitment and identification with the organisation (see Figure 13.2). Consideration is given here to symbolism and behaviour. Public relations is considered in Chapter 19 and internal marketing communications is explored in Chapter 30.

Symbolism

Symbolism refers to the visual aspect of identity and was once regarded as the sole aspect of corporate identity management. Salame and Salame (1975) were some of the first researchers to consider visual identity in this way. Indeed, there are many today who regard visual identity as the only real element of corporate identity, mentioned earlier as the visual school of corporate identity. Schein (1985), in his hierarchy of corporate culture, determines 'visible artefacts' as the first level. These are the more immediately observable aspects of the culture, such as the letterheads, logos, signage, emblems, colour schemes, architecture and the overall appearance of all the design aspects associated with the company. Dowling (1994) refers to visual identity and its composition consisting of four key elements: corporate names, logos and symbols, typefaces and colour. It is thought that through the use of symbolism a level of harmonisation can be achieved by bringing all of these identity cues together. To these elements should be added architecture and physical location (Melewar *et al.* (2006)).

> Visual identity consists of four keying in point for elements: corporate names, logos and symbols, typefaces and colour.

Visual identity is also an important element in an organisation's international strategy and the way in which it wishes to be perceived in different countries and regions. In particular, multinational organisations need to find new ways of identifying themselves as a result of merger, acquisition, technological developments, restructuring and other changes in their various marketplaces (Melewar, 2001).

Van den Bosch *et al.* (2004) found in their research that a large number of organisations use templates and corporate identity manuals to help manage their visual identities and that to a large extent these were accepted by both employees and managers as appropriate tools to manage what was agreed to be an important subject. However, there is little evidence to show whether this energy is well directed and importantly it appears that many managers are not consistent in their approach to managing visual identity and that they do not always 'do as they say'.

Corporate branding and names

Associated with the symbolism used by organisations is the name and how this is presented. The constituent parts of a corporate brand are many and varied. One interpretation suggests that a brand consists of the following variables: reputation, product and service performance, product brand and customer portfolio and networks in the sense of positioning (Knox and Maklan, 1998). Another interpretation is that each brand is perceived with varying degrees of intensity depending on the level of involvement customers have with the brand itself. According to Kunde (2000), brands can range from a product base where there is little value other than the name, through to a corporate concept brand where there is a strong and consistent relationship between the consumers, the company and the brand itself. At the highest level is brand religion, where the brand is paramount for consumers, a belief or a religion that enables a range of other products to be introduced within the same 'religious' environment. He quotes Body Shop, Harley-Davidson and Coca-Cola. What is noticeable about this approach is the importance attached to the internal culture and the need to balance the internal and external positioning, a view echoed throughout contemporary corporate branding literature and one thoroughly endorsed and supported in this text.

> The name of an organisation is a strong corporate cue as it is often people's first contact with the organisation.

The name of an organisation is a strong corporate cue as it is often people's first contact with the organisation.

Abbey National changed its name to *Abbey* in 2003 and at the same time removed a series of sub-brands such as Scottish Provident, Scottish Mutual and Inscape. The change also offered the opportunity to remove its strapline, 'because life's complicated enough'. The change in name accompanies a change in business strategy as the organisation attempts to re-establish itself.

Names used in the telecommunications sector were for a long time dominated by purely descriptive, functionally oriented titles. In 1994 this started to change when Wolff Olins created the Orange brand for Hutchinson Telecom. Orange offered instant differentiation that also reflected the 'different' service being offered for the first time. Owning a 'colour' offered a sense of exclusivity and allowed for a number of creative advertising opportunities (Murphy, 1999).

Some names need to change as a result of a strategic development such as when Group 4 merged with Securicor. The new name G4S, needed to reflect the dimensions of the new global company and its activities in all markets. Some new company names, such as Accenture, which means ascent to the future (see Viewpoint 13.3), have to be developed quickly. Sims (2008) reports that the Andersen Consulting rebrand into Accenture was achieved in just 147 days. Some new names just do not work, such as the new name for the Post Office 'Consignia', which was rejected by many stakeholder groups for many reasons. Some names just fade if not looked after and refreshed. For example, P&O was found to mean slow, had not moved with the times, lacked investment in people and infrastructure and had strong links to the colonial past. Not surprising then that their new owners, DPWorld, concluded that the P&O name lacked brand equity (Sims, 2008).

Behaviour

The behavioural aspect is largely concerned with the way in which employees and managers interact with one another and, more importantly, with external members of the organisation.

The behavioural aspect is largely concerned with the way in which employees and managers interact with one another and, more importantly, with external members of the organisation. The tone of voice used and the actions and consideration of customer needs by employees are often represented within a customer service policy, which is an important part of an organisation's interface with various stakeholder groups.

ViewPoint 13.3 Symbolic Tiger Swings in for Accenture

Accenture is a global management consulting, technology services and outsourcing company. After renaming itself in 2001, Accenture launched a highly successful rebranding campaign. The new name, derived from 'Accent on the future', was meant to reinforce its new positioning and reflected the organisation's further growth and broadened set of capabilities.

In 2003, Accenture announced that it had entered into an agreement with the world's number one golfer, Tiger Woods. He agreed to represent the company as a symbol of its new high performance business strategy, and the line, 'Go on. Be a Tiger.'

The campaign used pictures of Tiger Woods in golfing situations that demand optimum performance in competitive environments with a focus on winning. The campaign explained how Accenture helps its clients achieve superior economic performance. The campaign utilises the modern-day personification of high performance: Tiger Woods, the world's most iconic golfer.

Following a successful three-year run with the 'Go on. Be a Tiger' campaign, Accenture embarked on a new global campaign based around the line 'We know what it takes to be a Tiger.' This campaign used television, print, outdoor and online advertising to direct audiences to Accenture's High Performance Business site, where the campaign continues with more in-depth educational and interactive components online. The new site includes case studies, podcasts and client success stories designed to substantiate the high performance claim. See Exhibit 13.2 to see how Tiger Woods is used as a metaphor for superior business performance.

Source: http://www.accenture.com/Global/About_Accenture/Sponsorships/AccentureAndTigerWoods.htm

Question

What communication-related risks do you believe Accenture perceived when they signed Tiger Woods in 2003?

Task

If you ran a major consultancy, who would you choose to endorse your business, and why?

Exhibit 13.2 Working together: Accenture and Tiger Woods

These print ads demonstrate the skills and aptitudes that Tiger Woods brings to golf in order to be successful. These are also the high performance attributes that Accenture offers client organisations.

Courtesy of Young and Rubicam New York and Accenture.

Communication is used to inform stakeholders quickly of episodes concerning products and the organisation. This is normally achieved through the use of visual and verbal messages. However, a broad use can be seen in communicating not only values but also the direction the organisation is taking and notable traits of which the organisation wishes to inform its audiences. For example, in the United Kingdom Volvos were seen as very safe but very dull cars, driven by people who were similarly uninteresting. Communication was used to convey interest and excitement without the loss of the stable and important 'safe' attribute.

When considering the development of a corporate brand, the stewardship dimension also needs to be considered. This refers to the degree of importance that a company places on the development and maintenance of a corporate brand. The steward of the corporate brand is responsible for the consistency of the brand, in terms of the way it is presented, and for the way in which external members develop their images of the organisation. The chairman of British Airways, Willie Walsh, might be accused of not stewarding the British Airways brand appropriately during the company's transition to Terminal 5 in March 2008. This was manifest in the initial chaos, mountain of lost baggage, cancelled flights, staff unrest and swathes of customer anger. Vision and responsibility for this function often reside with 'the chairman' but many companies who successfully take care of their identity also have one communications professional charged with the task (Ferguson, 1996), operating at a very senior level within the organisation.

Much of this is an external perspective of identity, whereas much of the organisational behaviour literature sees identity as embedded within the organisation, with employees. Employees are members who sense identity and who are responsible for projecting their group identity to non-members, those outside the organisation. Identity develops through feelings about what is central, distinctive and enduring (Albert and Whetten, 1985) about the character of the organisation, drawn from the personality (see Chapter 30 for greater detail).

> Identity develops through feelings about what is central, distinctive and enduring.

ViewPoint 13.4 Time to close and no sense of responsibility?

In 2007 the Royal Mail announced that 2,500 UK post offices were to close, on the grounds that they were inefficient and lost money. The announcement triggered a huge amount of public controversy and debate because of the impact on older people and the effect the closures would have on the rural communities, among others.

Just after the announcement the Post Office ran a television campaign featuring the services targeted at the over 50s, one of the segments it was about to deprive of its services.

In much the same way the CEO of Barclays Bank decided in the summer of 2000 to announce closures to the branch network (retail outlets). One of the problems with this was that the closures affected many rural communities and attracted a great deal of hostile publicity and negative media comment. This should have been anticipated and measures put in place to ameliorate the damage. Unfortunately, the bank authorised an advertising campaign to run at exactly the same time. The problem was that the corporate branding campaign was national and it focused on functional positioning issues, namely the size of the bank.

The timing of both these announcements was 'unfortunate' as the credibility of the messages was lost in the welter of negative comment about the closures. Perhaps a different approach to social responsibility might have avoided the negative impact on both organisations' reputation.

Question

Is this an example of symbolism or behaviour? Why?

Task

Makes notes about how organisations should conduct themselves with regard to social responsibility.

Corporate communication enables stakeholders to form images about the organisation, from the various corporate communication cues. Therefore, corporate identity is the way the organisation presents itself to its stakeholders.

Corporate image

The third and final element is corporate image. This is the perception that different audiences have of an organisation and results from the audience's interpretation of the cues presented by an organisation. As Bernstein (1984) says, 'the image does not exist in the organisation but in those that perceive the organisation'. This means that an organisation cannot change its image in a directly managed way, but it can change its identity. It is through the management of its identity that an organisation can influence the image held of it.

The image stakeholders hold of an organisation is a result of a particular combination of a number of different elements, but is essentially a distillation of the values, beliefs and attitudes that an individual or organisation has of the focus organisation. The images held by members of the distribution network, for example, may vary according to their individual experiences, and will almost certainly be different from those that management thinks exists. This means that an organisation does not have a single image, but may have multiple images.

For an image to be sustainable, the identity cues around which the image is fashioned must be based on reality and reflect the values and beliefs of the organisation. Images can be consistent, but are often based on a limited amount of information. Images are prone to the halo effect, whereby stakeholders shape images based on a small amount of information. The strategic credibility of Microsoft may be based largely on the image of Bill Gates rather than the current financial performance of Microsoft and the actual strategies being pursued by the organisation. Stakeholders extrapolate that Bill Gates has a high reputation for business success, therefore, anything to do with Bill Gates is positive and likely to be successful.

Corporate images are shaped by stakeholder interpretations of the identity cues they perceive at an individual level. These cues are the identity signals transmitted by organisations, either deliberately planned and timed or accidental, often unknown to the organisation and very often unwelcome. Planned corporate communications reflected through symbolism, communication and behaviour are accompanied by unplanned communications such as those generated by competitors, through word-of-mouth and the personal experiences and memories of the individual (Cornelissen, 2000).

> Corporate images are shaped by stakeholder interpretations of the identity cues they perceive.

Corporate image is what stakeholders perceive the organisation to be.

Dimensions of corporate image

The image that stakeholders have of organisations is important for many reasons. The main ones are listed in Table 13.4, where it can be observed that the dimensions of corporate image are quite diverse.

The relational dimension refers to the exchange of attitudes and perceptions with stakeholders of the organisation itself. As will be seen later, organisations consider who they are and what they would like to be, and then project identity cues to those stakeholders who it is believed need to be informed. A more advanced understanding then allows for the adaptation of the organisation based on the feedback or the dialogue thus created.

Management also benefits from corporate identity programmes as they encourage senior staff to reflect on the organisation's sense of purpose and then provide a decision framework for the decisions that management and others, perhaps functional managers, follow.

The final dimension refers to the advantages that a strong positive identity can give products and services. It is possible to develop more effective and efficient promotional programmes by focusing on the organisation's distinctiveness and then allow for the ripple to wash over the

Table 13.4 Dimensions of corporate image

Image dimension	Elements of perception
Relational	Government, local community, employees, network members.
Management	Corporate goals, decision-making, knowledge, understanding.
Product	Product endorsement and support, promotional distinctiveness, competitive advantages.

variety of offerings. Banks have traditionally used this approach, and car manufacturers have also partially attempted this strategy. Although the car marque (brand) is a very important decision determinant (e.g. BMW, Audi, Honda, VW, Toyota), it is common for particular models within the marque to be featured heavily.

Apart from a positive relationship between reputation and corporate performance, the principal reasons for managing corporate identity are to make clear to all stakeholders what the values and beliefs of the organisation are and how it is striving to achieve its objectives. In addition, a strong reputation provides better opportunities to develop lasting relationships with key stakeholder groups and improved access to resources. There are a number of secondary benefits, but these distil down to creating a supportive environment for the offerings, employees and external stakeholders associated with the organisation. Finally, a strong reputation can provide some protection should an organisation encounter environmental turbulence or crisis.

Corporate reputation

Corporate reputation refers to an individual's reflection of the historical and accumulated impacts of previous identity cues, fashioned in some cases by near or actual transactional experiences.

A deeper set of images constitute what is termed corporate reputation. This concept refers to an individual's reflection of the historical and accumulated impacts of previous identity cues, fashioned in some cases by near or actual transactional experiences. It is much harder and takes a lot longer to change reputation, whereas images may be influenced quite quickly. The latter is more transient and the former more embedded.

This view of reputation, that image is different to reputation, is regarded as part of the 'differentiated' school of thought, but is a view not held by all writers. Gotsi and Wilson (2001) argue that although in the minority, authors such as Kennedy (1977) see the two terms as having the same meaning while authors such as Alvesson (1998), Dichter (1985) and Dutton *et al.* (1994) regard the terms as interchangeable. The view held here is that they are not interchangeable but interrelated, if only because reputations are developed through time, whereas images can be instantaneous and reality superficial. A strong reputation is considered strategically important for four main reasons:

A strong reputation is considered strategically important for four main reasons.

- a primary means of differentiation when there is little difference at product level;
- a support facility during times of turbulence and as a measure of corporate value (Greyser, 1999);
- the effect on a company's share price, perhaps as much as 15 per cent (Cooper, 1999);
- the higher the quality of customer relationships, the higher the reputation afforded the organisation (Broon, 2007).

In a survey reported by Gray (2000) the importance of a company's reputation was regarded by 1,005 CEOs consulted to be either important or very important. Fombrun (1996) claims that in order to build a favourable reputation four attributes need to be developed. These are credibility, trustworthiness, reliability and responsibility. Using these criteria it may be possible to speculate about the reputation developed by a company such as Nokia, the mobile phone manufacturer. Credibility is established through its range of products, which are perceived to be of high quality and branded. Trustworthiness has been developed through attention to customer service and support. Reliability and consistency have been achieved by setting and adhering to particular standards of quality, and responsibility is verified through a strong orientation to service and values manifested through the company's strong product development and innovation policy.

Reputation itself is developed through a number of variables. Greyser (1999) suggests that the key drivers are competitive effectiveness, market leadership, customer focus, familiarity/favourability, corporate culture and communications. It is the combination of these elements that drives corporate reputation. However, he states that the most important dimension impacting on reputation is the relationship between expectation and action. Whether this be at corporate level or at product/brand level, the brand promise must be delivered if reputation is to be enhanced, otherwise damage to the corporate reputation is most likely.

Despite their overall and continued marketing success, it would appear that the reputation of corporate brands can be tarnished. However, it is the strength of the brand, management's flexibility and willingness to be open and transparent with inquisitive publics that can protect reputation in the long run.

ViewPoint 13.5 Who cracked the Egg?

McDonald's, British Airways, Microsoft, Nike, Coca-Cola and Perrier are just some of the leading global brands that have been subject to media or judicial investigation. As a result of being in the public spotlight, their corporate reputation might be questioned, spoof web sites created and doubt expressed about their integrity and well-being.

Many of these brands represent a benchmark for marketing performance. Using highly recognisable visual identity cues (e.g. 'golden arches', 'national flags', packaging or unique logos) consistently throughout the world, these brands are normally associated with high standards of service, good value for money and wide availability. To help maintain their identity, huge sums are spent each year on advertising, public relations and relevant in-house training and support.

In 2008, Egg decided to withdraw the credit cards of 161,000 of its customers. It was claimed that the credit profiles of these customers had deteriorated. However, counter-claims were made by many of the affected customers, who stated that they paid off their credit bills promptly. This action is all the more remarkable as the Egg brand was developed by providing a high-quality customer service and by making the brand accessible. The enormous publicity accompanying the 'sacking of its customers' was thought to have severely damaged the brand.

Source: Odal (2008).

Question

Were Egg right to get rid of their unprofitable customers?

Task

Find a brand whose reputation has been damaged and determine how management have tried to restore their reputation.

Understanding the tasks of corporate identity

The gap between organisational image and identity, often uncovered during research, determines the nature of the communications task. A communications strategy is required to address all matters of structure and internal communications and the conflicting needs of different stakeholders so as to produce a set of consistent messages, all within the context of a coherent corporate identity programme. The British Broadcasting Corporation (BBC) changed its identity partly as a means of enabling it to compete more effectively in an environment that was changing quickly. With the then emergence of digital television, the developing international competitive arena and the impending launch a range of new services it was important that the BBC logo became distinctive and reflected the BBC core values of quality, fairness, accuracy and artistic integrity. The previous identity was expensive (four-colour), not suitable for the increasing volumes and range of applications, had become fragmented and reproduced in an inconsistent manner. In addition, it did not work on digital formats and was technically difficult to integrate with other graphics. The new identity signalled changes about the BBC and the culture, attitudes and behaviour of the people who work there.

Analysis of the perceptions and attitudes of stakeholders towards an organisation will often reveal the size of the gap between actual and desired perception.

Analysis of the perceptions and attitudes of stakeholders towards an organisation will often reveal the size of the gap between actual and desired perception. The nature and size of the gap will determine the task and objectives necessary to close the gap. This corporate perception gap may be large or small, depending upon who the stakeholder is. Organisations have multiple images and must develop strategies that attempt to stabilise, and if possible equalise, the images held.

Using a four-cell matrix (see Figure 13.3), where the vertical axis scales the size of the perceived gap and the horizontal axis the number of stakeholders who share the same perception, a series of strategies can be identified. Should a large number of stakeholders be perceived to hold an image of an organisation that is a long way from reality, then a correction strategy is required to communicate the desired position and performance of the focus organisation. Most common of these is the gap between perceived corporate

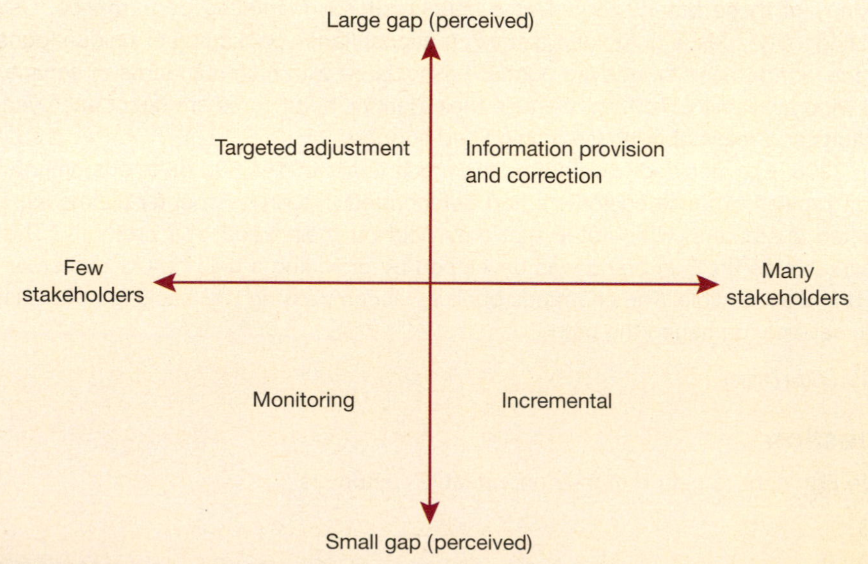

Figure 13.3 Corporate perception gap

performance and the real performance of the organisation when put in the context of the actual trading conditions.

If a small number of stakeholders perceive a large gap, then a targeted adjustment strategy would be required, aimed at particular stakeholder groups and taking care to protect the correct image held by the majority of stakeholders. For example, some students perceive some financial institutions (e.g. banks) as not particularly attractive for career progression or compatible with their own desired lifestyles. A targeted adjustment strategy would be necessary by the banks to alter this perception in order that they attract the necessary number of high-calibre graduates.

Should research uncover a small number of stakeholders holding a relatively small disparity between reality and image, a monitoring strategy would be appropriate and resources would be better deployed elsewhere. The best position would be if the majority of stakeholders perceived a small difference, in which case a maintenance strategy would be advisable and the good corporate communications continued. The natural extension of this approach is to use it as a base tool in the determination of the communication budget. Funds could be allocated according to the size of the perceived perception gap.

The reasons for the gap do not necessarily rest solely with stakeholders. If the image they hold is incorrect and the organisation's performance is good, then it is poor communications that are to blame, which are the fault of the organisation. If the image is correct and accurately reflects performance, then management must take the credit or the criticism for their performance as managers (Bernstein, 1984).

Strategy and corporate identity/image

It is taken for granted that measurements of the perceptions that consumers have of brands and offerings are taken periodically. This practice varies with each organisation and industry, but the overall tendency is to take such measurements on an ad hoc basis. As well as measuring the strength of perception of the organisation's offerings, measurements should also be taken of the perceptions that stakeholders have of the organisation. It may be that the marketing communications have to realign perceptions of the organisation before new offerings can be launched successfully.

In Figure 13.4 the perceptions that customers have of four recruitment companies are presented. The axes used show the levels of awareness and attitude towards the service provided by each of the companies, and for the sake of discussion each company is depicted in one of the four quadrants. Company A is in the strongest position and its communications should be aimed at maintaining its current position. Company B is liked just as much as A, but known only to a limited audience. Work needs to be undertaken to improve levels of awareness by reaching a larger number of stakeholders. Company C, to those that are aware of it, is seen as a poor organisation, but fortunately only a few know about it. Management's task is to bring about improvements to its offering and delay informing stakeholders until the level of service is satisfactory. Company D is seen to suffer from poor service delivery and everyone knows about it. Management's task is to lower the level of awareness, or not actively increase it, and put right the service offering before seeking stakeholder attention.

This depiction is obviously a simplification, as corporate image is multidimensional (Dowling, 1986) and there is no single indicator that can adequately reflect the corporate personality. As different stakeholders will inevitably have different images, the measurement of corporate image is made difficult.

Various models have been developed to provide a visual interpretation of the elements involved in corporate identity (Kennedy, 1977; Dowling, 1986; Abratt and Shee, 1989; Stuart, 1999b). These models reflect the development of the subject and the growing integrative nature

Various models have been developed to provide a visual interpretation of the elements involved in corporate identity.

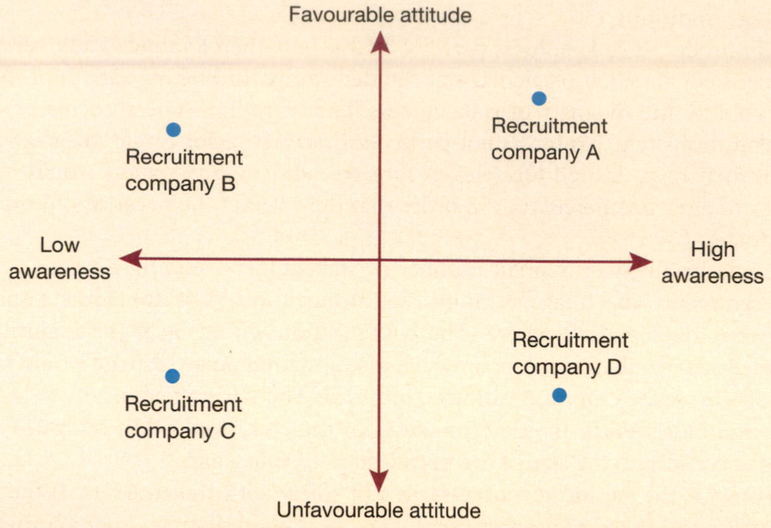

Figure 13.4 Images held by stakeholders of four recruitment companies
Source: Adapted from Barich and Kotler (1991).

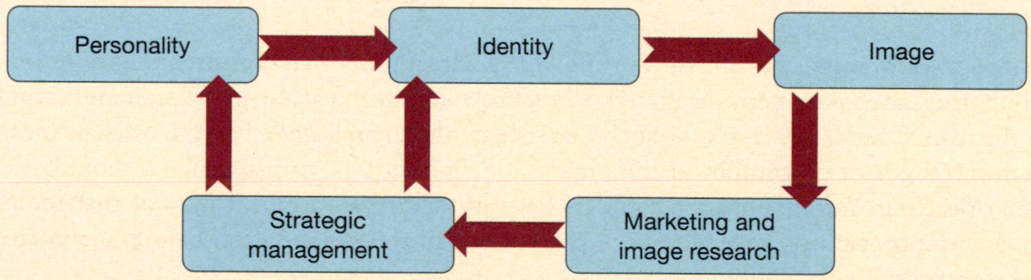

Figure 13.5 The corporate identity management process
Source: Adapted from Markwick and Fill (1997).

of corporate identity within an organisation's overall strategy. One such framework, presented by Markwick and Fill (1997), is entitled the corporate identity management process (CIMP) (see Figure 13.5), which depicts the three main elements of the process as identified by Abratt and Shee (1989): corporate personality, corporate identity and corporate image. In order for management to be able to use such a model there must be understanding of the linkages between the components. Just as the linkages in the value chain determine the extent of competitive advantage that may exist, so the linkages within the corporate identity process need to be understood in order to narrow the gap between reality and perception.

To assist with the linking process, van Riel's (1995) composition of corporate communication is used. These are marketing, management and organisational communications. The first linkage is to transpose, through self-analysis, the corporate personality so that management, or those responsible for the management of the corporate identity, have a realistic perception of the corporate personality. This can be assumed to be what management thinks the personality is and the principal method is through management communication.

The second linkage is between corporate identity and the corporate image. In order that stakeholders are able to perceive and understand the organisation, the corporate identity is projected to them. The identity can be projected with orchestrated cues, planned and delivered to a timed schedule, or it can be projected as a series of random, uncoordinated events and observations. In virtually all cases, corporate identity cues are a mixture of the planned (e.g. literature, telephone style and ways of conducting business) and the unplanned (e.g. employees' comments, media views and product failures). The principal linkages are through organisation and marketing communications.

> The second linkage is between corporate identity and the corporate image.

All organisations communicate all the time; everything they make, do, say or do not say is a form of communication. The totality of the way the organisation presents itself, and is visible, can be called its identity (Olins, 1989). Corporate image is how stakeholders actually perceive the identity. It is, of course, unlikely that all stakeholders will hold the same image at any one point in time. Owing to the level of noise and the different experiences stakeholders have of an organisation, multiple images of an organisation are inevitable (Dowling, 1986). It is important that organisations monitor these images to ensure that the (corporate) position is maintained.

> The totality of the way the organisation presents itself, and is visible, can be called its identity.

The third linkage is between the image that stakeholders have of an organisation and the corporate strategy formulation and implementation processes that an organisation adopts. This research-based linkage provides feedback and enables the organisation to adjust its personality and its identity, thus consequently affecting the cues presented to stakeholders. Image research is an important method of linking back into the strategy process.

The cues used to project the corporate identity are many and varied; some are controllable and others beyond the reach of management. These cues include the logo and letterheads, the way employees speak of the organisation, the buildings and architecture, the perception of the ability of the organisation to fulfil its obligations, its technical skills, prices, dress code, competitor communications, word-of-mouth and the way the telephone is answered. Of all these and the many others, however, research needs to determine those attributes that key stakeholders perceive as important.

Having determined the important attributes, stakeholders should be asked to evaluate how well the organisation rates on each of them and how well it performs on each attribute in comparison with competitors.

ViewPoint 13.6 Shell reserves, restructures and confuses

Shell announced in 2004 that it was to restructure itself in the light of the catastrophe relating to the organisation's overstated oil reserves and the subsequent impact on its share price and obvious perceived value for shareholders.

This example demonstrates the principles of the CIMP framework cycle rather neatly. The 100-year-old company had operated a dual structure based on the joint venture between Shell Transport and Trading (the UK arm) and the Royal Dutch of the Netherlands. The announcement saw an end to this structure and a single organisation established, making it leaner, tighter and much more capable of making faster decisions. However, the cycle of poor performance, damaged reputation, structural and strategy change will impact on the culture and values of the organisation and alter, in some way, the personality of the organisation. This in turn will feed through to the identity and branding cues and the images that stakeholders form of the new Shell organisation.

From an identity perspective Shell celebrated its 60-year technical partnership with the Ferrari Formula One team with a campaign that shows Formula One cars racing around city circuits, apparently using Shell's high performance fuel. Considering the environmental pressures, the green claims of BP and a subsequent

Shell campaign that focused on the organisation's environmental awareness, this identity strategy appears to be sending contradictory messages.

Sources: Various; Quilter (2007); www.shell.co.uk.

Question

Are there any simple rules in order to manage corporate reputation?

Task

Visit the Shell web site and view their online videos on their approach to the environment.

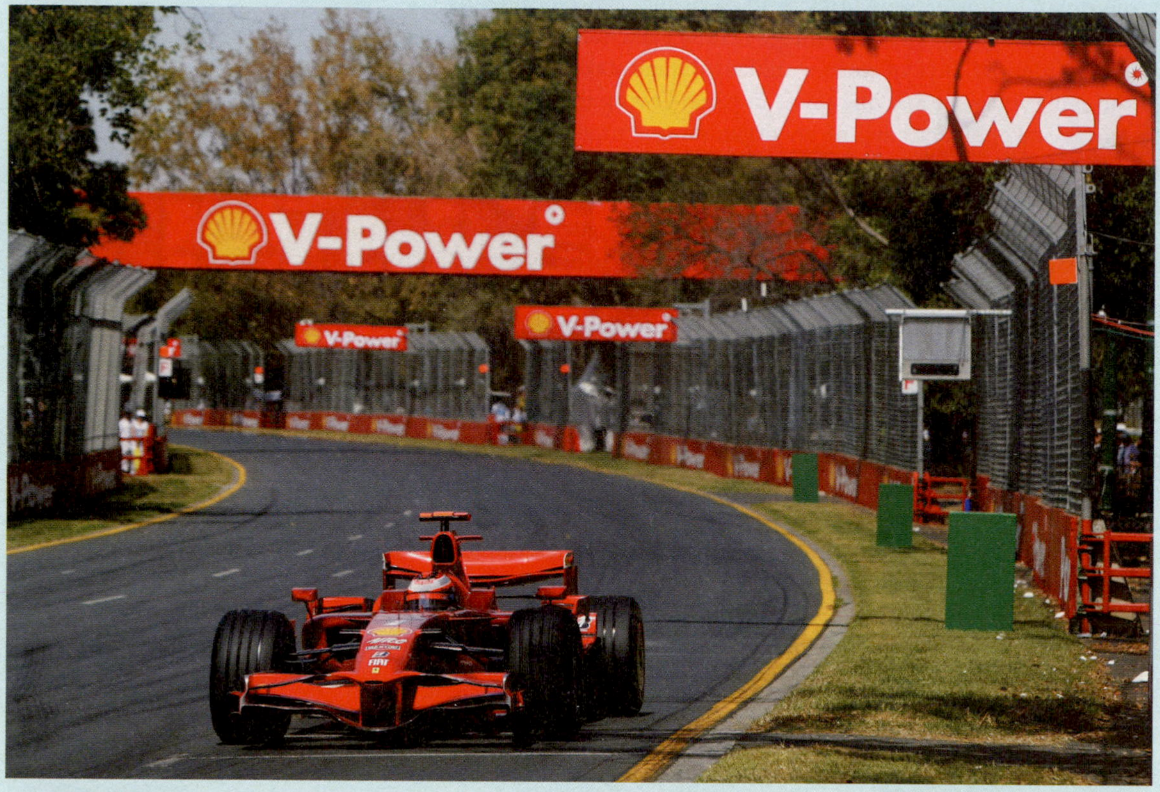

Exhibit 13.3 Shell's sponsorship and support of Formula One racing is compatible with the company's core business activities and provides opportunities to reach a global audience.
Courtesy of Shell Brands International AG.

Stakeholder images can also be determined on three dimensions: the importance of attributes, organisational performance against the attributes and performance with respect to competitors on the same attributes. A three-dimensional perception matrix (Figure 13.6) draws out the significant points. The ideal position occurs when high customer and competitor ratings are recorded for important attributes. When the attribute has a low level of importance it may be that the organisation's effort is misdirected, and management should reduce the effort spent on developing this image or seek alternative markets where this attribute has higher levels of importance. The worst position occurs when the organisation underperforms with respect to the customers' requirements and the competition on an attribute that is important. A change of strategy is required.

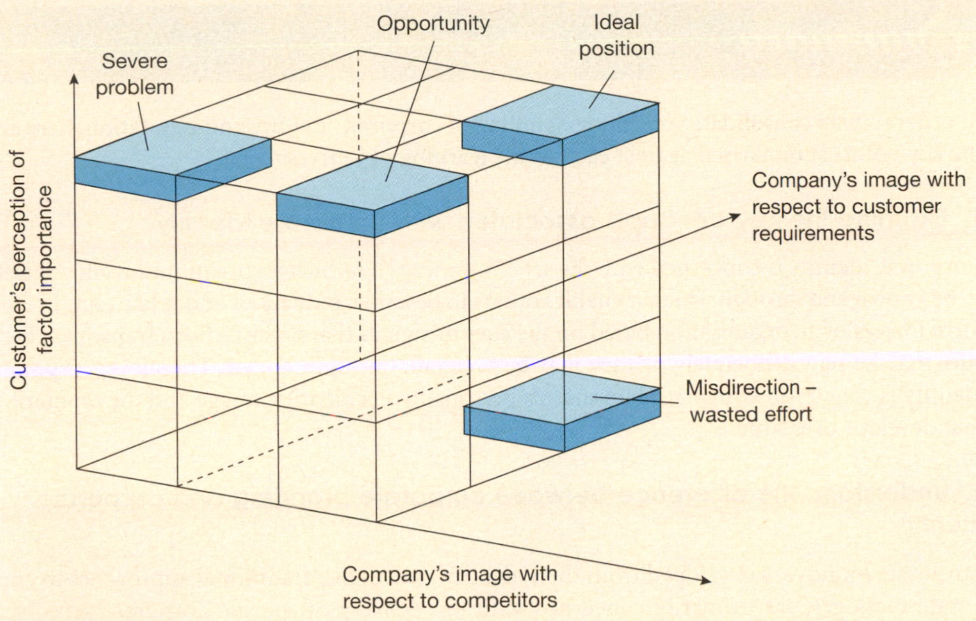

Figure 13.6 A three-dimensional attribute perception matrix
Source: Markwick (1993). Used with kind permission.

Effort should be concentrated on developing either corporate identity or personality in areas where the customer rating is poor and competitor rating is high on a factor that is important.

This model reveals that, by understanding the strength of images held by key stakeholders across attributes that are important to them, corrective action may be required to the personality and cues presented to stakeholders as part of the identity process. Strategic development therefore can result from an understanding of the images held about an organisation by its stakeholders.

Therefore, for the CIMP framework to be complete, management is required to analyse and interpret the research data and then use management and marketing communications either to develop the personality or to provide adjusted corporate identity cues for positioning and goal-setting purposes. This is not the only corporate identity framework to have been developed. For example, Stuart (1999b) developed the CIMP framework and offered a composite framework drawing on a variety of models and Balmer and Gray (1999) formulated a new model of the corporate identity–corporate communications process. Each of these has developed our understanding of this subject and extended the breadth and depth of corporate identity, branding and reputation management.

It may be concluded that corporate identity is not a peripheral tool to be used ad hoc, but is a component that is central to the strategic management process. It should be used regularly by managers to understand how the organisation is being interpreted and understood by different stakeholders and to understand the essence of the organisation and whether the symbolic, behavioural and communication cues are contextually appropriate. Managing an organisation's identity and reputation is a complex, variable and necessary aspect of developing stakeholder relationships in the twenty-first century.

Summary

In order to help consolidate your understanding of corporate identity and reputation, here are the key points summarised against each of the learning objectives:

1. Examine the key concepts associated with corporate identity.

Corporate identity is concerned with the set of meanings by which an organisation allows itself to be known and through which it enables others to describe, remember and relate to it. People form images of an organisation based on the cues or signals that organisations transmit. These cues may be sent deliberately or they may be accidental or unintended. Therefore, corporate identity is concerned with an organisation's personality, its identity, image and the reputation that develops over time.

2. Understand the difference between corporate branding and corporate identity.

Corporate brands are developed from their identity and, unlike traditional approaches to corporate messages, are primarily concerned with the delivery of specific corporate promises. Corporate brands are a complex form of identity but not all organisations need a corporate brand, if, for example, they are a public utility, monopoly or work in commodities.

3. Consider some of the ideas and issues associated with corporate communications.

Organisations project themselves (as they want to be seen/understood) through a series of 'cues'. These are then interpreted by stakeholders and used to create an image of the organisation. This corporate image may or may not be the intended interpretation but this perception is an important one and must be treated seriously. Reputations are developed over time from the image and can be seen to feed back to the corporate personality and impact on the way members of an organisation think about themselves and determine what is central, distinctive and enduring.

Communication strategies need to encompass the communication needs of all those other stakeholders, those other constituencies that might influence the organisation or be influenced by it. These approaches are referred to as the profile strategy and so complete the 3Ps for communication: push, pull and profile.

Profile strategies are essentially concerned with communication about the organisation itself rather than its products and/or services. The focus rests with the corporate body: who it is, what it is, what it is seeking to do and how it is important to other stakeholders.

4. Understand the core elements associated with corporate identity.

There are three main elements central to the corporate identity process. These are corporate personality, identity and image. Individuals and organisations project their personalities through their identity. The audience's perception of the identity is the image they have of the object, in this case, the corporate body. The identity is communicated through symbolism and behaviour.

5. Explain the meaning and importance of corporate reputation.

Corporate reputation is concerned with the deeper set of images and refers to an individual's reflection of the historical and accumulated impacts of previous identity cues, fashioned in some cases by near or actual transactional experiences. It is much harder and takes a lot longer to change reputation, whereas images may be influenced quite quickly. The latter is more transient and the former more embedded.

A strong reputation is considered strategically important for three main reasons: as a primary means of differentiation when there is little difference at product level, as a support facility during times of turbulence and as a measure of corporate value.

6. Introduce a framework incorporating corporate identity into the process of strategic management.

The corporate identity management process (CIMP) depicts the three main elements corporate personality, corporate identity and corporate image. These are supplemented by research data and information that is then used by management to develop the personality or to provide adjusted corporate identity cues for positioning and goal-setting purposes.

In order for management to be able to use such a model there must be understanding of the linkages between the components. Just as the linkages in the value chain determine the extent of competitive advantage that may exist, so the linkages within the corporate identity process need to be understood in order to narrow the gap between reality and perception.

Review questions

1. What are the main elements within corporate communications.
2. Explain what a corporate brand is. How does it differ from a product brand?
3. Discuss the differences between corporate branding and corporate identity. Are the differences of any value?
4. What are the main facets of corporate personality?
5. Describe the personality or defining characteristics of five organisations. What are their distinctive differences?
6. Prepare brief notes explaining what corporate identity is. Set out the differences between personality and identity.
7. Suggest ways in which planned and unplanned corporate identity cues are presented to stakeholders. Use an organisation with which you are familiar to illustrate your answer.
8. What is corporate image and how does it differ from corporate identity?
9. Draw the CIMP model, paying particular attention to the linkages between the components.
10. Discuss the view that there is nothing intrinsically different between corporate image and reputation.

MiniCase Just how branded is the NHS?

Karl Milner: Director of Communications and Public Relations, NHS Yorkshire and the Humber
Graham Hughes: Leeds Metropolitan University

Background – the changing environment

By its very nature, the NHS continues to operate in a complex and changing environment, which it can be argued is becoming more competitive both internally and externally. This clearly represents something of a challenge in corporate branding terms. The success of the NHS is crucially significant to the government and to all those who rely on its effective performance. Prime Minister, Gordon Brown (2007) states,

> No institution touches the lives of the British people like the NHS. It is part of what makes Britain the place it is. Yet, no modern health service that aspires to respond to its citizens' needs and expectations can afford to stand still.

More recent announcements by both the Prime Minister and the Health Secretary highlight the focus on the NHS agenda as a major government priority.

The differing NHS regions and providers attract people to the services they offer. Private providers, BUPA *et al.*, are becoming more aggressive in targeting customers often disenchanted with the offerings from the public sector. This is in part aided by growth in the provision of private health insurance. Some patients are seeking treatment in other parts of Europe and further afield. There is a significant body of service users who hold negative perceptions and attitudes toward the NHS (MRSA, waiting lists, service closures and reductions, meeting of treatment targets). These perceptions and attitudes may be based on actual experience or as a result of information gained from various media sources, some of which come officially and unofficially from NHS staff. There is a shift toward the more social aspects of the service provision, promotion of healthier lifestyles and personal well-being. Life expectancy levels are extending.

There is a changing shift in NHS strategic agenda to be:

- patient centred;
- clinically led;
- locally accountable.

The NHS brand

Peoples' expectations of getting good 'customer service' are increasing all the time. This is not just applicable in situations where there might be a direct alternative choice but in all those situations where service is provided in both public and private sectors. This might include services provided by local authorities as well as the myriad of other public service offerings, including those of the NHS. There is an increasing need to recognise that just because service users may not have a choice, they should (and will) expect and receive a service that will not only satisfy their needs, but also that they will feel positively toward the provider on an ongoing basis.

These issues are clear indicators that the NHS needs to rethink its position as a health service provider and the relationships it has with a range of different stakeholders.

What is the current position?

The diagram below, *the NHS brand spheres*, indicates the scope of the brands directly and indirectly associated with the NHS. At a 'macro' level, NHS as a central, government-controlled service is well known. The concept that people pay a proportion of their earnings through taxation and national insurance contributions which funds the NHS and other services, again is well known but perhaps not well understood in terms of its detailed structures. Expectations that the service is 'free' have become increasingly blurred as some aspects of the service have changed the focus and nature of their provision, dentistry for example. The spheres identify the range of brand levels, those that might be considered to be corporate in nature to those at a product or service level.

For some users, the NHS brand is seen as their known service provider, the GP or the local hospital. Others might recognise it through the sound and visual impact of the ambulance service. These are tangible and real points of service recognition and identity. The media provides for a whole range of NHS-related points of identity. Some might be news and information sources specific to actual parts of the NHS service provision at a local or national level. Further complexities

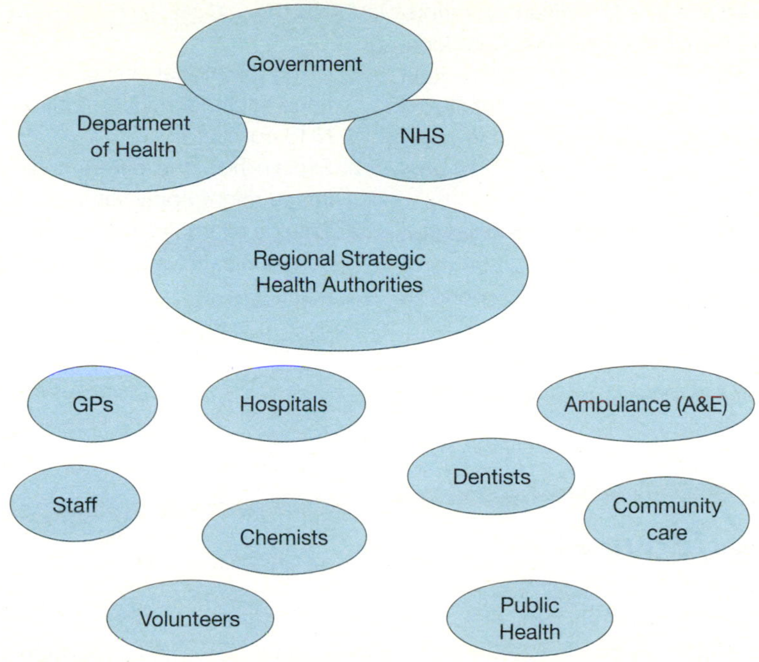

Figure 13.7 NHS brand spheres

arise when considering the growth in and popularity of health drama series such as *Casualty* or *Holby City* and the impact they can have on peoples' knowledge and understanding of the NHS, perception and reality. We live in an information-rich society in which so-called word-of-mouth (driven by Internet and mobile technologies) communication plays a significant role in providing information to large numbers of people very rapidly.

In addition to the corporate NHS brand(s), the service ranges provide for another level of service and brand structure at regional/local level including:

- GP services;
- hospital outpatient services;
- A & E;
- hospital in-patient services;
- ambulance service;
- dentist service;
- community care;
- walk-in centres.

Each of these services might be considered differently in terms of how the brand essence is made up. Brand attributes, benefits and personality traits might vary significantly.

There are individual parts of the service that have themselves developed a form of brand recognition as a result of developing a reputation for some part or the whole of their provision. For some this might be at a local, regional or national level. Examples might include individual hospitals – Great Ormond Street, Addenbrooke's in Cambridge, or St James in Leeds. Two of these provide interesting aspects of branding in that they are well known nationally in 'shorthand'- as *GOSH* and *Jimmys* with subsequent emotional legacies.

The regional geographic structure NHS could facilitate another level of brand perspectives. This could form the basis of creating a decentralised brand identity that would be something that individuals might recognise and associate with as a basis for forming a relationship – disaggregated from nationally driven issues. This might also have benefits in attempting to '*de-politicise*' perceptions of the NHS, for it to be considered on the basis of the services provided and away from the national media glare. This would not mean that major issues could be ignored, but presented in a more focused regional/local context allowing for more a more rational and meaningful approach.

Medical treatments quite clearly form the basis of the NHS raison d'être. As such they form an integral element of the brand. How, by whom and where these treatments are delivered are also significant contributors to the brand identity. Thus the staff and operational environments play an important role, just as they do in more commercially based branded sectors, retail and financial service sectors for example. This in itself provides a platform for brand development – *internal branding.*

The NHS brand development needs to be based on a time perspective that is sustainable, both in terms of maintaining core values and being able to respond to significant change.

MiniCase questions

1. Using the model associated with corporate perceptions gaps, identify how this might apply within the NHS context.
2. Explain how the different dimensions of corporate image might apply within the NHS.
3. Provide examples of planned and unplanned cues in communications associated with corporate identity management process of the NHS.

References

Albert, S. and Whetten, D.A. (1985) Organisational identity. In *Research in Organizational Behavior* (eds L.L. Cummings and B.M. Straw) 239–95, Greenwich, CT: JT Press.

Alvesson, M. (1998) The business concept as a symbol. *International Studies of Management and Organisation*, **28**(3), 86–108.

Anisimova, T.A. (2007) The effects of corporate brand attributes on attitudinal and behavioral consumer loyalty. *Journal of Consumer Marketing*, **24**(7), 395–405.

Balmer, J.M.T. (1998) Corporate identity and the advent of corporate marketing. *Journal of Marketing Management*, **14**(8), 963–96.

Balmer, J.M.T. and Gray, E.R. (1999) Corporate identity and corporate communications: creating a competitive advantage. *Corporate Communications, An International Journal*, **4**(4), 171–6.

Balmer, J.M.T. and Gray, E.R. (2003) Corporate brands: what are they? What of them? *European Journal of Marketing*, **37**(7/8), 972–97.

Barich, H. and Kotler, P. (1991) A framework for marketing image management. *Sloan Management Review*, **94** (Winter), 94–104.

Bernstein, D. (1984) *Company Image and Reality: A Critique of Corporate Communications.* London: Holt, Rinehart & Winston.

van den Bosch, A.L.M., de Jong, M.D.T. and Elving, W.J.L. (2004) Managing corporate visual identity: use and effects of organisational measures to support a consistent selfpresentation. *Public Relations Review*, **30**(2) (June), 225–34.

Broon, P.S. (2007) Relationship outcomes as determinants of reputation. *Corporate Communications: An International Journal*, **12**(4), 376–93.

Cooper, A. (1999) What's in a name? *Admap*, **34**(6), 30–2.

Cornelissen, J. (2000) Corporate image: an audience centred model. *Corporate Communications: An International Journal*, **5**(2), 119–25.

Cornelissen, J., Haslam, S.A. and Balmer, J.M.T. (2007) Social identity, organisational identity and corporate identity: towards an integrated understanding of processes, patternings and products. *British Journal of Management*, **18**(1) (March), 1–16.

Cowlett, M. (2000) Buying into brands. *PR Week*, 24 November, 13.

Dichter, E. (1985) What's in an image? *Journal of Consumer Marketing*, **2**, 75–81.

Dowling, G.R. (1986) Measuring your corporate images. *Industrial Marketing Management*, **15**, 109–15.

Dowling, G.R. (1993) Developing your company image into a corporate asset. *Long Range Planning*, **26**(2), 101–9.

Dowling, G.R. (1994) *Corporate Reputations: Strategies for Developing the Corporate Brand.* London: Kogan Page.

Dunnion, B. and Knox, S. (2005) *Organisation Brands: Meeting the Challenge of Complexity*, The 5th American Marketing Association/Academy of Marketing Joint Biennial Conference, Dublin Institute of Technology, Dublin, Ireland, 5–8 July.

Dutton, J.E., Dukerich, J.M. and Harquail, C.V. (1994) Organisational images and member identification. *Administrative Science Quarterly*, **39**, 239–63.

Ferguson, J. (1996) The image. *Communicators in Business*, **9** (Summer), 11–14.

Fombrun, C. (1996) *Reputation: Realising Value from the Corporate Image.* Cambridge, MA: Harvard Business School Press.

Gorb, P. (1992) The psychology of corporate identity. *European Management Journal*, **10**(3) (September), 310–13.

Gotsi, M. and Wilson, A.M. (2001) Corporate reputation: seeking a definition. *Corporate Communications: an International Journal*, **6**(1), 24–30.

Gray, R. (2000) The chief encounter. *PR Week*, 8 September, 13–16.

Greyser, S.A. (1999) Advancing and enhancing corporate reputation. *Corporate Communications: An International Journal*, **4**(4), 177–81.

Hatch, M.J. and Schultz, M. (2000) Scaling the Tower of Babel: relational differences between identity, image and culture in organisations. In *The Expressive Organisation: Linking Identity, Reputation and the Corporate Brand* (eds M. Schultz, M.J. Hatch and M.H. Larsen). Oxford: Oxford University Press.

He, H-W. and Balmer, J.M.T. (2007) Identity studies: multiple perspectives and implications for corporate level marketing. *European Journal of Marketing*, **41**(7/8), 765–85.

Ind, N. (1992) *The Corporate Image: Strategies for Effective Identity Programmes.* London: Kogan Page.

Keller, K.L. (1999) Brand mantra: rationale, criteria and examples. *Journal of Marketing Management*, **15**(1–3) (January–April), 43–51.

Kennedy, S. (1977) Nurturing corporate images. *European Journal of Marketing*, **11**(3), 120–64.

Knox, S. and Maklan, S. (1998) *Competing on Value: Bridging the Gap Between Brand and Customer Value.* London: Financial Times.

Kunde, J. (2000) *Corporate Religion.* London: Financial Times.

Leuthesser, L. and Kohli, C. (1997) Corporate identity: the role of mission statements. *Business Horizons*, **40**(3) (May–June), 59–67.

Markwick, N. (1993) Corporate image as an aid to strategic development. Unpublished MBA project, University of Portsmouth.

Markwick, N. and Fill, C. (1997) Towards a framework for managing corporate identity. *European Journal of Marketing*, **31**(5/6), 396–409.

Melewar, T.C. (2001) Measuring visual identity: a multi-construct study. *Corporate Communications: An International Journal*, **6**(1), 36–42.

Melewar, T.C. (2003) Determinants of the corporate identity construct: a review of the literature. *Journal of Marketing Communications*, **9**, 195–220,

Melewar, T.C., Bassett, K. and Simões, C. (2006) The role of communication and visual identity in modern organisations. *Corporate Communications: An International Journal*, **11**(2), 138–47.

Mintzberg, H. and Quinn, J. (1988) *The Strategy Process: Concepts, Contexts and Cases.* 3rd edn. Englewood Cliffs, NJ: Prentice-Hall.

Murphy, C. (1999) The real meaning behind the name. *Marketing*, 14 October, 31.

Odal, A. (2008) Egg brand tarnished by storm over credit cards. *Marketing*, 6 February, 1.

Odoi, A. (2008) Banking on a shift in perception. *Marketing*, 9 April, 19.

Olins, W. (1989) *Corporate Identity: Making Business Strategy Visible Through Design*. London: Thames & Hudson.

Quilter, J. (2007) Contradiction in terms. *Marketing*, 31 January, 14.

van Riel, C.B.M. (1995) *Principles of Corporate Communication*. Hemel Hempstead: Prentice-Hall.

Salame, E. and Salame, J. (1975) *Developing a Corporate Identity: How to Stand out in the Crowd*. New York: Wiley.

Schein, E.H. (1985) *Organizational Culture and Leadership*. San Francisco, CA: Jossey-Bass.

Shee, P.S.B. and Abratt, R. (1989) A new approach to the corporate image management, process. *Journal of Marketing Management*, **5**(1), 63–76.

Sims, J. (2008) Ditch the name, not the customers. *Marketing*, 8 August, 24–6.

Stuart, H. (1999a) The effect of organisational structure on corporate identity management. *Corporate Reputation Review*, **2**(2), 151–64.

Stuart, H. (1999b) Towards a definitive model of the corporate identity management process. *Corporate Communications: an International Journal*, **4**(4), 200–7.

Williams, P. (2006) Case study: rebranding success for ITN Source. *Admap*, 478 (December), 56–7.

Chapter 14

Financial resources for marketing communications

Organisations need to ensure that they achieve the greatest possible efficiency with each unit of resource (e.g. pounds sterling, dollars, yuan, euros, rubles, Swedish kronor) they allocate to promotional activities. They cannot afford to be profligate with scarce resources and managers are accountable to the owners of the organisation for the decisions they make, including those associated with the costs of their marketing communications.

Aims and learning objectives

The aim of this chapter is to examine the financial context within which organisations undertake promotional campaigns.

The learning objectives of this chapter are to:

1. determine current trends in advertising and promotional expenditure;
2. explain the role of the communication budget;
3. clarify the benefits of using budgets for communication activities;
4. examine various budgeting techniques, both practical and theoretical;
5. provide an appreciation of the advertising-to-sales (A/S) ratio;
6. set out the principles concerning the strategic use of the share of voice (SOV) concept;
7. appreciate how budgets might be set for the other elements of the communication mix.

For an applied interpretation see the MiniCase entitled ***Spending on breakfast can be cereal*** at the end of this chapter.

Introduction

Before examining some of the issues concerned with investing in marketing communications, consider how an organisation might decide on the amount they should spend on marketing communications? Also, how should organisations divide this sum across their brands, regions, territories and various activities? These two questions underpin the setting of communication budgets and the allocation of the budget once it is agreed. According to White (2007) the answers to these questions can lead directly to operational success or failure.

The rate at which advertising and associated media costs outstripped the retail price index, especially around the turn of the century, was regarded as both alarming and troublesome. This disproportionate increase in the costs of advertising served to make it increasingly less attractive to some clients. Consequently, this has spurred the increased use of other tools such as direct marketing, and new media formats, especially online- and interactive-based marketing communications media.

Levels of advertising spend have continued to grow although the growth has not been evenly distributed across all media.

Some advertising agencies have argued that this disproportionately high increase was necessary because of the increasing number of new products and the length of time it takes to build a brand. Levels of advertising spend have continued to grow although the growth has not been evenly distributed across all media. Between 2003 and 2006 cinema advertising expenditure grew 20 per cent. Outdoor has grown significantly, fuelled largely by demand for six-sheet posters. Procter & Gamble spent £181 million in Britain across their product portfolio, while O_2 spent £53 million and HSBC invested £33 million on their brands respectively (see Table 14.1).

Large investment and commitment are required over a period of years if long-term, high-yield performance is to be achieved. Many accountants, however, view advertising from a different perspective. For a long time, their attitude has been to consider advertising as an expense, to be set against the profits of the organisation. Many see planned marketing communications as a variable, one that can be discarded in times of recession (Whitehead, 2008).

These two broad views of advertising and of all marketing communications activities, one as an investment to be shown on the balance sheet and the other as a cost to be revealed in the profit and loss account, run consistently through discussions of how much should be allocated to the promotional spend. For management, the four tools of the communication mix are often divided into two groups. The first contains advertising, sales promotion and public relations, while the second group contains the financial aspects that relate to personal selling.

This division reflects not only a functional approach to marketing but also the way in which, historically, the selling and marketing departments have developed. This is often observed in older, more established organisations, those that find innovation and change a seriously difficult and challenging aspect of development. Accountability and responsibility for

Table 14.1 Top five UK advertisers January–December 2006

Organisation	£ million total (2006)
Procter & Gamble	188.9
Unilever	177
Central Office of Information	140.7
L'Oréal	120.1
BSkyB	118.3
Total	**3,189.3**

Source: ACNielsen MMS.

communications expenditure in the first group often fall to the brand or product manager. In the second group, this aspect is managed by sales managers who often, at national level, report to a sales director.

The communication costs that need to be budgeted include the following. First, there is the airtime on broadcast media or space in print media that has to be bought to carry the message to the target audience. Then there are the production costs associated with generating the message and the staff costs of all those who contribute to the design and administration of the campaign. There are agency and professional fees, marketing research and contributions to general overheads and to expenses such as cars, entertainment costs and telephones that can be directly related to particular profit centres. In addition to all of these are any direct marketing costs, for which some organisations have still to find a suitable method of cost allocation. In some cases a particular department has been created to manage all direct marketing activities, and in these cases the costs can be easily apportioned.

The budget for the sales force is not one that can be switched on and off like an electric light. Advertising budgets can be massaged and campaigns pulled at the last minute, but communication through personal selling requires the establishment of a relatively high level of fixed costs. In addition to these expenses are the opportunity costs associated with the lengthy period taken to recruit, train and release suitably trained sales personnel into the competitive environment. This process can take over 15 months in some industries, especially in the fast-changing, demanding and complex information technology markets.

Strategic investment to achieve the right sales force, in terms of its size, training and maintenance, is paramount. It should be remembered, however, that managing a sales force can be rather like turning an ocean liner: any move or change in direction has to be anticipated and actioned long before the desired outcome can be accomplished. Funds need to be allocated strategically, but for most organisations a fast return on an investment should not be expected.

This chapter concentrates on the techniques associated with determining the correct allocation of funds to the first group of communication tools and, in particular, emphasis will be placed upon advertising. Attention will then be given to the other measures used to determine the correct level of investment in sales promotion, public relations and the field sales force. Finally, in an era in which shareholder value is becoming increasingly prominent and a means of distinguishing between alternative strategic options, the question of how a brand's value might influence the budget setting is considered.

Trends in communication expenditure

It was stated earlier that advertising expenditure in the United Kingdom rose faster for a while than consumer expenditure. While this is true, the rapid increases in advertising spend in the 1980s slowed at the beginning of the 1990s, then speeded up again as the economy recovered only to waver again in 2001 after a buoyant previous year fuelled by the dot-com excitement. After a few years during which the advertising spend levels stabilised, only online advertising has grown substantially, in percentage terms. There has been considerable speculation that offline advertising revenues were about to plummet as organisations moved their spend online. Although many organisations have increased their online investment by some considerable amount and have reduced their offline, especially television spend, the impact has not been as great as some commentators had feared. In 2005 there were signs that real growth was emerging once again, especially in the United Kingdom, but this was not continued and stabilisation of the top-line figures has been the norm.

> The cutback in offline advertising expenditure when trading conditions tighten reflects the short-term orientation that some organisations have towards brand development or advertising.

The cutback in offline advertising expenditure when trading conditions tighten reflects the short-term orientation that some organisations have towards brand development or advertising. The IPA warn that budget reductions can lead to a 'loss of market share, a decline in brand image and long term sales damage', as reported by Donnelly (2008: 4). The report suggests that if a company cuts its advertising to zero it could take five years to recover whereas a budget slashed by 50 per cent will take three years to recover.

What is also of interest is the way in which the communication mix has been changing over the past 20 years. For a long time the spend on media advertising dominated the promotional budget of consumer products and services. Sales promotion became a strong influence but spend on this tool has stagnated over the past few years. Now sponsorship, direct marketing and digital activities show greatest investment. The reasons for this shift are indicative of the increasing attention and accountability that management is attaching to marketing communications. Increasingly, marketing managers are being asked to justify the amounts they spend on their entire budgets, including advertising and sales promotion. Senior managers want to know the return they are getting for their communication investments, in order that they meet their business objectives and that scarce resources can be used more efficiently and effectively in the future.

At the beginning of 2008, with the concern about impending recession, there was significant evidence of organisations deliberately reducing their communication budgets and for some, reallocating their budgets in order to make more funds available for price-cutting and discounting. In addition to this, the previous two years had seen many organisations move their advertising budgets away from television and put more into online and digital work.

It is not uncommon to find companies that are experiencing trading difficulties deciding to slash their adspend, if only on a temporary basis. Exceptions to this have been companies such as Marks & Spencer and Sainsbury's, who although experiencing difficulties, either increased or maintained their above-the-line spend and improved brand and share value. In anticipation of an impending recession the Institute of Practitioners in Advertising (IPA) launched a book of case studies in early 2008. This was sent to the CEOs of 350 FTSE companies and opinion formers such as journalists in the financial sector, fund managers and analysts. The 38 cases demonstrated how the use of advertising can improve brand value (Whitehead, 2008).

ViewPoint 14.1 Slashed mail

The Royal Mail announced in May 2004 that it was cutting back on its advertising by at least 40 per cent, approximately £8 million. It also announced that it was postponing further marketing activities, including £5 million assigned to promote its Parcelforce brand.

These cuts were made in the light of strikes the previous autumn, a series of reported financial losses and the reduction in headcount of about 350 staff.

The news of the reduction in communications spend coincided with a report from the industry watchdog Postwatch that over 14 million items of post are lost each year.

While the cuts affect a number of roster agencies and the brand was receiving poor publicity, the Royal Mail was under huge pressure to turn the operation around. Interestingly, in November 2004, the Royal Mail reported that its six-monthly results had shown a turnaround from a previous loss to a profit of £217 million. So, were the £8 million cuts in advertising really necessary? Perhaps it was the need to avoid publicity when so many items were not being delivered?

Question

To what extent is advertising spend used to disguise or deflect from other commercial issues?

Task

Find out what the Royal Mail spent on advertising relative to its turnover last year and how does this ratio compare with another postal operator (of your choice)?

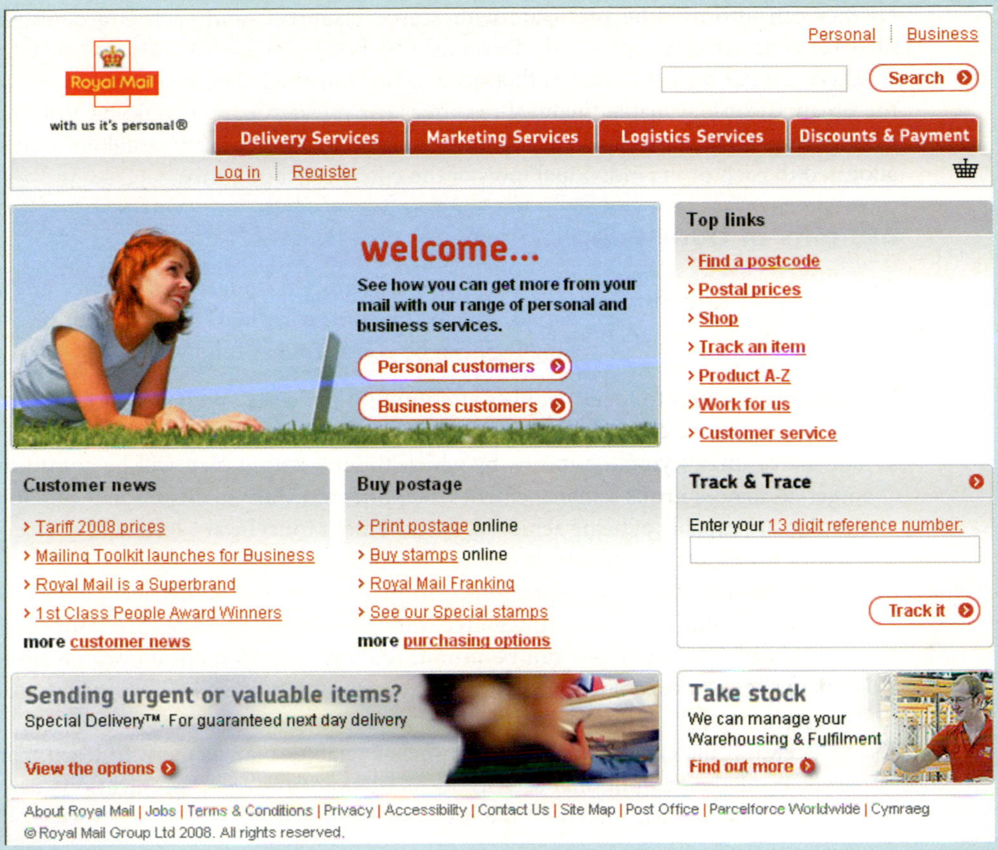

Exhibit 14.1 Royal Mail web site home page, www.royalmail.com

According to Hall (1999: 18), Procter & Gamble set 'strict guidelines about how much can be spent below-the-line if a brand's equity is to be maintained'. Research by Profit Impact on Market Strategy (PIMS) (Tomkins, 1999; Tylee, 1999) found that companies that maintain or even increase their adspend during a recession are likely to grow three times faster than those companies that cut the adspend when the economy turns round. The Renault Clio and the Nescafé Gold Blend brands were cited as examples of advertisers that had increased their adspends during the last downturn and succeeded in increasing their profitability and market performance.

A report undertaken for the Advertising Association (2004), however, found that the majority of brand leaders that use advertising as a substantial proportion of the communication mix continue to dominate their markets, just as they did 30 years ago. In doing so, the report concludes, they have thwarted the challenge of own brands. In other words, advertising can protect brands, as long as the adspend is substantial.

The role of the communication budget

The role of the communication budget is the same whether the organisation is a multinational, trading from numerous international locations, or a small manufacturing unit on an industrial estate outside a semi-rural community. Both types of organisation want to ensure that they achieve the greatest efficiency with each euro they allocate to promotional activities. Neither can afford to be profligate with scarce resources, and each is accountable to the owners of the organisation for the decisions it makes.

There are two broad decisions that need to be addressed. The first concerns how much of the organisation's available financial resources (or relevant part) should be allocated to promotion over the next period. The second concerns how much of the total amount should be allocated to each of the individual tools of the communication mix.

Benefits of budgeting

The benefits of engaging in budgeting activities are many and varied.

The benefits of engaging in budgeting activities are many and varied, but in the context of marketing communication planning they can be considered as follows:

1. The process serves to focus people's attention on the costs and benefits of undertaking the planned communication activities.
2. The act of quantifying the means by which the marketing plan will be communicated to target audiences instils a management discipline necessary to ensure that the objectives of the plan are capable of being achieved. Achievement must be at a level that is acceptable and will not overstretch or embarrass the organisation.
3. The process facilitates cross-function coordination and forces managers to ensure that the planned communications are integrated and mutually supportive. The process provides a means by which campaigns can be monitored and management control asserted. This is particularly important in environments that are subject to sudden change or competitive hostility.
4. At the end of the campaign, a financial review enables management to learn from the experiences of the promotional activity in order that future communications can be made more efficient and the return on the investment improved.

The process of planning the communications budget is an important one.

The process of planning the communications budget is an important one. Certain elements of the process will have been determined during the setting of the campaign objectives. Managers will check the financial feasibility of a project prior to committing larger resources. Managers will also discuss the financial implications of the communication strategy (that is, the push/pull positioning dimension) and those managers responsible for each of the individual tools will have estimated the costs that their contribution will involve. Senior management will have some general ideas about the level of the overall appropriation, which will inevitably be based partly upon precedent, market and competitive conditions and partly as a response to the pressures of different stakeholders, among them key members of the distribution network. Decisions now have to be made about the viability of the total plan, whether the appropriation is too large or too small and how the funds are to be allocated across the promotional tools.

Communication budgets are not formulated at a particular moment in a sequence of management activities. The financial resources of an organisation should be constantly referred to, if only to monitor current campaigns. Therefore, budgeting and the availability of financial resources are matters that managers should be constantly aware of and be able to tap into at all stages in the development and implementation of planned communications.

Difficulties associated with budgeting for communications

There are a number of problems associated with the establishment of a marketing communications budget. Of them all, the following appear to be the most problematic. First, it is difficult to quantify the precise amount that is necessary to complete all the required tasks. Second, communication budgets do not fit neatly with standard accounting practices. The concept of brand value is accepted increasingly as a balance sheet item, but the concept of investment in communication to create value has only recently begun to be accepted, for example by Jaguar and Nestlé. Third, the diversity of the tools and the means by which their success can be measured renders like-for-like comparisons null and void. Finally, the budget-setting process is not as clear-cut as it might at first appear.

The concept of investment in communication to create value has only recently begun to be accepted.

ViewPoint 14.2 What is the right level of spend?

Tiger Beer increased its UK spend up in 2008 from £85K to £5.5 million. This was partly because the owner wants to develop the brand away from its Asian origins.

Back in 1987 Nike's marketing president was pitching to the board for a revised advertising budget. The previous year Nike had spent $8 million, and the marketing chief wanted to raise this to $34 million, an astronomical increase, particularly for a company that was just getting going. The CEO, Philip Knight, turned to the marketing man and asked the question: 'How do I know if you are asking for enough?'

Sources: Holmes (2004), Charles (2008).

Question

Why did Tiger Beer settle at a £5.5 million investment? Why not £7m or £3m?

Task

Which brand invested the most in advertising last year and were they successful?

There are four main stakeholder groups that contribute to the budget decision. These are the organisation itself, any communication agencies, the media whose resources will be used to carry designated messages and the target audience. It is the ability of these four main stakeholders to interact, to communicate effectively with each other and to collaborate that will impact most upon the communications budget. However, determining the 'appropriate appropriation' is a frustrating exercise for the marketing communications manager. The allocation of scarce resources across a communication budget presents financial and political difficulties, especially where the returns are not easily identifiable. The development and significance of technology within marketing can lead to disputes concerning ownership and control of resources. For example, in many companies management and responsibility for the web site rests with the IT department, which understandably takes a technological view of issues. Those in marketing, however, see the use of the web site from a marketing perspective and need a budget to manage it. Tension between the two can result in different types of web site design and effectiveness and this leads to different levels of customer support.

There are four main stakeholder groups that contribute to the budget decision.

Smallbone (1972) suggested a long time ago that the allocation of funds for promotion is one of the primary problems facing marketers, if not one of the major strategic problems. Audience and media fragmentation, changed management expectations and a more global orientation have helped ensure that budgeting remains problematic.

Models of appropriation

At a broad level there are a number of models proposed by different authors concerning the appropriation of the communication mix. In particular, Abratt and van der Westhuizen (1985) who refer, among others, to Smallbone's (1972) and Gaedeke and Tootelian's (1983) models of promotional appropriation. Abratt and van der Westhuizen have determined, among other things, that personal selling dominated the mix of all their respondents in a particular study of business-to-business markets and that the models themselves were too simplistic to be of any direct benefit.

These broad approaches to budget allocation are not therefore appropriate, and it is necessary to investigate the value of using particular techniques. It is useful to set out the theoretical approach associated with the determination of communication and, in particular, advertising budgets.

Techniques and approaches

Theoretical approaches: marginal analysis and response curves

This method is normally depicted as a tool for understanding advertising expenditures but, as Burnett (1993) points out, it has been used for all elements of the communication mix, including personal selling, so it is included here for understanding the overall promotional allocation.

Marginal analysis (or response curve analysis) enables managers to determine how many extra sales are produced from an extra unit of communication spend. A point will be reached when an extra pound spent on communication will generate an equal amount (a single pound's-worth) of revenue. At this point marginal revenue is equal to marginal costs, the point of maximum communication expenditure has been reached and maximum profit is generated.

Another way of looking at this approach is to track the path of sales and communication expenditure. Even with zero promotional effort some sales will still be generated. In other words, sales are not totally dependent upon formal communication activity, a point that will be returned to later. When there is a small amount of promotion effort, the impact is minimal, as the majority of potential customers are either unaware of the messages or they do not think the messages are sufficiently credible for them to change their current behaviour. After a certain point, however, successive increments in communication expenditure will produce more than proportionate increments in sales. The sales curve in Figure 14.1 can now be seen to rise steeply and the organisation moves into a position where it can begin to take advantage of the economies of scale in communication. Eventually the sales curve starts to

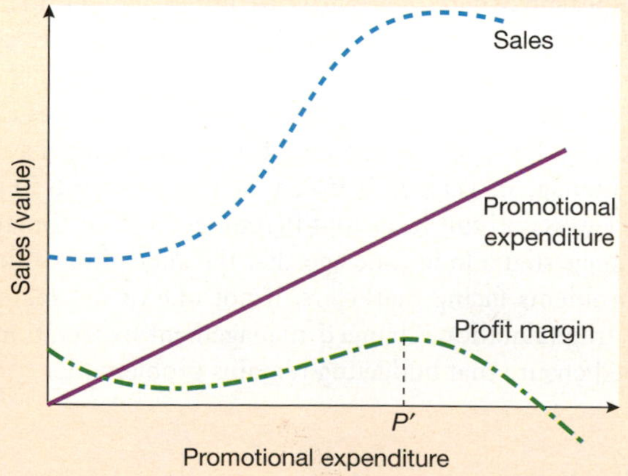

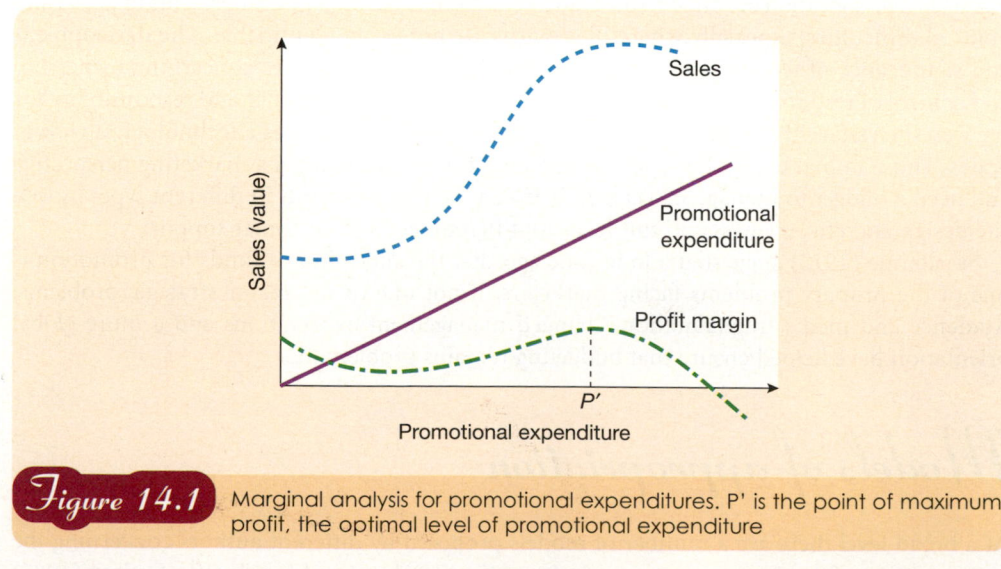

Figure 14.1 Marginal analysis for promotional expenditures. P' is the point of maximum profit, the optimal level of promotional expenditure

Table 14.2 Difficulties with the marginal analysis as a way of setting communication budgets

Assumes communication activities can be varied in a smooth and uniform manner.
Requires perfect data that in reality are very difficult to obtain.
Assumes only communication activities impact upon sales.
Does not consider all the costs associated with communication activities.
No account is made of the actions of direct and indirect competitors.
Adstock effects are ignored.
All messages are regarded as having equal impact. No consideration is given to the quality of messages.

flatten out as diminishing returns to promotion begin to set in. This is because the majority of the potential target market have become aware of the offering and have decided whether or not to become customers.

This model suffers from a number of disadvantages (Table 14.2). First, it assumes that communications can be varied smoothly and continuously. This is not the case. Second, it assumes that communications are the only influence upon sales. As discussed previously, sales are influenced by a variety of factors, of which planned communication is but one. Controllable and uncontrollable elements in the environment influence sales. Next, no account is taken of the other costs associated indirectly with the presentation of the offering, such as those allied to distribution. Each communication thrust will often be matched, or even bettered, by the competition. Furthermore, the actions of rivals may even affect the sales performance of all products in the same category.

The model assumes that communications can be varied smoothly and continuously. This is not the case.

It is fair to say, therefore, that the marginal approach fails to account for competitor reactions. The model assumes that sales are the result of current communication campaigns. No attempt is made to account for the effects of previous campaigns and that adstock (or carryover) may well be a prime reason for a sale occurring. The time parameters used to compute the marginal analysis could be totally inaccurate.

One of the most important shortcomings of the theory is its failure to account for the qualitative effects of the messages that are transmitted. It is assumed that all messages are of a particular standard and that relative quality is unimportant. Clearly this cannot be the case.

The marginal approach is suspect in that it operates outside the real world, and it requires data and skill in its implementation that are difficult and expensive to acquire. Theoretically, this approach is sound, but the practical problems of obtaining the necessary information and the absence of qualitative inputs render the technique difficult for most organisations to implement.

However, before moving to some of the more pragmatic approaches, it should be noted that marginal analysis is not entirely without practical foundation. For example, Weaver and Merrick (2004) consider ways in which response-curve approaches can be combined with econometrics and management judgement and through the merged processes a more accurate and meaningful budget can be determined.

Practical approaches

If the marginal approach is not practical then a consideration of the alternative approaches is necessary. Practitioners have developed a range of other methods that tend to reflect simplicity of deduction and operation but raise doubts over their overall contribution and effectiveness.

Practitioners have developed a range of other methods that tend to reflect simplicity of deduction and operation but raise doubts over their overall contribution.

The following represent some of the more common approaches. It should be noted, at this point, that none of the techniques should be seen in isolation. Organisations should use a variety of approaches and so reduce any dependence, and hence risk, on any one method. The main methods are arbitrary, inertia, media multiplier, percentage of sales, affordable, quantitative, and objective and task.

Arbitrary

Sometimes referred to as 'chairperson's rules', this is the simplest and least appropriate of all the techniques available. Under chairperson's rules, what the boss says or guesses at is what is implemented. The fact that the boss may not have a clue what the optimal figure should be is totally irrelevant. Very often the budget is decided on the hoof, and as each demand for communication resources arrives so decisions are made in isolation from any overall strategy.

Apart from the merit of flexibility, this method has numerous deficiencies. It fails to consider customer needs, the demands of the environment or marketing strategy, and there is an absence of any critical analysis. Regretfully this approach is often used by many small organisations.

Inertia

An alternative to guesswork is the 'Let's keep it the same' approach. Here all elements of the environment and the costs associated with the tasks facing the organisation are ignored. Not an impressive approach.

Media multiplier

One step more advanced is the method that recognises that media rate card costs may have increased. So, in order to maintain the same impact, the media multiplier rule requires last year's spend to be increased by the rate at which media costs have increased.

Percentage of sales

One of the more common and thoughtful approaches is to set the budget at a level equal to some predetermined percentage of past or expected sales. Invariably, organisations select a percentage that is traditional to the organisation, such as 'We always aim to spend 5.0 per cent of our sales on advertising.' The rationale put forward is that it is the norm for the sector to spend about 4.5–5.5 per cent or that 5.0 per cent is acceptable to the needs of the most powerful stakeholders or is set in recognition of overall corporate responsibilities. For example, a local authority will be mindful of the needs of its council taxpayers, whose finances contribute to the funding and maintenance of local tourism activities, for example a museum or park facilities.

There are a number of flaws with this technique. It is focused upon the sales base on which the budget rests. Planned communications, and advertising in particular, are intended to create demand, not to be the result of past sales. If the demand generators of the communication mix are to be based on the last period's performance, then it is likely that the next period's results will be similar, all things being equal. This must be the logical implication when the percentage is based on past performance.

Another way of looking at this method is to base the spend on a percentage of the next period's sales. This overcomes some of the problems, but still constrains the scope and the realistic expectations of a budget. No consideration is given to the sales potential that may exist, so this technique may actually limit performance.

Affordable

This approach is still regarded by many organisations as sophisticated and relatively free of risk. It requires each unit of output to be allocated a proportion of all the input costs and all the costs associated with the value-adding activities in production and manufacturing, together with all the other costs in distributing the output. After making an allowance for profit, what is left is to be spent on advertising and communication. In other words, what is left is what we can afford to spend.

The affordable technique is not in the least analytical, nor does it have any market or task orientation. It is a technique used by organisations of differing sizes (Hooley and Lynch, 1985), that are product-rather than customer-oriented. Their view of advertising is that it is a cost and that the quality of their product will ensure that it will sell itself. Organisations using this technique will be prone to missing opportunities that require advertising investment. This is because a ceiling on advertising expenditure is set and borrowings are avoided. As sales fluctuate in variable markets, the vagueness of this approach is unlikely to lead to an optimal budget.

The affordable technique is not in the least analytical, nor does it have any market or task orientation.

Quantitative approaches

Various quantitative approaches have been offered in an attempt to determine a precise, all-encompassing model to derive a budget. Weaver and Merrick (2004) refer to Dyson (1999), who published a mathematical model to help apportion a budget within a brand portfolio. They also mention Harper and Bridges (2003), whose scoring system approach was offered as a contrast to the algorithms of Dyson. Neither is entirely satisfactory, if only for their lack of flexibility and interpretation of the competitive environment.

Objective and task

The methods presented so far seek to determine an overall budget and leave the actual allocation to products and regions to some arbitrary method. This is unlikely to be a realistic, fair or optimal use of a critical resource.

The objective and task approach is different from the others in that it attempts to determine the resources required to achieve each objective. It then aggregates these separate costs into an overall budget. For example, the costs associated with achieving a certain level of awareness can be determined from various media owners who are seeking to sell time and space in their media vehicles. The costs of sales promotions and sales literature can be determined and the production costs of these activities and those of direct marketing (e.g. telemarketing) and PR events and sponsorships can be brought together. The total of all these costs represents the level of investment necessary to accomplish the promotion objectives that had been established earlier in the marketing communications plan. This approach is sometimes referred to as zero-based budgeting.

The objective and task approach is different from the others in that it attempts to determine the resources required to achieve each objective.

The attractions of this technique are that it focuses management attention on the goals to be accomplished and that the monitoring and feedback systems that have to be put in place allow for the development of knowledge and expertise. On the downside, the objective and task approach does not generate realistic budgets, in the sense that the required level of resources may not be available and the opportunity costs of the resources are not usually determined. More importantly, it is difficult to determine the best way to accomplish a task and to know exactly what costs will be necessary to complete a particular activity. Very often the actual costs are not known until the task has been completed, which rather reduces the impact of the budget-setting process. What is also missing is a strategic focus. The objective and task method deals very well with individual campaigns, but is not capable of providing the overall strategic focus of the organisation's annual (period) spend. The case of Procter & Gamble illustrates this point.

The use of this approach leads to the determination of a sum of money. This sum is to be invested, in this case in promoting the offerings of the organisation, but it could equally be a new machine or a building. To help discover whether such a sum should be invested and whether it is in the best interests of the organisation, a 'payout plan' can be undertaken.

Payout plans

These are used to determine the investment value of the advertising plan. This process involves determining the future revenues and costs to be incurred over a two- or three-year period. The essential question answered by such an exercise is 'How long will it take to recover the expenditure?'

Sensitivity analysis

Many organisations use this adjusting approach to peg back the advertising expenditure because the payout plan revealed costs as too large or sales developing too slowly. Adjustments are made to the objectives or to the strategies, with the aim of reducing the payback period.

Competitive parity

In certain markets, such as the relatively stable FMCG market, many organisations use communication appropriation as a competitive tool. The underlying assumption is that advertising is the only direct variable that influences sales. The argument is based on the point that while there are many factors that impact on sales, these factors are all self-cancelling. Each factor impacts on all the players in the market. The only effective factor is the amount that is spent on planned communications. As a result, some organisations deliberately spend the same amount on advertising as their competitors spend: competitive parity.

Competitive parity has a major benefit for the participants. As each organisation knows what the others are spending and while there is no attempt to destabilise the market through excessive or minimal communication spend, the market avoids self-generated turbulence and hostile competitive activity.

There are, however, a number of disadvantages with this simple technique. The first is that, while information is available, there is a problem of comparing like with like. For example, a carpet manufacturer selling a greater proportion of output into the trade will require different levels and styles of advertising and promotion from another manufacturer selling predominantly to the retail market. Furthermore, the first organisation may be diversified, perhaps importing floor tiles. The second may be operating in a totally unrelated market. Such activities make comparisons difficult to establish, and financial decisions based on such analyses are highly dubious.

The competitive parity approach fails to consider the qualitative aspects of the advertising undertaken by the different players.

The competitive parity approach fails to consider the qualitative aspects of the advertising undertaken by the different players. Each attempts to differentiate itself, and very often the communication messages are one of the more important means of successfully positioning an organisation. It would not be surprising, therefore, to note that there is probably a great range in the quality of the planned communications. Associated with this is the notion that, when attempting to adopt different positions, the tasks and costs will be different and so seeking relative competitive parity may be an inefficient use of resources. The final point concerns the data used in such a strategy. The data are historical and based on strategies relevant at the time. Competitors may well have embarked upon a new strategy since the data were released. This means that parity would not only be inappropriate for all the reasons previously listed, but also because the strategies are incompatible.

The competitive parity approach fails to consider the qualitative aspects of the advertising undertaken by the different players.

Advertising-to-sales ratio

An interesting extension of the competitive parity principle is the notion of advertising-to-sales (A/S) ratios. Instead of simply seeking to spend a relatively similar amount on communication as one's main competitors, this approach attempts to account for the market shares held by the different players and to adjust communication spend accordingly.

If it is accepted that there is a direct relationship between the volume of advertising (referred to as weight) and sales, then it is not unreasonable to conclude that if an organisation spends more on advertising then it will see a proportionate improvement in sales. The underlying principle of the A/S ratio is that, in each industry, it is possible to determine the average advertising spend of all the players and compare it with the value of the market. Therefore, it is possible for each organisation to determine its own A/S ratio and compare it with the industry average. Those organisations with an A/S ratio below the average may conclude either that they have advertising economies of scale working in their favour or that their advertising is working much harder, pound for pound, than some of their competitors.

Organisations can also use A/S ratios as a means of controlling expenditure across multiple product areas. Budgets can be set based upon the industry benchmark, and variances spotted quickly and further information requested to determine shifts in competitor spend levels or reasons leading to any atypical performance.

Budgets can be set based upon the industry benchmark, and variances spotted quickly.

Each business sector has its own characteristics, which in turn influence the size of the advertising expenditure. In 2006 the A/S ratio for female fragrances was 8.96 per cent, chewing gum 4.3 per cent, analgesics 5.1 per cent, digital cameras 2.19 per cent, toilet tissue 1.52 per cent, cereals 6.38 per cent and shampoo 4.95 per cent (Advertising Association). It can be seen that the size of the A/S ratio can vary widely. It appears to be higher (that is, a greater proportion of revenue is used to invest in advertising) when the following are present:

- the offering is standardised, not customised;
- there are many end-users;
- the financial risk for the end-user customer is small;
- the marketing channels are short;
- a premium price is charged;
- there is a high gross margin;
- the industry is characterised by surplus capacity;
- competition is characterised by a high number of new product launches.

A/S ratios provide a useful benchmark for organisations when they are trying to determine the adspend level. These ratios do not set out what the communication budget should be, but they do provide a valuable indicator around which broad commercial decisions can be developed.

A/S ratios provide a useful benchmark for organisations.

Share of voice

Brand strategy in the FMCG market has traditionally been based on an approach that uses mass media advertising to drive brand awareness, which in turn allows premium pricing to fund the advertising investment (cost). The alternative approach has been to use price-based promotions to drive market share. The latter approach has often been regarded as a short-term approach that is incapable of sustaining a brand over the longer term.

The concept underlying the A/S ratio can be seen in the context of rival supporters chanting at a football match. If they chant at the same time, at the same decibel rating, then it is difficult to distinguish the two sets of supporters, particularly if they are chanting the same song. Should one set of supporters shout at a lower decibel rating, then the collective voice of the other supporters would be the one that the rest of the crowd, and perhaps any television audience, actually hears and distinguishes.

This principle applies to the concept of share of voice (SOV). Within any market the total of all advertising expenditure (adspend), that is, all the advertising by all of the players, can be analysed in the context of the proportions each player has made to the total. Should one advertiser spend more than any other then it will be its messages that are received and stand a better chance of being heard and acted upon. In other words, its SOV is the greater. This implies, of course, that the quality of the message transmitted is not important and that it is the sheer relative weight of adspend that is the critical factor.

This concept can be taken further and combined with another, share of market (SOM). When a brand's market share is equal to its share of advertising spend, equilibrium is said to have been reached (SOV = SOM).

Strategic implications of the SOV concept

> These concepts of SOV and SOM frame an interesting perspective of competitive strategy based upon the relative weight of advertising expenditure.

These concepts of SOV and SOM frame an interesting perspective of competitive strategy based upon the relative weight of advertising expenditure. Schroer (1990) reports that, following extensive research on the US packaged goods market (FMCG), it is noticeable that organisations can use advertising spend to maintain equilibrium and to create disequilibrium in a market. The former is established by major brand players maintaining their market shares with little annual change to their advertising budgets. Unless a competitor is prepared to inject a considerable increase in advertising spend and so create disequilibrium, the relatively stable high spend deters new entrants and preserves the status quo. Schroer claims that if the two market leaders maintain SOV within 10 per cent of each other then competitive equilibrium will exist. This situation is depicted in Figure 14.2. If a market challenger launches an aggressive

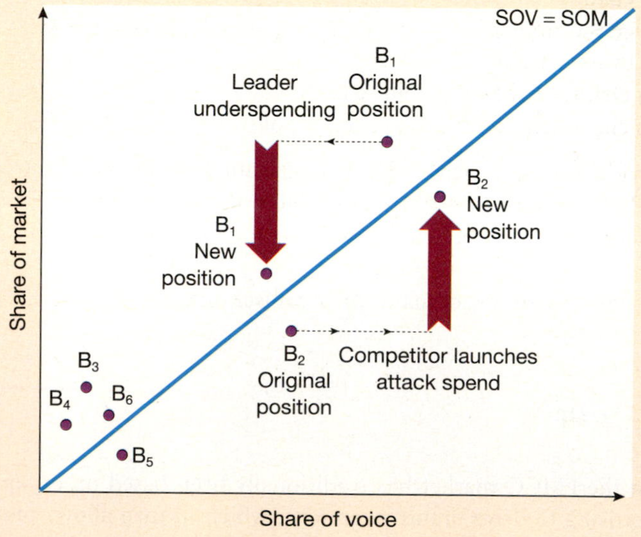

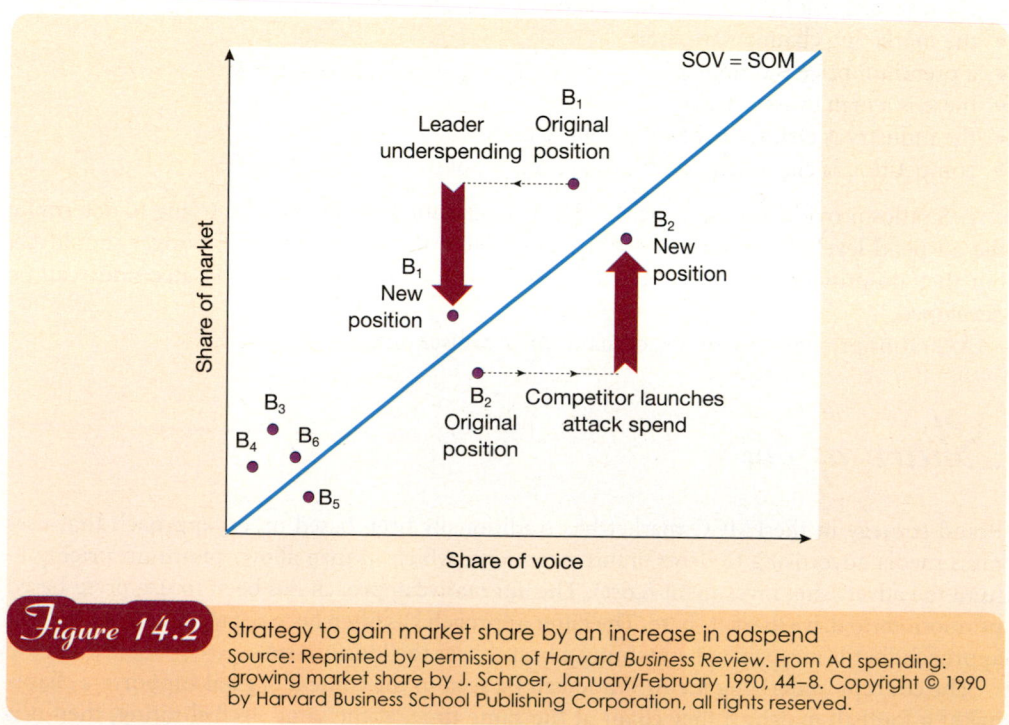

Figure 14.2 Strategy to gain market share by an increase in adspend
Source: Reprinted by permission of *Harvard Business Review*. From Ad spending: growing market share by J. Schroer, January/February 1990, 44–8. Copyright © 1990 by Harvard Business School Publishing Corporation, all rights reserved.

assault upon the leader by raising advertising spend to a point where SOV is 20–30 per cent higher than the current leader, market share will shift in favour of the challenger.

In Figure 14.2, brands 1, 3, 4 and 6 have an SOM that is greater than their SOV. This suggests that their advertising is working well for them and that the larger organisations have some economies of scale in their advertising. Brands 2 and 5, however, have an SOM that is less than their SOV. This is because brand 2 is challenging for the larger market (with brand 1) and is likely to be less profitable than brand 1 because of the increased costs. Brand 5 is competing in a niche market and, as a new brand, may be spending heavily (relative to its market share) to gain acceptance in the new market environment.

ViewPoint 14.3 Gauging brand success

One of the (many) problems associated with digital media is that there has been very little activity on which to build knowledge about how to optimise its use.

Brand Gauge is a propriety tool developed to assist both budgeting and media planning. Incorporating the goals of particular campaigns, this system stores online competitive data regarding particular expenditure on ads and market share across different categories. This enables it to generate share-of-voice and share-of-market calculations. These data are filtered through reach and effective frequency figures and compute the size of market covered, awareness levels and from this is delivered a figure that is equated to a 'positive brand reaction' score or PBR. The PBR is related to a campaign's objectives and therefore provides a measure of the value a campaign has delivered, whether this be a shift in brand perception, awareness or behaviour.

Of the many benefits of this approach one of the key ones is that wastage is reduced as the system advises when exposure is optimised and budget well spent.

Source: Longhurst (2006).

Question

Can these types of systems replace the human touch when devising budgets?

Task

Find out other methods used or recommended to set digital budgets.

This perspective brings implications for advertising spend at a strategic level. This is shown in the matrix, Figure 14.3, which shows that advertising spend should be varied according to the spend of the company's competitors in different markets. The implications are that advertising budget decisions should be geared to the level of adspend undertaken by competitors in particular markets at particular times. Decisions to attack or to defend are also set out. For example, communication investments should be placed in markets where competitors are underspending. Furthermore, if information is available about competitors' costs, then decisions to launch and sustain an advertising spend attack can be made in the knowledge that a prolonged period of premium spending can be carried through with or without a counter-attack.

This traditional perspective of static markets being led by the top two brands using heavy above-the-line strategies and the rest basing their competitive thrusts on price-based promotions was challenged by Buck (1995) through reference to a study of Superpanel data by Hamilton. It was found that the brand leaders in many FMCG markets spent nearly 50 per cent more than the industry average on advertising, while the number two brand spent about 8 per cent less than the industry average. In addition, the gap with the other actors was not as significant as Schroer reported. This is, of course, a comparison of European and US markets, and there is no reason why they should be identical or at least very similar. However, the data

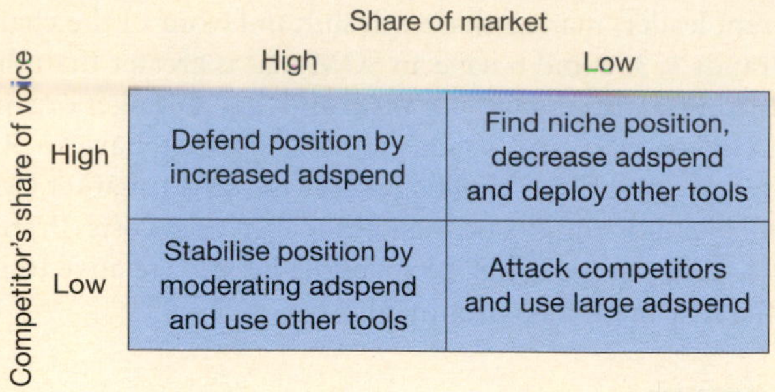

Figure 14.3 Strategies for advertising spend

Source: Reprinted by permission of *Harvard Business Review*. From Ad spending: growing market share by J. Schroer, January/February 1990, 44–8. Copyright © 1990 by Harvard Business School Publishing Corporation, all rights reserved.

are interesting in that the challenge of brand 2, postulated by Schroer, is virtually impossible in many of the UK, if not also in continental European, markets.

The concepts of SOV and SOM have also been used by Jones (1990) to develop a new method of budget setting. He suggests that those brands that have an SOV greater than their SOM are 'investment brands', and those that have a SOV less than or equal to their SOM are 'profit-taking brands'.

There are three points to notice. First, the high advertising spend of new brands is an established strategy and represents a trade-off between the need for profit and the need to become established through advertising spend. The result, invariably, is that smaller brands have lower profitability because they have to invest a disproportionate amount in advertising. Second, large brands are often 'milked' to produce increased earnings, especially in environments that emphasise short-termism. The third point is that advertising economies of scale allow large brands to develop with an SOV consistently below SOM.

Using data collected from an extensive survey of 1,096 brands across 23 different countries, Jones 'calculated the difference between share of voice and share of market and averaged these differences within each family of brands' (p. 40). By representing the data diagrammatically (Figure 14.4), Jones shows how it becomes a relatively simple task to work out the spend required to achieve a particular share of market. The first task is to plot the expected (desired) market share from the horizontal axis; then move vertically to the intersect with the curve and read off the SOV figure from the vertical axis.

Appropriation brand types

Using this approach it is possible to determine three main types of brands, based upon the amount of advertising investment. In each market there are brands that are promoted without the support of any advertising. These small niche players can be regarded as zero-based brands.

Using this approach it is possible to determine three main types of brands, based upon the amount of advertising investment.

Where brands are supported by token advertising, represented by a small SOV, the brand is probably being milked and the resources are being channelled into developing other brands. New launches are typified by the heavy advertising investment, which is necessary to get them off the ground. Here the SOV will be larger than the SOM and these can be referred to as investment brands.

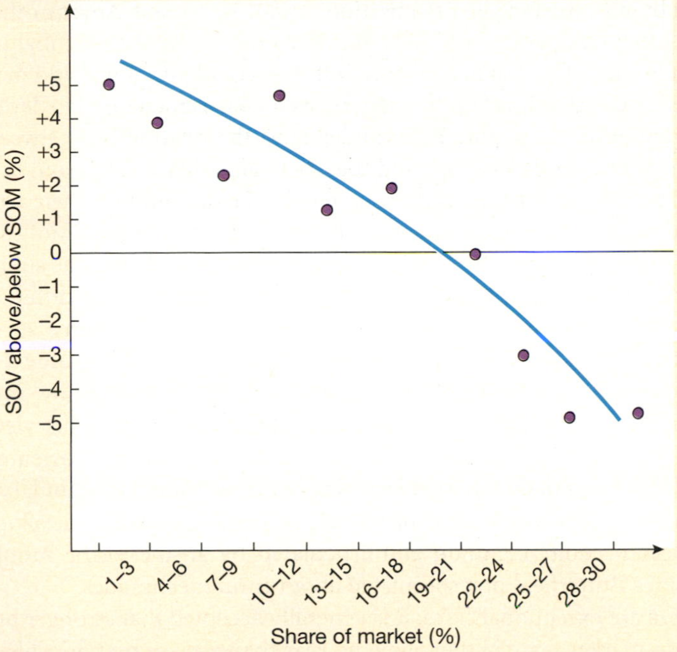

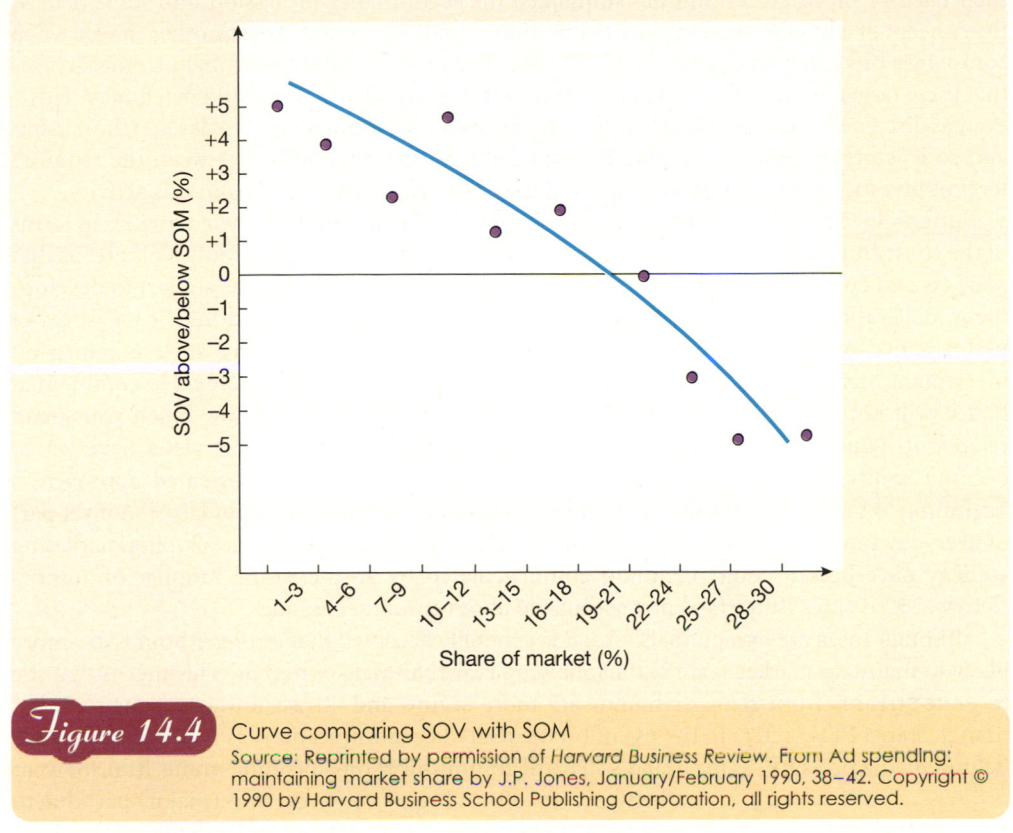

Figure 14.4 Curve comparing SOV with SOM

Source: Reprinted by permission of *Harvard Business Review*. From Ad spending: maintaining market share by J.P. Jones, January/February 1990, 38–42. Copyright © 1990 by Harvard Business School Publishing Corporation, all rights reserved.

In situations where the SOM is very large and the SOV much smaller, these profit-taking brands are running a risk of losing market share if a competitor spots the opportunity to invest a large sum in a prolonged attack. Finally, there is a group of brands that maintain stability by respecting each other's positions and by not initiating warfare. These brands can be referred to as equilibrium brands.

- Investment brands – SOV > SOM; heavy advertising to drive growth.
- Milking brands – SOV < SOM; low-level advertising to take profits out of the brand.
- Equilibrium brands – SOM = SOV; steady-level advertising to maintain position and avoid confrontation.

Assessing brands in the context of the advertising resources they attract is a slightly different way of reflecting their power and importance to their owners. If the SOV approach is limited by its applicability to stable, mature market conditions then at least it enables the communication spend to be seen and used as a competitive weapon.

The value of brand communications

The ideas and principles associated with the SOV concept provide a foundation upon which to consider the value of marketing communications as an aid to brand development. The importance of brands cannot be understated. Indeed, many organisations have attempted (and succeeded) in valuing the worth of their brands and have had them listed as an asset on

The ideas and principles associated with the SOV concept provide a foundation upon which to consider the value of marketing communications as an aid to brand development.

their balance sheets. While this has stimulated the accountancy profession into some debate, the concept of a brand's worth to an organisation cannot be refuted. Among other things, when companies buy other companies or brands, they are purchasing the potential income streams that these target brands offer, not just the physical assets of plant, capital and machinery. However, as discussed in Chapter 14, communications are a vital element used to develop these assets and so it is organisationally important to understand the relationship between the required level of investment in communications and the asset value that results from this activity.

Butterfield (1999) argued that marketers are required to account for their activities in terms of the contribution they make to the financial performance of an organisation. This means that markets and customers will be viewed as assets, which in turn will become subject to development, cultivation and leverage. Marketers will also be required to use different measures of performance. Market share, margin and revenues will give way to terms such as return on investment, net present value of future cash flows or just shareholder value. He commented that it will not be just a question of how much your adspend is, but how much you spend relative to your main competitors' market share. Although some of his views have yet to become reality there are signs that this longer-term, strategic value-oriented approach is beginning to become part of the overall marketing communications vocabulary, if not yet part of everyday practice. Ideas concerning shareholder value as a means of developing marketing strategy have become quite common and articulated by an increasing number of authors (Doyle, 2000) since Butterfield first speculated about future techniques.

Although there are exceptional cases, it is generally accepted that stronger brands are more likely to maintain market share in the following year than weaker brands. This means that the revenue streams from stronger brands are more secure and attract lower risk than weaker brands. Farr (2004) refers to the use of brand-related communications as media pressure. He defines media pressure 'as the brand's share of communications spending minus its prior-year market share' (p. 30). A brand's strength is in (major) part due to the accumulated investments and activities in the past. It follows therefore that these investments in communications should be continued rather than truncated. Figure 14.5 shows the relationship between risk (of share loss) and media pressure.

A brand's strength is in (major) part due to the accumulated investments and activities in the past.

Farr uses data from 350 brands, across a range of categories that have been divided into 20 groups based on media pressure. As media pressure grows so the risk (per cent) of losing share declines. This approach can be used to determine media budgets. Using discounted cash flows

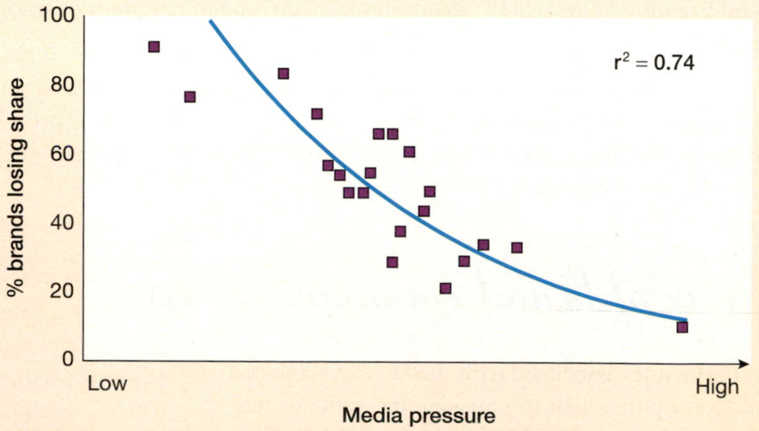

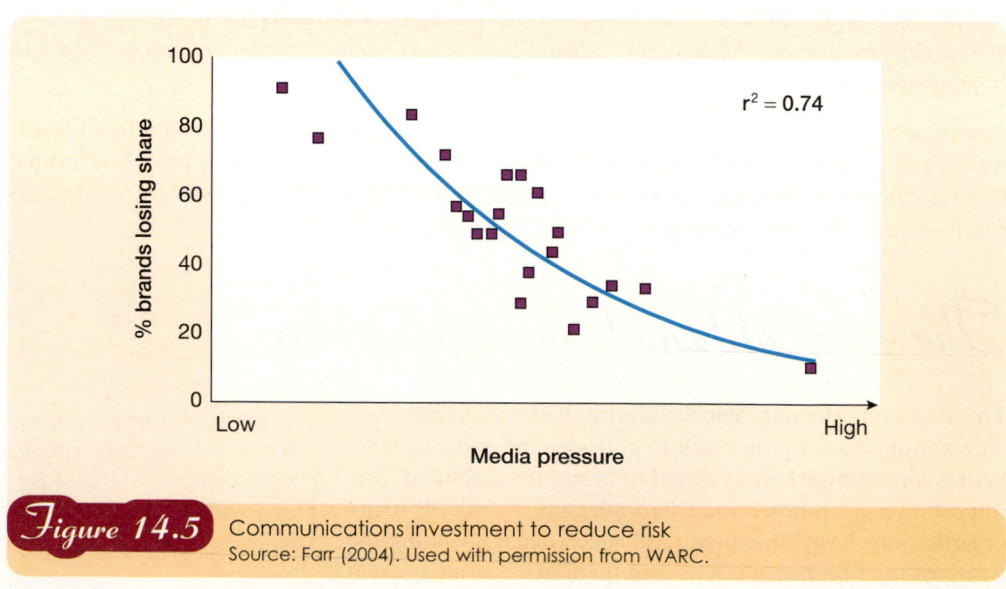

Figure 14.5 Communications investment to reduce risk
Source: Farr (2004). Used with permission from WARC.

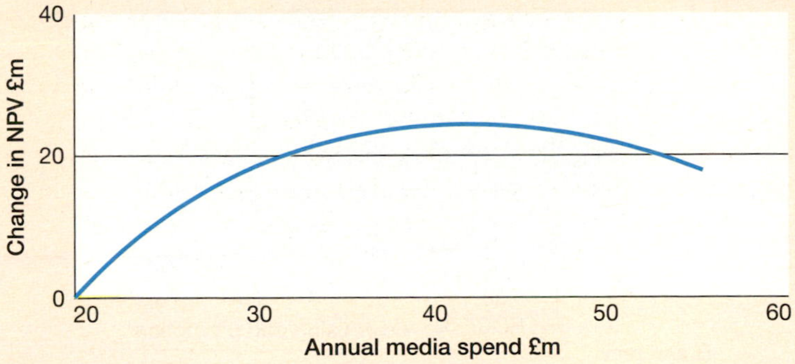

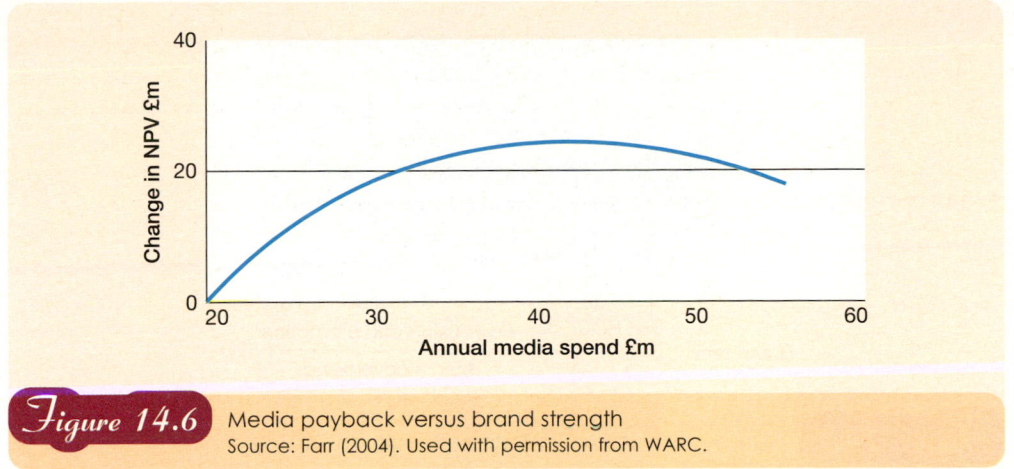

Figure 14.6 Media payback versus brand strength
Source: Farr (2004). Used with permission from WARC.

(DCFs) Farr shows that it is possible to estimate changes in the net present value (NPV) of the cash flows arising from different levels of media pressure. In the example depicted in Figure 14.6, investments up to around £40 million provide a positive impact on NPV but further investments fail to increase the value of future earnings, and should therefore not be utilised. He acknowledges that the assumption that investments in stronger brands will be more profitable may be misleading and other approaches to budget setting may need to be used when weaker (smaller) brands launch new variants or extensions.

At the end of the communication process one of the benefits that management hopes will emerge is an overall increase in the valuation of the brand. This net value arises as a result of the investment (for example, communication expenditures) generating a return to reward those who risked the capital invested in the brand. Some believe that this value arises from these activities and that the brand itself is worth £*x*; this should therefore be regarded as an asset and be placed on the balance sheet.

Profit impact on market strategy (PIMS)

One of the problems with the SOV and media pressure approaches is that they fail to take into account how much of a finite budget should be allocated to the other elements of the communication mix. Considering the relative amounts that are spent on advertising and sales promotions, let alone direct marketing, it is important to try to understand and determine how much of the budget should be spent on the other tools. In many markets a more useful strategic approach is to determine the relative spend of above- to below-the-line communication activities. As noted earlier, Procter & Gamble actually sets limits on what proportion of a brand can be spent below-the-line.

An alternative approach is the impact of marketing communications on profitability. One of the more notable commercial research organisations is PIMS. PIMS is a major database of the performance of 3,500 business units and includes profiles of over 200 variables measured over a rolling four-year period. The database records data of business performance, enabling managers to understand and develop strategies based on empirical results of businesses in particular sectors. One of the major findings is that total advertising spend is not correlated with profitability. What has emerged is that profitability is related to an optimum communication mix that is dependent on a number of key factors: again, an argument for integrated marketing communications.

PIMS is a major database of the performance of 3,500 business units and includes profiles of over 200 variables measured over a rolling four-year period.

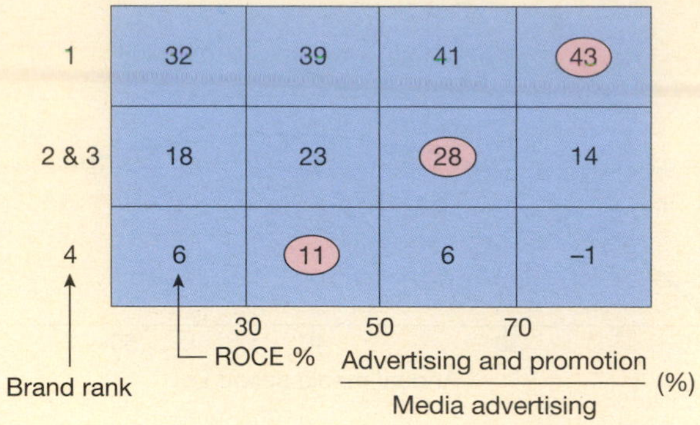

Figure 14.7 Brand leaders to concentrate on media advertising
Source: PIMS (2000).

The questions that brand managers need to answer are 'Should communication investment be used to build brand image or should the goal be to drive sales off the shelf?', and 'Where is the balance?'

According to PIMS, brand leaders spend 70 per cent plus above-the-line and make 43 per cent return on capital employed (ROCE). As if to make the point, Mistry (2001) reports that market leader snack food manufacturer Walkers spends approximately 33 per cent of its overall marketing budget below-the-line. Brands ranked 2 or 3 should invest a smaller amount above-the-line but above 50 per cent, whereas brands ranked 4 or lower should only really use below-the-line investments if they are to be less than moderately successful (see Figure 14.7).

The evidence from the database reveals many statistical relationships, too many to present here. Some of the other pointers are that brands should use advertising in declining markets and use sales promotions in expanding or rapid growth markets. One other outcome appears to be that above-the-line advertising should be used when there are many distributors and where there is little innovation or sister brands.

There is some debate about the applicability and real usefulness of the PIMS data and PIMS itself points out the limitations of its work. However, the database serves to counter the arguments of the SOV school of thought that media advertising alone is the only significant variable that determines performance. One measures market share, and the other uses market share to determine ROCE.

Which methods are most used?

From this review and commentary it is necessary to draw out the degree to which these particular tools are used in practice. Mitchell's (1993) study to determine the methods and criteria used by companies to determine their advertising budgets found that 40 per cent of respondents claimed to use the objective and task approach, 27 per cent used percentage of future sales (8 per cent used past sales) and 19 per cent used a variety of company-specific methods that do not fit neatly within any one item from the list presented above.

Although the figures resulting from the study can only be used to indicate trends of overall preferences, another set of important factors also emerged from this study. These are the range of organisational influences that impact on individual organisations. Over half the respondents reported that the method used to set these budgets actually varied, internally, across product categories. Different methods were used for new and established products.

The criteria used by organisations to set their communication budgets are many and varied. Mitchell suggests that the criteria used could be grouped as *controllables* (41 per cent), such as financial, product, production and goals; *uncontrollables* (41 per cent), such as sales, competition, market, media and distribution and *signals* (18 per cent), such as national activities, experience, effectiveness of expenditures and awareness. He reported that the processes used to determine the budgets were found as either essentially centralised or top down (52 per cent), decentralised or bottom up (13.5 per cent) or bargaining (top down and bottom up) (21 per cent). Gullen (2003) suggests ways in which all of the techniques can be grouped but concludes that management judgement based on weighting key criteria is required to determine the optimal budget. The main factors associated with the determination of marketing communications (advertising) budgets are:

Management judgement based on weighting key criteria is required to determine the optimal budget.

- organisational strategy and direction, values and cultural perspective;
- the relative amount of financial resources that are available;
- competitive activities and market conditions;
- the overall level of economic confidence felt by buyers and sellers;
- the level of product/brand development and the marketing objectives.

Over time a number of models and methods have been developed to manage these criteria to enable an appropriation to be determined.

Budgeting for the other elements of the communication mix

The methods presented so far have concentrated on the FMCG sector. The assumption has been that only one product has been considered. In reality, a range of products will need investment for communication and the allocation decision needs to reflect the requirements of an organisation's portfolio of brands. Broadbent (1989) suggests that this situation and others (e.g. direct marketing, corporate advertising) require particular combinations of the approaches presented so far. The recommendation again is that no single method will help organisations to determine the optimal investment sum.

Sales promotion activities can be more easily costed than advertising in advance of a campaign. Judgements can be made about the expected outcomes, based upon experience, competitive conditions and the use of predictive software tools. The important variable with sales promotion concerns the redemption rate. How many of the extra pack, price deals and samples will customers demand? How much extra of a brand needs to be sold if all the costs associated with a campaign are to be covered? The production and fulfilment costs can also be determined, so in general terms a return can be calculated in advance of a sales promotion event. However, there are a large number of sales promotion activities and these will often overlap. From a management perspective the brand management system is better, since a single person is responsible for the budget, one who is able to take a wider view of the range of activities. While the objective and task approach appears to be more easily applied to this element of the mix other methods, such as competitive parity and fixed ratios, are often used.

The costs of *public relations* activities can also be predicted with a reasonable degree of accuracy. The staffing and/or agency costs are relatively fixed and, as there are no media costs involved, the only other major factor is the associated production costs. These are the costs of the materials used to provide third parties with the opportunity to 'speak' on the organisation's behalf. As with sales promotion, if a number of public relations events have been calculated as a necessary part of the overall communication activities of the organisation, then the costs of the different tasks need to be anticipated and aggregated and a judgement made about the impact the events will make. The relative costs of achieving a similar level of impact through advertising or other elements of the mix can often be made, and a decision taken based on relative values.

It has already been stated that the costs associated with the *sales force* can be the highest of all the elements of the mix, especially in business-to-business situations. This would indicate that the greatest degree of care needs to be taken when formulating the size and deployment of the sales force. The different approaches to the determination of the sales force are covered in Chapter 22. The costs associated with each activity of personal selling and the support facilities (e.g. car, expenses, training) can be calculated easily, but what is more difficult to predict is the return on the investment.

These approaches to calculating the amount that should be invested in communication activities vary in their degree of sophistication and usefulness. Of all these methods, none is the ideal answer to the question of how much should be allocated to marketing communications or, more specifically, the advertising spend. Some of the methods are too simplistic, while others are too specific to particular market conditions. For example, formulating strategy to gain market share through increasing SOV seems to ignore the dynamic nature of the markets and the fact that organisations need to satisfy a range of stakeholders and not concentrate solely on winning the greatest market share.

Setting budgets specifically across digital media has not yet been well researched.

Setting budgets specifically across digital media has not yet been well researched. Renshaw (2008) offers advice for those with and without digital budgets. Where there is a digital budget he advocates 70 per cent allocated to 'emerged' digital media, 20 per cent to media 'going mainstream' and the remaining 10 per cent going to emerging digital media (see Table 14.3 and Viewpoint 14.4).

Organisations that do have a digital marketing budget are advised to consider a step process.

- Audiences – what do they do, when do they do it, when and what media/content do they consume?
- Media – which media has worked in the past? performance
- Competitors – use media that deliver results but are there media which present opportunities for advantage?
- Be bold – Consider all digital opportunities not just the Internet.

Table 14.3 Lea Burnett's recommended allocations for digital media budgets

Status of digital media	Explanation
Emerged digital media 70%	These media can be optimised and will provide results. Key media include: broadband video, rich media/video-based ads and search marketing.
Going mainstream 20%	These are media that are not as well proven as emerged media but which are increasingly prominent and appear to be emerged media at some point in the future. These include: mobile marketing, online social networks and specific types of gaming.
Emerging digital media 10%	These media are just appearing and are not well known either by large audiences or by researchers in terms of their commercial potential and performance.

Source: Renshaw (2008). Used with permission from WARC.

ViewPoint 14.4 Indy racing with cats and dogs?

Most organisations need to keep pace with the changing technological environment. To that extent Leo Burnett advocate that 10 per cent of the digital marketing budget should be allocated to testing new and developing digital areas and to treat the spend as an experiment and to not expect to measure for a return on investment.

As an example, they refer to the work they undertook for Nestlé Purina Petcare in conjunction with Joost, the Internet-based video television channel that can reach global audiences and is said to be the next generation of television for viewers, content owners and advertisers. Material was made available on Joost as a branded channel by reusing TV content from the Purina Incredible Dog Channel. So, when Joost broadcast the Indy 500 motor race an 'overlay' of the Purina content appeared so that when clicked viewers were taken to the Purina site.

Source: Renshaw (2008).

Question

The use of overlays can be distracting (annoying) to viewers. So, is this approach merely experimenting old interruptive techniques with contemporary technology?

Task

Next time your screen time is interrupted with an overlay or pop up, click through and consider the degree to which the programme content and advertised brand complement each other.

Readers may well have reached the conclusion that the most appropriate way forward for management is to consider several approaches in order to gather a ball-park figure. Such a composite approach negates some of the main drawbacks associated with particular methods. It also helps to build a picture of what is really necessary if the organisation is to communicate effectively and efficiently.

Of all the methods and different approaches, the one constant factor that applies to them all concerns the objectives that have been set for the campaign. Each element of the communication mix has particular tasks to accomplish and it is these objectives that drive the costs of the promotional investment. If the ultimate estimate of the communication spend is too high, then the objectives, not the methods used, need to be revised.

Summary

In order to help consolidate your understanding of some of the financial matters associated with marketing communications, here are the key points summarised against each of the learning objectives:

1. Determine current trends in advertising and promotional expenditure.

The decision to invest in marketing communications is relatively easy. The real difficulty lies in determining just how much to invest and in which tools and media. This is because the direct outcomes are intangible and often distant, as the advertising effects may be digested by potential buyers immediately but not acted upon until some point in the future.

Current trends in communication are a general move away from offline advertising and sales promotion and an increase in direct marketing and online investments, particularly advertising.

2. Explain the role of the communication budget.

The role of the communication budget is to ensure that the organisation achieves the greatest efficiency with each euro allocated to communication activities. Managers cannot be profligate with scarce resources, and they are accountable to the owners of the organisation for the decisions made. The budgeting process provides for internal coordination and helps ensure that communications support the marketing strategy.

3. Clarify the benefits of using budgets for communication activities.

There are many benefits associated with marketing communication budgets among which the following are significant. The process serves to focus people's attention on the costs and benefits of undertaking the planned communication activities. The act of quantifying the means by which the marketing plan will be communicated to target audiences instils a management discipline necessary to ensure that the objectives of the plan are achievable. The process facilitates cross-function coordination and forces managers to ensure that the planned communications are integrated and mutually supportive. The process provides a means by which campaigns can be monitored and management control asserted. This is particularly important in environments that are subject to sudden change or competitive hostility.

4. Examine various budgeting techniques, both practical and theoretical.

Marginal analysis provides a theoretical basis to determine the 'right' budget. However, this approach is impractical so organisations use a variety of practical approaches. These range from guesswork, a percentage of sales, what is affordable, inertia and objective and task. The last is considered to be the most appropriate.

5. Provide an appreciation of the advertising-to-sales (A/S) ratio.

If it is accepted that there is a direct relationship between the weight of advertising and sales, then if an organisation spends more on advertising it will see a proportionate improvement in sales. The underlying principle of the A/S ratio is that, in each industry, it is possible to determine the average advertising spend of all the players and compare it with the value of the market. Therefore, it is possible for each organisation to determine its own A/S ratio and compare it with the industry average.

6. Set out the principles concerning the strategic use of the share of voice (SOV) concept.

Within any market the total of all advertising expenditure (adspend), that is, all the advertising by all of the players, can be analysed in the context of the proportions each player has made to the total. Should one advertiser spend more than any other then it will be its messages that are received and stand a better chance of being heard and acted upon. In other words, its SOV is the greater. This implies, of course, that the quality of the message transmitted is not important and that it is the sheer relative weight of adspend that is the critical factor.

This concept can be taken further and combined with another, share of market (SOM). When a brand's market share is equal to its share of advertising spend, equilibrium is said to have been reached (SOV = SOM).

7. Appreciate how budgets might be set for the other elements of the communication mix.

In reality, a range of products will need investment and the allocation decision needs to reflect the requirements of an organisation's portfolio of brands. The recommendation is that no single method will help organisations to determine the optimal investment sum and that a combination of approaches is necessary. Each of the remaining tools requires different approaches.

There are specific techniques available to determine the optimum sales force size and costs. The size of the public relations effort depends on usage but the financial investment can be reduced to a judgement. Sales promotions and direct marketing are project-oriented and can be costed accordingly.

Review questions

1. How might organisations benefit from adopting an appropriation-setting process?
2. What problems might be encountered when setting them?
3. Write a brief paper outlining the essence of marginal analysis. What are the main drawbacks associated with this approach?
4. Why is the objective and task method gaining popularity?
5. What is a payout plan?
6. Discuss the view that if the A/S ratio only measures average levels of spend across an industry then its relevance may be lost as individual organisations have to adjust levels of promotional spend to match particular niche market conditions.
7. How might the notion of SOV assist the appropriation-setting process?
8. What are 'profit-taking' and 'investment' brands?
9. Determining the level of spend for sales promotion is potentially difficult. Why?
10. How might understanding brand value assist in developing a communications budget?

MiniCase Spending on breakfast can be cereal

The UK Ready-to-Eat (RTE) breakfast cereal market is worth £1,080 million and is dominated by three main manufacturers, Kellogg's, Weetabix and Cereal Partners. They hold 69 per cent market share but are faced with a number of competitive pressures, one of which is the 21 per cent share held by the own-label distributors that is growing at 5 per cent each year. The market is mature and is characterised by strong competition. Growth in the market has been slow with only product innovation and segmentation activities (e.g. chocolate flavours and children's products) showing above average performance. Branding in the RTE sector is extremely important.

With high penetration levels (90 per cent of UK households hold stock and 73 per cent of consumers claiming to eat them for breakfast) opportunities for real growth appear to be limited. However, research has shown that regular eating of the right sort of breakfast can help us get the right balance of foods we need. The nutritional value of breakfast cereals and their impact on health, diet and weight combined with their convenience, suggests that there are new opportunities for product development and marketing communications. This health orientation has helped broaden market opportunities through new products (e.g. the very successful launch of Nutrigrain cereal bars from Kellogg's for those who need to eat a mobile breakfast, for example when travelling to work) and the promotion of breakfast cereals as an all-day snack food (which has

Table 14.4 Market share and advertising spend for three leading UK cereal manufacturers

Manufacturer	Market share by volume %	UK advertising spend £m
Kellogg Co UK	42	55
Weetabix Ltd	15	15
Cereal Partners Ltd	12	18
Own-label	21	0
Others	10	14
Total	**100%**	**£102m**

Table 14.5 Market share and advertising spend for three leading UK cereal brands

Manufacturer	Leading brands	Brand market share by value (%)	Brand advertising spend £Ms
Kellogg Co UK	Kellogg's Cornflakes	9	8
Weetabix Ltd	Weetabix	7	9
Cereal Partners Ltd	Shredded Wheat	4.5	5

Note: Information for this case has been collected from a variety of public sources. The figures have been adjusted to enable clearer relationships to be observed. The material is not intended to imply good or bad management practice. This mini-case is presented as illustrative material and is suitable for teaching purposes only.

been referred to as guilt-free snacking). The development of the Nutrigrain bars also demonstrates how Kellogg's have moved into new marketing channels (e.g. petrol forecourts) and are reaching new audiences. The different strategies adopted by the leading brand manufacturers suggest that there is no single best way to use marketing communications in this market.

Kellogg's are the leading brand manufacturer, but have been most affected by the growth of own-label brands. Faced with declining market share they have just announced an aggressive marketing policy, by slashing prices by 12 per cent on its top six brands. They also intend to increase its advertising spend by 40 per cent. In the past their advertising has been based around a benefit-oriented message that aims to educate audiences about the nutritional values of their products. In doing so, Kellogg's acknowledge the role parents play in the decision-making process. Kellogg's also collaborate with the government's Health Education Authority to raise awareness of the need for a balanced diet and the important role breakfast plays in our daily food intake.

The **Weetabix** company is privately owned and discloses very little about its activities. The Weetabix biscuit, the company's main brand, has a unique characteristic in that it turns very soft and mushy when milk is poured on it. Rather than work as a product disadvantage it increases the product's utility as it makes the product a suitable food for all ages: from babies as a weaning food, to young people as a quick and convenient snack food through to those in their later years. In addition to specific brand advertising that has been largely attribute-based, Weetabix aim to add value to their brands through the use of sales promotions rather than focus on price reductions and discounts. For example, one promotion used 40 free drawstring teabags banded on top of a Weetabix 48-pack while another linked into an offer with Maxwell House coffee. Weetabix have been very profitable and they do not want to be drawn into a price war.

Cereal Partners was formed through an alliance between General Mills and Nestlé and is the single largest producer of own label products. The core part of their activities has been brand extensions and relaunches of established brands. This is demonstrated through the extensions of their largest single brand, Shredded Wheat, into Fruitful, Honey Nut and Bitesize. They do not see price as a significant factor in the decision-making process as they claim that research indicates that breakfast cereals are perceived to be a good value food. Their advertising messages are often directed at children and stress the taste and fun properties of their main line brands.

MiniCase questions

1. Evaluate the marketing communications strategy of each of the three main brand manufacturers.
2. Discuss how application of the SOV principles to the determination of advertising budgets might be applied to this case.
3. Suggest how Weetabix Ltd might use marketing communications to counter the new promotional strategy announced by Kellogg's.

References

Abratt, R. and van der Westhuizen, B. (1985) A new promotion mix appropriation model. *International Journal of Advertising*, **4**, 209–21.

Advertising Association (2004) *Advertising Statistics Year Book*. Henley: World Advertising Research Centre.

Broadbent, S. (1989) *The Advertising Budget*. Henley: NTC Publications.

Buck, S. (1995) The decline and fall of the premium brand. *Admap* (March), 14–17.

Burnett, J. (1993) *Promotion Management*, New York: Houghton Mifflin.

Butterfield, L. (1999) *Excellence in Advertising: The IPA Guide to Best Practice*. Oxford: Butterworth Heinemann.

Charles, G. (2008) Tiger Beer plans UK spending hike to £5.5m, *Marketing*, 19 March, 5.

Donnelly, A. (2008) Cut spend, damage the brand, *Marketing*, 19 March, 4.

Doyle, P. (2000) *Value-based Marketing: Marketing Strategies for Corporate Growth and Shareholder Value*. Chichester: Wiley.

Dyson, P. (1999) How to manage the budget across a brand portfolio. *Admap*, **37**(10) (December), 39–42.

Farr, A. (2004) Managing advertising as an investment. *Admap*, **39**(7) (July/August), 29–31.

Gaedeke, R.M. and Tootelian, D.H. (1983) *Marketing: Principles and Application*. St Paul, MN: West.

Gullen, P. (2003) 5 steps to effective budget setting, *Admap* (July/August), 22–4.

Hall, E. (1999) When advertising becomes an expensive luxury. *Campaign*, 10 December, 18.

Harper, G. and Bridges, D. (2003) Budgeting for healthier ROI. *Admap*, **38**(7) (July/August), 25–7.

Holmes, S. (2004) What happened to 'just do it'? *Independent on Sunday*, 12 September, 8–9.

Hooley, G.J. and Lynch, J.E. (1985) How UK advertisers set budgets, *International Journal of Advertising*, **3**, 223–31.

Jones, J.P. (1990) Ad spending: maintaining market share. *Harvard Business Review* (January/February), 38–42.

Longhurst, P. (2006) Budgeting for online: is it any different? *Admap* (November), 36–7.

Mistry, B. (2001) Walkers revives Tazo route, *Promotions and Incentives* (March), 26–8.

Mitchell, L.A. (1993) An examination of methods of setting advertising budgets: practice and literature. *European Journal of Advertising*, **27**(5), 5–21.

PIMS (2000) www.PIMS-Europe.com.

Renshaw, M. (2008) How to set digital media budgets. *WARC Exclusive*. Retrieved 20 March 2008 from www.warc.com.

Schroer, J. (1990) Ad spending: growing market share. *Harvard Business Review* (January/February), 44–8.

Smallbone, D.W. (1972) *The Practice of Marketing*. London: Staple Press.

Tomkins, R. (1999) If the return is right, keep spending. *Financial Times*, 19 March, 8.

Tylee, J. (1999) Survey warns against adspend cuts. *Campaign*, 12 March, 10.

Weaver, K. and Merrick, D. (2004) Budget allocation revisited, *Admap*, **39**(7) (July/August), 26–8.

White, R. (2007) How to use the budget better. *Admap*, July/August, 14–15.

Whitehead, J. (2008) IPA backs ads in face of downturn. *Marketing*, 9 January, 4.

Chapter 15

Evaluating marketing communications

As part of the marketing communication process it is necessary to evaluate the overall impact and effect that a campaign has on a target audience. It needs to be reviewed in order that management can learn and better understand the impact of its communications and its audiences.

Aims and learning objectives

The aims of this chapter are to review the ways in which marketing communications activities can be evaluated.

The learning objectives of this chapter are to:

1. discuss the role of evaluation as part of marketing communications;
2. explore the value and methods of pre-testing and post-testing advertisements;
3. explain the main ideas behind different physiological measures of evaluation;
4. provide an insight into the way in which each of the tools of the communication mix can be evaluated;
5. consider other ways in which the effectiveness of marketing communications can be evaluated;
6. measure the fulfilment of brand promises;
7. consider some of the issues associated with evaluating the effectiveness of digital and online communications.

For an applied interpretation see Jill Brown's MiniCase entitled ***Measuring communication effectiveness at the Salvation Army*** at the end of this chapter.

Introduction

All organisations review and evaluate the performance of their various activities. Many undertake formal mechanisms, while others review in an informal, ad hoc manner, but the process of evaluation or reflection is a well-established management process. The objective is to monitor the often diverse activities of the organisation so that management can exercise control. It is through the process of review and evaluation that an organisation has the opportunity to learn and develop. In turn, this enables management to refine its competitive position and to provide for higher levels of customer satisfaction.

The use of marketing communications is a management activity, one that requires the use of rigorous research and testing procedures in addition to continual evaluation. This is necessary because planned communications involve a wide variety of stakeholders and have the potential to consume a vast amount of resources.

The evaluation of planned marketing communications consists of two distinct elements. The first element is concerned with the development and testing of individual messages. For example, a particular sales promotion (such as a sample pack) has individual characteristics that may or may not meet the objectives of a sales promotion event.

An advertising message has to achieve, among other things, a balance of emotion and information in order that the communication objectives and message strategy be achieved. To accomplish this, testing is required to ensure that the intended messages are encoded correctly and are capable of being decoded accurately by the target audience and the intended meaning is ascribed to the message. The second element concerns the overall impact and effect that a campaign has on a target audience once a communications plan has been released. This post-test factor is critical, as it will either confirm or reject management's judgement about the viability of its communications strategy. The way in which the individual components of the communications mix work together needs to be understood so that strengths can be capitalised on and developed and weaknesses negated.

> Testing is required to ensure that the intended messages are encoded correctly and are capable of being decoded accurately by the target audience.

Prediction and evaluation require information about options and alternatives. For example, did sales presentation approach A prove to be more effective than B and, if so, what would happen if A was used nationally? Predictably, the use of quantitative techniques is more prevalent with this set of reasons. This concluding chapter of Part 3 examines the testing and evaluation methods that are appropriate to all the tools of the communications mix and introduces ideas relevant to the measurement of online communications.

The role of evaluation in planned communications

The evaluation process is a key part of marketing communications. The findings and results of the evaluative process feed back into the next campaign and provide indicators and benchmarks for further management decisions. The primary role of evaluating the performance of a communications strategy is to ensure that the communications objectives have been met and that the strategy has been effective. The secondary role is to ensure that the strategy has been executed efficiently, that the full potential of the individual promotional tools has been extracted and that resources have been used economically.

Research activity is undertaken for two main reasons. The first is guidance and development and the second is prediction and evaluation (Staverley, 1993). Guidance takes the form of

Table 15.1 Four dimensions of IMC

Dimension of IMC	Explanation
Unified communications for consistent messages and images	Activities designed to create a clear, single position, in the target market, delivering a consistent message through multiple channels.
Differentiated communications to multiple customer groups	The need to create different marketing communications campaigns (and positions) targeted at different groups (in the target market) who are at different stages of the buying process. Sequential communication models based on the hierarchy of effects or attitude construct apply.
Database-centred communications	This dimension emphasises the need to generate behavioural responses through direct marketing activities created through information collected and stored in databases.
Relationship fostering communications for existing customers	The importance of retaining customers and developing long-term relationships is a critical element of marketing communications.

Source: Lee and Park (2007). Used with permission from WARC.

shaping future strategies as a result of past experiences. Development is important in the context of determining whether the communications worked as they were intended to.

One of the predominant issues surrounding the development of IMC is the difficulty and lack of empirical evidence concerning the measurement of this concept.

The prevalence and acceptance of the integrated marketing communications concept (Chapter 9) suggests that its measurement should be a central aspect when evaluating marketing communications activities. One of the predominant issues surrounding the development of IMC is the difficulty and lack of empirical evidence concerning the measurement of this concept. In an attempt to resolve this Lee and Park (2007) provide one of the first multidimensional-scaled measures of IMC. Their model is based on four key dimensions drawn from the literature. These are set out in Table 15.1.

Each of these dimensions is regarded as separate yet integral elements of IMC. Lee and Park developed an 18-item scale, derived from the literature, to measure these dimensions. The use of this approach may advance our understanding of IMC and provide a substantial basis on which IMC activities can be measured. It is interesting to note that Lee and Park see IMC as a customer-only communication activity and choose to exclude other critical stakeholders from their measurement model.

Advertising

There have been four main stages to the measurement of advertising effectiveness.

An IPA report in 1998 stated that 23 per cent of finance directors said that if business costs were under pressure they would cut marketing and advertising before anything else (Farrow, 1999). Among the reasons offered for this view was the feeling that advertising was extremely difficult to measure and thus problematic in terms of its overall contribution to the organisation. If in doubt, cut it. On a more optimistic note Fendwick (1996) suggests that there have been four main stages to the measurement of advertising effectiveness.

1. Direct response – coupon response.
2. Executions – measurement of consumer psychological responses to the way individual ads are executed. The recognition and recall techniques were developed and refined to reflect this approach.

3. Campaign evaluation (current age) – the evaluation of campaigns working over a period of time. The use of econometrics and modelling techniques to examine the influence of key variables typifies this approach.
4. Research nirvana (future age) – through the use of computers and vast data sets it will become possible to evaluate specific individual and panel data regarding various emotional and rational impacts of a variety of marketing communication messages. The effect will be to enable managers to adjust their communications messages and media quickly, efficiently and much more effectively.

The techniques used to evaluate advertising are by far the most documented and, in view of the relative sizes of the communication tools, it is not surprising that slightly more time is devoted to this tool. This is not to disregard or disrespect the contribution each of the communication tools can make to an integrated campaign. Indeed, it is the collective measure of success against the goals set at the outset that is the overriding imperative for measurement, as will be seen later.

Pre-testing

Advertisements can be researched prior to their release (pre-test) or after they have been released (post-test). Pre-tests, sometimes referred to as copy tests, have traditionally attracted more attention, stimulated a greater variety of methods and generated much controversy, in comparison with post-tests.

The effectiveness of *pre-testing*, that is the practice of showing unfinished commercials to selected groups of the target audience with a view to refining the commercial to improve effectiveness, is still subject to debate. Reid (2000) argues that pre-testing can be used positively to support campaign development, predictively to gauge likely audience response and generally to improve advertising performance.

The methods used to pre-test advertisements are based upon either qualitative or quantitative criteria. The most common methods used to pre-test advertisements are concept testing, focus groups, consumer juries, dummy vehicles, readability, theatre and physiological tests. Focus groups are the main qualitative method used and theatre or hall tests the main quantitative test. Each of these methods will be discussed later.

The primary purpose of testing advertisements during the developmental process is to ensure that the final creative work will meet the advertising objectives. It is better to help shape the way an advertising message is formed, rather like potters continuously review their progress as they craft their vases, than to make a pot and then decide that it is not big enough or that the handle is the wrong shape. The practical objectives of pre-testing creative work are to provide opportunities to optimise ads before publication and second, and if necessary, to terminate an advertisement before costs become so large and commitment too final. Changes to an advertisement that are made too late may be resisted partly because of the sunk costs and partly because of the political consequences that 'pulling' an advertisement might have. The Newspaper Marketing Agency (NMA) in conjunction with Millward Brown has pre-tested a large number of newspaper ads and has found that pre-testing newspaper ads can more than double ad recognition levels. See www.nmauk.co.uk.

The primary purpose of testing advertisements during the developmental process is to ensure that the final creative work will meet the advertising objectives.

Once a series of advertisements has been roughed or developed so that its messages can be clearly understood, advertisers seek reassurance and guidance regarding which of the alternatives should be developed further. Concept tests, in-depth interviews, focus groups and consumer juries can be used to determine which of the proposed advertisements are the better ones by using ranking and prioritisation procedures. Of those selected, further testing can be used to reveal the extent to which the intended message is accurately decoded. These comprehension and reaction tests are designed to prevent inappropriate advertisements reaching the finished stage.

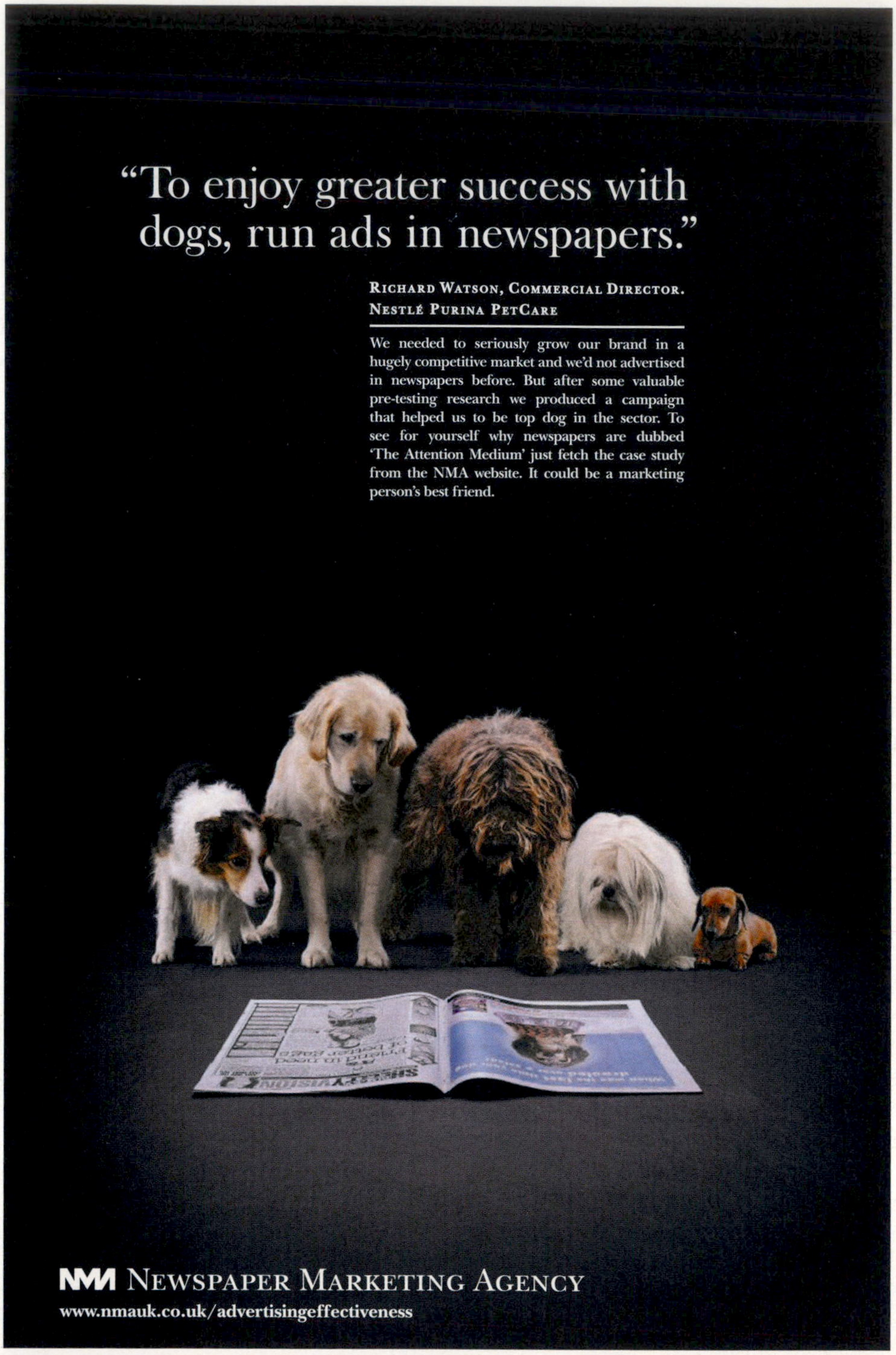

Exhibit 15.1 Newspaper Marketing Agency
A newspaper ad, placed in The Independent, promoting Nestlé Purina Petcare, the virtues of pre-testing and the NMA.
Created for The Newspaper Marketing Agency by VCCP Blue; copyright VCCP Ltd.

Pre-testing unfinished advertisements

Concept testing

The concept test is an integral part of the developmental stage of advertising strategy. The purpose is to reduce the number of alternative advertising ideas, to identify and build upon the good ideas and to reject those that the target audience feel are not suitable.

The concept test is an integral part of the developmental stage of advertising strategy.

Concept testing can occur very early on in the development process, but is usually undertaken when the target audience can be presented with a rough outline or storyboard that represents the intended artwork and the messages to be used. There are varying degrees of sophistication associated with concept testing, from the use of simple cards with no illustrations to photomatics, which are films of individual photographs shot in sequence, and livematics, which are films very close to the intended finished message. Their use will reflect the size of the advertiser's budget, the completion date of the campaign and the needs of the creative team.

Concept testing, by definition, has to be undertaken in artificial surroundings, but the main way of eliciting the target's views is essentially qualitatively oriented, based on group discussion. This group discussion is referred to as a focus group and is a technique used by most agencies.

Once a client has approved the agency's plans, ad production can begin. Very often the creative team or an independent artist will produce roughs or drawings for the agency and advertiser to see before the final artwork is finished. This is seen as necessary as the costs of producing finished work and going live without any pre-testing can be critical, and expensive.

Storyboards are a way in which it is possible to inexpensively simulate a 'rough' version of the advertisement. Pen-and-ink line drawings, animatics or cartoons and photoboards are some of the more common approaches. Some storyboards will consist of as many as 20 sketches, depicting key scenes, camera and product shots, close ups, along with background scenery and essential props.

Storyboards are a way in which it is possible to inexpensively simulate a 'rough' version of the advertisement.

Focus groups

When a small number (8–10) of target consumers are brought together and invited to discuss a particular topic a focus group is formed. By using in-depth interviewing skills a professional moderator can probe the thoughts and feelings held by the members of the group towards a product, media vehicles or advertising messages. One-way viewing rooms allow clients to observe the interaction without the focus group's behaviour being modified by external influences.

The advantage of focus groups is that they are relatively inexpensive to set up and run and they use members of the target audience. In this sense they are representative and allow true feelings and emotions to be uncovered in a way that other methods deny. They do not attempt to be quantitative and, in that sense, they lack objectivity. It is also suggested that the group dynamics may affect the responses in the 'artificial' environment. This means that there may be in-built bias to the responses and the interaction of the group members. Focus groups are very popular, but they should not be used on their own.

Consumer juries

A 'jury' of consumers, representative of the target market, is asked to judge which of a series of paste-ups and rough ideas would be their choice of a final advertisement. They are asked to rank in order of merit and provide reasons for their selections.

There are difficulties associated with ranking and prioritisation tests. First, the consumers, realising the reason for their participation, may appoint themselves as 'experts', so they lose

Exhibit 15.2 A focus group in operation
© Helen King/Corbis

Emotional advertisements tend to receive higher scores than informational messages.

the objectivity that this process is intended to bring. Second, the halo effect can occur, whereby an advertisement is rated excellent overall simply because one or two elements are good and the respondent overlooks the weaknesses. Finally, emotional advertisements tend to receive higher scores than informational messages, even though the latter might do better in the marketplace.

Pre-testing finished advertisements

When an advertisement is finished it can be subjected to a number of other tests before being released.

Dummy vehicles

Many of the pre-testing methods occur in an artificial environment such as a theatre, laboratory or meeting room. One way of testing so that the reader's natural environment is used is to produce a dummy or pretend magazine that can be consumed at home, work or wherever participants normally read magazines. Dummy magazines contain regular editorial matter with test advertisements inserted next to control advertisements. These 'pretend' magazines are distributed to a random sample of households, which are asked to consume the magazine in their normal way. Readers are encouraged to observe the editorial and at a later date they are asked questions about both the editorial and the advertisements.

The main advantage of using dummy vehicles is that the setting is natural but, as with the focus group, the main disadvantage is that respondents are aware that they are part of a test and may respond unnaturally. Research also suggests that recall may not be the best measure for low-involvement decisions or where motivation occurs through the peripheral route of the elaboration likelihood model (ELM). If awareness is required at the point of sale, then recognition may be a more reliable indicator of effectiveness than recall.

Readability tests

Rudolph Flesch (1974) developed a formula to assess the ease with which print copy could be read. The test involves, among other things, determining the average number of syllables per 100 words of copy, the average length of sentence and the percentage of personal words and sentences. By accounting for the educational level of the target audience and by comparing results with established norms, the tests suggest that comprehension is best when sentences are short, words are concrete and familiar, and personal references are used frequently.

Projective techniques

Projective techniques are used to probe the subconscious and have close associations with Freudian thinking and the motivation school advocated by Dichter (1966) (see Chapter 5). Individuals or groups can be encouraged through projective techniques to express their inner thoughts and feelings about brands, products, services and organisations, among others. Four main projective techniques can be identified (see Table 15.2).

Projective techniques are used to probe the subconscious.

Projective techniques have been used by many leading brands to understand how their brands are perceived, to test advertising and creative ideas and to segment their markets. For example, Guinness used projective techniques to understand how to position their brand and how advertising should be used to develop the ideal position.

Table 15.2 Projective techniques

Projective technique	Explanation
Association	Free word association tests require respondents to respond with the first word that comes to mind in response to a stimulus word. Often used in when naming brands.
Completion	Spontaneous sentence or story-telling completion are the most used methods. Responses can be graded as approval, neutral or disapproval enabling attitudes towards brands to be determined.
Transformation	These are also known as 'expressible' techniques and involve techniques such as psychodrawing. This requires respondents to express graphically their inner feelings about a brand or event (e.g. a shopping trip, holiday or purchase process).
Construction	This approach can involve role playing where respondents are asked to act out their feelings towards a purchase, a brand, event or organisation.

Source: Based on Robson (2002).

ViewPoint 15.1 Projective engagement with Sony Bravia

Projective testing techniques were used to measure the positioning success and the impact of the Sony Bravia 'Paint' ads. Sony wanted to use a creative that symbolised the technical colour development represented by the Bravia television.

Based on exploding colours around a council housing estate, Paint represented a radically different and unexpected creative, if only because there was no voice-over, no mention of attributes, features or benefits, in either copy or voice, and there were no visuals depicting the product or people consuming (watching) the television.

Paint was designed to communicate the point that the Bravia and SXRD range provide the 'colour that you'll see on these screens will be like no other' (www.Sony.com).

Part of the testing undertaken by TNS, using their AdEval™ methodology, included the use of people photosets. These are pictures of groups of personality types, used and validated internationally. Respondents were shown various different ads and asked which group of people they thought each would appeal to most. Many people have reported finding the Paint ads confusing and difficult to relate to. However, all the respondents were able to assign a personality type and the majority categorised the ads to people who were carefree, lively and bold. In terms of brand images the respondents reported vibrant colour, lively, outgoing, dynamic and cool/trendy as the key attributes (see Figure 15.1).

The claim made is that projective techniques can discover ways in which an ad engages with a consumer's emotions.

Source: Burden (2007).

Question

Which of the types of projective techniques set out in Table 15.2 do photosets best accompany?

Task

Try an informal word association test with your friends based around brands they enjoy.

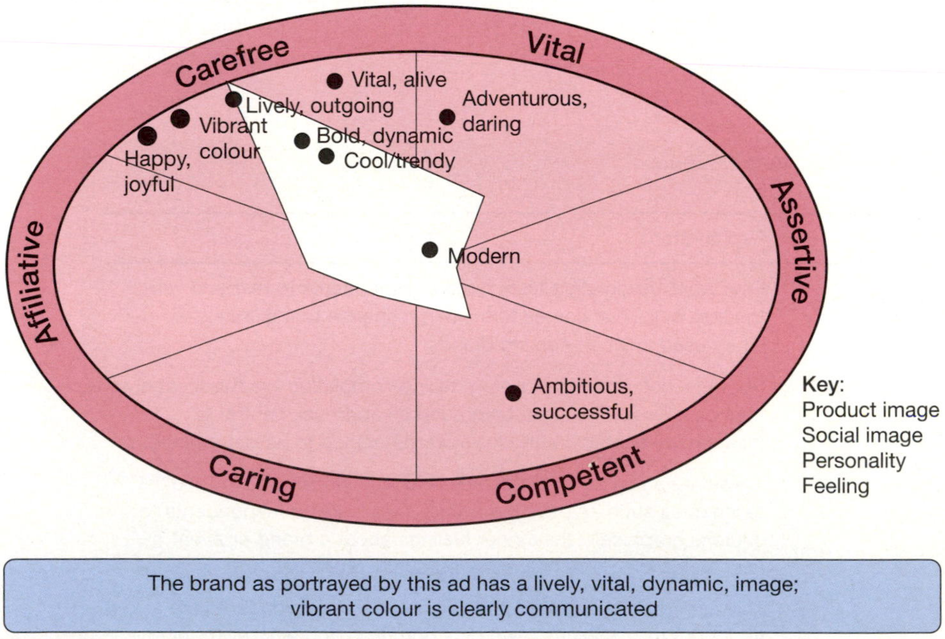

Figure 15.1 Results from projective technique for Sony Bravia television ad
Source: Burden (2007). Used with permission from WARC.

Theatre tests

As a way of testing finished broadcast advertisements, target consumers are invited to a theatre (laboratory or hall) to preview television programmes. Before the programme commences, details regarding the respondents' demographic and attitudinal details are recorded and they are asked to nominate their product preferences from a list. At the end of the viewing their evaluation of the programme is sought and they are also requested to complete their product preferences a second time.

As a way of testing finished broadcast advertisements, target consumers are invited to a theatre (laboratory or hall) to preview television programmes.

There are a number of variations on this theme: one is to telephone the respondents a few days after the viewing to measure recall and another is to provide joysticks, push buttons and pressure pads to measure reactions throughout the viewing. The main outcome of this process is a measure of the degree to which product preferences change as a result of exposure to the controlled viewing. This change is referred to as the persuasion shift. This approach provides for a quantitative dimension to be added to the testing process, as the scores recorded by respondents can be used to measure the effectiveness of advertisements and provide benchmarks for future testing.

It is argued that this form of testing is too artificial and that the measure of persuasion shift is too simple and unrealistic. Furthermore, some believe that many respondents know what is happening and make changes because it is expected of them in their role of respondent. Those in favour of theatre testing state that the control is sound, that the value of established norms negates any 'role play' by respondents and that the actual sales data support the findings of the brand persuasion changes in the theatre.

A major evaluation of 400 individual advertising tests in the United States found, among many other things, that there is no clear relationship between measures of persuasion shift and eventual sales performance. This questions the use of an organisation's scarce resources and the viability of using these techniques (Lodish and Lubetkin, 1992).

This technique is used a great deal in the United States, but until recently has had limited use in Britain. However, Mazur (1993) reports that theatre testing is increasing in Britain. Agencies are concerned that the simplistic nature of recording scores as a means of testing advertisements ignores the complex imagery and emotional aspects of many messages. If likeability is an important aspect of eventual brand success then it is unlikely that the quantitative approach to pre-testing will contribute any worthwhile information.

The increasing use of, or at least interest in, theatre tests and the movement towards greater utilisation of quantitative techniques in pre-testing procedures runs concurrently with the increasing requirements of accountability, short-termism and periods of economic downturn. As no one method will ever be sufficient, a mix of qualitative and quantitative pre-test measures will, inevitably, always be required.

Physiological measures

A bank of physiological tests has been developed, partly as a response to advertisers' increasing interest in the emotional impact of advertising messages and partly because many other tests rely on the respondents' ability to interpret their reactions. Physiological tests are designed to measure the involuntary responses to stimuli that avoid the bias inherent in other tests. There are substantial costs involved with the use of these techniques, and the validity of the results is questionable. Consequently they are not used a great deal in practice, but, of them all, eye tracking is the most used and most reliable (see Table 15.3).

Physiological tests are designed to measure the involuntary responses to stimuli that avoid the bias inherent in other tests.

Table 15.3 Physiological tests

Pupil dilation
Pupil dilation is associated with action and interest and is used to measure a respondent's reaction to a stimulus. If the pupil is constricted then interest levels are low and energy is conserved. The level of arousal is used to determine the degree of interest and preference in a particular advertisement or package design.
Eye tracking
This technique requires the use of eye movement cameras that fire an infrared beam to track the movement of the eye as it scans an advertisement. The sequence in which the advertisement is read can be determined and particular areas that do or do not attract attention can be located.
Galvanic skin response
This measures the resistance the skin offers to a small amount of current passed between two electrodes. Response to a stimulus will activate the sweat glands, which in turn will increase the resistance. Therefore the greater the level of tension induced by an advertisement the more effective it is as a form of communication.
Tachistoscopes
These measure the ability of an advertisement to attract attention. The speed at which an advertisement is flashed in front of a respondent is gradually slowed down until a point (about 1/100 second) is reached at which the respondent is able to identify components of the message. This can be used to identify those elements that respondents see first as a picture is exposed, and so facilitates the creation of impact-based messages.
Electroencephalographs
This involves the use of a scanner that monitors the electrical frequencies of the brain. Hemispheric lateralisation concerns the ability of the left-hand side of the brain to process rational, logical information and the right-hand side handles visual stimuli and responds more to emotional inputs.
Brain activation measures the level of alpha-wave activity, which indicates the degree to which the respondent is aroused by and interested in a stimulus. Therefore, the lower the level of alpha activity the greater the level of attention and cognitive processing. It would follow that, by measuring the alpha waves while a respondent is exposed to different advertisements, different levels of attention can be determined.

On the surface, pupil dilation has a number of attractions, but it is not used very much as research has shown little evidence of success. The costs are high and the low number of respondents that can be processed limits the overall effectiveness. Eye tracking can be a useful means of reviewing and amending the layout of an advertisement. Galvanic skin response is flawed because the range of reactions and emotions, the degree of learning and recall, and aspects of preference and motivation are all ignored. When these deficiencies are combined with the high costs and low numbers of respondents that can be processed, it is not surprising that this method of pre-testing has little value. The hemispheric lateralisation theory has been rejected by many researchers. Although the right side of the brain is best for recognition, and the left better for recall, only Vaughn (1980) has developed this approach in terms of advertising theory (Chapter 16).

Although now superseded, his grid was regarded as an important breakthrough in our understanding of how advertising works. However, while the grid has been used extensively, there is little evidence of any commercial application of electro-encephalographs. Advertisements should be designed to appeal to each hemisphere, but recent research now appears to reject this once-popular notion.

Post-testing

Testing advertisements that have been released is generally more time-consuming and involves greater expense than pre-testing. However, the big advantage with post-testing is that advertisements are evaluated in their proper environment, or at least the environment in which they are intended to be successful.

There are a number of methods used to evaluate the effectiveness of such advertisements, and of these inquiry, recall, recognition and sales-based tests predominate.

Inquiry tests

These tests are designed to measure the number of inquiries or direct responses stimulated by advertisements. Inquiries can take the form of returned coupons and response cards, requests for further literature or actual orders. They were originally used to test print messages, but some television advertisements now carry 0800 (free) telephone numbers. An increase in the use of direct-response media will lead to an increase in the sales and leads generated by inquiry-stimulating messages, so this type of testing will become more prevalent.

Inquiry tests can be used to test single advertisements or a campaign in which responses are accumulated. Using a split run, an advertiser can use two different advertisements and run them in the same print vehicle. This allows measurement of the attention-getting properties of alternative messages. If identical messages are run in different media then the effect of the media vehicles can be tested.

> Inquiry tests can be used to test single advertisements or a campaign.

Care needs to be given to the interpretation of inquiry-based tests, as they may be misleading. An advertisement may not be effective simply because of the responses received. For example, people may respond because they have a strong need for the offering rather than the response being a reflection of the qualities of the advertisement. Likewise, other people may not respond despite the strong qualities of the advertisement, simply because they lack time, resources or need at that particular moment.

Recall tests

Recall tests are designed to assess the impression that particular advertisements have made on the memory of the target audience. Interviewers, therefore, do not use a copy of the advertisement as a stimulus, as the tests are intended to measure impressions and perception, not behaviour, opinions, attitudes or the advertising effect.

Normally, recall tests require the cooperation of several hundred respondents, all of whom were exposed to the advertisement. They are interviewed the day after an advertisement is screened, hence the reference to day-after-recall (DAR) tests. Once qualified by the interviewer, respondents are first asked if they remember a commercial for, say, air travel. If the respondent replies 'Yes, Virgin', then this is recorded as unaided recall and is regarded as a strong measure of memory. If the respondent says 'No', the interviewer might ask the question 'Did you see an advertisement for British Airways?' A positive answer to this prompt is recorded as aided recall.

These answers are then followed by questions such as, 'What did the advertisement say about British Airways?', 'What did the commercial look like?' and 'What did it remind you of?' All the answers provided to this third group of questions are written down word for word and recorded as verbatim responses.

The reliability of recall scores is generally high. This means that each time the advertisement is tested, the same score is generated. Validity refers to the relationship or correlation between recall and the sales that ultimately result from an audience exposed to a particular advertisement. The validity of recall tests is generally regarded by researchers as low (Gordon, 1992).

> The reliability of recall scores is generally high.

Recall tests have a number of other difficulties associated with them. First, they can be expensive, as a lot of resources can be consumed by looking for and qualifying respondents. Second, not only is interviewing time expensive, but the score may be rejected if, on examination of the verbatim responses, it appears that the respondent was guessing.

It has been suggested by Zielske (1982) that thinking/rational messages appear to be easier to recall than emotional/feeling ones. Therefore, it seems reasonable to assume that recall scores for emotional/feeling advertisements may be lower. It is possible that programme content may influence the memory and lead to different recall scores for the same offering. The use of a preselected group of respondents may reduce the costs associated with finding a qualified group, but they may increase their attention towards the commercials in the knowledge that they will be tested the following day. This will inevitably lead to higher levels of recall than actually exist.

On-the-air tests are a derivative of recall and theatre tests. By using advertisements that are run live in a test area, it is possible to measure the impact of these test advertisements with DAR. As recall tests reflect the degree of attention and interest in the advertisement, this is a way of controlling and predicting the outcome of a campaign when it is rolled out nationally.

Recall tests are used a great deal, even though their validity is low and their costs are high. Wells *et al.* (1992) argue that this is because recall scores provide an acceptable means by which decisions to invest heavily in advertising programmes can be made. Agencies accumulate vast amounts of recall data that can be used as benchmarks to judge whether an advertisement generated a score that was better or less than the average for the product class or brand. Having said that, and despite their popularity, they are adjudged to be poor predictors of sales (Lodish and Lubetkin, 1992).

ViewPoint 15.2 Total Recall

The techniques available to measure the ability of most media to deliver on core attributes such as reach and frequency is well rehearsed and understood. However, what is more problematic is measuring whether any particular variation or format within a type of media can impact on a viewer's/reader's attention or as some would have it, engagement with a medium and message.

Research has shown that people standing on London Underground stations and travelling in tube trains accumulate considerable more dwell time with respect to the ads they are exposed to. However, it was not known how dwell time might affect recall or the extent to which dwell time might impact on brand perceptions.

A research project, call Total Recall, was created. This exercise sought to measure the extent to which recall improves with length of exposure and whether positive perceptions (brand empathy) improves.

Using various poster ads, some complex with extensive copy and some using simple visual branding techniques, respondents were exposed to these ads and to the control ads within a managed testing environment. The results were quite clear. Respondents who were exposed to the ads for longer periods of time were more likely to remember what they had seen and were more likely to develop more positive feelings towards the brands.

Source: Cox (2007).

Question

Are the results of this research exercise surprising or could they have been confidently anticipated?

Task

Make a list of the ways in which people might be exposed to billboard and magazine ads more frequently?

Recognition tests

Recall tests are based upon the memory and the ability of respondents to reprocess information about an advertisement. A different way of determining advertising effectiveness is to ask respondents if they recognise an advertisement. This is the most common of the post-testing procedures for print advertisements. One of the main methods used to measure the readership of magazines is based on the frequency-of-reading and generally there are three main approaches:

One of the main methods used to measure the readership of magazines is based on the frequency-of-reading.

- *recency:* reading any issue during the last publishing interval (e.g. within the last seven days for a weekly magazine);
- *specific issue:* reading of a specific issue of a publication;
- *frequency-of-reading*: how many issues a reader has read in a stated period (such as a month in respect of a weekly magazine).

Worldwide, the recency approach is the most widely used method in national readership surveys (www.roymorgan.com). Of the many services available, perhaps the Starch Readership Report is the best known. These recognition tests are normally conducted in the homes of approximately 200 respondents. Having agreed that the respondent has previously seen a copy of the magazine, it is opened at a predetermined page and the respondent is asked, for each advertisement, 'Did you see or read any part of the advertisement?' If the answer is yes the respondent is asked to indicate exactly which parts of the copy or layout were seen or read.

Four principal readership scores are reported: noted, seen-associated, read most and signature (see Table 15.4).

The reliability of recognition tests is very high, higher than recall scores. Costs are lower, mainly because the questioning procedure is simpler and quicker. It is also possible to deconstruct an advertisement into its component parts and assess their individual effects on the reader. As with all interviewer-based research, bias is inevitable. Bias can also be introduced by the respondent or the research organisation through the instructions given or through fatigue of the interviewer.

The validity of recognition test scores is said to be high, especially after a number of insertions. However, there can be a problem of false claiming, where readers claim to have seen an advertisement but, in fact, have not. This, it is suggested, is because when readers confirm they have seen an advertisement the underlying message is that they approve of and like that sort of advertisement. If they say that they have not seen an advertisement, the underlying message is that they do not usually look at that sort of advertisement. Wells *et al.* (1992) report on the view expressed by Krugman (1988), that readers are effectively voting on whether an advertisement is worth spending a moment of their time to look at. It might be that readers' memories are a

The validity of recognition test scores is said to be high.

Table 15.4 Principal readership scores

Readership scores	Explanation
Noted	The percentage of readers who remember seeing the advertisement.
Seen-associated	The percentage of readers who recall seeing or reading any part of the advertisement identifying the offering.
Read most	The percentage of readers who report reading at least 50 per cent of the advertisement.
Signature	The percentage of readers who remember seeing the brand name or logo.

reliable indicator of what the reader finds attractive in an advertisement and this could be a surrogate indicator for a level of likeability. This proposition has yet to be fully investigated, but it may be that the popularity of the recognition test is based on the validity rating and the approval that high scores give to advertisers.

Sales tests

If the effectiveness of advertisements could be measured by the level of sales that occurs during and after a campaign, then the usefulness of measuring sales as a testing procedure would not be in doubt. However, the practical difficulties associated with market tests are so large that these tests have little purpose. Counting the number of direct response returns and the number of enquiries received are the only sales-based tests that have any validity.

Practitioners have been reluctant to use market-based tests because they are not only expensive to conduct but they are also historical by definition. Sales occur partly as a consequence of past actions, including past communication strategies, and the costs (production, agency and media) have already been sunk. There may be occasions where it makes little political and career sense to investigate an event unless it has been a success, or at the very least reached minimal acceptable expectations.

ViewPoint 15.3 Ford measure their media

Measuring the return on their investment in marketing communications is really important to Ford. In addition to specific sponsorships Ford use a wide range of media, such as press, television, radio and online. It is critical that they understand what works and what does not work for them.

When Ford buy media space it is important that they achieve leverage. For example, when they launched the S-Max they took space in *The Observer* on- and offline as the readership profile matched that of the car.

Ford measure two key elements. The first concerns performance outputs or market measures such as market share at the retail level, profitability and ROI. They also measure the ROI on their direct mail and data-rich online activities. The second element concerns softer measures such as brand likeability, directly associated with some of their more emotionally oriented marketing goals.

However, the interesting aspect of Ford's media measurement activities concerns not what they measure but who actually does the measurement. All media buying and associated purchases are undertaken by MindShare but Ford then use the consulting company Accenture to measure the efficiency with which Mindshare buy media on Ford's behalf.

Source: Ovenden (2007).

Question

Why do Ford use Accenture to measure their own suppliers media buying effectiveness?

Task

Visit the Accenture web site www.accenture.com. How else do they contribute to the world of marketing communications?

For these reasons and others, advertisers have used test markets to gauge the impact their campaigns have on representative samples of the national market.

Simulated market tests

By using control groups of matched consumers in particular geographic areas, the use of simulated test markets permits the effect of advertising on sales to be observed under controlled market conditions. These conditions are more realistic than those conducted within a theatre setting and are more representative of the national market than the limited in-house tests. This market representation is thought by some to provide an adequate measure of advertising effect. Other commentators, as discussed before, believe that unless advertising is the dominant element in the marketing mix, there are usually too many other factors that can affect sales. It is therefore unfair and unrealistic to place the sole responsibility for sales with advertising.

Single-source data

With the development and advances in technology it is now possible to correlate consumer purchases with the advertisements they have been exposed to. This is known as single-source data and involves the controlled transmission of advertisements to particular households whose every purchase is monitored through a scanner at supermarket checkouts. In other words, all the research data are derived from the same households.

The advent of cable television has facilitated this process. Consumers along one side of a street receive one set of control advertisements, while the others on the other side receive test advertisements. Single-source data provide exceptionally dependable results, but the technique is expensive, is inappropriate for testing single advertisements and tends to focus on the short-term effect, failing, for example, to cope with the concept of adstock.

In the United Kingdom facilities such as Adlab, then ScatScan and Homescan have helped advertisers assess their advertising effectiveness in terms of copy testing, weight testing and even the use of mixed media. The use of split regions can be very important, allowing comparisons to made of different strategies.

Other tests

There is a range of other measures that have been developed in an attempt to understand the effect of advertisements. Among these are tracking studies and financial analyses.

Tracking studies

A tracking study involves interviewing a large number of people on a regular basis, weekly or monthly, with the purpose of collecting data about buyers' perceptions of marketing communication messages, not just advertisements and how these messages might be affecting buyers' perceptions of the brand. By measuring and evaluating the impact of a campaign when it is running, adjustments can be made quickly. The most common elements that are monitored, or tracked, are the awareness levels of an advertisement and the brand, image ratings of the brand and the focus organisation, and attributes and preferences.

Tracking studies can be undertaken on a periodic or continuous basis. The latter is more expensive, but the information generated is more complete and absorbs the effect of competitor's actions, even if the effects are difficult to disaggregate. Sherwood *et al.* (1989) report that, in a general sense, continuous tracking appears more appropriate for new products and periodic tracking more appropriate for established products.

> Tracking studies can be undertaken on a periodic or continuous basis.

A further form of tracking study involves monitoring the stock held by retailers. Counts are usually undertaken each month, on a pre- and post-exposure basis. This method of measuring sales is used frequently. Audited sales data, market share figures and return on investment provide other measures of advertising effectiveness.

Tracking studies are also used to measure the impact and effectiveness of online activities. These may be applied to banner ads, email campaigns and paid-for search engine placements and have for a long time been geared to measuring site visitors, clicks through or pages visited. Increasingly these studies are attending to the volume and value of traffic with regard to the behaviour undertaken by site visitors. Behaviour, or the more common term, call-to-action, can be considered in terms of the engagement through exchanges or transactions, the number of site or subscription registrations, the volume of downloads requested or the number of offline triggers such as 'call me buttons' that are activated.

Financial analysis

The vast amount of resources that are directed at planned communications, and in particular advertising, requires that the organisation reviews, on a periodic basis, the amount and the manner in which its financial resources have been used. For some organisations the media spend alone constitutes one of the major items of expenditure. For example, many grocery products incur ingredient, packaging and distribution plus media as the primary costing elements to be managed.

Variance analysis enables a continuous picture of the spend to be developed and acts as an early warning system should unexpected levels of expenditure be incurred. In addition to this and other standard financial controls, the size of the discount obtained from media buying is becoming an important and vital part of the evaluation process.

Increasing levels of accountability and rapidly rising media costs have contributed to the development of centralised media buying. Under this arrangement, the promotion of an organisation's entire portfolio of brands, across all divisions, is contracted to a single media-buying organisation. Part of the reasoning is that the larger the account the greater the buying power an agency has, and this in turn should lead to greater discounts and value of advertising spend.

The point is that advertising economies of scale can be obtained by those organisations that spend a large amount of their resources on the media. To accommodate this, centralised buying has developed, which in turn creates higher entry and exit barriers, not only to and from the market but also from individual agencies.

Likeability

A major study by the American Research Foundation investigated a range of different pretesting methods with the objective of determining which were best at predicting sales success. The unexpected outcome was that, of all the measures and tests, the most powerful predictor was likeability: 'how much I liked the advertisement'.

From a research perspective, much work has been undertaken to clarify the term 'likeability', but it certainly cannot be measured in terms of a simple Likert scale of 'I liked the advertisement a lot', 'I liked the advertisement a little', etc. The term has a much deeper meaning and is concerned with the following issues (Gordon, 1992):

- personally meaningful, relevant, informative, true to life, believable, convincing;
- relevant, credible, clear product advantages, product usefulness, importance to 'me';
- stimulates interest or curiosity about the brand; creates warm feelings through enjoyment of the advertisement.

The implication of these results is that post-testing should include a strong measure of how well an advertisement was liked at its deepest level of meaning.

> There are four main elements associated with likeability. These are entertainment, relevance, clearness (or clarity) and pleasantness.

Research by Smit *et al.* (2006) determined that there are four main elements associated with likeability. These are entertainment, relevance, clearness (or clarity) and pleasantness. Of these they found relevance to be the most important for changing viewer's opinions and entertainment for explaining how people process ads.

There are two main approaches to measuring likeability. One seeks to isolate what it is that viewers think and feel after seeing particular ads, i.e. how they feel. The other measures attitudes toward the ad itself. Essentially likeability is concerned with the affective element of the attitude construct. Indeed, some researchers argue that likeability is a suitable response to the cognitive processing school of thought where individuals are considered to be rational problem-solvers.

Cognitive response analysis is an attempt to understand the internal dynamics of how an individual selects and processes messages, of how counter-arguing and message bolstering, for example, might be used to retain or reject an advertisement (see Chapter 17). Back in 1993, Biel reported a growing body of research evidence linking behaviour, attitude change and cognitive processing. He went on to predict, correctly, that this approach, unlike many of the others, was not restricted to FMCG markets and would be deployed across service markets, durables and retailers.

One of the important points to be made from this understanding of likeability is the linkage with the concept of 'significant value' considered in Chapter 8. The degree to which advertising works is a function of the level of engagement a message creates. This engagement is mediated by the context in which messages are sent, received and personally managed. The main factors are that the product in question should be new or substantially different, interesting, stimulating and personally significant. For advertising to be successful, it must be effective, and to be effective it should be of personally significant value to members of the target audience (those in the market to buy a product from the category in the near future).

The future use of technology will help the measurement and evaluation of advertising. The technology is now in place to meter what people are watching, by appending meters not to sets, but to people. Strapped-on mobile people meters can pick up signals indicating which poster site, television or radio programme is being walked past, seen or heard respectively.

Sales promotion

The measurement and evaluation of sales promotions are similar in principle to those conducted for advertising. The notion that some piloting should occur prior to launch in order that any wrinkles can be ironed out still holds strong, as does the need to balance qualitative with quantitative data. However, advertising seeks to influence awareness and image over the long term, whereas sales promotions seek to influence behaviour over the short term. As discussed earlier in this chapter, the evaluation of advertising can be imprecise and is subject to great debate. In the same way, the evaluation of sales promotions is subject to debate, but the means by which they are measured is not as ambiguous or as difficult as advertising (Shultz, 1987).

The use of quantitative methods as a testing tool leads to directly measurable and comparable outcomes, in comparison with the more subjective qualitative evaluations. Notionally, the balance in testing advertising is to use a greater proportion of qualitative than quantitative methods. The balance with sales promotions is shifted the other way. This is because the object being measured lends itself more to these kinds of measurement. If the purpose of sales promotion is to influence purchasing behaviour, then a measure of sales performance is necessary in addition to the evaluation of individual promotions.

If the purpose of sales promotion is to influence purchasing behaviour, then a measure of sales performance is necessary in addition to the evaluation of individual promotions.

The different types of sales promotion are discussed in Chapter 24, where it is identified that there are a number of different target audiences for sales promotions activities; these are resellers, consumers and the sales force.

Manufacturer to reseller

The main objectives are to stimulate the resellers to try new products and to encourage them to allocate increased shelf space for established products. If campaigns are devised to meet these objectives, then a pre- and post-test analysis of the amount of allocated shelf space and the number of new products taken into the reseller's portfolio needs to be completed. These processes are called retail audits (such as those undertaken by Nielsen Marketing Research), and although the information about changes in distribution and stock levels is not usually available until after the promotion has finished, it does provide accurate information concerning the effects that the event had on these variables.

Resellers to consumers

By generating higher levels of store traffic and moving stock from the store shelves to the consumers, sales promotions in this context require two main forms of evaluation. The first requires measures of the image held of the retailer, and this needs the use of tracking studies. The second requires measures of stock turnover per product category or brand against a predetermined planned level of turnover.

Manufacturers to consumers

The objectives are to encourage new users to try a product or to increase the amount that current users consume. Targets can be set for the number of coupons to be redeemed, sales generated during and after a price deal, the volume of bonus packs sold, the speed and volume of premiums disposed of and other direct measures of activity. Consumer audits reveal changes in the penetration and usage patterns of consumers. Redemption levels give some indication of participation levels, but should not be considered as the sole method of evaluation, as there are many people who might be encouraged to purchase by the promotion, but who then fail to participate for a variety of reasons.

Redemption levels give some indication of participation levels.

Manufacturers to sales forces

The objectives of these activities are to build performance, morale and allegiance to the manufacturers and their products. Apart from measuring sales performance, the effectiveness of these activities can be expensive and difficult to measure. Attitude studies of the sales force can indicate the degree to which a contest has been influential, but it is hard to isolate the effects from those of other variables acting on them.

Through systematic tracking of sales and market share, products in mature markets can be evaluated in terms of their responsiveness to sales promotions. This type of information must be treated carefully, as the impact of other environmental factors has not been determined. Redemption rates allow for quantitative analysis, that, through time, leads to the establishment of a database from which benchmarks for promotional measurement and achievement can be obtained.

Using technology to evaluate sales promotions

It was noted in a previous section on advertising that advances in IT have radically altered the way in which advertising and product purchases can be evaluated. The same applies to sales promotions. It is now possible to predict with a high level of accuracy the impact on sales of different combinations of in-store promotions and price deals (Nielsen, 1993). This permits greater understanding of the way in which different sales promotions work and when they are most effective. This has two main benefits: the first is to focus promotions on activities that are effective; the second is to help target the communication spend on periods of the year, month and week that consumers are most responsive.

Homescan is an electronic household panel offered by ACNielsen that tracks day-to-day shopping patterns. It measures the household penetration and the retail distribution of a product. ACNielsen uses the system to analyse trial and repeat use and it provides data on consumer buying behaviour across most types of channel. These range from warehouse clubs and convenience stores to supermarkets, mass merchandisers, mail order and the Internet. It can measure the number of households that use the product once and it can then determine how many of these trialists adopt a product through repeat purchase activity. It follows that test promotions can be used in particular stores or geographic areas, and control promotions can be used to test impact and effectiveness. What might work in one area might be unsuccessful elsewhere.

Coupons need not only be distributed via products and media. Technology has been developed that allows coupons of competitive brands to be automatically dispensed at the checkout once a product has been scanned. This information, together with the demographics and psychographic details compiled for panel members, enables detailed profiles to be built up about the types, timing and value of sales promotions to which different consumers respond.

Sales promotions are a competitive tool that allows for swift reaction and placement. In that sense, they are not being used as part of an overall campaign, more as an ad hoc sales boost. This implies that the manageability of sales promotions is very high relative to the other elements of the promotions mix and that the opportunity to pre-test might not be as large in practice as is theoretically possible (Peattie and Peattie, 1993).

The evaluation of sales promotion is potentially fast, direct, precise and easily comprehended (Doyle and Saunders, 1985). However, evaluation is not necessarily that clear cut. The synergistic qualities of the promotion mix inevitably lead to cross-over effects where the impact of other communications influences responses to particular sales promotion events. Promotions may also bring about increased awareness in addition to the trial, use and switching activities. Peattie and Peattie suggest that not only might brand and product substitution result from promotions, but store loyalty patterns might also be affected.

Of all the tools in the promotions mix, sales promotions lend themselves more easily to evaluation rather than to testing. Testing is not realistically possible in the time frames in which some organisations operate, particularly those in the FMCG sector. Activities should be planned and research built into campaigns, but it is the availability of improved IT that will continue to improve and accelerate the quality of information that management has about its sales.

Of all the tools in the promotions mix, sales promotions lend themselves more easily to evaluation rather than to testing.

Public relations

Each of the two main forms, corporate and marketing public relations, seeks to achieve different objectives and does so by employing different approaches and techniques. However, they are not mutually exclusive and the activities of one form of public relations impact upon the others; they are self-reinforcing.

Corporate public relations (CPR)

The objectives that are established at the beginning of a promotional campaign must form the basis of any evaluation and testing activity. However, much of the work of CPR is continuous, and therefore measurement should not be campaign-oriented or time-restricted but undertaken on a regular, ongoing basis. CPR is mainly responsible for the identity cues that are presented to the organisation's various stakeholders as part of a planned programme of communications. These cues signal the visibility and profile of the organisation and are used by stakeholders to shape the image that each has of the focus organisation.

CPR is, therefore, focused on communication activities, such as awareness, but there are others such as preference, interest and conviction. Evaluation should, in the first instance, measure levels of awareness of the organisation. Attention should then focus on the levels of interest, goodwill and attitudes held towards the organisation as a result of all the planned and unplanned cues used by the organisation.

Traditionally these levels were assumed to have been generated by public relations activities. The main method of measuring their contribution to the communication programme was to collect press cuttings and to record the number of mentions the organisation received in the electronic media. These were then collated in a cuttings book that would be presented to the client. This would be similar to an explorer presenting an electric toaster to a tribe of warriors hitherto undisturbed by other civilisations. It looks nice, but what do you do with it and is it of any real use? Despite this slightly cynical interpretation, the cuttings book does provide a rough and ready way of appreciating the level of opportunities to see created by public relations activities.

The cuttings book provides a rough and ready way of appreciating the level of opportunities to see created by public relations activities.

The content of the cuttings book and the recorded media mentions can be converted into a different currency. The exchange rate used is the cost of the media that would have been incurred had this volume of communication or awareness been generated by advertising activity. For example, a 30-second news item about an organisation's contribution to a charity event may be exchanged for a 30-second advertisement at rate card cost. The temptation is clear, but the validity of the equation is not acceptable. By translating public relations into advertising currency, the client is expected not only to understand, but also to approve of the enhanced credibility that advertising possesses. It is not surprising that the widely held notion that public relations is free advertising has grown so substantially when practitioners use this approach.

A further refinement of the cuttings book is to analyse the material covered. The coverage may be positive or negative, approving or disapproving, so the quality of the cuttings needs to be reviewed in order that the client organisation can make an informed judgement about its next set of decisions. This survey of the material in the cuttings book is referred to as a content analysis. Traditionally, content analyses have had to be undertaken qualitatively and were therefore subject to poor interpretation and reviewer bias, however well they approached their task. Today, increasingly sophisticated software is being used to produce a wealth of quantitative data reflecting the key variables that clients want evaluated.

Hauss (1993) suggests that key variables could include the type of publication, the favourability of the article, the name of the journalist, the audiences being reached and the type of coverage. All these and others can be built into programmes. The results can then be cross-tabulated so that it is possible to see in which part of the country the most favourable comments are being generated or observe which opinion formers are positively or negatively disposed.

Corporate image

The approaches discussed so far are intended to evaluate specific media activity and comment on the focus organisation. Press releases are fed into the media and there is a response that is measured in terms of positive or negative, for or against. This quality of information, while useful, does not assist the management of the corporate identity. To do this requires an evaluation of the position that an organisation has in the eyes of key members of the performance network. In addition, the information is not specific enough to influence the strategic direction that an organisation has or the speed at which the organisation is changing. Indeed, most organisations now experience perpetual change; stability and continuity are terms related to an environment that is unlikely to be repeated.

The evaluation of the corporate image should be a regular exercise, supported by management. There are three main aspects. First, key stakeholders (including employees, as they are an important source of communications for external stakeholders), together with members of the performance network and customers, should be questioned regarding their perceptions of the important attributes of the focus organisation and the business they are in (Chapter 12). Second, how does the organisation perform against each of the

The evaluation of the corporate image should be a regular exercise.

attributes? Third, how does the organisation perform relative to its main competitors across these attributes?

The results of these perceptions can be evaluated so that corrective action can be directed at particular parts of the organisation and adjustments made to the strategies pursued at business and functional levels. For example, in the computer retailing business, prompt home delivery is a very important attribute. If company A had a rating of 90 per cent on this attribute, but company B was believed to be so good that it was rated at 95 per cent, regardless of actual performance levels, then although A was doing a superb job it would have to improve its delivery service and inform its stakeholders that it was particularly good at this part of the business.

Recruitment

Recruitment for some organisations can be a problem. In some sectors, where skills are in short supply, the best staff gravitate towards those organisations that are perceived to be better employers and provide better rewards and opportunities. Part of the task of CPR is to provide the necessary communications so that a target pool of employees is aware of the benefits of working with the focus organisation and develops a desire to work there.

Measurement of this aspect of CPR can be seductive. It is tempting just to measure the attitudes of the pool of talent prior to a campaign and then to measure it again at the end. This fails to account for the uncontrollable elements in CPR, for example the actions of others in the market, but, even if this approach is simplistic and slightly erroneous, it does focus attention on an issue. A major chemical-processing company found that it was failing to attract the necessary number of talented undergraduates, partly because the organisation was perceived as unexciting, bureaucratic and lacking career opportunities. A coordinated marketing communications campaign was targeted at university students, partly at repositioning the organisation in such a way that the students would want to work for them when they finished their degrees. The results indicated that students' approval of the company as a future employer rose substantially in the period following the campaign.

Crisis management

During periods of high environmental turbulence and instability, organisations tend to centralise their decision-making processes and their communications (Quinn and Mintzberg, 1992). When a crisis occurs, communications with stakeholders should increase to keep them informed and aware of developments. In Chapter 19, it will be observed that crises normally follow a number of phases, during which different types of information must be communicated. When the crisis is over, the organisation enters a period of feedback and development for the organisation. 'What did we do?', 'How did it happen?', 'Why did we do that?' and 'What do we need to do in the future?' are typical questions that socially aware and mature organisations, which are concerned with quality and the needs of their stakeholders, should always ask themselves.

When a crisis occurs, communications with stakeholders should increase to keep them informed and aware of developments.

Pearson and Mitroff (1993) report that many organisations do not expose themselves to this learning process for fear of 'opening up old wounds'. Those organisations that do take action should communicate their actions to reassure all stakeholders that the organisation has done all it can to prevent a recurrence, or at least to minimise the impact should the origin of the crisis be outside the control of management. A further question that needs to be addressed concerns the way the organisation was perceived during the different crisis phases. Was the image consistent? Did it change, and if so why? Management may believe that it did an excellent job in crisis containment, but what really matters is what stakeholders think – it is their attitudes and opinions that matter above all else.

The objective of crisis management is to limit the effect that a crisis might have on an organisation and its stakeholders, assuming the crisis cannot be prevented. The social system in which an organisation operates means that the image held of the organisation may well change as a result of the crisis event. The image does not necessarily become negative. On the contrary, it may be that the strategic credibility of the organisation could be considerably enhanced if the crisis were managed in an open and positive way. However, it is necessary that the image that stakeholders have of an organisation should be tracked on a regular basis. This means that the image and impact of the crisis can be monitored through each of the crisis phases. Sturges *et al.* (1991) argue that the objective of crisis management is to influence public opinion to the point that 'post-crisis opinions of any stakeholder group are at least positive, or more positive, or not more negative than before the crisis event'. This ties in with the need to monitor corporate image on a regular basis. The management process of scanning the environment for signals of change, along with change in the attitudes and the perception held by stakeholders towards the organisation, make up a joint process that public relations activities play a major role in executing.

Marketing public relations (MPR)

It was identified earlier that there is evidence of the increasing use of MPR. There are many reasons for this growth, but some of the more important ones quoted by organisations are rising media costs, audience fragmentation, changing consumer attitudes and increasing educational needs (Kitchen, 1993). By using public relations to support the marketing effort in a direct way, organisations are acknowledging that the third-party endorsement provided by MPR delivers a high level of credibility and cost effectiveness, which the other elements of the promotions mix fail to provide.

As Kitchen rightly argues, MPR cannot exist in a vacuum; it must be integrated with the other elements of the mix and provide complementarity. It is the use of MPR as a form of product support and as part of a planned communications mix that makes this a source of high-quality leads. However, evaluating the contribution of MPR is problematic.

Some practitioners believe that this can be overcome by coding press releases as a campaign, and with the use of particular software, leads can be tracked and costed. With the right software, the actual cost of a press release can be input and the number of leads that come back can be measured against sales on the database.

The software can not only estimate sales but also work out the number of leads required to make quota. The formula used is based on the rule that 45 per cent of leads turn into sales for someone in the market within the year. The organisation's own conversion rate can be used to adjust the 45 per cent and the quality of its lead conversion process can also be input. One of the benefits of this approach is that quantitative outcomes provide a measure of effectiveness, but not necessarily the effectiveness of the MPR campaign.

Pre- and post-test measures of awareness, preference, comprehension and intentions are a better measure of quality and impact.

Pre- and post-test measures of awareness, preference, comprehension and intentions are a better measure of the quality and impact that an MPR campaign might have on a target audience. Measuring the conversion ratio of leads to sales is not the only measure, as it fails to isolate the other forces that impact on market performance.

MPR in business-to-business markets is directly targeted at members of the performance network. The objectives are many and include building awareness, reducing costs, satisfying educational needs and enhancing image through improving credibility. The overriding need, however, is to improve the relationship between members of the network and to provide them with a reason to continue transactions with the focus organisation. The reasons are similar to those in the personal selling/buying formula (Chapter 22), namely to associate product adequacy when the appropriate problem is surfaced and to create pleasant feelings when the name of the product or the organisation is mentioned in the same context. MPR in this situation is being used as a competitive tool

Measurement of the effectiveness of MPR should be undertaken by evaluating the degree to which members support, like, endorse or prefer an organisation.

to defend established positions. Measurement of the effectiveness of MPR, therefore, should be undertaken by evaluating the degree to which members support, like, endorse or prefer an organisation and the products it offers. This can be achieved through the use of tracking studies that plot attitudes and opinions, against which the timings of campaigns and MPR activities can be traced and evaluated.

Other measuring techniques – PR

Of all the tools available to practitioners, Goften (1999) reports the following as the most common approaches to measuring public relations:

- *set objectives* and agree the criteria in advance of a campaign;
- *press cuttings*, radio and television tapes, but this is a measure of volume and not quality of impact. A media equivalent value is then applied;
- *media evaluation* through commercial systems such as CAMMA, impact, precis. Under this approach, panels of readers judge whether a mention is positive or negative and whether the client's key message has been communicated. Computer programmes then cut through the data;
- *tracking studies* are expensive but important when changing a perception of a brand, etc.

Both CPR and MPR are difficult and elusive elements of the promotional mix to test, measure and evaluate. Practitioners use a variety of methods, but few provide the objectivity and validity that is necessary. For example, Comic Relief monitored the impact of media coverage on the organisation in the run-up to Red Nose Day. It was able to track which initiatives were failing to attract attention and which issues were attracting negative coverage. It evaluated coverage over six key areas: television initiatives, education, grants (Africa and the United Kingdom), special projects, public fundraising and corporate fundraising.

The variety of measurement devices is increasing, especially as technology advances.

ViewPoint 15.4 Watching over TeleTrax

TeleTrax is an electronic tagging system that can monitor broadcast use of its footage. Using an indelible code embedded within video tapes and through the use of approximately 100 listening posts across Europe, the company is alerted as soon as the tape is broadcast. Unfortunately it does not track the tone of the content. Monitoring the Internet for PR coverage is more taxing.

Net.Cut was set up originally to provide early warning of unfavourable corporate comment on the Internet. It can monitor comment in Internet publications, UK newsgroups and the world-wide web by searching the world-wide web at night and saving company mentions. The cuttings are then reviewed the following morning for key messages prior to warning the client as necessary.

Question

What advantages do you believe TeleTrax offers clients?

Task

Make a list of the types of information you would like TeleTrax to find.

If, at the end of the process, evaluation and testing lack objectivity, then the method should not be used. As a greater number of organisations are beginning to recognise the impact that public relations can provide and establish a more credible balance for the promotional mix, so there is a greater requirement for planning and evaluation to be built into the process from the beginning (Watson, 1992).

Sponsorship

Both academics (Armstrong, 1998) and practitioners (Ovenden, 2007) agree that the measurement of sponsorship activities is problematic, although the importance of doing so is recognised and accepted. The problem concerns the ability to separate the impact of the various elements of the promotional mix, which can be expensive and beyond the reach of smaller brands.

Many organisations attempt to measure the size of the media audience and then treat this as an indicator of effectiveness. This is misleading, as advertising and sponsorship are considered to work in different ways and cannot be measured in a similar way. Audiences consider events (a sports match, exhibition or television programme) as their primary focus, not which organisation is sponsoring the activity, unlike advertising, where the message either dominates the screen or a page of a magazine and viewers attend according to their perceptual filters. The focus of attention is different, as should be the means of evaluation.

Marshall and Cook (1992) found that sports sponsors preferred to use consumer surveys to examine customer (not audience) profiles, brand-related images, attitudes and purchasing activities. This was accomplished through the use of personal interviews and telephone and postal surveys. Because the level of funding in many of the smaller sponsorships is relatively low, few if any resources are allocated to evaluative practices.

Taylor Nelson Sofres provides a single-source data panel through which the viewing habits and purchase behaviour of a representative panel of consumers are monitored through a system called TVSpan 3000. Unlike similar competitive offerings, TVSpan 3000 uses data from 3,000 homes where television set meters are installed that monitor each household's live television viewing, minute by minute. These homes are also equipped with AGB Superpanel scanning equipment for recording details of purchases of FMCG products. One of its prime tasks is to enable clients to monitor purchase behaviour and test advertisements at either pre- or post-test stage. Further uses are to test new creative ideas, to test the effects of advertising with or without below-the-line support and, interestingly, to test the interaction between advertising and sponsorship (Thorncroft, 1996).

The main way in which sponsorship activities should be measured is through the objectives set at the outset.

The main way in which sponsorship activities should be measured is through the objectives set at the outset. By measuring performance rigorously against clearly defined sales and communication-based measures it is more likely that a reasonable process and outcome to the sponsorship activity will be established.

Personal selling

In contrast to the other elements of the promotional mix, personal selling requires different methods of evaluation. Pre- and post-testing the performance of each salesperson is impractical and inappropriate. What is more pertinent for evaluation are the inputs and the effectiveness (measured as outcomes) of the personal selling process. Oliver (1990) suggests that performance can be seen as a factor of the effort and costs (inputs) that an organisation contributes. Outputs can be regarded as sales and profits resulting from exchanges with customers, while productivity can be deemed to be the ratio of inputs to outputs (see Figure 15.2).

This is a useful approach because it focuses attention on aspects of the promotional process that can be measured with the use of quantitative tools. This contrasts with the other tools, where qualitative measures generally predominate. In addition to this framework, it is necessary to measure the effectiveness of the sales force as a unit and the degree to which interdepartmental cooperation is achieved in synchronising the activities of the mix.

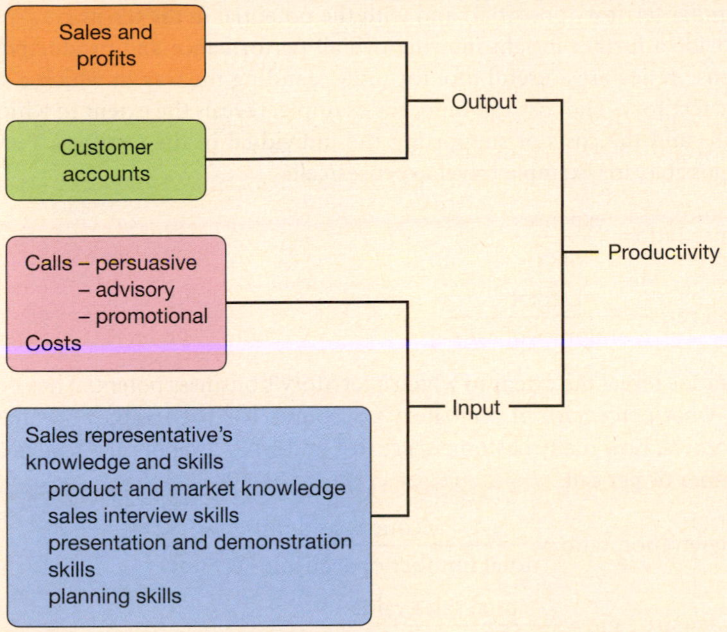

Figure 15.2 Methods for evaluating the performance of personal selling activities
Source: From Oliver (1990).

Evaluating the performance of a salesperson

The performance of a salesperson requires the use of both qualitative and quantitative methods. There are two main types of inputs to the sales process. The first of these consists of the activities undertaken and the costs incurred as a result. The second type of input concerns the knowledge and skills necessary to achieve the required outputs. These will be examined in turn.

Measuring and then evaluating the activities of each salesperson, the inputs, is an important and frequently used measuring stick. The number of planned and unplanned sales calls, the number of presentations, the frequency with which the showroom has been used and the mix of accounts visited, plus the expenses, cost of samples used and time associated with these activities, can be measured and evaluated against organisational standards and expectations. These simple quantitative measures provide for objectivity and measurement; what they do not do is provide an insight into why the input and the ultimate performance rating did or did not achieve the required standard.

Measuring and evaluating the knowledge component of the input dimension require greater subjectivity and reliance on qualitative measures. How well a sales-person uses their selling skills and presents themselves to customers is vitally important. In addition, the depth of knowledge that the subject has of the products, customers, territory and market will probably have a greater bearing on the performance outcome than the number of visits made. In other words, it is the quality of the sales call that is important, not the number of sales calls made. The measurement of these qualitative aspects relies on the individual judgement of the people responsible for the evaluation process (Churchill *et al.*, 1990).

Outputs are more easily measured than inputs. The most common technique used is that of the ratings attached to the volume or value of sales generated in a particular period in a designated area. Using a quota to measure achievement can be important for consistent tracking of performance and for motivational purposes. Volume analysis allows management to measure the effectiveness of the

Outputs are more easily measured than inputs.

sales process, as comparisons can be drawn with last year's performance, with other salespersons (with similar territory potential) and with the potential in the territory.

Ratios provide a further insight into the overall performance and productivity of a salesperson. Expense ratios are a useful tool for understanding the way in which a salesperson is managing the territory. The cost/call ratio, for example, reveals the extent to which the subject is making calls and the costs of supporting the individual in the territory. Further detailed analyses are possible, for example travel expenses/call:

$$\text{sales expense ratio} = \frac{\text{expenses}}{\text{sales}}$$

$$\text{cost per call ratio} = \frac{\text{total}}{\text{number of calls}}$$

Servicing ratios reveal the extent to which a territory's business potential has been acquired, for example, what percentage of a territory's accounts has been won, how many prospects become customers, how many customers are lost and what level of sales is achieved on average per customer or per call:

$$\text{account penetration ratio} = \frac{\text{accounts sold into}}{\text{total number of available accounts}}$$

$$\text{average order size ratio} = \frac{\text{total sales value}}{\text{total number of orders}}$$

$$\text{new account ratio} = \frac{\text{number of accounts}}{\text{total number of accounts}}$$

The final group, activity ratios, determines the effort that is put into a territory. Calls/day, calls/account type and orders/call reveal the amount of planning and thought that is being put into an area:

$$\text{calls/accounts ratio} = \frac{\text{number of calls made}}{\text{total number of accounts}}$$

$$\text{orders/calls ratio} = \frac{\text{number of orders}}{\text{total number of calls}}$$

$$\text{calls/week ratio} = \frac{\text{number of calls}}{\text{number of weeks worked}}$$

In isolation these ratios provide some objectivity when attempting to measure the performance of a salesperson. Used in combination they become a more powerful tool, but only to the extent that they are an aid to decision-making. One major advantage of ratio analysis is the benchmarking effect. Comparisons become possible not only across the sales force but also across the industry, as norms become established through time.

While the traditional measure has been volume, emphasis has been increasingly placed on measures of profitability, an efficiency measure. The level of gross margin achieved by each salesperson and the contribution each makes to the overall profitability of the organisation are regarded by many organisations as more important than measures of volume. The approach requires the involvement of each salesperson not only in achieving the outcomes but also in the process of setting the appropriate performance targets in the first place. This requires different types of training and skills development, which in turn will affect the expectations held by each member of the sales force.

Evaluating the performance of a sales force

The methods looked at so far have been used to evaluate the performance of individual salespersons. An overall measure of the effectiveness of the larger unit, the sales force, is also necessary. The following constitute the main areas of evaluation: the objectives set in the promotion mix, the level of interaction with the other elements of the promotion mix, activity measures and achievement against quota, the effectiveness of the sales channels used and the quality of the relationships established with customers.

The sales force, as a part of the promotion mix, has a responsibility to achieve the sales objectives set out in the promotion objectives. To do this the sales force needs the support of the other elements of the mix. Measuring this interdisciplinary factor is extremely difficult, but there is no doubt that each of the elements works more efficiently if they are coordinated with one another and the messages conveyed dovetail and reinforce each other.

The sales force has a responsibility to achieve the sales objectives.

Many of the measures used to evaluate the performance of individual salespersons can also be aggregated and used to evaluate the performance of the sales force as a whole. The sales force will have an overall sales budget, usually by volume and value, against which actual performance can be measured. The sales force will also be expected to open an agreed number of accounts each period and the value of business as a proportion of the potential will be watched closely.

There is no doubt that the role of the sales force is changing. If the expectations of the sales force are being adapted to new environmental conditions, it is probable that alternative measures will be required to determine the progress that a sales force is making. For example, in business-to-business markets, the traditional approach of the sales force is to manage products and their allocation to selected customers. The sales force of the future is going to be responsible, to a much greater degree, for the management of customer relationships (Wilson, 1993) and the maintenance of relational transactions that will provide organisations with strategic advantage. The use of simple quantitative techniques to measure the performance of the sales force will decline, the use of qualitative techniques will become more prevalent and the techniques themselves will become sophisticated. Measures will be required to evaluate the quality of the relationships developed by the sales force rather than the quantity of outputs achieved in a particular period. The traditional emphasis on short-term quota achievement may well change to a focus on long-term customer alliances and an evaluation of the strength of the relationship held between partners.

One further area of evaluation that is necessary is that of the sales channels themselves. The increased use of multiple sales channels and the contribution that direct marketing will make to the sales force cannot be ignored. Measures are required of the effectiveness of the field sales force, the key account selling team and the array of direct marketing techniques. Constant monitoring of the market is required to judge whether the classification of an account should be changed, and whether different combinations of selling approaches should be introduced.

Finally, customers need to be involved in the sales channel decision process and in the evaluation of the field sales force. If customers are happy with a sales channel, then they are more likely to continue using it. It is vital that the views of customers are monitored regularly and that they contribute to the evaluation process.

The evaluation of the sales force and its individual members has long been oriented to quantitative measures of input and output productivity. These are useful, as they provide for comparison within the organisation and with the industry norms. However, in future, evaluation will move from a revenue to a profit perspective and much greater emphasis will be placed on the quality of the relationships that the sales force develops with their customers. The current imbalance between the use of quantitative and qualitative measures will shift to a position where qualitative measures become more important in evaluating the performance of the sales force.

Evaluation will move from a revenue to a profit perspective.

Measuring the fulfilment of brand promises

Brands make promises and communicate them in one of two main ways. One is to make loud claims about the brand's attributes and the benefits these deliver to customers. This approach tends to rely on advertising and the strength of the brand to deliver the promise. The alternative is not to shout, but to whisper, and then surprise customers by exceeding their expectations when they experience the brand. This is an under promise/over deliver strategy, one which reduces risk and places a far greater emphasis on word-of-mouth communication, and brand advocacy. This in turn can reduce an organisation's investment in advertising and lead to a redirection of communication effort and resources in order to improve the customer experience.

It follows therefore that there are measurable gaps between the image and perceptions customers have of brands and their actual experiences. Where expectations are exceeded the promise gap is said to be positive. Where customers feel disappointed through experience of a brand, a negative promise gap can be identified. These gaps are reflected in the financial performance of brands.

The Promise Index reported by Simms (2007) found that although 66 per cent of the brands surveyed had positive promise gaps only 15 per cent had gaps that impacted significantly on business performance. Other research by Weber Shandwick found that the main factor for creating brand advocacy was the ability to 'surprise and delight customers'. This survey of 4,000 European consumers, reported by Simms, found that brand advocacy is five times more likely to prompt purchase than advertising.

A related metric, the Net Promoter Score (NPS), seeks to identify how likely an individual is to recommend a brand. Again, a key outcome is that brand growth is driven principally by surprising and delighting customers.

On the basis that brand advocacy is of major importance, two key marketing communication issues emerge. The first concerns how the marketing communications mix should be reformulated in order to encourage brand advocacy. It appears that advertising and mass media have an important role to play in engaging audiences to create awareness and interest. However, more emphasis needs to be given to the other tools and media in order to enhance each customer's experience of a brand beyond their expectations.

The second issue concerns identifying and communicating with passive rather than active advocates. Encouraging customers to talk about a brand means developing content that gives passive advocates a reason to talk about a brand. This means that the message component of the mix needs to be designed away from product attributes and towards stories and memorable events that can be passed on through all customer contact points. This in turn points to a greater use of public relations, viral and the use of user-generated-content, networks and communities and the use of staff in creating brand experiences.

ViewPoint 15.5 Measuring gorillas

For Cadbury the news had not been very good in 2006 and the first part of 2007. A salmonella scare in 2006 had resulted in more than 1 million bars of chocolate (including Dairy Milk) being removed from shelves accompanied by considerable negative media comment. In Februrary 2007, Cadbury spent £10 million launching the US chewing-gum Trident but then became enmeshed in controversy after the Advertising Standards Authority reprimanded the company for an ad featuring an Afro-Caribbean poet which was perceived to be racially offensive. This was followed by the news that Cadbury Schweppes was having to shed staff in a £300 million cost-cutting exercise.

In the autumn however it launched an ad that propelled its reputation in the opposite direction. The ad featured a man in a gorilla suit playing the drums to the Phil Collins hit 'In the Air Tonight'.

The ad caught the public's imagination, if only because there is no reason for a gorilla to play the drums, there is no connection between Cadbury's and a gorilla (at the time) and the ad says nothing about Dairy Milk apart from a shot of the brand name at the end. The ad was relatively inexpensive to produce and was released through a spoof real film production company, A Glass and a Half Full Productions.

The ad featured in a pre-ad teaser campaign in television listings that resembled a film. The Glass and a Half Full Productions web site helped to sustain dialogue with fans while 90-second spots during the Rugby World Cup and Big Brother Finals delivered the ad to huge audiences.

The ad was not part of an integrated campaign and the support might have been stronger. However, it was a one-off masterpiece of creativity that resonated with the nation. Sales rose 7 per cent by the end of October 2007 in value terms, and weekly sales were up 9 per cent year on year during the period 'gorilla' was on air. The ad generated the highest recognition scores ever recorded by Hall & Partners.

Sources: Various including Campaign (2007).

Question

How should the 'Gorilla' ad be evaluated, and how would you measure its success?

Task

Gorillas feature in other ways for some other brands. Find two other campaigns that feature gorillas.

Exhibit 15.3 The Cadbury gorilla in action
Image courtesy of The Advertising Archives.

Online communications

Online research has grown as the Internet population has soared and the measures used have developed through trial and experience. However, the notion that measurement of online communications is easy simply because all that is necessary is 'counting clicks' is misleading. Indeed, when speaking about marketing communications, Roisin Donnelly, UK & Ireland Corporate Marketing Director and Head of Marketing for Procter & Gamble, states that measurement is their biggest difficulty. It is not an issue to measure the overall impact of a campaign but when measuring the return generated by integrated campaigns, the contribution that word-of-mouth, blogging, online and public relations make, for example, is extremely difficult to isolate (Lannon, 2007).

Banner ads

Traditional measurement techniques of reach, frequency and target audience impressions are not capable of being readily transferred to the Internet.

Not surprisingly there is disagreement about whether it is possible to measure effectively online advertising. Dreze and Zurfryden (1998) rightly point out that as a viable advertising media, Internet advertising must be subject to suitable measurement standards to gauge the effectiveness of the medium. Web servers can indicate how many pages have been requested, the time spent on each page and even the type of computers that were used to request the page. However, this type of information is largely superficial and fails to provide insight into the user, their motivation to visit the site or the behavioural or attitudinal outcomes as a result of the interaction. Traditional measurement techniques of reach, frequency and target audience impressions are not capable of being readily transferred to the Internet.

Others argue that it is possible to measure online tools. For example, Briggs and Hollis (1997) point out that one of the more common measures used is the click-through rate. They indicate, however, that this normally only measures behaviour, whereas what is needed is an indicator of the user's attitudes. They claim to have developed a technique to measure attitudes (online) and show that banner advertising can be one of the most effective forms of advertising and brand development.

Web site effectiveness

Johnston cited by Gray (2000) reports that ACNielsen offers a 9,000 strong panel in the United Kingdom. The panel consists of Internet users who have special software loaded on their PCs that records every web page they visit. The strengths and weaknesses of online qualitative and quantitative research are shown in Tables 15.5 and 15.6.

Good marketing management practice suggests that evaluation of any management activity should always include a consideration of the degree to which the objectives have been satisfied.

However, the reasons organisations have for setting up a web site are many and varied: these might be to establish a web presence, to move to new methods of commercial activity, to enter new markets, to adhere to parent company demands or to supplement current distribution channels. Consequently, it is not practicable to set up a definitive checklist to use as a measure of web site effectiveness, although certain principles need to be followed (see Table 15.7).

One of the basic approaches is to develop profiles of web site visitors built up by presenting every tenth visitor with a questionnaire. The next stage will be to provide media planners with these data to optimise banner ad placement. Based on the work of Berthon *et al.* (1996), Table 15.6 suggests the criteria that might be used to test a site's effectiveness, but different criteria will have a different impact depending upon each organisation's situation.

Table 15.5 Online quantitative research

Strengths	Weaknesses
Relatively inexpensive	Respondent universe
Fast turnaround	Sampling issues: narrow target audience and difficult to identify
Automated data collection	Often self-completion, hence subject to self-selection
Can show graphics and video	Technical problems
No interviewer bias	
Quality of data	
Seamless international coordination	

Table 15.6 Online qualitative research

Strengths	Weaknesses
Slightly faster and cheaper than traditional focus group	Loss of non-verbal communications
Avoids the dominance of loud personalities	Less useful for emotional issues
More client control	Online moderation requires new skills pattern
Can show concepts and/or web sites	Slow keyboard skills can hamper some respondents
Allows for international coordination and permits mixed nationalities	Sampling issues: difficult to identify a narrow target audience

Table 15.7 Criteria to assess web site effectiveness

Visitor type	Cognitive state	Management action
All surfers	Level of awareness that a site exists: aware or not aware	Provide offline and online information and directions
Those aware	Level of interest in the site: interested or not interested	Create interest and curiosity
Those interested	Known route to the site: determined or accidental	Enable greater opportunities for site hit
Determined visitors	Was the visit completed successfully? Transaction or no transaction	Encourage bookmarking and post-purchase communication to permit legitimate dialogue
Those who transacted	Will these visitors return to the site? Retained or not retained	Maintain and enhance top-of-mind site recall

Source: Adapted from Berthon *et al.* (1996). Used with kind permission from WARC.

Dreze and Zurfryden (1998) were apprehensive of the difficulties associated with measuring the number of unique site visitors, mainly because of various technology-related factors and the difficulties of isolating who is a unique visitor.

As mentioned earlier in this chapter, tracking studies are used to measure online brand values (site visits) and various forms of calls-to-action.

Summary

In order to help consolidate your understanding of the methods and approaches used to evaluate marketing communications, here are the key points summarised against each of the learning objectives:

1. Discuss the role of evaluation as part of marketing communications.

The evaluation of a marketing communications plan, once implemented, is an essential part of the total system. The evaluation provides a potentially rich source of material for the next campaign and the ongoing communications that all organisations operate, either intentionally or not.

The evaluation of planned marketing communications consists of two distinct elements. The first element is concerned with the development and testing of individual messages. For example, a particular sales promotion (such as a sample pack) has individual characteristics that may or may not meet the objectives of a sales promotion event.

The second element concerns the overall impact and effect that a campaign has on a target audience once a communications plan has been released. This post-test factor is critical, as it will either confirm or reject management's judgement about the viability of its communications strategy. The way in which the individual components of the communications mix work together needs to be understood so that strengths can be capitalised on and developed and weaknesses negated.

2. Explore the value and methods of pretesting and post-testing advertisements.

Pretesting is the practice of showing unfinished commercials to selected groups of the target audience with a view to refining the commercial to improve effectiveness, it is still subject to debate about its effectiveness. Many practitioners feel that pretesting limits creativity. The most common methods used to pretest advertisements are concept testing, focus groups, consumer juries, dummy vehicles, projective assessments, readability, theatre and physiological tests.

Post-testing is the practice of evaluating ads that have been released. The main advantage with post-testing is that advertisements are evaluated in their proper environment. There are a number of methods used to evaluate the effectiveness of such advertisements, and of these inquiry, recall, recognition and sales-based tests predominate.

3. Explain the main ideas behind different physiological measures of evaluation.

A bank of physiological tests has been developed, partly as a response to advertisers' increasing interest in the emotional impact of advertising messages and partly because many other tests rely on the respondents' ability to interpret their reactions. Physiological tests have been designed to measure the involuntary responses to stimuli and so avoid the bias inherent in the other tests. There are substantial costs involved with the use of these techniques, and the validity of the results is questionable. Consequently they are not used a great deal in practice, but, of them all, eye tracking is the most used and most reliable.

4. Provide an insight into the way in which each of the tools of the communication mix can be evaluated.

Each of the tools of the mix require different forms of evaluation or testing, simply because of the way they work. Sales promotion and direct marketing provide relatively easy forms of measurement and evaluation based on quantitative methods. Public relations however, is far more subjective and measurement is much more problematic. The effectiveness of personal selling can be measured at an individual sales person level or in aggregate form, the sales team level.

5. Consider other ways in which the effectiveness of marketing communications can be evaluated.

Tracking studies involve interviewing a large number of people on a regular basis, weekly or monthly, with the purpose of collecting data about buyers' perceptions of marketing communication messages. Perceptions, attitudes and meanings attributed to campaigns can be tracked and adjustments made to campaigns as necessary.

Considering the vast amount of resources that are directed at planned communications, and in particular advertising, it is important to review, on a periodic basis, the amount and the manner in which its financial resources have been used. For some organisations the media spend alone constitutes one of the major items of expenditure.

Likeability refers to the deep seated set of meanings and associations an individual makes with particular ads and its measurement has proven to be a good indicator of an ad's performance.

6. Measure the fulfilment of brand promises.

There are measurable gaps between the image and perceptions customers have of brands and their actual experiences. Where expectations are exceeded the promise gap is said to be positive. Where customers feel disappointed through experience of a brand, a negative promise gap can be identified. These gaps are reflected in the financial performance of brands.

The Promise Index and the Net Promoter Score (NPS) are two approaches to measuring the success of delivering brand promises.

7. Consider some of the issues associated with evaluating the effectiveness of digital and online communications.

Online communications are perhaps the easiest to measure as web servers can indicate which and how many pages have been requested, the time spent on each page and even the type of computers that were used to request the page. However, this type of information is largely superficial and fails to provide insight into the user, their motivation to visit the site or the behavioural or attitudinal outcomes as a result of the interaction. Traditional measurement techniques of reach, frequency and target audience impressions are not readily transferrable to the Internet.

Review questions

1. If the process is difficult and the outcomes imprecise, why should organisations evaluate and monitor their marketing communications?
2. What are pre- and post-testing?
3. Write a brief report comparing recall and recognition tests.
4. What are the principal dimensions of likeability as a measure of advertising effectiveness?
5. Identify four ways in which sales promotions can be evaluated.

6. Write brief notes explaining why the use of media comparison techniques are insufficient when measuring the impact of public relations.
7. Why should the measurement of sales results be considered an inadequate measure of personal selling performance?
8. What are the techniques used to measure web site effectiveness? Are they any good?
9. Many organisations fail to undertake suitable research to measure the success of their campaigns. Why is this and what can be done to change this situation?
10. Comment on the view that, if a method of evaluation and testing lacks objectivity and testing, then the method should not be used.

MiniCase

Measuring communication effectiveness at the Salvation Army: A bunch of well meaning amateurs or a leading-edge social relief organisation?

Jill Brown: University of Portsmouth

Founded in London, England, in 1865 by William and Catherine Booth, the Salvation Army is a distinctive and instantly recognisable Christian Church with its military uniform, bands and ranks. It is also one of the United Kingdom's largest charities.

As a global organisation, the Salvation Army operates throughout the world and delivers services ranging from community development, education, social and medical care and disease prevention among the world's poor, to international emergency services.

The Salvation Army seeks to communicate with a variety of diverse audiences. In the United Kingdom and the Republic of Ireland, there are the members (Salvationists) and clergy (officers) associated with around 700 churches, members of other Christian denominations, actual and potential donors (who may be individuals or businesses), grant-making foundations, journalists, local authorities and other social work funding bodies. In addition the Salvation Army also works at public affairs level, including working with MPs, because much of its work is related to the government's social welfare policies and with other relevant services including the medical profession and social services due to its pioneering work in the area of addictions and provision for the socially excluded.

In Britain, a major piece of marketing research undertaken in 1999 helped the Salvation Army to understand how it was perceived by its various audiences. Results showed that the organisation was respected and liked. It was seen as down to earth, action-oriented and honest but rather old-fashioned and amateur. The key images triggered by the brand 'Salvation Army' were of a homeless person being given a cup of soup, and people in military-type uniform playing in a band.

The challenge for this organisation is how to convey the diversity and professionalism of its worldwide social care activities and persuade people to look beyond its stereotypical image. Measuring the effectiveness of its communication activity is an essential part of this task.

Communications strategy

Following on from the perceptions research a communications strategy has been developed that aims to achieve a consistency of message when communicating with all the different audiences, and a vocabulary that emphasises a modern, professional, caring, results-driven organisation. In addition, a set of non-negotiable brand guidelines is being developed for churches to ensure greater consistency of logo, letter heading, name and signage. The Salvation Army has central control over fundraising, media relations and public affairs, but unlike the branches of a commercial organisation, the communications activities of its member churches are largely devolved to local level.

The Salvation Army's communication strategy is focused on three main areas: direct marketing, public and media relations and online communications.

Direct marketing

The Salvation Army's direct marketing activity reaches up to 25 million people a year and raises around £20 million. Its primary aim is fundraising but there are subsidiary objectives related to recruiting new donors and raising awareness of the Salvation Army and its activities. Direct mail, door drops, magazine inserts, direct response television and radio advertising and online approaches are the main techniques used.

A specialist web media planner/buyer is employed to negotiate the best deals on a limited budget. Banner ads have been placed on Yahoo, television soap opera update websites and other sites frequented by the target donor audiences – typically people in their fifties and sixties. Pay per click deals were favoured until recently, but now a variety of deals are sought to give the best value for money in this rapidly evolving medium.

There is extensive measurement of direct marketing effectiveness including pretesting, marketing research and calculation of response rates and return on investment. Those who respond to the annual Christmas appeal for example, are sent a thank you letter that includes a questionnaire inquiring about their giving preferences and what further information they would like to receive from the Salvation Army. Focus groups composed of actual and potential supporters are used to check the likely effectiveness of direct mail messages or to test creative ideas for a poster and press advertising campaign.

Public and media relations

Good relations with the various media are very important to the Salvation Army but they are wary of making frequent, ill-judged public announcements. Instead, they seek to comment selectively on issues where they have expertise and something of value to say. Exposure in the local press has been found to be very effective and is linked with preparedness to give, so media awareness training is provided to church leaders and key people at local level to help them to deliver the Salvation Army's key messages to journalists.

Much of the Salvation Army's public relations activity is media-based but emphasis is also placed on personal influence. In addition, attendance at party political and other conferences, together with exhibitions is used to communicate with key opinion formers. The key objective here is 'to reinforce positive perceptions' according to Julius Wolff-Ingham, the Salvation Army's Head of Fundraising and Marketing.

The Salvation Army seeks to measure the effectiveness of its PR activity by participating in syndicated surveys undertaken by NFP Synergy, a marketing research agency that specialises in the not-for-profit sector. The quarterly awareness monitor asks a representative sample of the UK population questions such as, 'What are the top three UK charities which come to mind?', and 'Which charities work in the field of child protection?' The Salvation Army also undertakes surveys among two of its key audiences – MPs and journalists – to determine awareness levels and perceptions.

Online communications

The Salvation Army's web sites seek to serve a diverse range of people including donors, prayer supporters, school children studying the Salvation Army within the National Curriculum, potential service users, people seeking family members with whom they have lost contact, those exploring the Christian faith and looking for a Church, partner agencies, local authorities, journalists and professional practitioners.

There are separate web sites for young people (www.salvationarmy.org.uk/alove) and children (www.salvationarmy.org.uk/kids).

The current objectives for the web sites are:

(a) to emphasise that the Salvation Army is a worldwide evangelical Christian Church, as well as a human service provider, whose mission is to offer salvation in Christ to all;
(b) to offer relevant, accurate and up-to-date information about the Salvation Army in the United Kingdom to external enquirers, presented in an attractive, modern and user-friendly fashion;
(c) to provide news of Salvation Army activities and issues for an external audience;
(d) to reinforce the Salvation Army's identity and brand on the Internet in an attractive, dynamic, secure and consistent pattern, emphasising its contemporary relevance as well as its professional reliability;
(e) to provide an easy and inviting means for interested persons to contribute financially, in kind and as volunteers to the work of the Salvation Army in the United Kingdom, and so become and feel involved in its wider family;
(f) to create and serve an interactive online community of Salvationists and friends of the Salvation Army, encouraging them to welcome and support external visitors to the site.

The Salvation Army recognises the importance of developing a profile of its web site users. A recent survey of visitors to the youth web site sought to verify web analytics data that the primary users are youth leaders rather than young people themselves. Simple polls are regularly undertaken on the main web site to understand better who is visiting the site; Christian/non-Christian, views on ecology, moral issues, etc.

Web site performance is tracked primarily through analysing traffic data. The key metrics include number of visitors, page views, time on site, single-page bounces and errors encountered. Referrals from search engines and other web sites are monitored to identify common keywords in order to optimise performance. Visitors are encouraged to use Web 2.0 tools such as Facebook and Stumbleupon to share the Salvation Army's web content virally, and the number of click-throughs from social networking web sites is increasing.

Cookies are used sparingly and do not persist for repeat visits (except for the sole purpose of preventing multiple voting in polls).

Constraints

Lack of money is a common reason for avoiding the evaluation of marketing communications, but in the not-for-profit sector where every penny is raised by voluntary donation, the issue is particularly acute. The Salvation Army operates under tight financial constraints but prides itself on reinvesting a very small amount of funds raised back into its fundraising activity.

It is constantly looking for cost-effective communication solutions. Even with major projects such as a web site relaunch, care is taken to spend donated money wisely and in-house focus groups are often used to verify web site useability. Staff numbers are low and so time resource is another constraint.

The well-meaning amateur image may persist but this is an organisation that understands the significance of measuring the effectiveness of its communication activity and does so rigorously.

MiniCase questions

1. Appraise the methods that the Salvation Army uses to monitor its corporate image.
2. To what extent do the Salvation Army's online communication evaluation techniques adequately measure the achievement of its web site objectives?
3. Suggest other ways in which the Salvation Army could measure the effectiveness of its promotional activity.
4. Should charitable organisations use donated funds to measure marketing communication effectiveness? Justify your response.

References

Armstrong, C. (1998) Sport sponsorship: a case study approach to measuring its effectiveness. *European Research*, **16**(2), 97–103.

Berthon, P., Pitt, L. and Watson, R. (1996) The world wide web as an advertising medium: toward an understanding of conversion efficiency. *Journal of Advertising Research*, **6**(1) (January/February), 43–53.

Biel, A.L. (1993) Ad research in the US. *Admap* (May), 27–9.

Briggs, R. and Hollis, N. (1997) Advertising on the web: is there response before click-through? *Journal of Advertising Research*, **37**(2), 33–46.

Burden, S. (2007) Case study: pre-testing mould-breaking ads. *Admap*, July/August, 48–9.

Campaign (2007) Cadbury 'gorilla' wins Campaign of the Year, *Campaign*, 13 December. Retrieved 16 January 2008 from http://www.brandrepublic.com/InDepth/Features/773064/Cadbury-gorilla-wins-Campaign-Year/.

Churchill, G.A., Ford, N.M. and Walker, C. (1990) *Sales Force Management*. Homewood, IL: Irwin.

Cox, S. (2007) Total recall: advertising exposure and engagement. *Admap*, 480, (February), 44–6.

Dichter, E. (1966) How word-of-mouth advertising works. *Harvard Business Review*, 44 (November/December), 147–66.

Doyle, P. and Saunders, J. (1985) The lead effect of marketing decisions. *Journal of Marketing Research*, **22**(1), 54–65.

Dreze, X. and Zurfryden, F. (1998) Is internet advertising ready for prime time? *Journal of Advertising Research* (May/June), 7–18.

Farrow, C. (1999) If it doesn't sell it isn't creative . . . true or false? *Marketing News* (October/November), 4–5.

Fendwick, P. (1996) The four ages of ad evaluation. *Admap* (April), 25–7.

Flesch, R. (1974) *The Art of Readable Writing*. New York: Harper & Row.

Goften, K. (1999) The measure of PR. *Campaign Report*, 2 April, 13.

Gordon, W. (1992) Ad pre-testing's hidden maps. *Admap* (June), 23–7.

Gray, R. (2000) The relentless rise of online research. *Marketing*, 18 May, 41.

Hauss, D. (1993) Measuring the impact of public relations. *Public Relations Journal* (February), 14–21.

Jones, J.P. (1990) Ad spending: maintaining market share. *Harvard Business Review* (January/February), 38–42.

Kitchen, P.J. (1993) Public relations: a rationale for its development and usage within UK fast-moving consumer goods firms. *European Journal of Marketing*, **27**(7), 53–75.

Krugman, H.E. (1988) Point of view: limits of attention to advertising. *Journal of Advertising Research*, **38**, 47–50.

Lannon, J. (2007) Marketing is the Boss, *Market Leader*, **39** (Winter). Retrieved 27 February 2008 from www.warc.com.

Lee, D.H. and Park, C.W. (2007) Conceptualization and measurement of multidimensionality of integrated marketing communications. *Journal of Advertising Research*, (September), 222–36.

Lodish, L.M. and Lubetkin, B. (1992) General truths? *Admap* (February), 9–15.

Marshall, D.W. and Cook, G. (1992) The corporate (sports) sponsor. *International Journal of Advertising*, **11**, 307–24.

Mazur, L. (1993) Qualified for success? *Marketing*, 23 January, 20–2.

Nielsen, A.C. (1993) Sales promotion and the information revolution. *Admap* (January), 80–5.

Oliver, G. (1990) *Marketing Today*, 3rd edn. Hemel Hempstead: Prentice-Hall.

Ovenden, M. (2007) 21st century media: right on target. *Marketing*, 5 December, 6–7.

Pearson, C.M. and Mitroff, I. (1993) From crisis prone to crisis prepared: a framework for crisis management. *Academy of Management Executive*, **7**(1), 48–59.

Peattie, K. and Peattie, S. (1993) Sales promotion: playing to win. *Journal of Marketing Management*, **9**, 255–69.

Quinn, J.B. and Mintzberg, H. (1992) *The Strategy Process*, 2nd edn. Englewood Cliffs, NJ: Prentice-Hall.

Reid, A. (2000) Testing Times, *Campaign*, 22 September, 40.

Robson, S. (2002) Group discussions. In *The International Handbook of Market Research Techniques* (ed. Robin Birn) Kogan Page, London.

Sherwood, P.K., Stevens, R.E. and Warren, W.E. (1989) Periodic or continuous tracking studies: matching methodology with objectives. *Market Intelligence and Planning*, **7**, 11–13.

Shultz, D.E. (1987) Above or below the line? Growth of sales promotion in the United States. *International Journal of Advertising*, **6**, 17–27.

Simms, J. (2007) Bridging the gap. *Marketing*, 12 December, 26–8.

Smit, E.G., van Meurs, L. and Neijens, P.C. (2006) Effects of advertising likeability: a 10-year perspective. *Journal of Advertising Research*, **46**(1) (March), 73–83.

Staverley, N.T. (1993) Is it right . . . will it work? *Admap* (May), 23–6.

Sturges, D.L., Carrell, B.J., Newsom, D.A. and Barrera, M. (1991) Crisis communication management: the public opinion node and its relationship to environmental nimbus. *SAM Advanced Management Journal*, (Summer), 22–7.

Thorncroft, A. (1996) Business arts sponsorship: arts face a harsh set of realities. *Financial Times*, 4 July, 1.

Vaughn, R. (1980) How advertising works: a planning model. *Journal of Advertising Research* (October), 27–33.

Watson, T. (1992) Evaluating PR effects. *Admap* (June), 28–30.

Wells, W., Burnett, J. and Moriarty, S. (1992) *Advertising: Principles and Practice*, 2nd edn. Englewood Cliffs, NJ: Prentice-Hall.

Wilson, K. (1993) Managing the industrial sales force of the 1990s. *Journal of Marketing Management*, **9**, 123–9.

Zielske, H.A. (1982) Does day-after recall penalise 'feeling' ads? *Journal of Advertising Research*, **22**(1), 19–22.

Part 4
The tools of marketing communications

Chapters 16–23

This part of the book explores both the nature and characteristics of the primary tools or disciplines of the marketing communication mix. These are advertising, sales promotion, public relations, direct marketing and personal selling. Attention is also given to the main secondary tools including sponsorship, exhibitions, product placement, field marketing and packaging.

Chapter 16 builds on previous work in Chapter 8 and considers the various models and concepts that have been developed to explain advertising strategy. The following chapter complements this by examining the issues associated with the way in which messages are constructed in order that the intended meaning is conveyed and understood by the target audience. Issues concerning message construction and content, creativity and the emerging power of user-generated-content are reviewed.

Chapter 18 examines the management and techniques associated with sales promotion while Chapters 19 and 20 consider public relations and sponsorship respectively. Chapters 21 and 22 look at direct marketing and personal selling.

The final chapter in this part of the book looks at some of the remaining disciplines, albeit those that do not necessarily command the major share of most communication budgets. Nevertheless, they are important sub-disciplines and many clients are beginning to put an increasing amount of resources into exhibition work, product placement, field marketing and packaging.

Video Insight Part 4

Part 4 of the book considers the tools and messages of marketing communications. To assist your understanding, the Video Insight starts with Electrolux, highlighting the importance of knowing your target market and the use of tools, messages and media channels that match customer's needs. This fundamental principle of marketing communications is explained in the context of people planning to purchase white goods for a new kitchen or laundry room in comparison to those whose machines or equipment breaks down and which need to be replaced quickly.

In the Land Rover section of the Video Insight, Colin Green refers to their recent campaign to launch the Freelander. He also reflects upon their extensive use of sponsorship as a means of effective communication. He refers to the resonance that their sponsorship of rugby union and equestrianism has with many of its customers. The opportunity to set up mini exhibitions at the events they sponsor serves to reinforce customer attitudes towards the brand and provides a strong pull effect on potential customers. In addition, Land Rover provide 'Experience Centres' where customers can drive the vehicles and get first-hand knowledge of how the vehicles handle in a variety of conditions. These activities constitute what is referred to as 'experiential marketing', a rapidly growing aspect of contemporary marketing activity.

Go to **www.pearsoned.co.uk/fill** to watch the Video Insight, and then answer the following questions:

1. How do Electrolux communicate with its markets?
2. Why is experiential marketing important to Land Rover?
3. Land Rover use sponsorship as a major part of its marketing communications. Why is this and how might the other tools of the mix be used to support the brand?

Chapter 16

Advertising and strategy

An attempt to understand how advertising might work must be cautioned by an appreciation of the complexity and contradictions inherent in this commercial activity. Understanding how advertising might work, with its rich mosaic of perceptions, emotions, attitudes, information and patterns of behaviour, has been a challenge for many eminent researchers, authors and marketing professionals.

Aims and learning objectives

The aims of this chapter are to explore the different views about advertising strategy and to consider the complexities associated with understanding how clients can best use advertising.

The learning objectives of this chapter are to:

1. consider the role advertising plays in both consumer and business-to-business markets;
2. appraise the use of emotion in advertising and consider concepts associated with shock advertising;
3. explain the principal frameworks by which advertising is thought to influence individuals;
4. appraise the strong and weak theories of advertising;
5. consider ways in which advertising can be used strategically;
6. examine ideas concerning the use of advertising to engage audiences.

For an applied interpretation see Lorna Stevens' MiniCase entitled ***Tapping into a new zeitgeist: women consumers, lifestyle trends and the Red experience*** at the end of this chapter.

Introduction

The purpose of an advertising plan is to provide the means by which appropriate messages are devised and delivered to target audiences who then act in appropriate ways. This may be to buy a product, to enquire about a product or simply memorise a single aspect for future action. Guidelines for the content and delivery of messages are derived from an understanding of the variety of contexts in which the messages are to be used. For example, research might reveal a poor brand image relative to the market leader, or the different or changing media habits of target consumers. The nature of the messages and the problems to be addressed will be specified in the promotional objectives and strategy.

An advertising plan is composed, essentially, of three main elements:

- the message – what is to be said;
- the medium – how the message will be conveyed;
- the timing – manner in which the message will be carried.

This chapter is the first of two about advertising and several others in the next part of the book, about media. This chapter explores two main advertising issues, the first is about the way advertising might work, and consideration is given to some of the principal models and frameworks that have been devised to best describe the process by which advertising works. The second issue focuses on the strategic use of advertising, and the chapter is used to introduce a number of concepts and frameworks that have contributed to our understanding.

The chapter builds on the ideas about how marketing communications might work (Chapter 8) and shares some common thoughts. Chapter 17 considers the content of advertising messages, or what is to be said. In addition to these, Chapters 24–27 consider the media and ways in which advertising messages can be delivered.

The role of advertising

The role of advertising in most marketing communications campaigns is important. Advertising, whether it be on an international, national, local or direct basis, has the potential to engage audiences, albeit on a short-term basis. Engagement is enabled either by changing perceptions and building brand values or by encouraging a change in behaviour, often delivered through a call-to-action.

Advertising can reach huge audiences with simple messages that present opportunities to allow receivers to understand what a product is, what its primary function is and how it relates to all the other similar products. This is the main function of advertising: to communicate with specific audiences. These audiences may be consumer- or organisation-based, but wherever they are located, the prime objective is to build or maintain awareness of a product or an organisation.

Advertising cannot be said to have a single task as it can be used to achieve a number of DRIP-based outcomes. In can be used to differentiate and position brands, it can be used to reinforce brand messages, and it can easily inform and even persuade audiences to think and behave about and around products, services, brands and organisations. However, apart from its ability to reach large audiences, the key strengths of advertising have been to develop brand awareness, values and associations.

The key strengths of advertising have been to develop brand awareness, values and associations.

Management's control over advertising messages is strong; indeed, of all the elements in the communications mix, advertising has the greatest level of control. The message, once generated and signed off by the client, can be transmitted in an agreed manner and style and at times that match management's requirements. This means that, should the environment change unexpectedly, advertising messages can be 'pulled' immediately. For example, had a BA image campaign designed to build the reputation of the airline been planned for April 2008 in the United Kingdom, it would have had to have been 'pulled' (stopped) following the chaotic transfer to and opening of the new Terminal 5 building at Heathrow in March. Difficulties associated with redirecting over 15,000 pieces of lost baggage, clearing the check-in queues and restoring normal flight schedules, plus the wider debate concerning what caused the problem, and the potential of further 'disruption', would have prevented BA's messages from being received and processed normally. It is more likely that there would have been a negative effect had the planned advertising been allowed to proceed.

ViewPoint 16.1 Easy advertising

Rather than concentrate on differentiation or the development of brand awareness, the role of advertising at easyJet appears to be essentially about reinforcement. The airline undertakes substantial levels of in-house public relations. This is used to drive awareness levels, and is accomplished by the successful television docu-soap called 'Airline'. This reality television programme, which has drawn audiences of over 8 million, is about the everyday working life of easyJet's staff and customers at Luton airport.

All tickets are booked online so advertising's role is partly to drive site traffic. This is typified by the use of sales promotions, which are all linked to the Internet. This means customers must go online if they wish to take advantage of promotional fares.

Exhibit 16.1 easyJet use their aircraft to communicate their identity in a bold way
AFP/Getty Images.

The advertising strategy, therefore, is intended to reinforce the easyJet brand values that are based around the idea of 'consumer champion' and to drive customers to its web site. The advertising also serves to position the easyJet brand based slightly on anarchy as well as price and value for money. Interestingly, the media used are essentially press, outdoor and radio plus use of its own aircraft as flying billboards. Television is not used partly because of the positive exposure generated by the docu-soap, partly because of the targeting and costs, and partly because of the effectiveness of the media used.

Question

Would you increase or decrease easyJet's advertising in a recession. Why?

Task

Compare the advertising messages used by Ryanair and easyJet.

Advertising costs can be regarded in one of two ways. On the one hand, there are the absolute costs, which are the costs of buying the space in magazines or newspapers or the time on television, cinema or radio. These costs can be enormous, and they impact directly on cash flow. For example, the rate card cost of a full-page (colour) advertisement in the *Daily Mail* was £45,612 (April 2008). To show a 30-second ad each day for one week in the 365-seater Screen 6 at the Sheffield Vue Cinema multiplex, costs £175 (April 2008).

On the other hand, there are the relative costs, which are those costs incurred to reach a member of the target audience with the key message. So, if an audience is measured in hundreds of thousands, or even millions on television, the cost of the advertisement spread across each member of the target audience reduces the cost per contact significantly. This aspect is developed further in Chapter 27.

> The cost of the advertisement spread across each member of the target audience reduces the cost per contact significantly.

The main roles of advertising are to build awareness, induce engagement (if only on a cognitive basis) and to (re)position brands, by changing either perception or attitudes. The regular use of advertising, in cooperation with the other elements of the communication mix, can be important to the creation and maintenance of a brand personality. Indeed, advertising has a significant role to play in the development of competitive advantage. In some consumer markets advertising is a dominant form of promotion. Advertising can become a mobility barrier, deterring exit and, more importantly, deterring entry to a market by organisations initially attracted by the potential profits of the industry. Many people feel that some brands sustain their large market share by sheer weight of advertising; for example, the washing powder brands of Procter & Gamble and Unilever.

Advertising can create competitive advantage by providing the communication necessary for target audiences to frame a product. By providing a frame or the perceptual space within which to pigeonhole a product, target audiences are able to position an offering relative to their other significant products much more easily. Therefore, advertising can provide the means for differentiation and sustainable competitive advantage. It should also be appreciated, however, that differentiation may be determined by the quality of execution of the advertisements, rather than through the content of the messages.

Advertising in the business-to-business market is geared, primarily, to providing relevant factual information upon which 'rational' decisions can be made. Regardless of the target audience, all advertising requires a message and a carrier to deliver the message to the receiver. This text concentrates on these two main issues, while acknowledging the wider role that advertising plays in society.

Emotion in advertising

The preceding material, if taken at face value, suggests that advertising only works by people responding to advertising in a logical, rational and cognitive manner. It also suggests that people only take out the utilitarian aspect of advertising messages (cleans better, smells fresher). This is obviously not true and there is certainly a strong case for the use of emotion in advertising in order to influence and change attitudes through the affective component of the attitudinal construct (Chapter 6).

ViewPoint 16.2 An emotional M&S revival

In the late 1990s and early twenty-first century M&S experienced subsiding financial performance and a wealth of negative press comment. This in particular contributed to the public's loss of confidence in the brand.

The new CEO, Stuart Rose, revised the product range to make it more stylish and fashionable. He lowered some of the opening price points to be in line with the competition, improved service and started the process of refurbishing and redesigning the layout of stores. Only once these actions had been put in place could communications be used to re-engage customers with the brand and to rebuild their confidence. One of the first tasks that communications needed to achieve was to counter the negative public relations and give a reason for lapsed customers to reappraise and revisit the store. Food and womenswear were key to the revival, the former contributes 50 per cent of M&S turnover and the latter drives brand perceptions.

The strapline 'Your M&S' encapsulated the move to be audience-centred, was meaningful and could apply to a range of audiences. The choice of high visibility media was critical to conveying ideas about conviction and critical mass. The 'Your M&S' campaign sought to reassure customers, many of whom could identify with Twiggy, who fronted the womenswear ads. The food ads were underscored by the line 'This is not just food, this is M&S Food', which was backed by emotional, sultry music by Santana.

The success of the communications campaign can be demonstrated at various levels. For example, a blouse worn by Twiggy in one ad sold more in a single week than any other product in the whole history of M&S. The power of M&S' communications spawned press coverage said to worth an additional £6 million pounds in advertising space. The ROI on clothing was estimated at £2.61 for every £1 spent on media while the share price zoomed up to 595p, nearly 50 per cent above the price offered by Phillip Green when he attempted to buy the company in July 2004.

Sources: Sweney, *et al.* (2006); Thompson, *et al.* (2006).

Question

Discuss the view that once the M&S product range was corrected there was no real reason to use mass communications as word-of-mouth would have kicked in.

Task

Go to Youtube, find the 'This is not just food, this is M&S Food' ad. How else could food be conveyed emotionally?

Most advertised brands are not normally new to consumers as they have some experience of the brand, whether that be through use or just through communications. This experience affects their interpretation of advertising as memories have already been formed. The role of feelings in the way ads work suggests a consumerist interpretation of how advertising works rather than the rational, which is much more a researchers' interpretation (Ambler, 1998). Consumers view advertising in the context of their experience of the category and memories of the brand. Aligned with this approach is the concept of likeability, where the feelings evoked by advertising trigger and shape attitudes to the brand and attitudes to the advertisement (Vakratsas and Ambler, 1999). Feelings and emotions play an important role in advertising especially when advertising is used to build awareness levels and brand strength.

Consumers view advertising in the context of their experience of the category and memories of the brand.

Most of the models presented later in this chapter are developed on the principle that individuals are cognitive processors and that ads are understood as a result of information processing. The best examples of these are the hierarchy of effects or sequential models where information is processed step by step. This view is not universally accepted. Researchers such as Krugman (1971), Ehrenberg (1974), Corke and Heath (2004) and Heath and Feldwick (2007) dispute the importance of information processing, denying that attention is necessary for people to understand ads and that the creativity within an ad is more important in many circumstances, than the rational message the ad purports to deliver.

Shock strategy

Advertising strategy may also be considered in terms of the overall response a target audience might give on receipt of particular messages. Some organisations choose a consistent theme for their campaigns, one that is often unrelated to their products or services. One such strategy is the use of shock advertising. Shock advertising according to Venkat and Abi-Hanna (1995) 'is generally regarded as one that deliberately, rather than inadvertently, startles and offends its audience'.

Shock advertising is generally regarded as one that deliberately, rather than inadvertently, startles and offends its audience.

Dahl *et al.* (2003) suggest that shock advertising by definition is unexpected and audiences are surprised by the messages because they do not conform to social norms or their expectations. They argue that audiences are offended because there is 'norm violation, encompassing transgressions of law or custom (e.g., indecent sexual references, obscenity), breaches of a moral or social code (e.g., profanity, vulgarity), or things that outrage the moral or physical senses', for example gratuitous violence and disgusting images (p. 268). The clothing company French Connection's use of the FCUK slogan and the various Benetton campaigns depicting a variety of incongruous situations (for example a priest and a nun kissing and of a man dying of AIDS) are contemporary examples of norm violation. Shock advertising is not only used by commercial organisations such as Diesel, Egg and Sony Entertainment but is also used by not-for-profit organisations such as the government (anti-smoking), charities (child abuse) and human rights campaigners (Amnesty International) (see Viewpoint 16.3).

ViewPoint 16.3 Problem? What problem?

In a campaign designed to raise awareness and to shock the public into being less complacent about domestic violence, Amnesty International used posters in the style of cosmetics advertising, featuring models using make-up to hide the damage and injuries caused by violence.

The posters, used in over 100 tube stations, depict 'Cachez', a fictional cosmetics brand, and use the slogan 'Gentle skincare for bruising relationships'. The powerful messages show a smiling model with different injuries – a black eye, a cut cheek, a scar below her breast and three red marks on her shoulder. The aim is to address the complacency that exists about the issue and to make people think about the horror of domestic violence. Through the use of cosmetics to symbolically cover up the issue, Amnesty tried to shock people into not accepting this (or any) form of violence. (see Exhibit 16.2).

Source: www.amnesty.org.

Question

Do you believe that the use of advertising to shock people into a change of behaviour is morally wrong.

Task

Find an ad that uses shock techniques. What are the elements in the ad that generates the shock impact?

Exhibit 16.2 Amnesty International – Problem? What problem?

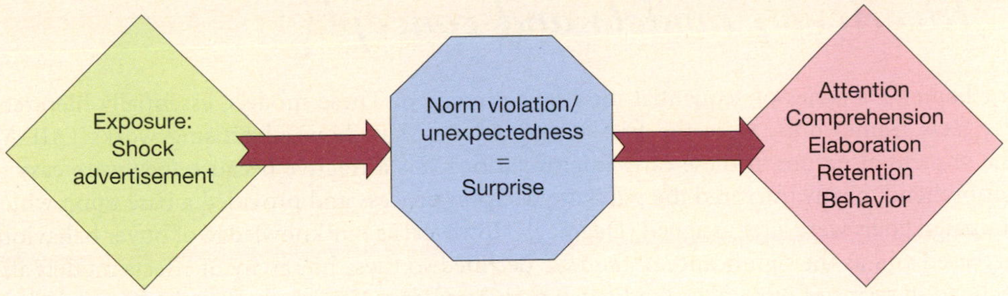

Figure 16.1 A preliminary model of consumer reactions to shock appeals
Source: Dahl *et al.* (2003). Used with kind permission from WARC.

The main reason for using a shock advertising strategy is that it is a good way to secure an audience's attention and achieve a longer-lasting impact than through traditional messages and attention-getting devices. The surprise element of these advertisements secures attention, which is followed by an attempt to work out why an individual has been surprised. This usually takes the form of cognitive engagement and message elaboration in order that the message be understood. Through this process a shocking message can be retained and behaviour influenced. This process is depicted in Figure 16.1.

Shocking ads also benefit from word-of-mouth communication as these messages provoke advertisement-related conversations (Dichter, 1966). The credibility of word-of-mouth communication impacts on others who, if they have not been exposed to the original message, often seek out the message through curiosity. Associated with this pass-along impact is the generation of controversy, which can lead to additional publicity for an organisation and its advertisements. This 'free' publicity, although invariably negative, is considered to be desirable as it leads to increased brand awareness without further exposure and associated costs. This in turn can give the organisation further opportunities to provide more information about the advertising campaign and generate additional media comment.

Shocking ads benefit from word-of-mouth communication as these messages provoke advertisement-related conversations.

The use of shock tactics has spread to viral marketing, a topic discussed in more detail in Chapter 26. Virals delivered through email communications have an advantage over paid-for advertising because consumers perceive advertising as an attempt to sell product, whereas virals are perceived as fun, can be opened and viewed (repeatedly) at consumer-determined times. Furthermore, virals are not subject to the same regulations that govern advertising, opening opportunities to convey controversial material. For example, a Volkswagon viral showed a suicide bomber exploding a device inside a car but the vehicle remained in one piece ('small but tough'). Another for Ford Ka showed a cat being decapitated by the sunroof. As Bewick (2006) suggests, joking with terrorism and pets is a sure-fire way of generating shock, and with that comes publicity.

Advertising models and concepts

In Chapter 7 a series of sequential models is presented. These models, essentially hierarchy of effects frameworks, were the first attempts to explain how advertising works (AIDA). The sequential nature of these early interpretations was attractive because they were easy to comprehend, neatly mirrored the purchase decision process and provided a base upon which campaign goals were later assigned (Dagmar). However, as our knowledge of buyer behaviour increased and as the significance of the USP declined so these hierarchy of effects models also declined in terms of our understanding about advertising. Now they are insignificant and are no longer used as appropriate interpretations of how advertising works.

In their place a number of new frameworks and explanations have arisen, all of which claim to reflect practice. In other words these new theories about how advertising works are a reflection of practice, of the way advertising is considered to work, or at least used by advertising agencies and interpreted by marketing research agencies. These are examples of information processing models, mentioned earlier in this chapter. The first to be considered here were developed by O'Malley (1991) and Hall (1992) and they suggest that there are four main advertising frameworks (Figure 16.2).

1. The sales framework
   This framework, oriented mainly to direct-response work, is based on the premise that the level of sales is the only factor that is worth considering when measuring the effectiveness of an advertising campaign. This view holds that all advertising activities are aimed ultimately at shifting product – generating sales. Advertising is considered to have a short-term direct impact on sales. This effect is measurable and, while other outcomes might also result from advertising, the only important factor is sales. On sales alone will the true effect of any advertising be felt.

Advertising is considered to have a short-term direct impact on sales.

2. The persuasion framework
   The second framework assumes advertising to work rationally, because messages are capable of being persuasive. Persuasion is effected by gradually moving buyers through a number of sequential steps. These hierarchy of effects models assume that buyer decision-making is rational and can be accurately predicted. As discussed earlier, these models have a number of drawbacks and are no longer used as the basis for designing advertisements, despite great popularity in the 1960s and 1970s.

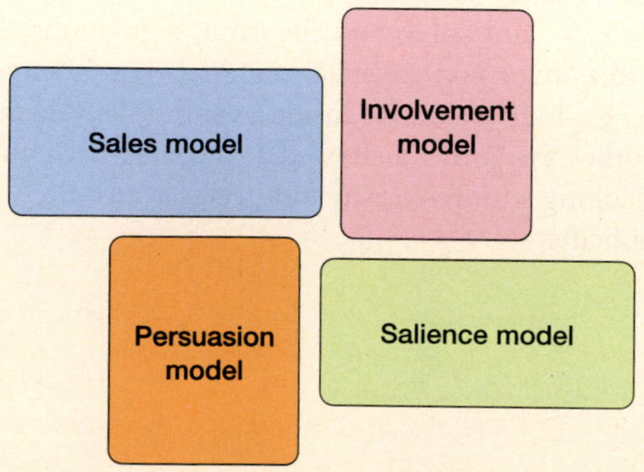

Figure 16.2 Four advertising frameworks
Source: After O'Malley (1991) and Hall (1992) .

ViewPoint 16.4 Persuasive mobiles

The use of advertising to persuade audiences can be key when launching new brands, when the competition becomes intensive or when the audience experiences high involvement.

In 2008 Sony Ericsson implemented a campaign designed to offset the threat of Apple and the iPhone, plus the push from market leaders Nokia. Sony Ericsson used campaigns to support its latest handsets, Cyber-Shot, Walkman, clamshell and touch-screen handsets. Included within this activity was support for their first sub-brand, Xperia and the first handset, X1.

Samsung were also experiencing pressure and used a £16m pan-European awareness campaign to introduce Soul, its key handset for 2008. Motorola meanwhile sought to back its Z10 kick-slider phone using television to demonstrate key attributes.

Source: Jones (2008).

Question

Why did Motorola use television to demonstrate the key attributes of their Z10 brand?

Task

Visit www.sonyericsson.com/x1/?lc=en&cc=gb. Watch the film for X1. Good?

3. The involvement framework

Involvement-based advertisements work by drawing members of the target audience into the advertisement and eliciting a largely emotional response. Involvement with the product develops as a consequence of involvement with the advertisement. Yellow Pages developed a highly successful series of television commercials that centred upon a fictional character called J.R. Hartley. This elderly gentleman was shown using Yellow Pages as a means of resolving a number of problems and served to provide warmth and character that involved people not only with J.R. Hartley but also helped establish brand values.

> Involvement-based advertisements work by drawing members of the target audience into the advertisement.

Another example of this approach can be observed in the Nescafé Gold Blend coffee advertisements. During the late 1980s and early 1990s, UK viewers witnessed the development of a relationship between an aspirational couple with a mutual liking for the Gold Blend brand of coffee. Each advertisement presented particular events in the development of the couple's relationship. Each ad was eagerly anticipated by audiences, many of whom were obsessive about the unfolding drama. By involving the target in the drama, the brand became part of the involvement, a crucial part of each of the ritualistic playlets. Later, the couple were reincarnated as a younger couple and presented in a more adventurous context. Again, the theme was romance, which was allowed to unfold over a series of different advertisements.

4. The salience framework

This interpretation is based upon the premise that advertising works by standing out, by being different from all other advertisements in the product class (see Exhibit 16.4). The launch of Radion, a soap powder that used the twin propositions of cleaning and removing odours, was remarkable because of its ability to 'shout' at the audience through the use of lurid colours and striking presentations. Cillit Bang, Injurylawyers4u, and Sheila's Wheels are some of the ads consumers report that they find irritating.

ViewPoint 16.5 The day Cillit went bang

Cillit Bang is a brand of household cleaner, owned by Reckitt Benckiser and introduced to the market in 2004. Since then the brand has been supported by a heavyweight ad campaign that features a fictional spokesperson, Barry Scott. The message is delivered through demonstration of the power of the brand to clean various surfaces, including a 1p coin dipped into the fluid. 'Members of the public' provide testimonials to the power of the cleaners and Barry Scott constantly repeats the brand name loudly, supported by heavy music, to the point that the message becomes annoying and for many, exceedingly irritating.

These ads are designed as if they are spoofing 1960s commercials. Yet despite the old-fashioned approach the brand became a market leader with a 12 per cent share (Mintel) and the ads have spawned a wave of look-alikes and remixes.

Sources: Various including Tiltman (2008).

Question

Why has an ad that irritates the audience so much become a market leader?

Task

Use Google to find some of the remixes of the Cillit Bang ads.

Acceptance of the persuasion and salience frameworks is based on the assumption that the audience are active, rational problem-solvers and are perfectly capable of discriminating among brands and advertisements. Furthermore, the models bring to attention two important points about people and advertising. Advertisements are capable of generating two very clear types of response: a response to the featured product and a response to the advertisement itself. As discussed earlier in Chapter 8, the cognitive responses that people make when exposed to marketing communication messages, in this case advertisements, and the elaboration likelihood model (ELM) are important means of understanding how different motivations affect decision-making.

The strong and the weak theories of advertising

The explanations offered to date are all based on the premise that advertising is a potent marketing force, one that is persuasive and which is done *to* people. More recent views of advertising theory question this fundamental perspective. Prominent among the theorists are Jones, McDonald and Ehrenberg, some of whose views will now be presented. Jones (1991) presented the new views as the strong theory of advertising and the weak theory of advertising.

The strong theory of advertising

All the models presented so far are assumed to work on the basis that they are capable of affecting a degree of change in the knowledge, attitudes, beliefs or behaviour of target audiences. Jones refers to this as the strong theory of advertising, and it appears to have been universally adopted as a foundation for commercial activity.

Exhibit 16.3 Cillit Bang
This brand uses a hard hitting, loud, and repetitive message to get attention and maintain awareness levels. Typical of the strong theory's persuasive approach.
Photo courtesy of Cillit Bang and Reckitt Benckiser.

According to Jones, exponents of this theory hold that advertising can persuade someone to buy a product that they have never previously purchased. Furthermore, continual long-run purchase behaviour can also be generated. Under the strong theory, advertising is believed to be capable of increasing sales at the brand and class levels. These upward shifts are achieved through the use of manipulative and psychological techniques, which are deployed against consumers who are passive, possibly because of apathy, and are generally incapable of processing information intelligently. The most appropriate theory would appear to be the hierarchy of effects model, where sequential steps move buyers forward to a purchase, stimulated by timely and suitable promotional messages.

Under the strong theory, advertising is believed to be capable of increasing sales at the brand and class levels.

The weak theory of advertising

Increasing numbers of European writers argue that the strong theory does not reflect practice. Most notable of these writers is Ehrenberg (1988, 1997), who believes that a consumer's pattern of brand purchases is driven more by habit than by exposure to promotional messages. The framework proposed by Ehrenberg is the awareness–trial–reinforcement (ATR) framework. Awareness is required before any purchase can be made, although the elapsed time between awareness and action may be very short or very long. For the few people intrigued enough to want to try a product, a trial purchase constitutes the next phase. This may be stimulated by retail availability as much as by advertising, word-of-mouth or personal selling stimuli. Reinforcement follows to maintain awareness and provide reassurance to help the customer to repeat the pattern of thinking and behaviour and to cement the brand in the repertoire for occasional purchase activity. Advertising's role is to breed brand familiarity and identification (Ehrenberg, 1997).

Advertising's role is to breed brand familiarity and identification.

Following on from the original ATR model (Ehrenberg, 1974), various enhancements have been suggested. However, Ehrenberg added a further stage in 1997, referred to as the nudge. He argues that some consumers can 'be nudged into buying the brand more frequently (still as part of their split-loyalty repertoires) or to favour it more than the other brands in their consideration sets' (p. 22). Advertising need not be any different from before; it just provides more reinforcement that stimulates particular habitual buyers into more frequent selections of the brand from their repertoire.

According to the weak theory, advertising is capable of improving people's knowledge, and so is in agreement with the strong theory. In contrast, however, consumers are regarded as selective in determining which advertisements they observe and only perceive those that promote products that they either use or have some prior knowledge of. This means that they

ViewPoint 16.6 Nudging chocolate

Our choice of preferred chocolate brands is fairly clear cut and considering that the amount we eat each year is so large, it is difficult to see how the volume of purchases or the frequency of consumption could be improved. The role of advertising in this market is not to inform or improve awareness, as these are high enough already. The real task in this market is to assist those who are lapsed brand users to try the brand again, in other words to nudge them back to the brand.

So, rather than build brand values the focus is on consolidating or changing behaviour. Consumer buying of chocolate has also changed as impulse buying has declined and been replaced by mass purchasing at supermarkets. Consumers get cost savings and control consumption through a single weekly purchase. This pressurises advertising into helping to secure the trade listings necessary to get product on to the supermarket shelves.

Question

Do you agree with this nudging perspective or does advertising really persuade us to buy more than we would normally purchase?

Task

Find out who the target market is for three different brands of chocolate.

already have some awareness of the characteristics of the advertised product. It follows that the amount of information actually communicated is limited. Advertising, Jones continues, is not potent enough to convert people who hold reasonably strong beliefs that are counter to those portrayed in an advertisement. The time available (30 seconds in television advertising) is not enough to bring about conversion and, when combined with people's ability to switch off their cognitive involvement, there may be no effective communication. Advertising is employed as a defence, to retain customers and to increase product or brand usage. Advertising is used to reinforce existing attitudes, not necessarily to drastically change them.

Unlike the strong theory, this perspective accepts that when people say that they are not influenced by advertising they are in the main correct. It also assumes that people are not apathetic or even stupid, but capable of high levels of cognitive processing.

In summary, the strong theory suggests that advertising can be persuasive, can generate long-run purchasing behaviour, can increase sales and regards consumers as passive. The weak theory suggests that purchase behaviour is based on habit and that advertising can improve knowledge and reinforce existing attitudes. It views consumers as active problem-solvers.

These two perspectives serve to illustrate the dichotomy of views that has emerged about this subject. They are important because they are both right and they are both wrong. The answer to the question 'How does advertising work?' lies somewhere between the two views and is dependent upon the particular situation facing each advertiser. Where elaboration is likely to be high if advertising is to work, then it is most likely to work under the strong theory. For example, consumer durables and financial products require that advertising urges prospective customers into some form of trial behaviour. This may be a call for more information from a sales representative or perhaps a visit to a showroom. The vast majority of product purchases, however, involve low levels of elaboration, where involvement is low and where people select, often unconsciously, brands from an evoked set.

> Where elaboration is likely to be high if advertising is to work, then it is most likely to work under the strong theory.

New products require people to convert or change their purchasing patterns. It is evident that the strong theory must prevail in these circumstances. Where products become established their markets generally mature, so that real growth is non-existent. Under these circumstances, advertising works by protecting the consumer franchise and by allowing users to have their product choices confirmed and reinforced. The other objective of this form of advertising is to increase the rate at which customers reselect and consume products. If the strong theory were the only acceptable approach, then theoretically advertising would be capable of continually increasing the size of each market, until everyone had been converted. There would be no 'stationary' markets.

Considering the vast sums that are allocated to advertising budgets, not only to launch new products but also to pursue market share targets aggressively, the popularity and continued implicit acceptance of the power of advertising suggest that a large proportion of resources are wasted in the pursuit of advertising-driven brand performance. Indeed, it is noticeable that organisations have been switching resources out of advertising into sales promotion activities. There are many reasons for this (Chapter 18), but one of them concerns the failure of advertising to produce the expected levels of performance: to produce market share. The strong theory fails to deliver the expected results, and the weak theory does not apply to all circumstances. Reality is probably a mixture of the two.

The alphabetical model

Prue (1998) presents a framework entitled the alphabetical model, based upon the premise that advertising should be interpreted from a customer orientation. His model is an attempt to return to the simplicity inherent in the AIDA and other sequential models (see Figure 16.3). This is not so much a theory as a rather wide depository for all known interpretations of how advertising might work.

Using advertising strategically

There are many varied and conflicting ideas about the strategic use of advertising. For a long time the management of the tools of the communication mix was considered strategic. Indeed, many practitioners still believe in this approach. However, ideas concerning integrated marketing communications and corporate identity (Chapters 9 and 13) have helped provide a fresh perspective on what constitutes advertising strategy, and issues concerning differentiation,

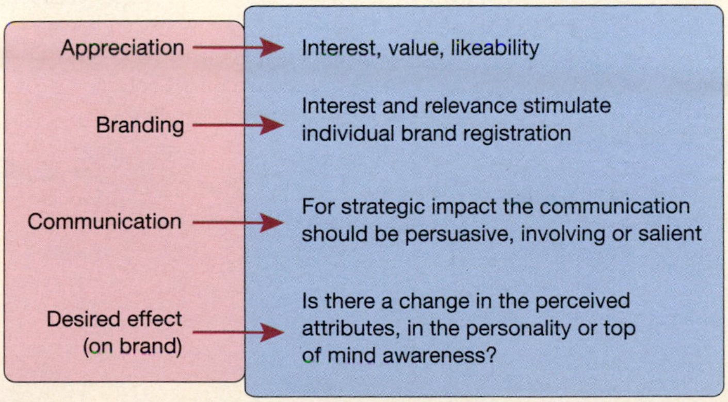

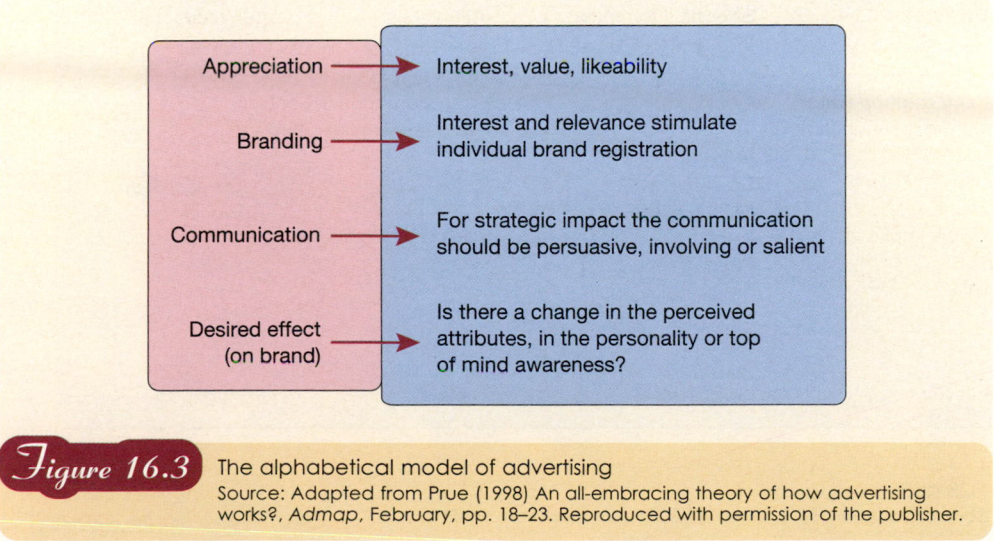

Figure 16.3 The alphabetical model of advertising
Source: Adapted from Prue (1998) An all-embracing theory of how advertising works?, *Admap*, February, pp. 18–23. Reproduced with permission of the publisher.

brand values and the development of brand equity have helped establish both strategic and a tactical or operational aspect associated with advertising.

One of the first significant attempts to formalise advertising's strategic role was developed by Vaughn when working for an advertising agency, Foote, Cone and Belding. These ideas (see below) were subsequently debated and an alternative model emerged from Rossiter and Percy. Both frameworks have been used extensively by advertising agencies, and although their influence has now subsided the underlying variables and approach remain central to strategic advertising thought.

The FCB matrix

Brain specialisation theory suggests that the left-hand side of the brain is best for handling rational, linear and cognitive thinking.

Vaughn (1980) developed a matrix utilising involvement and brain specialisation theories. Brain specialisation theory suggests that the left-hand side of the brain is best for handling rational, linear and cognitive thinking, whereas the right-hand side is better able to manage spatial, visual and emotional issues (the affective or feeling functions).

Vaughn proposed that by combining involvement with elements of thinking and feeling, four primary advertising planning strategies can be distinguished. These are informative, affective, habitual and self-satisfaction (see Figure 16.4). According to Vaughn, the matrix is intended to be a thought provoker rather than a formula or model from which prescriptive

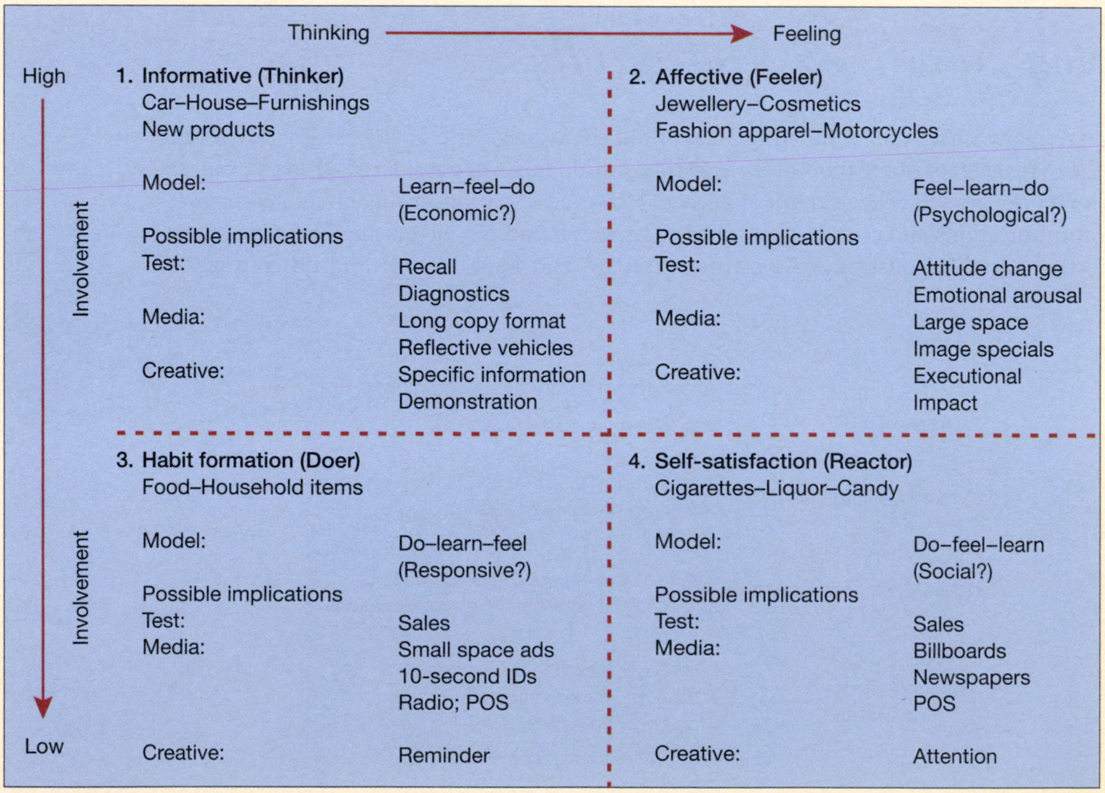

Figure 16.4 FCB grid
Source: Vaughn (1980). Used with kind permission from WARC.

solutions are to be identified. The FCB matrix is a useful guide to help analyse and appreciate consumer/product relationships and to develop appropriate communication strategies. The four quadrants of the grid identify particular types of decision-making and each requires different advertising approaches. Vaughn suggests that different orderings from the learn–feel–do sequence can be observed. By perceiving the different ways in which the process can be ordered, he proposed that the learn–feel–do sequence should be visualised as a continuum, a circular concept. Communication strategy would, therefore, be based on the point of entry that consumers make to the cycle.

Some offerings, generally regarded as 'habitual', may be moved to another quadrant, such as 'responsive', to develop differentiation and establish a new position for the product in the minds of consumers relative to the competition. This could be achieved by the selection of suitable media vehicles and visual images in the composition of the messages associated with an advertisement. There is little doubt that this model, or interpretation of the advertising process, has made a significant contribution to our understanding of the advertising process and has been used by a large number of advertising agencies (Joyce, 1991).

The Rossiter–Percy grid

Rossiter *et al.* (1991), however, disagree with some of the underpinnings of the FCB grid and offer a new one in response (revised 1997) (Figure 16.5). They suggest that involvement is not a continuum because it is virtually impossible to decide when a person graduates from high to low involvement. They claim that the FCB grid fails to account for situations where a person moves from high to low involvement and then back to high, perhaps on a temporary basis, when a new variant is introduced to the market. Rossiter *et al.* regard involvement as the level of perceived risk present at the time of purchase. Consequently, it is the degree of familiarity buyers have at the time of purchase that is an important component.

A further criticism is that the FCB grid is an attitude-only model. Rossiter *et al.* quite rightly identify the need for brand awareness to be built into such grids as a prerequisite for attitude development. However, they cite the need to differentiate different purchase situations. Some brands require awareness recall because the purchase decision is made prior to the act of purchasing. Other brands require

Some brands require awareness recall because the purchase decision is made prior to the act of purchasing.

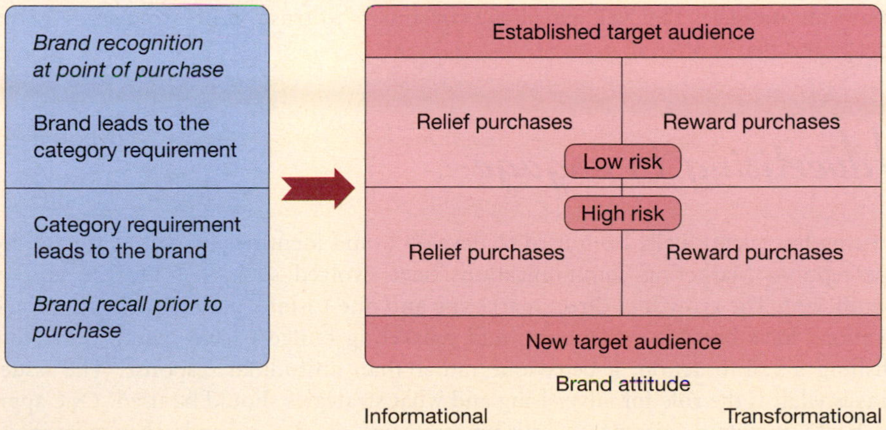

Figure 16.5 The Rossiter–Percy grid
Source: Adapted from Rossiter and Percy (1997). Used with kind permission.

awareness recognition at the point of purchase, where the buyer needs to be prompted into brand choice decisions. Each of these situations requires different message strategies, and these are explored in Chapter 17.

The other major difference between the two grids concerns the 'think–feel' dimension. Rossiter *et al.* believe that a wider spectrum of motives must be incorporated, as the FCB 'think–feel' interpretation fails to accommodate differences between product category and brand purchase motivations. For example, the decision to use a product category may be based on a strictly functional and utilitarian need. The need to travel to another country often designates the necessity of air transport. The choice of carrier, however, particularly over the North Atlantic, is a brand choice decision, motivated by a variety of sensory and ego-related inputs and anticipated outputs. Rossiter *et al.* disaggregate motives into what they refer to as informational and transformational motives. By detailing motives into these classifications, a more precise approach to advertising tactics can be developed (Chapter 17). Furthermore, the confusion inherent in the FCB grid, between the think and involvement elements, is overcome.

It should be understood that these 'grids' are purely hypothetical, and there is no proof or evidence to suggest that they are accurate reflections of advertising. It is true that both models have been used as the basis for advertising strategy in many agencies, but that does not mean that they are totally reliable or, more importantly, that they have been tested empirically so that they can be used in total confidence. They are interpretations of commercial and psychological activity and have been instrumental in advancing our level of knowledge. It is in this spirit of development that these models are presented in this text.

There are parts in both of these frameworks that have a number of strong elements of truth attached to them. However, for products that are purchased on a regular basis, pull strategies should be geared to defending the rationale that current buyers use to select the brand. Heavy buyers select a particular brand more often than light users do from their repertoire. By providing a variety of consistent stimuli, and by keeping the brand alive, fresh buyers are more likely to prefer and purchase a particular brand than those that allow their brands to lose purchase currency and the triggers necessary to evoke memory impressions.

For products purchased on an irregular basis, marketing communications need only touch the target audience on a relatively low number of occasions.

For products purchased on an irregular basis, marketing communications need only touch the target audience on a relatively low number of occasions. Strategies need to be developed that inform and contextualise the purchase rationale for consumers. This means providing lasting impressions that enable consumers to understand the circumstances in which purchase of a particular product/brand should be made once a decision has been made to purchase from the product category. Here the priorities are to communicate messages that will encourage consumers to trust and bestow expertise on the product/brand that is offered.

Advertising to engage

Advertising has traditionally been used to develop brand identities by stimulating awareness and perception. Marketing communications have evolved such that identity and values are insufficient. The growth of direct marketing and one-to-one, preferably interactive, communications have become paramount, and marketing budgets have swung more towards establishing a call-to-action, a behaviour rather than attitudinal response. The issue that remains is what is the role for advertising and what strategies should be used? One approach would be to maintain current advertising strategies on the grounds that awareness and perception are always going to be key factors. The other extreme approach would be to call for advertising to be used solely for direct-response work. Neither of these two options seems appropriate or viable in the twenty-first century.

In an age where values and response are both necessary ingredients for effective overall communication, advertising strategy in the future will probably need to be based on engagement. Customers will want to engage with the values offered by a brand that are significant to them individually. However, there will also be a need to engage with them at a behavioural level and to encourage them to want to respond to the advertising. Advertising strategy should therefore reflect a brand's context and be adjusted according to the required level of engagement regarding identity development and the required level of behavioural response. Advertising will no longer be able to rightly assume the lead role in a campaign and will be used according to the engagement needs of, first, the audience, second, the brand, and third, the communication industry, in that order.

Advertising strategy should reflect a brand's context.

ViewPoint 16.7 Ding Dong attacking advertising

Following BSkyB's share purchase of 18 per cent of ITV in 2007 a dispute erupted with its arch rival Virgin Media. Virgin claimed it was a move designed to prevent them from buying the organisation. Not long after this Sky and Virgin agreed to disagree about a fee for the Sky Basics TV package, which led to those channels being unavailable to Virgin Media viewers.

The dispute has two sides. Sky claim the dispute is about Virgin's refusal to pay the asking price to continue carrying the channels. Virgin on the other hand believe that Sky is trying to compel Virgin's customers into switching providers by denying them access to the basic channels (BBC).

Since then the two companies entered into a public spat and used adverting to make allegations and claims designed to inform the public of the real situation as each side saw it.

For example, Virgin Media used a print campaign to compare the TV, broadband and phone services of the two companies. Called 'The Real Deal' the campaign sought to show their superior service. However, Sky brought six complaints about the ads, claiming them as misleading or untrue. These were upheld by the Advertising Standards Authority (Sweney, 2007).

In November 2007 Virgin announced that it was to cease its campaign against Sky, after having spent £32 million on the advertising. James Kidd, Managing Director of Marketing at Virgin Media is reported to have said 'There's no point in spending any more time or money whacking the crap out of each other' (Jones, 2007).

Sources: BBC (2007); Jones (2007); and Sweney (2007).

Question

What value might Virgin have generated from this £32 million spend?

Task

Find two other brands that have been engaged in a public spat and what was the outcome?

Cohen (2003) refers to the gap between advertising used to develop brand identity and the need to encourage audience responses. He develops an OPC model where O refers to the offer, P to the product and C to the call-to-action. Advertising therefore should attempt to bring these elements together in a single, significant presentation. Key to his model is the brand/response (B/R) ratio, which relates to the relative levels of emphasis on the brand and response elements. The ratio refers to a line or spectrum of effects between these two elements. Traditional brand-based advertising equates with a B/R of 100/0 and direct response has a B/R of 0/100 where the sole intention is to maximise the likelihood of a response. The strategic claim behind this approach may be in need of elaboration to be operationally robust, but the principle of moving the focus of advertising strategy to one that recognises the need to incorporate brand experiences is essentially sound.

Summary

In order to help consolidate your understanding of advertising strategy, here are the key points summarised against each of the learning objectives:

1. Consider the role advertising plays in both consumer and business-to-business markets.

The role of advertising in most marketing communications campaigns is to engage audiences. Engagement is enabled either by informing, changing perceptions and building brand values or by encouraging a change in behaviour.

Advertising can reach huge audiences with simple messages that present opportunities to allow receivers to understand what a product is, what its primary function is and how it relates to all the other similar products. This is the main function of advertising: to communicate with specific audiences. These audiences may be consumer- or organisation-based, but wherever they are located the prime objective is to build or maintain awareness of a product or an organisation.

2. Appraise the use of emotion in advertising and consider concepts associated with shock advertising.

Advertising does not always work through rational information processing. Feelings and emotions play an important role, especially when advertising is used to build awareness levels and brand strength.

Audiences are offended by shock advertising because there is 'norm violation, encompassing transgressions of law or custom, breaches of a moral or social code, or things that outrage the moral or physical senses', for example gratuitous violence and disgusting image. The main reason for using a shock advertising strategy is that it is a good way to secure an audience's attention and achieve a longer-lasting impact than through traditional messages and attention-getting devices.

3. Explain the principal frameworks by which advertising is thought to influence individuals.

The hierarchy of effects frameworks (e.g. AIDA), were the first attempts to explain how advertising works. The sequential nature of these early interpretations was attractive because they were easy to comprehend, neatly mirrored the purchase decision process and provided a base upon which campaign goals were later assigned (Dagmar). However, as our knowledge of buyer behaviour increased and as the significance of the USP declined so these hierarchy of effects models also declined in terms of our understanding about advertising. Now they are insignificant and are no longer used as appropriate interpretations of how advertising works.

In their place a number of new frameworks and explanations have arisen, all of which claim to reflect practice. In other words these new theories about how advertising works are a reflection of practice, of the way advertising is considered to work, or at least used by advertising agencies and interpreted by marketing research agencies. The first of these information processing models were developed by O'Malley (1991) and Hall (1992) and they suggest that there are four main advertising frameworks: persuasion, sales, salience and involvement.

4. Appraise the strong and weak theories of advertising.

The strong theory of advertising reflects the persuasion concept, and has high credibility when used with new brands. However, the contrasting view is that advertising should be regarded as a means of defending customers' purchase decisions and for protecting markets, not building them. Reality suggests that the majority of advertising cannot claim to be of significant value to most people and that the strong and the weak theories are equally applicable, although not at the same time nor in the same context.

5. Consider ways in which advertising can be used strategically.

Advertising, once considered the prime form of mass persuasion, is now subject to many different views. Those who are sceptical of advertising's power to persuade consumers to change their purchasing habits now explore ideas concerning advertising's strategic role in reinforcing brand messages and repositioning brands.

The FCB and Rossiter–Percy grids represent formalised attempts to interpret the strategic use of advertising. Intended to provide agencies with a method that might ensure consistency, meaning and value with respect to their clients' brands, these are no longer considered by agencies to be sufficiently flexible, rigorous or representative of how contemporary advertising performs.

A more current perspective of advertising strategy suggests that advertising should become more engaged with the customer's experience of the brand and not be rooted just in the development of brand values.

6. Examine ideas concerning the use of advertising to engage audiences.

In an age where values and response are both necessary ingredients for effective overall communication, future advertising strategy will probably need to be based on engagement. Advertising strategy should therefore reflect a brand's context and be adjusted according to the required level of engagement regarding identity development and the required level of behavioural response. Advertising will no longer be able to rightly assume the lead role in a campaign and will be used according to the engagement needs of, first, the audience, second, the brand, and third, the communication industry, in that order.

Review questions

1. Find two advertisements and write notes explaining how they depict the roles of advertising.
2. Write brief notes outlining the difference between absolute and relative costs.
3. Name the three elements in advertising, identified by Dahl *et al.* (2003), which cause audiences to be offended. Find an example of each.
4. What are the essential differences between the involvement and salience frameworks of advertising? Find four advertisements (other than those described in the text) that are examples of these two approaches.
5. Write a short presentation explaining the differences between the strong and weak theories of advertising.
6. Select an organisation of your choice and find three ads it has used recently. Are the ads predominantly trying to persuade audiences or are they designed to reinforce brand values?
7. Evaluate the contribution of Prue's alphabetical model of advertising.
8. Draw the FCB grid and place on it the following product categories: shampoo, life assurance, sports cars, kitchen towels, box of chocolates.
9. Prepare a report explaining the differences between the Rossiter–Percy and FCB grids.
10. Write brief notes outlining the strategic role advertising plays within an organisation's overall promotional activities.

MiniCase Tapping into a new zeitgeist: women consumers, lifestyle trends and the *Red* Experience

Lorna Stevens: University of Ulster

In 1998, EMAP Elan launched a new woman's magazine called *Red* onto the already crowded UK women's monthly magazine market. The decision was based on the EMAP Elan's belief that there was an emerging sensibility in women in their thirties and forties that was not being catered for. This new 'zeitgeist' (spirit of the age) was the notion that age was a state of mind, and that contemporary women were taking youthful values and behaviours into their 30s and beyond. These 'middle-youth' women wanted a lively and vibrant magazine that helped them escape from their busy, day-to-day lives. EMAP Elan would offer women readers 'the precious experience of time to oneself' in a 'time poor world' (Rainey *et al.*, 1999).

The challenge for the *Red* team was to entice women in their 30s and 40s to buy the new magazine, and to do so they reckoned they would need to stress the pleasurable *experience* of consuming it. The advertising campaign revolved around three television ads, called 'Defining Moments', 'The Strip' and 'Me-Time'. Each of these advertisements made a direct appeal to the experiential aspects of consumption, namely the emotions and sensory feelings associated with the act of consumption (Holbrook and Hirschman, 1982).

Women's monthly magazines, while they are undeniably rich in information and advice for women, also have very strong experiential appeals for women. The editorial team at *Red* was convinced that women's magazines needed to provide an oasis of calm and pleasure in the midst of 'time-poor' everyday lives. Instead of addressing women in their 30s and 40s according to their numerous roles in life, then, the *Red* team decided that their unique proposition would be to focus on *Red* magazine as a self-indulgent, pleasurable *experience* that enabled women consumers to take time out from the demands of their daily, juggling lives. The name '*Red*' was chosen because it was considered 'quite sexy, quite glamorous, quite modern' (Anne-Marie Lavin, EMAP Elan). It also conjures up passion, warmth, feistiness, challenge, readability and simplicity. The focus of the marketing strategy would be on attitude and lifestyle, encapsulated by the core concept '*Red* Time is Me Time'.

The first television ad, 'Defining Moments' comprised a series of fleeting and evocative images, filmed in black-and-white, of a woman at work and at play, with soothing, classical music in the background. Its emphasis was on lifestyle rather than demographics. A female voiceover relates the following lines as the various scenes unfold:

> 'If you think life's too short for communal changing rooms/If you're madly in love with your garden/If you buy things and hide the receipts/If you're having an affair, or not/If you've grown up without growing old/And you don't want to have it all, you just want to have what you want/Then it's probably time you saw *Red*.

The ad has an almost documentary quality as we see a quick succession of scenes from the woman's life. She is slim and attractive, dressed simply in a white shirt and dark trousers. We see her dining with friends, out of doors with her red setter dog; driving her car; dancing in a glamorous cocktail dress. We see her pensively looking out the window at bare winter branches, and a man leaving the house – an illicit lover or a devoted husband? Then we see her at a drawing board, talking on the phone; having her back scrubbed in a bath tub; on a bicycle with a child. The final image is the front cover of *Red*'s first issue, with the caption 'Go on, treat yourself.'

The advertisement's attractive and evocative cinematic style and its romantic images are clearly designed to appeal to women consumers' senses and emotions. By the end of the ad nothing is known about the magazine's contents, but the ad is designed to enable the target market to recognise aspects of themselves in the series of so-called 'defining moments'. Anne-Marie Lavin, the then marketing manager of *Red*, observes: 'I think you can launch a magazine quite easily, but it's more difficult to launch a brand, and everything that we do – and that's everything in the magazine used to market it – reflects those values.'

The second advertisement in the series is called 'The Strip', which was launched a year after 'Defining Moments'. This ad caused considerable debate at its inception stage, as it shows a woman doing a striptease. The *Red* team were somewhat anxious about this concept, and were worried that if the ad was too sexually suggestive it might alienate the target market. They therefore worked closely with the ad agency to ensure that the ad portrayed the woman in a humorous way, as a likeable, human subject, rather than an objectified sex object.

An attractive 30-something woman enters a dark room wearing a black coat and high-heeled shoes. She switches on a lamp, and picks up a red note from the console table. Grinning, she tosses the note away from her, and her bag. Next she slowly removes her coat, shoulder by shoulder, and we realise she is doing a striptease. A woman's smoky voice sings *'I dreamt that I was chasing – the monster out of me'*. There are several cream sofas in the room, with scarlet cushions. The woman strikes various exaggerated, humorous poses as she gradually strips off to her underwear. At one point she kicks off one of her shoes, and it flies through the air, knocking over a tall vase of white lilies. She pulls a face, but continues to smile. We notice a bright green toy on the floor behind her. One of her stockings drifts onto a console table beside a framed photograph of a man, and she blows an exaggerated kiss at it. She walks over towards a sofa, tripping over the soft toy as she does so. She laughs and makes a face at herself in the mirror, and snatches some clothing from the back of the sofa. The next scene is of her reclining on the cream sofa, surrounded by rich red cushions, dressed in tracksuit bottoms and a fleecy top, smiling and reading a copy of *Red* magazine. A woman's voice now says '*Red* magazine – drop everything', underlining the humour that pervades the ad. Despite its somewhat risky and indeed risqué marketing strategy, the ad worked, and indeed sales of the magazine increased by 30,000 on the previous month.

The third advertisement, 'Me-Time', was launched a year after 'The Strip'. This ad was very different from the two previous ads, but once again there was a clear focus on the concept of 'me-time'. The ad focuses on ideal reading scenarios, and gives centre stage to a red sofa, which is used in every frame in the ad to symbolise the concept of 'me-time'. An elegant scarlet sofa is shown in a variety of idyllic places: a lush, flower-filled summer meadow, complete with butterflies; a sandy beach by moonlight; the sofa surrounded by a circle of candles; a sunny Mediterranean terrace; a rugged, mountain landscape overlooking a still lake, against a backdrop of a blue and white streaked sky. The final image is of a woman sitting on the sofa in an Italianate-style terrace, complete with elegant columns, urns and a water fountain. She sits, her bare feet drawn up beside her, absorbed in a copy of *Red* magazine, smiling. At the end of the ad a woman's voice says '*Red* magazine – your sofa awaits.' We are then shown the current issue of *Red*, against a luxurious red satin background, underlining its magical and precious qualities, and its associations with sensuous pleasure and relaxation. 'Your sofa awaits' clearly recalls the famous line from the Cinderella fairytale 'Your carriage awaits'. And just as a pumpkin can become a glass carriage, a sofa can become a magic carpet when combined with a very special ingredient, *Red* magazine. In short, it can carry its readers off to better places!

The *Red* marketing campaign was a great success: against the odds, the magazine was able to squeeze its way into the crowded women's magazine market, and more importantly, hold its own there, a feat it has continued to perform in the 10 years since its launch. Much of *Red*'s success is down to the clear focus of EMAP Elan's marketing strategy, and its memorable TV ads, all of which were based on the concept of 'me-time'. The *Red* case is testimony to the fact that consumers are very receptive to ads that appeal to their emotions, feelings and senses. *Red* magazine's development team recognised that it was not just about getting the contents of the magazine right; it was about creating the right ambiance around the magazine, and developing a strong and appealing brand image and personality for *Red*. It was also about understanding its market, and positioning the brand in such a way as to reflect current lifestyle trends. By creating a brand that encapsulated the notion of me-time and self-indulgence, *Red* appealed to 'middle-youth' women in their 30s and 40s who wanted a lively and pleasurable read, *and* the chance to put their feet up and indulge in some 'me-time'!

MiniCase questions

1. Can you think of other marketing campaigns that have recognised a new consumer trend or 'zeitgeist' and developed their campaign around this?
2. Do you think that experiential appeals have become more commonplace than informational ones in advertising? If so, why do you think this is the case?
3. The women's magazine market is holding its own in the face of increased competition from the Internet, TV and newspapers, and in fact magazine readership is rising, with Keynote predicting that this trend will continue. Why do you think women's magazines continue to appeal to women?

References

Ambler, T. (1998) Myths about the mind: time to end some popular beliefs about how advertising works. *International Journal of Advertising*, **17**, 501–9.

BBC (2007) *Q&A: Sky and Virgin Media TV row*, 24 May. Retrieved from http://news.bbc.co.uk/1/hi/business/6390655.stm.

Bewick, M. (2006) Pushing the boundaries. *The Marketer*, September, 25.

Cohen, A. (2003) Closing the brand/response gap. *Admap*, (September), 20–2.

Corke, S. and Heath, R.G. (2004) The hidden power of newspaper advertising. *Media Research Group Conference*, Madrid, (November).

Dahl, D.W., Frankenberger, K.D. and Manchanda, R.V. (2003) Does it pay to shock? Reactions to shocking and nonshocking advertising content among university students. *Journal of Advertising Research*, **43**(3) (September), 268–81.

Dichter, E. (1966) How word-of-mouth advertising works. *Harvard Business Review*, **44** (November/December), 147–66.

Ehrenberg, A.S.C. (1974) Repetitive advertising and the consumer. *Journal of Advertising Research*, **14** (April), 25–34.

Ehrenberg, A.S.C. (1988) *Repeat Buying*, 2nd edn. London: Charles Griffin.

Ehrenberg, A.S.C. (1997) How do consumers come to buy a new brand? *Admap* (March), 20–4.

Hall, M. (1992) Using advertising frameworks. *Admap* (March), 17–21.

Heath, R. and Feldwick, P. (2007) 50 years using the wrong model of TV advertising. *Admap*, (March), 36–8.

Jones, G. (2008) Handset manufacturers plot response to iPhone. *Marketing*, 13 February, 1.

Jones, J.P. (1991) Over-promise and under-delivery. *Marketing and Research Today* (November), 195–203.

Jones, G. (2007) Virgin Media pulls ads attacking rival Sky service. *Marketing*, 7 November, 3.

Joyce, T. (1991) Models of the advertising process. *Marketing and Research Today* (November), 205–12.

Krugman, H.E. (1971) Brain wave measurement of media involvement. *Journal of Advertising*, **11**(1), 3–9.

O'Malley, D. (1991) Sales without salience? *Admap* (September), 36–9.

Prue, T. (1998) An all-embracing theory of how advertising works? *Admap* (February), 18–23.

Rossiter, J.R. and Percy, L. (1997) *Advertising Communications & Promotion Management*, 2nd edn. New York: McGraw-Hill.

Rossiter, J.R., Percy, L. and Donovan, R.J. (1991) A better advertising planning grid. *Journal of Advertising Research* (October/November), 11–21.

Sweney, M. (2006) A successful ad campaign has revived the fortunes of Marks & Spencer. *The Guardian*, Monday, 6 November. Retrieved 15 January 2008 from www.guardian.co.uk/retail/story/0,,1940204,00.html.

Sweney, M. (2007) Sky wins ad wrangle with Virgin. *The Guardian*, 1 August. Retrieved 4 December 2007 from http://www.guardian.co.uk/media/2007/aug/01/advertising.news.

Thompson, M., Neal, J., Threadgould, S. and Lema Trillo, S. (2006) Marks & Spencer, This is not just advertising, this is M&S advertising: how confident communications helped restore public confidence in M&S. *Institute of Practitioners in Advertising*, www.ipa.co.uk, Retrieved 25 September 2007 from www.warc.com.

Tiltman, D. (2008) People's choice: most irritating ads of 2007. *Marketing*, 8 January. Available at www.brandrepublic.com/Marketing/News/774978/Peoples-choice-irritating-ads-2007/.

Vakratsas, D. and Ambler, T. (1999) How advertising works: what do we really know? *Journal of Marketing*, **63** (January), 26–43.

Vaughn, R. (1980) How advertising works: a planning model. *Journal of Advertising Research* (October), 27–33.

Venkat, R. and Abi-Hanna, N. (1995) *Effectiveness of Visually Shocking Advertisements: Is it Context Dependent?* Administrative Science Association of Canada Proceedings, **16**(3), 139–46.

Chapter 17

Messages, content and creative approaches

The message an organisation conveys through its marketing communications is critical. This means considering what organisations say and how they say it. However, in an age of interaction, individual consumers can also create and share content with others. In both cases, ensuring that the right balance of information and emotions is achieved and that the presentation of the message is appropriate for the target audience represents a critical part of the creative process for agencies, clients and individuals.

Aims and learning objectives

The aim of this chapter is to consider some of the ways in which advertising and promotional messages can be created by focusing on some of the principal aspects of message construction, presentation and user-generated-content.

The learning objectives of this chapter are to:

1. show how messages can be constructed to account for the context in which they are to be received;
2. examine the importance and characteristics of using source credibility;
3. explore the advantages and disadvantages of using spokespersons in message presentation;
4. discuss the impact of user-generated-content;
5. examine ideas concerning message framing;
6. consider how advertising messages might be best presented;
7. examine the use of emotions and feelings in advertising messages;
8. indicate how informational and transformational motives can be used as tactical tools in an advertising plan.

For an applied interpretation see Poonam V. Kumar and Prasad Narasimhan's MiniCase entitled ***The Apache motorcycle advertising campaign in India*** at the end of this chapter.

Introduction

Whether advertising converts people into becoming brand-loyal customers or acts as a defensive shield to reassure current buyers, and whether central or peripheral cues are required, there still remains the decision about the nature and form of the message to be conveyed: the creative strategy. In practice, the generation of suitable messages is derived from the creative brief. For the sake of discussion and analysis, four elements will be considered. First, considerable attention is given to the source of a message and issues relating to source credibility. This is followed by a consideration of the *balance*, *structure* and *presentation* of the message itself to the target audience.

Message source

Messages are perceived in many different ways and are influenced by a variety of factors. However, a critical determinant concerns the credibility that is attributed to the source of the message itself. Kelman (1961) believed that the source of a message has three particular characteristics. These are: the level of perceived credibility as seen in terms of perceived objectivity and expertise; the degree to which the source is regarded as attractive and message recipients are motivated to develop a similar association or position; and the degree of power that the source is believed to possess. This is manifest in the ability of the source to reward or punish message receivers. The two former characteristics are evident in various forms of marketing communications, but the latter is directly observable in personal selling situations, and perhaps in the use of sales promotions.

The source of a message has three particular characteristics.

Following this work on source characteristics three key components of source credibility can be distinguished:

- What is the level of perceived expertise (how much relevant knowledge the source is thought to hold)?
- What are the personal motives the source is believed to possess (what is the reason for the source to be involved)?
- What degree of trust can be placed in what the source says or does on behalf of the endorsement?

No matter what the level of expertise, if the level of trust is questionable, credibility will be adversely affected.

Establishing credibility

Credibility can be established in a number of ways. One simple approach is to list or display the key attributes of the organisation or the product and then signal trustworthiness through the use of third-party endorsements and the comments of satisfied users.

A more complex approach is to use referrals, suggestions and association. Trustworthiness and expertise are the two principal elements of source credibility. One way of developing trust is to use spokespersons to speak on behalf of the sponsor of an advertisement and in effect, provide a testimonial for the product in question. Credibility, therefore, can be established by the initiator of the advertisement or by a spokesperson used by the initiator to convey the message.

Credibility can be established by the initiator of the advertisement or by a spokesperson.

Effectively, consumers trade off the validity of claims made by brands against the perceived trustworthiness (and expertise) of the individuals or organisations who deliver the message. The result is that a claim may have reduced impact if either of these two components is doubtful or not capable of verification but, if repeated enough times, will enable audiences to accept that the products are very effective and of sufficiently high performance for them to try.

Credibility established by the initiator

The credibility of the organisation initiating the communication process is important. An organisation should seek to enhance its reputation with its various stakeholders at every opportunity. However, organisational credibility is derived from the image, which in turn is a composite of many perceptions. Past decisions, current strategy and performance indicators, the level of perceived service and the type of performance network members (e.g. high-quality retail outlets) all influence the perception of an organisation and the level of credibility that follows.

One very important factor that influences credibility is branding. Private and family brands in particular allow initiators to develop and launch new products more easily than those who do not have such brand strength. Brand extensions (such as Mars ice-cream) have been launched with the credibility of the product firmly grounded in the strength of the parent brand name (Mars). Consumers recognise the name and make associations that enable them to lower the perceived risk and in doing so provide a platform to try the new product.

The need to establish high levels of credibility also allows organisations to divert advertising spend away from a focus on brands to one that focuses on the organisation. Corporate advertising seeks to adjust organisation image and to build reputation.

ViewPoint 17.1 Max Factor use a source of credibility

Max Factor claims that its products are so good that they are used by the experts in their industry: 'The make-up of make-up artists'. Many of its recent campaigns feature expert make-up artists who work on blockbuster Hollywood movies. However, many of these experts are not known by the general public. The development of 'trustworthiness' therefore relies on the film credential.

As with all use of spokespersons, Max Factor needs to ensure that when using experts their target audiences perceive the messages to be genuinely believable. In this case, Max Factor uses these experts because they are perceived to be objective and independent simply because their job gives them freedom of choice with regard to the products they use.

Potential new customers seeing these advertisements are challenged on the grounds that if the brand is good enough for these experts then it should be good enough for them. If a viewer is already a Max Factor customer, then product experience will contribute to a support argument and these advertising messages are used to reinforce previous brand choice decisions. Either way these Max Factor advertisements are extremely powerful.

Question

To what extent does the use of experts evade focus on product attributes and quality?

Task

Using various magazine ads for fragrances and cosmetics, make a list of the different ways source credibility is established.

Credibility established by a spokesperson

People who deliver the message are often regarded as the source, when in reality they are only the messenger. These people carry the message and represent the true source or initiator of the message (e.g. manufacturer or retailer). Consequently, the testimonial they transmit must be credible. There are four main types of spokesperson: the expert, the celebrity, the chief executive officer and the consumer.

There are four main types of spokesperson: the expert, the celebrity, the chief executive officer and the consumer.

The expert has been used many times and was particularly popular when television advertising first established itself in the 1950s and 1960s. Experts are quickly recognisable because they either wear white coats and round glasses or dress and act like 'mad professors'. Through the use of symbolism, stereotypes and identification, these characters (and indeed others) can be established very quickly in the minds of receivers and a frame of reference generated that does not question the authenticity of the message being transmitted by such a person. Experts can also be users of products, for example professional photographers endorsing cameras, secretaries endorsing word processors and professional golfers endorsing golf equipment.

Entertainment and sporting celebrities are being used increasingly, not only to provide credibility for a range of high-involvement (e.g. David Beckham for Vodafone and Linda Barker for DFS) and low-involvement decisions (e.g. Jamie Oliver for Sainsbury's) but also to grab the attention of people in markets where motivation to decide between competitive products may be low. The celebrity enables the message to stand out among the clutter and noise that typify many markets. It is also hoped that the celebrity and/or the voice-over will become a peripheral cue in the decision-making process: Joanna Lumley for Privilege car insurance, Alan Hansen for Morrison's and as shown at Exhibit 17.1, Nicole Kidman for Chanel No. 5.

Exhibit 17.1 Nicole Kidman endorsing Chanel No 5
Image courtesy of The Advertising Archives.

Consideration needs to be given to the longer-term relationship between the celebrity and the brand.

There are some potential problems that advertisers need to be aware of when considering the use of celebrities. First, does the celebrity fit the image of the brand and will the celebrity be acceptable to the target audience? Consideration also needs to be given to the longer-term relationship between the celebrity and the brand. Should the lifestyle of the celebrity change, what impact will this change have on the target audience and their attitude towards the brand?

ViewPoint 17.2 Kate Moss: winner or loser?

The sparkling career of superstar model Kate Moss was brought to an abrupt halt in 2005 when pictures of her were published in a national newspaper allegedly showing her taking drugs. This was followed shortly by another newspaper that published other lurid stories about her private life. The impact of the widespread publicity was devastating. First, H&M, at that time Europe's largest clothing chain, cancelled her £500,000 contract to be the brand's 'face'. After initially tolerating the tabloid attack the company decided that because of the close association with a charity dedicated to the prevention of drug abuse, the contract had to be cancelled. Consequently months of work and a £1 million advertising campaign, scheduled to be featured in glossy magazines, were abandoned.

Exhibit 17.2 Supermodel Kate Moss has been used to the face of a number of brands during her career, stretching from the 1990s (left) to the current day (right)
Jim Smeal/Wire Image/Getty Images; Leon Neal/AFP/Getty Images.

Her contracts with the French fashion house Chanel, for whom she had been the face of Coco Mademoiselle perfume for four years, Rimmel and Burberry were all terminated.

However, her career was resurrected in 2006 when she first secured a lucrative contract to front a new campaign as the 'face' of Calvin Klein. This was followed by the announcement that she was to work with Topshop, not as a model and not as a conventional endorser. Her role was to be the designer for a new collection to be sold in all 309 branches of the High Street chain. This represented a significant shift for the superstar, from brand endorser to brand architect.

When the first collections went on sale there was a frenzy of activity. Some shoppers queued for eight hours to get first sight of the brand, the media gave the brand a mass of free publicity as they reported the opening event and Topshop themselves benefited through positive communications and sales and profits even though they had to limit individuals to buying just five items. This was to prevent exploitation of the Moss brand through sales on eBay.

Topshop appear to have struck gold with Kate Moss, and Moss herself has done nicely. As Armstrong (2006) commented, her earnings have been rumoured to have quadrupled since the allegations in 2005.

Sources: Various including Alleyne (2005), Anon. (2006), Armstrong (2006) and Rushton (2007).

Question

Consider the view that the use of celebrities who have a controversial and high media profile is potentially damaging for a brand in the long run.

Task

Think of three brands and find out who is used to endorse them.

The second problem concerns the impact that the celebrity makes relative to the brand. There is a danger that those receiving the message remember the celebrity but not the brand that is the focus of the advertising spend. The *celebrity* becomes the hero, rather than the product being advertised. Loveless (2007) reports on the financial services company First Plus who used celebrity mathematician Carol Vorderman to endorse their loan products. Some saw a discontinuity between this celebrity's values, and the possibility that the company she was endorsing might make some people worse off was highlighted. In these situations the endorser can overshadow the product to the extent that consumers might have trouble recalling the brand.

Some CEOs have relished the chance to sell their own products and there have been some notable business people who have 'fronted' their organisation. Richard Branson used to promote Virgin Financial products and Victor Kiam 'so liked the razor that he bought the company' (Remington). Here, the CEO openly promotes his company. This form of testimonial is popular when the image of the CEO is positive and the photogenic and on-screen characteristics provide for enhanced credibility. Until recently, Bernard Matthews has established authenticity and trustworthiness with his personal promotion of Norfolk Turkey Roasts.

When using consumers as the spokesperson to endorse products, the audience is being asked to identify with a 'typical consumer'. The identification of similar lifestyles, interests and opinions allows for better reception and understanding of the message. Consumers are often depicted testing similar products, such as margarine and butter. The Pepsi Challenge required consumers to select Pepsi from Coca-Cola through blind taste tests. By showing someone using the product, someone who is similar to the receiver, the source is perceived as credible and the potential for successful persuasion is considerably enhanced.

Sleeper effects

When the receiver's position is favourable to the message, a moderate level of credibility may be more appropriate.

The assumption so far has been that high credibility enhances the probability of persuasion and successful communication. This is true when the receiver's initial position is opposite to that contained in the message. When the receiver's position is favourable to the message, a moderate level of credibility may be more appropriate.

Whether source credibility is high, medium or low is of little consequence, according to some researchers (Hannah and Sternthal, 1984). The impact of the source is believed to dissipate after approximately six weeks and only the content of the message is thought to dominate the receiver's attention. This sleeper effect (Hovland *et al.*, 1949) has not been proved empirically, but the implication is that the persuasiveness of a message can increase over time. Furthermore, advertisers using highly credible sources need to repeat the message on a regular basis, in order that the required level of effectiveness and persuasion be maintained (Schiffman and Kanuk, 1991).

User-generated-content (UGC)

Before considering ways in which messages are designed, framed and presented for target audiences it is important to consider that today, many messages are developed and communicated by individuals. These are used to communicate with organisations of all types and sizes but they are also shared with peers, family, friends and others in communities such as social networks and specialist interest online communities (e.g. reunion and family history sites). What is interesting is that although people understand the rules and norms associated with communicating across peer groups and social networks, organisations have yet to be entirely successful. To date, they do not appear to be able to communicate as freely or with as much credibility and authority as individuals regularly do within these new environments. One of the reasons for this is the democratisation of the media and the language codes that have emerged. A simple example is SMS texting. Used by millions everyday to great effect, mobile communications and text messaging have yet to become as commercially prominent.

In December 2006, *Time* named 'you' (the consumer) as its Person of the Year and in January 2007 *Advertising Age* followed suit when it named 'the consumer' as its Advertising Agency of the Year. Simms (2007a) reports that both awards were made on the basis that consumers were regarded as responsible for making and generating more engaging brand communications than any one agency, during the previous year. It has to be said that most of this content was online but this is changing as the offline world becomes a target for content generation. See Viewpoint 17.3 for an example of how brands are trying to generate UGC offline.

ViewPoint 17.3 YouTo content

Deliberately inviting customers to create content is now quite commonplace. For example, Cadbury have run an offline campaign 'how do you eat yours?' about their creme eggs, for a few years. However, in 2007 it went online as they invited customers to send in videos along the same theme and to post them on its 'Gootube' site.

Doritos, Chevrolet and the NFL offered consumers prizes in order to attract ads for use at the 2007 SuperBowl. Those sent in to Doritos highlighted some very varied uses of the brand. These ranged from a middle-aged man who dances for 30 seconds clutching three bags of Doritos, to the a video of a young man who films his naked girlfriend writhing in a bath of crisps.

Unilever (US) held a competition that invited women to create their own 30-second ad to launch the Dove Cream Oil Body Wash Collection. The best ad was said to capture the 'essence of the products and its philosophy'. More than 700 entries were received and the winning entry was premiered in an ad break during the Oscars.

Source: Simms (2007a).

Question

Are there areas or subjects where user-generated-content might not be helpful?

Task

If some of your friends offered to create online content for you, which three topics would you request?

UGC can appear in many ways and in a variety of formats. The original format for UGC can be seen in letters to newspapers. The letter becomes part of the content of the newspaper and sits alongside the editorial and journalist written copy. More recently however, digitisation has enabled faster, more immediate posting opportunities for UGC.

Email enables viewers to interact with television and radio programmes, with presenters encouraging audiences to write and tell them 'what you think' about a topic. Discussion boards and online forums can only work through consumer participation and user-generated-content. One of the common and developing forms of UGC is blogging. Here individuals, sometimes in the name of organisations but more often as independent consumers, post information about topics of personal interest. Very often these people develop opinion leader status and are used by organisations to feed information about the launch of new brands, to educate opinion followers or to reposition brands.

Email enables viewers to interact with television and radio programmes.

Social networks thrive on the shared views, opinions and beliefs, often brand-related, of networked friends. YouTube and Flickr provide opportunities for consumers to share video and photos respectively, with all material posted by users. Users post their content and respond to the work of others, often by rating the quality or entertainment value of content posted by others.

Muňiz and Schau (2007) refer to what they call vigilante marketing. In these circumstances, consumers create self-generated advertising content to promote brands with which they have a strong affiliation. They refer to a brand community site based on the Apple Newton. This was an early PDA launched in 1993 and discontinued by Apple in 1998 as Palm Pilot undercut on price and exceeded the Newton on quality, size and overall value. Many users at the time blamed Apple for poor communications and not explaining the Newton accurately enough to attract more customers. Roughly 3–4,000 Newton users still participate in online forums. They create what the authors label as brand artefacts, some of which closely resemble ads, all for a brand that ceased production nearly a decade earlier. Their actions serve to maintain a brand that has a special meaning for them.

Marketers should use the increasing occurrence of UGC as an opportunity to listen to and observe consumers and to find out what meanings they attribute to a brand. Some companies invite consumers to offer content (ads). According to Bosman (2006) cited by Muňiz and Schau (2007), Mastercard created a web site called www.priceless.com and invited customers to submit copy for two television ads they were running in the Priceless campaign.

Message framing

The vast majority of messages are generated professionally, not by users, and there various strategies and tactics that are used to develop effective messages. One of these is message framing, which has long been used as a strategy to present brand messages. However, as Tsai (2007) indicates it is controversial and empirically unproven. Message framing works on the hedonic principles of our motivation to seek happiness and to avoid pain. So messages can be framed to either focus a recipient's attention to positive outcomes (happiness) or take them away from the possible negative outcomes (pain). For example, a positively framed message might be a yoghurt that is presented as 'contains real fruit' or a car as 'a stylish design'. Conversely messages could be presented as 'contains only 5 per cent fat' and 'low carbon emissions', these are regarded as negatively framed.

Message framing works on the hedonic principles of our motivation to seek happiness and to avoid pain.

Many practitioners work on the basis that positive are better than negative messages whereas others believe negative framing promotes deeper thinking and consideration. However, there is little empirical evidence to support any of these views. Therefore, in an attempt to understand when it is better to use positive or negative framing Tsai argues that it is necessary to develop a holistic understanding of the target audience. This involves considering three factors: self-construal; consumer involvement; and product knowledge. These are explained at Table 17.1.

Tsai believes that these three factors moderate an individual's response when they are exposed to positively or negatively framed brand messages. In turn these influence the three main dimensions of a brand's communication. These are generally accepted by researchers such as Mackenzie and Lutz (1989) and Lafferty *et al.* (2002) to be attitude to the ad, attitude to the brand and purchase intention (see Chapter 8 for a consideration of these dimensions). Tsai develops a conceptual model to demonstrate this through which he argues brand communication persuasiveness is moderated by these three factors.

His research concludes that positive message framing should be used when the following exists:

Independent self-construal × low consumer involvement × low product knowledge

Table 17.1 Factors associated with message framing

Factor		Explanation
Self construal	Independent	Individuals (the self) seek to distinguish themselves from others. These individuals respond best to positive framing.
	Interdependent	Individuals (the self) try not to distinguish themselves from others. These individuals respond best to negative framing.
Consumer involvement	High involvement Low involvement	Refers to the extent to which personal relevance and perceived risk influences decision-making within a product category. When high, negative framing is preferred; when low, positive framing is preferred.
Product knowledge	High Low	Product knowledge consists of two elements: behavioural (usage) experience and mental (search, exposure and information). Message framing is more suitable where product knowledge is low.

Source: Based on Tsai (2007).

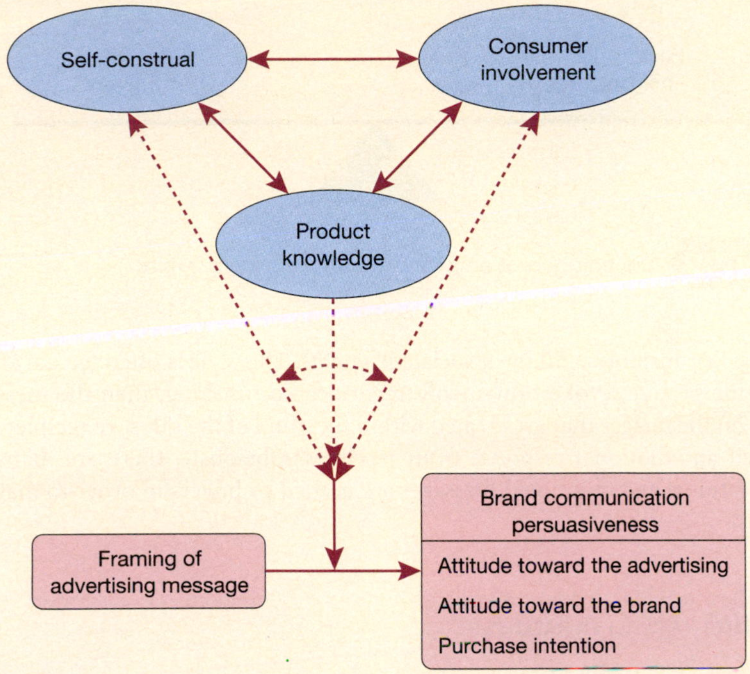

Figure 17.1 Message framing for brand communication (MFBC) model
Source: Tsai (2007). Used with permission from WARC.

Negative framing should be used when:

Interdependent self-construal × high consumer involvement × low product knowledge

While message framing may provide a strategic approach to the way in which messages should be presented, it is also necessary to consider how the detail of a message should be included in order to maximise effectiveness. Consideration is now given to the balance of information and emotion in a message, the structure in terms of how an argument should be presented and the actual appeal, whether it be based on information or emotion.

Message balance

It is evident from previous discussions that the effectiveness of any single message is dependent on a variety of issues. From a receiver's perspective, two elements appear to be significant: first, the amount and quality of the information that is communicated and, second, the overall judgement that each individual makes about the way a message is communicated.

This suggests that the style of a message should reflect a balance between the need for information and the need for pleasure or enjoyment in consuming the message. Figure 17.2 describes the two main forms of appeal. Messages can be product-oriented and rational or customer-oriented and based on feelings and emotions.

> Where persuasion occurs through a central processing route, the emphasis of the message should be on the information content.

It is clear that when dealing with high-involvement decisions, where persuasion occurs through a central processing route, the emphasis of the message should be on the information content, in

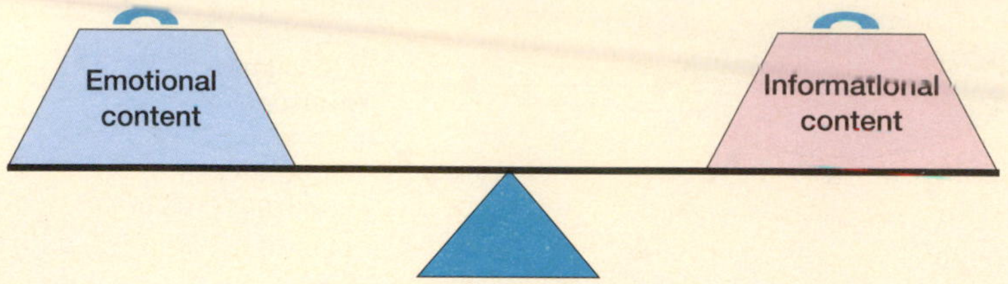

Figure 17.2 The balance of emotions and information provision

particular the key attributes and the associated benefits. This style is often factual and product-oriented. If the product evokes low-involvement decision-making, then the message should concentrate on the images that are created within the mind of the message recipient. This style seeks to elicit an emotional response from receivers. Obviously, there are many situations where both rational and emotional messages are needed by buyers in order to make purchasing decisions.

ViewPoint 17.4 Hair-raising messages

Salon brands of haircare products, such as Toni & Guy, Paul Mitchell, Fudge and Tigi, are distributed through hair salons and use the credibility that consumers bestow upon their 'regular' hairdressers as an important means to judge salon brands. Consumers delegate decision responsibilities to their professional.

Decisions about salon brands are made as a result of interpreting both rational and emotional messages. Rational messages are driven by the superior quality of the product, the strength of the relationship held with their hairdresser and the diagnosis that hairdressers provide. Emotional messages are derived from the packaging, the quality of the relationship with the hairdresser and the imagery associated with the relative exclusivity that salon brands afford. Younger buyers perceive increased 'shower cred' and older customers perceive indulgence and a treat factor.

Question

To what extent is a visit to a hair salon a low or high involvement decision? Why?

Task

Select three salon brands, consider their promotional materials (e.g. ads, packaging, salon design) and determine their message balance.

Message structure

An important part of any message strategy is a consideration of the best way of communicating the key points or core message. This needs to be accomplished carefully to avoid encouraging objections and opposing points of view. The following are regarded as some of the important structural features that can shape the pattern of a message.

Conclusion drawing

Should the message draw a firm conclusion for the audience or should people be allowed to draw their own conclusions from the content? Explicit conclusions are more easily understood and stand a better chance of being effective (Kardes, 1988). However, it is the nature of the issue, the particular situation and the composition of the target audience that influence the effectiveness of conclusion drawing (Hovland and Mandell, 1952). Whether or not a conclusion should be drawn for the receiver depends upon the following:

1. *The complexity of the issue*
   Healthcare products, central heating systems and personal finance services, for example, can be complex, and for some members of the target audience their cognitive ability, experience and motivation may not be sufficient for them to draw their own conclusions. The complexity of the product requires that messages must draw conclusions for them. It should also be remembered that even highly informed and motivated audiences may require assistance if the product or issue is relatively new.

The complexity of the product requires that messages must draw conclusions for them.

2. *The level of education possessed by the receiver*
   Better-educated audiences prefer to draw their own conclusions, whereas less-well-educated audiences may need the conclusion drawn for them because they may not be able to make the inference from the message.
3. *Whether immediate action is required*
   If urgent action is required by the receiver, then a conclusion should be drawn very clearly. Political parties can be observed to use this strategy immediately before an election.
4. *The level of involvement*
   High involvement usually means that receivers prefer to make up their own minds and may reject or resent any attempt to have the conclusion drawn for them (Arora, 1985).

ViewPoint 17.5 A Sure conclusion

The deodorant brand Sure used screen icons Steve McQueen, Elvis and James Dean to promote its Crystal for Men range. The message was that this simple antiperspirant product minimises the white marks on clothes and to convey this it used doctored pictures of the celebrities showing white stains on their clothes.

The message drew a conclusion for the audience whose low involvement required a clear one-sided message: white stains are bad, so use this product and you will avoid such problems.

Question

Discuss the view that as people generally process ads in a passive mode, only a one-sided message is necessary to be effective.

Task

Using brands that you like, what conclusions do they draw in the advertising?

One- and two-sided messages

This concerns how the case for an issue is presented. One approach is to present the case for and against an issue – a two-sided message. Alternatively just the case in favour of an issue can be presented – a one-sided message. Research indicates that one-sided messages are more effective when receivers favour the opinion offered in the message and when the receivers are less well-educated.

Two-sided messages, where both the good and the bad points of an issue are presented, are more effective when the receiver's initial opinion is opposite to that presented in the message and when they are well-educated. Credibility is improved by understanding the audience's position and then fashioning the presentation of the message. Faison (1961) found that

Two-sided messages tend to produce more positive perceptions of a source than one-sided messages.

two-sided messages tend to produce more positive perceptions of a source than one-sided messages.

Order of presentation

Further questions regarding the development of message strategy concern the order in which important points are presented. Messages that present the strongest points at the beginning use what is referred to as the *primacy* effect. The decision to place the main points at the beginning depends on whether the audience has a low or high level of involvement. A low level may require an attention-getting message component at the beginning. Similarly, if the target has an opinion opposite to that contained in the message, a weak point may lead to a high level of counter-argument.

A decision to place the strongest points at the end of the message assumes that the *recency* effect will bring about greater levels of persuasion. This is appropriate when the receiver agrees with the position adopted by the source or has a high positive level of involvement.

The order of argument presentation is more relevant in personal selling than in television advertisements.

The order of argument presentation is more relevant in personal selling than in television advertisements. However, as learning through television is largely passive, because involvement is low and interest minimal, the presentation of key selling points at the beginning and at the end of the message will enhance message reception and recall.

Message appeal

The presentation of a message requires that an appeal be made to the target audience. The appeal is important, because unless the execution of the message appeal (the creative) is appropriate to the target audience's perception and expectations, the chances of successful communication are reduced.

There are two main factors associated with the presentation. Is the message to be dominated by the need to transmit product-oriented information or is there a need to transmit a message that appeals predominantly to the emotional senses of the receiver? The main choice of presentation style, therefore, concerns the degree of factual information transmitted in a message against the level of imagery thought necessary to make sufficient impact for the message to command attention and then be processed. There are numerous presentational or executional techniques, but the following are some of the more commonly used appeals.

Information-based appeals

Factual

Sometimes referred to as the 'hard sell', the dominant objective of these appeals is to provide, often detailed, information. This type of appeal is commonly associated with high-involvement decisions where receivers are sufficiently motivated and able to process information. Persuasion, according to the ELM, is undertaken through the central processing route. This means that ads should be rational and contain logically reasoned arguments and information in order that receivers are able to complete their decision-making processes.

Slice of life

As noted earlier, the establishment of credibility is vital if any message is to be accepted and processed. One of the ways in which this can be achieved is to present the message in such a way that the receiver can identify immediately with the scenario being presented. This process of creating similarity is used a great deal in advertising and is referred to as slice-of-life advertising. For example, many washing powder advertisers use a routine that depicts two ordinary women (assumed to be similar to the target receiver), invariably in a kitchen or garden, discussing the poor results achieved by one of their washing powders. Following the advice of one of the women, the stubborn stains are seen to be overcome by the focus brand.

Creating similarity is used a great deal in advertising and is referred to as slice-of-life advertising.

On successful decoding of this message the overall effect of this appeal is for the receiver to conclude the following: that person is like me; I have had the same problem as that person; they are satisfied using brand X, therefore I, too, will use brand X. This technique is simple, well-tried, well-liked and successful, despite its sexist overtones. It is also interesting to note that a number of surveys have found that a majority of women feel that advertisers use inappropriate stereotyping to portray female roles, these being predominantly housewife and mother roles.

Demonstration

A similar technique is to present the problem to the audience as a demonstration. The focus brand is depicted as instrumental in the resolution of a problem. Headache remedies, floor cleaners and tyre commercials have traditionally demonstrated the pain, the dirt and the danger respectively, and then shown how the focus brand relieves the pain (Panadol), removes the stubborn dirt (Flash or Cillit Bang) or stops in the wet on a coin (or the edge of a rooftop – Continental tyres). Whether the execution is believable is a function of the credibility and the degree of life-like dialogue or copy that is used.

Comparative advertising

Comparative advertising is a popular means of positioning brands. Messages are based on the comparison of a brand with either a main competitor brand or all competing brands, with the aim of establishing and maintaining superiority (see Exhibit 17.3). The comparison may centre on one or two key attributes and can be a good way of entering new markets. Entrants keen to establish a presence in a market have little to lose by comparing themselves with market leaders. However, market leaders have a great deal to lose and little to gain by comparing themselves with minor competitors (see Viewpoint 17.6).

ViewPoint 17.6 Comparative bunnies

Duracell has established itself as the leading battery manufacturer in many markets, including the United Kingdom. Its advertising messages are information-based and use the strength and longevity of its batteries as the key attribute upon which it wants to be evaluated. Independent tests verify the Duracell attribute claims and prevent any counter-claim by competitors. Its positioning, with regard to ordinary zinc carbon batteries, is emphasised through the use of the strapline 'Duracell . . . lasts longer, much longer'.

One of the interesting aspects of Duracell's approach is its use of pink bunnies to symbolise the attribute. From a consumer perspective, batteries evoke little enthusiasm or engagement, yet the use of the bunnies as peripheral cues (see Chapter 7) enables consumers to connect with the Duracell brand, provides stand-out in the category and enables consumers to remember the key brand messages.

Question

Appraise the view that the use of comparative advertising should be encouraged as it provides consumers with a more balanced view of a brand.

Task

Visit an online comparison site (e.g. Kelco) and determine the extent to which the information provided is of practical assistance to consumers.

Exhibit 17.3 Duracell using comparative messages.
Duracell 'Mountain' ad image © Duracell 2006. Used with permission.

Emotions- and feelings-based appeals

Appeals based on logic and reason are necessary in particular situations, especially where there is high involvement. However, as products become similar and as consumers become more aware of what is available in the category, so the need to differentiate becomes more important. Increasing numbers of advertisers are using messages that seek to appeal to the target's emotions and feelings, a 'soft sell'. Cars, toothpaste, toilet tissue and mineral water often use emotion-based messages to differentiate their products' position.

There are a number of appeals that can be used to elicit an emotional response from an individual receiver. Of the many techniques available, the main ones that can be observed to be used most are fear, humour, animation, sex, music and fantasy and surrealism.

Fear

Fear is used in one of two ways. The first type demonstrates the negative aspects or physical dangers associated with a particular behaviour or improper product usage. Drink driving, life assurance and toothpaste advertising typify this form of appeal. For example, Scottish Widows, a financial services brand belonging to Lloyds TSB has used a lady dressed in a black cape to symbolise the 'Widow'. The 'Widow' has become synonymous with the brand – even taking on iconic status – especially as research shows that four out of five people can link the image with the company.

The second approach is the threat of social rejection or disapproval if the brand is not used. This type of fear is used frequently in advertisements for such products as anti-dandruff shampoos and deodorants and is used to support consumers' needs for social acceptance and approval.

Fear appeals need to be constrained, if only to avoid being categorised as outrageous and socially unacceptable. There is a great deal of evidence that fear can facilitate attention and interest in a message and even motivate an individual to take a particular course of action: for example to stop smoking. Fear appeals are persuasive, according to Schiffman and Kanuk (1991), when low to moderate levels of fear are induced. Ray and Wilkie (1970), however, show that should the level of fear rise too much, inhibiting effects may prevent the desired action occurring. This inhibition is caused by the individual choosing to screen out, through perceptive selection, messages that conflict with current behaviour. The outcome may be that individuals deny the existence of a problem, claim there is no proof or say that it will not happen to them.

Fear appeals need to be constrained, if only to avoid being categorised as outrageous and socially unacceptable.

Humour

If receivers are in a positive mood they are more likely to process advertising messages with little cognitive elaboration (Batra and Stayman, 1990). The use of humour as an emotional appeal is attractive because it can attract attention, stimulate interest and foster a positive mood. This can occur because there is less effort involved with peripheral rather than central cognitive processing, and this helps to mood protect. In other words, the positive mood state is more likely to be maintained if cognitive effort is avoided. Both Yellow Pages and 118 118 have used humour to help convey the essence of their brand and to help differentiate it from the competition.

The use of humour as an emotional appeal is attractive because it can attract attention, stimulate interest and foster a positive mood.

Zhang and Zinkhan (2006) found that humour is more effective when there is low rather than high involvement. They also consider whether the media used also influences the influence of humour. For example, television and radio demand less effort to process messages compared with print work. The choice of media used to deliver humorous content can therefore be critical.

It is also argued that humour is effective because argument quality is likely to be high. That is, the level of counter-argument can be substantially reduced. Arguments against the use of humour concern distraction from the focus brand, so that while attention is drawn, the message itself is lost. With the move to global branding and standardisation of advertising messages, humour does not travel well. While the level and type of humour are difficult to gauge in the context of the processing abilities of a domestic target audience, cultural differences seriously impede the transfer of jokes around the world.

Visual humour such as that generated by Catherine Tate, Little Britain and the older lavatorial humour that made Benny Hill so popular, is according to Archer (1994) more universally acceptable than word-based humour. This is partly because word-based humour can get lost in translation, without local references to provide the clues in order to decipher the joke. Humour, therefore, is a potentially powerful yet dangerous form of appeal. Haas (1997) reports that UK advertising executives have significantly higher confidence in the use of humour than their US counterparts, but concludes that 'humour is a vague concept and [. . .] its perception is influenced by many factors' (p. 15). These factors shape the context in which messages are perceived and the humour conveyed.

Animation

Animation techniques have advanced considerably in recent years, with children as the prime target audience. However, animation has been successfully used in many adult-targeted advertisements, such as those by Schweppes, Compaq, Tetley Tea, Direct Line Insurance and British Gas. The main reason for using animation is that potentially boring and low-interest/involvement products can be made visually interesting and provide a means of gaining attention. A further reason for the use of animation is that it is easier to convey complex products in a way that does not patronise the viewer.

Sex

Sexual innuendo and the use of sex as a means of promoting products and services are both common and controversial. Using sex as an appeal in messages is excellent for gaining the attention of buyers. Research shows, however, that it often achieves little else, particularly when the product is unrelated. Therefore, sex appeals normally work well for products such as perfume, clothing and jewellery but provide for poor effectiveness when the product is unrelated, such as cars, photocopiers and furniture. Häagen Dazs premium ice-cream entered the UK market using pleasure as central to the message appeal. This approach was novel to the product class and the direct, natural relationship between the product and the theme contributed to the campaign's success.

Using sex as an appeal in messages is excellent for gaining the attention of buyers.

The use of sex in advertising messages is mainly restricted to getting the attention of the audience and, in some circumstances, sustaining interest. It can be used openly, as in various lingerie, fragrance and perfume advertisements, such as WonderBra and Escape; sensually, as in the Häagen Dazs and Cointreau campaigns; and humorously in the Locketts brand.

Music

Music can provide continuity between a series of advertisements and can also be a good peripheral cue. A jingle, melody or tune, if repeated sufficiently, can become associated with the advertisement. Processing and attitudes towards the advertisement may be directly influenced by the music. Music has the potential to gain attention and assist product differentiation. Braithwaite and Ware (1997) found that music in advertising messages is used primarily either to create a mood or to send a branded message. In addition, music can also be used to signal a lifestyle and so communicate a brand identity through the style of music used.

Processing and attitudes towards the advertisement may be directly influenced by the music.

Many advertisements for cars use music, partly because it is difficult to find a point of differentiation (*Independent*, 18 October 1996), and music is able to draw attention, generate mood and express brand personality (e.g. BMW, Nissan Micra, Peugeot, Renault).

Some luxury and executive cars are advertised using commanding background music to create an aura of power, prestige and affluence, which is combined with strong visual images in order that an association be made between the car and the environment in which it is positioned. There is a contextual juxtaposition between the car and the environment presented. Readers may notice a semblance of classical conditioning, where the music acts as an unconditioned stimulus. Foxall and Goldsmith (1994) suggest that the stimulus elicits the unconditioned emotional responses that may lead to the purchase of the advertised product.

When David Cameron spoke at the Conservative Party conference in October 2006 he walked onto the stage accompanied by the rock music 'All these things I have done' by The Killers. He then proceeded to set out the new values held by the party and to urge them forward with purpose (WNIM, 2007). Music was used contextually, to suggest change and manage expectations.

Fantasy and surrealism

By using fantasy appeals, associations with certain images and symbols allow the advertiser to focus attention on the product.

The use of fantasy and surrealism in advertising has grown partly as a result of the increased clutter and legal constraints imposed on some product classes. By using fantasy appeals, associations with certain images and symbols allow the advertiser to focus attention on the product. The receiver can engage in the distraction offered and become involved with the execution of the advertisement. If this is a rewarding experience it may be possible to affect the receiver's attitudes peripherally. Readers may notice that this links to the earlier discussion on 'liking the advertisement'.

Finally, an interesting contribution to the discussion of message appeals has been made by Lannon (1992). She reports that consumers' expectations of advertisements can be interpreted on the one hand as either literal or stylish and on the other as serious or entertaining, according to the tone of voice. This approach vindicates the view that consumers are active problem-solvers and willing and able to decode increasingly complex messages. They can become involved with the execution of the advertisement and the product attributes. The degree of involvement (she argues implicitly) is a function of the motivation each individual has at any one moment when exposed to a particular message.

Advertisers can challenge individuals by presenting questions and visual stimuli that demand attention and cognitive response. Guinness challenged consumers to decode a series of advertisements that were unlike all previous Guinness advertisements and, indeed, all messages in the product class. The celebrity chosen was dressed completely in black, which contrasted with his blond hair, and he was shown in various time periods, past and future, and environments that receivers did not expect. He was intended to represent the personification of the drink and symbolised the individual nature of the product. Audiences were puzzled by the presentation and many rejected the challenge of interpretation. 'Surfer' and 'Bet on Black' are more recent Guinness campaigns that seek to convey the importance and necessity to wait (for the drink to be poured properly). To accomplish this, it portrays a variety of situations in which patience results in achievement.

When individuals respond positively to a challenge, the advertiser can either provide closure (an answer) or, through surreal appeals, leave the receivers to answer the questions themselves in the context in which they perceive the message. One way of achieving this challenging position is to use an appeal that cognitively disorients the receiver (Parker and Churchill, 1986). If receivers are led to ask the question 'What is going on here?' their involvement in the message is likely to be very high. Benetton consistently raises questions through its advertising. By presenting a series of messages that are socially disorienting, and for many disconcerting, Benetton continually presents a challenge that moves away from involving individuals into an approach where salience and 'standing out' predominates. This high-risk strategy, with a risk of rejection, has prevailed for a number of years.

The surrealist approach does not provide or allow for closure. The conformist approach, by contrast, does require closure in order to avoid any possible counter-arguing and message rejection. Parker and Churchill argue that, by leaving questions unanswered, receivers can become involved in both the product and the execution of the advertisement. Indeed, most advertisements contain a measure of rational and emotional elements. A blend of the two elements is necessary and the right mixture is dependent upon the perceived risk and motivation that the target audience has at any one particular moment.

The message appeal should be a balance of the informative and emotional dimensions.

The message appeal should be a balance of the informative and emotional dimensions. Furthermore, message quality is of paramount importance. Buzzell (1964) reported that, 'Advertising message quality is more important than the level of advertising expenditure' (p. 30). Adams and Henderson Blair (1992) confirm that the weight of advertising is relatively unimportant, and that the quality of the appeal is the dominant factor. However, the correct blend of informative and emotional elements in any appeal is paramount for persuasive effectiveness.

Copycat messaging

There are certain occasions where the appeal used by a follower brand can be judged to mimic that of the brand leader. The reasoning for adopting a copycat approach may be that the category has been revolutionised by the brand leader. For example, Magners revitalised the stagnant UK cider market by demonstrating its refreshment property through television and poster ads that showed the drink being poured over ice. Sales boomed to £17m in 2006 with the result that competitors are copycatting the approach. For example, Bulmers now claim their cider brand is 'Born for Ice' and a new brand, Maguires, has entered the market, also based on the over-ice proposition (Bowery, 2007).

Using a similar style of message can be used strategically, to diffuse the potency of the brand leader's marketing communications. Bowery refers to Matalan's use of four models that aped Marks & Spencer's iconic campaign based around Twiggy and three other models. Matalan did not reinforce their approach with a subsequent high-profile campaign but M&S have continued the message strategy to great effect.

Advertising tactics

The main creative elements of a message need to be brought together in order for an advertising plan to have substance. The processes used to develop message appeals need to be open but systematic.

The level of involvement and combination of the think/emotional dimensions that receivers bring to their decision-making processes are the core concepts to be considered when creating an advertising message. Rossiter and Percy (1997) have devised a deductive framework that involves the disaggregation of the emotional (feel) dimension to a greater degree than that proposed by Vaughn (1980) (see Chapter 16 for details). They claim that there are two broad types of motive that drive attitudes towards purchase behaviour. These are informational and transformational motives and are now considered in turn.

Informational motives

Individuals have a need for information to counter negative concerns about a purchase decision. These informational motives (see Table 17.2) are said to be negatively charged feelings. They can become positively charged, or the level of concern can be reduced considerably, by the acquisition of relevant information.

Transformational motives

Promises to enhance or to improve the user of a brand are referred to as transformational motives. These are related to the user's feelings and are capable of transforming a user's emotional state, hence they are positively charged. Three main transformational motives have been distinguished by Rossiter *et al.* (1991) (see Table 17.3). Various emotional states can be associated with each of these motives, and they should be used to portray an emotion that is appropriate to the needs of the target audience.

> Promises to enhance or to improve the user of a brand are referred to as transformational motives.

For example, Cancer Research UK changed the approach it used to communicate with donors. For a while, its campaigns used to

Table 17.2 Informational motives

Motive	Possible emotional state
Problem removal	Anger–relief
Problem avoidance	Fear–relaxation
Incomplete satisfaction	Disappointment–optimism
Mixed approach–avoidance	Guilt–peace of mind
Normal depletion	Mild annoyance–convenience

Table 17.3 Transformational motives

Motive	Possible emotional state
Sensory gratification	Dull–elated
Intellectual stimulation	Bored–excited
Social approval	Apprehensive–flattered

convey messages about family loss and in that sense adopted a negative approach. The charity then adopted an 'All Clear' campaign. This conveyed messages about people diagnosed with cancer and their improved chances of recovery due to the benefits of the research. For many people this is low-involvement with transformational motives. This means that the use of an emotional-based claim in the message is important. The happy ending, based on people surviving, achieves this while the endline uses a voice-over that requests a donation so that the words 'all clear' can be heard by more people in the future.

One of the key communication objectives, identified earlier, is the need to create or improve levels of awareness regarding the product or organisation. This is achieved by determining whether awareness is required at the point of purchase or prior to purchase. Brand recognition (at the point of purchase) requires an emphasis upon visual stimuli, the package and the brand name, whereas brand recall (prior to purchase) requires an emphasis on a limited number of peripheral cues. These may be particular copy lines, the use of music or colours for continuity and attention-grabbing frequent use of the brand name in the context of the category need, or perhaps the use of strange or unexpected presentation formats.

ViewPoint 17.7 Messaging functional foods

Increasingly, food manufacturers are redeveloping foods so that they provide functional benefits. These products claim to improve a person's health, by lowering their cholesterol level for example, or by improving their digestive systems, providing extra energy or even making people cleverer. Brands such as a Tropicana juice drink contain extra calcium to build bone health and strength. Kingsmill make Head Start, a bread that contains Omega-3, designed to improve brain health. The success of Actimel yoghurt drinks is based on its probiotic content that provides immunity and eases the digestive tract. These and many other products are based on scientific developments and are proving to be popular.

One of the problems facing functional food manufacturers is how best to communicate the benefits. By providing too much scientific information audiences become confused and switch off. Providing too little information about the benefits can result in the message not getting through. When Kellogg's launched Rice Crispies Muddles, a prebiotic for children the message failed to penetrate the market and the brand was altered to Rice Krispies Multigrain (Bashford, 2007).

There is an argument that in the future, specialist functional foods need to be targeted at specific niche, lifestage segments, middle-agers with high cholesterol, and older women with brittle bones. These need to be coupled with simplified messages that convey particular health benefits.

Sources: Adapted from Bashford (2007); Simms (2007b).

Question

Should functional foods provide for transformational or informational messages?

Task

Select a grocery product of your choice, visit the web site and determine whether the overall message is informational or transformational. Justify your response.

Exhibit 17.4 Functional foods, such as Actimel and Branston Baked Beans, need to communicate their key benefits clearly and in an unscientific manner
Courtesy of Danone; Paul Mogford/Alamy.

Advertising tactics can be determined by the particular combination of involvement and motives that exist at a particular time within the target audience. If a high-involvement decision process is determined, with people using a central processing route, then the types of tactics shown in Figures 17.3 and 17.4 are recommended (Rossiter and Percy, 1997). If a

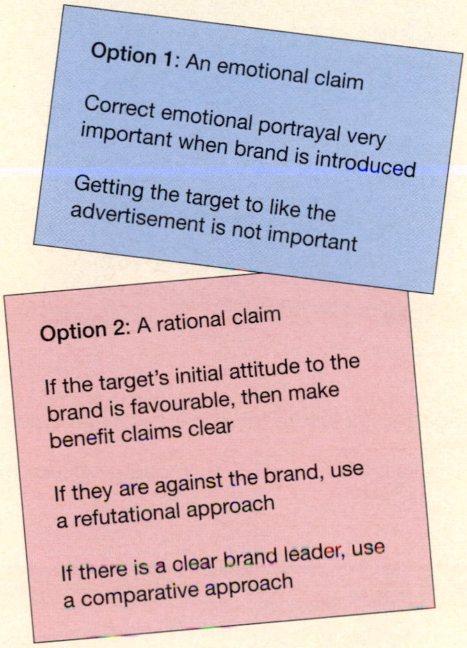
Option 1: An emotional claim
Correct emotional portrayal very important when brand is introduced
Getting the target to like the advertisement is not important
Option 2: A rational claim
If the target's initial attitude to the brand is favourable, then make benefit claims clear
If they are against the brand, use a refutational approach
If there is a clear brand leader, use a comparative approach

Figure 17.3 Message tactics where there are high involvement and informational motives
Source: After Rossiter and Percy (1997). Used with kind permission.

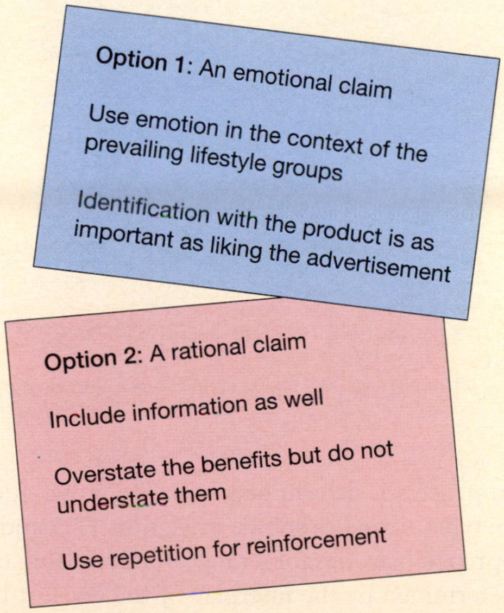
Option 1: An emotional claim
Use emotion in the context of the prevailing lifestyle groups
Identification with the product is as important as liking the advertisement
Option 2: A rational claim
Include information as well
Overstate the benefits but do not understate them
Use repetition for reinforcement

Figure 17.4 Message tactics where there are high involvement and transformational motives
Source: After Rossiter and Percy (1997). Used with kind permission.

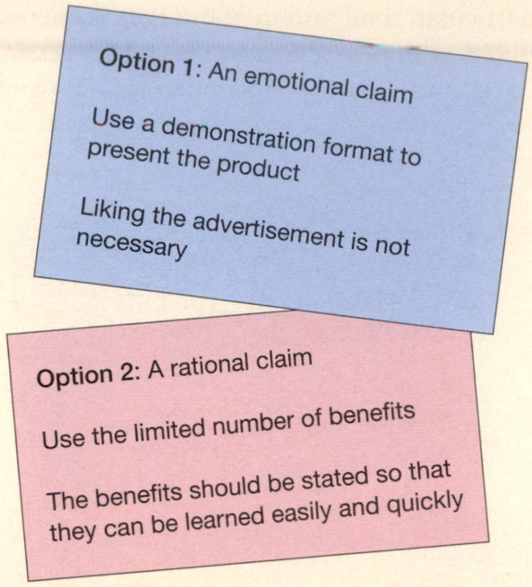
Option 1: An emotional claim
Use a demonstration format to present the product
Liking the advertisement is not necessary
Option 2: A rational claim
Use the limited number of benefits
The benefits should be stated so that they can be learned easily and quickly

Figure 17.5 Message tactics where there are low involvement and informational motives
Source: After Rossiter and Percy (1997). Used with kind permission.

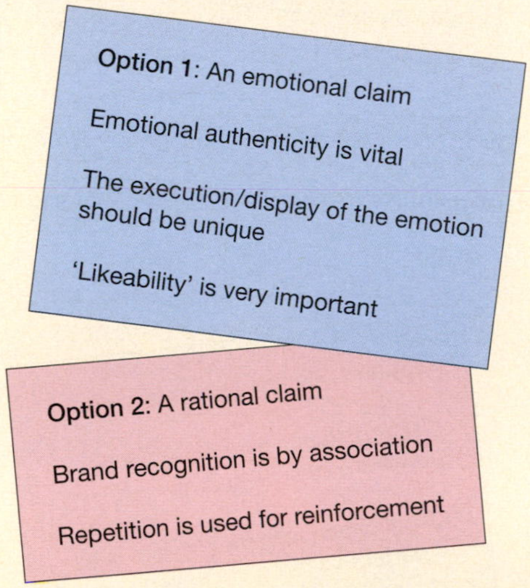
Option 1: An emotional claim
Emotional authenticity is vital
The execution/display of the emotion should be unique
'Likeability' is very important
Option 2: A rational claim
Brand recognition is by association
Repetition is used for reinforcement

Figure 17.6 Message tactics where there are low involvement and transformational motives
Source: After Rossiter and Percy (1997). Used with kind permission.

low-involvement decision process is determined, with the target audience using a peripheral processing route, then the types of tactics shown in Figures 17.5 and 17.6 are recommended.

The Rossiter–Percy approach provides for a range of advertising tactics that are oriented to the conditions that are determined by the interplay of the level of involvement and the type of dominant motivation. These conditions may only exist within a member of the target audience for a certain period. Consequently, they may change and the advertising tactics may also have to change to meet the new conditions. There are two main points that emerge from the work of Rossiter and Percy. The first is that all messages should be designed to carry both rational, logical information and emotional stimuli, but in varying degrees and forms. Second, low-involvement conditions require the use of just one or two benefits in a message, whereas high-involvement conditions can sustain a number of different benefit claims. This is because persuasion through the central processing route is characterised by an evaluation of the alternatives within any one product category.

Summary

In order to help consolidate your understanding of messages and content, here are the key points summarised against each of the learning objectives:

1. Show how messages can be constructed to account for the context in which they are to be received.

Messages need to be developed based on the needs of the target audience and the environment in which they will consume the communication. Issues such as their level of knowledge about the brand, involvement and education affect the way messages are presented.

2. Examine the importance and characteristics of using source credibility.

Source credibility consists of three key elements: the level of perceived expertise; the personal motives for the source is believed to possess; and the degree of trust that can be placed in what the source says or does on behalf of the endorsement. Consumers trade off the validity of claims made by brands against the perceived trustworthiness (and expertise) of the individuals or organisations who deliver the message.

3. Explore the advantages and disadvantages of using spokespersons in message presentation.

The use of spokespersons can draw attention and publicity to a brand, but should they fail to provide credibility or contravene a society's norms then the brand may be harmed.

4. Discuss the impact of user-generated-content.

The use of user-generated-content is increasing as communication becomes more democratised and technology advances. Information is increasingly being shared by consumers and content created in many different ways, including blogs, discussion boards and social networks.

5. Examine ideas concerning message framing.

Message framing works on the hedonic principles of our motivation to seek happiness and to avoid pain. Messages can be framed to either focus attention on positive outcomes (happiness) or take them away from the possible negative outcomes (pain).

Three factors (self-construal, consumer involvement and product knowledge) moderate an individual's response when they are exposed to a positively or negatively framed brand message. In turn these influence the brand communication persuasiveness.

6. Consider how advertising messages might be best presented.

Attention to message balance, structure and the form of the appeal is important if a message is to be successful and help achieve a campaign's goals.

7. Examine the use of emotions and feelings in advertising messages.

Increasing numbers of advertisers are using messages that seek to appeal to a target audience's emotions and feelings. This is necessary when products become similar and as consumers become more aware of what is available in the category. Of the many techniques available, the main ones used are fear, humour, animation, sex, music and fantasy and surrealism.

8. Indicate how informational and transformational motives can be used as tactical tools in an advertising plan.

It is claimed that there are two broad types of motive that drive attitudes towards purchase behaviour. These are informational and transformational motives. Individuals have a need for information to counter negative concerns about a purchase decision. These informational motives are said to be negatively charged feelings. They can become positively charged, or the level of concern can be reduced considerably, by the acquisition of relevant information.

Promises to enhance or to improve a brand are referred to as transformational motives. These are related to the user's feelings and are capable of transforming a user's emotional state, hence they are positively charged.

Review questions

1. Describe each of the four elements needed to create promotional messages.
2. Explain the concept of source credibility.
3. Discuss what is meant by the term 'balance' when applied to an advertising message.
4. How might an understanding of conclusion drawing assist the development of an advertising message?
5. Select five print advertisements and comment on the nature and extent to which the order of presentation features in each of them.
6. Why do advertisers use spokespersons in their advertising? Find examples of each type of spokesperson.
7. Why is the use of user-generated-content increasing?
8. What are the main types of appeal that are used by advertisers?
9. Find examples of advertising messages for each of the main appeals identified.
10. Explain the difference between informational and transformational motivations.

MiniCase The Apache motorcycle advertising campaign in India

Poonam V. Kumar: TNS – Asia Pacific & Middle East
Prasad Narasimhan: TVS Motor Company India
Adapted by
Clive Nancarrow: University of the West of England

This minicase is the second of two. It is advised that the first case is read before this one. Please see the case at the end of Chapter 6, p. 191.

Liberation – Life, Here I come!!!

With increasing competition, the dialogue between the consumer and marketer grows in sophistication and the balance of power shifts to the consumer. Marketing then has to shift from push to pull. From selling and product-focused marketing, the market moves to a need for brands that connect with consumer emotion. The Indian two-wheeler market was waiting for brands like Apache that understood this and met not only the need for great mileage and reliability, but also emotional needs.

NeedScope, through the use of a needs-based model, identified the discriminating needs. The underlying motivations were validated and quantified in terms of the commercial opportunity offered. Brands were mapped and measured on the same frame of reference and market gaps identified. TNS, a leading global marketing research agency, partnered the client in bringing the segments to life and in the development of concepts and guidance to the advertising and design team.

On the basis of the customer research described more fully earlier in this text (see p. 191) an opportunity for marketing a motorbike was identified – that of fulfilling a desire for freedom – the need for 'Liberation'.

The next step was to understand all the nuances and layers of Liberation. Based on their research, the following analysis was completed to guide the creative development.

- Emotively, Liberation represents the wonder years in a man's life. The first taste of freedom, the first coming into adulthood. A time of freedom, fun, exploration of the world and experiences before responsibility and the realities of life take over. The bike in this need state symbolises a rite of passage – the boy becomes a man – and is the ideal partner with which to explore spaces, both physically and emotively. In the physical sense it is about mobility. Emotionally it is about reaching places you have never been.
- Liberation evokes the heady kick and excitement of youth, the exciting discovery of adulthood and the bike is integral as a source of pleasure.
- There was a definite younger demographic skew, but the need also extended to the 'Young at Heart'. For the young man, the motorbike is a symbol used to flaunt his adult status. With older men it is about recapturing moments gone by, the wish for eternal youth.
- The social values of the need state are younger men in the golden period between boys and adult men. The need has a strong peer context, typical to that life stage. The need for affiliation, togetherness is also reflected in the relationship with the bike – a buddy to share the fun with.
- With every brand boasting of an international collaboration, this was not a differentiating nor for that matter a motivating proposition. International technology is obviously desirable, but there is also an emerging pride and comfort, especially among the youth about being Indian and Indianness.
- Functional delivery needs to live up to the vibrant need for a trendy, cool experience – a combination of speed, power, pick-up and trendy looks – advanced technology to reflect the fast-paced lifestyles of the emerging Indian youth.

Two concepts were developed and tested on the same frame of reference.

And so the Apache was born!

It's now or never!!!

The Apache operates at all levels, fulfilling emotional needs through relevant symbolic and social values and meeting functional needs:

Symbolic values – Living life in the moment. Targeting that part of every man that brings back the wonder years – of Freedom, of Irresponsibility, of LIVING!! A sense of release, exploration and the anticipation that the world is waiting for you! For the newly initiated, the

Exhibit 17.5 Apache advertising uses emotion to position the brand, rather than the traditional promises of functional endurance
Courtesy of TVS Motor Company Ltd.

promise of discovering a new world, for the young at heart, the recapturing of a time gone by, a retreat to Ladland!! About living life to the fullest and making most of the moment.

Social values – Unattached, young, popular men with lots of friends and popular with the girls.

Functional promise – Easy maintenance and great accessories (coupled with stylish looks), power and pick-up, lightness to reflect the mood.

How is this delivered in communications?

It is driven by those whom young people identify with and resemble (not celebrities). The brand has to be the rage of the moment – something that everyone is talking about. This was brought about by innovative co-sponsorship and partnership of events and promotions – on Channel V and MotoGP.

The tone of advertising is irreverent, but inoffensively so. It is fun, easygoing, defying conventions and conservatism without becoming rebellious or edgy.

The television commercial is set to a rap tune, but the words are in an Indian language – in tune with the current youth's desire for a blend of the international with the Indian – a distinct flavour of modern India.

The strongly evocative emotional proposition was also translated into trendy style and irresistible features. Notably, the much-used propositions of reliability and mileage promises were absent (see Exhibit 17.5).

The seeming purposelessness about the functional promises reinforced the indulgent, wonderful irresponsibility of the carefree, fun emotive positioning.

All activities and touch points were aligned with the symbolic positioning – partnership promotion with a trendy retail outlet, sponsorship on MotoGP sports (see Exhibit 17.6).

In all, Apache is a brand where all layers of needs and all marketing touch points were in perfect harmony and therefore the rewards, recognition and success inevitably had to follow.

The taste of success

Apache has been voted as the bike of the year by almost all stakeholder groups. The brand struck a deep chord with the auto experts, the auto media and most importantly with the consumers.

A final word

This case is not just about bold decision-making and creating the right concept. The execution and implementation remained true to the archetypal positioning and delivered the perfect tonality. The advertising created was completely different from both anything TVS had done before and a complete break from the corporate image. To ensure that the planners remained true to the archetype and did not give in to the temptation of resorting to a comfortable direction that had worked before, a principle of NOTness was used to develop the advertising and marketing communication.

Apache is . . .

- *Not* doing stuff by himself, but with a group – to be different from Potency and to avoid the temptation

Exhibit 17.6 Carefree emotional advertising was used with co-sponsorship activities to stimulate word of mouth communication
Courtesy of TVS Motor Company Ltd.

Exhibit 17.7 Apache advertising was used to create associations with liberation and freedom
Courtesy of TVS Motor Company Ltd.

of showing an all-man, rugged terrain bike that conquers elements and space.

- *Not* with a girlfriend – to keep away from the hackneyed boy–girl story that all youth brands tell. Instead, the bike was about having NO commitments.
- *Not* aspirationally upwardly mobile, or about success at work – again a temptation of all new launches to ride the optimism of the 'Shining India' mood. The bike was not about status or success – instead the optimism was captured by a carefree attitude that enables living of life without worrying about tomorrow.
- *Not* about family and the responsibilities that come with family – to avoid temptation to capture not just the youth, but family people as well.
- *Not* overtly premium – although modernity and premiumness were conveyed through features and styling rather than by exclusivity. The bike SPOKE the archetype.

And finally, there was realisation that to target Liberation, the planners and brand managers had to feel and live the archetype. They had to break out of their Brahmin engineering, rooted in rationality mindset. The team therefore had fun spending several Friday afternoons observing young people and testing the waters at the several pubs and cafes of Bangalore.

Note: This minicase is based on a paper given at ESOMAR Annual Congress, Berlin, September 2007 by Poonam Kumar, Motivational Research, APAC Region, TNS Asia, India & Prasad Narsimhan TVS Motor Company, India (ESOMAR Copyright).

MiniCase references and further reading

Gladwell, M. (1997) *The Coolhunt, New Yorker*, March 17, 78.

Knobil, M. (2002) What makes a brand cool? Market Leader, *Journal of the Marketing Society*, **18**, 21–5.

Nancarrow, C. and Nancarrow, P. (2007) Hunting for Cool Tribes. In *Consumer Tribes* (eds Cova, B., Kozinets, R.V. and Shankar, A.). Oxford: Butterworth Heinemann.

Robbins, D. (1991) *The Work of Pierre Bourdieu*. Milton Keynes: Open University Press.

Smith, S. (2003) *How to Bottle Cool, Sunday Times Style*, 10 August, 24–5.

Thornton, S. (1995) *Club Cultures: Music, Media and Subcultural Capital*. Cambridge: Polity Press.

MiniCase questions

1. Would word-of-mouth (WoM) be important in this case and how might you stimulate this?
2. What research would you carry out to determine if the advertising was working, which executions work particularly well and with whom? What would be the key questions the research should address?
3. Being cool is often important in youth markets. Does Apache have the ingredients to be 'cool' and is the concept of consumer tribe relevant?
4. Can you think of any cool brands?

References

Adams, A.J. and Henderson Blair, M. (1992) Persuasive advertising and sales accountability. *Journal of Advertising Research*, **32**(2) (March/April), 20–5.

Alleyne, R. (2005) Kate Moss is dropped as the face of H&M, *Daily Telegraph*, 21 September. Retrieved 13 November 2007 from www.telegraph.co.uk/fashion/main.jhtml?xml=/fashion/2005/09/21/efkate21.xml.

Alleyne, R. (2005) Kate Moss apologises as Rimmel expresses 'shock and dismay'. *Daily Telegraph*, 23 September. Retrieved 13 November 2007 from www.telegraph.co.uk/fashion/main.jhtml?xml=/fashion/2005/09/23/efkate23.xml.

Anon. (2006) Kate Moss is the new face of Calvin Klein. *The Times*, 10 April. Retrieved 13 November from http://entertainment.timesonline.co.uk/tol/arts_and_entertainment/article703897.ece.

Archer, B. (1994) Does humour cross borders? *Campaign*, 17 June, 32–3.

Armstrong, L. (2006) Topshop deal keeps Kate Moss at the height of fashion. *The Times*, 21 September. Retrieved 13 November from http://women.timesonline.co.uk/tol/life_and_style/women/fashion/article646025.ece.

Arora, R. (1985) Consumer involvement: what it offers to advertising strategy. *International Journal of Advertising*, **4**, 119–30.

Bashford, S. (2007) Functional foods: Now with added . . . *Marketing*, 29 August, 26–9.

Batra, R. and Stayman, D.M. (1990) The role of mood in advertising effectiveness. *Journal of Consumer Research*, **17** (September), 203–14.

Bosman, J. (2006) Chevy tries a write-your-own-ad approach and the potshots fly. *New York Times*, 4 April, B3.

Bowery, J. (2007) Haven't I seen you before? *Marketing*, 6 June, 17.

Braithwaite, A. and Ware, R. (1997) The role of music in advertising. *Admap* (July/August), 44–7.

Buzzell, R. (1964) Predicting short-term changes in market share as a function of advertising strategy. *Journal of Marketing Research*, **1**(3), 27–31.

Faison, E.W. (1961) Effectiveness of one-sided and two-sided mass communications in advertising. *Public Opinion Quarterly*, **25** (Autumn), 468–9.

Foxall, G.R. and Goldsmith, R.E. (1994) *Consumer Psychology for Marketing*. London: Routledge.

Haas, O. (1997) Humour in advertising. *Admap* (July/August), 14–15.

Hannah, D.B. and Sternthal, B. (1984) Detecting and explaining the sleeper effect. *Journal of Consumer Research*, 11 September, 632–42.

Hovland, C.I., Lumsdaine, A. and Sheffield, F.D. (1949) *Experiments on Mass Communication*. New York: Wiley.

Hovland, C.I. and Mandell, W. (1952) An experimental comparison of conclusion drawing by the communicator and by the audience. *Journal of Abnormal and Social Psychology*, **47** (July), 581–8.

Kardes, F.R. (1988) Spontaneous inference processes in advertising: the effects of conclusion omission and involvement on persuasion. *Journal of Consumer Research*, **15** (September), 225–33.

Kelman, H. (1961) Processes of opinion change. *Public Opinion Quarterly*, **25** (Spring), 57–78.

Lafferty, B.A., Goldsmith, R.E. and Newell, S.J. (2002) The dual credibility model: the influence of corporate and endorser credibility on attitudes and purchase intentions. *Journal of Marketing Theory and Practice*, **10**(3), 1–12.

Lannon, J. (1992) Asking the right questions – what do people do with advertising? *Admap* (March), 11–16.

Loveless, H. (2007) Our Carol Vorderman loan nightmare, *Mail on Sunday*, 28 October. Retrieved 26 March 2008 from www.thisismoney.co.uk/campaigns/loansinsu/article.

MacKenzie, S.B. and Lutz, R.L. (1989) An empirical examination of the structural antecedents of attitude toward the ad in an advertising pretesting context. *Journal of Marketing*, **53**, 48–65.

Muñiz, A.M. and Schau, H.J. (2007) Vigilante marketing and consumer-created content communications. *Journal of Advertising*, **36**(3), (Autumn), 35–50.

Parker, R. and Churchill, L. (1986) Positioning by opening the consumer's mind. *International Journal of Advertising*, **5**, 1–13.

Ray, M.L. and Wilkie, W.L. (1970) Fear: the potential of an appeal neglected by marketing. *Journal of Marketing*, **34** (January), 54–62.

Rossiter, J.R. and Percy, L. (1997) *Advertising and Promotion Management*, 2nd edn. New York: McGraw-Hill.

Rossiter, J.R., Percy, L. and Donovan, R.J. (1991) A better advertising planning grid. *Journal of Advertising Research* (October/November), 11–21.

Rushton, S. (2007) The big question: how did Topshop become the high street's dominant fashion brand? *The Independent*, 1 May. Retrieved 13 November 2007 from http://news.independent.co.uk/uk/this_britain/article2499332.ece.

Schiffman, L.G. and Kanuk, L. (1991) *Consumer Behavior*, 4th edn. Englewood Cliffs, NJ: Prentice-Hall.

Simms, J. (2007a) Advertising: and now a word from our customers. *Marketing*, 31 January. Retrieved 16 September 2007 from http://www.brandrepublic.com/News/629458/Advertising-word-customers/.

Simms, J. (2007b) Biggest brands. *Marketing*, 22 August 2007. Retrieved 6 November 2007 from www.brandrepublic.com/InDepth/Features/734340/Functional-foods-added/.

Tsai, S.-P. (2007) Message framing strategy for brand communication. *Journal of Advertising Research*, **47**(3), (September), 364–77.

WNIM (2007) The sound of music. *What's New in Marketing*, **57** (May). Retrieved 4 November 2007 from www.wnim.com/archive/issue0507/index.htm.

Vaughn, R. (1980) How advertising works: a planning model. *Journal of Advertising Research*, **20**(5), 27–33.

Zhang, Y. and Zinkhan, G.M. (2006) Responses to humorous ads: does audience involvement matter? *Journal of Advertising*, **35**(4) (Winter), 113–27.

Chapter 18

Sales promotion: principles and techniques

Sales promotion seeks to offer additional value as an inducement to generate an immediate sale. Sales promotions can form an important part of the communication mix and are often of strategic importance. By adding value to the offer and hoping to bring forward future sales, these techniques are a source of competitive advantage, one that is invariably short-rather than long-run. The range and sophistication of the main sales promotion techniques reflect the variety of audiences, their needs and the tasks that need to be accomplished.

Aims and learning objectives

The aims of this chapter are twofold. The first is to consider the nature and role of sales promotion and to appraise its position within the marketing communications mix. The second is to consider the nature and characteristics of the main sales promotion tools and techniques.

The learning objectives of this chapter are to:

1. understand the value of sales promotions;
2. consider the role of sales promotion;
3. explain the objectives associated with using sales promotion;
4. describe the ways in which sales promotion is thought to work;
5. evaluate the merits of loyalty and retention programmes;
6. argue the case for a strategic orientation towards sales promotions;
7. explain the different sales promotions methods and techniques.

For an applied interpretation see Mary Hedderman's MiniCase entitled ***Could online coupons save the High Street?*** at the end of this chapter.

Introduction

The main task of sales promotion is to encourage the target audience to behave in a particular way, often to buy a product. Advertising, on the other hand, is usually geared towards developing market awareness. These two tools set out to accomplish tasks at each end of the attitudinal spectrum: the conative and cognitive elements respectively. Just as advertising is used to work over the long term, sales promotion can achieve short-term, upward shifts in sales.

Sales promotion offers buyers additional value, as an inducement to generate an immediate sale.

Sales promotion offers buyers additional value, as an inducement to generate an immediate sale. These inducements can be targeted at consumers, distributors, agents and members of the sales force. A whole range of network members can benefit from the use of sales promotion.

This promotional tool is traditionally referred to as a form of below-the-line communication because, unlike advertising, there are no commission payments from media owners with this form of communication. The promotional costs are borne directly by the organisation initiating the activity, which in most cases is a manufacturer, producer or service provider.

Understanding the value of sales promotions

Sales promotion is used principally as a means to accelerate sales.

There are many sales promotion techniques, but they all offer a direct inducement or an incentive to encourage receivers of these promotional messages to buy a product/service sooner rather than later. The inducement (for example, price deals, coupons, premiums) is presented as an added value to the basic product, one that is intended to encourage buyers to act 'now' rather than later. Sales promotion is used, therefore, principally as a means to accelerate sales. The acceleration represents the shortened period of time in which the transaction is completed relative to the time that would have elapsed had there not been a promotion. This action does not mean that an extra sale has been achieved, just that a potential future exchange is confirmed and transacted upon now.

Sales promotions consist of a wide range of tools and methods. These instruments are considered in more detail at the end of this chapter, but consideration of what constitutes sales promotion methods is important. In many cases, price is the determinant variable and can be used to distinguish between instruments. Sales promotions are often perceived purely as a price discounting mechanism through price deals and the use of coupons. This, however, is not the whole picture, as there are many other ways in which incentives can be offered to buyers.

Reference has already been made to the idea that sales promotions are a way of providing value, and it is this value orientation that should be used when considering the nature and essential characteristics of sales promotions. Peattie and Peattie (1994) established a useful way of discriminating between price and non-price sales promotion instruments. They refer to sales promotions that are value increasing and sales promotions that are value adding (see Table 18.1).

This demarcation is important because a large amount of research into sales promotion has been based on value-increasing approaches, most notably price deals and coupons (Gupta, 1988; Blattberg and Neslin, 1990; Krishna and Zhang, 1999). This tends to distort the way sales promotions are perceived and has led to some generalisations about the overall impact of this promotional discipline. There is a large range of other sales promotion instruments that add value and enhance the offering and which provide opportunities to drive longer-term benefits (see Table 18.2). However, research into these is limited (Gilbert and Jackaria, 2002).

Table 18.1 A value orientation of sales promotions

Value element	Explanation
Value-increasing	Value is increased by offering changes to the product quantity/quality or by lowering the price. Generally used and perceived as effective over the short term.
Value-adding	Value is added by offering something to augment the fundamental product/price offering. Premiums (gifts), information or opportunities can be offered as extras and the benefits realised over different periods of time: delayed (postal premiums), accumulated (loyalty programmes) or instant (scratch and win competitions). These have the potential to add value over the longer term.

Source: Peattie and Peattie (1994).

Table 18.2 A sales promotion typology as used in the commercial sector

Value-increasing (alters price/quantity or price/quality equation)	Value-adding (offers 'something extra' while leaving core product and price unchanged)
Discount pricing	Samples
Money-off coupons	Special features (limited editions)
Payment terms (e.g. interest-free credit)	Valued packaging
Refunds	Product trial
Guarantees	In-pack gifts
Multipack or multi-buys	In-mail gifts
Quantity increases	Piggy back gifts
Buybacks	Gift coupons
	Information (e.g. brochure, catalogue)
	Clubs or loyalty programmes
	Competitions/prize draws

As a result of this diversity of sales promotion instruments it should be no surprise to learn that they are used for a wide range of reasons. Sales promotions can be targeted, with considerable precision, at particular audiences and there are three broad audiences at whom sales promotions can be targeted: consumers, members of the distribution or channel network, and the sales forces of both manufacturers and resellers. It should be remembered that the accuracy of these promotional tools means that many sub-groups within these broad groups can be reached quickly and accurately.

Sales promotions can be targeted, with considerable precision.

Lee (2002) suggests that the main reasons for the use of sales promotions can be reduced to four:

- as a reaction to competitor activities;
- as a form of inertia – this is what we have always done;
- as a way of meeting short-term sales objectives;
- as a way of meeting long-term objectives.

Table 18.3 Reasons for the use of sales promotions

Reach new customers	They are useful in securing trials for new products and in defending shelf space against anticipated and existing competition.
Reduce distributor risk	The funds that manufacturers dedicate to them lower the distributor's risk in stocking new brands.
Reward behaviour	They can provide rewards for previous purchase behaviour.
Retention	They can provide interest and attract potential customers and in doing so encourage them to provide personal details for further communications activity.
Add value	They can encourage sampling and repeat purchase behaviour by providing extra value (superior to competitors' brands) and a reason to purchase.
Induce action	They can instil a sense of urgency among consumers to buy while a deal is available. They add excitement and interest at the point of purchase to the merchandising of mature and mundane products.
Preserve cash flow	Since sales promotion costs are incurred on a pay-as-you-go basis, they can spell survival for smaller, regional brands that cannot afford big advertising programmes.
Improve efficiency	Sales promotions allow manufacturers to use idle capacity and to adjust to demand and supply imbalances or softness in raw material prices and other input costs, while maintaining the same list prices.
Integration	They can provide a means of linking together other tools of the promotional mix.
Assist segmentation	They allow manufacturers to price discriminate among consumer segments that vary in price sensitivity. Most manufacturers believe that a high-list, high-deal policy is more profitable than offering a single price to all consumers. A portion of sales promotion expenditures, therefore, consists of reductions in list prices that are set for the least price-sensitive segment of the market.

ViewPoint 18.1 Positioning cameras with sales promotions

The Fujifilm Finepix Z10fd digital camera was designed to appeal to the 16–25-year-old youth market. Its launch in the autumn of 2007 reflected this positioning as a huge emphasis was given to Facebook. A group called 'Be part of the Seen' was created.

The musician Patrick Wolf became part of the campaign and as he was on tour at the time of the launch, he posted blogs about the tour and associated events. The number of contacts or friends within the group increased as fans of Patrick Wolf were invited to join up. By joining the group they were entered into a competition, whereby 40 winners won tickets to attend a private gig at London's Grill Room along with members of the music and entertainment press. In addition, key opinion formers and celebrity endorsers were invited to use the camera to create photo blogs. Meanwhile targeted lifestyle media were encouraged to position the camera as a Christmas 'must buy'.

The results indicated that the campaign worked. The camera appeared in 35 different titles, including a range of newspapers, lifestyle and specialist interest magazines. Interviews with Patrick Wolf appeared in the mainstream press and the gigs received coverage in a range of tabloids and other print vehicles.

Sales reached 100,000 in just three months and enabled Fujifilm to reach a new audience.

Source: Anon. (2008).

Question

The competition provided the sales incentive. What were the other tools and media used in this integrated event?

Task

Consider the tools and techniques of sales promotion in the table at the end of this chapter and then make a list of the ways Fujifilm might had delivered the launch of the Finepix.

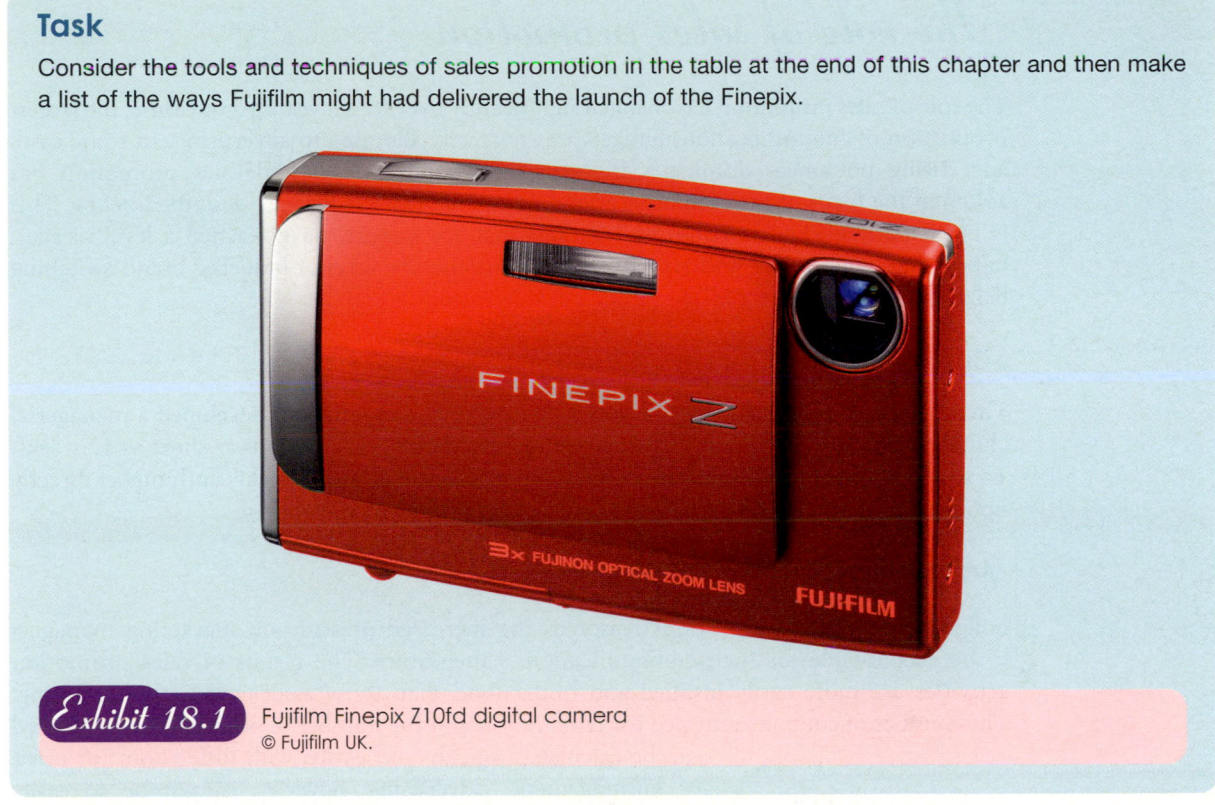

Exhibit 18.1 Fujifilm Finepix Z10fd digital camera

It appears that the first three are used widely and Lee comments that many brand owners use sales promotion as a panic measure when competitors threaten to lure customers away. Cutting prices is undoubtedly a way of prompting a short-term sales response but it can also undermine a longer-term brand strategy.

Not too many years ago sales promotions were regarded as a key way of developing sales, particularly in the grocery market. However, the use of sales promotions has stagnated and in particular the use of on-pack promotions, bonus packs, competitions and price deals have failed to maintain the growth of previous years. Reasons for the decline include changing consumer behaviour, the rise of new media and a distinct lack of innovation in the industry. Another important factor has been the expectations and drive of resellers, and the main supermarket chains in particular. They desire sales promotion programmes that are exclusive to them as this is seen as a major way of developing their retail brands. Supermarkets have effectively become media owners as their store space represents an opportunity for brand owners to promote their brands. On-pack promotions for individual stores are often too expensive and uneconomic so this form of promotion has suffered a great deal. Therefore, any form of sales promotion activity within their environments should be exclusive and tied into their brand.

New solutions have had to be found and as Barrand (2004) suggests, the use of digital media and the integration of sales promotion within other campaigns has been successful. The use of SMS, email, viral campaigns and the Internet are being used increasingly to drive sales by providing the veritable 'call-to-action', for a long time the province of sales promotion activities.

The use of digital media and the integration of sales promotion within other campaigns has been successful.

In the 1990s sales promotions were a potent part of the marketing communications mix. Today, their use has diminished as most major supermarkets try to control their in-store environments, reduce the amount of clutter and run their own promotions, designed to generate store traffic.

The role of sales promotion

The role of sales promotion has changed significantly over recent years. At one time, the largest proportion of communications budgets was normally allocated to advertising. In some cases advertising no longer dominates the communications budget and sales promotion has assumed the focus of the communications spend, for reasons that are described below. This is particularly evident in consumer markets that are mature, have reached a level of stagnation, and where price and promotion work are the few ways of inducing brand switching behaviour.

Short termism

The short-term financial focus of many industrialised economies has developed a managerial climate geared to short-term performance and evaluation, over periods as short as 12 weeks. To accomplish this, communications tools are required that work quickly and impact directly upon sales. Many see this as leading to an erosion of the brand franchise.

Managerial accountability

Following on from the previous reason is the increased pressure on marketing managers to be accountable for their communications expenditure. The results of sales promotion activities are more easily justified and understood than those associated with advertising. The number of coupons returned for redemption and the number of bonus packs purchased can be calculated quickly and easily, with little room for error or misjudgement. Advertising, however, cannot be so easily measured in either the short or the long term. The impact of this is that managers can relate the promotional expenditure to the bottom line much more comfortably with sales promotion than with advertising.

The number of coupons returned for redemption and the number of bonus packs purchased can be calculated quickly and easily.

Brand performance

Technological advances have enabled retailers to track brand performance more effectively. This in turn means that manufacturers can be drawn into agreements that promulgate in-store promotional activity at the expense of other more traditional forms of mass media promotion. Barcode scanners, hand-held, electronic shelf-checking equipment and computerised stock systems facilitate the tracking of merchandise, meaning that brand managers can be held responsible much more quickly for below-par performance.

Brand expansion

As brand quality continues to improve and as brands proliferate on the shelves of increasingly larger supermarkets, so the number of decisions that a consumer has to make also increases. Faced with multiple-brand decisions and a reduced amount of time to complete the shopping expedition, the tension associated with the shopping experience has increased considerably over the last decade.

Promotions make decision-making easier for consumers: they simplify a potentially difficult process. Thus, as brand choice increases, so the level of shopping convenience falls. The conflict this causes can be resolved by the astute use of sales promotions. Some feel that the cognitive shopper selects brands that offer increased value, which makes decision-making easier and improves the level of convenience associated with the shopping experience. However, should there be promotions on two offerings from an individual's repertoire then the decision-making is not necessarily made easier.

ViewPoint 18.2 Using nostalgia to reward cake eaters

In an attempt to reward existing customers and in doing so drive brand loyalty, Premier Foods Group Limited launched a sales promotion in 2008. The campaign was designed to engage and retain core customers rather than explicitly grow market share.

The promotion consisted of an on-pack campaign, targeted squarely at parents, not children. The mechanic consisted of on-pack voucher codes that were redeemable through two channels, online and by phone. There was no form of postal redemption. The reward itself was the chance to win various iconic toys and gifts from the past, a nostalgia based campaign. The gift products, all branded with Mini Rolls logos, included the Lava Lamp, Rubik's Cube, a 1960s retro radio, a Yo-Yo and an adult-sized Space Hopper. These prizes were derived from research into what consumers said were their favourite gifts or toys from when they were young.

The campaign used a bespoke microsite, which contained various elements designed to reflect the nostalgia theme. The online feature was important as it helped add a new dimension. Consumers were driven online to redeem their vouchers but when on the site they were then entertained.

Source: Quilter (2008).

Question

Do promotions such as this one build real brand value or just provide short term sales lifts?

Task

When you are next visiting a supermarket, make a note of any brands using an on-pack promotion.

Exhibit 18.2 Cadbury Cake promotion
Courtesy of Premier Foods Group Ltd.

Competition for shelf space

The continuing growth in the number of brands launched and the fragmentation of consumer markets mean that retailers have to be encouraged to make shelf space available. Sales promotions have helped manufacturers win valuable shelf space and assist retailers to attract increased levels of store traffic and higher utilisation of limited resources, but this approach is not always viable today.

The credibility of this promotional tool is low, as it is obvious to the receiver what the intention is of using sales promotion messages. However, because of the prominent and pervasive nature of the tool, consumers and members of the trade understand and largely accept the direct sales approach. Sales promotion is not a tool that hides its intentions, nor does it attempt to be devious (which is not allowed, by regulation).

The absolute costs of sales promotion are low, but the real costs need to be evaluated once a campaign has finished and all redemptions received and satisfied. The relative costs can be

> The real costs need to be evaluated once a campaign has finished and all redemptions received and satisfied.

high, as not only do the costs of the premium or price discount need to be determined, but also the associated costs of additional transportation, lost profit, storage and additional time spent organising and administering a sales promotion campaign need to be accounted for.

In its favour, sales promotion allows for a high degree of control. Management is able to decide just when and where a sales promotion will occur and also estimate the sales effect. Sales promotions can be turned on and off quickly and adjusted to changed market conditions.

The intended message is invariably the one that is received, as there is relatively little scope for it to be corrupted or damaged in transmission. However, this view needs to be tempered by some of the problems companies have experienced by not thinking through the sales promotion exercise in the first place, only to find themselves exposed to exploitation and financial embarrassment.

Sales promotion plans: the objectives

The objectives of using this tool are sales-oriented and geared to stimulating buyers either to use a product for the first time or to encourage use on a routine basis.

One objective of sales promotion activity is to prompt buyers into action, to initiate a series of behaviours that result in long-run purchase activity. These actions can be seen to occur in the conative stage of the attitudinal set. They reflect high or low involvement, and indicate whether cognitive processing and persuasion occur via the central or peripheral routes of the ELM (Chapter 8). If the marketing objectives include the introduction of a new product or intention to enter a new market, then the key objective associated with low-involvement decisions and peripheral route processing is to stimulate trial use as soon as possible. When high-involvement decisions and central route processing are present, then sales promotions need to be withheld until a suitable level of attitudinal development has been undertaken by public relations and advertising activities.

If a product is established in a market, then a key objective should be to use sales promotions to stimulate an increase in the number of purchases made by current customers and to attract users from competing products (see Figure 18.1). The objectives, therefore, are either

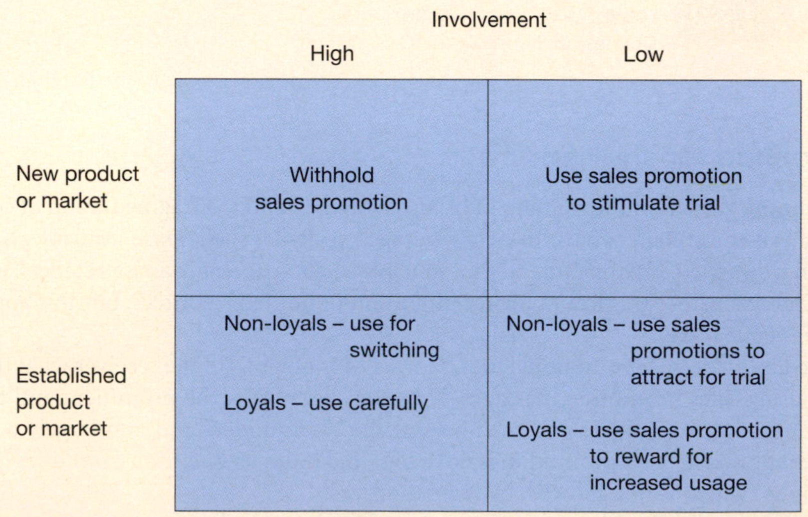

Involvement
High
Low
New product or market
Withhold sales promotion
Use sales promotion to stimulate trial
Established product or market
Non-loyals – use for switching
Loyals – use carefully
Non-loyals – use sales promotions to attract for trial
Loyals – use sales promotion to reward for increased usage

Figure 18.1 A sales promotion objectives grid

to increase consumption for established products or to stimulate trial by encouraging new buyers to use a product. Once this has been agreed, the desired trial and usage levels need to be determined for each of the target audiences. Before discussing these aspects, it is necessary first to review the manner in which sales promotions are thought to influence the behaviour of individuals.

An overview of how sales promotions work

If the overriding objectives of sales promotions are to accelerate or bring forward future sales, the implication is that a behavioural change is required by the receiver for the sales promotion to be effective. The establishment of new behaviour patterns is the preferred outcome. If sales promotions are to work over the longer term, that is, to bring about repeat purchase behaviour, then the new behaviour patterns need to be learned and adopted on a permanent basis.

This is a complex task, and is referred to by behaviourists as shaping. The behaviourists' view is advocated by Rothschild and Gaidis (1981). They suggest that by breaking the overall task into its constituent parts a series of smaller sequential tasks can be learned. When the successive actions are aggregated the new desired pattern of behaviour emerges. This view emphasises the impact of external stimuli in changing people's behaviour.

> The behaviourists' view emphasises the impact of external stimuli in changing people's behaviour.

The cognitive view of the way sales promotions operate is based on the belief that consumers internally process relevant information about a sales promotion, including those of past experiences, and make a reasoned decision in the light of the goals and objectives that individuals set for themselves.

The ELM suggests that individuals using the peripheral route will only consider simplistic cues, such as display boards and price reduction signs. Individuals using the central route of the ELM have a higher need for information and will develop the promotional signal to evaluate the value represented by the relative price and the salient attributes of the promoted product, before making a decision (Inman *et al.*, 1990).

The main difference between the views of the behaviourists and those of the cognitive school of thought is that the former stress the impact of externally generated stimuli, whereas the latter emphasise the complexity of internal information processing.

> The views of the cognitive school of thought emphasise the complexity of internal information processing.

ViewPoint 18.3 Walkers Crispy iPods

Walkers Crisps have used Gary Lineker to front its marketing communications for some time. Although still highly effective, it was important that the brand reached new younger customers, some of whom may not know who Gary Lineker is, let alone what he achieved on the football field.

To reach the younger, trendy and aspirational group, Walkers developed a sales promotion competition. Crisp eaters needed to text in a code that was to be found inside crisp packets. A prize draw was held and the winners won an iPod. In effect one iPod was won every five minutes.

A microsite designed to support the competition contained usage graphs. This enabled people to time their text submissions at quiet times and so improve their chances of winning. Over the three months the competition ran, over 7 million entries were received.

Source: Orton-Jones (2007).

Question

To what extent does this type of promotion build or devalue the brand?

Task

Find out who Walker's main competitor is. What promotions do they use?

Exhibit 18.3 Walkers competition crisp packet
Courtesy of Walkers and AMVBBDO.

The increasing proportion of budgets being allocated to sales promotions, and temporary price reductions (TPRs) in particular, has prompted concern about the costs and overall impact of these activities. It might be reasonable to expect that the sales curve following a price-based promotion would look like that depicted in Figure 18.2. There is plenty of evidence that sales volumes can be increased following use of a TPR (Ehrenberg, 2000). However, a long-term upward shift in demand is unrealistic, particularly in mature markets. Extra stock is being transferred to consumers, and therefore they have more than they require for a normal purchase cycle. Ehrenberg suggests that most people who use TPRs are actually infrequent purchasers of a given category. Research suggests that these types of promotion do not attract new buyers.

The graph shown in Figure 18.3 is more likely to occur, with sales volume falling in the period when buyers are loaded with stock and temporarily removed from the market. However, Dawes (2004) found that there were as many buyers in a market in the period following a promotion as there were when the TPR was running.

Promotional activity does not take place in a vacuum.

Promotional activity does not take place in a vacuum with new products: competitors will be attracted and some customers lost to competitive offerings; in mature markets, non-loyals will take advantage of a sales promotion and then revert to competitors' sales promotions when they re-enter the market. So, the third scenario is shown in Figure 18.4. The result is that overall demand for a brand *may* be reduced owing to the combined effects of competitive promotional activity. However, Dawes found that price promotions have a neutral impact on a brand, with

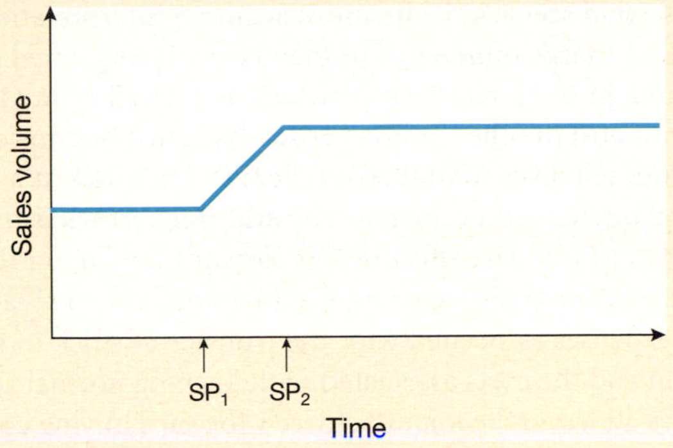

Figure 18.2 Expected response to a sales promotion event: SP_1 is the start of the event; SP_2 is the end

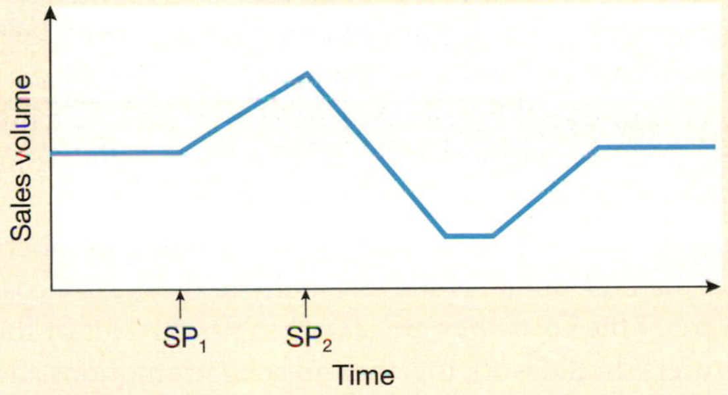

Figure 18.3 Realistic response to a sales promotion event

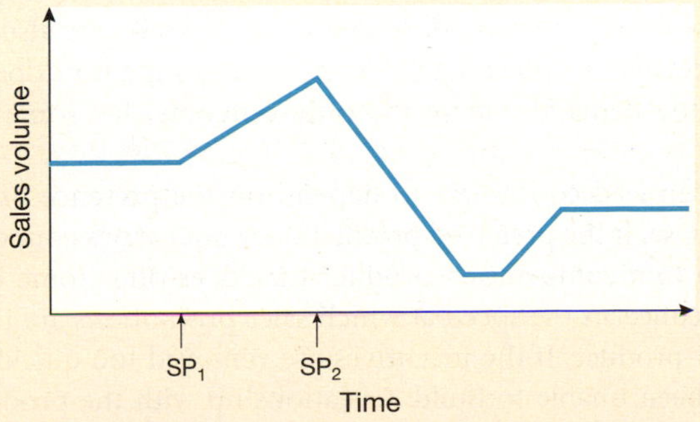

Figure 18.4 The destructive effect of competitive sales promotions

the benefits of volume increases being countered by the consequent fall in profitability. It may be, therefore, that the second scenario is the more accurate interpretation.

Sales promotions incur a large number of hidden costs. It was stated earlier that the cost of a sales promotion is thought to be relatively low but, as Buzzell *et al.* (1990) and others have demonstrated, there are a host of other indirect costs that must be considered. Manufacturers, for example, use promotional deals to induce resellers to buy stock at a promotional price, in addition to their normal buying requirements. The additional stock is then held for resale at a later date, at regular retail prices. The effect of this forward buying on the costs of the reseller can be enormous. Buzzell *et al.* point out that the promotional stock attracts higher interest charges, storage costs, expenses associated with the transfer of stock to different geographical areas of the organisation and the costs associated with keeping normal and promotional stock separate. When these are added to the manufacturer's forward buying costs it is probable, they conclude, that the costs outweigh the benefits of the sales promotion exercise.

As if to demonstrate this point the use of sales promotions and BOGOFS in particular, are used by supermarkets and brand owners because they can change consumer purchasing patterns and can get consumers to try a new product. Indeed, Simms (2007) reports that they are just as effective as television advertising in encouraging trial. There are, however, several problems with BOGOFS. According to Binet, cited by Simms, 84 per cent of trade promotions are unprofitable. This year's volumes get added into next year's targets, so manufacturers chase increased volumes as average prices fall, with the net effect of diluting profits.

Promotions give a brand presence through extra facings, but they also incur difficulties for retailers. This is because of the impact promotions can have on the relatively stable logistics associated with normal trading patterns. The capacity that stores and lorries have is finite and known. Goods are moved from warehouses, with lorries to stores whose sales performance is known. If a promotion is added to this mix these logistics patterns are thrown into temporary chaos as both the stores and the transportation create room for the promotion at the expense of other items and higher margins.

These activities suggest that the relationship between the members of the network is market-oriented rather than relational. However, many of these extra costs are unknown, and the resellers are unaware of the costs they are absorbing as a result of the deal. In the future, resellers and manufacturers should work together on such promotions and attempt to uncover all the costs involved to ensure that the exercise is successful for both parties.

Not only the short-term costs associated with a sales promotion but also the long-term costs must be evaluated. Jones (1990) refers to this as the double jeopardy of sales promotions. He argues that manufacturers who participate extensively in short-term sales promotions, mainly for defensive reasons, do so at the expense of profit. The generation of sales volume and market share is at the expense of profit. The long-term effects are equally revealing. As the vast majority of sales promotions are TPRs, the opportunity to build a consumer franchise, where the objective is the development of brand identity and loyalty, is negated. Evidence shows that as soon as a sales promotion is switched off, so any increased sales are also terminated until the next promotion. The retaliatory effect that TPRs have on competitors does nothing to stabilise what Jones calls volatile demand, where the only outcome, for some products, is decline and obscurity.

> The vast majority of sales promotions are TPRs.

Sales promotions can lead consumers to depend on the presence of a promotion before committing to a purchase. If the preferred product does not carry a coupon, premium or TPR, then they may switch to a competitor's product that does offer some element of increased value. A related issue concerns the speed at which sales promotions are reduced following the introduction of a new product. If the incentives are removed too quickly, it is probable that consumers will have been unable to build a relationship with the product. If the incentives are sustained for too long, then it is possible that consumers have only identified a product by the value of the incentive, not the value of the product itself. The process by which a sales promotion is removed from a product is referred to as fading, and its rate can be crucial to the successful outcome of a product launch and a sales promotion activity.

Loyalty and retention programmes

Despite questions about the use of sales promotions to build loyalty, the growth of loyalty programmes has been a significant promotional development in recent years. One of the more visible schemes has been the ClubCard offered by Tesco, which has been partly responsible for Tesco dominating the UK retail market (see ViewPoint 18.5). The response of its nearest rival Sainsbury's, at the time of launch, was to publicly reject loyalty cards, but some 18 months later it launched its Reward Card and then subsequently joined the group scheme, Nectar.

Loyalty schemes have been encouraged through the use of swipe cards. Users are rewarded with points each time a purchase is made. This is referred to as a 'points accrual programme', whereby loyal users are able to build up the necessary points, which are stored (often) on a card, and 'cashed in' at a later date for gifts or merchandise. The benefit for the company supporting the scheme is that the promised rewards motivate customers to accrue more points and in doing so increase their switching costs, effectively locking them into the loyalty programme and preventing them from moving to a competitor brand.

Recent technological developments mean that smart cards (a card that has a small microprocessor attached) can record enormous amounts of information, which is updated each time a purchase is made.

ViewPoint 18.4 Loyalty, values and points make proper prizes?

Harrods launched an in-store, points-based loyalty programme that members convert into discounts. The guiding principle was to reward customers because this mirrors the strategy used by Harrods. The two main goals were to enrol 1 million members by 2009 and to collect data in order to develop a better insight into the behaviour of their high-value customers.

Part of BMW's brand-stretching strategy involved launching its own credit card. This was undertaken in conjunction with American Express, a strong premium brand in its own right. BMW's brand values encompass integrity, quality, service and recognition so their loyalty scheme needed to reinforce these principles. The monthly prize draw offered by BMW to customers who spend £10 to win a trip to a Grand Prix event, may not be seen to be sufficiently in keeping with the brand's values and hence not strong enough to attract customers.

Virgin Atlantic used a 'member-get-member' scheme within its Flying Club. It offered bonus air miles not only to members who attracted new members but also rewarded new members when they flew for the first time. The success of the Virgin Atlantic scheme, which was designed to deliberately acquire customers, was mainly because the scheme provided value that was directly related to flying.

Sources: Whitson (2006); McLuhan (2007).

Question

Why do you think it is important that a loyalty scheme should reflect a brand's values?

Task

Check out the values of any brand you are associated with and its loyalty scheme.

Exhibit 18.4 Virgin Atlantic Flying Club
Courtesy of Virgin Atlantic.

Not only have loyalty schemes for frequent flyers been very successful, but the cards are also used to track individual travellers. Airlines are able to offer cardholders particular services, such as special airport lounges and magazines. Through its links to a database, the card also enables a traveller's favourite seat and dietary requirements to be offered. In addition, the regular accumulation of air miles fosters continuity and hence loyalty, through which business travellers can reward themselves with leisure travel. However, the airlines' desire to develop relationships with their customers might not be fully reciprocated as many customers seek only convenience.

Perhaps the attention given to loyalty and retention issues is misplaced because marketing is about the identification, anticipation and satisfaction of customer needs (profitably). If these needs are being met properly it might be reasonable to expect that customers would return anyway, reducing the need for overt 'loyalty' programmes. The withdrawal by Debenhams from the Nectar scheme in 2008 was made in order to better reward store-card holders, at a time when the trading environment was getting tighter. There is an argument that these schemes are important not because of the loyalty aspect but because the programme allows for the collection of up-to-date customer information and then the use of the data to make savings in the supply chain.

There has been a proliferation of loyalty cards, reflecting the increased emphasis on keeping customers rather than constantly finding new ones and there is evidence that sales lift by about 2 or 3 per cent when a loyalty scheme is launched. However, there is little evidence to support the notion that sales promotions, and in particular the use of premiums, are capable of encouraging loyalty, whether that be defined as behavioural and/or attitudinal. Loyalty schemes do enable organisations to monitor and manage stock, use direct marketing to cross- and up-sell customers, and manage their portfolio in order to consolidate (increase?) customer's spending in a store. Whether loyalty is being developed by encouraging buyers to make repeat purchases, or whether the schemes are merely sales promotion techniques that encourage extended and consistent purchasing patterns is debatable. Customer retention is a major issue and a lot of emphasis, possibly misplaced, has been given to loyalty schemes as a means of achieving retention targets.

There is little evidence to support the notion that sales promotions, and in particular the use of premiums, are capable of encouraging loyalty.

There are views that loyalty schemes are not only misguided but have cost industry a huge amount of money. Hastings and Price (2004), for example, have expressed strong views about the notion and viability of so-called loyalty and points-based schemes. They claim that loyalty schemes are misunderstood for two main reasons. First, is the assumption that loyalty can be bought when, like love, true loyalty can only be given. Second, there is an assumption that points-based schemes can be profit centres.

Hallberg (2004) reports a major study involving in excess of 600,000 in-depth consumer interviews. The study identifies different levels of loyalty and concludes that significant financial returns are gained only when the highest level of loyalty is achieved. These levels of loyalty are set out in Figure 18.5. Hallberg refers to the impact of emotional loyalty, a non-purchase measurement of attachment to a brand:

- At the 'no presence' level consumers are unaware of a brand and so there is no emotional loyalty.
- At the 'presence' level there is awareness but emotional loyalty is minimal.
- At the 'relevance and performance' level the consumer begins to feel that the brand is acceptable in terms of meeting their needs.
- At the 'advantage' level consumers should feel that the brand is superior with regard to a particular attribute.
- At the 'bonding' level emotional loyalty is at its highest because consumers feel the brand has several unique properties. They love the brand.

Loyalty schemes are exponentially effective when consumers reach the bonding stage. Although sales generally increase the further up the pyramid consumers move, it is only at the 'bonding' stage that sales start to reflect the emotional attachment people feel towards the brand. Hallberg refers to the success and market leadership that Tesco has achieved, but the principles established through this study should apply to loyalty programmes regardless of category or sector.

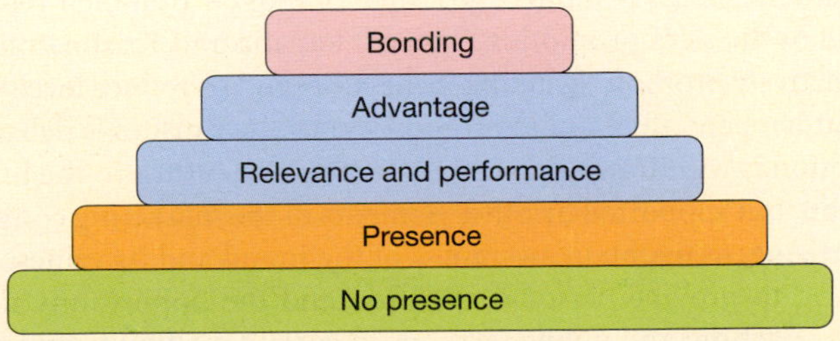

Figure 18.5 The brand emotional loyalty pyramid
Source: Hallberg, (2004). Used with permission.

Table 18.4 Five loyalty trends

Trend	Explanation
Ubiquity	Loyalty programmes have proliferated in most mature markets and many members have little interest in them other than the functionality of points collection. Managers are trying to reduce communication costs by moving the scheme online but also need to be innovative.
Coalition	Schemes run by a number of different organisations in order to share costs, information and branding (e.g. Nectar) appear to be the dominant structure industry model.
Imagination	Opportunities to exploit technologies and niche markets will depend on creativity and imagination in order to get customer data to feed into the loyalty system. Employ IST imaginatively.
Wow	To overcome consumer lethargy and boredom with loyalty schemes, many rewards in future will be experiential, emotional, unique in an attempt to appeal to life stage and aspirational lifestyle goals – wow them. Differentiate to stand out.
Analysis	To be competitive the use of customer data analytics and business intelligence is becoming critical, if only to feed CRM programmes. Collect and analyse customer information effectively.

Source: Adapted from Capizzi *et al.* (2004).

There is a proliferation of loyalty programmes to the extent that Capizzi *et al.* (2004) suggest that the market is mature. They also argue that five clear trends within the loyalty market can be identified (see Table 18.4).

These trends suggest that successful sales promotions schemes will be those that enable members to perceive significant value associated with their continued association with a scheme. That value will be driven by schemes run by groups of complementary brands, which use technology to understand customer dynamics and communications that complement their preferred values. The medium-term goal might be that these schemes should reflect customers' different relationship needs and recognise the different loyalty levels desired by different people.

The strategic use of sales promotions

Sales promotions have long been regarded as a short-term tactical tool whose prime purpose is to encourage customers to try a brand or to switch brands (within their repertoire), attracted by the added value of the sales promotion. Indeed, Papatia and Krishnamurthi (1996) claim that coupons can actively promote switching behaviour and so reduce levels of loyalty. As discussed earlier, what happens after a sales promotion activity finishes is debatable. Some claim that once a promotion is withdrawn satisfied customers will return to the brand unsupported by a sales promotion, but supported by other elements of the marketing communications mix: in particular advertising, to maintain awareness of the brand and its values; direct marketing, to provide personal attention and the opportunity to take immediate action; and public relations to sustain credibility and relevance.

> It can be argued that sales promotion serves to discount a brand.

By way of contrast it can be argued that sales promotion serves to discount a brand, either directly through price-based reductions or indirectly through coupons and premiums. Customer alignment is to the deal rather than to the brand itself. This serves to lower expectations of what a brand stands for and what it is capable of delivering. So, once a sales promotion is removed, the normal price is perceived as representing inferior value and so repeat purchase behaviour is deterred.

However, despite these less than positive views, some writers (Davis, 1992; O'Malley, 1998) argue that sales promotions have a strategic role to play in the promotional mix. Traditionally they have been viewed as short-term, tactical tools that can be used offensively to induce the trial of new products, or defensively for established products to retain shelf space and consumers. Sales promotions that do not work as intended may have been used to support inappropriate products or may have been devised without adequate planning. An example of the latter issue may be the Hoover free flights misjudgment and the associated over-subscription that followed the launch of that particular sales promotion activity. There can be no doubt that sales promotions oriented to consumer deals and TPRs, in particular, do little to contribute to the overall strategy adopted for an organisation or even a product.

One of the consequences of competitive sales promotions, especially in consumer markets, is the spiral effect that retaliatory actions can have on each organisation. A sales promotion 'trap' develops when competitors start to imitate each other's activities, often based on price reductions. This leads eventually to participants losing profitability and consumers losing value and possibly choice as some products are forced to drop out of the market. Meyers and Litt (2008) found that timing was crucially important. Their research discovered that coupon redemption was improved considerably when the coupon value and the expiration date (the redemption period) hit what they call the 'sweet spot',

With the development of relationship marketing and the move towards integrated marketing communications has come the realisation that employees are an important target audience.

There is a strong need to motivate the workforce and sales promotion activities have an important role to play. However, employee incentives need to be made accessible to everyone and not just a few (such as the sales force). This means that rewards need to be more broadly spread and there needs to be choice. Vouchers, for example, enable the prizewinner to make a choice based on their circumstances and they are easier to administer than many of the other types of reward. Incentive schemes should be designed in such a way that they do not fall into the trap of creating winners and losers, which can be the case when, for example, the top 20 in a scheme win a prize, which effectively creates 80 losers out of every 100 employees.

ViewPoint 18.5 Tesco score the strategic points

Clubcard is the vehicle Tesco use for their loyalty programme. The success of the scheme has been attributed to many factors but the evidence suggests that the UK's largest retailer has demonstrated that their strategic orientation towards loyalty has been significant. Humby *et al.* (2003) cited by Rowley (2007), found that the commitment of the directors and employees to the scheme is critical as they recognise that customers have opportunities to shop elsewhere.

Tesco Clubcard is integral to the business, its operations and the brand strategy. This was noticeable on the day the scheme was launched in 1995. It changed the way decisions were made by Tesco, the way they developed products, served their customers and managed their stores. The visual identity of the Clubcard complements the identity of the Tesco brand and both are heavily co-branded. The data collected through the card enabled Tesco to launch the right products at the right customers. This can be seen in the success of their financial services and their online and home delivery service.

The scheme is geared to both behaviour and attitudinal factors and notification of the rewards are delayed until four occasions in the year when Tesco send out the Clubcard magazine.

The final strategic link concerns the way the company's customer focus is used within the design and management of the information systems. This covers data collection, customer interaction and data analysis.

Sources: Humby *et al.* (2003); Rowley (2007).

Question

Tesco claim that Clubcard is not a reward scheme, but more an opportunity to demonstrate their appreciation to their customers. Is this a workable idea?

Task

Go to **Tesco.com** and find out about the multidimensional nature of the Clubcard scheme.

Exhibit 18.5 Tesco Clubcard
Courtesy of Tesco Stores Ltd (owner of all IP rights in the image).

Many schemes are based around product prizes, typically electrical goods. However, for many people these are no longer attractive (or sufficiently motivating) as rewards. Virgin vouchers provide activity-based rewards where there is an experience that gives the recipient a memory. Activities such as hot-air ballooning, sky diving, visits to the theatre or to health farms appeal to a wide cross-section of people.

The true strategic effect of sales promotion activities can only be achieved if they are coordinated with the other activities of the communications mix, and this requires planning. In particular, the complementary nature of sales promotion and advertising should be exploited through the use of common themes and messages, timing, targeting and allocation of resources (in particular budgets). Sales promotions that are planned as a sequence of predetermined activities, reflecting the promotional requirements of a product over the longer term, are more likely to be successful than those sales promotions that are simply reactions to competitors' moves and market developments.

The strategic impact of sales promotions is best observed when they are designed or built into a three- to four-year plan of promotional activities, coordinated with other communication tools and integrated with the business strategy.

The manner in which many of the loyalty programmes are managed signals a move from pure sales promotion to direct marketing.

The manner in which many of the loyalty programmes are managed signals a move from pure sales promotion to direct marketing. The integration of these two approaches has become necessary in order that the advantages of both are realised. This does raise an interesting conflict, in that sales promotion is essentially a short-term tool, and direct marketing needs to work over the long term. The former is product-oriented (albeit giving added value to consumers) and often oriented to mass audiences, whereas the latter is based on developing a personal dialogue (Curtis, 1996).

A further strategic issue concerns the use of joint promotions with other leading brands. By twinning brand names, increased promotional impact can assist both partners. However, there is a danger that such a pairing will be short lived, and hence the strategic perspective may be limited.

The use of sales promotions within marketing channels can lead to tension. For example, hostaging is a process whereby a retailer/reseller is able to exert power over a manufacturer in order to pressurise or force it into providing trade promotions on a more or less continual basis. A less dependent firm may use influence strategies, such as requests and information exchange (Anderson and Narus, 1990). In contrast, the more dependent firm should seek to add value (or reduce costs) to the exchange for the partner firm, at a relatively small cost to itself.

The more dependent firm in a working relationship needs to protect its transactions-specific assets by taking various actions, such as close bonding with end-user firms. Strategies to avoid 'hostaging' would include reducing the frequency of trade deals, converting trade spending into advertising and consumer promotions, and focusing on differentiating the brand with less reliance on price (Blattberg and Neslin, 1990).

Brito and Hammond (2007) demonstrate the variation and complexity of the different sales promotion tools and techniques. They also draw attention to the important point that some tools are best suited for a tactical short-term use (e.g. temporary price cuts) while others have a strategic, medium- to longer-term orientation (e.g. sweepstakes, competitions and contests). In other words, sales promotions can be considered as either strategic or tactical, depending on the tools used and whether the promotion is incorporated within an integrated programme, which by definition usually signifies a strategic approach.

Finally, the huge sums of money involved in some of the mainstream loyalty or reward-based programmes suggest that these should be seen as longer-term promotional investments. As the return will spread over many years, a medium-term perspective may be more appropriate than a short-term view based on a sales 'blip'.

Sales promotions: methods and techniques

As established earlier, sales promotions seek to offer buyers additional value, as an inducement to generate an immediate sale. These inducements can be targeted at consumers, distributors, agents and members of the sales force. A whole range of network members can benefit from the use of sales promotion.

The techniques considered in this section attempt to reflect the range and variety of techniques that are used to add value and induce a sale sooner rather than later. The nature and characteristics of the target audiences mean that different techniques work in different ways to achieve varying objectives. Consideration is given to the range of tasks that need to be accomplished among two key audiences: resellers and consumers.

> The nature and characteristics of the target audiences mean that different techniques work in different ways.

The range of techniques and methods used to add value to offerings is enormous but there are growing doubts about the effectiveness and profitability associated with some sales promotions. Sales promotions used by manufacturers to communicate with resellers are aimed at encouraging resellers to either try new products or purchase more of the ones they currently stock. To do this, trade allowances, in various guises, are the principal means.

The majority of sales promotions are those used by manufacturers to influence consumers. Again, the main tasks are to encourage trial or increase product purchase. A range of techniques, from sampling and coupons to premiums, contests and sweepstakes, are all used with varying levels of success, but there has been a distinct shift away from traditional promotional instruments to the use of digital media in order to reflect consumers' preferences and media behaviour.

ViewPoint 18.6 Digital sampling by Brylcreem

Brylcreem used sampling and SMS to launch its Next Generation Ultra Gel product. Samples of the brand were handed out to young males at welcome meetings at Club 18–30 holiday destinations. Each sample pack carried a code, encouraging recipients to text in for a chance to win prizes such as holidays and PlayStation games and consoles. They were also asked to text in their opinions on Brylcreem.

The simplicity of the campaign was intended to reflect Brylcreem's brand values and was designed to complement the fact that increasingly people are taking their phones on holiday and using SMS.

Question

Which element of the attitude construct does sampling influence?

Task

Find another example of a sampling programme.

The following two tables set out information about key sales promotions techniques used between manufacturers and their intermediary partners, and with consumers. It should also be appreciated that sales promotions are used by retailers to influence consumers and between manufacturers and dealer sales force teams, although these are not itemised here. Table 18.5 depicts information about the audiences and reasons for using sales promotions. Table 18.6 provides information about the various sales promotion methods and techniques.

Table 18.5 Principal audiences and sales promotion goals

Audience	Objectives	Explanation	Methods
Manufacturers to resellers	For new products: *Sampling and trial*	For new products it is important to create adequate channels of distribution in anticipation of consumer demand. The task of marketing communications is to encourage resellers to distribute a new product and to establish trial behaviour.	Allowances: *Buying* *Count and recount* *Buy-back* *Advertising*
	For established products: *Usage*	One of the key objectives of manufacturers is to motivate distributors to allocate increased shelf space to a product thereby (possibly) reducing the amount of shelf space allocated to competitors. The task of marketing communications, therefore, is to encourage resellers to buy and display increased amounts of the manufacturer's products and establish greater usage.	Dealer contests dealer Conventions and meetings Training and support
Manufacturers to consumers	For new users: *Stimulate trial*	Before a customer buys a product they need to test or trial the product. Through the use of coupons, sampling and other techniques (see below), sales promotions have become an important element in the new product launch and introduction processes.	Sampling Coupons Price offs Bonus packs Refunds and rebates
	For established customers: *Increase product usage*	In mature markets customers need to be encouraged to keep buying a product. This can be achieved by attracting users from competitive brands, by converting non-users and by developing new uses.	Premiums Contests and sweepstakes

Table 18.6 Principal audiences and sales promotion methods

Audience	Method	Explanation
Manufacturers to resellers	Advertising allowance	A percentage allowance is given against a reseller's purchases during a specified campaign period. Instead of providing an allowance against product purchases, an allowance can be provided against the cost of an advertisement or campaign.
	Buying allowance	In return for specific orders between certain dates, a reseller will be entitled to a refund or allowance of *x* per cent off the regular case or carton price.
	Count and recount	Manufacturers may require resellers to clear old stock before a new or modified product is introduced. One way this can be achieved is to encourage resellers to move stock out of storage and into the store. The count and recount method provides an allowance for each case shifted into the store during a specified period of time.
	Buy-back	Purchases made after the count and recount scheme (up to a maximum of the count and recount) are entitled to an allowance to encourage stores to replenish their stocks (with the manufacturer's product and not that of a competitor).
	Dealer contests	Used to hold a reseller's attention by focusing them on a manufacturer's products not a competitor's.
	Dealer conventions and meetings	These enable informal interaction between a manufacturer and its resellers and can aid the development and continuance of good relations between the two parties.
	Training and support	This is an important communications function, especially when products are complex or subject to rapid change, as in IT markets. This can build stronger relationships and manufacturers have greater control over the messages that the reseller's transmit.
Manufacturers to consumers	Sampling	Although very expensive, sampling is an effective way of getting people to try a product. Trial-size versions of the actual product are given away free. Sampling can also take the form of demonstrations, trial-size packs that have to be purchased or free use for a certain period of time.
	Coupons	These are vouchers or certificates that entitle consumers to a price reduction on a particular product. The value of the reduction or discount is set and the coupon must be presented at purchase.
	Price offs	These are a direct reduction in the purchase price with the offer clearly labelled on the package or point of purchase display.
	Bonus packs	These offer more product for the regular pack price, typically a 2 for 1 offer. They provide direct impact at the point of purchase and represent extra value.
	Refunds and rebates	Used to invite consumers to send in a proof of purchase and in return receive a cash refund.
	Premiums	Items of merchandise that are offered free or at a low cost in return for product purchase.
	Contests and sweepstakes	A contest is a customer competition based on skill or ability. Entry requires a proof of purchase and winners are judged against a set of predetermined criteria. A sweepstake determines winners by chance and proof of purchase is not required. There is no judging and winners are drawn at random.

Other sales promotion devices

Table 18.6 provides a list of the main sales promotion devices used by organisations. In addition to these are various other sales promotion approaches, used either for particular audiences or situations.

The good old fashioned 'brochure' is a sales promotion device that can be used to assist consumers, resellers and sales forces. Apart from the ability of the brochure to impart factual information about a product or service, brochures and sales literature stimulate purchase and serve to guide decisions. For service-based organisations, the brochure represents a temporary tangible element of the product. Inclusive tour operators, for example, might entice someone to book a holiday, but consumption may take place several months in the future. The brochure acts as a temporary product substitute and can be used to refresh expectations during the gestation period and remind significant other people of the forthcoming event (Middleton, 1989). Just as holiday photographs provide opportunities to relive and share past experiences, so holiday brochures help people to share and enjoy pre-holiday experiences and expectations. Consumption of inclusive tours, therefore, can be said to occur at the booking point, and the brochure extends or adds value to the holiday experience.

For service-based organisations, the brochure represents a temporary tangible element of the product.

Sales literature can trigger awareness of potential needs. As well as this, it can be useful in explaining technical and complex products. For example, leaflets distributed personally at DIY stores can draw attention to a double-glazing manufacturer's products. Some prospective customers may develop an initial impression about the manufacturer, based on past experiences triggered by the literature, the quality of the leaflet and the way it was presented. The leaflet acts as a cue for the receiver to review whether there is a current need and, if there is, then the leaflet may be kept longer, especially where high involvement is present; value is thus added to the purchase experience.

Financial services companies use sales literature at various stages in the sales process. Mailers are used to contact prospective customers, corporate brochures are used to provide source credibility, booklets about the overall marketplace are left with clients after an initial discussion and product guides and brochures are given to customers after a transaction has been agreed. To help prevent the onset of cognitive dissonance, a company magazine is sent soon after the sale and at intermediate points throughout the year to cement the relationship between client and company.

Financial services companies use sales literature at various stages in the sales process.

An increasingly important and expensive approach is to license a TV cartoon character from *The Simpsons*, *Rugrats* or *South Park* or a cyber person such as Lara Croft who was used by Lucozade. These characters are used strategically to build brands and part of the approach is to attract the attention of children and provide the parental agreement necessary for a purchase to be made. For example, Ribena wanted to exploit the license they held on Shrek 2. They selected a donkey character, which was used across the entire range. The prize was a real donkey with £1,000 for the winner to travel to see the donkey (at the sanctuary). In addtion, there were thousands of prizes of cinema tickets and three-foot inflatable donkeys. The whole scheme was supported with PR, cinema, viral, web site, in-store and TV advertising. The result was incremental sales of £6.86 million, 22.5 per cent over target (Mistry, 2006).

Inevitably, there are issues concerning consistency of brand values and the need to prevent competitors using the same or similar characters to support their brands. It is also argued that apart from a short-term sales increase there is a residual sales increase following promotions utilising these prime characters, especially if the promotion is based on a free gift or the chance to win an instant gift.

Summary

In order to help consolidate your understanding of sales promotion, here are the key points summarised against each of the learning objectives:

1. Understand the value of sales promotions.

Sales promotions offer a direct inducement or an incentive to encourage audiences to buy a product/service sooner rather than later. The inducement (for example, price deals, coupons, premiums) is presented as an added value to the basic product, one that is intended to encourage buyers to act 'now' rather than later.

2. Consider the role of sales promotion.

The role of sales promotion is to engage audiences and to motivate them so that they are persuaded to behave now rather than at a later stage.

3. Explain the objectives associated with using sales promotion.

The objective of sales promotion is to stimulate action. This can be to initiate a series of behaviours that result in long-run purchase activity, but the goal of sales promotion is to drive short-term shifts in sales. These actions can be seen to occur in the conative stage of the attitudinal set.

4. Describe the ways in which sales promotion is thought to work.

The cognitive view of the way sales promotions operate is based on the belief that consumers internally process relevant information about a sales promotion, including those of past experiences, and make a reasoned decision in the light of the goals and objectives that individuals set for themselves. The behaviourists' view is that when the various actions that are embedded within a sales promotion activity are aggregated, a new desired pattern of behaviour emerges.

5. Evaluate the merits of loyalty and retention programmes.

Many organisations have developed schemes designed to retain customers based on the notion that they, the customers, are loyal. This brings into debate the notion of what is loyalty. In many ways these schemes are a function of customer convenience and all that they achieve is sufficient leverage to hold on to a customer a fraction longer than might have been possible in the absence of the scheme.

6. Argue the case for a strategic orientation towards sales promotions.

It is argued that sales promotions have a strategic role to play in the communication mix. Traditionally, they have been viewed as short-term, tactical tools that can be used offensively to induce the trial of new products, or defensively for established products to retain shelf space and consumers.

The true strategic effect of sales promotion activities can only be achieved if they are co-ordinated with the other activities of the communications mix, and this requires planning. In particular, the complementary nature of sales promotion and advertising should be exploited through the use of common themes and messages, timing, targeting and allocation of resources (in particular budgets). Sales promotions that are planned as a sequence of predetermined activities, reflecting the promotional requirements of a product over the longer term, are more likely to be successful than those sales promotions that are simply reactions to competitors' moves and market developments.

7. Explain the different sales promotions methods and techniques.

The range of techniques and methods used to add value to offerings is enormous and range from sampling and coupons to premiums, contests and sweepstakes, all used with varying levels of success. However, there has been a distinct shift away from traditional promotional instruments to the use of digital media in order to reflect consumers' preferences and media behaviour.

Review questions

1. What are the purposes of using sales promotion and why has it assumed such a large share of promotional expenditure?
2. Write a brief note explaining how shaping works.
3. Identify the major differences between the behavioural and the cognitive explanations of how sales promotions work.
4. Write brief notes outlining some of the issues associated with loyalty programmes and customer retention initiatives.
5. How would you advise a newly appointed assistant brand manager on the expected outcomes of a sales promotion programme? (Choose any sector/industry of your choice.)
6. Find three examples of sales promotion activity and determine the extent to which they are strategic or tactical.
7. List the main sales promotion methods used by manufacturers and targeted at consumers.
8. Consider whether hostaging is conducive to relationship marketing.
9. What might be the value of joint sales promotion activities?
10. How might use of technology assist the development of loyalty and retention programmes?

MiniCase Could online coupons save the High Street?

Mary Hedderman: University of Wales, Newport

In recent times, newspapers seem to have featured stories about the 'death' of the High Street and the 'phenomenal growth' in online shopping in equal measure. Must High Street shopping and a growth in online shopping be mutually exclusive or does this increased use of the Internet by UK shoppers present an as yet, little exploited communication opportunity for High Street retailers?

UK consumers spent £13 billion online in the first three months of 2008, equal to £213 for every member of the population and showing an increase of 50 per cent for the same period in 2007, according to a report by IMRG Capgemini eRetail Sales Index. Recent research by Logan Tod Online Shopping Index, an independent digital consultancy, also suggests that while the 35–44-year-old age group are the consumers doing the most shopping online, the growth opportunity lies with the 44+ age group. Surely a drive to secure online business from the older target audience would present a very real threat to the High Street?

Bricks-and-mortar retailers are fighting back with a focus on providing a more positive and exciting experience for their instore customer. In fact, there are signs in the United States that suggest that online sales are tailing off, with shoppers returning to bricks-and-mortar outlets as they prefer the experience and more sociable aspect of shopping. This may provide some hope for High Street retailers in the United Kingdom but Internet sites are rapidly developing their own 'online experiences' through the inclusion of clubs, forums, competitions and other innovative interactive activities. The key question also remains – while shoppers might still prefer an instore experience, how do you ensure you get them there in the first place?

Several UK retailers have successfully forged strong links between their online and offline operations – Argos, for instance, offers customers the opportunity of reserving products online from home and then going and collecting their goods instore that day or the next. There is a strong possibility that once instore, customers will browse the catalogue, view goods on display and further purchases may be made. Could such buying behaviour suggest that people do not view virtual shopping and bricks-and-mortar as an either/or situation but more as complementary elements within the buying process? Could the Internet then be used as a communications channel to pull shoppers back to the High Street? The answer is yes, but today's marketing-savvy consumer would expect an incentive.

UK consumers love a bargain, they know their BOGOF's from their money off's and have a long history of coupon redemption. However, while coupons have traditionally been seen as the preserve of those on a budget, higher income individuals have also been introduced to the delights of the 'discount voucher'. Coupon company Valassis UK, which processes in excess of 5 billion coupons and vouchers a year, acting as a broker between issuer and redeemer, state on their web site that the image of couponing has moved away from 'penny pinching' and more towards 'a good way of saving money'. Many an office in the United Kingdom has experienced the frisson of excitement when a 'secret' email voucher is passed around for an appealing High Street store – a recent example being 'an invitation' to receive 25 per cent off at Monsoon, to be used instore only and for one weekend only (the restriction seems to only add to the thrill). In fact, in recent months online newspapers such as *Timesonline* and Guardian.co.uk have been featuring stories about 'secret sales', discussing the online pass codes and email vouchers that are widely available on the Internet if you know where to look. It appears that while vouchers and codes are being quietly sent to registered customers such as loyalty and account card holders, some of these shoppers are passing them on within Internet forums and posting them onto one of the many specialist coupon aggregation sites that are now in existence. Once a code is posted viral marketing seems to take over with consumers happily firing the information off to friends and colleagues.

Although Monsoon's invitation applied to instore sales only, a close inspection of the specialist coupon aggregation sites such as SendMeDiscounts.co.uk and My Voucher Codes.co.uk indicates that the vast majority of the publicised discounts are for online stores only. This suggests that offline stores could be missing out on a very real opportunity to exploit both available technology and current trends to transform their sales promotions and drive traffic back instore.

While online discount vouchers present a great marketing opportunity, as with sales promotions of any kind, each offer would have to be managed very carefully – canny consumers are on the look out for mistakes in codes to reap the benefits of even greater discounts. *Timesonline* reported in December 2006 how a computer error on the Hamleys web site had allowed customers to benefit from 60 per cent discount when shoppers were able to input three codes, each worth a discount of 20 per cent, simultaneously. One customer claimed that he had managed to buy a £13,000 snooker table for £5,000. There is also concern about the lack of control over redemption levels and the fear that response will be far in excess of what is desired by the retailer. However, technology is available to limit such events; the relatively new 2D barcodes which are currently being used for purchasing 'printed' postage online can be used to produce a voucher that can be downloaded once only, and that cannot be photocopied, since each barcode is unique. An inherent problem of the Internet will always be the issue of out-of-date offers remaining on sites and Internet forums, leading to disappointment and frustration among consumers, but as users become accustomed to such promotions they are likely to be alert to such errors.

A further advantage of online couponing and discount vouchers is that they present a very real opportunity for data capture and analysis. While sales promotions are traditionally viewed as largely tactical tools, online promotions allow close tracking and monitoring of buyer behaviour, providing greater customer insight which could be used to shape future strategic decision-making.

Since so few bricks-and-mortar retailers have embraced this sales promotions opportunity, it is worth considering one of the best-known to date – the Threshers discount voucher promotion which ran in 2006. The discount for 40 per cent off wine and champagne bought in store was reportedly intended for staff only but it has been rumoured that the voucher was downloaded more than 1 million times. Was this a disaster for Threshers or were they simply ahead of the game and knew how to exploit the power of the Internet to drive traffic back instore way before the rest of us?

MiniCase questions

1. Explain how the use of online discount vouchers and coupons might be viewed as a strategic rather than tactical promotional tool.
2. Suggest other appropriate marketing communications tools that could be used alongside online discount vouchers as part of an integrated marketing communications campaign.
3. Discuss the possible ethical issues that would need to be considered when engaging in a sales promotion using online discount vouchers and coupons.

References

Anderson, J.C. and Narus, J.A. (1990) A model of distributor firm and manufacturer firm working partnerships. *Journal of Marketing*, **54** (January), 42–58.

Anon. (2008) Facebook helps launch Fujifilm youth camera. *PR Week*, 11 January. Retrieved 19 February 2008 from www.brandrepublic.com/News/776265/CAMPAIGN-Facebook-helps-launch-Fujifilm-youth-camera/.

Barrand, D. (2004) Promoting change. *Marketing*, 6 October, 43–5.

Blattberg, R.C. and Neslin, S.A. (1990) *Sales Promotion: Concepts, Methods and Strategies.* Englewood Cliffs, NJ: Prentice-Hall.

Brito, P.Q. and Hammond, K. (2007) Strategic versus tactical nature of sales promotion. *Journal of Marketing Communications*, **13**(2), 131–48.

Buzzell, R.D., Quelch, J.A. and Salmon, W.J. (1990) The costly bargain of trade promotion. *Harvard Business Review* (March/April), 141–9.

Capizzi, M., Ferguson, R. and Cuthbertson, R. (2004) Loyalty trends for the 21st century. *Journal of Targeting Measurement and Analysis for Marketing*, **12**(3), 199–212.

Curtis, J. (1996) Opposites attract. *Marketing*, 25 April, 28–9.

Davis, M. (1992) Sales promotions as a competitive strategy. *Management Decision*, **30**(7), 5–10.

Dawes, J. (2004) Assessing the impact of a very successful price promotion on brand, category and competitor sales. *Journal of Product and Brand Management*, **13**(5), 303–14.

Ehrenberg, A.S.C. (2000) Repeat buying: facts, theory and applications. *Journal of Empirical Generalizations in Marketing Science*, **5**, 392–770.

Gilbert, D.C. and Jackaria, N. (2002) The efficacy of sales promotions in UK supermarkets: a consumer view. *International Journal of Retail and Distribution Management*, **30**(6), 325–32.

Gupta, S. (1998) Impact of sales promotions on when, what and how much we buy. *Journal of Marketing Research*, **25**(4), 342–55.

Hallberg, G. (2004) Is your loyalty programme really building loyalty? Why increasing emotional attachment, not just repeat buying, is key to maximizing programme success. *Journal of Targeting Measurement and Analysis for Marketing*, **12**(3), 231–41.

Hastings, S. and Price, M. (2004) Money can't buy me loyalty. *Admap*, **39**(2) (February), 29–31.

Humby, C., Hunt, T. and Phillips, T. (2003) *Scoring Points: How Tesco is Winning Customer Loyalty*, London: Kogan Page.

Inman, J., McAlister, L. and Hoyer, D.W. (1990) Promotion signal: proxy for a price cut? *Journal of Consumer Research*, **17**(June), 74–81.

Jones, P.J. (1990) The double jeopardy of sales promotions. *Harvard Business Review*, (September/October), 145–52.

Krishna, A. and Zhang, Z.J. (1999) Short or long duration coupons: the effect of the expiration date on the probability of coupon promotions. *Management Science*, **45**(8), 1041–57.

Lee, C.H. (2002) Sales promotions as strategic communication: the case of Singapore. *Journal of Product and Brand Management*, **11**(2), 103–14.

McLuhan, R. (2007) Is loyalty a myth? *Marketing*, 15 August, 29–30.

Meyers, P. and Litt, S. (2008) Finding the redemption sweet spot: debunking the top ten myths about couponing. *Journal of Consumer Marketing*, **25**(1), 57–9.

Middleton, V.T.C. (1989) *Marketing in Travel and Tourism*. Oxford: Heinemann.

Mistry, B. (2006) Live issue: Best SP ever – Weetabix takes the best SP accolade. *Promotions and Incentives*, 14 December. Retrieved 16 April 2008 from www.brandrepublic.com/News/610080/Live-issue-Best-SP-ever---Weetabix-takes-best-SP-accolade/.

O'Malley, L. (1998) Can loyalty schemes really build loyalty? *Marketing Intelligence and Planning*, **16**(1), 47–55.

Orton-Jones, C. (2007) How to . . . exploit digital media, *The Marketer*, November, 32–7.

Papatia, P. and Krishnamurthi, L. (1996) Measuring the dynamic effects of promotions on brand choice. *Journal of Marketing Research*, **33**(1) (February), 20–35.

Peattie, S. and Peattie, K.J. (1994) Sales promotion. In *The Marketing Book* (ed. M.J. Baker), 3rd edn. London: Butterworth-Heinemann.

Quilter, J. (2008) Cadbury goes back to the future. *Promotions and Incentives*, 2 January. Retrieved 21 February 2008 from www.brandrepublic.com/pAndI/Features/774307/Cadbury-goes-back-future/.

Rothschild, M.L. and Gaidis, W.C. (1981) Behavioural learning theory: its relevance to marketing and promotions. *Journal of Marketing Research*, **45**(2), 70–8.

Rowley, J. (2007) Reconceptualisng the strategic role of loyalty schemes. *Journal of Consumer Marketing*, **24**(6), 366–74.

Simms, J. (2007) Scant value in BOGOFS. *Marketing*, 7 November, 18.

Whitson, C. (2006) BMW's loyalty is too rewarding. Retrieved 20 March 2008 from http://www.mycustomer.com/cgi-bin/library.cgi?action=detail&id=5784?.

Chapter 19
Public relations

Public relations is a management activity that attempts to shape the attitudes and opinions held by an organisation's stakeholders. Through interaction and dialogue with these stakeholders an organisation seeks to adjust its own position and/or strategy. Therefore, there is an attempt to identify with, and adjust an organisation's policies to the interests of its stakeholders. To do this it formulates and executes a programme of action to develop mutual goodwill and understanding. Profile communication strategies make substantial use of public relations when developing understanding about their intentions and who they are.

Aims and learning objectives

The aim of this chapter is to explore the role and characteristics of public relations in the context of profiling organisations and their products.

The learning objectives of this chapter are to:

1. explain the nature and characteristics of public relations;
2. highlight the main audiences to which public relations activities are directed;
3. discuss the role of public relations in the communications mix;
4. appreciate ways in which public relations works;
5. provide an overview of some of the main tools used by public relations;
6. examine the nature and context of crisis management;
7. determine ways in which public relations can be integrated with the other tools of the marketing communications mix.

For an applied interpretation see Peter Betts' MiniCase entitled ***British Airways: the world's least favourite airline?*** at the end of this chapter.

Introduction

The shift in the degree of importance given by organisations to public relations over recent years is a testimony to its power and effectiveness. An increasing number of organisations are now recognising that the role that public relations can play in the external and internal communications of organisations is a tool for use by all organisations, regardless of the sector in which they operate. Therefore all organisations in the public, hybrid, not-for-profit and private sectors can use this tool to raise visibility, interest and goodwill.

Traditionally, public relations has been perceived as a tool that dealt with the manner and style with which an organisation interacted with its major 'publics'. It sought to influence other organisations and individuals through public relations, projecting an identity that would affect the image that different publics held of the organisation. By spreading information and improving the levels of knowledge that people held about particular issues, the organisation sought ways to advance itself in the eyes of those it saw as influential. This approach is reflected in the definition of public relations provided by the Institute of Public Relations: 'Public Relations practice is the planned and sustained effort to establish and maintain goodwill and mutual understanding between an organisation and its publics.' Another definition has been provided by delegates attending a world convention of public relations associations in 1978, entitled the Mexican Statement: 'Public Relations is the art and social science of analysing trends, predicting their consequences, counselling organisations' leadership and implementing planned programmes of action which will serve both the organisation's and the public interest' (Public Relations Educational Trust, 1991). A more recent definition from Bruning and Ledingham (2000) is that public relations is the management of relationships between organisations and their stakeholders (publics). This last definition indicates the direction in which both public relations and marketing theory is moving.

Public relations is the management of relationships between organisations and their stakeholders.

Public relations has long been concerned with the development and communication of corporate and competitive strategies. Public relations provides visibility for an organisation, and this in turn, it is hoped, allows it to be properly identified, positioned and understood by all of its stakeholders. What some definitions do not emphasise or make apparent is that public relations should also be used by management as a means of understanding issues from a stakeholder perspective. Good relationships are developed by appreciating the views held by others and by 'putting oneself in their shoes'.

Through this sympathetic and patient approach to planned communication, a dialogue can be developed that is not frustrated by punctuated interruptions (anger, disbelief, ignorance and objections). Public relations is a management activity that attempts to shape the attitudes and opinions held by an organisation's stakeholders. It attempts to identify its policies with the interests of its stakeholders and formulates and executes a programme of action to develop mutual goodwill and understanding, and in turn develop relationships that are in the long-term interests of all parties.

Characteristics of public relations

Public relations should, therefore, be a planned activity, one that encompasses a wide range of events. However, there are a number of characteristics that single out this particular tool from the others in the marketing communications mix. The use of public relations does not require the purchase of airtime or space in media vehicles, such as television or magazines. The decision on whether an organisation's public relations messages are transmitted or not rests with those charged with

Public relations should be a planned activity.

managing the media resource, not the message sponsor. Those messages that are selected are perceived to be endorsements or the views of parties other than management. The outcome is that these messages usually carry greater perceived credibility than those messages transmitted through paid media, such as advertising.

The degree of trust and confidence generated by public relations singles out this tool from others in the marketing communications mix as an important means of reducing buyers' perceived risk. However, while credibility may be high, the amount of control that management is able to bring to the transmission of the public relations message is very low. For example, a press release may have been carefully prepared in-house, but as soon as it is passed to the editor of a magazine or newspaper, a possible opinion former, all control is lost. The release may be destroyed (highly probable), printed as it stands (highly unlikely) or changed to fit the available space in the media vehicle (almost certain, if it is decided to use the material). This means that any changes will not have been agreed by management, so the context and style of the original message may be lost or corrupted.

The costs associated with public relations also make this an important tool in the marketing communications mix. The absolute costs are minimal, except for those organisations that retain an agency, but even then their costs are low compared with those of advertising. The relative costs (the costs associated with reaching each member of a target audience) are also very low. The main costs associated with public relations are the time and opportunity costs associated with the preparation of press releases and associated literature. If these types of activity are organised properly, many small organisations could develop and shape their visibility much more effectively and in a relatively inexpensive way.

This tool can be used to reach specific audiences in a way that paid media cannot.

A further characteristic of this tool is that it can be used to reach specific audiences in a way that paid media cannot. With increasing media fragmentation and finer segmentation (customisation) of markets, the use of public relations represents a cost-effective way of reaching such markets and audiences.

ViewPoint 19.1 Kittens in need

The KittenAid appeal in 2007, run by the Cats Protection charity, was designed to generate funds from the donors on the charity's database. The number of kittens delivered to the charity was exceptionally large in 2007 due to un-neutered cats breeding in the warm weather.

The campaign was started with a vismail teaser, showing video clips of the charity's kittens and announcing the arrival of kitten season. This was sent to the charity's 18,000 esubscribers. This activity was then followed by direct mail activity, this time targeted at their 94,000 donors. The mailer was used to tell the story of the recovery of two very ill kittens, now in the care of the charity. The charity's magazine *The Cat* ran the story while their 29 adoption centres and 252 branches actively discussed the story and associated issues with local media.

As a result of this public relations campaign the appeal generated 40 items of coverage in the media. On the morning of the first broadcast, the KittenAid message reached 1.5 million people and featured on various BBC Radio programmes. After just six weeks the donations reached £244,000, 15 per cent up on the whole of the previous year's fund raising.

Source: Anon. (2007).

Question

What role did the vismail play in generating donations?

Task

Identify the direct marketing and public relations activities in the KittenAid example.

New technology has played a key role in the development and practice of public relations. Gregory (2004) refers to the Internet and electronic communication 'transforming public relations'. With regard to the use of the Internet by public relations practitioners she identifies two main schools. One refers to those who use the Internet as an extension to traditional or pre-Internet forms of communication. The second sees opportunities through the Internet to develop two-way, enhanced communication. There can be little doubt that new technology has assisted communication management in terms of improving the transparency, speed and reach of public relations messages, while at the same time enabling interactive communication between an organisation and its specific audiences.

New technology has played a key role in the development and practice of public relations.

The main characteristics of public relations are that it represents a very cost-effective means of carrying messages with a high degree of credibility. However, the degree of control that management is able to exert over the transmission of messages can be limited.

Publics or stakeholders?

The first definition of public relations quoted earlier uses, as indeed does most of the public relations industry, the word *publics*. This word is used traditionally to refer to the various organisations and groups with which an organisation interacts. So far, this text has referred to these types of organisation as *stakeholders*. 'Stakeholders' is a term used in the field of strategic management, and as public relations is essentially concerned with strategic issues the word 'stakeholders' is used in this text to provide consistency and to reflect the strategic orientation and importance of this marketing communications tool.

The stakeholder concept recognises that various networks of stakeholders can be identified, with each network consisting of members who are oriented towards supporting the organisation either in an indirect way or directly through the added-value processes. For the purposes of this chapter it is useful to set out who the main stakeholders are likely to be. Stakeholder groups, it should be remembered, are not static and new groups can emerge in response to changes in the environment. The main core groups, however, tend to be the following.

Employees (internal public relations)

The employees of an organisation are major stakeholders and represent a major opportunity to use word-of-mouth communications. It has long been established that employees need to be motivated, involved and stimulated to perform their tasks at a high level. Their work as external communicators is less well-established, but their critical role in providing external cues as part of the corporate identity programme was discussed in Chapter 13.

Financial groups (financial or investor relations)

Shareholders require regular information to maintain their continued confidence in the organisation and to prevent them changing their portfolios and reducing the value of the organisation. In addition to the shareholders, there are those individuals who are either potential shareholders or who advise shareholders and investors. These represent the wider financial community, but nevertheless have a very strong influence on the stature, strength and value of an organisation. Financial analysts need to be supplied with information in order that they be up to date with the activities and performance outcomes of organisations, but also need to be advised of developments within the various markets that the organisation operates.

Organisations attempt to supply analysts with current information and materials about the organisation and the markets in which they are operating, to ensure that the potential and value of publicly quoted organisations is reflected in the share price. The success of any further attempts to increase investment and to secure any necessary capital will be determined

The perception of risk held by investors can be lowered, funds are released and new products developed.

by the confidence that the financial community has in the organisation. Public relations, or investor relations, is an important form of communication in that it can create and shape these relationships. By developing confidence in this way the perception of risk held by investors can be lowered, funds are released and new products are developed and launched.

Customers (media relations)

The relationships that organisations develop with the media are extremely important in ensuring that their messages reach their current and potential customers. Customers represent a major stakeholder audience and are often the target of public relations activities, because although members of the public may not be current customers the potential they represent is significant. The attitudes and preferences towards the organisation and its products may be unfavourable, in which case it is unlikely that they will wish to purchase the product or speak positively about the organisation. By creating awareness and trust it is possible to create goodwill and interest, which may translate into purchase activity or favourable word-of-mouth communications. This is achieved through media relations.

ViewPoint 19.2 Promoting cream for salads

Established food brands need to be refreshed and repositioned on a regular basis in order to be of value to successive generations. Heinz Salad Cream, for example, is a brand that has been around for over 90 years and was generally perceived as a salad dressing preferred mainly by the older generation. Many adults have not even tried it, as they have been brought up using mayonnaise.

Rather than discontinue the brand, Heinz decided to reposition the product by introducing it to a new generation of young adults and surrounding it with a new set of associations and brand values. This was accomplished using public relations, advertising, radio and in-store promotions in concert with the web site. A launch event involving Denise van Outen and Graham Norton was used to generate media attention and, through sponsorship of a comedy tour, tasting opportunities were increased among the target audience.

Question

This example shows how public relations can help reposition a brand. Isn't this the work of advertising?

Task

Why do you believe Denise van Outen and Graham Norton were used for this campaign?

Of all the media, the press is the most crucial, as it is always interested in newsworthy items and depends to a large extent on information being fed to it by a variety of corporate press officers. Consequently, publicity can be generated for a range of organisational events, activities and developments.

Organisations and communities (corporate public relations)

There are a variety of public, private, commercial and not-for-profit organisations and communities with whom organisations need to communicate and interact on a regular basis. Corporate public relations (sometimes referred to as corporate communications) are used to reach this wide spectrum of audiences and cover a range of activities. Each audience and set of issues have particular characteristics that lead to individual forms of public relations practice:

- *public affairs* – government and local authorities;
- *community relations* – members of local communities;
- *industry relations* – suppliers, associations and other trade stakeholders;
- *issues management* – various audiences concerning sensitive industries (e.g. tobacco or pharmaceuticals).

Organisations should seek to work with, rather than against, these stakeholder groups. As a result, public relations should be aimed at informing audiences of their strategic intentions and seeking ways in which the objectives of both parties can be satisfied.

A framework of public relations

Communications with such a wide variety of stakeholders need to vary to reflect different environmental conditions, organisational objectives and forms of relationship. Grunig and Hunt (1984) have attempted to capture the diversity of public relations activities through a framework. They set out four models to reflect the different ways in which public relations is, in their opinion, considered to work. These models, based on their experiences as public relations practitioners, constitute a useful approach to understanding the complexity of this form of communication. The four models are set out in Figure 19.1.

	Model			
Characteristic	**Press agentry/publicity**	**Public information**	**Two-way asymmetric**	**Two-way symmetric**
Purpose	Propaganda	Dissemination of information	Scientific persuasion	Mutual understanding
Nature of communication	One way; complete truth not essential	One way; truth important	Two way; imbalanced effects	Two way; balanced effects
Communication model	Source → Rec.*	Source → Rec.*	Source ⇄ Rec.* Feedback	Group ⇄ Group
Nature of research	Little; 'counting house'	Little; readability, readership	Formative; evaluative of attitudes	Formative; evaluative of understanding
Leading historical figures	P.T. Barnum	Ivy Lee	Edward L. Bernays	Bernays, educators, professional leaders
Where practised today	Sports, theatre, product promotion	Government, not-for-profit associations, business	Competitive business, agencies	Regulated business, agencies
Estimated percentage of organisations practising today	15%	50%	20%	15%

* Receiver.

Figure 19.1 Models of public relations
Source: Grunig and Hunt (1984). Used with kind permission.

The press agentry/publicity model

The essence of this approach is that communication is used as a form of propaganda. That is, the communication flow is essentially one way, and the content is not bound to be strictly truthful as the objective is to convince the receiver of a new idea or offering. This can be observed in the growing proliferation of media events and press releases.

The public information model

Unlike the first model, this approach seeks to disseminate truthful information. While the flow is again one way, there is little focus on persuasion, more on the provision of information. This can best be seen through public health campaigns and government advice communications in respect of crime, education and health.

The two-way asymmetric model

Two-way communication is a major element of this model.

Two-way communication is a major element of this model. Feedback from receivers is important, but as power is not equally distributed between the various stakeholders and the organisation, the relationship has to be regarded as asymmetric. The purpose remains to influence attitude and behaviour through persuasion.

The two-way symmetric model

This represents the most acceptable and mutually rewarding form of communication. Power is seen to be dispersed equally between the organisation and its stakeholders and the intent of the communication flow is considered to be reciprocal. The organisation and its respective publics are prepared to adjust their positions (attitudes and behaviours) in the light of the information flow. A true dialogue emerges through this interpretation, unlike any of the other three models, which see an unbalanced flow of information and expectations.

The model has attracted a great deal of attention and has been reviewed and appraised by a number of commentators (Miller, 1989). As a result of this and a search for excellence in public relations, Grunig (1992) revised the model to reflect the dominance of the 'craft' and the 'professional' approaches to public relations practices. That is, those practitioners who utilise public relations merely as a tool to achieve media visibility can be regarded as 'craft'-oriented.

Those organisations whose managers seek to utilise public relations as a means of mediating their relationships with their various stakeholders are seen as 'professional' practitioners. They are considered to be using public relations as a longer-term and proactive form of planned communication. The former see public relations as an instrument, the latter as a means of conducting a dialogue.

These models are not intended to suggest that those responsible for communications should choose among them. Their use and interpretation depend upon the circumstances that prevail at any one time. Organisations use a number of these different approaches to manage the communication issues that exist between them and the variety of different stakeholder audiences with whom they interact. However, there is plenty of evidence to suggest that the press/agentry model is the one most used by practitioners and that the two-way symmetrical model is harder to observe in practice.

These four models are not independent but coexist with one another.

These models have been subjected to further investigation and Grunig (1997) concluded that these four models are not independent but coexist with one another. Therefore, it is better to characterise public relations as dimensions of communication behaviour (Yun, 2006). These dimensions are direction, purpose, channel and ethics, and are explained at Table 19.1.

Table 19.1 Dimensions of public relations

Dimension of public relations	Explanation
Direction	Refers to whether communication is one-way (disseminating) or two-way (exchange).
Purpose	Purpose refers to degree to which there are communication effects on both parties. Symmetry refers to communications effects on both sides leading to collaboration whereas asymmetry leads to one-sided effects and in turn advocacy.
Channel	Interpersonal communication refers to direct, face-to-face communication. Mediated communication is indirect and routed through the media.
Ethics	The degree to which public relations-based communications are ethical. Grunig refers to three sub-dimensions: teleology (the consequences), disclosure (whose interests does the communication serve?) and social responsibility (who is affected?).

Source: After Yun (2006).

Public relations and relationship management

In addition, it is important to remember that the shift to a relationship management perspective effectively alters the way public relations is perceived and practised by organisations. Ehling (1992) suggests that instead of trying to manipulate audience opinion so that the organisation is of primary importance, the challenge is to use symbolic visual communication messages with behaviour such that the organisation–audience relationship improves for all parties. Kent and Taylor (2002) and Bruning and Ledingham (2000) develop this theme by suggesting that it is the ability of organisations to encourage and practise dialogue that really enables truly symmetrical relationships to develop. What follows from this is a change in evaluation, from measuring the decimation of messages to one that measures audience influence and behavioural and attitudinal change and, of course, relationship dynamics. Bruning and Ledingham describe this as a change from measuring outputs to one that measures outcomes.

A change from measuring outputs to one that measures outcomes.

In addition to this discernible shift in emphasis there has been a change in the way public relations is used by organisations. Traditionally, public relations has been used as a means of managing communication between parties, whereas now communication is regarded as a means of managing relationships (Kent and Taylor, 2002). In order to use communication to develop the full potential within relationships many argue that dialogic interaction should be encouraged. In Chapter 8 five tenets of dialogue were presented: mutuality, empathy, propinquity, risk and commitment. These have been offered by Kent and Taylor as the elements that may form a framework through which dialogue may be considered and developed. On a practical level they argue that organisations should place email, web addresses, 0800 telephone numbers and organisational addresses prominently in all forms of external communication, most notably advertisements and web sites, to enable dialogue.

In consideration of the role of public relations, namely to build relationships that are of mutual value, Bruning *et al.* (2008) conclude that input, interaction and participation of key public members in the organisation–public dynamic is critically important. In other words dialogue, arising through interaction, and the personalisation of communications is important for relationship development.

Corporate public relations and marketing public relations

Many writers and organisations are now challenging the traditional view of public relations. The marketing dimension of public relations has been developed considerably in recent years. This is a response to media rates increasing ahead of inflation, media and markets becoming increasingly fragmented and marketing managers seeking more effective communication mixes. As a result, public relations is being used actively to support and reinforce other elements of the communications mix (Kitchen, 1991).

The development of integrated marketing communications has helped bring marketing and public relations closer together. The advantage of utilising a number of tools together is that through coordination message impact is improved. For example, the Prostate Cancer Research Foundation's campaign, featuring the deceased comedian Bob Monkhouse, generated additional exposure worth over £3m (Allen, 2008).

A performance network consists of those organisations (stakeholders) who directly influence or are influenced by the value-added processes of the focus organisation. They can engage in relational exchanges and often seek to develop long-term collaborative relationships. The support network consists of those organisations that influence, and are influenced by, the value-adding processes in an indirect way. They tend to engage in market exchanges that encourage a short-term perspective.

Both these networks require public relations, but in different ways. The support network needs public relations to help build and sustain goodwill between members and to create relationships that acknowledge the direction and intent of the strategy being pursued by each of them. This requires the work of a more traditional approach to public relations. The performance network needs public relations to sustain an environment where there is not only goodwill but also collaboration and trust, one where the satisfaction of particular target segments is the goal of all members. This requires a marketing orientation where there is a greater emphasis on the need to achieve certain levels of profitability as a result of meeting and satisfying customer needs.

Bearing these points in mind and recalling the professional and craft designations set out previously, it is not surprising that two types of public relations have begun to emerge: corporate public relations and marketing public relations. Corporate public relations, according to Cutlip *et al.* (2006: 6), is 'a function of management that establishes and maintains mutually beneficial relationships between an organisation and the various publics on whom its success and failure depend'. They regard marketing public relations as activities associated with specific publics, such as customers, consumers and clients, characterised by exchange transactions.

> Two types of public relations have begun to emerge: corporate public relations and marketing public relations.

This dichotomy is not intended to suggest that these are mutually exclusive forms of public relations, since they are not, and, as Kitchen and Proctor (1991) rightly point out, they are mutually interactive. The use of corporate communications has an effect similar to that of ink being injected into a bottle of water: the diffusion produced can assist all parts of an organisation and its stakeholders, whether they be in the performance or support networks. Similarly, public relations at the product level can have an immediate effect on the goodwill and perspective with which stakeholders perceive the whole organisation.

For example, an airline opening a new route and using marketing PR activities focused on customers in the hinterland of each destination will impact on both the product and the airline as a whole. Further examples of MPR can be observed by companies installing 'carelines' that can be used by customers to contact them (to seek advice and complain) about aspects of the company's products and services. The telephone number, which can be made visible on posters, receipts, catalogues, advertisements and shopping bags, serves to feed negative and positive aspects and, through the use of data analysis, can assist the development of new products and services. Indeed, Burger King has used this to develop new menus and merchandising items.

The net impact of either approach has to be reflected in the performance of the organisation, and for many that is the profitability of the unit. The identification of these two forms of public relations does not mean that this approach is a widely used practice. Indeed, at this stage only a minority of organisations recognise the benefits that this approach can bring. However, as an increasing number of organisations, in a variety of sectors, are expanding their use of PR, so more sophisticated approaches are likely to emerge, aimed at improving product, corporate and overall performance and satisfaction levels.

Objectives of a public relations plan

It can be seen that the main broad objectives of public relations activities are to provide visibility for the corporate body and support for the marketing agenda at the product level. The marketing communications objectives, established earlier in the plan, will have identified issues concerning the attitudes and relationships stakeholders have with an organisation and its products. Decisions will have been made to build awareness and to change perception, preferences or attitudes. The task of the public relations plan is to provide a series of coordinated programmes that complement the overall marketing communications strategy and develop and enhance some of the identity cues used by stakeholders. The overall goal should be to develop the relationship between the organisation and its different audiences.

> The overall goal should be to develop the relationship between the organisation and its different audiences.

Public relations can be used to address issues identified within the support and performance networks (Chapter 7). These will be concerned with communications that aim to develop positive attitudes and dispositions towards the organisation and generally concern strategic issues. Public relations can also contribute to the marketing needs of the organisation and will therefore be focused at the product level in the performance network and on consumers, seeking to change attitudes, preferences and awareness levels with respect to products and services offered. Therefore, a series of programmes is necessary – one to fulfil the corporate requirements and another to support the marketing of products and services.

Cause-related marketing

One major reason for the development of public relations and the associated corporate reputation activities, has been the rise in importance and use of cause-related marketing activities. This has partly been due to the increased awareness of the need to be perceived as credible, responsible and ethically sound. Developing a strong and socially oriented reputation has become a major form of differentiation for organisations operating in various markets, especially where price, quality and tangible attributes are relatively similar. Being able to present corporate brands as contributors to the wider

> One major reason for this is the rise in importance and use of cause-related marketing activities.

social framework, a role beyond that of simple profit generators, has enabled many organisations to achieve stronger, more positive market positions.

Cause-related marketing is a commercial activity through which profit-oriented and not-for-profit organisations form partnerships to exploit, for mutual benefit, their association in the name of a particular cause.

The benefits from a properly planned and constructed cause-related campaign can accrue to all participants. Cause-related marketing helps improve corporate reputation, enables product differentiation and appears to contribute to improved customer retention through enhanced sales. In essence, cause-related marketing is a means by which relationships with stakeholders can be developed. As organisations outsource an increasingly larger part of their business activities and as the stakeholder networks become more complex, so the need to be perceived as (and to be) socially responsible becomes a critically important dimension of an organisation's image.

ViewPoint 19.3 Pouring water on troubled Coke

Although WWF and the Coca-Cola Corporation had been working together for several years on a number of projects to conserve water and address water efficiency in the company's operations, the announcement of a formal agreement between the two organisations marked a critical point for Coke.

The vast amount of water consumed by the Coca-Cola Corporation had led to widespread comment and criticism. In an attempt to change the perception held by the company's stakeholders, the announcement in 2007 that they were pledging to invest $20m in WWF freshwater schemes, wherever they had a bottling plant, represented a public commitment to change.

Exhibit 19.1 WWF visual representing the drive to save freshwater ecosystems
© Brent Stirton/Getty Images.

Neville Isdell, then Chairman of Coca-Cola, stated:

> Our goal is to replace every drop of water we use in our beverages and their production. For us that means reducing the amount of water used to produce our beverages, recycling water used for manufacturing processes so it can be returned safely to the environment, and replenishing water in communities and nature through locally relevant projects.

As part of the deal WWF provide Coca-Cola with advice on a range of related environmental topics, including water conservation, usage and recycling in manufacturing, how to cut its energy and carbon footprint and how the organisation can replenish water in local communities. In addition, the agreement involves joint communications programmes and campaigns, framing the relationship under cause for water conservation.

This scheme enables Coca-Cola to be seen as a more environmentally aware and socially responsible company. The scheme helps WWF achieve its goals and move towards encouraging other leading companies to become involved in similar schemes.

Sources: Bokaie (2007); Kleinman (2007); WWF Pressroom: www.panda.org/news_facts/newsroom/index.cfm?uNewsID=104940.

Question

To what extent is this scheme a cynical ploy to soften Coke's reputation?

Task

Find out how Pepsi are meeting the environmental challenge.

A public relations programme consists of a number of planned events and activities that seek to satisfy communication objectives. The following represent some of the broad tools and techniques associated with public relations, but it should be noted that the list is not intended to be comprehensive.

Public relations: methods and techniques

An organisation's corporate identity consists of those activities that reflect, to a large extent, the personality of an organisation (see Chapter 13). Public relations provides some of the deliberate cues that enable stakeholders to develop images and perceptions through which they recognise, understand, select and converse with organisations.

The range of public relations cues or methods available to organisations is immense. Different organisations use different permutations in order that they can communicate effectively with their various stakeholder audiences. For the purposes of this text a general outline is provided of the more commonly used methods.

A consideration of the differences between corporate and marketing public relations would reveal that many organisations use media and sports sponsorships, publicity and sales promotion tie-ups in the name of marketing public relations. Corporate public relations activities revolve around corporate publicity, issues management, public affairs, lobbying, financial/investor relations and corporate advertising (Kitchen and Moss, 1995). This demarcation is not up to date and should not be regarded as typical or indeed desirable, but it serves as a useful means of understanding the focus of these two types of public relations. What also emerges is a profound recognition of the need to integrate the various communication activities, which itself requires objective and coordinated management attention.

No further attempt is made in this book to segregate the cues used by organisations for either marketing or corporate public relations. The main reason for this is that there is no

Table 19.2 Cues used by PR to project corporate identity

Cues to build credibility	Cues to signal visibility
Product quality	Sales literature and company publications
Customer relations	Publicity and media relations
Community involvement	Speeches and presentations
Strategic performance	Event management
Employee relations	Marketing communications/messages
Crisis management skills	Media mix
Third-party endorsement	Design (signage, logo, letterhead)
Perceived ethics and environmental awareness	Dress codes
Architecture and furnishing	Exhibitions/seminars; sponsorships

useful benefit from such a sub-division. Cues are interchangeable and can be used to build credibility or to provide visibility for an organisation. It is the skill of the public relations practitioner that determines the right blend of techniques. The various types of cue are set out in Table 19.2.

While there is general agreement on a definition, there is a lower level of consensus over what constitutes public relations. This is partly because the range of activities is diverse and categorisation problematic. The approach adopted here is that public relations consists of a range of communication activities, of which media relations, publicity and event management appear to be the main ones used by practitioners.

Media relations

Media relations consist of a range of activities designed to provide media journalists and editors with information. The intention is that they relay the information, through their media, for consumption by their audiences. Obviously, the original message may be changed and subject to information deviance as it is processed, but audiences perceive much of this information as highly credible simply because opinion formers (Chapter 2) have bestowed their judgement on the item. Of the various forms of media relations, press releases, interviews, press kits and press conferences are most used.

> The intention is that media relations relay the information, through their media, for consumption by their audiences.

Press releases

The press release is a common form of media relations activity. A written report concerning a change in the organisation is sent to various media houses for inclusion in the media vehicle as an item of news. The media house may cover a national area, but very often a local house will suffice. These written statements concern developments in the organisation, such as promotions, new products, awards, prizes, new contracts and customers. The statement is deliberately short and written in such a style that it attracts the attention of the editor. Further information can be obtained if it is to be included within the next publication or news broadcast.

Press conferences

Press conferences are used when a major event has occurred and where a press release cannot convey the appropriate tone or detail required by the organisation. Press conferences are mainly used by politicians, but organisations in crisis (e.g. accidents and mergers) and individuals appealing for help (e.g. police requesting assistance from the public with respect to a particular incident) can use this form of communication. Press kits containing a full reproduction of any statements, photographs and relevant background information should always be available.

Press kits containing a full reproduction of any statements, photographs and relevant background information should always be available.

Interviews

Interviews with representatives of an organisation enable news and the organisation's view of an issue or event to be conveyed. Other forms of media relations concern bylined articles

ViewPoint 19.4 Press for Dyson

When James Dyson launched his revolutionary, upright vacuum cleaner he did not have the resources to fund an advertising campaign to support the launch. Although the design enabled the product to stand out in showrooms there was little to inform customers of the advantages of the product and to justify the starting price, which was double that of the competition.

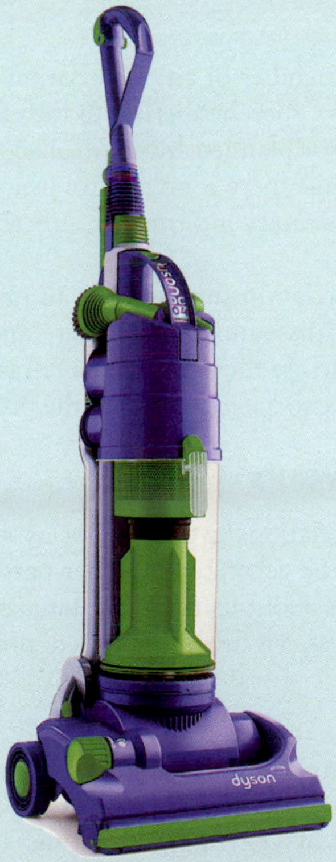

Exhibit 19.2 Dyson
The manufacturer of this revolutionary new domestic appliance uses marketing communications to differentiate, remind, inform and persuade audiences.
Picture reproduced with the kind permission of Dyson.

One solution was to hang a brochure and a point-of-sales tag on the handle of each machine. The brochure folded out, provided basic information about each component and avoided any superlatives or attempts at persuasion. The sales tag, however, was used to tell the story about the experiences Dyson encountered trying to design and bring the new product to the market. People would be seen bending over avidly reading the Dyson story.

The second solution was to use press journalists to recall the same story because they could reach the target market and their messages would be highly credible in the eyes of the target audience. Rather than write press releases Dyson gave interviews to selected reporters, many of whom were from the quality press. The articles tended to be extremely positive about the product but concentrated more on the life experiences of James Dyson himself, and reinforced the messages conveyed through the sales tags. The personalised account of the development process and the frequency with which these articles appeared, provided readers with a way of identifying and becoming emotionally engaged with the whole Dyson experience. The language used and the repetition of the messages only served to increase the overall intensity of these marketing communication messages.

Source: Based on Boyle (2004).

Question

Why did retailers decide to stock Dyson when there was no advertising to pull consumers into the store?

Task

Storytelling can be powerful. Find another campaign in which storytelling was a central feature.

(articles written by a member of an organisation about an issue related to the company and offered for publication), speeches, letters to the editor, and photographs and captions.

Media relations can be planned and controlled to the extent of what is sent to the media and when it is released. While there is no control over what is actually used, media relations allow organisations to try to convey information concerning strategic issues and to reach particular stakeholders.

The quality of the relationship between an organisation and the media will dramatically affect the impact and dissemination of news and stories released by an organisation. The relationships referred to are those between an organisation's public relations manager and the editor and journalists associated with both the press and the broadcast media.

Publicity and events

Control over public relations events is not as strong as that for media relations. Indeed, negative publicity can be generated by other parties, which can impact badly on an organisation by raising doubts about its financial status or perhaps the quality of its products. Three main event activity areas can be distinguished: product, corporate and community events.

Product events

Product-oriented events are normally focused on increasing sales. Cookery demonstrations, celebrities autographing their books and the opening of a new store by the CEO or local MP are events aimed at generating attention, interest and sales of a particular product. Alternatively events are designed to attract the attention of the media and, through stories and articles presented in the news, are able to reach a wide audience. For example, the public's attention was drawn to the launch of *The Simpsons Movie* in July 2007, by a stunt involving the painting of a giant Homer Simpson next to the 180-foot chalk cut Cerne Abbas giant in Dorset. News coverage of the new work of art, Homer holding a doughnut, was in most national newspapers, on ITV, Sky and BBC television, plus radio coverage (see Exhibit 19.3).

Exhibit 19.3 A paint line drawing of Homer Simpson next to the chalk cut Cerne Abbas Giant, used to attract media attention prior to the launch of *The Simpsons Movie* in July 2007
PA Photos.

Corporate events

Events designed to develop the corporate body are often held by an organisation with a view to providing some entertainment. These can generate considerable local media coverage, which in turn facilitates awareness, goodwill and interest. For example, events such as open days, factory visits and donations of products to local events can be very beneficial.

Community events

These are activities that contribute to the life of the local community. Sponsoring local fun runs and children's play areas, making contributions to local community centres and the disabled are typical activities. The organisation attempts to become more involved with the local community as a good employer and good member of the community. This helps to develop goodwill and awareness in the community.

The choice of events an organisation becomes involved with is critical. The events should have a theme and be chosen to satisfy objectives established earlier in the communications plan. See Chapter 20 for an example of sponsorship of local community events.

Events should have a theme and be chosen to satisfy objectives.

In addition to these key activities the following are important forms of public relations:

- lobbying (out of personal selling and publicity);
- sponsorship (out of event management and advertising) (see Chapter 26);
- corporate advertising (out of corporate public relations and advertising);
- crisis management (which has developed out of issues management, a part of corporate public relations).

Lobbying

The representation of certain organisations or industries within government is an important form of public relations work. While legislation is being prepared, lobbyists provide a flow of information to their organisations to keep them informed about events (as a means of scanning the environment), but they also ensure that the views of the organisation are heard in order that legislation can be shaped appropriately, limiting any potential damage that new legislation might bring.

Lobbyists provide a flow of information to their organisations to keep them informed about events.

Moloney (1997) suggests that lobbying is inside public relations as it focuses on the members of an organisation who seek to persuade and negotiate with its stakeholders in government on matters of opportunity and or threat. He refers to in-house lobbyists (those members of the organisation who try to influence non-members) and hired lobbyists contracted to complete specific tasks.

His view of lobbying is that it is one of

> *monitoring public policy-making for a group interest; building a case in favour of that interest; and putting it privately with varying degrees of pressure to public decision makers for their acceptance and support through favourable political intervention.*
> *(p. 173)*

Where local authorities interpret legislation and frame the activities of their citizens and constituent organisations, the government determines legislation and controls the activities of people and organisations across markets.

This control may be direct or indirect, but the power and influence of government are such that large organisations and trade associations seek to influence the direction and strength of legislation, because any adverse laws or regulations may affect the profitability and the value of the organisation. Recent initiatives by the UK government to reduce the length of time that new drugs are protected by patent were severely contested by representatives from drug manufacturers and their trade association, the Association of British Pharmaceutical Industries. Despite a great deal of lobbying the action was lost, and now manufacturers have only eight years to recover their investment before other manufacturers can replicate the drug. The pharmaceutical industry has also been actively lobbying the European Union with respect to legislation on new patent regulations and the information that must be carried in any marketing communications message. The tobacco industry is well known for its lobbying activities, as are chemical, transport and many other industries.

The pharmaceutical industry has been actively lobbying the European Union.

Corporate advertising

In an attempt to harness the advantages of both advertising and public relations, corporate advertising has been seen by some as a means of communicating more effectively with a range of stakeholders. The credibility of messages transmitted through public relations is high, but the control that management has over the message is limited. Advertising, however, allows management virtually total control over message dispersion, but the credibility of these messages is usually low. Corporate advertising is the combination of the best of advertising and the best of public relations.

Corporate advertising, that is advertising on behalf of an organisation rather than its products or services, has long been associated with public relations rather than the advertising department. This can be understood in terms of the origins and former use that organisations made of corporate advertising (Figure 19.2). The first major period was the 1960s, when

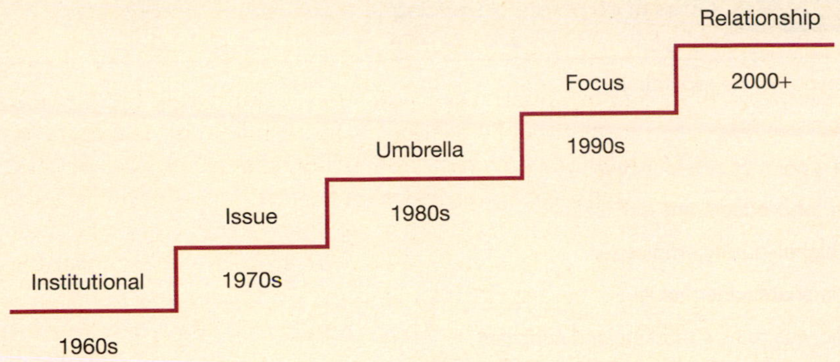

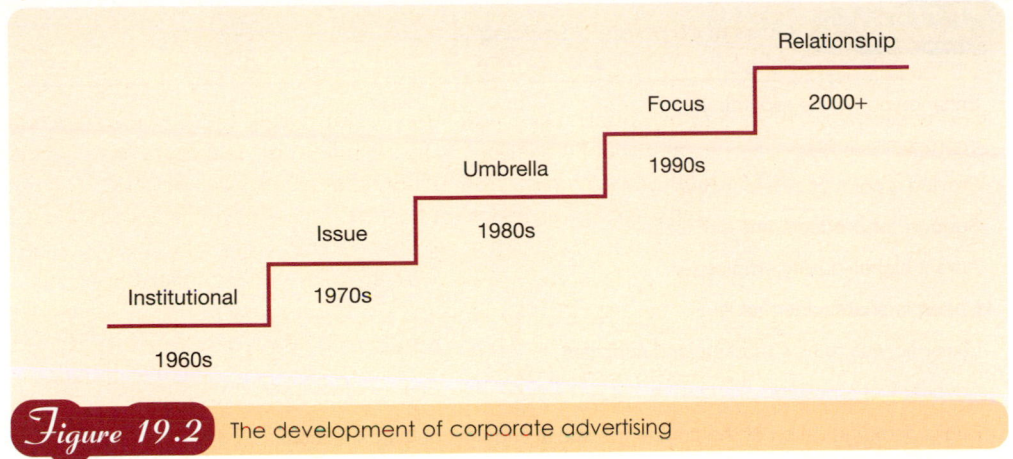

Figure 19.2 The development of corporate advertising

institutional advertising became prominent. According to Stanton (1964), the primary task of institutional advertising was to create goodwill. The next period was the 1970s, when corporate image advertising became popular. During this decade, organisations used issue and advocacy advertising as a means of promoting political and social ideas in an attempt to generate public support for the position adopted by an organisation.

During the 1980s, which witnessed a large number of mergers and takeovers, there was an increase in the use of umbrella advertising. Organisations used the name of the organisation as a broad banner, under which a range of products and services was promoted. As discussed previously, there has been a movement towards the incorporation of products and services in the use of public relations. This is reflected in the use of corporate advertising in the 1990s. Although the generation of goodwill continues to be a dominant theme, there is also a need to focus on organisations as discrete units. As many organisations de-layer and return to core business activities, so there is a need to focus communications on what they do best. Such focusing also enables them to reduce advertising expenditure on products because of increased media costs. Corporate advertising provides some opportunity for organisations to achieve these objectives.

However, the main purpose of corporate advertising appears to be the provision of cues by which stakeholders can identify and understand an organisation. This is achieved by presenting the personality of the organisation to a wide range of stakeholders, rather than presenting particular functions or products that the organisation markets. Schumann *et al.* (1991) conclude that a number of US studies indicate that the first goal of corporate advertising is to enhance the company's reputation and the second is to provide support for the promotion of products and services. Table 19.3 sets out the most important goals that executives see corporate advertising as responsible for satisfying.

Reasons for the use of corporate advertising

The need to improve and maintain goodwill and to establish a positive reputation among an organisation's stakeholders has already been mentioned. These are tasks that need to be undertaken consistently and continuously, with the aim of building a reputational reservoir. In addition, however, there are particular occasions when organisations need to use corporate advertising:

- during change and transition;
- when the organisation has a poor image;
- for product support;
- recruitment;

Table 19.3 Goals of corporate advertising

Enhance corporate reputation
Improve credibility
Provide a point of differentiation
Support for products and services
Attract higher-quality employees
Underpin shareholder value
Easier access to new markets and suppliers
Advocacy of a position
Public communication of the company's social and environmental actions

- repositioning;
- advocacy or issues.

Change

When an organisation experiences a period of major change, perhaps the transition before, during and after a takeover or merger, corporate advertising can be used in a variety of ways. The first is defensively, to convince stakeholders, particularly shareholders, of the value of the organisation and of the need not to accept hostile offers; second, to inform and to advise of current positions; finally to position any 'new' organisation that may result from the merger activity. The defence of Marks & Spencer led by Stuart Rose, when Philip Green attempted a takeover in 2004, was based around messages communicated to current shareholders of the superior future value of the business under the current ownership and managers. This was intended to raise credibility and hence prevent a takeover based on differing projected values.

Poor image

Corporate advertising can also be used to correct any misunderstanding that stakeholders might have of corporate reality (Reisman, 1989). For example, financial analysts may believe that an organisation is underperforming, but reality indicates that performance is good. As we have seen before, this can be a result of poor communication, and through corporate advertising the organisation can correct such misunderstandings and help establish strategic credibility with the financial community and other stakeholders.

Corporate advertising can be used to correct any misunderstanding.

Product support

Corporate advertising can also assist the launch of new products. The costs normally associated with a launch can be lowered, and it is feasible to assume, although difficult to measure, that the effectiveness of a product launch can be improved when corporate advertising has been used to establish good reputational equity.

Recruitment

Corporate advertising is used to recruit employees by creating a positive and attractive image of the organisation. The development of source credibility, in particular trust, is fundamental, and through the process of identification individuals can become attracted to the notion of working for a particular organisation and are stimulated to seek further information.

8lbs.
3oz.
poweredbycisco.
Ambulances outfitted with smart technology
connected to hospital admissions
connected to a bouncing bundle of joy in Sheffield.
And the myriad sonograms, lab tests and medication regimes
that make it all happen – now found in seconds.
In real time. On one secure, converged network.
Learn how Cisco is helping to change all kinds of business at
cisco.com/uk/poweredby, or by calling 00800 9999 0522.
CISCO SYSTEMS
collaboration. powered by

Exhibit 19.4 A corporate ad used by Cisco Systems. Used as a part of their repositioning to convey a more caring, human side of their technical capability and expertise
Courtesy of Cisco Systems, Inc. © 2007.

Repositioning

Organisations periodically undergo self-review that may lead to repositioning. Hewlett-Packard launched its 'Invent' campaign as part of a process of preparing stakeholders for the future. The campaign sought to take the company back to its roots, its original ideology 'the rules of the garage', in which the founders first developed the organisation and the values that are part of the corporate philosophy. The campaign sought to encourage invention and to legitimise exploration and risk taking, remembering, of course, that the HP way determines how employees work and that the customer defines whether the job is well done.

Organisations can be repositioned by the activities of competitor organisations. New products, new corporate messages, an improved trading performance or the arrival of a new CEO and the implementation of a new strategy can displace an organisation in the minds of its different stakeholders. This may require an adjustment by the focus organisation to re-establish itself. The Pepsi Challenge, referred to earlier, effectively dislodged Coca-Cola from its position as brand leader and led to a stream of product adjustments and messages from Coca-Cola aimed at repositioning itself.

Advocacy

The reasons presented so far for the use of corporate advertising are strongly related to image. A further traditional reason for the use of this tool is the opportunity for the organisation to inform its stakeholders of the position or stand that it has on a particular issue. This is referred to as advocacy advertising. Rather than promoting the organisation in a direct way, this form of corporate advertising associates an organisation with an issue of social concern, which public relations very often cannot achieve alone.

The organisation can be seen as a brand in much the same way as products and services are branded. Just as a product-based brand can be tracked, so can the corporate entity be tracked for levels of awareness, attitudes and preferences held by stakeholders.

Crisis communications

A growing and important part of the work associated with public relations is crisis communications. At one time, when a crisis such as a threat of takeover or workplace accident struck an organisation, the first stakeholders to be summoned by the CEOs were merchant bankers. Today the public relations consultant is first through the door. The power of corporate and marketing communications is beginning to be recognised and appreciated. Indeed, the astute CEO summons the public relations consultant in anticipation of crisis, on the basis that being prepared is a major step in diffusing the energy with which some crises can affect organisations.

Organisational crises can be usefully considered in the context of chaos theory (Seeger, 2002). Chaos occurs when complex systems break down and the established order and equilibrium is broken by events that are often abrupt and discontinuous. Chaos theory considers system breakdown as a necessary event in order that the system be refreshed. Seeger phrases this process as 'disorder necessary for order, decay a precursor to renewal, decline a step in growth and collapse a prelude to rebuilding as one of the most attractive and optimistic features of chaos theory' (p. 331).

> Organisational crises can be usefully considered in the context of chaos theory.

Crises can occur because of a simple or minor managerial mistake, an incorrect decision or because of a seemingly distant environmental event. All organisations face the prospect of managing a crisis, indeed, some commentators ominously suggest that all organisations have a crisis just around the corner (Fink, 2000). Crises are emerging with greater frequency as a result of a number of factors. Table 19.4 sets out some of the main factors that give rise to crises for organisations.

Figure 19.3 describes organisational crises in the context of two key variables. On the horizontal axis is the degree to which management has control over the origin of the crisis. Is the origin of the crisis outside management's control, such as an earthquake, or is it within its control, such as those crises associated with poor trading results? The vertical axis reflects the potential impact that a crisis might have on an organisation. All crises, by definition, have a potential to inflict damage on an organisation. However, some can be contained, perhaps on a geographic basis, whereas others have the potential to cause tremendous damage to an organisation, such as those experienced through product tampering and environmental pollution.

Table 19.4 Common causes of disasters

Origin of crisis	Explanation
Economic	As the Western world currently experiences growth and high levels of employment and countries in the developing world follow a fluctuating path of revitalisation and competition, this has brought some organisations and industries in the West to collapse (e.g. UK shipbuilding).
Managerial	Human error and the pursuit of financial goals by some organisations give rise to the majority of disasters. For example, cutting costs at the expense of safety and repair of systems.
Political	Issues concerning war and terrorism have encouraged kidnapping, as well as organisations having to change the locations of their business.
Climate	The climate is changing substantially in certain parts of the world, and this has brought disaster to those who lie in the wake of natural disturbances. For example, the hurricanes in 2004 that decimated the Cayman Islands and Grenada in the Caribbean; south-east Asia's December 2004 tsunami.
Technology	The rate at which technology is advancing has brought about crises such as those associated with transportation systems and aircraft disasters. Human error is also a significant factor, often associated with the rate of technological change.
New media	The age of electronic media and instant communication means that information can be disseminated throughout the world within 30 minutes of an event occurring.
Consumer groups	The rise of consumer groups (e.g. Amnesty International and Greenpeace) and their ability to investigate and publicise the operations and policies of organisations.

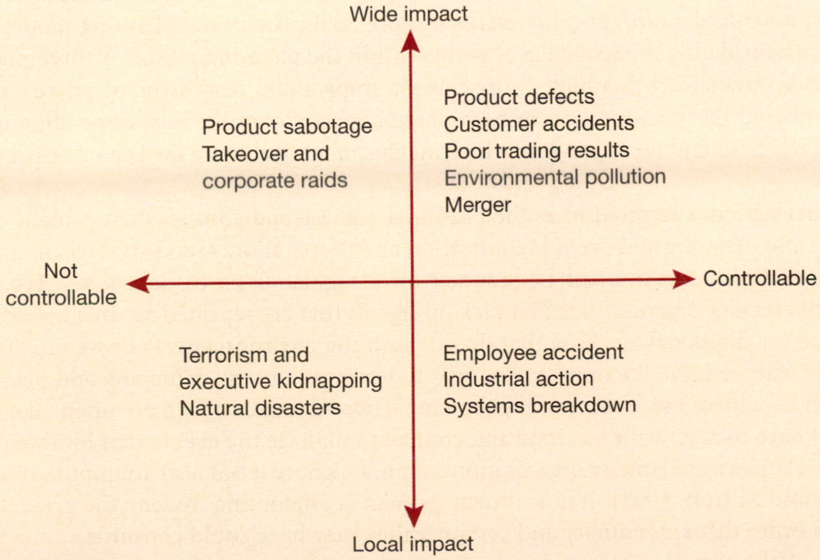

Figure 19.3 An organisational crisis matrix

The increasing occurrence of crises throughout the world has prompted many organisations to review the manner in which they anticipate managing such events, should they be implicated. It is generally assumed that those organisations that take the care to plan in anticipation of disaster will experience more favourable outcomes than those that fail to plan. Quarantelli (1988) reports that there is only a partial correlation between those that plan and those that experience successful outcomes. He attributes this to the fact that only some of the organisations that take care to prepare do so in a professional way. Poor planning can only deliver poor results. Fink (2000) reports that organisations that do not plan experience crises that last over twice as long as those that do plan.

Poor planning can only deliver poor results.

The second reason concerns the expectations of those who design and implement crisis plans. It is one thing to design a plan; it is entirely another to implement it. Crisis planning is about putting into position those elements that can effect speedy outcomes to the disaster sequence. When a crisis strikes, it is the application of contingency-based tactics by all those concerned with the event that will determine the strength of the outcome. Spillan (2003) sought to determine whether the experience of a crisis encourages concern and attention to preventing further crisis events. This was based on the evidence of Barton (2001) and Mitroff and Anagnos (2001) that most organisations only prepare crisis management plans after suffering and then recovering from a disaster. The central issue appears to revolve around the need to assess an organisation's vulnerabilities at the earliest opportunity, before a crisis occurs (Caponigro, 2000, as cited by Spillan, 2003).

Crisis phases

The number of phases through which a crisis passes varies according to author and the management model they are proposing. For example, Penrose (2000) mentions Littlejohn's six-step model, Fink's audit, Mitroff's portfolio planning approach and Burnett's crisis classification matrix. The number of phases is also influenced by the type of crisis management an organisation uses. Essentially there are two main models: organisations that plan in order to manage crisis events and in doing so attempt to contain the impact; secondly there are organisations that fail to plan and manage by reacting to crisis events (see Figure 19.4).

The differences between these two approaches are that there are fewer phases in the shorter 'reactionary' model and that the level of detail and attention given to the anticipation, management and consideration of crisis events is more deliberate in the planning model. Time is spent here considering the sequence of events within the planning model. A three-phase (and five-episode) framework is adopted: pre-impact, impact and readjustment phases. It should be remembered that the duration of each phase can vary considerably, depending upon the nature of the crisis and the manner in which management deals with the events associated with the crisis.

The first period is referred to as the pre-impact phase and consists of two main episodes, Scanning and planning and event identification and preparation. Good strategic management demands that the environment be scanned on a regular basis to detect the first signs of significant change. Organisations that pick up signals that are repeated are in a better position to prepare for disaster than those that do not scan the environment. Penrose (2000) reports that those who perceive the impact of a crisis to be severe or very damaging and plan accordingly tend to achieve more successful outcomes. Those that fail to scan are often taken by surprise and have to react with less time and control to manage the events that hit them. Even if they do pick up a signal, many organisations not only ignore it but also attempt to block it out (Pearson and Mitroff, 1993). It is as if management is attempting to deny the presence of the signals in order that any stability and certainty they may have could continue.

Many of the signals detected during the pre-impact phase wither and die. Some gather strength and develop with increasing force. The next episode is characterised by the identification of events that move from possible to probable status. There is increasing activity and

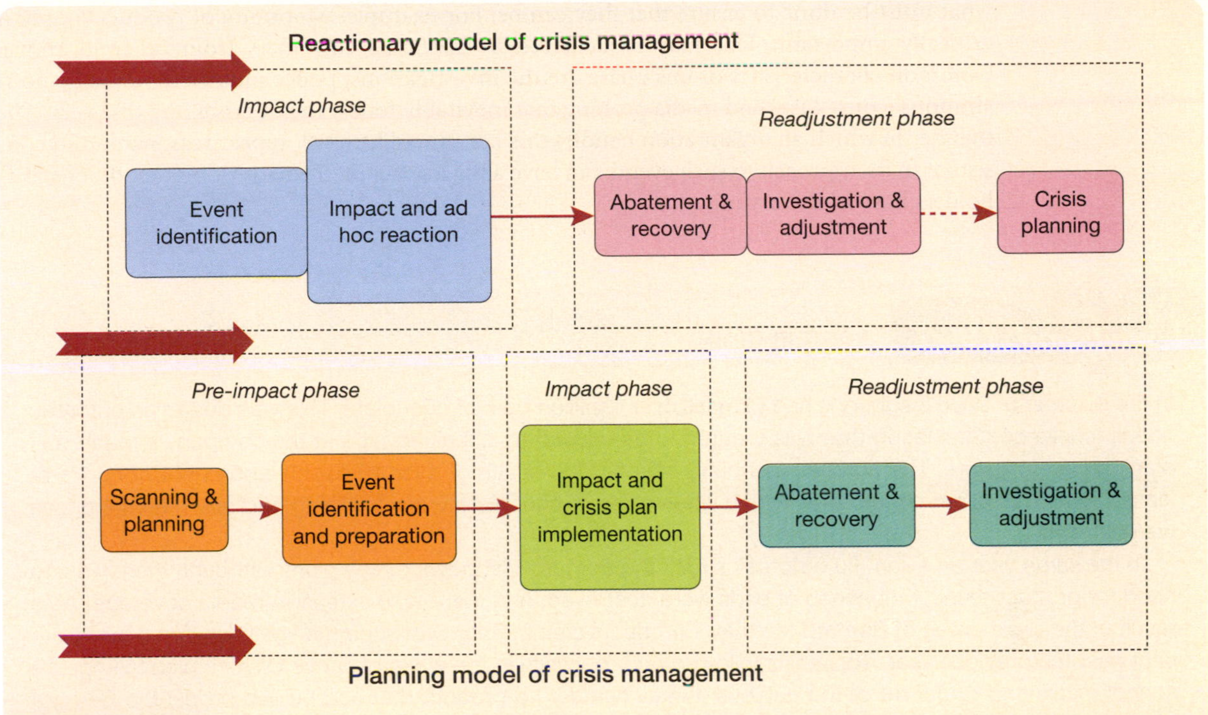

Figure 19.4 Twin models of crisis management

preparation in anticipation of the crisis, once its true nature and direction have been determined. Much of the activity should be geared to training and the preparation and deployment of crisis teams. The objective is not to prevent the crisis but to defuse it as much as possible, to inform significant stakeholders of its proximity and possible effects, and finally to manage the crisis process.

The impact phase is the period when the 'crisis breaks out' (Sturges *et al.*, 1991). Management is tested to the limit and if a plan has been developed it is implemented with the expectation of ameliorating the damage inflicted by the crisis. One method of reducing the impact is to contain or localise the crisis. By neutralising and constraining the event it can be prevented from contaminating other parts of the organisation or stakeholders. Pearson and Mitroff (1993) suggest that the containment of oil spills and the evacuation of buildings and aircraft are examples of containment and neutralisation. Through the necessity to talk to all stakeholders, management at this point will inevitably reveal its attitude towards the crisis event. Is its attitude one of genuine concern for the victims and stakeholders? Is the attitude consistent with the expectations that stakeholders have of the management team? Alternatively, is there a perception that management is making lame excuses and distancing itself from the event, and is this consistent with expectations? Readers should note that within the reactionary model the pre-impact and impact phases are merged into one, simply because there is little or no planning, no scanning and, by definition, no preparation in anticipation of a crisis.

By neutralising and constraining the event it can be prevented from contaminating other parts of the organisation.

The readjustment phase within the planning model consists of three main episodes. The period concerns the recovery and realignment of the organisation and its stakeholders to the new environment, once the deepest part of the crisis event has passed. The essential tasks are to ensure that the needs of key stakeholders can still be met and, if they cannot, to determine what must be done to ensure that they can be. For example, continuity of product supply is critically important. This may be achieved by servicing customers from other locations. Common characteristics of this phase are the investigations, police inquiries, public demonstrations, court cases and media probing that inevitably follow major crises and disasters. The manner in which an organisation handles this fall-out and tries to appear reasonable and consistent in its approach to such events can have a big impact on the perception that other stakeholders have of the organisation.

ViewPoint 19.5 Food in crisis!

In the summer of 2006 Cadbury's had to recall over 1 million bars of chocolate. This was due to an outbreak of salmonella contamination that was thought to be caused by a leaking pipe at the company's Marlbrook plant in Herefordshire. The outbreak seriously affected the health of over 40 people and cost Cadbury's at least £30m. This event occurred at a time when sales of chocolate were declining and raw material prices were climbing.

In the same year an avian 'flu outbreak struck the Bernard Matthews turkey plant. Although there was no need for product recall, thousands of birds were destroyed, and there was extensive media coverage. As a result of the crisis, sales of Bernard Matthews products plummeted, with supermarket sales down by 17 per cent over the previous year. This crisis followed poor publicity in the wake of Jamie Oliver's plea to improve school meals and to get rid of the dubious 'turkey twizzler', a product that had helped propel the Bernard Matthews brand.

Both these brands had previously held a great deal of consumer trust but much of this was lost following these scares as confidence drained and reputation tumbled.

Sources: Booth (2006); Murray-Wilson (2007); Tiltman (2007).

Question

How would you use public relations to rebuild trust in these brands?

Task

Identify another brand that experienced a crisis and track the way it used public relations to recover its position.

The rate at which organisations readjust depends partly on the strength of the image held by stakeholders prior to the crisis occurring. If the organisation had a strong reputation then the source credibility attributed to the organisation will be high. This means that messages transmitted by the organisation would be received favourably and trusted. However, if the reputation is poor, the effectiveness of any marketing communications is also going to be low. The level of source credibility held by the organisation will influence the speed with which stakeholders allow an organisation to readjust and recover after a crisis.

Benoit (1997) developed a theory concerning image restoration in the light of an organisational crisis. The theory states that there are five general approaches: denial, evade responsibility, reduce offensiveness, use corrective action and lastly mortification (see Table 19.5). Benoit has used these approaches to evaluate the responses given by a variety of organisations when faced by different disasters and crises (see Viewpoint 19.6).

Organisations that have not planned their management of crisis events and have survived a disaster may decide to instigate a more positive approach in order to mitigate the impact of future crisis events. This is not uncommon and crisis management planning may occur at the end of this cycle.

Table 19.5 Image restoration approaches

Damage retrieval	Explanation
Simple denial	Outright rejection that the act was caused by them or even occurred in the first place, or shifting the blame by asserting that another organisation (person) was responsible for the act.
Evasion (of responsibility)	Provocation . . . a reasonable response to a prior act.
	Defeasibility . . . the act occurred because of a lack of time or information.
	Accident . . . the act was not committed purposefully.
	Good intentions . . . the wrongful act was caused despite trying to do well.
Reducing offensiveness	This involves demonstrating that the act was of minor significance or by responding so as to reduce the impact of the accusor.
Corrective action	This may involve putting right what was damaged and taking steps to avoid a repeat occurrence.
Mortification	An apology or statement of regret for causing the act that gave offence.

Source: Benoit (1997).

Internet crisis

The development of the Internet may have forced many organisations to reconsider the significance of corporate reputation as part of their communication strategies. With so much information about each organisation available instantaneously, it is important that brands that have gone online be transparent and open in the way they communicate. The problem is that they are prone to attack from a variety of stakeholders. There are customers who have gripes, and there are others who despise the company on trading, moral and ethical stances. There are others who enjoy the fun of the chase. Hollingworth (2000) lists the areas of attack in Table 19.6.

Other potential public relations-related problems have arisen as a result of the development of Web 2.0. The use of blogs, wikis and podcasts along with the influence of online communities and user-generated-content presents a series of new issues for the management of public relations. These tools have facilitated a steep rise in the use of word-of-mouth communication and the promotion of citizen journalism. People are now much more able than they used to be, and more willing, to comment on brands, organisations and events that affect their lives. One of the implications of this concerns the way in which brands are perceived (see Chapter 12). Another is the way in which organisations use public relations. Gray (2007) claims that organisations need to provide training and guidelines or policies for employees who blog. Organisations also need to ensure that blog sites provide transparency, full disclosure and are honest. Some companies have tried to create artificial blogs and deceive readers. These 'floggs' risk damaging the very entity they are trying to promote and endorse. One-way communications enable organisations a degree of control over what is said about a brand. Web 2.0 empowers interaction, which means reduced control over communications and an increased need to be prepared to deal with

Organisations need to ensure that blog sites provide transparency, full disclosure and are honest.

Table 19.6 Forms of cyber attack

Method	Explanation
Cyber squatting	By registering and setting up domain names similar to established brand names, an attempt is made to mislead (gone out of business signs), misdirect (send them to other sites) or exploit (extract personal details) users.
Anti-corporate sites	Sometimes referred to as 'suck sites', these attempt to niggle large corporations (e.g. Mcspotlight) to extend their complaint or gripe.
Distributed denial of service	A DDOS attack comprises several hijacked computers simultaneously feeding information requests to a single site. This causes it to slow down or deny access.
Firewall attack	The defence shield surrounding a site becomes insecure and the host prone to data loss, misuse and corruption.
IP and web spoofing	These sites look and feel just like the master site. However, the intention may be to use the customer data fraudulently, to spy on the host site or just present a nuisance factor.
Direct/indirect site attacks	There are a number of forms of attack that vary from the indirect form by changing the style of the site text (e.g. to a biblical style) or by using Post-it style notes (e.g. 'Will never use this xxxx service again') to the more direct approach such as rewriting the web pages in real time and changing the prices.
Email	This is a potential problem for organisations – cyber harassment, defamation and the spread of viruses by email are unfortunately quite common.
Password capture	Entering networks with fake identities is a problem for companies as data destruction, corruption and misuse can seriously undermine customer confidence.

Source: Hollingworth (2000).

more controversy and even digitally enabled brand-related crises. However, Kent (2008) claims that the role of blogs within public relations is not as extensive as suggested by many commentators.

Who is affected by crisis events? When a crisis hits an organisation, many different stakeholders are vulnerable to the repercussions. Pearson and Mitroff (1993) suggest that stakeholders may perceive the focus organisation adopting a particular role. This role may be as a hero, villain or even protector. Figure 19.5 depicts some of the roles that the focus organisation might be cast in; in much the same way, stakeholders themselves might be cast in a role that reflects the perception of the focus organisation. It is interesting to monitor the ascribed roles and to see whether stakeholders actually fulfil their designated role or perhaps another when crisis strikes. Perhaps a move from rescuer to enemy is not uncommon.

The importance of this perspective is that attention has to be focused on the different organisations, not just the one on which the crisis has had immediate impact. The stakeholder net is wide and the sensitivity among cohesive groups in particular can be acute. The organisation that has a crisis plan of value is one that has considered the impact upon its stakeholders.

Internet-based communications have radically altered the way in which previous communication processes were deemed to operate (Springston, 2001). Now anyone with Internet access can post and compare information while remaining anonymous if they wish. While the Internet has provided a valuable new form of external communication, users are also more open, more exposed and more vulnerable to a range of stakeholders. The Internet provides for crisis potential (ICP) as critical information about them, whether true or false, can erupt at anytime and spread rapidly around the globe.

Although measures to manage ICP should include managing stakeholders, preparing an Internet crisis communication plan and regularly monitoring the online environment, Conway *et al.* (2007) found that 77 per cent of organisations do not manage the ICP.

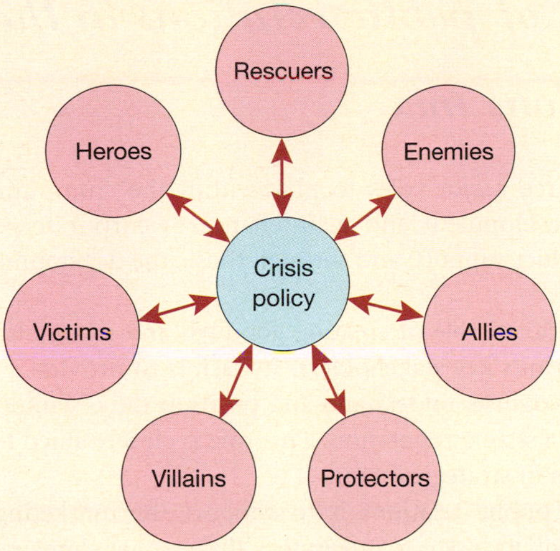

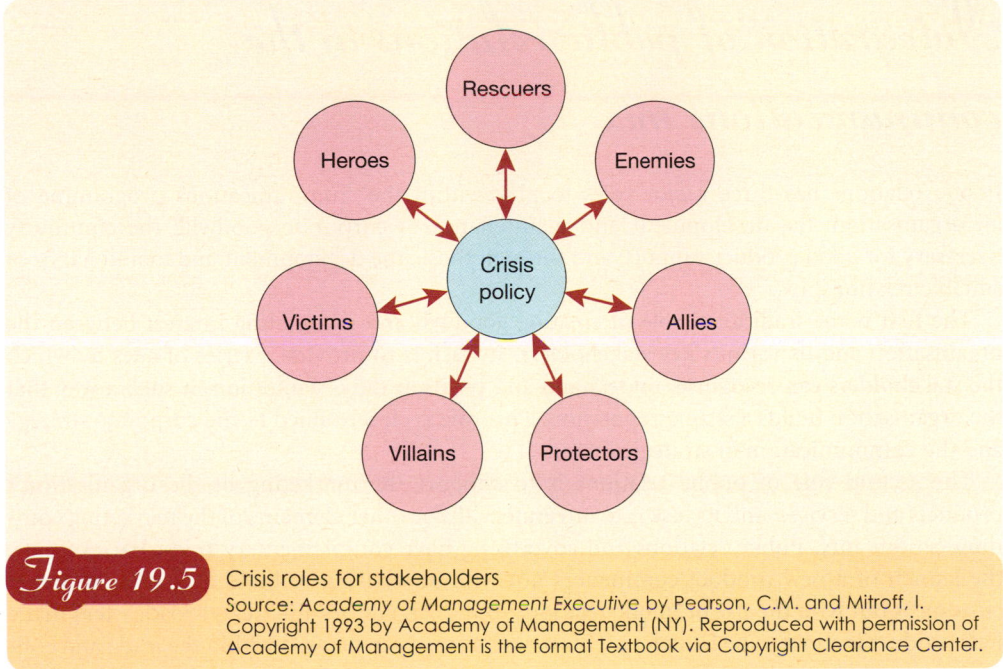

Figure 19.5 Crisis roles for stakeholders

Source: *Academy of Management Executive* by Pearson, C.M. and Mitroff, I. Copyright 1993 by Academy of Management (NY). Reproduced with permission of Academy of Management is the format Textbook via Copyright Clearance Center.

ViewPoint 19.6 Online protests

In 2007 many students not only used Facebook to maintain and develop their networks of friends and contacts, but some of them also used it to protest against the actions of the bank HSBC.

Faced with a perceived injustice, the National Union of Students decided to take action against the HSBC bank. The issue was that the bank had announced in the summer that it was to scrap the free £1,500 overdraft facility that it awarded to recent graduates. As a result 5,000 students signed up to group on the social network site 'Stop the Great HSBC Rip-Off'. With offline public comment beginning to take a critical stance, the bank decided to reverse the decision by the end of August, as the bank decided to avoid a rough public debate and possible damage to its reputation.

The UK's Labour Government, in conjunction with the mysociety.org political scrutiny charity, set up a petitions web site to engage further with the public. 1.79 million people signed the petition against proposed road pricing, and then received a four-page personal email response from the then Prime Minister Tony Blair, justifying his position.

The celebrity television chef Jamie Oliver collected 271,677 signatures via his Feed Me Better web site. His goal was to improve the quality of school meals and he succeeded in getting extra cash from the government (£280 million over three years) two hours before he handed in the petition to Downing Street.

Sources: Naughton (2005); Byers (2007); Gray (2007).

Question

Is the use of petitions merely a simple means of demonstrating volume of opinion or do they serve to bind communities together?

Task

Visit the government petition site (www.petitions.pm.gov.uk/) and see the range of topics currently available. Think of a petition you would like to post.

Integration of public relations in the communications mix

Public relations has three major roles to play within the communications programme of an organisation: the development and maintenance of corporate goodwill; the continuity necessary for good product support; and through these, the development and maintenance of suitable relationships.

The first is the traditional role of creating goodwill and stimulating interest between the organisation and its various key stakeholders. Its task is to provide a series of cues by which the stakeholders can recognise, understand and position the organisation in such a way that the organisation builds a strong reputation. This role is closely allied to the corporate strategy and the communication of strategic intent.

The second role of public relations is to support the marketing of the organisation's products and services, and its task is to integrate with the other elements of the marketing communications mix. Public relations and advertising have complementary roles. For example, the launch of a new product commences not with advertising to build awareness in target customers but with the use of public relations to inform editors and news broadcasters that a new product is about to be launched. This news material can be used within the trade and consumer press before advertising occurs and the target buyers become aware (when the news is no longer news). To some extent this role is tactical rather than strategic, but if planned, and if events are timed and coordinated with the other elements of the marketing communications mix, then public relations can help build competitive advantage.

The third role is to provide the means by which relationships can be developed. To do this public relations has a responsibility to encourage dialogue to provide the means through which interaction, discourse and discussion can occur and to play a full part in the communication process and the messages that are conveyed, listened to, considered and acted upon.

Summary

In order to help consolidate your understanding of public relations, here are the key points summarised against each of the learning objectives:

1. Explain the nature and characteristics of public relations.

Public relations is a communication discipline that can develop and maintain a portfolio of relationships with a range of key stakeholder audiences. The use of public relations does not require the purchase of airtime or space in media vehicles, such as television or magazines. The decision on whether an organisation's public relations messages are transmitted or not rests with those charged with managing the media resource, not the message sponsor. The main characteristics of public relations are that it represents a very cost-effective means of carrying messages with a high degree of credibility. However, the degree of control that management is able to exert over the transmission of messages can be limited.

2. Highlight the main audiences to which public relations activities are directed.

Public relations can be used to communicate with a range of publics (or stakeholders). These vary from employees (internal public relations), financial groups (financial or investor relations), customers (media relations) and *organisations and communities* (*corporate public relations*).

3. Discuss the role of public relations in the communications mix.

Public relations enables organisations to position themselves and provide stakeholders with a means of identifying and understanding an organisation. This may be accomplished inadvertently through inaction or deliberately through a planned presentation of a variety of visual cues. Using predetermined campaign objectives, these range from publicity through press releases, to the manner in which customers are treated, products perform, events are managed and expectations are met.

4. Appreciate ways in which public relations works.

Public relations can be seen to work at a practitioner level where the tool is used as a tool to achieve media visibility. At a different level public relations is seen as a means of mediating the relationships organisations develop with various stakeholders. Here, public relations is perceived as a longer-term and proactive form of planned communication. The former see public relations as an instrument, the latter as a means of conducting a dialogue (Ehling, 1992).

Public relations can be regarded as a dimension of communication behaviour. These dimensions are direction, purpose, channel and ethics (Yun, 2006).

5. Provide an overview of some of the main tools used by public relations.

Public relations consists of a range of communication activities, of which media relations, publicity and event management appear to be the main ones used by practitioners. However, in addition lobbying, corporate advertising and crisis communications form an important aspect of public relations activities.

6. Examine the nature and context of crisis management.

Public relations plays an important role in preparing for and constraining the impact of a crisis and re-establishing an organisation once a crisis has passed. Crisis planning is about putting into position those elements that can effect speedy outcomes to the disaster sequence.

7. Determine ways in which public relations can be integrated with the other tools of the marketing communications mix.

Public relations has three major roles to play within the communications programme of an organisation: the development and maintenance of corporate goodwill; the continuity necessary for good product support; and through these, the development and maintenance of suitable relationships. These roles can be accomplished more easily when public relations is integrated with the other tools and media of the communication mix.

Review questions

1. Define public relations and set out its principal characteristics.
2. Using an organisation of your choice, identify the main stakeholders and comment on why it is important to communicate with each of them.
3. Highlight the main objectives of using public relations.
4. What is the difference between corporate public relations and marketing public relations? Is this difference significant?
5. Write a brief paper describing the main methods of publicity.

6. Why do you think an increasing number of organisations are using sponsorship as a part of their marketing communications mix?
7. Suggest occasions when corporate advertising might be best employed.
8. Identify the main phases associated with crisis management.
9. What roles might stakeholders adopt when a crisis occurs?
10. Discuss the view that public relations can only ever be a support tool in the marketing communications mix.

MiniCase British Airways: the world's least favourite airline?

Peter Betts: University of Central Lancashire

Turbulence Ahead

In the words of Willie Walsh, the CEO of British Airways [BA], 27 March 2008 was to be a 'once in a lifetime' opportunity to transform the passenger experience at Britain's Heathrow airport. Heathrow had long been recognised as being one of the worst airports in the world. According to the Association of European Airlines, during 2007 Heathrow suffered the most delays with over 35 per cent of flights delayed for more than 15 minutes; lost the most passenger baggage and was rated by passengers to have the worst level of customer service. BA recognised the need to improve the Heathrow experience for its customers, especially if it was to live up to the company's acclaimed positioning as the 'World's Favourite Airline'. While Heathrow is the world's busiest international airport, handling over half of the passenger traffic between North America and the European Union, its excessive use of capacity and the impending start to the open skies agreement in 2008 would further stretch its limited capacity and resources. As the home of BA, much depends on how Heathrow can adequately and competitively respond to the challenges it faces in the global passenger airline market.

Open skies agreement

The opening of Terminal 5 was seen as the start of a new era. Indeed, it was seen as being so integral to BA's future, that the airline successfully lobbied the British government to delay the introduction of the open skies agreement between Europe and the United States so that it could move to the new terminal first. The introduction of the open skies agreement between Europe and the United States effectively allows any European airline to fly to any US city, effectively eliminating the long-standing Heathrow cartel. As a consequence, competition between airlines will increase to the particular benefit of business class passengers who will hopefully expect to see a reduction in prices. The arrival of new competitors at Heathrow would be of particular concern to BA who control over 40 per cent of the slots at the airport.

In response BA announced that it would be taking advantage of the open skies agreement by launching a new low-cost service to New York, flying out of Paris and Brussels. This new service to be operated by a BA subsidiary, ironically called Open Skies, would operate with a pilot workforce separate from its mainline operations. This announcement gave rise to the British Airline Pilots Association (Balpa) threatening strike action prior to, and on the day of, the launch of Terminal 5. The union argued that the new company would effectively drive down salaries and that jobs at the main company BA would ultimately be threatened. In order to forestall an impending pilot's strike and to mitigate against a major disaster on the day of the opening of Terminal 5, BA sought to use European law to prevent the pilot's strike. Balpa, in acknowledging that the company had a serious claim against it in terms of strike action, were disappointed that the company failed to negotiate through the normal channels and instead resorted to adopting the protection afforded through the European Courts.

A new dawn?

With a pilot's strike for the moment successfully averted, BA was ready to take 'delivery' of its new flagship Terminal 5.

The building, one of the largest infrastructure projects ever undertaken in the United Kingdom was built on time and in budget at a cost £4.3bn. Its opening on 27 March 2008 was to be the dawn of a new era and in the words of Willie Walsh, the opportunity for BA to restore its 'tarnished reputation'.

The omens, however, were not good. The notorious opening of Hong Kong's Chek Lap Kok airport in 1998 led to severe mechanical, technical and organisational problems that hindered the airport for months after its launch. For BA, shifting 70 per cent of its flight capacity almost overnight was always going to be a major challenge. From the commencement of opening, Terminal 5 was geared to handling 30 million passengers per year, up to 12,000 bags an hour at peak time and be the home for up to 6,700 BA staff.

However, within hours of opening on 27 March, chaos reigned as aircraft were delayed and the baggage system ground to a halt, forcing BA to cancel flights and allow only hand baggage onto flights. Problems for BA started even before the first passengers entered the new terminal. Staff arriving for work at 4a.m. found queues for the car-parks which were filling up with passengers and sight-seers. When overflow car parks were finally opened, staff and passengers were left waiting for buses to ferry them to the new terminal.

Inside the new terminal building, lifts and escalators failed to operate while staff had to wait for their computer check-in facility to warm up. One of the biggest problems was the failure of the automated work-allocation system, which was meant to give staff instructions via hand-held computers on where they should be stationed. The system sent staff to the wrong places and many were unable to find the correct loading bays via the maize of corridors inside the terminal. BA and the British Airports Authority (BAA), the Spanish company that operate the airport, held a press conference two weeks prior to the opening stating that the state-of-the-art baggage system had back-up facilities that could cope with any problems. Mike Forster of BAA stated that they would have a 'world class baggage handling system working perfectly on day one'.

At 6p.m. on the first evening, BA was faced with announcing the depressingly embarrassing statement that flights from Terminal 5 would depart with hand baggage only, due to the problems associated with processing customer's baggage. The baggage system designed to handle 12,000 bags an hour automatically shuts off when it is full. Thousands of bags were arriving at multiple locations and yet there were not enough staff to unload them. This accounted for up to 14,000 bags being stuck in the system in the first two days of operation. Passengers with check-in baggage were turned away and offered only refunds or a chance to rebook their flights for another day.

The blame game

In the immediate aftermath of the Terminal 5 debacle, neither BA nor BAA offered any explanation for the breakdown in the baggage system. Colin Matthews, BAA Chief Executive said there was nothing to be gained in finger pointing saying that 'jointly we shoulder the responsibility for providing good passenger service, and therefore we jointly need to solve the problem'. Willie Walsh acknowledged that both BA and BAA made mistakes but that he would 'take responsibility for the mistakes we made'.

None the less, in the early days of the Terminal 5 disaster, accusations and counter-accusations started to surface. Jim McAusian, general secretary of Balpa said the T5 problems were 'symptomatic of BA's loss of focus on delivering a sound operation'. One BAA official claimed that apart from short-lived BAA system problems early in the day, the baggage systems had been functioning properly. Indeed, senior management at BA had been warned that staff familiarisation issues would be central to a smooth functioning terminal. Jonathan Counsell, Head of T5 development identified the need to familiarise more than 10,000 people with the building before it opened. Union leaders questioned whether this had been achieved with a considerable number of staff effectively finding themselves lost on day one inside the terminal.

By 7 April 2008, 11 days after the opening of Terminal 5, BA had been forced to cancel 501 flights because of operational problems in one of the biggest public relations disasters suffered by the airline. BA put the initial cost to the company of the cancelled flights at £16 million although conservative estimates put the cost in excess of £25 million. This was further compounded by the announcement that business class passengers had fallen by 5 per cent during March.

By now, BA had been hoping to operate a full schedule of flights after the initial problems with baggage handling in the first week and the airline now laid the blame for the problems firmly at the door of BAA. Furthermore, and in an attempt to diffuse the issues surrounding the opening of T5, Willie Walsh announced the departures of two senior executives inside BA. Operations Director Gareth Kirkwood and Customer Services Director David Noyes were both relieved of their responsibilities two weeks after the opening of T5. This after Walsh himself declared that 'the buck stops with me'. In the city, BA's share price, already under pressure from the surge in fuel costs and concerns regarding the underlying weakness in the UK and US economies, continued to fall sharply and at 208.5p was at its lowest since October 2004.

The knock-on effect of the T5 disaster further resulted in BA announcing on 11 April that the transfer of its long-haul flights from T4 to T5 would be delayed by up to five weeks. This would have an adverse effect on other airlines planning to move into the spaces vacated as a result of BA's transfer to T5. Nigel Turner, Chief Executive of BMI, commented that 'BAA and BA had shown a total disregard for all other airlines and their passengers at Heathrow in coming to this decision because of their own shortcomings and their inability to implement an agreed plan'.

David Frost, Director General of the British Chamber of Commerce said, 'This shambles is yet another depressing chapter for the UK's crumbling transport system and sends a depressing message to businesses around the world.' Moreover for BA, the impact of the operational failures that plagued the opening of T5 were compounded by the lack of clear communication during the opening and subsequent days. Ironically, Gareth Kirkwood, the now ex-director of operations at Heathrow in the hours following the opening, read a statement apologising to customers but refused to take any question from journalists.

MiniCase questions

1. The operational failures at the opening of Heathrow's Terminal 5 were a PR disaster for BA. Analyse the situation from a PR perspective and identify the key communication issues for BA immediately after the opening and going forward.
2. Identify, prioritise and justify the key stakeholders with whom BA needs to develop its communications after the opening of Terminal 5.
3. While there are always going to be teething problems with any major infrastructure project such as Terminal 5, nevertheless, both BA and BAA should have had a well-rehearsed 'crisis plan' to deal with all eventualities. Outline the main elements of a 'crisis communication plan' and consider the varying scenarios such a plan should have covered in relation to Terminal 5.

References

Allen, A. (2008) A positive diagnosis. *The Marketer*, May, 20–2.

Anon. (2007) KittenAid hits hard to save unwanted cats. Retrieved 16 January 2008 from http://www.prweek/uk/thisweek/campaigns/article/766679/CAMPAIGN-KittenAid.

Barton, L. (2001) *Crisis Organisations II*. Cincinnati, OH: South Western Publishing.

Benoit, W.L. (1997) Image repair discourse and crisis communication. *Public Relations Review*, **23**, 177–86.

Bokaie, J. (2007) Coke commits to global water conservation drive. *Marketing*, 6 June, 1.

Booth, J. (2006) Cadbury's salmonella testing procedures 'inadequate'. *Timesonline*, 4 July 2006. Retrieved from www.timesonline.co.uk/tol/news/uk/article682877.ece.

Boyle, E. (2004) Press and publicity management: the Dyson case. *Corporate Communications: an International Journal*, **9**(3), 209–22.

Bruning, S.D. and Ledingham, J.A. (2000) Perceptions of relationships and evaluations of satisfaction: an exploration of interaction. *Public Relations Review*, **26**(1), 85–95.

Bruning, S.D., Dials, M. and Shirka, A. (2008) Using dialogue to build organisation–public relationships, engage publics, and positively affect organizational outcomes. *Public Relations Review*, **34**, 25–31.

Byers, D. (2007) Conservatives warn Blair over petitions site. *Timesonline*, 21 February. Retrieved 25 Februrary 2008 from www.timesonline.co.uk/tol/news/politics/article1419651.ece.

Caponigro, J.R. (2000) *The Crisis Counsellor: A-Step-by-Step Guide to Managing a Business Crisis*. Chicago, IL: Contemporary Books.

Conway, T., Ward, M., Lewis, G. and Bernhardt, A. (2007) Internet crisis potential: the importance of a strategic approach to marketing communications. *Journal of Marketing Communications*, **13**(3) (September), 213–28.

Cutlip, S., Center, A.H. and Broom, G.J. (2006) *Effective Public Relations*, 9th edn, Englewood Cliffs, NJ: Prentice-Hall.

Ehling, W.P. (1992) Estimating the value of public relations and communication to an organisation. In *Excellence in Public Relations and Communication Management* (eds J.E. Grunig, D.M. Dozier, P. Ehling, L.A. Grunig, F.C. Repper and J. Whits), 617–38. Hillsdale, NJ: Lawrence Erlbaum.

Fink, S. (2000) *Crisis Management Planning for the Inevitable*. New York: AMACON.

Gray, R. (2007) Rapid response. *Marketing*, (November), 48–9.

Gregory, A. (2004) Scope and structure of public relations: a technology driven view. *Public Relations Review*, **30**(3) (September), 245–54.

Grunig, J. (1992) Models of public relations and communication. In *Excellence in Public Relations and Communications Management* (eds J.E. Grunig, D.M. Dozier, P. Ehling, L.A. Grunig, F.C. Repper and J. Whits), 285–325. Hillsdale, NJ: Lawrence Erlbaum.

Grunig, J.E. (1997) A situational theory of publics: Conceptual history, recent challenges and new research. In *Public Relations Research: An International Perspective* (eds D. Moss, T. MacManus and D. Vercic), 3–48. London: International Thomson Business.

Grunig, J. and Hunt, T. (1984) *Managing Public Relations*. New York: Holt, Rineholt & Winston.

Hollingworth, C. (2000) *Cyber-Attack*, Communications Directors Forum, June.

Kent, M. (2008) Critical analysis of blogging in public relations. *Public Relations Review*, **34**, 32–40.

Kent, M.L. and Taylor, M. (2002) Toward a dialogic theory of public relations. *Public Relations Review*, **28**(1) (February), 21–37.

Kitchen, P.J. (1991) Developing use of PR in a fragmented demassified market. *Marketing Intelligence and Planning*, **9**(2), 29–33.

Kitchen, P.J. and Moss, D. (1995) Marketing and public relations: the relationship revisited. *Journal of Marketing Communications*, **1**, 105–19.

Kitchen, P.J. and Proctor, R.A. (1991) The increasing importance of public relations in FMCG firms. *Journal of Marketing Management*, **7**(4) (October), 357–70.

Kleinman, M. (2007) Coca-Cola commits $20m for water aid. *Daily Telegraph*, 5 June 2007. Retrieved 5 December 2007 from http://www.telegraph.co.uk/money/main.jhtml?xml=/money/2007/06/05/cncola05.xml.

Miller, G. (1989) Persuasion and public relations: two 'Ps' in a pod. In *Public Relations Theory* (eds C. Botan and V. Hazelton). Hillsdale, NJ: Lawrence Erlbaum.

Mitroff, I. and Anagnos, G. (2001) *Managing Crises Before They Happen*. New York: American Management Association.

Moloney, K. (1997) Government and lobbying activities. In *Public Relations: Principles and Practice* (ed. P.J. Kitchen). London: International Thomson Press.

Murray-Wilson, A. (2007) Salmonella scare diminishes confidence in Cadbury brand. *Daily Telegraph*, 15 August 2006. Retrieved from www.telegraph.co.uk/money/main.jhtml?xml=/money/2006/07/16/cncadb16.xml.

Naughton, P. (2005) Jamie Oliver wins school food fight. *Timesonline*, 30 March. Retrieved 25 February 2008 from www.timesonline.co.uk/tol/life_and_style/food_and_drink/article440436.ece.

Pearson, C.M. and Mitroff, I. (1993) From crisis prone to crisis prepared: a framework for crisis management. *Academy of Management Executive*, **7**(1), 48–59.

Penrose, J.M. (2000) The role of perception in crisis planning. *Public Relations Review*, **26**(2), 155–71.

Public Relations Educational Trust (1991) *The Place of Public Relations in Management Education*. London: Institute of Public Relations.

Quarantelli, E.L. (1988) Disaster crisis management: a summary of research findings. *Journal of Management Studies*, **25**(4), 373–85.

Reisman, J. (1989) Corporate advertising in disguise. *Public Relations Journal* (September), 21–7.

Schumann, D.W., Hathcote, J.M. and West, S. (1991) Corporate advertising in America: a review of published studies on use, measurement and effectiveness. *Journal of Advertising*, **20**(3), 35–56.

Seeger, M.W. (2002) Chaos and crisis: propositions for a general theory of crisis communication. *Public Relations Review*, **28**(4) (October), 329–37.

Spillan, J.E. (2003) An exploratory model for evaluating crisis events and managers' concerns in non-profit organisations. *Journal of Contingencies and Crisis Management*, **11**(4) (December), 160–9.

Springston, J. (2001) Public relations and new media technology: the impact of the internet, in *Handbook of Public Relations* (ed. R. Heath), 603–14. London: Sage Publications.

Stanton, W.J. (1964) *Fundamentals of Marketing*. New York: McGraw-Hill.

Sturges, D.L., Carell, B.J., Newsom, D.A. and Barrera, M. (1991) Crisis communication management: the public opinion node and its relationship to environmental nimbus. *SAM Advanced Management Journal* (Summer), 22–7.

Tiltman, D. (2007) Touch of flu costs Bernard Matthews 17% of sales. *Marketing*, 21 August 2007. Retreived from www.brandrepublic.com/News/732522/Touch-flu-costs-Bernard-Matthews-17-sales/.

WWF Pressroom (2007) WWF and Coca-Cola announce partnership to conserve freshwater resources, http://www.panda.org/news_facts/newsroom/index.cfm?uNewsID=104940 serve freshwater resources 5 June 2007.

Yun, S.-H. (2006) Toward public relations theory-based study of public diplomacy: testing the applicability of the excellence study. *Journal of Public Relations Research*, **18**(4), 287–312.

Chapter 20

Sponsorship

Sponsorship is a commercial activity whereby one party permits another an opportunity to exploit an association with a target audience in return for funds, services or resources. Organisations are using sponsorship activities in a variety of ways to generate awareness, brand associations and to cut through the clutter of commercial messages.

Aims and learning objectives

The aim of this chapter is to introduce and examine sponsorship as an increasingly significant form of marketing communications.

The learning objectives of this chapter are to:

1. explain how sponsorship activities have developed and provide an insight into the main characteristics of this form of communication;
2. consider reasons for the use of sponsorship and the types of objectives that might be set;
3. understand how sponsorship might work;
4. explain some of the conceptual and theoretical aspects of sponsorship;
5. appreciate the variety and different forms of sponsorship activities;
6. understand the reasons why sponsorship has become an important part of the communication mix.

For an applied interpretation see Katy Lahiffe and Tony Garry's MiniCase entitled ***Sponsorship and the British Superbike (BSB) Championship: a sport in transition?*** at the end of this chapter.

Introduction

There is a commonly held expectation that organisations should contribute to their local communities with a view to being seen as participative, caring and involved with local affairs. One of the drawbacks of this tie-up is that the degree of control that can be levied is limited once a commitment has been made. By adopting a more commercial perspective, some organisations have used sponsorship, particularly of sports activities, as a means of reaching wider target audiences. Sponsorship can provide the following opportunities for the sponsoring organisation:

1. Exposure to particular audiences that each event attracts in order to convey simple awareness-based brand messages.
2. To suggest to the target audiences that there is an association between the sponsored and the sponsor and that by implication this association may be of interest and/or value.
3. To allow members of the target audiences to perceive the sponsor indirectly through a third party and so diffuse any negative effects associated with traditional mass media and direct persuasion.
4. Sponsorship provides sponsors with the opportunity to blend a variety of tools in the communication mix and use resources more efficiently and arguably more effectively.

Sponsorship can be defined as a commercial activity, whereby one party permits another an opportunity to exploit an association with a target audience in return for funds, services or resources.

From this it is possible to define sponsorship as a commercial activity, whereby one party permits another an opportunity to exploit an association with a target audience in return for funds, services or resources.

It is necessary to clarify the distinction between sponsorship and charitable donations. The latter are intended to change attitudes and project a caring identity, with the main returns from the exercise being directed to society or the beneficiaries. The beneficiaries have almost total control over the way in which funds are used. When funds are channelled through sponsorship the recipient has to attend to the needs of the sponsor by allowing it access to the commercial associations that are to be exploited, partly because they have a legal arrangement, but also to ensure that the exchange becomes relational and longer-term; in other words, there is repeat purchase (investment) activity. The other major difference is that the benefits of the exchange are intended to accrue to the participants, not society at large.

Normally sponsorship involves two parties, the sponsor and the sponsee, although many sponsors may be assigned to a single sponsee. The degree of fit between these two parties partly determines the relative effectiveness of the relationship (Poon and Prendergast, 2006). The degree of fit, or product relevance as proposed by McDonald (1991) cited by Poon and Prendergast, can be considered in terms of two main dimensions. Function-based similarity occurs when the product is used in the event being sponsored. For example, the piano manufacturer *Bösendorfer*, sponsoring a Viennese' piano recital. The second dimension concerns image-based similarities, which reflects the image of the sponsor in the event. Here Airbus's sponsorship of a major technical or even artistic exhibition serves to bestow prestige on all parties. Poon and Prendergast discuss the literature on these topics and suggest that rather than treat these as mutually exclusive elements, there can be four interconnected dimensions. Figure 20.1 serves to illustrate their intentions.

Function-based similarity occurs when the product is used in the event being sponsored.

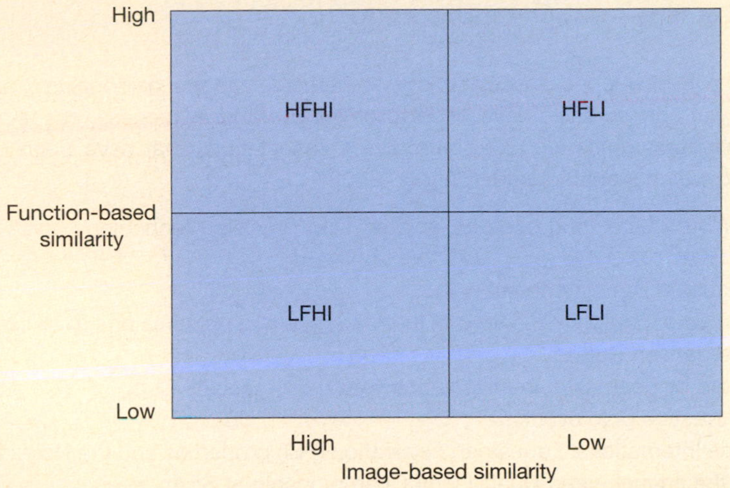

Figure 20.1 Dimensions of sponsorship interaction
Source: After Poon and Prendergast (2006). Used with kind permission from WARC.

The growth and development of sponsorship

Many researchers and authors agree that the use of sponsorship by organisations is increasing (Sneath *et al.*, 2005; Harvey *et al.*, 2006; Lacey *et al.*, 2007; Wakefield *et al.*, 2007) and that it is becoming a more significant part of the marketing communications mix. The development of sponsorship as a communication tool has been spectacular since the early 1990s. This is because of a variety of factors, but among the most important are the government's policies on tobacco and alcohol, the escalating costs of advertising media during the 1990s, the proven ability of sponsorship, new opportunities due to increased leisure activity, greater media coverage of sponsored events and the recognition of the inefficiencies associated with the traditional media (Meenaghan, 1991). In addition to this list of drivers can be added regulations and technology. The Independent Television Commission, which is now subsumed with Ofcom, acted to restrict the nature and form of programme (or broadcast) sponsorship. However, a relaxation in the regulations has allowed for the development of this type of sponsorship.

The reference to technology concerns digital video recorders, such as TiVo and PVRs that allow users to skip over advertising breaks (and eventually block them out altogether). Should these machines achieve strong consumer penetration then the sponsorship credits could become more important than advertising in achieving brand presence (see Table 20.1).

Table 20.1 Growth and development of sponsorship

Increased media coverage of events
Relaxation of government and industry regulations
Increased incidence of sponsorship event supply (and demand)
Relationship orientation and association between sponsorship participants
Positive attitude change toward sponsorship by senior management
Awareness and drive towards integrated marketing communications
Increasing rate of other media costs
Need to develop softer brand associations and to reach niche audiences

ViewPoint 20.1 On time for sports sponsorship

Many watch manufacturers have developed associations with particular sports personalities or sporting events. The main goals of these sponsorships have been to develop brand awareness, associations and favourable values. The following examples are just some of the associations that have been developed between particular events and watch manufacturers (Balfour, 2000):

Motor racing: The TAGHeuer brand has long been associated with precision technology and Grand Prix motor racing.

Certina sponsors the BMW Sauber Formula 1 team.

Chopard makes the Mille Liglia chronograph at the time of the road race and presents one to all competitors.

Seiko sponsors Honda F1 and Jenson Button.

Water sports: Omega promotes its Seamaster in association with the America's Cup.

Polo: Cartier sponsors many prestige polo events.

Equestrian: Rolex sponsors the International Equestrian Federation (FEI) properties and the Rolex Rankings.

Golf: Alfred Dunhill sponsors the annual Alfred Dunhill Golf Championship at St Andrews.

Football: Tissot sponsors Michael Owen, the Newcastle and England footballer.

Cricket: Citizen sponsor Kevin Pietersen, the Hampshire and England cricketer.

Aviation: Breitling has developed an association with aviation.

Question

If timing and sporting achievement are the key associations for watch houses, what might be important for fashion designers?

Task

Find a watch house that associates itself with the Olympic Games.

Exhibit 20.1 Lewis Hamilton, Formula 1 World Champion 2008, used to endorse the TagHeuer watch brand

Image courtesy of The Advertising Archives.

Sponsorship, a part of public relations, should be used as part of an integrated approach to an organisation's communications. In other words, sponsorship provides a further tool that, to be used effectively, needs to be harnessed strategically. For example, many companies and brands originating in south-east Asia and the Pacific regions have used sponsorship as a means of overseas market entry in order to develop name or brand awareness (e.g. Panasonic, JVC and Daihatsu).

Sponsorship, a part of public relations, should be used as part of an integrated approach.

In addition, many sponsorship arrangements have survived recessionary periods. This may be because of the two- to three-year period that each sponsorship contract covers and the difficulty and costs associated with terminating such agreements. It may also be because of the impact that sponsorship might have on the core customers who continue to buy the brand during economic downturns. Easier targeting through sponsorship can also assist the reinforcement of brand messages. Readers are reminded of the weak theory of advertising (Chapter 16), and it may be that sponsorship is a means of defending a market and providing additional triggers to stimulate brand recall/recognition.

Sponsorship objectives

There are both primary and secondary objectives associated with using sponsorship. The primary reasons are to build awareness, developing customer loyalty and improving the perception (image) held of the brand or organisation. Secondary reasons are more contentious, but generally they can be seen to be to attract new users, to support dealers and other intermediaries and to act as a form of staff motivation and morale building (Reed, 1994).

The primary reasons are to build awareness, developing customer loyalty and improving the perception (image) held of the brand or organisation.

Sponsorship is normally regarded as a communications tool used to reach external stakeholders. However, if chosen appropriately sponsorship can also be used effectively to reach internal audiences. Care is required because different audiences transfer diverse values (Grimes and Meenaghan, 1998). According to Harverson (1998), one of the main reasons IT companies sponsor sports events is that this form of involvement provides opportunities to 'showcase' their products and technologies, in context. Through application in an appropriate working environment, the efficacy of a sponsor's products can be demonstrated. The relationship between sports organisers and IT companies becomes reciprocal as the organisers of sports events need technology in order for the events to run. Corporate hospitality opportunities are often taken in addition to the brand exposure that the media coverage provides. EDS claims that it uses sponsorship to reach two main audiences, customers (and potential customers) and potential future employees. The message it uses is that the EDS involvement in sport is sexy and exciting.

EDS uses sponsorship to reach two main audiences, customers and potential future employees.

A further interesting point arises from a view of a company sponsor through time. Meenaghan (1998) suggests that, at first, the sponsor acts as a donor, through the pure exchange of money in order to reach an audience. The next stage sees the sponsor acting as an investor, where, although large sums of money may well be involved, the sponsor is now actively involved and is looking for a return on the investment made. The third stage is reached when the sponsor assumes the role of an impresario. Now the sponsor is vigorously involved and seeks to control activities so that they reflect corporate/brand values and thus assist the positioning process.

A further important characteristic concerns the impact of repeat attendance on brand image. Work by Lacey *et al.* (2007) found that a car manufacturer's image improved modestly by sponsoring a sporting event. However, through repeat attendance positive opinion scores towards the sponsor improved. The obvious implication for marketing is that it is important to attract attendees back to sporting events.

ViewPoint 20.2 Sponsors Simply Sailing Along

Ellen MacArthur's second place in the Vendée Globe solo round-the-world yacht race that ended in February 2001 resulted in considerable media exposure for her main sponsor, the Kingfisher Group, after whom her boat was named. The Group's purchases, at the time, of several French companies (France being a country enthusiastic about sailing) meant that the heroism and media interest in MacArthur's achievement was extremely high.

Kingfisher's investment was easily recouped if the strong positive media coverage was correctly valued at about £50 million media equivalents. However, as Hill (2001) reports, the overall success of the sponsorship lay in the supporting promotional campaign.

This success was followed up in 2005 when Ellen MacArthur smashed the world record for the solo navigation of the planet in a boat sponsored by B&Q. The 75-foot record-breaking trimaran B&Q lapped the planet in a record time of 71 days, 14 hours, 18 minutes and 33 seconds finishing on 7 February 2005.

Question

What attributes might Kingfisher have observed in MacArthur that led them to sponsor her?

Task

Discover three activities that other retailers sponsor.

Exhibit 20.2 B&Q's sponsorship of Ellen MacArthur's round the planet record breaking trip in 2004/05
Benoit Stichelbaut/DPPI/Offshore Challenges. Courtesy of B&Q.

Following on from this is the issue about whether sponsorship is being used to support a product or the organisation. Corporate sponsorships, according to Thwaites (1994), are intended to focus on developing community involvement, public awareness, image, goodwill and staff relations. Product- or brand-based sponsorship activity is aimed at developing media coverage, sales leads, sales/market share, target market awareness and guest hospitality. What is important is that sponsorship is not a tool that can be effective in a stand-alone capacity. The full potential of this tool is only realised when it is integrated with some (or all) of the other tools of the communication mix. As Tripodi (2001) comments, the implementation of integrated marketing communications is further encouraged and supported when sponsorship is an integral part of the mix in order to maximise the full impact of this communication tool.

How sponsorship might work

Interpretations about how sponsorship might work are varied, and research limited. However, assuming a cognitive orientation, sponsorship works through associations that consumers make with a brand (which will be an accumulation of previous advertising and other promotional activities) and the event being supported. In addition, people make a judgement based on the fit between the event and sponsorship such that the greater the degree of compatibility the more readily acceptable the sponsorship will be. Poon and Prendergast (2006) argue that sponsorship outcomes can best be understood in terms of the attitude construct and cite product quality, attitude to the brand and purchase intention as representative of the cognition, affection and conation components.

If a behavourist orientation is used to explain how sponsorship works, then the Sponsorship will be perceived as a reinforcement of previous brand experiences. An event generates rewards by reminding individuals of pleasurable brand experiences. However, this assumes that individuals have previous brand experience and fails to explain adequately how sponsorship works when launching new products.

> Sponsorship will be perceived as a reinforcement of previous brand experiences.

Generally, sponsorship plays a supporting or secondary role in the communication mix of many organisations and is not an important source of corporate information. This is largely because the communication impact of sponsorship is limited, as sponsorship only reinforces previously held corporate (or product) images (positive or negative) rather than changing them (Javalgi *et al.*, 1994). It is also suggested that the only significant relationship between sponsorship and corporate image occurs where there has been direct experience of the brand. This in turn raises questions about whether sponsorship should be used to influence the image of the product category and its main brands in order to be of any worthwhile effect (Pope and Voges, 1999).

As Dolphin (2003) suggests, the range of activities, events, goals and the variety of ways in which it is used by organisations suggest that it is not entirely clear how sponsorship might best be used to help an organisation achieve its business goals. It is used to shape and assist corporate image, develop name association and awareness, drive product sales, build brands, help with recruitment, defend against hostile competitors and as a means of developing and providing opportunities for corporate hospitality. However, the primary goal for its use will generally reflect the context within which it is used. In situations where transactional exchanges are predominant within the target audience, broad-based sponsorship activities are likely to be preferred. In contexts where the target audience is relatively small or geographically discrete and where relational exchanges are preferred or sought, then relationship development sponsorship activities are more likely to be successful.

ViewPoint 20.3 An Xceptional branded sponsorship

Nokia's share of the UK mobile market started to fall in 2000 as competition increased. The company's response either had to address long-term sales and reposition the brand as an aspirational brand for the youth market or drive short-term sales by appealing to the mass market. Its decision was to go for both and decided to sponsor the X Factor, a television show that attracted 10 million viewers, many of whom were in the youth market.

A range of activities designed to reinforce the sponsorship were implemented. These included the usual television bumpers, promotions, prizes and ads but also included an in-store promotion with Carphone Warehouse. This involved an exclusive X-Factor 3220 packaged handset tone. In addition to this a microsite was developed, Club Nokia, for X-Factor fans.

20,000 viewers entered competitions, 82,000 visited the microsite, sales doubled on the promoted handsets and brand preference ratings rose 5 per cent.

Source: Kolah (2008).

Question

To what degree is Nokia's sponsorship just about reaching the X-Factor audience or is it more than that?

Task

When the X-Factor or a favourite entertainment programme next goes on air, identify the sponsors and follow through any links and consider the range and quality of their involvement.

Theoretical aspects of sponsorship

The limited amount of theoretical research into sponsorship, suggests that the role of sponsorship within the marketing communications mix has not been clearly understood. Problems associated with goals, tools and measurement methods and approaches have hindered both academics and practitioners. However, two developments have helped resolve some of these dilemmas. First, the development of relationship marketing and an acknowledgement that there are different audiences, each with different relationship needs, has helped understanding about which types of sponsorship should be used with which type of audience. Second, our understanding of the nature and role of integrated marketing communications within relationship marketing has helped focus thinking about the way in which sponsorship might contribute to the overall communication process.

> The role of sponsorship within the marketing communications mix has not been clearly understood.

Relationship marketing is concerned with the concept of mutual value rather than the mere provision of goods and services (Gummesson, 1996) and is therefore compatible in many ways with the characteristics and range of benefits, both expected and realised, associated with sponsorship (Farrelly *et al.*, 2003). Sponsorship represents a form of collaborative communication, in the sense that two (or more) parties work together in order that one is enabled to reach the other's audience. Issues regarding the relationship between the parties involved will impact on the success of a sponsorship arrangement and any successive arrangements. As Farrelly *et al.* quite rightly point out, further work concerning the key drivers of sponsorship and relationship marketing is required as sponsorship matures as an increasingly potent form of marketing communications.

Table 20.2 Basic variables underpinning interorganisational networks

Network variable	Explanation
Actors	These are organisations and individuals who are interconnected; they control the other two variables.
Activities	Activities are created through the use of resources, and complex activity chains arise with different organisations (actors) contributing in different ways.
Resources	There are many different types of resource that can be combined in different ways to create new resources. The relationships that organisations develop create resource ties and these ties become shaped and adapted as the relationship develops.

Source: Based on Olkkonen (2001).

Olkkonen (2001) adopted a similar approach as he considered sponsorship within interactional relationships and ultimately a network approach. The network approach considers the range of relationships that impact on organisations within markets and therefore considers non-buyers and other organisations, indeed all who are indirectly related to the exchange process. This approach moves beyond the simple dyadic process adopted by the interaction interpretation. Some scholars have advanced a broad conceptual model within which to consider interorganisational networks (Hakansson and Snehota, 1995, cited by Olkkonen). These are actors, activities and resources (see Table 20.2).

A relationship consists of activity links based on organisations working together. Some of the activities will use particular resources in different configurations and differing levels of intensity. These activities will impact on other organisations and affect the way they use resources. In addition, organisations try to develop their attractiveness to other organisations in order to access other resources and networks. This is referred to as network identity and is a base for determining an organisation's value as a network partner. Sponsorship, therefore, can be seen as a function of an organisation's value to others in a network. The sponsored and the sponsor are key actors in sponsorship networks but agencies, event organisers, media networks and consultancies are also players, each of whom will be connected (networked) with the sponsor and sponsored.

> Sponsorship can be seen as a function of an organisation's value to others in a network.

Sponsorship has, traditionally, lacked a strong theoretical base, relying on managerial cause-and-effect explanations and loose marketing communications mix interpretations. The network approach may not be the main answer but it does advance our thought, knowledge and research opportunities with respect to this subject.

One concept that has been established in the literature concerns emotional intensity. This concerns the audience's attention (and associated cognitive orientation) toward the stimulus that is provoking the emotion (Bal *et al.*, 2007). So, if the event becomes dramatic and highly engaging then it is probable that attention will be diverted from the sponsors and any information they might provide (e.g. ads). What this means is that a strongly emotional event (sport, exhibition, programme, film) is likely to reduce the awareness scores associated with the sponsor.

Research by Farrelly *et al.* (2006), undertaken to better understand how value is perceived by parties to sponsorship agreements, has identified three key marketing competences necessary for the maintenance of successful sponsorship relationships. These are, reciprocal commitment, building capabilities and collaborative capabilities. These are set out in Table 20.3.

ViewPoint 20.4 Flora runs away from the London Marathon

Flora had sponsored the London Marathon for 11 years when it unexpectedly announced that it was giving it up in 2007. The tie-up had been regarded as one of the most successful sponsorship relationships, as it had driven high levels of heart health awareness and had enabled the brand to own 'heart health'.

In addition, the sponsorship had been used to launch new products and as a part of various integrated campaigns run by the brand's parent, Unilever. Charles (2007) suggested that the relationship had reached the stage experienced by some other long-standing sponsorship arrangements, where people stopped associating the name with a product. Other commentators speculated that Flora had been outbid by a rival.

Source: Charles (2007).

Question

To what extent can individual sponsorship arrangements, however successful, cease to contribute sufficient value?

Task

Find another long-lasting sponsorship arrangement and find out the history and how the sponsorship has evolved.

Table 20.3 Sponsorship relationship capabilities

Competence	Explanation
Reciprocal commitment	This is demonstrated by the reaction that one party makes to any additional investment in the sponsorship by the other. Sponsors expect the sponsee to reciprocate the investments (e.g. advertising) that the sponsor makes in the relationship. The greater the reciprocity, the greater the commitment.
Building capabilities	Sponsorship is increasingly perceived to be of value in terms of strategic branding rather than mere exposure. To what extent, therefore, do the parties link their sponsorship to broader marketing objectives?
Collaborative capabilities	This concerns the extent to which the sponsee is proactive within the relationship and sets out the ways in which the relationship and the sponsor's brand will be developed in the future. In effect this is about collaboration.

Source: Farrelly *et al.* (2006).

The greater the reciprocity, the greater the commitment.

Types of sponsorship

It is possible to identify particular areas within which sponsorship has been used. These areas are sports, programme/broadcast, the arts and others that encompass activities such as wildlife/conservation and education. Of all of these, sport has attracted most attention and sponsorship money.

Sports sponsorship

Sports activities have been very attractive to sponsors, partly because of the high media coverage they attract. Sport is the leading type of sponsorship, mainly for the following reasons:

> Sports activities have been very attractive to sponsors, partly because of the high media coverage they attract.

- Sport has the propensity to attract large audiences, not only at each event but more importantly through the media that attach themselves to these activities.
- Sport provides a simplistic measure of segmentation, so that as audiences fragment generally, sport provides an opportunity to identify and reach often large numbers of people who share particular characteristics.
- Visibility opportunities for the sponsor are high in a number of sporting events because of the duration of each event (e.g. the Olympics or the FIFA World Cup).

Barclaycard's sponsorship of the football Premier League and Coca-Cola's sponsorship of the football championship have been motivated partly by the attraction of large and specific target audiences with whom a degree of fit is considered to exist. The constant media attention enables the sponsors' names to be disseminated to distant audiences, many of them overseas. Marshall and Cook (1992) found that event sponsorship (e.g. the Olympics or the Ideal Home Exhibition) is the most popular form of sponsorship activity undertaken by organisations. This was followed by team, league and individual support.

Vodafone sponsored Manchester United in order to boost global awareness. Then the company bought Mannesman and found it then sponsored Benfica, Porto, Olympiakos and teams in La Liga in Spain and the Bundesliga in Germany. Rationalisation was necessary and wanting to maintain an association with football, it then became a Champions League sponsor (Murphy, 2007).

Golf has attracted a great deal of sponsorship money, mainly because it has a global upmarket appeal and generates good television and press coverage. Golf clubs are also well suited for corporate entertainment and offer the chance of playing as well as watching. Volvo sponsored the European Golf Championship for the period 1996–2000 for £20 million. Johnny Walker continues to sponsor major golfing championships. Toyota used to support the World Matchplay Championship at Wentworth each year because the tournament fitted into a much wider promotion programme. Toyota dealers sponsored competitions at their local courses, with qualifiers going through to a final at Wentworth. The winner of that played in the pro-am before the World Matchplay. Toyota incorporated the tournament into a range of incentive and promotional programmes and flew in top distributors and fleet customers from around the world. In addition, the environment was used to build customer relationships. This championship is now supported by HSBC.

ViewPoint 20.5 World Cup Rugby says Cheers

The Rugby World Cup finals held in Australia in 2003 and France in 2007 attracted a number of different sponsors, each termed official worldwide partners. Heineken was the official beer and one of its goals was to add to the experience of the event for rugby fans and beer drinkers all over the world, regardless of whether they are at the game, at home or at their local bar or pub.

In 2007, Heineken used a global advertising campaign prior to the event in order to draw attention to the event and the sponsorship. The ad featured rugby fans pushing continents across the globe in the form of a scrum. The campaign 'included 10-second break bumpers, print advertising, a cinema spot and a dedicated website featuring an interactive game as part of a wider campaign called "One World, One Cup, One Beer" ' (Davidson, 2007).

The English Rugby Football Union generates nearly £14 million from sponsorship each year (Farmer, 2007), and a successful tournament only serves to attract new sponsors. O_2, the mobile phone company, are a major sponsor of the England team, investing £3 million a year (see Exhibit 20.3).

Sources: Davidson (2007); Farmer (2007).

Question

What are the risks associated with being a major sponsor of a major global sporting event?

Task

What other events do Heineken sponsor?

Programme sponsorship

Television programme sponsorship began to receive serious attention in Britain in the late 1990s. The market has grown, as reflected in TV sponsorship revenues, from £81.2 million in 2000 to £176 million in 2006. This growth has occurred partly because of a relaxation in the regulations. For example, the visibility that each sponsor is allowed was strictly controlled to certain times, and before, during the break and after each programme with the credits. This was changed so that while sponsors are not allowed to influence the content or scheduling of a programme so as to affect the editorial independence and responsibility of the broadcaster, it is now permissible to allow the sponsor's product to be seen along with the sponsor's name in bumper credits and to allow greater flexibility in terms of the use of straplines. There is a requirement on the broadcaster to ensure that the sponsored credit is depicted in such a way that it cannot be mistaken as a spot advertisement. So, Hedburg (2000) gives the example of Nescafé sponsoring *Friends* showing a group of people sitting on a sofa and drinking coffee and of *Coronation Street* and former sponsor Cadbury's, which presented a whole chocolate street and set of chocolate characters.

Sponsors are not allowed to influence the content or scheduling of a programme.

Masthead programming, where the publisher of a magazine such as *Amateur Photographer* sponsors a programme in a related area, such as *Photography for Beginners*, is generally not permitted, although the regulations surrounding this type of activity are being relaxed. There are a number of reasons why programme sponsorship is appealing. First, it allows clients to avoid the clutter associated with spot advertising. In that sense it creates a space, or mini-world, in which the sponsor can create awareness and provide brand identity cues unhindered by other brands. Second, it represents a cost-effective medium when compared with spot advertising. Although the cost of programme sponsorship has increased as the value of this type of communication has appreciated, it does not command the high rates required for spot advertising. Third, the use of credits around a programme offers opportunities for the target audience to make associations between the sponsor and the programme.

Research by the Bloxam Group suggests that for a sponsorship to work there needs to be a linkage between the product and the programme. Links that are spurious, illogical or inappropriate are very often rejected by viewers. For example, a branded soft drink might work well

Toyota Auris sponsors ITV Mystery Drama.
TOYOTA

Exhibit 20.3 Toyota Auris's sponsorship credits for ITV Mystery Drama
Courtesy of Toyota and CHI and Partners.

with a youth-oriented programme, but a financial services brand supporting a sports programme or film series would not have a strong or logical linkage.

The same research suggests that viewers claim to own their favourite programmes. Therefore, sponsors should acknowledge this relationship and act accordingly, perhaps as a respectful guest, and not intrude too heavily on the programme. The line between product placement, brand entertainment and programme sponsorship becomes increasingly blurred. They should certainly resist any active participation in the programme unless using branded entertainment (Hudson and Hudson, 2006).

Programme sponsorship should not be seen as a replacement for advertising.

Programme sponsorship should not be seen as a replacement for advertising. The argument that sponsorship is not a part of advertising is clearly demonstrated by the point that many sponsors continue with their spot advertising when running major sponsorships.

Cadbury's sponsorship of the premier UK soap opera, *Coronation Street*, which ceased in 2006, is reported to have cost £10 million each year, when all the additional promotional activities and requirements are considered. The linkage established between the two parties (Cadbury's and *Coronation Street*) exemplifies the view about the relationship and the linkages. Research indicates that those aware of the sponsorship regarded the chocolate and the company more positively than those unaware of the linkage. When Cadbury's won the sponsorship they were awarded higher marks for being up to date and a supporter of the local community (Smith, 1997).

ViewPoint 20.6 The Sky's the Limit for Ford

Ford has been involved with Sky's sponsorship of football's Premier League since its inception in 1992. In 2007 the contract was extended to 2010, making this a good example of a long-term relationship forged through marketing communications.

Sponsorship activities are important to Ford and they believe that it is necessary to take a long-term perspective otherwise the full potential may not be realised. So, their involvement with Sky and football has enabled them, or they have been given permission, as Ovenden (2007) puts it, to sponsor the UEFA Champions League and also support the Kick-It Out anti-racism campaign. Each sponsorship opportunity is considered on its own merits and not, for example, on the basis of what competitors are doing.

Sponsorships are developed by Ford when there is a fit between a brand's values and those of the audience. Thus, Ford has traditionally developed very strong rational attributes such as good value for money, a strong dealer network and functional performance. In recent years, the marketing communications challenge has been to add more emotional values and they see sponsorship as a means of injecting this new dimension.

Source: Ovenden (2007).

Question

Why do Ford not consider what sponsorships their competitors are involved with or developing?

Task

Find out what sponsorships GM are involved with in your country.

Arts sponsorship

Arts sponsorship was very successful in the 1980s and 1990s, as responsibility for funding the arts in Britain has shifted from the government to the private sector and business in particular. Growth has slowed down partly because of the increasing need to justify such investments, partly because of the increasing opportunities to reach target audiences in other ways and also because it is difficult to engage in these very visible activities when profits are declining and company restructuring activities are of greater concern to those being made redundant or being displaced.

Arts sponsorship, according to Thorncroft (1996), began as a philanthropic exercise, with business giving something back to the community. It was a means of developing corporate image and was used extensively by tobacco companies as they attempted to reach their customer base. It then began to be appreciated for its corporate hospitality opportunities: a cheaper, more civilised alternative to sports sponsorship, and one that appealed more to women.

> Many organisations sponsor the arts as a means of enhancing their corporate status.

Many organisations sponsor the arts as a means of enhancing their corporate status and as a means of clarifying their name. Another important reason organisations use sponsorship is to establish and maintain favourable contact with key business people, often at board level, together with other significant public figures. Through related corporate hospitality, companies can reach substantial numbers of their targeted key people.

NTL used the benefits of sponsorship to enhance the corporate body, to increase awareness of the company and to change part of the corporate image. Others use sponsorship to influence image and awareness factors at the brand level, such as 7-Up, Foster's and Budweiser (Meenaghan, 1998).

Most recently, sponsorship has been used to reach specific groups of consumers. Orange sponsors a range of music-related events, one of them being the Glastonbury Festival. One of the key facilities is the 'chill n'charge' tent. This is a bright orange-coloured tent in which people can use the phone-charging equipment or the Internet facilities to pick up their email and over 50,000 people used the tent at the 2007 festival. Orange see their sponsorship of the festival as a way to develop their brand and purchase consideration, but not as a means of directly acquiring customers (Bartlett, 2007).

The sponsorship of the arts has moved from being a means of supporting the community to a sophisticated means of targeting and positioning brands. Sponsorship, once part of corporate public relations, has developed skills that can assist marketing public relations.

The sponsorship of the arts has moved from being a means of supporting the community to a sophisticated means of targeting and positioning brands.

These three main forms of sponsorship, sports, arts and programme, are not mutually exclusive and use of one does not necessarily prevent use of either of the others. Before NTL was merged into the Virgin Media dynasty, it sponsored four major English and Scottish football teams in order to drive brand awareness, and particularly in areas where it hoped to develop cable services. NTL also used programme sponsorship supporting *Who Wants to Be a Millionaire?* in an attempt to develop brand values. In addition to these two major sponsorships, NTL also supported the MacMillan Cancer Relief fund, perhaps to present a more caring or balanced identity for its various audiences. However, because of targeting issues,

Exhibit 20.4 Virgin's sponsorship of music festivals is an integral part of their communications strategy
© Tim Mosenfelder/Corbis.

many organisations find it more efficient to use one major form of sponsorship, supported by a range of secondary sponsorship activities.

Other forms of sponsorship

It has been argued that there is little opportunity to control messages delivered through sponsorship, and far less opportunity to encourage the target audiences to enter into a dialogue with sponsors. However, the awareness and image opportunities can be used by supporting either the local community or small-scale schemes. Whitbread has been involved in supporting school programmes, environmental developments and other locally oriented activities because that is where its customers are based. Volkswagen wanted to be associated with the motoring environment rather than just the motorist. To help achieve this goal it sponsored the jackets worn by road-crossing wardens (lollipop people) so that the local authority was free to use the money once spent on uniforms on other aspects of road safety (Walker, 1995).

Samsung Electronics use sponsorship to link up with a variety of activities. From being the shirt sponsor for Chelsea FC, and an official sponsor for the Olympic Games to the sponsor of the Crufts dog show (Murphy, 2007). However, they do feel that the greater the number of sponsors tied to an event the less opportunity there is to leverage the linkage. The one exception to this rule is the Olympics. This event involves all nations and Samsung is everywhere.

> The greater the number of sponsors tied to an event the less opportunity there is to leverage the linkage.

The majority of sponsorships, regardless of type, are not the sole promotional activity undertaken by the sponsors. They may be secondary and used to support above-the-line work or they may be used as the primary form of communication but supported by a range of off-screen activities, such as sales promotions and (in particular) competitions.

This section would not be complete without mention of the phenomenon called 'ambush marketing'. This occurs when an organisation deliberately seeks an association with a particular event but does so without paying sponsorship fees. Such hijacking is undertaken with the purpose of influencing the audience to the extent that they believe the ambusher is legitimate. According to Meenaghan (1998), this can be achieved by overstating the organisation's involvement in the event, perhaps through major communication activity using theme-based advertising or by sponsoring the media coverage of the event.

The role of sponsorship in the communication mix

Whether sponsorship is a part of advertising, sales promotion or public relations has long been a source of debate. It is perhaps more natural and comfortable to align sponsorship with advertising. Since awareness is regarded as the principal objective of using sponsorship, advertising is a more complementary and accommodating part of the mix. Sales promotion from the sponsor's position is harder to justify, although from the perspective of the sponsored the value-added characteristic is interesting. The more traditional home for sponsorship is public relations (Witcher *et al.*, 1991). The sponsored, such as a football team, a racing car manufacturer or a theatre group, may be adjudged to perform the role of opinion former. Indirectly, therefore, messages are conveyed to the target audience with the support of significant participants who endorse and support the sponsor. This is akin to public relations activities.

Hastings (1984) contests that advertising messages can be manipulated and adapted to changing circumstances much more easily than those associated with sponsorship. He suggests that the audience characteristics of both advertising and sponsorship are very different. For advertising there are viewers and non-viewers. For sponsorship there are three groups of people that can be identified. First, there are those who are directly involved with the sponsor or the event, the active participants. The second is a much larger group, consisting of those who attend sponsored events, and these are referred to as personal spectators. The third group is normally the largest, comprising all those who are involved with the event through various media channels; these are regarded as media followers.

As if to demonstrate the potential sizes of these groups, estimates suggest that in excess of 4 million people attend the Formula 1 Grand Prix championship races (active participants) and over half a billion people (media followers) watch the races on television.

Exploratory research undertaken by Hoek *et al.* (1997) suggests that sponsorship is better able to generate awareness and a wider set of product-related attributes than advertising when dealing with non-users of a product, rather than users. There appears to be no discernible difference between the impact that these two promotional tools have with users.

The authors claim that sponsorship and advertising can be considered to work in approximately the same way if the ATR (attention, trial, reinforcement) model developed by Ehrenberg (1974) is adopted (Chapter 16). Through the ATR model, purchase behaviour and beliefs are considered to be reinforced by advertising rather than new behaviour patterns being established. Advertising fulfils a means by which buyers can meaningfully defend their purchase patterns. Hoek *et al.* regard this approach as reasonably analogous to sponsorship. Sponsorship can create awareness and is more likely to confirm past behaviour than prompt new purchase behaviour. The implication, they conclude, is that, while awareness levels can be improved with sponsorship, other communication tools are required to impact upon product experimentation or purchase intentions.

Sponsorship can create awareness and is more likely to confirm past behaviour than prompt new purchase behaviour.

It was suggested earlier in this chapter that one of the opportunities that sponsorship offers is the ability to suggest that there is an association between the sponsored and the sponsor which may be of value to the message recipient. This implies that there is an indirect form of influence through sponsorship. This is supported by Crimmins and Horn (1996), who argue that the persuasive impact of sponsorship is determined in terms of the strength of links that are generated between the brand and the event that is sponsored.

These authors claim that sponsorship can have a persuasive impact and that the degree of impact that a sponsorship might bring is as follows:

$$\text{persuasive impact} = \text{strength of link} \times \text{duration of the link} \times \left\{ \text{gratitude felt due to the link} + \text{perceptual change due to the link} \right\}$$

The strength of the link between the brand and the event is an outcome of the degree to which advertising is used to communicate the sponsorship itself. Sponsors that failed to invest in advertising during the Olympic Games have been shown to be far less successful in building a link with the event than those who chose to invest.

The *duration* of the link is also important. Research based on the Olympic Games shows that those sponsors who undertook integrated marketing communications long before the event itself were far more successful than those who had not. The use of mass media advertising to communicate the involvement of the sponsor, the use of event graphics and logos on packaging, and the creative use of promotional tie-ins and in-store, event-related merchandising facilitated the long-term linkage with the sponsorship and added value to the campaign.

The *duration* of the link is important.

Gratitude exists if consumers realise that there is a link between a brand and an event. For example, 60 per cent of US adults said that they 'try to buy a company's product if they support the Olympics'. They also stated that 'I feel I am contributing to the Olympics by buying the brands of Olympic sponsors'.

Perceptual change occurs as a result of consumers being able to understand the relationship (meaning) between a brand and an event. The sponsor needs to make this clear, as passive consumers may need the links laid out before them. The link between a swimwear brand and the Olympics may be obvious, but it is not always the case. Crimmins and Horn (1996) describe how Visa's 15 per cent perceived superiority advantage over MasterCard was stretched to 30 per cent during the 1992 Olympics and then settled at 20 per cent ahead one month after the Games had finished. The perceptual change was achieved through the messages that informed audiences that Visa was the one card that was accepted for the Olympic Games; American Express and MasterCard were not accepted.

This research, while based only upon a single event, indicates that sponsorship may bring advantages if care is taken to invest in communications long before and during the event to communicate the meaning between the brand and the event, which will leverage gratitude from a grateful audience.

Summary

In order to help consolidate your understanding of sponsorship, here are the key points summarised against each of the learning objectives:

1. Explain how sponsorship activities have developed and provide an insight into the main characteristics of this form of communication.

Sponsorship permits one party an opportunity to exploit an association with a target audience of another organisation, in return for funds, services or resources. This form of communication has developed partly as a result of the government's policies on tobacco and alcohol, the escalating costs of advertising media during the 1990s, the proven ability of sponsorship, new opportunities due to increased leisure activity, greater media coverage of sponsored events, recognition of the inefficiencies associated with the traditional media, a relaxation in the regulations and the advances in digital technology.

2. Consider reasons for the use of sponsorship and the types of objectives that might be set.

Some organisations use sponsorship, particularly sports activities, as a means of reaching wider target audiences. Sponsorship can provide exposure to particular audiences that each event attracts in order to convey simple, awareness-based brand messages. It can be used to suggest to the target audiences that there is an association between the sponsored and the sponsor and that by implication this association may be of interest and/or value.

3. Understand how sponsorship might work.

Sponsorship works through associations that consumers make with a brand (which will be an accumulation of previous advertising and other promotional activities) and the event being supported. In addition, people make a judgement based upon the fit between the event and sponsorship such that the greater the degree of compatibility the more readily acceptable the sponsorship will be.

An alternative view holds that a sponsorship can be perceived as a reinforcement of previous brand experiences. An event generates rewards by reminding individuals of pleasurable brand experiences.

4. Explain some of the conceptual and theoretical aspects of sponsorship.

Sponsorship represents a form of collaborative communication, in the sense that two (or more) parties work together in order that one is enabled to reach the other's audience. Issues regarding the relationship between the parties concerned will impact on the success of a sponsorship arrangement and any successive arrangements.

Sponsorship can be seen as a function of an organisation's value to others in a network. The sponsored and the sponsor are key actors in sponsorship networks, but agencies, event organisers, media networks and consultancies are also actors, each of whom will be connected (networked) with the sponsor and sponsored.

5. Appreciate the variety and different forms of sponsorship activities.

Sponsorship is used in three key areas. These are sports, programme/broadcast, and the arts. There is also growing interest in other activities such as wildlife/conservation and education. Of all of these, sport has attracted most attention and sponsorship money.

6. Understand the reasons why sponsorship has become an important part of the communication mix.

Sponsorship has become an important part of the mix as it allows brands to be communicated without the clutter and noise associated with advertising. At the same time sponsorship enables associations and linkages to be made that add value for all the participants to the communication process.

There seems little doubt that the introduction of new products and brands can be assisted by the use of appropriate sponsorships. Indeed, it appears that sponsorship, in certain contexts, can be used to prepare markets for the arrival and penetration of new brands.

It is perhaps more natural and comfortable to align sponsorship with advertising but it has also been associated with sales promotion and public relations. Since awareness is regarded as the principal objective of using sponsorship, advertising is a more complementary and accommodating part of the mix.

Review questions

1. What are the main opportunities that sponsorship opens up for organisations?
2. Why has sponsorship become such a major promotional tool in recent years?
3. If the objective of using sponsorship is to build awareness (among other things), then there is little point in using advertising. Discuss this view.
4. Name four types of sponsorship.
5. Why is sport more heavily sponsored than the arts or television programmes?
6. Choose eight sporting events and name the main sponsors. Why do you think they have maintained their associations with the events?
7. Consider five television programmes that are sponsored and evaluate how viewers might perceive the relationship between the programme content and the sponsor.
8. How might sponsorship have a persuasive impact on its target audiences? What is the formula used to measure this impact?
9. Explain the role of sponsorship within the promotional mix.
10. How might sponsorship develop in the future?

MiniCase Sponsorship and the British Superbike (BSB) Championship: a sport in transition?

Katy Lahiffe: DeMonfort University and Tony Garry: DeMonfort University

Introduction

The historical view of sponsorship was often perceived to be one of a '*a philanthropic gesture*' (Hoek and Gendall, 2003: 1) by the owner of a business to one of their favourite causes. However, many now believe sponsorship has evolved into a mainstream component of the marketing mix to the extent that it is now considered to be a strategic tool that managers leverage to provide sustainable competitive advantage and a resultant financial return. Indeed, sponsorship of sporting events globally has risen exponentially in recent years with worldwide global sponsorship of such events estimated by the International Events Group (IEG) to have grown by 25 per cent from $24.4 billion to $30.5 billion in the three years up to 2005 alone. Motorsports in particular have been successful at attracting corporate sponsorship revenue because of their globally popular appeal.

The British Superbike Championship

The British Superbike (BSB) Championship is the United Kingdom's leading domestic series. Superbikes are essentially production motorcycles. This means motorcycles are modified to comply with BSB rules specified by the MCRCB (Motorcycle Racing Control Board) and effectively allows participants to produce highly tuned, race-specification machines that resemble on-road models. As a result, the BSB Championship attracts manufacturers from around the world who are keen to use the series to showcase their latest models. Brands such as Honda, Suzuki, Kawasaki, Yamaha, Ducati and Triumph are all officially backing a number of 'factory teams'.

The roots of BSB Championship sponsorship may be traced back to the 1950s when sponsors would pool their resources to create individual championship events based at particular racing circuits. This would entice riders to participate with large start-money and winning bonuses. However, this resulted in a rather fragmented racing calendar and in 1966 a more formalised and season-long series was established. As the Championship evolved, a multi-classification structure was adopted with a variety of different titles and sponsors. In 1989 Superbike machines ran in the Shell Oil ACU Supercup Series for the first time. From this, the BSB Championship series evolved and while the title has changed several times (the HEAT Super-cup Series (1994–95), the MCN British Superbike Championship (1996–2002), 'Think! British Superbike Championship' (2003–04)) the format has essentially remained the same. Today the series is named 'Bennett's British Superbike Championship'.

The season is organised by the MCRCB and consists of 12 rounds hosted by a number of venues across the United Kingdom including Brands Hatch, Donington Park and Silverstone Race Circuit. There are five classes: the British Superbike Championship, the British Supersport Championship, the National Superstock 600 Championship, the British 125ccGP and the Yamaha R6 Cup. Points are awarded to the top 15 riders to cross the finishing line with the winning rider being awarded the most points and the 14 subsequent riders receiving less and less points. At the end of each season the points are totalled up to determine the overall champions. In addition, each class complies with international regulations on bike modification, which enables wild-card entries from around the world to compete at particular events.

The changing nature of BSB championship sponsorship

The BSB Championship is an attractive proposition to potential sponsors. Recent years have seen an exponential growth in the popularity of the BSB Championship. Official promoters of the 2007 BSB Championship, Dorna UK Ltd, recorded hefty increases in track-side and televised viewing. The 2007 series attracted event crowds of an estimated 355,000 spectators during the season (almost twice the figure recorded in 1999). Brands Hatch attracted 34,000 visitors and the season averaged over 27,000 at each event (up 11 per cent year-on-year) despite poor weather. An estimated 12.7 million adults watched dedicated BSB programmes on terrestrial and Sky channels. The BSB Championship outperformed all other national motorsport series on television. The reason for this growth in popularity may be attributable to a number of interrelated reasons:

- the increasing popularity of extreme sports in general;

- interest in motorcycles as a leisure pursuit particularly among older males;
- motorcycle sales are increasing, benefitting from escalating personal disposable incomes;
- Superbike popularity has also been boosted by the success of a number of British World Champions in recent years.

The BSB Championship also has a number advantages over other sporting events. While motor-sport in general is perceived as being an expensive sponsorship activity, motorcycle racing is less expensive than motorcar racing. To place a competitive Superbike on the British Superbike circuit for one season costs an estimated £750,000. The sport enjoys a significant level of exposure, but is still affordable and relatively low in 'sponsorship clutter'. In return for funding, sponsors can attain considerable benefits such as team association (e.g. Redbull Honda, Rizla Suzuki, etc.), corporate hospitality venues, full team livery and naming rights. The top teams have carefully coordinated uniforms, race leathers, race bikes and their transporters and pit equipment incorporating unique and striking designs based upon sponsor imagery. For example, Rizla Suzuki, with its distinctive blue and yellow logo, have engendered a strong, fan-based following. Regardless of the riders, thousands of supporters purchase merchandise ranging from comedy blue and yellow wigs to complete race-specification motorcycle replicas. However, the changing environment of the BSB Championship in recent years has meant the nature of the relationship between some sponsors and sponsored teams has changed. As competitive teams are acquiring more exposure for sponsors, they are able to command greater sums of money in selling sponsorship rights. Also, as the sport has witnessed increasing at-track attendance and media coverage there has been a marked increase in the number of potential sponsors. Finally, as a result of the increased popularity of the BSB Championship, the organisational profile of many sponsors has changed from that of a small to medium-sized enterprise, often producing products and services related to motorcycling, to one of the large companies dominated by professional marketers. Sponsors now include global brands such as Red Bull, Virgin and Rizla.

Historically, a proportion of the sponsors had a prior interest in motorcycle racing. Similarly, most racing teams are established by ex-racers and/or enthusiasts. Consequently, there is an emotional attachment and 'sharing of passion' for the sport. This often manifests itself in mutual understanding and respect between sponsor and rider. Indeed, such sponsors seek to develop relationships with riders other than those that

Exhibit 20.5 Sponsorship of the bike and rider is an integral part of superbike racing

they sponsor primarily to reinforce the 'community of emotion or passion' found within the sport. However, the motivations of more recent sponsors are primarily commercial and tend to focus on two broad objectives:

- First, 'exposure-seeking' whereby sponsorship is essentially perceived as an advertising forum to enhance corporate/brand image among a diverse range of stakeholders; and second,
- An attempt to develop close associations between a brand and/or company and a particular event so as to increase goodwill among opinion formers and leaders.

Related to this, such events as the BSB Championship provide a valuable platform for corporate hospitality. Such hospitality activities are viewed by sponsors as part of the wooing of relevant and influential corporate customers. The goodwill generated by the attendance of a select customer group at such sporting events as the BSB Championship may become a key factor in improving the subsequent interactions between individuals from both the customer and sponsoring firm. Corporate hospitality is not just perceived as maintaining brand reputation and presenting a window on to the sponsor's corporate values, it attempts to generate a 'feel good factor' among corporate customers when they think about the sponsoring organisation.

The expectations of sponsors in terms of the role the sponsored teams are expected to play in the corporate hospitality process vary. Those sponsors who are more commercially driven tend to have differing expectations of what the sponsored teams should deliver, and indeed, in their ability to deliver it. In some situations, the sponsored teams are perceived as lacking the interpersonal skills and/or the motivation required to support the aspirations of sponsors. As one sponsor comments: 'You ultimately feel taken for granted . . . just money bags . . . I gave and they took . . . and yet the [sponsored] team said they were doing what they were expected to do . . . to ride . . . without tenting and trees [corporate hospitality].' In contrast, sponsors that are largely motivated by non-commercial drivers often do not believe participation in the corporate hospitality process is a priority. As one sponsor states: 'I don't think that my loyalty to my riders is different because of their ability to promote themselves. They aren't asked to promote me, anyway, so marketing isn't an issue . . . I'd rather they focus on riding.'

Related to this, there appears to be a growing general spectator backlash at the extent and nature of corporate sponsorship within other sporting contexts such as soccer. Particular issues cited include a preoccupation with commercial rather than sporting objectives; the 'prostitution' of teams in terms of excessive expectations related to promotional activities and the perception of corporate entertainment 'squeezing out' genuine supporters. Sponsors will have to tread carefully if they are to maintain the support of the various stakeholder groups.

Source: Based on 'The role of commitment and trust in a sponsorship dyad', Katy Lahiffe (2004), Unpublished Undergraduate Dissertation, De Montfort University (UK).

MiniCase references

Hoek, J. and Gendall, P. (2003) How does sponsorship work. ANZMAC Conference Proceedings , Adelaide, 1–3 December.

Sports Business.com (2006) Member press release – 30 January 2006.

A bright future for sports sponsorship. Retrieved 26 February 2007 from http://www.sponsorship.org/membPressDetail.asp?id=91.

MiniCase questions

1. List four sponsorship objectives that may be adopted by a sponsoring organisation within this context and what metrics could be adopted to evaluate whether these are being achieved?
2. Supposing you have just taken over the sponsorship of one of the more successful BSB Championship teams. What steps would you take to ensure a positive and ongoing relationship with the riders? And team (?)
3. Given the increasing spectator backlash against many forms of corporate sports sponsorship, what steps would you suggest a sponsoring organisation should take to avoid becoming the focus of such negative attention?

References

Bal, C., Quester, P.G. and Boucher, S. (2007) *Admap*, **486** (September), 51–2.

Balfour, M. (2000) Precision technology delivered in record time. *Financial Times*, 25 March.

Bartlett, M. (2007) Glowing at Glastonbury. *The Marketer* (September), 20–3.

Charles, G. (2007) Flora's race exit branded 'bizarre'. *Marketing*, 12 December, 6.

Crimmins, J. and Horn, M. (1996) Sponsorship: from management ego trip to marketing success. *Journal of Advertising Research* (July/August), 11–21.

Davidson, D. (2007) Heineken backs Rugby World Cup with earth-moving ad. *Brand Republic*, 13 June. Retrieved 9 January 2008 from http://www.brandrepublic.com/News/664266/Heineken-backs-Rugby-World-Cup-earth-moving-ad/

Dolphin, R.R. (2003) Sponsorship: perspectives on its strategic role. *Corporate Communications: An International Journal*, **8**(3), 173–86.

Ehrenberg, A.S.C. (1974) Repetitive advertising and the consumer. *Journal of Advertising Research*, **14** (April), 25–34.

Farmer, B. (2007) ITV and RFU set for Rugby World Cup windfall. *Daily Telegraph*, 20 October 2007. Retrieved 9 January 2008 from www.telegraph.co.uk/news/.

Farrelly, F., Quester, P. and Mavondo, F. (2003) Collaborative communication in sponsor relations. *Corporate Communications: An International Journal*, **8**(2), 128–38.

Farrelly, F. Quester, P. and Burton, R. (2006) Changes in sponsorship value: competencies and capabilities of successful sponsorship relationships. *Industrial Marketing Management*, **35**(8) (November), 1016–26.

Grimes, E. and Meenaghan, T. (1998) Focusing commercial sponsorship on the internal corporate audience. *International Journal of Advertising*, **17**(1), 51–74.

Gummesson, E. (1996) Relationship marketing and imaginary organisations: a synthesis. *European Journal of Marketing*, **30**(2), 31–45.

Hakansson, H. and Snehota, I. (1995) *Developing Relationships in Business Networks*. London: Routledge.

Harverson, P. (1998) Why IT companies take the risk. *Financial Times*, 2 June, 12.

Harvey, B., Gray, S. and Despain, G. (2006) Measuring the effectiveness of true sponsorship. *Journal of Advertising Research*, **46**(4) (December), 398–409.

Hastings, G. (1984) Sponsorship works differently from advertising. *International Journal of Advertising*, **3**, 171–6.

Hedburg, A. (2000) Bumper crop. *Marketing Week*, 19 October, 28–32.

Hill, A. (2001) On the crest of a sponsorship wave. *PR Week*, 23 February, 9.

Hoek, J., Gendall, P., Jeffcoat, M. and Orsman, D. (1997) Sponsorship and advertising: a comparison of their effects. *Journal of Marketing Communications*, **3**, 21–32.

Hudson, S. and Hudson, D. (2006) Branded entertainment: a new advertising technique or product placement in disguise? *Journal of Marketing Management*, **22**, 489–504.

Javalgi, R.G., Traylor, M.B., Gross, A.C. and Lampman, E. (1994) Awareness of sponsorship and corporate image: an empirical investigation. *Journal of Advertising*, **24** (June), 1–12.

Kolah, A. (2008) Sponsorship 2.0. *The Marketer* (December/January), 28–31.

Lacey, R., Sneath, J.Z., Finney, R.Z. and Close, A.G. (2007) The impact of repeat attendance on event sponsorship effects. *Journal of Marketing Communications*, **13**(4) (December), 243–55.

Marshall, D.W. and Cook, G. (1992) The corporate (sports) sponsor. *International Journal of Advertising*, **11**, 307–24.

McDonald, C. (1991) Sponsorship and the image of the sponsor. *European Journal of Marketing*, **25**(11), 31–8.

Meenaghan, T. (1991) The role of sponsorship in the marketing communications mix. *International Journal of Advertising*, **10**, 35–47.

Meenaghan, T. (1998) Current developments and future directions in sponsorship. *International Journal of Advertising*, **17**(1), 3–28.

Murphy, D. (2007) Lost in the crowd. *Marketing*, 29 August, 36–7.

Olkkonen, R. (2001) Case study: the network approach to international sport sponsorship arrangement. *Journal of Business and Industrial Marketing*, **16**(4), 309–29.

Ovenden, M. (2007) 21st century media: right on target. *Marketing*, 5 December, 6–7.

Poon, D.T.Y and Prendergast, G. (2006) A new framework for evaluating sponsorship opportunities. *International Journal of Advertising*, **25**(4), 471–87.

Pope, N.K.L. and Voges, K.E. (1999) Sponsorship and image: a replication and extension. *Journal of Marketing Communications*, **5**, 17–28.

Reed, D. (1994) Sponsorship. *Campaign*, 20 May, 37–8.

Smith, A. (1997) UK sponsors look to US. *Financial Times*, 24 March, 16.

Sneath, J.Z., Finney, R.Z. and Close, A.G. (2005) An IMC approach to event marketing: the effects of sponsorship and experience on customer attitudes. *Journal of Advertising Research*, **45**(4) (December), 373–81.

Thorncroft, A. (1996) Business arts sponsorship: arts face a harsh set of realities. *Financial Times*, 4 July, 1.

Thwaites, D. (1994) Corporate sponsorship by the financial services industry. *Journal of Marketing Management*, **10**, 743–63.

Tripodi, J.A. (2001) Sponsorship: a confirmed weapon in the promotional armoury. *International Journal of Sports Marketing and Sponsorship*, **3**(1) (March/April), 1–20.

Wakefield, K.L., Becker-Olsen, K. and Cornwell, T.B. (2007) Spy a sponsor: the effects of sponsorship level, prominence, relatedness, and cueing on recall accuracy. *Journal of Advertising*, **36**(4) (Winter), 61–74.

Walker, J.-A. (1995) Community service. *Marketing Week*, 20 October, 85–90.

Witcher, B., Craigen, G., Culligan, D. and Harvey, A. (1991) The links between objectives and functions in organisational sponsorship. *International Journal of Advertising*, **10**, 13–33.

Chapter 21

Direct marketing

Direct marketing is a strategy used to create a personal and intermediary-free dialogue with customers. This should be a measurable activity and it is very often media-based, with a view to creating and sustaining a mutually rewarding relationship. The development and use of direct marketing principles by a variety of organisations are testimony to the power of this personal form of communication.

Aims and learning objectives

The aims of this chapter are to explore the characteristics of direct marketing and to develop an understanding of interactive marketing communications.

The learning objectives of this chapter are to:

1. consider the role and characteristics of direct marketing;
2. examine the types of direct brands and their relationship with direct response media and their role within the marketing communications mix;
3. consider the reasons behind the growth and development of this new marketing communications tool;
4. appreciate the significance of the database in direct marketing;
5. explore issues associated with permission-based marketing;
6. identify and consider different direct response media;
7. consider the value of integrating the activities of direct marketing with other elements of the mix.

For an applied interpretion see the MiniCase entitled ***Recovering cars with direct marketing*** at the end of this chapter.

Introduction

From previous discussions about relational and marketing exchanges (Chapters 1 and 7), it should be apparent that the long-term goal of most organisations is to build a long-term relationship with each of their customers. Most of the marketing communications disciplines use mass media to address huge audiences, in what is essentially one-way communication – not an ideal way of developing relationships. Advertising communicates with large audiences and primarily seeks to provide certain information, affect emotions and frame intentions when the next purchase opportunity arises. Advertising is not capable of talking personally to individual customers, nor is it used to generate personal responses. Furthermore, those who choose to use advertising are constrained by the page sizes, paper types, fonts and style or the available spots, the skill of the media planner and the programmes that are available.

The long-term goal of most organisations is to build a long-term relationship with each of their customers.

Sales promotions are designed to generate an immediate sale, but the information is not stored or used in such a way that a relationship is deliberately created and sustained and the perceived value of a brand can be diluted. Public relations seeks to develop favourable interest and goodwill by piggy-backing on other media. Personal selling is certainly founded upon the need to establish long-term, personal relationships. However, the range of tasks that the sales force is expected to complete means that only a small percentage of its time can be focused on generating an immediate response. Personal selling is expensive and there is variable control over the messages that are transmitted by individual members of the sales force.

In addition to these promotional tool deficiencies, the distribution element of the marketing mix was the last to receive attention. Faced with an increasing lack of product/service differentiation and margins being eroded through price competition, the marketing channel was ripe for investigation and review. It became clear that many cost advantages could be achieved through a more direct approach to the market. This meant side-lining or avoiding expensive intermediaries (channel members) and providing opportunities to improve quality and service provision. For these main reasons, direct marketing has developed and flourished.

The role of direct marketing

Direct marketing is a term used to refer to all media activities that generate a series of communications and responses with an existing or potential customer. Early on there was considerable debate about the term 'direct marketing' itself. It was often referred to as direct mail or as 'curriculum marketing, dialogue marketing, personal marketing and database marketing' (Bird, 1989). This proliferation of terms reflects the range of activities that are undertaken in an attempt to prompt a response from a customer. Terminology has settled in favour of direct marketing, and this broad approach will be adopted here. However, readers are advised that this chapter on direct marketing should not be read in isolation, as issues concerning direct communications are embedded throughout this text. Particular reference should be made to Chapters 1, 7, 9, 24 and 26.

Direct marketing is a term used to refer to all media activities that generate a series of communications and responses with an existing or potential customer.

Primarily, direct marketing is concerned with the management of customer behaviour and is used to complement the strengths and weaknesses of the other communication disciplines. To put this another way, advertising and public relations provide information and develop brand values but sales promotion and direct marketing drive response, most notably behaviour.

Direct marketing is concerned with the management of customer behaviour.

Half price.
All yours.
Hurry, offer ends soon
Our Conservatory Blinds are now up to half-price in our spectacular Spring Sale.
For your FREE home presentation or brochure
Call 0800 220 603
or visit www.thomas-sanderson.co.uk
ThomasSanderson
An expression of individuality
Quote Ref: 811BC

Exhibit 21.1 This Thomas Anderson print ad appeals directly to customers offering a telephone number and a web site address to drive action
Courtesy of Thomas Sanderson.

For a long time direct mail was the main tool of direct marketing but the development of information technology and, in particular, the database, have enabled the introduction of a range of other media. These are used to communicate directly with individual customers and often carry a behavioural (call-to-action) message. Typically, direct marketing agencies work across a variety of media including the telephone, Internet, direct mail, email, press and posters. No single media channel dominates their work. In an era where the talk is about integration and media neutrality (Chapter 9) the direct marketing industry is in a strong position to provide a wide range of client communication services. All the elements of the communication mix can be used with direct marketing to support and build meaningful relationships with consumers and members of the various stakeholder networks.

ViewPoint 21.1 A&L value the direct approach

A&L is the seventh largest UK bank and like many other banks was hit by the credit crunch that emerged in 2007. The banking industry also suffers from a negative customer perception, with many customers cynical about over-promise and under-delivery.

It is said that A&L had failed to invest in their brand in recent years although traditionally A&L was perceived to be a strong brand. To help differentiate itself now it follows a low-cost business strategy, based around four core brand values: attracting new customers by offering better value products and services; being simple and straightforward; offering a friendly and approachable service; and 'recognising' existing customers.

To deliver the business objectives, A&L use direct marketing to reach their target audience. They simply refuse to spend huge amounts on brand advertising just so they can compete with the bigger banks. If they did it would undermine their value proposition. In addition to the branch network, A&L use direct channels, such as the Internet and telephone banking.

Source: Turner (2008).

Question

If A&L do not want to compete using advertising or direct marketing, what other methods could they use?

Task

Make a list of the various forms of direct communications A&L could use to reach their markets.

Direct marketing is a strategy used to create and sustain a personal and intermediary-free dialogue with customers, potential customers and other significant stakeholders. In most cases this is a media-based activity and offers great scope for the collection and utilisation of pertinent and measurable data. There are a number of important issues associated with this definition. The first is that the activity should be measurable. That is, any response(s) must be associated with a particular individual, a particular media activity and a particular outcome, such as a sale or inquiry for further information. The second issue concerns the rewards that each party perceives through participation in the relationship. The customer receives a variety of tangible and intangible satisfactions. These include shopping convenience, time utility and the satisfaction and trust that can develop between customers and a provider of quality products and services when the customers realise and appreciate the personal attention they appear to be receiving.

Underpinning the direct marketing approach are the principles of trust and commitment, just as they support the validity of the other promotional tools. If a meaningful relationship is to be developed over the long term and direct marketing is an instrumental part of the dialogue, then the pledges that the parties make to develop commitment and stability are of immense importance (Ganesan, 1994).

> Underpinning the direct marketing approach are the principles of trust and commitment.

Indeed, the concept of establishing trust is vital if relational exchanges are to be developed. Trust is a multidimensional construct (Morgan and Hunt, 1994) and the need to ensure that it is recognised and accepted by parties where direct marketing is used is highly important (Fletcher and Peters, 1997).

The direct marketer derives benefits associated with precision target marketing such as minimised waste, increased profits and the opportunities to provide established customers with other related products, without the huge costs of continually having to find new customers. In addition, direct marketing represents a strategic approach to the market. It actively seeks to remove channel intermediaries, reduce costs and improve the quality and speed of service for customers. Through this bundle of attributes, direct marketing can itself present a new offering for the market, one that may provide competitive advantage. For example, First Direct, Virgin Direct and the pioneer, Direct Line, all provide these advantages, which have enabled them to secure strong positions in the market.

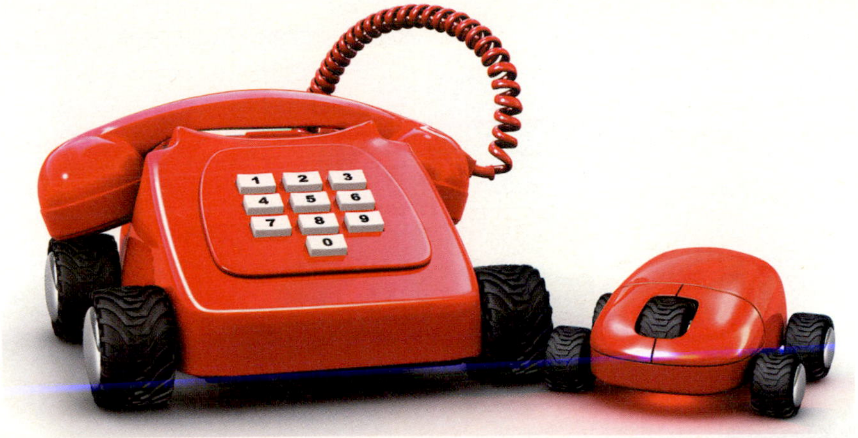

Exhibit 21.2 Direct Line telephone
The red telephone identifies Direct Line, one of the first to establish direct marketing as its principal form of marketing communications.
Picture reproduced with the kind permission of Direct Line Insurance.

Types of direct brand

Direct marketing is assumed to refer to direct promotional activity, but this is only part of the marketing picture. Using direct response media in this way is an increasingly common activity used to augment the communication activities surrounding a brand and to provide a new dimension to the context in which brands are perceived.

In addition to these promotional advantages there are two main types of direct brands: *pedigree direct* brands and *hybrid direct* brands (Foster, 1996). These reflect the origins of a brand in the sense that the pedigree direct brand is developed to exploit a market-positioning opportunity. Hybrid direct brands are essentially the same except that the brand heritage is rooted in traditional distribution channels, which may well continue to be a route to market, used in parallel to the direct route. Therefore, as Foster points out, the main difficulty facing the hybrid direct brand is the organisational culture: its context and heritage. With these brands there is a generally accepted approach to the market and commonality as to the way things should be done. Even the systems and processes associated with the intermediary-based approach are established and need to be altered to meet the needs of a new type of customer.

However, there is further difficulty, which lies with the image that the customer base and other stakeholders have of the hybrid direct brand. It represents a change from the frame in which stakeholders expect to see the brand. Care therefore, needs to be taken with the marketing communications to ensure that the transition is carried out in such a way that the credibility of the brand is maintained.

From this review it is possible to see direct marketing as part of one of the types shown in Figure 21.1. These are not hierarchical in the sense that there has to be progression from one type to another. They are reflections of the way different organisations use direct marketing and the degree to which the tool is used strategically.

Type 1: complementary tool

Direct response media are used to complement the other promotional activities.

At this level, direct response media are used to complement the other promotional activities used to support a brand. Their main use is to generate leads and to some extent provide awareness, information

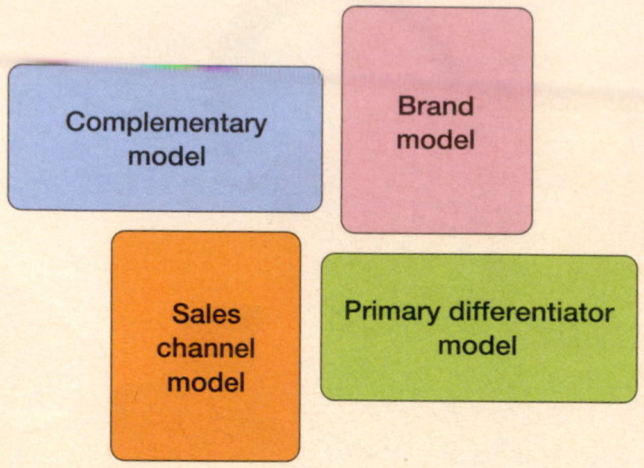

Figure 21.1 Types of direct marketing

and reinforcement. For example, financial services companies, tour operators and travel agents use direct response television (DRTV) to stimulate enquiries, loans and bookings, respectively.

Type 2: primary differentiator

Rather than be one of a number of promotional tools, at this level direct response media are the primary form of communication. They are used to provide a distinct point of differentiation from competitor offerings. They are the principal form of communication. In addition to the Type 1 advantages they are used to cut costs, avoid the use of intermediaries and reach precisely targeted audiences, for example book, music and wine clubs.

Type 3: sales channel

A third use for direct marketing and telemarketing in particular concerns its use as a means of developing greater efficiency and as a means of augmenting current services. By utilising direct marketing as a sales tool, multiple sales channels can be used to meet the needs of different customer segments and so release resources to be deployed elsewhere and more effectively. This idea is developed further later in this chapter.

Type 4: brand vehicle

Organisational brands are developed to exploit market space opportunities.

At this final level, organisational brands are developed to exploit market space opportunities. These may be the pedigree or hybrid brands identified earlier (for example, Direct Line, Virgin Direct and Eagle Star Direct). The strategic element is most clearly evident at this level. Indeed, the entire organisation and its culture are oriented to the development of customer relationships through direct marketing activities.

ViewPoint 21.2 ING Direct . . . literally

In just under three years, ING Direct took on the UK savings market and became the UK's fastest growing bank with over 1 million customers and £25 billion funds under management.

One of the goals at launch was to become a direct banking brand but not an ordinary one. ING Direct had to be perceived as highly differentiated from the current offerings. This required the brand to be positioned clearly and the platform for this was to be a straightforward, fair 'no catches' financial player. However, this would not be enough to grow quickly so there was a need to drive high levels of response.

Once a gap had been spotted in the market, a communications strategy was developed, built on a multi-channel approach, yet targeted at mainstream savers. The creative was based on the premise that the brand was 'for everyone' and that ING Direct offered simple products and that ING were no clutter and simple messages.

To grow rapidly, ING Direct needed to establish brand awareness across their target market and then drive high levels of response. First, a communications plan was established that included television, press, outdoor and direct mail. In addition, an online presence was imperative so a web site was developed, which was used in conjunction with telemarketing in order to create the accounts for new customers.

Sources: VCCP (2008), Gall *et al*. (2006).

Question

What might be the role of the web site in ING Direct's direct marketing other than to help create accounts?

Task

Go to the ING Direct web site and then to each of three of their competitors. What colours have each of the brands adopted?

ING
Direct
no catches
Open a Savings Account in minutes
No penalties and no catches
Open with £1
ingdirect.co.uk
0800 561 8831
ING DIRECT
savings

Exhibit 21.3 ING Direct print ad
ING Direct.

The growth of direct marketing

There can be little doubt that, of all the tools in the marketing communications mix, direct marketing has experienced the most growth in the last 15 years. The reasons for this growth are many and varied, but there have been three essential drivers behind the surge in direct marketing: technological advances; changing buyer lifestyles and expectations; and organisational expectations (see Figure 21.2). These forces for change demonstrate quite dramatically how a change in the context can impact on marketing communications.

There have been three essential drivers behind the surge in direct marketing.

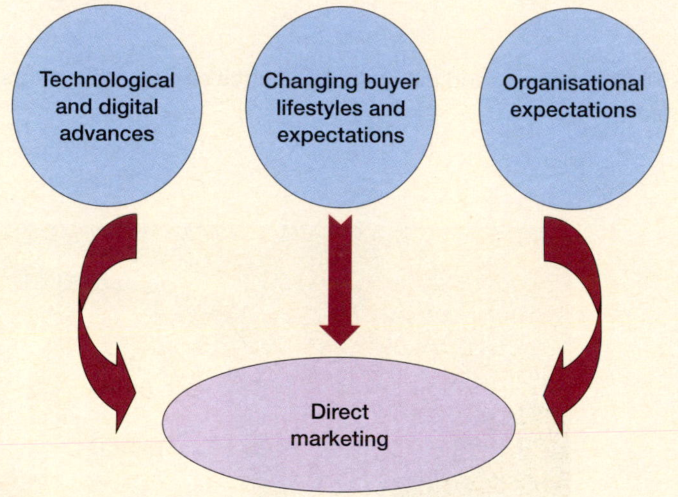

Figure 21.2 Three forces for direct marketing

Growth driver 1: technology

Rapid advances in technology have heralded the arrival of new sources and forms of information. Technology has enabled the collection, storage and analysis of customer data to become relatively simple, cost-effective and straightforward. Furthermore, the management of this information is increasingly available to small businesses as well as the major blue chip multinational organisations. Computing costs have plummeted, while there has been a correspondingly enormous increase in the power that technology can deliver.

The technological surge has in turn stimulated three major developments: first, the ability to capture information; second, the capacity to process and analyse it; and third, the capability to represent part or all of the information as a form of communication to stimulate dialogue and interaction to collect further information (see Table 21.1).

Organisations have been able to make increasing use of technological developments within marketing communications. Indeed, all areas of the mix have benefitted as new and more effective and efficient processes and methods of communication evolve. Advances in technology are responsible for the demise of some traditional forms of communication. For example, the impact of mass communications and advertising in particular as a single device has diminished in favour of a more personalised and

Advances in technology are responsible for the demise of some traditional forms of communication.

Table 21.1 Advances in technology

Data capture and collection	
	Web site registration data, scanners, smart cards, loyalty schemes, marketing research
Information processing	
	Database marketing, warehousing, mining
Communication and interaction	
	Greater precision in segmentation and targeting effectiveness, direct mail, telemarketing, SMS and mobile marketing plus a simultaneous decline in traditional media consumption/effectiveness.

Table 21.2 Changing market context

Lifestyles and expectations	
	Inner directedness, pluralism, individualism
Fragmentation	
	Audience, media
Market expectations	
	Increased competition, faster speed of response, shorter lifecycles, move to premium products.

integrated approach to communications, enabled by technology. This gives the ability to target potential customers much more precisely, at any location and at lower cost.

Growth driver 2: changing market context

The lifestyles of people in industrialised economies in particular, have evolved and will continue to do so. Generally, the brash phase of *selfishness* in the 1980s gave way to a more caring, society-oriented *selflessness* in the 1990s. The first decade of the twenty-first century suggests that a *self-oriented* lifestyle was prominent, reflected in short-term brand purchase behaviour and self-centred brand values and society behaviour. Perhaps the second decade will see further change as the global economy and forces for environmental adaptation bring about change to the way societies interact and individuals perceive their role within any one society. However, it seems as if there will be continued fragmentation of the media and finely tuned segmentation and communication devices will be necessary to communicate with discrete audiences.

Growth driver 3: changing organisational expectations

Organisations can expect to continue experiencing performance pressures. These vary from the expectations of shareholders as they demand short-term returns on their investments to the impact this can have on managers. They are having to cope with an increasing cost base caused by demands on fuel and other resources by developing economies and a downward pressure on prices due to intense competition. This pressure on margins requires new routes to markets to reduce costs. Direct marketing addresses some of these changing management

> There are no intermediary costs, there is fast access to markets (and withdrawal) plus opportunities to respond quickly to market developments.

Table 21.3 Changing organisational context

Shareholder requirements	
	Faster returns on investment, increased performance, increased propensity to switch funding
Management expectations	
	More accountability, increased costs, intense pressure on prices, shortening performance windows.

needs as there are no intermediary costs, there is fast access to markets (and withdrawal) plus opportunities to respond quickly to market developments and also justify their use and allocation of resources (see Table 21.3).

The impact of these three drivers can be seen within the emergence of ideas about integrated marketing communications and an overall emphasis on relationship marketing principles. The enhanced ability of organisations to collect, store and manage customer lifestyle and transactional data, to generate personalised communications and their general enthusiasm for retention and loyalty schemes have combined to provide a huge movement towards an increased use of direct and interactive marketing initiatives.

The role of the database

A database is a collection of files held on a computer that contain data that can be related to one another.

At the hub of successful direct marketing and customer relationship management (CRM) activities is the database. A database is a collection of files held on a computer that contain data that can be related to one another and that can reproduce information in a variety of formats. Normally the data consist of information collected about prospects and customers that are used to determine appropriate segments and target markets and to record responses to communications conveyed by the organisation. A database therefore plays a role as a storage, sorting and administrative device to assist direct and personalised communications.

Age and lifestyle data are important signals of product usage. However, there will be attitudinal variances between people in similar groups demanding further analysis. This can, according to Reed (2000), uncover clues concerning what the direct mail piece should look like. So, older customers do not like soft colours and small type and sentences should not begin with 'and' or 'but'.

The information stored in databases is gathered from transactions undertaken with customers, and this is known as the recency/frequency/monetary (RFM) model. On its own this information is not enough and further layering of data is required (Fletcher, 1997). Lifestyle data, often bought in from a list agency, can be used to further refine the information held. Response analysis requires the identification of an organisation's best customers, and then another layer of data can be introduced which points to those that are particularly responsive to direct mail, mail order, telephone or online communications. It is the increasing sophistication of the information held in databases that is enabling more effective targeting and communications. The database consists of several layers of information whereby traditional segmentation data, which set out customer profiles, could be fused with transactional data so that biographics (Evans, 1998) emerged as a radically new approach to developing interaction and dialogue with individual customers.

The information stored in databases is gathered from transactions undertaken with customers.

ViewPoint 21.3 Tesco watches Your Trolleys

Tesco announced in the Spring of 2008 that they were going to monitor and record the shopping habits of over 60 million people in nine of the countries in which it operates.

Tesco Clubcard has 13.5 million current users in the United Kingdom, and versions of the card are available in South Korea, China and Malaysia. Each day an analysis is undertaken of their purchases. This data are then used to target discount coupons and promotions based on an individual's purchase patterns. The Clubcard is to be made available in Thailand, Hungary, Turkey, Slovakia, the Czech Republic and Poland.

Dunnhumby, who operate the database, have identified different types of shoppers:

- Price sensitive shoppers – uses reward vouchers, few fresh foods, value lager
- Traditional shoppers – oldest group, buys small number of items from a list
- Mainstream shoppers – prefers easy-to-prepare family meals, saves Clubcard points for deals
- Healthy shoppers – any age but buys wholesome food, counts calories and fat
- Convenience shoppers – buys quick meals, often ready meals, prepared salads
- Finer foods shopper – affluent, older adults who prefer to cook with organic foods, exotic fruits and ovenware.

Source: Hawkes (2008).

Question

To what extent does database information of this type provide Tesco with a competitive advantage?

Task

Visit dunnhumby.com and find out what they call relevance marketing.

However, the merging of data generated through transactions with attitudinal and lifestyle data poses a further problem. In essence, this paints a picture of what has been achieved, it describes behaviour. What it does not do is explain why the behaviour occurred. It may be possible to track back through a campaign to examine the inputs, isolate variables and make a judgement, but the problem remains that the data itself, what has been collected, does not provide insight into what underpins the behaviour. Pearson (2003) suggests that direct marketing and market research data sets should be brought together into what has been referred to as 'consilience' (Wilson, 1998) or a unity of knowledge. This data-rich information should then be capable of providing organisations with data intelligence and an opportunity to predict behaviour and offer a new form of data value.

Databases provide the means by which a huge range of organisations, large and small, can monitor changes in customer lifestyles and attitudes. In the business-to-business sector, the changing form of the interorganisational relationships and their impact on other members in the network, as well as the market structure and level of competitive activity, requires better management. It is through the use of the database that relationships with participants can be tracked, analysed and developed. Very importantly, database systems can be used not only to identify strategically important customers and segments but also to ascertain opportunities to cross-sell products (Kamakura *et al.*, 2003).

> Databases provide the means by which a huge range of organisations can monitor changes in customer lifestyles and attitudes.

Permission marketing

However, there are a number of tensions associated with the use of the database. These tensions can be related to concerns about privacy and the need to communicate sensitively with audiences who experience varying needs for privacy (Dolnicar and Jordaan, 2007). For example, customers have varying tolerances regarding the level of privacy that a database can exploit. These tolerances or thresholds (Goodwin, 1991) vary according to the nature of the information itself, how it was collected and even who collected it. The information on a database very often exists simply because a customer entered into a transaction. The business entity that received the information as part of a transaction has a duty to acknowledge the confidential nature of the information and the context in which it was collected before selling the details to a third party or exploiting the information to the detriment of the individual who provided it in the first place. Breaking privacy codes and making unauthorised disclosures of personal details lays open the tenuous relationship an organisation thinks it has with its 'loyal' customers. These tensions have given rise to regulations requiring customers to provide organisations with their formal, express permission to use their personal data in particular ways.

It is commonly agreed that Godin (1999) is the pioneer of permission marketing (PM) (Krishnamurthy, 2001; Gomez and Hlavinka, 2007) and that the aim of PM is to 'initiate, sustain and develop a dialogue with customers, building trust and over time lifting the levels of permission, making it a more valuable asset' (Kent and Brandal, 2003: 491). To put it another way, PM is about 'getting the okay from individuals to market to them' (Smith, 2004: 52).

PM occurs when consumers give their explicit permission for marketers to send them various types of promotional messages (Krishnamurthy, 2001). Essentially customers authorise a marketer to transmit promotional messages in certain 'interest' categories. This is usually obtained when a customer registers to enter a web site or completes a survey indicating their interests when registering for a service. Marketers are then able to target advertising messages more closely with the interests and needs of their registered customers. Definitions of PM vary according to the focus of the researchers, but they range from education, trust and share of wallet, to enticement and clutter.

Customers authorise a marketer to transmit promotional messages in certain 'interest' categories.

Tezinde *et al.* (2002) examine PM in relation to the Internet and more specifically, email. They suggest the 'permission relationship' commences when customers give their 'explicit' and 'active' consent to receive commercial messages. Moustakas *et al.* (2006) agrees that a firm must obtain permission from a customer before contact through a direct marketing medium and concur that with every 'communication sent, the firm must provide consumers with an opportunity to rescind permission' (Dreze, 2005: 444).

Customers benefit from using PM through:

- a reduction in search costs and clutter (Lehman, 2004);
- better organisation of the information search processes (Dufrene *et al.*, 2005);
- improved message relevance through personalisation, customisation and recognition (Milne and Gordon, 1993, Reynolds *et al.*, 1995, Grunert, 1996 and Soars, 2001).

For organisations the benefits of using PM are related to:

- improved segmentation and targeting precision (Tezinde *et al.*, 2002 and Thomas, 2007);
- the acquisition of new customers, an increase of sales and the development of long-term, loyal customers (Kavassalis *et al.*, 2003);
- flexibility, resulting in: improved interactivity, lower sales costs, enhanced direct communication with customers and increased profitability (Dreze, 2005).

Levels of permission marketing

Godin (2002) identifies five distinct levels or types of permission marketing. These are set out in Table 21.4.

Godin's levels appear to be more of a hierarchical progression than a series of informed levels. Kent and Brandal (2003) suggest there are two levels of permission; 'basic permission' and 'extended permission'. Basic permission refers to individuals that have consented to receive information via email. Extended permission, involves 'asking the members in an email

Table 21.4 Levels of permission marketing

Level of PM	Explanation
Intravenous	A marketer makes buying decisions on behalf of consumers. Often granted by consumers to save time, save money, avoid making a choice and avoid stock-outs.
Points	Once a pre-determined number of points (or coupons) are accumulated consumers are entitled to a free gift and further patronage.
Personal relationships	The value of personal relationships is used to grant permission and is used to refocus consumers attention and modify their behaviour. It is used to move people to higher levels.
Brand trust	The next level of PM is termed the 'brand trust' level (Godin, 2002). It is depicted as 'the tried-and-true branding that is the mantra of most interruption marketers' (p. 123). Godin believes that it is largely overrated, as it is expensive to establish, time-consuming to progress, difficult to measure and even harder to influence. Godin believes that it leads to brand extensions, and can potentially hold a high degree of significance.
Situation	The final level of PM is the 'situational' level. Godin maintains that it occurs when 'the consumer and the salesperson/marketer have very high physical and social proximity' (p. 105). The process is usually initiated by the consumer, typically because there is money involved.

Source: Adapted with the permission of The Free Press, a division of Simon & Schuster, Inc., from *Permissions Marketing: Turning Strangers into Friends and Friends into Customers* by Seth Godin.

survey whether they would give information on their personal interests and preferences' (p. 493).

Direct response media

The choice of media for direct marketing can be very different from those selected for general advertising purposes. The main reason for using direct response media is that direct contact is made with prospects and customers in order that a direct response can be generated, interaction stimulated and hopefully a dialogue established. In reality, a wide variety of media can be used, simply by attaching a telephone number, web site address or response card. However, if broadcast media such as television and radio are the champions of the general advertiser, their adoption by direct marketers in the United Kingdom has been relatively slow. Direct mail, telemarketing and door-to-door activities are the main direct response media, as they allow more personal, direct and evaluative means of reaching precisely targeted customers.

Direct mail, telemarketing and door-to-door activities are the main direct response media.

Direct mail

The largest direct response media expenditure is direct mail, which has grown steadily year on year. However, the industry has since struggled to maintain momentum and fell back to £2.32 billion in 2006 (Advertising Association, 2008). Direct mail refers to personally addressed advertising that is delivered through the postal system. It can be personalised and targeted with great accuracy, and its results are capable of precise measurement.

The generation of inquiries and leads, together with the intention of building a personal relationship with customers, are the most important factors contributing to the growth of direct mail. However, the intention to build loyalty is not always that clear as many mailings appear to be focused on customer acquisition, not retention. Other factors include the increased market and media fragmentation, which have combined to reduce the overall effectiveness of general advertising. Direct mail can be expensive, at anything between £250 and £500 per 1,000 items dispatched. It should, therefore, be used selectively and for purposes other than creating awareness.

In 2000 the volume of direct mail equated to nearly half of the overall letterbox (DMIS, 2000) and 15 per cent of total promotional expenditure (Ridgeway, 2000). Volumes however, reached a peak in 2003 and since then have been falling, reaching 5,028 million pieces in 2006. This is due to increased use of email and digital communications and the associated falling levels of opening and reading of direct mail items. This apparent behavioural response to technological development, the move from offline to online behaviours and media preferences, suggests that direct mail activity may never be as high again.

Organisations are the main users of direct mail.

Organisations in the financial services sectors are the main users of this medium and the financial health of the sector is dependent to a large extent on some of the major financial services companies maintaining their spend on direct mail. However, an increasing number of other organisations are experimenting with this approach, as they try to improve the effectiveness of their promotional expenditure and reduce television advertising costs.

Telemarketing

The prime qualities of the telephone are that it provides for interaction, is flexible and permits immediate feedback. In addition, it offers users the opportunity to overcome objections raised by others within the same communication event. Other dimensions of telemarketing include the development and maintenance of customer goodwill, allied to which is the increasing need to provide high levels of customer service. Telemarketing also allows organisations to undertake marketing research that is both highly measurable and accountable in that the effectiveness can be verified continuously and call rates, contacts reached and the number and quality of positive and negative responses are easily recorded and monitored.

Telemarketing allows organisations to undertake marketing research.

Originally customer contact centres (CCC) were designed for in-house use to handle a large volume of telephone calls. They became a largely outsourced facility and managed high volumes of incoming calls through automatic call distribution (ACD) technology. ACDs distribute incoming calls to predetermined groups of agents. An ACD can hold calls in queues if necessary and play music and make announcements. Now CCCs are Internet-enabled communication solutions, designed to process and integrate a variety of media using voice messaging, interactive voice response, outbound calling and fax.

CCCs do not need to be tied to a particular physical location and agents work either from home or in various offices around the globe, each connected through a voice-over-IP network. CRM software can be integrated with computer–telephone integration (CTI), which means that each interaction is immediately reported (to the database) so updated information is available to agents right away.

Growth in telemarketing activity in the business-to-business sector has been largely at the expense of personal selling. The objectives have been to reduce costs and to utilise the expensive sales force and their skills to build on the openings and leads created by telemarketing and other lead generation activities. These operations are often conducted through outsourcing as mentioned above, however, the emergence of contract sales organisations (CSOs) is interesting. Although the use of CSOs is commonplace in the pharmaceutical business, little is documented about their operations or development. CSOs are not contact centres, they represent a core part of their partners organisation and strategic activities. As a result, CSOs represent a strategic development, one in which partnerships are established and whose goal is to create of value for both parties. CSOs enable change, are flexible and can be quickly implemented (Rogers, 2008).

Some of the advantages of using the telephone as part of the media mix are that it allows for interaction between participants, it enables immediate feedback and sets up opportunities to overcome objections, all within the same communication event when both the sender and the receiver are geographically distant.

> The advantages of using the telephone as part of the media mix are that it allows for interaction between participants.

All of these activities can be executed by personal selling, but the speed, cost, accuracy and consistency of the information solicited through personal visits can often be improved upon by telemarketing. The complexity of the product will influence the degree to which this medium can be used successfully. However, if properly trained professional telemarketers are used, the sales results, if measured on a call basis, can outperform those produced by personal selling.

Contact centres use a variety of IST with the prime goals of reducing costs, improving efficiency and improving the client's reputation through quality of customer interaction. The following are just a few of the ways in which technology is used in these environments:

- Automatic call distribution systems enable inbound calls to be distributed efficiently among contact centre operators. Interactive voice response (IVR) systems allow callers to perform self-help functions without speaking with an individual. Using simple phone keypad selections these systems have the capability to connect calls to employees who may be working at home or in remote geographic offices.
- Call recording systems, which consist of voice recording, logging, monitoring and call management that can be vital in a CRM environment.

Exhibit 21.4 A typical call centre layout and design
Stan Gamester/Photofusion.

- Computer–telephone integration (CTI) allows telephone applications and services to be merged with computer applications. CTI enables the simultaneous arrival of a call and associated caller data to be displayed on an agent's desktop.
- Customer interaction management (CIM) systems are used to support the contact centre's operations. Technologies such as predictive dialling, live chat applications as well as email response systems are often used together with conventional communications technology.
- Predictive diallers (PDs) are used in outbound telemarketing to increase the number of successful calls and optimise the operators time speaking to customers. PDs enable engaged lines, no response and answering machines to be avoided (ignored), thus allowing operators to spend an increased proportion of their time talking to potential customers rather than wasting time dialling and listening to telephones ringing. Estimates vary, but now operators can talk for 45 minutes in every hour, compared with 25 minutes before the development of predictive dialling facilities.

Operator contact with customers can be also be supported by technology. Computer-assisted telephone interviewing (CATI) can provide varying degrees of technical support. The degree to which this is used depends on the task, the product and the nature of the target audience. Calls might be driven through a prepared script, often regardless of the interjections of the receiver. This rather crude approach can be quite sophisticated, as software prepares scripts that 'branch', as in a decision tree, to respond to a prospect's different answers.

Another approach is to use a semi-structured interview, where the caller has a number of topics that need to be covered but the order and the style in which the issues are dealt with are immaterial. A third method is based on a personal sales presentation. Undertaken by professionally trained callers, the conversation is tuned to the needs of the receiver, not those of the caller. When the call is completed, regardless of whether an order has been placed, it is intended that recipients finish the call feeling satisfied that they have used their time appropriately and in full expectation that they will receive further calls.

The behaviour of call centre employees is a function of service quality.

The behaviour of call centre employees, however much they are regulated or controlled by various software applications, is a function of service quality, as perceived by callers. Referred to as customer orientation behaviours, Rafaeli *et al.* (2008) identify five COBs that are related to service quality. These are:

- anticipating customer requests;
- offering explanations and justifications;
- educating customers;
- providing emotional support;
- offering personalised information.

When these five COBs are used by call centre employees, customers perceive a high level of service quality. The implication of this, as pointed out by the researchers, is that as call centre managers invariably seek to minimise call length in order to reduce costs and increase the number of transactions, their actions appear to endanger service quality.

The costs of telemarketing are high. It is estimated for example, that is costs £15–£20 to reach a decision-maker in an organisation. When this is compared with £5 for a piece of direct mail or £150+ for a personal sales call to the same individual, it is the effectiveness of the call and the return on the investment that determines whether the costs are really high.

Carelines

Another reason to use telemarketing concerns the role carelines can play within the consumer brand relationships. Manufacturers use contact centres to enable customers to:

- complain about a product performance and related experience;
- seek product-related advice;

- make suggestions regarding product or packaging development;
- comment about an action or development concerning the brand as a whole.

What binds these together is the potential all of these people have for repurchasing the brand, even those who complain bitterly about product performance and experience. If these people have their complaints dealt with properly then there is a reasonable probability that they will repurchase.

The previous letter-based mechanism did not encourage customer response, especially when research by Sitel (McLuhan, 2000) found that 98 per cent of customers switched brands rather than complain. Telephone and email encourage greater contact and the chance to talk to customers because it is easier and quicker to implement. The majority of the careline calls are not about complaints but seek advice or help about products. Food manufacturers can provide cooking and recipe advice, cosmetic and toiletries companies can provide healthcare advice and application guidelines while white goods and service-based organisations can provide technical and operational support.

The majority of the careline calls are not about complaints but seek advice or help about products.

Carelines are essentially a post-purchase support mechanism that facilitates market feedback and intelligence gathering. They can warn of imminent problems (product defects), provide ideas for new products or variants and provide a valuable method to reassure customers and improve customer retention levels. Call operators, or agents as many of them are now being called, have to handle calls from a variety of new sources – web, email, interactive television and mobile devices – and it is appreciated that many are more effective if they have direct product experience. Instant messaging channels enable online shoppers to ask questions that are routed to a call centre for response. Sales conversion ratios can be up by 40–50 per cent and costs are about £1 to answer an inbound question, compared with £3.50 by phone (Murphy, 2000). Kellogg's report that its careline makes a 13:1 return on investment (Bashford, 2004).

Expenditure on telemarketing increased rapidly in the late 1980s and early 1990s, but this rapid growth then subsided. Some organisations began undertaking their outbound calls themselves rather than using tele-agencies to do the work on their behalf, but as technology improved outsourcing resumed normal growth. In recent years the telemarketing sector has experienced huge growth. There were signs of oversupply in the market and so there is huge pressure on costs and margins.

As the application of digital technologies gathered pace, so telemarketing and call centres became threatened. Rather than persist in a potentially declining business activity, call centres repositioned themselves so that they could provide multimedia support services such as eCRM, Internet and even email management. The name has changed to (customer) contact centres and the accent is now on strategic partnerships to assist clients develop customer relationships. Bashford (2004) explains that L'Oréal runs a careline staffed by former hairdressers and skincare consultants. This first-hand product knowledge reflects the attention given to understanding the brand and being able to relate to customer questions. In order that staff can communicate effectively they must believe in the brand values themselves. Davenge refers to the current terminology that expresses this level of involvement as 'emotional connectivity' and 'emotional congruence'. This may be a new form of temporary hyper-language, but at least this idea of involvement in the brand or category should be of comfort to customers in need.

While the Internet has provided further growth opportunities, it will also take on a number of the tasks currently the preserve of telemarketing bureau. Web sites enable product information and certain support advice to be accessed without the call centre costs and focus attention on other matters of concern to the customer. Chat room discussions, collaborative browsing and real-time text conversations are options to help care for customers in the future. However, it is probably the one-to-one telephone dialogue between customer and agent that will continue to provide satisfaction and benefits for both parties.

ViewPoint 21.4 Making contact

BAA, who operate several premier airports across Britain have used call centres as a means of driving increased revenue. The majority of calls BAA receives are about car parking, so they decided to use these calls to promote a range of additional services. This was achieved by redirecting calls to a contact centre.

The contact centre handles a range of inquiries delivered through web, phone and email. Travellers have their questions answered but they are also informed about travel insurance, hotels and foreign currency.

Approximately 500,000 individual contacts are managed each year and BAA uses the information not only to provide feedback but to inform direct marketing campaigns, targeted at 250,000 active customers. This contact centre activity generates in excess of £10 million revenue per annum.

Nestlé Purina, whose petfood brands include Purina ONE, Felix, Go Cat, Bakers and Winalot, refers to its contact centre as a relationship centre. Using a strapline 'Your pet, our passion™', the careline is used not only to get feedback on campaigns and products, but is used by a variety of people internally who 'listen in' in an attempt to get close to the consumer.

The extent of the company's involvement with consumers is demonstrated by the fact that contact staff have been trained in bereavement counselling, to help people who have recently lost a pet.

Sources: Bashford (2004); McLuhan (2006).

Question

To what extent should contact centres drive an organisation's entire direct marketing programme?

Task

Find out how many contact centres there are in the United Kingdom and what proportion are located outside the United Kingdom?

Inserts

Inserts are media materials that are placed in magazines or direct mail letters. These not only provide factual information about the product or service but also enable the recipient to respond to the request of the direct marketer. This request might be to place an order or post back a card for more information, such as a brochure.

The popularity of inserts is based on their effectiveness as a lead generator.

Inserts have become more popular, but their cost is substantially higher than a four-colour advertisement in the magazine in which the insert is carried. Their popularity is based on their effectiveness as a lead generator, and new methods of delivering inserts to the home will become important to direct mailing houses in the future. Other vehicles, such as packages rather than letter mail, will also become important.

Print

There are two main forms of direct response advertising through the printed media: first, catalogues and, second, magazines and newspapers. Catalogues mailed direct to consumers have been an established method of selling products for a long time. Mail order organisations such as Freeman's, GUS and Littlewoods have successfully exploited this form of direct marketing. Organisations such as Tchibo and Kaleidoscope have successfully used mini-catalogues, but instead of providing account facilities and the appointment of specific freelance agents, their business transactions are on a cash-with-order basis.

Business-to-business marketers have begun to exploit this medium, and organisations such as Dell and IBM now use online and offline catalogues, partly to save costs and partly to free valuable sales personnel so that they can concentrate their time on selling into larger accounts.

Direct response advertising through the press is similar to general press advertising, except that the advertiser provides a mechanism for the reader to take further action. The mechanism may be a telephone number (call free) or a coupon or cut-out reply slip requesting further information. Dell changed to a direct marketing strategy, which was based around direct response advertising promoting its core offer of customised built products. Consumer direct response print ads, such as the one for the Kitchen Restoration Company at Exhibit 21.5 can signal and develop brand value but can also be used to drive readers to either the telephone or their web site so that they can find out more, at no additional cost to the company, and to become more involved with the brand.

Transform
your Kitchen
from old to new
TOP QUALITY ACCESSORIES
• Sinks • Taps
• Door & Drawer Handles, etc
WIDE RANGE OF WORKTOPS
New doors and drawer-fronts made to your units' measurements – designed and fitted by our own expert team with the minimum of fuss and upheaval at DIRECT FROM FACTORY PRICES.
Wide range of top quality accessories to choose from – sinks, taps, door and drawer handles, worktops and top-named appliances to complete the look.
Replace the doors and drawer fronts to give your kitchen a completely NEW LOOK
At a fraction of the cost
of refitting your whole kitchen
FREE SURVEY
FREE NO OBLIGATION QUOTATION
Call for a FREE colour brochure
Freephone
0800 917 7238
24 Hour, 7 day service
OVER 400 STYLES
TRADITIONAL
CONTEMPORARY
SOLID WOODS
VENEERS
LAMINATES
PAINTED FINISHES
STAINLESS STEEL
GLASS
OVER 200 COLOURWAYS
THE New Kitchen RESTORATION Company
The experts in kitchen facelifts
or post the coupon to: The New Kitchen Restoration Company FREEPOST NAT 22741, Birmingham B2 2BR
visit our website:
www.kitchen-restoration.com
To: The New Kitchen Restoration Company
[ ] Please send me your latest FREE COLOUR BROCHURE
[ ] Please phone to arrange a FREE SURVEY and NO OBLIGATION QUOTATION
Name Mr/Mrs/Miss/Ms
Address
Post Code
Tel.No
Email
The New Kitchen Restoration Company, FREEPOST NAT 22741, Birmingham B2 2BR

Exhibit 21.5 A direct response print ad promoting the benefits (financial and emotional) of a kitchen update at a fraction of the normal cost. Response mechanisms include telephone, web site and coupon (post)
Designed and produced by Lavery Rowe Advertising London. www.laveryrowe.com.

Door-to-door

Responses are lower because door-to-door drops cannot be personally addressed.

This delivery method can be much cheaper than direct mail as there are no postage charges to be accounted for. However, if the costs are much lower, so are the response rates. Responses are lower because door-to-door drops cannot be personally addressed, as can direct mail, even though the content and quality can be controlled in the same way.

Avon Cosmetics and Betterware are traditionally recognised as professional practitioners of door-to-door direct marketing. Other organisations, such as the utility companies (gas, electricity and water), are using door-to-door drops to create higher levels of market penetration. For more information on this see Chapter 27.

Radio and television

Of the two main forms discussed earlier, radio and television, the former is used as a support medium for other advertising, often by providing enquiry numbers. Television has greater potential because it can provide the important visual dimension, but its use in the United Kingdom for direct marketing purposes has been limited. One of the main reasons for this has been the television contractors' attitude to pricing. However, the industry has experienced a period of great change and has introduced greater pricing flexibility, and a small but increasing number of direct marketers have used the small screen successfully, mainly by providing freephone numbers for customers. The business model established by Direct Line based on its outstanding use of television has since been copied by many other financial services organisations. For example, Churchill, Privilege and Esure have all made substantial use of television within its direct response strategy.

The Internet and new media

The explosion of activity around new media and the Internet has been quite astonishing in recent years and now represents a major new form of interactive marketing communications. The development of digital television services has generated a new form of interactivity during a period when analogue services are being withdrawn. Home shopping, tourism and banking facilities are attractive to those whose lifestyles complement the benefits offered by the new technology. In the longer term fully interactive services will bring increased leisure and entertainment opportunities to a greater number of people. A much fuller consideration of interactive communications can be found in Chapter 26.

Integration and direct marketing

This brief review of the media used in direct marketing activities has tended to present them as separate, independent resources. Increasingly, successful direct marketing programmes are using these media in combination, as a team of complementary or even integrated tools. Many organisations, regardless of whether their marketing activities are oriented solely to direct marketing or not, are using direct response media to support and supplement their other promotional activities.

Other organisations are using integrated direct marketing, which Eisenhart (1990) originally identified as 'the orchestration of various direct marketing vehicles so that they work together in a synergistic fashion' (p. 27). An example of this orchestration might be the dispatch of a direct mailing using a well-qualified list followed by contacting addresses through a telemarketing programme within 24 hours of the mailing arriving. In some cases response rates have doubled by using telemarketing in this way.

Some doubt whether organisations can justify the cost and the administrative and managerial implications of complex integrated direct campaigns. Advocates of the approach claim that each contact with a prospect helps to create a wave effect, with response rates increasing at each contact. According to a Royal Mail report, advertisers who combine direct mail with digital advertising can increase customer spending by up to 25 per cent (Frost, 2007). The report holds that consumers who prefer this channel combination spend an average of £105 a month on goods and services. This represents £19 more than those who prefer just online ads, and £34 more than consumers who only prefer direct mail.

Another interesting point point to emerge from those surveyed was that direct mail gives a better impression of a company than email but 69 per cent feel that email is best for supporting or clarifying the mail they receive. Consumers appear to recognise how online, email and direct mail work together and the different benefits they bestow.

Advertisers who combine direct mail with digital advertising can increase customer spending by up to 25 per cent.

Consumers appear to recognise how online, email and direct mail work together.

ViewPoint 21.5 Multichannel BUPA Wellness

BUPA Wellness offers an onsite corporate dental service. Rather than use the expensive and time-poor field sales force to generate leads and new business it decided to manage the process of customer acquisition through technology. BUPA outsourced the task to Inbox Media, whose goals were to develop a database as a foundation for the project, create awareness and impact in the market and generate leads for the sales force to convert. Inbox Media used telemarketing to create a list of HRM managers who agreed to receive emails from it in the future. Their details were used in the database and then each was sent personalised video emails informing them about the services of BUPA Wellness and, more particularly, the number of days that their organisation lost each year through dental visits and associated oral health problems.

While the results were entirely satisfactory (52 per cent of emails were opened, 21 per cent clicked through and approximately 50 leads were turned into appointments), one of the interesting elements of the campaign concerned the dynamics associated with the email part of the programme. Inbox Media was able to monitor who opened the emails, how long they spent reading them and who they forwarded them to. It thus built a picture of email opening and behaviour characteristics.

Although the opportunity was declined, it was technically possible to use the sales team to call recipients as they opened their video email or even when or just after it had been played. However, this coordinated approach was considered inappropriate as it would raise strong concerns about privacy, trust, intrusion, reputation and the ethics associated with over-aggressive selling strategies.

Source: Adapted from Anon. (2003).

Question

Do you agree that contacting recipients in the way suggested above would be an invasion of privacy?

Task

What other professions might benefit from this approach?

There are two aspects to direct marketing integration. One is the integration of direct marketing activities themselves and the other concerns the integration of direct marketing within wider marketing communications activities. Acland (2003) suggested there was plenty of evidence to support the view that the distinction between above- and below-the-line communications was blurring and that this was reflected in the structure and the work of agencies operating in the market. This blurring has continued as media continues to fragment and agencies of all disciplines diversify in an attempt to grow and meet their own goals. There is no doubt that the pattern of communications spend is continuing to move from above- to below-the-line channels and that there is substantial movement from offline to online communications.

There can be little doubt, therefore, that integrated direct response media will be used increasingly in the future as organisations realise its power and continue to build the direct approach. As general media rates continue to increase ahead of inflation, and as managers seek new ways of providing evidence of their astute use of marketing and, in particular, promotional resources, so direct response media will play an increasingly important role in the marketing activities of a large number of organisations. It is highly unlikely that direct marketing agencies have the necessary credentials, in particular the account planning skills necessary, to attract clients completely away from brand-based agencies and the media budgets that are attached to them. However, it is probable that direct marketing will play a more influential role within the marketing communications industry as it seeks to become more integrated and offer a more integrated range of services for its clients.

Integrated direct response media will be used increasingly in the future.

It should not be forgotten, however, that commitment to the direct route or to a combination of general and direct response media means that organisations must ensure that they are transmitting a consistent or complementary message through each medium used.

Supporting the sales force

In an effort to increase the productivity of the sales force and to use their expensive skills more effectively, direct marketing has provided organisations with an opportunity to improve levels of performance and customer satisfaction. In particular, the use of an inside telemarketing department is seen as a compatible sales channel to the field sales force. A telemarketing team can accomplish the following tasks:

- they can search for and qualify new customers, thereby saving the field force from cold calling;
- they can service existing customer accounts and prepare the field force should they be required to attend to the client personally;
- they can seek repeat orders from marginal or geographically remote customers, particularly if they are low-unit-value consumable items;
- they can provide a link between network members that serves to maintain the relationship, especially through periods of difficulty and instability.

Many organisations prefer to place orders through telesales teams, as it does not involve the time costs associated with personal sales calls. The routine of such orders gives greater efficiency for all concerned with the relational exchange and reduces costs.

Direct mail activities are also becoming more important in areas where personal contact is seen as unnecessary or where limited field sales resources are deployed to key accounts. As with telesales, direct mail is often used to supplement the activities of the field force. Catalogue and electronic communications such as fax can be used for accounts, which may be regarded as relatively unattractive.

In addition to this, use of the Internet and mobile-based communications have provided new opportunities to reach customers. The web site itself symbolises the changing orientation of marketing communications. Whereas once the brochure, mass media advertising and perhaps a promotional incentive represented the central channel of communication, now the web site and the database serve to integrate directed, sometimes interactive, one-to-one communications. These are supported in many cases by more call-to-action messages channelled through a variety of coordinated offline and digital media.

All of these activities free the field sales force to increase their productivity and to spend more time with established customers or those with high profit potential.

Multichannel selling

A number of different sales channels have been identified so far and many organisations, in their search to reduce costs, have restructured their operations in an attempt to meet better the 'touchpoints' of their different customers.

Restructuring has often taken the form of introducing multiple sales channels with the simple objective of using less expensive channels to complete selling tasks that do not require personal, face-to-face contact. Technology-enhanced channels, mainly in the form of web-based and email communications, have grown considerably, often at the expense of telephone and mail facilities. Payne and Frow (2004) have developed a categorisation of sales channels, which are depicted in Table 21.5.

Restructuring has often taken the form of introducing multiple sales channels.

In order to meet better the needs of customers, organisations need to evolve their mix of channels. Customers will then be able to interact with their supplying organisations using the mix of channels that they prefer to use. Therefore, marketing communications needs to be used in order to complement best the different audiences, channel facilities and characteristics. Through mixing channels and communications in a complementary way higher levels of customer service can be achieved. The proliferation of channels may, however, lead organisations to believe that the greater the number of channels the greater the chances of commercial success. In addition to the view that multichannel customers are known to spend up to 30 per cent more than single channel customers, the Internet and overseas call centres also offer substantial (short-term) cost savings (Myers *et al.*, 2004). However, there is a word of caution, which is that although cost savings per transaction might be achieved, the use of multiple channels can incur higher overall costs. Myers *et al.* (2004) cite retail offline banks as an example of false economies. The introduction of ATMs helped reduce the average transaction cost by 15 per cent but the number of transactions more than doubled compared with the times when queuing in a bank represented the only operating format. As a result, they argue, the cost of serving customers has actually increased.

Multichannel customers are known to spend up to 30 per cent more than single channel customers

Table 21.5 Comparison of channel characteristics

Channel	Breadth	Dominant form of communication	Cost/contact
Field sales	Key account, service and personal representation	Dialogue	High
Outlets	Retail branches, stores, depots and kiosks	Interactive	Medium
Telephony	Traditional telephone, facsimile, telex and contact centres	One-way and two-way	Low to medium
Direct marketing	Direct mail, radio and traditional television	One-way and two-way	Low
ecommerce	Email, Internet, interactive television	Interactive	Very low
mcommerce	Mobile telephony, SMS, WAP and 3G	Interactive	Very low

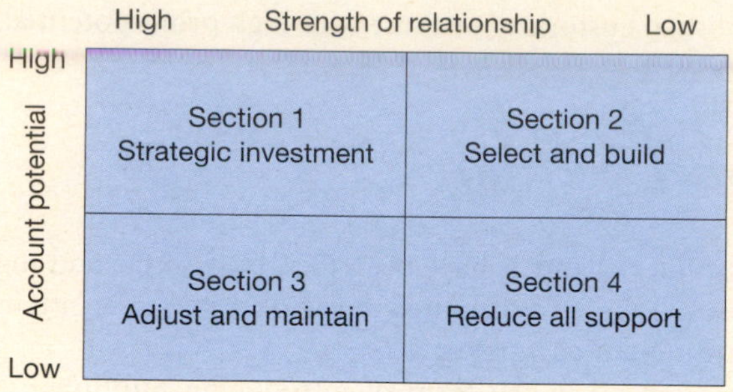

Figure 21.3 Account investment matrix

This may or may not be true, but what is not accounted for is the value customers place on the convenience of the services provided, the closer the organisation is able to get to customers increases the opportunities to cross-sell and develop new products. The move from a cost to a customer perspective is readily made, although the banks have some way to go before they are truly customer-oriented.

Categorising customers

One simple approach to managing channels is to categorise accounts (customers) according to their potential attractiveness and the current strength of the relationship between supplier and buyer (see Figure 21.3). A strong relationship, for example, is indicative of two organisations engaged in mutually satisfying relational exchanges. A weak relationship suggests that the two parties have no experience of each other or, if they have, that it is not particularly satisfying. If there have been transactions, it may be that these can be classified as market exchange experiences. Attractiveness refers to the opportunities a buying organisation represents to the vendor: how large or small the potential business is in an organisation.

For reasons of clarity, these scales are presented as either high or low, strong or weak. However, they should be considered as a continuum, and with the use of some relatively simple evaluative criteria accounts can be positioned on the matrix and strategies formulated to move accounts to different positions, which in turn necessitate the use of different sales channel mixes.

ViewPoint 21.6 Getting licensed on campus

To watch television in the United Kingdom each separately occupied household needs a television licence. This licence covers all appliances used to receive and watch television programmes, such as laptops, PCs, mobiles and of course, all television sets. The problem, of course, is that certain sections of society believe they are exempt and fail to buy a licence and end up being fined (up to £1,000 at the time of writing).

One of the princpal groups of licence dodgers are students. Living in a hall of residence or a shared flat does not provide immunity. Many reasons are offered by those caught without a licence, two of which are 'I live in a shared house. It's not my TV.' and 'I refuse to pay for a whole year when I'm only here for nine months.' The first is contestable and the second, rebates can be obtained. However, the real issue concerns a lack of awareness among university students that they need to buy a licence if they want to watch television.

A direct campaign was developed to inform students about the need for a television licence, and about how and where to buy one. The campaign combined direct mail material sent through the post, posters, leaflets and stickers around campus plus digital media to encourage word-of-mouth communications and active participation.

The campaign had to be multichannel in order to make contact with first-time students as they entered academic life. Students were targeted at three key stages: in their parents' homes (prior to univerity life), when they arrived at university, and later in the first semester or term.

The campaign was based on a message that turned on the joke that 'It's not funny watching TV without a licence' and used word-of-mouth communication to spread the 'joke'. Posters were put up on 250 university sites, each residential bedroom had stickers and post-it notes informing them about the need to get a licence, and a 'good luck' television awareness card awaited each student when they entered their room for the first time. The agency behind the campaign also used digital media such as email, SMS and banner ads on student sites to convey the message. Some students filmed their un-funny jokes and made their own 'It's not funny . . .' programmes and then aired these on televisions all around their campus.

Sales increased 25 per cent and generated an ROI of 12:1. See also Chapter 15 to see how this campaign was evaluated.

Source: Anon. (2007).

Question

How might knowledge of integrated marketing communications have helped this campaign?

Task

Check that you have a TV licence!

Based on the original approach developed by Cravens *et al.* (1991) appropriate sales channels are superimposed on the grid so that optimum efficiency in selling effort and costs can be managed (Figure 21.4). Accounts in Section 1 vary in attractiveness, as some will be assigned key account status. The others will be very important and will require a high level of selling effort (investment), which has to be delivered by the field sales force. Accounts in Section 2 are essentially prospects because of their weak relationship but high attractiveness. Selling effort should be proportional to the value of the prospects: high effort for good prospects and low for the others. Care should be given to allocating a time by which accounts in this section are moved to other parts of the grid, and in doing so save resources and maximise opportunities for growth. All the main sales channels should be used, commencing with direct and email to

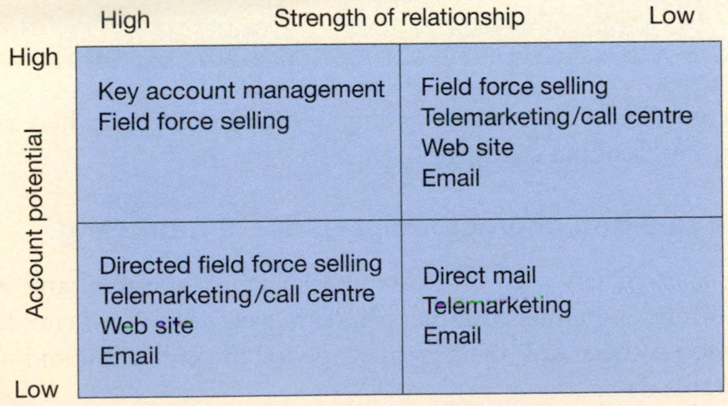

High
Strength of relationship
Low
High
Account potential
Low
Key account management
Field force selling
Field force selling
Telemarketing/call centre
Web site
Email
Directed field force selling
Telemarketing/call centre
Web site
Email
Direct mail
Telemarketing
Email

Figure 21.4 Multichannel mix allocation

identify prospects, telesales for qualification purposes, field sales force selling directed at the strong prospects and telesales and web site for the others. Web site details provide support and information for those accounts that wish to remain distant. As the relationship becomes stronger, so field selling takes over from telemarketing and the coordinating activities of the contact or call centre. If the relationship weakens, then the account may be discontinued and selling redirected to other prospects.

If the relationship weakens, then the account may be discontinued and selling redirected to other prospects.

Accounts in Section 3 do not offer strong potential and, although the relationship is strong, there are opportunities to switch the sales channel mix by reducing, but not eliminating, the level of field force activity and to give consideration to the introduction of telemarketing for particular accounts. Significant cost reductions can be achieved with these types of accounts by simply reviewing the means and reasoning behind the personal selling effort. Accounts in Section 4 should receive no field force calls, the prime sales channels being telesales, email, the web site and perhaps catalogue selling depending on the nature of the web site.

Establishing a multiple sales channel strategy based on the grid suggested above may not be appropriate to all organisations. For example, the current level of performance may be considered as exceeding expectations, in which case there is no point in introducing change. It may be that the costs and revenues associated with redeployment are unfavourable and that the implications for the rest of the organisation of implementing the new sales channel approach are such that the transition should be either postponed or rejected.

Payne and Frow (2004) suggest a range of channel options or strategies can be identified that relate to the channel needs of target segments. These range from a single dominant channel such as those used by Amazon and Egg; a customer segment approach designed for use with different channel types such as intermediaries, b2b end-user customers and consumers; one based on the different activity channels that customers prefer to use, such as a mix of online and offline resources to identify, see, demonstrate, select and pay for a computer; and finally a truly integrated multichannel strategy utilising CRM systems to integrate all customer information at whichever contact point the customer chooses to use. These strategies reflect some of the approaches that can be used and, indeed, various combinations can be used to meet customers' channel needs. However, experience has shown that costs can be reduced through the introduction of a multiple sales channel approach and that levels of customer satisfaction and the strength of the relationship between members of the network can be improved considerably. In addition, it is vital to remember that customers will move into and use new channel mixes over the customer lifecycle and that channel decisions should be regarded as fluid and developmental.

Summary

In order to help consolidate your understanding of direct marketing, here are the key points summarised against each of the learning objectives:

1. Consider the role and characteristics of direct marketing.

Direct marketing is a strategy used to create and sustain a personal and intermediary-free dialogue with customers, potential customers and other significant stakeholders. In most cases this is a media-based activity and offers great scope for the collection and utilisation of pertinent and measurable data.

For a long time direct mail was the main tool of direct marketing, but the development of information technology and, in particular, the database, have enabled the introduction of a range of other media. These are used to communicate directly with individual customers and often carry a behavioural (call-to-action) message. Typically, direct marketing agencies work across a variety of media including the telephone, Internet, direct mail, email, press and posters.

2. Examine the types of direct brands and their relationship with direct response media and their role within the marketing communications mix.

There four main types of brand within which direct marketing plays a significant role. These are as a *complementary tool* where direct response media are used to complement the other promotional activities used to support a brand. As a *primary differentiator*, direct response media is the primary form of communication. A third use for direct marketing is its use as a *sales channel* and the final type is as an *organisational brand* developed to exploit market space opportunities.

3. Consider the reasons behind the growth and development of this new marketing communications tool.

The reasons for the growth and development of direct marketing are many and varied, but three essential drivers behind the surge in direct marketing can be identified: technological advances; changing buyer lifestyles and expectations; and organisational expectations.

4. Appreciate the significance of the database in direct marketing.

The database is the hub of contemporary marketing communications. Whereas the database used to contain records of segmentation data, they now consist of several layers of information whereby customer profiles can be fused with transactional and lifestyle data. This information can be used to customise and personalise direct marketing activities, providing for accuracy, minimal wastage and reduced costs.

5. Explore issues associated with permission-based marketing.

The aim of permission marketing is to get individuals to agree that organisations can communicate with them. Permission marketing occurs when consumers give their explicit permission for marketers to send them various types of promotional messages.

6. Identify and consider different direct response media.

A wide variety of direct response media can be used simply by attaching a telephone number, web site address or response card. However, direct mail, telemarketing and door-to-door activities are the main direct response media, as they allow more personal, direct and evaluative means of reaching precisely targeted customers.

7. Consider the value of integrating the activities of direct marketing with other elements of the mix.

Successful direct marketing programmes are using media in combination, as a team of complementary or even integrated tools. Many organisations, regardless of whether their marketing activities are oriented solely to direct marketing or not, are using direct response media to support and supplement their other promotional activities.

There are two aspects to direct marketing integration. One is the integration of direct marketing activities themselves and the other concerns the integration of direct marketing within wider marketing communications activities.

Review questions

1. Set out a definition of direct marketing and consider the key words in the definition.
2. Explain the differences between direct response media and direct marketing.
3. Direct response media have many advantages over general mass advertising. What are they and why is this form of promotional communication increasing so quickly?
4. What are the different levels of direct marketing? What is the fundamental difference between levels?
5. Evaluate the main drivers behind the growth of direct marketing. How might these drivers change in the future?
6. Discuss the role of the database as the hub of marketing communications.
7. Telemarketing has become an integral feature of the promotional mix for reaching consumer and business-to-business markets. Why is this and what particular features of telemarketing attract clients?
8. Identify and then evaluate three different media for delivering direct response communications.
9. Find two examples of organisations using carelines. Comment on their effectiveness.
10. Explain why direct marketing activities should be integrated with other elements of the promotional mix.

MiniCase **Recovering cars with direct marketing**

In the UK car recovery and breakdown market the Royal Automobile Club (RAC) is regarded as the challenger brand with the Automobile Association (AA) as the undisputed market leader. In addition, Direct Line Rescue (DLR) has entered the market and taken a 10 per cent market share.

Customers in this market are no longer simply users of the vehicle breakdown services but expect a broad range of products and services, which the motoring organisations aim to satisfy in different ways.

Traditionally, marketing communications messages have been based on advertising and the development of brand values. Messages have been very product-focused, typified by ads for speed of recovery, get you home services, helpfulness of staff and a range of ancillary products such as car finance, legal and advisory services.

The perceived benefits of motor organisation membership have changed. Factors concerning reassurance have become more important while economic factors have become less so. For example, research shows that many motorists are more concerned about getting home, with or without their car, than they are with the relative merits of membership costs and the variety of ad hoc services most motoring organisations now provide.

One of the main reasons for the change in attitude towards motor organisation membership is the change in profile of the UK motorist. The dominance of middle-aged, male drivers has diminished as the percentage of young and female drivers has increased. Drivers are less willing to perform roadside repairs while, at the same time, cars are becoming more complex. Cars are becoming more reliable but it is becoming increasingly difficult for drivers to repair them by the roadside, partly as a result of sealed accessories and the need for specialised diagnostic equipment.

During the 1990s, the promotional emphasis of the main motoring organisations changed from one that emphasised economic and tangible attributes to ones that gave higher prominence to driver safety and re-assurance. In addition to changes in the core messages used by the RAC and AA, greater emphasis has been placed on the other promotional tools, partly in response to the entry and aggression of DLR.

One of the strategies used by both the AA and RAC has been to change the organisational culture, although some commentators feel this has been at the expense of customer service. A recently published *Which?* magazine survey revealed that the RAC fared badly against the AA. In addition, a BBC consumer affairs programme, *Rogue Traders*, revealed that some RAC patrolmen were selling car batteries to stranded drivers who did not need them.

In the face of competitive pressures, profit margins declining on recovery services and private membership rising only slightly, the RAC has moved into direct response television to support its ancillary services. This required a move to a more emotionally based message to convey the idea that the RAC can help people afford their dream car, regardless of what it is, and secure the finance from a trusted brand to help them buy it. The ads encouraged viewers to call an 0800 number to apply for a loan and get an instant decision. Every successful loan applicant received free RAC breakdown cover. In addition, the RAC has developed its 36-page *RAC Magazine* as a means of communicating with its different markets. In several million copies mailed out three times a year everyone receives the standard 20 pages of content but, in addition, there is also a 16-page insert that takes account of a person's lifestage and their length of membership.

Direct Line Rescue (DLR) is a very strong brand that lends itself to strong imagery and no-nonsense messaging. DLR wants to develop a much closer relationship with its customers and it too has strategies that are designed to offer more than just vehicle breakdown services. A recent campaign was designed to target customers of the RAC and AA and to reinforce the Rescue brand, which has nearly 1 million customers. Through its DM agency DLR developed a series of mail packs, each containing a letter, envelope and insert, targeting different messages to existing AA and RAC members. These messages instructed recipients to 'Stop paying too much' by switching to Direct Line. The company's own car insurance customers received a third pack which said that 'First we save u money, then we save u'. This was intended to highlight the breakdown cover offer from £35 and to reassure people about the high level of service while prompting them to respond through bold calls-to-action and guaranteed low prices.

Source: http://www.warc.com/ArticleCenter/Default.asp?CType=A&AID=WORDSEARCH79886&Tab=A.

MiniCase questions

1. Explain ways in which use of a database might assist the RAC with its direct marketing programme.
2. Prepare a list of sales channels that the RAC could use to reach its different types of customers. Select the four top channels and explain their advantages in respect of the RAC.
3. Discuss the role of the telephone in the RAC's marketing communications programme.

References

Acland, H. (2003) Direct marketing: championing the direct route. *Campaign*, 5 December. Retrieved 7 January from www.brandrepublic.co.uk/news/newsArticle.

Advertising Association (2008) *Advertising Statistics Year Book*. Henley: NTC. Also at www.adassoc.org.uk/inform/.

Anon. (2003) Royal Mail. Data 2003. *Marketing Direct*, Sponsored Supplement.

Anon. (2007) BBC TV Licensing marketing reaches university students. Retrieved 12 February 2008 from http://www.utalkmarketing.com/Pages/Article.aspx?.

Bashford, S. (2004) Telemarketing: customers calling. *Marketing*, 8 September. Retrieved 16 October 2004 from www.brandrepublic.com/news/.

Bird, D. (1989) *Commonsense Direct Marketing*, 2nd edn. London: Kogan Page.

Cravens, D.W., Ingram, T.N. and LaForge, R.W. (1991) Evaluating multiple channel strategies. *Journal of Business and Industrial Marketing*, **6**(3/4), 37–48.

DMIS (2000) *Letterbox Fact File*. Bristol: Direct Mail Information Service.

Dolnicar, S. and Jordaan, Y. (2007) A market-orientated approach to responsibly managing information privacy concerns in direct marketing. *Journal of Advertising*, **36**(2) (Summer) 123–49.

Dreze, X. (2005). Lessons from the front line: two key ways in which the internet has changed marketing forever. *Applied Stochastic Models in Business and Industry*, **21**, 443–8.

DuFrene, D.D., Engelland, B.T., Lehman, C.M. and Pearson, R.A. (2005) Changes in consumer attitudes resulting from participation in a permission e-mail campaign. *Journal of Current Issues and Research in Advertising*, **27**(1).

Eisenhart, T. (1990) Going the integrated route. *Business Marketing* (December), 24–32.

Evans, M. (1998) From 1086 and 1984: direct marketing into the millennium. *Marketing Intelligence and Planning*, **16**(1), 56–67.

Fletcher, K. (1997) External drive. *Marketing*, 30 October, 39–42.

Fletcher, K.P. and Peters, L.D. (1997) Trust and direct marketing environments: a consumer perspective. *Journal of Marketing Management*, **13**, 523–39.

Foster, S. (1996) Defining the direct brand. *Admap* (October), 33–6.

Frost, V. (2007) Royal Mail champions integrated approach, *Brand Republic*, 16 August. Retrieved 18 October 2007 from http://www.brandrepublic.com/News/731760/Royal-Mail-champions-integrated-approach/.

Gall, D., Stokes, M., Lynch, V., Perella, J. and Cook, L. (2006) ING Direct – Taking the savings market by storm, *IPA Effectiveness Awards*. Retrieved 21 February 2008 from http://www.warc.com/Search/Browse/Marketing_Intelligence/Brands/I_-_J/ING_Direct/.

Ganesan, S. (1994) Determinants of long-term orientation in buyer–seller relationships. *Journal of Marketing*, **58** (April), 1–19.

Godin, S. (1999) *Permission Marketing: Turning Strangers into Friends, and Friends into Customers*. New York: Simon & Schuster.

Godin, S. (2002) *Permission Marketing: Turning Strangers into Friends, and Friends into Customers*. New York: Simon & Schuster.

Gomez, L. and Hlavinka, K. (2007) The total package: loyalty marketing in the world of consumer packaged goods (CPG). *Journal of Consumer Marketing*, **24**(1), 48–56.

Goodwin, C. (1991) Privacy: recognition of a consumer right. *Journal of Public Policy and Marketing*, **10**(1), 149–66.

Grunert, K.G. (1996). Automatic and strategic processes in advertising effects. *Journal of Marketing*, **60**(4), 88–101.

Hawkes, S. (2008) Tesco rolls out trolley watch around the world, *The Times*, 12 April, 51.

Kamakura, W.A., Wedel, M., de Rosa, F. and Mazzon, J.A. (2003) Cross-selling through database marketing: a mixed factor analyzer for data augmentation and prediction. *International Journal of Research in Marketing*, **20**(1) (March), 45–65.

Kavassalis, P., Spyropoulou, N., Drossos, D., Mitrokostas, E., Gikas, G. and Hatzistamatiou, A. (2003) Modile permission marketing: framing the market inquiry. *International Journal of Electronic Commerce*, **8**(1), 55–79.

Kent, R. and Brandal, H. (2003) Improving email response in a permission marketing context. *International Journal of Market Research*, **45**(4), 489–503.

Krishnamurthy, S. (2001) A comprehensive analysis of permission marketing. *Journal of Computer-Mediated Communication*, **6**(2) (January). Retrieved 8 March 2008 from www.jcmc.indiana.edu/vol6/issue2/krishnamurthy.html.

Lehman, J. (2004). Permission marketing personalises the sales pitch. *Crain's Cleveland Business*, **25**(37), 23–4.

McLuhan, R. (2000) How a complaint can offer insights. *Marketing*, 3 August, 25–6.

McLuhan, R. (2006) The power of the phone, *Marketing*, 13 December, 41–2.

Milne, G.R. and Gordon, M.E. (1993) Direct mail privacy-efficiency trade-offs within an implied social contract framework. *Journal of Public Policy and Marketing*, **12**(2), 206–13.

Morgan, R.M. and Hunt, S.D. (1994) The commitment–trust theory of relationship marketing. *Journal of Marketing*, **58** (July), 20–38.

Moustakas, E., Ranganathan, C. and Duquenoy, P. (2006) E-mail marketing at the crossroads: a stakeholder analysis of unsolicited commercial email (spam). *Internet Research*, **16**(1), 38–52.

Murphy, D. (2000) Call centres ponder price of technology. *Marketing*, 14 September, 43–4.

Myers, J.B., Pickersgill, A.D. and Metre van, E.S. (2004) Steering customers to the right channels, *McKinsey Quarterly*, **4**, 16 November. www.mckinsey.com/practices/marketing/ourknowledge/pdf/Steering_customers_to_the_right_channel.pdf.

Payne, A. and Frow, P. (2004) The role of multichannel integration in customer relationship management. *Industrial Marketing Management*, **33**(6) (August) 527–38.

Pearson, S. (2003) Data takes centre stage. Data 2003. *Marketing Direct*, Sponsored Supplement.

Rafaeli, A., Ziklik, L. and Doucet, L. (2008) The impact of call center employees' customer orientation behaviors on service quality. *Journal of Service Research*, **10**(3) (February), 239–55.

Reed, D. (2000) Too much, too often. *Marketing Week*, 12 October, 59–62.

Reynolds, T.J., Gengler, C.E. and Howard, D.J. (1995) A means–end analysis of brand persuasion through advertising. *International Journal of Research in Marketing*, **12**(3), 257–67.

Ridgeway, J. (2000) Direct watch in 2000. *Marketing*, 21 December, 24–5.

Rogers, B. (2008) Contract sales organisations: making the transition from tactical resource to strategic partnering. *Journal of Medical Marketing*, **8**(1), 39–47.

Smith, J.W. (2004) Permission is not enough: empowerment and reciprocity must be included, too. *Marketing Management*, **13**(3), 52.

Soars, B. (2001) Let's get personal. *In-Store Marketing*, 31–4.

Tezinde, T., Smith, B. and Murphy, J. (2002) Getting permission: exploring factors affecting permission marketing. *Journal of Interactive Marketing*, **16**(4), 28–36.

Thomas, A.R. (2007) The end of mass marketing or, why all successful marketing is now direct marketing. *Direct Marketing: An International Journal*, **1**(1), 6–16.

Turner, C. (2008) Ready for takeover? *Marketing Week*, 10 January. Retrieved 8 February 2008 from www.marketingweek.co.uk/cgi-bin/item.cgi?id=59192&d=259&h=263.

VCCP (2008) www.utalkmarketing.com/Pages/Article.aspx?ArticleID=1512&Title=ING_Direct_case_study.

Wilson, E.O. (1998) *Consilience: The Unity of Knowledge*. New York: Random House.

Chapter 22

Personal selling

This form of marketing communication involves a face-to-face dialogue between two persons or by one person and a group. Message flexibility is an important attribute, as is the immediate feedback that often flows from use of this promotional tool.

Aims and learning objectives

The aims of this chapter are to examine personal selling as a promotional tool and to consider management's use of the sales force.

The learning objectives of this chapter are to:

1. consider the different types, roles and tasks of personal selling;
2. determine the strengths and weaknesses of personal selling as a form of communication;
3. explore the ways in which personal selling is thought to work;
4. establish the means by which management can organise a sales force;
5. compare some of the principal methods by which the optimum size of a sales force can be derived;
6. discuss the future role of the sales force.

For an applied interpretation see David Stringer's MiniCase entitled ***Selling the benefits of personal selling*** at the end of this chapter.

Introduction

In an era when relationship marketing has become increasingly understood and accepted as the contemporary approach to marketing theory and practice, so personal selling characterises the importance of strong relationships between sellers and buyers.

The traditional image of personal selling is one that embraces the hard sell, with a brash and persistent salesperson delivering a volley of unrelenting, persuasive messages at a confused and reluctant consumer. Fortunately, this image is receding quickly as the professionalism and breadth of personal selling has become more widely recognised and as the role of personal selling becomes even more important in the communications mix.

> The association of personal selling with the hard sell is receding as the role of personal selling becomes more important in the communications mix.

Personal selling activities can be observed at various stages in the buying process of both the consumer and business-to-business markets. This is because the potency of personal communications is very high, and messages can be adapted on the spot to meet the requirements of both parties. This flexibility, as shall be seen later, enables objections to be overcome, information to be provided in the context of the buyer's environment and the conviction and power of demonstration to be brought to the buyer when they request it.

Personal selling is different from other forms of communication in that the transmitted messages represent, mainly, dyadic communications. This means that there are at least two persons involved in the communication process. Feedback and evaluation of transmitted messages are possible, more or less instantaneously, so that these personal selling messages can be tailored and be made much more personal than any of the other methods of communication.

Types of personal selling

One way of considering the types of personal selling is to examine the types of customer served through this communication process:

1. *Intermediaries*
   This involves selling offerings onward through a particular channel network to other resellers. They in turn will sell the offering to other members who are closer to the end-user. For example, computer manufacturers have traditionally distributed their products through a combination of direct selling to key accounts and through a restricted number of dealers, or value-added resellers. These resellers then market the products (and bundle software) to their customers and potential customer organisations.
2. *Industrial*
   Here the main type of selling consists of business-to-business marketing and requires the selling of components and parts to others for assembly or incorporation within larger offerings. Goodman manufactures car radio systems and sells them to Ford, which then builds them into its cars as part of the final product offering.
3. *Professional*
   This type of selling process requires ideas and offerings to be advanced to specifiers and influencers. They will in turn incorporate the offering within the project(s) they are developing. For example, a salesperson could approach an architect to persuade them to include the alarm system made by the salesperson's organisation within the plans for a building that the architect has been commissioned to design.
4. *Consumer*
   This form of personal selling requires contact with the retail trade and/or the end-user consumer.

It will be apparent that a wide range of skills and resources is required for each of these types of selling as a result of which, salespersons usually focus their activities on just one of these types.

The tasks of personal selling

The generic tasks to be undertaken by the sales force have been changing because the environment in which organisations operate is shifting dramatically. These changes, in particular those associated with the development and implementation of new technologies, have had repercussions on the activities of the sales force and are discussed later in this chapter.

The tasks of those who undertake personal selling vary from organisation to organisation, and in accord with the type of selling activities on which they focus. It is normally assumed that they collect and bring into the organisation orders from customers wishing to purchase the offering. In this sense the order aspect of the personal selling tool can be seen as one of four order-related tasks:

- *Order takers* are salespersons to whom customers are drawn at the place of supply. Reception clerks at hotels and ticket desk personnel at theatres and cinemas typify this role.
- *Order getters* are sales personnel who operate away from the organisation and who attempt to gain orders, largely through the provision of information, the use of demonstration techniques and services and the art of persuasion.
- *Order collectors* are those who attempt to gather orders without physically meeting their customers. This is completed electronically or over the telephone. The growth of telemarketing operations was discussed in the previous chapter, but the time saved by both the buyer and the seller using the telephone to gather repeat and low-value orders frees valuable sales personnel to seek new customers and build relationships with current customers.

Order getters are sales personnel who operate away from the organisation.

- *Order supporters* are all those people who are secondary salespersons in that they are involved with the order once it has been secured, or are involved with the act of ordering, usually by supplying information. Order processing or financial advice services typify this role. In a truly customer-oriented organisations all customer-facing employees will be order supporters.

However, this perspective of personal selling is too narrow as it fails to set out the broader range of activities that a sales force can be required to undertake. Salespersons do more than get or take orders. The tasks listed in Table 22.1 provide direction and purpose, and also help to establish the criteria by which the performance of members of the personal selling unit can be evaluated. The organisation should decide which tasks it expects its representatives to undertake.

One view of personal selling is that the sales force is responsible for selling, installing and upgrading customer equipment and another is they are responsible for developing, selling and protecting accounts. The interesting point from both of these views is that responsibilities, or rather objectives, are extended either vertically upstream, into offer design, or vertically downstream, into the development and maintenance of long-term customer relationships, or both. It is the last point that is becoming increasingly important. In the business-to-business sector the sales activity mix is becoming much more oriented to the need to build and sustain the relationships that organisations have with their major customers. This will be discussed later. Some of the key questions that need to be addressed when preparing a communications plan are 'What will be the specific responsibilities of the sales force?' and 'What role will personal selling have relative to the other elements of the mix?'

Personal selling is the most expensive element of the communications mix. The average cost per contact can easily exceed £150 when all markets and types of businesses are considered. It

Table 22.1 Tasks of personal selling

Prospecting	Finding new customers
Communicating	Informing various stakeholders and feeding back information about the market
Selling	The art of leading a prospect to a successful close
Information gathering	Reporting information about the market and reporting on individual activities
Servicing	Consulting, arranging, counselling, fixing and solving a multitude of customer 'problems'
Allocating	Placing scarce products and resources at times of shortage
Shaping	Building and sustaining relationships with customers and other stakeholders

is generally agreed that personal selling is most effective at the later stages of the hierarchy of effects or buying process, rather than at the earlier stage of awareness building. Therefore, each organisation should determine the precise role the sales force is to play within the communication mix.

Personal selling is the most expensive element of the communications mix.

The role of personal selling

Personal selling is often referred to as interpersonal communication and from this perspective Reid *et al.* (2002) determined three major sales behaviours, namely getting, giving and using information:

- Getting information refers to sales behaviours aimed at information acquisition, for example gathering information about customers, markets and competitors.
- Giving information refers to the dissemination of information to customers and other stakeholders, for example sales presentations and seminar meetings designed to provide information about products and an organisation's capabilities and reputation.
- Using information refers to the sales person's use of information to help solve a customer's problem. Associated with this is the process of gaining buyer commitment through the generation of information (Thayer, 1968, cited by Reid *et al.*, 2002).

These last authors suggest that the using information dynamic appears to be constant across all types of purchase situations. However, as the complexity of a purchase situation increases so the amount of giving information behaviours decline and getting information behaviours increase. This finding supports the need for a sales person to be able to recognise particular situations in the buying process and then to adapt their behaviour to meet buyer's contextual needs.

As the complexity of a purchase situation increases so the amount of giving information behaviours decline.

However, sales people undertake numerous tasks in association with communication activities. Guenzi (2002) determined that some sales activities are generic simply because they are performed by most sales people across a large number of industries. These generic activities are selling, customer relationship management and communicating to

Sales people undertake numerous tasks in association with communication activities.

customers. Other activities such as market analysis, pre-sales services and the transfer of information about competitors to the organisation are industry-specific. Interestingly, he found that information-gathering activities are more likely to be undertaken by organisations operating in consumer markets than in b2b, possibly a reflection of the strength of the market orientation in both arenas.

The role of personal selling is largely one of representation.

The role of personal selling is largely one of representation. In business-to-business markets sales personnel operate at the boundary of the organisation. They provide the link between the needs of their own organisation and the needs of their customers. This linkage is absolutely vital, for a number of reasons that will be discussed shortly, but without personal selling, communication with other organisations would occur through electronic or print media and would foster discrete closed systems. Representation in this sense therefore refers to face-to-face encounters between people from different organisations. Wright and Fill (2001) found that doctors used the sales representatives of pharmaceutical companies as a means of forming images of the companies themselves. In other words, the sales force, whether intentionally or not, served as a corporate identity cue and provided valuable signals.

Many authors consider the development, organisation and completion of a sale in a market exchange-based transaction to be the key part of the role of personal selling. Sales personnel provide a source of information for buyers so that they can make the right purchase decisions. In that sense they provide a good level of credibility, but they are also perceived, understandably, as biased. The degree of expertise held by the salesperson may be high, but the degree of trustworthiness will vary, especially during the formative period of the relationship, unless other transactions with the selling organisation have been satisfactory. Once a number of transactions have been completed and product quality established, trustworthiness may improve.

As the costs associated with personal selling are high, it is vital that sales personnel are used effectively and efficiently. To that end, some organisations are employing other methods to decrease the time that the sales force spends on administration, travel and office work and to maximise the time spent in front of customers, where they can use their specific selling skills.

The amount of control that can be exercised over the delivery of the messages through the sales force depends on a number of factors. Essentially, the level of control must be regarded

ViewPoint 22.1 Hayfever under control

It can be argued that members of the sales team must be free to adapt messages at the point of delivery because individual clients are themselves different and have different needs and requirements. Lloyd (1997) believes that, when selling to doctors, medical representatives enter into conversations that are appropriate for individual doctors.

An example concerns two products manufactured by Schering-Plough. They have two hayfever products (one nasal and the other an oral antihistamine), and sales representatives are expected to decide which to present (in detail) to doctors, based on the representatives' knowledge and experience of each individual doctor's preferences and the needs of their patients.

This flexibility is framed within the context of the product strategy. Decisions that impact upon strategy are not allowed. There is freedom to adapt the manner in which products are presented, but there is no freedom for the sales representatives to decide the priority of the products to be detailed.

Question

Why do you believe the presentation of medical products is controlled so strictly?

Task

Next time you come into contact with a sales person, in a non-work situation, find out if the products or service they sell are prioritised.

as low, because each salesperson has the freedom to adapt messages to meet changing circumstances as negotiations proceed. In practice, however, the professionalism and training that many members of the sales force receive and the increasing emphasis on measuring levels of customer satisfaction mean that the degree of control over the message can be regarded, in most circumstances, as very good, although it can never, for example, be as high as that of advertising.

Strengths and weaknesses of personal selling

There are a number of strengths and weaknesses associated with personal selling. It is interesting to note that some of the strengths can in turn be seen as weaknesses, particularly when management control over the communication process is not as attentive or as rigorous as it might be.

Strengths

Dyadic communications allow for two-way interaction that, unlike the other communication tools, provides for fast, direct feedback. In comparison with the mass media, personal selling allows for the receiver to focus attention on the salesperson, with a reduced likelihood of distraction or noise.

There is a greater level of participation in the decision process by the vendor than in the other tools. When this is combined with the power to tailor messages in response to the feedback provided by the buyer, the sales process has a huge potential to solve customer problems.

Weaknesses

One of the major disadvantages of personal selling is the cost. Costs per contact are extremely high, and this means that management must find alternative means of communicating particular messages and improve the amount of time that sales personnel spend with prospects and customers. Reach and frequency through personal selling are always going to be low, regardless of the amount of funds available.

Control over message delivery is very often low and, while the flexibility is an advantage, there is also the disadvantage of message inconsistency. This in turn can lead to confusion (a misunderstanding perhaps with regard to a product specification), the ramifications of which can be enormous in terms of cost and time spent by a variety of individuals from both parties to the contract.

Costs per contact are extremely high.

The quality of the relationship can, therefore, be jeopardised through poor and inconsistent communications.

When personal selling should be a major part of the communications mix

In view of the role and the advantages and disadvantages of personal selling, when should it be a major part of the communications mix? The following is not an exhaustive list, but is presented as a means of considering some of the important issues: complexity, network factors, buyer significance and communication effectiveness.

Complexity

Personal selling is very important when there is a medium to high level of relationship complexity. Such complexity may be associated either with the physical characteristics of the product, such as computer software design, or with the environment in which the negotiations

Personal selling is very important when there is a medium to high level of relationship complexity.

are taking place. For example, decisions related to the installation of products designed to automate an assembly line may well be a sensitive issue. This may be due to management's attitude towards the operators currently undertaking the work that the automation is expected to replace. Any complexity needs to be understood by buyer and seller in order that the right product is offered in the appropriate context for the buyer. This may mean that the buyer is required to customise the offering or provide assistance in terms of testing, installing or supporting the product.

When the complexity of the offering is high, advertising and public relations cannot always convey benefits in the same way as personal selling. Personal selling allows the product to be demonstrated so that buyers can see and, if necessary, touch and taste it for themselves. Personal selling also allows explanations to be made about particular points that are of concern to the buyer or about the environment in which the buyer wishes to use the product.

Buyer significance

Significance can be measured as a form of risk.

The significance of the product to the buyers in the target market is a very important factor in the decision on whether to use personal selling. Significance can be measured as a form of risk, and risk is associated with benefits and costs.

The absolute cost to the buyer will vary from organisation to organisation and from consumer to consumer. The significance of the purchase of an extra photocopier for a major multinational organisation may be low, but for a new start-up organisation or for an established organisation experiencing a dramatic turnaround, an extra photocopying machine may be highly significant and subject to high levels of resistance by a number of different internal stakeholders.

The timing of a product's introduction may well be crucial to the success of a wider plan or programme of activities. Only through personal selling can delivery be dovetailed into the client's scheme of events.

Communication effectiveness

There may be a number of ways to satisfy the communication objectives of a campaign, other than by using personal selling. Each of the other communication tools has strengths and weaknesses; consequently differing mixes provide different benefits. Have they all been considered?

One of the main reasons for using personal selling occurs when advertising alone, or any other tool or medium, provides insufficient communications. The main reason for this inadequacy surfaces when advertising media cannot provide buyers with the information they require to make their purchasing decisions. For example, someone buying a new car may well observe and read various magazine and newspaper advertisements plus information on the web. The decision to buy, however, requires information and data upon which a rational decision can be made. This rationality and experience of the car, through a test drive perhaps, balances the former, more emotional, elements that contributed to the earlier decision.

The decision to buy a car normally evokes high involvement, and motivation occurs through the central route of the ELM. Therefore, car manufacturers provide a rich balance of emotional and factual information in their literature, from which a prospective buyer seeks further information, experience and reassurance from car dealers, who provide a personal point of contact. Car buyers sign orders with the presence and encouragement of sales persons. Very few cars are bought on a mail order basis, although some are bought over the Internet.

Personal selling provides a number of characteristics that make it more effective than the other elements of the mix. As discussed, in business-to-business marketing the complexity of many products requires salespeople to be able to discuss with clients their specific needs; in other words, to be able to talk in the customer's own language, to build source credibility through expertise and hopefully trustworthiness, and build a relationship that corresponds with the psychographic profile of each member of the DMU. In this case, mass communications would be inappropriate.

There are two further factors that influence the decision to use personal selling as part of the communications mix. When the customer base is small and when it is dispersed across a wide geographic area, it makes economic sense to use salespersons, as advertising in this situation is inadequate and ineffective. However, web sites and the use of interactive marketing communications can provide increased communication richness and obviate the need for sales representatives in some situations.

Web sites and the use of interactive marketing communications can provide increased communication richness

Channel network factors

If the communications strategy combines a larger amount of push rather than pull activities, then personal selling is required to provide the necessary communications for the other members of the channel network. Following on from this is the question regarding what information needs to be exchanged between members and what form and timing the information should be in. Handling objections, answering questions and overcoming misconceptions are also necessary information exchange skills.

When the number of members in a network is limited, the use of a sales force is advisable, as advertising is inefficient. Furthermore, the opportunity to build a close collaborative relationship with members may enable the development of a sustainable competitive advantage. Cravens (1987) suggested that the factors in Table 22.2 are important and determine when the sales force is an important element of the communications mix.

The roles of personal selling and the sales force are altering because the environment in which organisations operate is changing dramatically. The repercussions of these changes will become evident following the discussion of the tasks that personal selling is expected to complete.

Table 22.2 When personal selling is a major element of the communications mix

	Advertising relatively important	Personal selling relatively important
Number of customers	Large	Small
Buyers' information needs	Low	High
Size and importance of purchase	Small	Large
Post-purchase service required	Little	A lot
Product complexity	Low	High
Distribution strategy	Pull	Push
Pricing policy	Set	Negotiate
Web-enabled communications and exchanges	High	Low
Resources available for promotion	Many	Few

Source: Adapted from Cravens (1987).

How personal selling works: sales processes

A number of conceptual schemes have been proposed to explain the various stages in the sales process. These can be distilled into nine main stages, set out in Figure 22.1. The alignment and rigidity of the sequence should not be overstated, as the actual activities undertaken within each of these stages will vary not only from organisation to organisation but also between salespeople.

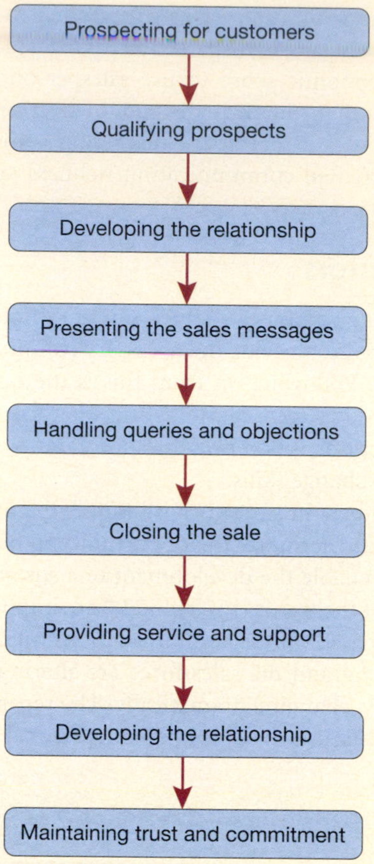

Figure 22.1 The main stages in the sales process

This rather simplistic approach to the sales process fails to explain how a salesperson should approach a customer or why some negotiations are successful and others are not. There have been many attempts to explain how the personal selling process works. One of the first methods proposed was discussed in Chapter 8 when exploring the hierarchy of effects models. The AIDA sequence put forward by Strong (1925) says that prospects must be drawn along a continuum of mental states, from attention to interest, desire, and finally stimulation to act in accordance with the vendor's wishes. This approach allows for a good deal of flexibility in the salesperson's approach and permits movement around a central theme.

The stimulus–response model suggests that if a salesperson can create the right set of circumstances then it is probable that the buyer will react in a particular way.

A further model, the stimulus–response model, suggests that if a salesperson can create the right set of circumstances then it is probable that the buyer will react in a particular way. Therefore, by controlling the circumstances of the sales process it is possible to induce the desired response. The salesperson is trained to deliver a particular stimulus (that is, what to say) and the buyer provides predictable responses, to which the salesperson has a number of expected responses. The sales presentation is therefore 'canned', ensuring that all aspects of the sale are covered in a logical order.

Jolson (1975) studied the results of such canned or prepared presentations with those that are personalised and determined more 'on the hoof'. His results indicated that buyers learned more through on-the-hoof presentations, but revealed that buyers had greater intentions to buy after the prepared presentation. This behavioural view is vendor-led and discounts the cognitive processes of the buyer in its attempt to control the process and the differing needs of different buyers.

A third model focuses on buyers and their needs. The role of the salesperson is to assist buyers to find solutions to their problems. According to Still *et al.* (1988), the salesperson needs to understand the cognitive processes of buyers in respect of their decision to buy or not to buy. This approach has been termed the 'buying formula' and is based on the satisfactions that a buyer experiences when placing orders as a solution to perceived problems (from work based on Strong, 1938).

The 'buying formula' is based on the satisfactions that a buyer experiences when placing orders as a solution to perceived problems.

The sequence of the model, therefore, is that a buyer first recognises a problem or a need. A solution is then found, which is purchased, and the buyer experiences a level of satisfaction. This formula can be seen in Figure 22.2. The solution contains two components, the product or service and the name of the organisation or the salesperson who facilitated the solution. When a buying habit is formed, the formula adjusts to that in Figure 22.3. To complete the formula, buyers must regard the product and the source as adequate and experience pleasant feelings when thinking of the components to the solution (see Figure 22.4).

Still *et al.* (1988) emphasise the need for salespersons to ensure that all the components of the buying habit are in place. For example, it is important that the buyer knows why the

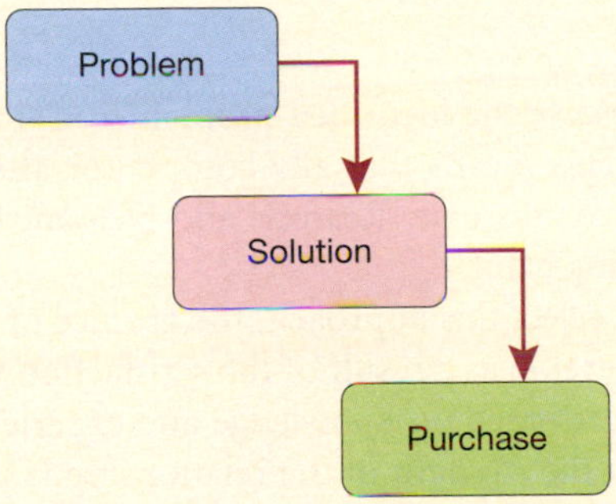

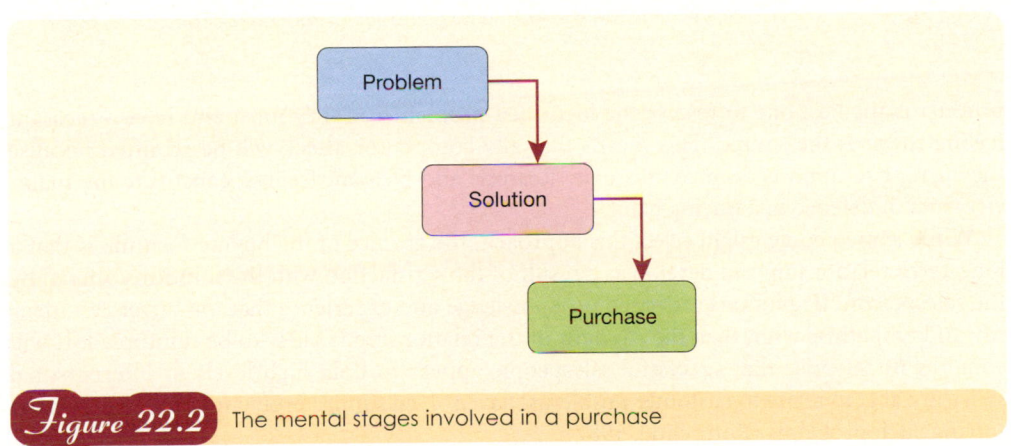

Figure 22.2 The mental stages involved in a purchase

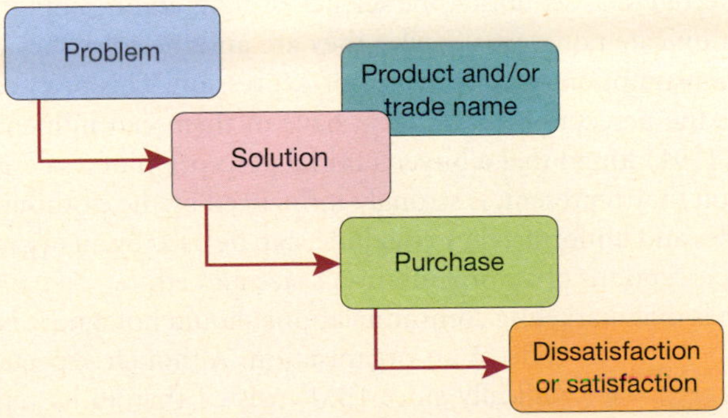

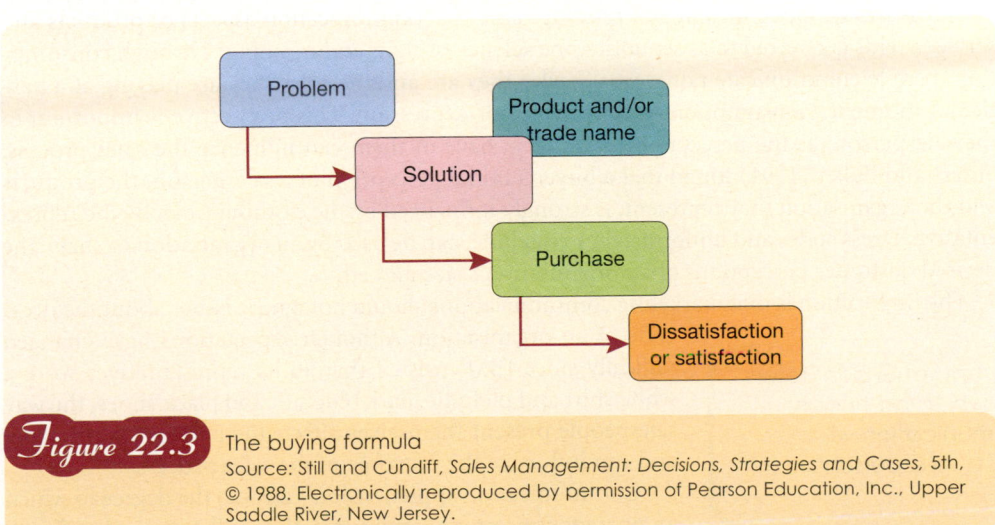

Figure 22.3 The buying formula
Source: Still and Cundiff, *Sales Management: Decisions, Strategies and Cases*, 5th, © 1988. Electronically reproduced by permission of Pearson Education, Inc., Upper Saddle River, New Jersey.

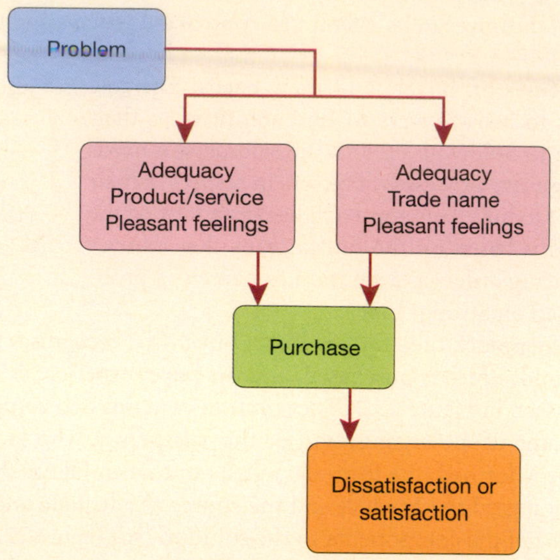

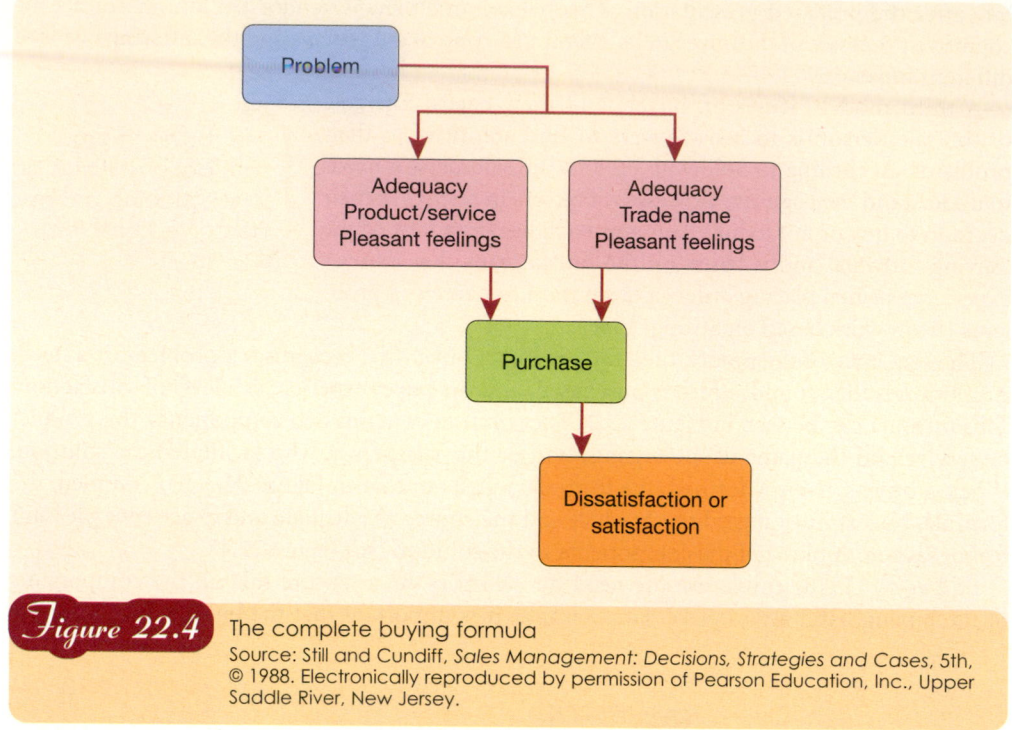

Figure 22.4 The complete buying formula

Source: Still and Cundiff, *Sales Management: Decisions, Strategies and Cases*, 5th, © 1988. Electronically reproduced by permission of Pearson Education, Inc., Upper Saddle River, New Jersey.

product is the best one to resolve the identified problem and they must also have a pleasant feeling towards the source. This means that any competitor attack will be rebuffed because the current solution is deemed adequate. Reasons and pleasant feelings constitute the major elements of defence in a buying habit.

While some people might reject this approach, the essence of the buying formula is that a long-term relationship can develop as a result of the satisfaction with the solutions offered by the salesperson. If solutions are based on knowledge and experience that the buyer can identify and empathise with, then the strength of the relationship is likely to be reinforced. It will come as no surprise that successful salespeople appear to hold high levels of interpersonal skills, are able to relate to customer problems, have solved similar problems and are experts at solving such problems (Rothschild, 1987).

A host of factors can influence the buying process, but one growing area of interest concerns the symbolic meaning of offerings and the communication aspects of products and services. This is referred to as semiotics, the science of signs and meaning. Through consumption, people communicate non-verbally who they are and the roles they are playing at a particular moment. Consumption allows people self-expression. This perspective is important to the salesperson, as the perception that buyers have of them can influence the sales process. Stuart and Fuller (1991) found that a buyer's initial perception of a salesperson, the products and the organisation they represent, is strongly influenced by the clothing worn by the representative. Dress codes and uniforms, they conclude, can be used by an organisation to shape the desired customer perceptions of an organisation's size and ethics.

The implication is that marketing communications should not ignore issues about the dress code of an organisation. Although expectations have changed radically since IBM insisted that all its representatives wore a white shirt and plain tie, dark blue suit and black shoes, the way salespeople present themselves affects the perception of others and can influence the outcome of the sales process.

'Communication apprehension' refers to the degree to which an anxiety concerning communication will negatively affect a salesperson's performance.

'Communication apprehension' refers to the degree to which an anxiety concerning communication will negatively affect a salesperson's performance. There appears to be a range of situations in which apprehension might be observed. McCroskey (1984) developed a framework depicting different apprehension levels. Essentially there are two main conditions. One is a condition that affects individuals in situations that normal people would not consider threatening. The other is a state that refers to the normal apprehension felt by people when speaking in meetings, group situations, dyadic communications and public speaking situations. Generally speaking, it is not uncommon to find that above-average sales performance is achieved by individuals who have the lowest level of communication apprehension. Not surprisingly, those with low levels of sales performance tend to have high levels of communication apprehension (Pitt *et al.*, 2000).

ViewPoint 22.2 Different selling approaches

Having repeatedly failed to get appointments with major organisations in order to sell his services about compliance with the regulations in the technology sector, Steve Kerner tried a different approach. He wrote to Dell and offered to pay for their time if they agreed to meet him. Not only did they meet but he got the job, didn't have to pay and they gave him a referral to AT&T.

Richard Knight runs an advertising agency in Hampshire, which concentrates on poster-sized advertisements. However, he sensed that prospects were bored and cynical of standard presentations so he has adopted a number of different approaches. One of these requires him to fold a poster until it is small and proclaim that this size will cost £300 (in a local paper). He unfolds it once and announces that will cost £600 and then completely unfolds it and states that he will put this at bus stops for just £40. The response is immediate and based on the visual impact of the value that was so clearly demonstrated.

Source: Armistead (2002).

Question

Do you think these examples of alternative selling approaches can only be applied by small and medium-sized organisations?

Task

Think through how you would present an air conditioning system and a new brand of fruit juice.

A further issue concerns the degree of ambiguity that both parties to a sales meeting might experience. Such ambiguity might refer to specific product-related information, failure to understand the problem that needs to be resolved, the time available to resolve it or the impact on other stakeholders related to the specific situation.

Sales force management and organisation

The target market and profile of the customer will have been established previously during the development of the communication plan. In particular, the communication strategy should have indicated the degree of push and pull to be used and will have illuminated detail about the nature of the channels in which the salesperson is to operate. Such information is important, as it helps to shape the sales strategy and the messages to be transmitted. Essentially, the salesperson acts as a link between a supplier and a customer, the primary role being to arrange matters so that the relationship can be continued and developed to the mutual benefit of both organisations and their participants.

The primary and traditional sales channel is the field sales force.

The primary and traditional sales channel is the field sales force. These are people who are recruited and trained to find prospective customers, to demonstrate or explain the organisation's products and services and to persuade prospects that they should buy the offering. Orders are then signed, and the salesperson reports the order to their organisation, which then fulfils the details of the customer's order, as agreed. However, while life is not this simple, this broad perspective is assumed to be the primary sales channel of many organisations, particularly those operating in the business-to-business sector.

In some ways, salespersons are like any other unit of resource in that they need to be deployed in a way that provides maximum benefit to the organisation. Grant and Cravens (1999) suggest that the effectiveness of the sales organisation (or unit) is determined as a result of two main antecedents: the sales manager and the sales force itself. These are shown in Figure 22.5.

An organisation is linked to its customers through three main processes that Srivastava *et al.* (1999) refer to as core business capabilities, namely product development management, supply chain management and customer relationship management (see Table 22.3). Ingram *et al.* (2002) make the point that the centrality of the customer to the organisation highlights the crucial role of sales strategy with regard to the organisation's overall customer interaction process.

In order to decide on an appropriate sales strategy, the nature of the desired communication needs to be examined. Are there to be salespersons negotiating individually, or as a team with a single buyer or buying team? Is a sales team required in order to sell to buying teams or will conference and seminar selling achieve the desired goals? What is the degree of importance of the portfolio of accounts, and how should the organisations be contacted?

The primary, and traditional, sales channel is the field sales force. These are people who are fully employed by the organisation and are referred to as the direct sales force. Salespersons, like any other unit of resource, should be deployed in a way that provides maximum benefit to the organisation. Sales organisation effectiveness results from the performance of salespeople, organisational factors and various environmental factors (Baldauf *et al.*, 2002).

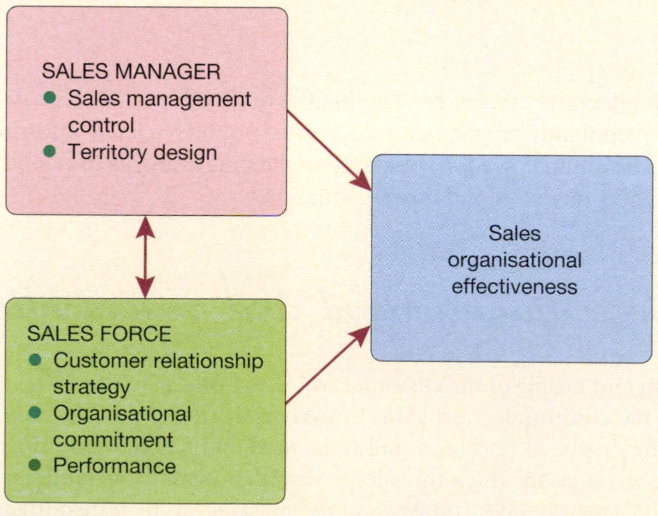

Figure 22.5 Antecedents of sales organisational effectiveness
Source: Grant and Cravens (1999). Used with kind permission.

Table 22.3 Core business capabilities

Category	Explanation
Product development management	Developing and maintaining suitable products and services to meet customer needs and provide customer value
Supply chain management	The acquisition and transformation of resources (inputs) into valued customer offerings, throughout the supply chain
Customer relationship management	Creating, sustaining and developing customer relationships for mutual benefit.

Source: Adapted from Srivastava *et al.* (1999) by permission of American Marketing Association.

The performance of salespeople is a measure of their work or task-related behaviours, and the results of their activities and inputs. Therefore, a sales management control strategy should refer to the degree to which sales managers actively manage the inputs as a well as reward against targeted outcomes (sales, market share, etc.).

From this it is possible to identify two main sales management approaches, behaviour based- and outcome-based control systems (Baldauf *et al.*, 2002). Essentially, control through behaviour-based systems is founded upon managing the inputs or processes to a salesperson and rewarding them with a high fixed salary and low commission. Conversely, control through outcome-based approaches is characterised by a focus on results, little managerial supervision and direction and high levels of commission as an incentive to perform. Some see the outcome–behaviour systems as a continuum (Anderson and Oliver, 1987) whereas others see these as two discrete activities (Piercy *et al.* 2004).

Control through outcome-based approaches is characterised by a focus on results, little managerial supervision and direction and high levels of commission as an incentive to perform.

Many organisations use a hybrid approach, but research by Baldauf *et al.* indicates that sales managers appear to utilise a 'coaching rather than command and control management styles'. The emphasis appears to be on the long term and the value of developing relationships. The performance of salespeople is therefore enhanced by sales management strategies that are based on generating positive behaviour. However, results from previous work undertaken by Piercy *et al.* (1998) supported many previous findings that salespeople with high levels of behaviour performance also exhibit high levels of outcome performance. This implies that sales managers should spend a greater amount of their time selecting, training and developing salespeople rather than just selecting, directing and measuring results. Further research by Piercy *et al.* (2004) indicates that the way sales managers emphasise outcome or behaviour controls needs to reflect region or country differences, local personnel inputs and the need for flexibility in the implementation of control strategies.

From this brief overview of sales management responsibilities it can be concluded that they are responsible for five broad activities associated with salespeople. These are:

- selection and recruitment;
- training;
- size and deployment;
- motivation and supervision;
- evaluation, control and reward.

Of these space is devoted only to the issue of size and deployment.

Sales force size and structure

One of the first questions that needs to be addressed concerns the type of sales force to be used (assuming the decision has been made that some form of personal selling is required in the communications mix). Further questions are concerned with how many salespersons are required and where and how they should operate. Decisions regarding the type, structure, size and territory of the sales force will be discussed on the basis that this is the only sales channel used by an organisation.

There are a number of ways in which an organisation can structure the sales force, but there are three broad approaches (geographic, product and market/customer) that most organisations have used. The following examples are based upon Tgi PLC, which designs, manufactures and distributes loudspeaker products. These are purely examples of how it might organise its sales force and are not intended to represent the way in which Tgi approaches its markets.

Geographic-based sales force

The most common and straightforward method of organising a sales force is to assign individuals to separate geographic territories

The most common and straightforward method of organising a sales force is to assign individuals to separate geographic territories (see Figure 22.6). In this type of sales force the salesperson is responsible for all the activities necessary to sell all products to all potential customers in the region or area in which the territory is located. This method of assignment is used by new companies, in situations where customers tend to buy a range of products, where there is little difference in the geographic spread of the products or when resources are limited.

Strengths

This approach provides for the lowest cost, concentrates the selling effort throughout the territory and allows for a quick response to regional or local needs. This structure also ensures that customers only see one person from the selling organisation and are not at risk of becoming the recipient of multiple and conflicting messages.

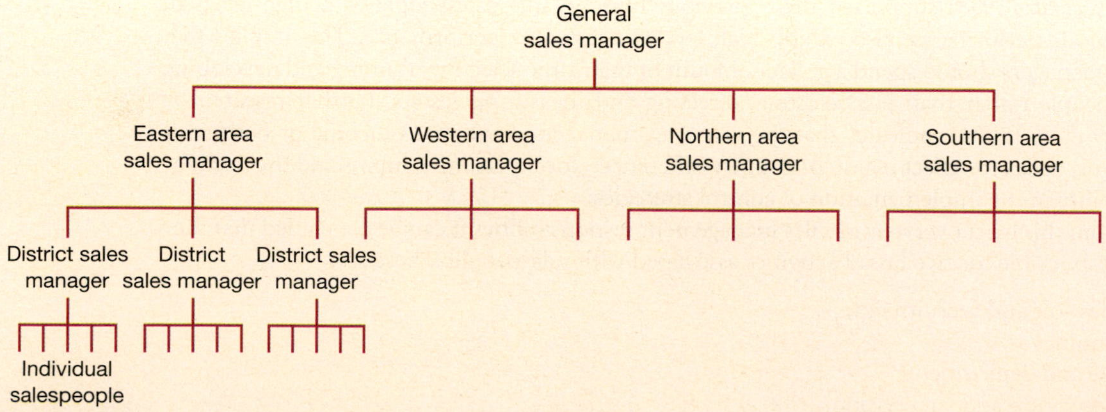

Figure 22.6 A geographically based sales force structure

Weaknesses

The level of specialised knowledge is reduced, as many products have to be promoted by each salesperson. Furthermore, salespeople under this structure tend to be allowed greater freedom in the design and execution of their working day. Consequently, the number of new customers is often low and the line of least resistance is usually pursued. This may also conflict with the objectives of the organisation, as, for example, call patterns may not be compatible with the overall goals of the sales force.

Product-based sales force

Under this type of structure, the organisation has different sales teams, each carrying a particular line of products (see Figure 22.7). This is often used by organisations with large and diverse product lines. Also, organisations with highly technical and complex products, which require specialist knowledge and particular selling techniques, prefer this form of sales force structure.

Strengths

The most important advantage of this approach is that it allows the development of product knowledge and technical expertise. In business-to-business markets this factor can lead to improved source credibility, since the level of expertise, and possibly trustworthiness, can be important if the messages are to be persuasive and effective. If the organisation's production facilities are organised by product (separate factories), each with a sales team operating out of the unit, then there can be increased cooperation, which in turn benefits the customer.

Sales management is better able to control the allocation of the selling effort across all products under this type of structure. If greater focus on a particular product is required, then more salespersons can be allocated appropriately.

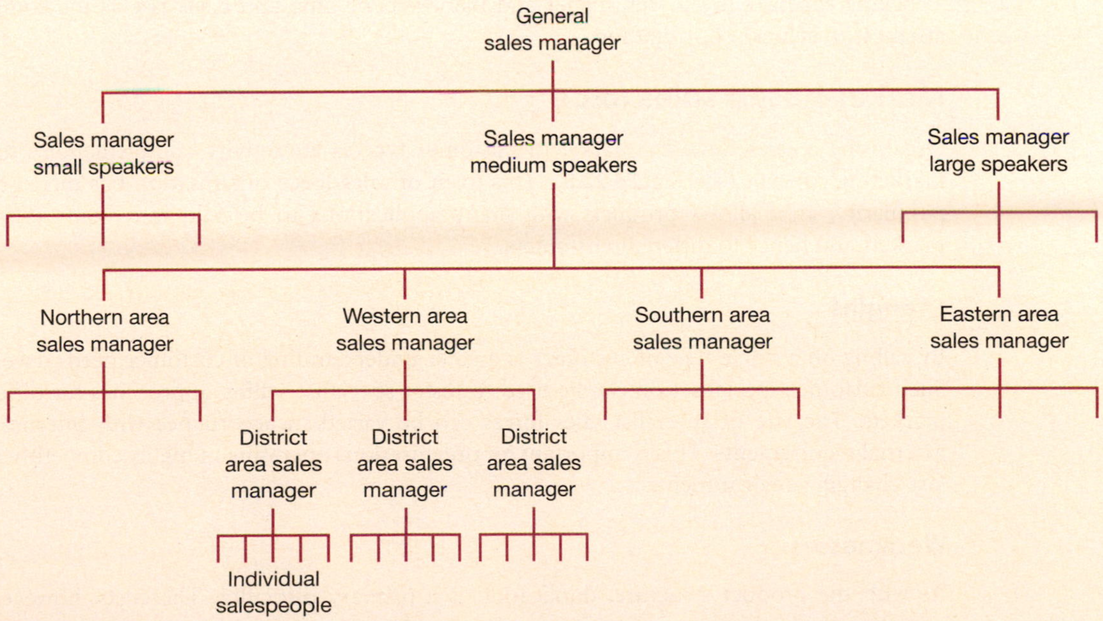

Figure 22.7 A product-based sales force structure

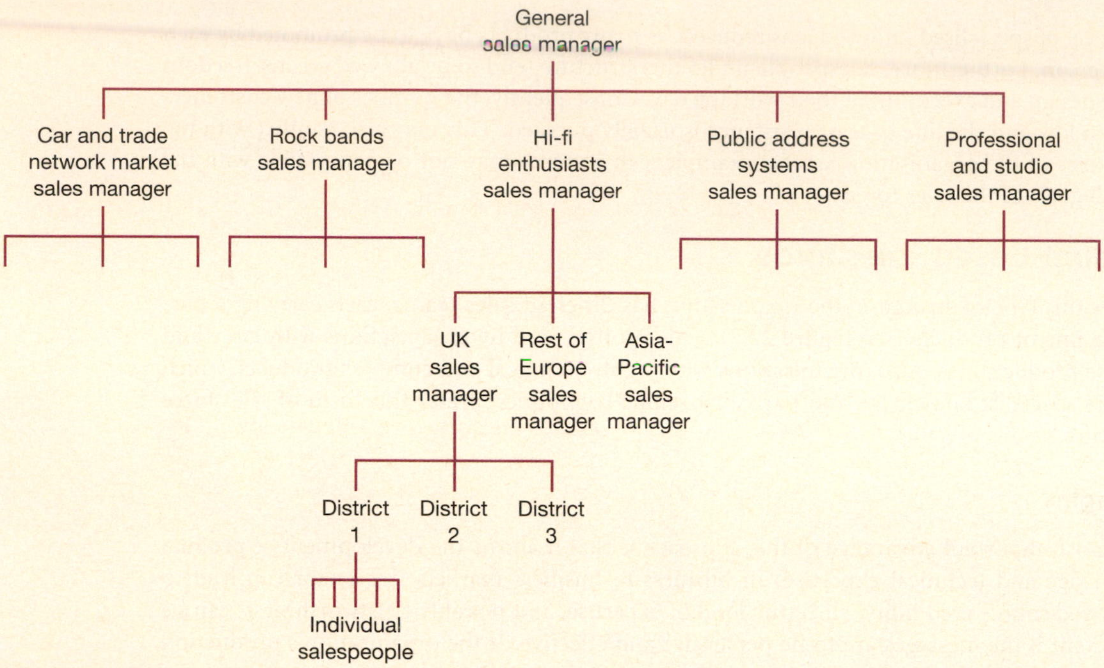

Figure 22.8 A market-based sales force structure

Weaknesses

The major disadvantage is that there is a high probability that there will be duplication of sales effort. A customer could be called on by a number of different salespeople, all from the same organisation.

Selling expenses are driven higher and management time and costs rise as the company attempts to achieve coordination.

Market-based sales force

Organising a sales force by market or customer type is an activity complementary to the marketing concept (see Figure 22.8). This form of sales force organisation has increased in popularity, as it allows products with many applications to be sold into many different markets and hence to different customers.

Strengths

By calling on a single type of customer, a greater understanding of customer needs develops. Such customer specialisation can be used to foster specialist selling approaches for different markets. The size of specialist sales forces can be varied in accordance with internal and external requirements. This is important for organisations operating in highly competitive and fast-changing environments.

Weaknesses

As with the product structure, duplication is a primary difficulty. The costs, however, of operating under this form of structure are higher than any of the others.

These three approaches to sales force design are not mutually exclusive, and most major organisations use a combination of the three to meet the needs of their various stakeholders.

As Still *et al.* (1988) state, the sub-division of the structure is usually related to primary and secondary needs for marketing success. Most organisations use geography as a sub-division, but whether this is a primary or secondary sub-division depends largely on the importance of customer or product sub-divisions for the achievement of competitive advantage. Such hybrid structures are not static and should evolve as the organisation and the environment in which it operates develop. Tgi uses the customer approach not only for the sales force but at an SBU (strategic business unit) level as well.

The three approaches to sales force design are not mutually exclusive.

Sales force size and shape

The size of the sales force needs to be determined on a regular basis because the environments in which sales forces are operating are changing rapidly. The decision regarding the size of the sales force presents a dilemma. Increasing the size of the sales force will increase sales revenue, but it will also increase costs. A balance needs to be achieved and the decision is often a blend of market and resource factors. Market-related issues concern the number of potential customers, the sales potential of each of these accounts, the geographic concentration of the customers and predictions concerning the strength and volatility of the economy. Resource-related issues concern the corporate and marketing strategy, competitive conditions and the availability of financial resources.

There are many different approaches to the determination of the appropriate sales force size. Many of the more recent ones are based on sophisticated software, but these are derived essentially from three main approaches: the *breakdown, workload* and *sales potential* methods.

The intuitive method is a label for all of the methods not based on reason, logic, market information or, in some cases, sense. At one extreme are the hunch and the 'I have been in this business for x years' approach, while at the other extreme there is the 'If it is good enough for the competition, then it is good enough for us' approach. These are to be rejected.

The breakdown method

This is the simplest method. Each salesperson is viewed as possessing the same sales productivity potential per period. Therefore, divide the total expected sales by the sales potential and the resultant figure equates to the number of salespeople required:

$$n = \frac{sv}{sp}$$

where n is the number of salespeople required, sv is the anticipated sales volume and sp is the estimated sales productivity of each salesperson/unit.

This technique is flawed in that it treats sales force size as a consequence of sales, yet the reverse is probably true. A further difficulty concerns the estimate of productivity used. It fails to account for different potentials, abilities and levels of compensation. Furthermore, there is no account of profitability as it treats sales as an end in itself.

The workload method

Underlying this method is the premise that all salespeople should bear an equal amount of the work necessary to service the entire market. The example offered here is based on work by Govoni *et al.* (1986).

The first task is to classify customers into categories based on the level of sales to each account. The ABC rule of account classification holds that the first 15 per cent of customers account for 65 per cent of sales (A accounts), the next 20 per

The premise is that all salespeople should bear an equal amount of the work necessary to service the entire market.

cent will produce 20 per cent of sales (B accounts) and the final 65 per cent will yield only 15 per cent (C accounts).

- *Task 1*. Classify customers into categories:
  Class A: large/very attractive = 300
  Class B: medium/moderately attractive = 400
  Class C: small/unattractive = 1,300
- *Task 2*. Determine the frequency and desired duration of each call for each type of account:
  Class A: 15 times/pa 95 mins/call = 23.75 hours
  Class B: 10 times/pa 63 mins/call = 10.50 hours
  Class C: 6 times/pa 45 mins/call = 4.50 hours
- *Task 3*. Calculate the workload in covering the market:
  Class A: 300 accounts 23.75 hours/account = 7,125 hours
  Class B: 400 accounts 10.50 hours/account = 4,200 hours
  Class C: 1,300 accounts 4.50 hours/account = 5,850 hours
  Total workload = 17,175 hours
- *Task 4*. Determine the time available per salesperson:
  40 hours/week × 46 weeks/pa = 1,840 hours
- *Task 5*. Determine selling/contact time per salesperson:
  Contact: 45% = 828 hours
  Travelling: 31% = 570 hours
  Non-selling: 24% = 442 hours
- *Task 6*. Calculate the number of salespersons required:

$$\text{number of salespersons} = \frac{\text{total work load}}{\text{contact hours}} \frac{17{,}175}{828} = 20.74$$

A total of 20 or 21 salespeople would be required using this method. While this technique is easy to calculate, it does not allow for differences in sales response among accounts that receive the same sales effort. It fails to account for servicing and assumes that all salespersons have the same contact time. This is simply not true. One further shortcoming is that the profitability per call is neglected.

The sales potential method

The principle recognises that there will be diminishing returns as extra salespeople are added to the sales force.

Semlow (1959) was one of the earliest to report the decreasing-returns principle when applied to sales force calculations. The principle recognises that there will be diminishing returns as extra salespeople are added to the sales force. For example, one extra salesperson may generate £120,000, but two more may only generate a total of £200,000 in new sales. Therefore, while the first generates £120,000, the other two only generate £100,000 each.

Semlow found, for example, that sales in territories with 1 per cent potential generated £160,000, whereas sales in territories with 5 per cent averaged £200,000. Therefore, 1 per cent potential in the second territory equates to £40,000 (200,000/5) and £160,000 (160,000/1) in the first.

The conclusion reached was that a higher proportion of sales per 1 per cent of potential could be realised if the territories were made smaller by adding salespeople. As asked above, what is the optimum number of salespersons, because costs rise as more salespeople are added?

Semlow's work provides the basis for some of the more sophisticated techniques and derivatives of the incremental or marginal approach. It is relatively simple in concept but exceedingly difficult to implement. The conclusion, that a salesperson in a low-potential territory is expected to achieve a greater proportion of the potential than a colleague in a high-potential territory is, as Churchill *et al.* (1990) say, 'intuitively appealing'.

Territory design

Having determined the number of salespeople that are necessary to achieve the set promotion objectives, attention must be given to the shape, potential and equality of the territories to be created. The decomposition of the total market into smaller units facilitates easier control of the sales strategy and operations. A sales territory is a grouping of customers and prospects assigned to an individual or team of salespeople. The reason for the establishment of sales territories is mainly oriented to aspects of planning and control. Sales territories enable the organisation to cover the designated market, to control costs, to assist the evaluation of salesperson performance, to contribute to sales force morale and to provide a bridge with other promotional activities, most notably advertising (Still *et al.*, 1988).

Churchill *et al.* (1990) suggest that the steps depicted in Figure 22.9 are the most appropriate. The objective is to make all territories as equal as possible with respect to, first, sales potential, as this facilitates performance evaluation, and, second, work effort, as this tends to improve morale and reduce levels of conflict.

The most basic unit is a small geographic area. Small units permit easier adjustments to be made and allow for the reassignment of accounts from one salesperson to another. Units can

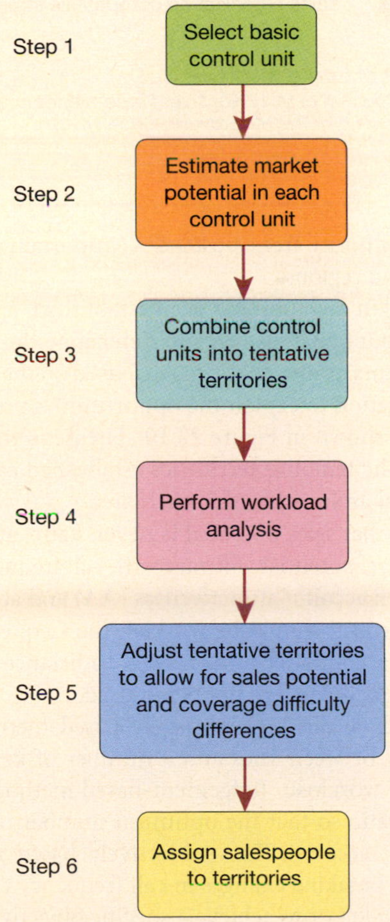
Step 1
Select basic control unit
Step 2
Estimate market potential in each control unit
Step 3
Combine control units into tentative territories
Step 4
Perform workload analysis
Step 5
Adjust tentative territories to allow for sales potential and coverage difficulty differences
Step 6
Assign salespeople to territories

Figure 22.9 Key steps in territory design
Source: Churchill *et al.* (1990) *Sales Force Management*, 3rd edition. Reproduced with permission of The McGraw-Hill Companies.

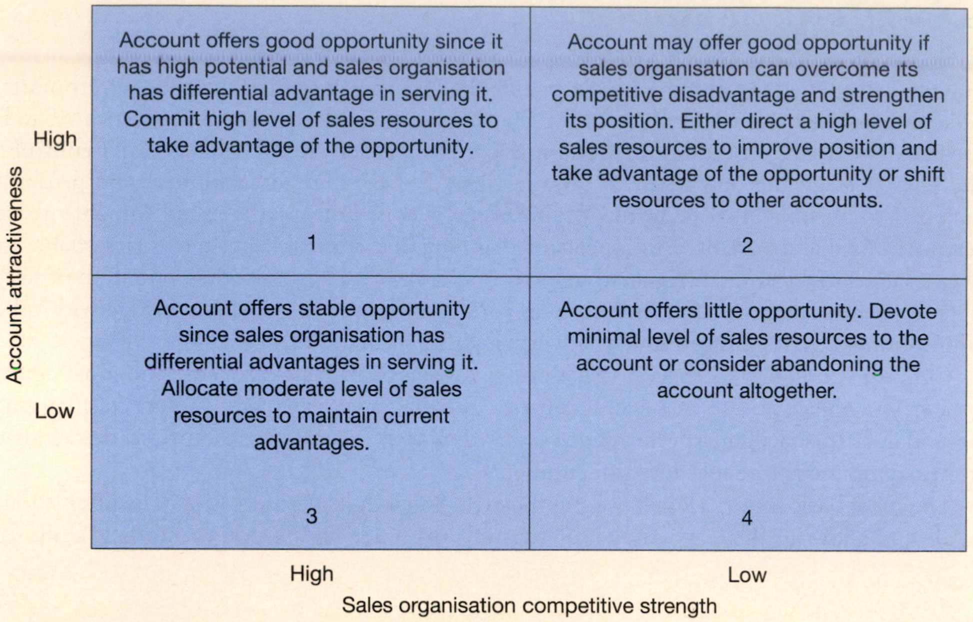

Figure 22.10 Account planning matrix
Source: Churchill *et al.* (1990) *Sales Force Management*, 3rd edition. Reproduced with permission of The McGraw-Hill Companies.

be based on counties, local authority areas, postcodes (important in Greater London and other metropolitan areas), cities and regions.

Once the market potential in each unit has been established, approximate territories can be set up. From this point, account analysis helps to determine the call frequency and duration necessary for the larger accounts. A matrix approach, based on the attractiveness of the account and the ability of the organisation to exploit the opportunities presented, can help this part of the management process, as shown in Figure 22.10. The penultimate step is to make adjustments to the boundaries of the tentative territories established earlier. These adjustments are designed to equalise potential and workload in each area.

It should be remembered that sales potential is never static, at the market, the territory or the account level. In particular, potential will vary with call frequency. It will be apparent that there is a relationship between account attractiveness (AA) and account effort (AE). While AA determines how hard the account should be worked, the frequency and duration will affect the sales derived from each account. There is a need to balance potentials and workloads if computer programs, such as CallPlan, are not being used.

There are several methods available. Empirically based methods use regression analysis to represent the relationship between sales and a number of key sales variables such as the number of calls, potential or workload. Judgement-based methods require the salesperson to estimate the sales/sales call ratio so that the optimum number of calls can be made on each account. The subjectively based method involves executives making changes in call frequency to reflect changes in the market or to achieve a specific objective.

Judgement-based methods require the salesperson to estimate the sales/sales call ratio so that the optimum number of calls can be made on each account.

The final task is to assign salespeople to territories. It should be remembered that salespeople have varying levels of ability. To overcome this disparity, the most able is allocated an index of 1.00 and all others rated relative to that individual. For example, an index of 0.75 means that a salesperson could achieve 75 per cent of the business that a salesperson with an index of 1.0 could achieve in the same territory. Salespeople can then be allocated on a basis that maximises the return to the organisation.

Grant and Cravens (1999) found that the effectiveness of a sales organisation is partly determined by the design of sales territories. For sales organisations that place high value on directing, evaluating, rewarding and monitoring, territory design and sales force commitment appear to be linked to sales unit effectiveness. From their research they state that territory design plays a 'pivotal role in sales unit effectiveness'. Decisions regarding the size, shape and form of the sales force need to be made once a strategic decision has been made to employ a sales force. An alternative approach is to hire or rent a sales force, by region, product or time, to suit the needs of the task at hand. These temporary sales forces are recruited from companies in the field marketing sector. This sector has grown in significance and stature over the past few years, and more detail is provided in Chapter 29.

Changing channels

The previous discussion of the role of the field sales force was pre-empted by the statement that this is the primary sales channel for many organisations in the business-to-business sector. There are, however, a growing number of organisations that see a different role for the sales force and which are introducing other sales channels in order to improve productivity and the bottom line. These have been explored in other parts of the book, most notably Chapter 21. There are many implications for organisations arising from the development of a multichannel approach. Two of these include team selling and sales force automation, which are discussed below. Others include key and global account management, which are discussed in Chapter 29, and direct marketing, which is the subject of Chapter 21.

Team selling

Three distinct selling strategies can be identified: transactional, consultative and alliance sales (Rackham and DeVincetis, 1999) (see Table 22.4). These strategies represent different eras of thought and approaches to selling and sales management. However, they also represent phases through which individual organisations can develop their selling practices.

Three distinct selling strategies can be identified: transactional, consultative and alliance sales.

Table 22.4 Three selling strategies

Selling strategy	Explanation
Transactional selling	This is the traditional form of selling and the strategy is characterised by the planned development of a large volume of sales accounts, each of which has individual and unrelated buyers
Consultative selling	Due to better understanding about relationships and the need to limit the number of buyers, consultative selling evolved in the mid 1980s. Partnerships were formed with customers and a form of preferred supplier status was established. Sometimes referred to as solution selling
Alliance sales	An alliance sales strategy was developed when various processes of the selling organisation were integrated with those of the partner. Sales moved from a quantitative perspective (transactional) to a qualitative perspective (both consultative and alliance-based).

Source: Adapted from Rackham and DeVincetis (1999).

In order that partnership and more collaborative selling approaches be implemented it has become increasingly necessary and common for organisations to assign a team of salespeople to meet the needs of key account customers. A variety of different skills are thought necessary to meet the diversity of personnel making up the DMUs of the larger organisations. Consequently, a salesperson may gain access to an organisation, after which a stream of engineers, analysts, technicians, programmers, training executives and financial experts follow.

For example, when one of Goodman's (a division of Tgi discussed earlier) car-manufacturing clients plans a new model, a salesperson opens the door to provide a communication link between the two organisations. Soon, a project team evolves, consisting of engineering, manufacturing, purchasing, production and quality staff, all working to satisfy the needs of their client. Goodman even uses the same project code number as the client to provide for clarity and avoid confusion. It also helps to build the relationship and identification between the partners.

Most leading IT-based organisations used to sell the hardware and then leave the customer to work out how to use it. Team selling is now used by Digital, Hewlett-Packard, IBM and others to provide customised combinations of hardware, software and technical support as solutions to their customers' business problems. This requires teams of salespeople and technical experts working closely with the customer's DMU throughout the sales/purchasing cycle and beyond.

The sales team approach requires high levels of coordination and internal communication if it is to be successful and sell across product lines from various locations (Cespedes *et al.*, 1989). In addition, the range of activities associated with team selling requires a culture that is focused on customers' needs and the team must be supported and self-driven to deliver on these internally recognised performance barriers. Indeed, Workman *et al.* (2003) refer to the need to develop an *esprit de corps* in order that selling teams, primarily used for key accounts, be successful. Team selling requires a different approach to both the customer and also the associated internal activities from those required for regular field force selling. Both the levels of commitment and costs associated with cross-functional team selling are large, and these reasons alone restrict the use of this selling approach to those accounts that are strategically important.

Both the levels of commitment and costs associated with cross-functional team selling are large.

Sales force automation (SFA)

The use of technology to assist field force selling has grown substantially, and 3G technology has accelerated usage of digital technology in the sales and selling context. There are a number of reasons for this interest, most notably the attraction of lower selling costs, improved communication effectiveness and enhanced market and customer information. Various forms of technology have been employed (Engle and Barnes, 2000). What constitutes sales force automation is questionable, simply because of the breadth of internal and external activities undertaken in the name of selling. One perspective is that such technology embraces sales force automation, communication technology and customer relationship management (Widmier *et al.*, 2002). These authors identify six main sales-related functions, namely organising, presenting, reporting, communicating, informing and supporting transactions. These are set out in Table 22.5.

Six main sales-related functions are identified, namely organising, presenting, reporting, communicating, informing and supporting transactions.

Research by these authors shows that technology is used extensively to assist all of the selling functions, but is used least by salespersons when in the field for actually supporting transactions (e.g. order status and stock enquiries and qualifying customers). It also indicates that technology is more likely to be used by salespersons in the office (preparing presentations, proposals, route planning, scheduling and reporting) than the field.

The deployment of SFA varies among organisations and its effectiveness will, to a large extent, be dependent upon appropriate implementation, proper utilisation by the sales force

Table 22.5 The use of technology in sales

Sales function	Use of technology
Organising	Call schedules, route plans, contacts, sales plans
Presenting with	Portable multimedia presentations, customised proposals
Reporting on	Call reports, expense claims, monthly performance
Informing about	Prospecting, product performance and product configuration information
Communicating via	Mobile phones, pagers, the Internet, email, personal organisers, fax machines
Supporting transactions	Order status and tracking, stock control, stock availability

Source: Adapted from Widmier *et al.* (2002).

and suitable support processes. However, SFA has not been entirely successful (Honeycutt *et al.*, 2005) and Morgan and Inks (2001) report SFA failure rates between 25 and 60 per cent, a large proportion of which can be accredited to poor management of change and sales force resistance to change.

The factors that relate to the successful implementation of SFA will vary according to industry and organisation and perhaps even individual salespeople. Research by Morgan and Inks identified four main elements associated with the successful implementation of SFA: management commitment, training, user involvement and accurate expectation setting. They also determined that implementation will be less than satisfactory when there are fears of technology, of interference in an individual's selling activities, or a loss of power (over the information they have on their customers), and where there is a general resistance to change.

It would appear logical that the adoption of SFA should lead to substantial productivity gains. However, high implementation costs, sales force resistance and under-utilisation have been cited as some of the key reasons for the failure to substantially increase productivity. This apparent conflict of views should be considered in the light of varying industry characteristics, operational circumstances and different definitions of SFA and technology. To date, there is little research evidence to show the impact of SFA on relationships. In addition to this are emerging ethical issues concerning SFA. For example, issues relating to sales force exploitation and control were identified by Bush *et al.* (2007) while they also found that SFA 'helps efficiency but hinders effectiveness aspects of sales force productivity' (p. 1203).

There can be little doubt that most salespeople use technology much more in their work than their counterparts of 20 years ago. However, it may be that technology is used by sales force personnel to engage with internal colleagues more than their customers. The greater adoption of SFA will only come through appropriate management leadership, training, accurate expectations and the influence and encouragement of users themselves (Morgan and Inks, 2001).

The future role of the sales force

For several years the performance networks of many markets have been in transition. This has influenced the structure and strategy of organisations and has stimulated recognition that organisations should seek cooperative relationships (Jarillo, 1993) rather than be competitive in the manner that Porter (1985) and the Design School advocates.

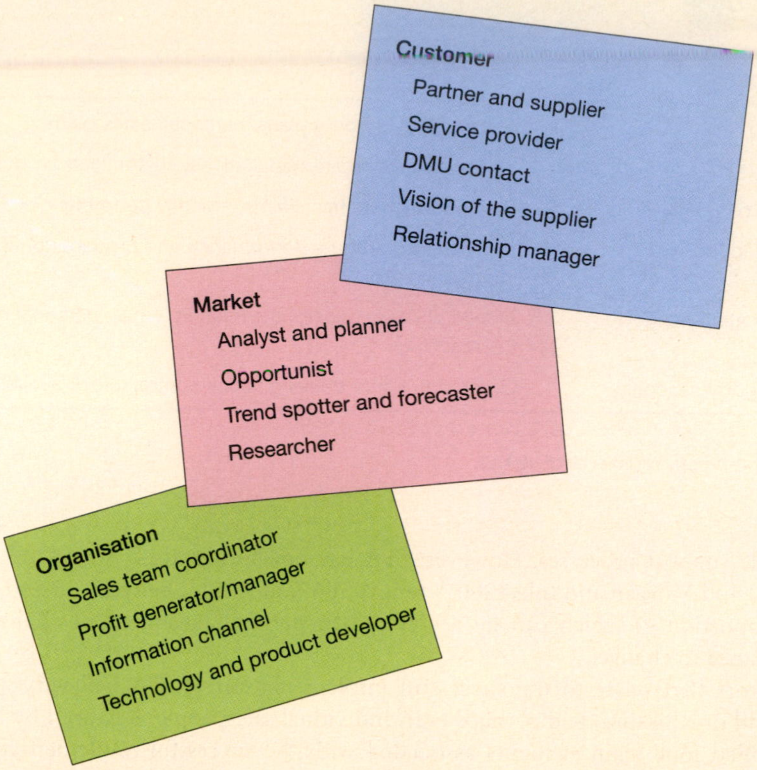

Figure 22.11 Changing roles for the sales force
Source: Adapted from Wilson (1993) and Anderson and Rosenbloom (1982).

Transition has also been brought about because of changing customer needs, the overall general health of the European economy and the shifting balance of key stakeholders. The expectations of organisational buyers and consumers have shifted so that new skills are required of a salesperson. Internally, organisations have moved their focus. For example, the manner in which performance is measured and resources are deployed has moved from a sales to a profit basis, while the sharp rise in costs of personal selling has required organisations to seek new ways of reaching and communicating with customers.

In consideration of the multiple sales channel approach and the factors that have brought significant change to the way in which field sales forces are organised, it is not surprising that the roles salespeople are expected to undertake are changing. Some of these roles are set out in Figure 22.11.

When these factors are brought together the salesperson, seen earlier as working at the boundary of the organisation to generate sales, is now expected to act as a network coordinator and as a manager of customers (Wilson, 1993). In Chapters 10 and 29 it is identified that a collaborative communication strategy seeks to establish long-term, relational transactions. The short-term, market exchange perspective hinders the development of strategic advantage. Strong personal interaction with clients, based on a problem–solution perspective to buyer needs, can provide a source of sustainable competitive advantage for organisations.

Integrating and coordinating the efforts of both the buying and the selling teams will become an important role for the salesperson, particularly as the effects of concentration lead to even greater levels of centralisation of the buying function.

The integration of personal selling with the other elements of the communications mix

Personal selling cannot work effectively in isolation from the other elements in the marketing communication mix. For example, members of the sales force are literally representative of the organisation for whom they work: they are mobile PR representatives. Stakeholders perceive them and partly shape their image of the selling organisation on the way in which, for example, the salesperson dresses, speaks and handles questions, the type of car driven and the level of courtesy displayed to the support staff.

> Personal selling cannot work effectively in isolation from the other elements in the marketing communication mix.

The integration and compatibility of direct marketing with the sales force have been discussed and the degree of impact should not be underestimated. The sales force's role within sales promotions can be strong, especially with activities directed at members of the performance network. Members of the sales force are often used to distribute promotional merchandise to both consumers and the trade.

It is with advertising that the strongest degree of integration with personal selling can be observed. As determined earlier, it would appear that these two elements of the communications mix complement each other in many ways. Advertising is more effective at the initial stages of the response hierarchy, but the later stages of inducing trial and closing for the order are more appropriate for personal selling.

As long ago as 1967, Levitt found that organisations that invest in advertising to create awareness are more likely to create a favourable reception for their salespeople than those organisations that do not invest in awareness-building activities. However, those that had invested were also expected to have a better-trained sales force.

Morrill (1970) found that selling costs were as much as 28 per cent lower if the customer had been made aware of the salesperson's organisation prior to the call. Swinyard and Ray (1977) determined that even if a sale was not made for reasons other than product quality, further use of advertising increased the probability of a future sale.

All these findings suggest that, by combining advertising with personal selling, costs will be reduced, reach extended and the probability of a sale considerably improved.

Summary

In order to help consolidate your understanding of personal selling, here are the key points summarised against each of the learning objectives:

1. Consider the different types, roles and tasks of personal selling.

The types of personal selling can be understood through the types of customer served, namely, *intermediaries*, *industrial*, *professional* and *consumers*. The tasks can be seen as one of four order-related tasks: *order takers*, *order getters*, *order collectors* and *order supporters*. The role of personal selling is largely one of representation.

2. Determine the strengths and weaknesses of personal selling as a form of communication.

Personal selling epitomises dyadic communications, allows for the receiver to focus attention on the salesperson and provides for fast, direct feedback. There is a greater level of participation in the decision process by the vendor than in the other tools and there is a reduced likelihood of distraction or noise.

Reach and frequency through personal selling are always going to be low, regardless of the amount of funds available. Control over message delivery is very often low and, while the flexibility is an advantage, there is also the disadvantage of message inconsistency. The costs per contact are extremely high, and this means that management must find alternative means of communicating particular messages and improve the amount of time that sales personnel spend with prospects and customers.

3. Explore the ways in which personal selling is thought to work.

Apart from the AIDA model, which is rather too simplistic, two other frameworks are considered. The stimulus–response model suggests that if a salesperson can create the right set of circumstances then it is probable that the buyer will react in a particular way. Therefore, by controlling the circumstances of the sales process it is possible to induce the desired response.

The problem–solution model works on the basis that a buyer first recognises a problem or a need. A solution is then found, which is purchased, and the buyer experiences a level of satisfaction. The solution contains two components, the product or service and the name of the organisation or the salesperson who facilitated the solution. To complete the formula, buyers must regard the product and the source as adequate and experience pleasant feelings when thinking of the components to the solution.

4. Establish the means by which management can organise a sales force.

Once an organisation has decided that a sales force is required the next decision concerns how many salespersons are required and where and how they should operate. Decisions regarding the type, structure, size and territory of the sales force will be discussed on the basis that this is the only sales channel used by an organisation.

Sales teams can be organised on a geographic product or market basis. These three approaches to sales force design are not mutually exclusive, and most major organisations use a combination of them to meet the needs of their various stakeholders.

5. Compare some of the principal methods by which the optimum size of a sales force can be derived.

Increasing the size of the sales force will increase sales revenue, but it will also increase costs. A balance needs to be achieved and the decision is often a blend of market and resource factors. Market-related issues concern the number of potential customers, the sales potential of each of these accounts, the geographic concentration of the customers and predictions concerning the strength and volatility of the economy. Resource-related issues concern the corporate and marketing strategy, competitive conditions and the availability of financial resources.

There are many different approaches to the determination of the appropriate sales force size. Many of the more recent ones are based on sophisticated software, but these are derived essentially from three main approaches: the *breakdown*, *workload* and *sales potential* methods.

6. Discuss the future role of the sales force.

The role of personal selling in the promotional mix is changing. As organisations move to more relational exchanges, so the sales force will need to play a complementary role. The sales force will need to be deployed in a way that optimises the resources of the organisation and realises the greatest possible percentage of the available sales and profit potential that exists in the defined area of operation. This will result in a continuance of the growth of key accounts.

The use of the field sales force as the primary means of communication is unlikely to remain. Technological advances and the need for increasing levels of promotional effectiveness and accountability, together with tighter cost constraints, indicate that the more progressive organisations will employ multiple sales channels. This may mean the use of telemarketing and direct mail to free the sales force from non-selling activities, which will allow management to focus the time of the sales force on getting in front of customers and prospects, with a view to using their particular selling skills.

Review questions

1. What are the different types of personal selling?
2. Describe the role of personal selling and highlight its main strengths and weaknesses.
3. Which factors need to be considered when determining the significance of personal selling in the promotional mix?
4. What are the tasks that salespersons are normally expected to accomplish?
5. Describe two ways in which the personal selling process is thought to work.
6. Write a brief report highlighting the strengths and weaknesses of each of the main ways of structuring the sales force.
7. Identify the principal differences between the workload and the sales potential methods of determining sales force size.
8. Write brief notes outlining the way in which direct marketing might be used to assist personal selling activities.
9. Suggest four new roles that salespersons might be required to adopt in the future.
10. If an organisation seeks to establish relational exchanges with its partner organisations and customers, the size of the field sales force should be increased. Discuss.

MiniCase Selling the benefits of personal selling

David Stringer: Business Development Director

Introduction

With twenty-first-century technology it might be thought that personal selling would be redundant. In the world of business sales, where companies operate professional procurement departments, the buyer can gather all information via the web, request a brochure, develop an evaluation matrix, make their decision and place their order online.

For simple commodities this may be applicable, but when the purchasing decision is associated with risk, with many stakeholders an assurance is needed through the development of business relationships, which is where personal selling has many advantages.

Johnson & Johnson Orthopaedics (JJO) specialise in the production of artificial knee caps and hips. Their main UK customer, the NHS, hold minimal stock levels at each hospital. Once this stock is exhausted, i.e. through unforeseen Accident & Emergency requirements, it needs to be replenished quickly.

The products are small and their customer's are spread nationwide. It is neither practical, nor cost-effective, for JJO to operate their own transport fleet. They rely on third-party transport companies to provide a reliable, nationwide parcel delivery service. In order to avoid operations being cancelled, product is often needed first thing in the morning. Failure to deliver on time could result in loss of reputation and customers to

Johnson & Johnson and negate their own sales force's good work.

As part of their own sales activity JJO employ technically skilled account managers, who even observe operations and work closely with orthopaedic consultants developing new products.

JJO's incumbent parcel company had become unreliable, manifest through complaints to the sales force, who in turn placed pressure on customer services and the despatch department.

JJO's procurement department became involved and evaluated the market. They invited ten companies to tender on a contractual basis. They first courted the opinions of the sales force, customer services and the despatch department to identify the elements each deemed important in a delivery service.

The evaluation process began at the enquiry stage. They measured the quality of response to their initial enquiry, as communication skills were deemed important, as was time-keeping. Each company was invited to an initial briefing with the procurement manager, to understand the client's requirement and to offer a suitable solution.

Amazingly, of the ten companies who were invited to attend, only two arrived on time for their appointment. Two arrived late, but rang ahead to advise they had been delayed. The other six were late. As the procurement manager later alluded, 'If they can't arrive on time for the appointment, what hope have they of delivering my parcels?' The six late companies were excluded.

Following the first initial meetings three companies were short-listed and invited to make a formal presentation of the key benefits they would provide. The presentation was to be made to the procurement, customer services and despatch managers.

One of these companies was TNT Express. Their salesman had made an extremely positive first impression, being one of the two to arrive on time for his appointment. He was professionally dressed in a smart business suit and was standing when he met the procurement manager. He made immediate eye contact and greeted the procurement manager confidently. Unlike some other salesmen who went through a regimented, set presentation in the hope of stumbling across an area of interest, he spent most of the initial meeting listening and asking questions. He was able to ascertain that although price was important, reliability, ease of communication and flexibility were of greater importance.

The invitation was communicated by telephone, as the salesman had proactively phoned to ask whether he had been short-listed. He also ascertained who would be at the meeting and their roles.

For the presentation, the salesman also invited the regional director of TNT Express to attend. The participation of a senior decision-maker further enhanced trust and demonstrated commitment.

At the meeting the salesmen outlined the benefits that TNT could provide. He focused on reliability and quality. TNT were the first UK parcel carrier to obtain the BS5750 quality accreditation and this reinforced their quality ethos. Through their innovative 'hub and spoke' distribution system, he also emphasised the enhanced delivery services they offered.

JJO's current parcel carrier offered a next-day service with the option of before 10 a.m. and 12 noon deliveries to England only. TNT Express offered next-day, but also offered before noon, before 10.30 a.m. and before 9 a.m. deliveries including the major cities of Scotland (including Aberdeen) and Belfast. These services appealed to the customer services manager, as often their account managers would request early deliveries to their homes, before they left for appointments. A before 9 a.m. delivery service would also be beneficial for emergency deliveries. The salesman also provided a complete telephone list of all the key staff at the local depot, to enhance the relationship between the companies.

TNT has a telephone policy that all calls are directly routed, without the customer name or purpose of the call being requested. This enables a culture of empowerment and responsibility among their staff, focused on total customer satisfaction.

This commitment to quality was reinforced by the offer to provide a weekly report of the times and details of every delivery made the previous week. This report was normally only provided to the local depot's largest customers. Again, this offered benefits to the customer services department as they were able to pass on this information both to the sales team and to the accounts department, enabling the latter to invoice promptly.

A total of an hour was allocated for the presentation and questions. The salesman deliberately kept his presentation short, at 15 minutes, thereby allowing for a thorough questions and answers session, in which he hoped that further key issues could be explored. It was ascertained that the current delivery company called quite early in the afternoon to collect the parcels. This effectively meant that orders could only be accepted in the morning, as it took, on average, two hours for the despatch department to accurately process orders.

TNT allocated delivery vehicles to defined postcode areas, as they did for their salesmen. This encouraged the forming of relationships between drivers and customers, as well as strengthening internal relationships.

The salesman knew each of his drivers (for example, where they stopped for lunch) as they were a great source of local knowledge. He knew that he could offer a later collection time of 4 p.m.

After 40 minutes, he summarised the current situation and offered a solution. The use of a summary gave both parties the opportunity to check understanding and ensure the proposal fully met Johnson & Johnson requirements. Competitor analysis and market knowledge had led him to believe that the prices he would offer would be substantially higher than his competitor's. His summary emphasised quality, communication and flexibility and the additional sales, both new and retained, which Johnson & Johnson would gain through a reliable service.

He offered his best available price and went for a conditional close by asking 'When would you like collections to commence?'. Deliberately asking an open question to identify any objections. The procurement manager replied that although they were impressed with the service package, they could not justify such a large increase in price, which amounted to nearly 30 per cent.

Here the involvement of the regional director was beneficial. He offered a lower price, above the salesman's authority level, but still 20 per cent higher than the incumbent. He also asked what time customer services and despatch worked too. This was 6 p.m. The regional director then offered to speak to the local operations manager and request that a second collection vehicle call at 6 p.m. for 'emergency' collections.

This again reinforced customer confidence, as they knew that the request (order) would be implemented. The customer services and despatch manager clearly saw the benefits of the TNT proposal, through a reduction in complaints and enhanced flexibility. The procurement manager's responsibility was to minimise risk and maximise value.

On an 'apples to apples' comparison TNT was still 20 per cent higher, but by offering additional features, especially the second collection vehicle, she was rightly able to state that she had gained additional benefits and concessions, thereby justifying the additional cost.

The regional director made no apology for being the most expensive, justifying not only the ongoing investment made in the national infrastructure, but also the training and recruitment of quality staff. He stated that 'quality was remembered long after price was forgotten', and that TNT had a responsibility to be profitable, to be able to form long-term partnerships with their customers.

The meeting closed with a commitment to ring the procurement manager to confirm the availability of the second collection vehicle, while JJO reviewed the presentation and evaluated the offer.

After the other two companies were interviewed, the JJO team evaluated the benefits of each company. The revised TNT offer was the most expensive, but offered the most reliability. It crucially extended the working day by four hours, with the option for customers to receive items before 9 a.m. These were major benefits to the customer services and sales teams. Due to the delivery difficulties, the procurement process was accelerated and took less than two weeks.

As promised, the salesman rang the procurement manager the following morning, to confirm the availability of the second collection vehicle. He then asked whether they had reviewed all three companies and made a decision. The procurement manager responded 'yes', and they would like to start collections the following Monday.

MiniCase questions

1. What were the criteria Johnson & Johnson deemed important in a parcel carrier? Whose opinion was sought by the procurement department?
2. What techniques did the TNT salesman use to create trust and develop a relationship?
3. How did the TNT salesman identify and overcome objections at the final interview?

References

Anderson, R.E. and Oliver, R.L. (1987) Perspectives on behavior-based versus outcome-based salesforce control systems. *Journal of Marketing*, **51** (October), 76–88.

Anderson, R.E. and Rosenbloom, B. (1982) Eclectic sales management: strategic responses to trends in the 1980s. *Journal of Personal Selling and Sales Management* (November), 41–6.

Armistead, L. (2002) Forms sold short by bad sales technique. *Sunday Times*, 20 October, 17.

Baldauf, A., Cravens, D.W. and Grant, K. (2002) Consequences of sales management control in field sales organisations: a cross-national perspective. *International Business Review*, **11**(5) (October), 577–609.

Bush, A.J., Bush, V.D., Orr, L.M. and Rocco, R.A. (2007) Sales technology: help or hindrance to ethical behaviours and productivity? *Journal of Business Research*, **60**(11) (November), 1198–1205.

Cespedes, F.V., Doyle, S.X. and Freedman, R.J. (1989) Teamwork for today's selling. *Harvard Business Review* (March/April), 44–55.

Churchill, G.A., Ford, N.M. and Walker, C. (1990) *Sales Force Management*. Homewood, IL: Irwin.

Cravens, D.W. (1987) *Strategic Marketing*. Homewood, IL: Irwin.

Engle, R.L. and Barnes, M.L. (2000) Sales force automation usage, effectiveness and cost benefit in Germany, England and the United States. *Journal of Business and Industrial Marketing*, **15**(4), 216–42.

Govoni, N., Eng, R. and Galper, M. (1986) *Promotional Management*. Englewood Cliffs, NJ: Prentice-Hall.

Grant, K. and Cravens, D.W. (1999) Examining the antecedents of sales organisation effectiveness: an Australian study. *European Journal of Marketing*, **33**(9/10), 945–57.

Guenzi, P. (2002) Sales force activities and customer trust. *Journal of Marketing Management*, **18**, 749–78.

Honeycutt, Jr. E.D., Thelen, T., Thelen, S.T. and Hodge, S.K. (2005) Impediments to sales force automation. *Industrial Marketing Management*, **34**(4) (May), 313–22.

Ingram, T.N., LaForge, R.W. and Leigh, T.W. (2002) Selling in the new millennium. *Industrial Marketing Management*, **32**(7) (October), 559–67.

Jarillo, J.C. (1993) *Strategic Networks: Creating the Borderless Organisation*. Oxford: Butterworth-Heinemann.

Jolson, M.A. (1975) The underestimated potential of the canned sales presentation. *Journal of Marketing*, **39** (January), 75.

Levitt, T. (1967) Communications and industrial selling. *Journal of Marketing*, **31** (April), 15–21.

Lloyd, J. (1997) Cut your rep free. *Pharmaceutical Marketing* (September), 30–2.

McCroskey, J.C. (1984) The communication apprehension perspective. In *Avoiding Communication* (ed. J.A. Daley), 13–38, Beverly Hills, CA: Sage.

Morgan, A.J. and Inks, S.A. (2001) Technology and the sales force: increasing acceptance of sales force automation. *Industrial Marketing Management*, **30**(5) (July), 463–72.

Morrill, J.E. (1970) Industrial advertising pays off. *Harvard Business Review* (March/April), 159–69.

Piercy, N.F., Cravens, D.W. and Morgan, N.A. (1998) Salesforce performance and behaviour-based management processes in business-to-business sales organisations. *European Journal of Marketing*, **32**(1/2), 79–100.

Piercy, N.F., Low, G.S. and Cravens, D.W. (2004) Consequences of sales management's behavior- and compensation-based control strategies in developing countries. *Journal of International Marketing*, **12**(3), 30–57.

Pitt, L.F., Berthon, P.R. and Robson, M.J. (2000) Communication apprehension and perceptions of salesperson performance: a multinational perspective. *Journal of Managerial Psychology*, **15**(1), 68–97.

Porter, M.E. (1985) *Competitive Advantage: Creating and Sustaining Superior Performance.* New York: Free Press.

Rackham, N. and DeVincetis, J.R. (1999) *Rethinking the Sales Force: Redefining Selling to Create and Capture Customer Value.* New York: McGraw-Hill.

Reid, A., Pullins, E.B. and Plank, R.E. (2002) The impact of purchase situation on salesperson communication behaviors in business markets. *Industrial Marketing Management*, **31**(3), 205–13.

Rothschild, M.L. (1987) *Marketing Communications.* Lexington, MA: D.C. Heath.

Semlow, W.E. (1959) How many salesmen do you need? *Harvard Business Review* (May/June), 126–32.

Srivastava, R.K., Shervani, T.A. and Fahey, L. (1999) Marketing, business process and shareholder value: an organizationally embedded view of marketing activities and the discipline of marketing. *Journal of Marketing*, **63**, 168–79.

Still, R., Cundiff, E.W. and Govoni, N.A.P. (1988) *Sales Management*, 5th edn. Englewood Cliffs, NJ: Prentice-Hall.

Strong, E.K. (1925) *The Psychology of Selling.* New York: McGraw-Hill.

Strong, E.K. (1938) *Psychological Aspects of Business.* New York: McGraw-Hill.

Stuart, E.W. and Fuller, B.K. (1991) Clothing as communication in two business-to-business sales settings. *Journal of Business Research*, **23**, 269–90.

Swinyard, W.R. and Ray, M.L. (1977) Advertising–selling interactions: an attribution theory experiment. *Journal of Marketing Research*, **14** (November), 509–16.

Thayer, L. (1968) *Communication and Communication Systems.* Homewood, IL: Irwin.

Widmier, S.M., Jackson Jr, D.W. and McCabe, D.B. (2002) Infusing technology into personal selling. *Journal of Personal Selling and Sales Management*, **22**(3) (Summer), 189–99.

Wilson, K. (1993) Managing the industrial sales force of the 1990s. *Journal of Marketing Management*, **9**, 123–39.

Workman Jr, J.P., Homburg, C. and Jensen, O. (2003) Interorganisational determinants of key account management effectiveness. *Journal of Academy of Marketing Science*, **31**(1), 3–21.

Wright, H. and Fill, C. (2001) Corporate images, attributes, and the UK pharmaceutical industry. *Corporate Reputation Review: An International Journal*, **4**(2) (Summer), 99–112.

Chapter 23

Exhibitions, product placement, field marketing and packaging

The five major tools of the communications mix work better if supported by other secondary or support tools and media. Exhibitions are a significant part of b2b promotional work, and packaging is vital to the fast-moving consumer goods sector as the majority of product decisions are made at the point of purchase. Product placement enables brands to be seen in the correct context and used by appropriate celebrities in order to help form brand associations for consumers. Field marketing offers a range of merchandising and brand experience opportunities often necessary to cut through the clutter of competitive and distracting messages.

Aims and learning objectives

The aims of this chapter are to consider a range of marketing communications activities that have no specific designation, yet which can make a major contribution to a promotional campaign. These activities are applied to both the b2b and b2c markets.

The learning objectives of this chapter are to:

1. explain the significance of exhibitions and trade shows;
2. consider the main advantages and disadvantages of using exhibitions as part of the communication mix;
3. understand the concept and issues associated with product placement;
4. explore ideas associated with field marketing and related activities;
5. examine the role and key characteristics of packaging as a form of marketing communication.

For an applied interpretation see Jim Blythe's MiniCase entitled ***Sustainability*live!** at the end of this chapter.

Introduction

The majority of marketing communications presented so far focus on the five primary tools and both traditional and digital media. However, in order to provide a difference and to cut through the noise of competing brands it is necessary to provide additional resources and communications right up to the point when customers make decisions. This chapter considers several other important means of communicating with both customers and distributor: exhibitions, product placement, field marketing and packaging.

Exhibitions fulfil a role for customers by enabling them to become familiar with new developments, new products and leading-edge brands. Very often these customers will be opinion leaders and use word-of-mouth communications to convey their feelings and product experiences to others. In the b2b market, exhibitions and trade shows are very often an integral and important component in the communications mix. Meeting friends, customers, suppliers, competitors and prospective customers is an important sociological and ritualistic event in the communication calendar for many companies. In the consumer sector, and in particular the FMCG market, it is important to provide a point of difference and offer continuity for those people who make the brand choice decisions at the point of purchase.

> In the b2b market, exhibitions and trade shows are very often an integral and important component in the communications mix.

Product placement enables a brand to be observed in a more natural environment than if viewed on a shelf. This part of marketing communications is growing and provides income for film producers, authenticity for brand managers and relief from advertising for consumers. Field marketing has emerged out of what was formally referred to as merchandising but now encompasses a wider range of activities, one of which is experiential marketing, again a growing and important aspect of marketing communications for several product categories.

Finally, this chapter considers the impact of packaging as a form of marketing communication. Not only does packaging fulfil the role of protecting a product, it also conveys associations and brand cues, many of which are important means by which consumers make brand choice decisions.

Trade shows and exhibitions

The idea of many suppliers joining together at a particular location in order to set out their products and services so that customers may meet, make comparisons and place orders is far from new. Indeed, not only does this form of promotional activity stretch back many centuries, it has also been used to explain the way the Internet works (Bertheron *et al.*, 1996). They refer to the Internet as a virtual flea circus, a forum where buyers and sellers can meet, browse, discuss, find out more information and buy products and services if appropriate.

At a basic level, trade fairs can be oriented for industrial users or consumers and the content or purpose might be to consider general or specialised products/markets. According to Boukersi (2000), consumer-oriented general fairs tend to be larger and last longer than the more specialised industrial fairs and it is clear that this more highly segmented and focused approach is proving more successful, based on the increasing number of these types of exhibitions.

> Trade fairs can be oriented for industrial users or consumers.

Reasons to use exhibitions

There are many reasons to use exhibitions, but the primary reasons appear not to be 'to make sales' or 'because the competition is there' but because these events provide opportunities to meet potential and established customers and to create and sustain a series of relational exchanges. The main aim, therefore, is to develop long-term partnerships with customers, to build upon or develop the corporate identity and to gather up-to-date market intelligence (Shipley and Wong, 1993). This implies that exhibitions should not be used as isolated events, but that they should be integrated into a series of activities, which serve to develop and sustain buyer relationships.

After a tentative start to the 1990s, the exhibition industry has grown and is now experiencing real growth. With managers increasingly accountable for their promotional spend, a greater number of budgets are now channelled into exhibitions and related events. In 1995, visitors attended 773 exhibitions in the United Kingdom, where venues exceeded 2,000 square feet. By 2005, the number had risen to 944 exhibitions (Advertising Association, 2008).

Costs can be reduced by using private exhibitions.

Costs can be reduced by using private exhibitions. The increased flexibility allows organisations to produce mini or private exhibitions for their clients at local venues (e.g. hotels). This can mean lower costs for the exhibitor and reduced time away from their businesses for those attending. The communication 'noise' and distraction associated with the larger public events can also be avoided by these private showings.

Characteristics of exhibitions and trade shows

Exhibitions and trade fairs enable organisations to meet customers, place/take orders generate leads and gather market information.

The main reasons for attending exhibitions and trade fairs are that they enable organisations to meet customers (and potential customers) in an agreeable environment, one where both have independently volunteered their time to attend; to place/take orders; to generate leads; and to gather market information. The reasons for attending exhibitions are set out in Table 23.1.

From this it is possible to distinguish the following strengths and weaknesses of using exhibitions as part of the marketing communications programme.

Strengths

The costs associated with exhibitions, if controlled properly, can mean that this is an effective and efficient means of communicating with customers. The costs per inquiry need to be calculated, but care needs to be taken over who is classified as an inquirer, as the quality of the audience varies considerably. Costs per order taken are usually the prime means of evaluating the success of an exhibition. This can paint a false picture, as the true success can never really be determined in terms of orders because of the variety of other factors that impinge upon the placement and timing of orders.

Table 23.1 Reasons exhibitors choose to attend exhibitions

To meet existing customers
To take orders/make sales
To get leads and meet prospective new customers
To meet lapsed customers
To meet prospective members of the existing or new marketing channels
To provide market research opportunities and to collect marketing data.

ViewPoint 23.1 Making a fishy exhibition of themselves

Too many exhibitors fail to stand out on their stands, to the extent that staff are very often indistinguishable from visitors. When a new company attended its first two exhibitions it made a deliberate effort to stand out.

No Catch, a supplier of sustainable organic cod, needed to reach retailers of various shapes and sizes and so decided to use two exhibitions to achieve their objectives. One of these was a trade show, the biggest seafood show in the world, namely the Brussels European Seafood Exposition. The other was a consumer show, the BBC Good Food Show.

As there were over 1,800 exhibitors at Brussels it was vital that No Catch stood out. This they achieved by building a stand based on a Caribbean beach shack and dressing staff in surfer clothes. The stand was complemented with graffiti, beach balls, reggae music and a barbecue cooking Caribbean-style organic fish recipes.

The same approach had been used previously at the BBC Food Show and the results from the two exhibitions were quite clear. They made contact with all the European distributors and even won the vote by journalists and consumers as the best product at the BBC Food Show.

Source: Allen (2007).

Question

What do you think is the main reason to attend exhibitions; to make sales or to meet contacts, friends and others in the industry?

Task

Choose a product and then consider how you would present the brand at a consumer or trade show.

Exhibit 23.1 The No Catch exhibition stand
ING MEDIA.

ViewPoint 23.2 Making an exhibition of Ireland

The development of Ireland's tourism market involves attracting both individuals for vacations and also the business market in terms of conferences, events and meetings. One thing that is common to both groups is the opportunity to visit and enjoy the breathtaking scenery and the warmth and friendliness of the people.

Some of Ireland's recent economic changes included an advantageous set of tax breaks designed to encourage investment in the construction industry. One of the results of this initiative has been the development of a huge number of recently completed high quality hotels, many with conference centres. Thus, with a wealth of excellent suppliers, the challenge for Tourism Ireland at the International Confex 2007 exhibition was to stand out among the other 1,075 exhibitors and attract conference organisers to their exhibition platform.

To encourage visitors it was decided to send out mailers to key conference organisers prior to the exhibition and give them a reason to visit the Tourism Ireland stand. These mailers were designed to be personal invitations and included an invitation to experience some genuine Irish hospitality in the form of a Hot Irishman (coffee liqueur) or a Guinness. This was to be symbolic of the opportunities to relax away from a conference. Normally a return of 3 per cent might be expected for a mailer of this type. However, 2.9 per cent responded asking for more information because they were unable to attend the exhibition, while a further 7.1 per cent attended the stand. An overall response rate of 10 per cent was achieved.

Source: UTalk (2007).

Question

Why was direct mail used to reach conference organisers?

Task

How would you attract business people to attend an exhibition on office equipment?

Products can be launched at exhibitions, and when integrated with a good PR campaign a powerful impact can be made. This can also be used to reinforce corporate identity. Exhibitions are an important means of gaining information about competitors, buyers and technical and political developments in the market, and they often serve to facilitate the recruitment process. Above all else, exhibitions provide an opportunity to meet customers on relatively neutral ground and, through personal interaction, develop relationships. Products can be demonstrated, prices agreed, technical problems discussed and trust and credibility enhanced.

Weaknesses

One of the main drawbacks associated with exhibition work is the vast and disproportionate amount of management time that can be tied up with the planning and implementation of exhibitions. However, good planning is essential if the full potential benefits of exhibition work are to be realised.

Taking members of the sales force 'off the road' can also incur large costs. Depending on the nature of the business these opportunity costs can soar. Some pharmaceutical organisations estimate that it can cost approximately £5,000 per person per week to divert salespeople in this way.

The expected visitor profile must be analysed in order that the number of quality buyers visiting an exhibition can be determined. The variety of visitors attending an exhibition can be misleading, as the vast majority may not be serious buyers or, indeed, may not be directly related to the industry or the market in question.

Exhibitions as a form of marketing communications

As a form of marketing communications, exhibitions enable products to be promoted, they can build brands and they can be an effective means of demonstrating products and building industry-wide credibility in a relatively short period of time. Attendance at exhibitions may also be regarded from a political standpoint, in that non-attendance by competitors may be taken as an opportunity by attendees to suggest weaknesses.

In the b2b sector new products and services are often introduced at exhibitions, especially if there are to be public relations activities and events that can be spun off the launch. In other words, exhibitions are not activities independent of the other communication tools. Exhibitions, if used effectively, can be part of an integrated communications campaign. Advertising prior to, during and after a trade show can be dovetailed with public relations, sponsorship and personal selling. Sales promotions can also be incorporated through competitions among customers prior to the show to raise awareness, generate interest and to suggest customer involvement. Competitions during a show can be focused on the sales force to motivate and stimulate commercial activity and among visitors to generate interest in the stand, raise brand name awareness and encourage focus on particular products (new, revised or revolutionary) and generate sales leads and enquiries.

Exhibitions are not activities independent of the other communication tools.

New media and exhibitions

In many ways the use of the Internet and a web site as brochureware represented a first attempt at an online exhibition. In these situations, commercial organisations provided opportunities for people who physically could not get to see a product to gain some appreciation of its size, configuration and capability (through text). However, the development of multimedia technologies has given not only commercial but also not-for-profit organisations the opportunity to showcase their wares on a global basis. One type of organisation to explore the use of this technology has been museums and art collections (static exhibits). Khoon *et al.* (2003) refer to the American History Documents (at www.indiana.edu/liblilly/histy/), Exploring Africa (at www.sc.edu/library/spcoll/sccoll/africa) and SCRAN (at www.scran.ac.uk) (which is a multimedia resource for Scottish history and culture) as examples of previous work and facilities in this area. The use of multimedia technologies enables audiences across the world to access these collections and with the use of audio, video clips and streaming video, in addition to pictures and extensive text, these exhibitions can be brought to life, visited repeatedly, focus given to particular exhibits, materials updated quickly and unobtrusively and links made to other similar facilities. The key difference between this development and previous brochureware-type facilities is the feeling of virtual reality, the sense that a digital visitor is actually in the exhibition, even though seated several thousand miles away.

The use of ecommerce and digital media in the management and presentation of exhibitions is likely to increase. It is unlikely that online exhibitions will ever replace the offline, real-world version, if only because of the need to form relationships and to network with industry members, to touch and feel products and to sense the atmosphere and vitality that exhibitions generate. However, there is huge scope to develop specialised exhibitions, to develop online showcases that incorporate exhibits (products and services) from a variety of geographically dispersed locations.

Marketing management of exhibitions

Good management of exhibitions represents some key aspects of marketing communications in general. Successful events are driven by planning that takes place prior to the exhibition,

Stands should be designed to deliver key messages.

with communications inviting a range of stakeholders, not just customers, in advance of the exhibition event. Stands should be designed to deliver key messages and press releases and press information packs should be prepared and distributed appropriately.

During the event itself staff should be well briefed, trained and knowledgeable about their role in terms of the brand and in the exhibition process. After the exhibition it is vital to follow up on contacts made and discussions or negotiations that have been held. In other words, the exhibition itself is a planned marketing communications activity, one where activities need to be planned prior to, during and after the event. What is key is that these activities are coordinated, themed and supported by brand-oriented staff.

Above all else, exhibitions are an important way of building relationships and signalling corporate identity. Trade shows are an important means of providing corporate hospitality and showing gratitude to all an organisation's customers, but in particular to its key account customers and others of strategic interest. Positive relationships with customers, competitors and suppliers are often reinforced through face-to-face dialogue that happens both formally in the exhibition hall and informally through the variety of social activities that surround and support these events.

Product placement

One way of overcoming the irritation factor associated with advertisements screened in cinemas prior to a film showing is to incorporate the product in the film that is shown. This practice is referred to as product placement, which is the inclusion of products and services in films (or media) for deliberate promotional exposure, often, but not always, in return for an agreed financial sum. It is regarded by some as a form of sales promotion, by others as sponsorship, but for the purposes of this text it is treated as an advertising medium because the 'advertiser' pays a third party for the opportunity to present the product in their channel.

Product placement is the inclusion of products and services in films (or media) for deliberate promotional exposure.

A wide variety of products can be placed in this way, including drinks (both soft and alcoholic), confectionery, newspapers, cars, airlines, perfume and even holiday destinations and sports equipment. However, the development of product placement has inevitably led to new formats and fresh approaches, some of which only serve to muddy the waters.

Hudson and Hudson (2006) set out the development of product placement. Early forms of product placement concerned brand owners making deals with film producers and film stars to openly endorse the brand. The brand owner would fund props and facilities for the film in return for spoken and visual endorsement. Some of the first television programmes were named after the brands that sponsored them, for example, *The Colgate Comedy Hour* and the *Kraft Television Theatre* (Hudson and Hudson, 2006).

The establishment of product placement agencies in the 1980s helped formalise the process and removed much of the barter and haggling that had typified arrangements. The turning point occurred when the film *ET* depicted an alien being lured by Reese's Pieces. Hershey, the manufacturer, saw sales rise 65 per cent following the release of the film and since then product placement has grown year on year.

Two distinct forms of product placement-related activity have emerged.

Two distinct forms of product placement-related activity have emerged, partly as a result of the proliferation of the media, the consequential surge in the production of entertainment programmes and the media industries, need to generate income streams. Rather than place a product within a film, television or radio programme where it assumes a passive role, hoping to get noticed, a new approach sees whole entertainment programmes built around a single product. In contrast to the passivity of product placement, here a brand is actively woven into the theme or the plot of the programme. This latter approach has been labelled 'branded entertainment'. Hudson and Hudson (2006) depict this as a continuum, represented at Figure 23.1.

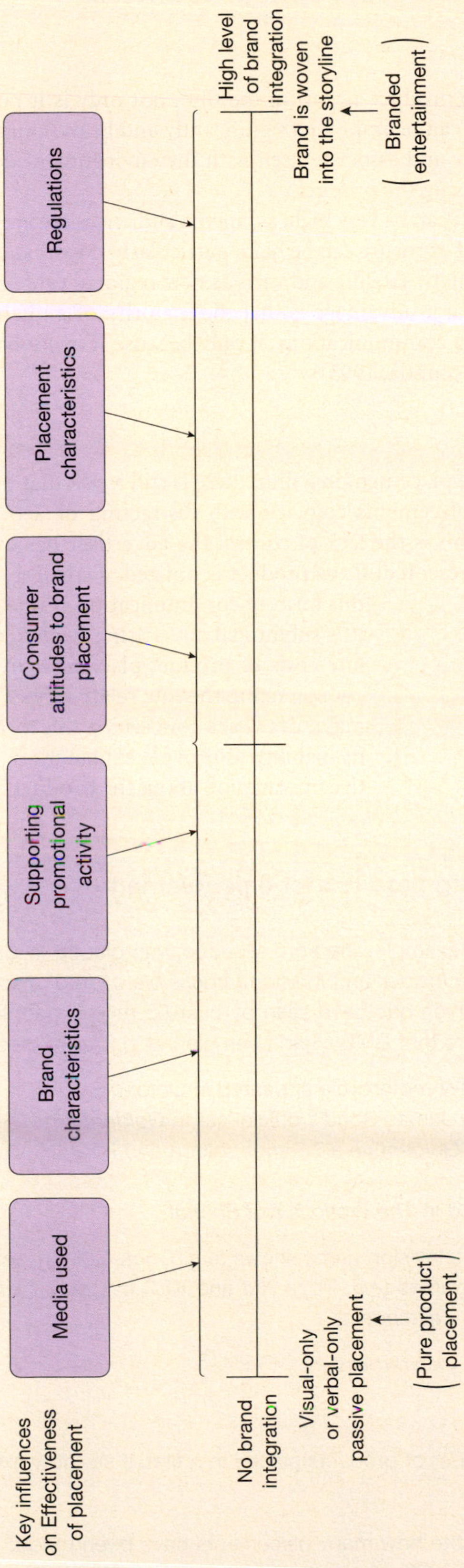

Figure 23.1 The product placement-branded entertainment continuum
Source: Hudson and Hudson (2006). Reproduced by permission of Westburn Publishers Ltd.

Characteristics of product placement

Strengths

By presenting the product as part of the film, not only is it possible to build awareness, but source credibility can be improved significantly and brand images reinforced. The audience is assisted to identify and associate itself with the environment depicted in the film or with the celebrity who is using the product.

Levels of impact can be very high, as cinema audiences are very attentive to large-screen presentations. Rates of exposure can be high, particularly now that cinema films are being released through video outlets, satellite and various new regional cable and television organisations.

Perhaps the major advantage is that the majority of audiences appear to approve of this form of marketing communications, if only because it is unobtrusive and integral to the film (Nebenzahl and Secunda, 1993).

Weaknesses

Having achieved a placement in a film, there is still a risk that the product will run unnoticed, especially if the placements coincide with distracting or action-oriented parts of the film. Associated with this is the lack of control the advertiser has over when, where and how the product will be presented. If the product is noticed, a small minority of audiences claim that this form of communication is unethical; it is even suggested that it is subliminal advertising, which is, of course, illegal. The absolute costs of product placement in films can be extremely high, counteracting the low relative costs or cost per contact. The final major drawback concerning this form of communication concerns its inability to provide explanation, detail, or indeed any substantive information about the product. The product is seen in use and

The product is seen in use and is hopefully associated with an event, person(s) or objects that provide a source of pleasure, inspiration or aspiration for the individual viewer.

ViewPoint 23.3 Placing products for entertainment

Cars are often placed in films, for example, the Ford Mondeo was placed in *Casino Royale* and Audi has placed cars in the films *Ronin*, *The Insider* and *Mission Impossible II*. Audi also developed a futuristic car especially for the film *I, ROBOT* which has been seen by over 55 million people. Aston Martins feature in recent James Bond films, but before that BMWs had been placed in four of these films:

- 1983 – BMW 5 Series and a BMW motorcycle appeared in *Octopussy*;
- 1994 – the Z3 Roadster became James Bond's official car in *GoldenEye*;
- 1997 – following the success of *GoldenEye* a 7 Series saloon and R1200C Cruiser motorcycle appeared in *Tomorrow Never Dies*;
- 1999 – the Z8 sports car featured in *The World is Not Enough*.

Products can also be placed in television game shows (e.g. Coca-Cola in *American Idol*), in books (e.g. *The Bulgari Connection*), in video games (e.g. Pizza Hut and KFC in *Crazy Taxi*) in TV dramas and soaps (Audi in *Silent Witness* and Saab in *Eastenders*).

Sources: Various including Plaut (2004); www.bmw.com/.

Question

Should there be a limit on the number of products placed in a film, if so, how many and why?

Task

Watch *Casino Royale* (again) and note how many placements have been made.

is hopefully associated with an event, person(s) or objects that provide a source of pleasure, inspiration or aspiration for the individual viewer.

Product placement is not confined to cinema films. Music videos, television plays, dramas and soap operas can also use this method to present advertisers' products. The novel *The Sweetest Taboo*, written by novelist Carole Matthews, includes frequent references to various Ford cars, which is not surprising as Ford paid her to mention their cars in her work (Plaut, 2004). Pervan and Martin (2002) found that product placement in television soaps was an effective communications activity. They also concluded that the way a product is used in the soap, i.e. positive and negative outcomes, may well have important implications for the attitudes held towards these brands. In addition, they suggested that organisations should study the consumption imagery associated with placed products as this might yield significant information about the way in which these products are actually consumed. Product placement is not confined to offline communications. For example, the toothpaste brand Pearl Drops has been written into the plotline and integrated into the social network Bebo's interactive drama called *Sofia's Diary*, a teen-targeted programme.

Product placement is not confined to cinema films. Music videos, television plays, dramas and soap operas can also use this method.

Placement issues

The nature of a placement and the impact it has on the audience appear to be affected by a number of variables. Important issues concern: the placement and its association with the storyline; whether the actors use the product or it remains a background object; if the product fits the plot; the degree to which the product is prominently displayed; and the amount of time that the product is actually exposed. Karrh *et al.* (2003) refer to the relative lack of control that marketers have over product placement activities, but confirm that in comparison to advertising equivalents, product placement can have a far greater impact on audiences and in most cases at a fraction of the cost of a 30-second advertisement. Russell and Belch (2005) refer to difficulties relating to the way the value of product placement is perceived. There is a view, held by creative and media agencies that the 'number of seconds on screen' is a valid measurement of effectiveness. Many do not agree and prefer to consider the context of the placement and the level of continuity within a defined communications strategy as more meaningful measures.

Field marketing

Field marketing is a relatively new sector of the industry and seeks to provide support for the sales force and merchandising personnel along with data collection and research facilities for clients. The sector started as a way of ensuring that products were accessible in retail outlets (McLuhan, 2007). Based on merchandising and shelf-positioning skills, this aspect of field marketing remains important. McLuhan reports that 'at least 4 per cent of an fmcg's product's sales depend on getting this right; the rate is higher for other product types' (p. 9). Although this element remains important, field marketing has evolved so that it now encompasses ways in which people can experience a brand. This reflects an overall shift in marketing communications from one based largely on developing brand values through an emotional proposition, to one that emphasises changes in behaviour and calls-to-action.

The Field Marketing Council (FMC) states that the sector is about the use of people to communicate sales and marketing messages. This is quite an open remit and reflects the wide range of activities that practitioners within the area have recently encompassed. At a basic level, field marketing is concerned with getting free samples of a product into the hands of potential customers. At another level, field marketing is about creating an interaction between

The sector is about the use of people to communicate sales and marketing messages.

the brand and a new customer. At yet another level, it is about creating a personal and memorable brand experience for potential customers. The key to field marketing is the flexibility of services provided to clients. Sales forces can be hired on short-term contracts and promotional teams can be contracted to launch new products, provide samples (both in-store and door-to-door) and undertake a range of other activities that are not part of an organisation's normal promotion activities.

The decision about whether to own or to hire a sales force has to be based on a variety of criteria, such as the degree of control required over not only the salesperson, but also the message to be transmitted. A further criterion is flexibility. Ruckert *et al.* (1985) identified that in environments subject to rapid change, which brings uncertainty (for example because of shortening product lifecycles or major technological developments), the ability to adjust quickly the number of representatives in the distribution channel can be of considerable strategic importance. A further criterion is cost; for some the large fixed costs associated with a sales force can be avoided by using a commission-only team of representatives.

A large number of organisations choose to have their own sales force, but of these many use the services of a manufacturer's agent to supplement their activities. A number of pharmaceutical manufacturers use independent sales forces to supplement the activities of their own sales teams.

Range of FM activities

At the turn of the century, research undertaken by the FMC found that there was a serious misunderstanding by clients and agencies concerning what constitutes field marketing activities (McLuhan, 2000). Since them, this situation has not changed a great deal, although there is now greater acceptance that field marketing should be a part of the marketing communications mix for most organisations. Table 23.2 sets out the range of activities undertaken in the name of field marketing. To some extent it consists of tasks pulled from some of the five main promotional tools, repackaged and presented under a more contemporary title; for example, door-to-door and sales activities from personal selling, merchandising from both personal selling and sales promotion, sampling (which is a straight sales promotions task) and event

Table 23.2 Essential features of field marketing activities

Core activities	Essential features
Sales	Provides sales force personnel on either a temporary or a permanent basis. This is for business-to-business and direct to the public.
Merchandising	Generates awareness and brand visibility through point-of-purchase placement, in-store staff training, product displays and leaflets.
Sampling	Mainly to the public at shopping centres and station concourses but also for business-to-business purposes.
Auditing	Used for checking stock availability, pricing and positioning.
Mystery shopping	Provides feedback on the level and quality of service offered by retail- and services-based staff.
Event marketing	Used to create drama and to focus attention at sports events, open-air concerts and festivals. Essentially theatrical or entertainment-based.
Door-to-door (home calls)	A form of selling where relatively uncomplex products and services can be sold through home visits.

Source: Adapted from McLuhan (2000). Reproduced from *Marketing* magazine with the permission of the copyright owner, Haymarket Business Publications Limited.

marketing from public relations. Field marketing is a response to market needs and is a development practitioners have pioneered to fulfil a range of customer needs that presumably had not been adequately satisfied.

Field marketing can take place virtually anywhere, but common locations are in shopping centres and supermarkets where footfall is greatest. Typically these events require agency staff to dress up in an eye-catching way in order to form associations between the clothing and the brand (e.g. dressed in Mexican ponchos and sombreros to give out free samples of Pot Noodle in a supermarket). It is regarded as a cost-effective way of demonstrating a product, getting stand-out and creating opportunities for customers to trial a product with minimum risk. Field marketing is also used to sell relatively complex products where a degree of explanation is required (e.g. computers, hi-fis or mobile phones).

Field marketing can take place virtually anywhere, but common locations are in shopping centres and supermarkets where footfall is greatest.

A key aspect of field marketing concerns the growing interest in what is referred to as experiential marketing or brand experience. Many in the industry see their role as delivering brand experience opportunities for their clients' customers. Others would argue that brand experience occurs through various interactions with a brand, namely purchasing, consumption and consideration. However, the term 'brand experience' appears to be owned by those in the field marketing industry and has evolved through the development of both sampling and event/roadshow activities. Unsurprisingly therefore, mystery shopping has developed as an important aspect of field marketing. Used increasingly by service-based operations, such as airlines, travel agents, restaurants and hotels, the intention is to understand how a customer experiences the service or purchase encounter and then feed the information into training and service improvements.

A key aspect concerns the growing interest in what is referred to as experiential marketing or brand experience.

Whether the brand experience industry lies inside or outside field marketing is not particularly critical. However, what differentiates the experiential aspect from other FM activities is that it requires more precise targeting (not mass market) and it is more emotionally and physically engaging than sampling and many events or roadshows, which in turn Bashford (2004) claims can lead to stronger (positive) memories. She quotes Paul Ephremsen, a leading industry practitioner who says that field marketing is 'all about the numbers and not the interaction, and is driven by cost per sample' whereas brand experience is about 'creating an emotional bond between the brand and the consumer'.

The debate about what constitutes field marketing and experiental marketing is explored by Bashford (2007). She provides two definitions, set out in Table 23.3.

Table 23.3 Two aspects of field marketing

Element	Explanation
Field marketing	The use of promotional staff in a marketing campaign to boost sales of a brand. Typically the field force will distribute product samples and carry out non-brand-related tasks that must be in place to maximise sales, such as compliance, auditing and merchandising.
Experiential marketing	The creation is a campaign delivered face-to-face, that engages the target audience in the brand through stimulation of some or all of the senses. This technique strives to forge a deeper connection with individuals and convey a sense of the brand's values.

Source: Bashford (2007). Reproduced from *Marketing* magazine with the permission of the copyright owner, Haymarket Business Publications Limited.

One of the essential tasks of field marketing is to continue to make brand signals available to consumers so that they can make the necessary brand associations that they have developed through advertising, brand and category experience. It is a matter of keeping brand values alive at the point of purchase (Kemp, 2000). Field marketing has undoubtedly expanded its role in recent years and in doing so has begun to establish itself as a core marketing support activity. Indeed, Moyies (2000) claims that field marketing should be cross-fertilised with direct marketing and sales promotion, and in doing so would not only benefit clients but also enhance the credibility of the industry.

ViewPoint 23.4 Enhancing the driving experience

Car manufacturers are fully aware of the benefits of getting prospective customers to test drive a vehicle. The hands-on driving experience has the potential to advance the purchase decision process considerably. Some manufacturers have developed car experience centres where customers can drive a range of vehicles. Here various terrains are available and the experience is a day-long event.

Car dealerships are environments often associated with alienation and pressure. Most are located in the suburbs, if only for cost and access reasons. Experience centres have to be located further away from city centres due to the need for land and resources. Both of these locations mean that customer footfall is limited and that marketing communications are required to drive visitors to these locations.

In an effort to generate footfall and create brand awareness, Fiat have opened a showroom, or experience centre, in central London. The centre has an innovative (non-traditional) design, where visitors view the cars on giant video screens. Visitors interact with the screens through hand motions in order to view particular elements in more detail. There are no sales people. One of the goals is to introduce people to Fiat and to encourage them to talk about their experience at the centre. The centre can also be used for conferences, fashion shows and events, all of which draw consumers closer to Fiat.

Source: McLuhan (2008).

Question

How can service brands develop if experience is a key element in the purchase decision process?

Task

Make a list of three product categories in which it is possible to generate relevant prior experience of the brand.

Packaging

Packaging has long been considered a means of protecting and preserving products during transit and while they remain in store or on the shelf prior to purchase and consumption. As Stewart (1995) aptly suggests, the function of packaging is to 'preserve product integrity'. In this sense, packaging can be regarded as an element of product strategy. To a certain extent this is still true; however, technology has progressed considerably and, with consumer choice continually widening, packaging has become a means by which buyers, particularly in consumer markets, can make significant brand choice decisions. Indeed, recent research by Silayoi and Speece (2007) has found that the way Asian consumers perceive the convenience of a package can be the most important factor in the decision-making process for some segments. To that extent, because packaging can be used to convey persuasive information and be part of the decision-making process, yet still protect the contents, it is an important means of marketing communications in particular markets, such as FMCG.

Packaging can be used to convey persuasive information and be part of the decision-making process.

Low-involvement, decision-making requires peripheral cues to stimulate buyers into action. It has already been noted that decisions made at the point of purchase, especially those in the FMCG sector, often require buyers to build awareness through recognition. The design of packages and wrappers is important, as continuity of design, combined with the power to attract and hold the attention of prospective buyers, is a vital part of point-of-purchase activity. The degree of importance that manufacturers place upon packaging and design was seen in 1994, when Sainsbury's introduced its own cola. The reaction of the Coca-Cola company to the lookalike design of the own-label product is testimony to the value placed on this aspect of brand personality. There should be no doubt that packaging can provide a strong point of differentiation, one that is increasingly recognised by food manufacturers and producers (Wells *et al.* 2007).

ViewPoint 23.5 Bottling it

Volvic's 'Touch of Fruit' brand had 47 per cent of the UK market, but as part of a strategy to build market share the bottle and labelling were redesigned in 2008. Coloured caps to emphasise product differentiation and bigger labels to attract attention and encourage product and flavour trial were key aspects of the redesign. However, the new packaging was woven into a campaign to highlight the brand. This involved, radio, online and a series of print ads in consumer magazines such as *Marie Claire* and various grocery trade press vehicles.

An innovative approach to bottle design was undertaken by Guinness in Asia. In a region where awareness of the Guinness brand is as high as that of Carlsberg and Heineken, beer drinkers were asked to vote for their favourite bottle design. The campaign featured four different designs, one of which was based on the god of thunder, Thor, to provide a 'witty parody of conventional drinking attitudes'.

To help promote the redesign a campaign involving print ads was run in *Today*, *Shin Min*, *Lianhe Wanbao* and mainstream magazines such as *FHM*, *8 Days*, *Juice*, *Men's Health*, *IS* and *Banter* in Singapore. This was supported with outdoor work in Hong Kong, with the posters carrying a toll-free number inviting consumers to vote for their favourite design. Guinness used mobile billboards, with fully plastered trucks driving through Singapore.

Sales promotions using tent cards, column posters, table standees and coasters were used across the city. The winning bottle design was taken out on the street with promoters dressed in life-sized bottle costumes, pitching themselves to the public as 'the better, more attractive bottle'.

Sources: Hargrave-Silk (2003); Odol (2008a).

Question

To what degree should the design of a bottle be determined by the positioning strategy for the brand?

Task

Using the bottle of a brand you use, make notes about how you could improve its design.

The communication dimensions of packaging

There are a number of dimensions that can affect the power and utility of a package. Colour is influential, as the context of the product class can frame the purchase situation for a buyer. This means that colours should be appropriate to the product class, to the brand and to the prevailing culture if marketing overseas. For example, red is used to stimulate the appetite, white to symbolise purity and cleanliness, blue to signal freshness, and green is increasingly being used to denote an environmental orientation and natural ingredients. From a cultural aspect, colours can be a problem. In China red is used to depict happiness, in Germany bright bold colours are regarded as appropriate for baby products, whereas in the United Kingdom pastel shades are more acceptable.

The shape of the packaging can be a strong form of persuasion.

The shape of the packaging can be a strong form of persuasion. Verebelyi (2000) suggests that this influence may be due to the decorative impact of some brands (see Exhibit 23.2).

Various domestic lavatory cleaners have a twist in the neck or a trigger action, facilitating directable and easier application.

The shape may also provide information about how to open and use the product, while some packages can be used after the product has been consumed for other purposes. For example, some jars can be reused as food containers, thereby providing a means of continual communication for the original brand in the home. Packaging can also be used as a means of brand identification, as a cue by which buyers recognise and differentiate a brand. The supreme example of this is the Coca-Cola contour bottle, with its unique shape and immediate power for brand recognition at the point of purchase (see Exhibit 23.4).

Package size is important, as different target markets may consume varying amounts of product. Toothpaste is available in large-size family tubes and in smaller containers for those households that do not use so much. However, the size of a package can also be important perceptual stimuli. Research by Raghubir and Krishna (1999) found that the height of a container

Exhibit 23.2 A packaging example
Toblerone and the Toblerone Triangular Packaging are the registered trademarks owned and licensed by Kraft Foods.

Exhibit 23.3 Coca-Cola contour bottle

Packaging is an important aspect of marketing communications in many sectors. Depicted here is the Coca-Cola bottle with its unique (and well-protected) shape.

Coca-Cola is a registered trade mark of the Coca-Cola Company. This image has been reproduced with the kind permission of the Coca-Cola Company.

was an important variable that consumers used to make judgements about the volume of the container.

However, Folkes and Matta (2004) counter this by referring to *Gestalt* theory, which is concerned with holistic perspectives, and say that consumers use multiple dimensions to make judgements about objects (packages). Their research suggests that there is a relationship between the attractiveness of a package and the volume of the package. As a broad generalisation, the greater the attractiveness, the greater the perceived volume. The implications of this insight have been implicitly known by marketing management for years, judging by the effort that is given to create attractive packaging and shelf stand-out.

Packaging can be strategically important as it can affect positioning.

In certain markets packaging can be strategically important as it can affect positioning. Ampuero and Vial (2006) identify colour, typography, graphical forms and images as the key packaging variables from a design perspective. They then consider how these combine to produce optimum positioning conditions. They conclude that dark-coloured cold packaging, which show, the product, is perceived to be associated with products that are elegant and expensive. The packaging for products targeted at customers for whom a low price is important should be light-coloured and show illustrations of people.

Washing and dishwasher powder manufacturers now provide plastic refill packs that are designed to provoke brand loyalty. These packs are cheaper than the original pack, partly because some of the packaging expense has been reduced as the customer has been introduced to the product at an earlier time. Purchase of the refill pack is dependent on product quality and customer satisfaction and, as long as the brand name is prominent for identification and reminder purposes, the decision to select the refill is quicker, as most of the risk (financial, physical and social) has been removed through previous satisfactory usage.

ViewPoint 23.6 Beware of men bearing gift trays

Milk Tray is a well-known brand of chocolate, selling over 8 million packs each year. It was launched by Cadbury in 1915 and its packaging has evolved, often reflecting changing values and brand positioning. The name was derived from the way in which it was originally packed and delivered to shops. Milk Tray chocolates were arranged in five-and-a-half pound boxes, arranged on trays and then sold loose to customers. Since then Milk Tray has been presented in packs and positioned as an assortment for everyday, use not just special occasions. Just as the contents have been regularly updated, so has the packaging in order to maintain its position and modernity. The design is essentially stylish but with no frills or frivolity.

In the period 1980–2000 the advertising used to support the brand featured a James Bond character who undertook various daring stunts in order to deliver a box of Milk Tray. This epitomised the position that Milk Tray was something men gave to women.

In 2003, the brand underwent a makeover to bring it up-to-date as the light-hearted token of affection. The brand was relaunched again in 2008, this time to reposition the brand as a gift for men to give to 35–45-year-old women. Following research, the contents were revised, and updated packaging was introduced. The traditional purple colour was retained but with an embossed typeface, partly in an attempt to provide in-store, stand-out and point-of-purchase attention, to help compete with Terry's All Gold.

Sources: Odol (2008b); www.cadbury.co.uk/.

Question

To what extent is packaging the most important element in the communication mix for grocery and FMCG products?

Task

How would you use colour as a point of differentiation in the gift chocolate market? Choose four different segments (e.g. grannies, mums, dads and girl/boy-friends), and decide which colour you would use for each segment. Justify your selection.

All packages have to carry information concerning the ingredients, nutritional values and safety requirements, including sell-by and use-by dates. Non-food packages must also attempt to be sales agents and provide all the information that a prospective buyer might need, while at the same time providing conviction that this product is the correct one to purchase. Labelling of products offers opportunities to manufacturers to harmonise the in-store presentation of their products in such a way that buyers from different countries can still identify the brand and remain brand loyal. For example, Buckley (1993) reported that Unilever decided not to change its different brands of washing powder in favour of a pan-European brand. It decided instead to retain the existing names (Omo, Skip, Via, Persil and All) and to package them in a similar way, using similar visual devices, typography and colours. This not only allows customers to remain loyal but also presents opportunities to save on advertising and design costs and gain access to satellite and other cross-border media.

> The psychological impact that packages can have should not be underestimated.

Packages carry tangible and intangible messages. The psychological impact that packages can have should not be underestimated. They convey information about the product, but they also say something about the quality of the product (Hall, 1991) and how it differs from competitive offerings. In some cases, where there is little to differentiate products, buyers may use the packaging on its own for decision-making purposes.

Gordon and Valentine (1996) argue that the market, competitive and associated products, provide a context within which a brand's packaging communicates. This is achieved by using packaging that conforms to a design code that has been established for the category. This permits consumers to identify quickly the range of brands in the product field, but does not necessarily allow for the identification of individual brands. They make the important point that it is this process that allows own-label brands to become part of a category without the support of advertising to establish credibility.

Packaging has been termed passive and active (Southgate, 1994). Passive packaging relies on vast amounts of advertising to infuse the design to create interest (e.g. Heinz). This is similar to the above-the-line approach to branding. Active packaging is more demonstrative and tends to work with the other marketing and communication elements. Connolly and Davison (1996) cite Tango as an example of this type of packaging.

Summary

In order to help consolidate your understanding of these various forms of marketing communications, here are the key points summarised against each of the learning objectives:

1. Explain the significance of exhibitions and trade shows.

The main reasons for attending exhibitions and trade fairs are that: it enables organisations to meet customers (and potential customers) in an agreeable environment, one where both have independently volunteered their time to attend; to place/take orders; to generate leads; and to gather market information.

2. Consider the main advantages and disadvantages of using exhibitions as part of the communication mix.

As a form of marketing communications, exhibitions enable products to be promoted, they can build brands and they can be an effective means of demonstrating products and building industry-wide credibility in a relatively short period of time. Positive relationships with customers, competitors and suppliers are often reinforced through face-to-face dialogue that happens both formally in the exhibition hall and informally through the variety of social activities that surround and support these events.

3. Understand the concept and issues associated with product placement.

Product placement is the inclusion of products and services in films (or media) for deliberate promotional exposure, often, but not always, in return for an agreed financial sum. It is regarded by some as a form of sales promotion, by others as sponsorship, but the most common linkage is with advertising, because the 'advertiser' pays a third party for the opportunity to present the product in their channel.

There are distinct forms of product placement. One involves the passive placement of a product within the media; the other sees whole entertainment programmes built around a single product, one where it is actively woven into the theme or the plot of the programme. This is known as 'branded entertainment'.

4. Explore ideas associated with field marketing and related activities.

Field marketing is a relatively new sector and seeks to provide support for the sales force and merchandising personnel along with data collection and research facilities. A key aspect of field marketing concerns the growing interest in what is referred to as experiential marketing or brand experience.

What differentiates the experiential aspect from other FM activities is that it requires more precise targeting (not mass-market) and it is more emotionally and physically engaging than sampling and many events or road shows.

5. Examine the role and key characteristics of packaging as a form of marketing communication.

Packaging has become a means by which buyers, particularly in consumer markets, can make significant brand-choice decisions and constitutes more than preserving product integrity. Packages carry tangible and intangible messages. The psychological impact that packages can have is important. Packaging conveys information about the product, but it also makes a statement about the quality of the product and how it differs from competitive offerings. In some cases, where there is little to differentiate products, buyers may use the packaging on its own for decision-making purposes.

Review questions

1. Evaluate the differences between consumer- and business-oriented trade shows.
2. As sales manager for a company making plastic mouldings for use in the manufacture of consumer durables, set out the reasons for and against attendance at trade shows and exhibitions.
3. Write brief notes explaining the role exhibitions might play in a company's integrated marketing communications strategy.
4. The development of interorganisational relationships is best undertaken through personal selling rather than through exhibitions and trade shows. Discuss.
5. Explain how packaging can be an integral part of a consumer's brand experience.
6. Find three brands where the shape of a package is an integral part of the product.
7. What is the difference between active and passive packaging?
8. Name two strengths and two weaknesses of product placement.
9. Identify four examples of product placement. Evaluate their effectiveness.
10. Name five core activities associated with field marketing and explain their essential features. Do not refer to Table 23.2 until you have attempted the exercise from memory.

MiniCase Sustainability*live!*

Jim Blythe: Visiting Reader at Plymouth Business School

In May 2008, Sustainability*live!* was held at the National Exhibition Centre in Birmingham, UK. The exhibition attracted over 7,000 visitors, and 450 exhibitors: it was the largest exhibition on environmental issues in the United Kingdom. Given the current prominence of environmentalism in both business- and public-sector thinking, the exhibition could hardly be more relevant, but the definition of 'environmental issues' had clearly been widely cast by many exhibitors and visitors.

Sustainability*live!* was actually a combination of four already-successful shows: the National Energy Management Exhibition (NEMEX), the Environmental Technology and Environmental Services Exhibition (ET&ES), Brownfield Expo and the International Water and Effluent Exhibition (IWEX).

Exhibitors ranged from companies selling water coolers for offices through to government organisations such as the British Geological Survey. A sample of exhibiting companies is as follows:

- CDR Pumps Ltd. This company specialises in pumps for moving toxic waste, as well as other liquids.
- Climate Change Solutions Ltd. This is a non-profit organisation dedicated to facilitating synergies

between companies and public bodies concerned about climate change.

- City University. This university attended with the aim of promoting its new MSc in energy, environmental technology and economics. This degree is aimed at middle managers in industry. Cranfield University also exhibited, promoting their environmental consultancy services as well as their range of degrees.
- The Environment Agency. This is the government department charged with responsibility for environmental issues, in particular, the agency has recently been interested in flood defences.
- Executive Futures. An employment agency, Executive Futures exhibited on the basis that they can locate people with specific environmental credentials.
- Lighting Solutions UK Ltd. This company provides energy-efficient lighting systems.
- Meteo France. The French government weather-forecasting service, this agency seeks to provide weather-forecasting services for industry. For some industries (notably airlines and shipping) weather forecasting is crucial, but it is certainly also useful in predicting demand for some products and services.

Some companies, perhaps surprisingly, provided few details about their activities for the exhibition web site. Global Water Intelligence, Gazprom and Kingspan Renewables were all reticent about what they actually do. This was despite exhortations from the exhibition organisers to provide as much information as possible – obviously information provided on the web site would be used by potential visitors to decide whether or not to attend. Other companies provided extremely detailed information, including contact details and links to their own web sites.

Exhibitors were encouraged to attend on the basis that they would increase their networking possibilities, would meet potential buyers and broaden their client base, would be able to launch new products, and would be able to reach new sectors due to cross-marketing between the four exhibitions making up Sustanability*live!* The emphasis was thus firmly on selling activities – finding new buyers, launching new products and reaching new sectors. In fact, the organisers' PR agents (Mistral Public Relations) even sent out a press release promoting the 'Meet the Buyer' event, at which buyers from over 35 countries were present to discuss their needs and purchasing processes. For this event, the UK Department of Trade and Industry sent advisers along to provide information about foreign business cultures and assistance that could be made available for exporting firms.

Exhibition organisers Faversham House Group established partnerships with several trade organisations: the British Pump Manufacturers' Association, the Chemical Industries Association and the Environmental Services Association were just 3 of the 30 associations and organisations who sponsored the exhibition. Forming a partnership with Faversham House meant that these organisations could have some input into the running and promotion of the exhibition, as well as the fact that activities such as promoting exhibitions form part of their reason for existing – trade associations are all about networking and promoting their industries. However, on the downside, Faversham House were obliged to issue a warning to potential exhibitors as a result of an Austrian publishing firm approaching exhibitors with an offer to be included in a 'directory' about the exhibition. This directory purported to offer free publicity, but in fact concealed a charge of €971. Such scams are not uncommon at exhibitions, and are, obviously, potentially damaging for the reputation of the exhibition organisers.

Faversham House Group encouraged visitors to attend by promoting the benefits of attendance – specifically, their publicity referred to the networking opportunities, the free seminar and masterclass presentations, the opportunities to discuss specific requirements (i.e. to meet potential suppliers) and (perhaps controversially) the opportunity to meet prospective clients. This last opportunity is controversial because it implies that visitors might attend in order to sell to exhibitors – something that exhibitors might resent, since they were paying for stand space and visitors were not. Visitors were offered the opportunity to register on-line for the show, thus flagging up their specific interests and reasons for attending: failing this, they could register on arrival, thus adding their names to a mailing list and ensuring that exhibitors could contact them with specific advice and solutions.

A notable feature for adding value to the visitor experience was the wide range of free seminars on offer. These included subjects such as environmental law changes, waste-to-energy conversion technology, recycling of industrial waste, and human health issues arising from exposure to toxins. Over 80 seminars were run over the three days of the exhibition, mainly offered free by exhibiting companies as a way of promoting their own products and services, but at the same time offering visitors the latest information on sustainability.

Adding value for visitors was a key feature of the exhibition. For an exhibition organiser, the first priority was to ensure that as many visitors as possible attend: the next priority was that they should be the right kind of visitors, but this was harder to achieve. If there are plenty of visitors, exhibitors will want to book stand space, and in many cases will not be aware of the types of visitor attending. The only restriction the organisers placed on visitors was that under-16s were refused entry: all others were welcomed. Obviously, screening of visitors is extremely difficult to achieve in practice – so organisers simply allow everyone in, and accept that some at least are less than truthful when filling in the registration forms.

Despite the problems, however, the vast majority of exhibitors and visitors came away satisfied with their time at the exhibition. Approached with the right attitude and objectives, Sustainability*live!* proved to be an excellent showcase for a variety of industries involved in environmental areas of activity: it also proved to be an excellent source of information for visitors.

MiniCase questions

1. What was the role of public relations in the exhibition?
2. What do you conclude from the fact that some firms did not provide much detail about themselves for the exhibition web site?
3. How might a company maximise the effectiveness of its activities at the exhibition?

References

Allen, A. (2007) How to . . . score a hit at trade shows, *The Marketer*, September, 34–7.

Advertising Association (2008) *Advertising Statistics YearBook 2008*, Henley on Thames: Advertising Association.

Ampuero, O. and Vial, N. (2006) Consumer perceptions of product packaging. *Journal of Consumer Marketing*, **23**(2), 100–12.

Bashford, S. (2004) Field marketing: The great divide? *Event*, 8 September. Retrieved 14 October from www.brandrepublic.com/news.

Bashford, S. (2007) Which way forward? *Marketing*, 13 December, 12.

Bertheron, P., Pitt, L.F. and Watson, R.T. (1996) The World Wide Web as an advertising medium. *Journal of Advertising Research*, **6**(1) (January/February), 43–54.

Boukersi, L. (2000) The role of trade fairs and exhibitions in international marketing communications. In *The Handbook of International Marketing Communications* (ed. S. Moyne), 117–35. London: Blackwell.

Buckley, N. (1993) More than just a pretty picture. *Financial Times*, 13 October, 23.

Connolly, A. and Davison, L. (1996) How does design affect decisions at point of sale? *Journal of Brand Management*, **4**(2), 100–7.

Folkes, V. and Matta, S. (2004) The effect of package shape on consumers' judgments of product volume: attention as a mental contaminant. *Journal of Consumer Research*, **31**(2) September, 390–402.

Gordon, W. and Valentine, V. (1996) Buying the brand at point of choice. *Journal of Brand Management*, **4**(1), 35–44.

Hall, J. (1991) Packaged good. *Campaign*, 18 October, 21–3.

Hargrave-Silk, A. (2003) Guinness builds buzz with bottle's new look. *Media Asia*. Retrieved 31 October from www.brandrepublic.co.uk/news/newsArticle.

Hudson, S. and Hudson, D. (2006) Branded entertainment: a new advertising technique or product placement in disguise? *Journal of Marketing Management*, **22**(5–6), 489–504.

Karrh, J.A., McKee, K.B., Britain, K. and Pardun, C.J. (2003) Practitioners' evolving views of product placement effectiveness. *Journal of Advertising Research*, **43**(2) (June), 138–50.

Kemp, G. (2000) Elastic brands. *Marketing Business*, (October), 40–1.

Khoon, L.C., Ramaiah, C. and Foo, S. (2003) The design and development of an online exhibition for heritage information awareness in Singapore. *Program: Electronic Library and Information Systems*, **37**(2), 85–93.

McLuhan, R. (2000) Fighting for a new view of field work. *Marketing*, 9 March, 29–30.

McLuhan, R. (2007) Face value. *Marketing*, 13 December, 9–10.

McLuhan, R. (2008) Plan now, enjoy later. *Marketing*, 20 February, 33–4.

Moyies, J. (2000) A healthier specimen. *Admap* (June), 39–42.

Nebenzahl, I.D. and Secunda, E. (1993) Consumer attitudes toward product placement in movies. *International Journal of Advertising*, **12**, 1–11.

Odol, A. (2008a) Bottling it. *Marketing*, 2 April, 8.

Odol, A. (2008b) Cadbury Milk Tray to focus on gift appeal. *Marketing*, 2 April, 8.

Pervan, S.J. and Martin, B.A.S. (2002) Product placement in US and New Zealand television soap operas: an exploratory study. *Journal of Marketing Communications*, **8**, 101–13.

Plaut, M. (2004) Ford advertises the literary way. *BBC News/Business*. Retrieved 20 March 2008 from http://news.bbc.co.uk/1/hi/business/3522635.stm.

Raghubir, P. and Krishna, A. (1999) Vital dimensions in volume perception: can the eye fool the stomach? *Journal of Marketing Research*, **36** (August), 313–26.

Ruckert, R.W., Walker, O.C. and Roering, K.J. (1985) The organisation of marketing activities: a contingency theory of structure and performance. *Journal of Marketing* (Winter), 13–25.

Russell, C.A. and Belch M. (2005) A managerial investigation into the product placement industry. *Journal of Advertising Research*, **45**(1) (March), 73–92.

Shipley, D. and Wong, K.S. (1993) Exhibiting strategy and implementation. *International Journal of Advertising*, **12**(2), 117–30.

Silayoi, P. and Speece, M. (2007) The importance of packaging attributes: a conjoint analysis approach. *European Journal of Marketing*, **41**(11/12), 1495–517.

Southgate, P. (1994) *Total Branding by Design*. London: Kogan Page.

Stewart, B. (1995) *Packaging as an Effective Marketing Tool*, Surrey: Pira International.

Utalk (2007) How direct mail boosted Tourism Ireland's conference market. Retrieved 4 January 2008 from www.utalkmarketing.com/pages/article.aspx?.

Verebelyi, N. (2000) The power of the pack. *Marketing*, 27 April, 37.

Wells, L.E., Farley, H. and Armstrong, G.A. (2007) The importance of packaging design for own-label food brands. *International Journal of Retail and Distribution Management*, **36**(9), 677–90.

Part 5 The media

Chapters 24–27

This part of the book is new to this edition and is used to bring together different aspects and forms of the media. It should be regarded as complementary to the previous part on the tools of the marketing communications mix, and advertising in particular.

Chapter 24 considers the characteristics and key developments associated with traditional media. It examines print, broadcast, outdoor, in-store and other types such as cinema and ambient media.

Chapters 25 and 26 use similar materials to consider digital media. The first part of Chapter 25 examines the functionality and opportunities digital media provide. The second part of this chapter explores what these features and benefits mean. For example, interactivity, mobility and the personalisation associated with marketing communications.

Chapter 26, which should be read after Chapter 25, examines interactive marketing communications. This is a new chapter and considers how digital technology has been used in marketing communications. Here consideration is given to online applications of the tools of the mix but, in addition, explores search engine marketing, communities and social networks, digital aspects of word-of-mouth communications (viral, podcasting and blogging) and other aspects of social media.

The final chapter in this part is given to the principles and concepts associated with media planning. Although the tradition and development of the subject is rooted in offline media planning, consideration is also given to online media planning issues.

Video Insight Part 5

Part 5 of the book focuses on the use and variety of the media as an integral aspect of marketing communications. The Video Insight features three brands. Firstly, we begin by looking at the way Land Rover work with the motoring press and the relationships they form with motoring journalists such as Jeremy Clarkson. Perhaps you can see the link to the role of opinion formers examined in Chapter 2 on communication theory?

Royal Enfield provide an insight into the way a motorcycle manufacturer targets particular motorcycle magazines to reach fairly discerning audiences. Reference is made to press and magazines in addition to the increasing importance of web sites.

Ikea describe their use of television and print media, essentially as a means to provide awareness and information. However, they are also increasing their dot.com business and this inevitably involves improving and developing the web site. One of their goals is to enable people to experiment with their brand and to use the web site as a means of getting closer to the brand.

Go to **www.pearsoned.co.uk/fill** to watch the Video Insight, and then answer the following questions:

1. How do Land Rover use the motoring media to develop their brand?
2. What are the primary media used by Royal Enfield and how do they use magazines to promote their brand?
3. To what extent will the development of the web site to enable people to play with the Ikea brand make offline advertising redundant?

Chapter 24
Traditional media

The use of particular media is required in order that client messages are delivered to specific target audiences. The array of available media is continually growing but each has strengths and weaknesses that impact on the quality, effectiveness and the meaning attributed to the message by the audience. This chapter focuses on the nature and characteristics of traditional, offline media.

Aims and learning objectives

The aim of this chapter is to establish the principal characteristics of each type of offline media. This will assist understanding of the management processes by which media are selected and scheduled to deliver advertiser's messages. Digital media are explored in the following chapter and media planning and scheduling processes are looked at in Chapter 27.

The learning objectives of this chapter are to:

1. determine the variety and types of traditional media;
2. explain the main criteria used to evaluate media and their use;
3. establish the primary characteristics of each type of medium;
4. examine the strengths and weaknesses of each type of medium;
5. provide a brief summary of the main UK trends in advertising expenditure on each type of medium;
6. consider the dynamics associated with direct response media;
7. explore ways in which media can be integrated.

For an applied interpretation see Nicola Robinsonova's MiniCase entitled ***For different types of wood: the Pila Pasak (Shepherd's Sawmill) campaign*** at the end of this chapter.

Introduction

Organisations use the services of a variety of media in order that they can deliver their planned messages to target audiences. Of the many available media, six main *classes* can be identified. These are broadcast, print, outdoor, digital, in-store and other media classes. Within each of these classes there are particular *types* of media. For example, within the broadcast class there are television and radio, and within the print class there are newspapers and magazines.

Six main classes can be identified: broadcast, print, outdoor, digital, in-store and other media.

Within each type of medium there are a huge number of different media *vehicles* that can be selected to carry an advertiser's message. For example, within UK television there are the terrestrial networks (Independent Television Network, Channel 4 and Channel 5) and the satellite (BSkyB) and cable (e.g. Virgin Media) networks. In print, there are consumer and business-oriented magazines and the number of specialist magazines is expanding rapidly. These specialist magazines are targeted at particular activity and interest groups, such as *Amateur Photographer*, *Golf World* and the infamous *Sponge Divers Gazette*! This provides opportunities for advertisers to send messages to well-defined homogeneous groups, which improves effectiveness and reduces wastage in communication spend. Table 24.1 sets out the three forms of media – classes, types and vehicles – with a few examples.

Table 24.1 Summary chart of the main forms of media

Class	Type	Vehicles
Broadcast	Television	*Coronation Street, X Factor*
	Radio	Virgin Radio, Classic FM
Print	Newspapers	The *Sunday Times*, *The Mirror*, *The Daily Telegraph*
	Magazines: Consumer	*Cosmopolitan*, *Woman*, *The Grocer*, *Plumbing News*
	Business	
Outdoor	Billboards	96-, 48- and 6-sheet
	Street furniture	Adshel
	Transit	London Underground, airport buildings, taxis, hot-air balloons
Digital media	Internet	Web sites, email, intranets
	Digital television	Teletext, SkyText,
	CD-ROM	Various including music, educational, entertainment
In-store	Point-of-purchase	Bins, signs and displays
	Packaging	The Coca-Cola contour bottle
Other	Cinema	Pearl & Dean
	Exhibitions	Ideal Home, The Motor Show
	Product placement	Films, TV, books
	Ambient	Litter bins, golf tees, petrol pumps
	Guerrilla	Flyposting

Evaluative criteria

One of the key marketing tasks is to decide which combination of vehicles should be selected to carry the message to the target audience. The means by which this decision is reached is the subject of Chapter 27. First, however, it is necessary to consider the main characteristics of each type of media in order that media planning decisions can be based on some logic and rationale. The fundamental characteristics concern the costs, the richness of the communication, the interactive properties and audience profile associated with a communication event.

Costs

One of the important characteristics that needs to be considered is the costs that are incurred using each type of medium. There are two types of cost: absolute and relative. Absolute costs are the costs of the time or space bought in a particular media vehicle. These costs have to be paid for and directly impact upon an organisation's cash flow. Relative costs are the costs of contacting each member of the target audience. Television, as will be seen later, has a high absolute cost but, because messages are delivered to a mass audience, when the absolute cost is divided by the total number of people receiving the message the relative cost is very low.

Communication richness

The use of sight, sound and movement can generate great impact with a message.

The way in which a message is delivered and understood by a target audience varies across types of media. Certain media, such as television, are able to use many communication dimensions, and through the use of sight, sound and movement can generate great impact with a message. Other types of media have only one dimension, such as the audio capacity of radio or the written word on a page of text. The number of communication dimensions that a media type has will influence the choice of media mix. This is because certain products, at particular points in their development, require the use of different media in order that the right message be conveyed and understood. A new product, for example, may require demonstration in order that the audience understands the product concept. The use of television may be a good way of achieving this. Once understood, the audience does not need to be educated in this way again and future messages need to convey different types of information that may not require demonstration, so radio or magazine advertising may suffice (see Chapter 27, where media richness theory is explored).

Interactive properties

Following on from the previous element is the important issue of interactive communications. The development of digital media has enabled interaction, which we know can lead to dialogue, and this in turn enables relationship development (Ballantyne, 2004). However, there are some circumstances in which interaction is not required due to the nature of the market, the product or the objectives of the campaign. In these circumstances the mix will need to consist of media that primarily deliver messages through a one-way, or monologic, communication format.

Those that deliver a call-to-action will need to use media that enable interaction.

Marketing communications that seek to engage audiences through interaction, in particular those that deliver a call-to-action, will need to use media that enable interaction and to be used where support facilities are in place to facilitate interactive communications.

Audience profile

The profile of the target audience (male, female, young or old) and the number of people within each audience that a media type can reach are also significant factors in media decisions. For example, 30 per cent of adults in the socioeconomic grade A read the *Sunday Times*. Only

4 per cent of the C2 group also read this paper. Messages appropriate to the A group would be best placed in the *Sunday Times* and those for the C2 group transmitted through the *News of the World*, which 34 per cent of the C2 group read. It is important that advertisers use media vehicles that convey their messages to their target markets with as little waste as possible. Newspapers enable geographically dispersed audiences to be reached. The tone of their content can be controlled, but the cost per target reached is high. Each issue has a short lifespan, so for positive learning to occur in the target audience a number of insertions may be required.

A large number of magazines contain specialised material that appeals to particular target groups. These special-interest magazines (SIMs) enable certain sponsors to reach interested targets with reduced wastage. General-interest magazines (GIMs) appeal to a much wider cross-section of society, to larger generalised target groups. The life of these media vehicles is generally long and their 'pass along' readership high. It should not be forgotten, however, that noise levels can also be high owing to the intermittent manner in which magazines are often read and the number of competing messages from rival organisations.

Television reaches the greatest number of people, but although advertisers can reach general groups, such as men aged 16–24 or housewives, it is not capable of reaching specific interest groups and it incurs high levels of wastage. This blanket coverage offers opportunities for cable and satellite operators to offer more precise targeting, but for now television is a tool for those who wish to talk to mass audiences. Television is expensive from a cash-flow perspective but not in terms of the costs per target reached.

Radio offers a more reasonable costing structure than television and can be utilised to reach particular geographic audiences. For a long time, however, this was seen as its only real strength, particularly when its poor attention span and non-visual dimensions are considered. Although radio will never overtake television in terms of usage and overall popularity, radio has been shown to be capable of generating a much closer personal relationship with listeners, witnessed partly by the success of Classic FM and local radio stations, than is possible through posters, television or print.

The interesting point about outdoor and transit advertising is that exposure is only made by the interception of passing traffic. Govoni *et al.* (1986) make the point that such interception represents opportunistic coverage. Consequently the costs are low, at both investment and per contact levels.

The use of direct marketing has grown in recent years, as technology has developed and awareness has increased. The precise targeting potential of direct mail and its ability to communicate personally with target audiences is impressive. In addition, the control over the total process, including the costs, remains firmly with the sponsor.

The size of the industry should not be underestimated as UK advertising expenditure reached £19.1 billion in 2006 (see Table 3.1 in Chapter 3).

Print media

Of the total amount spent on advertising, across all media, most is spent on the printed word. Newspapers and magazines are the two main types of media in this class. They attract advertisers for a variety of reasons, but the most important is that print media are very effective at delivering a message to a target audience.

Print media are very effective at delivering a message to a target audience.

Most people have access to either a newspaper or a magazine. They read in order to keep up to date with news and events or to provide themselves with a source of entertainment. People tend to have consistent reading habits and buy or borrow the same media vehicles regularly. For example, most people read the same type of newspaper(s) each day and their regular choice of magazine reflects either their business or leisure interests, which are normally quite stable. This means that advertisers, through marketing research, are able to build a database of the main characteristics (a profile) of their readers. This in turn allows advertisers to buy space in those media vehicles that will be read by the sort of people they think will benefit from their product or service.

The printed word provides advertisers with the opportunity to explain their message in a way that most other media cannot. Such explanations can be in the form of either a picture or a photograph, perhaps demonstrating how a product is to be used. Alternatively, the written word can be used to argue why a product should be used and detail the advantages and benefits that consumption will provide the user. In reality, advertisers use a combination of these two forms of communication.

The print media are most suitable for messages designed when high involvement is present in the target market.

The print media are most suitable for messages designed when high involvement is present in the target market. These readers not only control the pace at which they read a magazine or newspaper, but also expend effort to read advertisements because they care about particular issues. Where elaboration is high and the central processing route is preferred, messages that provide a large amount of information are best presented in the printed form.

Magazines are able to reach quite specialised audiences and tend to be selective in terms of the messages they carry. In contrast, newspapers reach a high percentage of the population and can be referred to as a mass medium. The messages that newspapers carry are usually for products and services that have a general appeal.

Print media is often regarded as a secondary medium to television. There are several reasons for this, but one of them is linked to the perceived 'emotional power' of television. However, Heath and McDonald (2007) report research by OTX using the CEP®Test, which demonstrates that emotive power of print and television ads are basically the same. Their research suggests strongly that press is just as effective as television in building brands and is, in fact, superior with regard to attention-getting and communicating information. What this means is that advertisers can seriously reduce their media costs simply by switching some of their budget out of television and into print and still achieve the same impact.

Newspapers

In general, newspaper readership is in decline and has been falling since the mid 1980s. This is most starkly visible among the young as they gather their news from other sources, most notably the television and now the Internet. The biggest shift has been away from the popular press with some movement towards the quality press. As a result advertising expenditure has not grown in this medium. In 2006, expenditure on national newspaper advertising reached £1.9 billion, down from the £2.3 billion in 2003 (Advertising Association, 2007).

Newspapers are repositioning themselves as multi-platform publishing entities.

Faced with a declining market newspapers are repositioning themselves as multi-platform publishing entities. In addition to the change from broadsheet to compact formats and the provision of online papers, innovation in the newspaper sector is critical. This is reflected in the growth of free papers, the growing interest in local news and a cross-media orientation (WARC, 2007). This requires major structural change and some risk in anticipating consumer needs.

Strengths

Readers are in control when reading a newspaper and as a result newspaper advertisements are seen positively. This means that readers choose which advertisements are read, how long they consider them (dwell time) and how often they are read. This facilitates 'comparison shopping' and is useful when readers experience high involvement. Newspapers provide wide exposure for advertisements, and market coverage in local, regional or national papers can be extensive. These media vehicles are extremely flexible as they present opportunities for the use of colour and allow advertisements of variable sizes, insertions and coupons.

Weaknesses

The combination of a high number of advertisements and the small amount of genuine reading time that many readers give to newspapers, means that most newspaper advertisements receive little exposure. Statistics show that newspaper circulation has fallen behind population growth; furthermore, teenagers and young adults generally do not read newspapers.

Advertising costs have risen very quickly and the competition to provide news, not just from other newspapers, but also from other sources such as cable, satellite and terrestrial television, means that newspapers are no longer one of the main providers of news. Printing technologies advanced considerably during the 1980s and 1990s, but the relatively poor quality of reproduction means that the impact of advertisements can often be lost.

Magazines

For some time the circulation of monthly magazines was larger than weekly magazines. This has changed as weeklies now have the dominant share of the circulation. Magazine advertising revenue has been fairly static at around £812 million in 2006 (Advertising Association, 2008), whereas advertising in business magazines fell by 7 per cent in 2006. However, business magazines attract substantially more advertising revenue than the consumer sector, despite being highly fragmented and complex.

Strengths

The visual quality of magazines is normally very high, a result of using top-class materials and technologies. This provides advertisers with great flexibility with the visual dimension of their messages. The visual element of magazines is a real strength as it can be used to create impact and demand the attention of readers.

The large number and wide range of specialised titles means that narrow, specific target audiences can be reached much more successfully than with other media vehicles. For example, messages concerning ski equipment, clothing and resorts will be best presented in specialist ski magazines on the basis that they will be read by those who have an interest in skiing, rather than, for example, knitting, snooker or fishing. Magazines can provide a prestigious and high-quality environment, with the editorial providing authority, reassurance and credibility to the advertising that they contain.

Magazines are portable, can be read nearly anywhere and some have the potential to bestow status on the reader. Magazines are often passed along to others to read once the original user has finished reading it. This longevity issue highlights the difference between circulation (the number of people who buy or subscribe to a magazine) and readership (the number of people who actually read the vehicle, perhaps as a friend or partner at home, in a doctor's waiting room or at the instigation of a department head or workplace superior).

Magazines are often passed along to others to read.

Weaknesses

Magazine audience growth rates have fallen behind the growth in advertising rates. Therefore the value of advertising in magazines has declined relative to some other types of media. The long period of time necessary to book space in advance of publication dates and to provide suitable artwork means that management has little flexibility once it has agreed to use magazines as part of the media schedule. Apart from specialist magazines, a single magazine rarely reaches the majority of a market segment. Several magazines must be used to reach potential users. Having reached the target, impact often builds slowly, as some readers do not read their magazine until some days after they have received it. The absolute and relative costs associated with magazines are fairly high, particularly costs associated with general-interest magazines. Special-interest magazines, however, allow advertisers to reach their target audiences with little waste and hence high levels of efficiency.

ViewPoint 24.1 Land Rover's adventurous publications

The psychological issues associated with owning a 4 × 4 are probably quite complex. At one level the rationale for ownership is that they are practical, roomy and safe. At another more emotional level, owners gain a spirit of adventure and perhaps feel that this type of car enables them to project a slightly different dimension of their personality.

Loyalty towards the Land Rover brand is strong, with many customers purchasing these vehicles for many years. At the heart of Land Rover's loyalty programme are two publications. **Onelife** is a customer-focused publication, mailed to existing Land Rover owners. It provides an introduction to Land Rover's world of adventure and features expeditions and more local outdoor activities closer to home. This is a biannual magazine that generates a 6.8 per cent response rate.

The other publication is sent to dealers. This is a communication pack that contains sets of letters, post-cards and mailing materials all designed to help Land Rover dealers manage their particular customers through each of the stages of their vehicle ownership. Both publications are supported by the Land Rover web site, which develops the adventures theme with the G4 Challenge and Go Beyond. The latter pages enable people to upload their own adventures, which do not necessarily feature Land Rover.

Land Rover's customer loyalty programme provides an unrivalled ownership experience. All of Land Rover's marketing communications develop their customers' thirst for adventure and knowledge about their vehicles. They also encourage them to become life-long advocates of the brand. Not surprising then that Land Rover has one of the highest repurchase rates of any vehicle manufacturer.

Question

Why do you think print media are so effective in this context?

Task

Get a copy of any customer magazine sent direct to a household, and compare the content with a consumer magazine bought off the shelf of a retail store.

Exhibit 24.1 *OneLife* is Land Rover's customer magazine that is sent twice a year, to encourage engagement with the brand and eventual repurchase
Courtesy of Land Rover.

Customer magazines differ from consumer magazines because they are sent to customers direct, often without charge, and contain highly targeted and significant brand-related material. These have made a big impact in recent years and, partly because of high production values, have become a significant aspect of many direct marketing activities.

The number of customer magazines has grown in recent years across a variety of sectors. *M&S Magazine*, Waitrose's *Food Illustrated*, Honda's *Dream* and Boots' *Health and Beauty* are just some of the more prevalent titles. In Spring 2005, the NSPCC, in a co-branding alliance with Woolworths, launched *Your Family*. This is a quarterly magazine and is part of the charity's positive parenting campaign. Distributed free through Woolworths' stores, the magazine is funded through advertising and competes against paid-for consumer magazine titles such as *Practical Parenting* and *BBC Parenting*.

One final form of print media yet to be discussed concerns directories. Advertising expenditure on directories has continued to increase. One of the largest consumer directories is Yellow Pages, or Yell as they are now called, as they have diversified across new media (e.g. Yell.com).

Broadcast media

Fundamentally, there are two main forms of broadcast media, television and radio. Advertisers use this class of media because this class of media can reach mass audiences with their messages at a relatively low cost per target reached.

Advertisers can reach mass audiences with their messages at a relatively low cost per target reached.

Approximately 99 per cent of the population in the United Kingdom has access to a television set and a similar number have a radio. The majority of viewers use television passively, as a form of entertainment; however, new technological applications, such as digitalisation, indicate that television will be used proactively for a range of services, such as banking and shopping. Radio demands active participation, but can reach people who are out of the home environment.

Broadcast media allow advertisers to add visual and/or sound dimensions to their messages. The opportunity to demonstrate or to show the benefits or results that a particular product can bring gives life and energy to an advertiser's message. Television uses sight, sound and movement, whereas radio can only use its audio capacity to convey meaning, but it does stimulate a listener's imagination and thus can involve audiences in a message. Both media have the potential to tell stories and to appeal to people's emotions. These are dimensions that print media find difficulty in achieving effectively within the time allocations that advertisers can afford.

Advertising messages transmitted through the broadcast media use a small period of time, normally 60, 30 or 20 seconds, that are bought from the owners of the medium. The cost of the different time slots varies throughout a single transmission day and with the popularity of individual programmes. The more listeners or viewers that a programme attracts, the greater the price charged for a slice of time to transmit an advertising message. This impacts on the costs associated with such advertising. The time-based costs for television can be extremely large. For example, as at April 2008, the rate card cost of a nationwide 30-second spot in the middle of *Coronation Street* was £95,042 (www.itvsales.com). However, this large cost needs to be put in perspective. The actual cost of reaching individual members of the target audience is quite low, simply because all the costs associated with the production of the message and the purchase of time to transmit the message can be spread across a mass of individuals, as discussed earlier.

The costs associated with radio transmissions are relatively low when compared with television.

The costs associated with radio transmissions are relatively low when compared with television. This reflects the lack of prestige that radio has and the pervasiveness of television. People are normally unable, and usually unwilling, to become actively involved with broadcast advertising messages. They cannot control the pace at which they consume such advertising and as time is expensive and short, so advertisers do not have the opportunity to present detailed information. The result is that this medium is most suitable for low-involvement messages. Where the need for elaboration is low and the peripheral processing route is preferred, messages transmitted through electronic media should seek to draw attention, create awareness and improve levels of interest.

As the television and radio industries become increasingly fragmented, so the ability to reach particular market segments has become more difficult, as the target audience is often dispersed across other media. This means that the potential effectiveness of advertising through these media decreases. These media are used a great deal in consumer markets, mainly because of their ability to reach large audiences, but there is often considerable wastage and inefficiency. The result is that advertisers are moving their advertising spend to other media, most notably, online.

Television

For a number of years there was above inflation growth in television advertising expenditure, but annual growth since 2003 has been moderate. When the dot-com bubble burst, revenue growth stopped abruptly and station average prices have been falling by anything up to 30 per cent, causing major difficulties for the various station owners. The value of television advertising in 2006 was £4,594 million and showing little growth. This has prompted a review of the capacity of television advertising. The current regulations allow for a maximum of 12 minutes advertising an hour. However, the overall average must be seven minutes an hour, with a specific average of eight minutes an hour between 6p.m. and 11p.m. Ofcom are about to change this, although at the time of writing it is not clear whether the average will be increased by one or two minutes. The change is designed to bring the public service broadcasters (ITV1, Channel 4, Five, GMTV and S4C) into line with EU rules, which govern multi-channel television stations. Such a change will reduce prices and provide better opportunities for smaller business to use the medium.

The number of households connected to cable networks represented 13.0 per cent of all homes by December 2006. This is now a static figure even though cable television is now more established, stable and attractive to advertisers, who are able to target their audiences easily and communicate with less wastage. More importantly, the percentage of homes with a satellite dish is now 32 per cent.

Strengths

From a creative point of view, this medium is very flexible and the impact generated by the combination of sight and sound should not be underestimated. Consumer involvement and likeability of an advertisement is dependent upon the skill of the creative team. The prestige and status associated with television advertising is higher than that of other media: in some cases, the credibility and status of a product or organisation can be enhanced significantly just by being seen to be advertising on television.

The prestige and status associated with television advertising is higher than that of other media. The costs of reaching members of large target segments are relatively low, so the medium is capable of a high level of cost efficiency.

Weaknesses

Because the length of any single exposure is short, messages have to be repeated on television.

Because the length of any single exposure is short, messages have to be repeated on television in order to enhance learning and memory. This increases the absolute costs of producing and transmitting television commercials, which can be large, making this medium the most expensive form of advertising.

Television audiences are increasingly fragmented as the number of entertainment and leisure opportunities expands. For example, terrestrial television networks are suffering from the competition from cable and satellite broadcasters plus video recorders and other sources of entertainment. This proliferation of suppliers has led to television clutter. In order to keep viewers, programmes are now promoted vigorously by television companies and a variety of techniques are being used to prevent viewers from channel grazing (switching).

The trend towards shorter messages has led to increased clutter. Management flexibility over the message is frustrated, as last-minute changes to schedules are expensive and difficult to implement. The only choices open to decision-makers are either to proceed with an advertisement or to 'pull' it, should circumstances change in such a way that it would be inappropriate to proceed.

Technological developments, most notably the development of interactive television (iTV), have been slow to be adopted. However, this is changing as iTV is increasingly recognised as the way forward (see Chapter 25 for more on iTV). However, as technology advances to create better, more commercially viable interactive opportunities so it also develops disruptive potential to benefit viewers who dislike advert interruptions. First, there was TiVo, a device to blank out ads when recording programmes, which was slow to catch on but is now gathering momentum. Now there are personal video recorders (PVRs) that enable viewers to pause live programmes, 'time-shift' programming to suit their own lifestyles and convenience and to fast forward through commercial breaks in six seconds (Sherwin, 2004). He reports that advertisers are developing 'intelligent' ads that impart information, so that they are recognised when the fast forward button is activated.

ViewPoint 24.2 Eating Weetabix with the help of television

Weetabix is a premier brand among breakfast cereals. Many people have experienced the brand as a child, often as a baby, as the biscuit reduces to a mush when soaked with milk and becomes an ideal food for weaning. Weetabix is well established and market penetration rates of 40 per cent mean there is little room for growth and development. In addition, the breakfast market was experiencing change in the 2003–05 and the plainer products such as Cornflakes and Shredded Wheat were losing share.

Weetabix commissioned qualitative research and asked a group of lapsed users to eat the brand for a week and keep a diary. Two of the more startling results were that many of the group soon reported health benefits (no snacking before lunch. In addition, others had started to add 'things' to the cereal to overcome the monotony of its blandness. Here lay the foundation for the advertising campaign, to reveal the variety, interest and added value by using different toppings. A 'Weetabix Week' advertising campaign was devised, which provided the basis for an event designed to stimulate and motivate people to use the brand. First, to encourage them to experiment with different toppings by showing them ways others approached their Weetabix. Second, to provide motivation for people to try the brand for long enough (3/4 days) so that they started to feel the health benefits.

Television was the critical media because it allowed the audience to see the different toppings the participants used to decorate their Weetabix. The second benefit was that television enabled the audience to see 'real people' trying the Weetabix Week. These testimonials provided source credibility and opportunities to link consumption into lifestyle (e.g. children at breakfast, students late at night).

Source: Okin and Robothan-Jones (2007).

Question

What might have been the impact had celebrities been used rather than normal consumers?

Task

Which tools and media would you have used to to support the Weetabix Week?

Radio

There has been a rapid increase in the number of commercial radio services offered in the United Kingdom since 1973. Advertising expenditure on radio reached £582 million in 2003, a growth of 6.8 per cent on the previous year, but has since fallen back to £534 million in 2006. This renewed interest in radio is possibly due to a trend away from television and a recognition of the versatility of what is often regarded as a secondary medium.

Strengths

Radio permits specialised programming, which in turn attracts selective audiences.

Radio permits specialised programming, which in turn attracts selective audiences. Radio is a mobile medium (that is, one that can travel with audiences), so that messages can be relayed to them, for example, even when shoppers are parking their cars near a shopping precinct. The production costs are low and radio has great flexibility, which management can use to meet changing environmental and customer needs. If it is raining in the morning, an advertiser can implement a promotional campaign for umbrellas in the afternoon.

From a creative point of view the medium needs the active imagination of the listener. Radio has a high level of passive acceptance and the messages that are received are more likely to be retained than if they were delivered via a different medium. This combination of features makes radio an excellent support medium.

Weaknesses

Because there is an absence of visual stimuli, the medium lacks impact and the ability to hold and enthuse an audience. Levels of inattentiveness can be high, which means that a high number of messages are invariably ignored or missed. When this is combined with low average audiences, high levels of frequency are required to achieve acceptable levels of reach.

Outdoor media

The range of outdoor media encompasses a large number of different media, each characterised by two elements. First, they can be observed at locations away from home. For this reason some refer to this medium as 'out-of-home'. Second, they are normally used to support messages that are transmitted through primary media: broadcast and print. Outdoor media can therefore, be seen to be a secondary but important support media for a complementary and effective communications mix.

One of the common strands that bind these diverse media together is that they are all used to reach consumers who are themselves in transit, moving from one place to another, even if this is a shopping trip, going to/from work or taking a holiday. Fitch (2007) comments that this class of media is not associated with any particular content. Advertising in television, radio, magazines, newspapers, cinema and the Internet media involves interrupting or accompanying editorial, informational or entertainment material. This is not the case with outdoor media.

There is a balance to be achieved between reaching people and enriching their landscape and annoying those who do not like to see commercial messages on every available space. In Fitch's view, the use of outdoor media must take into account the following variables: 'the length of the ad exposure (viewer "dwell time" in relation to the ad), the ad's intrusiveness on the surrounding environment, and the likely mood and mindset of the consumers who will encounter the ad'. It is the interaction of these variables that shape each individual's experience of outdoor media and hence the effectiveness of each communication.

Media spend on outdoor advertising declined in the earlier 1990s after steady growth in the 1980s. Growth returned once again to the sector as the UK economy moved out of recession

ViewPoint 24.3 A laddering brand

The use of large or intriguing outdoor media simply to attract the attention of passers-by is a technique that has been employed by advertisers over the years. One of the more noticeable advertisers in recent years has been hosiery manufacturer Pretty Polly. In 2007, the brand wanted to stir a little bit of controversy and at the same time re-establish its credentials as a fashion brand for women.

Using an internationally recognised fashion photographer (Georges Antoni) they developed an eye-catching image of a model's long legs on a ladder. Referred to as 'Stairway to Heaven', the image was used in a variety of places: the web site, buses, billboards, in-store, through direct marketing and to support retailers.

In order to attract real media attention the image was placed on a temporary 64 ft high tower that was placed on the Chiswick Tower roundabout, a very busy traffic route to the west of London. The stunt achieved placement in several London newspapers, three national women's magazines, one national newspaper and several fashion web sites.

Source: Cowlett (2007).

Question

Is the use of this type of outdoor media likely to cause accidents rather than promote brand recall?

Task

Choose a brand and think of interesting ways in which outdoor media might be used to attract attention.

Exhibit 24.2 'Stairway to Heaven' for the Pretty Polly brand and Britain's largest billboard
Courtesy of Pretty Polly.

and has since grown consistently. In 2007, steady growth helped advertising revenues to £1,084 million (Advertising Association, 2008).

Outdoor media consist of three main formats.

Outdoor media consist of three main formats: street furniture (such as bus shelters); billboards (consisting primarily of 96-, 48- and 6-sheet poster sites); and Transit (which covers the Underground, buses and taxis). Outdoor media accounted for approximately 5.7 per cent of total advertising expenditure in 2006, and has been taking an increasing percentage of organisations' media spend. Recent growth has been due to a 34 per cent increase in the growth of 6-sheet posters (Advertising Association, 2007).

Other reasons for the growth in outdoor expenditure are that it can reinforce messages transmitted through primary media, act as a substitute media when primary media are unavailable (e.g. tobacco organisations deprived of access to television and radio) and provide novelty and interest (electronic, inflatable and three-dimensional billboards), which can help avoid the clutter caused by the volume of advertising activity.

Billboards and street furniture

These are static displays and, as with outdoor media generally, are unable to convey a great deal of information in the short period of time available in which people can attend to the messages. However, advances in technology permit precise targeting of poster campaigns on a national, regional or individual audience basis, or by their proximity to specific outlets, such as banks, CTNs (confectioner, tobacconist and newsagent) and off-licences. There are two key developments in the industry that concern the replacement of the traditional bucket-and-paste production process. The first is the use of biodegradable one-sheet posters. The second concerns the use of high definition (HD) billboards, which are glue-less vinyl posters that can be clipped in and out of a frame, reused and eventually recycled (Gray, 2008). Evaluation using the POSTAR system allows for measurement of not only the size and type of audience but also the traffic flows, travel patterns and even how people read posters.

Strengths

One of the main advantages of this medium springs from its ability to reach a large audience. This means that most members of a target audience are likely to have an opportunity to see the message, so the cost per contact is very low. It is generally recognised that outdoor media can provide tremendous support to other tools in the media mix, particularly at product launch, as back-up and when attempting to build brand name recognition.

The medium is characterised by its strong placement flexibility. Messages can be placed geographically, demographically or by activity, such as on the main routes to work or shopping. The potential impact is high, as good sites can draw the eye and make an impression. Gross rating points (GRPs; see Chapter 27) can be developed quickly by reaching a large percentage of the target audience many times in a short period.

Weaknesses

Messages transmitted by this medium do not allow for the provision of detailed information. Posters are passed very quickly and the potential attention span is therefore brief. This means that the message must be short, have a high visual impact and be capable of selling an idea or concept very quickly. Printing and production lead times are long; therefore, while control over message content is high, the flexibility in delivery once showings are agreed can be a limiting factor. The final disadvantage of outdoor media to be mentioned is that the effectiveness of message delivery is very difficult to measure, and in an age when accountability is becoming an increasingly important factor, this drawback does not help to promote the usage of this medium.

Transit

The names, signs and symbols that are painted on the sides of lorries and taxis can best represent transit or transport advertising. These moving posters, which travel around the country, serve to communicate names of organisations and products to all those who are in the vicinity of the vehicle. Indeed, transport advertising includes all those vehicles that are used for commercial purposes. In addition to lorries and taxis, transit media include buses, the Underground (trains, escalators and walkways), airplanes, blimps and balloons, ferries and trains, plus the terminals and buildings associated with the means of transport, such as airports and railway stations. For example, at Milan airport, the walls of terminal 1 are dominated by huge advertisements for the Giorgio Armani brand. The difference between outdoor and transport media is arbitrary, although the former are media static and the latter are media mobile.

The difference between outdoor and transport media is arbitrary.

Transit, and in particular taxi advertising, has been found to have very good reach and that its main role should be as a support medium (Veloutsou and O'Donnell, 2005). Messages can be presented as inside cards, where the messages are exposed to those using the vehicle. An example of this would be the small advertising messages displayed on the curvature of the roof of London Underground trains. Outside cards are those that are displayed on the exterior of taxis, buses and other commercial vehicles.

Strengths

The exposure time given to messages delivered via transport media can be high, but is dependent upon the journey time of the reader. The high readership scores that are recorded are due, possibly, to the boredom levels of travellers. The cost is relatively low, mainly because no extra equipment is necessary to transmit the message. Local advertisers tend to benefit most from transport advertising, as it can remind buyers of particular restaurants, theatres and shops.

Weaknesses

The medium fails to cover all market segments, as only particular groups use transportation systems. In comparison with other media it lacks status, is difficult to read (particularly in the rush hour) and suffers from the high level of clutter associated with inside cards.

In-store media

As an increasing number of brand choice decisions are made during the shopping experience, advertisers have become aware of the need to provide suitable in-store communications. The primary objective of using in-store media is to direct the attention of shoppers and to stimulate them to make purchases. The content of messages can be easily controlled by either the retailer or the manufacturer. In addition, the timing and the exact placement of in-store messages can be equally well controlled.

As mentioned previously, both retailers and manufacturers make use of instore media although, of the two main forms (point-of-purchase displays and packaging), retailers control the point-of-purchase displays and manufacturers the packaging. Increasingly, there is recognition of the huge potential of retail stores becoming an integrated media centre, with retailers selling and managing media space and time. Attention is given here to in-store media and the retail media format, while a consideration of packaging issues can be found in Chapter 23.

Point-of-purchase (POP)

There are a number of POP techniques, but the most used are window displays, floor and wall racks to display merchandise, posters and information cards, plus counter and checkout displays. The most obvious display a manufacturer has at the point of purchase is the packaging used to wrap and protect the product until it is ready for consumption. This particular element is discussed in Chapter 23.

Supermarket trolleys with a video screen attached have been trialled by a number of stores. As soon as the trolley passes a particular infrared beam a short video is activated, promoting

Indirect messages can play a role in in-store communications.

brands available in the immediate vicinity of the shopper. Other advances include electronic overhead signs, in-store videos at selected sites around the store and coupons for certain competitive products dispensed at the checkout once the purchased items have been scanned. Indirect messages can also play a role in in-store communications: for example, fresh bread smells can be circulated from the supermarket bakery at the furthest side of the store to the entrance area, enticing customers further into the supermarket. Some aroma systems allow for the smell to be restricted to just 45 cm (18 inches) of the display.

End-of-row bins and cards displaying special offers are POP media that aim to stimulate impulse buying. With over 75 per cent of supermarket buying decisions made in store, a greater percentage of communication budgets will be allocated to POP items.

ViewPoint 24.4 Thorntons keep it in-store

Valentine's Day is an important day for chocolate manufacturers and retailers. For Thorntons, who have 600 retail outlets, Valentine's Day in 2008 was approached without any advertising work. Apart from product-oriented PR work, all the communications were kept in store with a heavy emphasis on merchandising.

Thorntons use email to deliver catalogues to b2b customers, while their web site is used to support the flowers, champagne and hampers ranges that complement their gift portfolio.

Source: Jacob (2008).

Question

Why do you think Thorntons have pulled out of any above-the-line work for Valentine's Day?

Task

Think of another gift-oriented brand, and find out what communications are used to support it.

Exhibit 24.3 A Thorntons store
Courtesy of Thorntons.

Strengths

Point-of-purchase media are good at attracting attention and providing information. Their ability to persuade is potentially strong, as these displays can highlight particular product attributes at a time when shoppers have devoted their attention to the purchase decision process. Any prior awareness a shopper might have can be reinforced.

From management's point of view, the absolute and relative costs of POP advertisements are low. Furthermore, management can easily fine tune a POP ad to reflect changing conditions. For example, should stock levels be high and a promotion necessary to move stock out, POP displays can be introduced quickly.

The absolute and relative costs of POP advertisements are low.

Weaknesses

These messages are usually directed at customers who are already committed, at least partly, to purchasing the product or one from their evoked set. POP messages certainly fail to reach those not actively engaged in the shopping activity.

There can be difficulties maintaining message continuity across a large number of outlets. Signs and displays can also be damaged by customers, which can impact upon the status of a product. Shoppers can therefore be negatively influenced by the temporary inconvenience of damaged and confusing displays. Unless rigorously controlled by store management, the large amount of POP materials can lead to clutter and a deterioration in the perception shoppers have of a retail outlet.

Retail media centres

Traditionally retailers allow their stores to be used in a variety of ways by a variety of organisations to communicate messages to their audiences. These audiences are jointly owned, not necessarily in equal proportion, by the branded food manufacturers that use stores for distribution purposes, and the retailers that try to build footfall or store traffic through retail branding approaches. As a result, the management of the media opportunities and the messages that are communicated are uncoordinated, inconsistent and the media potential, to a large extent, ignored. In the past, retailers will have argued that their core business rests with retailing, not selling and managing media. However, the media world has developed considerably in recent years, often in tandem with developments in technology. For a long time, retailers have built databases using customer information and developed sales promotion-based loyalty programmes as a result.

Street furniture has been used in the immediate vicinity of supermarkets and shopping centres and malls to drive local traffic. In-store radio has been used, first as background and now, in many cases, as a radio station based on entertainment. In-store posters, promotions, merchandising and various ambient media opportunities have been used haphazardly or, at best, in an uncoordinated way. All of these have been managed by a variety of specialists, typical of the way in which the marketing communications industry has developed (see Chapter 3). However, as Reid (2004) pointed out, Tesco and Asda-Walmart installed various in-store plasma television screens. The intention was to sell television time according to product category, some of which equates directly with particular aisles and store space. In addition, Asda has created its own media (or sales) centre through which media activities are coordinated. Tesco understands the media potential of each of its stores and the opportunities that advertisers value by reaching the 27 per cent of all UK shoppers who visit Tesco each week. Indeed, some of the time sold on the Tesco television channels has been sold to advertisers that are not stocked in store (e.g. finance, travel and cars). It was hoped that this retail channel would grow in volume, value and media presence. However, the experiments are reported not to have been entirely successful and in some cases the screens have been removed.

Cinema

There has been a revival in the level of expenditure on cinema advertising, reflecting the trends in audience sizes.

There has been a revival in the level of expenditure on cinema advertising, reflecting the trends in audience sizes. In 2007 cinema advertising was worth £203 million (Esposito, 2008) or approximately 1 per cent of total advertising spend. Advertisers used to be reluctant to use this medium, but as the number of people visiting cinemas in the United Kingdom grew considerably since 1998 reaching 167 million in 2003. However, attendances have fallen back since then and although they were 156 million in 2007 (CAA/EDI), this was partly because of the wet summer which served to boost cinema attendance. The growth in attendances was linked to the increase in multiplex cinemas (multiple screens at each site) and as Esposito reports, the appalling summer weather in 2007 that drove many people into the cinema for their entertainment. Advertisers have followed the crowds but have also listened to the research that shows that cinema audiences remember more detail than television audiences and as a captive audience there are no distractions.

With customer satisfaction levels improving, advertisers have consistently increased the adspend in this medium. Advertising messages transmitted in a cinema have all the advantages of television-based messages. Audio and visual dimensions combine to provide high impact. However, the audience is more attentive because the main film has yet to be shown and there are fewer distractions or noise in the communication system. The implication is that cinema advertising has greater power than television advertisements. This power can be used to heighten levels of attention and, as the screen images are larger than life and because they appear in a darkened room that is largely unfamiliar to the audience, the potential to communicate effectively with the target audience is strong.

Strengths

The mood of the audience is generally positive, particularly at the start of a show.

The mood of the audience is generally positive, particularly at the start of a show. This mood can be carried over into the commercials. Furthermore, the production quality of cinema messages is usually very high and transmission is often assisted by high-quality audio (digital surround-sound systems) that is being installed in the new multiplex arenas.

The production and transmission costs are quite low, which makes this an attractive media vehicle. The attention-getting ability and the power of this medium contribute to the high recall scores that this medium constantly records, often four times higher than the average recall scores for television commercials.

Weaknesses

The costs associated with reaching local audiences are low; however, if an advertiser wishes to reach a national audience, the costs can be much higher than those for television. The audience profile for UK cinema admissions indicates that approximately 80 per cent of visitors are aged 15 to 34. With an increasing proportion of the population aged over 55 (the grey market), cinema advertising is limited by the audience profile and the type of products and services that can be realistically promoted.

The third and final weakness is, to some, the most important. The irritation factor associated with viewing advertising messages when customers have paid to see a film has been found to be very high. Some respondents, to a number of studies, have expressed such an intensity of feeling that they actively considered boycotting the featured products. So despite the acclaim and positive reasons for using cinema advertising, advertisers are advised to be careful about the films they select to run their commercials against (audience profile will also be affected) and whether they should use this medium.

Advertisers are advised to be careful about the films they select to run their commercials against.

ViewPoint 24.5 Orange cinemas?

Orange are the only mobile operator to work with cinema (at the time of writing). In addtion to their considerable £13.5m spend on cinema advertising in 2007 they also sponsored the Bafta film awards. The reason for this activity is that the main cinema audience is the 16- to 34-year-old demographic and that matches Orange's target market. Interestingly they do not use cinema for product-based communications, but use the medium to develop a strong link between Orange and the cinema. Research indicates that Orange are perceived to be the number-one brand associated with film in the United Kingdom.

Mobile brand Orange have used a cinema campaign called 'The Film Board'. For several years 'The Film Board' has occupied the 'gold spot' – the last ad spot before the main feature film begins. The Board is a fictional panel, obsessed with product placement, who listen to famous people and celebrities pitch their ideas for movies. For example, John Cleese pitched his idea for a dramatic war film, but he is not taken seriously by the Board, who even get one of their executives to watch the pitch on their Orange 3G Mobile phone.

Sources: Esposito (2008); www.visit4info.com/details.cfm?adid=24648.

Question

Although Orange have developed strong associations with cinema could it be said that they 'own the media' as they do not use the medium to promote products?

Task

Next time you visit the cinema make a note of the Film Board spot and consider how prominent Orange is.

Exhibit 24.4 Vue Entertainment has 63 state-of-the-art multiplex cinemas with over 615 screens and 136,000 seats. Vue alone attracts over 32 million customers every year
Freud Communications.

Ambient media

Ambient media are a fairly recent innovation and represent a non-traditional alternative to outdoor media. Ambient media are regarded as out-of-home media that fail to fit any of the established outdoor categories. Ambient media can be classified according to a variety of factors (see Table 24.2). Of these, standard posters account for the vast majority of ambient activity (59 per cent) with distribution accounting for 24 per cent and the four remaining categories just 17 per cent.

Guerrilla tactics

Guerrilla media tactics are an attempt to gain short-term visibility and impact in markets where the conventional media are cluttered and the life of the offering is very short.

Traditionally, flyposting was the main method, practised most often by the music business. Now the term refers to a range of activities that derive their power and visibility from being outside the jurisdiction of the paid-for media. Sabotage is a stronger interpretation, as the tactics require the hijacking of conventional media events. Lanigan (1996) reports on the use of spray paint to sabotage other advertisers' posters, while the launch of the *Blah Blah Blah* music magazine involved sticking speech bubbles over posters carrying messages for other advertisers.

Sabotage is a stronger interpretation of guerrilla tactics.

Table 24.2 Ambient media categories

Ambient category	Explanation
Standard posters	Washrooms, shopping trolleys, phone boxes
Distribution	Tickets, receipts, carrier bags
Digital	Video screens, projections, LED screens
Sponsorships	Playgrounds, golf holes, petrol pump nozzles
Mobile posters	Lorries, barges, sandwich boards
Aerials	Balloons, blimps, towed banners

Source: Advertising Association (2003) *Advertising Statistics Yearbook*. Used by permission of WARC.

Direct response media

This chapter on the media would not be complete without reference to direct response media. The principal use of the media is to convey one of two types of message: one is oriented towards the development of brands and attitudes; the other is aimed at provoking a physical (and mental) response. It follows that attitude and response-based communications require different media.

Conventional media (television, print or radio) once used just to develop brands and attitudes are now used as a mechanism or device to provoke a response, through which consumers/buyers can follow up a message, enter into an immediate dialogue and either request further information or purchase goods. The main difference with new media is the time delay or response pause between receiving a message and acting on it. Through direct response mechanisms, the response may be delayed for as long as it takes to make a telephone call, press a button or fill out a reply coupon. However, the response pause and the use of a separate form of communication highlight the essential differences.

Estimates vary, but somewhere between 30 per cent and 40 per cent of all television advertisements now carry a telephone number or web address. Direct response television (DRTV) is attractive to those promoting service-based offerings and increasingly travel brands and some FMCG brands are using it. Reid (1996) argues that DRTV can be likened to a video game. Level 1 is viewing the commercial, while level 2 requires the respondent to phone in and receive more information and derive greater entertainment value. Only at level 3 will there be an attempt to sell directly to the respondent. The main purpose for advertisers using this route is to extract personal information for the database and subsequent sales promotion and mailing purposes.

One aspect that is crucial to the success of a direct response campaign is not the number of responses but the conversion of leads into sales. This means that the infrastructure to support these promotional activities must be thought through and put in place, otherwise the work and resources put into the visible level will be wasted if customers are unable to get the information they require – the provision of the infrastructure alone is not sufficient – the totality of the campaign should support the brand. Indeed, this is an opportunity to extend brand opportunities and provide increased brand experiences.

Integrated media

This chapter has considered the merits of different media and has considered them as single media as if they operate in environments unaffected by each other, or indeed aloof from any other influence. Obviously, this is far from reality, and in a world of integrated marketing communications, media neutral planning and open planning approaches each medium needs to be considered in the light of its effectiveness when deployed with other media.

There is a growing body of evidence that shows that the effectiveness of the media increase considerably when media are used in combination. Just as it was shown in Chapter 20 that the impact of sponsorship improves when advertising is used before, during and after the sponsored event, so the impact of particular media can improve when they are used collectively within a campaign. Of course, the possible number of media combinations is huge and too numerous for each to be considered here.

> The effectiveness of the media increase considerably when media are used in combination.

ViewPoint 24.6 Golfing media

Sports events often represent prime promotional opportunities, if only because of the television coverage. For example, major golf tournaments attract huge global television audiences and as a result attract advertisers. The placement of billboards and posters around a golf course are restricted but the tees, where golfers drive off for each hole, are prime points for advertisers. Sometimes these are restricted to the sole use of the tournament's sponsors but it is possible to see a wide array of brands as the camera focuses on the golfers preparing to play. In some cases flowers on the surrounding grassy banks can be used to remind audiences of the location, and the perimeter boards reinforce brand messages or the main sponsors of the event. Very often a clock is used to remind viewers just who is sponsoring the event, while the caddies' bibs carry advertising messages and even the waste bins receive financial support.

All of these are different types of media and they are used to deliver a variety of messages.

Question

To what extent are this cluster of messages likely to cut through or are there just too many?

Task

Choose a sporting event of your choice and note the various promotional opportunities.

It is now commonly accepted that online advertising in general works best with offline media. The main reason for this is that it is necessary to drive people to a particular web site. To date, there is no firm evidence to show that any one type of offline media is best suited to this task and a great deal depends on the nature of the product or service, as well as the audience's involvement in the category.

Snoddy (2007) reports on research referred to as 'brain fingerprinting' (see Chapter 12 for more details). This technical study claims to have scientifically proven that when newspaper advertising is used with television ads, the brand impact scores rise by 72 per cent. As a result, the Newspaper Marketing Agency claims that newspapers provide a complement impact for, and improve, the impact and response to television ads.

Catalogues, once a popular way of buying clothes and household items, is no longer a fashionable marketing channel and has faded with the development of the Internet and online shopping. While the huge bulky catalogues have all but disappeared, they have been replaced with newer, slimmer and highly targeted catalogues. The product scope is narrow and the aim is to drive people to the brand's web site. The new slim-line catalogues contain a fraction of the products available, but provide a preview and an incentive to visit the web site. Referred to as 'flick-to-click' this approach reflects changing consumer behaviour. Research reported by Murphy (2007) found that 66 per cent of consumers prefer the combination of catalogue to view and online to buy. The most popular categories were clothing, travel, cosmetics and gardening. It is suggested that this behaviour is a function of time-poor customers who prefer to read something offline, at a time convenient to them, perhaps late at night when relaxing (not in front of a computer screen).

> The new slim-line catalogues contain a fraction of the products available, but provide a preview and an incentive to visit the web site.

Outdoor has long been seen as an important support for television and print media, often used to reinforce brand messages or to create attention. What is key of course is to understand how, when and which media people use. Before the arrival of digital media individuals used a limited media mix. This was often based around a few television channels, a Sunday and a weekday paper, maybe a couple of magazines and perhaps cinema. This mix has been transformed so that today research indicates that adults consume a portfolio of media that embraces 10–15 television channels, 10–15 web sites and a similar number of magazines. This does not account for a wealth of other media such as radio and cinema. In addition, people are consuming media through time and place shifting and using their portfolio of media in an integrated format (WARC, 2007).

Summary

In order to help consolidate your understanding of traditional media, here are the key points summarised against each of the learning objectives:

1. Determine the variety and types of traditional media.

Of the many available media, six main classes can be identified. These are broadcast, print, outdoor, new, in-store and other media classes. Within each of these classes there are particular types of media. For example, within the broadcast class there are television and radio, and within the print class there are newspapers and magazines.

Within each type of medium there are a huge number of different individual media vehicles that can be selected to carry an advertiser's message.

2. Explain the main criteria used to evaluate media and their use.

Understanding of the key characteristics of each type of media assists media selection and planning. The fundamental characteristics concern the costs, the richness of the communication, the interactive properties and audience profile associated with a communication event.

3. Establish the primary characteristics of each type of medium.

The rich array of characteristics that each type of media possesses serve to engage audiences in different ways.

4. Examine the strengths and weaknesses of each type of medium.

These were detailed in the chapter and represent opportunities for organisations to make sure they use the right media to deliver against different goals.

5. Provide a brief summary of the main UK trends in advertising expenditure on each type of medium.

The overall trend in media spend is that organisations are increasingly moving funds from offline to online media. Digital media spend is increasing and is increasing at a rate far faster than any other type or class of media. Although digital spend is greater than print, most of the large grocery firms allocate less than 1 per cent of their total budget to online resources.

6. Consider the dynamics associated with direct response media.

The principal use of the media is to convey one of two types of message: one is oriented towards the development of brands and attitudes; the other is aimed at provoking a physical (and mental) response. It follows that attitude- and response-based communications require different media. One aspect that is crucial to the success of a direct response campaign is not the number of responses but the conversion of leads into sales.

7. Explore ways in which media can be integrated.

There is a growing body of evidence that shows that the effectiveness of the media increases considerably when media are used in combination. The possible number of media combinations is huge and too numerous for each to be considered here. It is important to understand how, when and which media people use. Before the arrival of digital media, individuals used a limited media mix. This was often based around a few television channels, a Sunday and a weekday paper, maybe a couple of magazines and perhaps cinema. This mix has been transformed so that today research indicates that adults consume a portfolio of media that embraces 10–15 television channels, 10–15 web sites and a similar number of magazines. This does not account for a wealth of other media such as radio and cinema. In addition, people are consuming media through time and place shifting and using their portfolio of media in an integrated format.

Review questions

1. Explain the differences between media classes, types and vehicles. Give two examples of each to support your answer.
2. Describe the main characteristics of the print media. Find examples to illustrate your points.
3. Compare and contrast newspapers and magazines as advertising media.

4. What do you think will be the impact on broadcast television of the growth in penetration by cable television? How will this affect advertisers?
5. If radio is unobtrusive, why should advertisers use it?
6. What are the strengths and weaknesses of outdoor advertising media? Why is it sometimes referred to as the last true broadcast medium?
7. Why are the relative costs of each medium different?
8. Under what conditions might cinema be used as the primary medium?
9. List the main types of ambient media.
10. Explain the role of primary and secondary media. Is this a valid demarcation in a period of media-neutral planning?

MiniCase For different types of wood: The Pila Pasak (Shepherd's Sawmill) campaign

Nicola Robinsonova: Freelance Marketing Consultant

The Sawmill

Pila Pasak is a small, but growing sawmill based in the Czech Republic. The company was established in the 1940s and was nationalised during the communist era, before being restituted to a descendant of the founder in 1994. When Pasak first started renting the sawmill, the only advertising consisted of hand-painted signs. There are competitors to Pila Pasak located in the same geographical area. Potential customers need to know about Pila Pasak and actively choose to purchase from the sawmill in preference to a competitor.

Lubos Pasak bought the sawmill in 2003. It now has a staff of 43 (unusually for the industry type, more than 50 per cent of the workforce is female). The sawmill is located in South Bohemia, a landscape of forests and lakes, close to the E55 (European motorway) linking Prague with Linz in Austria. Wood arrives at the plant as tree trunks, and leaves in a variety of forms. There is no waste, tree bark is sold to garden centres, the woodchip is bought by a wood pellet manufacturer. Any other waste is sold as fuel for wood-burning stoves.

The product itself is essentially a commodity and not capable of differentiation. Pila Pasak would claim to have a higher quality of product than its competitors, but this would be hard to justify. There is not a lot of difference between one sawmill and another. The tree trunks are bought from the same central supplier. The Czech forestry is state owned and state operated, and sets the price and quantity of wood for each year. Wood prices can vary in response to supply and demand – for example the price fell in 2007 partly because of strong storms that blew down many trees.

Pila Pasak's customers are mainly from the building trade, with a limited number of private purchasers. A notable recent customer was the producer of the movie Oliver Twist. Antique timber from Pila Pasak featured in the film, which was filmed partly in the Czech Republic.

About Czech media

Since communism ended in 1989, there has been a rapid transformation of the Czech media industry. Previously, no advertising was allowed, whereas now there is a range of newspapers and magazines (*Tyden* 150k daily readership and *Respekt* 70k) and an active trade press. Broadcast media includes four national television stations and a range of local and national radio stations. There is less regulation of outdoor media, so many prominent adverts, including huge (aesthetically challenging) 3-D sculptures appear beside the major roads of the country. The Czech parliament is now debating the safety issues of such advertising structures.

Ice hockey is the national sport and so billboard ads surround ice hockey pitches in the same way as can be observed at football matches in the United Kingdom. Transport advertising is well established, one notable example being the Zappa cement factory, which uses a highly original livery for their vehicles, as well as a quite extraordinary level of decoration on the plant itself.

The infrastructure supporting Internet use in the Czech Republic is very developed, and so the Internet (and Internet marketing) is a normal part of life. Instore media, such as point-of-purchase and packaging is perhaps somewhat less prominent than in more consumerist societies (or countries with a longer consumerist history), and most Czechs prefer to spend weekends in their country cottages rather than shopping. Other media such as cinema, exhibition and ambient advertising can all be found in the Czech Republic, though product placement is not quite so common in the film industry.

One option used by retail advertisers in the Czech Republic is a weekly broadsheet delivered to the door of every customer, seemingly from every supermarket and chain store.

These free-sheets contain only limited amounts of product- and price-based information. However, people in the Czech Republic do not complain about it, not because they are unsophisticated about advertising, or naive about the purpose of free-sheets, but because many homes in this region are still heated by log-burning stoves, and stoves need fire-lighters, and what better way to acquire them than to have them delivered by a free 'just-in-time' mechanism.

Marketing communications and Pila Pasak

Pila Pasak has a web site (www.pasak.cz), which is visited by around 1,200 people a month. It is a brochure site, with no online shop or additional functionality. Pasak estimates that only 10 per cent of his customers have Internet access and he feels that so far the site has not been of great interest to his customers.

The current marketing communications strategy of Pila Pasak aims to differentiate and remind customers. The marketing budget is 0.7 per cent of turnover, reflecting the growth of the company since a more standard 2–3 per cent budget was set in 2003. Regional advertising agencies are used, but only to print and position the billboard adverts, which are produced in-house.

The campaign was launched in November 2007. The main strap line of the advertising campaign translates as 'For different types of wood' and features three women, each of different size, shape and skin tone, and there is a great deal of exposed flesh (see Exhibit 24.5). Pasak selected four billboard locations within 10 kilometres of the premises to display Eurotype 5.4 × 2.8 m print ads (see Exhibit 24.5).

Media choices

For reasons of cost and practicality, there are no press or radio adverts, and the web site has not been made a part of the campaign. The monthly cost of the billboard equals that of a one-eighth of a page ad in a regional daily, with an estimated readership of 20,000 people. The only point of sale is the sawmill itself, and there is no packaging. Newspaper ads are comparatively expensive when considered alongside billboards.

The sawmill is passed by 30,000 vehicles daily and is on the main road between Prague and Austria. For Pila Pasak, the one clear advantage of this position is that advertising can be created over time by trial and error. The ads can be changed regularly and the effects measured. For example, 'normal'-looking women are used in this campaign because more glamorous models were not so effective. Pasak explains that the more glamorous models did not attract as many new customers because they were not seen as a potentially realistic part of the life of the average Pila Pasak customer.

Exhibit 24.5 Outdoor advertising used by Pila Pasak

Promotional materials

The campaign was not carried over to the corporate gifts distributed over the Christmas period by Pila Pasak. The calendar, which was sent out to key business contacts, featured a collection of historic photos of moustaches. The 'different kinds of wood' calendar cards were given to customers at the payment counter. A more special corporate gift was a bottle of Borovicka, a locally produced spirit flavoured with Juniper berries. The text on the labels had been amended to read 'Pasakova Borovicka'.

Some measures of campaign success include awareness levels among potential customers. For example, people from outside the geographical area of South Bohemia recall the campaign when the name Pila Pasak is mentioned to them. The campaign also received coverage in the national press. For example, a full-page article in *Respekt* with a half-page image of the Pila Pasak advert. When customers visit the premises of Pila Pasak, they can see images from previous adverts over the last 15 years, perhaps a form of strategic brand reinforcement.

MiniCase questions

1. If the Shepherd's Sawmill was based in the United Kingdom, how would you redesign this marketing campaign?
2. What reaction would you imagine if you were to run the campaign as it stands in the United Kingdom?
3. Find out what 'Pasak' means (both literally and in Czech slang), how does this impact on perceptions of the campaign?

References

Advertising Association (2004) *Advertising Statistics Year Book*. Henley: NTC. Also at www.adassoc.org.uk/inform/.

Advertising Association (2007) *Advertising Statistics Year Book*. Henley: NTC. Also at www.adassoc.org.uk/inform/.

Advertising Association (2008) *Advertising Statistics Year Book*. Henley: NTC. Also at www.adassoc.org.uk/inform/.

Ballantyne, D. (2004) Dialogue and its role in the development of relationship specific knowledge. *Journal of Business and Industrial Marketing*, **19**(2), 114–23.

Cowlett, M. (2007) Pretty Polly replicates success of 'Hello Boys', Campaign, 14 March. Retrieved 25 January 2008 from www.prweek.com/uk/search/article/643525/.

Esposito, M. (2008) Cinema advertising: stars of the silver screen. *Marketing*, 9 January. Retrieved 19 January from www.brandrepublic.com/InDepth/Features/775594/Cinema-advertising-Stars-silver-screen/.

Fitch, D. (2007) Outdoor advertising. Retrieved 20 January 2008 from www.millwardbrown.com/Sites/MillwardBrown/Content/News/EPerspectiveArticles.aspx?id=%2f200711010001.

Govoni, N., Eng, R. and Galper, M. (1986) *Promotional Management*. Englewood Cliffs, NJ: Prentice-Hall.

Gray, R. (2008) Green credentials on display. *Marketing*, 9 April, 33–4.

Heath, R. and McDoanld, S. (2007) Press advertising: equal to TV in building brands. *Admap*, (April) 482, 34–6.

Jacob, R. (2008) How personalisation has helped build Thorntons. *UtalkMarketing.com*. Retrieved 26 Februray 2008 from www.utalkmarketing.com/Pages/Article.aspx?ArticleID=4353&Title.

Lanigan, D. (1996) Guerrilla Media. *Campaign*, 5 April, 26–7.

Murphy, D. (2007) Off the page, on to the web, *The Marketer*, (October) 31–3.

Okin, G. and Robothan-Jones, R. (2007) Weetabix – The Weetabix Week: turning a barrier into a benefit. *Institute of Practitioners in Advertising*, IPA Effectiveness Awards. Retrieved 18 April 2008 from www.ipa.co.uk.

Reid, A. (1996) FMCG advertisers are starting to wise up to DRTV. *Campaign*, 26 April, 15.
Reid, A. (2004) Asda leads charge as retail media comes of age. *Campaign*, 2 July, 15.
Sherwin, A. (2004) Instant adverts to counter digital TV viewers. *The Times*, 24 July, 15.
Snoddy, R. (2007) A potent brain wave for newspapers, *Marketing*, 2 May, 18.
Veloutsou, C. and O'Donnell, C. (2005) Exploring the effectiveness of taxis as an advertising medium. *International Journal of Advertising*, **24**(2), 217–39.
WARC (2007) WARC Media report the newspaper market in 2007. Retrieved 21 January 2008 from www.warc.com.

Chapter 25

Digital media

The development of digital-based technologies and web-enabled communications has had a profound effect on marketing communications. However, the full potential of these new technologies has yet to be realised as customer behaviour adapts and learns new ways of incorporating these facilities. Interactivity and rapid two-way communications enabled by technology require the development of new communication strategies and a fresh understanding of how best to communicate with target audiences.

Aims and learning objectives

The aim of this chapter is to consider the nature and characteristics of digital media. The intention is to examine the many aspects and features of digital media and to consider its potential to assist marketing communications. It is recommended that this chapter be read prior to Chapter 26 where the application of these tools and devices is considered in greater detail.

The learning objectives of this chapter are to:

1. explain the key forms of digital media;
2. understand what digital media enables users to do;
3. examine some of the issues arising from the design and use of web sites;
4. explain the key differences between traditional and digital media;
5. consider future technologies and their impact on marketing communications;
6. explain what convergence means and how it influences marketing communications.

For an applied interpretation see Matt King's MiniCase entitled ***Integrating traditional and digital media*** at the end of this chapter.

Introduction

The dramatic impact that digital technologies have had on people does not need amplification here. However, digitisation has provided marketers with the opportunity to develop new ways of communicating with a variety of audiences. This chapter starts by setting out the main types of digital media. It then proceeds to explain what they are and examines the generic benefits that each of these types of digital media can bring, that is, what it enables users to do. Part of this enabling concerns the creation of web sites, and this chapter explores their design and marketing functionality, before comparing some of the key characteristics of traditional and digital media. The chapter concludes with a consideration of the future of digital media, the associated convergence issues that are evolving and how these might impact on marketing communications in the future.

Chapter 26 then explores the various ways in which marketers have used digital media to communicate effectively with their various audiences.

Key forms of digital media

As suggested above, the range of digital media is vast and is growing rapidly. However, the following section considers some of the key types or forms of digital media and should not be considered comprehensive.

The Internet

The Internet provides a wide variety of activities, including electronic mail, global information access and retrieval systems, discussion groups, multiplayer games and file transfer facilities, all of which not only help to transform the way we think about marketing communications, but also impact on business strategy, marketing channel structures, interorganisational relationships and the configuration of the marketing communications mix.

The Internet impacts upon marketing in two main ways: distribution and communication. The first concerns distribution and marketing channels. The Internet provides a new, more direct route to customers, which can either replace or supplement current distribution/channel arrangements. The second element concerns the Internet as a communication medium. It provides a means of reaching huge new audiences and enabling the provision of vast amounts of information. These two elements, distribution and communication, combine as ebusiness and ecommerce to provide benefits for both buyers and sellers.

The Internet is an important way of providing product and service information and can enable organisations to provide frequent and intensive levels of customer support. With it come doubts about its ability to deliver competitive advantage and whether it could offer suitable levels of privacy, security and measures of advertising effectiveness.

The Internet is not a panacea for a manager's marketing communications problems. It is a relatively new and different means of communication, one that should be integrated into the marketing communications mix. Offline communications are used to raise site awareness and interest among a wide audience and to provide them with the site address. Once at the web site, in-depth product information can be exchanged for customer-specific details to refresh the database and fuel future communication activities. It is this holistic perspective of the new media that should be developed.

Traditional marketing communications strategies employ a mix of tools and normally involve an emphasis on one type of communication device, depending on the context. Broadly speaking, it has been the norm to weight advertising over the other tools when dealing with consumer markets, and to weight personal selling when operating in the b2b sector. This reflects advertising's ability to raise awareness and develop brands and personal selling's prime skill at provoking behavioural action and closing orders. These general approaches have begun to be relaxed as audience and media fragmentation gathers speed and new ways of doing business (e.g. ecommerce) are developed.

The Internet is the fastest growing advertising medium.

The Internet is the fastest growing advertising medium, attracting revenues from a range of sources, some of which are investments previously devoted to television. Online advertising now equates to 10.6 per cent of total adspend and grew at 47.5 per cent in 2006 (Advertising Association, 2008). To demonstrate this extraordinary growth, online advertising attracted £153 million in 2000. By 2006 this figure had reached £2,016 million.

Adverting online takes one of two main forms.

Adverting online takes one of two main forms, display advertising, which includes, banners, interruptive, sponsorships, tenancies and display on email. Classified advertising is principally concerned with paid for search (see later in this chapter), but also includes recruitment and classifieds (including b2b).

The development of Web 2.0 or social media has added a new and critical dimension to the Internet. Web 2.0 represents a step change in the development and use of the Internet and even at the time of writing, Web 3.0 looms. Constantinides and Fountain (2008) argue that there are three main principles associated with Web 2.0:

- there is a focus on service-based, simple, open source solutions as online applications;
- it represents continual and incremental application development which requires users to participate and interact in new ways. So, from a position of consuming media, users are now contributors, reviewers and content editors;
- Web 2.0 also represents a new service business model that has created new opportunities to reach small, individual business customers with low-volume products.

Many of the applications associated with Web 2.0 (social networks, RSS (really sample syndication), Viral marketing etc.) are explored in Chapter 26.

The prime benefit of the Internet, as a hybrid medium, is that it is good at all of these activities, but it is not as good for any one task as a single communication tool might be. Interestingly, it excels as a part of the communication and decision-making process that the established communication tools fail to properly address, namely the search for, and retrieval of, information pertinent to purchase behaviour. It might be said, therefore, that the Internet provides a complementary facility to the marketing communication tools and as such should be used with, and not instead of, the established means of marketing communication. Above all else, the Internet is a medium, not a tool.

The Internet provides a complementary facility to the marketing communication tools and as such should be used with the established means of marketing communication.

Database technologies

A marketing database is a collection of records that can be related to one another in multiple ways and from which information, usually customer-related, can be obtained in a variety of formats. This can be analysed to determine appropriate segments and target markets and used to stimulate and record individual responses to marketing communications. It therefore plays a role as a storage, sorting and administrative device to assist direct, personalised communications.

When customer-related transactional and response data are combined with additional information from external sources, such as a list broker, the database can become a potent source for marketing communication activities. Indeed, the increasing sophistication of information retrieval from databases enables much more effective targeting and communications.

Databases provide a means of monitoring changes in customer behaviour, identifying new target markets, and cross-selling products and services. The purpose of cross-selling is to reduce customer churn and increase switching costs (Kamakura *et al.*, 2003). While increasing a customer's potential switching costs may not be compatible with relationship marketing principles, the result of successful implementation may be improved levels of customer retention and satisfaction where relationships are more discrete and transactional rather than collaborative in nature.

There are many potential operational problems associated with interrogating and processing information within live databases. Ryals and Payne (2001) point out that the transaction processing performance may be slowed down when interrogating customer information and the structure of the database itself is constantly changing in response to the large volume of transactions. Many organisations use data warehouses (and smaller data marts). These are integrated stores of data collected from a variety of sources (e.g. customer contact centres, the sales force and market research) and are updated at intervals, making it non-volatile and easier for interrogating customer information.

Multimedia

The term multimedia has not achieved universal agreement. Strictly speaking, the term refers to any presentation of information or material that uses two or more media. However, the term multimedia has only gained prominence since the advent of digital technologies. So, multimedia is generally assumed to refer to the integration of text, audio and images in order to enhance the user interface with computer-based applications. As a result 'streaming' of video and 'audio over the Internet' typify multimedia applications. As hardware and communications technology evolve, so new systems and applications develop to provide delivery of personalised email and marketing communication messages.

Multimedia is generally assumed to refer to the integration of text, audio and images in order to enhance the user interface.

Mobile technologies

Mobile phone technologies have advanced considerably and have enjoyed huge commercial success. Wireless application protocol, or WAP, phones possess the usual email and text information services, but they also have an Internet browser facility. As a result, messages can be not only location- but also time-specific. For example, a message can be sent when someone is in a town centre at lunch time, promoting a cafe, restaurant or shop. However, market growth in WAP technologies has been far less than originally expected, partly because of the text input facilities and the need for improved information displays.

New and faster technologies, such as general packet radio service (GPRS) and third-generation (3G) services enabling sound and image transfers, are expected to herald a successful relaunch of m-commerce. For example, in September 2007, Mazda used mobile advertising to drive awareness of their new Mazda2 model and to position the car as a stylish, bold new car. Video ads over 3 and T-Mobile networks were used to reach their core market, 25–34-year-old adults (Utalkb, 2007).

A further important development has been Bluetooth, the name given to a short-range radio technology that enables any kind of electronic equipment to be connected. Bluetooth's founding members include Ericsson, IBM, Intel, Nokia and Toshiba and their goal is to let Bluetooth's radio communications take the place of wires for connecting peripherals, telephones and computers.

Mobile marketing communications (to give it its full title) involves the delivery of direct marketing messages to mobile devices using wireless technologies. The prevailing usage is built around short message services (SMS), multimedia messaging services (MMS – which combines text with simple graphics and sound), wireless application protocol (WAP) mobile Internet and WAP push services and full multimedia third-generation (3G) services for both product promotion and entertainment purposes (MMA, 2007).

The more common title for this activity is mobile marketing, while some in the industry refer to it as proximity marketing. These titles are misleading because marketing is more than just communications, if only because this is primarily a communications medium, nothing more. In view of this discrepancy and to avoid misunderstanding, the phrase mobile communications is used here.

Apart from the sheer volume of users, 150 million in the European Union alone (www.bbc.co.uk) there are several reasons why the use of mobile communications has grown in recent years:

- *Interactivity*: the use of SMS provides recipients with the opportunity to respond directly to incoming requests. Simple yes/no answers are quick and easy to execute while opportunities to encourage interaction with brands exist 24/7, whether that be in- or out-of-home.
- *Personalisation*: mobile communications can enable messages that are customised to the personal needs of users. This means information can be highly targeted and contain relevant information.
- *Ubiquity*: the portability of mobiles means that it is possible to reach users at virtually any location, at any time and send them location-specific information.
- *Integration*: the effectiveness of mobile communications is optimised when it is used as a part of an integrated communications campaign.
- *Accountability*: the volume and nature of SMS responses can be measured, which is important from an investment perspective. In addition, it is possible to measure the contribution that different media make to drive responses. This in turn helps organisations to optimise their offline media spend and pursue integrated communications.
- *Cultural expectations*: as the number of mobile phones in circulation reaches saturation point, and as technology develops enabling more efficient communication, so peer group pressure and the entertainment industry encourage use of mobile phones. For example, presenters of television and radio programmes encourage their audiences to engage with them through text and mobile facilities in response to news items, quizzes and general topics of current interest. For many this form of communication and involvement has become a normal element of their leisure and entertainment expectations.

The key attributes of mobile communications are that it is a personal channel, one which enables direct, targeted and interactive communications and which can occur at any time and any place. SMS communications have underpinned its growth and are used not just for brand awareness-based advertising, but also as an effective way of delivering sales promotions, such as announcing special offers and 'text and win' events. This again reflects the contemporary role of mobile communications. However, as with email, it is also important to consider the potential privacy concerns of customers, especially as the receipt of unwanted messages (i.e. spam) may well increase.

It is also important to consider the potential privacy concerns of customers.

One of the difficulties facing the mobile communications industry has been how to provide a direct link between the offline and online environments. One possible solution is to use quick response or QR codes. These are two dimensional barcodes as represented at Exhibit 25.1.

By taking a picture of a QR code with a camera phone with a built in QR code reader, consumers can access further brand-related material that is linked to the code. Used with great success in Japan, some believe the use of QR codes will transform mobile marketing in Europe. Murphy (2008) reports that others are not so positive, citing differences in the Japanese technology infrastructure, which serves to facilitate this type of use and Britain's less than favourable disposition towards the use of Java software.

The potential to develop mobile communications is enormous, simply because the channel can deliver direct marketing messages related to advertising, sales promotion and public relations to individuals regardless of location. These messages can be used to develop brand awareness, support product launches, incentivise customers through competitions and promotions and promote trade and distributor involvement, as well as provide branded entertainment.

The potential to develop mobile communications is enormous.

ViewPoint 25.1 Mobile health

A large number of Health and Fitness Clubs, such as LA Fitness, Bannatynes, Greens, Village, Aquaterra and Esporta use mobile communications regularly. For example, Cannons Health Clubs, who manage 67 sites across the United Kingdom serving 165,000 members, have used mobile and email communications for customer acquisition and retention. In particular, they have found it very effective as part of their CRM programme by providing an effective delivery channel for time-sensitive issues, such as appointment reminders.

The effectiveness of mobile communications is demonstrated by Cannon's use of it for customer acquisition and their response rate is said to be 10 per cent. Text campaigns cost approximately £2 per response and they have found that text-only-generated new members regularly drive revenues exceeding £500 per member.

Mobile communications are used to reduce the number of no-shows and so increase conversion rates. Health Clubs can send SMS reminders to advise prospective members of gym tours, remind new joiners of induction training and members of classes and events. The gym manager, personal trainer or receptionist will book a text message reminder for the time required at the point of initial contact. This also gives the customer the opportunity to cancel in advance, thereby allowing the Club to fill the space.

SMS campaigns can be used to convert prospects once they have been informed by local offline media. By sending them a message using the keywords 'Offer' or 'Join' it is possible to track which offline media they might have been exposed to and from this data set switch their advertising between local press, radio and poster media according to which generates the highest response levels.

Source: Thurner (2007).

Question

Why have organisations been slow to develop mobile communication opportunities?

Task

Think about those organisations that contact you through SMS. How do you react and why?

Exhibit 25.1 A QR code

Source: Murphy (2008). Reproduced from *Marketing* magazine with the permission of the copyright owner, Haymarket Business Publications Limited.

Business applications

The phrase 'information systems and technology' (IST) is used to embrace the wide variety of new technologies that have been developed to improve the quality of life for the people who use IST and for those who benefit from their deployment. Ryssel *et al.* (2004: 197) refer to information technology as a term that embraces 'all forms of technology utilized to create, capture, manipulate, communicate, exchange, present and use information in its various forms (business data, voice conversations, still images, motion pictures, multimedia presentations and other forms, including those not yet conceived)'. They conceptualise the range of IST in terms of where the IST are used (internal or external) and across which broad functions (information, communication and decision support) (see Figure 25.1).

However, it is not the intention to provide a detailed examination of each of these systems or of the various technologies, as that is beyond the scope of this book. Readers interested in this aspect of technology are referred to Chaffey *et al.* (2006) or Rayport and Jaworski (2004).

A raft of increasingly sophisticated application programmes have evolved to meet the needs of the market. Initially electronic data interchange (EDI) via public networks, and now the Internet, managed the direct transmission between different companies' computer systems of data relating to business transactions. The applications tended to focus on systems designed by suppliers to assist customers in their purchasing procedures, processes and overall decision-making. The level of sophistication and scope of these applications now embrace a network of transactions and flow of information between a number of organisations. Radjou (2003: 25) refers to 'supply network processes', which encompass the following categories:

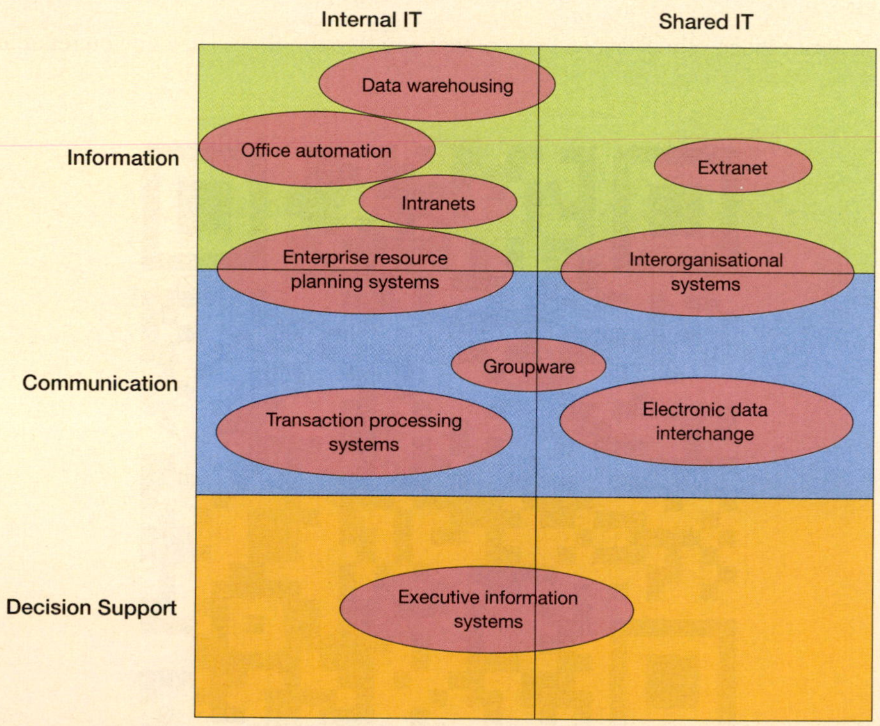

Figure 25.1 Types of information systems and their classification
Source: Ryssel *et al.* (2004).

- product lifecycle management;
- supply chain management;
- enterprise asset management;
- production network management;
- continuous demand management;
- order fulfilment and distribution management;
- aftermarket service management.

These applications serve to reduce costs, speed up processes, improve accuracy and provide added value for end-user customers. In terms of the relationships between organisations and their customers, these applications can serve to improve collaboration, both internally and externally. For example, enterprise-wide solutions such as complete enterprise resource planning (ERP) systems attempt to integrate all business processes across an organisation's accounting, manufacturing, sales and human resource departments. Further downstream, electronic point of sale (EPOS), which involves computerised tills linked back to a company's central computer(s), enables the data of every retail sale to be transmitted back to the organisation to facilitate sales and inventory management and, in a marketing context, can be used to better understand customer demand and buying behaviour. As networks, including the Internet, have extended to connect multiple businesses in the supply chain, sophisticated point-of-sale data have enabled collaborative marketing. For example, the leading supermarkets have systems that enable selected suppliers to 'find out information such as the repeat purchase rate of individual products, profiles of customers purchasing particular products and the most appropriate tools to attract customers' (Thomas, 2003).

These applications serve to reduce costs, speed up processes, improve accuracy and provide added value for end-user customers.

Interorganisational use of network technologies to share business information and coordinate supply chain activities has been termed 'ecollaboration' and represents a major area of development, particularly for high-technology-based companies.

Interactive television

Another important technological development is digital broadcasting and the opportunities for interactive television. Digital television and interactive services are two related but different facilities. Digital television is well established, but full interactivity has yet to be delivered to the majority of the population. Potential advantages are consumer familiarity, the full-screen, high-quality sound and picture format, fast channel and picture/text 'hopping', combining entertainment and shopping. The disadvantages include the current high cost of the sets to consumers and of broadcasting for companies. Also, it cannot deal with individual customers until TV-based email is widely established. Penetration rates will rise as analogue services in the United Kingdom are phased out.

Digital services provide many benefits for consumers, one of which will be the opportunity to screen out current intrusive advertising. Interactive, or red button advertising has to be driven by consumers who decide which advertisements they want to watch, when, and how long they will stay involved. The creative possibilities are far ranging, but in order to retain audiences it will become increasingly important to develop creative ideas based on a sound understanding of the target audience and their interactive and buying patterns. In January 2008, Andy Duncan, Channel 4's CEO, is reported to have claimed that red button technology is 'slow', 'basic' and 'clunky' (Jones, 2008). Their exit was followed in April 2008 by Channel 5. They announced it was abandoning its interactive red button adverting facility, citing that it was too costly (the return was poor) and that it did not fit the organisation's strategy.

Digital services provide many benefits for consumers.

Currently on UK teletext there are pages about holiday bargains that direct potential users to the Internet (www.teletext.co.uk/holidays) where they will find a searchable database, plus weather reports, resort reviews and advice. This service claims a choice of preferred operators, competitive pricing, confidence – full financial protection, up-to-date offers and human interaction at the point of sale. It states that, in the future, customers will be able to access the full functionality of the web site via digital television and/or mobile phone.

Digital television and interactive marketing communications are unlikely to thrive in isolation from other methods of communication.

The point is that digital television and interactive marketing communications are unlikely to thrive in isolation from other methods of communication. Just as online facilities need offline drivers, and just as bricks and clicks appear to be a more profitable format than clicks only, so an integrated perspective is required if digital television and interactive advertising are to be successful.

The BBC iPlayer and 4Odemand are hybrid applications (databases, television content, interactivity and broadband) that have quickly become popular forms of access to entertainment content material. These facilities enable people to watch recently transmitted television programmes (usually a week old) on their computers.

Video conferencing

There are currently two main types of video conferencing systems: PC-based and room-based. PC-based, or desktop, systems are suitable for a small number of people, for short time periods. The cameras are usually fixed focus, with small field capability, and viewing screens are also small. Transmission speeds are limited by modem and telephone line capabilities. An advantage is that software applications and files can be shared and viewed jointly.

Room-based systems use large, sophisticated (pan–tilt–zoom) cameras and wide television screens, which means that more people can participate. Transmission via ISDN (integrated services digital network), including satellite links, facilitates better picture/sound quality. Video conferencing can be used in marketing communications for research (audience polling), product promotion/launch, training, employee and/or channel member briefings and sales negotiations. The advantages of video conferencing include speed and convenience as travel costs, carbon footprints and time away from core tasks are minimised; there is potential to reduce message ambiguity as there is joint and simultaneous viewing of materials and instant feedback; and relationships with customers and stakeholders can be improved through increased more personal communication.

One of the disadvantages is that all participants have to be available at the same time, which can be difficult across time zones. The connections are not always reliable and room time-slots often cannot be extended beyond the original booking. Some people are uneasy in front of cameras, which may impair effectiveness.

The use of video conferencing has increased because the cost of the equipment has plummeted and there have been major technical advances.

The use of video conferencing has increased because the cost of the equipment has plummeted and there have been major technical advances, which have improved the clarity and reliability of many commercial systems. In addition, there have been periods of major global crisis, and an increasing number of messages about global warming, all of which have led some organisations to reduce their volume of air travel, and spurred the use of video conferencing.

Kiosks

Electronic kiosks are terminals that can be accessed by the public for information and services. Very often, kiosks are operated via touch-screens and video displays and incorporate card readers, coupon printers and other devices specific to their application. Increasingly, electronic kiosks provide not only multimedia facilities but also enable access to the Internet (www.scala.com).

ViewPoint 25.2 **REI in kiosks**

The outdoor climbing, hiking and mountain biking clothes made by REI require a high degree of touch and trial as well as significant information prior to purchase. REI has exploited these characteristics by building in-store climbing walls as well as hiking boot and mountain bike test areas. Due to limited retail floor space, REI installed web kiosks through which customers research 68,000 items as well as 45,000 web pages of product information.

By exploiting the fundamental nature of its products and through the instalment of kiosks in its stores, REI has effectively engaged its customers in a multi-channel experience. Kiosk implementation has allowed it to dedicate floor space to test areas while simultaneously attending to its breadth of inventory. Customers can utilise the strength of each channel and have consequently increased their spending. According to Jupiter Communications, existing REI customers who shopped online for the first time increased their store spending by 22 per cent and customers shopping on more than one channel spent overall more than in the previous year.

Question

If kiosks free up floor space for customer experience should not all shops move in this direction?

Task

Think of a product category that you are interested in, and make notes about how kiosks might enhance customers' experiences.

What digital media enables users to do

The various technologically-driven facilities referred to above can influence an organisation's marketing communications in many different ways. The implementation and benefits derived from technology will vary across organisations. This is because the level of strategic significance afforded to these investments, the culture, managerial skills, resources and degree to which the organisation has a true customer orientation differ widely. This section considers some of the generic ways in which digital media can influence marketing communications, but readers should be aware that the intensity of the influence is variable and far from uniform.

Interactivity

> Digital technology allows for true interactively based communications.

Digital technology allows for true interactively based communications, where messages can be responded to more or less instantly. Although there has been considerable media attention given to the development and potential of interactive services, the reality is that only a relatively small proportion of the public has become immersed in interactive environments, measured in terms of advertising space sold, usage and attitude research, and the number of transactions undertaken interactively. The development of interactive services may well be best served by the identification of those most likely to adopt such services and who will encourage others in their social orbits to follow their actions. This strategy would require communication with innovators and early adopters to speed the process of adoption (Rogers, 1983). This is quite crucial, as the infrastructure and associated heavy costs require an early stream of cash flows (Kangis and Rankin, 1996). The cost of equipment and time taken to learn and utilise interactive services does represent a barrier to adoption. These barriers might be substantial, depending on the background characteristics, education, personality, propensity to take risks and willingness to develop new skills and patterns of behaviour. This reinvention process can take individuals varying amounts of time to accomplish and hence impact on the speed of adoption.

Technological advances have enabled a range of other interactive communication opportunities. So far, emphasis has been placed on the Internet, but there have been many other imaginative and exciting developments and applications. One area where interactivity has been subject to experimentation is television, and some organisations have experimented with interactive messages, most notably the very first interactive advertisement for Chicken Tonight, plus Dove, Mazda and Tango.

One of the biggest factors accelerating the consumer use of digital television will be the variety of entertainment possibilities that the Internet can provide. The development of the BBC iPlayer facility has helped stimulate computer-based viewing of television programmes, which in turn may change consumer behaviour with regard to the consumption of this form of entertainment. This in turn may assist online shopping behaviour.

Home shopping represents a significant change in buyer behaviour.

Home shopping represents a significant change in buyer behaviour that may affect a range of ancillary activities. Several UK supermarket operators have invested heavily in shopping channels and they have had to learn new fulfilment operations and new processes and procedures to meet customer expectations. Although Tesco appears to have been particularly successful, there is little evidence to suggest that retailers will give up their high street presence, as predicted in the later 1990s. The physical shopping experience provides many consumers with significant entertainment and social interaction satisfactions and these are unlikely to be discarded for total virtual shopping.

The financial services sector can be expected to undergo further change as home banking in particular becomes a secure and more convenient transaction context. Entertainment possibilities will be even more attractive, as interactive games and interactive viewing through pay-per-view, video on demand and time shifting (which is, as Rosen pointed out as long ago as 1997, the option to view yesterday's programmes today) become easily accessible.

The new technology and the new communication infrastructure offer increasing numbers of people the opportunity to experience interactive marketing communications. This may impact on their expectations and bring changes to the way in which people lead their lives.

Intuitive software is used to monitor a visitor's movement around a site, store it and then adjust the site to meet the preferred pattern each time that visitor enters the site. The implications for targeting advertising are enormous. However, despite all these developments, it appears that Cohen (1995) was quite prophetic when he commented that there was 'great uncertainty as to the level of consumer demand' (p. 8). In 1995, technology and demand were uncertain, but even at the beginning of the twenty-first century online profitability remains elusive to many virtual traders. The reality must be that technological advances and changes in buyer behaviour are more severely lagged than originally realised. While some consumers are ready and eager to take advantage of the new opportunities, many are not, and the process of diffusion needs to move forward in order that an increasing proportion of customers has the means and motivation to participate in the interactive environments.

Multichannel marketing

Although not entirely responsible, new technology has enabled organisations to reach new markets and different segments using more than a single marketing channel. Database-generated telemarketing, direct mail, email and Internet channels now complement field sales, retail and catalogue selling and have allowed organisations to determine which customers prefer which channels, and which are the most profitable. This in turn enables organisations to allocate resources far more effectively and to spread the customer base upon which profits are developed. A multichannel strategy should accommodate customers' account channel preferences, their usage patterns, needs, price sensitivities and preferred point of product and service access. So, as Stone

A multichannel strategy should accommodate customers' account channel preferences, their usage patterns, needs and price sensitivities.

and Shan (2002) put it, the goal is to manage each channel profitably while optimising the attributes of each channel so that they deliver value for each type of customer.

Multichannel strategies have added new marketing opportunities, and enabled audiences to access products and services in ways that best meet their own lifestyle and behavioural needs. For organisations this has reduced message wastage, used media more efficiently and, in doing so, reduced costs and improved communication effectiveness.

ViewPoint 25.3 Multichannel NME

NME is a long-term music brand launched in magazine format in 1953 (as *New Music Express*). Among its claims are that it helped develop the careers of many bands and artists, including the Stones, Beatles, Bowie and the Sex Pistols. However, as the magazine market as whole continues to slide so NME was not immune especially as many of the readership are digital natives and generally averse to magazines.

Part of the remedy was to launch new media channels. The first of these was NME.com which now draws 1.8 million unique users. The web site is used to complement the magazine, although it provides increased depth and covers content not always suitable for the print version and enables blogging from music events.

A further channel, NMETV, was launched in 2007. Available to 9 million homes, the programme content includes video and interviews, and can be used to enhance material in the magazine channel.

NME Radio was launched in the summer of 2008 and is available on a number of national digital broadcast platforms.

Each of the media channels offers different opportunities, but NME have been able to integrate them so that each one reinforces the other. The television channel draws a different audience to the magazine, the former claiming 25–34-year-olds and the latter 15–24-year-olds. The obvious remaining question is, which of these channels is the most profitable?

The answer is magazines, even though circulation fell 12 per cent in the second half of 2007.

Source: Turner (2008).

Question

Is there an optimum number of channels that brands should use?

Task

Choose a grocery brand and find out how many channels are used to reach you.

Retailers are faced with particular problems that concern the amount of property/freehold they possess and the as yet unknown pattern of consumer shopping behaviour in the light of multichannel opportunities. The Arcadia Group (which owns Dorothy Perkins, Miss Selfridge, Wallis, Topshop, etc.) made a significant attempt to make its own name synonymous with online shopping through the development of Zoom, an online shopping mall. Some people might think that retailers should dispose of their fixed assets and move into the Internet or perhaps reconfigure their store layouts. In most cases, the optimum solution is to develop a multichannel solution whereby a range of media and experiences is offered to consumers. So, some prefer the Internet, some traditional shopping, some will use interactive television and some will prefer catalogue shopping. Many prefer a mix of these. This approach puts customers' needs first by determining their preferred marketing channels and also enables organisations to reconfigure their cost structures.

What may happen is that shopping activities become divided into categories that reflect particular channel options. So routine, unexciting purchases may be consigned to online and interactive channels, and the more explorative, stimulating and perhaps socially important purchases are prioritised for shopping expeditions. Many stores have recognised the

> Unexciting purchases may be consigned to online and interactive channels, and the more explorative, stimulating and perhaps socially important purchases are prioritised for shopping expeditions.

need to adapt themselves to provide more value (than a current product focus). Related benefits and enhanced services are important as they help differentiation and attract customers. For example, the bookstore Waterstones provides coffee bars and comfortable seating, an environment in which customers are encouraged to relax and consider their possible purchases. Larger stores and mainstream brands may need to establish themselves as 'destination' stores where the attraction for consumers is bound by excitement, entertainment and a brand experience. In some destination stores it is possible to test products in simulated but related environments. For example, attending cookery classes in supermarkets or test driving a range of cars in the countryside.

In the United States these types of store are now relatively common, and experience shows that High Street shopping is not about to die, but take a revised shape, form and role. Mercedes has a cafe on the Champs-Elysées in Paris but its role is to remind, differentiate and bring the brand into people's consciousness away from the traditional frame of reference. There is no persuasion as cars cannot be bought (or sold), but the brand is reinforced. See Chapter 21 for more on multichannel strategies.

Personalisation

For the first time, digital technology has empowered organisations to personalise messages and communicate with stakeholders on a one-to-one basis, on a scale that is commercially viable. This has driven the dramatic development of direct marketing, reshaped the basis on which organisations target and segment markets, stimulated dialogue, brought about a raft of new strategies and challenged the conventional approach to mass marketing and branding techniques.

The use of email communications is now extensive and viral marketing campaigns are gaining increasing acceptance. As with all forms of communication, the successful use of email requires an understanding of the recipient's behaviour. Email communication enables a high degree of personalisation, and in order to personalise messages it is necessary to understand the attitudinal and behavioural characteristics of each email audience (Chaffey, 2003). He suggests that the following need to be considered:

The successful use of email requires an understanding of the recipient's behaviour.

- How many recipients read their emails from home and at work?
- Which times of the day and days of the week do they read their email?
- How soon after receipt is email read?
- How do recipients configure their email readers?

Understanding the email behaviour of different audiences can influence the degree of personalisation that is given to email communications and web site welcome messages. However, email communication that is based on an understanding of the audience's email behaviour should influence the message content, the time when it should be sent and, most importantly, the keys to encouraging recipients to open the email and not delete it. These keys are the 'header' of the email, which contains the subject matter, and the 'from' address, which signifies whether the sender is known and hence strongly determines whether the email is perceived positively at the outset. If it is, then there is a stronger chance that the email will be opened and hence a greater opportunity for response and interactivity. A deeper consideration of email communication can be found in Chapter 26.

However, many people now expect a high level of personalisation and virtual recognition as opportunities arising through 'personalisation' reach beyond email communication. Personalisation is a sensitive area, often twinned with privacy issues. Indeed there appears to be little agreement about what constitutes personalisation and to that end Vesanen (2007) identifies five types of personalisation. These are shown at Table 25.1.

Personalisation is a sensitive area, often twinned with privacy issues.

Table 25.1 Types of personalisation

Type of personalisation	Segment marketing	Adaptive personalisation	Cosmetic personalisation	Transparent personalisation	Collaborative customisation
Typical actor	Reader's Digest	Yahoo.com	Google.com	Amazon.com	Hairdresser
Basic idea	To match customer preferences better than with mass-marketing	To let customers choose from different options	The organisation changes the package of standard good	The organisation changes the content of a good with a standard look	The organisation and customer are together building the product
When to use	Little customer knowledge, cheap	A lot of choices to choose from	Customer sacrifice is due to presentation	Customer contacts are repetitive	Determining either-or choices
Customer information	Purchase-/ demographic information	Direct choice by customer	Purchase-/ demographic-/ behavioural information	Purchase-/ demographic-/ behavioural information	Direct interaction
Learning opportunity	Low	Medium	Medium	Medium	High
Customer interaction	None	High	Low	Low	High
Change in presentation	Possibly	No	Yes	No	Likely
Variation of product	Possibly	No	No	Yes	Likely

Source: Reprinted by permission of Harvard Business School Press. From *The Experience Economy: Work is theatre and every business is a stage* by J. Pine and J. Gilmore. Boston, MA 1999. Copyright © 1999 by the Harvard Business School Publishing Corporation; all rights reserved.

Personalisation should be an integral aspect of relationship marketing, especially in b2b markets. The degree of personalisation will inevitably vary over the customer lifecycle and become more intimate as a relationship matures.

Personalisation should be an integral aspect of relationship marketing.

Mobility

Digital technologies now support a range of devices and applications that enable mobile communications. Mobile commerce (or mcommerce) refers to the use of wireless devices such as mobile phones for transactional activities; and because the wireless facility enables transactions to be undertaken in real time and at any location, a feature referred to as 'ubiquity', the impact on marketing communications could be huge. Because of the reachability, the opportunity to keep in touch, increased convenience, localisation and personalisation opportunities offered by this new technology, theoretically it will soon be possible to track people to particular locations. Then the delivery of personalised and pertinent information plus inducements and promotional offers in order to encourage specific purchase behaviour can have greater impact.

SMS communications are used increasingly not just for brand awareness-based advertising but also as an effective way of delivering sales promotions, such as announcing special offers. This again reflects the increasing ubiquity of contemporary mobile communications. However, as with email, it is also important to consider the potential privacy concerns of customers, especially as the receipt of unwanted messages (i.e. spam) may well increase.

Speed

IST has enabled aspects of marketing communications to be conducted at much faster, indeed electronic speeds. This impact is manifest in direct communications with end-users and in the production

IST has enabled aspects of marketing communications to be conducted at much faster, indeed electronic speeds.

process itself. Draft documents, film and video clips, contracts, address lists and research and feedback reports, to name but a few, can all now be transmitted electronically, saving processing time and reducing the elapsed production time necessary to create and implement marketing communication activities and events.

Efficiency

Efficiency is a broad term used to encompass a wide array of issues. New technology helps organisations to target their messages accurately to discrete groups or audiences. Indeed, one-to-one marketing is possible, and when compared with mass communications and broad audiences it is clear that IST offers huge opportunities for narrow casting and reduced communication waste. Rather than shower audiences with messages that some of them do not wish to receive, direct marketing should, theoretically, enable each message to be received by all who are favourably disposed to the communication.

This principle of narrow casting applies equally well to communication costs. Moving away from mass media to direct marketing and one-to-one communications reduces the absolute costs associated with campaigns. The relative costs may be higher but these richer communications facilitate interactive opportunities with a greater percentage of the target audience than previously experienced in the mass broadcast era.

A further type of efficiency can be seen in terms of the accuracy and precision of the messages that are delivered. Marketing communications delivers product information, specifications and service details, contracts, designs, drawings and development briefs when customising to meet customer needs. The use of IST can help organisations provide customers with precise information and reduce opportunities for information deviance.

A further type of efficiency can be seen in terms of the accuracy and precision of the messages that are delivered.

Enhanced relationships

As mentioned previously, new technology is now used by organisations to gather and use information about customers in order to better meet their needs. Through the use of the database, organisations now seek to develop longer-term relationships with customers, with programmes and strategies that are dubiously termed as customer loyalty schemes. While there may be doubt about the term loyalty, there can be no doubt that IST has helped develop new forms of sales promotion and influenced customer relationships. What should also be clear is that the existence of IST in an organisation or relationship is no guarantee that additional value will be created (Ryssel *et al.*, 2004).

Some customer service interface functions have been replaced with technology in the name of greater efficiency, cost savings and improved service. Financial services organisations are able to inform customers of their bank balances automatically without human intervention. Meyronin (2004: 222) refers to this as an 'infomediation' strategy and suggests that this neglect of the human interaction in the creation of joint value in service environments may be detrimental.

Relationships with intermediaries have also been affected by new technology. The development of ecommerce has given rise to channel strategies that either result in channel functions and hence members being discarded, or give rise to opportunities for new functions and members. These processes, disintermediation and reintermediation respectively, are both dynamic and potentially destabilising for organisations and their channel partners.

Strategic implications

Organisations have had to adapt to new technologies as a means of delivering value to their stakeholders. The strategic implications are very significant although it should be noted that not all organisations have recognised or responded adequately to the strategic challenge, witnessed by the problems associated with customer relationship management (CRM) systems. IST has not changed the value propositions or the assumptions of the value chain itself (Porter, 1985). Apart from enabling organisations to adopt a customer focus, what IST has done is change the way in which the primary and support activities work in order that value be generated. New technology has enabled organisations to reach new markets, work with different channel partners and provide value and satisfaction for a range of new audiences.

Web sites

Web sites are the cornerstone of Internet activity for organisations, regardless of whether they are operating in the b2b, b2c or not-for-profit sectors and whether the purpose is merely to offer information or provide fully developed embedded ecommerce (transactional) facilities. The design characteristics of a web site can be crucial in determining the length of stay, activities undertaken and the propensity for a visitor to return to the site at a later time. When the experience is satisfactory, then both the visitor and the web site owner might begin to take on some of the characteristics associated with relationship marketing.

To understand the characteristics associated with web site interaction, consideration will first be given to their strengths and weaknesses, then the issues associated with the development of a web site will be identified and finally the processes involved in attracting and managing web site activity will be examined.

Web sites can be used for a variety of purposes but essentially they are either product-oriented or corporate-oriented. Product-oriented web sites aim to provide product-based information such as brochureware, sales-based enquiries, demonstrations and endorsements through to online transactions and ongoing technical support as the main activities.

Corporate-oriented web sites aim to provide information about the performance, size, prospects, financial data and job opportunities relating to the organisation. They also need to relate to issues concerning the ethical expectations and degree of social responsibility accepted by the company, if only to meet the needs of prospective investors and employees. The demarcation is not necessarily as clear cut as this might suggest, but the essence of a site's orientation is largely derived from the organisation's approach to branding.

The strengths and weaknesses of web site facilities are set out in Table 25.2; however, it should be remembered that these are generalised comments and that some organisations have attended to these issues and have been able to develop the strengths and negate some of the weaknesses such that their web sites are particularly attractive, user friendly and encourage repeat visits.

Strengths

Any www user can create a web site, consisting of a home page and a number of linked pages. Business pages can carry advertising, product catalogues, descriptions, pricing, special offers, press releases – all forms of promotional material. They can link to online order pages, so that potential customers can order directly, or to email facilities for requesting further information or providing feedback. Consumer interest and activity can be monitored easily, allowing for timely market research, rapid feedback and strategy adaptation.

Barriers to entry are low, it is relatively inexpensive to create/maintain a site and share of voice is theoretically equal for all participants, although in practice this is clearly not the case. Large organisations can buy banner ads and have a better chance of appearing in the first few results presented by search engines (see Chapter 26 for more detail on Search). Good design can add to brand appeal and recognition.

Barriers to entry are low, it is relatively inexpensive to create/maintain a site and share of voice is theoretically equal for all participants.

Table 25.2 Strengths and weaknesses of web site-based communications

Strengths	Weaknesses
Quick to set up and easy to maintain	Slow access and page downloading speeds, but increasing broadband access has reduced this type of problem
Flexibility	Huge variability in web site design and user friendliness
Variety of information	Attract large amounts of unsolicited email
High level of user involvement	Security and transaction privacy issues
Potentially high level of user convenience (and satisfaction)	Variable levels of Internet penetration across UK households
Range of service facilities	Inconsistent fulfilment standards (online transactions only)
Global reach and equal access opportunities	Variability and speed of technology provision
Open all hours – reduced employment costs	Lack of regulation concerning content and distribution
Very low relative costs (per person reached)	Online search time costs prohibitive for many users
Can provide cost efficiencies in terms of marketing research	

Potential customers actively seek products and services, which is both time- and cost-effective from a company's point of view, and indicative of positive attitudes, perception and involvement. Channel communications can also be swift and supportive. Coverage is global, without the need for huge investment or expensive staff to be employed around the clock. Savings can be made in advertising budgets, travel, postage and telephone costs. Different time zones no longer matter in the virtual environment, and language barriers are less of an issue.

Weaknesses

For some the disadvantages are that the speed of access, page location and loading are still too slow for many users, especially from home PCs. However, as broadband penetration increases, so these problems disappear. Perversely however, even broadband and the extra bandwidth brings other difficulties. The launch of the BBC iPlayer in 2008 resulted in over 17 million users in the first seven weeks (BBC Radio) and people are downloading greater and greater volumes of material such that the infrastructure was, even then, starting to creak.

Potential customers are easily put off by slow or unreliable connections and this frustration can result in negative images of the company or product. Poorly designed web sites, which confuse rather than clarify, also create a poor impression, one that can deter a return visit.

Unsolicited email is extremely annoying to many users and may be counterproductive. Worries over the security of financial details and transactions online, while not discouraging people from seeking information, may still be a barrier to full ecommerce. Fulfilment issues, principally delivery problems (such as long delays), wrong items, incorrect billing, plus the associated inconvenience of returning products or otherwise seeking resolution, may deter repeat purchase.

Some regard ecommerce as transactional web sites or extended enterprises, but it is more to do with information/communication management and the impact on relationships.

eCommerce should be aimed at building new relationships with established customers and providing potential customers with a reason to change. The idea that eCommerce provides process efficiencies is correct but these features need to be transformed into benefits for customers.

Web site design

The design and functionality of a web site is now recognised as an important integral aspect of an organisation's communication strategy. Indeed many organisations now update their sites on a regular basis. What constitutes a suitable web site has also been the subject of much debate and speculation, marked by a lack of substantial empirical work to determine a common framework. Of the many ideas available two are featured here, if only because of their currency at the time of writing and the background of the researchers involved.

The design and functionality of a web site is now recognised as an important integral aspect of an organisation's communication strategy.

Karayanni and Baltas (2003) suggest that web sites have four main characteristics. These are set out in Table 25.3 and were presented in the context of b2b markets.

This breakdown is useful because it indicates the main facilities that a successful site should provide. However, what it does not provide is a depth of insight and balance that would help organisations design their sites more appropriately. Rayport and Jaworski (2004) offer a 7Cs framework, which they subsequently develop into a map that can be used to analyse sites and to design sites more effectively.

The 7Cs of the customer interface design are intended to cover the range of elements necessary for good web site design. These are set out in Table 25.4.

The 7Cs of the customer interface design are intended to cover the range of elements necessary for good web site design.

Table 25.3 Four aspects of web site design

Web site characteristic		Explanation
Interactivity		The provision of solutions in response to the provision of personal information and the ability of users to customise preferences. This can be delivered through memory storage/organisation and response to individual needs.
Navigability		The structure and organisation of the site combined with the ease with which information can be retrieved.
Multimedia design		The Internet offers all the facilities that each of the other media provide individually. This provides opportunities for stimulation as well as flexibility and visitor involvement with a site.
Content	Company content	Information relating to the organisation, its markets, culture and values are important to establish credibility and reduce risk.
	Customer content	This concerns both the provision of information, for example a *frequently asked questions* facility, and the collection of information about customers and the market.

Source: Karayanni and Baltas (2003)

Table 25.4 The 7Cs of the customer interface

Type of community	Explanation
Context	Layout and design of web site
Content	Text, sound, pictures and video material
Community	Site-enabled, user-to-user communication
Customisation	Site facilities to tailor itself to user needs
Communication	The ways in which two-way communication is enabled
Commerce	Ability to enable commercial transactions
Connection	The number of other linked sites

Source: Rayport and Jaworski (2004).

Context

The context of a site is concerned with the balance between the functional and aesthetic look and feel. Some sites will be designed such that their functionality dominates the aesthetic and will try to provide text-based information rather than emphasising the visual elements of the site. Conversely other sites attempt to provide warm feelings for visitors and use multimedia facilities to create an emotional engagement with the site, often at the expense of long loading times. The balance between the functional and emotional can be termed balanced (although Rayport and Jaworski call it integrated). In this approach, visitors experience a site that provides a suitable level of information, is easy to navigate and yet is interesting and stimulating in terms of the emotional satisfaction derived from using the site. This need not be the optimal site design for all organisations, as the context should reflect the values and purpose of the organisation itself. At one extreme, high fashion and luxury brands will focus on aesthetic styled sites while the Driving Vehicle Licensing Agency would be expected to be predominately functional.

Content

This refers to what is presented on the site in terms of audio, text, graphics, images and video. The content can be considered in terms of the following:

- *offering mix* – the balance between information, products and services;
- *appeal mix* – the balance between functional (attribute and benefits) and the emotional (feelings and brand engagement) appeals;
- *multimedia mix* – the selected combination of audio, text, graphics, images and video;
- *timeliness mix* – the time sensitivity of the information determines how often a site needs to be updated. For example, www.BBC.co.uk/news has to be updated on a frequent and regular basis, whereas a site dealing with largely historical or archive data (e.g. family trees) needs less regular attention.

Community

The increasing role and significance of online communities indicates that site design should reflect the needs and significance of these communities to organisations. Online communities are about the interaction between the users of a site, not between the site and users. These interactions may be one-to-one (email) or among many (chat rooms) but are significant to organisations as they can be a source of information about customer feelings and attitudes that may be strong or weak. A deeper consideration of these communities can be found at the end of this chapter.

ViewPoint 25.4 Gorilla games

When ZSL London Zoo developed their campaign to launch Gorilla Kingdom in 2007 they used a variety of media to reach their target audience. These included outdoor, especially the London Underground sites, radio, using sponsorship of the Travel and Transport element of Magic FM, and digital in the form of both web and email.

Gorilla Kingdom was a major investment project and so it was important to attract visitors to the 'new green oasis within London'. In addition to strong branding, work with the travel trade and several important joint promotions and partnerships plus heavy public relations activities and events, the ZSL web site had an important role to play as the fulcrum for the launch.

The web site carried a microsite for Gorilla Kingdom. This held information about gorillas, pictures and visuals about the development of the new exhibit through the various phases of construction and video interviews with the keepers. Email banners were developed and all staff were encouraged to incorporate them in their electronic signatures.

However, one particular development attracted considerable attention. Radio presenter and celebrity Chris Evans apparently spent seven minutes on his Radio 2 programme discussing the merits of their 'gorilla game'. This required players to download a virtual gorilla and then look after it for three weeks. The three people who looked after their gorilla best won the opportunity to meet the real gorilla behind the scenes.

Source: Winner of the Best Marketing Project at the BIAZA awards 2007.

Question

To what extent did the emotional element of the gorilla game complement the more informative aspects of the ZSL web site?

Task

Make a list of some of the other ways a web site can be used to attract, retain and encourage visitors to return.

Customisation

This is concerned with the extent to which a site is capable of being adapted to the individual needs of visitors. When customisation is initiated by customers it is referred to as personalisation, but when driven and managed by the organisation it is called tailoring. Obviously, different sites will provide varying levels of customisation, from low through medium to high levels, and this will be reflected in the users' site experience.

Communication

The type of communication provided by a site is to some extent a reflection of the type of relationship offered by the organisation. The communication may be broadcast (content update reminders or mass mailings), in which case one-way communication prevents user response and with it opportunities for dialogue. Alternatively, interactive communication (user ratings or feedback) enables user response that can lead to dialogue.

The type of communication provided is to some extent a reflection of the type of relationship offered by the organisation.

Connection

Connection is concerned with the degree to which a site is linked or connected to other sites. These links may be located on other web pages and, when clicked, take the user to another site. If a transaction then occurs a commission is payable to the affiliate site. Outside links make it

Table 25.5 7Cs framework map

Context	Aesthetically dominant		Functionally dominant	Integrated
Content	Product-dominant		Information-dominant	Service-dominant
Community	Nonexistent		Limited	Strong
Customisation	Generic		Moderately customised	Highly customised
Communication	One-to-many, nonresponding user	One-to-many, responding user	One-to-one, nonresponding user	One-to-one, responding user
Connection	Destination		Hub	Portal
Commerce	Low		Medium	High

Source: Rayport and Jaworski (2004).

difficult for the user to return to the original page and are therefore not used a great deal. Framed links attempt to overcome this problem. Pop-up windows present a new site within the original site but can be annoying to users.

Commerce

The ability of a site to support financial transactions is an important feature of product-dominated web sites. Apart from the need to provide a secure and risk-free trading environment, the key activities associated with these sites are: registration, shopping carts, credit card approval, one-click shopping, orders through affiliate sites, configuration facilities (different combinations of products and services), order tracking and delivery options. All of the 7Cs can be mapped and a site analysed against this criteria (see Table 25.5). Use of this mapping approach, that is the identification of which element applies to a web site, can enable web site designers to better understand how their site appears to visitors and enables sites to be developed according to the planned needs of organisations.

> There is little empirical research that shows how different web site design features impact on visitor responsiveness.

To conclude this section it should be noted that there is little empirical research that shows how different web site design features impact on visitor responsiveness. Indeed Kent *et al.* (2003) make the point that there is a gulf between what many organisations expect of a web site capability to foster relationships and the actual web sites that are designed to facilitate these relationships. They argue that there is an inconsistency in what is thought to be possible through a web site and practice, that it is generally recognised that web sites are all too often poorly used dialogic tools, and that the actual design of a web site can have a strong impact on the way in which visitors perceive the organisation and hence influence its relationship-building potential.

Web sites – visitor behaviour

It is possible to deconstruct users' web site behaviour into a number of discrete activities, but the resultant list would be far too complex to be of any practical assistance. However, several authors have tried to discriminate among Internet users and segment the market accordingly. For example, Lewis and Lewis (1997) were one of the first and they segmented the Internet on the basis of people who use the Internet. Later Forsyth *et al.* (2000) grouped users on the basis of those who are active online consumers, a behavioural approach to segmentation.

> The design of web sites should account for the needs of different types of users.

The design of web sites should account for the needs of these different types of users and also the different stages each has reached in terms of their experience in using the Internet, their stage in the adoption

Table 25.6 Online segments

	Group of Internet users	Explanation
Lewis and Lewis (1997)	Directed information seekers	Experienced users who know what information they require and where to find it.
	Undirected information seekers	Inexperienced users (generally) who surf looking for information or who browse for leisure and pleasure.
	Directed buyers	Experienced users who are online with the express intention of purchasing specific goods/services.
	Bargain hunters	Users in search of free offers and sizeable discounts.
	Entertainment seekers	Users whose intentions are primarily to exploit sales promotions and competition opportunities and use chat rooms.
Forsyth *et al.* (2000)	Simplifiers	Simplifiers like readily available product information, reliable customer service and easy returns, and they respond positively to any evidence conveyed through advertising or on-site messages.
	Surfers	Surfers move quickly among sites, continually seeking new online experiences. Sites must offer a strong online brand, cutting-edge design and features, constant updates, and a rich variety of products and services.
	Bargainers	Bargainers care mainly about getting a good deal and enjoy the search for a good price, control over transactions, and the sense of community that sites such as eBay offer.
	Connectors	Connectors tend to be novices who use the Internet mainly to relate to other people through chat services.
	Routiners	Routiners use the Internet for news and financial information and spend more than 80 per cent of their online time surfing through their 10 favourite sites.
	Sportsters	Sportsters behave like Routiners but gravitate to sports and entertainment sites. They view content as entertainment, so sites must be fresh, colourful and interactive to attract them.

process (see Chapter 2) and different stages users have reached in the buying process. For the purposes of the rest of this text, reference is made to two broad categories, active (goal-directed) and passive (experiential) information seekers.

The initial goal is to generate awareness of the web site and this needs to be understood in the knowledge that there are many web users who have no interest in a particular (your) web site and those who do are said to have a potential interest. The task is therefore to drive awareness levels among those who might find the site useful.

The second phase is to encourage the potential segment to actually visit the site. The problem is that there are two types of information seeker, passive and active. Passive seekers have no intention of hitting any particular site, whereas active seekers do have the express intention of visiting a particular site. Part of the communication strategy must therefore be geared to facilitating active seekers and attracting passive information seekers.

The next phase is to ensure that active seekers, once on the web site, are able to find the information they need quickly and efficiently so that they are inclined to revisit. This entails good site access and, once found, good site design so that navigation is easy, simple and fast. This normally means that the design of the site is simple and is user-, rather than technology-oriented. Passive information seekers, on the other hand, need to be made curious and stimulated to want to know more about the site and the products and services available. Here the objective is to convert hitters into visitors. A site registration book, supported perhaps with sales promotion devices, or a site design that is sufficiently intriguing, may allow these goals to be met. Research suggests that there are three main elements that strongly influence the perceived quality of a web site visit (Oxley and Miller, 2000):

- all are content-oriented and refer to whether the site material is relevant to the needs of the visitor;
- the degree to which the content (and design) encourages curiosity to explore the site;
- whether the content is presented in an interesting way.

These three points correlate strongly with the idea of 'likeability', that advertising effectiveness improves when an individual assigns significant value (represented by relevance, curiosity and interest) to any particular form of marketing communication discipline, but advertising in particular in this case (Chapters 8 and 16). Therefore, the main factors that might influence the way an individual perceives a web site may be similar to the way they process and evaluate other marketing communications and, in particular, advertising messages. Goldsmith and Lafferty (2002) have made similar observations and consider theories concerning attitudes towards the ad as developed by Lutz *et al.* (1983) and Bruner and Kumar (2000). Attitudes developed towards advertisements can also impact on attitudes towards the brand and hence are better indicators of purchase intentions (see Chapter 5). Goldsmith and Lafferty also refer to ad brand recall and the fact that those consumers who have strong emotional feelings towards a brand (a positive attitude) are more likely to be able to recall it. Therefore, investment in marketing communications that seeks to establish top-of-mind awareness of a brand and also creates positive attitudes are more likely to be successful.

Attitudes developed towards advertisements can impact on attitudes towards the brand.

Key differences between traditional and digital media

Having considered the characteristics of traditional media in the previous chapter, this appears to be the right point at which to bring traditional and digital media together. In comparison with traditional media, the Internet and digital media facilities provide an interesting contrast (see Table 25.7). Space (or time) within traditional media is limited and costs rise as demand for the limited space/time increases. On the Internet, space is unlimited so absolute costs remain very low and static, while relative costs plummet as more visitors are recorded as having been to a site. Another aspect concerns the focus of the advertising message. Traditionally, advertisers tend to emphasise the emotional rather than information aspect, particularly within low-involvement categories. Digital media allow focus on the provision of information and so the emotional aspect of advertising messages tends to have a lower significance. As branding becomes a more important aspect of Internet activity, it is probable that there will be a greater use of emotions, especially when the goal is to keep people at a web site, rather than driving them to it.

Digital media allow focus on the provision of information and so the emotional aspect of advertising messages tends to have a lower significance.

Apart from the obvious factor that digital media, and the Internet in particular, provide interactive opportunities that traditional media cannot provide, it is important to remember

Table 25.7 Comparison of new and traditional media

Traditional media	New media
One-to-many	One-to-one and many-to-many
Greater monologue	Greater dialogue
Active provision	Passive provision
Mass marketing	Individualised marketing
General need	Personalised
Branding	Information
Segmentation	Communities

that opportunities-to-see are generally driven by customers rather than by the advertiser that interrupts viewing or reading activities. People drive the interaction at a speed that is convenient to them; they are not driven by others.

Management control over internet-based marketing communications is relatively high, as not only are there greater opportunities to control the position and placement of advertisements, promotions and press releases, but it is also possible to change the content of these activities much more quickly than is possible with traditional media. The goals outlined above indicate the framework within which advertising needs to be managed.

In addition to considering the attributes of the two different forms of media, it is also worth considering the content of the information that each is capable of delivering. These are set out in Table 25.8.

As mentioned earlier, digital media are superior at providing rational, product-based information whereas traditional media are much better at conveying emotional brand values. The former have a dominant cognition orientation and the latter an emotional one. There are other differences, but the predominant message is that these types of media are, to a large

Table 25.8 Comparison of information content

Web sites/Internet	Traditional media
Good at providing rational, product-based information	Better at conveying emotional brand values
More efficient as costs do not increase in proportion to the size of the target audience	Costs are related to usage
Better at prompting customer action	Less effective for calling to action except point-of-purchase and telemarketing
Effective for short-term, product-oriented brand action goals and long-term corporate identity objectives	Normally associated with building long-term values
Poor at generating awareness and attention	Strong builders of awareness
Poor at managing attitudes	Capable of changing and monitoring attitudes
Measures of effectiveness weak and/or in the process of development	Established methodologies, if misleading or superficial (mass media); direct marketing techniques are superior
Dominant orientation – cognition	Dominant orientation – emotion

extent, complementary, suggesting that they should be used together, not one independently of the other.

Future technologies and marketing communications

The Internet lies at the heart of current and future marketing applications of new technology but Karnell (2004) suggests that future developments will be based around three main themes: wireless networking, smart devices and intelligent communications services.

Wireless networking refers to communication between computers and related devices that does not require the use of cables and wires. It works through the use of low-powered radio frequency and infrared waves. Protocols such as Wi-Fi (wireless fidelity) means that wireless-enabled computers or personal digital assistants (PDAs) can connect to the Internet if they are within 15 metres of an access point.

Radio frequency identification (RFID) tags contain chips and work on the basis that a radio signal, received by an antenna, activates the chip, which in turn transmits a unique code identifying the object to which the tag is attached (Blau, 2003). In addition to security applications, retail staff are able to use handheld devices to check stock and to assemble orders in the established way, but these tags are also used to trigger screens within changing rooms, enabling customers to view video clips of the merchandise. Using video cameras and plasma screens, in place of mirrors, customers are able to see themselves from behind (Dean, 2003).

RFID tags do not need line-of-sight reading, as with barcodes, which means that hundreds of tags can be read in a second, saving considerable amounts of time. In addition, these radio tags are capable of providing not only the universal product codes as used in barcodes, but also a unique identifying code. This means that promotions can be based on particular groups of items purchased and changed very quickly in response to changing market or competitive conditions. Consumers can use this technology to sample games and music CDs.

ViewPoint 25.5 Store into the future

The building used by the Metro Future Store in Germany is completely covered by a wireless network. Through this network, various mobile devices such as personal shopping assistants (PSAs) and personal digital assistants (PDAs) and static devices such as electronic shelf labels (ESLs), check-out points and flat-screen displays for product promotion are all interlinked.

PSAs are for the use of shoppers whose shopping trolleys have a touch screen mini-computer linked to the network and an integrated scanner. This is referred to as a PSA and allows shoppers to scan their own purchases, and the data to be transmitted to the checkout in advance of the shopper.

The PDAs are also linked to the network and are used by store employees to check stock by directly accessing Metro's merchandise management system at any time and at any point in the store. Using VoIP (Voice over Internet Protocol) technology, it is planned for the PDAs to receive 'soft phone' functionality, enabling staff to make calls in addition to sending messages or downloading information.

Source: Adapted from Fill (2005).

Question

Is this use of technology of real value to customers?

Task

Find one piece of new technology that has a retail application.

Barcode technology is a mature technology and will gradually be replaced by radio tags as the cost of the embedded chips decreases. RFID technology is being used to develop electronic labelling systems and smart shelves. Connected to the store network, smart shelves have readers embedded in them that will enable the main system to be informed when merchandise is removed, and will then automatically trigger a request for shelf replenishment.

Out-of-store applications of wireless technologies will grow as the Internet becomes an information utility where corporations, individuals and governments will access and interact with information anywhere, anytime and, most importantly, with any device. For marketers, this increased access means greater scope for targeted and personalised delivery of timely marketing communications messages and increased opportunities for co-branding and marketing alliances.

Out-of-store applications of wireless technologies will grow as the Internet becomes an information utility.

Smart devices, or information-powered devices, have continuous Internet access and can be incorporated within furniture and furnishings, clocks and watches, carpets, refrigerators and freezers, and lighting and security systems. These devices can process information, signals, graphics, animation, video and audio and have the ability to exchange such information with another smart device. These devices, which will be able to receive up-to-date news, traffic, weather and sports information, have the potential to radically change the way consumers interact with brands. In addition to obvious above-the-line communications, this technology opens up opportunities for sponsorship and promotional programmes.

Intelligent communication services are smart devices that are integrated with the Internet. This will enable them to detect changes in their environment and in doing so prompt users to act in particular ways. Karnell suggests that this will enable marketers to track products and consumers and deliver intelligent real-time, proximity-specific and ultra-personalised information. So, as a freezer senses that the last pizza (previously tagged) has been removed it will prompt, via text, visuals or voice that a new pizza is required. This may in time be remotely linked through to a specified store, which will automatically add the item to the consumer's standing order for home delivery.

These devices could be used in-store enabling retailers and brand owners to interact with consumers while they are shopping or they might be used to make purchasing and brand choice decisions in the home. Used as the ultimate form of personalised marketing communications, messages can be delivered, at the appropriate time in the consumption cycle, about products and services, lower prices or promotional offers (e.g. time-based electronic coupons); all driven by each customer's individual consumption patterns and transaction history, they have the potential to transform the shopping experience.

These devices could be used in-store enabling retailers and brand owners to interact with consumers while they are shopping.

Biometrics

The film *Minority Report* contains a sequence in which Tom Cruise enters a futuristic store, at which point his iris/retina is scanned, checked, cross-referenced and a stream of products and services related to his preferences are then presented to him. While this futuristic view of technology-enabled, personalised marketing communications has yet to be commercially resolved and implemented, the concept and use of biometric technology applications are currently being developed. At present a range of applications are available or are at an advanced stage of development. Das (2004) refers to hand geometry, fingerprint, voice/speech, iris/retinal and face recognition facilities with earlobe, brain mapping, odour and gait recognition at an early stage of development. For example, the WatchPad uses a fingerprint sensor to identify the owner of a watch, thus replacing the need for passwords, improving security and with it trust, and reducing perceived risk and reasons not to buy.

Many of these biometric technologies have been used within security-related environments to identify and authenticate individuals. Some voice recognition technologies have been used successfully in back-office situations and are currently considered to be best used to gather simple information such as names, addresses and/or supporting applications such as voicemail account management through a preset menu of choices (Rockwell, 2004).

Although these voice recognition technologies have the potential to reduce customer contact centre costs there are difficulties associated with dialects and regional accents (Rockwell, 2004). In addition, it is not yet possible to induce real-time dialogue with smart devices in order to communicate personalised product offers. Although in development it should be remembered that the advent of these facilities will also prompt a series of privacy- and personal freedom-related issues.

Industry issues

New technology has led to changes in the balance of the tools used by many organisations. Most notably, those operating in the FMCG sector that spend vast sums on above-the-line media in order to develop brand values have begun to spend more below-the-line in an effort to impact on behaviour rather than just brand development. Direct marketing has also impacted on the advertising spend, and with the development of IMC and related concepts such as media-neutral planning, the balance of the communications spend has moved towards either sales promotions and/or direct marketing.

The content of many marketing communication messages has therefore swung, and with it the work of advertising agencies. Agencies have had to adapt to a new environment, one in which clients expect their agencies to present strategies that involve a much broader range of tools and media and to offer new skills and resources. This has been achieved mainly through acquisition and the development of international networks of agencies, from all disciplines, pooling their talents in order to secure domestic and international business.

Tapp and Hughes (2004) refer to the impact of IST on the company–customer interface and on the internal processes and marketing resources within client companies. They report on the major impact IST has had internally, and the struggle organisations have experienced coping with the disruption new technology has stimulated. In terms of marketing communications, this disruption is potentially enormous. With web sites becoming the focus of much internal communication activity; forces propelling ideas concerning the desire to integrate marketing communications and planning; and strategy processes having to accommodate uncertain industry, media and audience expectations, marketing communications has been severely buffeted by IST.

However, while the changes driven by new technology might bring about an unwelcome internal production focus, these changes should be seen positively, as a primary means of moving organisations forward. New technology can help organisations communicate more effectively and more efficiently, both internally and externally. By adopting a stronger customer focus, organisations can deliver improved levels of customer value and be better placed to meet their marketing goals and improve shareholder value.

New technology can help organisations communicate more effectively.

Convergence in marketing communications

Ideas concerning the nature and characteristics of the concept of integrated marketing communications, previously explored in Chapter 9, continue to be discussed. There can be little doubt that there are genuine benefits for organisations and their stakeholders by striving to achieve the principles of IMC. More recently, however, there is a growing body of thought concerning media convergence. At one level convergence refers to a technological 'bringing

Table 25.9 Dimensions of media convergence

Convergence dimension	Explanation
Media technology	Digitalisation and a reduction in number of technological devices necessary to send and receive a variety of streams of information
Media content	Almost all media content can now be produced, edited, distributed and stored digitally. This negates any need to keep media (and devices) separate
Media economics	The increasing horizontal concentration of media ownership, typified by the mergers of different media companies across different sectors, plus the re-organisations experienced by several media organisations.

together' of digital devices. So, information in different formats such as audio, text, search, still and moving pictures, which previously required multiple devices to receive, such as an individual computer, television, radio or newspaper, is accessed through a single (converged) device. However, at another level convergence refers to what Murdock (2000), cited by Herkman (2007) sees as three different dimensions, or what Murdock refers to as levels. These are media technology, media forms (and contents) and media economics. These are explained in Table 25.9.

At one level convergence refers to a technological 'bringing together' of digital devices.

New technology has driven the IMC concept not only through the development of direct marketing opportunities but also through ecommerce. Guens argues that IMC provides the *opportunity* for organisations to integrate their communications and that ecommerce has provided the *ability* for organisations to integrate their communications (2005). The proposition is that these two streams converge at the organisation's web site. The web site has become a central point for an organisation's digital communications. It is a point at which the complexity of messages that arise from different functional areas and departments can be integrated and managed together with the array of messages emanating from a variety of external stakeholders.

It may be that centralising marketing communications in this way has not helped to draw the offline and online communications into an integrated whole. Indeed, it appears that if marketing communications is to be audience-centred then it is crucial that the apparent focus on the technology and digitisation gives way to a more considered understanding of the meaning and interpretation that audiences give to the array of branded messages they receive, whether they be channelled through offline or online media.

ViewPoint 25.6 Integrated travel?

WAYN (Where Are You Now?) is a social network for travellers around the world. The network has over 8 million unique users, many of whom are young travellers and backpackers.

WAYN introduced streamed video ads in June 2007, partly to add value and partly to supplement their existing online ad strategy, including banner ads, skyscrapers and text ads. The aim is to enable users to view each other's video clips and click-on streaming ad 'tickers' with targeted travel and lifestyle products, services, deals and competitions. It is hoped that the integrated approach to site advertising will help WAYN's advertising partners provide relevant content without disrupting the viewing experience and flow of the social network.

However, WAYN also entered into a short-term sponsorship deal with the travel company Thomas Cook, who in return received exclusive branding rights on the network in exchange for providing competitions and special discounts. At first glance, the fit between the two organisations is quite clear and makes sense. However, in reality backpackers are not interested in the niceties of organised travel and prefer to make their own arrangements, picking and choosing deals off the Internet, many of which are more advantageous than those offered by Thomas Cook. What this experience makes abundantly clear is the need to ensure there is a tight fit between the sponsor and the needs of the target audience.

Sources: Anon (2007); Crow (2007).

Question

What value does WAYN bring to the site's users?

Task

The sponsorship with Thomas Cook was not a success. Which brand might be more successful in this type of arrangement?

At a macro level, media convergence and integrated marketing communications present an interesting context. Convergence should propel integration but evidence suggests that truly integrated marketing communications is not taking place at a level or consistency that some popular commentators suggest is happening or necessary. Apart from the technological, content and economic convergence, integrated marketing communications needs to adopt an audience-centred approach, one that accounts for the meaning different audiences bestow on the messages they receive.

Summary

In order to help consolidate your understanding of digital media, here are the key points summarised against each of the learning objectives:

1. Explain the key forms of digital media.

The range of digital media is vast and is growing rapidly but consideration was given to some of the key types or forms of digital media. The Internet, databases, multimedia, mobile phone technologies, business applications (software), interactive television, video conferencing and electronic kiosks were examined.

2. Understand what digital media enables users to do.

The benefits arising from using digital media are many, but consideration has been given to interactivity, multichannel marketing, personalisation, speed, mobility, efficiency, enhanced relationships and issues relating to strategy.

3. Examine some of the issues arising from the design and use of web sites.

The web site has become the fulcrum for many organisations and their marketing communications. The design characteristics of a web site can therefore be crucial in determining the length of stay, activities undertaken and the propensity for a visitor to return to the site at a later time. The 7Cs framework by Rayport and Jaworski provides a useful design checklist.

When the experience is satisfactory, then both the visitor and the web site owner might begin to take on some of the characteristics associated with relationship marketing.

4. Explain the key differences between traditional and digital media.

Space is unlimited on the Internet, so absolute costs remain very low and static, while relative costs plummet as more visitors are recorded as having been to a site. Digital media are superior at providing rational, product-based information, whereas traditional media are much better at conveying emotional brand values. The former have a dominant cognition orientation and the latter an emotional one. There are other differences, but the predominant message is that these types of media are, to a large extent, complementary, suggesting that they should be used together, rather than independently of each other.

5. Consider future technologies and their impact on marketing communications.

The Internet lies at the heart of current and future marketing applications of new technology, but as Karnell (2004) suggests, future developments are likely to be based around three main themes: wireless networking, smart devices and intelligent communications services. In addition, biometrics and issues arising within the industry will also impact significantly on the shape of future marketing communications.

6. Explain what convergence means and how it influences marketing communications.

At one level convergence refers to a technological 'bringing together' of digital devices. This means that information, in different formats such as audio, text, search, still and moving pictures, which previously required multiple devices, such as an individual computer, television, radio or newspaper are accessed through a single (converged) device. At another level convergence refers to media technology, media forms (and content) and media economics.

It is also argued that IMC provides the *opportunity* for organisations to integrate their communications and that digital media, albeit in the form of ecommerce or emarketing, provides the *ability* for organisations to integrate their communications, and in doing so converge systems, processes, structures and messages.

Review questions

1. Prepare brief notes explaining how the database has influenced marketing communications.
2. Discuss ways in which use of the Internet has assisted organisations to develop their marketing communications.
3. Identify different ways in which multimedia applications might be configured.
4. Why has the use of mobile communications been slow but is now about to increase rapidly?
5. Why is interactivity so important in contemporary marketing communications?
6. How would you advise a web site be designed from a marketing perspective?
7. To what extent does multichannel marketing assist marketing?
8. Prepare notes identifying how digital media have affected the structure of the marketing communications industry.
9. Explain the meaning of biometrics and consider how biometrics and wireless technologies might affect marketing communications in the future.
10. What is convergence and how might this affect marketing communications?

MiniCase Integrating traditional and digital media

Matt King: Co-founder and Director of Media Safari

Introduction

The days when a marketing campaign ran a set number of times a year, in a pre-agreed format and through a pre-determined channel are long gone. Customers have moved on, and now prefer interactive communications and an ongoing dialogue that contains a sequence of personalised messages delivered in a way that is convenient to them. This process usually involves a combination of offline and online media, otherwise referred to as 'traditional' and 'digital' media, to engage and educate consumers and ultimately influence their purchase decisions.

The volume of competition, the limited shelf space retailers have to maximise their revenues and the short attention spans of many consumers, mean that bringing a product to market successfully does not happen by chance. It requires a meticulously planned and well-executed campaign, which involves close working relationships with all parties in the channel, to ensure that every aspect is brought together at exactly the right time.

Two cases are considered. Media Safari works with Avanquest Software (www.avanquest.com), a leading developer and publisher of personal and professional software for the global PC market. Avanquest markets a product called 'Radiotracker', a software title that legally downloads music from Internet radio stations to MP3 players, for free.

Ascaron Entertainment (www.ascaron.com) is one of the leading European 'boutique' developers and publishers of games. Ascaron launched a new game for PCs called 'Hard to be a God' and Media Safari managed the launch campaign.

The brief – setting objectives

Having established the product's target 'street date', i.e. launched to UK consumers in retail, e.g. PC World or Game, and online e.g. www.Amazon.co.uk or www.Play.com, the key task was to develop a marketing communications strategy and plan, incorporating a variety of tools, tactics and media. This included advertising, (full-colour, half-page ads) public relations (news releases) and direct marketing (e-shots), all delivered in a selection of target print and online magazines.

Achieving the right balance and mix of tools, tactics and media generally depends on the target audience and available budget, but will include both 'push' and 'pull' activity to satisfy trade and end-user needs. It is also at this stage that particular communications objectives are set, for example, the number of news releases and e-shots in the campaign, the levels of expected coverage in certain magazines or the anticipated number of downloads of a trial version or 'demo' directly from the company's web site.

Campaign commencement – creating awareness

Activity for the 'Hard to be a God' campaign began 17 weeks from its target street date. This gave Media Safari sufficient time to build the hype within the gaming industry, educate buyers within key retailers and to distribute the game's 'assets'. The 'assets' are the elements of the game, like the box shot, screen shots or trailers that are drip-fed to the Press to create excitement and anticipation for the launch of the game.

At this early stage, PR and 'media relations' play a crucial element in most launches, with advertising in key trade titles providing support. Particular magazines such as PC Gamer and www.gamespot.com (online) were targeted, offering them a 'preview' of the product. Preview coverage serves several important purposes. First, it assists the sales team to sell the game into the channel. The size of the pre-order gives the publisher an early indication of how many copies it is likely to sell. Second, it acts as a tool to sell into other media including the national newspapers and consumer lifestyles. Finally, it begins to populate gaming web sites and seeds consumer demand.

The third element is an essential part of any campaign and confirms the interdependence of traditional and online media. As consumers move to an increasing reliance on search engines as 'fact finding' tools, it is necessary to feed relevant web sites with 'optimised' news releases. 'Optimised' refers to the way a news release is written in order to enhance its chances of being picked up by the leading search engines.

The advantage of this in the context of 'Hard to be a God' is that when a consumer heard or read about the game and wanted to find out more, they searched

Exhibit 25.2 'Hard to be a God'

for the game and were presented with a selection of links that connect with sites carrying the previews and reviews. Online coverage of this kind also found its way into online gaming forums that helped stimulate word-of-mouth communication and viral marketing.

At this stage, consumers would also be likely to supplement their understanding by buying a gaming magazine. So the PR coverage and advertising in 'traditional' gaming magazines is used to support the 'digital' online coverage. Working with the editorial teams within the magazines to secure a review, Media Safari also provided them with a relevant and specific web address. Consumers were then guided to a web page containing additional information, opportunities to download screen savers and trailers etc., plus links to where it could be pre-ordered and purchased.

Engaging the consumer

Initial interest was therefore generated with the use of PR and advertising in both traditional and online media, the focus being to generate awareness and drive consumer traffic to a specific web site. At that stage, the balance of activity moved towards educating end-users to ensure that the resellers and retailers actually sold the product that they committed to stocking and promoting in-store or online.

In the case of 'Radiotracker', the PR and advertising coverage aimed to drive consumers to a particular space on the web. Once there, the emphasis shifted to engaging the consumer, capturing their information for use in future campaigns and to maintain the current dialogue. This was achieved by offering the customer

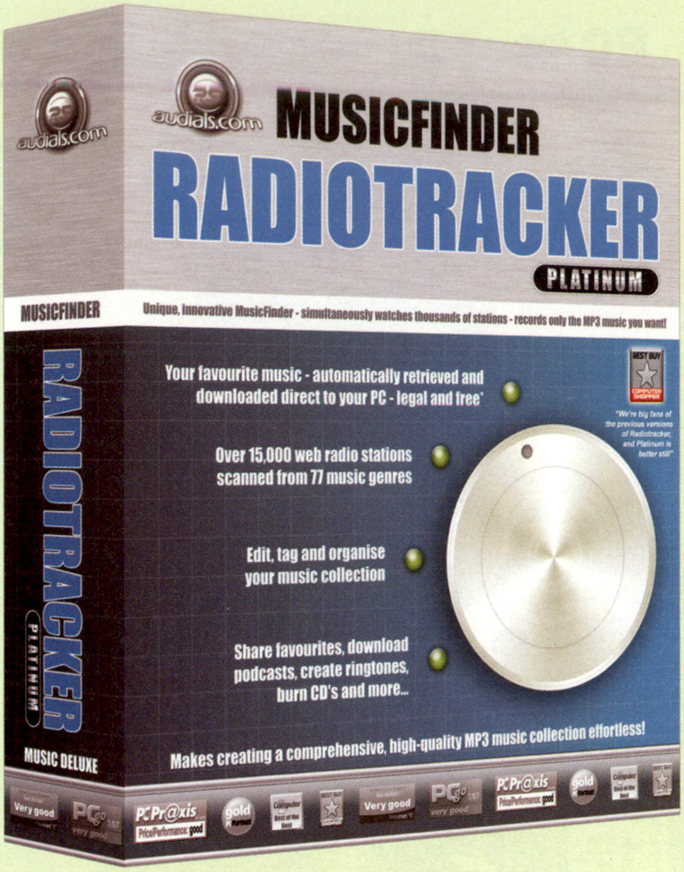

Exhibit 25.3 'Radiotracker'

access to similar or related products for free, a trial download lasting a set period of time and discounts on future purchases, all in return for registering and opting into the Avanquest database. This process of capturing customer data is continuous and serves to convert 'prospects' into 'customers'. It is the ability to segment the database and target specific groups with particular offers via email, a cost-effective and highly targeted method of direct marketing, that demonstrates the power of the digital environment.

Having registered and opted in, Avanquest then used these data to email the prospective customers regular updates on 'Radiotracker' containing specific offers to purchase the product. Avanquest continues to send regular e-newsletters containing information about other related products. The use of sales promotion here is used to drive the sale, as well as cross-sell or up-sell other products within the Avanquest range. All correspondence includes reference codes to trace the sale and links to a support page, in case the transaction online becomes problematic or the consumer has any last minute questions.

Evaluation

With an ever-increasing need for consultancies to demonstrate a return on investment, evaluation of the communications activity and its relationship with sales is essential. Historically, traditional media would have to carry response codes, but this relied on the individual remembering where they saw the information and customer services asking for that code. This was invariably inconclusive, meaning that it was difficult to relate the sale to any meaningful marketing activity.

The Internet has changed all this. Now both traditional print PR and advertising activity carry specifically created URLs that drive traffic to particular pages on the web. So a news piece or promotion for 'Radiotracker' organised in a music magazine might use www.avanquest.co.uk/Mojo or www.radiotracker.co.uk/Mojo. This allows hit rates to be monitored, customer registrations to be counted, downloads to be assessed and click-through rates to ecommerce sites to be tracked. These are critical data and are used to demonstrate the effectiveness of the communications activity.

Last words

The interdependence of offline and online activity has become increasingly pronounced, with the digital environment being central to what Media Safari now does. By using PR and advertising to increase awareness and capture customer data, we can drive sales using direct marketing and sales promotion. Traditional and digital media can obviously operate in isolation, but by integrating the two environments, and allowing them to work off each other rather than in competition with each other, the potential for greater penetration and more effective evaluation will be greatly enhanced.

mediasafari
exploring communication™

Media Safari is a marketing communications consultancy specialising in the technology sector. It provides the communications plans and activities for a number of global software developers and games publishers in the United Kingdom.

Source: www.mediasafari.co.uk.

MiniCase questions

1. What benefits do Avanquest achieve from building a customer database?
2. In the case of 'Radiotracker', what areas of media would you suggest targeting?
3. What methods can be used to evaluate the success of marketing communications activity and what new ways of evaluation could you look to introduce using digital media?

References

Advertising Association (2008) *Advertising Statistics Year Book*. NTC. Also at www.adassoc.org.uk/inform/.

Anon. (2007) WAYN streams ads through VideoEgg. *Revolution UK*, 4 June. Retrieved 15 August from http://www.brandrepublic.com/News/662000/WAYN-streams-ads-VideoEgg/.

Blau, J. (2003) Supermarket tunes into wireless. Retrieved 19 April 2004 from www.computerweekly.com/articles/.

Bruner, G.C. and Kumar, A. (2000) Web commercials and advertising hierarchy of effects. *Journal of Advertising Research*, January/April, 35–42.

Chaffey, D. (2003) E-marketing insights: what's new in marketing. Retrieved 27 August 2004 from www.wnim.com/archive/issue1903/emarketing.htm.

Chaffey, D., Mayer, R., Johnston, K. and Ellis-Chadwick, F. (2003) *Internet Marketing*. 2nd edn. Harlow: Pearson.

Chaffey, D., Mayer, R., Johnston, K. and Ellis-Chadwick, F. (2006) *Internet Marketing Strategy, Implementation and Practice*, 3rd edn. Harlow: Pearson Education.

Cohen, R. (1995) Interactive demand is not as high as believed. *Precision Marketing*, 25 September, 8.

Constantinides, E. and Fountain, S.J. (2008) Web 2.0: Conceptual foundations and marketing issues. *Journal of Direct, Data and Digital Marketing Practice*, **9**, 231–44.

Crow, D. (2007) Sponsorship can take online advertising to the next level. *The Business*, 30 June, 32.

Das, R. (2004) The application of biometric technologies: 'The Afghan Girl-Sharbat Gula'. Available online at: http://technologyexecutivesclub.com/articles/artbiometricsapplications.htm.

Dean, A. (2003) High street: the new technological battleground. Retrieved 18 April 2004 from www.raeng.org.uk/news/publications/ingenia/issue18.

Fill, C. (2005) Recent developments in below-the-line communications. In *Marketing Communication: New Approaches, Technologies and Styles* (ed. A. Kimmel). Oxford: Oxford University Press.

Forsyth, J.E., Lavoie, J. and McGuire, T. (2000) Segmenting the e-market. *The McKinsey Quarterly*, **4**. Retrieved 10 November 2004 from www.mckinseyquarterly.com/article.

Goldsmith, R.E. and Lafferty, B.A. (2002) Consumer response to web sites and their influence on advertising effectiveness. *Internet Research: Electronic Networking Applications and Policy*, **12**(4), 318–28.

Guens, T.W. (2005) Current and future developments in electronic commerce. In *Marketing Communication: Emerging Trends and Developments* (ed. A. Kimmel). Oxford: Oxford University Press.

Herkman, J. (2007) Current Trends in Media Research. Retrieved 18 January 2008 from www.nordicom.gu.se/common/pub1_pdf/261.

Jones, G. (2008) iTV returns will be worth the wait. *Marketing*, 9 April, 21.

Kamakura, W.A., Wedel, M., de Rosa, F. and Mazzon, J.A. (2003) Cross-selling through database marketing: a mixed factor analyzer for data augmentation and prediction. *International Journal of Research in Marketing*, **20**(1) (March), 45–65.

Kangis, P. and Rankin, K. (1996) Interactive services: how to identify and target the new markets. *Journal of Marketing Practice: Applied Marketing Science*, **2**(3), 44–67.

Karayanni, D.A. and Baltas, G.A. (2003) Web site characteristics and business performance: some evidence from international business-to-business organizations. *Marketing Intelligence and Planning*, **21**(2), 105–14.

Karnell, I. (2004) Tech watch: the future of one-to-one marketing. Retrieved 3 May 2004 from www.the-dma.org.

Kent, M.L., Taylor, M. and White, W.J. (2003) The relationship between web site design and organisational responsiveness to stakeholders. *Public Relations Review*, **29**(1) (March), 63–77.

Lewis, H. and Lewis, R. (1997) Give your customers what they want. Cited in Chaffey *et al.* (2003).

Lutz, J., Mackensie, S.B. and Belch, G.E. (1983) Attitude toward the ad as a mediator of advertising effectiveness. *Advances in Consumer Research*, **10**. Ann Arbor, MI: Association for Consumer Research.

Meyronin, B. (2004) ICT: the creation of value and differentiation in services. *Managing Service Quality*, **14**(2/3), 216–25.

MMA (2007) Mobile Marketing, *Alumni Briefing Paper*, May, Cambridge: Cambridge Marketing Colleges.

Murdock, G. (2000) Digital Futures: European Television in the Age of Convergence. In *Television Across Europe: A Comparative Introduction* (eds J. Wieten, G. Murdock and P. Dahlgren), 35–8. London: Sage.

Murphy, D. (2008) Crack the code. *Marketing*, 6 February, 30–1.

Oxley, M. and Miller, J. (2000) Capturing the consumer: ensuring website stickiness. *Admap* (July/August), 21–4.

Porter, M.E. (1985) *Competitive Advantage: Creating and Sustaining Superior Performance.* New York: Free Press.

Radjou, N. (2003) Supply chain processes replace applications: 2003 to 2008. In *Achieving Supply Chain Excellence through Technology* (ed. N. Mulani), 24–8. San Francisco, CA: Montgomery Research.

Rayport, J.F. and Jaworski, B.J. (2004) *Introduction to E-Commerce.* Boston, MA: McGraw-Hill/Irwin.

Rockwell, M. (2004) Can voice recognition answer the call? Retrieved 17 April 2004 from www. wirelessweek.com/article/.

Rogers, E.M. (1983) *Diffusion of Innovations*, 3rd edn. New York: Free Press.

Rosen, E.M. (1997) Digital TV will soon overtake the Internet. *Revolution* (July), 6–7.

Ryals, L. and Payne, A. (2001) Customer relationship management in financial services: towards information-enabled relationship marketing. *Journal of Strategic Marketing*, **9**, 3–27.

Ryssel, R., Ritter, T. and Gemunden, H.G. (2004) The impact of information technology deployment on trust, commitment and value creation in business relationships. *Journal of Business and Industrial Marketing*, **19**(3), 197–207.

Stone, M. and Shan, P. (2002) Transforming the bank branch experience for customers. *What's New in Marketing*, **10** (September). Retrieved 23 August 2004 from http://www.wnim.com/archive/.

Tapp, A. and Hughes, T. (2004) New technology and the changing role of marketing. *Marketing Intelligence and Planning*, **22**(3), 284–96.

Thomas, D. (2003) Sainsbury's boosts supplier collaboration. *ComputerWeekly.com*, 24 October 2003. Retrieved 10 November 2003 from http://www.computerweekly.com/articles/.

Thurner, R. (2007) *FitPr*, Retrieved 18 August 2007 from www.incentivated.com/PDFs/Feature_FitPro0707.pdf.

Turner, C. (2008) How NME achieved multi-platform success. *Utalk Case Studies.* Retrieved 28 February 2008 from www.utalkmarketing.com/pages/.

Utalkb (2007) Mazda2 mobile marketing campaign, *Utalk Case Studies.* Retrieved 9 November from www.utalkmarketing.com/pages/.

Vesanen, J. (2007) What is personalization? A conceptual framework. *European Journal of Marketing*, **41**(5/6), 409–18.

Chapter 26

Interactive marketing communications

For many organisations the use of digital, interactive marketing communications has become an important channel to reach and communicate effectively with specific audiences. The ability to target individuals, often unreachable through conventional approaches, with messages and media that are related to their needs, to personalise communications, to encourage interactivity and to reflect their lifestyle and communication needs has become a critical aspect of contemporary marketing communications.

Aims and learning objectives

The aims of this chapter are to explore the essential characteristics associated with interactive marketing communications and to understand the key tools and applications used by organisations in order that they communicate effectively in a digital environment.

The learning objectives of this chapter are to:

1. appraise the nature and characteristics of interactive marketing communications;
2. describe the primary techniques and issues relating to online advertising;
3. consider some of the issues relating to the way in which each of the tools of the communications mix can be used interactively;
4. explain the key features associated with mobile communications;
5. evaluate search engine marketing and distinguish the main features of both pay-per-click and search engine optimisation;
6. discuss the features of email marketing communications for both customer acquisition and retention;
7. evaluate the role of electronic word-of-mouth communications, and consider applications such as viral marketing communications, podcasting, RSS feeds and web logs;
8. identify the characteristics of online communities and consider how social networks and affiliate marketing can be used to develop marketing communications opportunities.

For an applied interpretation see Nicola Robinsonova's MiniCase entitled ***How Learnit uses Web 2.0 to engage audiences*** at the end of this chapter.

Introduction

The title of this chapter is *interactive* marketing communications. The use of the word interactive is important as it denotes the key characteristic of this form of marketing communications. It is key because it signifies the functionality that is available, namely the ability of all participants in a communication network to respond to messages, often in real time. This is not a feature of most offline marketing communications such as radio or billboards and posters. It is also key because it indicates that this type of communication environment is open, that is, more democratic than conventional marketing communications. The latter tend to be one-sided and driven primarily by organisations and the satisfaction of their more overt needs. The word interactive suggests that all parties to a communication event are enabled to communicate. Finally, the word interactive is used to cover a wide spectrum of electronic environments, one that is not limited or defined by the Internet. For example, mobile communications do not operate online, yet can be used to reach people digitally wherever they are and engage them interactively.

Back in 1995, Deighton and Grayson speculated correctly about the impact of the move towards digital-based marketing communications and how electronic dialogue would make marketing communications more conversational. Well, the movement has gained considerable impetus and is now a central marketing communications activity for many organisations. Before examining the elements of interactive marketing communications it is necessary to determine what interactive marketing communications is thought to be. Two researchers based in Zagreb, Vlasic and Kesic (2007) review different interpretations and at a simple level suggest it is about the interchanging roles of senders and receivers within a communication event. However, this view casts little light on the depth and significance of the topic. They cite Hoey (1998) who among others, sees it as direct communication without time–space constraints. Some authors stress the measurability element (Morowitz and Schmittlein, 1998) and others focus on the communication and information control perspective (Liu and Shrum, 2005; Lockenby, 2005) and the influence the communication bestows on parties to the communication process. Vlasic and Kesic (2007: 111) deduce that interactivity brings benefits concerning 'convenience, diversity, relationship and intellectual challenges alongside the very important aspect of control of communication and relationships'.

The movement is now a central marketing communications activity for many organisations.

Interactivity brings benefits concerning 'convenience, diversity, relationship and intellectual challenges alongside the very important aspect of control of communication and relationships'.

Considering these perspectives, it can be concluded that interactive marketing communications concerns the process whereby organisations attempt to engage individuals with messages that are delivered through electronic channels, and which offer all parties the opportunity to respond. Interaction can occur through the same or different media as the original message, but the purpose is to build and sustain relationships that are based on mutual satisfaction achieved through the exchange of information, goods or services that are of value to those involved.

Perhaps the strongest characteristic of interactive marketing communications is that it enables communications to move from one-way and two-way models to one that is literally 'interactive'. Interactivity normally precedes the establishment of dialogue between participants in the communication process. This in turn enables all participants to contribute to the content that is used in the communication process. This is referred to as user-generated-content, as demonstrated by people uploading videos to YouTube or even emailing comments to television news programmes. This symbolises a shift in the way in which marketing communications has developed, especially in the online environment. So, when the maintenance of 'relationships' is a central marketing activity it is possible to conclude that interactive marketing communications has an important role to play.

When the Internet began to be developed commercially in the early 1990s, organisations attempted to use the traditional offline promotional tools and processes in the new online context. This was understandable, as it was all that was known at the time. However, lessons were quickly learned, as it soon became apparent that marketing communications worked differently in an electronic environment. It was also realised that it was necessary to integrate offline communications with the online version in order to maximise returns. In this chapter consideration is given first to the way in which the communication tools can be used online and interactively. This is followed by an examination of particular aspects of interactive marketing communications. These include mobile, search, email, viral and community aspects of marketing communication in a digital environment.

Interactive online advertising

Online advertising expenditure is growing.

Online advertising expenditure is growing. It is growing faster than any other sector in the marketing communications industry. It was worth more than £2 billion in 2006 (IAB) a rise of 42 per cent on the previous year and the expectation is that it will continue to grow at a rate of around 30 per cent. In 2006, television advertising revenue fell by over 4 per cent, reflecting current perspectives on the value of these two media.

Advertising, and indeed all digital promotional activity, needs to be planned and managed in just the same way as traditional media. Setting suitable goals is part of this process and Cartellieri *et al.* (1997), consultants with McKinsey, provide a useful set of objectives in this context:

- *delivering content*: click-through to a corporate site that provides more detailed information (e.g. health advice at www.nhsdirect.co.uk/);
- *enabling transactions*: a direct response that leads to a sale (e.g. air travel at www.easyjet.com/);
- *shaping attitudes*: development of brand awareness such as product launches (e.g. http://www.hillaryclinton.com/?splash=1);
- *soliciting response*: encouraging interaction with new visitors (e.g. www.towards-sustainability.co.uk/).
- *improving retention*: reminding visitors and seekers of the organisation and developing reputation and loyalty (e.g. www.ferrymiles.com/).

First, it is necessary to consider the scope of interactive online advertising, or what Goldsmith and Lafferty (2002), two marketing professors based in Florida, refer to as Internet advertising. Two different issues can be identified. One concerns all offline media that is used to drive traffic to an interactive site. The second concerns advertising material that only appears in an online environment. Both need to be used together in an integrated manner if a web site is to be successful, as they are complementary forms of advertising.

Traffic needs to be directed from other sites.

Interactive online advertising is not confined to an organisation's web site. Traffic needs to be directed from other sites (where target customers are thought to visit), to the destination or advertiser's home page. To achieve this, these advertisements need to be placed on other suitable web sites where it is thought the target audience is most likely (or known) to visit. For example, links from Harry Potter pages to Warner Bros. Therefore, advertisements are bought and placed on other web sites and, through careful analysis, it is possible to place the ads on sites where it is thought that members of the target market will pass and be prompted to click the banner and be taken to the advertiser's own corporate or microsite.

Just like offline ads, interactive online ads are used to achieve one of two main tasks:

- to create brand awareness and make a favourable impression such that the reader develops a positive image of the brand;
- to maintain brand awareness and to provoke the reader to behave in particular ways. This is direct response advertising, and it is used to provide readers with a call-to-action. This may be in the form of a click-through to the advertiser's destination site or to a purchase or phone call.

The vast majority of interactive online ads are direct response, making use of the interactive capacity to provide immediate measurement of the success or otherwise of each campaign. For many brands, offline communications are used to create brand images while online ads are used to generate the call-to-action.

The most common form of ads are referred to as banner ads (see below), but as technology and marketing knowledge has improved, so more sophisticated versions of the banner ad have evolved. Some of these are outlined below.

Banner ads

These are the dominant form of paid-for interactive online communications. Fifty-five per cent of all web ads are banner ads, which are responsible for 96 per cent of all Internet ad awareness. Although effective as a stand-alone ad, banner ads are linked through to an advertiser's chosen destination and therefore can act as a gateway to other web sites. Banner ads are linked to keywords submitted by a searcher into a search engine. The ad should therefore be strategically positioned to catch the optimum, or even greatest, traffic flow. Certain product groups, such as computer-related products represent 56 per cent of all banner ads, whereas financial products account for only 7 per cent. Therefore banners are said to signpost, whereas media-rich content provides action. These allow for a depth of material and even ecommerce transactions.

> Banners are said to signpost, whereas media-rich content provides action.

Instead of transferring visitors to an orthodox web site, banner ads can also be used to transfer visitors to a games or a competition site. These games provide entertainment, seek to develop user involvement and can act as an incentive to return to the site at a later date. In addition, data about the user can be captured in order to refine future marketing offers. These ads can be saved for later use and are, therefore, more adaptable and convenient than interstitial ads (ones that pop up as users move between web sites) and cannot be controlled by the user (see p. 776). Banner ads can also be used to transfer users to an interactive microsite.

The aim of banner ads is to attract attention and stimulate interest, but the problem is that click-through rates are very low, at just 0.18 per cent (Mathews, 2007). This leads to the question of whether banner ads are worthwhile. Briggs and Hollis (1997) wrote a seminal paper on the topic in which they reported their finding that click-through rates are determined by five main factors (see Table 26.1).

> The aim of banner ads is to attract attention and stimulate interest.

Table 26.1 Determinants for click-through

Source of predisposition	Factor
Audience-related	Innate tendency to click through
Audience-related	Immediate relevance of product
Audience-related	Pre-existing source appeal (product or organisation)
Advertising-related	Immediate relevance of the message
Advertising-related	Level of curiosity generated by the banner

Source: Briggs and Hollis (1997). Used with kind permission from WARC.

An interesting outcome from Briggs' and Hollis' work was that banner ads were regarded as an important and effective form of online communication. Making allowances for the scope of their research, click-through was seen as unnecessary for the development of brand awareness and even the development of brand attitudes. Click-through rates can be improved when online ads are integrated with a sales promotion device that is designed to reward the behaviour. Special offers, competitions and other incentives can increase rates by as much as 10 per cent. However, it should always be remembered that incentives cost money, and these costs should be considered when analysing the overall return from a banner-based campaign. Another way of improving click-through is to consider not only the design and attractiveness of the ad, but also its placement and timing. This is because audience volumes and composition vary throughout any month or day period (Chaffey *et al.*, 2006).

Since the leading work of Briggs and Hollis, banners have declined in importance to the extent that they are not well regarded, either by customers or clients. However, they continued to be used with many incorporating Flash, rich media, multipurpose units and skyscrapers (very tall banner ads) as these formats generate better recall scores than the standard banner.

Pop-ups

Also known as transitional online ads, pop-ups appear in separate browser windows, when web pages are being loaded or closed. Technically, *interstitials* appear during web page loading and *superstitials* appear during closing (Gay *et al.*, 2007). Originally they are intended to appear as a relief to the boredom that can set in when downloading files took a long time. In that sense, they were regarded as supportive communications. However, as broadband speeds and computer technology has accelerated, so the 'waiting' times experienced by users have been minimised, to the extent that pop-ups are now generally regarded as an intrusive pain.

Microsites

Microsites are much less expensive to set up than a traditional site.

This type of site is normally product- or promotion-specific, and is often run as a joint promotion with other advertisers. Creating a separate site avoids the difficulty of directing traffic to either of the joint partners' sites. Microsites are much less expensive to set up than a traditional site and are particularly adept at building awareness as click-throughs to microsites are higher than through just banners.

Rich media ads

The essential difference between regular and rich media banner ads is that the latter allow for significantly more detailed and enhanced messages to be accessed by the target audience. Rich media ads closely resemble offline ads and this helps to move online ads from a largely informational perspective to one that is much more emotional. This suggests that rich media are more likely to deliver stronger branding messages than in the past, which of course would negate the behavioural advantage inherent in this interactive environment.

Media-rich banner ads are highly effective, if only because the medium is said to be the message.

Streaming video and other more visitor-engaging material, such as Flash and Shockwave, provide depth and interest for users. It is accepted that media-rich banner ads are highly effective, if only because the medium is said to be the message.

Online video

One area that is expected to grow quickly in the next few years is online video advertising. To date, there have been a number of technical issues that have impeded its use, but the growth in broadband connections enabling users to download the data required to view online video, and the increasing use of TiVo and devices that let users fast-forward through television commercials, are encouraging the development of online video advertising.

Online video ads can be used in a number of different ways apart from simply showing ads at the beginning or end of programmes. Online video content normally plays in an unstoppable loop, so the ads are unavoidable. In addition, advertisers will be able to place ads within video streams, another reason preventing users from avoiding them. Also, video ads can be embedded within web pages and online articles, relating closely to the site content. To date, many online ads are directly derived from television ads, but the 30-second format is not appropriate for the online environment. This means specific content for online ads needs to be developed. See the *Guardian* film site for some examples of this (www.http://film.guardian.co.uk/Featurepages/).

It was mentioned earlier that there have been some difficulties associated with the development of online video advertising. One of these concerns the difficulties controlling online content. There is a risk that ads can show up on pages that include content with which they may not want to be associated. For example, in August 2007 some major brands, including Virgin Media, AA, Vodafone and Direct Line all withdrew their advertising from Facebook. Their actions were a response to their ads being positioned next to communications for the British National Party (BNP), the controversial, far right political party. Their withdrawl represented a response to the lack of control that brands have in certain online environments when buying space through media-buying agencies. In this particular instance, Facebook reacted swiftly by introducing a blocking process that enables advertisers to opt out of different parts of the site (Davidson, 2007a). In much the same way, advertisers do not want to be associated with illegally uploaded, copyrighted content, often a problem on some user-generated-content sites.

The development of video advertising has also been frustrated by the difficulties associated with searching online video. Video-search engines currently index content through the use of 'tags', which are supplied by content producers or users. However, this tagging process is not always used properly and some tags are too general to attach appropriate advertising (Holahan, 2006).

One technical development reported by a commercial journalist concerns a video-search feature that allows advertisers to append messages to particular points within videos (Holahan, 2007). So, as an example, users on a La Liga football web site will, at some point in the future, be able to search for videos of particular players performing certain shots, tricks, celebrations, tackles or scoring goals. Advertisers could pay to be linked with particular players, teams or actions, and their ads would play at certain points when the video is requested.

Interactive online sales promotions

Sales promotions play just the same marketing communications role online as they do offline, namely to provoke a behavioural response. Indeed, sales promotions are so good at provoking responses they can be up to five times more effective than direct mail. Using sales promotions online enables the interactive functionality of the web to be developed and this is important when attempting to engage customers with a brand for the first time. Some would argue that a more appropriate term for this activity is interactive sales promotions. This is because this tool can be used in a mobile arena and is not restricted to an online context.

> Using sales promotions online enables the interactive functionality of the web to be developed.

The main aims of using interactive sales promotion are first, that they can either attract or retain customers, and second, that they provide interest and involvement with the brand by encouraging interaction and return visits. In reality, sampling, free gifts, e-coupons, price deals and competitions are the main incentives used interactively.

Organisations use incentive-based interactive promotions because they are capable of delivering two main sources of value. First, they engage customers, providing them with a reason to stay on a site or return to it more frequently than they might otherwise have done. Second, because interactive promotions require customers to opt-in and give permission they deliver huge amounts of pertinent data about customers, potential customers and the market, without too much effort on the behalf of the customer or the organisation.

Online sales promotions are generally less expensive than hard-copy versions, but to date web-based sales promotions have not been used extensively to develop brand differentiation or add value. The issue here is that sales promotions are normally used to bring forward future sales, to provide a reason to buy now. On the Internet this motivation does not exist in the same way, and for many people the only reason to use the Internet is to find information and to compare prices. However, digital media are being used increasingly to deliver sales promotion activities. Indeed, there has been a decline in the use of traditional, on-pack promotions (Barrand, 2004) and a significant growth in the use of SMS, email and the Internet as means of delivering interactive sales promotions (see Chapter 22). If traditional forms of sales promotion might be in need of innovation, the use of the Internet to deliver risk-free sampling and trial opportunities, involving trivia games, interactive loyalty programs, instant-win gratification experiences, plus other opportunities to earn points and prizes, reflects an industry determined to adapt and reinvent itself.

ViewPoint 26.1 Interactive promotional teeth?

In September 2006, an innovative campaign was launched to help promote Colgate's Oral Health Month. The campaign used interactive mobiles and red button ads on Channel 4 and E4 to involve consumers. The red button ads linked through to a Colgate microsite and the linear ads invited people to text 'Smile' to 80889.

Both the mechanic and message 'Colgate would love you to reply with pictures of your smile to 07738 000222 to win a day for two at a health spa', were developed specifically to build closer relationships with consumers, and were based on the principle of incorporating user-generated-content. The best pictures were published on the 'Your smile on TV' section of the microsite every couple of days.

The microsite played an important part in the campaign, not just as a destination site for traffic driven from other parts of the web, but also in giving viewers information about brushing and tips on how to maintain healthy teeth.

Source: Farey-Jones (2006).

Question

To what extent might online sales promotions only attract price hunters and discount seekers?

Task

Choose another toothpaste brand and find out if they run an online sales promotion.

Sampling can be an important stage in customer relationship development and in certain markets the Internet enables this admirably. For example, music and software can be downloaded for trial purposes, while services such as photo processing can be tested risk-free through introductory offers. Another area experiencing growth is the rather oddly termed 'e-coupons'. Downloaded coupons can be redeemed online using a code at checkout, or printed off and used offline in-store.

Interactive online direct marketing

Direct marketing is a primary online communications tool because it can be used interactively to generate both transactional- and relational-based responses within a target audience. Direct marketing activities are often used to integrate a range of activities, but when used to lead campaigns, either offline or online, they should be based on database technologies that target the right audience, shape the creative, are deliverable through appropriate channels and can measure responses.

Interactive direct marketing underpins the majority of communication activities in the online environment. There are some branding-based communications, but the majority of activity is wrapped up as direct marketing, whether that be in the form of direct response advertising (e.g. banners or rich media), sales promotion (e-coupons or sampling) or public relations (e.g. sponsorship, blogs and podcasts).

> Interactive direct marketing underpins the majority of communication activities in the online environment.

Offline direct marketing is used to drive traffic to a web site. This might be undertaken by branding or by providing incentives. For example, many insurance companies use direct response television ads to inform consumers of their low cost/high value insurance deals to be found at their web site. Originally, advertising was the primary offline tool used to drive traffic. Following the reassessment and consolidation of dot-com growth at the beginning of 2000, direct marketing (and direct mail in particular) became the key primary traffic generator. It does this in one of two main ways: the first is to launch a teaser campaign appealing to people's innate curiosity or, second, the direct mail piece is part of a sales promotion campaign in which the promise of a reward lures people to a web site.

The most obvious form of online direct marketing is email and a close application, viral marketing, both of which are discussed later in this chapter. Direct marketing used to revolve around direct mail and telemarketing with a view to acquiring new, 'cold' customers. Now direct marketing is used to converge different media in order to convert warm prospects. See Viewpoint 26.2 for an example of how this works.

ViewPoint 26.2 Man. Utd play the direct card

In an attempt to improve the volume and speed of season ticket renewals, Manchester United used a combination of offline and online direct marketing activities. They sent a personalised direct mail CD card to season ticket holders just after the end of the season. The card delivered an enormous call-to-action in the form of United-branded downloads, video clips including a specially recorded message from the club manager Alex Ferguson, and ticket holder information. The card also enabled a click-through to the club's web site, which achieved a response rate of over 40 per cent. This made the whole process of ticket renewal easy for customers and for those who renewed by a specific date, there was a prize draw contest.

The average play time per card was 10–15 minutes and 43 per cent of those who clicked onto the web site clicked to the ticket area on manutd.com. Click-throughs were experienced from 36 different countries and 259 cities worldwide. The net result was that the season tickets sold out in weeks rather than months and the scheme saved money because the whole process was automated. What does this demonstrate? Well, the campaign was interactive and was based on the convergence of several media formats, not just one. It was designed to meet the perceived needs of the target audience who were 'hot' prospects and already engaged with the brand. The campaign was personalised and sought to convert rather than acquire customers.

Source: Media Week (2007).

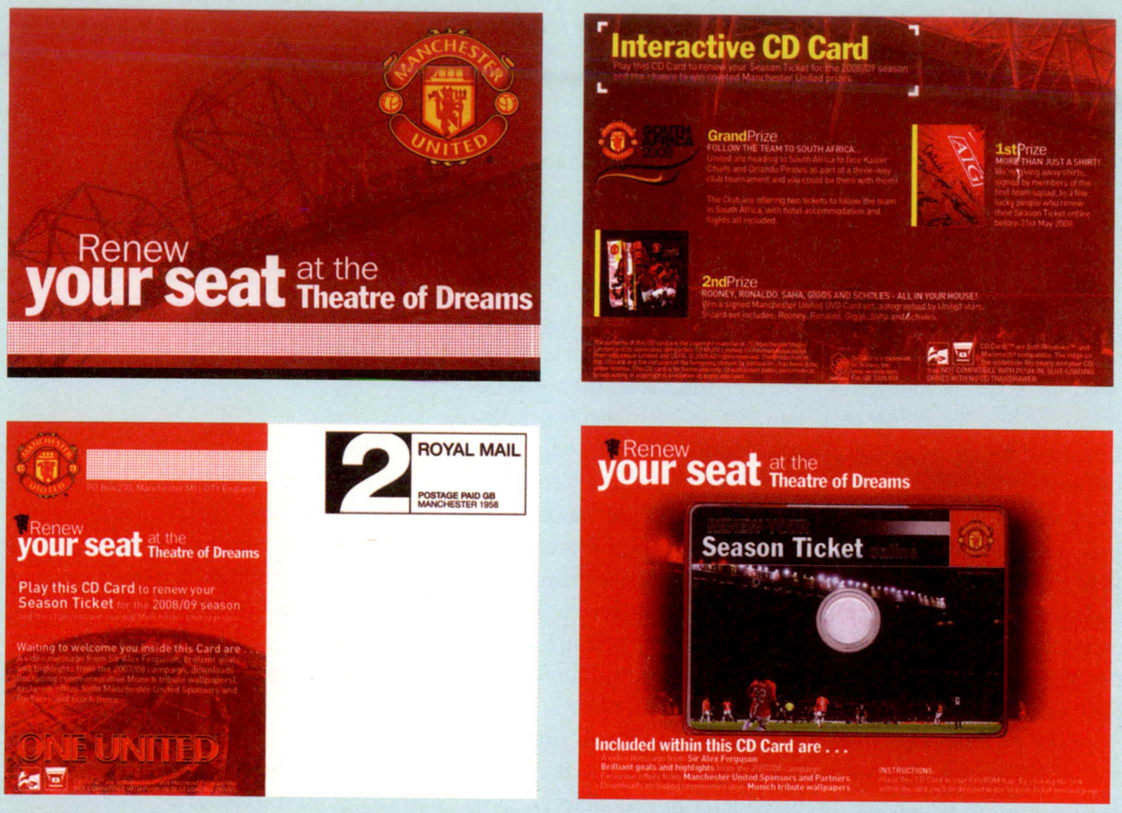

Exhibit 26.1 Manchester United CD Card
Courtesy of Manchester Utd Ltd.

Question

What do you believe was the prime motivation for Man. Utd to adopt this approach. Drive cash flow or further engage season ticket holders?

Task

Make a list of some other ways a sports brand might use a CD card.

Interactive online public relations

The use of interactive online public relations, and extranets in particular, is an increasingly important part of an organisation's marketing communications. Online public relations is concerned with maximising opportunities to present the organisation (and its products and services) in a positive manner. The goal is to create 'mentions' in both traditional media and online on other web sites, which is important for establishing links and achieving higher search engine rankings (see p. 782).

Developments in digital media have been instrumental in assisting public relations move from a predominantly one-way model of communication to an interactive model. In 2001, Hurme suggested that public relations practitioners can be divided into two broad groups: those that predominantly use traditional media and those that adopt online communications. Since that article was written, an increasing number of practitioners have moved over to online communications, but the realisation of the potential to develop true dialogue with stakeholders remains unfilled in many cases. Therefore, opportunities for interactivity and dialogue have increased even if web sites are not being designed to fulfil this requirement completely.

Developments in digital media have been instrumental in assisting public relations move from a predominantly one-way model of communication to an interactive model.

Web site hosts are able to sell advertising space and they also have opportunities to engage with public relations activities. This might lead to the conclusion that owners of web sites have evolved into surrogate media owners, in the sense that they are free to publish content without recourse to the origin of the material. The problem is that the content they present (on their own behalf) has not been influenced by an independent third party, such as an opinion former, and may be no more than brochureware. However, the role is more complex than this, because web sites can now fulfil the role of fax machines. Previously, press releases were faxed to designated journalists. Now press releases are posted on the web site and emailed as attached files to specified individuals on mailing lists so that those interested can view the files (at their discretion and initiative) and then choose to enter into an interaction or even dialogue, in order to expand on the information provided. See the Nokia press release centre at http://www.nokia.com/A4126602.

An associated activity concerns the distribution of e-newsletters and white papers. In many ways e-newsletters and white papers are a natural extension of email communications. The differences concern content and goals. Email communications are sales-driven with product-related content. Newsletters and white papers are reputation-driven with a diverse range of content concerning organisational and/or technical-related material. These communications can be an essential part of the 'stickiness' that good web sites seek to develop. Recipients who find these communications of value either anticipate their release or return to the host's web site to search in archived files for past copies and items of interest.

Other forms of public relations are more easily observable. Statements concerning an organisation's position on an issue of public interest, corporate social responsibility or environmental matters can be published, while investor relations and public affairs issues are easily accommodated. Sponsorship activities are an important part of interactive online marketing communications, whether they be in the form a partnership deal or direct sponsorship of a social networking site. Web sites can also play an important role in terms of crisis management. In the event of an organisational crisis or disaster, up-to-date information can be posted quickly, either providing pertinent information or directing visitors to offline information and associated facilities.

Interactive online personal selling

Face-to-face personal communications are, by definition, always interactive. However, the online application for the purposes of buying and selling remains the one part of the mix that cannot be addressed. Video conferencing does provide this facility but costs and logistics limit the practical application of this tool to conferencing and non-sales meetings. Although the Skype telephone software enables people to talk over the Internet using their PCs free of charge, using next-generation peer-to-peer software, the online environment is an impersonal medium and, as such, does not allow for direct personal communication.

The recognition of this limitation should direct management attention to the use of the Internet as a complementary role within the promotional mix. However, it has been determined that the Internet can impact upon sales performance indirectly through sales management activities (Avlonitis and Karayanni, 2000). They demonstrate how managing and analysing data can refine segmentation and customer classification schemes, allowing sales people to spend more time on core activities.

Search engine marketing

Web sites need visitors and the higher the number of visitors the more effective the web site is likely to be. Many people know of a particular site and simply type in the address or use a bookmark to access it. However, it is estimated that nearly 80 per cent of people (Haig, 2001) arrive at sites following a search using particular key words and phrases to search for products, services, entertainment and the information they need. They do this through search engines and the results of each search are displayed in rank order. It is understandable therefore, that those ranked highest in the results lists are visited more often than those in lower positions.

There are two main search engine marketing techniques; search engine optimisation (SEO) and pay-per-click (PPC).

Therefore, from a marketing perspective it is important to undertake marketing activities to attain the highest possible ranking position, and this is referred to as search engine marketing (SEM). There are two main search engine marketing techniques; search engine optimisation (SEO) and pay-per-click (PPC) with the latter outweighing the former quite substantially (Jarboe, 2005).

Search engine optimisation

Search engine optimisation (SEO), or as it used to be referred, organic search, is a process used to get a high ranking position on major search engines and directories. To achieve top-ranking positions, or least a first page listing, involves designing web pages and creating links with other quality web sites, so that search engines can match closely a searcher's key words/phrases with the content of registered web pages.

Each search engine, such as Google, MSN Search and Yahoo, uses an algorithm to compare the content of relevant site pages with the key words/phrases used to initiate the search. Search engines use robotic electronic spiders to crawl around registered sites and from this compile an index of the words they find, placed there by the designer of each web site. When a search is activated, it is the database housing these keyword/phrases that is searched, not the millions of world wide web pages.

In order to get a high ranking it is important for a site to be registered, which is normally achieved by adding the URL of a site directly into a search engine. Some sites are automatically registered if there are links with another company that is already registered. Once registered, a high ranking is best achieved by attaining a match between the search words/phrases entered by the searcher and the words/phrases on the pages stored in the index. Achieving a good match can be helped by understanding, if not anticipating the words and phrases that are likely to be used by individual searchers. Through web analytics, the study of web site visitors' behaviour, it is possible to analyse the search terms used by current visitors. This can also help improve the matching process, however, there are some fundamental activities that can influence ranking positions.

Through web analytics, the study of web site visitors', behaviour, it is possible to analyse the search terms used by current visitors.

The first important factor is referred to as 'keyphrase density', which refers to the number of times a key phrase is repeated in the text of a web page. The next concerns the number of

ViewPoint 26.3 Searching for quality chocolat

Luxury chocolate retailer Hotel Chocolat began as a mail-order business. However, the company's marketing strategy involved the development of a multichannel approach. This was realised through the launch of an online store and then through the opening of various offline stores.

The design and opening of its online store required that the company consider its search engine marketing and in particular SEO. In order to determine the key search words and phrases that customers for high quality chocolates would use, rather than just chocolate, they used a mind mapping process. Phrases such as 'Gifts for Christmas' and 'Gifts for Valentines' emerged, complementing their peak sales periods.

The company has bought a cocoa plantation in the West Indies and both text and video content was added to the site. This material was reflected in the site's tags so that a range of related ethical key phrases was built into its SEO work and Hotel Chocolat's search ratings improved.

Question

Why do people search for chocolate . . . don't we know where to buy our preferred chocolate?

Task

Choose a product category you are interested in and list some of the keywords that should assist SEO.

inbound links from what are regarded as good-quality sites. The greater the number of quality links, the higher the ranking is likely to be. Two further factors that affect a page's ranking concern the use of tags. The use of keywords in the *title tag* of a web page and the *meta tags*, which signify the content and describe what searchers will find when they click on the site, are embedded by web page designers and read by some search engine spiders. When key words and phrases used by searchers match those in these tags, it is likely that the site will have a higher ranking. For example, the airline easyJet, who sell more than 98 per cent of its seats via the www.easyjet.com web site, use search engine optimisation to drive traffic to its web sites across Europe. It is vital that easyJet appears when the search phrases associated with the discount airlines business are used.

Pay-per-click searches

Pay-per-click (PPC) is similar to display advertising found in offline print formats. Ads are displayed when particular search terms are entered into the search engine. These ads appear on the right-hand side of the results page and are often referred to as sponsored links. However, unlike offline display ads, where a fee is payable in order for the ad to be printed, here a fee is only payable once the display ad is clicked, and the searcher is taken through to the company's web page. See Exhibit 26.2 for an example of these sponsored links displayed as a result of the keyphrase 'cheap airline tickets' input to Google.

It is important for organisations to maintain high visibility, especially in competitive markets, and they cannot rely on their search engine optimisation skills alone. PPC is a paid search list and once again, position in the listings (on the right-hand side of the page) is important. The position in the list is determined mainly through a bidding process. Each organisation bids an amount they are willing to pay for each searcher's click, against a particular key word or phrase. Unsurprisingly, the higher the bid the higher the position on the page. To place these bids, brokers (or PPC ad networks) are used and their role is to determine what a competitive cost per click should be for their client. They achieve this through market research to determine probable conversion rates, and from this deduce what

> Each organisation bids an amount they are willing to pay for each searcher's click, against a particular key word or phrase.

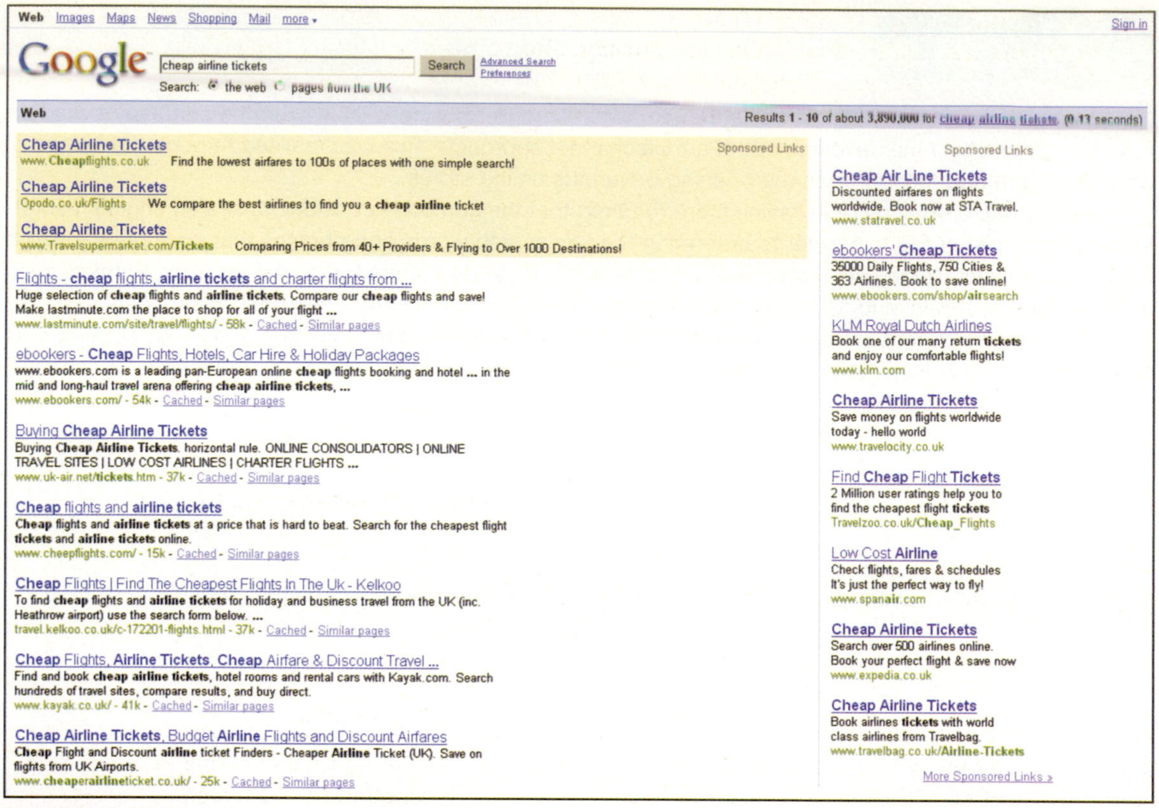
Web Images Maps News Shopping Mail more
Sign in
Google
cheap airline tickets
Search
Advanced Search
Preferences
Search: the web pages from the UK
Web
Results 1 - 10 of about 3,890,000 for cheap airline tickets. (0.13 seconds)
Sponsored Links
Cheap Airline Tickets
www.Cheapflights.co.uk Find the lowest airfares to 100s of places with one simple search!
Cheap Airline Tickets
Opodo.co.uk/Flights We compare the best airlines to find you a cheap airline ticket
Cheap Airline Tickets
www.Travelsupermarket.com/Tickets Comparing Prices from 40+ Providers & Flying to Over 1000 Destinations!
Flights - cheap flights, airline tickets and charter flights from ...
Huge selection of cheap flights and airline tickets. Compare our cheap flights and save! Make lastminute.com the place to shop for all of your flight ...
www.lastminute.com/site/travel/flights/ - 58k - Cached - Similar pages
ebookers - Cheap Flights, Hotels, Car Hire & Holiday Packages
www.ebookers.com is a leading pan-European online cheap flights booking and hotel ... in the mid and long-haul travel arena offering cheap airline tickets, ...
www.ebookers.com/ - 54k - Cached - Similar pages
Buying Cheap Airline Tickets
Buying Cheap Airline Tickets. horizontal rule. ONLINE CONSOLIDATORS | ONLINE TRAVEL SITES | LOW COST AIRLINES | CHARTER FLIGHTS ...
www.uk-air.net/tickets.htm - 37k - Cached - Similar pages
Cheap flights and airline tickets
Cheap flights and airline tickets at a price that is hard to beat. Search for the cheapest flight tickets and airline tickets online.
www.cheepflights.com/ - 15k - Cached - Similar pages
Cheap Flights | Find The Cheapest Flights In The Uk - Kelkoo
To find cheap flights and airline tickets for holiday and business travel from the UK (inc. Heathrow airport) use the search form below. ...
travel.kelkoo.co.uk/c-172201-flights.html - 37k - Cached - Similar pages
Cheap Flights, Airline Tickets, Cheap Airfare & Discount Travel ...
Find and book cheap airline tickets, hotel rooms and rental cars with Kayak.com. Search hundreds of travel sites, compare results, and buy direct.
www.kayak.co.uk/ - 41k - Cached - Similar pages
Cheap Airline Tickets, Budget Airline Flights and Discount Airfares
Cheap Flight and Discount airline ticket Finders - Cheaper Airline Ticket (UK). Save on flights from UK Airports.
www.cheaperairlineticket.co.uk/ - 25k - Cached - Similar pages
Sponsored Links
Cheap Air Line Tickets
Discounted airfares on flights worldwide. Book now at STA Travel.
www.statravel.co.uk
ebookers' Cheap Tickets
35000 Daily Flights, 750 Cities & 363 Airlines. Book to save online!
www.ebookers.com/shop/airsearch
KLM Royal Dutch Airlines
Book one of our many return tickets and enjoy our comfortable flights!
www.klm.com
Cheap Airline Tickets
Save money on flights worldwide today - hello world
www.travelocity.co.uk
Find Cheap Flight Tickets
2 Million user ratings help you to find the cheapest flight tickets
Travelzoo.co.uk/Cheap_Flights
Low Cost Airline
Check flights, fares & schedules It's just the perfect way to fly!
www.spanair.com
Cheap Airline Tickets
Search over 500 airlines online. Book your perfect flight & save now
www.expedia.co.uk
Cheap Airline Tickets
Book airlines tickets with world class airlines from Travelbag.
www.travelbag.co.uk/Airline-Tickets
More Sponsored Links »

Exhibit 26.2 Google™ search engine results for Keyphrase 'cheap airline tickets'. Google is a trademark of Google Inc.

the purchase and lifetime value of customers are likely to be. Consideration needs to be given to the quality of the landing page to which searchers are taken (not the home page), and whether the call-to-action is sufficiently strong.

The cost of each click normally starts at $0.20 or 10p and can reach several dollars, euros or pounds depending on the item and its competitive context. In many sectors, bidding for a paid listing has become a serious competitive activity. For example, a competitor who bids $0.05 more than the current top-ranked company, will assume top position and the previous incumbent then gets relegated in the rankings. Their response might be to increase their bid and so a 'bidding war' might emerge and the cost per click might rise to a point that is not economic for either party. One of Yahoo!'s search marketing strengths is that they guarantee that advertisers will not pay a penny more than the advertiser immediately below them (Gay *et al.*, 2007). This means that if two advertisers use bid management software, set the desired ranking to number 1 and set a bid price maximum of $0.40, even though they might both start with a click cost of $0.25 and $0.27 respectively, the software will ensure that the maximum bid of $0.40 will be achieved quite quickly.

Bidding is just one part of the arithmetic associated with PPC. What is actually at stake is the cost for *converting* a searcher who is interested enough to click on a site, into a paying customer. The cost per customer acquisition (CPA) will vary for a range of reasons but the main one relates to how specific the keywords/phrases are. General search terms such as 'mobile phones' will attract a large number of responses and subsequent clicks and so the cost per click will be generally low. However, searches on '3G' or specific brands such as *Samsung*, *Motorola* or *Nokia* will produce a lower number of clicks, but in competitive markets each click will indicate higher levels of interest and hence be of increased financial potential. As a result, the fee or cost per click will be correspondingly higher. According to Chaffey *et al.* (2006), two generic marketing strategies can be identified in PPC search engine advertising. The first, a premium strategy, involves bidding high amounts on popular keywords in order to generate high volumes of traffic to a web site. The requirement is that the web site has a sufficiently strong call-to-action to achieve suitable conversion rates. A low-cost strategy focuses on keywords and phrases that are not commonly used and hence do not attract high bids. As the traffic generated is lower (than the premium strategy) it is necessary to use a number of these less popular terms to generate sufficient web site visitors.

Search engine marketing is important if only because of the relative ineffectiveness of other online marketing activities. The goal of SEM is to drive traffic to web sites, and ranking on the search-results page is achieved in two fundamentally different ways. In SEO ranking searches are based on content while the PPC approach relies entirely on price as a ranking mechanism. Of these two main approaches, research indicates that the PPC model attracts far more investment (by advertisers) than the SEO model. This indicates that paid ads or sponsored links have low credibility and do not carry high levels of trust. Added to this is the overwhelming research that shows that SEO is more effective in terms of recall and driving site traffic (Jansen and Molina, 2006).

In SEO ranking searches are based on content while the PPC approach relies entirely on price as a ranking mechanism.

So, as Sen (2005) pondered, why is it that advertisers do not invest more in SEO? The answer to this rests partly with the costs associated with SEO. Optimising a site to meet search needs is fine, but optimisation has to take place for each different search engine and the needs of each search engine are different. It is here that costs escalate and the returns diminish in comparison to the performance of PPC. As Sen indicates, SEM is not the dominant form of online marketing communication and the reason for this lies within the searcher's online buying and search characteristics. He suggests SEM would not be useful when a high ranking is probable and the site would become part of the searcher's consideration set. This could occur when there are few relevant web sites associated with the search terms used, as a result of which a searcher has the opportunity to visit each listed site that is returned.

The second reason is associated with a searcher's level of search intensity. This is linked to the opportunity cost of time, perceived price dispersion, the anticipated savings arising from the search, consumer characteristics (e.g. search skills, experience) and the importance or value of the product or information sought (Sen, 2005; Zhang *et al.*, 2007). So, a low opportunity cost, high levels of perceived price dispersion or when an expensive product is to be purchased will result in high search intensity and a site will be uncovered regardless of position in the search-results page. In this circumstance SEM is not likely to provide a suitable return on investment. However, when intensity is low, typified by a purchase that can be made from a number of different sites, such as a music CD or book purchase, a high ranking is important and so investment in SEM is advisable.

The second reason is associated with a searcher's level of search intensity.

Email marketing

There are two key characteristics associated with email communications. First, it can be directed at clearly defined target groups and individuals. Second, email messages can be personalised and refined to meet the needs of individuals. In this sense email is the antithesis of broadcast communications, which are scattered among a mass audience and lack any sense of individualisation, let alone provide an opportunity for recipients to respond. In addition, email can be used with varying levels of frequency and intensity, which is important when building awareness, reinforcing messages or when attempting to persuade someone into a trial or purchase.

Table 26.2 Three measures of email campaign success

Email measure	Explanation
Delivery rate	This concerns the deliverability of email messages and is a measure of the number of messages that fail to be delivered. This may be because the email address is no longer valid or has been has been bounced through a spam filter.
Open rate	This is an attempt to measure the number of messages that are opened and is often based on the number of downloaded images. This measure is not entirely accurate for various reasons, including preview panes and systems that automatically block the receipt of images.
Click-through rate	This measures the percentage of email messages clicked open. It does not measure whether the messages are actually read in part or in full, or what is understood as a result of reading the email message.

Organisations need to manage two key dimensions of email communications; outbound and inbound email. Outbound email concerns messages sent by a company often as a part of a direct marketing campaign, designed to persuade recipients to visit a web site, to take a trial or make a purchase. The inbound dimension concerns the management of email communications received from customers and other stakeholders. These may have been stimulated either by an individual's use of the web site or through product experience, which often entails a complaint. Managing inbound email represents a huge opportunity not only to build email lists for use in outbound campaigns, but also to provide high levels of customer service interaction and satisfaction. If undertaken properly and promptly this can help to build trust and reputation, which in turn can stimulate word-of-mouth communication, all essential aspects of marketing communication.

In order to manage outbound email and realise its potential three key factors need to be measured. These are explained in Table 26.2.

The key attribute of email communications is that it is generally very effective at stimulating responses. Another characteristic is that it is extremely cost effective, with both the absolute and relative costs lower than other forms of communication. As mentioned earlier, email communications are easily customised, enabling tailored messages to be delivered to different segments.

The use of email to attract and retain customers has become a main feature of many organisations' marketing communications campaigns. Using appropriate email lists is a fast, efficient and effective way to communicate regularly with a market. Email-based marketing communication enables organisations to send a variety of messages concerning public relations-based announcements, newsletters and sales promotions, to distribute online catalogues and to start and manage permission-based contact lists. Many organisations build their own lists using data collected from their CRM system. By acquiring email responses and other contact mechanisms, addresses and contact details can be captured for the database and then accessed by all customer support staff. The use of email to attract and retain customers has become a main feature of many organisations' marketing communications campaigns. Indeed, email can be used to deliver messages at all points in the customer relationship lifecycle.

Many organisations build their own lists using data collected from their CRM system.

Customer acquisition

To generate customer acquisition, email house lists of prospects are used to convert people who have come into contact with the organisation but who have yet to make a purchase. So, people who visit a web site and who give their permission to receive email communications, will receive automated emails prompting them to trial a product or service. In this circumstance the web site will provide the information and serve to differentiate the brand, while email is used to encourage trial and purchase. Email can be used to deliver newsflashes, product offers and availability notices, newsletters, white papers, press releases and event reminders. In addition to this, acquisition can be assisted through email delivered via another company, one with which the target has a reasonable relationship. Clickable links enable potential customers to connect with the main web site and so the conversion process kicks in once again.

Customer retention

As far as retention strategies are concerned, house lists can be used to reinforce customer relationships and so retain customers and prevent defection to a rival brand. Email messages can be used operationally to reassure customers and to build customer confidence at the order stage. For example, orders can be confirmed and updates on the delivery status can be provided. Email can also be used strategically to build and reinforce relationships. Established customers can be reached with email messages that remind them about the brand and in doing so keep it in the mind of customers. Messages about product and brand offers, company developments, personalised greetings, technical support, expiration of contracts and significant personal events are used with increasing sophistication, all designed to retain customers and to realise their potential value.

Short message services (SMS)

Although different in format, short message services (SMS), or 'texting', can be regarded as an extension of email communication. SMS is a non-intrusive but timely way of delivering information and as Doyle (2003) points out, the global system for mobile communication (GSM) has become a standard protocol, so that users can send and receive information across geographic boundaries. Apart from pure text, other simple applications consist of games, email notifications and information-delivery services such as sports and stock market updates.

Organisations have been relatively slow at adopting SMS despite the low costs and high level of user control (target, content and time). It is these types of benefits that are attracting marketing professionals to consider SMS for more complex services. However, marketers also need to consider the potential concerns of consumers, most notably security and privacy. Just as with email, there is the potential for unwanted messages (i.e. spam) and Internet service providers (ISP) need to manage the increasing numbers of unsolicited messages through improved security systems as SMS becomes more widespread. Given that most consumers pay for SMS functionality, marketers should realise that invading personal privacy greatly reduces the potential value and effectiveness of SMS.

Word-of-mouth communication

It was established in Chapter 2 that people use word-of-mouth recommendations to provide information and to support and reinforce their purchasing decisions. The impact of personal influences on the offline communication process can be important if communication is to be successful. Opinion leaders and formers were identified as significant personal influencers, simply because organisations target these individuals with messages knowing that they will transmit messages onwards to the organisation's target audience. The same principle is true of digital communications where the popular term 'word-of-mouse' is used to reflect personal, electronic recommendation and endorsement. However, the role of opinion formers is much diminished in the online world, especially with the predominant 18–25-year-old user group. For them expert opinion, as represented by opinion formers, is rejected in favour of peer group recommendation. For example, www.last.fm, a social music platform, tracks individual music preferences based on what people play on their computers or iPods, locates individuals into neighbourhoods who share similar tastes and then wait for them to interact. People share views, interests and favourite music and then make recommendations to others in their neighbourhood, based on shared preferences (Crow, 2007). Although there is a hint of social engineering, the power of peer group and opinion leader recommendation has seen this model copied by others, including book libraries.

People share views, interests and favourite music and then make recommendations to others in their neighbourhood, based on shared preferences.

In 2000, Malcolm Gladwell, a writer with the *New Yorker* magazine, published a book entitled *The Tipping Point*. In it he considers the power personal recommendation. He refers to the 'tipping point', to explain the way in which ideas, products and behaviour can spread through a population. Marketers are advised to create 'tipping points' such that new ideas multiply and accelerate through a population, similar to the way in which a falling domino can trigger a chain reaction. Tipping points are governed by three elements. The first concerns the initial adoption of the idea by socially connected individuals who use word-of-mouth to propagate the news. These 'connectors' often use blogs, podcasts and email newsletters to seed their views and opinions. A second element concerns the 'stickiness' of the idea or product, or the extent to which an individual feels attached to a brand. The strength of the stickiness can be influenced by many factors, ranging from the uniqueness and aesthetic of a brand through to the cost, level of personification and the expressive and functional values the brand represents (Morris and Martin, 2000). The third element concerns the context in which a communication event occurs. Viruses and diseases are most virulent when the physical context is conducive to multiplication and development. In just the same way, products and ideas are more likely to spread when the physical, mental and social contexts are receptive.

Four main aspects of electronic word-of-mouth communication are considered here: viral marketing; podcasts; web logs (or blogs); and RSS feeds.

Viral marketing

Viral marketing involves the use of email to convey messages to a small part of a target audience where the content is sufficiently humorous, interesting or persuasive that the receiver feels emotionally compelled to send it on to a friend or acquaintance. For example, marketing journalist Davidson, reports that Triumph, the British motorcycle manufacturer, distributed a viral message based on the Triumph Rocket III, the world's largest production motorcycle (2007b). The humorous film showed the bike being built on the production line and then being tested by factory workers. One of the scenes showed the factory workers risking their lives to test the speed of the bike's brakes. The viral was aimed at motorcycle enthusiasts and was made available on YouTube and biker-related online communities and social networks. The goals were to show a more irreverant side of Triumph, and to raise the profile of the Rocket III while drawing attention to the bike's key attributes, in an entertaining way (http://www.youtube.com/watch?v=HKEuzxC4eGc).

The term, 'viral marketing' was developed by a venture capital company, Draper Fisher Juvertson (Juvertson and Draper, 1997). The term was used to describe the Hotmail email service, one of the first free email address services offered to the general public and one that has grown enormously. According to Juvertson (2000: 1, 2) they defined the term simply as 'network-enhanced word-of-mouth'. However, although the literature contains a variety of terminology used to explain what viral marketing is, for example *stealth marketing* (Kaikati and

Kaikati, 2004), *interactive marketing* (Blattberg and Deighton, 1991) and *referral marketing* (De Bruyn and Lilien, 2004), viral marketing (communications) is the term used here.

Welker (2002), from the German Institute of Information Management, was one of the first to see an analogy between this type of communication and a living biological virus. He stresses the power of the contagious nature of a virus and suggests that a 'virus replicates [itself] with geometrically increasing power, doubling with each interaction' (p. 4). Ecommerce consultant, Ralf Wilson defines viral marketing more simply as 'any strategy that encourages individuals to pass on a marketing message to others, creating the potential for exponential growth in the message's exposure and influence' (2000: 1). By understanding the properties of a biological virus, he argues that it becomes clear just how powerful, yet completely uncontrollable, this form of communication is.

> It becomes clear just how powerful, yet completely uncontrollable, this form of communication is.

Porter and Golan (2006: 33) suggest that viral advertising is 'unpaid peer-to-peer communication of provocative content originating from an identified sponsor using the Internet to persuade or influence an audience to pass along the content to others'. They argue that these materials are usually seeded through the Internet, are often distributed through independent third-party sites, are usually personal, more credible than traditional advertising and humour is almost unanimously employed in executions. Kirby, a leading viral marketing consultant, agrees indicating that there are three key elements associated with viral marketing (2003):

- *content*, which he refers to as the 'viral agent' is the quality of the creative material and whether it is communicated as text, image or video;
- *seeding*, which requires identifying web sites or people to send email in order to kick start the virus;
- *tracking*, or monitoring, the impact of the virus and in doing so provide feedback and a means of assessing the return on the investment.

However, although these qualities might be present, it is necessary that receivers of viral messages are predisposed to open the message, derive value from the message and be sufficiently engaged to become a part of the virus campaign by sending it on to others.

There is no doubt that viral marketing is difficult to control and can be very unpredictable, yet despite these characteristics organisations are incorporating this approach within their marketing communications in order to reach their target audiences.

ViewPoint 26.4 Flying with Irn Bru's snowman

In December 2006, Irn Bru ran an animated ad based on the classic Christmas story *The Snowman*, by Raymond Briggs. The ad was screened only on Scottish television, where the drink is extremely popular, and depicted a little boy who refused to give his Irn Bru to the Snowman as they flew over the snowy Scottish landscape. It had been planned to release the ad as a viral as it was thought it would appeal to the large Irn Bru online community. However, production over ran and the ad was only finished the day before the first screening. The ad was a huge success and attracted interest from national newspapers, which led to extensive public relations and media comment.

As soon as the ad was put on YouTube a far wider audience enjoyed the short story and soon there had been over 1 million YouTube downloads. It also won awards such as the Grand Prix at the Scottish Advertising Awards.

Based on this success, the ad returned to television during Christmas 2007, but this time was screened throughout the United Kingdom, with strategic placement in cinemas. Whereas normally viral is used to leak an ad *prior* to a national launch, this 'conventional' pattern was changed as the Irn Bru Snowman went viral *after* a television launch.

Sources: Davidson (2007c); Turner (2007).

Exhibit 26.3 Irn Bru used the Snowman animated character to reinforce its Scottish credentials and create awareness for the brand
Produced by Jayne Bevitt, directed by Robin Shaw for Sherbet.

Question

What might have been the motivation to use animation to promote a soft drink?

Task

Make a list of four product categories. How many of the brands use animation? Are they successful?

Widgets

A relatively recent addition to the array of interactive marketing communications media is the widget. These are stand-alone applications that enable users to interact with the owner of the widget. As Chaffey (2008) suggests, the applications can provide functionality such as a calculator or real-time information, as in travel updates or weather forecasts. Widgets sit on a desktop, are relatively cheap to develop and manage and ideally are distributed virally.

The real benefit of widgets is that they provide a way of advertising a brand.

The real benefit of widgets is that they provide a way of advertising a brand, delivering online public relations or even driving direct response sales via affiliate marketing.

Blythe (2008) sees the real potential of widgets as sponsored entities on social networking sites. To date, attempts by brands to derive commercial benefit from social networking sites have been thwarted by the prevailing network culture that is essentially one that rejects advertising and outright commercialism. Sponsored widgets might provide a means of overcoming these difficulties as widgets offer benefits that might appeal to social network users. For example, Jamiroquai use a widget that allows their fans to keep up-to-date on video releases, tour dates and tracks. Cadbury have created a game called 'Room with a Goo'. In it players are required to stop creme eggs being smashed, blended and splattered. A widget on the Bebo site enables users to destroy or rebuild others Cadbury's Creme Eggs by either hugging or karate-chopping the eggs, virtually. A whole range of widget applications can be seen at www.directory.snipperoo.com.

Web logs

Web logs, or blogs as they are commonly known, are personal online diaries. Although personal issues are recorded and shared, a large proportion of blogs concern organisations and public issues, and they are virtually free. As Wood *et al.* (2006) conclude, blogging represents a simple, straightforward way of creating a web presence. Even if the quality and content of some blogs varies considerably, their popularity has grown enormously. The informality of blogs enables information to be communicated in a much more relaxed manner than most other forms of marketing communication. This is typified by the use of podcasting and the downloading of blogs to be 'consumed' at a later, more convenient time or while multi-tasking. Blogs represent user-generated-content (for more on UGC see Chapter 2) and are often a key indicator of the presence of an opinion leader or former.

Blogging represents a simple, straightforward way of creating a web presence.

Blogs can be understood using a number of criteria, other than the basic consumer or corporate demarcation. Typically, the content and the type of media are the main criteria. A blog can be categorised by its content or the general material it is concerned with. The breadth of content is only limited by the imagination, but some of the more mainstream blogs tend to cover topics such as sport, travel, music, film, fashion and politics. Blogs can also be categorised according to the type of media. For example, 'vlogs' contain video collections, whereas a 'photoblog' is a collection photos and a 'sketchblog' contains sketches.

Business-related or corporate blogs represent huge potential as a form of marketing communications for organisations. This is because blogs reflect the attitudes of the author, and these attitudes can influence others. As consumers write about their experiences with brands, opportunities exist for organisations to identify emerging trends, needs and preferences, and to also understand how brands are perceived. Sony used blogging as a integral part of its campaign to establish the Handycam and Cybershot brands. When shooting the ad in Miami, dubbed as 'Sony Foam City', Sony invited 200 visitors, mainly bloggers. Each was equipped with Sony cameras and encouraged to capture the soapy event which involved covering parts of Miami with foam. Clips of the ad and the making of the ad were then leaked onto the Internet in advance of the launch of the ad being released and in doing so created a buzz around the brands.

Organisations can set up *external* corporate blogs to communicate with customers, channel partners and other stakeholders. Cisco Systems use external blogs to provide information about company issues (Wood *et al.*, 2006) and other organisations use blogs to launch brands or attend to customer issues. The other form of corporate blog is the *internal* blog. Here the focus is on enabling employees to write about and discuss corporate policies, issues and developments. Some organisations encourage interaction between their employees and customers and the general public. Although problems can arise through inappropriate comments and observations, blogging is an informal communication device that can serve to counter the formality often associated with planned marketing communications.

Cisco Systems use external blogs to provide information about company issues.

Therefore, enabling people to blog, perhaps by creating dedicated web space, facilitates interaction and communication through people with similar interests. There is also an added attraction in that communities of bloggers can attract advertisers and form valuable revenue streams. Blogs can be used by organisations as a form of public relations in order to communicate with a range of stakeholders. For example, a blog on an intranet can be used to support internal communications, on an extranet to support distributors and on the Internet to reach consumers. In 2007, King of Shaves (www.shave.com) rolled out a series of blogs in order to improve their image and offer customer service online. A series of eight blogs including a community blog, a design blog and a digital blog, were supplemented with a blog from the company founder Will King, generating news on the brand's parent company KMI (McCormick, 2007).

One novel use of blogging concerned the Taxi Challenge campaign that was acclaimed a major success (see Viewpoint 26.5).

ViewPoint 26.5 Travelling through Irish blogs

Tourism Ireland developed an intriguing campaign to promote Ireland as a tourist destination. The winners of a competition, Ken and Shamilla, won a 10-day trip around Ireland in a luxury taxi. Not only did they visit major tourist attractions and places of interest, they also had to complete various daily tasks for which they received £1,000 each time they were successful. Hence the name of the promotion, the Taxi Challenge.

The clever twist to the campaign was the use of a web site to which daily video reports were posted as the journey progressed. This enabled people to follow the couple's trip, keep up with their progress, adventures and success in completing the tasks. In addition, the site contained a wealth of tourist information so that people interested in visiting Ireland could access tourist information on all of the places the couple visited, see the places on video clips and download each day's fact sheets. All of this added to the web site's stickiness, engaged people and potential tourists over a period of time and provided huge interest and added value.

Source: www.tourismirelandtaxichallenge.com.

Question

In your opinion, what was the main reason for the success of this campaign?

Task

Browse the web and try to find a similar competition site that involves viewers in the core activity. Once you have found one, post the details on the companion web site for this book and invite feedback.

Exhibit 26.4 Taxi Challenge home page

Podcasting

Podcasting emerged as a major new form of communication in 2005 and has grown significantly since then. This is mainly because of the huge growth in the adoption of MP3 players and the desire for fresh, up-to-date or different content.

Podcasting is a process whereby audio content is delivered over the Internet to iPods, MP3 players and computers, on demand. A podcast is a collection of files located at a feed address, which people can subscribe to by submitting the address to an aggregator. When new content becomes available it is automatically downloaded using an aggregator or feed reader which recognises feed formats such as RSS (see below).

In many ways podcasting is similar to radio broadcasts, yet there are a couple of major differences. First, the material is pre-recorded and time-shifted so that material can be listened to at a user's convenience, that is, on demand. The second difference is that listeners can take the material they have chosen to listen to, and play it at times and locations that are convenient to them. They can listen to the content as many times as they wish simply because the audio files can be retained.

Podcasting is relatively inexpensive and simple to execute. It opens up publishing to a host of new people, organisations as well as individuals, and it represents a new media channel for audio content. Users have control over what they listen to, when they listen to it and how many times they listen to the content.

Users have control over what they listen to, when they listen to it and how many times they listen to the content.

RSS

RSS stands for 'really simple syndication' and refers to the distribution of news content on the web. Rather than trawl all relevant web pages to find new content and updates, RSS allows for specific content to be brought together and made available to an individual without their always having to return to numerous sites. Just checking the RSS feed to see whether something new has been posted online can save huge amounts of time.

Originally email was the preferred way of notifying people of breaking news and information updates. The problem with email is that not only has the user to sort out and organise the separate strands of information, they also have to contend with increasing amounts of spam and unwanted material that accompanies it. In addition, RSS feeds allow content updates to be read in a reader, not online.

From a publisher's point of view RSS feeds enable information to reach a wide audience. This is because of syndication. Once content has been created, RSS feeds allow the content to be grouped (syndicated) with web sites that publish similar content. These are referred to as aggregator web sites. Each feed consists of brief information about headlines, a summary of the content and a link to the article on the requisite web site.

From a marketing perspective RSS Feeds act as a media channel delivering a variety of information about news stories, events, headlines, project updates and even corporate information, often as press releases. This information is delivered quickly and efficiently to audiences who have signed up and effectively given express permission to be sent the information.

RSS Feeds act as a media channel delivering a variety of information about news stories, events, headlines, project updates and even corporate information, often as press releases.

Interactive online communities

Armstrong and Hagel (1996) were two of the first researchers to propose the benefits of virtual communities. They also saw that the development of these communities is one of the key elements that differentiate interactive from traditional media. Communities of people who share a common interest(s), who interact, share information, develop understanding and build relationships all add value, in varying degrees, through their contribution to others involved with the web site. In a sense, user groups and special interest groups are similar facilities, but the key with all these variations is the opportunity to share information electronically, often in real time.

Chaffey *et al.* (2006) refer to Durlacher (1999), who argues that there are four main types of community defined by their purpose, position, interest and profession (see Table 26.3). Communities can be characterised by several determining elements. Muniz and O'Guinn (2001), assistant professors of marketing at DePaul and Temple Universities respectively when they wrote the paper, identify three core components:

- consciousness of kind: an intrinsic connection that members feel towards one another;
- the presence of shared rituals and traditions that perpetuate the community's history, culture and consciousness;
- a sense of moral responsibility, duty or obligation to the community as a whole and its individual members.

Within these online or virtual communities five particular characteristics can be identified. The first concerns the model of communication, which is essentially visitor-to-visitor and in some cases customer-to-customer. Second, communities create an identity that arises from each individual's involvement and sense of membership and belonging. The more frequent and intense the interaction, the stronger the identity the participants feel towards the community. Third, relationships, even close friendships develop among members, which in turn can facilitate mutual help and support. The fourth characteristic concerns the language that the community adopts. Very often specialised languages or codes of (electronic) behaviour emerge that have particular meaning to members. The fifth and final characteristic refers to the methods used to regulate and control the behaviour and operations of the community. Self-regulation is important in order to establish acceptable modes of conduct and interaction among the membership.

Table 26.3 Four types of virtual community

Type of community	Explanation
Purpose	Those attempting to achieve the same goal or who are experiencing a similar process
Position	Those experiencing particular circumstances. These might be to do with life-stage issues (the old or the young), health issues or perhaps career development opportunities
Interest	Those sharing a hobby, pastime or who are passionately involved with, for example, sport, music, dance, family trees, jigsaws, gardening, film, etc.
Profession	Those involved with the provision of b2b services. Often created by publishers these portals provide information about jobs, company news, industry issues and trading facilities (e.g. auctions).

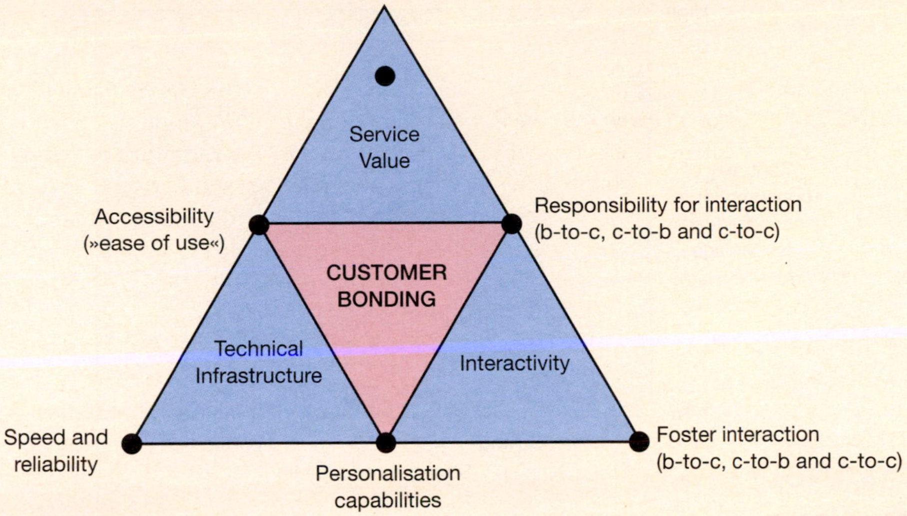

Figure 26.1 The Customer Bonding Triangle framework
Source: Szmigin and Reppel (2004). © Emerald Group Publishing Limited. All rights reserved.

The role that members assume within these communities and the degree to which they participate also varies. There are members who attend but contribute little, those who create topics, lead discussion, those who summarise and those who perform brokerage or intermediary roles among other members.

According to Jepsen (2006) the number of consumers undertaking product information search within virtual communities can be expected to develop simply because the number of experienced Internet users will grow. The provision and form of online communities will inevitably develop and frameworks will emerge in order that understanding about the way they operate (effectively) is disseminated. Szmigin and Reppel (2004) have offered their customer bonding triangle framework, which is built on interactivity, technical infrastructure and service value elements (see Figure 26.1). It is argued by the authors of this framework that it is the fit between the elements that determine the level of bonding between community members. Further work is required in this area, but this framework provides an interesting conceptualisation of the elements that characterise this relatively new relationship developing approach.

> The provision and form of online communities will inevitably develop.

The knowledge held in virtual communities can be expected to be of significant value when searching for product information. Community-based information can be expected to be rich, up-to-date and dynamic, reflecting the involvement of members. In 1999, Kozinets presented four segments related to virtual communities, based around two dimensions. The first dimension relates to the extent to which the consumption activity is central to an individual's self-image. Reference is made to Chaudhuri (2000) who holds that consumers tend to be more knowledgeable about products that are important to them individually. The second dimension concerns the strength of social ties between an individual and other community members. Where tie strength is strong, so trust in the information provided by that person may be sufficient to replace offline commercial sources.

The four segments identified by Kozinets, based around these dimensions, are referred to as insiders, devotees, minglers and tourists. Insiders have strong social ties to other members of the community and consumption is central to their self-image. Devotees only have ties to the product, minglers are tied to the members and tourists do not have ties to the product or other members. Jepsen speculates that information provided by the virtual community may

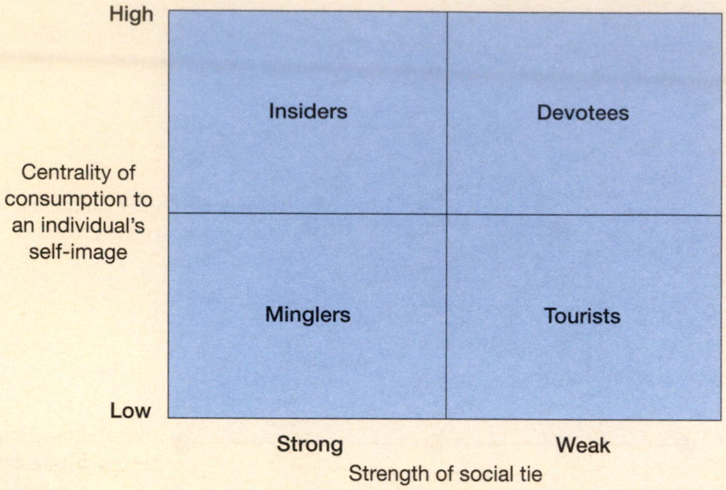

Figure 26.2 Four segments within virtual communities
Source: Kozinets (1999).

be sufficiently strong for insiders that it replaces information from offline sources. This is probably not the case for any of the other three segments.

Social networks

One particular interpretation of online communities is the relatively recent evolution and rapid development of social networks. Social networks are about people using the Internet to share lifestyle and experiences. The participants in these networks not only share information and experiences, but they can also use the interactive capacity to build new relationships. The critical aspect of social networks is that the content is user-generated and this means users own, control and develop content according to their needs, not those of a third party.

Social networks concern the Internet's ability to enable people to share experiences. Typical sites include MySpace, Bebo, YouTube and Facebook, each of which has experienced rapid growth in recent years. These sites provide certain segments of the population, mainly the 16–25-year-old group, an opportunity to use online networks to reach their friends, generate new ones and share experiences, information and insights. The activity might also be regarded as a supplement to their offline social networks. Some sites encourage ranking and rating of content that has been added to the site by others, for example Digg and Flickr. What is happening is that social networks are helping to re-engineer the way in which parts of society link together and share information (Walmsley, 2007).

The results of a European-wide study undertaken by Forrester Research reveal that there are six key characteristics that typify the dominant usage by online consumers of social media (Pinkerfield, 2007a). There are those whose core activity on these sites is to publish content (9 per cent); those who prefer to comment (18 per cent); networkers (1 per cent); those who gather information (12 per cent); people who prefer to listen and observe interaction (49 per cent); and finally a large group who ignore all these activities (41 per cent).

When these data are aggregated on a country by country basis, it is revealed that the Dutch are the most active users publishing the most blogs and web pages. The Spanish prefer to comment, while the Italians actively gather information. French users are most likely to read blogs and reviews (are listeners), while UK users prefer to visit social media sites and make comments, typical of networkers. The study found that the Germans tend to ignore most social media.

Competition among the various social networking sites has intensified, fuelled by the knowledge that users are not loyal to a single site but often have space on two or three sites simultaneously (Blakely, 2007). MySpace, owned by the News Corp, is reported to have had 6.5m unique UK visitors in May 2007, and although this represents considerably more participants than those attached to Facebook, it is the latter that has been developing rapidly in 2007. Facebook, originally the most popular site with US college students, has now been opened up globally and their rate of new registrations grew at a rate of 81 per cent during June and July 2007 whereas MySpace only grew 7 per cent (Hicks, 2007). In Britain alone, Facebook saw a 523 per cent increase in UK visitors compared to MySpace's rise of just 28 per cent in 2006 (Crow, 2007). The growth of these two main sites is partly a reflection of the relative investment made in them. MySpace has seen little investment and attracts widespread criticism, whereas Facebook is innovative and eager to meet the needs of its target audience. For example, as part of its strategic development in May 2007, Facebook allowed its users to build and install applications within the social network. The more obvious marketing strategy would have been to charge developers the opportunity to access Facebook's users. However, by opening the site up in this way, and free of charge, huge numbers of people switched to the site and within a couple of months over 1,700 new applications such as SuperPoke, which encourages users to 'slap, chest-bump or headbutt' their friends (Hicks, 2007), photo slideshows and online data storage, had been developed, integrated and accessed by site visitors (Walmsley, 2007).

Competition among the various social networking sites has intensified.

Social networking sites make money by selling advertising space. Advertisers are attracted to the large numbers of visitors frequenting these sites, and the profiles they are able to build up about the target audience. However, the relative immaturity of these sites means that some rules and codes of behaviour are evolving, the Facebook example mentioned earlier is a good example of the developing behavioural infrastructure.

The relative immaturity of the social networking arena and the way in which content is developed raises challenges about how organisations can best use marketing communications to reach their target audiences. It has been mentioned earlier that site users are less than loyal as many have own multiple sites, so the challenge is to persuade users to visit their sites as often as possible and to encourage them to attract new users. The key therefore, is to create sites that are 'sticky', that is, contain sufficient content and facilities that engage users and give them reason to stay on the site for longer periods of time and also give them reason to return on a regular basis. If this works and the number of users increases then this should attract advertisers who are willing to pay premium rates.

The key is to create sites that are 'sticky', that is, contain sufficient content and facilities that engage users and give them reason to stay on the site for longer periods of time.

However, questions then arise about the effectiveness of online ads in a social networking environment. Many users do not like brand advertising and prefer to take advice from their online peers in these communities when deciding what to buy, rather than listen to advertisers. Social networking is becoming a media channel in its own right and it is one that is reflecting the voice of consumers instead of those of brand owners.

An understanding of social media reveals that brand communications should not be invasive, intrusive or interruptive. In order to work, marketing communications need to become part of the context in which site users are interacting. Online advertising will continue to form a major revenue stream for the owners of these social networking sites, but increasingly this needs to be supplemented with the use of a mixture of sponsorship, product placement and public relations. For example, sponsored groups, such as Apple's 'Apple Students' group, with 400,000 members, have been developed (Hicks, 2007).

In April 2007 iVillage launched what was claimed to be the first UK social network designed specifically for women. The iVillage Connect platform serves a community of 3.5 million monthly women readers, enabling them to build groups for people interested in areas such as fashion, health, television soaps, motherhood and cookery. Users can create profiles, post blogs, upload photos and invite friends and family to join (Pinkerfield, 2007b). See also Viewpoint 26.6 for two examples of the way in which brands are beginning to be involved with social networks.

ViewPoint 26.6 Networked brands

The communications potential represented by social networking sites has started to attract some major brand manufacturers. For example, the Starburst, McDonald's, Haribo and Skittles brands have all used the Internet to reach children, especially since the regulations concerning advertising during children's television have been strengthened.

In July 2007, the owners of the Skittles confectionary brand paid a substantial six-figure sum to set up a profile on Bebo, the social networking site. The Skittles profile attracted 50,000 visitors in the first month and enlisted over 3,500 'friends'. A Bebo spokesman described these 'friends' as 'brand ambassadors', individuals who endorse a brand and speak positively about it to others.

At around the same time Canon rolled out a pan-European campaign, called 'We speak image' to encourage consumers to to go online to upload fashion images that they believe represent the spirit of their nation. Canon created a branded social network to generate a community of interest around the photos. The intention was to allow consumers to view each other's photos, for them to co-create 'mood boards' and vote for their favourite image in a series of weekly competitions. The user with the most popular photo in each country won a Canon IXUS 70 digital camera.

Sources: Jones (2007); Pidd (2007).

Question

What are the key difficulties faced by brands attempting to use social networks to reach their target markets?

Task

Ask your networked friends what they feel about brands using social networks to reach them.

Using social networks to promote brands has to be undertaken carefully.

Using social networks to promote brands has to be undertaken carefully, mainly because users of these sites do not appreciate blatant commercial activity. As a result, organisations are experimenting with different ideas to see what does and does not work. The social networking site Bebo launched one such experiment in the summer of 2007. Called 'KateModern', this online soap opera was based on a video diary of a fictional character, an art student (Kate), and traced her lifestyle and adventures. Targeted at young teenagers, audiences could interact with the characters and even help shape the script (co-created content).

There is no advertising on the KateModern site, simply because it was realised that it would be a turn-off for the target audience. However, companies such as Procter & Gamble (who own major brands such as Gillette, Pantene and Tampax), MSN, Orange Mobile, Paramount and Disney/Buena Vista each paid £250,000 for six months of name-checking and product placement opportunities in KateModern. For example, Buena Vista used the site to promote their film, *Hallam Foe*. This was achieved by allowing the film's star, Jamie Bell to make a cameo appearance in the KateModern drama. By allowing viewers to post messages about his involvement in the plot and to interact with his character, the goal is to attract attention and visitors, which in turn will raise the reputation of both Bebo and KateModern.

KateModern represents an opportunity to capitalise on the power word-of-mouth communications simply because if the soap is successful, people will talk. As more people are attracted to the site (and Bebo) so these larger audiences will attract commercial money and advertisers in particular. As audiences watch Kate's videos, read her blog, post messages and pictures on her page, suggest story lines and interact with the characters so their engagement with and stickiness to the site will be prolonged (Beale, 2007).

Affiliate marketing

Affiliate marketing has become an essential aspect of online marketing communications.

Associated with the concepts of communities and networks, affiliate marketing has become an essential aspect of online marketing communications and ecommerce. Affiliate schemes are based on a network of web sites on which advertisements or text links are placed. Those who click on them are taken directly to the host site. If this results in a sale, only then will the affiliate receive a commission (payment for the ad). Cookies, information generated by a web server and stored in the user's computer, ready for future access (http://www.cookiecentral.com/c_concept.htm), are used to track, monitor and record transactions and pay commission plus any agreed charges. As with many online marketing schemes, management can be undertaken in-house or outsourced. If the latter approach is adopted then many of the relationship issues discussed earlier need to be considered and managed.

Amazon is probably one of the best examples of affiliate marketing schemes. Amazon has thousands of affiliates who all drive visitors to the Amazon web site. If a product is sold to the visitor as a result of the click-through, then the affiliate is rewarded with a commission payment. Affiliate schemes are popular because they are low-cost operations, paid on a results-only basis and generating very favourable returns on investment. Rigby, a marketing journalist, reports that the low-cost airline Flybe has an affiliate network of over 1,450 web sites, which generate 10 per cent of sales, an ROI twice that earned through direct response press activity and all at zero risk (2004).

Summary

In order to help consolidate your understanding of interactive marketing communications, here are the key points summarised against each of the learning objectives:

1. Appraise the nature and characteristics of interactive marketing communications.

Interactive marketing communications allows participants in the communication process to interact with one another. Rather than passive one-way communication that characterises much of offline marketing communications, interactivity is inclusive, engages audiences and can lead to dialogue and the development of meaningful relationships.

2. Describe the primary techniques and issues relating to interactive online advertising.

As offline revenues from television and print advertising decline, so money is being switched into interactive budgets and online advertising. Direct response advertising is the primary approach used in this environment as advertisers seek to encourage users to click-through to destination web pages and microsites. Banner ads and sponsored link ads form the backbone of advertising in this fast-growing environment but online video advertising is set to grow.

3. Consider some of the issues relating to the way in which each of the tools of the communications mix can be used interactively.

Online sales promotions, public relations and direct marketing all have key roles to play in a converging multimedia environment. Sales promotions and direct marketing provide incentives and motivation for people to become interactive and to become involved with a campaign or brand. Personal selling has the least application of all the traditional tools in an online environment.

4. Explain the key features associated with mobile communications.

The key attributes of mobile communications are that it is a personal channel, one which enables direct, targeted and interactive communications, which can occur at any time and any place. SMS communications have underpinned its growth and are used not just for brand awareness-based advertising but also as an effective way of delivering sales promotions, such as announcing special offers and 'text and win' events.

5. Evaluate search engine marketing and distinguish the main features of both pay-per-click and search engine optimisation.

There are two types of search engine marketing techniques: search engine optimisation (SEO) and pay-per-click (PPC). The latter outweighs the former quite substantially in terms of investment but the former is superior in terms of quality of results.

6. Discuss the features of email marketing communications for both customer acquisition and retention.

Email communications can be directed at clearly defined target audiences, even individuals; they can be personalised and refined to meet the needs of individuals. In addition, email can be used with varying levels of frequency and intensity, which is important when building awareness, reinforcing messages or when attempting to persuade someone into a trial or purchase. It is a particularly useful way of provoking responses and can be used for customer acquisition and retention.

7. Evaluate the role of electronic word-of-mouth communications, and consider applications such as viral marketing communications, podcasting, RSS feeds and web logs.

Word-of-mouth communications in an online environment is fast becoming a major form of communication. Viral marketing, podcasting and blogging are three key ways in which word-of-mouth is being used.

8. Identify the characteristics of online communities and consider how social networks and affiliate marketing can be used to develop marketing communications opportunities.

The development of online communities of people who share a common interest(s), interact, share information, develop understanding and build relationships has been a major characteristic of what is referred to as Web 2.0. In particular, social networks such as Facebook, MySpace and Bebo have millions of registered users and present major opportunities for communicating brands. The problem, however, is that conventional offline marketing communications, and advertising in particular, do not work in these environments. Alternative, more subtle and supportive communication strategies are required, such as sponsorship, product placement and public relations.

Review questions

1. Define interactive marketing communications and explain its key characteristics. What might go wrong with the use of interactive marketing communications?
2. Identify reasons why organisations use interactive online advertising. Name three types of online ad formats.
3. Identify the two main types of value derived by organisations when using sales promotions online.
4. To what extent is online public relations just online advertising?
5. Identify five reasons why mobile marketing communications activities have grown in recent years.
6. Explain the basic principles underpinning the way in which both search engine optimisation and pay-per-click systems operate.
7. Write a report examining the use of email as a form of marketing communications. Find examples to support the points you make.
8. Discuss the three key elements that Kirby associates with successful viral marketing.
9. Make brief notes concerning the ways in which marketing communications should be used within online communities.
10. Appraise the concept of word-of-mouth communication and consider its use within social networks.

MiniCase How *Learnit* uses Web 2.0 to engage audiences

Nicola Robinsonova: Freelance Marketing Consultant

Learnit is a widget that helps people learn a foreign language. It uses the principles of the advertising industry namely 'brand exposure leads to brand recall', to teach people new vocabulary. *Learnit* works by placing a daily list of the same 10 words in many frequently visited locations around the Internet. These include blogs, banner adverts, search engines and social network sites such as Facebook, Bebo and MySpace. The *Learnit* widget can be put on a desktop or used as a screen saver.

Learnit can be used by both English learners and speakers. It offers 20 language pairs with more planned. *Learnit* also includes endangered languages via an integrated open source Wiki project. The *Learnit* development team consists of four people, and within two months of inception, they had a working demo with 10,000 registered users. With limited resources, an online audience and Web 2.0 functionality, their marketing communications strategy had to be strongly online. Of the options available, they use search marketing, affiliate advertising, link strategies, blogging, social network marketing and publicity via 'expertise'. These are now considered in turn.

Web 2.0 is the collective name given to the second generation of www, both in terms of technology and design. Web 2.0 is the active use of technologies such as social networking, Wikis, blogs and crowd filtration to create web-based communities who collaborate, create and share content. Web-based marketing is both softer and harder than traditional marketing. It is softer because there is far more user interaction, and harder because the numbers talk loudly. There is immediate access to data about the effects of a marketing strategy, so it is possible to know which campaigns work and which need to be amended. It is also easier to make and track the effects of changes in strategy, in real time. For example, some companies pay to advertise on search engines. The more they pay, the higher their ads appear on the list. However, if the Web 2.0 marketing strategy is good enough, this is not always necessary.

Search marketing is the single most important online communication strategy and content on the *Learnit* lists web site was written with an awareness of the key words people use when they are searching for information about learning a language. Key words are important, as these are what search engine spider bots look for when they crawl around the Internet assessing content. This influences the ranking of a site in any search results. Key words can be appropriately included into the text of a web site, though this is not always the case, which is why online e-books have descriptions written in a slightly odd style. These pages are the online equivalent of a man with an open suitcase standing on a street corner, shouting very loudly at passers by. What sellers are doing is maximising the number of key words in their text. Content needs to be carefully written with key words as it is easy to sound unnatural with key word over-use. This is often not a consideration for self-appointed experts selling expensive ebooks about emarketing, but most companies, including *Learnit*, will have brand values to protect, so they must integrate key words with care.

Though there are many language learners, the market of language provision is very crowded: if 'learn English', is 'googled', 24 million pages are listed. Therefore, there is a really strong need to differentiate products. One way to do this is through the name of the product itself. A unique name is a common strategy with Web 2.0 projects and the key advantage is that it is possible to track precisely any Internet activity about a site or product.

An affiliate advertising programme can be immensely effective for SMEs with small marketing budgets. Instead of being charged by page impression, advertisers can elect to pay publishers a percentage of any sale made, so there is no out-of-pocket expense for the advertiser. Publishers like to have adverts on their site that are effective and aesthetic, so *Learnit* produced a range of banner adverts in different colours and sizes. *Learnit* lists offer a commission of 15 per cent. They can offer a high commission because additional sales do not generate very much additional workload.

As well as looking at web site content in terms of key words, spider bots will follow links to and from websites. If there are many links, this may influence the search engine ranking. Used intelligently, links can enhance brand values and the visitor experience.

Many blogs encourage meaningful discussion by allowing comments and trackbacks (a link to a page which references an article), as well as link exchanges with other like-minded bloggers. Unscrupulous e-marketers spam many different sites with irrelevant comments along with a link to their site, in order to improve their page ranking. Luckily, as the logarithms used by search engines increase in sophistication, this technique becomes less effective.

During the development phase of the *Learnit* widget, user opinions were crucial. After a single press release, a site called 'Mashable' picked up the story. The steady trickle of comments became a wash-out and they found their in-boxes full of requests for additional languages, sound and tonal markers. At the point when they became inundated with comments, so that they could not manage to write a personal reply, they added an FAQs section. These were based on common themes, and signposted users to a support forum for responses to queries.

Learnit then added salient market research questions in the form of a daily 10-second survey. The data gathered via the research questions and the individual comments, reinforced knowledge about the need for sound, grammar and pronunciation. The day after the 'Mashable' coverage, users were invited to vote on a list of possible features to be included in the future. The most frequently requested were sound (34 per cent) and a test function (26 per cent). It was then decided not to publicise *Learnit* lists until these features had been developed and made available.

The use of web page content that motivates people either to dwell on a site or keep returning to it is important. Sites that enable these behaviours are referred to as 'sticky' and blogging can create stickiness. The *Learnit* blog has the following characteristics: analysis of the daily market research results; media coverage; a tally of users/countries/languages/site visitors; as well as ongoing news about their progress and developments, such as new features and languages. Although content in a business blog could be very similar to a daily newsletter, successful corporate or business blogs have the following characteristics: they are slightly less formal; provide useful and interesting information for readers; the content is fresh and the delivery professional.

Learnit is part of UNESCO 2008, Year of Languages project. The UNESCO scheme lead to the *Learnit* Wiki language project, so that volunteers who wished to add an endangered language could add the basic 1,000 word list plus sound, thereby sharing their language with a wide audience of language learners. Being involved in a Wiki project is an opportunity for any company as there are wide variety of topics on which expertise can be shared. Wiki projects will not let a business directly publicise themselves, but useful and relevant paragraphs or pages in a Wiki site with a user name relevant to your business can be added. No advertising is permitted and any direct promotion is usually swiftly removed.

Other forms of online marketing communication using 'expertise' are also available, at little cost. These include the active use of relevant professional forums to offer help and advice. There are also outlets for articles about specialist subjects. Work is copyright-free on condition that a link to a web site is published with the text: 'find out more at www.learnitlists.com'. Contributions to specialist publications, such as case studies for marketing web sites are also possible. Similarly, video tutorials are becoming popular and can be used as viral marketing. For a good example, see 'top 5 ways to learn foreign languages for free online' on youtube.com.

The development and marketing communications used by *Learnit* has been based on a range of Web 2.0 applications and facilities.

MiniCase questions

1. Identify a business or organisation whose stakeholders do not have Internet access.
2. Draft an online marketing strategy for a local not-for-profit organisation in your geographical area. Assume that the NFP has no budget, but some willing marketing student volunteers to offer their time.
3. How does your company use social networks such as LinkedIn, Facebook and MySpace?
4. Research the most important key words for your business and industry.

References

Armstrong, A. and Hagel III, J. (1996) The real value of on-line communities. *Harvard Business Review*, **74**(3) (May/June), 134–41.

Avlonitis, G.J. and Karayanni, D. (2000) The impact of Internet use on business-to-business marketing. *Industrial Marketing Management*, **29**, 441–59.

Barrand, D. (2004) Promoting change. *Marketing*, 6 October, 43–5.

Beale, C. (2007) The online soap has arrived, and it's broadening advertisers' horizons. *The Independent*, 6 August 2007. Retrieved 27 August 2007 from www.news.independent.co.uk/media/article2836676.ece.

Blakely, R. (2007) Social network site users 'are chronically unfaithful', *Timesonline*, 25 June. Retrieved 27 July 2007 from business.timesonline.co.uk/tol/business/industry_sectors/media/article1984032.ece.

Blattberg, R.C. and Deighton, J. (1991) Interactive marketing: exploiting the age of addressability. *Sloan Management Review*, **33**(1), 5–14.

Blythe, A. (2008) How can brands exploit widgets? *Revolution*, (April), 13.

Briggs, R. and Hollis, N. (1997) Advertising on the web: is there response before click-through? *Journal of Advertising Research*, (March/April), 33–45.

Cartellieri, C., Parsons, A., Rao, V. and Zeisser, M. (1997) The real impact of Internet advertising. *McKinsey Quarterly*, **3**, 44–63.

Chaffey, D., Ellis-Chadwick, F., Johnston, K. and Meyer, R. (2006) *Internet Marketing*, 3rd edn. Harlow: Pearson.

Chaffey, D. (2008) Using branded widgets, gadgets and buttons for web marketing. Retrieved 8 April 2008 from www.davechaffey.com/Internet-Marketing/C8-Communications/E-tools/Online-PR/Using-Widgets-Marketing.

Chaudhuri, A. (2000) A macro analysis of the relationship of product involvement and information search: the role of risk. *Journal of Marketing Theory and Practice*, **8**(1), 38–52.

Crow, D. (2007) Talking about my generation. *The Business*, 28 July, 18–20.

Davidson, D. (2007a) Advertisers back Facebook move. *Brand Republic*, 9 August 2007. Retrieved 13 August 2007 from http://www.brandrepublic.com/News/730452/Advertisers-back-Facebook-move/.

Davidson, D. (2007b) Triumph launches viral film to promote Rocket bike. *Brand Republic* 10 July 2007. Retrieved 16 August 2007 from www.brandrepublic.com/News/669638/Triumph-launches-viral-film-promote-Rocket-bike/.

Davidson, D. (2007c) Irn-Bru enlists Snowman in animated Christmas push. 2 December 2007. Retrieved 14 January 2008 from www.brandrepublic.com/News/.

De Bruyn, A. and Lilien, G.L. (2004). A multi-stage model of word-of-mouth through electronic referrals. *eBusiness Research Centre Working Paper*, February.

Deighton, J. and Grayson, K. (1995) Marketing and seduction: building exchange relationships by managing social concensus. *Journal of Consumer Research*, **21**(4), 660–76.

Doyle, S. (2003) The big advantage of short messaging. Retrieved 16 May from www.sas.com/news.

Durlacher (1999) UK on-line community. *Durlacher Quarterly Internet Report*, **Q3**, 7–11. London.

Farey-Jones, D. (2006) Colgate runs 'smile to win' interactive promotion with C4. *Brand Republic*, 7 September 2006. Retrieved 16 August 2007 from www.brandrepublic.com/News/591366/Colgate-runs-smile-win-interactive-promotion-C4/.

Gay, R., Charlesworth, A. and Esen, R. (2007) *Online Marketing: A Customer Led Approach*. Oxford: Oxford University Press.

Gladwell, M. (2000) *The Tipping Point: How Little Things Can Make a Big Difference*. New York: Little Brown.

Goldsmith, R.E. and Lafferty, B.A. (2002) Consumer response to web sites and their influence on advertising effectiveness. *Internet Research: Electronic Networking Applications and Policy*, **12**(4), 318–28.

Haig, M. (2001) *The E-Marketing Handbook*. London: Kogan Page.

Hicks, R. (2007) All About . . . Facebook. *Media Asia*, 3 August 2007. Retrieved 13 August 2007 from http://www.brandrepublic.com/News/675228/About-Facebook/.

Holahan, C. (2006) Up next: online video ad boom? *Business Week*, 7 November. Retrieved 26 October 2007 from www.businessweek.com/technology/content/nov2006/tc20061106_523381.htm

Hoey, C. (1998) Maximizing the effectiveness of web based marketing communications. *Marketing Intelligence and Planning*, **16**(1), 31–7.

Hurme, P. (2001) On-line PR: emerging organisational practice. *Corporate Communications: an International Journal*, **6**(2), 71–5.

Jansen, B.J. and Molina, P.R. (2006) The effectiveness of web search engines for retrieving relevant e-commerce links. *Information Processing and Management*, **42**(4) (July), 1075–98.

Jarboe, G. (2005) Why does search engine marketing look like a penny-farthing bicycle? *Internet Search Engine Database*, 11 January. Retrieved 27 July 2007, from www.isedb.com/news/article/1086/.

Jepsen, A.L. (2006) Information search in virtual communities: is it replacing use of offline communication? *Journal of Marketing Communications*, **12**(4) (December), 247–61.

Jones, G. (2007) Digital: Canon set for fashion drive. *Marketing*, 2 May 2007. Retrieved 13 August 2007 from http://www.brandrepublic.com/News/654310/Digital-Canon-set-fashion-drive/.

Juvertson, S. and Draper, T. (1997) *Viral marketing*. Draper Fisher Juvertson website. Retrieved 12 March 2006 from http://www.dfj.com/cgi-bin/artman/publish/printer_steve_tim_may97.html.

Juvertson, S. (2000) *What is Viral Marketing?* Draper Fisher Juvertson website. Retrieved March 12 2006 from http://www.dfj.com/cgi-bin/artman/publish/printer_steve_may00.shtml.

Kaikati, A.M. and Kaikati, J.G. (2004) Stealth marketing: how to reach consumers surreptitiously. *California Management Review*, **46**(4), 6–22.

Kirby, J. (2003) The message should be used as a means to an end, rather than just an end in itself. *VM-People*, 16 October. Retrieved 31 August 2007 from http://www.vm-people.de/en/vmknowledge/interviews/interviews_detail.php?id=15.

Kozinets, R.V. (1999) E-tribalized marketing?: the strategic implications of virtual communities on consumption. *European Management Journal*, **17**(3), 252–64.

Liu, Y. and Shrum, L.J. (2005) Rethinking interactivity. In *Advertising, Promotion and New Media* (eds M.R. Stafford and R.J. Faber), 103–24. New York: M.E. Sharpe.

Lockenby, J.D. (2005) The interaction of traditional and new media. In *Advertising, Promotion and New Media* (eds M.R. Stafford and R.J. Faber), 13. New York: M.E. Sharpe.

Mathews, K. (2007) Is branding best and are click throughs through? *Internet Advertising Bureau*. Retrieved 31 August 2007 from http://www.iabuk.net/en/1/isbrandingbestand areclickthroughsthrough.mxs.

McCormick, A. (2007) Shaving brand to roll out application on Facebook, *Media Week*, 7 August 2007. Retrieved 13 August 2007 from http://www.brandrepublic.com/News/730028/Shaving-brand-roll-application-Facebook/.

Media Week (2007) Direct marketing in a digital world. *Media Week*, 31 July. Retrieved 16 August 2007 from www.brandrepublic.com/InDepth/Analysis/674135/Direct-marketing-digital-world/.

Morowitz, V.G. and Schmittlein, D.C. (1998) Testing new direct marketing offerings: the interplay of management judgement and statistical models. *Management Science*, **44**(5), 610–28.

Morris, R.J. and Martin, C.L. (2000) Beane Babies: a case study in the engineering of an involvement/relationship-prone brand. *Journal of Product and Brand Management*, **9**(2), 78–98.

Muniz Jr, A.M. and O'Guinn, T.C. (2001) Brand community. *Journal of Consumer Research*, **27**(4), 412–32.

Pidd, H. (2007) Food manufacturers target children on internet after regulator's TV advertising clampdown, *The Guardian*, 31 July. Retrieved 13 August from http://www.guardian.co.uk/uk_news/story/0,,2138123,00.html#article_continue.

Pinkerfield, H. (2007a) New social media user types unveiled. *Revolution*, 28 June 2007. Retrieved 13 August 2007 from http://www.brandrepublic.com/News/667634/New-social-media-user-types-unveiled/.

Pinkerfield, H. (2007b) New women's social network offers targeted digital marketing. *Revolution UK*, 5 April 2007. Retrieved 13 August 2007 from http://www.brandrepublic.com/News/649065/New-womens-social-network-offers-targeted-digital-marketing/.

Porter, L. and Golan, G.J. (2006) From subservient chickens to brawny men: a comparison of viral advertising to television advertising. *Journal of Interactive Advertising*, **6**(2), 30–8.

Rigby, E. (2004) E-tail affiliate marketing. *Revolution*, (October), 66–9.

Sen, R. (2005) Optimal search engine marketing strategy. *International Journal of Electronic Commerce*, **10**(1) (Fall), 9–25.

Szmigin, I. and Reppel, A.E. (2004) Internet community bonding: the case of macnews.de. *European Journal of Marketing*, **38**(5/6), 626–40.

Turner, C. (2007) How Irn-Bru viral success prompted a national campaign. Retrieved 8 January 2008 from www.utalkmarketing.com/.

Vlasic, G. and Kesic, T. (2007) Analysis of customers' attitudes toward interactivity and relationship personalization as contemporary developments in interactive marketing communications. *Journal of Marketing Communications*, **13**(2) (June), 109–29.

Walmsley, A. (2007) Social networks are here to stay. *Marketing*, 27 June, 15.

Welker, C.B. (2002) The paradigm of viral communications. *Information Services and Use*, **22**, 3–8.

Wilson, R.F. (2000) The six simple principles of viral marketing. *Web Marketing Today*, **70**, 1–3.

Wood, W., Behling, R. and Haugen, S. (2006) Blogs and business: opportunities and headaches. *Issues in Information Systems*, **V11**(2), 312–16.

Zhang, J., Fang, X. and Liu Sheng, R. (2007) Online consumer search depth: theories and new findings. *Journal of Management of Information Systems*, **23**(3) (Winter), 71–95.

Chapter 27

Media planning and behaviour: delivering the message

Media planning is essentially a selection and scheduling exercise. The selection concerns the choice of media vehicles to carry the message on behalf of the advertiser. With media fragmentation, audiences are switching between media with greater regularity, which impacts on media scheduling. Decisions regarding the number of occasions, timing and duration that a message is exposed, in the selected vehicles, to the target audience have become increasingly critical.

Aims and learning objectives

The aims of this chapter are to introduce the fundamental elements of media planning and to set out some of the issues facing media planners.

The learning objectives of this chapter are to:

1. explain the role of the media planner and highlight the impact of media and audience fragmentation;
2. consider various theories concerning the content of different media and related media switching behaviours;
3. examine the key concepts used in media selection: reach and cover, frequency, duplication, rating points and CPT;
4. appreciate the concept of repetition and the debate concerning effective frequency and recency planning;
5. understand the concepts of effectiveness and efficiency when applied to media selection decisions;
6. introduce media source effects as an important factor in the selection and timing of advertising in magazines and television programmes;
7. explore the different ways in which advertisements can be scheduled.

For an applied interpretation see Yasmin Sekhon's MiniCase entitled ***Targeting the 'brown pound' – an untapped market*** at the end of this chapter.

Introduction

Once a message has been created and agreed, a media plan should be determined. The aim of the media plan is to devise an optimum route for the delivery of a message to the target audience. This function is normally undertaken by specialists, either as part of a full-service advertising agency or as a media independent whose primary function is to buy air time or space from media owners (e.g. television contractors or magazine publishers) on behalf of their clients, the advertisers. This traditional role has changed since the mid 1990s, and many media independents now provide consultancy services, particularly at the strategic level, plus planning and media research and auditing services.

The aim of the media plan is to devise an optimum route for the delivery of a message.

Media departments are responsible for two main functions. These are to 'plan' and to 'buy' time and space in appropriate media vehicles. There is a third task – to monitor a media schedule once it has been bought – but this is a function of buying. Planners define the target audience and choose the type of medium. Buyers choose programmes, frequencies, spots and distribution and assemble a multichannel schedule (Armstrong, 1993). In the past the media planner has been pre-eminent, but the role of the buyer is changing. Some feel the role of the buyer is in the ascendancy, but there are others who feel that the role is capable of increased automation and that many software packages already fulfil many functions of the media buyer. Such a move has implications for the type of person recruited. In the United States, for example, many semi-skilled people have been recruited on a part-time basis to do many parts of the traditional media planner's job.

As mentioned earlier, media planning is essentially a selection and scheduling exercise. The selection refers to the choice of media vehicles to carry the message on behalf of the advertiser. Scheduling refers to the number of occasions, timing and duration that a message is exposed, in the selected vehicles, to the target audience. However, there are several factors that complicate these seemingly straightforward tasks. First, the variety of available media is huge and increasing rapidly. This is referred to as media fragmentation. Second, the characteristics of the target audience are changing equally quickly. This is referred to as audience fragmentation. Both these fragmentation issues are discussed later in this chapter. The job of the media planner is complicated by one further element: money. Clients have restricted financial resources and require the media planner to create a schedule that delivers their messages not only effectively but also efficiently, which means within the parameters of the available budget.

Scheduling refers to the number of occasions, timing and duration that a message is exposed.

The task of the media planner, therefore, is to deliver advertising messages through a selection of media that match the viewing, reading or search habits of the target audience at the lowest possible cost. In order for these tasks to be accomplished, three sets of decisions need to be made about the choice of media, vehicles and schedules.

Decisions about the choice of media are complex. While choosing a single one is reasonably straightforward, choosing media in combination and attempting to generate synergistic effects is far from easy. Advances in technology have made media planning a much faster, more accurate process, one that is now more flexible and capable of adjusting to fast-changing market conditions.

One of the key tasks of the media planner is to decide which combination of vehicles should be selected to carry the message to the target audience. In addition, McLuhan (1966) said that the medium is the message, that is, the choice of medium (or vehicle) says something about the brand and the message itself. He went on to say that the medium is the *massage*, as each medium massages the recipient in different ways and so contributes to learning in different ways. For example, Krugman (1965) hypothesised that television advertising washes over individuals. He said that viewers, rather than participate actively with

The medium is the *massage*.

television advertisements, allow learning to occur passively. In contrast, magazine advertising requires active participation if learning is to occur. Today, online and interactive advertising actively promotes involvement and participation.

The various media depicted in Table 27.1 have wide-ranging characteristics. These, and the characteristics of the target audience, should be considered when deciding on the optimal media mix. It should be clear that simply deciding on which media to use is fraught with difficulties, let alone deciding on the optimal combination – how much of each media should be used – before even considering the cost implications.

Table 27.1 A summary of media characteristics

Type of media	Strengths	Weaknesses
Print		
Newspapers	Wide reach High coverage Low costs Very flexible Short lead times Speed of consumption controlled by reader	Short lifespan Advertisements get little exposure Relatively poor reproduction, gives poor impact Low attention-getting properties
Magazines	High-quality reproduction that allows high impact Specific and specialised target audiences High readership levels Longevity High levels of information can be delivered	Long lead times Visual dimension only Slow build-up of impact Moderate costs
Television	Flexible format, uses sight, movement and sound High prestige High reach Mass coverage Low relative cost, so very efficient	High level of repetition necessary Short message life High absolute costs Clutter Increasing level of fragmentation (potentially)
Radio	Selective audience, e.g. local Low costs (absolute, relative and production) Flexible Can involve listeners	Lacks impact Audio dimension only Difficult to get audience attention Low prestige
Outdoor	High reach High frequency Low relative costs Good coverage as a support medium Location-oriented	Poor image (but improving) Long production time Difficult to measure
Digital media	High level of interaction Immediate response possible Tight targeting Low absolute and relative costs Flexible and easy to update Measurable	Segment-specific Slow development of infrastructure High user set-up costs Transaction security issues
Transport	High length of exposure Low costs Local orientation	Poor coverage Segment specific (travellers) Clutter
In-store POP	High attention-getting properties Persuasive Low costs Flexible	Segment-specific (shoppers) Prone to damage and confusion Clutter

Media switching behaviour

The range of media has grown dramatically in the past 30 years and is continuing to grow as technology, in particular, advances. However, even before digital media started to change the media landscape, researchers had recognised that different media have different capabilities and that media were not completely interchangeable. In other words, different tasks can be accomplished more effectively using particular media. This implies that there is a spectrum of media depending on the content they carry.

Daft and Lengel (1984) were the first to propose that this content issue concerned the richness of the information conveyed through each medium. As a result, the tasks facing managers should be considered according to the degree of fit with the most appropriate media based on the richness of the information. Communication media help resolve ambiguity and facilitate understanding in different ways and to different degrees. They established that there were four main criteria that determined what level of richness a medium possessed:

> The tasks facing managers should be considered according to the degree of fit with the most appropriate media based on the richness of the information.

- the availability of instant feedback;
- the capacity to transmit multiple cues;
- the use of natural language;
- the degree of personal focus.

Media richness theory (MRT) holds that there is a hierarchy or spectrum of media ranging from personal or face-to-face encounters as the richest media through to single sheets of text-based information as lean media at the other end. Rich media facilitate feedback, dialogue iteration and an expression of personal cues such as tone of voice, body language and eye contact that in turn help establish a personal connection. In descending order of richness the other media are telephone, email, letter, note, memo, special report, fliers and bulletins. At this end of the richness scale numeric and formal written communication is slow, often visually limited and impersonal.

> Rich media facilitate feedback, dialogue iteration and an expression of personal cues.

MRT suggests that rich media reduce ambiguity more effectively than others, but are more resource-intensive than lean media. If rich media allow for more complex and difficult communications, then lean media are more cost-effective for simple or routine communications. McGrath and Hollingshead (1993) developed a matrix showing the levels of richness required to perform certain tasks successfully and efficiently. Their media richness grid identifies the level of fit between the information richness requirements of the tasks and the information richness capacity of the media (see Table 27.2).

Social influence theory (SIT) was developed by Fulk *et al.* (1990). This is intended to complement MRT as it also assumes that the relatively objective features of media do influence how individuals perceive and use media. However, these researchers argue that SIT has a strong social orientation because different media properties (such as ability to transmit richness) are subjective and are influenced by attitudes, statements and the behaviour of others. This approach recognises that members of groups influence other people in terms of their perceptions of different media. The main difference between MRT and SIT is that MRT identifies rich media as inefficient for simple or routine communication whereas SIT suggests rich media can be just as appropriate for simple messages as it is for ambiguous communication.

A third approach, the technology acceptance model (TAM) relates to the utility and convenience a medium offers. The perceived usefulness and perceived ease of use are regarded as the main issues that are considered when selecting media (King and Xia, 1997). Perceived usefulness refers to the user's subjective assessment

> The technology acceptance model (TAM) relates to the utility and convenience a medium offers.

Table 27.2 Media richness grid

	Computer text systems	Audio systems	Video systems	Face-to-face communication
Generating ideas and plans	Good fit	Marginal fit: medium too resource-intense	Poor fit: medium too resource-intense	Poor fit: medium too resource-intense
Choosing correct answer: intellective tasks	Marginal fit: medium too constrained	Good fit	Good fit	Poor fit: medium too resource-intense
Choosing preferred answer: judgement tasks	Poor fit: medium too constrained	Good fit	Good fit	Marginal fit: medium too resource-intense
Negotiating conflicts of interest	Poor fit: medium too constrained	Poor fit: medium too constrained	Marginal fit: medium too constrained	Good fit

Source: Adapted from McGrath and Hollingshead (1993).

Table 27.3 Factors influencing the choice of technology

Factor	Explanation
Experience and familiarity	With virtual operations the amount of experience using a particular interactive medium
Permanence	The degree to which users need an historical record of team interactions or decisions
Symbolic meaning	The subjective meanings attached to the use of a particular medium
Time constraints	The amount of time available to the user to use a medium in order to execute their tasks
Access to technology and/or support	The number of and access to available media influences media choice

that using a specific computer application will improve their job performance. Perceived ease of use addresses the degree to which a user expects the identified application to be free of effort.

Influential factors for media selection

In addition to these richness, social and utility issues of media selection, other factors are also important. Duarte and Snyder (2001) propose a list of factors influencing technology selection (see Table 27.3).

Switching behaviour

It is clear that different media have different properties and that people switch between media according to their tasks, social environment, familiarity and access to different media. What is important, therefore, is to understand switching behaviour and the decision-making process that people use. Decisions are made through *rational* and *systematic* processes or alternatively there are unaccountable factors that 'bound' decision-making. The classic, eight-stage rational–linear decision-making model (situation analysis, objectives setting, through to choosing and

Table 27.4 Reasons for moving to richer or leaner media

Movement	Reasons
Towards a richer medium	Message complexity Increased comfort Time pressure Timely discussion required Need to rest from computer-based medium
Towards a leaner medium	Desire for written record Reducing cost Convenience (of being asynchronous or distant) Share individual written work (attachment) External pressure or requirement

evaluating alternatives, making the decisions, evaluation and consequences) is well known and its criticisms well documented. Simon (1972, 1987) showed that people make decisions within 'bounded rationality', performing limited searches and accepting the first acceptable alternative, what is regarded as 'satisficing behaviour'.

Srinavasan (1996) developed a satisfaction–loyalty curve whereby an individual's level of satisfaction is the biggest determinant of their switching behaviour. As their satisfaction increases, so does loyalty, and the reverse is equally true. For each person there is a point at which decreasing satisfaction intersects with the decreasing loyalty levels. This is the point at which switching occurs and the current brand is abandoned in favour of another.

For each person there is a point at which decreasing satisfaction intersects with the decreasing loyalty levels.

Keaveney (1995) distinguishes between involuntary, simple and complex switching behaviours. Involuntary switching may be due to factors beyond an individual consumer's control (e.g. business liquidated), whereas simple switching is characterised by individual events where consumers can identify a single incident or factor causing the switch, for example a price change. Complex switching behaviour occurs when a customer's loyalty has decreased due to a variety of factors, which might include core product failure, price changes and poor service. It should be noted that switching is very often a routine behaviour influenced by the expectations of the context in which the media decision is made. For example, when sending text-based documents to team members, most people would select email and use file attachments.

As a final comment on media switching behaviour it is useful to return to MRT and to consider the reasons why individuals move towards rich or lean media. These are set out in Table 27.4. Therefore, movement between media is based on a range of criteria and will vary according to the context and individual skills and preferences.

Vehicle selection

The discussion so far has explored unpaid media, and increasingly the Internet and the use of email communications fit this range. However, organisations need to use media that are owned by others in order to convey their messages. These paid-for media have particular characteristics and ability to deliver rich or lean content. The discussion now moves on to consider different paid-for media and the ways in which organisations develop a media mix to meet their communications needs.

Increasingly, organisations are required to prove how advertising adds value to the bottom line. While this is not a new question, it is one that is being asked more often and in such a way that answers are required. As advertisers attempt to demonstrate effectiveness, contribution and return on investment, senior managers are increasingly haunted by questions concerning the choice of media, how much should be spent on message delivery and how financial resources are to be allocated in a multichannel environment.

ViewPoint 27.1 Media vehicles for 'You & Us'

When UBS launched their 'You & Us' global campaign, advertising played an important role in communicating what UBS stands for to its clients. The aim was to help support their efforts to build stronger client relationships, and help them to make more confident financial decisions, hence the phrase 'You & Us'. With television and print their aim was to increase relevance in specific markets. Regional variations are also being created.

The television spot, titled 'Everywhere', emphasises the global/personal dimension and follows meetings between two people that occur in interesting, unusual locations around the world. This speaks of the benefits that accrue from being able to access the resources of a global financial firm through a strong, personal relationship.

The advertising focuses on two key themes: globality and understanding. Both strands of communication support the core message of proactively finding solutions to our customers' needs, but each does so in a slightly different way that makes the overall message accessible.

The print advertising reflects the visual tones and style used in the television work, and places an increased graphic emphasis on 'You & Us'. Importantly, the new press ads were designed to enable the reader to project themselves into the situation depicted, thus fostering empathy.

In order to deliver these messages a media plan was established. This set out the specific types of media the campaign was to use and where possible certain types of media and specific vehicles. One of the first

Exhibit 27.1 Although this is not an actual shot used by UBS, this picture represents the essence of the core message that the 'You & Us' campaign sought to deliver. See the UBS web site for actual pictures used in their campaign

decisions was whether television, a class of media, had a role to play. Once the answer was yes, particular television channels in the target countries, such as the USA, UK, Germany, France, Italy and in Asia were selected. This was then followed by the selection of print and outdoor media and particular vehicles were then determined.

Question

Why do you believe UBS used television in order to reach high net worth individuals and businesses?

Task

Visit the site www.ubs.com and follow the links through 'About Us' and then 'You & Us'. View the campaign detail and see the television and print ads. Make notes on what impresses you and what you might have done differently.

Management's attention towards media decision-making has increased as the media have become more visible and significantly more important. For example, Brech (1999) reports that companies need to make choices about the split between the Internet, mass media, digital TV, outdoor and print media. Companies such as BT, IKEA and ScottishPower need to use media strategically in order that they reach the right audience, in the right context, at the right time and at an acceptable cost. To help organisations achieve these goals a variety of approaches have been adopted. For example, New PHD is an agency retained by BT to advise about strategic (media) planning and budget allocation. However, ZenithOptimedia implements decisions for press and radio and the Allmond Partnership manages television and cinema, while Outdoor Connections handles poster-buying. This division provides objectivity, reduces partisan approaches and can deliver more effective media plans. Cost per response is certainly one way of measuring effectiveness, but the communication impact, or share of mind, is also important. There has also been a move away from volume of media to one where media decisions are made by looking at media in the context of the brand's total communications.

> Cost per response is certainly one way of measuring effectiveness.

A further problem facing clients and media concern the integrated media experience. For a long time, some organisations have used above-the-line media to reach audiences of 20 million people. With fragmented media it is difficult to generate consistent levels and types of impact. Increasingly, media management is being outsourced so there are fewer in-house areas of expertise. All this means that, to forge appropriate solutions, advertisers and media agencies need to work closely together so that the relationship becomes so close that it acts more as an extension to the marketing department. Decisions regarding which vehicles are to carry an advertiser's message depend on an understanding of a number of concepts: reach and coverage, frequency, gross rating points, effective frequency, efficiency and media source effects.

Media planning concepts

There are several fundamental concepts that underpin the way in which traditional media should be selected and included in the media plan. These are reach, frequency, gross rating points, duplication and effective frequency.

Reach and coverage

Reach refers to the percentage of the target audience exposed to a message at least once during the relevant time period. Where 80 per cent of the target audience has been exposed to a message, the figure is expressed as an '80 reach'.

Coverage, a term often used for reach, should not be confused or used in place of reach. Coverage refers to the size of a potential audience that might be exposed to a particular media vehicle. For media planners, therefore, coverage (the size of the target audience) is very important. Reach will always be lower than coverage, as it is impossible to reach 100 per cent of a target population (the universe).

Building reach within a target audience is relatively easy, as the planner needs to select a range of different media vehicles. This will enable different people in the target audience to have an opportunity to see the media vehicle. However, there will come a point when it becomes more difficult to reach people who have not been exposed. As more vehicles are added, so repetition levels (the number of people who have seen the advertisement more than once) also increase.

Frequency

Frequency refers to the number of times a member of the target audience is exposed to a media vehicle.

Frequency refers to the number of times a member of the target audience is exposed to a media vehicle (not the advertisement) during the relevant time period. It has been stated that targets must be exposed to the media vehicle, but to say that a target has seen an advertisement simply because they have been exposed to the vehicle is incorrect. For example, certain viewers hop around the channels as a commercial break starts. This has been referred to as 'channel grazing' by Lloyd and Clancy (1991). Individuals have different capacities to learn and to forget, and how much of a magazine does a reader have to consume to be counted as having read an advertisement? These questions are still largely unanswered, so media planners have adopted an easier and more consistent measure – opportunities to see (OTS).

This is an important point. The stated frequency level in any media plan will always be greater than the advertisement exposure rate. The term OTS is used to express the reach of a media vehicle rather than the actual exposure of an advertisement. However, a high OTS could be generated by one of two different events. First, a large number of the target audience are exposed once (high reach) or second, a small number are exposed several times (high frequency).

This then raises the first major issue. As all campaigns are restricted by time and budget limitations, advertisers have to trade off reach against frequency. It is impossible to maximise both elements within a fixed budget and set period of time.

ViewPoint 27.2 Haier than the weather

Haier, the major Chinese global manufacturer of consumer durables, uses television in China to reach its main audiences. In a country where it is estimated that over 250 million Chinese families watch CCTV programmes, Haier sponsors the weather forecast, which is the highest-rated programme in China. Guaranteeing large audiences on a repeat basis ensures Haier achieves high OTS based on a large frequency.

Source: Adapted from unpublished student coursework and www.zaobao.com/.

Question

As there is little natural fit between Haier and the weather forecast is this a good use of marketing communications?

Task

Pick a leading brand in a country of your choice and find out if it is involved in any sponsorship arrangements. If they are, what do think the goal might be, reach or frequency, or indeed something else?

To launch a new product, it has been established that a wide number of people within the target audience need to become aware of the product's existence and its salient attributes or benefits. This means that reach is important but, as an increasing number of people become aware, so more of them become exposed a second, third or fourth time, perhaps to different vehicles. At the outset, frequency is low and reach high, but as a campaign progresses so reach slows and frequency develops. Reach and frequency are inversely related within any period of time, and media planners must know the objective of a campaign: is it to build reach or develop frequency?

Reach and frequency are inversely related within any period of time.

Gross rating point

To decide whether reach or frequency is the focus of the campaign objective, a more precise understanding of the levels of reach and frequency is required. The term gross rating point is used to express the relationship between these two concepts. GRPs are a measure of the total number of exposures (OTS) generated within a particular period of time. The calculation itself is simply reach × frequency:

reach × frequency = gross rating point

Media plans are often determined on the number of GRPs generated during a certain time period. For example, the objective for a media plan could be to achieve 450 GRPs in a burst (usually four or five weeks). However, as suggested earlier, caution is required when interpreting a GRP, because 450 GRPs may be the result of 18 message exposures to just 25 per cent of the target market. It could also be an average of nine exposures to 50 per cent of the target market.

Rating points are used by all media as a measurement tool, although they were originally devised for use with broadcast audiences. GRPs are based on the total target audience (e.g. all women aged 18–34, or all adults) that might be reached, but a media planner needs to know, quite rightly, how many GRPs are required to achieve a particular level of effective reach and what levels of frequency are really required to develop effective learning or awareness in the target audience. In other words, how can the effectiveness of a media plan be improved?

Effective frequency

There are a number of reasons why considering the effectiveness of a media plan has become more important in recent years. First, there is the combination of media and audience fragmentation plus increasing media costs. Second, there is short-termism, increased managerial accountability and intensifying competition. This last point about competition refers to the media planning industry itself and the restructuring and concentration of media buying points (centralisation) in response to clients' globalisation strategies and their need for more cost-effective ways of buying media.

Frequency refers to the number of times members of the target audience are exposed to the vehicle. It says nothing about the quality of the exposures and whether any impact was made. Effective frequency refers to the number of times an individual needs to be exposed to an advertisement before the communication is effective. Being exposed once or possibly twice is unlikely to affect the disposition of the receiver. But the big question facing media planners is, how many times should a message be repeated for effective learning to occur? The level of effective frequency is generally unknown, but there has been some general agreement following work by Krugman (1972) that, for an advertisement to be effective (to make an impact), a target should have at least three OTS, the three-hit theory. The first exposure provokes a 'What is this?' reaction, the second reaction is 'What does this mean to me?' The reaction to the third is 'Oh, I remember'

The big question facing media planners is, how many times should a message be repeated for effective learning to occur?

(du Plessis, 1998). The three-exposure theory is based on messages that first provide understanding, second, provide recognition and third, actually stimulate action. More than 10 exposures is regarded as an ineffective plan and hence a waste of resources.

Determining the average frequency partially solves the problem. This is the number of times a target reached by the schedule is exposed to the vehicle over a particular period of time. For example, a schedule may generate the following:

10 per cent of the audience is reached ten times ($10 \times 10 = 100$)
25 per cent of the audience is reached seven times ($25 \times 7 = 175$)
65 per cent of the audience is reached once ($65 \times 1 = 65$)
Total = 340 exposures

Average frequency = 340/100 = 3.4

This figure of average frequency is misleading because different groups of people have been reached with varying levels of frequency. In the example above, an average frequency of 3.4 is achieved but 65 per cent of the audience is reached only once. This means that the average frequency, in this example, may lead to an audience being underexposed.

Members of the target audience do not buy and read just one magazine or watch a single television programme. Consumer media habits are complex, although distinct patterns can be observed, but it is likely that a certain percentage of the target audience will be exposed to an advertisement if it is placed in two or more media vehicles. Those who are exposed once constitute unduplicated reach. Those who are exposed to two or more are said to have been duplicated. Such overlapping of exposure, shown in Figure 27.1, is referred to as duplicated reach.

Media plans need to specify levels of duplicated and unduplicated reach.

Duplication provides an indication of the levels of frequency likely in a particular media schedule. Duplication also increases costs, so if the objective of the plan is unduplicated reach, duplication brings waste and inefficiency. So media plans need to specify levels of duplicated and unduplicated reach.

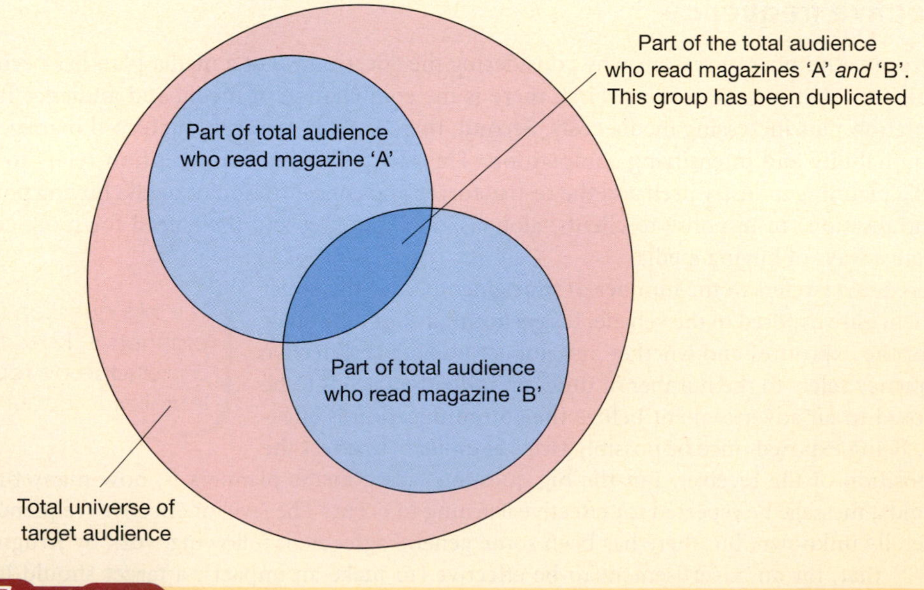

Figure 27.1 Duplication

ViewPoint 27.3 Optimising media schedules

Multi-media optimisers (MMO) are software programs that plan and schedule the placing of advertising campaigns across more than one medium. MMOs use single-source or fused database information rather than survey-based information, which is prone to inaccuracies.

MMOs take into account duplication rates when deciding which combination of media vehicles to use (not types such as television and magazines). They also facilitate media-neutral planning (see Chapter 9).

However, MMOs work on responses, and this can pose problems in terms of agreeing what form of response is valid, while audiences have to be converted to ad exposures/impacts in order to base evaluation on equivalent measures. Accounting for decay rates and adstock features (ad impact retention) by medium, through time is also problematic.

Sources: Adapted from Jarvis and McElroy (2004) and www.fipp.com/sadmin/1418.

Question

If media planning software works just on responses can this be an effective planning tool?

Task

Find out the training necessary to become a media planner.

Nevertheless, it is generally agreed that a certain level of GRPs is necessary for awareness to be achieved. It is also accepted that increased GRPs are necessary for other communication effects to be achieved. These levels of GRPs are referred to as weights, and the weight of a campaign reflects the objectives of the campaign. For example, a burst designed to achieve 85 per cent coverage with eight OTS would make a 680 rating, which is considered to be heavy. Such high ratings are often associated with car launches and, for example, products that are market leaders in their class, such as Nescafé or Pantene. An average rating would be one set to achieve a 400 rating, through 80 per cent coverage and five OTS over the length of a five-week period.

Our understanding about how learning works can assist the quest for effective frequency levels. The amount of learning in individuals increases up to a certain point, after which further exposure to material adds little to our overall level of knowledge. The same applies to the frequency level and the weightings applied to exposures.

Coverage and reach figures only show the numbers of people who are exposed to the vehicle. Effective reach measures those that are aware of the message. This ties in with the previous discussion on effective frequency levels. Essentially, media planners recognise that effective advertising requires that, in addition to the other aspects of advertising planning, a single transmission (reach) of an advertisement will be unproductive (Krugman, 1975; Naples, 1979). A minimum of two exposures and a reach threshold of 45 per cent of the target audience are required for reach to be regarded as effective (Murray and Jenkins, 1992).

Recency planning

A relatively new perspective to counter the effective frequency model has emerged from the United States. This is known as recency planning, and developed at a time when the weak theory of advertising started to gain greater acknowledgement as the most acceptable general interpretation of how advertising works. There is also a growing general acceptance that advertising is not the all-powerful communication tool it was once thought to be, and that the timing and presentation of advertising messages needs to be reconsidered in the light of the way advertising is currently thought to work.

If it is accepted that consumer decision-making is more heavily influenced by 'running out' of particular products (opening empty fridges and store cupboards), than by exposure to

Table 27.5 The differences between effective frequency and recency planning

Recency planning model	Effective frequency model
Reach goal	Frequency goal
Continuity	Burst
One-week planning cycle	Four-week planning cycle
Lowest cost per reach point	Lowest cost per thousand
Low ratings	High ratings

Source: Adapted from Ephron (1997). Used by permission of WARC.

advertising messages that are repeated remorselessly, then it follows that advertising needs to be directed at those people who are actually in the market and prepared to buy (Ephron, 1997).

As many fast-moving consumer goods products are purchased each week, Jones (1995) argues that a single exposure to an advertising message in the week before a purchase is to be made is more important than adding further messages, thereby increasing frequency. Recency planning considers reach to be more important than frequency.

The strategy requires reaching as many consumers as possible in as many weeks as possible.

The goal of this new approach is to reach those few consumers who are ready to buy (in the market). To do this the strategy requires reaching as many consumers as possible in as many weeks as possible (as far as the budget will extend). This requires a lower weekly weight and an extended number of weeks for a campaign. Advertising budgets are not cut; the fund is simply spread over a greater period of time. According to Ephron, this approach is quite different from effective frequency models and quite revolutionary (see Table 27.5).

This approach has been greeted with a number of objections. It has not been universally accepted, nor has it been widely implemented in the UK market. Gallucci (1997), among others, rejected the notion of recency planning because effectiveness will vary by brand, category and campaign. He claims that reaching 35 per cent of the Indonesian cola market once a week will not bring about the same result as reaching 65 per cent four times a week.

The development of banner advertising on the Internet raises interesting questions concerning effective frequency in new media. Is the frequency rate different and, if so, how many times is exposure required in order to be effective? Research into this area is in its infancy and no single, accepted body of knowledge exists. Broussard (2000) reports that, in a limited study concerning the comparison of a direct-response and a branding-based campaign on the Internet, the lowest cost per lead in the direct-response campaign was achieved with low frequency levels. Results from the branding campaign suggest that up to seven exposures were necessary to improve brand awareness and knowledge of product attributes.

The debate concerning the development of recency planning and effective frequency will continue. What might be instrumental to the outcome of the debate will be a better understanding of how advertising works and the way buyers use advertising messages that are relevant to them.

Media usage and attitudes

A large number of people have a negative attitude towards advertising, and TV ads in particular. Advertising is regarded as both intrusive and pervasive. Beale (1997) developed a four-part typology of personality types based upon respondents' overall attitudes towards advertising

Table 27.6 Advertising attitudes for media determination

Cynics (22 per cent) This group perceives advertising as a crude sales tool. They are resentful and hostile to advertisements, although they are more likely to respond to advertisements placed in relevant media.	**Enthusiasts (35 per cent)** Enthusiasts like to get involved with advertising and creativity is perceived as an important part of the process. Apart from newspapers, which are regarded as boring, most types of media are acceptable.
Ambivalents (22 per cent) While creativity is seen as superfluous and irrelevant, ambivalents are more disposed to information-based messages or those that promise cost savings. The best advertisements are those that use media that reinforce the message.	**Acquiescents (21 per cent)** As the name suggests, this group of people has a reluctant approach to advertising. This means that they see advertising as unavoidable and an inevitable part of their world. Therefore, they are open to influence through a variety of media.

Source: Adapted from Beale (1997). Used with kind permission.

(see Table 27.6). Through an understanding of the different characteristics, it is possible to make better (more informed) decisions about the most appropriate media channels to reach target audiences.

It is common for advertisers and media planners to discuss target markets in the context of heavy, medium, light and non-users of a product. It is only now that consideration is being given to the usage levels of viewers and readers. ZenithOptimedia has determined that television audiences can be categorised as heavy, medium and light users based on the amount of time they spend watching television. One of the implications of this approach is that if light users consume so little television, then perhaps it is not worthwhile trying to communicate with them and resources should be directed to the medium and heavy user groups. The other side of the argument is that light users are very specific in the programmes that they watch, therefore it should be possible to target messages at them and a heavy number of GRPs should be used. However, questions still remain about the number of ratings necessary for effective reach in each of these categories.

Light users are very specific in the programmes that they watch.

A more contemporary study by Schultz *et al.* (2006) sought to discover how media consumption is determined by an individual's need to access media. Using criteria based on the amount of time spent with all forms of media, the amount of simultaneous media usage, the need to provide or receive information and the speed at which a medium delivers the information, four clusters were identified. These were:

- Zeros – this group consists of people who are not active media consumers.
- Traditionals – this group use media sequentially, one form of media at a time.
- Information hounds – this group are heavy media users and information providers.
- Network creators – this group are heavy users but primarily use slow media and use the information largely for their own purposes.

The researchers believe this media consumption model should be used to enhance the media planning process by being used in addition to the general demographic-, geographic- and psychographic-based approaches. Further research was based around three key dimensions: media usage, media influence and simultaneous media usage.

Ostrow (1981) was the first to question how many rating points should be purchased. He said that, rather than use average frequency, a decision should be made about the minimum level of frequency necessary to achieve the objectives and then maximise reach at that level. Ostrow (1984) suggested that consideration of the issues set out in Table 27.8 would also assist.

Table 27.7 The SIMM database – media usage dimensions

Media dimension	Explanation
Media usage	Average usage of media, based on minutes, for both weekday and weekend consumption. Includes, newspaper, direct mail, magazines, radio, television and the Internet.
Media influence	The self-reported average for each media category across eight product groups: electronics, apparel, groceries, home improvement, cars, medicines, telecom services and eating out.
Simultaneous media usage	This is an average of all pairs of media that were reported as 'used simultaneously'. If a pair is reported as regularly consumed then it was assumed to be 70 per cent of the time. If reported as occasional, then it was defined as 30 per cent of the time.

Source: Schultz *et al.* (2006).

Table 27.8 Issues to be considered when setting frequency levels

Issues	Low frequency	High frequency
Marketing issues		
Newness of the brand	Established	New
Market share	High	Low
Brand loyalty	Higher	Lower
Purchase and usage cycle times	Long	Short
Message issues		
Complexity	Simple	Complex
Uniqueness	More	Less
Image versus product sell	Product sell	Image
Message variation	Single message	Multiple messages
Media plan issues		
Clutter	Less	More
Editorial atmosphere	Appropriate	Not appropriate
Attentiveness of the media in the plan	Holds	Fails to hold
Number of media in the plan	Less	More

Source: Adapted from Ostrow (1984).

The traditional approach of using television to reach target audiences to build awareness is still strong. For example, Procter & Gamble, Unilever, Nestlé, Kellogg's and BT all spend in excess of 70 per cent of their budgets on television advertising. However, many major advertisers have moved from a dominant above-the-line approach to a more integrated and through-the-line approach as a more effective way of delivering messages to target audiences. Nescafé now uses 48-sheet posters and Unilever, traditionally a heavy user of television, has begun to use radio and posters as support for its television work.

Efficiency

All promotional campaigns are constrained by a budget.

All promotional campaigns are constrained by a budget. Therefore a trade-off is required between the need to reach as many members of the target audience as possible (create awareness) and the need to repeat the message to achieve effective learning in the target audience. The decision about whether to emphasise reach or frequency is assisted by a consideration of the costs involved in each proposed schedule or media plan.

There are two main types of cost. The first of these is the *absolute cost*. This is the cost of the space or time required for the message to be transmitted. For example, the cost of a full-page, single-insertion, black-and-white advertisement, booked for a firm date in the *Sunday Times*, is £56,150 (November 2004). Cash flow is affected by absolute costs.

The cost of a full-page, single-insertion, black-and-white advertisement, booked for a firm date in the *Sunday Times*, is £56,150 (November 2004).

In order that an effective comparison be made between media plans the *relative costs* of the schedules need to be understood. Relative costs are the costs incurred in making contact with each member of the target audience.

Traditionally, the magazine industry has based its calculations on the cost per thousand people reached (CPT). The original term derived from the print industry is CPM, where the 'M' refers to the Roman symbol for thousand. This term still has limited use but the more common term is CPT: CPT = space costs (absolute) × 1,000/circulation. The newspaper industry has used the milline rate, which is the cost per line of space per million circulation.

Broadcast audiences are measured by programme ratings (United States), and television audiences in Britain are measured by television ratings or TVRs. They are essentially the same in that they represent the percentage of television households that are tuned to a specific programme. The TVR is determined as follows:

TVR = number of target TV households tuned into a programme
× 100/total number of target TV households

A single TVR, therefore, represents 1 per cent of all the television households in a particular area that are tuned into a specific programme.

A further approach to measuring broadcast audiences uses the share of televisions that are tuned into a specific programme. This is compared with the total number of televisions that are actually switched on at that moment. This is expressed as a percentage and should be greater than the TVR. Share, therefore, reveals how well a programme is perceived by the available audience, not the potential audience. The question of how to measure relative costs in the broadcast industry has been answered by the use of the rating point or TVR. Cost per TVR is determined as follows:

Cost per TVR = time costs (absolute costs)/TVR

Intra-industry comparison of relative costs is made possible by using these formulae. Media plans that only involve broadcast or only use magazine vehicles can be evaluated to determine levels of efficiency. However, members of the target audience do not have discrete viewing habits; they have, as we saw earlier, complex media consumption patterns that involve exposure to a mix of media classes and vehicles. Advertisers respond to this mixture by placing advertisements in a variety of media, but have no way of comparing the relative costs on an inter-industry basis. In other words, the efficiency of using a *News at Ten* television slot cannot be compared with an insertion in *The Economist*. Attempts are being made to provide cross-industry media comparisons, but as yet no one formula has yet been provided that satisfies all demands. The television and newspaper industries, by using CPT in combination with costs per unit of time and space respectively, have attempted to forge a bridge that may be of use to their customers.

Finally, some comment on the concept of CPT is necessary, as there has been speculation about its validity as a comparative tool. There are a number of shortcomings associated with the use of CPT. For example, because each media class possesses particular characteristics, direct comparisons based on CPT alone are dangerous. The levels of wastage incurred in a plan, such as reaching people who are not targets or by measuring OTS for the vehicle and not the advertisement, may lead to an overestimate of the efficiency that a plan offers.

There are a number of shortcomings associated with the use of CPT.

Similarly, the circulation of a magazine is not a true representation of the number of people who read or have an opportunity to see. Therefore, CPT may underestimate the efficiency unless the calculation can be adjusted to account for the extra or pass-along readership that occurs in reality. Having made these points, media buyers in the United Kingdom continue to use CPT and cost per rating point (CPRP) as a means of planning and buying time and space. Target audiences and television programmes are priced according to the ratings they individually generate. The ratings affect the cost of buying a spot. The higher the rating, the higher the price to place advertisements in the magazine or television programme.

Planning, placing and measuring ads online

The decision to place online ads is complicated not just by deciding which of the various formats discussed previously should be used, but also by where and when the ads need to be placed. Table 27.9 sets out the various options available for placing online ads.

Longhurst (2006) argues that much of the online media planning work is based on dividing the expenditure (investment) by the anticipated response (click-throughs) to determine a cost

Table 27.9 Online ad placement opportunities

Location for ad placement	Explanation
Portals	Major portals such as Google, Yahoo and MSN attract the majority of online ads. Smaller portals enable more specific targeting of messages to reach defined target audiences. For example, airlines or ferries on a travel portal.
Community web sites	Social networking sites consist of communities of people who share common pastimes, health geographic or other interests. These represent ideal opportunities to reach specific target audiences.
Search engines	Pay-per-click ads based on users searching on particular key words constitute a major source of revenue for each search engine. See p. 782 for more information.
Shopping comparison sites	Ads placed on sites where a comparison of shopping products has been requested is going to reach a high proportion of a target audience.
Chat rooms	In return for providing software and hosting, companies can place ads on relevant pages.
Online forums	Ads can be targeted to meet the needs and interests of the topics and subjects being discussed.
Blogs	Blog sites are provided for bloggers to write, but in order to sustain the site ads need to be placed, again targeted to the principle subjects under discussion.
Podcasts	Opportunities to place ads around specific podcasts are currently limited but will increase as podcasting becomes more mainstream.
RSS aggregators	These enable subscribers to receive specific information and short news updates from organisations that bring information together (aggregators) and feed it out. Some RSS aggregators are beginning to sell ad space on the various news feeds.
Mobile devices	Opportunities to reach audiences on the move increase as technology improves.
Newsletters	The content or theme of a newsletter will attract appropriate advertisers.
Online magazines	Whether a manufacturer or an association produces these they still provide good opportunities to reach audiences with specific interests.

Source: Based on Gay *et al.* (2007).

per response. This figure is then used to compare with other media combinations. The problem is that this approach is not market-oriented and the investment sum is all too often simply determined by taking a preset percentage of the main budget.

The media planning concepts referred to previously in this chapter (reach, frequency, etc.) evolved to help manage traditional media. The interruption model has been the main way traditional media has been used. This is predicated on the idea that the media manages audiences, influences what they see, when they see it and shapes the pattern of their media behaviour. Advertisers therefore, interrupted an audience's viewing or reading to deliver product messages, for which, according to the advertiser's segmentation analysis, they were suitable recipients.

However, technological advances have brought about huge changes in the types of available media and the way in which people now use media. As Moore (2007) rightly points out, people use traditional media for information and entertainment. Now they can be active participants as opportunities to be interactive enables user-generated-content (Chapter 2) through search, downloading, sharing, publication and involvement in virtual communities. Advertisers should not try to interrupt participants but facilitate interaction. Moore (2007), media manager for the drinks-based group, Diageo in the United Kingdom, suggests that, in addition to the need for information and entertainment, media now need to satisfy four new consumer motivations: to discover, participate, share and express (themselves). What he does not say is that these do not apply to all consumers in the same way. Most people consume a mixture of traditional and new media, with particular audiences skewed more to one rather than the other. The argument that mass media advertising is in permanent decline is a fallacy, proved by the continuing investment by a range of brands in television advertising. There has certainly been a readjustment of media budgets to reflect contemporary media usage, but the new is not going to wipe out the old.

Most people consume a mixture of traditional and new media.

The early years of digital and online media saw attempts to use the established methods of measurement and evaluation. However, it became clear that these methods were not entirely suitable, simply because digital media are used differently. Instead of measuring how often a message is delivered or the share of audience reached with a message, it becomes more important to measure a consumer's expectations of a brand and their interaction with brands. Put another way these might be considered as dwell time (the amount of time consumers spend with a brand), dwell quality (a consumer's perceived richness resulting from brand interaction) and dwell insight (what motivates a consumer to spend time with a brand).

Media source effects

CPT is a quantitative measure, and one of its major shortcomings is that it fails to account for the qualitative aspects associated with media vehicles. Before vehicles are selected, their qualitative aspects need to be considered on the basis that a vehicle's environment may affect the way in which a message is perceived and decoded.

An advertisement placed in one vehicle, such as *Cosmopolitan*, may have a different impact on an identical audience to that obtained if the same advertisement were placed in *Options*. This differential level of 'power of impact' is caused by a number of source factors, of which the following are regarded as the most influential:

- *vehicle atmosphere* – editorial tone, vehicle expertise, vehicle prestige;
- *technical and reproduction characteristics* – technical factors, exposure opportunities, perception opportunities;
- *audience and product characteristics* – audience/vehicle fit, nature of the product.

Vehicle atmosphere

Editorial tone

This refers to the editorial views presented by the vehicle and the overall tone of the material contained. Understandably, some clients do not want to be associated with particular television shows or certain specialist magazines that are characterised by sex or violence.

Vehicle expertise

Magazines and journals can reflect a level of expertise and represent source credibility. Readers who regard particular magazines, especially some of the consumer SIMs (e.g. *Golf Monthly*), business-to-business magazines (e.g. *Fire & Rescue*) and academic journals (e.g. *Harvard Business Review*), as important sources of credible information are more relaxed and open to persuasion.

Vehicle prestige

The message strategy adopted for each advertisement should be appreciated, as this can have a strong effect upon the scheduling. The prestige of a vehicle is important to some products, especially when targeted at audiences where vehicle status is important, for example *Country Life*. Transformational advertisements have been shown to be more effective in prestige-based vehicles than in expertise-based vehicles (and vice versa for information-based advertisements).

Transformational advertisements have been shown to be more effective in prestige-based vehicles.

Technical and reproduction characteristics of a vehicle

Technical factors

The technical characteristics of the vehicle, such as its visual capability, may influence the impact of the message. The use of colour, movement and sound may be necessary for the full effectiveness of a message to be realised. Other messages may need only a more limited range of characteristics, such as sound. For example, the promotion of inclusive tour holidays benefits from the communication of an impression (photograph/drawing) of the destination resort. This is important, as each destination needs to be differentiated, in the minds of the target audience, from competing destinations.

Exposure opportunities

The possibility that an advertisement will be successfully exposed to the target increases as more consideration is given to the likelihood of successful communication. Each vehicle has a number of time slots or spaces that provide opportunities for increased exposure. The back pages of magazines or facing matter often command premium advertising rates, just as prime-time spots or film premieres on television always generate extra revenue for the television contractors.

Perception opportunities

Being exposed to the message does not mean that the message is perceived. A reader may not perceive an advertisement when searching for the next page of an article. Similarly, a car driver may not 'hear' a radio message because their attention may be on a passing car or a strange engine noise. The solution is to use strong attention-grabbing materials, such as loud or distinctive music or controversial headlines. In addition, new, imaginative ways of attracting attention are being developed. Car dealers have used incentives to attract audiences to test drive a car and receive vouchers for a free video film or have free subscriptions to particular magazines.

ViewPoint 27.4 Digital perception at Terminal 5

When Heathrow airport opened Terminal 5 in March 2008, a raft of new advertising technology was released. Over 200 digital screens have been built into the infrastructure of the airport, all with strategic placement. Here the advertising panels have been sited alongside the path that passengers take from check-in to their flight. Some giant displays are referred to as 'global gateways' some dominating the security area. Some digital ads are incorporated into the flight-information screens.

The digital screens enable ad continuity so that a passenger may see a seemingly endless line of the same ads. This opportunity to reach a mass of people in this way is a first for this part of the advertising industry. Now the industry has the opportunity to use digital technology to deliver moving, interactive, responsive and time-specific advertising. This means that interactive ads can be changed for morning, noon and afternoon customers, unlike the traditional outdoor poster sites that need two weeks, several rolls of paper and a bucket of paste. Visa have taken four giant lightboxes that measure 29m × 36m and should be seen by all passengers as they move through to the departure areas.

Digital and interactive screens have been installed at other airports following the T5 launch, in the London Underground, in and around various new shopping centres and maybe even a bus shelter near you.

Sources: Bainbridge (2008); Bokaie (2008).

Question

To what extent are these digital screens and their location likely to aid the exposure and perception opportunities (to reach travellers with effective messaging)?

Task

Next time you visit an air or rail terminal look out for digital screens and make a note of which brands are using them.

Exhibit 27.2 T5 Visa's digital screens
Courtesy of JCDecaux Airport.

Audience/product characteristics

Audience/vehicle fit

The media plan should provide the best match between the target market and the audience reached by the vehicles in the media schedule. The more complex the target market description or consumer profile, the greater the difficulty of matching it with appropriate vehicles.

ViewPoint 27.5 Monday is Horlicks night

Horlicks is a rich milky drink made with malt that contains high levels of calcium and other vitamins. Traditionally, it is associated with older people and helps relaxation and inducing sleep. MediaCom was given the task of finding a new target audience and repositioning the brand. Planning and research identified women aged 35+ who were stressed trying to manage both their careers and their family. MediaCom also identified Mondays as the night when they were most likely to have a poor night's sleep.

This information enabled MediaCom to target the Monday night schedule, and the end of evening section, or the 'wind-down ritual' in particular. With a 13-week concentration Horlicks was able to target its customers at a time when they would be most receptive and as a result a new market was won. It was reported that sales climbed 28 per cent in the first four weeks of the campaign.

Source: Adapted from Grimshaw (2004).

Question

Although sales rose during the first four weeks, does this measure provide sufficient long-term optimism for the brand? If not, why not?

Task

Think of a product that you use, consider when you use it and try to identify communications that reflect your usage.

Exhibit 27.3 Horlicks
Horlicks, part of GSK Nutritional Healthcare U.K.

Weilbacher (1984) argues that media evaluation based on product usage may be better than using demographics and psychographics. These may be inappropriate and inefficient when matching markets with audiences. As advertising is directed at influencing consumer behaviour, product usage is a more logical measure of media evaluation. This view is supported by media planners targeting heavy, medium and light users.

This perspective contrasts with the view of Rothschild (1987). He regards demographic and psychographic factors as relatively stable and enduring factors, and thus suitable influences on the media selection decision. By contrast, the dynamic factors (those that vary within an individual with respect to brand choice, purchase behaviour and time of adoption between products) are seen as being more suitable for influencing media strategy.

Nature of the product

In addition to this, consideration needs to be given to the nature of the product itself. Audiences have particular viewing patterns, therefore it does not make sense to advertise when it is known that the target audience is not watching (for example, promoting children's sweets late at night or photocopiers in consumer-interest magazines).

Prime television spots such as *Coronation Street* or major sporting occasions such as the Olympic Games attract many major competitive brands. It may be wise to avoid competing for time and look for other suitable programmes.

Vehicle mood effects

The mood that a vehicle creates can also be an important factor. Aaker *et al.* (1992) report on the work of a number of studies in this area. These suggest that food advertisements using transformational appeals are more effective when placed in situation comedies than in thrillers and mystery programmes. Advertisements for analgesics work better in both adult westerns and situation comedies (Crane, 1964).

These qualitative, vehicle-related source effects need to be considered as support for the quantitative work undertaken initially. They should not be used as the sole reason for the selection of particular media vehicles, if only because they are largely subjective.

Scheduling

This seeks to establish when the messages are transmitted in order that the media objectives be achieved at the lowest possible cost. The first considerations are the objectives themselves. If the advertising objectives are basically short term, then the placements should be concentrated over a short period of time. Conversely, if awareness is to be built over a longer term, perhaps building a new brand, then the frequency of the placements need not be so intensive and can be spread over a period so that learning can occur incrementally.

The second consideration is the purchasing cycle. It has been noted before that the optimum number of exposures is thought to be between three and ten, and this should occur within each purchasing cycle. Obviously, this is only really applicable to packaged goods, and is not as applicable to white or brown goods or, indeed, the business-to-business sector. However, the longer the cycle, the less frequency is required.

> The optimum number of exposures is thought to be between three and ten.

The third consideration is the level of involvement. If the objective of the plan is to create awareness, then when there is high involvement few repetitions will be required compared with low-involvement decisions. This is because people who are highly involved actively seek information and need little assistance to digest relevant information. Likewise, where there is low involvement, attitudes develop from use of the product, so frequency is important to maintain awareness and to prompt trial.

Finally, the placement of an advertisement is influenced by the characteristics of the target audience and their preferred programmes. Selecting compatible 'spots' is likely to improve message delivery considerably.

Timing of advertisement placements

The timing of placements is dependent on a number of factors. One of the overriding constraints is the size of the media budget and the impact that certain placement patterns can bring to an organisation's cash flow. Putting cost to one side, many researchers have identified and labelled different scheduling patterns. Govoni *et al.* (1986), Sissors and Bumba (1989), Burnett (1993) and Kotler (1997) all suggest different approaches to scheduling. Figure 27.2 and the following are presented as a synthesis of the more common scheduling options.

Continuity patterns

Continuous patterns involve regular and uniform presentation of the message to the target audience. Over the long term, a continuous pattern is more appropriate for products and services where demand is crisis led, e.g. plumbing, or where there is a long purchase cycle. These continuous patterns are often used for mature products, where reminder advertising is appropriate. A rising pattern is used when activity centres around a particular event, such as the FA Cup Final, the Olympic Games or a general election. A fading pattern may follow an initial burst to launch a new product or to inform of a product modification.

A rising pattern is used when activity centres around a particular event.

Flighting patterns

Flighting allows advertisers the opportunity to spread their resources across a longer period of time.

Flighting allows advertisers the opportunity to spread their resources across a longer period of time. This may improve the effectiveness of their messages. A flighting pattern may be appropriate in situations where messages need to reflect varying demand, such as that experienced by the retail sector throughout the year. Flighting is also adopted as a competitive response to varying advertising weights applied by rivals. These schedules are used for specific events, such as support for major sales promotions and responses to adverse publicity or one-off market opportunities.

Flighting patterns can also be used in short and often heavy periods of investment activity. Because of the seasonality of the product (e.g. for inclusive tour operators), advertising at other times is inappropriate and a waste of resources. This approach can also be used to respond quickly to a competitor's potentially damaging actions, to launch new products or to provide unique information, such as the announcement of a new organisation as a result of merger activity, or to promote information about a particular event such as an impending share offer.

Pulsing patterns

Pulsing seeks to combine the advantages of both the previous patterns. As a result, it is the safest of all the options, but potentially the most expensive. It allows advertisers to increase levels of message activity at certain times of the year, which is important for times when sales traditionally increase, as with fragrance sales in December and ice-cream in June.

Whereas flighting presents an opportunity for individuals to forget messages during periods of no advertising, pulsing helps to prevent the onset of forgetting, to build high levels of awareness and to provide a barrier that holds back competitor attack.

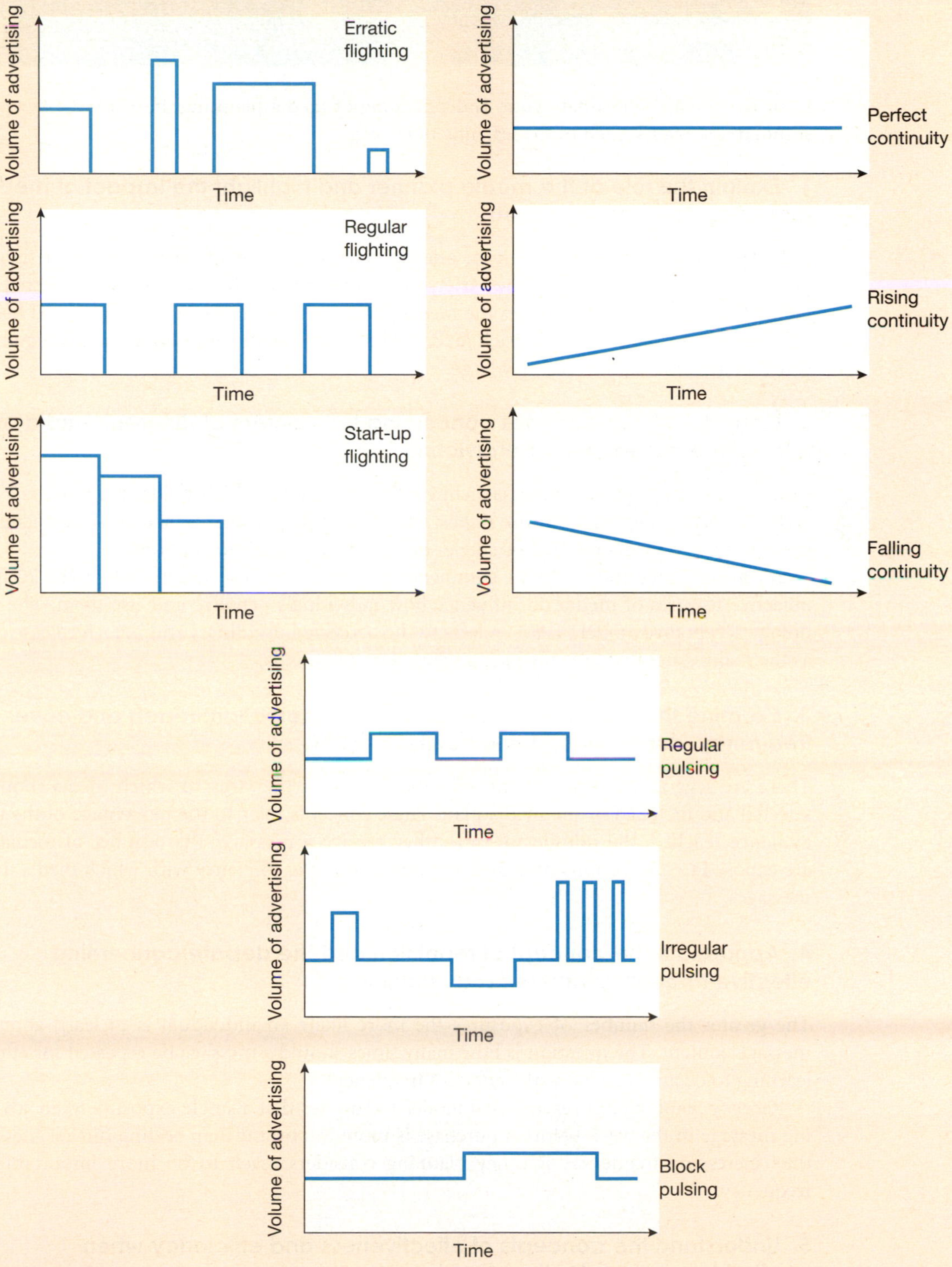

Figure 27.2 Media scheduling patterns

Summary

In order to help consolidate your understanding of media planning, here are the key points summarised against each of the learning objectives:

1. Explain the role of the media planner and highlight the impact of media and audience fragmentation.

Media planning is concerned with the selection and scheduling of media vehicles designed to carry an advertiser's message. The variety of media is rapidly increasing and is referred to as media fragmentation. This makes the media planner's task increasingly complicated because the size of audience available to each media reduces, making the number of media required to reach a target market increasingly large.

2. Consider various theories concerning the content of different media and related media switching behaviours.

Consideration was given to media richness theory (MRT), which holds that there is a hierarchy of media ranging from the richest media such as personal or face-to-face encounters through to lean media typified by single sheets of text-based information.

Social influence theory (SIT) complements MRT as it also assumes that the relatively objective features of media do influence how individuals perceive and use them. The technology acceptance model (TAM) relates to the perceived usefulness and perceived ease of use as the main issues that are considered when selecting media.

3. Examine the key concepts used in media selection: reach and cover, frequency, duplication, rating points and CPT.

There are several fundamental concepts that underpin they way in which media should be selected and included in the media plan. These concepts refer to the percentage of the target audience reached, the number of times they receive a message, the number of media they are exposed to and various measures associated with the efficiency with which media deliver messages.

4. Appreciate the concept of repetition and the debate concerning effective frequency and recency planning.

The greater the number of exposures the more likely an individual is to learn about the message content. The question is how many times should a message be repeated for effective learning to occur, i.e. what is the effective frequency?

Recency planning is a reach-based model and argues that a single exposure to an advertising message in the week before a purchase is more important than adding further messages, thus increasing frequency. Recency planning considers reach to be more important than frequency.

5. Understand the concepts of effectiveness and efficiency when applied to media selection decisions.

The efficiency of a schedule refers to the costs involved in delivering messages. There are two main types of cost. The first of these is the *absolute cost*, which is the cost of the space or time required for the message to be transmitted. The second concerns the costs incurred in making contact with each member of the target audience. These are refereed to as the *relative costs* and are used to compare different media schedules.

The magazine industry uses calculations based on the cost per thousand people reached (CPT). Broadcast audiences are measured by television ratings or TVRs. These represent the percentage of television households that are tuned to a specific programme.

6. Introduce media source effects as an important factor in the selection and timing of advertising in magazines and television programmes.

Different media impact on audiences in different ways because of three main factors. These are the *vehicle atmosphere* – editorial tone, vehicle expertise, vehicle prestige; their *technical and reproduction characteristics* – technical factors, exposure opportunities, perception opportunities; and finally their *audience and product characteristics* – audience/vehicle fit, nature of the product.

7. Explore the different ways in which advertisements can be scheduled.

The scheduling of a media plan seeks to establish when the messages are transmitted in order that the media objectives be achieved at the lowest possible cost. Various factors affect the schedule: the campaign objectives; the purchasing cycle; the level of involvement; and the characteristics of the target audience and their preferred programmes. The selection of compatible 'spots' is likely to improve message delivery considerably.

Review questions

1. Compare media richness theory, social influence theory and the technology adoption model.
2. What are the main tasks facing media planners?
3. If the rate at which information decays within individuals is known, then the task of the media planner is simply to place messages at suitable intervals in the path of decay. Discuss.
4. Why is it important that a media planner knows whether reach or frequency is the main objective of a media plan?
5. Why are frequency levels so important? Explain the concept of effective frequency.
6. How does recency planning differ from effective frequency?
7. What is a TVR and how does it relate to GRPs?
8. How does planning for digital media differ from that for traditional media?
9. Write a brief report outlining the principal characteristics of media source effects.
10. What are the main ways in which media plans can be scheduled?

MiniCase Targeting the 'brown pound' – an untapped market

Yasmin Sekhon: Bournemouth University

The fundamental aim of media planning is to formulate a strategy that will allow marketing communication messages to reach the target audience. This involves 'buying' time and space and utilising the appropriate media vehicles. However, for a media plan to work it has to be effective and efficient, having the relevant impact and getting the message across.

One key issue, as yet not properly resolved, concerns ways in which marketers can make the right decisions when targeting the 'brown pound'. That is, how to use the right media to reach ethnic markets, especially when these markets are generally under-researched and remain untouched.

Background

The combined disposable income of ethnic minorities in the United Kingdom is in the region of £32bn, according to the Institute of Practitioners in Advertising (IPA). However, businesses are generally guilty of not effectively promoting to these audiences and paying little or no attention to them. Often labelled as the 'hard-to-reach groups' it seems to be a self-fulfilling prophecy, it is hard to reach them so why bother?

The 'brown pound', and the ethnic communities that constitute it, have some key characteristics that must be understood and targeted accordingly. In planning to target these audiences once the appropriate message has been devised, the relevant media vehicle has to be chosen. This will involve choosing the right media and scheduling them according to the target market needs.

Characteristics

Based on the last census, South Asians represented 3 per cent of the UK population, which is approximately 1.6 million people. This segment consists of not only actual immigrants, but also second- and third-generation Asians born in this country. In the main, these group are highly educated, professional and some are business-owning individuals. The audience profile of this segment varies from male to female and young to old, with varying amounts of disposable income.

Distinguishing between the different generations is important. The first generation may have a greater affiliation with their home country – their cultural roots – and so consumption decisions are made according to their own level of acculturation in Britain. While the second generation, born and bred in the United Kingdom, will live a more bi-cultural lifestyle, mixing both Eastern and Western value systems.

So what is the optimal solution for reaching this diverse but potentially rich group? Many of the campaigns aimed at this audience are neither planned nor do they demonstrate consideration of the media and channels, which means that the right media space is not being bought, so it remains an untapped market.

The role of media

The choice of media has to meet the target audience's needs. Essentially, those targeting ethnic audiences have a plethora of media to choose from, encompassing radio or television stations, newspapers, magazines and also web sites.

However, when making decisions about which media to choose it may be more favourable to use a combination that will result in synergistic results. There are a number of media vehicles that can be selected to carry a company's promotional message. However, choices have to take account of the generation, the age, level of disposable income and levels of affiliation with the home and host countries.

Reaching and communicating to this audience, ethnic minority media often uses community-based methods of distribution, but organisations are really not tapping into these communities' related opportunities. Punjab Radio for instance, targets Britain's Punjabi community. Also, particular television programmes such as Zee TV and specialist magazines, for example, *Asiana*, *Asian Women* and *Asian Bride* are media where potential messages can reach ethnic audiences in a concentrated manner.

However, when selecting and scheduling media, organisations also need to think beyond the sole use of concentrated media. What about the more traditional and mainstream media? The integration of both would have a greater impact and allow a number of different touch points for the potential customer.

Companies that wish to tap into the 'brown pound' have a number of choices to make when planning their marketing communications campaigns. First, the objectives of the campaign have to be understood – what do you want to say to the consumers and what tools will be most effective for the message? In addition, issues concerning reach and frequency are important.

However, to tap into the 'brown pound' it may be a case of not only understanding the differences, but also recognising the similarities between consumers of an ethnic background compared to the indigenous population. Also, the message has to be relevant to the segment and how you can influence ethnic consumers: directly, indirectly, through reference groups or opinion leaders? Finally, the timing and scheduling of campaigns, in order to develop a consistent message and deliver it at times relevant to the target audience, is all-important in targeting what marketers have labelled as 'select audiences'.

The 'brown pound' still remains a fairly untapped market, it is worth millions, so planning the right message, and delivering it through the right media, at the right time, could bring lucrative returns for many companies.

MiniCase questions

1. Using a company or brand of your choice, plan an outline marketing communications campaign aimed at one specific ethnic group. Pay particular attention to media choice and the campaign schedule.
2. Which particular factors might need to be taken into account when planning campaigns to reach ethnic groups?
3. When planning a media mix to reach ethnic audiences, what do you believe might be the critical factors?

References

Aaker, D., Batra, R. and Myers, J.G. (1992) *Advertising Management*, 4th edn. Englewood Cliffs, NJ: Prentice-Hall.

Armstrong, S. (1993) The business of buying: time, lads, please. *Media Week*, 3 September, 26–7.

Bainbridge, J. (2008) Now ad campaigns can take off. *The Independent*, 17 March 2008, 10.

Beale, C. (1997) Study reveals negativity towards ads. *Campaign*, 28 November, 8.

Bokaie, J. (2008) Gateway to Britain. *Marketing*, 19 March, 16.

Brech, P. (1999) When the media buck stops with you. *Media Week*, 19 November, 22–3.

Broussard, G. (2000) How advertising frequency can work to build online effectiveness. *International Journal of Market Research*, **42**(4), 439–57.

Burnett, J. (1993) *Promotion Management*. New York: Houghton Mifflin.

Crane, L.E. (1964) How product, appeal, and program affect attitudes towards commercials. *Journal of Advertising Research*, **4** (March), 15.

Daft, R.L. and Lengel, R.H. (1984) Information richness: a new approach to managerial behavior and organizational design. In *Research in Organizational Behavior*, **6** (eds L.L. Cummings and B.M. Straw), 191–233. Homewood, IL: JAI Press.

Duarte, D.L. and Snyder, N.T. (2001) *Mastering Virtual Team*, 2nd edn. San Francisco, CA: Jossey-Bass.

Ephron, E. (1997) Recency planning. *Admap* (February), 32–4.

Fulk, J., Schmitz, J.A. and Steinfield, C.W. (1990) A social influence model of technology use. In *Organizations and Communication Technology* (eds J. Fulk and C. Steinfield). Newbury Park, CA: Sage.

Gallucci, P. (1997) There are no absolutes in media planning. *Admap* (July/August), 39–43.

Gay, R., Charlesworth, A. and Esen, R. (2007) *Online Marketing: A Customer Led Approach*. Oxford: Oxford University Press.

Govoni, N., Eng, R. and Galper, M. (1986) *Promotional Management.* Englewood Cliffs, NJ: Prentice-Hall.

Grimshaw, C. (2004) MediaCom – media agency of the year. *Marketing Agency*, December, 7.

Jarvis, T. and McElroy, B. (2004) Can optimisers provide a lifeline for media? *Admap*, **39**(2) (February), 32–5.

Jones, P. (1995) *When Ads Work: New Proof that Advertising Triggers Sales.* New York: Simon & Schuster, Free Press/Lexington Books.

Keaveney, S.M. (1995) Consumer switching behavior in service industries: an exploratory study. *Journal of Marketing*, **59**(2), 71–82.

King, R.C. and Xia, W. (1997) Media appropriateness: effects of experience on communication media choice. *Decision Sciences*, **28**(4), 877–909.

Kotler, P. (1997) *Marketing Management: Analysis, Planning, Implementation and Control*, 9th edn. Englewood Cliffs, NJ: Prentice-Hall.

Krugman, H.E. (1965) The impact of television advertising: learning without involvement. *Public Opinion Quarterly*, **29** (Fall), 349–56.

Krugman, H.E. (1972) How potent is TV advertising? Cited in du Plessis (1998).

Krugman, H.E. (1975) What makes advertising effective? *Harvard Business Review* (March/April), 96–103.

Lloyd, D.W. and Clancy, K.J. (1991) CPMs versus CPMis: implications for media planning. *Journal of Advertising Research*, **31**(4) (August/September), 34–44.

Longhurst, P. (2006) Budgeting for online: is it any different? *Admap*, November, 36–7.

McGrath, J.E. and Hollingshead, A.B. (1993) Putting the 'group' back into group support systems: some theoretical issues about dynamic processes in groups with technological enhancements. In *Group Support Systems: New Perspectives* (eds L.M. Jessup and J.S. Valacich, 78–9). New York: Macmillan.

McLuhan, M. (1966) *Understanding Media: The Extensions of Man.* New York: McGraw-Hill.

Moore, L. (2007) 21st century media: let your brand lose control. *Marketing*, 5 December, 10–11.

Murray, G.B. and Jenkins, J.R.G. (1992) The concept of effective reach in advertising. *Journal of Advertising Research*, **32**(3) (May/June), 34–42.

Naples, M.J. (1979) *Effective Frequency: The Relationship Between Frequency and Advertising Effectiveness.* New York: Association of National Advertisers.

Ostrow, J.W. (1981) What level of frequency? *Advertising Age* (November), 13–18.

Ostrow, J.W. (1984) Setting frequency levels: an art or a science? *Marketing and Media Decisions*, **24**(4), 9–11.

Plessis, E. du (1998) Memory and likeability: keys to understanding ad effects. *Admap* (July/August), 42–6.

Rothschild, M.L. (1987) *Marketing Communications.* Lexington, MA: D.C. Heath.

Shultz, D.E., Pilotta, J.P. and Block, M.P. (2006) Media consumption and consumer purchasing, ESOMAR, Worldwide Multi-media Measurement, Shanghai, Retrieved 12 March 2008 from http://www.bigresearch.com/esomar2006.pdf.

Simon, H. (1972) Theories of bounded rationality. In *Decision and Organisation* (eds C.B. McGuire and R. Radner), 161–76. London: North-Holland.

Simon, H. (1987) Bounded rationality. In *The New Palgrave* (eds J. Eatwell, M. Milgate and P. Newman). London: Macmillan.

Sissors, J.Z. and Bumba, L. (1989) *Advertising Media Planning*, 3rd edn. Lincolnwood, IL: NTC Business Books.

Srinivasan, M. (1996) New insights into switching behaviour: marketers can now put a numerical value on loyalty. *Marketing Research*, **8**(3), 26–34.

Weilbacher, W. (1984) *Advertising*, New York: Macmillan.

Part 6

Marketing communications for special audiences

Chapters 28–30

This last part of the book considers marketing communications in the context of special audiences.

These audiences are special in the sense that they are contextually different from mainstream audiences and can require particular strategies and configurations of the marketing communications mix. Chapter 28, for example, considers some of the issues arising when dealing with marketing communications in an international or even a global environment.

Chapter 29 looks at marketing communications in the business-to-business market. Here a different emphasis on communications is required simply because the purchase decision process and the focus on relationships is very different from consumer-based marketing communications.

The final chapter in the book, Chapter 30, looks at the important issue of marketing communications when targeted at internal audiences. Although touched on at different points in the book, this chapter considers more fully the role of employees in the branding process and the tasks marketing communications is expected to undertake.

Video Insight Part 6

This final part of the book is concerned with communications with special audiences. In this context, 'special' refers to customers other than domestic or regionally based consumers. The audiences featured here include international audiences, business-to-business customers and employees.

The Video Insight starts with a short clip from Land Rover that refers to the different perceptions different audiences can have of products and services. Reference is made to the perceptions held of the brand in the USA, Russia, China and the Middle East. Interestingly, the strength and form of these perceptions are linked to the experience each region has of the brand, whether it be through Range Rover or directly through the Land Rover brand.

Chapter 28 examines the issues associated with global marketing communications. The key argument concerns whether messages should be changed to reflect local preferences and cultural needs. One argument is that the message should be the same in all regions and countries, a standardised approach. The other argues that messages should be adapted to meet the cultural needs of local areas, an adapted strategy. The Royal Enfield section of the Video Insight explores their approach, an adaptation strategy, and examines the way they communicate in different countries and the reasoning behind the different approaches.

Finally, the Ikea section considers the importance of culture and how Swedish values have been used to augment the Ikea brand.

Go to **www.pearsoned.co.uk/fill** to watch the Video Insight, and then answer the following questions:

1. How might Land Rover benefit from using an adapted marketing communications strategy rather than a standardised one?
2. What risks might Royal Enfield incur if they leave the management of their dealers to the appointed local distributors? What might be the impact on their marketing communications and the brand?
3. To what extent might the prevailing Swedish culture impede the development of the Ikea brand?

Chapter 28

Marketing communications across borders

The management of marketing communications for audiences domiciled in two or more countries is haunted by the dilemma of whether to send the same message to all regions or adapt it to meet the needs of local markets, or do a little bit of both. The implications for messaging, branding and costs are substantial.

Aims and learning objectives

The aim of this chapter is to examine the impact that cross-border business strategies might have on marketing communications agencies and strategies.

The learning objectives of this chapter are to:

1. consider the development and variety of organisations operating across international borders;
2. examine the key variables affecting international marketing communications;
3. discuss the adaptation versus standardisation debate about marketing communications strategy;
4. explore issues concerning the international communication mix;
5. explain the ways in which advertising agencies have developed to meet the international communication requirements of their clients.

For an applied interpretation see Stefan Schwarzkopf's MiniCase entitled ***Procter & Gamble and the ethnology of markets: adapting a giant to emerging markets*** at the end of this chapter.

Introduction

For organisations the differences between operating within home or domestic markets as compared with overseas or international markets are many and varied. Most of these differences can be considered within an economic, cultural, legal, technological and competitive framework. If the core characteristics of a home market (such as prices, marketing channels, finance, knowledge about customers, legislation, media and competitors) are compared with each of the same factors in the international markets in which an organisation might be operating, the degree of complexity and uncertainty can be easily illuminated. Management might be conversant with the way of doing business at home but, as they move outside the country/regional borders/areas that represent their domain of knowledge, understanding and to some extent security, so levels of control decline and risk increases.

The objective of this chapter is not to consider these particular characteristics, as time and space restrict scope. Readers interested in these issues are recommended to consult some of the many international marketing or business texts that are available. The goal of this chapter is to consider some of the issues that impact on marketing communications when operating across international borders. To do this it is first necessary to consider the various environments and the types of organisation that operate away from their home markets.

Types of cross-border organisations

Organisations can be regarded as international, multinational, global or transnational (Keegan, 1989; Bartlett and Ghoshal, 1991) and each form is a reflection of their structure and disposition towards their chosen markets (see Table 28.1).

These organisations regard their overseas activities as feeders or delivery tubes for a unified global market.

Table 28.1 Organisational frameworks

International organisations	These organisations see their overseas operations as appendages or attachments to a central domestic organisation. The marketing policy is to serve customers domestically and then offer these same marketing mixes to other countries/areas.
Multinational organisations	These organisations see their overseas activities as a portfolio of independent businesses. The policy is to serve customers with individually designed country/area marketing mixes.
Global organisations	These organisations regard their overseas activities as feeders or delivery tubes for a unified global market. The policy is to serve a global market with a single, fundamental marketing mix.
Transnational organisations	These organisations regard their overseas activities as a complex process of coordination and cooperation. The environment is regarded as one where decision-making is shared in a participatory manner. The policy is to serve global business environments using flexible global resources to formulate different global marketing mixes.

Source: Based on Bartlett and Ghoshal (1991) and de Mooij (1994).

International organisations evolve from national organisations whose origins are to serve national customers.

International organisations evolve from national organisations whose origins are to serve national customers using domestic or 'home-grown' resources. Some of these organisations, either by accident or by design, begin to undertake a limited amount of work 'overseas'. They begin to become international, first by deploying their domestically oriented marketing mix and then later by adapting it to the needs of the new, local 'overseas' market. This adaption phase signals the commencement of a *multinational strategy*. What distinguishes these organisations is that they regard the world (or their parts of it) as having discrete regions. Each country/area reports to a world head office, and performance is normally geared to meet financial targets.

Organisations at this stage in the evolutionary process are referred to as *global*. This is characterised by centralised decision-making, where, unlike in multinational companies, the similarities as well as the differences of each country/area are sought. Customers are seen on a global rather than a country/area basis.

Transnational organisations are an extension of global organisations. These sophisticated organisations seek to develop advantages based on efficiencies driven by serving global customers. Using technology as a key part of the infrastructure, networks allow resources to be globally derived in response to local requirements.

Anholt (2000), among others, suggests that in recent years a new type of transnational organisation has emerged. Primarily as a result of the Internet, these organisations are conceived and born as global brands and therefore do not experience the slow development and evolution as suggested in the previous framework. These new *universal* brands, owned by either a global parent or a small independent operator, often from start-up, transcend established patterns by either minimising or negating the formal distribution channels. Dell computers, Microsoft and search engines such as Google and Yahoo! all require a global market. What characterises these organisations is that they are generally faster and more adaptable than the established organisations and they create new channels to market. In addition, although some might have a global business, they operate with a single office, can be based in third-world nations or are simply small global businesses in their own right.

Organisations are far from static and, as domestic markets may stagnate, and technology and communication opportunities in particular develop, so opportunities contract and expand. In addition, organisations seek efficiency and flexibility with regard to their use of materials and resources. The use of strategic alliances and outsourcing arrangements complements this goal, and network organisations, spanning the globe, emerge.

Appreciating the different types of worldwide organisation is important, not just from a structural perspective but also for the formulation and implementation of business strategy. In addition, other issues concerning the products, markets and the marketing communications used by these organisations also surface.

Key variables affecting international marketing communications

There are a large number of variables that can impact on the effectiveness of marketing communications that cross international borders. Many of these are controllable by either local or central management. However, there are a large number that are uncontrollable, and these variables need to be carefully considered before communications are attempted. The following variables (culture and media) are reviewed here because of their immediate and direct impact on organisations and their communication activities.

Culture

The values, beliefs, ideas, customs, actions and symbols that are learned by members of particular societies are referred to as culture. The importance of culture is that it provides individuals with identity and the direction of what is deemed to be acceptable behaviour. Culture is acquired through learning. If it were innate or instinctive, then everyone would behave in the same way. Human beings across the world do not behave uniformly or predictably. Therefore different cultures exist, and from this it is possible to visualise that there must be boundaries within which certain cultures, and hence behaviours and lifestyles, are permissible or even expected. These boundaries are not fixed rigidly, as this would suggest that cultures are static. They evolve and change as members of a society adjust to new technologies, government

The values, beliefs, ideas, customs, actions and symbols that are learned by members of particular societies are referred to as culture.

ViewPoint 28.1 Cultural euromales

With changes to expectations about a job for life, women's increasingly independent financial and social lifestyle, and media debates concerning the role of men in society, it is not surprising that international marketing communications targeted at men are unlikely to be based on common attitudes, values and beliefs. Research by RDSi revealed, for example, the following:

Italian men are comfortable in their relationships with women, unless they are their superiors at work. The family is very important, with men aspiring to beautiful wives, beautiful children and a beautiful home. Therefore, aspirational advertisements are favoured and scenes depicting family life are approved.

Spanish men are judged to have low morale, partly as a result of the country's relatively recent move towards democracy and the high levels of unemployment when compared with the rest of Europe. The family is an important unit and with it come high levels of respect for the older generation. Cross-generation advertisements that reflect bonding and family ties are well received. There is still a strong macho theme in society, with men seeking to prove themselves.

German men see these changes in society as a challenge and one that needs a disciplined approach. The family is high on their list of things to be openly valued but, unlike the Italians and the French, they are uncertain about how to achieve this as it conflicts with the German work ethic.

Frenchmen are the most self-assured of all European males. They are relaxed and confident about the changing role of women in society and see opportunities to change themselves. There are, however, some poorer sections of French society that do resent the changes and resort to displays of masculinity to reassert themselves.

British males retain a US-style work ethic and on the surface are comfortable with the changes in society. Underneath, however, research suggests that they are in denial, and it cites the successful 'lads' magazines (e.g. *Loaded*, *FHM*) as evidence. This complexity, when combined with the most sophisticated advertising literacy and cynicism, makes it difficult to communicate with British males.

Source: Adapted from Davies (2000).

Question

To what extent are these profiles a useful aid to marketing communications?

Task

Choose a male fragrance or deodorant and consider how you would communicate with each of the types of men listed above.

policies, changing values and demographic changes, to mention but a few dynamic variables. From a marketing communications perspective, the prevailing culture in a region must be respected, otherwise it is likely that a brand and or an organisation will be rejected. For example, the Dove ads in which happy women of all shapes and sizes pose in their underwear have had to be shown in different ways to meet the needs of different cultures. In Brazil the women are depicted hugging each other yet in the United States they stand slightly apart from each other, as body contact in the United States is not part of the culture (Laurance, 2007).

Culture is passed from generation to generation.

Culture is passed from generation to generation. This is achieved through the family, religion, education and the media. These conduits of social behaviour and beliefs serve to provide consistency, stability and direction. The extent to which the media either move society forward or merely reflect its current values is a debate that reaches beyond the scope of this book. However, there can be no doubt as to the impact that the media have on society and the important part that religion plays in different cultures around the world.

Culture has multiple facets, and those that are of direct relevance to marketing communications are the values and beliefs associated with *symbols*, such as language and aesthetics, *institutions* and *groups*, such as those embracing the family, work, education, media and religion, and finally *values*, which according to Hofstede *et al.* (1990) represent the core of culture. These will be looked at in turn.

Symbols

Language, through both the spoken and the non-spoken word, permits members of a society to enter into dialogue and to share meaning. Aesthetics, in the form of design and colour, forms an integral part of packaging, sales promotions and advertising. Those involved in personal selling must be aware of the symbolic impact of formal and informal dress codes and the impact that overall personal appearances and gestures (for example when greeting or leaving people) may have on people in different cultures. Advertisers need to take care that they do not infringe a culture's aesthetic codes when designing visuals or when translating copy into the local language.

Advertisers need to take care that they do not infringe a culture's aesthetic codes when designing visuals or when translating copy into the local language.

Institutions and groups

The various institutions that help form the fabric of societies and particular cultures provide a means by which culture is communicated and perpetuated through time. These groups provide the mechanisms by which the process of socialisation occurs. Of these groups, the family plays an important role. The form of the *family* is evolving in some Western cultures, such that the traditional family unit is declining and the number of single-parent families is increasing. In many developing economies the extended family, with several generations living together, continues to be a central, stable part of society. Marketing communication messages need to reflect these characteristics. The impact and importance of various decision-makers need to be recognised and the central creative idea needs to be up to date and sensitive to the family unit.

Work patterns vary across regions: not all cultures expect a 9-to–5 routine. This is breaking down in the United Kingdom as delayering pressurises employees to work increased hours, while in Asia-Pacific Saturday morning work is the norm.

Literacy levels can impact heavily on the ability of target audiences to understand and to ascribe meanings.

Literacy levels can impact heavily on the ability of target audiences to understand and to ascribe meanings to marketing communication messages. The balance between visual and non-visual components in messages and the relative complexity of messages should be considered in the light of the education levels that different countries and regions have reached. In addition to these factors, some target audiences in more developed economies have developed a high level of advertising

ViewPoint 28.2 Colourful communication

Colours must be treated with care depending on the particular country where communications are being conducted. Griffin (1993) sets out how the colour of flowers is used to depict death and or unhappiness in different countries:

purple flowers in Brazil;
white and yellow lilies in Taiwan;
yellow lilies in Mexico;
white lilies in Canada, Great Britain and Sweden;
yellow flowers stand for infidelity in France and disrespect for a woman in the (ex)-Soviet Union.

Question

Should these colours be avoided in packaging?

Task

Find out what colours symbolise happiness in various countries.

sophistication. The meaning given to messages is in some part a reflection of the degree to which individuals understand commercial messages and what the source seeks to achieve. This high level of interaction with messages or advertising literacy suggests that advertisers need to create a dialogue with their audiences that recognises their cognitive processing abilities and does not seek to deceive or misinform.

Religion has always played an important part in shaping the values and attitudes of society. Links between religion and authority have been attempted based on the highly structured nature of religion and the role that religion can play in the family, forming the gender, decision-making roles and nurturing the child-rearing process. While the results of research are not conclusive, there appears to be agreement that religion plays an important part in consumer buying behaviour and that marketing communications should take into account the level of religious beliefs held by the decision-maker (Delner, 1994).

Similarly, mass communication technologies provide audiences with improved opportunities to understand and appreciate different religious beliefs and their associated rituals and artefacts, so care needs to be taken not to offend these groups with upsetting or misinformed marketing communications.

Values

One of the most important international, culturally oriented research exercises, was undertaken by Hofstede (1980, 1991). Using data gathered from IBM across 53 countries, Hofstede's research has had an important impact on our understanding of culture (Hickson and Pugh, 1995). From this research, several dimensions of culture have been discerned. The first of these concerns the individualist/collectivist dimension. It is suggested that individualistic cultures emphasise individual goals and the need to empower, to progress and to be a good leader. Collectivist cultures emphasise good group membership and participation. Consequently, difficulties can arise when communications between these two types of culture have meanings ascribed to them that are derived from different contexts. To avoid the possible confusion and misunderstanding, an adapted communication strategy is advisable.

> Collectivist cultures emphasise good group membership and participation.

In addition to these challenges, comprehension (ascribed meaning) is further complicated by the language context. In high-context languages, information is conveyed through who is speaking and their deportment and mannerisms. Content is inferred on the basis that it is implicit: it is known and does not need to be set out. This is unlike low-context languages, where information has to be detailed and 'spelled out' to avoid misunderstanding. Not surprisingly, therefore, when (marketing) communications occur across these contexts, inexperienced communicators may be either offended at the blunt approach of the other (of the low-context German or French, for example) or intrigued by the lack of overt information being offered from the other (from the high-context Japanese or Asians, for example). Referring to advertising creative strategy, Okazaki and Alonso (2003) assert that the Japanese prefer a more subtle, soft approach. In contrast, North Americans prefer a more direct, hard-sell strategy with direct, explicit messages.

In high-power-distance cultures, authority figures are important.

A further cultural dimension concerns the role that authority plays in society. Two broad forms can be identified. In high-power-distance cultures, authority figures are important and guide a high proportion of decisions that are made. In low-power-distance cultures, people prefer to use cognitive processing and make reasoned decisions based on the information available. What might be deduced from this is that expert advice and clear, specific recommendations should be offered to those in high-power-distance cultures, while information provision should be the goal of marketing communications to assist those in low-power-distance cultures (Zandpour and Harich, 1996).

People in different cultures can exhibit characteristics that suggest they feel threatened or destabilised by ambiguous situations or uncertainty. Those cultures that are more reliant on formal rules are said to have high levels of uncertainty avoidance. They need expert advice, so marketing communications that reflect these characteristics and are logical, clear and provide information directly and unambiguously (in order to reduce uncertainty) are likely to be more successful.

From the adaptation/standardisation perspective, this information can be useful in order to determine the form of the most effective advertising messages. Zandpour and Harich used these cultural dimensions, together with an assessment of the advertising industry environment in each target country. The results of their research suggest that different countries are more receptive to messages that have high or low levels of logical, rational and information-based appeals (think). Other countries might be more receptive to psychological and dramatically based appeals (feel).

ViewPoint 28.3 Varying international regulations

Advertising of toys is not permitted in Sweden and is banned until 2200 hours in Greece. In France, all alcohol advertisements are banned, while in the Czech Republic, drink can be shown but it cannot be poured, nor can advertisements show people enjoying the product. In Mexico, the restrictions state that food must be visible, whereas the Costa Ricans are allowed to see a glass being filled or the drink being poured, but not both.

Tobacco advertising is banned across all EU countries while pet food advertisements are banned in Lithuania before 2300 hours. The reason for this strict ruling is that food is scarce and this type of commercial could be considered offensive to humans.

Question

Does legislation regarding the use of advertising infringe civil liberties?

Task

Find out the regulations concerning the use of advertising fast food in a country of your choice. Are these regulations self-imposed by the industry (voluntary) or are they enforced through law?

Research concerning the effectiveness of advertising strategies in the United States and Australia (Frazer and Sheehan, 2002) found that safety appeals were more frequently used in Australia than the United States. This may well reflect varying cultural values regarding concern for safety-related issues, concern for the environment and varying regulatory requirements.

Media

The rate of technological change has had a huge impact on the form and type of media that audiences can access. However, media availability is far from uniform, and the range and types of media vary considerably across countries. These media developments have been accompanied by a number of major structural changes to the industry and the way in which it is regulated. Many organisations (client brands, media and agencies) have attempted to grow through diversification and the development of international networks (organic growth and alliances), and there has been an increase in the level of concentration as a few organisations/individuals have begun to own, and hence control, larger proportions of the media industry. For example, Rupert Murdoch, Ted Turner, Time-Warner, Bertelsmann and Silvio Berlusconi now have substantial cross-ownership holdings of international media. This concentration is partly the result of the decisions of many governments to deregulate their control over the media and to create new trading relationships. As a result, this cross-ownership of the media (television, newspapers, magazines, cable, satellite, film, publishing, advertising, cinema, retailing, recorded music) has created opportunities for client advertisers to have to go to only one media provider, which will then provide access to a raft of media across the globe. For example, the Time-Warner/AOL merger was intended to take the concentration and cross-industry collaboration a stage further as positions for future markets are adopted. This facility, known as one-stop shopping, has been available in North America for some time, and was attempted by Saatchi & Saatchi and WPP in the 1980s from a European base, but it is only since the 1990s that this opportunity has been offered elsewhere. The failure of the Time-Warner/AOL merger is symptomatic of other cultural and business-related problems.

Deregulation has had a profound impact on media provision in nearly all parts of the world. This often manifests itself in terms of the growth in types of the media available and the number of media vehicles.

Table 28.2 sets out some of the more general worldwide trends in advertising media. The net impact of all these changes has been principally the emergence of satellite television and cable provision and the development of the international consumer press.

Table 28.2 General trends in worldwide media

Electronic media expenditure has grown at the expense of print.
The worldwide adspend on newspapers has fallen considerably.
The number of general-interest magazines has fallen and the number of specialist-interest magazines has grown.
The growth of satellite facilities has helped generate the development of television and cable networks.
Online adspend is increasing faster than for any other medium.
Television programming and distribution have become more important.
Cinema capacity is beginning to outstrip demand.
Out-of-home media, in particular outdoor and alternative new media (e.g. ambient), have grown significantly.

Cross-border communication strategy

The degree to which organisations should adapt their external messages to suit local or regional country requirements has been a source of debate since Levitt (1983) published his seminal work on global branding. The standardisation/adaptation issue is unlikely to be resolved, yet is an intuitively interesting and thought-provoking subject. The cost savings associated with standardisation policies are attractive and, when these are combined with the opportunity to improve message consistency, communication effectiveness and other internally related efficiencies such as staff morale, cohesion and organisational identity, the argument in favour of standardisation seems difficult to renounce. However, in practice there are very few brands that are truly global. Some, such as McDonald's, Coca-Cola and Levi's are able to capitalise on the identification and inherent brand value that they have been able to establish across cultures. The majority of brands lack this depth of personality, and because individual needs vary across cultures, so enterprises need to retune their messages in order that their reception is as clear and distinct as possible.

The cost savings associated with standardisation policies are attractive.

Adaptation

The arguments in favour of adapting messages to meet the needs of particular local and/or regional needs are as follows:

1. Consumer needs are different and vary in intensity. Assuming there are particular advertising stimuli that can be identified as having universal appeal, it is unlikely that buyers across international borders share similar experiences, abilities and potential either to process information in a standardised way or to ascribe similar sets of meanings to the stimuli they perceive. Ideas and message concepts generated centrally may be inappropriate for local markets.
2. The infrastructure necessary to support the conveyance of standardised messages varies considerably, not only across but often within broad country areas.
3. Educational levels are far from consistent. This means that buyers' ability to give meaning to messages will vary. Similarly, there will be differing capacities to process information, so that the complexity of message content has to be kept low if universal dissemination is to be successful.
4. The means by which marketing communications are controlled in different countries is a reflection of the prevailing local economic, cultural and political conditions. The balance between voluntary controls through self-regulation and state control through legislation is partly a testimony to the degree of economic and political maturity that exists. This means that what might be regarded as acceptable marketing communications activities in one country may be unacceptable in another. For example, cold calling is not permissible in Germany but, although not popular with either sales personnel or buyers, is allowed in the Netherlands and France.
5. Local management of the implementation of standardised, centrally determined messages may be jeopardised because of a lack of ownership. Messages crafted by local 'craftsmen' to suit the needs of local markets may receive increased levels of support and motivation.

Consumer needs are different and vary in intensity.

Standardisation

Just as the arguments for adaptation appear convincing at first glance, then so do those in favour of standardisation:

1. Despite geographical dispersion, buyers in many product categories have a number of similar characteristics. This can be supported by the various psychographic typologies that have

been developed by advertising agencies for their clients. As brand images and propositions are capable of universal meaning, there is little reason to develop a myriad of brand messages.

2. Many locally driven campaigns are regarded as being of poor quality, if only because of the lack of local resources, experiences and expertise (Harris, 1996). It is better to control the total process and at the same time help exploit the opportunities for competitive advantage through shared competencies.

Many locally driven campaigns are regarded as being of poor quality.

3. As media, technology and international travel opportunities impact on increasing numbers of people, so a standardised message for certain offerings allows for a strong brand image to be developed.
4. Just as local management might favour local campaigns, so central management might prefer the ease with which they can implement and control a standardised campaign. This frees local managers to concentrate on managing the campaign and removes from them the responsibility of generating creative ideas and associated issues with local advertising agencies.
5. Following on from this point is one of the more enduring and managerially appealing ideas. The economies of scale that can be gained across packaging, media buying and advertising message creation and production can be enormous. In addition, the prospect of message consistency and horizontally integrated campaigns across borders is quite compelling. Buzzell (1968) argued that these economies of scale would also improve levels of profitability.

ViewPoint 28.4 iPod = adaptive music

When Apple launched the iPod it received instant acclaim from both technical and music PR opinion formers. The problem facing Apple after the first year, however, was that the iPod was still perceived by consumers as a device just for techies and celebrities. The task, therefore, was to use communications to inform world audiences that the iPod was for everyone, not just a select few.

The campaign had to run in several countries, but its key challenge was to reach a predominantly Windows world and to inform them that this Apple product was actually accessible through PCs. At the same time it was important to retain the cool image of the iPod and the uniqueness of the Apple brand.

The target audience was music lovers, of all ages, denominations, colours, relations and cultures. What bound this group together was that iPod represented a way in which an individual's relationship with music was enhanced. The iPod provided freedom to enjoy music. The creative platform was developed from this insight, and that was to use music and dancing as this was a language common to all. The execution showed silhouettes of different types of people dancing in different ways, but each was shown holding an iPod in one hand . . . freedom. However, in order to provide local relevance, the campaign used music. By adapting the campaign through different types of music that appealed to a global youth culture, for example rock, hip hop and dance, it was possible to provide local relevance through a global strategy.

Sources: Anon. (2004) and www.nyama.org.

Question

Why did Apple not adapt its communications completely to each region's music preferences?

Task

How have MP3 players tried to compete against the market dominance of iPod?

Exhibit 28.1 iPod Silhouette ad
Image courtesy of The Advertising Archives.

Fielding (2000) and Hite and Fraser (1988) argue that the evidence indicates that, although organisations pursued standardisation strategies in the 1970s, the trend since then has been towards more local adaptation. Harris (1996) makes the point that, although the operation of a purely standardised programme is considered desirable, there is no evidence to suggest that standardisation actually works. There appears to have been little research to compare the performance of advertising that has been developed and implemented under standardisation policies with that executed under locally derived communications.

However, while a few organisations do operate at either end of the spectrum, the majority prefer a contingency approach. This means that there is a degree of standardisation, where for example creative themes, ideas and campaign planning are centrally driven and other campaign elements such as language, scenes and models are adapted to the needs of the local environment. The cosmetic manufacturer L'Oréal used to distribute its Studio Line of hair care products aimed at 18–35-year-olds, across 50 countries. 'These are the same products with the same formulation with the same attitudinal message of personal choice', (Sennett, in Kaplan, 1994). All the advertisements have the same positioning intentions, which are developed centrally, but the executions (featuring different hairstyles) are produced locally to reflect the different needs of different markets.

It is too easy to consider the internationalisation debate in terms of packaged goods companies when other sectors have approached the task in different ways. Bold (2000) refers to pharmaceutical companies that have generally made the product, as opposed to brands, the centre of their communication strategy. Drugs are launched in different countries using different names and different strategies targeted at the medical professionals. He comments that while this approach was prevalent, the structure of pharmaceutical companies tended to be nation-focused, even to the extent that there would be separate regionalised budgets. The merger and consolidation activity, together with the rapid rise in patient involvement in health care (e.g. AIDS), has resulted in the formation of centralised marketing departments and the development of multinational brands.

The argument for some form of standardisation is twofold. First, there is an increasing need for improved levels of internal efficiency (and accountability) in terms of the use of resources.

Second, there is an increasing awareness of the benefits that standardised advertising may have on organisational identity, employee morale and satisfaction. The pressure to make cost savings and to develop internal efficiencies, therefore, appears to override the needs of the market.

There is an increasing awareness of the benefits that standardised advertising may have on organisational identity, employee morale and satisfaction.

However, those who argue in favour of standardisation need to be aware that the information content will often need to be correspondingly low. Mueller (1991) observes that the greater the amount of information the greater the opportunity for buyers to discriminate among alternative purchases. Conversely, the emphasis with uninformative advertising is to use imagery and indirect (peripheral) cues. Multinational organisations prepare individual marketing mixes for individual countries/areas. Products and prices will be different, so comparisons are difficult. Likewise, key attributes will vary across countries/areas, so this means that organisations need to decide whether high levels of standardisation and low levels of information are preferable to adapted campaigns with higher levels of information content.

The criterion by which organisations should decide whether to adapt or standardise their marketing (communications) activities is normally the impact that the different strategies are likely to have on profit performance (Buzzell, 1968). The basis for these financial projections has to be a suitably sensitive segmentation analysis based on a layering of segment information. Country-only or arbitrary regional analysis is unlikely to be suitable. Cross-cultural and psychographic data need to be superimposed to provide the richness upon which to build effective communications.

Organisations rarely decide on a polarised strategy of total adaptation or complete standardisation. In practice, a policy of 'glocalisation' seems to be preferred. Under this approach, organisations develop standard messages centrally, but expect the local country areas to adapt them to meet local cultural needs by adjusting for language and media components. There are, of course, variations on this theme. For example, head office might decide on the strategic direction and thrust of the campaign and leave the local country management to produce its own creatives.

Tools of the international communication mix

International public relations

International public relations differs from domestically related activities only in the sense that it seeks to build cultural, geographical and linguistic bridges between stakeholders outside the country of origin. As if to continue the foregoing debate, issues remain about whether to standardise communications or adapt them to meet local needs. One complication to this approach concerns the development and prevalence of trading blocs and the degree to which individuals within these blocs retain notions of national identity. This in turn will influence the relationships formed between stakeholder groups.

Wherever it is practised, public relations needs to be based on a willingness and propensity to share information, to be prepared to adjust one's own position in the light of feedback, to be ethical in one's own behaviour.

Packaging

Product packaging fulfils two main functions. One is to protect the product so that the customer can consume the product in pristine condition at all times. The second function concerns the marketing communication needs and their potential impact on the purchase decision process. Packaging, especially in consumer markets for purchase decisions that generate low levels of involvement, needs to be protective (due to possibly longer distribution chains and variations in temperature/climate) and be persuasive in such a way that it reinforces the positioning requirements and the other activities of the promotional mix. Research by Berg-Weitzel and van de Laar (2000) states quite emphatically that a nation's culture has repercussions for the design of its packaging and, if standardised packaging is decided on, then a neutral design should be pursued. If the decision is to adapt, then local aspects of design should be 'exploited to gain the consumer's confidence'. Colour, shape and language issues need to be carefully considered, regardless of whether the decision is to standardise or localise packaging design.

Colour, shape and language issues need to be carefully considered.

Trade shows and exhibitions

This is a much underestimated aspect of marketing communications, but it is of great significance in an international dimension. The benefits for organisations attending trade fairs are basically the same whether they be domestic or international events. What is significant, however, is that exhibitions are important, especially in the b2b market, for building and maintaining relationships with customers and members of the marketing channel (horizontally and vertically). In an international arena, where the cultural backgrounds of visitors and exhibitors may be very diverse, it is essential not only that attendance occurs, but that visibility is high and hospitality compatible with the local environment and those of other significant visitors.

Personal selling

Local customs, culture, language and product attribute determine that a localised approach to personal selling techniques and content is vital and that a standardised approach to selling across international markets is for the vast majority of organisations a non-starter. Having said that, an international sales effort can be organised and managed with a degree of standardisation. There are four main approaches that can be used, either in sequence or simultaneously, as conditions permit.

The first approach, mainly applicable for small organisations beginning to operate in international markets, enables them to use spare domestic capacity. They use a sales force that is based in the home market and that either has some international responsibilities or operates exclusively abroad. This requires the sales personnel not only to be fully conversant with the entire product range, but also to understand the countries, organisations and cultures in which they seek to operate. If only from a time and expense perspective, there are strong limitations to the extent to which this approach can be realistically expected to work.

A second approach requires the use of manufacturers' representatives and agents. These organisations provide local knowledge of both competitors and culture that can cut considerably the length of time necessary to enter a new market. However, there are problems associated with the commitment and bias of such agents and the level of control that management can retain. For example, agents are paid on a commission-only basis and their allegiance to a product/manufacturer is thin, such that their desire to sort out local problems of logistics, finance or product operation is questionable.

A third approach is to establish a marketing channel and appoint distributors and dealers in the target country/regions. This allows management a greater level of control, but it does incur greater levels of management time and commitment to the international trade channel and the associated training if the strategy is to be successful.

The fourth and final approach is to establish a dedicated sales force in each of the countries/regions. This is expensive, and although control is considerably improved it is an approach only adopted once a market presence has been well established.

International sponsorship

Sponsorship, whether it be in a domestic (Serie A football in Italy) or an international context (Olympics 2012), enables support of the public relations activity either by providing a means to meet key customers or members of the marketing channel in an informal way or by improving awareness and attitudes towards the sponsor. In addition, sponsorship has an impact on the quality of relationships with a variety of stakeholders. Relations with employees, governments and local communities can all be enhanced through understanding and sympathetic alignment with the sponsor's position regarding their social responsibilities, ethical stance and overall role as a corporate citizen (Owusu-Frimpong, 2000).

It is not surprising that the costs associated with sponsorship activities vary according to the scale (size and duration) of the activities and the size of the audience. Global brands need sponsorship on an international basis in order to reinforce their market presence and to support and reinforce the other aspects of the promotional mix. Integrated marketing communications in an international context needs to use advertising (to promote awareness and to reinforce brand values); public relations (to provide understanding, interest and goodwill); sponsorship (to be seen to be involved); and personal selling (to enable and drive customer action) if a brand is to be established.

The costs associated with sponsorship activities vary according to the scale of the activities and the size of the audience.

Direct marketing

Most of the points concerning domestic direct marketing apply equally on the international stage. It would appear that there are four main factors that need to be considered:

1. Language is an important factor as most people prefer to receive (and give) communications in their own, first language. The focus organisation needs to consider translation costs (including time), list availability and making judgements about tone, humour and, indeed, what the most appropriate language might be.
2. The second factor is media availability. There may be wide variation in the range and quality of the media in the country/regions in which it wishes to trade. The quality and effectiveness of the telephone and postal services, the coverage of cable and satellite channels, the significance of magazines and the readership of the national, regional and local press all need to be carefully considered when developing an international direct marketing campaign.
3. The third factor to consider is the quality and breadth of the services and infrastructure necessary to support an international campaign. The quality of mailing lists, databases and supporting agencies needs to be carefully reviewed before committing to an international DM campaign.
4. The quality of management control is the final international factor to be considered. Most campaigns of this nature need to be controlled centrally by the focus organisation and/or their direct marketing agency. This centralised approach is important in the light of the need for integration, control of costs and data management. There may be conditions that allow for the development of a decentralised approach whereby the planning and implementation of these direct campaigns are delegated to local management.

The role of the Internet

The Internet has an important role to play for those organisations considering internationalisation or those who have already achieved transnational status. Hamill and Gregory (1997) found that smaller organisations view the Internet as a tool to enable them to develop network communications, sales promotion and market intelligence activities.

The Internet provides global market access for all organisations and each needs a strategy to determine the role of its web site and how it will interact with the organisation's current, established distribution and communication strategies.

The Internet provides global market access for all organisations.

ViewPoint 28.5 Beat the international cravings

Pharmaceutical brands tend to be country-specific due mainly to cultural attitudes towards healthcare, medicine and related activities. Regulations also pose problems as they vary across countries and restrict what messages can and cannot be said. Therefore, the task of converting a pharmaceutical brand into a global entity requires lateral thinking, something that Nicorette undertook in their quest to be a billion dollar brand by 2010.

The answer lay in repositioning Nicorette as a consumer brand, one imbued with emotion rather than one that conveyed rational, information health-dominated messages. This meant that rather than convey messages about how Nicorette could help a smoker give up completely, messages were designed to support smokers through each cigarette not smoked and overcoming the cravings.

The creative instrument used across the campaign was 'Cravings Man' . A 2.5 metre cigarette with a face, legs and arms. Each ad showed a smoker literally beating the craving for a cigarette. This creative idea travelled across all countries as the same underlying feelings are experienced by all smokers (see Exhibit 28.2).

Source: Horry and Miller (2006).

Question

How might 'Cravings Man' be used in other tools and media?

Task

Find one of Nicorette's competitors and compare the basic messages they convey with Nicorette's.

Exhibit 28.2 The Nicorette Cravings Man
Image courtesy of The Advertising Archives.

International advertising agencies

Just as many organisations have sought to expand internationally, so many advertising agencies have attempted to grow with their clients. This process gathered speed in the 1980s and 1990s, with varying levels of success. By trying to mirror client/brand needs and by expanding operations over increased geographic areas, organisations have experienced many financial and management challenges. These challenges have been met with varying degrees of success. The consequences of this 'natural' development are that aspects such as the structure of the industry, the configuration and work patterns of constituent agencies, the relationships between clients and advertisers and the form of advertising messages that are developed and given meaning by target audiences and agencies alike have evolved.

Agency development overseas

Operating overseas is not a recent phenomenon for advertising agencies. This strategy has been established for many decades. There are three primary routes that agencies have taken to secure international growth. These are *organic growth* through the creation of overseas subsidiaries, *acquisitive growth* through the purchase of established indigenous agencies and finally *cooperative growth*, where agencies collaborate through the formation of networks and strategic alliances.

> There are three primary routes that agencies have taken to secure international growth.

Organic growth requires the setting up of subsidiary offices in selected regions or countries. Costs and management can be controlled, but the relatively slow speed of development has deterred many from this approach. *Acquisitive growth*, involving the merger with, or purchase of, advertising agencies already operating in the required market, is attractive because it is possible to use the skills and established contacts of local managers. However, these overseas operations are relatively inflexible and can incur considerable overheads as well as high initial purchase costs.

Cooperative growth through strategic alliances and partnerships, often as part of global networks, can appear to be a more flexible and efficient approach to meeting a client's international marketing communications requirements. One of the potential problems with this approach is that the level of control over local actions can be reduced, but the reduced costs and increased speed of set-up and delivery make this an attractive option. A further variation of this method of expansion is the formation of networks of independent agencies. By contributing to a central financial fund, thereby giving the network a formal legal status, agencies are able to work together and provide flexibility for their clients.

International agency networks can provide clients with a number of advantages. These focus primarily on two main areas: resource utilisation and communication effectiveness.

Resource utilisation

1. Clients and agencies help each other by avoiding costly duplication of message development work and media buying.
2. Economies of scale can reduce costs for both parties.
3. By centralising decision-making, management has increased control over the direction of campaigns and their implementation such that clients have a single main point of contact.
4. Special resources and scarce creative expertise are made available to a client globally.

Communication effectiveness

1. Creative ideas from all parts of the network can be shared and, if a largely adaptive strategy is followed, good ideas can be replicated elsewhere. Good creative ideas are rare, so by using an international agency these highly prized gems can be used to the client's benefit worldwide.

2. Internal communications are improved by a common infrastructure and management information system.
3. By using a single agency, operating across many markets, feedback and market analyses can be standardised (process, timing and format), thus facilitating common reporting and fast feedback of audience and competitor actions.

Freeman (1996) argues that, as manufacturers are re-evaluating the way in which they approach their customers, changes are also being brought about at business-to-business advertising agencies. Rapid technological advances in communications, global marketing of brands, shorter purchase decision-making cycles and heightened competition are forcing agencies to re-evaluate their internal organisation and communications strategies. This, he suggests, has already led to a number of mergers with larger organisations and internal reorganisation to better handle clients' needs.

These developments have impacted on the pitching process. When WPP agreed a deal to manage the Boots global account, the decision was made between Martin Sorrell and Steve Russell, the respective CEOs of the two organisations. The agenda, to create a unified brand and save money (White, 2000) is clear and understandable. However, the process by which the agreement was reached signalled some concern for other agencies. As a result of this 'boardroom' deal, many roster agencies (e.g. OMD) lost substantial billings and did not have an opportunity to defend their business, even though their client had, at marketing manager levels, been more than satisfied with the relationship.

Global and multinational advertising agencies work with a variety of clients generating high volumes and a broad variety of materials.

Global and multinational advertising agencies work with a variety of clients generating high volumes and a broad variety of materials (e.g. storyboards, design and copy for print advertisements, media plans). Traditional methods of communication, such as telephone and mail, are often slow and inefficient. Faster alternatives, such as overnight delivery and couriers, can become expensive as projects pass through multiple review cycles. Even email has limited application.

The use of web-based portals has been instrumental in improving communications and developing relationships. The development and use of portals has been important when measured in terms of time savings and cost reductions. However, there are a range of other benefits associated with the ease of use and maintenance of a wide range of documents. In addition, there is improved collaboration and link management facilities, which are regarded as an important factor when attempting to improve agency performance and reduce client turnover. As part of the process of enhancing client interaction, a number of features and benefits accrue to the user and their networks. These can be seen at Table 28.3.

Table 28.3 Features and benefits of using a portal within an advertising agency

Feature	Benefit
Content organisation	Workspace views, links to other web pages, and news updates.
Productivity tools	Secure, threaded discussions to foster and enhance collaboration; directories with phone listings; calendar functions; templates for campaign tracking.
Document routing and management	Expedites the review and approval process and improves workflow. This includes document version controls, distribution list maintenance, and automated notification agents to alert clients and account teams when new content is added or modifications are made to existing content.
Server architecture	A distributed architecture that allows several GEM servers to function as a single server. This brings increased scalability, improved load balancing and distribution, and a higher degree of reliability to the agency's portal environment.
Administrative functions	Activity audit trail reports, user profile maintenance, user definitions and access privileges, and default view definitions.

Source: Adapted from Kanda Software.

Table 28.4 Criteria for agency/client portals

Criteria	Explanation
Simplicity of creation and operation	Client portals need to be easy for the company's account teams. A template-based system can save time, reducing duplication of effort and bringing consistency to the construction and ongoing management of such sites.
Low maintenance	The system should have built-in capabilities to keep every portal site organised and running properly with minimal intervention.
Flexible and comprehensive	The system must accommodate graphical images, audio and video files, and common office documents. In addition, multilingual capability is required.
Solid security	The system requires security features that instil confidence in the agency clients and guarantee that unauthorised personnel cannot see or access documents or collaborative areas.
Powerful and accurate searching	With the large number of documents, these systems require a powerful search capability for both document content and meta data.

Source: Adapted from Kanda Software.

When the advertising agency Havas developed a b2b portal, five key criteria were identified. These are set out in Table 28.4. Havas claims its portal has increased efficiency and saved time and money. Turnaround times for client approval of creative work have been significantly reduced by as much as 50 per cent. The ability to manage global research and creative materials within the agency's network has improved dramatically, as has staff's willingness to share knowledge among account teams. As a result, account teams now have more time to focus on strategic planning and delivering greater value to their clients. The agency can now communicate rapidly and more efficiently with clients, giving both the agency and its clients an improved quality of interaction and a positive working relationship. Through the use of IST this case demonstrates the opportunities to improve agency/client relationships and reduce client turnover.

The ability to manage global research and creative materials within the agency's network has improved dramatically.

Agency growth

The expansion of advertising agencies away from domestic markets is essentially an investment decision in which normal return on investment criteria need to be determined. Such decisions can be based upon the relative size of competitive advantage that an expanded operation might generate. Multinational agencies (MNAs) might be able to develop key advantages, such as size, access to capital, the loyalty given to them by multinational advertisers, their knowledge and skill, and their ability to use their foreign locations to service regional markets (West, 1996). Some of the growth has been motivated by the need to meet the expanding international requirements of clients. Kim (1995) cites Procter & Gamble's entry into Eastern Europe and the subsequent opening of offices in the same area by its advertising agency, Leo Burnett. Anholt (2000) refers to Lintas' development on the back of Unilever's growth. Offensive and defensive business strategies, to either capitalise on or counter competitor moves, can also be regarded as prime motivating factors.

A further explanation lies with the motivations of individual managers, or agency theory. This perspective suggests that managers seek growth in order to fulfil personal needs rather than those that may be in the best interests of the organisation. These advantages nevertheless have little distinguishing power if the MNA itself is unable to coordinate its activities and lever its resources to provide its clients with the benefits of speed, creativity and media purchasing power.

Some implications of international growth

One of the current dilemmas facing clients and agencies is that through consolidation the number of agencies capable of, and interested in, international work is declining. At the same time, the volume of work available is expanding as a greater number of clients seek to develop internationally. Indeed, the work is fragmenting and hence the value of individual pieces of work is getting smaller. As Anholt (2000) states quite succinctly, 'Global clients are getting more numerous, smaller and spending less, as global agencies are getting fewer, bigger and charging more.' (p. 20) What this means is that something has to change, probably in the way agencies think and act towards global business opportunities and the way in which they implement strategies, and involving more local creative experience to satisfy client needs.

Many advertisers have been comfortable with the way in which advertising agencies have attempted to build European and international networks to complement their own global branding initiatives. There is some evidence, however, that this one-stop shopping approach is not entirely satisfactory (*The Economist*, 1996). Some client organisations want access to a range of creative teams and, at the same time, want the benefits of consolidation. The response of some MNAs has been to reorganise internally. Many of the mega-mergers between major agency networks have resulted in further structural changes as agencies shed accounts that cause conflicts of interest. Those clients caught up in the restructuring and consequent consolidation of the industry may well regard themselves as unwitting participants.

The creation of the position of worldwide account director (Farrell, 1996) was an attempt to coordinate and control the global accounts of clients such as IBM and Reebok, which had centralised their international advertising activities. Another role that emerged was that of the worldwide creative director (Davies, 1996). This position, it is suggested, developed directly from clients' expectations for their agency networks to mirror their own global branding drives and management structures. But, as Martin (1996) points out, as these worldwide creative directors are invariably appointed with no department or resources and are inclined to meet resistance from local management teams, the positions appear to be irrelevant and impotent.

Media planning has become increasingly difficult, as not only has the provision of media services in particular regions (e.g. Asia) expanded rapidly, but, at the same time, there have been major social changes. Kilburn (1996) reports that, in Taiwan, Ogilvy & Mather and J. Walter Thompson have formed The Media Partnership from their media-buying operations, thus providing increased buying power for their clients in what is effectively a fragmented market.

Agency structures are evolving and adapting to the needs of their environments.

Agency structures are evolving and adapting to the needs of their environments. The traditional perspective of control by head office executives over the work of local network agencies, either by a disproportionate level of standardisation policies or by rather inflexible procedures that put bureaucratic needs before market requirements, is changing. Instead of control, coordination is one of the keys to competitive advantage in MNA/agency relationships. The one factor that distinguishes transnational organisations applies equally to advertising agencies. As Banerjee (1994) suggests, agency decision-making concerning the development of major multi-country brands will need to be collaborative in the future as 'agency power structures evolve to better reflect emerging revenue geographies' (p. 112).

Stages of cross-border advertising development

Cho *et al.* (1994) propose a framework whereby the type of advertising deployed can be considered in the context of the stage of internationalisation that organisations have reached. Based on studies of Korean firms, the authors propose that the advertising strategy is (or should be) a direct reflection of the marketing and business strategies employed. Therefore:

Table 28.5 Strategies associated with international advertising development

	Home	International	Multinational	Global	Transnational
Advertising stage	Domestic	Export	Multinational	Global	Transnational
Key message	Product or corporate	Product and brand	Corporate and brand	Corporate and brand	Corporate and/or brand
Management	Standardisation	Standardisation	Standardisation and adaptation	Regional adaptation	Global adaptation
Management structure/support	Centralised	Centralised	Decentralised	Grouped centralisation	Network
Agency	Domestic	Domestic	Domestic and foreign local	Global	Transnational network

Domestic marketing = Domestic advertising
Export marketing = Export advertising
Multinational marketing = Multinational advertising
Global marketing = Global advertising

From this, and utilising the information about international development, it is possible to establish the key characteristics and strategies associated with each stage of international growth (see Table 28.5).

Summary

In order to help consolidate your understanding of using marketing communications across borders, here are the key points summarised against each of the learning objectives:

1. Consider the development and variety of organisations operating across international borders.

As organisations saturate domestic markets and seek growth opportunities overseas, so they meet new challenges and embark upon fresh strategies. Organisations operating across a number of international and/or regional borders evolve through international, multinational, global and transnational phases and forms. The differentiating characteristics appear pronounced and convincing as growth drivers impel development.

2. Examine the key variables affecting international marketing communications.

Two of the main variables that impact on the marketing communications deployed by organisations across these different forms are culture and the media. Culture is a composite of a number of elements, ranging from symbols such as language, groups and education, through values represented in language context and power distance.

The media are also significant drivers that have been influenced by both technological drivers and political initiatives to deregulate and open up accessibility.

3. Discuss the adaptation versus standardisation debate about marketing communications strategy.

The strategies used to communicate with cross border audiences focus on either standardisation or total adaptation to the needs of the local audience. While the debate is interesting and practice varied, the evidence suggests that a mixture of the two approaches, glocalisation, is the preferred practice of many global and transnational organisations.

4. Explore issues concerning the international communication mix.

Each of the tools and media play an important role within the communications mix, when deployed across borders. Local rules, regulations, customs and values can impact the effectiveness of a campaign, so it is important to consider cultural and media-based issues when deciding the balance of a mix and the tools and media to be used.

5. Explain the ways in which advertising agencies have developed to meet the international communication requirements of their clients.

Advertising agencies have had to respond to the initiatives driven by their clients. Global advertising agency development has taken a variety of forms; however, there appears to be a match between the marketing strategies pursued by client organisations and the consequent advertising strategies to support them.

Review questions

1. There are four types of cross-border organisation, reflecting their structure and disposition to their markets. Name them and their key characteristics.
2. Prepare some brief notes explaining how culture impacts on an organisation's marketing communications.
3. Select two countries of your choice. Compare the significance of cultural symbols and provide examples of how these are used.
4. Explain high- and low-context languages.
5. Discuss how deregulation of media ownership has affected marketing communications.
6. You have been asked to make a presentation to senior managers on the advantages and disadvantages of standardising the marketing messages delivered for your brand throughout the world. Prepare notes for each of the slides you will use.
7. Evaluate the different ways in which advertising agencies can grow.
8. International advertising agencies provide resource utilisation and communication effectiveness as their main advantages. Explain the detail associated with these two characteristics.
9. Determine the four stages of cross-border advertising development.
10. What are the key differences between each of these four stages?

MiniCase

Procter & Gamble and the ethnology of markets: adapting a giant to emerging markets

Stefan Schwarzkopf: Queen Mary College, University of London

Procter & Gamble (f. 1837) is a US-based global consumer goods company, which counts brands such as Ariel, Bounty, Braun, Crest, Duracell, Gillette, Hugo, Max Factor, Olay, Oral-B, Pampers and Tide among its worldwide portfolio of almost 100 brands. The company operates in over 80 countries worldwide and employs 138,000 people, who provide products and services to consumers in 180 countries. Procter & Gamble markets 300 household goods products to more than 5 billion consumers, which makes it the world's largest consumer goods company ahead of Unilever, L'Oréal, Colgate-Palmolive, Johnson & Johnson and Kraft Foods (Dyer *et al.*, 2004). This unique position brings with it unique difficulties in managing brands in global markets that are characterised by vast differences in income levels, languages and, not least, in consumer expectations and local cultures.

Over the past twenty years or so, Procter & Gamble's (P&G) marketing strategy had to negotiate its way in between the two extremes of adaptation and standardisation of product development and marketing communications. On the one hand, the sunk costs involved in such activities are far too great to risk entering a market without trying to blend the marketing offering carefully into the cultures of a target market. On the other hand, the economies of scale afforded by standardised products and communication campaigns are too important for the economic bottom-line of global companies such as P&G. But how does a company know where to draw the line between the imperatives of cultural adaptation and the need to maintain high levels of standardisation? And how does a company know which elements of the target country's culture are actually worth taking into account? Increasingly, global companies look to the exciting field of consumer anthropology as a way of bridging the gap between marketing theory and practice. Anthropology is often defined as the scientific study of the origins and behaviour of man. But for the anthropologist Clifford Geertz (1973), culture is at the heart of this fascinating science. Anthropology thus studies culture as a form of practice, which consists of a dense network of stories, symbols and behaviours. In order to understand fully that network, the anthropologist actually has to take part in that culture and live it together with those people who are at the heart of it.

P&G realised as far back as the late 1980s that traditional market research tools were often unable to deliver insights that would have allowed it to understand a foreign society in depth. Ever since P&G planned its market entry into China, the company has used consumer anthropological methodologies that helped make its products a part of Chinese consumers' everyday life. P&G had been interested in China as a market since the early 1980s and began to conduct market research in Beijing in 1985. It began operations in China in 1988, initially producing and marketing its Head & Shoulders product in the Guangzhou area. Unlike other Western companies, P&G recognised very early the importance of language for its success in the Chinese markets. In itself, the name 'Procter & Gamble' is as meaningless in Chinese as the word 'Xiaoping' would be for Western ears – it does not convey any idea of what the word signifies. Therefore, P&G translated its own name into Chinese as 'Baojie', which means 'precious and clean' and successfully encapsulated the company's brand values. Other P&G brands are marketed using similarly careful translations, like 'Fafeisi' (Head & Shoulders), 'Panting' (Pantene) and 'Jilie' (Gillette).

Moreover, during the late 1990s, P&G sent out its product managers to actually live with Chinese families in their homes and observe housewives' behaviour. In their observations, the product managers began to realise fully, for example, that the central unit for much of the consumer decision-making in China was the collective (family) and not the individual, and whereas in the United States the kitchen is the centre of family activity, in most Chinese homes it is the living room. They also noted that the US obsession with whiteness and brightness as an outcome of the laundering process was not necessarily shared by all Chinese consumers, among whom a sense of 'normal' cleanliness prevailed. The Western obsession with cleanliness and the taboo of body fluids was not necessarily shared either: while Chinese people care a lot about the appearance and the health of their hair and teeth, even today, the use of antiperspirants/deodorants to 'combat' sweat is minimal. P&G now celebrates its twentieth year of operations in China, but it took the company at least 10 years to realise that not all Asian skin is the same. While its SK II face cream, for example, had been tested among hundreds of Japanese women without complications, a number of Chinese consumers showed adverse reactions.

This example shows that P&G's activities in China were not always a success story. Being part of the North American/European cultural hemisphere, P&G assumed, for example, that straightforward competitive messages on posters would convince Chinese consumers that its products provided better value than those of the competition. This, however, resulted in a clamp-down by the government in 1996 and some P&G posters were banned for making unfair comparisons (Gao, 2003). P&G had to learn that while Chinese street-peddlers and shopkeepers can be quite pushy in their sales efforts, posters are seen as part of a semi-official public sphere and are, therefore, expected to show restraint and dignity. Even more trouble lay ahead: after numerous problems with its SK II cosmetics brand in 2005 and 2006, the company decided to offer a refund to consumers who had purchased its face creams. However, instead of simply generously refunding consumers, P&G made consumers sign waivers stating that they recognised the products presented no harmful effects. Shaun Rein of the China Market Research Group compared this to the typical 'lawyerly' response of US companies. In China, this action caused outrage, as consumers felt mistreated (Rein, 2006). Thousands of Chinese rushed to voice their anger on the Internet and, at some point, the doors of Shanghai's P&G office were smashed by a mob of angry consumers.

P&G had to learn the hard way that in a family-based society, which is still largely ruled by *guanxi* and *renqing* (i.e., personal relationships and the moral obligation to invest in them) trust is an extremely rare commodity, which can be taken away by consumers at the drop of a hat – with sometimes devastating long-term effects, especially for Western companies, which had to work twice as hard to gain that trust in the first place.

MiniCase references

Dyer, D., Davis, D., Dalzell, F. and Olegario, R. (2004) *Rising Tide: Lessons from 165 Years of Brand Building at Procter & Gamble*. Cambridge, MA: Harvard Business School Press.

Gao, Z. (2003) The future of foreign advertising in China: the lessons of history. In *Advertising and Society Review*, 4(1). Retrieved from http://muse.jhu.edu/journals/asr/v004/4.1gao.html.

Geertz, C. (1973) *The Interpretation of Cultures*. Basic Books: New York. Retrieved 1 March 2008 from http://www.pg.com.cn/.

Rein, S. (2006) Procter & Gamble's China problem: the return of SK II. In *Seeking Alpha*, 9 November 2006. Retrieved http://seekingalpha.com/article/20248-procter-gamble-s-china-problem-the-return-of-sk-ii.

MiniCase questions

1. What do you think are the limits of anthropological methods in marketing research?
2. Discuss marketing communications tools that P&G can use in order to regain Chinese consumers' trust in their SK II cosmetics brand.
3. What are the social forces that shape the marketing ethical environment within which P&G operates in China? How do you think they are going to change over the coming 20 years?

References

Anon. (2004) Apple Computer: iPod Silhouettes, *New York American Marketing Association*, Effie Awards. Retrieved 12 Februray 2006 from www.nyama.org.

Anholt, S. (2000) Updating the international advertising model. *Admap* (June), 18–21.

Banerjee, A. (1994) Transnational advertising development and management: an account planning approach and a process framework. *International Journal of Advertising*, **13**, 95–124.

Bartlett, C. and Ghoshal, S. (1991) *Managing Across Borders: The Transnational Solution*. Cambridge, MA: Harvard Business School Press.

Berg-Weitzel, van den, L. and Laar, R. van de (2000) Local or global packaging. *Admap* (June), 22–5.

Bold, B. (2000) Unlocking the global market. *PR Week*, 11 August, 13–14.

Buzzell, R. (1968) Can you standardise multinational marketing? *Harvard Business Review*, **46** (November/December), 102–13.

Cho, D.-S., Choi, J. and Yi, Y. (1994) International advertising strategies by NIC multinationals: the case of a Korean firm. *International Journal of Advertising*, **13**, 77–92.

Davies, J. (1996) The rise of the super-creative. *Campaign*, 1 November, 18.

Davies, J. (2000) Euroman: warrior or wimp? *Campaign*, 15 October, 39.

Delner, N. (1994) Religious contrast in consumer decision behaviour patterns: their dimensions and marketing implications. *European Journal of Marketing*, **28**(5), 36–53.

Economist, The (1996) A passion for variety. *The Economist*, 30 November, 68–71.

Farrell, G. (1996) Suits: the world is their ad oyster. *Adweek*, **37**(8), 29–33.

Fielding, S. (2000) Developing global brands in Asia. *Admap* (June), 26–9.

Frazer, C.F. and Sheehan, K.B. (2002) Advertising strategy and effective advertising comparing the USA and Australia. *Journal of Marketing Communications*, **8**, 149–64.

Freeman, L. (1996) Client-driven change alters agency strategies. *Advertising Age – Business Marketing*, **81**(2), 1–20.

Griffin, T. (1993) *International Marketing Communications*. London: Butterworth-Heinemann.

Hamill, J. and Gregory, K. (1997) Internet marketing in the internationalisation of UK SMEs. *Journal of Marketing Management*, **13**, 9–28.

Harris, G. (1996) International advertising: developmental and implementational issues. *Journal of Marketing Management*, **12**, 551–60.

Hickson, D.J. and Pugh, D.S. (1995) *Management Worldwide*. London: Penguin.

Hite, R.E. and Fraser, C. (1988) International advertising strategies of multinational corporations. *Journal of Advertising Research*, **28** (August/September), 9–17.

Hofstede, G. (1980) *Culture's Consequences: International Differences in Work Related Values*. Thousand Oaks, CA: Sage.

Hofstede, G. (1991) *Cultures and Organisations*. London: McGraw-Hill.

Hofstede, G., Neuijen, B., Ohayv, D.D. and Sanders, G. (1990) Measuring organisational cultures: a qualitative and quantitative study across twenty cases. *Administrative Science Quarterly*, **35**(2), 286–316.

Horry, T. and Miller, J. (2006) Sold not dispensed – the power of consumer brands vs pharmaceutical brands, *Advertising Works* **15**, 333–4. Henley: NTC Publications.

Kaplan, R. (1994) Ad agencies take on the world. *International Management* (April), 50–2.

Keegan, W.J. (1989) *Global Marketing Management*. Englewood Cliffs, NJ: Prentice-Hall.

Kilburn, D. (1996) Asia rising. *Adweek*, **37**(34), 22–6.

Kim, K.K. (1995) Spreading the net: the consolidation process of large transnational advertising agencies in the 1980s and early 1990s. *International Journal of Advertising*, **14**, 195–217.

Laurance, B. (2007) Unilever learns to join the dots. *Sunday Times*, 18 March, 11.

Levitt, T. (1983) The globalization of markets. *Harvard Business Review* (May/June), 92–102.

Martin, M. (1996) How essential is the role of a worldwide creative director? *Campaign*, 9 February, 45.

Mooij, M. de (1994) *Advertising Worldwide*. Hemel Hempstead: Prentice-Hall.

Mueller, B. (1991) An analysis of information content in standardised vs. specialised multinational advertisements. *Journal of International Business Studies* (First Quarter), 23–39.

Okazaki, S. and Alonso, J. (2003) Right messages for the right site: online creative strategies by Japanese multinational corporations. *Journal of Marketing Communications*, **9**, 221–39.

Owusu-Frimpong, N. (2000) The theory and practice of sponsorship in international marketing communications. In *The Handbook of International Marketing Communications* (ed. S.O. Moyne). Oxford: Blackwell.

(Sennett, in Kaplan, 1994).

West, D.C. (1996) The determinants and consequences of multinational advertising agencies. *International Journal of Advertising*, **15**(2), 128–39.

White, J. (2000) Can agencies survive clients' global expansion? *Campaign*, 27 October, 24.

Zandpour, F. and Harich, K. (1996) Think and feel country clusters: a new approach to international advertising standardization. *International Journal of Advertising*, **15**, 325–44.

Chapter 29

Business-to-business marketing communications

Organisations have many reasons to enter into exchange relationships with one another, rather than with consumers. This is referred to as the business-to-business sector and marketing communications needs to reflect the characteristics of the buyer behaviour inherent in these relationships. Effective communications are important in helping to build long-term relationships, closer levels of collaboration and cooperative behaviours, and help secure some advantage in the market system.

Aims and learning objectives

The aims of this chapter are to introduce and explore business-to-business marketing communications and to consider the factors that influence and shape relationships between organisations.

The learning objectives of this chapter are to:

1. establish the principle characteristics of the b2b sector;
2. understand the concepts of networks and interorganisational relationships;
3. explore the key dynamics of b2b and interorganisational communications;
4. consider ecommerce and its impact on communications;
5. explore the main characteristics and issues relating to the b2b communication mix;
6. examine issues related to strategic account management.

For an applied interpretation see Jeremy Miles' MiniCase entitled ***Educating the educators about asbestos*** at the end of this chapter.

Introduction

The characteristics of the business-to-business market are very different from those of the consumer market. The larger size of markets, the lower number of customers, the high average spend per customer, the wider geographic spread and the relatively complex nature of buyer behaviour are significant differences. Of all of these factors, it is the buyer behaviour element that is the primary distinguishing element, and the one that impacts most on marketing communications. It should not be surprising therefore that the marketing communications in these two major sectors are very different.

The commercial b2b sector is made up of four main subsectors, all of which share common buyer behaviour characteristics and communication needs, i.e. goods/services for:

- *Own consumption* – vending machines, office furniture, stationery.
- *Incorporation and assembly* – materials and supplies necessary for the production of your products and services. The identity of the materials can be lost within the larger product. These organisations are sometimes referred to as original equipment manufacturers.
- *Resale to another organisation* – acting as a member of a marketing channel, perhaps taking ownership and possession, adding value before passing the products on to another organisation that will add value to it in some way.
- *Retail* – the most common example, where goods and services are sold to end-user consumers.

In all of the situations, organisations are involved in the buying of products, and only in the last situation are consumers at all involved. Therefore, the nature and form of the cooperation and the interorganisational relationships that develop from the exchanges influence the nature of the marketing communication activities used. The degree of cooperation between organisations will vary and part of the role of marketing communications is to develop and support the relationships that exist between partner organisations.

The degree of cooperation between organisations will vary and part of the role of marketing communications is to develop and support the relationships that exist between partner organisations.

In this sector, organisations buy products and services and they use processes and procedures that can involve a large number of people. Fuller details about these characteristics can be found in Chapter 6. What is central, however, is the decision-making unit and the complexities associated with the variety of people and processes involved in making organisational purchase decisions and the implications for suppliers in terms of the length of time, and nature of the communications mix and messages necessary to reduce the levels of risk inherent in these situations. Mitchell (1999) refers to Haakansson and Wootz (1979), who identified need, transaction and market uncertainties, and Valla (1982) who suggested that there are five categories of risk that must be addressed by buyers and suppliers. From these it is possible to identify seven types of risk that are relevant to organisational buyers. These are shown in Table 29.1.

Personal selling is very important in b2b markets, often because of the need to help build relationships with members of buying centres and the need to demonstrate and explain technicalities associated with the products and services being marketed. In support of the personal selling effort (and exhibitions), trade promotions, trade advertising, direct marketing and public relations all play important roles (see Exhibit 29.1 for an example of b2b advertising). Increasingly, the Internet provides not only new direct routes to customers and intermediaries but also a vibrant new communications medium.

Personal selling is very important in b2b markets.

Table 29.1 Seven types of organisational decision-making risk

Risk type	Explanation
Technical risk	Will the parts, equipment or product/service perform as expected?
Financial risk	Does this represent value for money? Could we have bought cheaper?
Delivery risk	Will delivery be on time, complete and in good order? Will our production schedule be disrupted?
Service risk	Will the equipment be supported properly and within agreed time parameters?
Personal risk	Am I comfortable dealing with this organisation? Are my own social and ego needs threatened?
Relationship risk	To what extent is the long-term relationship with this organisation likely to be jeopardised by this decision?
Professional risk	How will this decision affect my professional standing in the eyes of others and how might my career and personal development be affected?

Networks and interorganisational relationships

The strategic value of marketing channels, partnerships and alliances and business networks has become increasingly more significant in recent years. As channel networks have developed so has their complexity, which impacts on the marketing communications strategies and tools used to help reach these customers, partners and fellow intermediaries. The expectations of buyers in these networks have risen in parallel with the significance attached to them by manufacturers. The power of multiple retailers, such as Curry's, Comet, Boots and Superdrug, is such that they are able to dictate terms (including the marketing communications) to many manufacturers of branded goods. For example, many consumer-related sales promotion events are prompted by retailers in response to claims for shelf space and in-store visibility.

The basic structure of any network consists of an organisation that is tied with a number of other functionally specialised organisations. The network uses collaborative exchanges to regularise and sustain cooperative activities. This is a general view and it is recognised that there is a variety of network forms. However, to repeat an important point, it is necessary to distinguish the type of networks to which an organisation belongs from traditional perspectives, if only because it is now generally accepted that all organisations are networks in their own right, and that there is a variety of internal and external networks to which all organisations belong.

Therefore, network organisations can be distinguished from traditional organisational forms because the exchanges are based on membership, which encourages mutually determined relational transactions. This long-term perspective reflects the density, closeness and shared values that such networks seek to perpetuate.

Many commentators have observed that organisations are forging relationships with other organisations, which are based around a network in order to achieve new, fresh advantages. These advantages may be driven by competitive goals, but the behaviour exhibited is increasingly cooperative. These networks vary in the strength of their ties (degrees of interconnectedness), but success can be seen to be a function of the partnerships that are developed in these networks. A key question has to be, what determines a successful partnership and how is success characterised and replicated? An underlying principle of relational exchanges is the pivotal role of trust and commitment (Morgan and Hunt, 1994) (see Figure 29.1).

An underlying principle of relational exchanges is the pivotal role of trust and commitment.

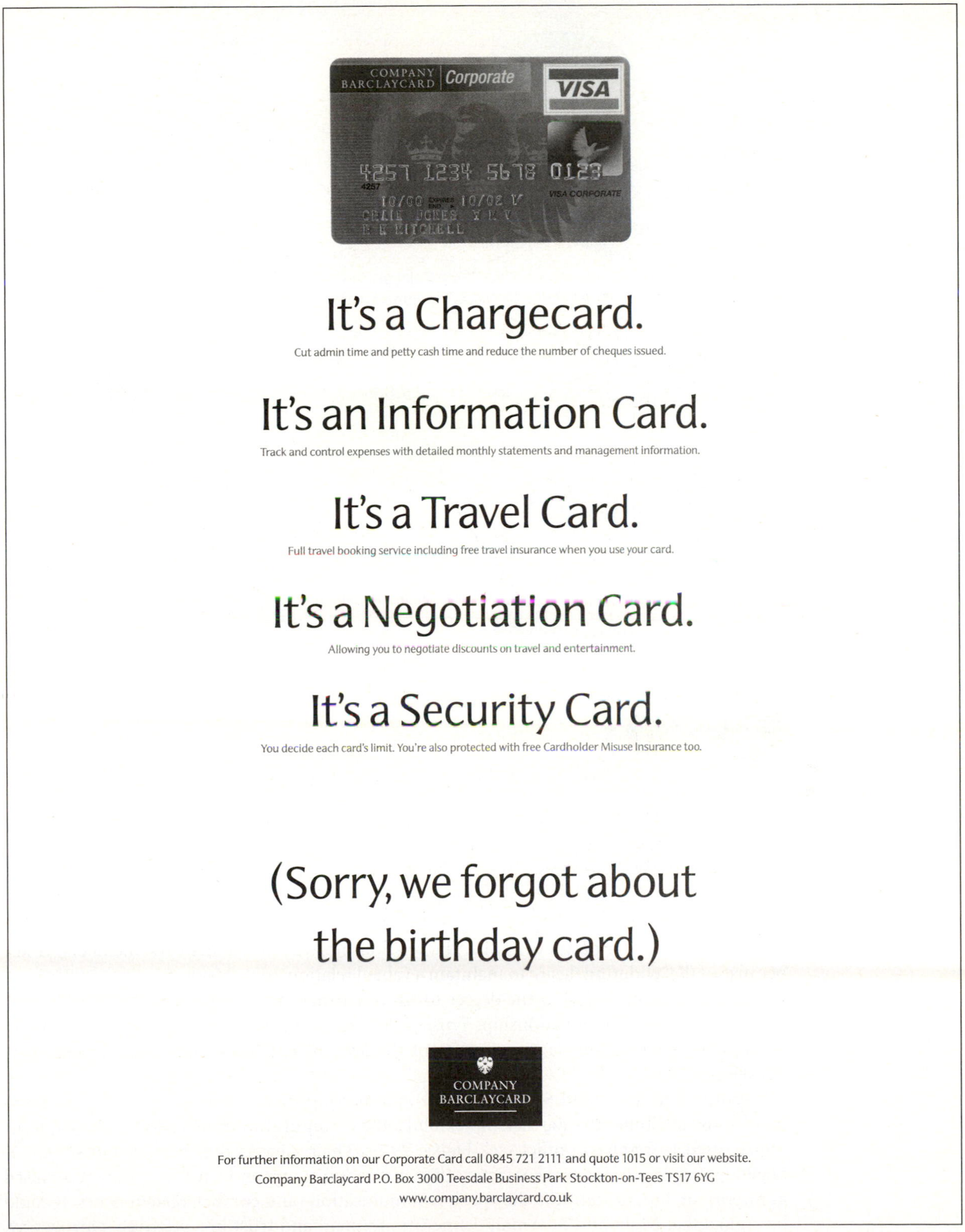
COMPANY BARCLAYCARD
Corporate
VISA
4257 1234 5678 0123
VISA CORPORATE
It's a Chargecard.
Cut admin time and petty cash time and reduce the number of cheques issued.
It's an Information Card.
Track and control expenses with detailed monthly statements and management information.
It's a Travel Card.
Full travel booking service including free travel insurance when you use your card.
It's a Negotiation Card.
Allowing you to negotiate discounts on travel and entertainment.
It's a Security Card.
You decide each card's limit. You're also protected with free Cardholder Misuse Insurance too.
(Sorry, we forgot about the birthday card.)
COMPANY BARCLAYCARD
For further information on our Corporate Card call 0845 721 2111 and quote 1015 or visit our website.
Company Barclaycard P.O. Box 3000 Teesdale Business Park Stockton-on-Tees TS17 6YG
www.company.barclaycard.co.uk

Exhibit 29.1 Company Barclaycard (this advertisement is pre-April 2004)
An example of B2B advertising.
Advertisement reproduced with the kind permission of Barclaycard.

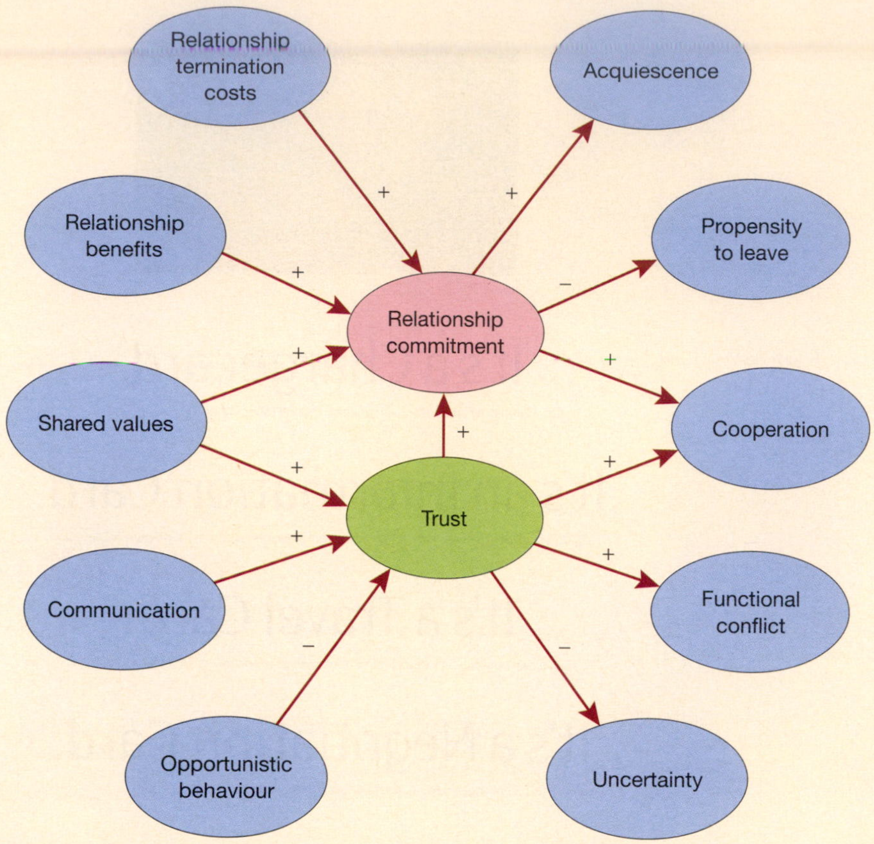

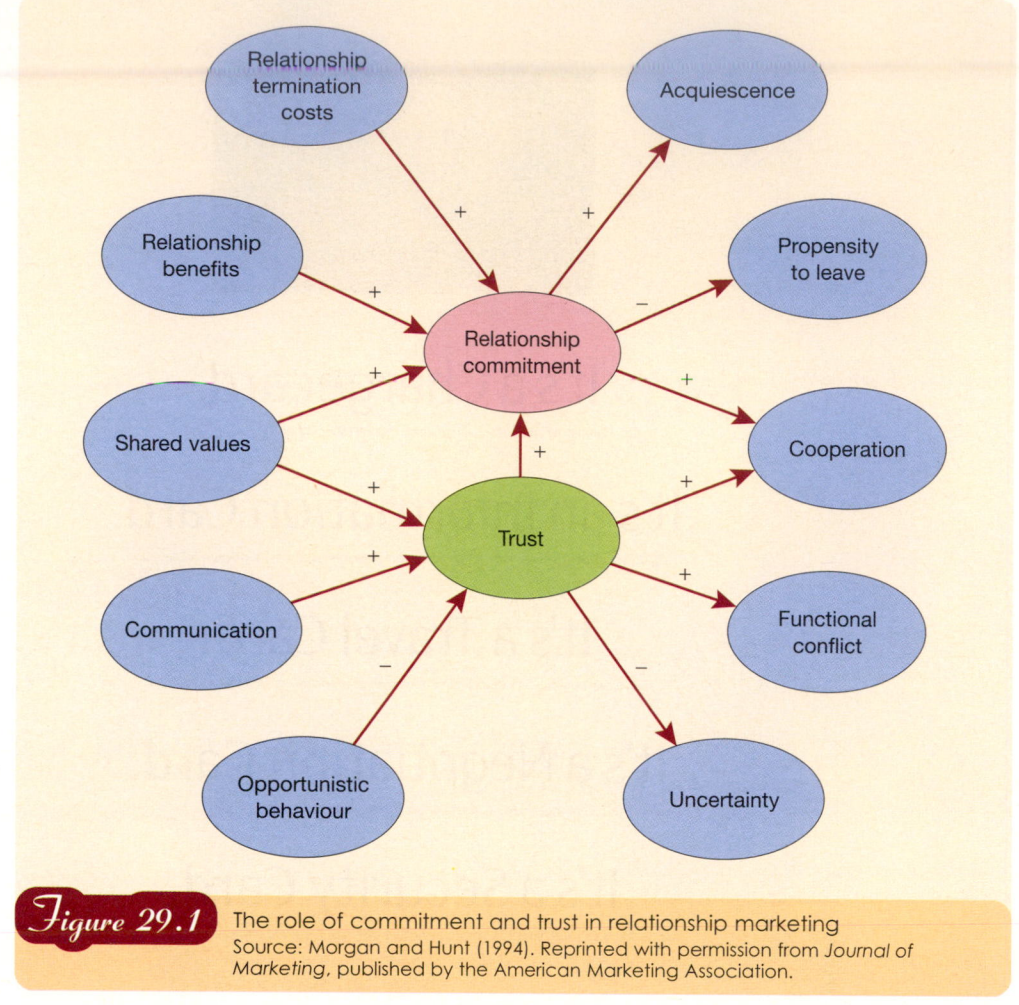

Figure 29.1 The role of commitment and trust in relationship marketing
Source: Morgan and Hunt (1994). Reprinted with permission from *Journal of Marketing*, published by the American Marketing Association.

Commitment to a partnership, i.e. the relationship with other network members, is key because of the 'enduring desire to maintain a valued relationship' (Moorman *et al.*, 1992: 316). Of comparable importance is the degree to which partners are confident that each will act in the best interests of the relationship. *Trust*, therefore, is also regarded as a key aspect of collaborative exchanges and is a composite of the level of reliability and integrity that exists between partners.

According to Mohr and Spekman (1994), partnership success is based on three key parameters: the attributes the partnership exhibits; the communication behaviour; and the techniques used to resolve conflict (see Figure 29.2). Their view is that partnership success is dependent upon a wider array of factors than just commitment and trust. These are recognised as important, but, in addition, they posit communication- and conflict-related issues. It could be argued that Mohr and Spekman define commitment and trust in a relatively narrow way, such that the other factors need to be made explicit. What is important, however, is that these authors state unequivocally that communication problems are associated with a lack of partnership success and that communication might be interpreted as an overt manifestation of more subtle phenomena, such as trust and commitment.

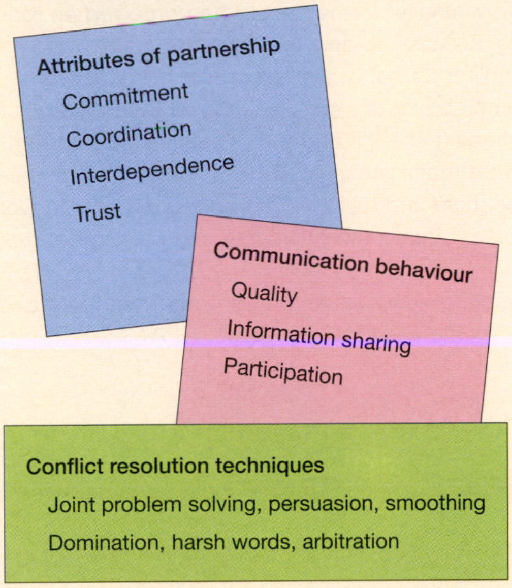

Figure 29.2 Characteristics of partnership success
Source: Mohr and Spekman (1994).

B2b communications

Effective communication is key to the satisfaction of buyer expectations and is the main link between an organisation and its environment. Indeed, the systems used to transfer information and meaning from people and machines, in both inter- and intraorganisational contexts, can advance or hinder the implementation of corporate and operational strategies. If the dynamics of an organisation are to be understood, for example, in order that effective and appropriate strategic change processes can be developed, then all its communication systems and networks need to be appreciated.

What are their communication requirements in the light of the objectives that have been set, and more importantly what are their communication expectations? Once these have been considered, it is possible to think about the communication strategies that may be best suited to achieving these goals and then determine the means by which strategies will be implemented.

ViewPoint 29.1 'Lloyds List' changes identity

Lloyds List is a daily newspaper that serves the maritime and transport market. It was first published in 1734 as a broadsheet newspaper and has become the leading paper of its kind. However, the paper was in danger of losing its place in the market because it was perceived as too traditional and not contemporary, especially as all of its competitors publish as a tabloid-sized paper.

Reader research showed that broadsheet-sized papers are perceived to be intellectual and 'high brow' so when the decision was made to switch to a Berliner format it was important to make the transition without alienating some of its current readers who might be regarded as 'old school traditionalists'.

Research also revealed that a move to a smaller format would be perceived as reducing the news content. Messages were developed informing business readers that there would be more pages and more news. It was also decided not to refer to the Berliner format but to a 'compact broadsheet'.

Direct mail was used prior to the relaunch and ads were placed in all the industry's leading titles informing and reassuring audiences of the impending change and the benefits it would bring.

The launch was timed to coincide with a major shipping show in Oslo with the sales team able to give out actual copies so customers could see, hold and feel the 'compact broadsheet'. Contact details for new users were collected and the telesales team offered them five free samples to get them to experience the paper.

During the six months since the relaunch, renewal rates are up 4 per cent, paid circulation figures went up over 8 per cent and advertising business increased 38 per cent.

Source: Anon. (2008).

Question

Using the DRIP format considered in Chapter 1, which elements could be considered to be working in this example?

Task

Find two other newspapers with a Berliner format and compare them to tabloid papers.

Gilliland and Johnston (1997) published a model of b2b marketing communication effects, which has been reproduced as Figure 29.3. In this model, the buy task involvement (BTI) represents the degree to which individual members of the DMU feel personal relevance (involvement) with each purchase decision. Gilliland and Johnston identify four main elements that can impact on an individual's level of personal involvement, as set out in Table 29.2.

The model then follows a similar path to the elaboration likelihood model, which is explained in a consumer market context in Chapter 8. Essentially, those involved with the purchase decision will process information via the central route, and will be more attentive to well-argued messages and look for rational, logical information in order to support their decision. Those less involved will use the peripheral route and not pay attention to the arguments or information provided. So for this group it will be the design and layout of the advertisement or the attractiveness of the expert sources used that will determine whether there is a change in attitude. Attitude change through the central route tends to be longer lasting than attitude change through peripheral cues.

The authors of this model also recognise that there are political dynamics associated with the roles each member of the DMU adopts. Indeed, there will be a degree of intergroup persuasion according to the degree of affiliation or identification with the products and brands being considered. The more positive the association and the higher the BTI, the more likely an individual will be to engage in behaviour that will seek more information and attempt to influence others.

The significance of this model is that it highlights the importance of emotion and feeling in b2b advertising messages. For a long time the focus of this work has been on producing information advertisements that present product-related information. This will be an effective appeal to those who have a higher BTI. However, there are many others involved with purchase decisions who have a low BTI, but who may have a significant input to the decision process. There are also implications for the media schedule, with more reason to use television and consumer print media in particular.

For a long time the focus of this work has been on producing information advertisements that present product-related information.

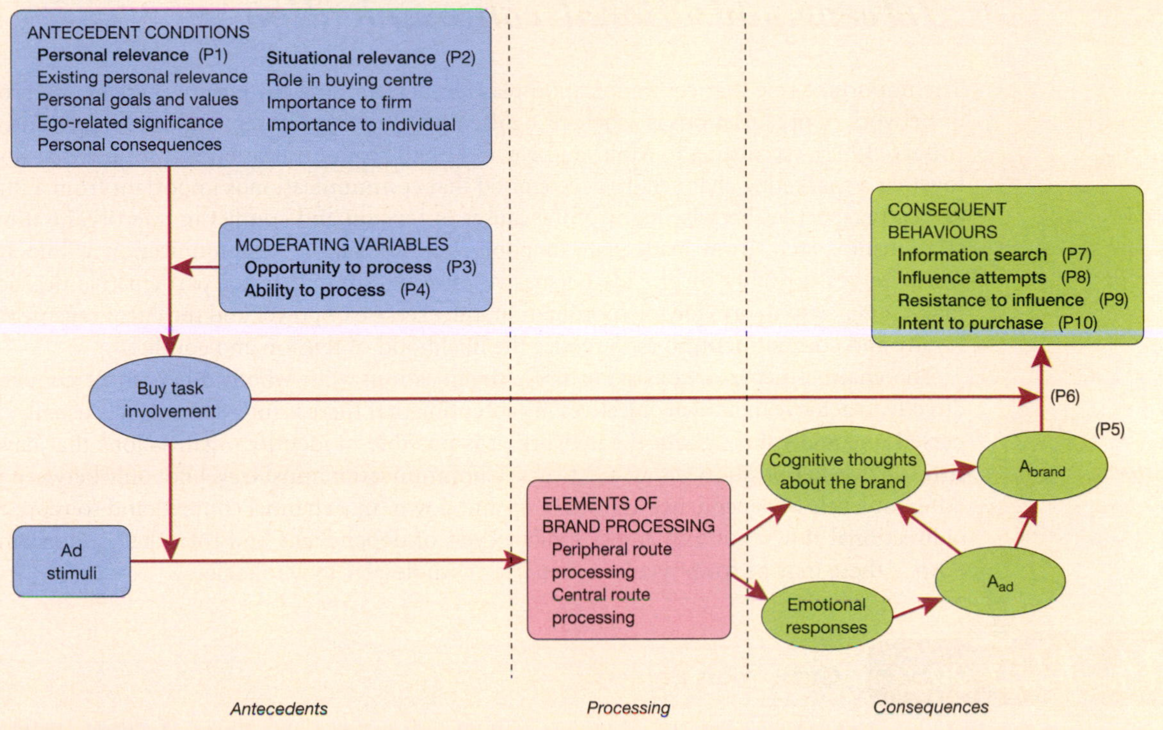

Figure 29.3 Model of business-to-business marketing communications
Source: Gilliland and Johnston (1997). Used with kind permission.

Table 29.2 The antecedents associated with BTI

Relevance factor	Explanation
Personal	Refers to personal goals, any ego-related significance and the perceived personal consequences of the purchase decision. The higher the personal relevance, the higher the BTI.
Situational	Refers to the importance of the decision to the individual and to the firm. The higher the situational relevance, the higher the BTI.
Opportunity to process	Refers to the level of distractions and noise that might impede exposure or prevent comprehension of a marketing message. The higher the number of opportunities to process information, the higher the BTI.
Ability to process	Refers to the knowledge an individual has about the product under consideration as the more the individual knows, the greater their ability to process information about it. The greater the ability to process information, the higher the BTI.

Source: Adapted from Gilliland and Johnston (1997). Used with kind permission.

Interorganisational communication

The important role that communication plays in determining the effectiveness of any group or network of organisations is widely recognised (Grabner and Rosenberg, 1969; Stern and El-Ansary, 1992). According to Mohr and Nevin (1990), communication is 'the glue that holds together a marketing channel'. It is recognised that communication is important from a managerial perspective, because many of the causes of tension and conflict in interorganisational relationships stem from inadequate or poor communication. Communication within networks serves not only to provide persuasive information and foster participative decision-making, but also to provide for coordination, the exercise of power and the encouragement of loyalty and commitment, so as to reduce the likelihood of tension and conflict.

The channel network consists of those organisations with whom others must cooperate directly to achieve their own objectives. By accepting that there is interdependence, usually dispersed unequally throughout the network, it is possible to identify organisations that have a stronger/weaker position within a network. Communication must travel not only between the different levels of dependence and role ('up and down' in a channel context) and so represent bidirectional flows, but also across similar levels of dependence and role, that is, horizontal flows – these may be from retailer to retailer or wholesaler to wholesaler.

ViewPoint 29.2 Grass-roots dealers

John Deere manufacture a range of quality lawn mowers and reach their customers through a well-established and valued dealer network. However, research showed that although the brand was strongly admired, only 40 per cent of consumers (those who wanted professionally specified equipment) ever thought of buying a John Deere machine. It was also found that women influenced 80 per cent of these types of purchases and that they were more likely to visit a mass retailer site than an out-of-town garden equipment dealer.

In order to reach the mass market, John Deere not only featured more women in their marketing communications, but they also entered into an agreement with Home Depot. Unlike the dealers who offered the full range, Home Depot just ran the entry level '100 range' of John Deere equipment. Each store was then paired with a local dealer who carries out the presales checks and all the servicing. The dealer was rewarded financially through each Home Depot sale.

It is also possible to buy John Deere equipment direct through the Internet. However, as a means of protecting the dealer network, and in order to provide important customer support and servicing, all machines purchased directly are delivered and supported by a local dealer. John Deere's marketing communications needs to work with the dealers, Home Depot, as well as with target market consumers.

Question

What do you consider would be the key goals for John Deere's marketing communications?

Task

Find a competitor to John Deere (or similar manufacturer in another country). What do you think are the key differences in their marketing communications?

Communication flows do not change radically over the short term.

There are some specialised messages that need to be distributed across a variety of networks, for example messages proclaiming technological advances, business acquisitions and contracts won. It is also apparent that communication flows do not change radically over the short term. On the contrary, they become established and regularised through use. This allows for the emergence of specialised communication networks (Chapter 2). Furthermore, it is common for networks to be composed of subnetworks, overlaying each other. The complexity of an organisation's networks is such that unravelling each one would be dysfunctional.

What is necessary is the establishment of those elements that contribute to the general communications in a b2b situation, and a marketing channel environment in particular. The development of a planned, channel-oriented communications strategy, a push strategy, should be based on identifiable elements that contribute to, and reinforce, the partnerships in the network. A number of these can be identified, namely a consideration of the movement of flows of information and, in particular, the timing and permanence of the flows (Stern and El-Ansary, 1992). It should also take into account the various facets of communication and the particular channel structures through which communications are intended to move (Mohr and Nevin, 1990). These will now be considered in turn.

Timing of the flows

Message flows can be either simultaneous or serial. Where *simultaneous* flows occur, messages are distributed to all members so that the information is received at approximately the same time. Business seminars and dealer meetings, together with direct mail promotional activities and the use of integrated IT systems between levels (overnight ordering procedures), are examples of this type of flow. *Serial* flows involve the transmission of messages so that they are received by a preselected number of network members who then transmit the message to others at lower levels within the network. Serial flows may lead to problems concerning the management of the network, such as those concerning stock levels and production.

Message flows can be either simultaneous or serial.

Permanence of the flows

The degree of permanence that a message has is determined by the technology used in the communication process. Essentially, the more a message can be recalled without physical distortion of the content, the more permanent the flow. This would indicate that the use of machines to record the message content would have an advantage over person-to-person messages transmitted at a sales meeting. Permanence can be improved by recording the meeting with a tape recorder or by putting the conversation on paper and using handouts and sales literature.

Essentially, the more a message can be recalled without physical distortion of the content, the more permanent the flow.

Mohr and Nevin (1990) suggest that the performance outcomes of a channel network are a result of the interaction of the communications strategy used within a network and the structure of the channel within which the communications flow. Figure 29.4 depicts the relationships between strategies and structure. Therefore, by examining the constituent elements and moulding the variables to meet the channel conditions, it may be possible to enhance the performance/success of the network.

Communication facets

Communication strategy results from a combination of four facets of communication: the frequency, direction, modality and content of communications.

Frequency

The amount of contact between members of the performance network needs to be assessed. Too much information (too frequent, aggregate volume or pure repetition) can overload members and have a dysfunctional effect. Too little information can undermine the opportunities for favourable performance outcomes by failing to provide necessary operational

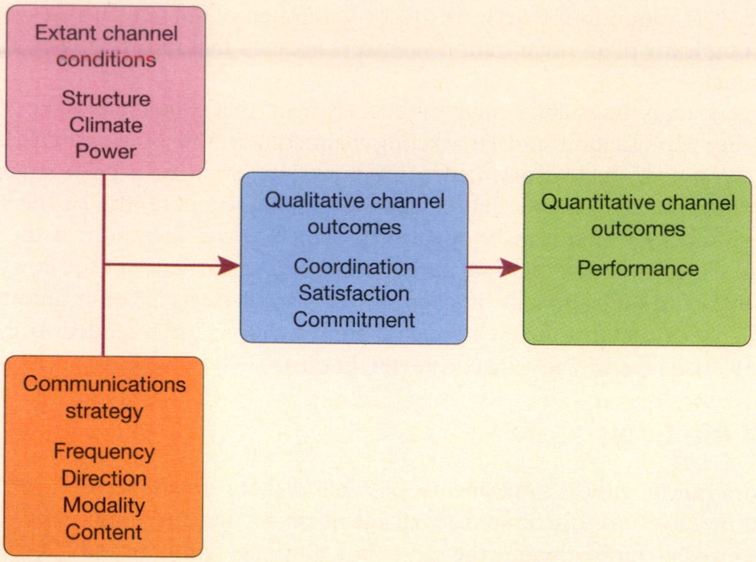

Figure 29.4 A model of communication for marketing channels
Source: After Mohr and Nevin (1990). Used with kind permission of the American Marketing Association.

It is important to identify the current volume of information being provided

information, motivation and support. As a consequence, it is important to identify the current volume of information being provided and for management to make a judgement about the desired levels of communication.

Direction

This refers to the horizontal and vertical movement of communication within a network. Each network consists of members who are dependent on others, but the level of dependence will vary, hence, the dispersion of power is unequal.

Communications can be unidirectional in that they flow in one direction only. This may be from a source of power to subordinate members (for example, from a major food retailer such as Sainsbury's or Tesco to small food manufacturers). Communications can also be bidirectional, that is, to and from powerful organisations. The relative power positions of manufacturer/producer and reseller need to be established and understood prior to the creation of any communication plan.

Modality

Modality refers to the method used to transmit information. Mohr and Nevin agree that there is a wide variety of interpretations of the methods used to convey information. They use modality in the sense that communications can be either formal and regulated, such as meetings and written reports, or informal and spontaneous, such as corridor conversations and word-of-mouth communications, often carried out away from an organisation's formal structures and environment.

Content

Direct strategies are designed to change behaviour by specific request.

This refers to what is said. Frazier and Summers (1984) distinguish between direct and indirect influence strategies. Direct strategies are designed to change behaviour by specific request (recommendations, promises and appeals to legal obligations). Indirect strategies attempt to change a receiver's beliefs and attitudes about the desirability of the intended behaviour. This may take the form of an information exchange, where the source uses discussions about general business issues to influence the attitudes of the receiver.

Channel structures

Communication facets can be seen in the light of three particular channel conditions: structure, climate and power.

Structure

Channel structure, according to Stern and El-Ansary (1988), can be distinguished by the nature of the exchange relationship. These are relational and market structure relationships. Relational exchanges have a long-term perspective and high interdependence and involve joint decision-making. By contrast, market exchanges are ad hoc and hence have a short-term orientation where interdependence is low (Chapter 1).

Climate

Anderson *et al.* (1987) used measures of trust and goal compatibility in defining organisational climate. This in turn can be interpreted as the degree of mutual supportiveness that exists between channel members.

Power

Dwyer and Walker (1981) showed that power conditions within a channel can be symmetrical (with power balanced between members) or asymmetrical (with a power imbalance). Table 29.3 shows the relationships between communication facets and channel conditions. This is the combination of elements identified above.

Two specific forms of communication strategy can be identified. The first is a combination referred to as a 'collaborative communication strategy' and includes higher-frequency, more bidirectional flows, informal modes and indirect content. This combination is likely to occur in channel conditions of relational structures, supportive climates or symmetrical power. The second combination is referred to as an 'autonomous communication strategy' and includes

Table 29.3 The relationships between channel conditions and the facets of communication

	Communication facets			
Channel conditions	Frequency	Direction	Content	Modality
Structure				
Relational	Higher	More bidirectional	More indirect	More informal
Market	Lower	More unidirectional	More direct	More formal
Climate				
Supportive	Higher	More bidirectional	More indirect	More informal
Unsupportive	Lower	More unidirectional	More direct	More informal
Power				
Symmetrical	Higher	More bidirectional	More indirect	More informal
Asymmetrical	Lower	More unidirectional	More indirect	More informal

Source: Mohr and Nevin (1990). Used with kind permission of the American Marketing Association.

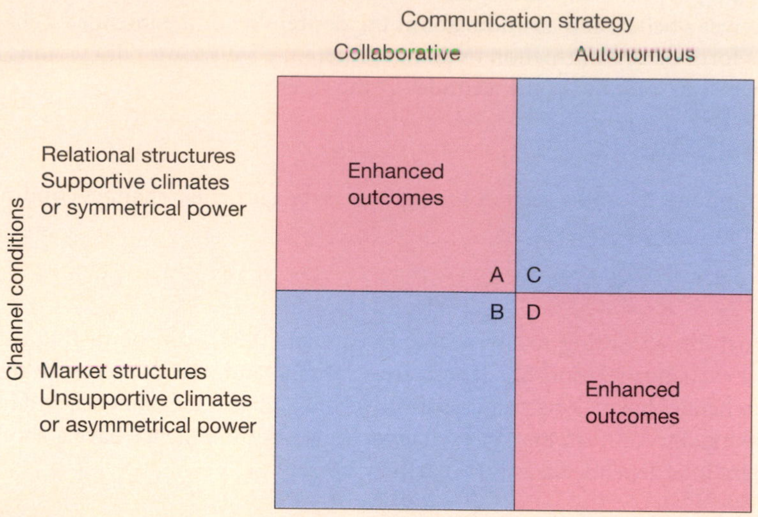

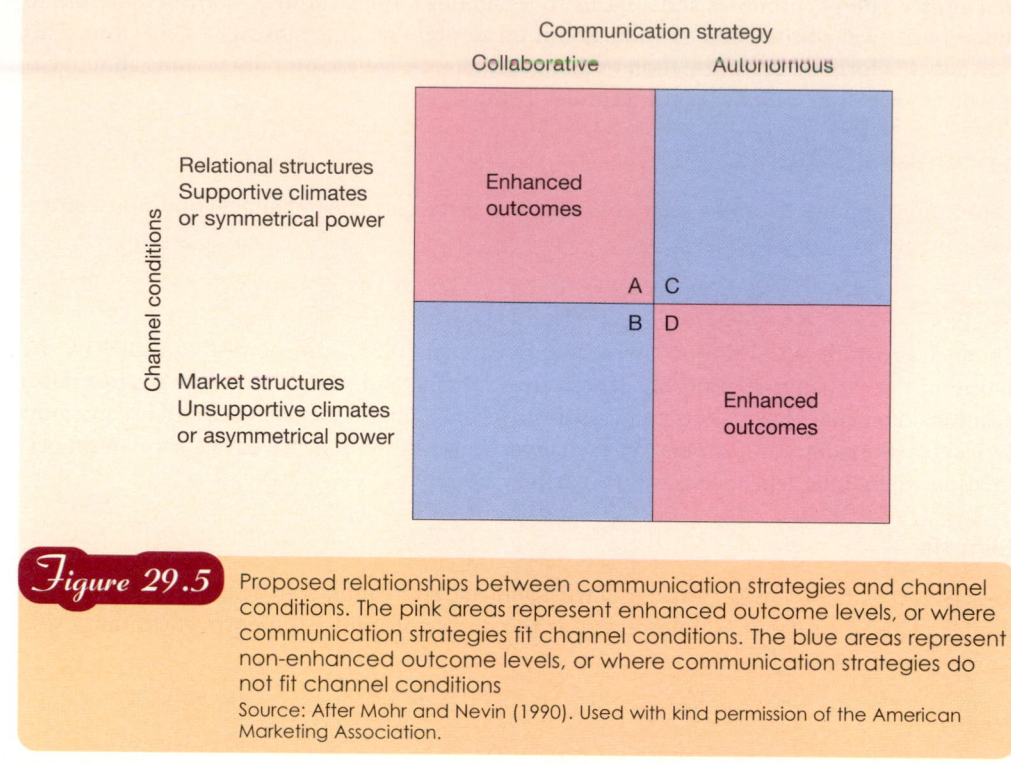

Figure 29.5 Proposed relationships between communication strategies and channel conditions. The pink areas represent enhanced outcome levels, or where communication strategies fit channel conditions. The blue areas represent non-enhanced outcome levels, or where communication strategies do not fit channel conditions

Source: After Mohr and Nevin (1990). Used with kind permission of the American Marketing Association.

lower-frequency, more unidirectional communication, formal modes and direct content. This combination is likely to occur in channel conditions of market structures, unsupportive climates and asymmetrical.

> Communication strategy should be built upon the characteristics of the situation facing each organisation in any particular network.

Communication strategy should, therefore, be built upon the characteristics of the situation facing each organisation in any particular network. Not all networks share the same conditions, nor do they all possess the same degree of closeness or relational expectations. By considering the nature of the channel conditions and then developing communication strategies that complement them, the performance of the focus organisation and other members can be considerably improved, and conflict and tension substantially reduced. Mohr and Nevin (1990) bring this together conceptually in Figure 29.5. Where channel conditions match communication strategy, the outcomes of the performance network will be enhanced. Likewise, when the communication strategy fails to match the appropriate channel conditions, the outcomes are unlikely to be enhanced.

Communication quality

Recently an interesting new perspective on marketing channel communications has emerged, namely issues concerning the quality of the communications and the success that might be attributed to the communication behaviours of the partners in any loose or tight networks.

Mohr and Sohi (1995) considered whether communication quality might be a function of the propensity to share information. The inclination among members to share information could be assumed to be positive in networks where members show high levels of trust and commitment. Frequency of communication flows, the level of bidirectional communications in a network and the level of communication formality are assumed to be the main elements of the propensity to share information.

Another aspect considered by the researchers was the degree to which information might be withheld or distorted (deviance). Information deviance might be high when there is an absence of rules (norms) determining what information needs to be communicated. Informality may lead to vagueness or inattentiveness and higher levels of deviance.

Information deviance might be high when there is an absence of rules.

The research sought to determine whether any (or all) of the three factors indicated that there was a linkage between the variables and the quality of information perceived by channel members. The results indicated that in the sample sector (computer dealers) the only significant variable was the frequency of information. The higher the frequency of communications received by channel members, the higher the perception of the quality of the communications. Issues concerning information overload and irritance are discounted.

Satisfaction levels appear to be correlated with higher levels of bidirectional communications. Thus, frequency impacts on perceived quality (and hence satisfaction) and the degree of bidirectional communications is significant in determining levels of satisfaction with the communications in a channel (network) environment.

The quality of communication messages can also be enhanced by communicating rich information through indirect channels. For example, although firms target communications at members of the decision-making unit, people in these units are themselves referring to a range of external sources for support and guidance. When organisations need to make significant decisions, they draw on a range of external opinions simply because the stakes are too high to get it wrong. Brown (2008: 33) reports that an ecosystem of influencers such as 'journalists and analysts . . . systems integrators, consultants, academics, authors, management gurus, purchasing cooperatives, regulators, government executives, resellers, standard setters, lobbyists, environmental activists and bloggers' emerge around each significant decision. Essentially this is about word-of-mouth and opinion formers (Chapter 2), but Brown refers to this as *influencer marketing*. Key to this process is understanding who are the key influencers, selecting influencers for particular projects and then designing and implementing communication strategies that help the influencer achieve their goals. The inference is that by assessing the market reach, the quality and frequency of impact, and how close an influencer is to a decision-maker, the impact of a potential influencer can be assessed.

eCommerce

Following on from the discussion about the propensity to share information is the rise of ecommerce and the opportunities to share information electronically. The development of extranets, in particular, enables organisations to share information for mutual benefit and to develop a form of competitive advantage through collaboration. Extranets allow organisations to work together in privacy and to deliver more efficient transactions. One of the difficulties experienced by extranet users is that all participants must use a common software system and those not hosting the system are invariably required to change the business operations behind their IT interface. New technology is changing that as ecollaboration was launched in 2000. This business model uses software that enables two different operating systems to talk to each other and to share information. All that is required is a portal through which all parties must pass.

A b2b communication strategy will often consist of a series of activities designed ultimately to influence the audience and persuade a percentage of it to take a particular action, very often to purchase the product/service itself. For example, a five-stage strategy to launch a new web site for the purchase of office services might be to:

- Build brand name awareness among the target audience. This would involve both offline and online communications. The goal would be to drive site traffic and to encourage site visitors.
- Drive site registration and generate reasons for visitors to return to the site.
- Convert registrations into purchasers and the use of online and offline sales promotions might be effective.
- Ensure that a certain percentage of purchasers are retained and are encouraged to return to the site. Not necessarily loyalty, but a retention facility based upon a points collection scheme could be useful.
- Build into the communication strategy a means of personalising communications such that each buyer would receive special offers and notices of products and services that reflect their purchase patterns to date.

To support this strategy, a creative proposition will need to be developed so that there is a central theme around which all communications are linked. This might be related to particular attributes such as product features, for example a colour, size or speed of service. The benefits of the attributes might also be used, for example no production downtime or improved staff efficiency might be valid claims. In contrast, an emotional feeling might be generated through the use of a tag line, gimmick, slogan, music or perhaps a mood. In other words, some form of branding needs to be used to differentiate the web site and create longer-lasting memories that can be easily recalled through the mention of the brand name or perhaps an attribute or central theme.

The b2b communication mix

As stated earlier, the use of the tools of the communication mix is very different from that in consumer markets. The prime tool is personal selling supported by both above- and below-the-line activities. The Internet and related digital technologies have played a very significant role in changing the way business is conducted and the speed at which transactions can be undertaken and costs reduced. The www is both a new distribution channel and communication medium. As a form of communication it is impersonal and more disposed to information search and retrieval than to information that is heavily branded and has emotional overtones. The nature of communications in b2b is that they are very personal, often require face-to-face interaction and the interactive nature lends itself to tailored messages and rapid feedback.

The rest of this chapter will be spent reviewing each of the tools and media of the mix and the role they play within a b2b context. For a fuller exposition of these tools, readers are advised to refer to Parts 4 and 5 of this text, commencing at Chapter 16.

Tools and b2b

As a general rule personal selling and direct marketing are the two most important tools in b2b marketing communications.

As a general rule personal selling and direct marketing are the two most important tools in b2b marketing communications. Advertising plays a relatively minor role, sales promotion is used but understated and public relations is being used more by organisations than in the past.

Advertising and b2b

Apart from increasing use of online advertising, the most important form is print advertising in trade journals and newspapers. Perhaps the most important role of advertising in this context is to inform and remind, whereas differentiation and persuasion are delivered through other tools of the communication mix, namely sales promotion and personal selling.

Direct marketing and b2b

Telemarketing has played an important role in recent years as a support mechanism to the sales force. It is used to facilitate customer enquiries, to establish leads, make appointments, and in certain circumstances provide a direct sales channel. One of the more common uses is as a sales order-processing system to collect routine low-value orders. This frees up the sales force to concentrate on other more profitable activities.

Direct mail has been an important part of the communications mix in b2b markets for some time. It can be used to support personal selling by building awareness, enhancing image, establishing credibility and taking orders, as well as providing levels of customer management. The significance of this part of the communications is not in doubt, even though some of it is being surpassed by the use of the Internet and ecommerce practices.

Therefore, it would appear sensible to be able to measure direct mail activities and in the b2b sector this is usually accomplished through measurement of response rates. However, this is not entirely satisfactory (Vöegle, 1992), because there are a number of stages through which a receiver of direct mail moves. These are the opening, scanning, (re)reading and response behaviours. Vriens *et al.* (1998) suggest that there are three main parts to the process. The first is the opening behaviour that is influenced by the attractiveness of the envelope and situational factors. Reading behaviour is influenced by the opening behaviour, the reader's situational characteristics and the attractiveness of the mailing and its contents. The final behaviour concerns the response generated, which is affected by the attractiveness of the offer, by the reading behaviour that preceded the response and the characteristics of the individual reader and their situation.

Wulf *et al.* (2000) used this framework to find ways in which response rates to direct mail could be increased. They found that the attractiveness of the envelope did impact on opening behaviour but so did the envelope size, material, colour and even type of postage. Surprisingly, the volume of direct mail each manager received had no impact on opening behaviour. With

ViewPoint 29.3 Viral gas

In an attempt to encourage businesses to switch electricity supplies, British Gas Business launched a humorous viral email campaign. According to British Gas Business, the clip aims to drive awareness of an incentive offer throughout the business community. It claims businesses are given the guarantee that any written quote for electricity supply will be either matched or bettered and they will receive free electricity for one month on switching.

The video clip shows a middle-aged, male business executive responding to a dismal weather forecast by rearranging all the lamps on his office desk. He then strips off, tilts back his chair and wallows in the increasing heat. The viral finishes with the line: 'The cheapest electricity online.'

The company tracked the video campaign via web analytics, measuring number of views and response rates. The results were not available at the time of writing.

Source: Anon. (2006).

Question

Is viral marketing a viable approach for businesses?

Task

Search the web for two other examples of businesses using viral marketing. Were they successful?

regard to reading behaviour, it was the attitudes of the reader that were found to be significant, not the situational factors. Finally, response behaviour appeared to be determined more by the reading behaviours of the individual rather than any other factor.

Sales promotions and b2b

The use of sales- or rather trade-based promotions very often goes unnoticed by consumers. However, trade promotions and interorganisational incentives are common and generally effective. Manufacturers will use competitions and sweepstakes to incentivise the sales forces of its distributors, to motivate technical and customer support staff in retail organisations and as an inducement to encourage other businesses to place orders and business with them.

Manufacturers will use competitions and sweepstakes to incentivise the sales forces.

ViewPoint 29.4 Decorating the trade

In an effort to consolidate its position as market leader and to increase sales, Dulux used a trade-based promotion. Targeting decorators who choose paints on behalf of their largely domestic customers, rather than contractors who work on commercial accounts where the brand choice of paint is decided by the customer, a cash prize fund of £2 million was a significantly attractive promotion. The sales promotion instrument or mechanic was a scratchcard that was distributed through 1,200 trade outlets across the United Kingdom. Rather than use premium giveaways or price cuts, the scratchcard was placed inside cans of white paint so that the benefit went to the buyer (the decorator) rather than the counter staff who tend to feed their largest, by volume, customers.

Source: Adapted from Mistry (2004) and Dulux-provided materials.

Question

How else could Dulux use sales promotions to good effect in the trade?

Task

Make a list of the benefits of using sales promotions with trade customers? Are they the same as those benefits experienced by consumers?

Price-based promotions and delayed discounts are used to encourage organisations to place business. Another popular approach is to discount technical support and bundle up a range of support facilities. Whatever the package, the purpose remains the same, to add value in order to advance (or gain) a purchase commitment.

Public relations and b2b

The effectiveness of public relations in a b2b context should not be underestimated. The range of public relations tools and techniques enables credibility to be developed in an environment where advertising is relatively ineffective, personal selling critical to the development of relationships and sales promotion limited to short-term sales shifts. Direct marketing and particularly interactively based communications are increasingly important in this sector, but public relations provides credibility and richness to an organisation's communications.

Personal selling and b2b

Personal selling is the most important tool of the marketing communications mix in b2b markets. Readers are referred to the substantial space that has been allocated to this topic in Chapter 28. In addition, exhibitions are a major part of the communication mix used in b2b work and this was examined in Chapter 28. However, one area that has developed in recent years, owing to the use of direct marketing and interactive technology, is the management of those customers who are of strategic importance to an organisation. This is explored in the sections that follow.

ViewPoint 29.5 B2b integrated channels

There is substantial evidence that b2b marketers are experimenting with more channels and are moving beyond a simple mix of advertising, direct mail and telesales. The use of an integrated marketing communications approach in b2b marketing has been growing in recent years, mainly due to the development of online marketing, which has made multichannel strategies more cost-effective.

Computer Associates (CA), providers of Internet security software, often have to wait up to three years for customers to make purchase decisions. Their communications are not helped by the complexity of their product messages. In an integrated multichannel campaign designed to keep CA's customers and their preferred channels at the centre of their activities, CA aimed to ensure that CA's messages remained consistent across the different channels.

Prospects were sent a direct mail pack, informing them of, and inviting them to attend, a seminar. Having then been signed up, they were sent an email in which was embedded a link to a microsite. Visitors to the web site could tailor their particular details via the microsite, after which they were sent email updates alerting them to updates and targeted product news. The microsite also held further information about the seminar, together with an invitation to dinner with some of the speakers.

Source: Benjamin (2007).

Question

To what extent do you think the role of direct mail in b2b communications is likely to diminish as environmentally sensitive communications policies become expected?

Task

Using the tools and media of marketing communications as your framework, list all the ways in which organisations can communicate with one another.

Media and b2b

On the basis that advertising plays a minor role within the B2B marketing communications mix, the use of media is restricted. The use of broadcast media in this context is limited as is outdoor work. However, two media are important, print and digital, especially the Internet.

Print and b2b

Print media are important for recruitment advertising, and for many larger organisations print is used to communicate corporate values and to enhance their reputation.

The use of catalogues in the b2b market is well established and even the rise of the Internet has not provided a huge distraction for organisational buyers. Catalogues provide a reference source for an organisation's range of products. One of their functions is that they provide fast access to a company's range of products, especially in comparison to a web site. Euroffice.co.uk are a online catalogue but now use a printed version in order to drive customers online and also provide an opportunity to introduce themselves to an organisation. The flick-to-click behaviour observed in consumer markets is not yet established in the b2b market but this may evolve (Murphy, 2007).

The use of catalogues in the b2b market is well established.

ViewPoint 29.6 Soliciting a mwah, mwah darling

In order to find a way into the media and entertainment market, commercial law firm Lewis Silkin had to find a way of differentiating themselves. They realised that they might be perceived as old-fashioned and an inappropriate business partner.

The result was a campaign that suggested empathy with the industry's culture yet maintained sufficient integrity. The core message was 'I love ME'. This was a tongue-in-cheek reference to media types who believe 'it's all about me' (aka the television hit programme, *Absolutely Fabulous*). This phrase was printed on tee shirts and badges and tested to sense if the right tone had been achieved. The campaign was launched at Britain's largest international music industry exhibition, 'London Calling'.

In addition, Lewis Silkin sponsored the 'Future of Music Business' event at the exhibition. The purpose was to demonstrate the company's credentials and knowledge of the industry. Banner advertising featuring the 'I love ME' slogan was placed on the 'London Calling' web site as a means of inviting clients to the show and their stand. Branded pill boxes were distributed to particular prospects. These were intended to allude to the media industry's party atmosphere and the need to have something for the morning after the night before. Branded memory sticks featuring information about Lewis Silkin and their new business sector were distributed to potential clients at the exhibition. This served to provide a reminder of their contact with Lewis Silkin and act as a prompt to consider Lewis Silkin, at a later date, away from the communication noise associated with these events.

Although the campaign consumed 50 per cent of the marketing budget in one fell swoop, the return was impressive. Thirty-three new clients were signed up with a substantial number of further prospects in the pipeline.

Source: Papas (2008). This case study first appeared in *The Marketer*, the magazine of The Chartered Institute of Marketing.

Question

To what extent do you believe firms should poke fun at an industry or its values?

Task

How would you extend the idea of 'I love ME' into the next phase of the Lewis Silkin campaign?

Exhibit 29.2 Branded materials used by Lewis Silkin
Photography: Redactive Media Group.

Digital and b2b

The development of digital media has helped transform b2b marketing communications. In particular, the Internet provides both a distribution channel and communication medium between organisations, as well as drastically improving productivity. eCommerce saves transaction time, lowers costs and can shorten the period between order and delivery. Digitally based communications can improve the accuracy of the information provided, thereby giving a good measure of the effectiveness of marketing communication activities. All of this can improve the quality of b2b relationships, but it can also serve to heighten expectations concerning service delivery and further innovation.

Just as sales literature and demonstration packs take time to prepare, even longer to change/update and are quite expensive with a great deal of wastage, brochureware on a web site is fast, easily accessible and adaptable. The collection of names and addresses, responses to email questions and the provision of rich data for the sales force are also more quickly and more accurately completed. If developed further, transactional web sites enable routine orders to be processed quickly and at a lower cost. As noted elsewhere, this can free up the sales force to visit established customers more often, open more new accounts and be more attentive to strategically important accounts.

There are some legal and information security issues that need to be addressed in order to reduce any risk to business partners. This is part of the development and maintenance of profitable relationships, and marketing communications has an important role to play in the development of these relationships by reducing perceived risk and uncertainty. Marketing communications also needs to provide clarity and fast, pertinent and timely information in order that decisions can be made. Through marketing communications (and operational efficiencies and political contingencies) the development of loyalty between organisations might be observed. By targeting information and customising messages for the right people within a partner organisation, via an extranet for example, the development of loyalty through trust and commitment might be possible.

A range of digital media are now used to enhance b2b relationships. In addition to the Internet, web site and email activities, organisations are using corporate blogging, video conferencing, mobile and CRM. Regularised, balanced communication, which is embedded within the operational interactions between organisations, is much more likely to lead to higher levels of customer (intermediary) satisfaction than when it is absent. The need to reduce the frequency and intensity of conflict that is inevitable in interorganisational relationships is paramount. The propensity to share information and to provide higher rather than lower volumes of information is perceived as an indicator of high quality (and therefore satisfying) communication. The Internet is an ideal resource for enabling these events to happen and in doing so bind partner organisations closer.

A range of digital media are now used to enhance b2b relationships.

Strategic account management

One of the major issues concerning the development and maintenance of interorganisational relationships is the method by which very important and/or valuable customers are managed. In many ways these methods are an extension of personal selling (Chapter 22) but as they are business-to-business matters, these issues are discussed in this chapter. Two main forms are considered here, key account management and the emerging global account management disciplines. These are considered in turn.

Key account management

The increasing complexity of both markets and products, combined with the trends towards purchasing centralisation and industrial concentration, mean that a small number of significant accounts have become essential for the survival of many organisations. The growth in the significance of key account management (KAM) is expected to continue and one of the results will be the change in expectations of buyers and sellers, in particular the demand for higher levels of expertise, integration and professionalism of sales forces.

It has long been recognised that particular customer accounts represent an important, often large, proportion of turnover. Such accounts have been referred to variously as national accounts, house accounts, major accounts and key accounts. Millman and Wilson (1995) argue that the first three are sales-oriented, tend to the short term and are often only driven by sales management needs. However, Ojasalo (2001) sees little difference in the terminology KAM, national account marketing (NAM) and strategic account management (SAM).

Key accounts may be of different sizes in comparison to the focus organisation, but what delineates them from other types of 'account' is that they are strategically important. Key accounts are customers who, in a business-to-business market, are willing to enter into collaborative exchanges and who are strategically important to the focus organisation.

There are two primary aspects of this definition. The first is that both parties perceive relational exchanges as a necessary component and that the relationship is long term. The second aspect refers to the strategic issue. The key account is strategically important because it might offer opportunities for entry to new markets, represent access to other key organisations or resources, or provide symbolic value in terms of influence, power and stature.

The key account is strategically important because it might offer opportunities for entry to new markets.

The importance of the long-term relationship as a prime element of key account identification raises questions about how they are developed, what resources are required to manage and sustain them, and what long-term success and effectiveness results from identifying them. Essentially, this comes down to who in the organisation should be responsible for these key accounts. Generally speaking, there are three main responses: to assign sales executives, to create a key account division or to create a key account sales force (see Table 29.4).

Table 29.4 Three ways of managing key accounts

Category	Explanation
Assigning sales executives	Common in smaller organisations that do not have large resources. Normally undertaken by senior executives who have the flexibility and can provide the responsive service often required. They can make decisions about stock, price, distribution and levels of customisation. There is a tendency for key accounts to receive a disproportionate level of attention, as the executives responsible for these major customers lose sight of their own organisation's marketing strategy.
Creating a key account division	The main advantage of this approach is that it offers close integration of production, finance, marketing and sales. The main disadvantage is that resources are duplicated and the organisation can become very inefficient. It is also a high-risk strategy, as the entire division is dependent upon a few customers.
Creating a key account sales force	This is adopted by organisations that want to differentiate through service and they use their most experienced and able salespersons and provide them with a career channel. Administratively, this structure is inefficient, as there is a level of duplication similar to that found in the customer-type structure discussed earlier. Furthermore, commission payable on these accounts is often a source of discontent, both for those within the key account sales force and those aspiring to join the select group.

The assignment of sales executives to these important accounts is common in smaller organisations. Those organisations that have the resources are able to incorporate the services of senior executives, who assume this role and bring to it the flexibility and responsive service that are required as the account grows in stature. They can make decisions about stock, price, distribution and levels of customisation.

These accounts may be major or national accounts, as very often their strategic significance is not recognised. There is a tendency for these accounts to receive a disproportionate level of attention, as the executives responsible for these major customers lose sight of their own organisation's marketing strategy.

A further way of managing these accounts is to create a key account division. The main advantage of this approach is that it offers close integration of production, finance, marketing and sales. The main disadvantage is that resources are duplicated and the organisation can become very inefficient. It is also a high-risk strategy as the entire division is dependent upon a few customers.

Should a key account sales force be preferred then issues concerning the management of this resource arise. Key account managers require particular skills, as, indeed, do the executives themselves.

Key account managers

Abratt and Kelly (2002) report Napolitano's (1997) work that found that, to be successful, a KAM programme requires the selection of the right key account manager. This person should possess particularly strong interpersonal and relationship skills and be capable of managing larger, significant and often complex customers. Key account managers act as a conduit between organisations, through which high-value information flows in both directions. They must be prepared and able to deal with organisations where buying decisions can be protracted and delayed (Sharma, 1997).

Benedapudi and Leone (2002) agree that the key account manager is vitally important to the success of a KAM relationship, but they also view the relationship differences between the organisations as distinct from the interpersonal relationships between the customer firm's contact person and the supply-side firm's key account manager, or contact employee as they refer to them. These relationships will vary in strength and there are differing consequences for the KAM relationship should the contact person leave the supply side organisation.

Among the key success factors, Abratt and Kelly report that, in addition to selecting the right key account manager, the selection of the right key account customers is also important for establishing KAM programmes. Not all large and high-volume customers are suitable for KAM programmes. Segmentation and customer prioritisation according to needs and an organisation's ability to provide consistent value should be used to highlight those for whom KAM would not be helpful.

In addition, particular sales behaviours are required at this level of operation. As the majority of key account managers are drawn internally from the sales force (Hannah, 1998, cited by Abratt and Kelly, 2002) it is necessary to ensure that they have the correct skills mix. It is also important to take a customer's perspective on what makes a successful KAM programme. Pardo (1997) is cited as claiming that the degree of impact a product has on the customer's business activity will determine the level of attention offered to the supplier's programme. Also, the level of buying decision centralisation will impact on the effectiveness of the KAM programme.

The level of buying decision centralisation will impact on the effectiveness of the KAM programme.

Abratt and Kelly found six factors were of particular importance when establishing a KAM programme: the 'suitability of the key account manager, knowledge and understanding of the key account customer's business, commitment to the KAM partnership, delivering value, the importance of trust and the proper implementation and understanding of the KAM concept' (p. 474).

One final point can be made concerning key account managers. The inference is that one, multitalented individual is the sole point of contact between the supplier and customer. This is not the case as there are usually a number of levels of interaction between the two organisations. Indeed, there could be 'an entire team dedicated to providing services and support to the key account' (Ojasalo, 2001: 210). Therefore, it is more appropriate to suggest that the key account manager should assume responsibility for all points of contact within the customer organisation.

Having established a KAM programme, one of the tasks that key account managers need to implement is to ensure the relationship benefits from a planned approach. The need for planning within key account relationships is argued by Ryals and Rogers (2007). They find that key account planning is not widely used and certainly fails to have a strategic focus. As if to try and remedy this situation, they also demonstrate the impact that key account planning can have on managers and their subsequent performance.

Key account relationship cycles

A number of researchers have attempted to gain a greater understanding of KAM by considering the development cycles through which relationships move. Millman and Wilson offer the work of Ford (1980), Dwyer *et al.* (1987) and Wotruba (1991) as examples of such development cycles (see Table 29.5).

Millman and Wilson have attempted to build on the work of the others (included in Table 29.5) and have formulated a model that incorporates their own research as well as that established in the literature. McDonald (2000) has since elaborated on their framework, providing further insight and explanation.

The cycle develops with the *exploratory KAM* level, where the main task is to identify those accounts that have key account potential, and those that do not, in order that resources can be allocated efficiently. Both organisations are considering each other: the buyer in terms of the supplier's offer in terms of its ability to match their own requirements; and the seller in terms of the buyer providing sufficient volumes, value and financial suitability.

Basic KAMTS is where both organisations enter into a transactional period, essentially testing each other as potential long-term partners.

The next level is *basic KAM*, where both organisations enter into a transactional period, essentially testing each other as potential long-term partners. Some relationships may stabilise at this level while others may develop as a result of the seller seeking and gaining tentative agreement with prospective accounts about whether they would become 'preferred accounts'.

At the *cooperative KAM* level, more people from both organisations are involved in communications. At the basic KAM level, both parties understand each other and, through experience, the selling company has established its credentials with the buying organisation. At this next level, opportunities to add value to the relationship are considered. This could be

Table 29.5 Comparison of relational models

Ford (1980), Dwyer *et al.* (1987)	Wotruba (1991)	Millman and Wilson (1995)	McDonald (2000)
Pre-relationship awareness	Provider	Pre-KAM	Exploratory
Early stage exploration	Persuader	Early KAM	Basic
Development stage expansion	Prospector	Mid-KAM	Cooperative
Long-term stage commitment	Problem solver	Partnership KAM	Interdependent
Final stage institutionalisation	Procreator	Synergistic KAM	Integrated
		Uncoupling KAM	Disintegrated

Source: Updated from Millman and Wilson (1995). Used with kind permission of Emerald Group Publishing Limited.

encouraged by increasing the range of products and services transacted, thereby involving more people in the relationship.

At the *interdependent KAM* level of a relationship both organisations recognise the importance of the other to their operations, with the supplier either first choice, or only, supplier. Retraction from the relationship is now problematic as 'inertia and strategic suitability', as McDonald phrases it, holds the partners together.

Integrated KAM is achieved when the two organisations view the relationship as consisting of one entity where they create synergistic value in the marketplace. Joint problem solving and the sharing of sensitive information are strong characteristics of the relationship and withdrawal by either party can be traumatic at a personal level for the participants involved, let alone at the organisational level.

The final level is *disintegrating KAM*. This can occur at any time for a variety of reasons, ranging from company takeover to the introduction of new technology. The relationship may return to another, lower level and new terms of business are established. The termination, or readjustment, of the relationship need not be seen as a negative factor as both parties may decide that the relationship holds no further value.

McDonald develops Millman and Wilson's model by moving away from a purely sequential framework. He suggests that organisations may stabilise or enter the model at any level, indeed, he states that organisations might readjust to a lower level. The time between phases will vary according to the nature and circumstances of the parties involved. The labels provided by McDonald reflect the relationship status of both parties rather than of the selling company (e.g. prospective) or buying company (e.g. preferred supplier). While the Millman and Wilson and McDonald interpretations of the KAM relationship cycle provide insight they are both primarily dyadic perspectives. They neglect to consider the influence of significant others, in particular those other network member organisations that provide context and interaction in particular networks and that do influence the actions of organisations and those key individuals who are strategic decision-makers.

Some final aspects of KAM

In mature and competitive markets, where there is little differentiation between the products, service may be the only source of sustainable competitive advantage. Key account management allows senior sales executives to build a strong relationship with each of their customers, thereby providing a very high level of service and strong point of differentiation.

This approach enables an organisation to select its most experienced and able salespersons and, in doing so, provide a career channel for those executives who prefer to stay in sales rather than move into management. Administratively, this structure is inefficient as there is a level of duplication similar to that found in the customer-type structure discussed earlier. Furthermore, commission payable on these accounts is often a source of discontent, both for those within the key account sales force and those aspiring to join the select group.

The development and management of key accounts is complex and evolving. Key account relationships are rarely static and should be rooted within corporate strategy, if only because of the implications for resources, which customers seek as a result of partnering in this way (Spencer, 1999). Key account relationships can generate positive financial value but not without considerable management effort (Kalwani and Narayanas, 1995; Ryals and Holt, 2007). Consideration of customer profitability appears to be the foundation for successful key account relationships.

The development and management of key accounts is complex and evolving.

Global account management

The development of key account management approaches highlighted the strategic importance that some customers represent to organisations. KAM represents an attempt to meet the needs of these customers in a customised and personal way. However, there are many organisations whose customers are located in many different countries, regions and even on different continents, and the management of their needs demands different skills and resources from those adopted for KAM. The management of these customers is referred to as global account management (GAM) and in many ways is evidence of a new strategic approach to business development and marketing management in b2b organisations.

Understanding the nature of GAM is helped by Hennessey and Jeannet, who provide a useful definition:

> *Global accounts are large companies that operate in multiple countries, often on two or more continents, are strategically important to the supplier and have some form of coordinated purchasing across different countries.*
> *(2003: 1)*

As if to reinforce the nature of GAM, Birkinshaw (2003) refers to Hewlett-Packard, which regards Boeing as a national (key) and not a global account as its decision-making is all US-centred. One of the characteristics of global accounts is that their decision-making units are influenced through inputs from various geographical locations. Wilson *et al.* (2000) highlight the important characteristic associated with the strategic coordination associated with GAM. To them, a strategic global account is characterised as representing a major part of a supplier's corporate objectives and where the account expects the supplier to offer an integrated global product service offering.

It would therefore be a mistake to think that KAM and GAM are the same. Indeed, Birkinshaw (2003) makes the point that global and key accounts are not identical. He argues that the roots of global account management are to be found in supply chain management, unlike KAM, which has been influenced by the sales management perspective. Hennessey and Jeannet (2003) believe that national account managers are relationship managers, whereas global account managers have a greater focus on strategic issues and coordination of personnel in different countries. Millman and Wilson (1998) refer to the importance and significance of cultural diversity and organisational issues when adopting a global account management programme.

The roots of global account management are to be found in supply chain management.

Wilson *et al.* (2000) consider how global account programmes can be delivered. They identified the need for three main global competences:

- a coordinated, globally competent supply chain;
- management of the interaction process *within* the supplying company, particularly the information and communication flows;
- the establishment of a forum, with the customer, of a collaborative design process.

This suggests that relationship management skills, in particular the use of interaction and collaboration to develop dialogue, are critical factors associated with GAM. Wilson *et al.* (2000) identify many competences that are necessary for GAM to be successful, ranging from strong communications and relationship management skills through cultural empathy and business and financial acumen. However, they make the point that global account managers need strong political skills, especially in view of the fact that they often operate without direct authority, particularly with regard to resources and processes. They refer to this role as 'political entrepreneur'.

Understanding the nature of GAM, its management and indeed associated research are at an early stage as the discipline is very young. Early work in the area suggests that there is no fixed strategic model that represents GAM, if only because GAM needs to be flexible and dynamic as engagement with key global customers evolves.

Summary

In order to help consolidate your understanding of business-to-business marketing communications, here are the key points summarised against each of the learning objectives:

1. Establish the principle characteristics of the b2b sector.

The b2b market is characterised by the decision-making processes that organisational buyers use. As these can be very different from those used by consumers, it is not surprising that the marketing communications will also vary in many ways. The b2b market consists of four main types of interorganisational relationships, reflecting the role the product/service plays in the business activity of the organisation (e.g. for resale, as OEM (original equipment manufacturer)).

Seven different types of risk were identified with organisational decision-making. Consequently, the marketing communications used to reach different organisations, predominantly personal selling, need to be adaptive to reduce different types of risk.

2. Understand the concepts of networks and interorganisational relationships.

The basic structure of any network consists of an organisation that is tied with a number of other functionally specialised organisations. The channel network consists of those organisations with which others must cooperate directly to achieve their own objectives. The network uses collaborative exchanges to regularise and sustain cooperative activities. This is a general view, and it is recognised that there is a variety of network forms.

As channel networks have developed so has their complexity, which impacts upon the marketing communications strategies and tools used to help reach these customers, partners and fellow intermediaries. The expectations of buyers in these networks have risen in parallel with the significance attached to them by manufacturers.

Commitment to a partnership, i.e. the relationship with other network members, is key because of the 'enduring desire to maintain a valued relationship'. Of comparable importance is the degree to which partners are confident that each will act in the best interests of the relationship. *Trust*, therefore, is also regarded as a key aspect of collaborative exchanges and is a composite of the level of reliability and integrity that exists between partners.

3. Explore the key dynamics of b2b and interorganisational communications.

Effective communication is key to the satisfaction of buyer expectations and is the main link between an organisation and its environment. A model of b2b marketing communications suggests that the level of involvement experienced by the main participants in the buying process will affect the level and type of communications used. However, while the simplicity and logical reasoning associated with the model are intuitively appealing, the authors of the model accept that the political ambience in which these decisions are made does in fact 'muddy' the view and reflect the complexity of network relationships.

Communication is 'the glue that holds together a marketing channel' and it is recognised that, from a managerial perspective, communication is important, because many of the causes of tension and conflict in interorganisational relationships stem from inadequate or poor communication. Communication within networks serves not only to provide persuasive information and foster participative decision-making, but also to provide for coordination, the exercise of power and the encouragement of loyalty and commitment, so as to reduce the likelihood of tension and conflict.

4. Consider ecommerce and its impact on communications.

Following on from the discussion about the propensity to share information is the rise of ecommerce and the opportunities to share information electronically. The development of extranets, in particular, enables organisations to share information for mutual benefit and to develop a form of competitive advantage through collaboration. Extranets allow organisations to work together in privacy and to deliver more efficient transactions.

5. Explore the main characteristics and issues relating to the b2b communication mix.

The tools of the communication mix are used very differently from those used in consumer markets. The prime tool is personal selling supported by both above- and below-the-line activities. Two media are important – print and digital. The Internet and related digital technologies have played a very significant role in changing the way business is conducted and the speed at which transactions can be undertaken and costs reduced. The www is both a new distribution channel and communication medium. As a form of communication it is impersonal and more disposed to information search and retrieval than to information that is heavily branded and has emotional overtones.

B2b communications are very personal, often require face-to-face interaction and the interactive nature lends itself to tailored messages and rapid feedback.

6. Examine issues related to strategic account management.

The strategic importance of key accounts and global accounts has gained increased attention in recent years. One of the prime dimensions of key accounts is the long-term relationship that can develop. McDonald (2000) has developed Millman and Wilson's (1995) interpretation of the different phases that can be associated with key account relationships. In addition, global account management has recently emerged as a new strategic approach to managing customers that are represented at various locations around the world. In both these cases, relationship marketing principles are important and marketing communications, principally through personal selling, is an important tool in fostering, nurturing and sustaining these strategically important accounts.

Review questions

1. Who are the principal target audiences for push-oriented communications and how do these communications differ from pull-based communication strategies?
2. Discuss the role that trust and commitment might play in marketing communications with intermediaries.
3. What are the three parameters upon which partnership success is built?
4. Prepare notes for a short article to be included in a marketing magazine about the importance of communications within marketing channels.
5. Describe the main elements of communication informational flows in performance networks.
6. How can communication facets and channel structures be effectively combined?
7. What are the differences between collaborative and autonomous communication strategies?
8. Outline the concept of communication quality and identify the main dimension upon which quality is perceived to be based.
9. Identify the main difference between house or major accounts, key accounts and global account management.
10. Explain the concept of key account relationship cycles using the McDonald (2000) framework.

MiniCase Educating the educators about asbestos

Jeremy Miles: Silverdell

Asbestos is a naturally occurring fibrous mineral and has been used commercially for about 150 years as a building material. It is versatile, plentiful and was ideal as a fireproofing and insulation material. Serious, often fatal diseases can be caused when asbestos fibres are released from materials, become airborne, and are inhaled.

The most likely way that asbestos in schools and colleges may become damaged is through the maintenance and repair of construction activities. This could occur when installing new computer cables, putting up shelving or installing new security systems. On a day-to-day basis, asbestos is a safe building material providing it is in good condition and not damaged.

School caretakers have been identified as a particularly important group. This is due to the nature of the risk, they are employed directly by the school and they have a duty of care for their employees and responsibility for the maintenance of the school. In addition, contractors who work in schools or colleges who may be IT technicians, electricians and other tradesmen are also considered at risk from asbestos.

Silverdell Plc are a group of companies that specialise in the management of asbestos. Three organisations make up the group. Redhill Analysts are asbestos consultants who identify where asbestos is located in buildings and advise on how the asbestos should be best managed. There are two asbestos removal contractors – Silverdell and Kitsons – who undertake the removal of asbestos throughout the United Kingdom, under license. The profile of asbestos in education has increased dramatically. As a response to this market opportunity, a specific campaign to target schools and their respective contractors employed in the upkeep of school and college buildings was developed.

The following sets out the details concerning the campaign that was implemented.

Managing the education sector campaign for the Silverdell group

Aims

- To increase turnover and market share in the public and private sector schools market.
- Increase the penetration of private and independent schools who use the Silverdell group for integrated asbestos solutions – asbestos surveying and removal.

Campaign objectives

Raise prompted awareness among headteachers, school business managers, bursars and local education authorities that the group provides innovative and cost-effective solutions for the schools market.

Promote services/solutions offered by Redhills in respect of consultancy and project management solutions.

Promote asbestos removal solutions by Silverdell and Kitsons as leading removal contractors in the education field.

Support the NUT (National Union of Teachers) as stakeholders and opinion formers within in advice given to head teachers.

Raise awareness of: communication need within each school, it's workforce and tradesmen appointed/monitoring; and safe systems of work.

What we know about them that helps us

- Asbestos is a high-profile subject, which is currently contentious among managers, teachers and the trade unions.
- Local practical knowledge of schools is a specialist area where staff need vetting before working in an environment with children.
- Head teachers are increasingly responsible for repairs and maintenance within the school. The implication is that they manage the budgets.

Key messages

Having identified several stakeholders, it is important to target key messages.

To the head teacher

1. Re-inspections are a critical part of asbestos management compliance.
2. A pro-active approach is significantly cheaper than the consequences of mistakes by tradesmen.
3. Integrated asbestos management and removal solutions are user-friendly, accountable and cost-effective.

Adopting a related creative principle of Redhill Analysts integrated approach designed to stimulate thought should include:

To the trade

1. A breath of fresh air – protect yourself and the children in your school.
2. Are you sure there is no asbestos where you are working?
3. Think before you do.

Why do we believe we are saying the right thing in the right way

- Evidence sourced from specialist researchers.
- Notes from the HSE sourced specifically about schools.
- The NUT has an agenda to raise profile – intelligence suggests a competitor to Redhill has agreed to support the NUT in producing 100 draft surveys to be published at the NUT conference in the summer.

Format

Design and print of e-flyer/adverts.

Print and design of quality 32-page advisory guide for head teachers.

Print and design of contractor cards.

Advertisements – educational press only.

Seminar costs – potential three seminars using the NUT/LEA (Local Education Authority) route to market.

Profile: PR support and article and *News at 10* should it be shown.

Additional web site pages as advisory support – www.asbestosinschools.co.uk.

Telephone calls to LEA's/local authorities in area responsible for education establishments.

Advisory helpline.

Tone of message and approach

Supportive and advisory.

Managed/integrated solutions.

Non-confrontational, sensitive to the fact that the HSE may have other agendas.

Point of differentiation – Ability to offer an integrated package nationally.
Ability to offer internal compliance training.

Remind – Reminding will be a key part of the campaign to target audiences a minimum of three times.

Inform – Offer advisory support to enable compliance to be achieved locally.

Persuade – Integrated solutions are easier to manage, and more cost effective.

Pilot

Regional campaign in the Midlands area by designated postcode: wider national campaign will follow based on pilot success to 7,000 decision-makers.

Routes to market

Direct: Direct mail and email to head teachers – they are ultimately responsible for financial activities in public-funded schools, and are the catalysts for distribution to their heads of department and to governors.

Trade Unions/LEA/local government: Use the NUT's profile within the sector to gain access and credibility of our service offerings through a series of awareness seminars for heads, LEA's and L/A's (Local Authorities).

Contractors: Information to contractors working in schools to be aware of asbestos.

Essential practical solutions

We should not compromise our trading position against any other opinion leaders.

Number of advisory sessions needs to be closely monitored – re cost implications.

Direct marketing campaign – limited regionally. (Opt-in required.) E-based campaign to reduce costs of postage, etc.

Logo – group.

Availability of email addresses (opt-in).

Support – education help-line – Redhill.

Timings/flighting

February/March:

Liaise with NUT/Trade Unions and Local Education Authorities re compliance training.

Run pilot.

March/April: Run primary campaign designed to fit with new fiscal year in schools and in time when preparations are being made for refurbishments during summer period.

Proposed flighting timescales:

Email 1, direct mail – hard copy to include contractor inserts.

Email 2 as a reinforcement.

Total budgets and costs – schools email campaign

Schools and colleges (private and public)
Schools and colleges – Art & Design
Schools and colleges – Commercial
Schools and colleges – Further Education
Schools and colleges – Foundation
Schools and colleges – Independent and Preparatory
Schools and colleges – Local Authority
Schools and colleges – Special
Head teacher or Bursar contact (default do decision-maker)
Cannot be split via private/state
UK-wide
Names, address and email contacts in total 7,130

Totals	
Direct marketing – flyer and contractor information	£2,500
Design and print	£6,000
Fulfilment and postages	£7,500 E
12-month licence (database)	£2,000
Web site	**£1,500**
Compliance road show (at cost)	£500
Total – Full campaign	**£20,000**

Managing quality and quantity of responses

Number of responses after three reminders
Number of seminars provided
Attendances at seminars
Volume of works commissioned

References

Abratt, R. and Kelly, P.M. (2002) Perceptions of a successful key account management program. *Industrial Marketing Management*, **31**(5) (August), 467–76.

Anderson, E., Lodish, L. and Weitz, B. (1987) Resource allocation behaviour in conventional channels. *Journal of Marketing Research* (February), 85–97.

Anon. (2006) British Gas Business switches on to viral campaign. Retrieved 4 April 2006 from http://www.b2bm.biz/.

Anon. (2008) Casting off the past. *The Marketer*, December/January, 21–2.

Benedapudi, N. and Leone, R.P. (2002) Managing business-to-business customer relationships following key contact employee turnover in a vendor firm. *Journal of Marketing*, **66** (April), 83–101.

Benjamin, K. (2007) Special report: The importance of being integrated. *Marketing Direct*, 6 February 2007. Retrieved 4 April 2007 from www.brandrepublic.com/InDepth/Features/631450/Special-report-importance-integrated/.

Birkinshaw, J.M. (2003) *The Blackwell Handbook of Global Management*. Boston, MA: Blackwell.

Brown, D. (2008) Under the influence. *Marketing*, 23 April, 33–4.

Dwyer, R. and Walker, O.C. (1981) Bargaining in an asymmetrical power structure. *Journal of Marketing*, **45** (Winter), 104–15.

Dwyer, F.R., Shurr, P.H. and Oh, S. (1987) Developing buyer–seller relationships. *Journal of Marketing*, **51**(2), 11–28.

Ford, I.D. (1980) The development of buyer–seller relationships in industrial markets. *European Journal of Marketing*, **14**(5/6), 339–53.

Frazier, G.L. and Summers, J.O. (1984) Interfirm influence strategies and their application within distribution channels. *Journal of Marketing*, **48** (Summer), 43–55.

Gilliland, D.I. and Johnston, W.J. (1997) Towards a model of marketing communications effects. *Industrial Marketing Management*, **26**, 15–29.

Grabner, J.R. and Rosenberg, L.J. (1969) Communication in distribution channel systems. In *Behavioral Dimensions in Distribution Channels: A Systems Approach* (ed. L. Stern). Boston, MA: Houghton Mifflin.

Haakansson, H. and Wootz, B. (1979) A framework of industrial buying and selling. *Industrial Marketing Management*, **8**, 28–39.

Hannah, G. (1998) From transactions to relationships: challenges for the national account manager. *Journal of Marketing and Sales* (SA), **4**(1), 30–3.

Hennessey, D.H. and Jeannet, J.-P. (2003) *Global Account Management: Creating Value*. Chichester: Wiley.

Kalwani, M.U. and Narayanas, N. (1995) Long-term manufacturer-supplier relationships: do they pay off supplier firms? *Journal of Marketing*, **59**(1), 1–16.

McDonald, M. (2000) Key account management: a domain review. *Marketing Review*, **1**, 15–34.

Millman, T. and Wilson, K. (1995) From key account selling to key account management. *Journal of Marketing Practice: Applied Marketing Science*, **1**(1), 9–21.

Millman, T. and Wilson, K. (1998) Global account management: reconciling organisational complexity and cultural diversity. *The 14th Annual Industrial Marketing and Purchasing (IMP) Group Conference*, Turku School of Economics and Business Administration.

Mistry, B. (2004) Dulux sets out to steal share. *Promotions and Incentives*, March, 32–3.

Mitchell, V.-M. (1999) Consumer perceived risk: conceptualisations and models. *European Journal of Marketing*, **33**(1–2), 163–95.

Mohr, J. and Nevin, J.R. (1990) Communication strategies in marketing channels. *Journal of Marketing* (October), 36–51.

Mohr, J. and Sohi, R.S. (1995) Communication flows in distribution channels: impact on assessments of communication quality and satisfaction. *Journal of Retailing*, **71**(4), 393–416.

Mohr, J. and Spekman, R. (1994) Characteristics of partnership success: partnership attributes, communication behaviour and conflict resolution techniques. *Strategic Management Journal*, **15**, 135–52.

Moorman, C., Zaltman, G. and Despande, R. (1992) Relationships between providers and users of marketing research: the dynamics of trust within and between organisations. *Journal of Marketing Research*, **29** (August), 314–29.

Morgan, R.M. and Hunt, S.D. (1994) The commitment–trust theory of relationship marketing. *Journal of Marketing*, **58** (July), 20–38.

Murphy, D. (2007) Off the page, on to the web. *The Marketer*, (October), 31–3.

Napolitano, L. (1997) Customer–supplier partnering: a strategy whose time has come. *Journal of Selling and Sales Management*, **17**(4), 1–8.

Ojasalo, J. (2001) Key account management at company and individual levels in business-to-business relationships. *Journal of Business and Industrial Marketing*, **16**(3), 199–220.

Papas, C. (2008) Lawyers for luvvies. *The Marketer*, (March), 20–2.

Pardo, C. (1997) Key account management in the business-to-business field: the key accounts point-of-view. *Journal of Selling and Sales Management*, **17**(4), 17–26.

Ryals, L.J. and Holt, S. (2007) Creating and capturing value in KAM relationships. *Journal of Strategic Marketing*, **15** (December), 403–20.

Ryals, L.J. and Rogers, B. (2007) Key account planning: benefits, barriers and best practice. *Journal of Strategic Marketing*, **15** (May–July), 209–22.

Sharma, A. (1997) Who prefers key account management program? An investigation of business buying behaviour and buying firm characteristics. *Journal of Personal Selling and Sales Management*, **17**(4), 27–39.

Spencer, R. (1999) Key accounts: effectively managing strategic complexity. *Journal of Business and Industrial Marketing*, **14**(4), 291–310.

Stern, L. and El-Ansary, A.I. (1988) *Marketing Channels*, Englewood Cliffs, NJ: Prentice-Hall.

Stern, L. and El-Ansary, A.I. (1992) *Marketing Channels*, 4th edn. Englewood Cliffs, NJ: Prentice-Hall.

Valla, J.-P. (1982) The concept of risk in industrial buying behaviour. Workshop on Organisational Buying Behaviour, European Institute for Advanced Studies in Management, Brussels, December, 9–10.

Vöegle, S. (1992) *Handbook of Direct Mail. The Dialogue Method of Direct Written Sales Communication*. Englewood Cliffs, NJ: Prentice-Hall.

Vriens, M., van der Scheer, H.R., Hoekstra, J.C. and Bult, J. (1998) Conjoint experiments for direct mail response optimisations. *European Journal of Marketing*, **32**(3/4), 323–40.

Wilson, K., Croom, S., Millman, T. and Weilbaker, D.C. (2000) *Global Account Management Study Report*. Southampton: The Sales Research Trust.

Wotruba, T.R. (1991) The evolution of personal selling. *Journal of Personal Selling and Sales Management*, **11**(3), 1–12.

Wulf, K.D., Hoekstra, J.C. and Commandeur, H.R. (2000) The opening and reading behaviour of business-to-business direct mail. *Industrial Marketing Management*, **29**(2) (March), 133–45.

Chapter 30

Internal marketing communications

The concept of 'internal marketing' recognises the importance of organisational members (principally employees) as important markets in their own right. These markets can be regarded as segments (and can be segmented), each of which has particular needs and wants that require satisfaction in order that an organisation's overall goals be accomplished. Internal (marketing) communications not only serve to convey managerial intentions and members' feelings, but in many circumstances represent an integral aspect of communications with external stakeholder groups.

Aims and learning objectives

The aim of this chapter is to examine the context of internal marketing and how such issues might impact on an organisation's overall marketing communications.

The learning objectives of this chapter are to:

1. introduce the concept of internal marketing;
2. consider the purpose of internal marketing and communication;
3. explore issues associated with organisational identity;
4. examine the impact of corporate culture on planned communications;
5. explain the intellectual and emotional dimensions of brand engagement;
6. develop an insight into the notion of strategic credibility and stakeholder perception of organisations;
7. explain how the use of communication audits can assist the development of effective marketing communications.

For an applied interpretation see Simon Hardaker's MiniCase entitled ***Valuing internal communication: why should companies invest in communicating with employees?*** at the end of this chapter.

Introduction

It was established earlier that marketing communications is concerned with the way in which various stakeholders interact with one another and with the organisation. Traditionally, external stakeholders, for example, customers, intermediaries and financiers, are the prime focus of marketing communications. However, recognition of the importance of internal stakeholders as a group who should receive marketing attention has increased, and the concept of *internal marketing* emerged in the 1980s. This developed with greater impetus in the 1990s and is becoming a major focus of attention for both academics and practitioners.

Berry (1980) is widely credited as the first to recognise the term 'internal marketing', in a paper that sought to delineate between product- and service-based marketing activities. The notion that the delivery of a service-based offering is bound to the quality of the personnel delivering it has formed the foundation of a number of research activities and journal papers.

The popular view is that employees constitute an internal market in which paid labour is exchanged for designated outputs. An extension to this view is that employees are a discrete group of customers with whom management interacts (Piercy and Morgan, 1991), in order that relational exchanges can be maintained (developed) with external stakeholders. Although care needs to be taken to ensure that different groups of employees are recognised, employees are, as Christensen and Askegaard (2001) state, the most central audience for organisational communication.

> The popular view is that employees constitute an internal market in which paid labour is exchanged for designated outputs.

Both employees and managers impose their own constraints upon the range and nature of the activities an organisation pursues, including its external 'promotional' activities. Employees, for example, are important to external stakeholders not only because of the tangible aspects of service and production that they provide, but also because of the intangible aspects, such as attitude and the way in which the service is provided: 'How much do they really care?' Images are often based more on the intangible than the tangible aspects of employee communications.

Management, on the other hand, is responsible for the allocation of resources and the process and procedures used to create added value. Its actions effectively constrain the activities of the organisation and, either consciously or unconsciously, shape the nature and form of the communications the organisation adopts. It is important, therefore, to understand how organisations can influence and affect the communication process.

Therefore, as a legitimate type of 'customer', they should be subject to similar marketing practices. Each organisation is a major influence on its own marketing communications. Indeed, the perception of others is influenced by the character and personality of the organisation.

It can be argued that the role of the employee has been changing. Once they could be just part of the company, but this role has been extended so that they are now recognised as, and need to adopt the role of, brand ambassadors (Freeman and Liedtka, 1997; Hemsley, 1998). This is particularly important in service environments where employees represent the interface between an organisation's internal and external environments and where their actions can have a powerful effect in creating images among customers (Schneider and Bowen, 1985; Balmer and Wilkinson, 1991). It is evident that many now recognise the increasing importance of internal communications (Storey, 2001).

> The role of the employee has been changing.

Member/non-member boundaries

The demarcation of internal and external stakeholders is not as clear as many writers suppose. The boundaries that exist between members and non-members of an organisation are becoming increasingly indistinct as a new, more flexible workforce emerges. For

> The boundaries that exist between members and non-members of an organisation are becoming increasingly indistinct.

example, part-time workers, consultants, outsourced workers and temporary workforces spread themselves across organisational borders (Hatch and Schultz, 1997) and in many instances assume multiple roles of employee, consumer (product) and financial stakeholder (e.g. Halifax or Standard Life employees, who may be borrowers or savers and are now also shareholders).

According to Morgan (1997), many organisations have a problem, as they do not recognise that they are themselves part of their environment. The context in which they see themselves and other organisations is too sharp. They see themselves as discrete entities faced with the problem of surviving against the vagaries of the outside world, which is often constructed as a domain of threat and opportunity. He refers to these as *egocentric* organisations. They are characterised by a fixed notion of who they are or what they can be, and are determined to impose or sustain that identity at all times. This can lead to an overplay of their own importance and an underplay of the significance of the wider system of relationships of which they are a part. In attempting to sustain unrealistic identities, they produce identities that end up destroying important elements of the context of which they are part. The example provided by Morgan is of typewriter manufacturers who failed to see technological developments leading to electronic typewriters and then word processors.

It would appear that by redrawing or even collapsing boundaries with customers, competitors and suppliers, organisations are better able to create new identities and use internal marketing communications to better effect.

Purpose of internal marketing and communication

Research by Foreman and Money (1995) indicates that managers see the main components of internal marketing as falling into three broad areas, namely development, reward and vision for employees. These will inevitably vary in intensity on a situational basis.

All of these three components have communication as a common linkage. Employees and management (members) need to communicate with one another and with a variety of non-members, and do so through an assortment of methods. Communication with members, wherever they are located geographically, needs to be undertaken for a number of reasons. These include the DRIP factors (Chapter 1), but these communications also serve the additional purposes of providing transaction efficiencies and affiliation needs (see Table 30.1).

Table 30.1 The roles of internal marketing communications

DRIP factors	To provide information To be persuasive To reinforce – reassure/remind To differentiate employees/groups
Transactional	To coordinate actions To promote the efficient use of resources To direct developments
Affiliation	To provide identification To motivate personnel To promote and coordinate activities with non-members

The values transmitted to customers, suppliers and distributors through external communications need to be reinforced by the values expressed by employees, especially those who interact with these external groups. Internal marketing communications are necessary in order that internal members are motivated and involved with the brand such that they are able to present a consistent and uniform message to non-members. This is an aspect of integrated marketing communications and involves product- and organisation-centred messages. If there is a set of shared values, then internal communications are said to blend and balance the external communications. This process whereby employees are encouraged to communicate with non-members so that organisations ensure that what is promised is realised by customers is referred to as 'living the brand'. Hiscock (2002) claims that employees can be segmented according to the degree and type of support they give a brand. He claims that, in the United Kingdom, 30 per cent of employees are brand neutral, 22 per cent are brand saboteurs and 48 per cent are brand champions, of whom 33 per cent would talk about the brand positively if asked, and 15 per cent spontaneously.

Internal marketing communications are necessary in order that internal members are motivated and involved with the brand.

In a large number of both b2b and b2c organisations new products and services are often developed through the use of project teams. According to Lievens and Moenart (2000), project communication is characterised by both flows of communication among project members (intra-project communication) and flows across boundaries with external members (extra-project communication). Boundary spanners act as mediators facilitating communications flows internally (for resources) and externally to customers, suppliers, competitors and technologies. Project teams perceive differing levels of uncertainty associated with their task and these are related to external (user needs, technologies and the competition) and internal (human and financial resources) factors.

Boundary spanners act as mediators facilitating communications flows.

Uncertainty about the resources needs to be reduced in order to reduce uncertainty associated with external stakeholders, improve communication effectiveness and achieve project tasks. As will be seen later, the integration of internal and external communications is a key factor in the development of integrated marketing communications. Project teams have an important role to play in enhancing corporate reputation, particularly in the b2b sector.

Welch and Jackson (2007) provide an interesting and helpful insight into some of the issues associated with understanding internal communication. Although they assume a stakeholder approach and refrain from considering any related marketing issues, they suggest that internal communication should be considered in terms of four dimensions: internal line management communication; internal peer communication; internal project communication and internal corporate communication. These are intended to provide a typology of internal communication and are set out in Table 30.2.

Attention is given to the fourth dimension, internal corporate communication. Welch and Jackson believe that this refers to communication between an organisation's strategic managers and its internal stakeholders, with the purpose of promoting *commitment* to the organisation, a sense of *belonging* (to the organisation), *awareness* of its changing environment and *understanding* of its evolving goals (2007: 186). These four goals are depicted in Figure 30.1.

These four goals serve to engage employees not only with their roles, tasks and jobs but also with the organisation. It is recognised that the internal environment incorporates the organisation's structure, culture, sub-cultures, processes, behaviour and leadership style and that this interacts with the external environment and provides context for the internal communication.

These four goals serve to engage employees not only with their roles, tasks and jobs but also with the organisation.

Some of these ideas about commitment, belonging and identity with an organisation are explored later in this chapter.

Table 30.2 Internal communication matrix

Dimension	Level	Direction	Participants	Content
1. Internal line management communication	Line managers/ supervisors	Predominantly two-way	Line managers-employees	Employees' roles Personal impact, e.g. appraisal discussions, team briefings
2. Internal team peer communication	Team colleagues	Two-way	Employee-employee	Team information, e.g. team task discussions
3. Internal project peer communication	Project group colleagues	Two-way	Employee-employee	Project information, e.g. Project issues
4. Internal corporate communication	Strategic managers/top management	Predominantly one-way	Strategic managers-all employees	Organisational/corporate issues, e.g. goals, objectives, new developments, activities and achievements

Source: Welch and Jackson (2007).

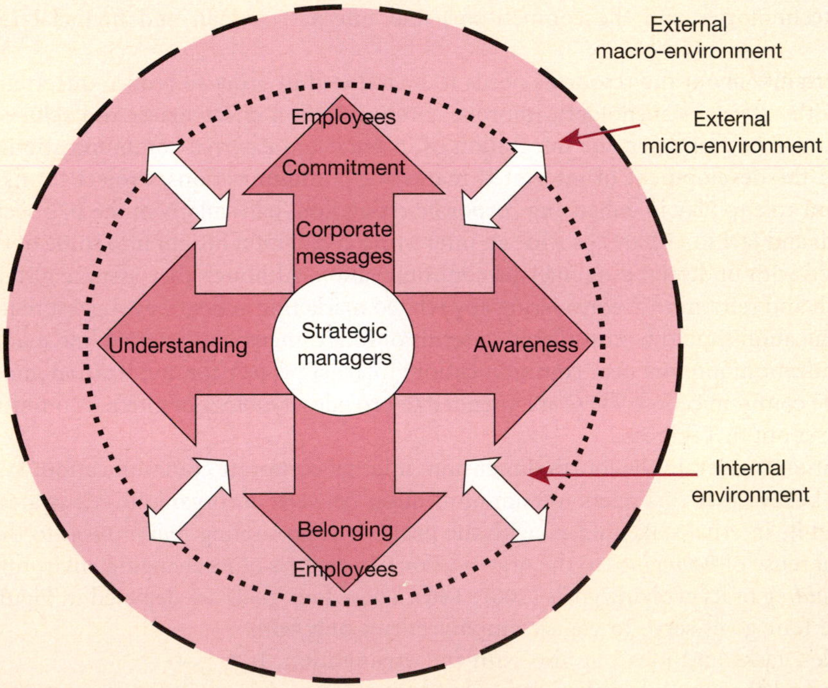

Figure 30.1 Internal corporate communication
Source: Welch and Jackson (2007).

Organisational identity

Organisational identity is concerned with what individual members think and feel about the organisation to which they belong. When their perception of the organisation's characteristics accords with their own self-concept then the strength of organisational identity will be strong (Dutton *et al.*, 1994). Organisational identity also refers to the degree to which feelings and thoughts about the distinctive characteristics are shared among the members (Dutton and Dukerich, 1991). There are, therefore, both individual and collective aspects to organisational identity.

There are both individual and collective aspects to organisational identity.

Mention was made earlier of brand ambassadors, people who identify closely with a brand and speak openly and positively about it. Albert and Whetten (1985) stated that organisations must make three main decisions: who they are, what business they are in and what they want to be. In order that these decisions be made, they claim that consideration must be given to what is central, what is distinctive and what is enduring about the character of the organisation.

Non-members of an organisation also develop feelings and thoughts about what are the central, enduring and distinctive characteristics of an organisation. It is highly probable that there will be variances between the perceptions and beliefs of members and non-members, and this may be a cause of confusion, misunderstanding or even conflict.

ViewPoint 30.1 Using people for strategic positioning

The role of employees within the strategic branding process is understood by some organisations. However, there is a big difference between understanding the issue and implementing a cohesive strategy designed to integrate the workforce.

One company to have successfully implemented a strategic approach is easyJet. Several directors visited Southwest Airlines and returned with fresh insight into how service can be used as a key point of differentiation. In what is referred to as the 'low cost' airline market, price is normally the discriminating attribute. Low costs are traditionally achieved by providing few elements of service. Indeed, easyJet helped pioneer the use of the web to drive bookings, and in doing stripped out a high level of service costs.

EasyJet reformulated their proposition to 'Low cost, with care and convenience'. This delivered messages about price, care and destination: i.e. they fly to recognised and accessible airports, at a low price but provide customers with a high level of care.

In order to provide customer care with credibility, the company sought to establish linkages through each point of customer interaction. However, early research found staff unhappy about the colour of the uniforms (bright orange) and structure of the shift rostas. The uniforms were redesigned with the help of staff and the shift system changed. The brand repositioning was explained in the staff magazine and discussed at internal workshops. This was supplemented with a revised incentive scheme designed to promote exceptional customer service.

The net result was that profits rose 56 per cent.

Source: Edwards (2008).

Question

To what extent is the emphasis on customer service and interaction a contradiction to the web-only booking system?

Task

Consider a flight you have taken and make a list of the customer/airline points of interaction. How would you improve them?

Table 30.3 When organisational identity is important

During the formation of the organisation
At the loss of an identity-sustaining element
On the accomplishment of an organisation's *raison d'être*
Through extremely rapid growth
If there is a change in the collective status
Retrenchment

Source: After Albert and Whetten (1985).

This discrepancy between what Goodman and Pennings (1977) termed private and public identities can impair the 'health' of the organisation. The 'unhealthier' or greater the discrepancy, the more will be the difficulty in generating the resources required to guarantee corporate survival. In other words, the closer the member/non-member identification, the better placed the organisation will be to achieve its objectives.

Organisational identity is deemed to be important at a collective level, when an organisation is formed or when there is a major change to the continuity of the goals of the organisation or when the means of accomplishment are hindered or broken (see Table 30.3). According to Dutton and Penner (1993), what an individual sees as important, distinctive and unique about an organisation will affect the individual's assessment of the importance of an issue facing the organisation and also the degree to which it is of personal importance.

For members, organisational identity may be conceptualised as their perception of their organisation's central and distinctive attributes, including its positional status and relevant compositional group. Consequently, external events that refute or call into question these defining characteristics may threaten the perception that organisational members have of their organisational identity (Dutton and Dukerich, 1991).

Research by Elsbach and Kramer (1996) found that members of a high-ranking organisation (MBA schools) perceived a threat because the ranking devalued their central and cherished identity dimensions and so refuted their prior claims of positional status.

Members used selective categorisations to re-emphasise positive perceptions of their organisational identities for both themselves and their non-member audiences by highlighting identity dimensions or alternative groups with which they should be compared and that were not previously identified, the intention being to deflect attention.

> There is a significant interdependence between individuals' social identities and their perceptions of their organisational identities.

Dutton and Dukerich state that there is a significant interdependence between individuals' social identities and their perceptions of their organisational identities. Thus, as they care about how their organisations are described and how they are compared with other organisations, so they experience cognitive distress (identity dissonance) when they think that their organisation's identity is being threatened by what they perceive as inaccurate descriptions or misleading (unfair) comparisons with other organisations.

In response to this distress, members restore positive self-perceptions by highlighting their organisation's membership in alternative comparison groups. It is normal to assume that identity is relatively static. However, just as organisations can experience strategic drift when the corporate strategy and performance move further away, each period, from the intended or expected pattern, so organisations can suffer from identity drift away from the expected lifecycle. Kimberley (1980) argues that this can occur for three main reasons: environmental complexity; identity divestiture; and organisational success.

This indicates that care must be given to understanding and managing the organisational identity to ensure that any discrepancy between members' and non-members' perceptions of what is central, enduring and distinctive is minimised and to be aware of identity dissonance should the organisation be threatened and the values upheld by its members challenged.

Organisational culture

According to Beyer (1981), organisational identity is a subset of the collective beliefs that constitute an organisation's culture. Indeed, internal marketing is shaped by the prevailing culture, as it is the culture that provides the context within which internal marketing practices are to be accomplished.

Corporate culture encompasses the basic assumptions and beliefs that members of an organisation take for granted, share and use to shape its view of itself (Schein, 2004). A more common view of organisational culture is 'the way we do things around here'. It is the result of a number of factors, ranging through the type and form of business the organisation is in, its customers and other stakeholders, its geographical position, and its size, age and facilities. These represent the more tangible aspects of corporate culture. There are a host of intangible elements as well, including the assumptions, values and beliefs that are held and shared by members of the organisation. These factors combine to create a unique environment, one where norms or guides to expected behaviour influence all members, whatever their role or position.

A more common view of organisational culture is 'the way we do things around here'.

ViewPoint 30.2 B&Q shares values

B&Q is part of Kingfisher plc, Europe's leading home improvement retail group and the third largest in the world, with over 800 stores in eight countries in Europe and Asia. In the UK B&Q has over 320 stores and employs over 34,000 people, which means that communicating a consistent message to these employees is a complex yet important task.

B&Q utilises a number of different internal communications tools to undertake this task, including magazines and newsletters, email and team briefs.

B&Q pioneered the use of real-life store staff in its advertising, back in 1996 and over the years more than 500 employees in orange aprons have featured in the popular B&Q ads. The ads were successful partly because they featured fallible, real life people and partly because they reflect the popularity of reality TV programmes.

In the autumn of 2008 B&Q launched a new advertising campaign 'Real Staff, Real Value' which featured real-life store staff. The multi million pound TV and print campaign also introduced an evolution of B&Q's end line from 'Let's do it' to 'Let's do it . . . let's B&Q it'.

The first execution in the TV campaign 'Kitchen' shows Lynne rehearsing her lines at home before she's filmed in store selling the kitchen range. Another execution features David rehearsing his lines on a park bench before doing a piece to camera on B&Q's bathroom range.

Research undertaken by B&Q reveals that in periods of financial uncertainty people feel more confident shopping in well-known, multiple retailers with expert staff. The B&Q campaign returns to the company's roots and taps into the existing goodwill people have for the brand.

B&Q recognises that their staff are a major part of the brand's success. It also recognises that the continuing commitment of its staff is essential, and effective internal communications are an important component in the process to gain this commitment.

Source: Material kindly provided by B&Q.

Question

How would you measure staff commitment?

Task

Can you think of other firms who have involved their employees in their promotional activities?

Exhibit 30.1 B&Q feature their staff in their advertising to provide credibility, boost morale and enhance customer perceptions
Picture reproduced with the kind permission of B&Q.

Levels of organisational culture

Corporate culture, according to Schein (1985), consists of a number of levels. The first of these, according to Thompson (1990), is the most visible level. This includes physical aspects of the organisation, such as the way in which the telephone is answered, the look and style of the reception area, and the general care afforded to visitors. Other manifestations of these visible aspects are the advertisements, logos, letterheads and other written communications that an organisation generates.

The second level consists of the values held by key personnel. For example, should particular sales teams who regularly better their targets have their targets increased or should certain members of the sales team be redeployed to less successful teams or new markets? If the decision is made to increase the target, and the outcome is successful, then the decision is more likely to be repeated when the same conditions arise again.

The third level in Schein's approach is achieved when the decision to increase the target becomes an automatic response to particular conditions. A belief is formed and becomes an assumption about behaviour in the organisation. This automatic approach can lead to complementary behaviour by members of the sales team. The placing of orders can become manipulated, to the extent that orders placed in month 6 may be 'delayed' or stuck in the top drawer of the sales representative's desk, until some point in month 7, when it is appropriate to release them.

The belief that the targets will be increased can lead to a behaviour that is referred to as 'the way we do things around here'. This behaviour leads to relative stability for all concerned and need not be disturbed unless a change is introduced, whose source is elsewhere in the system, i.e. outside the team.

ViewPoint 30.3 Changing values at QinetiQ

The Defence Evaluation and Research Agency (DERA) owned by the Ministry of Defence (MoD) in the United Kingdom has recently moved from public to private ownership. Many of the staff at the organisation are scientists and engineers who, under public ownership, had no real need to interact with a diverse external audience and, indeed knew little of the work in other divisions and parts of DERA. However, the success of the QinetiQ organisation depended on employees adopting a commercially focused value set, one that is very different from that engrained through working in a publicly owned organisation. They also needed to be committed and engaged with the new organisation.

This transformation was achieved partly through the use of CEO-led roadshows plus printed matter, cascade briefings, desk drop packs and online web chats (with the CEO). Internal, direct-looped radio, accessed through telephones and later desktop PCs, are used by the CEO to communicate key developments, to provide divisional results or just to encourage feedback. One broadcast attracted an audience of 2,000 people, of whom 300 provided immediate feedback. In addition, the use of an intranet, a variety of posters and notice boards plus face-to-face staff meetings all reflect the organisation's drive to reach employees, to actively encourage involvement and in doing so engage them within the QinetiQ brand.

Source: Hardaker and Fill (2005).

Question

To what extent is the choice of media important in internal communications?

Task

Choose three media and make a list of their qualities with regard to delivering internal communications.

Culture and communication

Corporate culture is not a static phenomenon; the stronger the culture, the more likely it is to be transmitted from one generation of organisational members to another, and it is also probable that the culture will be more difficult to change if it is firmly embedded in the organisation. Most writers acknowledge that effective cultural change is difficult and a long-term task. Achieving a cultural fit is necessary if an organisation wishes to embrace a strategy that is incompatible with the current mind set of the organisation. Hunger and Wheelan (1993), for example, state that, to bring about cultural change, good communication, throughout the organisation, is a prerequisite for success.

Mitchell (1998) considers the strong corporate culture that exists at Procter & Gamble. Depending upon one's perspective, this rigid formal hierarchical culture may be considered an advantage or a disadvantage. On the plus side it allows for strong identity, consistency and people development opportunities, as the company has a 'promote from within' policy. On the downside, the strength and penetration of the culture and need to toe the party line can restrict innovation, entrepreneurship and the use of initiative.

This strength of culture and the cautious approach to risk taking may be responsible for the consistent emphasis on product attributes, performance and pack shots in its advertising and communications, unlike its close rival Unilever, which makes greater use of emotions in its advertising. Procter & Gamble appears to recognise this as a limitation and has recently embarked on a change of emphasis and has incorporated a more emotional approach in its communications.

The strength of culture and the cautious approach to risk taking may be responsible for the consistent emphasis on product attributes.

Changing the culture will be a challenge, but to be successful senior management will, among other things, need to be 'obsessive' about communicating the following to all members of the organisation (Gordon, 1985):

1. the current performance and position of the organisation in comparison with its competition and the outlook for the future;
2. the vision of what the organisation was to become and how it would achieve it;
3. the progress the organisation had made in achieving those elements identified previously as important.

The focus of this communication is internal, usually through training and development programmes. Certain complex offerings, such as information technology-based products, require channel members to provide high levels of training and support. It is also important to communicate the objectives of the network and to share responsibility for the performance of the channel as a whole. This is partly achieved by members fulfilling their roles as successful dealers, retailers or manufacturers, but there is still a strong requirement for the channel leader to set out what is required from each member of its different networks and to report on what has been achieved to date.

Management of the communication finances, through time, will show the degree to which an organisation values such investments. Brands need time, the long term, to build and develop strength. Cutting back on investment in communications, especially advertising, in times of recession and difficulty, reveals management to view such activities as an expense, a cost against short-run needs. Furthermore, the expectation of channel members may be that a certain volume of marketing communications is necessary, not only to sustain particular levels of business, but also because competitors are providing established levels of communication activity. What is important is that the communications manager understands the culture of the organisation and the primary networks, values, styles, motivations and norms so that the communications work with, rather than against, the corporate will.

Brand engagement

The relationship between corporate strategy and communications is important. Traditionally, these communications are perceived as those that make the network between an organisation's employees and its managers. This internal perspective of communications is important, particularly when organisations are in transition (see the mini case at the end of the chapter). This is only one part of the communication process. Employees are just one of the many stakeholders each organisation must seek to satisfy. Communications regarding strategic issues should also be targeted at internal and external stakeholders in order to gain their goodwill, involvement and understanding.

> It is clear that long-term relationships cannot be sustained if the brand delivery is unsatisfactory.

It is clear that long-term relationships cannot be sustained if the brand delivery is unsatisfactory and where the people behind the brand do not match the expectation generated by the promise. Apart from computer-mediated communication, employees provide the main points of contact between organisations or with customers. These interactions or 'moments of truth' as Gummesson (1999) refers to them, need to be consistent and of high quality.

Intellectual and emotional aspects

Employees are required to deliver both the functional aspects of an organisation's offering and the emotional dimensions, particularly in service environments. By attending to these twin elements it is possible that long-term relationships between sellers and buyers can develop

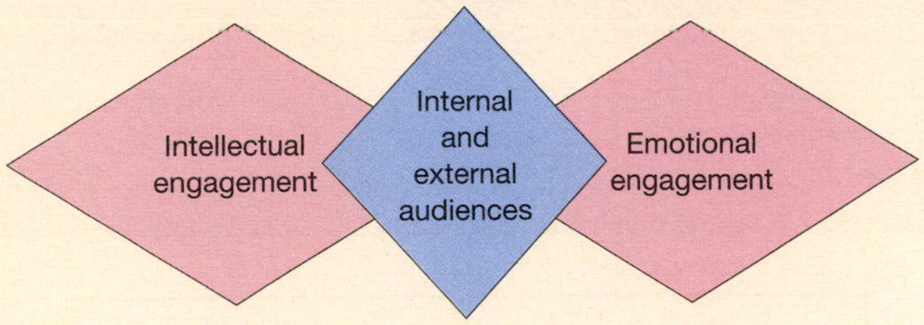

Figure 30.2 Brand engagement

effectively. Hardaker and Fill (2005) explore ideas concerning the notion that employees need to buy-in to organisational vision, goals and strategy (Thomson and Hecker, 2000). This buy-in, or engagement, consists of two main components, an intellectual and an emotional element (see Figure 30.2). The intellectual element is concerned with employees buying-in and aligning themselves with the organisation's strategy, issues and overall direction. The emotional element is concerned with employees taking ownership of their contribution and becoming committed to the achievement of stated goals. Communication strategies should be based on the information processing styles of employees and access to preferred media. Communications should reflect a suitable balance between the need for rational information to meet intellectual needs and expressive types of communication to meet the emotional needs of the workforce. It follows that the better the communication, the higher the level of engagement.

> Communication strategies should be based on the information processing styles of employees and access to preferred media.

The development of internal brands based around employees can be accomplished effectively and quickly by simply considering the preferred information-processing style of an internal audience. By developing messages that reflect the natural processing style and using a diversity of media that best complements the type of message and the needs of each substantial internal target audience, the communication strategy is more likely to be successful.

Advertising and the impact on employees

Gilly and Wolfinbarger (1998) concluded that an organisation's advertising can have both a positive and a negative effect on its employees. Such advertising can serve to clarify roles, make promises that can be realistically delivered and demonstrates that the organisation values its employees. These positive outcomes can be seen in terms of improved morale and commitment.

Conversely, negative effects ensue when the advertising promises are unrealistic and cannot be delivered, messages are not true or the roles portrayed are far from flattering. For example, Boots used a campaign to inform consumers about its 'mix-and-match' offer. The ads depicted a member of staff explaining the deal to a confused colleague, who then apologises announcing that it is her first day. Staff, according to Witt (2001), complained that they were made to look stupid and incompetent. The outcome is low morale, distrust and unfavourable attitudes that can be perceived by non-members. It seems important, therefore, to generate advertising messages that are perceived by employees to be transparently achievable and consistent, and this may involve the participation of a few staff in the development of advertising strategy.

Gilly and Wolfinbarger developed a framework that presents the impact of advertising on employees (see Figure 30.3). This model shows that employees use three main criteria when evaluating the advertising used by their employers, namely accuracy of the message, value

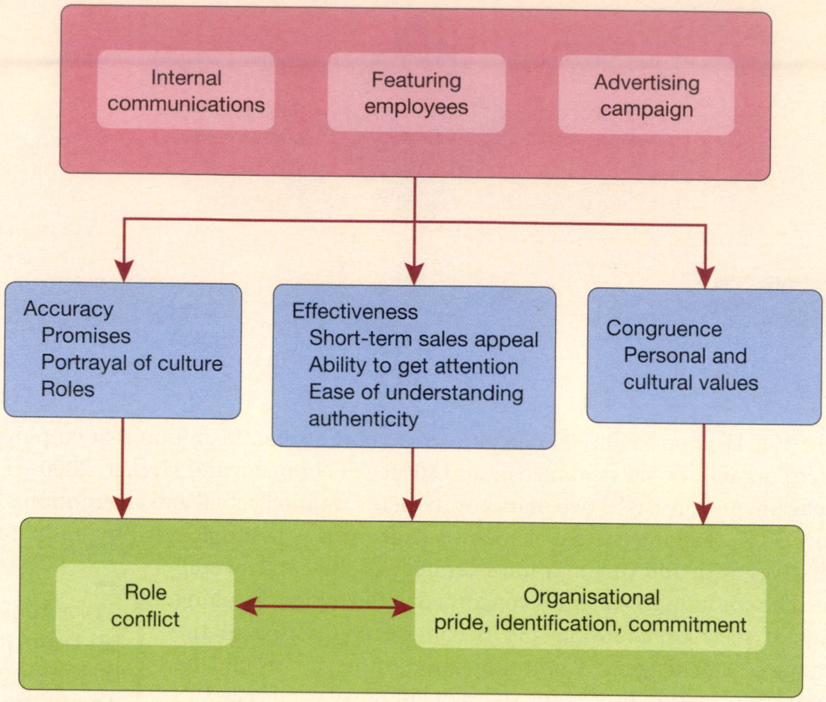

Figure 30.3 The impact of advertising on employees
Source: Adapted from Gilly and Wolfinbarger (1998). Used with kind permission.

congruence and effectiveness. In order to reduce any gap that might emerge as a result of an advertising campaign (and consequent deterioration in morale and commitment), increased vertical and horizontal communications are deemed necessary. This might require staff to be involved in both advertising development and in some cases actual participation in the advertisement, the pretesting of ideas and the dissemination of the advertising and the supporting rationale.

All stakeholders need to know what the objectives of the organisation are.

All stakeholders need to know what the objectives of the organisation are, particularly the organisation's mission and overriding vision, as this will impact on the other organisations in the performance network. For example, if Heinz or Pedigree Petfoods were to announce that, in the future, all their products were to be presented in recyclable containers, then current suppliers might need to reformulate their offerings and any future suppliers would be aware of the constraint this might place on them. The information is provided in order that others may work with them and continue supplying offerings to end-users with a minimum of interruption.

Barich and Kotler (1991) suggest that the concept of positioning (the process whereby offerings are perceived by consumers relative to the competition) applies at the brand and corporate levels. If an organisation is pursuing a generic strategy of differentiation, then the positioning statements of the organisation need to reflect this. The image that stakeholders have of an organisation and its offerings affects their disposition towards the organisation, their intentions to undertake market transactions and the nature of the relationships between members.

Good external communications are important because, among other benefits, they can provide a source of competitive advantage. Perrier has built its share of the mineral water market on the volume and style of its planned communications. It has dominated communications in the market and has effectively set a mobility barrier that demands that any major challenger must be prepared to replicate the size of Perrier's investment in communications. The quality of the Perrier communications has also led distributors and other network members to support and want to be involved with the organisation, as evidenced by the swift recovery in market share after all world stocks had to be withdrawn because a small number of bottles had been identified as 'contaminated'. Morden (1993) refers to these positive external perceptions as intangible benefits that help to differentiate the organisation from its competitors.

All marketing strategies, such as those to harvest, build, hold and divest, require different communication strategies and messages. Similarly, market penetration, product development, market development and product penetration strategies all require varying forms of support that must be reflected in the communications undertaken by the organisation.

Marketing research may indicate that different stakeholders do not perceive the corporate and marketing strategies of an organisation in the same way as that intended by management. Some stakeholders may perceive the performance of an organisation inaccurately. This means that the organisation is failing to communicate in an effective and consistent way, and any such mismatch will, inevitably, lead to message confusion and relative disadvantage in the markets in which the organisation operates.

The communication of strategic intent and corporate performance must be harmonised. Understating, or even misleading different stakeholders may influence performance, and if claims are made for an organisation that suggest a level of performance or intent beyond reality, then credibility may be severely jeopardised.

Strategic credibility

According to Higgins and Bannister (1992), strategic credibility refers to 'how favourably key stakeholders view the company's overall corporate strategy and its strategic planning processes'.

> Strategic credibility refers to 'how favourably key stakeholders view the company's overall corporate strategy and its strategic planning processes'.

If stakeholders perceive the focus organisation as strategically capable, it is suggested that it will accrue a number of benefits. The benefits vary from industry to industry and according to each situation, but it appears from the early research that those organisations experiencing transition and that are not regulated in any way have potentially the most to gain from open corporate communication with their stakeholders. The benefits from this open attitude include improved stock market valuations and price/earnings multiples, better employee motivation and closer relationships with all members of the performance and support networks, particularly those within the financial community. There are four main determinants of strategic credibility:

- an organisation's strategic capability;
- past performance;
- communication of corporate strategy to key stakeholders;
- the credibility of the CEO.

Strategic capability

Capability is a prerequisite for credibility. The perception that stakeholders have of the strategic processes within an organisation will influence their belief that the focus organisation can or cannot achieve its objectives. This is important in networks that are characterised by close working arrangements and high levels of interdependence. Should one organisation indicate that it lacks the necessary capability to perform strategically, then other members of the network are likely to be affected. The sharing of a strategic vision, one that may be common to all members of the stakeholder network, is a positive indicator of the acceptance that the focus organisation is strategically capable.

ViewPoint 30.4 **Virtual internal learning**

One critical part of the employee/customer interface is the customer's perception of the employee's knowledge of the organisation's products and services. It is therefore important to ensure that all employees have a comprehensive and up-to-date knowledge of the organisation's offerings.

Vodafone established an elearning facility designed to help employees understand the business and recent developments. The programme was based within a microsite on the web site facilitating employee interaction from wherever they were based. Once staff had become familiar with Vodafone's range of products and services they were required to complete an online assessment.

Source: Gardner (2007).

Question

What does the online assessment at Vodafone really achieve?

Task

Using an organisation you are familiar with, find out how they enable employees to develop their knowledge of the organisation's products and/or services.

Past performance

The maintenance of a sustained strategic capability profile depends partly on corporate performance. Poor performance does not sustain confidence, but even the existence of a strong performance is only worthwhile if it is communicated properly. The communication should inform the target audiences that the performance was planned and that there was sound reasoning and management judgement behind the performance.

Corporate communications

> Organisations should inform members of the network of their strategic intentions as well as their past performance.

Organisations should inform members of the network of their strategic intentions as well as their past performance. This requires the accurate targeting and timing of the messages at a pace suitable and appropriate to the target's requirements. Higgins and Bannister refer to financial analysts, in particular, as stakeholders in need of good information. They argue that trying to evaluate the performance of a diversified organisation operating in a number of different markets, of which many of the analysts lack knowledge and expertise, is frustrating and difficult. Good information delivered through appropriate media and at particular times can be beneficial in the development of the realm of understanding between parties.

By keeping financial analysts aware of the strategic developments and the strategic thinking of the organisation and the industries in which it operates, the value of the organisation is more likely to reflect corporate performance.

The credibility of the CEO

The fourth element proposed by Higgins and Bannister concerns the ability of the CEO to communicate effectively with a variety of audiences. By projecting strong, balanced and positive communications, it is thought that a visible CEO can improve the overall reputation of the organisation. Coupled with the improvement will be a perception of the strategic capability of the organisation. The CEO, can therefore, be regarded as a major determinant of the organisation's perceived strategic credibility.

Haji-Ioannou, Terence Conran, Alan Sugar, James Dyson and Richard Branson are some of the major CEOs to promote themselves on behalf of their organisations, but there are many others who have tried and failed. However, research by Newell and Shemwell (1995) suggests that care should be taken when using CEOs as endorsers. They argue that the impact of source credibility may be reduced because of beliefs about product attributes, and this in turn may affect behavioural intentions. Therefore, CEOs might be best used as endorsers when informational-, rather than emotional- or transformational-based messages predominate.

ViewPoint 30.5 A groce(ry) way of using CEOs?

The choice of CEO is normally based on a range of criteria. For most organisations the key criteria include a successful career track record, particular knowledge and insight to the market and industry, a strong network of influential contacts and that candidates be able to demonstrate excellence at a range of tasks. For most, one of these tasks concerns their media relations skills, their ability to manage the media and front-up the organisation, especially when events are not running well.

In 2004, Sainsbury's appointed Justin King as CEO, and he quickly established a recovery plan. Since its inception he has consistently been in the media, taking questions and putting forward a positive message about the organisation at all times. For example, he regularly appears on Breakfast Television commenting on the latest trading reports or discussing a supermarket-related issue.

In much the same way, Marks & Spencer appointed Stuart Rose as CEO at a time when the company was in crisis and under threat of a take-over. The success of his recovery plan has been even more astounding in comparison to Sainsbury's, and he too appears frequently in the media commenting on the latest results and future activities associated with M&S.

Question

Why do some companies prefer to use their CEOs as their lead media person when they could use trained actors, media-friendly staff or just not comment at all?

Task

Make notes listing reasons why Asda and Tesco do not use their CEOs in the same way as Sainsbury's and M&S.

Exhibit 30.2 CEO endorser for M&S – Stuart Rose
Courtesy of Marks and Spencer Group plc.

For example, Richard Branson has been used as CEO endorser of the Virgin Group. As chairman he has been a focal point in the promotion of Virgin financial products (mainly informational messages), but has not played such a central role in the planned communications concerning the airline Virgin Atlantic, where emotionally based messages have been used to influence brand choice decisions.

In addition to advertising, some CEOs are using personal blogs as a means of communications and standout. For example, Mark Price, Managing Director of Waitrose, launched a blog through the company's web site. His theme is healthy eating and the blogs monitor his attempt to lose weight. As Bokaie (2008) argues, this approach has difficulties because blogging requires answers and interaction. So when Charles Dunstone, CEO of Carphone Warehouse, started his blog he promised to keep everyone up-to-date.

Unfortunately he began just as the company had launched Talk Talk, a free broadband offer. The demand was so heavy that the company could not keep up. Thousands of customers became extremely frustrated and the media leveraged the story in their inimitable way. The result was that even though the connections were eventually made, the blogs stopped immediately.

Internal communications: auditing and planning

Increasingly, organisations understand the need to adopt a planned approach to the deployment of their employees in order to support the external brand. One such approach has been identified by Mahnert and Torres (2007) who offer a framework to the process of developing a internal brand. They identify seven key factors that influence the success or failure of internal branding. These are set out in Table 30.4.

Table 30.4 Seven factors for internal branding

Internal factors	Explanation
Organisation	Cultural change is difficult but may be necessary where there is no match with the objectives. Use cross-functional coordination and cooperation to reduce departmentalised thinking and internal competition.
Information	Important to provide in-depth knowledge of the external and internal environments. Changes to current programmes may emerge as a result.
Management	Senior management must not only support and actively endorse the internal programme, they must be *seen* to do so as well. Visibility is key.
Communication	Critical to keep everyone informed but without overloading them.
Strategy	Need to align strategies and programmes in order to reduce the potential for conflict where there is a poor fit between the brand and the objectives of the organisation.
Staff	Support at all levels internally is an antecedent for success. Therefore, recruiting, motivating and rewarding staff is important for internal branding.
Education	It is necessary to understand and monitor employee beliefs, attitudes and perceptions in order that an internal programme be kept on track.

Source: Based on Mahnert and Torres (2007).

STAGE	STEP	ELEMENTS
Stage 1: Planning	I Preparation	1 Decide on timing
		2 Establish quantifiable short- and long-term targets
		3 Gain managerial support and generate awareness
		4 Secure a suitable budget
	II Investigation	5 Constituency assessment
		6 Internal market research
		7 Cultural fit analysis
	III Configuration	8 Align business objectives and brand values
		9 Link external and internal messages
		10 Segment where appropriate
		11 Ensure appropriate frequency
		12 Decide on language and messages design
Stage 2: Executing	IV Facilitation	13 Decide on degree of staff empowerment
		14 Obtain and sustain staff involvement
	V Implementation	15 Utilise multiple channels in multiple directions
		16 Reduce hierarchical communicative and execulive boundaries to ensure organisational permeation
	VI Remuneration	17 Develop a fair bonus system
		18 Offer brand-oriented education and training
		19 Link measurable effective brand commitment and team spirit to promotional prospects
Stage 3: Evaluating	VII Quantification	20 Establish a coherent balanced scorecard measurement system
		21 Regularly assess internal brand commitment and external orientation
	VIII Reaction	22 Facilitate constant, multi-directional feedback
	IX Alteration	23 Conduct regular review of programme and alter where necessary

Figure 30.4 The consolidated internal branding framework
Source: Mahnert and Torres (2007).

Mahnert and Torres develop a consolidated internal branding framework, drawn from the key, salient and confirmed elements in the literature. These they group into the planning, execution and evaluation phases. Their framework is replicated at Figure 30.4.

Research is an important element in the design of communication plans. Associated with this should be an evaluation of the most recent attempts at communicating with target audiences. The accumulation of this type of short-run information is useful because it builds into a database that can be used to identify key factors over the long run. Regression analysis can eventually be used to identify key variables in the marketing communications and marketing plans.

The communications strategies of competitors should also be measured and evaluated. Organisations and offerings do not exist in isolation from each other and competitor activities; messages, styles and levels of spend should also be taken into account. If a differentiation strategy is being pursued it would appear pointless and wasteful to position an offering in the same way as a main competitor.

The process by which an organisation communicates with its target audiences is, as we have seen, extremely important. To assist the process of evaluating the effectiveness of past communication strategies, strategic credibility and the corporate image held by different members of all networks, a communications audit should be undertaken. Financial audits examine the processes by which organisations organise and systematically manage their financial affairs. Some of the underlying agenda items may be to prevent fraud and malpractice, but the positive aspects of the financial audit are to understand what is happening, to develop new ways of performing certain tasks and to promote efficiency and effectiveness. The same principle holds for the communications audit. How is the organisation communicating and are there better ways of achieving the communication objectives?

A communications audit is a process that can help assess whether an organisation is communicating with its consumers and other stakeholders in an effective and meaningful way. A further important goal of such an exercise is to determine whether the communications perceived and understood by the target audiences are the messages that were intended in the first place. Are the messages being decoded in the manner in which they were designed when they were encoded? This exercise helps organisations to develop their realm of understanding with their respective network members and includes all internal and external communications, whether overt or covert.

Procedures associated with a communications audit

> The task is to identify consistent themes and the logic of the organisation's communications.

All forms of printed and visual communications (brochures, leaflets, annual reports, letterheads, advertisements, etc.) need to be collected and assembled in a particular location. Examples of main competitors' materials should also be brought together, as this will provide benchmarks for market evaluation. Once collated, the task is to identify consistent themes and the logic of the organisation's communications.

Ind (1992) suggests that one way of accomplishing this is to develop a communications matrix (see Figure 30.5). Information needs to be grouped by type of offering (vertically) and then by each type of medium (horizontally). The vertical grouping helps determine the variety of messages that customers receive if they are exposed to all the communications relating to a single offering. Are the messages consistent? Are the messages logically related? Is the related logic one that is intended and what is the total impact of these communications? The horizontal grouping helps determine message consistency across a number of different offerings, perhaps from different divisions. If a single dealer or end-user receives the communications relating to a product line or even a particular product mix, is the perception likely to be confusing?

Internal communications should be included in the audit. An analysis of official publications, such as in-house magazines, is obvious, but materials posted on notice boards and the way in which the telephone is answered affect the perception that stakeholders have of the organisation.

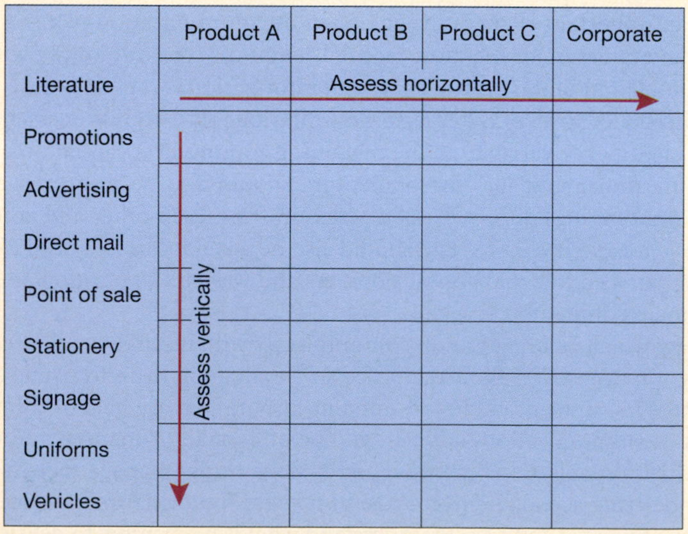

Product A
Product B
Product C
Corporate
Literature
Promotions
Advertising
Direct mail
Point of sale
Stationery
Signage
Uniforms
Vehicles
Assess horizontally
Assess vertically

Figure 30.5 A communications audit matrix
Source: Ind (1992). Used with kind permission.

The audit needs to incorporate research into the attitudes of employees to the organisation and the perceptions held by various stakeholders. This will involve both qualitative and quantitative research. The objective is to determine whether the image of the organisation reflects reality. If corporate performance exceeds the overall image, then corporate communications are not working effectively. If the image is superior to performance, then the operations of the organisation need to be improved.

The objective is to determine whether the image of the organisation reflects reality.

Organisations should understand how they are perceived by their stakeholders. A communications audit focuses attention on the totality of messages transmitted and provides a framework for corporate identity programmes.

Functional capability

The final elements to be reviewed as part of the internal marketing context are those relating to the individual functional areas within an organisation. A firm's overall core competence may be the result of a number of competences held at functional level. Internal marketing can be regarded as a key to providing strong external marketing performance (Greene *et al.*, 1994). This is achieved by releasing high levels of internal service provision within the functional areas. As Varey (1995: 42) confirms, 'Internal service quality is necessary for superior external service quality'.

Financial capability

Before any communications plan can be devised in any detail, it is necessary to have a broad understanding of the financial capability of the organisation; in other words, how much money is available for communications? This is important, as it affects the objectives that are to be set later and the choice of media necessary to carry the organisation's messages. For example, it is pointless asking dealers to undertake training programmes with end-users if the manufacturer does not have the sales representatives and training staff to instruct the dealers in the first place. Most medium-sized tour operators do not have the capital to fund television-based campaigns, even though some of the major national tour operators regularly use television.

Manufacturing capablility

One of the main aims of the communications plan is to stimulate and maintain demand. If production resources are limited the capacity needs to be aligned with the potential demand of a region or local area rather than nationally. Equally, the communications programme should be geared to the same area. All demand must be satisfied and likewise much of the communications programme will be ineffective in the short term if full production capacity has been reached.

Marketing capability

Discussion so far has assumed that the available corporate and marketing expertise is of sufficient calibre not only to formulate, but also to implement, a marketing strategy and its associated communications requirements. This raises questions about the customer orientation of the organisation, its attitude towards marketing and its general disposition towards the provision of a sustained level of customer service and satisfaction.

In a Research International study reported by Simms (2004) it was found that 47 per cent of respondents had little or no idea of what marketing does while 54 per cent believe that if marketing was abolished it would have little or no manageable impact on the company. This type of information is fairly typical of a number of studies in this area. Marketing appears to have difficulty establishing itself within many organisations, although its prominence in FMCG companies is high.

Many CEOs still have a poor understanding of what marketing is: to a number of them marketing is about selling and promotion. Such a shallow perspective is unlikely to lead to an organisational culture that will support a marketing orientation, especially when so few marketing directors have a main board position. The ability of an organisation to deliver consistently effective marketing communications is dependent upon many things, but among them are the presence of a customer-oriented organisational culture and leadership with a broad mix of marketing skills.

It seems reasonable to extend these conclusions by surmising that the same values and beliefs are necessary for the successful adoption of a planned approach to marketing communications, if only because it is a subsystem of marketing planning.

Summary

In order to help consolidate your understanding of internal marketing communications, here are the key points summarised against each of the learning objectives:

1. Introduce the concept of internal marketing.

Employees constitute a major stakeholder group, and an internal market based on the exchange of wages for labour. However, they have many other roles of varying complexity and they make a major contribution to the success and performance of the organisation. Their role in providing service and support for a brand has become increasingly recognised. The boundaries that exist between members and non-members of an organisation are becoming increasingly indistinct as a new, more flexible workforce emerges.

2. Consider the purpose of internal marketing and communication.

Managers see the main components of internal marketing as falling into three broad areas: development; reward; and vision for employees. These will inevitably vary in intensity on a situational basis. Internal communication can be considered in terms of four dimensions: internal line management communication; internal peer communication; internal project communication; and internal corporate communication.

The values transmitted to customers, suppliers and distributors through external communications need to be reinforced by the values expressed by employees, especially those who interact with these external groups. Internal marketing communications are necessary in order that internal members are motivated and involved with the brand such that they are able to present a consistent and uniform message to non-members.

3. Explore issues associated with organisational identity.

Organisational identity is concerned with what individual members think and feel about the organisation to which they belong. When their perception of an organisation's characteristics accords with that of an employee, the strength of organisational identity will be strong. Organisational identity also refers to the degree to which feelings and thoughts about the distinctive characteristics are shared among the members. There are, therefore, both individual and collective aspects to organisational identity.

4. Examine the impact of corporate culture on planned communications.

Corporate culture is concerned with the basic assumptions and beliefs that are shared by members of an organisation, that operate unconsciously and define an organisation's view of itself and its environment. A more common view of organisational culture is 'the way we do things around here'.

Both internal and external communications often reflect the prevailing and dominant culture, whether this be adventurous or cautious, innovative or solid, or pessimistic or optimistic the theme and tone of the communications is often mirrored.

5. Explain the intellectual and emotional dimensions of brand engagement.

Employees are required to deliver both the functional aspects of an organisation's offering and the emotional dimensions, particularly in service environments. By attending to these twin elements it is possible that long-term relationships between sellers and buyers can develop effectively. Engagement consists of two main components – an intellectual and an emotional element. The intellectual element is concerned with employees buying-in and aligning themselves with the organisation's strategy, issues and overall direction. The emotional element is concerned with employees taking ownership of their contribution and becoming committed to the achievement of stated goals.

6. Develop an insight into the notion of strategic credibility and stakeholder perception of organisations.

Strategic credibility refers to the extent to which key stakeholders favour the company's overall corporate strategy and its strategic planning processes.

If stakeholders perceive the focus organisation as strategically capable, it is suggested that the benefits include improved stock market valuations and price/earnings multiples, better employee motivation and closer relationships with all members of the performance and support networks, particularly those within the financial community. There are four main determinants of strategic credibility: an organisation's strategic capability; past performance; communication of corporate strategy to key stakeholders; and the credibility of the CEO.

7. Explain how the use of communication audits can assist the development of effective marketing communications.

A communications audit is a process that can assist marketing communications manager to assess whether an organisation is communicating with its consumers and other stakeholders in an effective and meaningful way. A further important goal is to determine whether the communications perceived and understood by the target audiences are the messages that were intended in the first place. Are the messages being decoded in the manner in which they were designed when they were encoded? This exercise helps organisations to develop their realm of understanding with their respective network members and includes all internal and external communications, whether overt or covert.

Review questions

1. Write a short definition of internal marketing and explain how marketing communications needs to assume both internal and external perspectives.
2. What is the role of internal marketing communications?
3. Write short notes explaining why organisational boundaries appear to be less clear than was once thought.
4. What is organisational identity and what do Albert and Whetten (1985) consider to be the three important aspects of identity?
5. Write a brief paper explaining why an understanding of corporate culture is important for successful marketing communications.
6. Why should marketing communications accommodate corporate strategy?

7. What are the elements of strategic credibility?
8. Select three different CEOs from a variety of organisations and evaluate their strategic credibility. What is your justification for selecting these individuals?
9. Prepare a communications matrix for an organisation (or brand/product) with which you are familiar.
10. Why might the functional capabilities of an organisation affect an organisation's marketing communications?

MiniCase Valuing internal communication: why should companies invest in communicating with employees?

Simon Hardaker: Group Head of Internal Communication at Rolls-Royce

Today's working environment is always changing. The job-for-life concept that our fathers may have anticipated when they left school is a rare one, both from an employee and from an employer perspective. Today's graduates join with a plan that rarely involves staying in the same company much beyond the completion of their graduate programme or apprenticeship. Employers since the 1980s have learned new vocabulary: downsizing; reengineering; right-sizing. All metaphors for shedding employees. The so-called psychological contract between employer and employee, 'I will do work in return for payment', has irrevocably changed.

In this environment, companies have had to find ways to recruit and hang on to the best employees. To this end, FTSE 100 companies such as Rolls-Royce are spending tens of millions of pounds, recruiting and training their workforce and expect a return on that investment over time.

Exhibit 30.3 The world's number two engine maker has over 12,400 jet engines in service
This photograph is reproduced with the permission of Rolls-Royce plc, copyright © Rolls-Royce plc 2006.

Since the early to mid 1990s, a concept known as employee engagement has been adopted to measure the amount of discretionary effort employees are prepared to expend at work; researched widely now for its affect on the employee/employer relationship, it is proving to be a popular metric to measure employees propensity to stay, give a 100 per cent to their work, and be positive about how they describe their employer. Research has highlighted a range of benefits to the company: improved performance and greater customer satisfaction and margins among others, that provide good reasons to invest in and pursue the idea of an engaged workforce. Communicating with employees is central to delivering this.

Rolls-Royce adopted the engagement measure in 2004, surveying a sample population, before doing a worldwide census of its workforce in 2006. While there were some variations in the levels of engagement, a consistent theme was repeated around the company, that of supervisor communication and the involvement of their staff in decision-making.

Some areas were better than others as might be expected. A range of approaches were adopted to address the engagement issues and one at the Rolls-Royce plant in Oakland, California, achieved particular distinction for the change in engagement. A programme called Winning Workplace was launched there in 2005 and moved engagement from bottom-quartile to top-quartile engagement levels.

Can engagement be improved by corporate initiatives?

There is a phrase in human resources management that 'employees don't leave their company, they leave their manager'. This is a good starting point for building engagement with employees. The relationship between staff and their manager is what motivates individuals and engages them with their work.

One of the drivers of engagement in individuals is the extent to which individuals have a say in 'how they complete the work they are allocated', something that is embedded in the relationship between supervisors and their staff and formed the basis of the Winning Workplace process.

The consultants LM Dulye and Co, along with the North America Internal Comms team, were engaged to support the programme, establishing a concept described as 'action-based teams'.

In simple terms, the plant's employees initially elected two groups, 13 employees in each, to form action teams. The first team looked at trust in leadership, the second

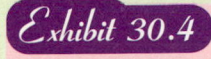

Exhibit 30.4 The Rolls-Royce Plant in Oakland, California
This photograph is reproduced with the permission of Rolls-Royce plc, copyright © Rolls-Royce plc 2006.

at knowledge of the business. Each followed a process facilitated by Dulye's team, through root-cause analysis, to develop a set of recommendations for each topic area.

Employees were recruited from all over the Oakland site, from all functions and all job levels. They had to commit 10 hours per week during business hours to supporting the programme; quite an investment from individuals and the business. The teams received training on how to analyse problems, come up with solutions and ways to implement these. They conducted 15-minute 'huddles' each week to discuss progress on the topic areas and gather new issues to be brought into the programme.

Another new feature was the introduction of a standard form of measuring meeting effectiveness to evaluate the quality of communication and recommend improvements. The programme has since introduced enhancements to the induction process that new employees go through and continuous leadership learning programmes for senior managers. The business knowledge team introduced a 'voice of the customer' programme to bring plant members face-to-face with the people using the engines they serviced, a powerful eye-opener for both parties.

The 'secret' of the success is that, unlike so many initiatives, this one is run by employees for employees. They are truly engaged in its outcome. What is more, it has transcended the 'initiative' label by continuing to thrive, with new team members being elected to new project issues continuing the work.

The case illustrates at a micro-level how the quality of a partnership approach between employees and managers can enhance the working environment. It demonstrates some of the key issues for internal communication: supervisors are a central element that can lift or lower engagement – their training, accountability and involvement will influence the level of engagement of their staff in a way that corporate initiatives and, indeed, corporate communications cannot. Clear feedback mechanisms provide for employee contributions or questions about their work environment, which involves them in contributing to the increased success of their team. So, can engagement be improved by corporate initiatives? Probably not, but in this case, the plant's management were courageous enough to initiate the programme and their support undoubtedly contributes to its continued success.

If supervisors have been shown to be central to the quality of engagement, what role does internal communication really play in developing engagement?

If engagement works broadly at two levels, the rational and the emotional, staff being aware and proud of the performance of their part of their business might be rationally engaged; being inspired by managers to understand and contribute to that success is the emotional element. This is particularly important as it provides for greater contribution of discretionary effort from employees.

The role of internal communication is to provide the bedrock for the rational communications; what the company is doing, what new policies are being introduced and why, how the company is performing and so on. It provides and regulates the major channels of employee communication from intranets to printed magazines, web casting to organising leadership road shows. All of which establishes the ground for supervisors to build on emotional engagement. Training managers to communicate in a compelling way locally, converting the company information into local meaning, is also a role for internal communication professionals.

Methods such as cascade or team briefing have been widely used in companies to distribute information from senior leaders to front-line employees through their supervisors. These are not always successful in the corporate environment on one of three levels: timeliness, not everyone receives information at the same time; the information is conveyed in such a way that employees cannot relate to or remember it; and the opportunity for any feedback or contributing through dialogue is very limited. Timing can be addressed through initiating the communications globally through mass media. The dialogue and feedback issue can be resolved through more use of action-based teams as described in the case above, but conveying a message in a memorable way, such as through story-telling, is another useful skill.

The use of story-telling is nothing new; hundreds of years ago, before the widespread use of printed material, it was the only way to convey information. It has, however, seen a resurgence in recent years. Communication with employees went through a period of becoming increasingly writing-based – through company magazines, intranets and emails etc. Although these media are able to convey information in a rational sense, none is able to engage employees in the way that a supervisor can.

The re-introduction of story-telling as a key skill to relate information to staff is having a positive effect on engagement in many companies.

Rolls-Royce made use of the method on a global scale to its 40,000 employees. Story-telling provided the method to inform employees about the strategy it was following, the competition it faces and the context for its business operations, putting the various change programmes into some perspective and engaging employees with the need for action.

Using 'storyboards' and 700 trained supervisor story-tellers from the business, every employee over a period of a few months was taken through the company in short stories. The supervisors, using their own experiences, or those learned from other story-tellers, conveyed the complete picture of the company in its competitive environment. The 90-minute sessions, involving up to a dozen employees, were widely acclaimed by employees, underlining the contribution a good story can make. Material was all prepared and standard, posted as 60 A3 graphics on a 10m long 'wall'. Facilitators were able to walk along the wall, picking relevant pieces of material to illustrate their points and making the connections between what happened elsewhere and what happened in their audience's local area. Employees could absorb the material at their own pace, asking questions throughout.

Two important outcomes were achieved in this project: supervisors learned the value of using this method to communicate sometimes quite complex material in an engaging way and employees know much more about the opportunities and challenges that the company faces.

Both these cases help to illustrate the changing role of internal communications in corporations today. The function can contribute much more than simply running a global survey and publishing the results in its in-house magazine. While the role of supporting a rational level of engagement is still an important part of the responsibility through traditional and new media channels, some argue that a greater need is served through supporting managers across the organisation in developing ways of emotionally engaging employees with their work, to deliver higher and more rewarding performance to companies and individuals.

MiniCase questions

1. Why should companies invest in communicating with employees?
2. Can engagement be improved by corporate initiatives?
3. If supervisors have been shown to be central to the quality of engagement, what role does internal communication really play in developing engagement?

References

Albert, S. and Whetten, D.A. (1985) Organisational identity. In *Research in Organizational Behavior* (eds L.L. Cummings and B.M. Staw), 263–95. Greenwich, CT: Jai Press.

Balmer, J.M.T. and Wilkinson, A. (1991) Building societies: change, strategy and corporate identity. *Journal of General Management*, **17**(2), 22–33.

Barich, H. and Kotler, P. (1991) A framework for marketing image management. *Sloan Management Review*, **94** (Winter), 94–104.

Berry, L.L. (1980) Services marketing is different. *Business* (May/June), 24–9.

Beyer, J.M. (1981) Ideologies, values and decision making in organisations. In *Handbook of Organisational Design* (eds P. Nystrom and W. Swarbruck). London: Oxford University Press.

Bokaie, J. (2008) Corporations get personal. *Marketing*, 6 February, 17.

Christensen, L.T. and Askegaard, S. (2001) Corporate identity and corporate image revisited. *European Journal of Marketing*, **35**(3/4), 292–315.

Dutton, J.E. and Dukerich, J.M. (1991) Keeping an eye on the mirror: image and identity in organisational adaptation. *Academy of Management Review*, **34**, 517–54.

Dutton, J.E. and Penner, W.J. (1993) The importance of organisational identity for strategic agenda building. In *Strategic Thinking: Leadership and the Management of Change* (eds J. Hendry, G. Johnson and J. Newton), 89–113. Chichester: Wiley.

Dutton, J.E., Dukerich, J.M. and Harquail, C.V. (1994) Organisational images and member identification. *Administrative Science Quarterly*, **39**, 239–63.

Edwards, H. (2008) The battle to harness people power. *Marketing*, 30 January, 26–7.

Elsbach, K.D. and Kramer, R.M. (1996) Members' responses to organisational identity threats: encountering and countering the *Business Week* rankings. *Administrative Science Quarterly*, **41**, 442–76.

Foreman, S.K. and Money, A.H. (1995) Internal marketing: concepts, measurements and application. *Journal of Marketing Management*, **11**, 755–68.

Freeman, E. and Liedtka, J. (1997) Stakeholder capitalism and the value chain. *European Management Journal*, **15**(3), 286–96.

Gardner, D. (2007) Engaging your most valuable asset. *What's New in Marketing*, **64** (December). Retrieved 15 January 2008 from http://www.wnim.com/archive/issue1207/index.htm.

Gilly, M.C. and Wolfinbarger, M. (1998) Advertising's internal audience. *Journal of Marketing*, **62** (January), 69–88.

Goodman, P.S. and Pennings, J.M. (1977) *New Perspectives on Organisational Effectiveness*. San Francisco, CA: Jossey-Bass.

Gordon, G. (1985) The relationship of corporate culture to industry sector and corporate performance. In *Gaining Control of the Corporate Culture* (eds R.H. Kilman, M.J. Saxton, R. Serpa, and associates), 103–25. San Francisco, CA: Jossey-Bass.

Greene, W.E., Walls, G.D. and Schrest, L.J. (1994) Internal marketing: the key to external marketing success. *Journal of Services Marketing*, **8**(4), 5–13.

Gummesson, E. (1999) *Total Relationship Marketing. Rethinking Marketing Management: From 4Ps to 30Rs*. Oxford: Butterworth-Heinemann.

Hardaker, S. and Fill, C. (2005) Corporate service brands: the intellectual and emotional engagement of employees. *Corporate Reputation Review: an International Journal*, **8**(1), 365–76.

Hatch, M.J. and Schultz, M. (1997) Relations between organisational culture, identity and image. *European Journal of Marketing*, **31**(5/6), 356–65.

Hemsley, S. (1998) Internal affairs. *Marketing Week*, 2 April, 49–53.

Higgins, R.B. and Bannister, B.D. (1992) How corporate communication of strategy affects share price. *Long Range Planning*, **25**(3), 27–35.

Hiscock, J. (2002) The brand insiders. *Marketing*, 23 May, 24–5.

Hunger, J.D. and Wheelan, T. (1993) *Strategic Management*, 4th edn. Reading, MA: Addison-Wesley.

Ind, N. (1992) The *Corporate Image: Strategies for Effective Identity Programmes*, rev. edn. London: Kogan Page.

Kimberley, J. (1980) Initiation, innovation and institutionalisation in the creation process. In *The Organizational Lifecycle* (eds J. Kimberley and R. Miles), 18–43. San Francisco, CA: Jossey-Bass.

Lievens, A. and Moenart, R.K. (2000) Communication flows during financial service innovation. *European Journal of Marketing*, **34**(9/10), 1078–110.

Mahnert, K.F. and Torres, A.M. (2007) The brand inside: the factors of failure and success in internal branding. *Irish Marketing Review*, **19**(1/2), 54–63.

Mitchell, A. (1998) P&G's new horizons. *Campaign*, 20 March, 34–5.

Morden, T. (1993) *Business Strategy and Planning*. London: McGraw-Hill.

Morgan, G. (1997) *Images of Organisation*, 2nd edn. New York: Sage.

Newell, S.J. and Shemwell, D.J. (1995) The CEO endorser and message source credibility: an empirical investigation of antecedents and consequences. *Journal of Marketing Communications*, **1**, 13–23.

Piercy, N. and Morgan, R. (1991) Internal marketing: the missing half of the marketing programme. *Long Range Planning*, 24 (April), 82–93.

Schein, E.H. (1985) *Organizational Culture and Leadership*. San Francisco, CA: Jossey-Bass.

Schein, E.H. (2004) *Organizational Culture and Leadership*, 3rd edn. San Francisco, CA: Jossey-Bass.

Schneider, B. and Bowen, D. (1985) Employee and customer perceptions of service in banks: replication and extension. *Journal of Applied Psychology*, **70**, 423–33.

Simms, J. (2004) You're not paranoid, they do hate you. *Marketing*, 19 May, 32–4.

Storey, J. (2001) Internal marketing comes to the surface. *Marketing Week*, 19 July, 22.

Thompson, J.L. (1990) *Strategic Management: Awareness and Change*. London: Chapman & Hall.

Thomson, K. and Hecker, L.A. (2000) The business value of buy-in. In *Internal Marketing: Directions for Management* (eds R.J. Varey and B.R. Lewis), 160–72. London: Routledge.

Varey, R.J. (1995) Internal marketing: a review and some interdisciplinary research challenges. *International Journal of Service Industry Management*, **6**(1), 40–63.

Welch, M. and Jackson, P.R. (2007) Rethinking internal communication: a stakeholder approach. *Corporate Communications: An International Journal*, **12**(2), 177–98.

Witt, J. (2001) Are your staff and ads in tune? *Marketing*, 18 January, 21.

Glossary

A

A la carte – drawn from the hospitality market, the term à la carte refers to each item on a menu having a separate charge. In advertising, à la carte refers to selecting services from a range of different providers.

Above-the-line – a term used to depict the use of advertising. The line refers to the commission payable to media agencies as a form of remuneration.

Account manager – a title given to agency staff who are responsible for representing the interests of the client. They have a key representational role in the client/agency relationship and have to ensure that all those working on a client's account are fully informed, working to deadline and to budget.

Account planner – a specific role within a communications agency. Their task is to understand the client's target consumers and develop strategies for the creative and media departments. Using research data to identify ideal audiences and optimum methods of communication, account planners develop ideas to enable the creative team to produce advertising ideas that resolve defined business problems.

Adoption – the sequential process through which individuals become committed to the use of a new product. The process consists of stages, each characterised by the different elements.

Adstock – a term used to refer to the residual, yet declining, value of advertising messages through time. Also known as carryover.

Advertising – a non-personal form of communication that uses paid-for media to deliver messages to target audiences.

Advertising-to-sales ratio – the relationship between an organisation's sales and the amount it spends on advertising, expressed as a percentage. This can then be compared with the average A/S ratio for the industry.

Advocacy advertising – used to promote an organisation's socially acceptable behaviour.

Affective component – is a part of the attitude construct, and refers to the feelings held about a product, object or person. This is concerned with feelings, sentiments, moods and emotions about an object.

Affiliate marketing – refers to a network of independent web sites that act as a 'sales force' to direct interested parties to a seller's site, in return for a commission on any revenue that results from a sale.

AIDA – a hierarchy of effects model, originally used to explain the key stages of personal selling. It stands for *awareness*, *interest*, *desire* and *action* (a sale) and was used in the 1960s–80s to explain how advertising works. No longer an acceptable interpretation.

Alphabetical model – a broad advertising framework based on sequential models, used to explain how advertising works.

Ambient media – are regarded as out-of-home media that fail to fit any of the established outdoor categories.

ATR – stands for awareness–trial–reinforcement, a framework developed by Ehrenberg to explain how advertising works.

Attitudes – are predispositions, shaped through experience, through which people respond in an anticipated way to an object or situation. Attitudes consist of three components: cognitive, affective and conative. They are learned through past experiences and serve as a link between thoughts and behaviour.

Audience fragmentation – the splintering of audiences into smaller groups as a result of the increasing number of available media and leisure opportunities.

B

Banner ad – A graphic image used on web sites to advertise a product or service. Typically these measure 468 pixels wide and 60 pixels tall (i.e. 468 × 60).

Below-the-line – a term used to depict the various marketing communication tools that do not attract commission payments.

Biometrics – refers to technologies that measure and analyse human body characteristics, such as fingerprints, eye retinas and irises, voice patterns, facial patterns and hand measurements. Often used for authentication purposes but it also provides potential for delivering personalised marketing communication messages.

Blog – refers to the term 'web log', which is a frequently updated journal intended for general public consumption.

Bonus packs – a sales promotion technique. Packs that offer more products for the regular pack price, typically a 2-for-1 offer.

Boutiques – comparatively small firms that provide a limited range of specialist or niche services, often at premium prices. An advertising boutique may offer either creative work or research services, but not both.

Brand architecture – the structure an organisation gives to its brand portfolio.

Brand equity – a measure of the value of a brand. It is an assessment of a brand's physical assets plus a sum that represents their reputation or goodwill.

Brand extensions – a term used when a successful brand launches a new product into a new market.

Brand portfolio – a collection of brands, under the ownership of a single organisation.

Branded entertainment – a term, derived from product placement, where a brand becomes a constituent element of a film and the storyline is woven together with a brand.

Branded house – a brand architectural form which uses a single (master) brand to cover a range or series of offerings that may operate within descriptive sub-brand names.

Brands – products and services that have been given added value by marketing managers in an attempt to augment the products with values and associations that are recognised by, and are meaningful to, their customers.

Breakdown method – is a means of devising the optimum size of a salesforce. It is based on the premise that each salesperson has the same sales productivity potential per period.

Briefs – written documents used to exchange information between parties involved with the development and implementation of a campaign.

Business markets – organisations that consume products and services for use within the manufacture/production of other products or for use in their daily operations.

Business-to-business – marketing activities undertaken by one company directed at another.

Buyclasses – the different types of buying situations faced by organisations.

Buying centre see **decision-making unit**.

Buyphases – the series of sequential activities or stages through which organisations proceed when making purchasing decisions.

C

Call-to-action – that part of a marketing communication message that explicitly requests the receiver to act (or behave) in a particular way.

Careline – a telephone service that enables customers to obtain information, advice, or assistance, usually from retailers.

Cause-related marketing – the cooperation between private sector companies and charities, whereby each party enjoys the various benefits arising through cooperation with the other sector.

Channel partners – see **intermediaries**.

Channel power – the ability of one organisation to influence another channel member's opportunity to achieve their goals.

Classical conditioning – a theory of learning based around the association between a stimulus and a response, within an existing relationship.

Client brief – a document used to inform agency personnel about a client's organisation, market, operations, contacts and campaign requirements.

Co-branding – occurs when two established brands work together, either on one product or service. The principle behind co-branding is that the combined power of the two brands generates increased consumer appeal and attraction.

Cognitive component – a part of the attitude construct, this refers to the level of knowledge and beliefs held by individuals about a product and/or the beliefs about specific attributes of the offering. This represents the learning aspect of attitude formation.

Cognitive learning – a theory of learning that assumes that individuals attempt to resolve problems by processing information stored in memory, that is pertinent to each situation.

Cognitive processing – the way in which individuals transform external information into meanings or patterns of thought and how these meanings are combined to form judgements.

Cognitive theory – the belief that information is given thought, processed, transferred into meanings or patterns and then combined to form judgements about behaviour.

Collaborative exchanges – a long-term series of exchanges of money for products or services, in which the relationship between buyer and seller is of central importance.

Commitment – the desire that a relationship continues in order that a valued relationship be maintained or strengthened.

Communication – the process by which individuals share meaning.

Communication networks – the regular use of patterned flows of information.

Communication objectives – goals used to gauge the success of a communication campaign in terms of non-related sales factors. Often these include levels of awareness, perception, comprehension/knowledge, attitudes and overall degree of preference for a brand.

Communication value – the extent to which individuals perceive an organisation's communication to be of significance to them. There are four key elements that constitute communication value: the content, presentation, location and timing.

Competitive parity – occurs when an organisation deliberately spends the same amount on advertising as their competitors.

Competitor advertising – undertaken as either a response to a competitor's actions or proactively to develop market performance. There are three main forms: defensive; comparative; and endorsement advertising.

Conative component – a part of the attitude construct, this refers to an individual's disposition or intention to behave in a certain way.

Concept testing – a part of researching ad effectiveness. It involves presenting the target audience with a rough outline or storyboard that represents the intended artwork and the messages to be used.

Conclusion drawing – the level of clarity used to conclude an ad's core message. The message may be explicitly concluded or it may allow people to draw their own conclusions.

Consumer juries – a small group of representative consumers, who are asked to judge which of a series of paste-ups and rough ideas would be their choice of a final advertisement.

Consumer marketing – marketing activities undertaken directly to influence consumers, as opposed to other businesses.

Content perspective – a term related to IMC that assumes message consistency is the primary goal in order to achieve the 'one voice, one look' position. IMC works when there is a consistency throughout the various materials and messages.

Contest – a sales promotion technique that requires customers to use skill or ability to win a competition. Entry requires a proof of purchase and winners are judged against a set of predetermined criteria.

Context analysis – the first stage of the marketing communications planning process. It involves the analysis of four main areas: the customer; business; internal; and external environmental contexts.

Convenience products – non-durable goods or services, often bought with little pre-purchase thought or consideration.

Corporate communication – refers to the process that translates corporate identity into corporate image. Corporate communications consists of three main elements: symbolism; behaviour; and different forms of planned communication.

Corporate identity – the planned and unplanned formation of cues by which stakeholders can recognise and identify an organisation.

Corporate image – the perception that different audiences have of an organisation. It results from the audience's interpretation of the identity cues presented by an organisation.

Corporate objectives – the mission and the business area that the organisation believes it should be in. These are derived from the business or marketing plan.

Corporate personality – the totality of the characteristics that identify an organisation. It can be considered to be composed of two main facets: the culture and overall strategic purpose.

Corporate reputation – an individual's interpretation and reflection of the historical and accumulated impressions of previous identity cues, fashioned, in some cases, by near or actual transactional experiences.

Coupons – are a sales promotion technique. Free vouchers or certificates are distributed entitling consumers to a price reduction on a particular product. The value of the reduction or discount is set and the coupon must be presented at purchase.

CPT – is an acronym for cost-per-thousand-impressions. A unit of measure typically assigned to the cost for each 1,000 viewers (readers).

Creative briefs – used to help the creative team develop ads that address the needs of the client.

Creative magnifier – parts of an advertisement that are of intrinsic value to the recipient, sometimes referred to as 'the take-out', and is the part that is remembered.

Creative teams – people responsible for translating a proposal into an advertisement. Normally composed of a copywriter and an art director, supported by a service team.

Credentials presentation – part of the process of selecting an adverting agency. Clients visit each of the short-listed agency candidates to evaluate the degree to which the agency fits the client's expectations and requirements.

CRM see **customer relationship management**.

Culture – the values, beliefs, ideas, customs, actions and symbols that are learned by members of particular societies.

Customer acquisition – the activities and strategies used by organisations to get new customers.

Customer portfolio matrix – the strength of the relationships between a buyer and seller and the profitability each account represents to the seller.

Customer relationship lifecycle – the stages an organisation's customer moves through during their relationship with one another. These stages are customer acquisition, development and retention.

Customer relationship management (CRM) – the delivery of customer value through the strategic integration of business functions and processes, using customer data and information systems and technology. Usually incorporated as a software system that provides all staff with a complete view of the history and status of each customer.

Customer relationship marketing – the marketing activities and strategies used to retain customers. This is achieved by providing customers with relationship enhancing products and/or services that are perceived to be superior to those offered by a competitor.

Customer retention – the activities and strategies used by organisations to keep current customers.

Customer satisfaction – a position reached when the provision of goods or services meet or exceed a customer's pre-purchase expectations of quality and service.

D

Dagmar – a model for setting advertising objectives and measuring the results. Stands for 'defining advertising goals for measured advertising results'.

Database – a collection of files held on a computer that contains data that can be related to one another and which can reproduce information in a variety of formats.

Decay – sometimes referred to as wear-out, decay refers to the rate at which individuals forget material.

Deciders – people who make purchasing decisions. Very often these people are the most difficult to identify.

Decision-making unit – a group of people who collectively make purchasing decisions on behalf of organisations.

Decoding – the process of transforming and interpreting a message into thought. Receivers unpack the various components of a message, and start to make sense of it and give it meaning.

Dialogue – the development of knowledge that occurs when all parties to a communication event listen, adapt and reason with one another, about a specific topic.

Differentiation – a strategy through which an organisation offers products and services to broad customer groups, who perceive the offering to be significantly different, and superior, to its competitors.

Diffusion – the process by which an innovation is communicated among members of a social system. Diffusion is the process of adoption in aggregate form.

Digital influencer – an online opinion leader.

Digital value – the means by which digital processes and systems can be used to provide customers with enhanced product and service value.

Direct marketing – a communication tool that uses non-personal media, to create and sustain a personal and intermediary free communication with customers, potential customers and other significant stakeholders. In most cases this is a media-based activity.

Direct response advertising – advertisements that contain mechanisms such as telephone numbers, web site addresses, email and snail mail addresses. These are designed to encourage viewers to respond immediately to the ads. Most commonly used on television as DRTV.

Distributor (or own-label) brands – brands developed by the wholesalers, distributors, dealers and retailers who make up the distribution channel. Sometimes referred to as own-label brands.

Distributors – organisations that buy goods and services, often from a limited range of manufacturers, and normally sell them to retailers or resellers.

Domain – an area, field or sphere of function undertaken by organisations. There are four main elements: population, territory, roles and issues.

DRIP – the tasks of marketing communications: to differentiate, reinforce, inform and persuade.

Dummy vehicles – a dummy or pretend magazine that contains regular editorial matter with test advertisements inserted next to control advertisements. These 'pretend' magazines are distributed to a random sample of households, which are asked to consume the magazine in their normal way.

Duplication – a media planning concept that refers to the percentage of a target audience who are exposed to a message through two or more media vehicles, in any one campaign.

Durable goods – goods bought infrequently and which involve a reasonably high level of consumer risk.

E

Early adopters – a group of people within the process of diffusion that contains a large proportion of opinion leaders. Early adopters tend to be younger than any other group and above average in education. This group is important to the marketing communications process because they can determine the speed at which diffusion occurs.

Early majority – a group of people within the process of diffusion who require reassurance that a product works and has been proven in the market before they are prepared to buy it. Mainly opinion followers, they are a little above average in age, education, social status and income. They rely on informal sources of information and take fewer publications than other groups.

Effective frequency – a media planning concept that refers to the number of times a message needs to be repeated for effective learning to occur.

Elaboration likelihood model (ELM) – elaboration refers to the extent to which an individual needs to develop and refine information necessary for decision-making to occur. This model is used to explain how cognitive processing, persuasion and attitude change occur when different levels of involvement are present.

Emergent networks – informal patterns of information flows which emerge as a response to the social and task-oriented needs of the participants.

Emergent school – considers strategy to develop incrementally, step-by-step, as organisations learn, sometimes through simple actions of trial and error. The core belief is that strategy is comprised of a stream of organisational activities that are continuously being formulated, implemented, tested, evaluated and updated.

Encoding – the process of selecting a combination of appropriate words, pictures, symbols and music to represent the message to be transmitted. Also, a stage in memory that involves the selection of an image to represent the perceived object.

Engagement – the use of communication tools, media and messages in order to captivate an audience, often achieved through a blend of intellectual and emotional content, delivery or stimulation.

Episode – a series of interrelated actions that form part of a relationship event. Interrelated episodes are referred to as *sequences*, which are time-specific.

Equilibrium brands – brands whose share of voice is equal to its share of market.

Exhibitions – events when groups of sellers meet collectively with the key purpose of attracting buyers.

Experiential marketing – is a face-to-face campaign, that tries to engage a target audience with a brand through the stimulation of some or all of the senses.

Expressive positioning – a brand promise, one which emphasises the ego, social and hedonic satisfactions that a brand can bring. See **functional positioning.**

Extended problem solving – occurs when consumers give a great deal of attention and care to a purchase decision that where there is no previous or similar product purchase experience.

Extrinsic attributes – those elements that are not intrinsic and if changed do not alter the material functioning and performance of the product itself: devices such as the brand name, marketing communications, packaging, price and mechanisms that enable consumers to form associations which give meaning to the brand.

F

Fantasy imagery – is experienced when an individual constructs an event, drawing together various colours, sounds and shapes to compose a mental experience of an event that has not occurred previously.

FCB grid – a matrix that uses involvement and brain specialisation theories to distinguish four primary advertising planning strategies: informative, affective, habitual and self-satisfaction. Used a great deal in the 1980s and 1990s.

Feedback – part of the response that is returned to the sender of a message.

Field marketing – a marketing communications activity concerned with providing support for the sales force and merchandising personnel.

Focus groups – a small number (8–10) of target consumers brought together and invited to discuss a particular topic.

Four Cs (4Cs) framework – a tool that depicts the key characteristics and the relative effectiveness of the primary communication tools across a number of different characteristics. These are the ability of each to communicate, the credibility they bestow on messages, the costs involved and the control that each tool can maintain.

Frequency – a media planning concept that refers to the number of times the target audience is exposed to a message within a campaign.

Fulfilment house – an organisation that provides services needed to support sales promotion and direct marketing activities. In particular these include, order picking and processing, packing and dispatch, brochure fulfilment, warehousing and storage, packaging and returns.

Full-service agency – typically an advertising agency that offers the full range of services that a client requires in order to advertise its products and services. Increasingly, full service implies the provision of other of marketing communication activities, such as public relations, sales promotion, direct marketing and Internet marketing.

Functional positioning – a brand promise, one which emphasises the attributes, features and benefits a brand offers. See **expressive positioning**.

G

Gatekeepers – people who control the type and flow of information into the organisation and the members of the DMU.

Global account management (GAM) – the collaborative and centralised processes necessary to coordinate the worldwide buying and selling activities between global customers and global suppliers.

Gross rating points – a media planning concept used to express the relationship between reach and frequency and is a means of deciding which of the two concepts is important in a campaign.

H

Hedonic consumption – a range of products and services that can evoke multi-sensory, fantasy and emotive feelings when purchasing and consuming certain products and services.

Hierarchy of effects (HoE) – sequential models used to explain how advertising works. Popular in the 1960s–1980s these models provided a template that encouraged the development and use of communication objectives.

High involvement – experienced by individuals when purchasing a product/service that has high levels of uncertainty attached to it.

Historical imagery – experienced when an event (e.g. smell, scene, colour) triggers an individual's memory to replay a similar sensation.

House of brands – a brand architecture characterised by a group or collection of brands that have no outward connections and which operate independently of each other. These are brands that stand alone.

Hybrid direct brands – a type of direct marketing brand which has its roots in traditional distribution channels, which may well continue to be a route to market, used in parallel to the direct route.

I

Iconic learning – a form of cognitive learning where the repetition of simple messages is used to develop understanding.

IMP – the Industrial Marketing and Purchasing Group. IMG represent a school of thought about relationship marketing. Sometimes referred to as the International Marketing and Purchasing group.

Influencers – people who help set the technical specifications for a proposed purchase and assist the evaluation of alternative offerings by potential suppliers.

Information deviance – refers to the accidental or deliberate delivery of information that may not be entirely truthful or wholly accurate. Sometimes observed through opportunistic behaviour.

Initiators – people who start the organisational buying process.

Innovators – a group of people within the process of diffusion, who like new ideas, are prepared to take risks with new products and have a large disposable income.

Inquiry tests – used to measure the number of inquiries or direct responses stimulated by a single advertisement or a campaign.

Inseparability – a characteristic of a service, that refers to their instantaneous production and consumption.

Inside-out – a term used to refer to the process whereby some managers first design strategies for the product and treat the market/audience as a secondary consideration. Can apply to a variety of marketing (including communication) activities. See **outside-in**.

Institutional-oriented Advertising – a general term used to describe advertising that promotes an organisation its, policies, attitudes and position on ecological, ethical and political issues.

Intangibility – a characteristic of a service, namely that they do not have physical attributes and so therefore cannot be perceived by the senses – cannot be tasted, seen, touched, smelt or possessed.

Integrated marketing communications (IMC) – a term used to explain the processes concerned with the consistent development and coordinated delivery of company's messages with its target audiences.

Intentions – refers to the underlying attitude towards the act of behaviour and the subjective norm. In other words, the context within which a proposed purchase is to occur is seen as important to the attitude that is developed towards the object.

Interaction – concerns the mutual interaction between interested parties and the act of reciprocating or exchanging information.

Interaction model – a communication model that depicts a flow of communication messages to and from respondents, that lead to mutual understanding about a specific topic.

Interactive marketing communications – the process whereby organisations attempt to engage individuals with messages that are delivered through electronic channels and which offer all parties an opportunity to respond.

Interactivity – a responsive form of communication, characterised as either mediated (through technology) or non-mediated (human) interaction.

Intermediaries – are members of the marketing channel, such as distributors, dealers, agents and others who add value to products and services before transferring them to others for sale to end-user customers.

Internal marketing – the application of marketing concepts and principles within an organisation. Normally targeted at employees with a view to encouraging them to support and endorse the organisation's strategy, goals and brands.

Interorganisational conflict – refers to the disagreements and tensions that can arise between organisations. In particular, channel conflict can arise in distribution channels when one organisation changes their role, scope or strategy.

Intrinsic attributes – the functional characteristics of a product such as its shape, performance and physical capacity. If any of these intrinsic attributes were changed, it would directly alter the product.

Investment brands – a brand whose share of voice is greater than its market share. Advertising is being used to invest in the brand to drive growth.

Involvement – the level of care an individual experiences when considering the purchase of products and services.

K

KAM development cycle – the development stages experienced as relationships with key account customers develop.

Key accounts – business customers who are strategically significant to the supplier and with whom it wishes to build long-lasting relationships through collaborate exchanges.

KMV – the 'key mediating variables', commitment and trust, used within the Morgan and Hunt model of relationship marketing.

L

Laggards – a group of people within the process of diffusion who are suspicious of all new ideas and who are set in their opinions. Lowest of all the groups in terms of income, social status and education, this group takes a long time to adopt an innovation.

Late majority – a group of people within the process of diffusion who are sceptical of new ideas and only adopts new products because of social or economic factors.

Licensing – a commercial process whereby the trademark of an established brand is used by another organisation over a defined period of time, in a defined area, in return for a fee, to develop another brand.

Likeability – the extent to which individuals like an advertisement. It is used as a predictor of sales and measures the degree of how meaningful, how relevant and how interesting an individual finds an ad.

Limited problem solving – occurs when consumers have some product and purchase familiarity.

Linear model of communication – the fundamental expression about how mass communication works. The model identifies various components that make up the communication process: source, encoding, signal, decoding, receiver, feedback and noise.

Long-term memory – a place in which information can be stored for extended periods.

Low involvement – experienced by individuals when purchasing a product/service that has low levels of uncertainty attached to it.

M

Manufacturer brands – created and sustained by producers who seek widespread awareness and distribution because these brands are sought after.

Marketing communications eclipse – a visual interpretation of the balance between the pull, push and profile strategies, the three strategic dimensions.

Marketing communications mix – the particular combination of tools, media and messages used by organisations to reach consumers and other organisations with product and organisation based messages.

Marketing communications planning framework (MCPF) – the sequential framework used to represent the series of decisions that marketing managers undertake when preparing, implementing and evaluating communication strategies and plans. This framework reflects a deliberate or planned approach to strategic marketing communications.

Marketing objectives – market share, sales revenues, volumes, ROI (return on investment) and other profitability indicators. They are derived from the marketing plan and are sales oriented.

Media – channels of communication that convey or deliver messages to target audiences. Media offer a variety of entertainment, the communication of news and information, and the display of advertising messages.

Media briefs – used to help the media planning process.

Media fragmentation – the break up of the available media from a few mainstream media channels into many different media and channels formats.

Media multiplier – a means of setting a media budget, based on increasing last year's spend by the percentage rate at which media costs have increased over the last 12 months.

Media-neutral planning (MNP) – attempts to stimulate the use of a communication mix that is not mass media-oriented. This means that rather than keep recommending that clients use mass media communications, which have traditionally rewarded agencies through a more than generous commission system, a more balanced mix of tools and media be adopted in order to be more effective and efficient. See **open planning**.

Media planning – the selection and choice of media vehicles that fit the target audience's preferred media mix. It is also concerned with determining when and how often the message should be exposed to the target audience, in each of the selected vehicles.

Media richness theory – provides a scale or ranking of different media concerning the richness of information each medium is capable of communicating. It suggests that there is a range or depth of message content embedded within different media. This influences the capacity of different types of media to process ambiguous communication in organisations.

Media teams – those responsible for media planning and media buying.

Media vehicle – a term that refers to an individual medium that can be selected to carry advertising messages.

Message balance – the effectiveness of any single message is partly dependent upon the balance between the amount and quality of the information that is communicated and the way a message is communicated.

Message content – the intellectual and emotional information contained within a message.

Message framing – A method of presenting advertising messages which works on the hedonic principles of our motivation to seek happiness and to avoid pain. Messages can be framed to either focus a recipient's attention to positive outcomes (happiness) or take them away from the possible negative outcomes (pain).

Message origin – the source of a message may be an organisation or a brand but increasingly can be consumer- or user-generated.

Message reception – the contextual conditions in which messages are received, processed and ascribed meanings.

Microsite – a small web site or a part of a web site that has a separate URL to its home page, but the content is related. Often used as a temporary web site to promote a new product or event.

Milking brand – a brand whose share of voice is less than its current market share. Advertising investment is being withheld and profits are being taken from the brand.

Modelling – a form of cognitive learning which involves the observation and imitation of others and the associated outcomes of their behaviour.

Modified rebuy – the infrequent purchase of products and services.

Multi-step flow of communications – a model that reflects the interaction of a range of respondents within a communication network.

Mystery shopping – research undertaken by unidentifiable individuals who provide feedback on the level and quality of service offered by retail- and services-based staff.

N

New task – the buying situation faced by organisations when they buy a product or service for the first time.

Noise – occurs when a receiver is prevented from receiving all or part of a message in full, due to the omission or distortion of information during transmission.

Non-durable goods – low priced products which are bought frequently and which incur low levels of risk.

O

Open planning – An approach to selecting a communication mix based on clients needs rather than industry drivers. See **media-neutral planning**.

Operant conditioning – a theory of learning based upon an individual operating or acting on some part of the environment. The response of the individual is instrumental in getting a positive reinforcement (reward) or negative reinforcement (punishment).

Opinion followers – the vast majority of people who receive messages via the media, and/or through personal influencers.

Opinion formers – individuals who are able to exert personal influence because of their formal expertise and gained through authority, education or status associated with the object of the communication process.

Opinion leader – an individual who reprocesses information in order to influence others. They are of the same social class as non-leaders, but may enjoy a higher social status within the group. They are regarded as more persuasive than information received directly from the mass media.

Organisational buyer behaviour – the purchase behaviour of producers, resellers, government units and institutions.

Organisational identity – the identity of an organisation or group as perceived by the members.

Original equipment manufacturers (OEMs) – to one company purchasing, relabelling a product and incorporating it within a different product in order to sell it under their own brand name.

Outside-in – a term used to refer to the process whereby some managers first design strategies based around market/audience needs, and treat the product/internal issues as a secondary consideration. Can apply to a variety of marketing (including communication) activities. See **inside-out**.

P

Packaging – activities associated with designing, protecting and communicating a product's container or wrapper.

Pay-per-click (PPC) – refers to the payment an advertiser makes when the ad is clicked on to the destination site, based on a predetermined per-click rate.

Pedigree direct brands – pedigree direct brands are deliberately developed to exploit a market-positioning opportunity.

Perceived risk – the real and imagined uncertainties that buyers consider when they purchase products and services.

Perceived value – a customer's estimate of the extent to which a product or service can satisfy their needs.

Perception – the selection, organisation and interpretation of stimuli, by individuals so that they can understand the world as they see it.

Perceptual maps – these represent a geometric comparison of how competing products are perceived. Using the key dimensions used by consumers when purchasing, each product is positioned on the map according to the perception that buyers have of the strength of each attribute, of each product.

Perishability – a characteristic of a service that recognises that spare or unused capacity cannot be stored for use at some point in the future.

Permission-based communications – the use of marketing communications with individuals who have already given their express approval that an organisation may communicate with them.

Personal selling – the use of personal communication with the goal of informing and persuading customers to purchase products and services.

Physiological tests – a range of tests designed to measure the involuntary responses made by individuals to stimuli (ads).

PIMS – stands for profit impact on marketing strategy and is a major database of the performance of 3,500 business units and includes profiles of over 200 variables measured over a rolling four-year period. One of the major findings is that total advertising spend is not correlated with profitability.

Pioneer advertising – advertising which seeks to inform and make audiences aware of a new product's existence.

Pitch – a presentation made by competing agencies, in order to win a client's account (or business).

Planning school – is based on the idea that strategy development and implementation, is explicit, rational and planned as a sequence of logical steps.

Podcasting is a process whereby audio content is delivered over the Internet to iPods, MP3 players and computers, on demand. A podcast is a collection of files located at a feed address, which people can subscribe to by submitting the address to an aggregator. When new content becomes available it is automatically downloaded using an aggregator or feed reader which recognises feed formats such as RSS (see below).

Pop up – an ad that appears in a window on top of the browser window of a web site.

Positioning – an activity designed to manage the way in which audiences perceive brands. Positioning is about visibility, recognition and understanding of what a brand represents to a buyer. Marketing communications strategy is fundamentally about positioning brands in the minds of the target audience.

Post-testing – tests undertaken to measure the effectiveness of ads once they have been released.

Premiums – a technique used in sales promotion. Items of merchandise are offered free or at a low cost in return for product purchase.

Prescribed networks – formalised patterns or flows of information, often established by management and organisations to provide order and control.

Pretesting – the practice of showing unfinished commercials to selected groups of the target audience with a view to refining the ad to improve effectiveness.

Primacy effects – refers to messages that present the strongest points at the beginning.

Process of adoption – the way in which individuals accept and use new products. The different stages in the adoption process are sequential and are characterised by the different factors that are involved at each stage.

Process of diffusion – the rate at which a market adopts an innovation. According to Rogers, there are five categories of adopters, innovators, early adopters, early majority, late majority and laggards.

Process perspective – a term related to IMC that assumes that a structural realignment of the communication disciplines within organisations, even to the point of collapsing all communications into a single department is necessary.

Product – anything that is capable of satisfying customer needs.

Product class – the broad category of products in which an individual product such as cat food, shampoo or cars belongs.

Product lifecycle – the pathway a product assumes over its lifetime. There are said to be five main stages: development, introduction, growth, maturity and decline.

Product lines – a group of brands that are closely related in terms of their functions and the benefits they provide.

Product mix – the set of all product lines and items that an organisation offers for sale to buyers.

Product-oriented advertising – a general term used to describe the advertising of products and services.

Product placement – the deliberate use of brands within films, television and other entertainment vehicles with a view to developing awareness and brand values.

Production house – a general term which refers to organisations who produce film and video, CDs and DVDs and other digital products, mailing and fulfilment houses, photographers and other activities necessary to support the generation of marketing communication activities.

Profile strategies – used to communicate with a range of stakeholders, such as the local community, trade unions, suppliers, local and national government.

Projective techniques – a research technique used to probe the subconscious in order that target consumers express their inner thoughts and feelings about brands, products, services and organisations, among others.

Promotion – the use of communication to inform and persuade individuals, groups or organisations to purchase a company's products and services.

Promotional mix – the combination of five key communication tools: advertising, sales promotion, public relations, direct marketing and personal selling.

Psychoanalytical theory – based on drives of two primary instincts: life and death, psychoanalytic theory holds that many of the motives for purchase are driven by deeply rooted sexual drives and/or death instincts.

Public relations – a non-personal form of communication used by companies to build trust, goodwill, interest and ultimately relationships, with a range of stakeholders.

Pull strategies – used to communicate directly with end-user customers. These may be consumers but they might also be other organisations within a business-to-business context.

Push strategies – used to communicate with channel intermediaries, such as dealers, distributors and retailers, otherwise referred to as the 'trade' or channel buyers.

Q

QR codes – or quick response codes, are two dimensional barcodes which enable faster, deeper and more information to be communicated through the use of mobile phones.

R

Reach – a media planning concept that refers to the percentage of the target audience who are exposed to the message at least once during the campaign.

Realms of understanding – concerns the areas in which a source and the receiver understand each other, where there is some common ground. This understanding can concern attitudes, perceptions, behaviour and experience.

Reasoning – the most complex form of cognitive learning where individuals reorganise information held in long-term memory and combine it with fresh inputs in order to generate new outputs.

Recall tests – used to assess the impression that particular advertisements have made on the memory of the target audience.

Receiver – the individuals or organisations, that have seen, heard, smelt or read a message.

Recency effect – the placement of the strongest points at the end of the message.

Recency planning – a media planning concept that requires reaching as many consumers as possible in as many weeks as possible.

Recognition tests – used to assess a respondent's ability to recognise an advertisement.

Rehearsal – a stage of memory during which information is repeated or related to an established category. This is necessary so that the second function, encoding, can take place.

Reinforcement advertising – a type of advertising that tries to reassure or remind audiences that they have made the right choice either recently or at some previous time.

Relational bonds – the three structural elements within a relationship: financial, structural and social bonds.

Relationship marketing – is a perspective that considers the relationship between buyers and sellers to be of central importance. It is concerned with the long-term frequency and intensity of exchanges, which seeks to retain customers by developing their loyalty or preference.

Resellers – people (organisations) who purchase goods and services from wholesalers, distributors or even direct from producers and manufacturers, and make these available to other organisations for resale or consumption.

Retailers – people (organisations) who purchase goods and services from wholesalers, distributors or even direct from producers and manufacturers, and make these available to consumers and business for consumption.

Retrieval – the final function in the memory process whereby information is recovered from storage.

Rossiter–Percy grid – an advertising framework developed as a response to the several perceived shortcomings of the FCB grid.

Routinised response behaviour – exists when consumers have much product and purchase experience and where they perceive low risk.

RSS – stands for Really Simple Syndication or Rich Site Summary. Refers to related web feeds which distribute frequently updated digital content, such as news, podcasts, blogs and videos.

S

Sales potential – a method of determining the optimum size of a sales force. It is based on premise that there will be diminishing returns as extra salespeople are added to the sales force.

Sales promotions – a marketing communications tool used to add value to a product or service, with the intention encouraging people to buy now rather than at some point in the future.

Salience advertising – advertising that is thought to work because it stands out and is different from all other advertisements in the product class.

Sampling – a technique used in sales promotion designed to encourage people to try a product/service. Trial-size versions of the actual product are given away free.

Search engine marketing – is a marketing activity designed to attain the highest possible ranking position. There are two main search engine marketing techniques: search engine optimisation (SEO) and pay-per-click (PPC).

Search engines – is a database of many web pages and 'ranks' the results of a search term according to predetermined algorithms.

Sensory storage – a stage in memory during which information is sensed for a split second, and if an impression has been made the information will be transferred to short-term.

Service encounter – when a customer interacts directly with a service.

Service failure – where a customer's expectations of a service are not met.

Service mix – refers to the various service/product combinations.

Service processes – the series of sequential actions that lead to predetermined outcomes when a service is performed correctly.

Service quality – refers to the extent to which service experience exceeds their expectations.

Service recovery – an organisation's systematic attempt to correct a service failure and to retain a customer's goodwill.

Services – any act or performance offered by one party to another, that is essentially intangible and where consumption does not result in any transfer of ownership.

SERVQUAL – a disconfirmation model designed to measure service quality. It is based on the difference between the expected service and the actual perceived service.

Share of voice (SOV) – the percentage share of an industry's total advertising investment made by any one organisation.

Shock advertising – advertising that deliberately, rather than inadvertently, startles and offends its audience. It is unexpected and audiences are surprised by the messages because they do not conform to social norms or their expectations.

Shopping products – those bought relatively infrequently and so consumers need updating when making these purchase decisions.

Short-term memory – a period in which a maximum of four or five items can be stored for no longer than approximately eight seconds.

Significant value – a message that is meaningful, relevant and is perceived to be suitably credible is said to be of significant value.

Six markets model – a relationship marketing framework which suggests that marketing relationships should be deliberately developed with recruitment, supplier, influence, internal, referral and customer markets.

SMART – a set of guidelines designed to assist the development of effective objectives. This acronym stands for specific, measurable, achievable, relevant, targeted and timed.

Social enterprise – a business whose primary objectives are essentially social and whose surpluses are reinvested for that purpose in the business or in the community, rather than dispersed to the owners.

Social exchange theory – states that relationships evolve from exchange behaviour which serves to provide the rules of engagement. They are socially constructed and are based on the exchange of values between two or more parties. Social norms drive exchange reciprocity within relationships, and serve to guide behaviour expectations.

Social identity – how members of an organisation or group see themselves as a social part of the organisation.

Social penetration theory – states that as relationships develop individuals begin to reveal more about themselves. Every encounter between a buyer and seller will allow each party to discover more about the other and make judgements about assigning suitable levels of relationship confidence.

Source credibility – the perception that the source of a message is credible in terms of their objectivity and expertise, their personal motives and reasons to be involved, and the level of trust that can be placed in what the source says or does.

Sponsorship – a commercial activity, whereby one party permits another an opportunity to exploit an association with a target audience in return for funds, services or resources.

Speciality products – represent very high risk, are extremely expensive and are bought very infrequently.

Stages theory – a view of the relationship continuum that holds that relationships can develop incrementally.

States theory – the belief that a relationship grows stronger or weaker as a result of a discrete event or specific set of circumstances, rather than move along a continuum.

Storyboards – an inexpensive way of simulating a 'rough' version of an intended advertisement. Pen-and-ink line drawings, animatics or cartoons and photoboards are some of the more common approaches.

Straight rebuy – the routine reordering of goods and services, often undertaken from an approved list of suppliers.

Strategic credibility – refers to how favourably key stakeholders view the organisation's overall corporate strategy and associated strategic planning processes.

Strategic school – one of two schools of thought about strategic identity management. The 'strategic' school, is concerned with an organisation's vision and aims, together with how it positions and distinguishes itself.

Strong theory – a belief that advertising works sequentially and that ads can persuade people to buy products by moving them forward to a purchase, stimulated by timely and suitable promotional messages.

Subjective norm – the relevant feelings others are believed to hold about the proposed purchase, or intention to purchase.

Supply chains – formed when organisations link their individual value chains.

Support activities – facilitate the primary activities within the value chain.

Sweepstake – a sales promotion technique where winners are selected by chance and proof of purchase is not required. There is no judging and winners are drawn at random.

Switching costs – all the direct and indirect costs incurred by buyers when they change supplier.

Symbolism – the visual aspect of identity and was once regarded as the sole aspect of corporate identity management.

T

Telemarketing – activities associated with selling, researching, soliciting or promoting a product or service over the telephone.

Test marketing – undertaken when a new product is tested with a sample of customers, or is launched in a specified geographical area, to judge customers' reactions prior to a national launch.

Theatre test – a method used to test finished broadcast advertisements. Consumers visit a theatre (laboratory or hall) to preview television programmes, into which are submitted test and control ads. A before and after preference measure is taken to judge the influence of the ads.

Theory of reasoned action – developed by Ajzen and Fishbein (1980) this theory holds that purchase intentions are composed of interrelated components. These are the subjective norms, and the beliefs about the probable outcomes that a behaviour will lead to.

Transactional (or market) exchanges – a single, one-off exchange of money for products or services where products and prices are of central importance.

Trust – the confidence a person has in another, an object, brand or organisation that they will behave appropriately or as promised.

Two-step flow of communication – a model which depicts information flowing via media channels to particular types of people (opinion leaders and opinion formers) to whom other members of a target audience refer for information and guidance.

Two-step model – a communication process when the receiver responds to the message received from the sender.

U

User organisations – companies who purchase goods and services and consume them as part of their production and manufacturing processes.

Users – people or groups who acquire and use products and services before evaluating their performance.

V

Value – a customer's estimate of the extent to which a product or service can satisfy their needs.

Value chain – a term determined by Michael Porter (1985) that refers to the various activities an organisation undertakes and links together in order to provide products and services that are perceived by customers to be different and of superior value.

Variability – the amount of diversity allowed in each step of service provision.

Viral marketing – the electronic version of word-of-mouth communication. This endorsement of a product or service is targeted at key individuals who voluntarily pass the message to friends and colleagues and in doing so bestow, endorse and provide the message with much valued credibility.

Virtual brand communities – is a group of individuals who interact online in order to share their interest in a brand or product.

Visual school – one of two schools of thought about strategic identity management. The 'visual' school is concerned with design and operational aspects of the way an organisation is presented, and the design.

W

Widgets – are typically buttons and windows that display information and invite users to act in a number of ways.

Wiki – refers to software that allows the co-creation and contribution of knowledge on a particular topic by a group of people. A wiki is a web publishing platform that makes use of technologies similar to blogs and also allows for collaboration with multiple users.

Word-of-mouth – communication undertaken voluntarily between people, concerning the quality or characteristics of products, services and organisations. The receiver regards the source as objective and impartial and not attempting to sell products or services.

Workload method – a means of devising the optimum size of the sales force, based on equalising the amount of work.

Author index

Subject index

N